FEDERAL RULES OF EVIDENCE

Rules, Legislative History, Commentary and Authority

FEDERAL RULES OF EVIDENCE

Rules, Legislative History, Commentary and Authority

Glen Weissenberger
Professor of Law
University of Cincinnati

Anderson Publishing Co. / Cincinnati

NOTICE

Amendments to the Federal Rules of Evidence were adopted by the Supreme Court and transmitted to Congress by the Chief Justice on March 2, 1987. These amendments will become effective on October 1, 1987, unless Congress takes further action with respect to them. Because these amendments are pending, but not in effect at the time of the publication of this treatise, they are set forth in the Appendix at page 873. With minor exceptions, these amendments are technical. As stated by the Advisory Committee in the context of technical amendments, "No substantive change is intended."

WEISSENBERGER'S FEDERAL RULES OF EVIDENCE

© 1987 by Anderson Publishing Co.

Library of Congress Cataloging in Publication Data

Weissenberger, Glen.
   Federal evidence.

   Includes index.
   1. Evidence (Law)—United States. 1. Title.

KF8935.W42 1987	347.73'6	87-17486
ISBN: 0-87084-923-9	347.3076	
ISBN: 0-87084-924-7	(PBK.)	

For Sarah, Geoff and Kim

Contents

V
PRIVILEGES

VI
WITNESSES

VIII
HEARSAY

IX
AUTHENTICATION AND IDENTIFICATION

Chapter 901. Requirement of Authentication or Identification

Chapter 901—*Concluded*

Chapter 902. Self-Authentication

XI
MISCELLANEOUS RULES

Preface

This is a comprehensive treatise on the Federal Rules of Evidence contained in one volume. It is designed to provide a succinct, yet scholarly analysis of the interpretation and application of each of the Federal Rules of Evidence. For the judge and practitioner, it contains practical direction for the application of federal evidentiary doctrines. For the student of evidence, it provides a discussion of the theory and purpose of our evidentiary system.

I sincerely hope that this book will make a significant contribution to the level of practice in federal courts and to the literature on the law of evidence.

Glen Weissenberger
University of Cincinnati
March 4, 1987

Acknowledgments

Professor Weissenberger would like to acknowledge the research contributions of Daniel J. Donnellon, Jean C. Donath, V. Ellen Graham, Carole Kellerman and Marilyn Maag. Wade Kocovsky served as the senior research associate. Substantive contributions were made by Susan Demidovich, Brenda N. Dunlap and Mark E. Elsener.

I
GENERAL PROVISIONS

Chapter 101

RULE 101. SCOPE

Rule 101 reads as follows:

These rules govern proceedings in the courts of the United States and before United States magistrates, to the extent and with the exceptions stated in rule 1101.

§ 101.1 General Applicability.

Rule 101 is fundamentally a statement of the scope of the Federal Rules of Evidence. Rule 101 provides that as a general principle, the Federal Rules of Evidence apply in all courts of the United States as well as proceedings before United States magistrates.[1] Rule 1101 must be consulted to determine the particular limitations and refinements of this statement.[2]

Rule 101 is designed to contain a general introduction to the applicability of the Rules of Evidence. The intent of the drafters was to provide detail in Rule 1101. Consequently, specific exceptions are set forth at the end of the Rules where, as the Advisory Committee has stated, they ". . . will not discourage the reader of the rules by confronting him at the outset with a rule filled with minute detail."[3]

It should be noted that the Rules of Evidence generally apply in both civil and criminal cases and in both jury and bench trials.

[1] *See, generally,* 1 WEINSTEIN ¶¶ 101[01]-[03]; 1 LOUISELL & MUELLER, § 1. *See also* Degnan, *The Law of Federal Evidence Reform,* 76 HARV. L. REV. 275 (1962); Goldberg, *The Supreme Court, Congress, and Rules of Evidence,* 5 SETON HALL L. REV. 667 (Spring, 1974); Powell and Burns, *A Discussion of the New Federal Rules of Evidence,* 8 GONZ. L. REV. 1 (1972); Weinberg, *Choice of Law and the Proposed Federal Rules of Evidence: New Perspectives,* 122 U. PA. L. REV. 594 (1974).

[2] *See* the discussion of Rule 1001, § 1001.1 Treatise.

[3] Rule 101, Advisory Committee's Note to first draft, cited in 1 WEINSTEIN, ¶ 101[01]. *See* Chapter 1101 for a discussion of the specific exceptions to the applicability of the Rules of Evidence.

3

Chapter 102

RULE 102. PURPOSE AND CONSTRUCTION

Rule 102 reads as follows:

These rules shall be construed to secure fairness in administration, elimination of unjustifiable expense and delay, and promotion of growth and development of the law of evidence to the end that the truth may be ascertained and proceedings justly determined.

§ 102.1 In General.

Federal Rule 102 directs courts to apply a construction to the Rules of Evidence which will attain the stated goals of fairness to the parties throughout the administration of proceedings and the elimination of unjustifiable expense and delay.[1] The Rule also provides courts with power to expand the Rules of Evidence through case law to insure growth and refinement of the Rules of Evidence in order that truth may be ascertained and fair results obtained.[2] By granting discretion to the trial court in admitting evidence, the drafters tacitly recognized that the inflexible application of any system of rules may result in unfairness.

A system of rules that does not allow for some discretion on the part of a trial judge in making evidentiary rulings lays the groundwork for its own obsolescence. As methods of communication and interaction between individuals change, the Rules of Evidence must accommodate this progress.

---

[1] *See, generally*, 1 WEINSTEIN ¶¶ 102[01]-[02]; 1 LOUISELL & MUELLER, §§ 3-4. *See also* Christian, *The Proposed Federal Rules of Evidence*, 33 FED. B.J. 96 (1974); Rothstein, *The Proposed Amendments to the Federal Rules of Evidence*, 62 GEO. L.J. 125 (1973); Ladd, *Some Highlights of the New Federal Rules of Evidence*, 1 FLA. ST. U.L. REV. 191 (1973); Atkins, *Significant Changes in the Proposed Federal Rules of Evidence*, 9 FORUM 175 (1973).

[2] *See* United States v. Bibbs 564 F.2d 1165, 1170 (5th Cir. 1977) (court is free to fashion an evidentiary procedure with regard to subsequent inconsistent statements which will accord with objectives of Rule 102); United States v. King, 73 F.R.D. 103, 105 (E.D.N.Y. 1977) (reliance on Rule 102 to hold that the need for full revelation of all pertinent evidence was the most powerful factor in privilege matter); United States v. Barbati, 284 F. Supp. 409, 413 (E.D.N.Y. 1968) (mechanical and unreasoned application of hearsay not permitted to deny evidence vital to search for truth). *See also* In re Richter & Phillips Jewelers & Dist., 31 B.R. 512, 514 (Bankr. Ct. S.D. Ohio 1983).

Rule 102 is designed to insure the continued viability of the Federal Rules of Evidence by providing that the evidence as to the disputed relationship between the parties is available to the trier of fact.

Rule 102 relies on the discretion of the trial court to fulfill its stated objectives. The court's discretion is, of course, subject to review under Rule 103.[3]

[3] *See, e.g.*, United States v. Thorne, 547 F.2d 56, 59 (8th Cir. 1976) (rules permit exercise of discretion by trial judge in finding witness rehabilitated, and therefore limiting cross-examination under Rule 609 so as to implement objectives of Rule 102). *See also* Weinstein & Berger, *Basic Rules of Relevancy in the Proposed Federal Rules of Evidence*, 4 GA. L. REV. 43 (1969).

Chapter 103

RULE 103. RULINGS ON EVIDENCE

Rule 103 reads as follows:

(a) **Effect of Erroneous Ruling.** Error may not be predicated upon a ruling which admits or excludes evidence unless a substantial right of the party is affected, and

(1) Objection. In case the ruling is one admitting evidence, a timely objection or motion to strike appears of record stating the specific ground of objection, if the specific ground was not apparent from the context; or

(2) Offer of proof. In case the ruling is one excluding evidence, the substance of the evidence was made known to the court by offer or was apparent from the context within which questions were asked.

(b) **Record of Offer and Ruling.** The court may add any other or further statement which shows the character of the evidence, the form in which it was offered, the objection made, and the ruling thereon. It may direct the making of an offer in question and answer form.

(c) **Hearing of Jury.** In jury cases, proceedings shall be conducted, to the extent practicable, so as to prevent inadmissible evidence from being suggested to the jury by any means, such as making statements or offers of proof or asking questions in the hearing of the jury.

(d) **Plain Error.** Nothing in this rule precludes taking notice of plain errors affecting substantial rights although they were not brought to the attention of the court.

§ 103.1   Rulings on Evidence—In General.

Rule 103 embodies the general procedures pertaining to errors on evidentiary objections and motions.[1] It should be noted that the Rule addresses only the issue of identifying evidentiary rulings which are subject to review, and it does not purport to provide substantive standards governing the circumstances under which a reversal is required.

§ 103.2   Effect of Erroneous Ruling: Timely Objection and Proffer Requirements.

Rule 103(a) identifies two situations in which the record of the trial proceedings must clearly reflect the alleged error if the appellate court is to review the propriety of the evidentiary ruling. These situations are, first, error predicated upon an admission of evidence where an objection is overruled improperly, and, second, error predicated upon an exclusion of evidence where an objection is sustained improperly and a proffer is made.

Errors in rulings which result in admitting evidence are deemed waived if not predicated on motions to strike or objections in the record stating the supporting reasons. [2] The Rule is derived from the general principle that a reviewing court will only consider an issue which has been raised in the lower court in a manner such that the lower court had ample opportunity to consider its own ruling and pass on the issue.[3] As a further qualification of the foregoing principle, harmless error will not serve as grounds for review on appeal, *i.e.*, a "substantial right" of a party must be affected.[4]

[1] *See, generally,* McCormick, § 51-52, 54-55; 1 Weinstein ¶¶ 103[01]-[08]; 1 Louisell & Mueller, §§ 6-23; 1 Wigmore, §§ 17, 18. *See also* Poulos, *The Trial of Celebrated Criminal Cases: An Analysis of Evidentiary Objections,* 56 Tul. L. Rev. 602 (1982); Note, *Harmful Use of Harmless Error in Criminal Cases,* 64 Cornell L. Rev. 538 (1979); Note, *Harmless Error: The Need for a Uniform Standard,* 53 St. John's L. Rev. 541 (1979); Note, *Ineffective Assistance of Counsel and the Harmless Error Rule: The Eighth Circuit Abandons Chapman,* 43 Geo. Wash. L. Rev. 1384 (1975).

[2] *E.g.,* United States v. Wilson, 690 F.2d 1267, 1273-74 (9th Cir. 1982); United States v. Collins, 690 F.2d 670, 674 (8th Cir. 1982); Espino v. Kingsville, 676 F.2d 1075, 1078 (5th Cir. 1982).

[3] *E.g.,* United States v. DeBiasi, 712 F.2d 785, 793-94 (2d Cir. 1983); United States v. Richardson, 562 F.2d 476, 478 (7th Cir. 1977), *cert. denied,* 434 U.S. 1072, 98 S.Ct. 1257, 55 L.Ed.2d 776 (1978).

[4] *E.g.,* Oberst v. International Harvester Company, Inc., 640 F.2d 863, 866 (7th Cir. 1981) (no substantial right of party affected by exclusion of evidence regarding post-accident repairs); United States v. Sarmiento-Perez, 633 F.2d 1092, 1104 (5th Cir. 1981) (admission of co-conspirator's confession "constituted reversible error as affecting the substantial rights of the accused"); Hill v. Polleri, 615 F.2d 886, 890 (9th Cir. 1980) (error harmless because it did not affect substantial right of a party); United States v. Lomax, 598 F.2d 582, 584-85 (10th Cir. 1979) (admitted evidence was cumulative and "no substantial right of the defendant was affected"). A "harmless error" is one found not to affect "substantial rights." 1 Weinstein, 103[01], at 103-7. *See, generally,* 1 Weinstein ¶ 103[06], at 103-50 *et*

Although the Rule does not define "substantial right," it may be stated at minimum that errors in the admission or exclusion of evidence, whether in a civil or criminal matter, which do not affect the final determination of the case, do not affect a substantial right. Such errors are not prejudicial.[5] It should be noted that under Rule 103(d), considered subsequently, error may be reviewed on appeal even if it has not been preserved where it falls within the category of "plain error."

Rule 103(a)(1) provides that in order to preserve the matter for appeal, the objecting party must state the ground for objecting unless the reason is apparent from the context. While Rule 103 only identifies errors that are subject to review, case law provides that the admission of evidence over a general objection is not a basis for reversal if any significant part of the evidence is admissible. Likewise, if it is admissible for any purpose, evidence admitted over a general objection will not constitute reversible error.[6] When a party advances certain grounds for objection to the admission of evidence, either at its own instance or at the request of the court, the party will be held to have waived all other grounds not so specified.[7] Where, however, the court assigns the wrong reason for receiving evidence and a proper reason exists, a reviewing court generally will not reverse since the lower court's receipt of the evidence was nevertheless proper.[8]

Much the same analysis may be applied to rulings which result in the exclusion of evidence. Again, the ruling must affect a substantial right, and the party offering such evidence must make a proffer of the evidence (alternately called an "offer of proof") to ensure that the reviewing court is presented with a complete record on appeal. If, however, the substance of the excluded evidence is apparent from the context within which the questions were asked, a proffer is unnecessary. Where the substance of the excluded evidence is not apparent from the context of the question and no proffer is made, the exclusion of evidence will not be entertained as a basis

---

seq. as to "harmless error." For a discussion of the subject, see Saltzburg, *Another Ground for Decision—Harmless Trial Errors*, 47 TEMP. L.Q. 1983 (1974).

[5] E.g., M/V American Queen v. San Diego Marine Const. Corp., 708 F.2d 1483, 1491-92 (9th Cir. 1983); Jordan v. Medley, 711 F.2d 211, 218-19 (D.C. Cir. 1983). The terms "prejudicial error" and "reversible error" are synonymous. 1 WEINSTEIN, ¶ 103[01], at 103-7.

[6] United States v. Gentile, 525 F.2d 252, 259 (2d Cir. 1975), cert. denied, 425 U.S. 903, 96 S.Ct. 1493, 47 L.Ed.2d 753 (1975) (no error in overruling *Miranda*-based defense objections in bribery prosecution,

since there was no warrant for suppression of all the statements and defendant made no effort to differentiate the statements at trial or on appeal; trial judge was not required to separate out the statements which were arguably excludable on the objection).

[7] E.g., Jay Edwards, Inc. v. New England Toyota Distributor, 708 F.2d 814, 825 (1st Cir. 1983); United States v. Auerbach, 682 F.2d 735, 738 (8th Cir.), cert. denied, 103 S.Ct. 219 (1982).

[8] 1 WIGMORE, § 18. But cf. MORGAN, BASIC PROBLEMS OF EVIDENCE 54 (1962). See also 1 WEINSTEIN, ¶ 103[02], at 103-24.

for appeal absent the extreme case of "plain error."[9] One pre-Rule exception to this general principle appears to have survived: If evidence is excluded during cross-examination, a proffer is not necessary in order to preserve the question on appeal since it would be impractical to speculate as to the potential answer.[10] Finally, no special form for a proffer is set forth in the Rules. The only requirement is that the substance of the excluded evidence must clearly appear in the proffer.[11]

Again, it should be noted that under the "plain error" provision of Rule 103(d), certain errors may be reviewed on appeal in absence of proper preservation in the record.

§ 103.3　Record of Offer and Ruling.

As a corollary to the duty of the parties to make a record concerning rulings on the admission and exclusion of evidence, Rule 103(b) provides that the court *may* comment for the record on the circumstances surrounding its ruling. This procedure is especially useful where evidence is received on a limited basis and the trial court feels constrained to instruct the jury accordingly. By so instructing the jury, the trial judge simultaneously ensures that the reasons for the ruling appear in the record for review on appeal.

[9] United States v. Hutcher, 622 F.2d 1083, 1087 (2d Cir. 1980), *cert. denied*, 449 U.S. 875, 101 S.Ct. 218, 66 L.Ed.2d 96 (1980) (mere statement of objection without stating grounds was insufficient to preserve error, where the specific ground was not apparent). *See also* United States v. Sumin, 567 F.2d 684, 688 (6th Cir. 1977).

[10] *See* Burr v. Sullivan, 618 F.2d 583, 587-588 (9th Cir. 1980); Fairfield Scientific Corp. v. United States, 611 F.2d 854, 862 (Ct. Cl. 1979). *But see* United States v. Lavallie, 666 F.2d 1217, 1220-21 (8th Cir. 1981); United States v. Nez, 661 F.2d 1203, 1205-06 (10th Cir. 1981).

[11] *See* Saltzman v. Fullerton Metals Co., 661 F.2d 647, 652-53 (7th Cir. 1981) (court refused to entertain plaintiff's argument that judge erroneously denied cross-examination where plaintiff's "conclusory offer of proof disclosed neither of plaintiff's particular needs for cross-examination argued on appeal and failed to set out any testimony

not cumulative of that already provided"); United States v. Winograd, 656 F.2d 279, 284 (7th Cir. 1981), *cert. denied*, 456 U.S. 202, 102 S.Ct. 1612, 77 L.Ed.2d 848 (1982) ("It is well-established . . . that the appellant cannot raise theories or issues for the first time on appeal, which were not presented to the trial court"); United States v. Winkle, 587 F.2d 705, 710 (5th Cir. 1979), *cert. denied*, 444 U.S. 827, 100 S.Ct. 51, 62 L.Ed.2d 34 (1979) (citing Treatise). *See also* Foster v. Ford Motor Co., 621 F.2d 715, 721 (5th Cir. 1980) (appellate court refused to consider whether deposition testimony had been improperly excluded where it had never formally been offered into evidence); Wright v. Hartford Accident & Indemnity Co., 580 F.2d 809, 810 (5th Cir. 1978) (defendant cannot on appeal argue that trial judge erroneously excluded evidence where trial judge had specifically asked counsel to provide support for admitting evidence, which counsel failed to provide).

§ 103.4　Hearing of Jury.

Rule 103(c) provides that, whenever practicable, discussions concerning rulings on evidence should be conducted outside the hearing of the jury. Quite obviously, the purpose of the procedures set out in Rule 103(a) and (b) could be wholly defeated if the jury were permitted to overhear a proffer of excluded evidence or a lengthy discourse on, *e.g.*, the highly prejudicial nature of evidence admitted over objection.

§ 103.5　Plain Error.

While the thrust of Rule 103(a) is to impose upon the parties the duty of making a complete record on evidentiary rulings, there are instances where the error complained of, though not raised at trial, is so egregious and so affects a substantial right of a party that an appellate court is empowered to review the issue and redress the wrong.[12] In this context, Rule 103(d) emphasizes that the doctrine of "plain error" applies to rulings on evidence.

The doctrine of plain error should not be confused with the concept of prejudicial error, although the similarities between the two are extensive. The doctrine of plain error, as embodied in Rule 103(d), is a specific appellate device for reviewing records in which, perhaps through inexperience or incompetence of counsel, the party adversely affected by significant evidentiary error has not properly preserved its position on the record. By comparison, the requirement that any error challenged on appeal must be prejudicial in order to justify a reversal applies equally to all appeals, whether the error is reviewed because it was properly preserved in the trial court record, or because the plain error doctrine is properly invoked.

The Rule itself does not define "plain error," and the definition must be derived from case law.[13] Generally, in order for the plain error doctrine to be satisfied, the error must be "obvious" and "fundamental."[14] It appears

---

[12] *E.g.*, Rojas v. Richardson, 703 F.2d 186, 190-92 (5th Cir. 1983); United States v. Escobar, 674 F.2d 469, 475-76 (5th Cir. 1982).

[13] Rogers v. United States, 422 U.S. 35, 40, 95 S.Ct. 2091, 2095, 45 L.Ed.2d 1, 7 (1975) (court, in absence of counsel, instructed jury on effect of a recommendation of mercy; "the combined effect of the District Court's errors was so fraught with potential prejudice as to require us to notice them, notwithstanding petitioner's failure to raise the issue in the court of appeals or in this court"). *See, generally*, 1 WEINSTEIN, ¶ 103[07], at 130-70 *et seq.*

[14] 1 LOUISELL & MUELLER, § 16, at 81, § 21, at 120, and § 22, at 129. *See* United States v. Check, 582 F.2d 668, 676-78 (2d Cir. 1978).

that the threshold for invocation of the plain error doctrine is higher in civil cases than in criminal cases,[15] and erroneous rulings are susceptible to plain error treatment in civil cases only in extreme situations.[16]

[15] As Professors Louisell & Mueller point out, "Rule 103 makes the plain error principle fully applicable to civil cases, where previously neither rule nor statute expressly accomplished this result." *Id.*, § 22, at 129.

[16] 1 LOUISELL & MUELLER, § 22, at 129-135. *See* Hormel v. Helvering, 312 U.S. 552, 557, 61 S.Ct. 719, 721, 85 L.Ed. 1037, 1041 (1941) ("Rules of practice and procedure are devised to promote the ends of justice, not to defeat them; orderly rules of procedure do not require sacrifice of the rules of fundamental justice".) *See, e.g.,* Silber v. United States, 370 U.S. 717, 718, 82 S.Ct. 1287, 1288, 8 L.Ed.2d 798, 799 (1962) (criminal case). *See also* Rule 103, Advisory Committee's Note (application of the plain error doctrine "more pronounced" in criminal cases). As to constitutional error, *see* Chapman v. California, 386 U.S. 18, 24, 87 S.Ct. 824, 828, 17 L.Ed.2d 705, 710-11 (1967) ("before a federal constitutional error can be held harmless, the court must be able to declare a belief that it was harmless beyond a reasonable doubt").

Chapter 104

RULE 104. PRELIMINARY QUESTIONS

Rule 104 reads as follows:

(a) **Questions of Admissibility Generally.** Preliminary questions concerning the qualification of a person to be a witness, the existence of a privilege, or the admissibility of evidence shall be determined by the court, subject to the provisions of subdivision (b). In making its determination it is not bound by the rules of evidence except with respect to privileges.

(b) **Relevancy Conditioned on Fact.** When the relevancy of evidence depends upon the fulfillment of a condition of fact, the court shall admit it upon, or subject to, the introduction of evidence sufficient to support a finding of the fulfillment of the condition.

(c) **Hearing of Jury.** Hearings on the admissibility of confessions shall in all cases be conducted out of the hearing of the jury. Hearings on other preliminary matters shall be so conducted when the interests of justice require or, when an accused is a witness, if he so requests.

(d) **Testimony by Accused.** The accused does not, by testifying upon a preliminary matter, subject himself to cross-examination as to other issues in the case.

(e) **Weight and Credibility.** This rule does not limit the right of a party to introduce before the jury evidence relevant to weight or credibility.

§ 104.1   Rule 104—In General.

Rule 104 governs the allocation of responsibility between judge and jury for determining questions of admissibility.[1] The primary focus of the Rule is on situations in which a preliminary showing must be made in order for certain evidence to be properly admitted or rejected. More specifically, the Rule governs the methodology and corollary issues surrounding the establishment of this prerequisite showing. In many contexts, this procedure is commonly described by the familiar phrase, "laying a foundation for the admission of evidence." In other situations, the process may apply to the opponent of evidence establishing the incidents of an evidentiary exclusionary principle or rule.

§ 104.2   Role of Judge in Determining Admissibility.

Rule 104(a) provides that preliminary questions regarding the admissibility of evidence shall be determined by the trial judge. As the Rule specifies, preliminary questions may involve the qualifications of a person to be a witness (*e.g.*, whether a person is qualified to testify as an expert, or whether a lay witness is competent or incompetent by virtue of the provisions of Rule 601); the existence of a privilege (*e.g.*, whether a communication was confidentially made); and questions of admissibility of the evidence itself (*e.g.*, criteria for the application of a hearsay exception).[2] In

---

[1] *See, generally*, McCORMICK, § 53, at 124; 1 WEINSTEIN, ¶ 104[01]-[14]; 1 LOUISELL & MUELLER, §§ 26-36; 9 WIGMORE, § 2550. *See also* Ball, *The Myth of Conditional Relevancy*, 14 GA. L. REV. 435 (1980); Haddad, *Post-Bruton Developments: A Reconsideration of the Confrontation Rationale and a Proposal for a Due Process Evaluation of Limiting Instruc-* *tions*, 18 AM. CRIM. L. REV. 1 (1980); Kaplan, *Of Mabrus and Zorgs — An Essay in Honor of David Louisell*, 66 CALIF. L. REV. 987 (1978); Bergman, *The Co-Conspirators' Exception: Defining the Standard of Independent Evidence Test Under the New Federal Rules of Evidence*, 5 HOFSTRA L. REV. 99 (1976).

[2] 1 LOUISELL & MUELLER, § 26, at 155.

each of the foregoing instances, the judge hears evidence on the underlying question and decides whether the elements are met. Rule 104 is in accord with the traditional view[3] which is summarized by McCormick:

> . . . under the traditional view and the generally accepted principle the trial judge decides with finality those preliminary questions of fact upon which depends the admissibility of an item of evidence that is objected to under an exclusionary rule of evidence.[4]

§ 104.3   Limitations on Trial Judge's Role in Making Preliminary Determinations.

The trial judge's role in deciding preliminary questions of admissibility is limited by the provisions of Rule 104(b) pertaining to conditional relevancy. This restriction is discussed in § 104.6 *et seq.* of this Treatise. Rule 104(a) is further limited by the provisions of Rule 1008, a constituent rule of the so-called "best evidence rule." The "best evidence rule" generally requires production of an original writing, recording or photograph where the contents thereof are sought to be proved.[5] In certain situations where the original item is not available, contents may be proved through other "secondary" evidence. Rule 1004 specifies situations in which the original is not required. Each of these situations identified in Rule 1004 may provide the foundation for using secondary evidence. Rule 1008 incorporates this practice but limits it by designating certain determinations as jury questions. Accordingly, the jury, rather than the judge, ultimately decides "(a) whether the asserted writing ever existed, or (b) whether another writing, recording or photograph produced at the trial is the original, or (c) whether other evidence of contents correctly reflects the contents."[6]

The purpose of the limitation in Rule 1008 is discussed in the Advisory Committee's Note to Rule 1008: "Questions may arise which go beyond the mere administration of the rule preferring the original and into the merits of the controversy." As an example, the Note describes the situation in which the party opposing the introduction of secondary evidence of a contract argues that the contract never existed. The operation of Rule 1008 prevents the judge from disposing of the entire case by an admissibility determination that production of the original contract is not excused, *i.e.*, by a determination that none of the conditions of Rule 1004 is satisfied.

---

[3] *See, generally,* 1 WEINSTEIN, ¶ 104[02]; 1 LOUISELL & MUELLER, § 26; McCORMICK, § 53, at 121; 9 WIGMORE, § 2550, at 501.

[4] McCORMICK, § 53, at 121.

[5] Rule 1002.

[6] Rule 1008.

§ 104.4   Inapplicability of Rules of Evidence to Preliminary Admissibility Determinations.

The second sentence of Rule 104(a) provides that in making admissibility determinations, the court "is not bound by the rules of evidence except those with respect to privileges." This principle is also reflected in Rule 1101 which establishes the scope of the Rules. Rule 1101(d) provides: "The rules (other than with respect to privilege) do not apply in the following situations: (1) *Preliminary question of fact*. The determination of questions of fact preliminary to admissibility of evidence when the issue is to be determined by the court under rule 104."

In application, Rule 104(a) provides that the court may base its determination of admissibility upon evidence that is itself inadmissible under the Rules.[7] For example, it may base its ruling on hearsay statements in an affidavit or on an unauthenticated document. McCormick has endorsed the position of inapplicability of evidentiary rules to this determination as a matter of "sound sense,"[8] and it has also been described as a matter of "practical necessity" in certain situations.[9] For example, a declarant's otherwise inadmissible out-of-court statements may be considered in determining satisfaction of the subjective contemplation of death requirement for dying declaration hearsay exception.[10] Also, a child's potential testimony must be considered in determining the child's competency to testify. The effect of privileges, however, is expressly left intact and may not be set aside in the court's preliminary determinations.[11]

§ 104.5   Comment by Court on its Admissibility Ruling.

The Rules empower the trial judge to make determinations of admissibility under Rule 104(a) and to comment on such rulings under Rule 103(b). The latter Rule provides, in part: "at the time of making the ruling admitting or excluding evidence," the court may add any other or further statement which shows the character of the evidence, the form in which it was offered, the objection made, and the ruling thereon.

§ 104.6   Conditional Relevancy—Definition and Examples.

Rule 104(b) governs conditional relevancy, *i.e.*, the relevancy of evidence

[7] United States v. Whitten, 706 F.2d 1000, 1019 (9th Cir. 1983).

[8] McCormick, § 53, at 122 n.91.

[9] Rule 104, Advisory Committee's Note.

[10] *See* Rule 804(b)(2).

[11] The emphasis on the uniform applicability of the law of privilege at all stages of a proceeding is apparent from its frequent mention. *See* Rule 1101(c) and Rule 104(a).

that depends upon the establishment of other factual evidence as a condition. Lilly has described conditional relevancy in these terms:

> This more demanding standard [of Rule 104(b)] applies whenever the existence of one fact, A, conditions (is necessary for) the relevance of evidence of an allied fact, B. Put conversely, the relevance of allied fact B is dependant (conditioned) upon the existence of underlying fact A. In this circumstance, it is necessary to provide sufficient evidence of fact A to enable the trier to use the evidence of fact B for a consequential (material) purpose.[12]

In McCormick's example, proof that a swaying automobile passed a given spot at a certain time may be relevant in a negligence action only if it is also shown that the automobile was operated by the defendant.[13] The relevancy of the swaying vehicle is conditional because it depends upon further evidence which is probative of the identity of the operator. Rule 104(b) addresses the question of the sequencing of evidence as well as the respective roles of judge and jury, and in the context of McCormick's example, it provides that the conditional evidence regarding the operator of the vehicle may be submitted prior to or subsequent to the evidence of negligent conduct. Additionally, Rule 104(b) provides that the jury is to determine the ultimate relevancy of the swaying automobile where sufficient evidence of the conditional fact is adduced.

The issue of conditional relevancy frequently arises due to the necessity of offering evidence at trial which is not in logical sequence.[14] From such practice arises the need of "connecting up" the conditionally relevant evidence at a subsequent point in the trial. It is the judge's responsibility to assure that the proponent's order of evidence is acceptable, and he or she should seek assurances from counsel that admissible connecting evidence is forthcoming where such subsequent evidence is not self-apparent.[15]

§ 104.7 Jury's Role with Regard to Conditional Relevancy.

Normally, foundational or conditional evidence is directed exclusively to the trial judge under Rule 104(a). Where the one item of evidence is integrally connected to the relevancy of another item of evidence, however,

---

[12] LILLY, § 14, at 35.

[13] McCORMICK, § 58, at 133. Another example of conditional relevancy involves documents, the relevancy of which depends upon a finding of authenticity. Upon the proper threshold showing, the document may be submitted to the jury for ultimate determination as to authenticity and resulting relevancy. See § 901.1 of this Treatise.

[14] Rule 104(b), Advisory Committee's Note. See also McCORMICK, § 227, at 555. See Article IX.

[15] LILLY, § 14, at 37.

Rule 104(b) applies, and under Rule 104(b) the jury plays a role in assessing the conditional evidence. Where the proponent of conditionally relevant evidence introduces evidence that meets the threshold standard, *i.e.*, "sufficient to support a finding," the question of relevancy of the primary fact is left to the jury.[16] The rationale is explained by McCormick:

> When the conditional fact determines merely the relevancy of the offered fact there is no need for any special safe-guarding procedure [*i.e.*, leaving the determination to the court], for relevancy is a mere matter of probative pertinence which the jury understands and is willing to observe.[17]

The probative value of the offered fact may be disputed by the opposing party and will be an issue which the jury must decide.

The policy behind the Rule is similar to that supporting Rule 1008 concerning jury determination of secondary evidence offered in lieu of an original, *i.e.*, the trial judge is prevented from usurping the fact-finding function of the jury in the process of determining a preliminary matter of admissibility.[18] In instances involving conditional relevancy, the jury considers both the conditional fact and the offered fact in ascribing weight to the evidence.

§ 104.8   Role of the Judge with Regard to Evidence Admitted Subject to the Fulfillment of Condition of Fact ("Connecting Up").

Where objection is made to evidence on the ground of relevancy, and where the proponent offers to establish relevancy through subsequent evidence, Rule 104(b) authorizes the admission of the initially offered evidence subject to control by the trial judge. The court must determine whether evidence subsequently introduced is sufficient to support a finding of the fulfillment of the condition on which the relevancy of the initial evidence was premised. If the court determines that no sufficient evidence is subsequently introduced, it should withdraw the conditionally relevant evidence from the jury's determination.[19] The burden for requesting such action is on the opponent of the evidence who should make a motion to strike or a motion to withdraw the conditionally relevant fact from the jury

---

[16] McCORMICK, § 58, at 134.

[17] *Id.* § 53, at 125.

[18] Rule 104(b), Advisory Committee's Note. For further discussion of the principles underlying Rules 104(a) and 104(b), *see* Morgan, *Functions of Judge and Jury in the Determination of Preliminary Questions of Fact*, 43 HARV. L. REV. 165 (1929). *See, generally*, Ball, *The Myth of Conditional Relevancy*, 14 GA. L. REV. 435 (1980).

[19] Rule 104(b), Advisory Committee's Note.

once the proponent has rested without making a sufficient showing as to the conditional evidence.[20]

§ 104.9   Standard for Conditional Evidence Under Rule 104(b): Function of the Court.

Regardless of whether the conditional evidence precedes or succeeds the primary evidence, Rule 104(b) provides that the condition of fact must be established by "evidence sufficient to support a finding of the fulfillment of the condition." The conditional evidence must be sufficient to support a rational jury decision as to the existence of the conditional evidence.[21] Absent satisfaction of this standard as to the conditional fact, the conditionally connected evidence should not be submitted to the jury. If it is already submitted, it should be withdrawn. It is, of course, the function of the court to determine whether this threshold standard has been met.

§ 104.10   Forum for Conducting Admissibility Determinations.

Rule 104(c) addresses the methodology of the court's preliminary determinations of the admissibility of evidence, and it indicates whether such matters should be considered in the jury's presence. The effect of the Rule is to prevent the jury from hearing matters which may not be admitted into evidence but which may nonetheless influence its decision. Of similar import is Rule 103(c) which specifically embodies this concern: "In jury cases, proceedings shall be conducted, to the extent practicable, so as to prevent inadmissible evidence from being suggested to the jury . . . ."

Rule 104(c) contains a mandatory provision and a permissible provision. The mandatory provision concerns hearings on the admissibility of confessions in criminal cases. In this area, constitutional protections of due process and guarantees against self-incrimination dictate that hearings on the voluntariness, and hence, the admissibility of confessions be conducted by the court out of the hearing of the jury.[22] Absent insulation from jury consideration, there is an unacceptable risk that a confession found to be unconstitutionally obtained, and therefore inadmissible, might nonetheless influence the jury's deliberations.[23] The court is also required, when the

---

[20] McCormick, § 58, at 134.

[21] United States v. Terebecki, 692 F.2d 1345, 1349 (11th Cir. 1982).

[22] See Jackson v. Deno, 378 U.S. 368, 377, 84 S.Ct. 1774, 1785, 12 L.Ed.2d 908, 919 (1964).

[23] See Id. (The Court held as unconstitutional New York's procedure of allowing the jury to determine the voluntariness of a confession.)

accused who is a witness requests, to hold a preliminary hearing outside of the jury's presence on matters other than confessions.

In all other cases presence of the jury on preliminary matters is within the discretion of the trial judge consistent with the interests of justice.[24] There are occasions when no harm will result from the jury hearing foundational matters, and in such cases, convenience and time considerations are better served by not excusing the jury. Moreover, in many instances, the same evidence which is relevant to the foundation requirements is also relevant to weight and credibility. Allowing the jury to hear such foundational evidence avoids duplication of effort and waste of time.[25]

§ 104.11   Testimony of the Accused on Preliminary Matters.

The protective provision of Rule 104(d) allows an accused to testify as to a preliminary matter without exposing himself to wide-ranging cross-examination on subjects beyond the preliminary matter. The limited scope of cross-examination adopted in Rule 611(b) discussed *infra*, will work concurrently with Rule 104(d). Rule 104(d) also operates in concert with the accused's privilege against self-incrimination.[26]

§ 104.12   Limitation on the Protection Offered to the Accused.

Rule 104(d) states that the accused does not subject himself to cross-examination as to other issues in the case merely by testifying upon a preliminary matter. The Rule does not provide, however, that the accused may offer gratuitous testimony that goes beyond preliminary matters and escape cross-examination on such matters. The accused is subject to cross-examination on any matters he or she introduces that exceed the evidence necessary to resolve the preliminary matter.[27]

§ 104.13   Scope of Rule 104(d).

Rule 104(d) is limited specifically to the scope of cross-examination of an accused who testifies as to preliminary matters of admissibility. It does not address the issue of the extent to which such testimony may be subse-

---

[24] Rule 104(c), Advisory Committee's Note.

[25] *Id.*

[26] *See* McCORMICK, § 26, at 54.

[27] *See* Rule 104, Report of Senate Committee on the Judiciary.

quently used. The availability of such prior testimony for impeachment purposes is left to judicial determination.[28]

§ 104.14 Effect of Admissibility Determinations upon Probative Value.

Rule 104(e) is a clarifying provision concerning the effect of the prior sections of Rule 104, and it serves to emphasize the preliminary function of admissibility determinations made under subdivisions (a) and (b).

The fact that a particular item of evidence is determined to be admissible does not determine the probative value of such evidence.[29] The determination of the extent of probative value, which relates to evaluating the weight or credibility of evidence, is left to the jury. Accordingly, the opponent of any evidence is always free to introduce evidence for the purpose of affecting the credibility and weight of the evidence that has been received.

[28] *See, e.g.,* Simmons v. United States, 390 U.S. 377, 392, 88 S.Ct. 967, 976, 19 L.Ed.2d 1247, 1256 (1968) (defendant's testimony in support of a motion to suppress evidence on fourth amendment grounds not admissible against him at trial on the issue of guilt where he makes an appropriate objection). *See also* Harris v. New York, 401 U.S. 222, 224, 91 S.Ct. 643, 645, 28 L.Ed.2d 1, 4 (1971); Walder v. United States, 347 U.S. 62, 66, 74 S.Ct. 354, 356, 98 L.Ed.2d 503, 505 (1954).

[29] This rule complements Rule 104(a) and (b) in preserving the fact-finding function of the jury.

Chapter 105

RULE 105. LIMITED ADMISSIBILITY

Rule 105 reads as follows:

> When evidence which is admissible as to one party or for one purpose but not admissible as to another party or for another purpose is admitted, the court, upon request, shall restrict the evidence to its proper scope and instruct the jury accordingly.

§ 105.1   The Concept of Limited Admissibility.

Rule 105 embodies the doctrine of "limited admissibility."[1] For example, under Rule 404(b) evidence of other crimes, wrongs or acts is admissible to prove motive, opportunity, intent, etc. Such evidence is not, however, admissible to prove the character of a person in order to show that he acted in conformity with his character on a given occasion. Other examples are collected in the footnote.[2] Consequently, evidence of extrinsic acts must be

---

[1] *See, generally,* McCORMICK, §§ 56, 59; 1 WEINSTEIN, ¶¶ 105[01]-[05]; 1 LOUISELL & MUELLER, §§ 40-45; 1 WIGMORE, §§ 13.215, 216.5. *See also,* Note, *Co-defendant's Confessions,* 3 COLUM. L.J. & SOC. PROBS. 80 (1967); Note, *The Limiting Instruction — Its Effectiveness and Effect,* 51 MINN. L. REV. 264 (1966); Note, *Evidence Admissible for a Limited Purpose — The Risk of Confusion Upsetting the Balance of Advantage,* 16 SYRACUSE L. REV. 81 (1964).

[2] For other examples, *see* Rule 407 (subsequent remedial measures); Rule 408 (compromise and offers to compromise); Rule 409 (payment of medical and similar expenses); Rule 411 (liability insurance); Rule 608 (evidence of character and conduct of witness); Rule 609 (impeachment by evidence of conviction of crime); Rule 801 (hearsay and non-hearsay applications of out-of-court statements). All of the foregoing Rules illustrate that evidence may be admissible for one purpose while simultaneously remaining inadmissible for another. Evidence admitted under any of these Rules is subject to a limiting instruction upon the request of the opposing party. *See, generally,* United States v. Baron, 707 F.2d 125 (5th Cir. 1983).

properly channeled for consideration by the trier of fact in cases in which it is admitted. Rule 105 provides the basis for controlling such restricted consideration.

When evidence of limited admissibility is admitted by the trial judge, there exists the almost certain risk that, unless instructed otherwise, the jury will consider such evidence broadly as it relates to any issue or any party. To prevent this result, Rule 105 provides the mechanism by which the court educates the jury as to the permissible use of the evidence it has heard or seen.[3]

§ 105.2   Limiting Instructions.

Rule 105 provides for the "limiting instruction." Pursuant to this technique, the court instructs the jury on the limited purpose for which it may consider the admitted evidence. The Rule is triggered by a request for a limiting instruction[4] and it imposes a mandatory duty upon the court to issue the instruction when such a request is made.[5] The request may be made during the course of the trial or prior to trial where a party anticipates that an issue of limited admissibility will arise. In either case the request should be specific and in conformity with the directives of Rule 103(a) pertaining to rulings on evidence.[6] Nothing in the Rule prevents the trial judge from providing a limiting instruction *sua sponte* in the absence of a request by a party.[7]

§ 105.3   Relationship With Rule 403.

The function of Rule 105 must be considered in light of Rule 403 which provides for the exclusion of otherwise relevant evidence where the proba-

---

[3] *See, e.g.,* United States v. Eddy, 597 F.2d 430, 434-35 (5th Cir. 1979) (testimony by agent that co-defendant had told him he received forged checks from defendants was admissible to impeach co-defendant who had testified that he received checks from someone else; evidence was therefore not hearsay; trial court had properly instructed jury twice not to use testimony as evidence of defendant's guilt). *See also* Inmates of Nebraska Penal and Correctional Complex v. Greenholtz, 567 F.2d 1368, 1381 (8th Cir. 1977) (where evidence was not produced until surrebutter portion of defendant's case and was offered by plaintiffs for impeachment purposes, evidence was not sub-

stantively available to support inference of purposeful discrimination; citing Rule 105).

[4] Federal Rule 105 does not specify that the request must be made by a party. However, it is not clear from the Rule or from the Advisory Committee's Note who, other than a party, might make such a request.

[5] The Rule uses the word "shall." *See* Lubbock Feed Lots, Inc. v. Iowa Beef Processors, 630 F.2d 250, 266 (5th Cir. 1980) *reh. denied,* 634 F.2d 1355 (5th Cir. 1980) (but finding error harmless).

[6] *See* United States v. Dozier, 672 F.2d 531, 543 (5th Cir. 1982).

[7] LILLY, § 5, at 7.

tive value is substantially outweighed by countervailing negative influences. Accordingly, where, for example, the admission of evidence would cause unfair prejudice or confusion of the issues, such evidence may be excluded under Rule 403.[8] Part of the court's consideration in deciding whether to exclude evidence under Rule 403 should address an evaluation of the effectiveness of a limiting instruction under Rule 105 if the evidence were admitted.[9] Consequently, the proponent of evidence who evokes an objection based on Rule 403 should suggest that the court may obviate the adverse effect by giving the jury a limiting instruction. Conversely, a party who requests the exclusion of evidence under Rule 403 should be prepared to seek a limiting instruction should the court overrule the initial objection.

It should be noted that a limiting instruction may not be used in criminal trials in situations where an accused's constitutional rights would be jeopardized by the admission of evidence for a limited purpose. For example, a limiting instruction will not correct the constitutional error of admitting into evidence the confession of a non-testifying co-defendant when that confession implicates another defendant.[10]

[8] Rule 403. *See also* 1 WEINSTEIN, ¶ 105[01], at 105-3; 1 LOUISELL & MUELLER, § 40, at 283; MCCORMICK, § 59, at 136. *But cf.* United States v. De Carlo, 458 F.2d 358, 368, (3d Cir. 1972), *cert. denied*, 409 U.S. 843, 93 S.Ct. 107, 34 L.Ed.2d 83 (1972) (in extortion prosecution, evidence that alleged victim died of arsenic poisoning was received to shed light on state of mind of alleged victim, who was portrayed by other testimony as being "possessed by fear and capable of taking extreme action to secure the money needed to pay his debt and to protect his family;" since victim's fear was provable as a necessary element of the crime, it was proper to receive this evidence even though it might lead jury to wonder if defendants had murdered the alleged extortion victim or played a role in having him killed).

[9] *See* Rule 403, Advisory Committee's Note. *See also* Mauldin v. Upjohn Co., 697 F.2d 644, 648 (5th Cir. 1983).

[10] Bruton v. United States, 391 U.S. 123, 131, 88 S.Ct. 1620, 1628, 20 L.Ed.2d 476, 484 (1968), *cert. denied*, 397 U.S. 1014, 90 S.Ct. 1248, 25 L.Ed.2d 428 (1968). For an extensive discussion of *Bruton* and its progeny, *see* 1 WEINSTEIN, ¶ 105(4), 105-21 *et seq.*

Chapter 106

RULE 106. REMAINDER OF OR RELATED WRITINGS OR RECORDED STATEMENTS

Rule 106 reads as follows:

> When a writing or recorded statement or part thereof is introduced by a party, an adverse party may require him at that time to introduce any other part or any other writing or recorded statement which ought in fairness to be considered contemporaneously with it.

§ 106.1 Remainder of, or Related Writings or Recorded Statements.

When a party introduces a writing or recording into evidence, or any part thereof, the adverse party may require the party to introduce any other recording or writing, or the remainder of the evidence introduced, which in fairness should be considered contemporaneously with the admitted evidence.[1] Rule 106 is procedural in nature, requiring only that the complementary evidence be introduced at a time when it is needed to place the primary writing or recording into proper context or perspective. The Rule is limited to writings and recordings and does not pertain to oral statements.[2]

In practice, Rule 106 operates to avoid the need for an adverse party to wait until cross-examination or rebuttal to introduce the writing or recording, and it is intended to prevent consideration of matters out of context.[3]

---

[1] *See, generally,* McCORMICK, § 56; 1 WEINSTEIN, ¶¶ 106[01]-[04]; 1 LOUISELL & MUELLER, §§ 49-52; 7 WIGMORE, §§ 2094-2125. *See* Rule 32(a)(4), Federal Rules of Civil Procedure as to depositions.

[2] United States v. Terry, 702 F.2d 299, 321 (2d Cir. 1938), *cert. denied sub nom.* Williams v. United States, 454 U.S. 866, 103 S.Ct. 2095, 77 L.Ed.2d 304 (1983). As to testimonial completeness, *see* Rule 611. *See also* United States v. Pintar, 630 F.2d 1270, 1283-84 (8th Cir. 1980) (doctrine of verbal completeness expressed in Rule 106

has no application where prosecution witness impeached for bias, and government witness seeks to show additional reasons for her hostility to defendants).

[3] *See, e.g.,* Huddleston v. Herman & MacLean, 640 F.2d 534, 553 (5th Cir. 1981), *mod. on other grounds, en banc,* 456 U.S. 914, 102 S.Ct. 1766, 72 L.Ed.2d 173 (1982) (since Rule 106 is made specifically applicable to depositions, defendants were entitled to introduce other portions of deposition relating to same matter dealt with in portion of deposition introduced by

Obviously, the Rule contemplates a very high degree of discretion to be exercised by the trial judge in applying the term "fairness" set forth in the Rule.[4]

Evidence admissible solely under Rule 106 is to be used for the limited purpose expressed in the Rule. A limiting instruction, if requested under Rule 105, is appropriate to prevent the jury from improperly using the evidence.[5]

---

plaintiff; hearsay objections may be made when deposition is introduced into evidence). *See, generally*, 1 WEINSTEIN, ¶ 106, at 106-15. *See also* United States v. Jamar, 561 F.2d 1103, 1108-1109 (4th Cir. 1977) (on perjury charge growing out of defendant's testimony at preliminary hearing it was not error for government to introduce transcript of defendant's testimony without introducing testimony of other witnesses, including defendant's daughter; "the purpose of Rule 106 . . . is to permit the contemporaneous introduction of recorded statements that place in context other writings admitted into evidence, which, viewed alone, may be misleading . . . there is no such problem here").

[4] United States v. Weisman, 624 F.2d 1118, 1128 (2d Cir. 1980) (trial court did not err in refusing to admit tape recordings introduced by the prosecution in their entirety where the omitted portions were not "necessary to clarify, or make not misleading, that which is introduced"). *See also*

United States v. Enright, 579 F.2d 980, 985-86 (6th Cir. 1978). *See, generally,* 7 WIGMORE, § 2094. Failure to apply Rule 106 into an accused's recorded statement can result in reversible error despite the high level of discretion afforded the trial judge. *See, e.g.,* United States v. Walker, 652 F.2d 708, 713-14 (7th Cir. 1981).

[5] See Chapter 105 of this Treatise. While this issue is not without debate, it appears that otherwise inadmissible evidence may be exposed to the jury where "in fairness" the trier of fact should receive the evidence under Rule 106. *See* 1 LOUISELL & MUELLER, § 49, at 356-57, noting that Rule 403 may operate to preempt the application of Rule 106 in this context. *But see* United States v. Costner, 684 F.2d 370, 373 (6th Cir. 1982) ("[R]ule 106 is intended to eliminate the misleading impression created by taking a statement out of context; the rule covers an order of proof problem; it is not designated to make something admissible that should be excluded").

II
JUDICIAL NOTICE

Chapter 201

RULE 201. JUDICIAL NOTICE OF ADJUDICATIVE FACTS

Rule 201 reads as follows:

(a) **Scope of Rule.** This rule governs only judicial notice of adjudicative facts.

(b) **Kinds of Facts.** A judicially noticed fact must be one not subject to reasonable dispute in that it is either (1) generally known within the territorial jurisdiction of the trial court or (2) capable of accurate and ready determination by resort to sources whose accuracy cannot reasonably be questioned.

(c) **When Discretionary.** A court may take judicial notice, whether requested or not.

(d) **When Mandatory.** A court shall take judicial notice if requested by a party and supplied with the necessary information.

(e) **Opportunity to be Heard.** A party is entitled upon timely request to an opportunity to be heard as to the propriety of taking judicial notice and the tenor of the matter noticed. In the absence of prior notification, the request may be made after judicial notice has been taken.

(f) **Time of Taking Notice.** Judicial notice may be taken at any stage of the proceeding.

(g) **Instructing Jury.** In a civil action or proceeding, the court shall instruct the jury to accept as conclusive any fact judicially noticed. In a criminal case, the court shall instruct the jury that it may, but is not required to, accept as conclusive any fact judicially noticed.

§ 201.1   Judicial Notice of Adjudicative Facts—In General.

Judicial notice is the evidentiary process by which a court recognizes a fact in the absence of any antecedent, formal proof.[1] It is a substitute for formal proof where, under the circumstances of a particular case, an adjudicative fact sought to be proved is reasonably beyond dispute. Where the fact sought to be noticed is reasonably indisputable, the normal standards of formal proof, if held to apply, would impede judicial efficiency by erecting unwarranted barriers to the party seeking to establish the fact. In this regard, the policy of judicial notice permits the court to accept evidence through an alternate process of admission without sacrificing the fundamental safeguards of the adversary system.[2] In operation, judicial notice does nothing to cast aside the basic standards upon which the system of evidence is predicated. Rather, judicial notice represents a realistic appraisal that certain facts present virtually none of the risks the usual safeguards are designed to protect, and consequently, the need for formal proof is largely absent where the standard of Rule 201 is satisfied.[3]

In essence, judicial notice supersedes formal proof, yet it carries equal force. As such, the doctrine of judicial notice is applicable to circumstantially relevant facts as well as to ultimate facts of any case, civil or criminal, although the jury may be under varying instructions depending upon the nature and significance of the fact judicially noticed.

[1] *See, generally,* McCORMICK, §§ 328-335; 1 WEINSTEIN ¶¶ 201[01]-[08]; 1 LOUISELL & MUELLER, §§ 56-60; 9 WIGMORE, §§ 2565-2583. *See also* O'Brien, *Of Judicial Myths, Motivations and Justifications: A Postscript on Social Science and the Law,* 64 JUDICATURE 285 (1981); Comment, *The Presently Expanding Concept of Judicial Notice,* 13 VILL. L. REV. 528, 530 (1969); Roberts, *Preliminary Notes Toward a Study of Judicial Notice,* 52 CORNELL L.Q. 210 (1967). As Rule 201(a) expressly provides, the Rule only pertains to judicial notice of "adjudicative facts." This chapter is likewise limited in scope. Rule 44.1, Federal Rules of Civil Procedure and Rule 26.1, Federal Rule of Criminal Procedure pertain to judicial notice of foreign law. Judicial notice of "legislative facts" is not codified. *See* Rule 201, Advisory Committee's Note. Other types of facts, of which a court may take cognizance in the absence of formal proof, are also outside the scope of the Rule. *See* Rule 201, Advisory Committee's Note. *See, generally,* Morgen, *Judicial Notice,* 36 HARV. L. REV. 269 (1944).

[2] *See* Rule 201, Advisory Committee's Note.

[3] *See* 1 LOUISELL & MUELLER, § 56, at 393-395; 1 WEINSTEIN, ¶ 201[01], at 201-14 to 201-15. *See also* Davis, *A System of Judicial Notice Based on Fairness and Convenience,* PERSP. OF LAW 69, 82 (1964); Davis, *Judicial Notice,* 55 COLUM. L. REV. 945 (1955).

§ 201.2 "Adjudicative" Versus "Legislative" Facts.

On its face, Rule 201(a) limits the scope of the Rule to the judicial notice of "adjudicative facts." Put simply, adjudicative facts are those facts which concern the burdens of proof of the case as they pertain to the immediate parties and to the outcome of the litigation. Such facts reveal who did what to whom, when and where it occurred, and how and why it occurred.[4] Adjudicative facts are normally established through formal proof and only exceptionally through judicial notice.

By comparison, "legislative" facts are those facts which are employed by the court in the decisional process of a case in the expansion of the common law or in the interpretation, construction and extension of legislative enactments.[5] When courts make new law, or "legislate," they inevitably rely upon policy assumptions concerning the operation of the law and its impact on society. These policy assumptions, which are largely factual in nature, are denominated "legislative facts." Generally, these factual assumptions are not made the subject of formal proof and the court takes cognizance of them merely by "noticing" them.

The label "legislative fact" is primarily significant in distinguishing such facts from adjudicative facts in the context of judicial notice. This distinction is important because "indisputably" is a requirement only for notice of adjudicative facts. The indisputability standard does not attach to legislative facts which a court might judicially notice in extending or expanding the law.[6]

§ 201.3 Qualification of Adjudicative Facts.

Subdivision (b) of Rule 201 delineates the necessary conditions for a court to take judicial notice of adjudicative facts. An adjudicative fact is subject to judicial notice if it is not subject to dispute or uncertainty[7] be-

---

[4] *E.g.*, Finley v. United States, 314 F. Supp. 905, 915-16 (1970); 2 DAVIS, ADMINISTRATIVE LAW TREATISE, § 15.03 (1958).

[5] Davis, *Judicial Notice*, 55 COLUM. L. REV. 945, 952 (1955). *See, generally,* 1 WEINSTEIN, ¶ 200[03], at 200-13 *et seq.* Judge Weinstein points out that: "Requiring formal proof of legislative facts would be inhibiting, time consuming and expensive. . . . The judges may seek information from the parties via briefs, request the aid of amicus curiae or conduct independent research of their own." *Id.* at 200-14. *See also* Personnel Adm. of Mass. v. Fenney, 442

U.S. 256, 99 S.Ct. 2282, 60 L.Ed.2d 870 (1979); Alexander v. Youngstown Bd. of Educ., 454 F. Supp. 985, 988 (D.C. Ohio 1978).

[6] *See* 1 WEINSTEIN, ¶ 200[03], at 200-15; 1 LOUISELL & MUELLER, § 56, at 395. *See also* Karst, *Legislative Facts in Constitutional Litigation*, 1960 SUP. CT. REV. 75. *See, generally,* McCORMICK, § 331, at 766-69.

[7] *See, e.g.*, Datlof v. United States, 252 F. Supp. 11, 23 (E.D. Pa. 1966) *cert. denied*, 387 U.S. 906, 87 S.Ct. 1688, 18 L.Ed.2d 624 (1967) (judicial notice taken

cause it is well-known within the trial court's jurisdiction.[8] In the alternative, notice is appropriate if the fact is capable of ready and accurate determination by resort to a reasonably reliable source.[9]

Rule 201(b)(1) applies to reasonably indisputable adjudicative facts generally known within the trial court's jurisdiction. Certain kinds of facts are part of the structure and function of the court itself and are peculiarly within the purview of judicial notice.[10] Beyond facts relating specifically to the court, the appropriateness of judicial notice is measured by the general notoriety of facts. The fact subject to notice must be within the general knowledge of reasonably well-informed people within the territorial jurisdiction of the trial court. The Rule should be interpreted to permit the court to take judicial notice of those adjudicative facts which are, or should be, known to people of reasonable intelligence within the trial court's jurisdiction.[11]

Where general notoriety within the jurisdiction does not attend the fact sought to be noticed, Rule 201(b)(2) provides for judicial notice if the fact is subject to accurate and ready determination. The critical feature of this provision is that it shifts the test from common knowledge to that of verifiable accuracy.[12] If the fact is not commonly known, it may nevertheless be

that October 5, 1955 was a Wednesday); Wansley v. Wilkerson, 263 F. Supp. 54, 58 (W.D. Va. 1967) (judicial notice taken of 4 year delay before trial being due to efforts of petitioner rather than the government).

[8] See Eden Toys, Inc. v. Marshall Field & Co., 675 F.2d 498, 500 n.1 (2d Cir. 1982). See also United States v. Blunt, 558 F.2d 1245, 1246 (6th Cir. 1977) (district court would have been correct in taking judicial notice that the Federal Correctional Institution at Lexington, Kentucky was within the territorial jurisdiction of the United States); United States v. Dolan, 544 F.2d 1219, 1223 n.8 (4th Cir. 1976) (judicial notice taken that PCP is another name for phencyclidine, a controlled substance). See, e.g., Otto v. Alper, 489 F. Supp. 953 (D. Del. 1980); Caufield v. Board of Ed. of City of New York, 486 F. Supp. 862, 864 (E.D.N.Y. 1980); United States v. Fatico, 441 F. Supp. 1285, 1288 (E.D.N.Y. 1977), rev'd on other grounds, 579 F.2d 707 (2d Cir. 1978), on remand, 458 F. Supp. 388 (E.D.N.Y. 1978).

[9] E.g., KVUE, Inc. v. Austin Broadcasting Corp., 709 F.2d 922, 929-30 (5th Cir. 1983); Reiner v. Washington Plate Glass

Co., Inc., 711 F.2d 414, 416 (D.C. Cir. 1983).

[10] Commodity Futures Trading Commission v. Co/Petro Marketing Group, Inc., 680 F.2d 573, 584 (9th Cir. 1982); ITT Rayonier, Inc. v. United States, 651 F.2d 343, 345 n.2 (5th Cir. 1981).

[11] McCORMICK, § 329, at 922.

[12] See Commonwealth of Massachusetts v. Wescott, 431 U.S. 322, 326, 97 S.Ct. 1755, 1760, 52 L.Ed.2d 349, 353 (1977) (judicial notice taken of Coast Guard Records); Coast Indian Community v. United States, 550 F.2d 639, 645 (Ct. Cl. 1977) (judicial notice taken of voter's roster that was published in the newspaper). See also Government of Canal Zone v. Burjan, V., 596 F.2d 690, 693 (5th Cir. 1979); Davis v. Freels, 583 F.2d 337, 339 (7th Cir. 1978); State v. Hawkins, 566 F.2d 1006, 1008 (5th Cir. 1978), cert. denied, 439 U.S. 848, 99 S.Ct. 150, 58 L.Ed.2d 151 (1978). Cf., Association Against Discrimination in Employment, Inc. v. City of Bridgeport, 647 F.2d 256, 277-78 (2d Cir. 1981), cert. denied, 455 U.S. 988, 102 S.Ct. 1611, 71 L.Ed.2d 847 (1982).

noticed so long as it is capable of instant and reasonable demonstration.[13] Most notably, this application of judicial notice has been used to obtain recognition of historical and geographical facts or scientific and medical principles. It has been used to justify, for example, the evidentiary use of dates, natural and political boundaries, positions of public figures, blood tests, ballistics, fingerprints, handwriting, and typewriter analysis.[14]

Representative authoritative sources for verification include such reference materials as historical works, science and art books, language and medical journals and dictionaries, calendars, encyclopedias, commercial lists and directories, maps and charts, statutes and legislative reports.[15]

§ 201.4   Judicial Knowledge Versus Judicial Notice.

Judicial notice of adjudicative facts in any particular case is not determined or circumscribed by the personal knowledge of the individual court. It is inconsequential that matters of judicial cognizance are actually known or unknown to the judge. As long as the facts are a proper subject for notice, the judge may be informed of the indisputability of the facts in any reasonable way. Likewise, facts which are not subject to judicial cognizance must be proved, even though personally known to the court to be true.[16]

The rule is similar with respect to jurors. Unlike the early stages of common law, under modern practice jurors are selected because of their supposed unfamiliarity with, and disinterest in the litigation. Accordingly, in the absence of admissible evidence on the subject, jurors may not predicate a finding of fact upon their peculiar knowledge or experience.[17] In according weight to the evidence and credibility to witnesses, however, jurors are expected to employ their own common experience and observation of human nature.

---

[13] United States v. Garcia, 672 F.2d 1349, 1356-57 (11th Cir. 1982); Terrebone v. Blackburn, 646 F.2d 997, 1000 n.4 (5th Cir. 1981).

[14] See 1 WEINSTEIN, ¶ 201[03], at 201-23 et seq. See also Patrick v. Sharon Steel Corp., 549 F. Supp. 1259, 1268-69 (N.D. W. Va. 1982). See, generally, 1 LOUISELL & MUELLER, § 57, at 440 et seq.

[15] Harrington v. Vandalia-Butler Bd. of Education, 649 F.2d 434, 441 (6th Cir. 1981); United States v. Salinas, 611 F.2d 128, 130 (5th Cir. 1980); Florida Power and Light Co. v. Castle, 650 F.2d 579, 589 (5th Cir. 1981).

[16] Hardy v. Johns-Manville Sales Corporation, 681 F.2d 334, 347-48 (5th Cir. 1982). See also United States v. Bramble, 641 F.2d 681, 683 (9th Cir. 1981) (no judicial notice taken that 21 marijuana plants in a hot house in defendant's yard must have been grown for purposes of sale; not common knowledge to members of panel); United States v. Baker, 641 F.2d 1311, 1313 (9th Cir. 1981) (no judicial notice taken that anyone who is a gill netter and resident of Washington knows of injunction).

[17] Beverly Hills Fire Litigation, 695 F.2d 207, 209 (6th Cir. 1982), cert. denied, 103 S.Ct. 2090 (1983).

§ 201.5   Discretionary Versus Mandatory Judicial Notice.

In subdivision (c), Rule 201 provides that the court may *sua sponte* take judicial notice of adjudicative facts under the proper circumstances at any time during the course of the proceedings.[18] The taking of judicial notice under this provision rests within the sound discretion of the trial court, and such determinations may only be disturbed upon a finding of an abuse of the discretion.[19]

Subdivision (d) places upon the trial court the express duty of taking judicial notice of any adjudicative fact where the proponent of the evidence advances information or documentation demonstrating the fact to be reasonably indisputable. Naturally, this provision operates almost exclusively within the context of proving those facts which are capable of ready and accurate verification, since, in the main, such supporting data would not be useful or required where the fact is commonly known by persons of reasonable intelligence in the community.[20] While Rule 201(d) mandates the court to take judicial notice when it is "supplied with the necessary information," the nature and quality of information or documentation that is sufficient to establish the veracity of a fact is, in the end, a matter of discretion with the trial court. As is the case under Rule 201(c), this function of the trial court, and any subsequent rulings on the admission of adjudicative facts, will not be invaded by a reviewing court absent a clear showing of an abuse of discretion and prejudice.[21]

§ 201.6   Hearing In Support Or Opposition.

Basic considerations of procedural fairness demand an opportunity to be heard on the propriety of taking judicial notice and the nature of the matter to be noticed. On its face, the Rule requires the granting of an opportunity to be heard upon request. The Rule is not limited to the party against whom the fact is offered, and it is equally available to the party offering the matter to be noticed. No formal scheme of hearing nor any procedure for giving notice to adverse parties is provided or contemplated.[22] Consequently, the Rule is flexible in its nonspecificity, and it is

[18] *See* Eden Toys, Inc. v. Marshall Field & Company, 675 F.2d 498, 500 (2d Cir. 1982) (summary judgment); United States v. Bliss, 649 F.2d 390, 392 n.2 (10th Cir. 1981) (court declined to take judicial notice at appellate level).

[19] Eagle-Picher Industries, Inc. v. Liberty Mutual Insurance Co., 682 F.2d 12, 22, n.8 (1st Cir. 1982).

[20] *See* Clark v. South Central Bell Tel. Co., 419 F. Supp. 697, 704 (W.D. L.A.

1976) (no judicial notice taken of black/white labor force in race employment discrimination case, since it was not a matter of general knowledge; no facts or reliable sources placed before the court).

[21] M/V American Queen v. San Diego Manne Const. Corp., 708 F.2d 1483, 1485 (9th Cir. 1983).

[22] *See* 1 Weinstein, ¶ 201[05], at 201-40; 1 Louisell & Mueller, § 59, at 461.

clearly intended to permit the trial court, in the exercise of its sound discretion, to manage such matters in an *ad hoc* fashion. Accordingly, the time for making a request to be heard on the subject, depending upon the peculiarities of any given case, is also flexible. Accordingly, in the absence of advance notice, an adversely affected party may request a hearing either contemporaneously with the taking of notice or even after the fact. And, in the absence of prior notice, a request made after the fact could not fairly be held to be untimely.[23]

The requirement that a hearing be afforded the affected parties is fundamentally consistent with the directive contained in Rule 201(b) which requires that only those adjudicative facts reasonably beyond dispute are amenable to judicial notice.

§ 201.7　Time Of Taking Judicial Notice.

In accord with the prevailing view and pre-Rule Federal law, judicial notice of adjudicative facts may be taken at any stage in the proceedings, whether during the trial or on appeal.[24] Judicial notice may be taken during the course of the presentation of formal evidence, during pretrial conference, or after the evidence is closed. Subdivision (f) is a natural complement to subdivision (e) in providing that judicial notice remains available to any court, subject only to subdivision (b)(1) on the appellate level, *i.e.*, the common knowledge basis for notice applies to the territorial jurisdiction of the trial court, not the appellate court.

Although the procedure may be applied to any adjudicative fact, reviewing courts frequently resort to judicial notice of adjudicative facts to fill in trivial factual gaps in the record as transmitted by the parties. An appellate court may judicially notice any fact which the lower court could have noticed, and where the appellate court is presented with an appeal from a judgment that is entirely correct, except for the absence of some indisputable but essential fact, the court may affirm the judgment by taking judicial notice of the missing fact.[25] This procedure is considered preferable to remanding the cause on the basis of the defect in the record; the trial court and the parties are not made to suffer an unreasonable and time-consum-

---

[23] 1 LOUISELL & MUELLER, § 58, at 445.

[24] United States v. Lavender, 602 F.2d 639, 641 (4th Cir. 1979); Jones v. Illinois Department of Rehabilitation Services, 689 F.2d 724, 728 (7th Cir. 1978).

[25] *See* Ives Laboratories, Inc. v. Darby Drug Co., 638 F.2d 538, 544 n.8 (2d Cir. 1981) (appellate court took notice of facts which indicated that premise of trial judge's decision had no support); Govern-

ment of Canal Zone v. Burjan, V., 596 F.2d 690, 692 (5th Cir. 1979) (appellate court took judicial notice of geographical boundaries). *But cf.*, Melong v. Micronesian Claims Commission, 643 F.2d 10, 12 n.5 (D.C. Cir. 1980) (appellate court did not take judicial notice of 172 pages of unauthenticated documentary material; material submitted did not satisfy Rule 201).

ing impediment to final disposition of the matter on the merits. However, where the adjudicative fact is of such magnitude as to be critical to the outcome of the case, and the fact is not commonly known but arguably capable of accurate demonstration, appellate courts tend to avoid the available curative route of judicial notice. Most frequently in this situation, the case is remanded so that a complete record may be presented to the reviewing court.[26]

§ 201.8 Jury Instructions.

Subdivision (g) of Rule 201 follows the common law principle that once a fact has been judicially noticed in a civil action, it is conclusive. The adverse party may not introduce evidence to contradict the noticed fact.[27] Accordingly, the jury in a civil case must be specifically instructed as to the conclusive nature of the evidence received pursuant to judicial notice. Because judicial notice of a given fact relieves the proponent of the burden of presenting formal proof, it might seem that the opposing party should be at liberty to present contradictory evidence to the trier of fact on the point in an attempt to defeat the noticed fact. Nevertheless, it is clear under the Rule that the appropriate time for such contradictory evidence is when the matter is heard by the trial judge in the first instance under Rule 201(e).

It should be noted that when the court hears evidence in opposition to judicial notice, the evidence heard in this context goes to the limited issue of whether or not notice should be made. Frequently, however, in addressing the issue, the opponent of the noticed fact will offer evidence which seeks to demonstrate the falsity of the fact in question. Consequently, the issue of appropriateness of judicial notice in a civil case is always won or lost before the judge, not the trier of fact. But in deciding whether notice is warranted, the court often considers whether the opponent of the fact has contradicting evidence available which might be presented through the medium of formal proof. Such contradicting evidence would demonstrate that the fact is disputable and not subject to notice. Nevertheless, in civil cases where the judge has ruled on the appropriateness of notice and has determined that notice is proper, the jury will be instructed that judicially noticed facts are conclusive upon the parties to the litigation.[28]

[26] E.g., Reiner v. Washington Plate Glass Co., Inc., 711 F.2d 414, 417 (D.C. Cir. 1983).

[27] 1 WEINSTEIN, ¶ 201[07], at 201-49 to 201-51; 1 LOUISELL & MUELLER, § 60, at 493-494. See also Davis, A System of Judicial Notice Based on Fairness and Convenience, PERSP. OF LAW 69, 77 (1964).

[28] 1 WEINSTEIN, ¶ 201[07], at 201-51. See, e.g., Morgan, Judicial Notice, 57 HARV. L. REV. 269, 279 (1944); Keefe, Landis, and Shaad, Sense and Nonsense About Judicial Notice, 2 STAN. L. REV. 664, 668 (1950). See also McCORMICK, § 332.

In a criminal case the Rule reinforces the principle that a conviction may only rest upon a finding that each element of the charged offense has been proved beyond a reasonable doubt and that a verdict will not be directed against the accused.[29] Accordingly, Rule 201 provides that where the judicially noticed fact represents an element of the charged crime, the jury must be instructed that the taking of judicial notice provides that the jury may, but is not required to, accept as conclusive any fact judicially noticed. Despite the conceptual foundation that judicially noticed facts are only those which are notorious or beyond reasonable dispute, the accused has the procedural opportunity to present evidence to the trier of fact which is directly contradictory to the judicially noticed fact. For example, where an essential element of rape is the fact that the victim is not the spouse of the accused, the court may take judicial notice of this fact based upon the absence of any record of a valid marriage license. Nonetheless, the accused may introduce evidence to contradict this fact by showing that the records were destroyed or that a common law marriage existed at the time of the alleged offense. Under the Rule, the jury may resolve this issue in favor of either party and the judge must instruct the jury accordingly.

§ 201.9   Selected Matters Judicially Noticed.

Under the rubric of judicial notice, courts have taken notice of facts concerning cities, towns, villages and school districts, such as their populations[30] or the effect of the national economy upon the region,[31] centers of specific types of industrial or commercial enterprises,[32] the rate or flow of vehicular or pedestrian traffic,[33] locations or buildings, parks, streets and commercial centers,[34] the condition of prisons,[35] and the incidence of tor-

---

[29] United Brotherhood of Carpenters & Joiners v. United States, 330 U.S. 395, 400, 67 S.Ct. 775, 779, 91 L.Ed. 973, 977 (1947) (the trial court cannot constitutionally direct a verdict of guilty against the accused). *See also* 9 Wigmore, § 2495, at 312.

[30] Castilleja v. Southern Pacific Co., 445 F.2d 183, 185 (5th Cir. 1971).

[31] Mainline Inv. Corp. v. Gaines, 407 F. Supp. 423, 426-27 (D.C. Tex 1976); Fox v. Kane-Miller Corp., 398 F. Supp. 609, 651 (D.C. Md. 1975).

[32] D.A. Shulte, Inc. v. Gangi, 328 U.S. 108, 113, 66 S.Ct. 925, 930, 90 L.Ed. 1114, 1119 (1946); Knollman v. United States, 214 F.2d 106, 108 (1954); United States v.

Underwood, 344 F. Supp. 486, 488 (D.C. Fla. 1972).

[33] See United States v. Dreos, 156 F. Supp. 200, 208 (D.C. Md. 1957) ("It is sufficient to show that the equipment has been properly tested and checked, that it was manned by a competent operator, that proper operative procedures were followed, and that proper records were kept").

[34] United States v. Hughes, 542 F.2d 246, 248 n.1 (5th Cir. 1976); Otto v. Alper, 489 F. Supp. 953, 954-55 (D. Del. 1980).

[35] Falzerano v. Collier, 535 F. Supp. 800, 801 (D.N.J. 1982); United States v. Lucchetti, 533 F.2d 28, 37-38 (2d Cir. 1976).

ture and murder in foreign countries.[36] Judicial notice may be taken either because the fact offered is commonly known within the jurisdiction or because it is readily capable of being accurately demonstrated to a reasonable certainty.

Similarly, facts relating to the course and laws of nature, qualities and properties of matter, organic or inorganic, scientific, technological, or mechanical, principles and processes and normal human experiences, are all readily susceptible to being noticed judicially as adjudicative facts in any appropriate case. Accordingly, notice has been taken of such things as the effects of certain drugs, alcohol and medicinal compounds,[37] properties of burning substances,[38] general statistical data on the distance required to permit a car to stop,[39] the phenomena of animal and vegetable life,[40] and the development of disease in humans.[41] Geographical, historical, and political and linguistic facts, such as the location and topographical characteristics of lakes, streams, mountains and navigable waters,[42] distance between places,[43] public events of local or worldwide notoriety,[44] time, days

[36] Orantes Hernandez v. Smith, 541 F. Supp. 351, 358 (C.D. Cal. 1982). *But see* Abu Eain v. Adams, 529 F. Supp. 685, 692 (N.D. Ill. 1980).

[37] Jaffe v. United States, 592 F.2d 712, 720 (3d Cir. 1979); Miller Brewing Co. v. G. Heilemann Brewing Co., 561 F.2d 75, 81 n.11 (7th Cir. 1977).

[38] Goodman v. Stalfort, Inc., 411 F. Supp. 889, 893-94 (D.C. N.J. 1976).

[39] Jamison v. Kline, 454 F.2d 1256, 1257 (3d Cir. 1972) (proper to receive in evidence testimony by a state trooper based in part upon a speed chart; the chart was a reduction to usable form of the speed of the vehicle, and was a proper subject for judicial notice). *See also* Clayton v. Rimmer, 262 N.C. 302, 304, 136 S.E.2d 562, 564 (1964); Brown v. Hale, 263 N.C. 176, 139 S.E.2d 210 (1964).

[40] Golaris v. Jewel Tea Co., 22 FRD 16, 20 (D.C. Ill. 1958) (user of pork charged with obligation of cooking meat to the point of killing the trichinae; courts adhere to the concept of caveat emptor in this particular circumstance); Long v. United States, 241 F. Supp. 286, 289 (D.C. S.C. 1965) (court took judicial notice of fact that livestock are easily frightened by sudden loud noises and by objects which are propelled directly over their heads, thereby making defendant guilty of negligence

which was the proximate cause of plaintiff's injuries when an armed forces helicopter passed overhead at tree level, the blades of a mule-drawn mower almost amputating plaintiff's leg).

[41] Bey v. Bolger, 540 F. Supp. 910, 916 (E.D. Pa. 1982). *See also* Franklin Life Insurance Co. v. William J. Champion & Co., 350 F.2d 115, 130 (6th Cir. 1965), *reh. denied*, 353 F.2d 919 (6th Cir. 1965), *cert. denied*, 384 U.S. 928, 86 S.Ct. 1445, 16 L.Ed.2d 531 (1966) (judicial notice taken of the fact that cancer does not manifest itself to the person afflicted with it until it suddenly affects a vital part of the body, rather than making itself known in the beginning stages; therefore it often results in death even though the best treatment available is given upon discovery of the disease). *See, e.g.*, Goodman v. Stalfort, Inc., 411 F. Supp. 889, 893-94 (D.C. N.J. 1976).

[42] United States v. Garcia, 672 F.2d 1349, 1356 (11th Cir. 1982); Farmland Preservation Asso. v. Goldschmidt, 611 F.2d 233, 237 (8th Cir. 1979).

[43] United States v. Baborian, 528 F. Supp. 324, 332 (D.R.I. 1981); United States v. Lavender, 602 F.2d 639, 641 (4th Cir. 1979).

[44] Pratt v. Kelly, 585 F.2d 692, 696-97 (4th Cir. 1978).

and dates,[45] weights, measures and values,[46] offices held by persons,[47] and meanings of abbreviations and definitions contained in standard dictionaries[48] are all subject to judicial notice. Further, notice may be taken of human life, health, habits, customs and usages as well as matters of art and skill.[49] The court may also be willing to take judicial notice of the doctrine or purpose of an organization.[50]

[45] *See* Allen v. Allen, 518 F. Supp. 1234, 1235-36 (E.D. Pa. 1981).

[46] *See* Varlack v. SWC Caribbean, Inc., 550 F.2d 171, 178 (3d Cir. 1977).

[47] Orlando v. Wizel, 443 F. Supp. 744, 749 (W.D. Ark. 1978).

[48] *See*, *e.g.*, Palmer v. Sun Oil Co., 78 F. Supp. 38, 52-53 (D.C. Ohio 1948).

[49] *See*, *e.g.*, Lucerne Products, Inc. v. Cutler-Hammer, Inc., 568 F.2d 784, 798 (6th Cir. 1977).

[50] United Klans of America v. McGovern, 453 F. Supp. 836, 838-39 (N.D. Ala. 1978), *aff'd*, 621 F.2d 152 (5th Cir. 1980); United States v. Crenshaw County Unit of United Klans, 290 F. Supp. 181, 182 n.1 (D.C. 1968).

III
PRESUMPTIONS

Chapter 301

RULE 301. PRESUMPTIONS IN GENERAL IN CIVIL ACTIONS AND PROCEEDINGS

Rule 301 reads as follows:

> In all civil actions and proceedings not otherwise provided for by Act of Congress or by these rules, a presumption imposes on the party against whom it is directed the burden of going forward with evidence to rebut or meet the presumption, but does not shift to such party the burden of proof in the sense of the risk of nonpersuasion, which remains throughout the trial upon the party on whom it was originally cast.

§ 301.1 Presumptions In Civil Actions—In General.

Rule 301 governs the effect of presumptions on the allocation of the burden of proof in civil actions and other civil proceedings.[1] Its scope is limited, and in conjunction with Rule 302, its provisions are inapplicable to: (a) presumptions governed by state law; (b) presumptions directed against a criminal defendant; and (c) presumptions governed by congres-

---

[1] See, generally, McCORMICK, §§ 336-348; 1 WEINSTEIN ¶¶ 301[01]-[04]; 1 LOUISELL & MUELLER, §§ 65-73; 9 WIGMORE, §§ 2483-2493. See also Allen, Presumptions, Inferences and Burden of Proof in Federal Civil Actions — An Anatomy of Unnecessary Ambiguity and a Proposal for Reform, 75 NW. U.L. REV. 892 (1983); Allen, Presumptions in Civil Actions Reconsidered, 66 IOWA L. REV. 843 (1981); Gordon and Tenebaum, Conclusive Presumption Analysis: The Principle of Individual Opportunity, 71 NW. U.L. REV. 579 (1977); Louisell, Construing Rule 301: Instructing the Jury on Presumptions in Civil Actions and Proceedings, 63 VA. L. REV. 281 (1977).

sional enactments.[2] Moreover, the Rule addresses only one aspect of the law of presumptions, *i.e.*, the question of the impact of a presumption on the burden of going forward and the burden of persuasion. The Rule leaves to case law the resolution of corollary issues that are raised by the invocation of a presumption.[3]

As enacted by Congress, Rule 301 greatly differs from the version of the rule recommended by the Advisory Committee and promulgated by the Supreme Court. The Supreme Court's rule followed the approach advocated by Professor Morgan, which shifted both the burden of going forward and the burden of persuasion to the opponent of the presumption after its proponent established the base facts.[4] Supporters of this rule argued that a rule which shifted only the burden of production gave too "slight and evanescent" an effect to a presumption because it disappeared from the case and was not mentioned to the jury once its opponent introduced evidence sufficient to support a finding of the nonexistence of the presumed fact.[5] Despite this criticism, Congress adopted a rule which shifts only the burden of going forward.

Under Rule 301 a presumption is a procedural device that operates to shift the evidentiary burden of producing evidence (*i.e.*, the burden of going forward) to the party against whom the presumption is directed.[6] The burden of producing evidence operates generally to expose a party to an adverse result on a directed verdict where evidence on the issue has not been advanced. The burden of persuasion, *i.e.*, the risk of nonpersuasion, is not affected under the Rule, and it remains on the party to whom it was originally allocated by the substantive law and the pleadings. Under Rule 301 a presumption has a modest effect; it is a device to be applied only where no substantial rebuttal evidence regarding the fact or facts to be presumed is provided by the opponent of the presumption.[7]

---

[2] 1 WEINSTEIN, ¶ 301[01], at 301-18. *See* § 301.4, *infra*, as to "Scope of the Rules."

[3] See § 301.4, *infra*.

[4] The Supreme Court's Rule 301 read:

In all cases not otherwise provided for by Act of Congress or by these rules a presumption imposes on the party against whom it is directed the burden of proving that the nonexistence of the presumed fact is more probable than its existence.

See 1 WEINSTEIN, ¶ 301[01], at 301-3.

[5] Rule 301, Advisory Committee's Note (quoting Morgan and Maguire, *Looking Backward and Forward at Evidence*, 50 HARV. L. REV. 909, 913 (1937)).

[6] Earlier versions of the Rule would have had a more dramatic effect on the burden of proof. *See* 1 LOUISELL & MUELLER, § 65, at 578.

[7] *See* MORGAN, BASIC PROBLEMS OF EVIDENCE, 32 (1962). *See also* United States v. Gaines, 690 F.2d 849, 853 (11th Cir. 1982). *See* § 301.5, *infra*.

§ 301.2   Definitional Distinctions.

Confusion in the area of presumptions has been generated by the imprecise usage of a variety of terms such as burden of persuasion, burden of production, rebuttable presumption, irrebuttable or conclusive presumption and inference. The terms should be distinguished as follows:

Burden of Persuasion.

The "burden of persuasion" is the "risk of non-persuasion." It is the burden of persuading the trier of fact of the elements of a claim or a defense in accordance with the degree of proof mandated by the substantive law, *i.e.*, "preponderance of the evidence," "clear and convincing evidence," or "beyond a reasonable doubt."[8] Under Rule 301 the burden of persuasion is not affected by a presumption, and it remains upon the party to whom it was originally allocated by the substantive law.

Burden of Going Forward.

The "burden of going forward" is the "burden of production" or the "burden of producing evidence." It is the burden to come forward with evidence to avoid an adverse resolution by the judge which would preempt consideration by the trier of fact of the issue,[9] usually through the device of a directed verdict.[10] It is the obligation, initially, to produce sufficient evidence to support a rational jury decision in favor of the factual element sought to be proven.[11] Under Rule 301 the burden of production may be affected by a presumption. A presumption operates to shift the burden of production on a factual element where the proponent of the presumption submits evidence as to the base facts (the fundament) of the presumption. Having proved the base facts of the presumption, the burden of production as to the presumed fact is satisfied for the proponent. The burden of production to disprove the presumed fact shifts to the opponent by virtue of the operation of the presumption, *i.e.*, the opponent risks a preemptive verdict if he fails to counter the presumption.

Inference.

An "inference" is a permissible deduction or induction which the trier of fact may draw from facts which are established according to the rules of evidence. An inference is typically based on logic or common human experience, and it is the essential component of circumstantial proof. A jury

---

[8] Lilly, § 15, at 41.
[9] Lilly, § 15, at 44.

[10] McCormick, § 337, at 784.
[11] McCormick, § 338, at 791.

may attach weight to the inferred fact in the same manner as it does to the direct evidence upon which the inferred fact is based.[12]

Rebuttable Presumption.

A "rebuttable presumption" is a presumption which the law requires the trier of fact to make where the prerequisite base facts have been established and where no contrary evidence has been produced.[13] A common example is the presumption of the delivery which arises upon establishment of the base facts of proper addressing and posting of a letter. Rule 301, which governs rebuttable presumptions, only directs the manner in which presumptions operate, and it does not dictate whether a particular presumption applies or obtains. Substantive law must provide a particular presumption. Presumptions are based upon a variety of rationales, and as creatures of deliberate legal formulation, presumptions may or may not coincide with logic or common experience. Consequently, while in some cases a presumption may be based upon or coincide with an inference indicated by logic and experience, the terms "inference" and "presumption" are not synonymous.

Conclusive Presumption.

The term "conclusive presumption" denotes what is more properly considered a rule of substantive law as opposed to an evidentiary, procedural device. For example, where the law declares that a child of less than seven years is incapable of committing a felony, such a rule forecloses the legal questions involved.[14] It raises no proof problems, and consequently is not within the purview of Rule 301.

§ 301.3   The Policy of Presumptions.

Presumptions are largely products of evidentiary necessity or convenience that operate to assist a party in satisfying the risk of nonpersuasion. They are derived from varied rationales and serve such purposes as: 1) counterbalancing one party's superior access to proof; 2) advancing deep-seated social or economic policies; 3) avoiding a legal impasse; and 4) acknowledging the high probability of a given conclusion which experience has demonstrated (*i.e.*, giving formal effect to an inference).[15] Frequently,

---

[12] *See, e.g.*, United States v. Roglieri, 700 F.2d 883, 887 (2d Cir. 1983); United States v. Leonard, 524 F.2d 1076, 1091-92 (2d Cir. 1975), *cert. denied*, 425 U.S. 958, 96 S.Ct. 1737, 48 L.Ed.2d 202 (1976). *See, generally*, 1 LOUISELL & MUELLER, § 67, at 535-536 *et seq.*

[13] Gausewitz, *Presumptions in a One Rule World*, 5 VAND. L. REV. 324, 327 (1952).

[14] MORGAN, BASIC PROBLEMS OF EVIDENCE, 31 (1962).

[15] *See* McCORMICK, § 343.

a presumption is based on some combination of the foregoing factors, and it almost always is indicated by a modicum of rational, intrinsic probability.

The common law doctrine of bailee liability is illustrative of the policy regarding accessibility of evidence: Where property is delivered to a bailee, and the bailee on demand fails to deliver the property to the bailor, a common law presumption of liability may arise on the part of the bailee. Social or economic policies supporting presumptions are reflected by the frequently recognized presumption of legitimacy that attaches to a child born during lawful wedlock. Likewise, the presumption against a finding of suicide is also illustrative of a social policy underpinning. Presumptions dealing with the order of death of persons involved in a common disaster illustrate the use of a presumption to avoid a legal impasse in a situation where the proof is equally inaccessible to all parties and the presumption is imposed to facilitate a final result.

§ 301.4   Effect of the Rule.

Rule 301 comes into play where the party bearing the burden of persuasion on a given issue introduces base facts which are supportive of a presumption supplied by substantive law. At this point the burden of production shifts to the opposing party requiring him to come forward with evidence which is contrary to the presumed fact. The risk of non-persuasion, however, is not affected, and it remains on the party to whom it was originally allocated.

In practice, this distinction between shifting the burden of production but not that of persuasion, translates into an evaluation of the quantity and quality of rebuttal evidence required of the party opposing the presumption in order to avoid an instruction to the trier of fact on the presumption. In accordance with the traditional Thayer-Wigmore theory of presumptions,[16] the opponent of the presumption need only offer credible evidence sufficient to support a finding that is contrary to the presumed fact in order to dislodge the presumption from the case.[17] The standard does not

---

[16] Wigmore, § 2490 *et seq*.

[17] *See* Breeden v. Weinberger, 493 F.2d 1002, 1005-06, (4th Cir. 1974) (court relied on proposed Rule 301 as persuasive, though not controlling, in an administrative proceeding concerning Social Security disability benefits, and noted that the party against whom the presumption operates need only persuade the trier that the con-

trary of the presumed fact is more probable than not; there is no increased measure of persuasion; "[A]s a general rule, presumptions do not operate to raise the standard of proof"); Sinatra v. Heckler, 566 F. Supp. 1354, 1359-60 (E.D. N.Y. 1983). *See, generally*, 1 Weinstein, ¶ 301[02] at 301-32; 1 Louisell & Mueller, § 70; McCormick, § 345, at 821. *See also* United States v. Chi-place upon the opponent the burden of proving the contrary finding by, for example, a preponderance of the evidence or beyond a reasonable doubt. In the language of the terms defined in Section 301.2 above, the opposing party must only satisfy its burden of going forward in order to defeat its operation.

Interestingly, Rule 301 itself does not dictate the procedural result which attends compliance or non-compliance with the requirement of producing evidence to rebut the presumption. Case law continues to govern in this regard, and case law provides that if the party opposing the presumption fails to come forward with sufficient credible evidence, as determined by the court, the presumption is crystallized, and the jury is instructed to find the presumed fact if it believes the base facts to be true.[18] If, however, the party against whom the presumption is directed produces sufficient rebuttal evidence, the presumption never takes effect and it is not mentioned to the jury. No instruction is given.[19] Fundamentally, the impact of a presumption turns on whether the instruction will be given: "If you find X (base facts), then you must find Y (presumed facts)."

Although internally consistent, application of the "bubble-bursting effect"[20] of presumptions under Rule 301 has been criticized for according too little weight to presumptions, many of which are forged of significant policy considerations. Consequently, proponents of such criticism would allow the presumption to be mentioned to the jury in such cases, even where evidence contrary to the presumed fact has been introduced.[21] The express language of Rule 301 does not prohibit courts from carving out limited areas where the existence of a presumption might be mentioned to the jury even though credible rebuttal evidence has been introduced.

cago, 411 F. Supp. 218, 231-33 (1976) (civil rights action involving sexual and racial discrimination in Chicago's police department, where employers argued that Rule 301 precluded the placement on them of the burden of persuasion respecting the job-relatedness of the questioned testing; the court rejected this contention on the ground that the pertinent provision of the Civil Rights Act of 1974, as interpreted by the Supreme Court, placed the burden of proof of job-relatedness of testing on the employer, and that the statutory prescription prevailed over Rule 301).

[18] WIGMORE, § 2490, at 287. See, generally, 1 WEINSTEIN ¶ 302[02]; 1 LOUISELL & MUELLER, § 70, at 568.

[19] Sprague v. Director, Office of Worker's Compensation Programs, United States Department of Labor, 688 F.2d 862, 865-66; n.7. (1st Cir. 1982).

[20] McCORMICK, § 345, at 821. See also 1 LOUISELL & MUELLER, § 70, at 563 et seq.

[21] See McCORMICK, § 345, at 822-23. McCormick goes so far as advocating that the burden of persuasion be shifted to the party against whom a presumption is offered. McCORMICK § 345, at 826. See also 1 LOUISELL & MUELLER, § 70, at 575.

Chapter 302

RULE 302. APPLICABILITY OF STATE LAW IN CIVIL ACTIONS AND PROCEEDINGS

SECTION
302.1   In general
302.2   Application of state law
302.3   Presumptions in criminal cases

Rule 302 reads as follows:

> In civil actions and proceedings, the effect of a presumption respecting a fact which is an element of a claim or defense as to which State law supplies the rule of decision is determined in accordance with State law.

§ 302.1   In General.

Rule 302 provides that a court must apply state law to determine the effect of a presumption where a fact to which the presumption applies is an element of a claim or defense as to which state law provides the rule of decision.[1] The Rule as enacted applies only to civil actions and proceedings.

Rule 302 is in essence an embodiment of the "*Erie* doctrine."[2] Under *Erie R. R. Co. v. Tomkins,* rules governing presumptions and burdens of proof

---

[1] *See, generally,* MCCORMICK, § 334, at 983; 1 WEINSTEIN, ¶¶ 302[01]-[02], at 302-6 to 302-10; 1 LOUISELL & MUELLER, §§ 74-75, at 591-617. *See also* Berger, *Privileges, Presumptions and Competency of Witnesses in the Federal Court: A Federal Choice of Laws Rule,* 42 BROOKLYN L. REV. 417 (1976); Wellborn, *The Federal Rules of Evidence and the Application of State Law in Federal Courts,* 5 Tex. L. Rev. 3 (1977); Weinstein, *The Uniformity-Conformity Dilemma Facing Draftsmen of Federal Rules of Evidence,* 69 COLUM. L. REV. 353 (1969).

[2] *See, generally,* WRIGHT, MILLER & COOPER, FEDERAL PRACTICE AND PROCEDURE, §§ 4501-15; WRIGHT, FEDERAL COURTS §§ 54-60 (4th Ed.):

> Except in matters governed by the Federal Constitution or by Acts of Congress, the law to be applied in any case is the law of the state. And whether the law of the state shall be declared by its legislature in a statute or by its highest court in a decision is not a matter of federal concern. There is no federal general common law. Congress has no power to declare

may in certain applications be treated as substantive because of a clear and direct effect on the litigation's outcome.[3] The *Erie* doctrine continues to control the circumstances under which a federal court is to apply a state-created presumption.[4]

The scope of Rule 302 is coextensive with the scope of the *Erie* doctrine. Therefore, Rule 302 requires application of state law to presumptions which affect claims or defenses arising from state law, regardless of the basis of federal jurisdiction. Rule 302 will not apply state law to cases involving federal claims or issues even if jurisdiction is based upon diversity. In actions not based on diversity jurisdiction, if the source of the claim is governed by state law, Rule 302 applies.[5]

§ 302.2   Application of State Law.

Rule 302 draws a distinction between presumptions which operate upon a substantive element of a claim or defense and those which serve only tactical purposes. Rule 302 requires application of state law only as to the former type of presumption.[6] Examples of presumptions which commonly relate to a substantive element of a claim or defense include the presumption that death resulted from accidental causes in an action to recover accidental death benefits[7] and the presumption of lack of consideration for

substantive rules of common law applicable in a state whether they be local in their nature or 'general.'
Erie Railroad Co. v. Tompkins, 304 U.S. 64, 78, 58 S.Ct. 817, 822, 82 L.Ed.2d 1188, 1194 (1938).

[3] Palmer v. Hoffman, 318 U.S. 109, 117, 63 S.Ct. 477, 482, 87 L. Ed. 645, 651 (1943) ("the question of the burden of establishing contributory negligence is a question of local law which federal courts in diversity of citizenship cases . . . must apply"); Johnson v. Pierce Packing Co., 550 F.2d 474, 476 n.1. (9th Cir. 1977) ("[R]ules governing presumptions and burdens of proof are generally regarded as substantive for purposes of *Erie*").

[4] 1 Louisell & Mueller, § 74, at 593 n.47.

[5] *See, e.g.,* Steele v. Richardson, 472 F.2d 49, 52-53 (2d Cir. 1972) (in action to review decision denying benefits under Social Security Act, New York law of presumptions as to validity of marriages applied; the court seemed affected by the general federal policy in favor of claimants

of the type involved); Maternally Yours, Inc. v. Your Maternity Shop, Inc., 234 F.2d 534, 540-41 n.1 (2d Cir. 1956) ("it is the source of the right sued upon, and the ground on which federal jurisdiction over the case is founded, which determines the governing law . . . thus the *Erie* doctrine applies, whatever the ground for federal jurisdiction to any issue or claim which has its source in state law").

[6] *See* Rule 302, Advisory Committee's Note. *See also* 1 Weinstein ¶ 302[01], at 302-4; 1 Louisell & Mueller, § 74, at 598; McCormick, § 347.

[7] Melville v. American Home Assur. Co., 584 F.2d 1306, 1311 (3d Cir. 1978) (following a forum non conveniens dismissal in New York state court, beneficiary under accident policy brought diversity action to recover proceeds following insured's death in airplane crash; insurance company claimed that insured had committed suicide; District Court found the Pennsylvania would classify presumption against suicide as substantive, and then found that Pennsylvania's choice of law in contract cases was in

a conveyance from a bankrupt to a family member in a proceeding to set aside the conveyance.[8] In comparison the following example illustrates a tactical use of a presumption:

> In an action upon an account, plaintiff, desiring to prove defendant's failure to deny as an admission of liability, may prove the mailing of a statement of account to defendant and rely upon the presumption that it was received by him in due course of the mails. The presumed fact of delivery is much smaller than an element in the case.[9]

Whether a presumption is of tactical or substantive importance may not at all times be clear, but there are characteristics which indicate a purely tactical use of a presumption. If the presumption can be raised by either a defendant or plaintiff in any factual context in which the presumption would be applicable, then the presumption probably does not attempt to create a substantive right in a particular type of plaintiff or defendant and was created by the state merely to facilitate the litigation process.[10] In this situation the state presumption would serve merely a tactical purpose in the federal litigation, and consequently, neither the *Erie* doctrine nor Rule 302 would require the federal court to apply state law.[11] In cases in which it remains unclear whether a presumption is substantive or tactical, the narrow interpretation of the *Erie* doctrine contained in Rule 302 suggests federal law should be applied to advance the policy of uniformity in federal courts.[12]

§ 302.3   Presumptions in Criminal Cases.

The procedures delineated in Rule 301 are inapplicable to criminal cases. Although the Supreme Court promulgated Proposed Rule 303 which, if adopted, would have governed the instructions attendant to and circumstances under which a presumption could be submitted to the jury in a criminal action, the Rule was deleted by Congress because the subject of presumptions in criminal cases was addressed in several bills pending to amend the pertinent provisions of the federal criminal code.[13] The revision

---

utter disarray and confusion and that either the traditional choice of law rule for contracts or an interest analysis-Restatement II approach would lead to choosing New York rather than Delaware or Pennsylvania law).

[8] In re Bahre, 23 B.R. 460, 462 (Bkrtcy. D. Conn. 1982).

[9] Cleary, *Presuming and Pleading: An Essay on Juristic Immaturity*, 12 Stan. L. Rev. 5, 26 (1959).

[10] 1 Weinstein, ¶ 302[01], at 302-4.

[11] *But cf.* Dodson v. Imperial Motors Inc., 295 F.2d 609, 614-15 (6th Cir. 1961) (court applied Michigan's statutory presumption that a notorial certificate constitutes presumptive evidence of the facts contained therein, and affirmed a judgment against defendant).

[12] 1 Weinstein, ¶ 302[01], at 302-5.

[13] Proposed Rule 303 (now Standard 303) reads:

of the federal code pertaining to these matters was not adopted, however, and thus in federal criminal cases the operation of presumptions currently is controlled by principles of federal common law as circumscribed by constitutional limitations.[14]

While a detailed discussion of presumptions in criminal cases is beyond the scope of the rules of evidence and this Treatise, the special limitations placed on presumptions in criminal cases should be mentioned. In criminal actions, due process prevents presumptions from operating to obviate the state's burden of proving each element of an offense to the requisite standard of "beyond a reasonable doubt."[15] Correlatively, in criminal cases the court may not direct the jury to make certain findings even where the base or supportive facts are conclusively established, because the court cannot direct a verdict against the accused.[16]

(a) **Scope.** Except as otherwise provided by Act of Congress, in criminal cases, presumptions against an accused, recognized at common law or created by statute, including statutory provisions that certain facts are prima facie evidence of other facts or guilt, are governed by this rule.

(b) **Submission to Jury.** The judge is not authorized to direct the jury to find a presumed fact against the accused. When the presumed fact establishes guilt or is an element of the offense or negatives a defense, the judge may submit the question of guilt or of the existence of the presumed fact to the jury, if, but only if, a reasonable juror on the evidence as a whole, including the evidence of the basic facts, could find the guilt or the presumed fact beyond a reasonable doubt. When the presumed fact has a lesser effect, its existence may be submitted to the jury if the basic facts are supported by substantial evidence, or are otherwise established, unless the evidence as a whole negatives the existence of the presumed fact.

(c) **Instructing the Jury.** Whenever the existence of a presumed fact against the accused is submitted to the jury, the judge shall give an instruction that the law declares that the jury may regard the basic facts as sufficient evidence of the presumed fact but does not require it to do so. In addition, if the presumed fact establishes guilt or is an element of the offense or negatives a defense, the judge shall instruct the jury that its existence must, on all the evidence, be proved beyond a reasonable doubt.

[14] 1 LOUISELL & MUELLER, § 66, at 524-25.

[15] Rose v. Clark, No. 84-1974 (U.S. July 2, 1986); Sandstrom v. Montana, 442 U.S. 510, 526, 99 S.Ct. 2450, 2458, 61 L.Ed.2d 39, 43 (1979); County Court of Ulster County, New York v. Allen, 442 U.S. 140, 149, 99 S.Ct. 2213, 2219, 60 L.Ed.2d 777, 782 (1979); Patterson v. New York, 432 U.S. 197, 215-16, 97 S.Ct. 2319, 2321, 53 L.Ed.2d 281, 292 (1977); Mullaney v. Wilbur, 421 U.S. 684, 693, 95 S.Ct. 1881, 1889, 44 L.Ed.2d 508, 517 (1975); In re Winship, 397 U.S. 358, 363, 90 S.Ct. 1068, 1072, 25 L.Ed.2d 368, 371 (1970).

[16] 1 WEINSTEIN, ¶ 303[03], at 303-17. See United Brotherhood of Carpenters and Joiners of America v. United States, 330 U.S. 395, 401, 67 S.Ct. 775, 779, 91 L.Ed. 973, 977 (1947); United States v. Hayward, 420 F.2d 142, 144 (D.C. Cir. 1969).

IV
RELEVANCY AND ITS LIMITS

Chapter 401

RULE 401. DEFINITION OF "RELEVANT EVIDENCE"

Rule 401 reads as follows:

> "Relevant evidence" means evidence having any tendency to make the existence of any fact that is of consequence to the determination of the action more probable or less probable than it would be without the evidence.

§ 401.1 Definition of Relevant Evidence—In General.

Considered in conjunction with Rule 402, Rule 401 constitutes the cornerstone of the Federal evidentiary system. In essence, Rule 401 provides that in order for evidence to qualify for admission, such evidence must meet the threshold test of relevancy.[1] Once relevancy is established, however, evidence may be excluded for affirmative reasons identified in Rule 402. The bases for exclusion identified in Rule 402 are the Constitution of

---

[1] See, generally, McCORMICK, § 185, at 541-48; 1 WEINSTEIN ¶¶ 401[01]-[10]; 1 LOUISELL & MUELLER, §§ 91-107; 1 WIGMORE, §§ 24-43. See also Kaye, The Numbers Game: Statistical Inference in Discrimination Cases, 80 MICH. L. REV. 833 (1982); Note, Diagnosing the Dead: The Admissibility of the Psychiatric Autopsy, 18 AM. CRIM. L. REV. 617 (1981); Lempert, Modeling Relevancy, 75 MICH. L. REV. 1021 (1977).

the United States, statutes enacted by the Congress, the Federal Rules of Evidence, and other rules prescribed by the Supreme Court pursuant to statutory authority.

Accordingly, relevant evidence is "assumptively" admissible.[2] The proponent of evidence must be prepared to establish its relevancy, and if appropriate, the opponent of the evidence must be prepared to establish its inadmissibility predicated on one of the bases cited in Rule 402.

§ 401.2   Determination of Relevancy.

Determining whether a particular item of evidence is relevant is ordinarily not a question of law. Rather, the process of determining relevancy is based on experience, logic, and common sense. Consequently, many cases applying the concept of relevancy fall into no set pattern, and the trial lawyer can only rarely rely upon specific precedent to establish the relevancy of a particular item of evidence. While certain cases tend to fall into recurring patterns from which some guidance can be gleaned,[3] cases deal-

---

[2] LILLY, § 12, at 28. Professor Lilly uses the term "assumptive," as opposed to "presumptive," admissibility in order to avoid confusion with the operation of "presumption" as a term of art.

[3] See 1 WEINSTEIN, ¶ 410[10] for a thorough discussion of the categories mentioned in this note. For example, evidence of similar accidents or incidents is frequently offered to establish notice, (Mauldin v. Upjohn Co., 697 F.2d 644, 648 (5th Cir. 1983)) the gravity of the danger involved, (Collins By and Through Kay v. Seaboard Coastline Railroad Co., 675 F.2d 1185, 1193-94 (11th Cir. 1982)) or the foreseeability of the product defect in question, (Wagner v. International Harvester Co., 611 F.2d 224, 230 (8th Cir. 1979)) or causation (Walker v. Fairchild Industries, Inc., 554 F. Supp 650, 658 (D. Nev. 1982)). In cases falling within these categories the similarity between the prior accident or incident and the present crime will be the determining factor of relevancy.

Evidence of a defendant's actions or speech may also be relevant as bearing on his consciousness of guilt. United States v. Rossbach, 701 F.2d 713, 719 (8th Cir. 1981). Also, physical evidence offered by the prosecution to show a defendant possessed a weapon used in a crime is highly relevant and falls into a category of generally admissible evidence. United States v. Arnott, 704 F.2d 322, 326 (6th Cir. 1983). Evidence of the defendant's acquisition of a large amount of wealth following a crime is relevant. United States v. Mangan, 575 F.2d 32, 45 (2d Cir.), cert. denied, 439 U.S. 931, 99 S.Ct. 320, 58 L.Ed.2d 325 (1978). Other categories of generally admissible relevant evidence include: Evidence of a party's wealth in assessing damages, Fury Imports Inc. v. Shakespeare Co., 554 F.2d 1376, 1389 (5th Cir. 1977) cert. denied, 450 U.S. 921, 101 S.Ct. 1369, 67 L.Ed.2d 349 (1981), including the future expected earnings of a party, Hysell v. Iowa Public Service Inc., 505 F.2d 665, 668-69 (5th Cir. 1974).

Governmental, industrial, or professional regulations, customs and practice are highly probative in some instances when a party's knowledge of such procedures is relevant. Johnson v. Nigeria Machine & Tool Works, 666 F.2d 1223, 1226 (8th Cir. 1981). Statistics are highly relevant in discrimination cases. Gay v. Waiter's and Dairy Lunchmen's Union, 694 F.2d 531, 549-50 (9th Cir. 1982), and the sale of a comparable piece of real estate may be relevant in judging the market value of a piece of real property. United States v. 79.20 Acres of Land, More or Less, 710 F.2d 1352 (8th Cir. 1983).

ing with relevancy more frequently involve the reasoning of the court in a specific instance that is of little precedential value because of its intimate relationship with the unique facts of the case.[4]

§ 401.3   Standard of Relevancy.

Evidence is relevant if it merely alters the probabilities of the existence or nonexistence of a fact properly before the court. The offered evidence need only make the fact sought to be proven more probable or less probable in order to satisfy Rule 401. A single item of relevant evidence need not in itself be sufficient to support a jury verdict in order to satisfy the threshold standard of relevancy. Accordingly, in stating, "[a] brick is not a wall,"[5] McCormick points out that each item of evidence need only alter the probabilities of a factual issue to a slight extent, whereas the totality of the evidence must support the factual proposition sought to be proven if the proponent is to prevail on the issue.

Evidence is not subject to exclusion solely because its probative value is extremely low. If evidence has any probative value whatsoever, it is relevant and admissible unless otherwise excludable for an affirmative reason.[6] The practical consequence is that the opponent of the evidence cannot properly argue exclusion on the basis of minimal probative value alone. Evidence with low probative value, however, may be subject to exclusion under Rule 403 which balances probative value against such countervailing considerations as unfair prejudice and confusion of the issues.[7] Consequently, where the probative value of evidence is low, an argument coupling the minimal probity with a counterweight, e.g. confusion, may justify exclusion under Rule 403.

The establishment of a connection between the evidence and the fact sought to be proved is usually not a scientific process.[8] The Rule is more

---

[4] See, e.g., Jay Edwards, Inc. v. New England Toyota Distributor, 708 F.2d 814, 824 (1st Cir. 1983); Gootee v. Colt Industries, Inc., 712 F.2d 1057, 1059 (5th Cir. 1983); United States v. Washington, 705 F.2d 489, 492 (D.C. Cir. 1983); United States v. Clifford, 704 F.2d 86, 90 (3d Cir. 1983).

[5] McCORMICK, § 135, at 436.

[6] See discussion of Rule 402, at § 402.1 et seq of this Treatise.

[7] See discussion of Rule 403, at § 403.1 et seq of this Treatise.

[8] See 1 WEINSTEIN, ¶ 401[07]. Scientific evidence may be admissible in some situations to enhance the relevancy of another piece of evidence. For example, statistical evidence of the small probability that a given disease would occur in a normal individual not exposed to a caustic substance would enhance the relevancy of a claim that X had been exposed to Y and had suffered a disease as a result. When statistical evidence of the probability of an occurrence is utilized, great care must be taken to lay a foundation which establishes the accuracy of the probability admitted into evidence. United States v. Green, 680 F.2d 520, 523 (7th Cir. 1982), cert. denied, 103 S.Ct. 493 (1982).

customarily applied by the trial judge in a highly discretionary manner based upon experiential perceptions of the way in which the world operates.[9] Application of the standard of relevancy consequently calls upon the trial lawyer to use persuasion in establishing the necessary logical or experiential nexus between the offered evidence and the consequential facts sought to be established.

§ 401.4   Direct and Circumstantial Evidence.

The definition of relevancy in Rule 401 comprehends both direct and circumstantial evidence. Direct evidence does not rely upon an inference; it usually involves an eyewitness account of the ultimate, consequential facts sought to be proven.[10] Circumstantial evidence consists of proof of facts from which other connected facts are established.[11] As noted by Professor Lilly, direct evidence raises only issues of credibility of the testifying witness, whereas circumstantial evidence additionally involves an assessment by the trier of fact of the inference connecting the evidence and the consequential fact sought to be proven.[12]

§ 401.5   Conditional Relevancy.

By its terms, Rule 401 does not purport to deal with the concept of "conditional relevancy." Where evidence is conditionally relevant, its probative value depends upon not only satisfying the basic requirement of relevancy, but also upon establishing the existence of some other fact. Under conditional relevancy one item of evidence is relevant only if another item of evidence is established. The discussion of conditional relevancy appears in connection with Rule 104 which specifically addresses the concept.[13]

[9] See, e.g., United States v. Sweeney, 688 F.2d 1131, 1144 (7th Cir. 1982); United States v. Bouye, 688 F.2d 471, 475-76 (7th Cir. 1982).

[10] See United States v. Brady, 579 F.2d 1121, 1127 (9th Cir. 1978); United States v. Pelton, 578 F.2d 701, 711 (8th Cir. 1978).

[11] See United States v. Bycer, 593 F.2d 549, 551 (3d Cir. 1979); United States v. Knife, 592 F.2d 472, 475 (8th Cir. 1979). See also United States v. Fairchild, 526 F.2d 185, 188-89 (7th Cir. 1975), cert. denied, 425 U.S. 942, 96 S.Ct. 1682, 48 L.Ed.2d 186 (1975) (illustrates use of circumstantial proof to support elements of prosecution's charges and to defeat elements of a defense).

[12] Lilly, § 9, at 20.

[13] See § 104.1 et seq of this Treatise. See, generally, Morgan, Basic Problems of Evidence, 45-46 (1962).

§ 401.6   Relevancy and Materiality.

Rule 401 designates a properly provable fact as one "that is of consequence to the determination of the action." "Of consequence" is a term of art which embraces the traditional concept of materiality.

Material evidence, under traditional terminology, is evidence offered to establish a matter that is properly an issue in the case according to the substantive law.[14] Analysis of the pleadings and substantive law generally indicates whether a fact is material. Under the traditional analysis, if the evidence offered is not directed to a factual proposition that substantive law indicates is a matter in issue, the evidence was said to be "immaterial."

Relevancy and materiality have frequently been used interchangeably because the concepts are nearly impossible to distinguish in many situations. Because of this blurring between relevancy and materiality, the Federal Rules of Evidence have abandoned the term materiality in favor of the more comprehensive term of relevancy. Accordingly, under the terminology of Rule 401, the term relevancy applies both to traditional relevancy and traditional materiality. The result is a change only in terminology, and as a result of this change, evidence may be irrelevant, and subject to exclusion on this basis, in two distinct ways. First, evidence may be irrelevant if it is directed to a fact not properly at issue under the substantive law of the case. This is the application of the concept of materiality under traditional terminology. Under modern federal terminology the factual proposition is said to be irrelevant because it is not "of consequence" or "consequential" in the law suit. Second, an item of evidence may fail to alter the probabilities of the existence or nonexistence of a consequential fact, *i.e.*, a fact to be proven pursuant to the substantive law. This evidence, while directed toward a proper factual target, is irrelevant because of a failure of logical or experiential connection with the target, consequential fact.[15]

Accordingly, a "fact of consequence" or a "consequential fact" is an ultimate fact because it is a substantive element of a charge, claim or defense,

---

[14] *See* United States v. Duff, 707 F.2d 1315, 1318-19 (11th Cir. 1983); Rossi v. Mobil Oil Corp., 710 F.2d 821, 830-31 (Temp. Emer. Ct. App. 1983). *See also* Stonehocker v. General Motors Corp., 587 F.2d 151, 153 (4th Cir. 1978) (in diversity action based on crashworthiness or second collision products liability theory, evidence of automobile manufacturer's compliance with subsequently enacted federal safety standard should have been admitted as relevant on issue of due care).

[15] United States v. Akers, 702 F.2d 1145, 1149 (D.C. Cir. 1983); United States v. Bifield, 702 F.2d 342, 350 (2d Cir. 1983), *cert. denied*, 103 S.Ct. 2095 (1983). *See also* discussion of Rule 401 n.9, *supra*.

or it is a fact which is logically or experientially connected with such an ultimate fact by an inference that satisfies the "more or less probable" standard.

§ 401.7   Relevant Facts Need not be Contested Facts.

Rule 401 presents no requirement that the consequential facts sought to be proved are contested or disputed in the law suit. Evidence is relevant even if it is directed to a fact that is conceded by the opposing party to be true. Background evidence, for example evidence of a person's name, address and profession, is undisputed and usually admitted without questions. Likewise, charts and illustrations are examples of evidence that usually involve undisputed matters which are yet relevant and admissible. Accordingly, if trial counsel wishes to exclude an opponent's evidence merely by conceding its truth, the evidence will not be rendered irrelevant and inadmissible. Nevertheless, evidence which is directed to a consequential fact that is not contested in the law suit has minimal probative value and may be subject to exclusion under Rule 403 where a stipulated counterweight is applicable.[16]

§ 401.8   Relevancy Compared with Competency.

Relevancy and competency are distinguishable. Relevancy, considered in Rule 401, is defined in terms of the minimal qualifications an item of evidence must possess in order to be admissible. "Competency" usually refers to the appropriateness of testimony from a particular witness. Competency is generally addressed in Rules 601 and 602.[17] Also, the term competency is occasionally used as a synonym for admissible evidence, *i.e.*, evidence that is admissible on a particular subject or in regard to a particular fact, as in the expression, "A is competent proof of B."

§ 401.9   Relevancy Compared with Weight and Sufficiency of the Evidence.

Relevancy, weight, and sufficiency should be distinguished. Relevancy, a standard to be administered by the trial judge, is the threshold qualification for evidence. Sufficiency, by comparison, is a term which refers to the

---

[16] *See* discussion of Rule 403, at § 403.1 of this Treatise.

[17] *See* discussion of Rule 601, at § 601.1 of this Treatise.

totality of the evidence that must be admitted in order to advance an issue to the jury.[18] Relevancy deals primarily with admissibility or inadmissibility. Sufficiency deals primarily with whether a party has submitted sufficient evidence to warrant jury consideration of the matter. The weight of evidence is the believability of the evidence as evaluated by the jury.[19]

[18] It is for the trial judge to determine if there is any evidence to establish a fact in issue which should go to the jury. To comply with the requirements of sufficiency is tantamount to the defeat of a motion for a directed verdict.

[19] Some courts have failed to observe these distinctions. United States v. Kreimer, 609 F.2d 126, 131 (1980) (confusion of relevancy with sufficiency); United States v. McCoy, 517 F.2d 41, 44 (7th Cir. 1975), *cert. denied*, 423 U.S. 895, 96 S.Ct. 195, 46 L.Ed.2d 127 (1975) (trial court confused relevancy with the weight of the evidence); Lehrman v. Gulf Oil Corp., 464 F.2d 26, 42 (5th Cir. 1972), *cert. denied*, 409 U.S. 1077, 93 S.Ct. 687, 34 L.Ed.2d 665 (1972) (confusion of relevancy with sufficiency to prove a contested proposition of fact).

Chapter 402

RULE 402. RELEVANT EVIDENCE GENERALLY ADMISSIBLE; IRRELEVANT EVIDENCE INADMISSIBLE

SECTION
402.1   Admissibility—In general
402.2   Conceptual basis for Rule 402
402.3   The Rules of Evidence: Constitutional inadmissibility
402.4   The Rules of Evidence: Statutory inadmissibility
402.5   Other rules of inadmissibility

Rule 402 reads as follows:

> All relevant evidence is admissible, except as otherwise provided by the Constitution of the United States, by Act of Congress, by these rules, or by other rules prescribed by the Supreme Court pursuant to statutory authority. Evidence which is not relevant is not admissible.

§ 402.1   Admissibility—In General.

Rule 402 is the pivotal provision of the federal evidentiary system by connecting Rule 401, which defines relevancy, with all rules of exclusion.[1] Thayer identified the concept embodied in Rule 402 as the "pre-supposition involved in the very conception of the rational system of evidence."[2] The essence of Rule 402 is that irrelevant evidence is not admissible, and that all relevant evidence will be admitted subject to specific identified exceptions. The opponent of relevant evidence must advance a specific exclusionary rule or principle in order to obstruct the admissibility of evidence.

---

[1] See, generally, 1 WEINSTEIN, ¶¶ 402[01]-[05]; 1 LOUISELL & MUELLER, §§ 111-114. See also Martin, *Inherent Judicial Power, Flexibility Congress Did Not Write Into the Federal Rules of Evidence*, 57 TEX. L. REV. 167 (1979).

[2] THAYER, PRELIMINARY TREATISE ON EVIDENCE, 264 (1898).

Rule 402 indicates that the bases for excluding evidence may be internal to the Rules or they may be extrinsic authority. In the latter category, Rule 402 specifically identifies authorities which are to be given the equivalent force of express exclusionary rules set forth in the Rules of Evidence.

§ 402.2   Conceptual Basis for Rule 402.

Most fundamentally, relevant evidence will be admitted to the trier of fact unless there is a specific reason to exclude it, and the policies supporting the exclusion of evidence are manifold. For example, exclusion may be predicated on social policy. Certain social policies are paramount to the accurate determination of the facts in a law suit and require suppression of relevant and otherwise trustworthy evidence. Obvious examples of such values are those associated with privileges, presumptions, subsequent remedial actions and compromise negotiations.[3] Other reasons for excluding evidence may relate to the inherent trustworthiness or lack of trustworthiness of the evidence, and obvious examples would include the authentication rules,[4] the hearsay rules,[5] and the so-called "best evidence rule."[6] Likewise, accuracy may be affected by the evidence's psychological or emotional impact on the trier of fact. Character evidence is an example of relevant evidence which may be excluded because of its untoward inflammatory effect upon the trier of fact.[7]

§ 402.3   The Rules of Evidence: Constitutional Inadmissibility.

Rule 402 implicitly indicates that no attempt is made within the Rules of Evidence to codify constitutional principles of exclusion. Evidence which is relevant may appear to be admissible because no specific Rule within the Rules of Evidence would require its exclusion. Nevertheless, the evidence may be subject to exclusion in order to protect the constitutional rights of a litigant. Consequently, constitutional inadmissibility may be a distinct basis for denying the admission of evidence, and like other bases, the opponent of the evidence generally must be prepared to assert the constitutional doctrine in an effort to exclude the evidence in question.[8] While there is no embodiment within the Rules of constitutional doctrines, such as those

---

[3] *See* Article V.
[4] *See* Article IX.
[5] *See* Article VIII.
[6] *See* Article X.
[7] *See* Article IV.

[8] *See, e.g.,* Katz v. United States, 389 U.S. 347, 356-57, 88 S.Ct. 507, 513-14, 19 L.Ed.2d 576, 584-85 (1967); Miranda v. United States, 384 U.S. 436, 492, 86 S.Ct. 1602, 1647, 16 L.Ed.2d 694, 737 (1966).

pertaining to unlawful search and seizure or self-incriminating statements, such doctrines of constitutional inadmissibility obviously may be the basis for excluding evidence in Federal Courts.[9]

§ 402.4   The Rules of Evidence: Statutory Inadmissibility.

Rule 402 provides that statutes governing the inadmissibility of evidence have not been abrogated by the adoption of the Rules.

Statutes which would commonly have the effect of rendering evidence inadmissible include: sections of the Omnibus Crime Control and Safe Streets Act of 1968 which refer to the admissibility of confessions and admissions of the accused in a criminal proceeding;[10] provisions of the same Act which determine the appropriateness of admitting wiretap evidence;[11] Section 605 of the Communications Act which protects individuals' privacy by preventing the unauthorized interception of wire or radio transmissions, or by an electronic means;[12] provisions in the Bankruptcy Act which render evidence given by a bankrupt in a bankruptcy proceeding inadmissible against him in a criminal trial;[13] and statutes which prevent the admissibility of originals as retained copies of data sheets submitted to the Census Bureau.[14]

§ 402.5   Other Rules of Inadmissibility.

Other Rules promulgated by the Supreme Court will render relevant evidence in a proceeding inadmissible. The Federal Rules of Criminal Procedure,[15] The Federal Rules of Civil Procedure,[16] The Bankruptcy Rules[17] and The Rules of Admiralty[18] are the most notable sources of Rules which determine the admissibility of evidence.

Also, in light of the incorporation of state law in Rule 501, state law may also render evidence inadmissible, when the state's law of privileges govern a claim as defense in a civil action.[19]

[9] *See* Weeks v. United States, 232 U.S. 383, 393-94, 34 S.Ct. 341, 346, 58 L.Ed. 576, 581 (1914). *But cf.* United States v. Grajeda, 587 F.2d 1017, 1019 (9th Cir. 1978) (court declined to consider whether Rule 402 altered the previous common-law rule in this circuit that the propriety of a stop or arrest by a state officer is subject to both state and federal standards).

[10] 28 U.S.C., § 3501 (1968).

[11] 28 U.S.C., §§ 2510-20 (1968). *See also* Weiss v. United States, 308 U.S. 321, 328, 60 S.Ct. 269, 275, 84 L.Ed. 298, 304 (1939); Nardone v. United States, 302 U.S. 379, 58 S.Ct. 275, 82 L.Ed. 314 (1937); United States v. Dote, 371 F.2d 176 (7th Cir. 1966).

[12] 47 U.S.C., § 605 (1970).

[13] 11 U.S.C., § 25(a) 10 (1970).

[14] 13 U.S.C., § 9(a) (1970).

[15] 18 U.S.C., § 3371 (1964).

[16] 28 U.S.C., § 2072 (1964).

[17] 11 U.S.C., § 53 (1964).

[18] 28 U.S.C., § 2073 (1964).

[19] See the discussion of Rule 501, *infra*.

Chapter 403

RULE 403. EXCLUSION OF RELEVANT EVIDENCE ON GROUNDS OF PREJUDICE, CONFUSION, OR WASTE OF TIME

Rule 403 reads as follows:

Although relevant, evidence may be excluded if its probative value is substantially outweighed by the danger of unfair prejudice, confusion of the issues, or misleading the jury, or by considerations of undue delay, waste of time, or needless presentation of cumulative evidence.

§ 403.1 In General.

Rule 403 codifies the long-standing authority of the trial judge to exclude relevant evidence where the probity of the offered evidence is outweighed by one or more of certain identified countervailing considerations.[1] The underlying premise of the Rule is that certain relevant

---

[1] *See, generally*, McCormick, § 180; 1 Weinstein, ¶¶ 403[01]-[06] at 403-1-61; 2 Louisell & Mueller, §§ 124-30; 2 Wigmore, §§ 443-44; 6 Wigmore, §§ 1904- 1907. *See also* Graham, *Observation,—The Relationship Among Federal Rules of Evidence 607, 801(d)(1)(A) and 403: A Reply to Weinstein's Evidence*, 55 Tex. L. Rev.

evidence should not be admitted to the trier of fact where the admission would result in an adverse effect upon the effectiveness or integrity of the fact finding process.[2] This same policy generally underpins the succeeding Rules contained in Article IV, and Rules 404 through 412 represent applications of the balancing of relevancy and countervailing adverse effects which have recurred with sufficient frequency to have resulted in a specific rule.

Like most rules of exclusion in the Federal Rules of Evidence, Rule 403 may be applied as the authority for objection at trial, or alternatively, it may be the basis for a motion in limine submitted prior to trial pursuant to Rule 104. A pretrial ruling on evidence potentially subject to exclusion under Rule 403 may be particularly desirable. If raised at trial as a basis for exclusion, objections citing prejudice and confusion — even if granted — may not absolutely prevent exposure to the jury of inflammatory or misleading evidence. Through the device of a pretrial motion in limine, *i.e.*, a motion for an advance ruling on the admissibility of evidence, the trial judge can consider both sides' positions on probative value as well as the counterweight in question without the risk of exposing the jury to evidence which may be ultimately excluded.[3]

§ 403.2 Balance of Probative Values Versus Counterweight, Discretion of Trial Judge.

When the court is requested to exclude evidence for one of the reasons specified under Rule 403, the trial judge must determine whether the adverse effect *substantially* outweighs the probative value of the evidence. The word "substantial" is undoubtedly a word of some elasticity, and ultimately in applying that standard, the trial judge has broad discretion. Consequently, it is generally held that a trial judge's determination based on Rule 403 will be overturned only upon a showing of abuse of his discretion.[4] No precise definition of the term "substantial" appears in the Rules,

---

573 (1977); Wellborn, *The Federal Rules of Evidence and the Application of State Law in Federal Courts*, 55 TEX. L. REV. 3 (1977); Travers, *An Essay on the Determination of Relevancy Under the Federal Rules of Evidence*, 1977 ARIZ. ST. L.J. 327 (1977); Weinstein & Berge, *Basic Rules of Relevancy in the Proposed Rules of Evidence*, 4 GA. L. REV. 43 (1969).

[2] Rule 611 codifies parallel authority regarding the trial judge's control of the interrogation of witnesses.

[3] *See, e.g.*, Litton Systems, Inc. v. American Telephone and Telegraph Co., 700 F.2d 785, 818 & n.45 (2d Cir. 1983); United States v. Southard, 700 F.2d 1, 13 (1st Cir. 1983), *cert. denied*, 104 S.Ct. 89 (1983); Maudlin v. UpJohn Co., 697 F.2d 644, 648 (5th Cir. 1983), *cert. denied*, 104 S.Ct. 155 (1983).

[4] *See, e.g.*, United States v. Abel, 469 U.S. 45, 105 S.Ct. 465, 83 L.Ed.2d 450 (1984) (no abuse of discretion to allow highly probative yet prejudicial testimony

yet it is clear that, at least symbolically, Rule 403 favors a presumption of admissibility by mandating that the negative attribute of the evidence must substantially outweigh its probative value before exclusion is justified.[5] At minimum, intelligent advocacy under the Rule suggests that a litigant seeking exclusion based on Rule 403 should never argue that the balance is a "close question."

As indicated by the Advisory Committee's Note, Rule 403 essentially states a principle broadly recognized in prior law.[6] While the trial judge has always possessed substantial discretion to exclude evidence, the Rule will undoubtedly sharpen analysis and provide a framework for clearer argument as to admissibility or inadmissibility. Prior case law often evaluated counterbalancing factors as merely part of the function of assessing probative value, and pre-Rule case law might, for example, assess probative value as non-existent because of concomitant unfair prejudice or confusion. As McCormick has stated, the better approach is to distinguish between probative value on one hand, and the counterbalancing danger on the other:

> "Legal relevancy" has been taken as a standard requiring "plus value"—more than a bare minimum of probative worth—a standard which is doubtless implicit in the balancing process. It seems better to discard the term "legal relevancy" altogether. Its use tends to emphasize conformity to precedent in an area where the need for discretionary responsibility for weighing of value against dangers in the particular case should be stressed.[7]

In applying Rule 403 the trial judge should consider alternate means by which the fact sought to be proven can be established. Obviously, if the same consequential fact can be proven by evidence unattended by the risk of prejudice, confusion or inefficiency, the trial court should exercise its inherent power under Rule 403 to compel the use of the alternate method

of membership in a prisoners' group dedicated to commit perjury on behalf of members where court took precautions, *i.e.*, limiting instruction, to prevent undue prejudice); United States v. Arnott, 704 F.2d 322, 326 (6th Cir. 1983); United States v. Birney, 686 F.2d 102, 106-07 (2d Cir. 1982); Forro Precision, Inc. v. International Business Machines Corp., 673 F.2d 1045, 1057 (9th Cir. 1982); United States v. Barletta, 652 F.2d 218, 220 (1st Cir. 1981); F & S Offshore, Inc. v. K. O. Steel Castings, Inc., 662 F.2d 1104, 1107 (5th Cir. 1982); Wade v. Haynes, 663 F.2d 778, 783 (8th Cir. 1981); United States v. MacDonald, 688 F.2d 224, 228-29 (4th Cir. 1982), *cert. denied*, 103 S.Ct. 726 (1983); United States v. Pomeranz, 683 F.2d 352 (11th Cir. 1982); Rovegno v. Geppert Brothers, Inc., 677 F.2d 327 (3d Cir. 1982); United States v. Serin, 707 F.2d 953 (7th Cir. 1983); United States v. Harris, 661 F.2d 138 (10th Cir. 1981).

[5] SALTZBEND & REDDEN, FEDERAL RULES OF EVIDENCE MANUAL, (2d ed.) at 115; LILLY, § 13, at 34.

[6] *See* Rule 403 Advisory Committee's Note. *See also* United States v. Brown, 547 F.2d 1264, 1266 (5th Cir. 1977).

[7] MCCORMICK, § 185, at 441.

of proof.[8] A judge should also determine whether or not a limiting instruction pursuant to Rule 105 would sufficiently diminish the danger of an adverse effect. Where the use of a limiting instruction cannot adequately neutralize the negative attribute of the evidence, exclusion under Rule 403 may be warranted.[9] In any case in which Rule 403 is invoked, it is appropriate for a trial lawyer to ask the trial judge to provide a statement on the record which explicates the court's analysis of probative value and the countervailing adverse effect.[10]

§ 403.3 Exclusion of Relevant Evidence Based Upon Unfair Prejudice.

Exclusion on the basis of unfair prejudice involves more than a balance of adverse prejudice. If unfair prejudice referred to any evidence prejudicial to a party's case, anything adverse to a litigant's position at trial would be excludable under Rule 403. Emphasis must be placed on the word "unfair." Unfair prejudice is that quality of evidence which might result in an improper, usually irrational, basis for a jury decision.[11] Consequently, if the evidence arouses the jury's emotional sympathies, evokes a sense of horror, or appeals to an instinct to punish, the evidence may be unfairly prejudicial.[12] Usually, although not always, unfairly prejudicial evidence appeals to the jury's emotions rather than intellect.[13]

Unfair prejudice may be present when inflammatory or otherwise shocking real proof or photographs are offered.[14] Likewise, the subject matter of testimony may be excessively prejudicial and subject to exclusion under Rule 403.[15] It must be remembered that Rule 403 calls for a balancing of probative value against the case counterweight, and no evidence is inadmissible simply because it is sensational or prejudicial.[16]

---

[8] Roshan v. Ford, 705 F.2d 102, 104-05 (7th Cir. 1981); United States v. Mills, 704 F.2d 1553, 1560 (11th Cir. 1980).

[9] Harris v. Illinois-California Express Inc., 687 F.2d 1361, 1369-71 (10th Cir. 1982); United States v. Figuero, 618 F.2d 934, 943 (2d Cir. 1980).

[10] See United States v. Dwyer, 539 F.2d 924, 926 (2d Cir. 1976).

[11] 2 LOUISELL & MUELLER, § 126, at 18.

[12] McCORMICK, § 185, at 439-40.

[13] Advisory Committee's Note to Rule 403. See, e.g., United States v. Abel, 469 U.S. 45, 105 S.Ct. 465, 83 L.Ed.2d 450 (1984); United States v. Mills, 704 F.2d 1553, 1559-60; Farrace v. Independent Fire Insurance Co., 699 F.2d 204, 210-11 (5th Cir. 1983); United States v. Booth, 669 F.2d 1231, 1234 (9th Cir. 1982). See generally, 2 LOUISELL & MUELLER, § 126.

[14] See, e.g., United States v. Quasar, 671 F.2d 732, 735 (2d Cir. 1982); United States v. Bowers, 660 F.2d 527, 529 (5th Cir. 1981).

[15] See, e.g., United States v. Abel, 469 U.S. 45, 105 S.Ct. 465, 83 L.Ed.2d 450 (1984) (use of name "Aryan Brotherhood" excluded as unduly prejudicial); United States v. Milstead, 671 F.2d 950, 953 (5th Cir. 1980); Cohn v. Papke, 655 F.2d 191, 194 (9th Cir. 1981); Ware v. Reed, 709 F.2d 345, 347 (5th Cir. 1983).

[16] See United States v. Dazzo, 672 F.2d 284, 288 (2d Cir. 1982); Ballou v. Henri Studios Inc., 656 F.2d 1147, 1155 (5th Cir. 1981); United States v. Thompson, 710 F.2d 915, 918 (2d Cir. 1983).

Rule 403 frequently operates in conjunction with other Rules of Evidence to fine tune their application, and reference will be made through this Treatise to interplay between Rule 403 and other Rules.

§ 403.4 Exclusion of Relevant Evidence Based Upon Confusion of the Issues or Misleading the Jury.

Exclusion based upon confusion usually is justified where the offered evidence would require the trier of fact to engage in intricate, extraordinary or impossible mental gymnastics in order to comprehend the import of the evidence or to assess its weight.[17] Likewise, if the jury is likely to ascribe excessive, unwarranted weight to the evidence, the offered proof is a candidate for exclusion under Rule 403.[18] In any situation in which the evidence must be accompanied by a limiting instruction so convoluted or tortured that the jury will be at a loss to gauge the proper application or weight of the evidence, Rule 403 may operate to exclude the offer.[19]

While the bases of exclusion relating to confusion of the issues or misleading of the jury finds precedent in pre-Rule case law,[20] some pre-Rule cases address the analysis in terms of "remoteness," *i.e.* remoteness resulting because the offered facts are temporarily or spatially separated from the event sought to be established.[21] In actuality, any evidence that alters the probabilities of a fact of consequence in the law suit is relevant even though substantial time or space separates the facts offered from the transaction or occurrence sought to be established. However, as a generalization, the more remote a fact from the event sought to be proven, the lower its probative value, and an extremely remote fact possessing extremely low probative value may be easily excluded under Rule 403 where an appropriate counterweight is present, *e.g.* confusion or prejudice. It should be emphasized, however, that no evidence is inadmissible simply because its probative value is extremely low. An express exclusionary rule must be invoked. Nevertheless, when probative value is extremely low, Rule 403

---

[17] United States v. Hartley, 678 F.2d 961, 980-81 (11th Cir. 1982), *cert. denied*, 103 S.Ct. 815 (1983); United States v. Schmidt, 711 F.2d 595, 598 (5th Cir. 1983).

[18] *See* Brumley Estate v. Iowa Beef Processors, Inc., 707 F.2d 1351, 1356-57 (5th Cir. 1983); United States v. Landes, 704 F.2d 152, 154 (5th Cir. 1983); Golden Bear Distr. Systems of Texas Inc. v. Chase Revel, Inc., 708 F.2d 944, 947 (5th Cir. 1983).

[19] Kim v. Coppin State College, 662 F.2d 1055, 1058 (4th Cir. 1981); United States v.

Steffen, 641 F.2d 591, 593 (8th Cir. 1980), *cert. denied*, 452 U.S. 943, 101 S.Ct. 3091, 69 L.Ed.2d 959 (1981); United States v. Ness, 665 F.2d 248, 250-51 (8th Cir. 1981).

[20] *See, e.g.*, Shepard v. United States, 290 U.S. 96, 101, 54 S.Ct. 22, 26, 78 L.Ed. 196, 200 (1933); United States v. 25.406 Acres of Land, 172 F.2d 990, 993 (4th Cir. 1949), *cert. denied*, 337 U.S. 931, 69 S.Ct. 1496, 93 L.Ed. 1738 (1949).

[21] *See, e.g.*, Cotton v. United States, 361 F.2d 673, 675 (8th Cir. 1966).

may be an appropriate basis for exclusion of the minimally helpful evidence where a negative attribute identified in Rule 403 can be cited.[22]

Confusion of the issues and misleading the jury may also be bases for exclusion of evidence in instances where evidence is inadmissible in part or where evidence is admissible for one purpose and not for another.[23] Pursuant to Rule 105, evidence is not rendered inadmissible simply because it is admissible for one purpose but not for another, and the court may admit such evidence subject to a limiting instruction to the jury. Rule 403 may be the basis for exclusion of evidence falling within this category where its admission would have such a misleading effect, that the jury's decision-making process would be compromised.[24] Again, it should be emphasized that the danger must *substantially* outweigh the probative value, and the mere possibility of confusion will not be a basis for exclusion of evidence under Rule 403.

§ 403.5   Exclusion of Relevant Evidence Based Upon Waste of Time, Undue Delay and Needless Presentation of Cumulative Evidence.

A trial judge possesses discretion under Rule 403 to exclude evidence based upon such efficiency and considerations as undue delay, needless presentation of cumulative evidence and waste of time.[25] Because of the similarity between waste of time, undue delay and presentation of cumulative evidence as grounds for exclusion, courts rarely distinguish among these factors.[26] Nevertheless, it is clear that in this context, Rule 403 may be the basis for limiting: the number of witnesses to prove a fact;[27] repetitious

---

[22] *E.g.*, Czajka v. Hickman, 703 F.2d 317, 320 (8th Cir. 1983); United States v. Akers, 702 F.2d 1145, 1149 (D.C. Cir. 1983). Rexrode v. American Laundry Press Co., 674 F.2d 826, 832 (10th Cir. 1982), *cert. denied*, 103 S.Ct. 137 (1982).

[23] Jamison v. Storer Broadcasting Co., 511 F. Supp. 1286, 1294-95 (E.D. Mich. 1981); United States v. Terebecki, 692 F.2d 1345, 1350 (11th Cir. 1982); United States v. Green, 548 F.2d 1261, 1270 (6th Cir. 1977).

[24] Larue v. National Union Electric Corp., 571 F.2d 51, 58 (1st Cir. 1978); Marx & Co. Inc. v. Diner's Club Inc., 550 F.2d 505, 511 (2d Cir. 1977), *cert. denied*, 434 U.S. 861, 98 S.Ct. 188, 54 L.Ed.2d 134 (1977).

[25] Abernathy v. Superior Hardwoods Inc., 704 F.2d 963, 968 (7th Cir. 1983); United States v. Baye, 688 F.2d 471, 476 (7th Cir. 1982).

[26] *See, e.g.*, United States v. Cole, 622 F.2d 98, 100 (4th Cir. 1980), *cert. denied*, 449 U.S. 956, 101 S.Ct. 363, 66 L.Ed.2d 221 (1980); United States v. Johnson, 605 F.2d 1025, 1030 (7th Cir. 1979).

[27] *See, e.g.*, Donovan v. Burger King Corp., 672 F.2d 221-25 (1st Cir. 1982); Wetherill v. University of Chicago, 565 F. Supp. 1553, 1555 (N.D. Ill. 1983).

evidence;[28] as well as evidence which represents an inefficient use of the court's time when compared with probative value.[29]

§ 403.6   Exclusion of Relevant Evidence and the Role of "Surprise."

In not designating unfair surprise as a ground for exclusion, Rule 403 comports with Wigmore's view rather than McCormick's.[30] While surprise may undoubtedly result in injustice in certain situations, the granting of a continuance is considered to be the more appropriate method of achieving fairness in this context.[31]

§ 403.7   Relationship of Rule 403 and Rule 105.

The interrelationship between Rule 105, "Limited Admissibility," and Rule 403 cannot be over emphasized. Rule 105 provides for a limiting instruction from the trial judge, and a limiting instruction is frequently used as the second line of defense when trial counsel has unsuccessfully attempted to exclude evidence under Rule 403.[32] Likewise, the trial judge should consider the efficacy of a limiting instruction in addressing the counterweight in evaluating a claim of exclusion based on Rule 403.

---

[28] *See, e.g.*, Gibson v. Mohawk Rubber Co., 695 F.2d 1093, 1101 (8th Cir. 1982); United States v. Ackal, 706 F.2d 523, 526 (5th Cir. 1983).

[29] *See* MCI Communications v. American Telephone & Telegraph Co., 708 F.2d 1081, 1084 (7th Cir. 1983); Koutz v. K-Mart Corp., 712 F.2d 1302, 1305 (8th Cir. 1983).

See also, Abernathy v. Superior Hardwoods, Inc., 704 F.2d 963, 968 (7th Cir. 1983).

[30] *Compare* 6 WIGMORE, § 1848 with McCORMICK, § 185. *See, generally*, 2 LOUISELL & MUELLER, § 130; LILLY, § 13, at 34.

[31] Rule 403, Advisory Committee's Note.

[32] *See* discussion of Rule 105, *supra*.

Chapter 404

RULE 404. CHARACTER EVIDENCE NOT ADMISSIBLE TO PROVE CONDUCT; EXCEPTIONS; OTHER CRIMES

Rule 404(a)   Character Evidence Generally

Rule 404(a) reads as follows:

(a) **Character Evidence Generally.** Evidence of a person's character or trait of his character is not admissible for the purpose of proving that he acted in conformity therewith on a particular occasion, except:

(1) **Character of accused.** Evidence of a pertinent trait of his character offered by an accused, or by the prosecution to rebut the same;

(2) **Character of victim.** Evidence of a pertinent trait of character of the victim of the crime offered by an accused, or by the prosecution to rebut the same, or evidence of a character trait of peacefulness of the victim offered by the prosecution in a homicide case to rebut evidence that the victim was the first aggressor;

(3) **Character of witness.** Evidence of the character of witness, as provided in Rules 607, 608 and 609.

§ 404.1   Character Evidence—In General.

Rule 404 addresses the circumstances under which evidence of character or a trait of character is admissible.[1] Once it is determined that character evidence is admissible, consideration of Rule 405 is necessary in order to determine the methodology of proof. Where character evidence is admissible in order to affect the credibility of a witness, however, Rule 608 and 609 should be considered for methodology of proof.

§ 404.2   Policy Supporting Rule 404(a).

Rules 401 through 403 define relevancy and provide for the function of relevancy as the threshold standard of admissibility.[2] The remainder of the Rules in Article IV relate to applications of relevancy in specific situations

---

[1] *See, generally,* McCormick, §§ 186-93; 2 Weinstein, ¶¶ 404[01]-[07]; 2 Louisell & Mueller, §§ 135-38; 1 Wigmore, §§ 52-81. *See also* Ulviller, *Evidence of Character to Prove Conduct: Illusion, Illogic and Injustice in the Courtroom,* 130 U. Pa. L. Rev. 845 (1982); Weissenberger, *Character Evidence under the Federal Rules; A Puzzle with Missing Pieces,* 48 U. Cin. L. Rev. 1 (1979); Comment, *Collateral Estoppel Ef-* *fect of Prior Acquittals: United States v. Mespoulede,* 46 Brooklyn L. Rev. 781 (1980); Annot., *When is evidence of a trait of accused character 'pertinent' for purposes of admissibility under Rule 404(a)(1) of the Federal Rules of Evidence,* 49 A.L.R. Fed. 478 (1980).

[2] *See, generally,* § 401.1 *et seq.* of this Treatise.

which have recurred with sufficient frequency that specialized principles have been developed. The considerations underlying the limited admissibility of character evidence embody the same policy contained in Rule 403. Essentially, character evidence is in many instances inadmissible because its probative value is substantially outweighed by its potential adverse effect upon the integrity of the litigation process. Accordingly, it should be recognized that character evidence may be highly relevant, but nevertheless inadmissible under Rule 404.[3]

§ 404.3   Definitions.

The term "character" refers to a generalized description of a person's disposition or a general trait such as honesty, temperance or peacefulness. Generally speaking, character refers to an aspect of an individual's personality which is usually described in evidentiary law as a "propensity."[4]

Habit is a distinguishable concept. Habit is a person's regular practice of meeting a particular kind of situation with a specific type of responsive conduct.[5] In behavioral terms, habit refers to the tendency of a person to exhibit a regular response to a specific stimulus. Habit is unquestionably a form of propensity, and consequently, it is in many cases difficult to distinguish habit from what evidentiary law would designate as character. The distinction, nevertheless, is important because the admissibility of character evidence is highly restricted by Rule 404 whereas the admissibility of habit evidence is authorized under Rule 406.[6] Where the propensity is general and represents a behavioral inclination, the propensity is character governed by Rule 404; where the propensity is specific and connected with an identifiable prompting circumstance, the propensity is habit governed by Rule 406.[7] While gradations of gray undoubtedly exist between these definitions, the law requires designation of the propensity as either habit or character in order to determine whether Rule 404 or Rule 406 applies. Consequently, sensitive appreciation of the policy of this sector of the law of evidence is important to ensure a proper resolution in difficult cases.

Despite occasional blurring of the concepts, reputation and character are distinguishable concepts. Character is a trait of personality whereas reputation is the collective perception of an individual by persons in an identifiable community.[8] As discussed in conjunction with Rule 405, repu-

[3] 2 LOUISELL & MUELLER, § 135, at 79.

[4] 2 WEINSTEIN, ¶ 404[04], at 404-25.

[5] See, generally, 2 WEINSTEIN, ¶ 404[01]; 2 LOUISELL & MUELLER, § 156; McCor-

MICK, § 195, at 462-65; 1 WIGMORE, §§ 92-97.

[6] See § 406.1 of this Treatise.

[7] McCORMICK, § 195, at 462.

[8] Rule 405, Advisory Committee's Note.

tation is one means of proving the character of an individual when character evidence is admissible.

§ 404.4 Exclusionary Rule as to Character Evidence.

Rule 404(a) codifies the basic principle that evidence of a person's character trait is not admissible for the purpose of proving that such person acted in conformity with his character on a particular occasion. This basic prohibition is often called "the propensity rule" because it prohibits the use of propensity to demonstrate actions conforming to the propensity.[9] In essence, the fundamental exclusion rule creates a forbidden inferential pattern.[10] Under the prohibition of Rule 404(a), a person's character or propensity to act in a particular way may not be offered as a basis for the inference that on a specific occasion he acted in accordance with his propensity or trait. It should be noted that subject to the express exceptions in Rules 404(a)(1) through (3), the prohibition applies to any person, party or non-party, principal actor or minor player.

Evidence of a person's character or character traits possesses the inherent risk of distracting the trier of fact from the primary issues of the case. Character evidence has a tendency to invite a finding based upon the trier's attitude toward a person's character, rather than upon an objective evaluation of the operative facts of the case.[11] Consequently, the prohibition of Rule 404(a) is aimed at the tactic of attempting to prove a person's action upon a particular occasion by offering evidence that the person has an ingrained tendency to act in a certain way.

In order to comprehend the application of Rule 404(a), it is important to recognize two considerations. First, a person's propensity, *e.g.* violence, is unquestionably (indeed, by definition) relevant to proving an act consistent with the propensity, *e.g.* murder. Consequently, the policy of Rule 404(a) is not based upon non-existent relevancy; rather, the policy is prejudice.[12] Second, where the proponent of evidence is seeking to prove an act, the proponent is not deprived of the totality of means to prove the act. Propensity to commit the act is but one item of relevant evidence that might be employed to substantiate the occurrence of the act. Other lines of proof remain available: *e.g.*, eyewitness testimony of the occurrence, circumstantial evidence such as motive, opportunity, etc. In the case of the proof of murder, for example, myriad forms of proof are available to prove the act

---

[9] 2 WEINSTEIN, ¶ 404[04], at 405-25.
[10] This forbidden inference can be diagrammed:

Character ⟶ Conforming
or Trait ⟶ Conduct

[11] McCORMICK, § 195, at 462-65.
[12] McCORMICK, § 195, at 463.

other than the violent propensity of the alleged perpetrator. Consequently, the effect of Rule 404(a) is to preclude but one line of circumstantial evidence to prove an act.

Rule 404(a) is applicable in both civil and criminal cases, but its prohibitory effect will most frequently arise in a criminal case. Accordingly, the prosecution may not offer evidence of a negative character trait of the accused in order to establish that the accused acted in conformity with his character trait and committed the crime in question. While, for example, a propensity to be violent is probative of an assault, such evidence is excluded under Rule 404(a) because it may unduly excite the emotions and prejudices of the jury and invite an irrational verdict. The trier of fact might seek to penalize a person who has a violent character rather than making a dispassionate and objective evaluation of the operative facts of the case. The doctrine embodied in Rule 404(a) has been generally recognized in pre-Rule case law.[13]

The basic proposition that propensity evidence is inadmissible has equal force in civil cases. Accordingly, accident proneness or a propensity toward negligence is not admissible to establish that a person failed to exercise due care on a particular occasion.[14]

Rule 404(a) sets forth three exceptions where the exclusionary principle will not apply and where character may be used to prove conforming conduct. In effect, these exceptions authorize use of the otherwise forbidden inference in limited contexts. The otherwise prohibited inferential pattern may be used only where these exceptions apply.

§ 404.5   Character of the Accused, Rule 404(a)(1).

Rule 404(a)(1) provides that an accused in a criminal case may introduce the issue of his character. In a criminal matter, the accused may seek to offer appropriate evidence supporting his good character in order to establish that on the particular occasion involving the facts of the crime charged, the accused acted in conformity with his good character and did not commit the crime in question.[15] Use of the word "accused" in Rule

---

[13] See WIGMORE, §§ 57, 64; McCORMICK, § 159.

[14] See Re Aircrash in Bali, Indonesia, 684 F.2d 1301, 1315 (9th Cir. 1982); Reyes v. Missouri Pacific Railroad Co., 589 F.2d 791, 794 (5th Cir. 1979); George v. Morgan Construction Co., 389 F. Supp. 253, 264-65 (E.D. Pa. 1975). But cf. Gray v. Sherrill, 542 F.2d 953, 954 (5th Cir. 1976) (civil rights action against police for arresting plaintiff for no apparent reason; court

stated that since plaintiff had put his character in issue by testifying that he was calm and temperate, no error in permitting testimony by witness concerning plaintiff's character trait of having emotional outbursts and being argumentative; no mention of Federal Rules).

[15] See, generally, McCORMICK, § 195. See also United States v. Lechoco, 542 F.2d 84, 88 n.5 (D.C. Cir. 1976).

404(a)(1) indicates that this exception is only available in a criminal matter. For example, where the criminal defendant is charged with an assault, he may offer evidence of a "pertinent trait" in accordance with Rule 404(a)(1). A pertinent trait in this context would be peacefulness, *i.e.* a propensity which is consistent with the accused's theory of the case and which is behaviorally incompatible with the crime which is charged. It should be noted that Rule 404(a)(1) requires evidence of a *pertinent* trait, and the accused proffer of evidence of his general, good character is inappropriate and tactically unwise.

It is universally the rule that the prosecution, as part of its case-in-chief, may not offer evidence of the accused's character in order to show his propensity to commit the acts underlying the crime that is charged. Only the accused may introduce character evidence by offering appropriate testimony in accordance with Rule 405 regarding this character in his case in defense. Once, however, the accused has introduced evidence as to his or her good character, the prosecution, in its case in rebuttal, may offer evidence attacking the character of the accused.[16] Again, this evidence must conform to the directives of Rule 405.

An accused will often elect to use character evidence where the prosecution's case is largely circumstantial. Use of character evidence in this situation seeks to establish a reasonable doubt as to whether the accused committed the crime. Reasonable doubt, of course, would be created by evidence which shows that it is unlikely that the accused is the type of person who would commit the crime in question, *i.e.*, that the accused lacks the propensity to commit such a crime.[17]

When an accused offers evidence of his good character and injects the issue of his propensities into the case, three critical tactical considerations must be addressed. First, consistent with Rule 405, any character witness offered may be cross-examined as to prior acts of the accused which are relevant to the pertinent trait advanced.[18] These acts may otherwise never

---

[16] *See* discussion of Rule 405, *infra*, which governs the methodology of proof by both the accused and the prosecution. *See also* Carson v. Polley, 689 F.2d 562, 576 (5th Cir. 1982). *See, e.g.,* United States v. Gilliland, 586 F.2d 1384, 1389 (9th Cir. 1978) (reversible error for court to have allowed defendant's purported eyewitness, who was also his stepson, to be cross-examined about defendant's prior convictions where witness had not been called as a character witness).

[17] Edgington v. United States, 164 U.S. 361, 366, 17 S.Ct. 72, 74, 41 L.Ed. 467, 469 (1896); Michelson v. United States, 335 U.S.

469, 479, 69 S.Ct. 213, 219, 93 L.Ed. 168, 176 (1948).

[18] Rule 405 reads as follows:

(a) **Reputation or Opinion.** In all cases in which evidence of character or a trait of character of a person is admissible, proof may be made by testimony as to reputation or by testimony in the form of an opinion. On cross-examination, inquiry is allowable into relevant specific instances of conduct.

(b) **Specific Instances of Conduct.** In cases in which character or a trait

be exposed to the jury. Second, the accused usually should seek to advance a narrow trait, rather than a general endorsement of good character; the narrower the trait, the narrower the rebuttal by the prosecution.[19] And third, the accused must weigh the possibility of negative character witnesses called by the prosecution during its case in rebuttal.[20] Pre-Rule case law generally supports the principles embodied in Rule 404(a)(1).[21]

§ 404.6   Character of Accused, Policy for Admissibility.

While character evidence is generally thought to affect adversely the fact finding process, character evidence is available to the accused on the theory that a criminal defendant should have every opportunity to disprove his guilt. In essence, Rule 404(a)(1) embodies a mercy principle. It must be emphasized, however, that if the accused exercises the option to utilize character evidence, he then exposes himself to prosecution evidence which would rebut the accused's evidence of good character.

When the accused offers evidence of his good character, the risk of prejudice is minimal. As stated by McCormick: "There may be some danger that the jury will be induced by the evidence of good character to outstep their function by pardoning a man whom they believe to be guilty, but this kind of equitable dispensing power is one that the community, while it does not explicitly sanction, probably does not disapprove."[22]

§ 404.7   Character of the Victim, Rule 404(a)(2).

The second exception to the exclusionary principle of Rule 404(a) provides that an accused may introduce pertinent evidence of the character of a victim of the charged crime.[23] Again, the term "accused" indicates that,

---

of character of a person is an essential element of a charge, claim, or defense, proof may also be made of specific instances of his conduct.
See United States v. Apfelbaum, 621 F.2d 62, 65 (3d Cir. 1980); United States v. Glass, 709 F.2d 669, 673 (11th Cir. 1983).

[19] See United States v. Reed, 700 F.2d 638, 645 (11th Cir. 1983).

[20] See United States v. Reese, 568 F.2d 1246, 1249-50 (6th Cir. 1976).

[21] See Michelson v. United States, 335 U.S. 469, 479, 69 S.Ct. 213, 219, 93 L.Ed. 168, 175 (1948); United States v. Lechoco, 542 F.2d 84, 88 n.5 (D.C. Cir. 1976).

[22] McCORMICK, § 191, at 454 n.61.

[23] United States v. Greschner, 647 F.2d 740, 742 (7th Cir. 1981); Lagasse v. Vestal, 671 F.2d 668, 669 (1st Cir. 1982), cert. denied, 102 S.Ct. 2939 (1982); Government of Virgin Islands v. Carino, 631 F.2d 226, 229-30 (3d Cir. 1980). See, generally, LILLY, § 40, at 117. See also United States v. Kelley, 545 F.2d 619, 623 (8th Cir. 1976), cert. denied, 430 U.S. 933, 97 S.Ct. 1555, 51 L.Ed.2d 777 (1977); Annot., Admissibility of Evidence as to Other's Character or Reputation for Turbulence on Question of Self-Defense by One Charged with Assault or Homicide, 1 A.L.R.3d 571 (1965).

like the first exception to Rule 404, Rule 404(a)(2) is applicable only in a criminal case.

Rule 404(a)(2) is triggered in largely the same way as Rule 404(a)(1): The accused offers a character witness in accordance with the procedures of Rule 405 who testifies to the "pertinent trait" of the victim of the charged crime. Additionally, a special application in homicide cases is provided in Rule 404(a)(1). In homicide prosecutions, "a plea of self-defense coupled with evidence that the deceased was the first aggressor is sufficient to trigger the prosecutor's right to offer rebuttal evidence that the victim was a person of peaceful character."[24] This provision is based on the special need for the evidence in situations in which the victim, by the nature of the crime, is unavailable.[25] The evidence that the victim was the first aggressor may be of any competent type in order to avail the prosecution of the opportunity to offer evidence of the victim's peaceful character, but the evidence so offered by the prosecution, of course, must conform to the methods of proof prescribed in Rule 405.

When an accused injects the issue of the victim's character into the case, either by offering character evidence in accordance with Rule 405 or by coupling self-defense with evidence of first-aggression of the victim in a homicide case, the accused does not by virtue of these elections open the issue of his own character.[26] The issue of the accused's own character is only introduced in accordance with the provisions of Rule 404(a)(1), *i.e.* when the accused offers positive character evidence as prescribed by the procedures delineated in Rule 405.

Rule 404 is not applicable to rape victims. Rule 412 preempts Rule 404 in governing the admissibility of a rape victim's reputation for past sexual behavior.[27]

§ 404.8   Character of Witness, Rule 404(a)(3).

The third exception to the exclusionary principle of Rule 404(a) relates to the character of a witness who takes the stand to testify. Rule 404(a)(3) provides that the character of a witness may be explored as to the witness's traits of veracity or truth-telling. This exception to the basic exclusionary rule is more specifically codified in Rules 607, 608 and 609, which relate to impeachment. It is significant to note, however, that the exception relating to the character of witnesses will apply to the accused if he takes the stand on his own behalf. Consequently, if the accused elects to testify in his or

---

[24] LILLY, § 40, at 118.
[25] *Id.*

[26] LILLY, § 40, at 119.
[27] *See* the discussion of Rule 412, *infra*.

her own case, certain aspects of his or her character are subject to exploration by the prosecution pursuant to Rules 608 and 609.

§404.9   Character in Issue—In General.

While the basic exclusionary principle of Rule 404(a) prohibits the use of a specific type of inference, it does not forbid the use of all character evidence. Consequently, when character evidence is offered to establish consequential facts other than conforming conduct of the person characterized, the character evidence is not proscribed by Rule 404(a).[28] The great majority of uses of character evidence, however, does capitalize upon the forbidden inference, and consequently, the prohibition and its limited exceptions will apply in most situations. While "character in issue" is not expressly addressed by Rule 404, the admissibility of such evidence arises by implication because it is relevant (indeed, substantively mandated), and not excluded under Rule 404.[29]

§ 404.10   Character in Issue—Test for Application.

The test for determining when character is in issue tends to be elusive. Essentially, character evidence is not caught in the net of the Rule 404(a) exclusionary principle wherever character evidence is offered to prove a consequential fact other than conforming conduct. Actions for libel, slander, malicious prosecution, seduction, and assault and battery have been identified as cases in which character may be in issue.[30] It should be emphasized, however, that the nature of the case is not determinative of whether character is in issue. Where character or a trait of character is an

---

[28] While character evidence which does not capitalize on the forbidden inference of Rule 404(a) usually falls within the category of "character in issue," a third relatively rare application of character evidence is also analytically possible. This third, distinct application of character evidence (*i.e.*, not "character in issue" and not the prohibited inference of Rule 404(a)), is the use of character as the basis for an inference other than conforming conduct. *See* LILLY, § 41, at 120. Accordingly, evidence of a victim's character may be relevant not by showing conforming conduct, but rather, to show the accused's reasonable reaction to the character trait known to the accused. *See* 1 WIGMORE, § 54; ". . . a deceased's character to show that the defendant was reasonably afraid of an attack by the deceased." This rare use of character evidence is admissible because it is not caught by the exclusionary net of Rule 404(a). *See* Weissenberger, *Character Evidence and the Federal Rules: A Puzzle with Missing Pieces*, 48 U. CIN. L. REV. 1 (1979).

[29] *See, generally,* Weissenberger, *Character Evidence Under the Federal Rules: A Puzzle with Missing Pieces*, 48 U. CIN. L. REV. 1 (1979).

[30] *See* McCORMICK, § 187; WIGMORE, § 66.

essential element of the crime, a claim, or defense, character is in issue. The ultimate question is whether character is the basis for an inference to prove conforming conduct. If character is used in an inferential manner to prove conforming conduct, then the prohibition of Rule 404(a) applies. If, on the other hand, character or a trait of character is an essential element of a party's case, character is in issue as compelled by the substantive law.

The "essential element" formulation, which finds its source in Rule 405, however, can be misleading if it is not fully appreciated. The source of the problem is that the term "essential" can have various meanings. For example, essential evidence could be construed to mean evidence that is necessary because alternative means of proof are unavailable. This, however, is not the intent of the Rule or the character in issue principle. The essential element test demands that character evidence be substantively required as a terminal point of proof. The substantive law must give the party no choice but to use the character evidence if his claim or defense is to be substantiated. For example, where plaintiff charges defendant with a slander claiming that the defendant said "Plaintiff is dishonest," and the defendant pleads truth as a defense, the defendant must prove plaintiff's dishonesty (a character trait) in order to prevail. The dishonest trait of the plaintiff becomes an element of the defendant's affirmative defense. Plaintiff's dishonesty is not being utilized as proof of conforming conduct. Rather, it is an essential element of the defense, and plaintiff's character trait is "in issue."

Rule 404(b)　　Other Crimes, Wrongs, or Acts

Rule 404(b) reads as follows:

(b) Other Crimes, Wrongs, or Acts. Evidence of other crimes, wrongs, or acts is not admissible to prove the character of a person in order to show that he acted in conformity therewith. It may, however, be admissible for other purposes, such as proof of motive, opportunity, intent, preparation, plan, knowledge, identity, or absence of mistake or accident.

§ 404.11　　Other Crimes, Wrongs, or Acts—In General.

Rule 404(b) codifies an extension of the exclusionary principle of Rule 404(a), and it is a restatement of implicit limitations on the proof of character evidence set forth in Rule 405. Rule 404(b) provides that evidence of other crimes, wrongs, or acts is not admissible to prove the character of a person in order to show that such person acted in conformity with his character on a particular occasion.[31] As in the application of Rule 404(a), Rule 404(b) embraces the customary construction of the term "character," i.e., "propensity." Accordingly, the term "character" essentially pertains to a person's distinct traits or propensities to act in a particular way, and it applies to such propensities as dishonesty, violence, peacefulness, and veracity.[32] It is important to note the Rule applies in both civil and criminal cases, and its scope encompasses any extrinsic act, not only acts resulting in criminal conviction or acts subject to criminal prosecution.

Like Rule 404(a), Rule 404(b) creates a prohibited inferential pattern.[33] The Rule in essence prohibits the argument which would suggest that because a person acted in a particular way on a distinct, specific occasion, she likely acted the same way in regard to the operative facts of the instant litigation.

Rule 404(b) is composed of two sentences, each with distinct functions. The first sentence sets forth the rule of exclusion. The second sentence is a clarifying provision which emphasizes the limited scope of the exclusionary rule contained in the first sentence.

§ 404.12   Policy of Rule 404(b) in Criminal Cases.

The prohibition of Rule 404(b) pertains to the establishment of extrinsic acts as a basis for the inference that an individual acted in conformity with his "other" act and the indicated propensity. The evidence of the extrinsic act is excluded because it is thought that the jury might punish or reward an individual for his distinct conduct rather than weighing only the evidence directly relevant to the specific occurrence. Another policy supporting Rule 404(b) is a recognition of the danger that the jury may misestimate the probative value of the extrinsic act evidence in evaluating its significance:

> [Extrinsic act evidence is excluded] not because it has no appreciable probative value, but because it has too much. The natural and inevi-

---

[31] *See, generally*, McCormick, §§ 190-94; 2 Weinstein, ¶¶ 404[8]-[20]; 2 Louisell & Mueller, §§ 140-44; 2 Wigmore, §§ 300-73. *See also* Weissenberger, *Making Sense of Extrinsic Act Evidence: Federal Rules of Evidence 404(b)*, 70 Iowa L. Rev. 579 (1985); Orfield, *The Defense of Entrapment in the Federal Courts*, 1967 Duke L.J. 39 (1978); Annot.,

Admissibility Under Rule 404(b) of Federal Rules of Evidence, of Evidence of Other Crimes, Wrongs, or Acts not Similar to Offense Charged, 41 A.L.R. Fed. 497 (1979).

[32] *See* discussion at § 404.1 of this Treatise.

[33] Here the forbidden inference can be diagrammed:

Extrinsic → Character → Conforming
Act   (Propensity)   Conduct

table tendency of the tribunal—whether judge or jury—is to give excessive weight to the vicious record of crime thus exhibited, and either to allow it to bear too strongly on the present charge, or to take the proof of it as justifying a condemnation irrespective of guilt of the present charge. . . .[34]

Rule 404(b) recognizes the frequent unpredictability of human behavior, and consequently excludes extrinsic act evidence to prevent the tendency for a jury to believe the defendant is guilty of committing the crime merely because he is purportedly a bad person with a criminal propensity.

Rule 404(b) also is based on the fundamental premise of our accusatory, as opposed to inquisitorial, mode of trial. The accusatory model generally embraces the policy that a person should be free from his past misdeeds in facing a charge for a specific criminal act and that the criminal defendant should not be expected to defend his entire past life. As Justice Rutledge has stated:

> General bad character, much less general bad reputation, has not yet become a criminal offense in our scheme. Our whole tradition is that a man can be punished by criminal sanctions only for specific acts defined beforehand to be criminal, not for general misconduct or bearing a reputation for such misconduct.[35]

It should be noted that the prohibition of the first sentence of Rule 404(b) applies to all parties, including the criminal defendant, and the Rule therefore operates to prevent the accused from introducing evidence of his extrinsic *good* acts to show he acted in conformity with his good character on the occasion in question. Consistent with the express provisions of Rule 405, character may never be established with specific act evidence where it is offered to prove conforming conduct.

§ 404.13　Admissible Extrinsic Acts—In General.

The second sentence of Rule 404(b) indicates that evidence of other crimes, wrongs, or acts may be admissible where offered to prove consequential facts other than conforming conduct. It should be appreciated that a specific inference involving extrinsic acts is prohibited in the first sentence of Rule 404(b), and the Rule does not by its terms absolutely prohibit the admissibility of extrinsic crimes, wrongs, or acts. A person's acts, including criminal acts, may be relevant for a purpose other than

[34] McCORMICK, § 190, at 447-48.
[35] 1 WIGMORE, § 194, at 646.

showing propensity to commit a similar act. Such acts would not be subject to the exclusionary principle expressed in the first sentence of Rule 404(b).[36]

The list of proper bases for offering an extrinsic act set forth in the second sentence of Rule 404(b) is not exhaustive, and the essential issue is whether the act is offered only to prove propensity and conforming conduct. If so, the evidence is rendered inadmissible by the first sentence of Rule 404(b). Moreover, the second sentence of Rule 404(b) should not be seen as a list of exceptions to the Rule, but rather as a suggestive, nonexhaustive catalogue of bases which do not violate the exclusionary principle of the first sentence of the Rule. The ultimate issue is a determination of the way in which the extrinsic act is relevant, and the Rule specifically authorizes the use of extrinsic acts where the evidence is offered to prove a relevant fact other than conforming conduct. The burden is consequently upon the proponent of the extrinsic act to demonstrate that the relevancy of the extrinsic act does not pertain to propensity and conforming conduct.[37]

The proponent must also prove the prior act has in fact occurred, and additionally in criminal cases where the alleged extrinsic act is that of the accused, that the criminal defendant in fact committed the act. The Circuits do not agree on the degree of proof necessary to establish the extrinsic act or crime and its connection with the accused. Some federal courts have limited the admissibility of extrinsic act evidence in criminal cases where the prosecution cannot establish by clear and convincing evidence that the extrinsic crime or act was committed by the accused.[38] Other federal courts have used a "preponderance of the evidence" test,[39] a "beyond a reasonable doubt" standard,[40] or a "sufficient for the jury to reasonably find that the offense occurred"[41] test. The most appropriate approach is that mandated

[36] *See, generally,* 2 WEINSTEIN, ¶ 404[09], at 404-49; 2 LOUISELL & MUELLER, § 140, at 144; MCCORMICK, § 194, at 574.

[37] *See, e.g.,* Morris v. Washington Metropolitan Area Transit Authority, 702 F.2d 1037, 1046-47 (D.C. Cir. 1983); United States v. Scott, 701 F.2d 1340, 1345 (11th Cir. 1983); United States v. Bice-Bey, 701 F.2d 1086, 1089 (4th Cir. 1983).

[38] *See* Manning v. Rose, 507 F.2d 889, 892 (6th Cir. 1971); United States v. Wormick, 709 F.2d 454, 459 (7th Cir. 1983); United States v. Evans, 697 F.2d 240, 249 (8th Cir. 1983), *cert. denied,* 458 U.S. 1131, 103 S.Ct. 1779, 77 L.Ed.2d 316 (1983).

[39] United States v. Kahan, 572 F.2d 923, 932 (2d Cir. 1978) (if a person within a short time of charged crime received a large shipment of stolen goods under strikingly similar circumstances, *i.e.,* similar documentation, receipt shortly after the hijacking, absence of demand by supposed consignee, ignorance of consignee's identity, the supposition that the warehouseman did not know the goods were stolen is greatly weakened).

[40] United States v. Testa, 548 F.2d 847, 852 n.1 (9th Cir. 1977) (court charged jury that "prior events could not be considered for any purpose unless the jury first found beyond a reasonable doubt that the accused did the act charged"). *Compare* United States v. Herrera-Medina, 609 F.2d 376, 379 (9th Cir. 1979) (clear and convincing).

[41] United States v. Mortazavi, 702 F.2d 526, 528 (5th Cir. 1983); United States v. Beechum, 582 F.2d 898, 913 (5th Cir. 1978).

by Rule 104(b), "Relevancy conditioned on fact."[42] The extrinsic act is only relevant if it can be shown, as a conditional matter, that the accused committed the act. Consequently, in accordance with Rule 104(b), the prosecution should demonstrate that it possesses evidence "sufficient to support a finding" that the accused committed the extrinsic act.[43] This determination of whether the prosecution possesses the requisite quantum of proof should occur outside the hearing of the jury to avoid any possible prejudice.[44]

§ 404.14   Extrinsic Act Evidence Offered to Show Intent in a Criminal Case.

Cases have generally held that extrinsic acts of the accused are admissible in order to establish the mental state of the accused in situations in which such issue is properly before the court, and while intent must be a genuine issue in the litigation before extrinsic acts may be admitted, courts differ in their determination of when intent is in issue.[45] Where admissible, the acts should tend to prove that the accused understood the wrongful nature of his act by virtue of the fact that prior similar wrongful conduct has been the subject of arrest or conviction.[46] Consequently, a disclaimer of

[42] Rule 104(b) provides:

Relevancy Conditioned on Fact. When the relevancy of evidence depends upon the fulfillment of a condition of fact, the court shall admit it upon, or subject to, the introduction of evidence sufficient to support a finding of the fulfillment of the condition.

[43] See United States v. Beechum, 582 F.2d 898, 911 (5th Cir. 1978) (court reserved decision on whether intent may be proved on direct case where clear before trial that accused would contest intent, and any objection to order of proof waived when he took stand and professed lack of criminal intent). The trial court will generally allow the introduction of evidence of a prior crime even though the party was acquitted or had the charges dropped against him. This is grounded on the premise that any acquittal does not indicate that the party charged was innocent of committing the crime but merely that the state failed to prove its case beyond a reasonable doubt. See United States v. Hill, 550 F. Supp. 983, 988 (E.D. Pa.), aff'd, 716 F.2d 893 (3d Cir. 1983).

[44] See, e.g., United States v. Harrison, 679 F.2d 942, 948 (D.C. Cir. 1982); United States v. Day, 591 F.2d 861, 873-74 (D.C. Cir. 1978). See also 103(c) which provides:

(c) Hearing of Jury. In jury cases, proceedings shall be conducted, to the extent practicable, so as to prevent inadmissible evidence from being suggested to the jury by any means, such as making statements or offers of proof or asking questions in the hearing of the jury.

[45] See United States v. Reed, 639 F.2d 896, 906 (2d Cir. 1981) (no issue of intent when defendant denies commission of the act instead of admitting the act occurred but he lacked the mental intent to commit the crime.); United States v. Franklin, 704 F.2d 1183, 1187-88, n.3 (10th Cir. 1983); United States v. Hamilton, 684 F.2d 380, 384 (6th Cir. 1982), cert. denied, 459 U.S. 976, 103 S.Ct. 312, 74 L.Ed.2d 291 (1982) (evidence of prior crimes is admissible when specific intent is an issue). See, generally, 2 WEINSTEIN, ¶ 404[09], at 404-52.

[46] See United States v. Nabors, 707 F.2d 1294, 1299-1300 (11th Cir. 1983); United States v. Dudley, 562 F.2d 965, 966 (5th Cir. 1977).

knowledge of the criminal nature of an act may be rebutted by proof of prior law enforcement encounters involving similar acts.[47]

When a party seeks to admit evidence of prior acts to prove intent, some courts have held that, to be probative, the prior act should have similar criminal elements to the crime with which the accused is charged. Courts vary in the degree of requisite similarity between the prior and charged crime as a precondition to admitting the evidence.[48]

§ 404.15 Extrinsic Act Evidence Offered to Show Motive in a Criminal Case.

Where an extrinsic act is used to establish motive, the act should demonstrate that the accused possesses a specific reason to commit the crime with which he is charged.[49] An extrinsic act used to prove motive is illustrated by the hypothetical fact pattern in which an accused is charged with the murder of a person who witnessed the commission of a prior crime. The fact that the victim is a known witness to the prior crime may be admissible, because it would be relevant in establishing a motive for the accused to murder the victim in question.

Although motive is usually relevant in all criminal cases, it is not a necessary element of the crime. Nevertheless, extrinsic act evidence of motive may be admissible in cases in which it is highly probative.[50]

§ 404.16 Extrinsic Act Evidence Offered to Show Knowledge, Absence of Mistake or Accident in a Criminal Case.

Extrinsic act evidence may be admissible to negate a mistake or accident, and obviously, this theory is closely linked with demonstrating intent.[51] Under this theory, the proponent must establish a relationship between the mode, time and situation involved in the extrinsic act and the act sought to be proven in order to show that the person in question acted purposefully, rather than by mistake or accident.[52] Professor Lilly provides this example:

[47] United States v. Wilford, 710 F.2d 439, 449 (8th Cir. 1983).

[48] E.g., United States v. Dixon, 698 F.2d 445, 447 (11th Cir. 1983); United States v. Evans, 697 F.2d 240, 247-48.

[49] See United States v. Fraser, 709 F.2d 1556, 1559 (6th Cir. 1983); Phillips v. Smalley Maintenance Services, Inc., 711 F.2d 1524, 1532 (11th Cir. 1983); Bohannon v. Pegelow, 652 F.2d 729, 731 (7th Cir. 1981).

[50] See, e.g., United States v. Birney, 686 F.2d 102, 106-07 (2d Cir. 1982); United States v. Englemen, 648 F.2d 473, 479 (8th Cir. 1981).

[51] See § 404.14, supra.

[52] See, e.g., United States v. Satterfield, 644 F.2d 1082, 1084 (5th Cir. 1981); United States v. Sciortino, 601 F.2d 680, 683 (2d Cir. 1979); United States v. Fairchild, 526 F.2d 185, 189 (7th Cir. 1975), cert. denied,

In the trial of D for receiving stolen property from A, evidence that on other occasions and under similar circumstances A had supplied D with goods known by D to have been stolen is relevant to show that D had "knowledge" that the goods in question were stolen.[53]

§ 404.17   Extrinsic Act Evidence Offered to Show Scheme, Plan, System, Modus Operandi or Identity in a Criminal Case.

Extrinsic acts may be part of the immediate background of the act which is the fundament of the crime charged. In this situation the extrinsic act evidence must show events which are "inextricably related" to the crime charged.[54] Occasionally, this admissibility theory is known as the "res gestae" doctrine.[55] Under this doctrine, the acts must rationally constitute the same transaction as the act that is the object of proof.[56]

Also, extrinsic act evidence may be used to establish the defendant's identity as the perpetrator of the offense in question by showing that he has committed similar crimes and that a distinct, identifiable scheme, plan or system was commonly utilized in the commission of the crimes.[57] A distinct modus operandi tends to show that the crimes were committed by the same person, and consequently, the defendant's extrinsic acts may be relevant to show his unique modus operandi where identity of the perpetrator is an issue.[58]

Finally, extrinsic acts may be admissible on a theory which utilizes the distinct acts as elements of a sequence of events leading up to the crime for which the accused is charged.[59] Consequently, where evidence is presented that the accused previously stole a gun to facilitate the commission of a robbery for which he is charged, the extrinsic act of the theft of the gun is probative of a plan to commit the armed robbery.[60] Cases applying this

---

425 U.S. 942, 96 S.Ct. 1682, 48 L.Ed.2d 186 (1976) (in prosecution for distributing counterfeit bills, no error to receive evidence that defendant had other bills in his possession, as tending to negative "mere accident or mistake").

[53] LILLY, § 45, at 134-35.

[54] E.g., United States v. Costa, 691 F.2d 1358, 1361 (11th Cir. 1982); United States v. Wooten, 688 F.2d 941, 948 (4th Cir. 1983).

[55] United States v. Blewitt, 538 F.2d 1099, 1101 (5th Cir. 1976), cert. denied, 429 U.S. 1026, 97 S.Ct. 650, 50 L.Ed.2d 629 (1976) (court properly admitted allegedly forged checks where payor, payee, and endorsement were the same as on checks which defendant was charged with aiding

and abetting their interstate transportation; all checks were negotiated during same time period and thus constituted part of the system of criminal action involved in the entire fraudulent scheme). See WIGMORE, § 218 for a criticism of this concept.

[56] McCORMICK, § 193, at 572-73.

[57] See e.g., United States v. Messersmith, 692 F.2d 1315, 1320 (11th Cir. 1982); United States v. Andrini, 685 F.2d 1094, 1096-97 (9th Cir. 1982).

[58] See, e.g., Adail v. Wyrick, 711 F.2d 99, 102 (8th Cir. 1983); United States v. Means, 695 F.2d 811, 816-17 (5th Cir. 1983).

[59] See, generally, 2 WEINSTEIN, ¶ 404[16], at 404-89.

[60] See LILLY, § 45, at 134-35.

basis for admissibility vary greatly in the range of acts constituting part of a scheme or plan relevant to the act constituting the crime which is charged.[61]

§ 404.18   Extrinsic Acts in Civil Cases.

While Rule 404(b) will most frequently arise in the context of a criminal case, the Rule is applicable in civil cases. For example, pursuant to the first sentence of Rule 404(b), evidence of other instances of negligence of a defendant is not admissible to establish the defendant's negligence on the particular occasion which forms the basis for the cause of action. Extrinsic acts may not be used to establish a person's negligent propensity or accident proneness. While the extrinsic acts might be relevant, such acts would fall squarely within the prohibition set forth in the first sentence of Rule 404(b).[62] Accordingly, in order to show a negligent propensity, distinct automobile accidents are not admissible against a civil defendant who is sued for vehicular negligence.

Under the second sentence of Rule 404(b), evidence of extrinsic acts of an individual are admissible in civil cases where the acts are not offered to establish conforming conduct. Again, Rule 404(b) does not prohibit evidence of all extrinsic acts; the Rule only prohibits use of a certain inferential pattern. Consequently, evidence of extrinsic acts may be offered to prove notice to the defendant that a dangerous condition or nuisance exists.[63] Likewise, evidence of extrinsic acts might be used to show the existence of a dangerous condition.[64]

§ 404.19   The Interplay of Rule 403 with Rule 404(b).

When evidence is facially admissible under Rule 404(b), the court should address the concerns expressed in Rule 403 before ruling on the

[61] *See, e.g.*, United States v. Nadler, 698 F.2d 995, 1000 (9th Cir. 1983); United States v. Roylance, 690 F.2d 164, 168 (10th Cir. 1982); United States v. McCroy, 699 F.2d 1308, 1311 (11th Cir. 1983).

[62] *See* Re. Aircrash in Bali, Indonesia, 684 F.2d 1301, 1315 (9th Cir. 1982); Reyes v. Missouri Pacific Railroad Co., 589 F.2d 791, 793 (5th Cir. 1979); George v. Morgan Construction Co., 389 F. Supp. 253, 264-65 (E.D. Pa. 1975). *See also* Trautman, *Logical or Legal Relevancy — A Conflict in Theory*, 5 VAND. L. REV. 385, 399-401 (1952); James and Dickinson, *Accident Proneness and Accident Law*, 63 HARV. L.

REV. 769 (1950).

[63] LILLY, § 47, AT 147-48. *See also* Louisville & N.R. Co., 115 F.2d 268, 275-77 (6th Cir. 1902) (in wrongful death action against railroad, no error to exclude evidence tending to show that the deceased was in the habit of jumping on trains near the place where the body was found).

[64] Young v. Illinois Central Gulf R.R. Co., 618 F.2d 332, 335 (5th Cir. 1980); Bailey v. Southern Pacific Transportation Co., 613 F.2d 1385, 1387 (5th Cir. 1980), *cert. denied*, 449 U.S. 836, 101 S.Ct. 109, 66 L.Ed.2d 42 (1980). *See, generally*, LILLY, § 47, at 146-48.

ultimate admissibility of the evidence. Because of the inevitable risk of prejudice and confusion presented by extrinsic act evidence, coupled with the varying degree of probative value of extrinsic acts, there is a special need for careful application of the Rule 403 balance in this context. The necessity for, and probative value of, the extrinsic act must be clear before any extrinsic act is admitted, and the balance of factors identified in Rule 403 should be addressed on the record before the act is admitted pursuant to the second sentence of Rule 404(b).[65]

§ 404.20   Limiting Instruction.

In any case in which the court accepts the proponent's theory of the admissibility of evidence of an extrinsic act and proceeds to admit the act, the trial judge should be requested to provide the jury with a limiting instruction pursuant to Rule 105.[66] Such a limiting instruction would restrict the jury's consideration to the proper basis for admission. The instruction would admonish the jury that the evidence of the extrinsic act may not be considered as a basis for an inference that the individual in question acted in conformity with his extrinsic conduct or with the indicated propensity.

[65] *E.g.*, United States v. Lewis, 693 F.2d 189, 195 (D.C. Cir. 1982); United States v. Melia, 691 F.2d 672, 677 (4th Cir. 1982); United States v. Baileaux, 685 F.2d 1105, 1112 (9th Cir. 1982).

[66] *See* United States v. Woods, 484 F.2d 127, 130 (4th Cir. 1973), *cert. denied*, 415 U.S. 979, 94 S.Ct. 1566, 39 L.Ed.2d 875 (1973); United States v. Phillips, 599 F.2d 134, 136 (6th Cir. 1979).

Chapter 405

RULE 405. METHODS OF PROVING CHARACTER

Rule 405 reads as follows:

(a) **Reputation or Opinion.** In all cases in which evidence of character or trait of character of a person is admissible, proof may be made by testimony as to reputation or by testimony in the form of an opinion. On cross-examination, inquiry is allowable into relevant specific instances of conduct.

(b) **Specific Instances of Conduct.** In cases in which character or a trait of character of a person is an essential element of a charge, claim, or defense, proof may also be made of specific instances of his conduct.

§ 405.1 Methods of Proving Character—In General.

The function of Rule 405 is to designate the permissible method of proving character or a character trait.[1] Rule 405 does not address the issue of the admissibility of character evidence, and Rule 404 should be consulted for determining whether character evidence may be introduced in a particular case.

---

[1] *See, generally,* McCormick, § 191, at 566; 2 Weinstein, ¶¶ 405[01]-[04]; 2 Louisell & Mueller, §§ 148-50; 7 Wigmore, §§ 1981-86. *See also* Dunforth, Jr., *Death Knell for Pre-Trial Mental Examination? Privilege Against Self-Incrimination,* 19 Rutgers L. Rev. 489 (1965); Slough, *Relevancy Unraveled — Part II,* *Character and Habit Evidence,* 5 U. Kan. L. Rev. 404, 415-20 (1957); Curran, *Expert Psychiatric Evidence of Personality Traits,* 103 U. Pa. L. Rev. 999 (1955); Falknor B. Steffey, *Evidence of Character: From the Crucible of the Community to the Couch of Psychiatrist,* 102 U. Pa. L. Rev. 980 (1954).

Rule 405 recognizes three devices for proving a person's character or character trait, but it should be noted that all methodologies of proof are not necessarily available to prove character in each instance in which it is admissible. First, reputation within a pertinent community may be used to establish circumstantially the character of an individual. Second, a person familiar with the character of an individual may provide opinion testimony as to the character in question. Third, specific instances of conduct may be offered to establish the character of an individual. The use of a particular methodology depends upon the way in which character is used in conjunction with the issues of a case. Where character is "in issue,"[2] all methodologies of proving character are available.[3] Where character is used circumstantially to establish conforming conduct, only reputation and opinion evidence are available.[4] Where, however, character evidence is utilized to impeach the credibility of a witness, methodology of proof is governed by Rules 608 and 609.

Specific instances of conduct are available to prove character only when character is in issue because, as a general proposition, proof of specific instances of conduct has the greatest capacity to arouse prejudice, to confuse, to surprise and to consume unnecessary time.[5] Consequently, such methodology of proof is reserved for the situation where character plays a pivotal role in the litigation, *i.e.*, when character is in issue.

§ 405.2　Reputation Evidence Used to Prove Character.

Reputation evidence is available to establish and rebut character in all situations where character is admissible under Rule 404. Reputation evidence, which is used to prove circumstantially the character trait sought to be proven, is the collective opinion of a particular community in regard to a person's character or trait.[6]

[2] See Chapter 404, §§ 404.9, 404.10 of this Treatise.

[3] *See, e.g.*, Crumpton v. Confederation Life Ins. Co., 672 F.2d 1248, 1252 (5th Cir. 1982); Christy v. United States, 68 F.R.D. 375, 377 (N.D. Tex. 1975); United States v. Dennis, 625 F.2d 782, 800 (8th Cir. 1980).

[4] *See* United States v. Bendetto, 571 F.2d 1246, 1250 (2d Cir. 1978) (fact that defendant improperly attempted to establish his good character by reference to specific good acts did not justify prosecution's use of testimony concerning bad acts either in its direct case or on rebuttal). *Accord*, United States v. Herman, 589 F.2d 1191, 1197 (3d Cir. 1978). *See also* 2 Weinstein, ¶ 405[01], at 405-14; McCormick, § 191, at 568.

[5] *See* United States v. Lewis, 693 F.2d 189, 192 (D.C. Cir. 1982); United States v. Cook, 558 F.2d 100, 1003-04 (3d Cir. 1976). *See also* 1 Wigmore, § 194.

[6] *See, e.g.*, United States v. Oliver, 492 F.2d 943, 945-47 (8th Cir. 1974), *cert. denied*, 424 U.S. 973, 96 S.Ct. 1477, 47 L.Ed.2d 743 ("courts have readily extended the concept of community to include the community in which one works, as well as where one lives"). *See also* United States v. Parker, 447 F.2d 826, 831 (7th Cir. 1971) (error to exclude evidence of defendant's reputation among his co-workers, which may well be more significant than his reputation among neighbors, particularly if they are apartment dwellers).

The reputation of a person sought to be characterized is established through the testimony of a character witness. A person qualifies as a character witness where he is a member of a pertinent community in which the person characterized is known, and the character witness must know the reputation of the person sought to be characterized and be prepared to testify to such reputation within the community.[7] Traditionally, character witnesses must be familiar with a person's reputation in his residential community, but contemporary practice permits knowledge of the person's reputation in any relevant community, for example, a business community.[8]

The character witness testifying as to reputation should provide testimony specifically directed to a "pertinent trait" of the person characterized.[9] Accordingly, character evidence of a defendant's truth or veracity is not probative in a case charging him with conspiracy to sell drugs.[10] Nor is evidence of a witness's illicit affair admissible in a case concerned with bank embezzlement.[11] Typically, evidence of a peaceful trait is appropriate for consideration in an assault case; similarly, the trait of honesty is pertinent in a perjury case.[12]

Limiting the scope of the character witness's testimony is critical, because it will ultimately define and limit the scope of cross-examination by opposing counsel. Reputation testimony should also relate to reputation at the time of the facts of the case rather than at the time of the trial.

§ 405.3 Opinion Evidence Used to Prove Character.

Federal Rule 405 departs from prior practice in providing for the availability of opinion testimony to establish and rebut the character of an individual. As stated in the Advisory Committee's Note to Rule 405: "It seems likely that the persistence of reputation evidence is due to its largely being opinion in disguise."

---

[7] *See, e.g.*, United States v. Perry, 643 F.2d 38, 52 (2d Cir. 1981).

[8] *See, e.g.*, United States v. Oliver, 492 F.2d 943, 945-47 (8th Cir. 1974); United States v. Parker, 447 F.2d 826, 831 (7th Cir. 1971).

[9] *See* United States v. Angelini, 678 F.2d 380, 381-82 (1st Cir. 1982); United States v. Hewitt, 634 F.2d 277, 278 (5th Cir. 1981), *See also* Chapter 404 and § 404.8 of this Treatise.

[10] United States v. Jackson, 588 F.2d 1046, 1055 (5th Cir. 1979) (in prosecution for conspiracy to distribute and possess her-

oin, trial judge did not err in excluding character evidence as to defendant's truth and veracity). *See also* Aaron v. United States, 397 F.2d 584, 585 (5th Cir. 1968) (false bank entries and embezzlement; improper to inquire of illicit affair with woman as wholly immaterial to the character traits involved, but instruction to disregard evidence cured error).

[11] Aaron v. United States, 397 F.2d 584, 585 (5th Cir. 1968).

[12] 1 Wigmore, § 59; McCormick, § 191, at 455.

The justification for opinion testimony is discussed by Wigmore:

> The Anglo-American rules of evidence have occasionally taken some curious twistings in the course of their development, but they have never done anything so curious in the way of shutting out evidential light as when they decided to exclude the person who knows as much as humanly can be known about the character of another [*i.e.*, firsthand opinion], and have still admitted the secondhand irresponsible product of multiplied guesses and gossip which we term "reputation."[13]

While the reputation is generally thought to be an effective method of proving character because it collects and summarizes all the minute details of a person's life, opinion evidence can be more effective in situations where a person is not well known within a community or where the community is so large that an individual's reputation is only minimally developed.

Opinion evidence is available in all cases where evidence of character or a trait of character is admissible. Like reputation evidence, opinion evidence must be offered through the testimony of a properly qualified character witness who possesses a first hand basis for his opinion. A substantial familiarity with the person characterized is necessary.[14]

§ 405.4　Cross-examination of a Character Witness.

The cross-examination of a character witness is governed by the second sentence of Rule 405(a), and on cross-examination, inquiry into relevant specific instances of conduct of the person characterized is permissible. The purpose of cross-examination relating to specific instances of conduct is to test the qualifications of the character witness as to the basis for the reputation or opinion testimony. As stated by Lilly:

> Note that if the character witness has not heard of an unfavorable event, his familiarity with the accused's character is brought into question; if he has heard of the unfavorable event, but nonetheless states that the accused enjoys a good reputation, his standard for determining that the reputation is favorable is brought into question.[15]

Specific instances of conduct may be inquired into on cross-examination only if two criteria are satisfied. First, the instance of conduct must be

[13] 7 WIGMORE, § 1986, at 167.
[14] *See, e.g.*, United States v. Perry, 643 F.2d 38, 52 (2d Cir. 1981); United States v. Straughan, 453 F.2d 422, 424-27 (8th Cir. 1972).
[15] LILLY, § 39, at 114.

relevant to the pertinent character trait in question. Accordingly, an act of marital infidelity would not be appropriate for inquiry where the essential issue in the case is embezzlement.[16] Second, before cross-examination, the opponent of the character witness must satisfy the judge that he is proceeding in good faith in inquiring into the specific event. The cross-examiner must have a good faith basis for the contention that the event actually occurred.[17] It should be noted that the cross-examiner may not introduce into evidence independent proof that the events occurred, and he is limited to inquiring about such events on cross-examination of the character witness where he has a good faith basis for the inquiry.[18]

Questioning the character witness concerning prior instances of conduct of the person characterized may assume the traditional form: "Have you heard that Mr. X was terminated from his job in December of 1980 because of embezzlement?" Alternately the cross-examiner may use the more contemporary form: "Do you know that Mr. X was terminated from his job in December of 1980 because of embezzlement?"[19]

Specific instances of conduct, where pertinent and supported by a demonstration of good faith, may include acts,[20] arrests,[21] and convictions.[22]

[16] Aaron v. United States, 397 F.2d 584, 585 (5th Cir. 1968) (false bank entries and embezzlement; improper to inquire of illicit affair with woman, since it was wholly immaterial to the character traits involved).

[17] United States v. Bright, 588 F.2d 504, 511-12 (5th Cir. 1979). *See also* United States v. Reese, 568 F.2d 1246, 1250 (6th Cir. 1977) (court suggested that before permitting character witnesses to be asked whether they had heard of defendant previously buying stolen merchandise, better practice would have been for the trial judge to have had a voir dire examination to determine whether there were actually such rumors before permitting the cross-examination).

[18] *See* Michelson v. United States, 335 U.S. 469, 477, 69 S.Ct. 213, 219, 93 L.Ed. 168, 174-75 (1948) (the Supreme Court, in a case which approaches constitutional significance, thoroughly discussed the theory and procedure for the cross-examination of character witnesses in criminal cases).

[19] *See* Advisory Committee's Note, Rule 405. *See also* McCormick, § 569.

[20] United States v. Glass, 709 F.2d 669, 673-74 (11th Cir. 1983); Hendrix v. United States, 547 F.2d 438, 440 (8th Cir. 1977), *cert. denied*, 430 U.S. 937, 97 S.Ct. 1566, 51 L.Ed.2d 784 (1977).

[21] United States v. Watson, 587 F.2d 365, 367 (7th Cir. 1978) (where defendant's character witness was asked about honesty of defendant, door was opened to cross-examination of witness concerning defendant's arrests; no error where defendant then withdrew character witness' testimony on direct and court advised jury of its final rule); United States v. Duhon, 565 F.2d 345, 353-54 (5th Cir. 1978), *cert. denied*, 435 U.S. 952, 98 S.Ct. 1580, 55 L.Ed.2d 802 (1978) (within trial judge's discretion to decide whether character witness could be cross-examined about defendant's arrest and indictment on an independent charge subsequent to events in instant case); United States v. Bermudez, 526 F.2d 89, 95 (2d Cir. 1975), *cert. denied*, 475 U.S. 970, 96 S.Ct. 2166, 48 L.Ed.2d 793 (1976) (proper to ask character witnesses in a cocaine case whether they had heard that defendant had been arrested the year before on a marijuana charge).

[22] Government of Virgin Island v. Roldan, 612 F.2d 775, 778 (3d Cir. 1979) (where limiting instruction not requested, failure to give an instruction does not constitute plain error); United States v. Edwards, 549 F.2d 362, 367 (5th Cir. 1977), *cert denied*, 434 U.S. 828, 98 S.Ct. 107, 54 L.Ed.2d 87 (1978) (court on cross-examination permitted character witness who testi-

§ 405.5   Cross-examination of a Character Witness; Rule 105 and Rule 403.

The questioning of a character witness concerning prior instances of conduct of the person characterized may result in unfair prejudice, confusion of the issues, and misleading the jury, *i.e.* the trier of fact may inappropriately consider the prior instances of conduct in conjunction with making a determination of the operative facts of the case, rather than merely considering the conduct in ascribing weight to the testimony of the character witness. To minimize the prejudicial impact, a limiting instruction under Rule 105 may be requested.[23]

Alternately, Rule 403 may be invoked in an attempt to preclude the inquiry entirely. Where the probative value of the evidence is extremely low in assessing the credibility of the character witness, and the risk of prejudice is high, exclusion under Rule 403 is appropriate.[24]

§ 405.6   Prior Instances of Conduct to Prove Character.

According to Rule 405(b), prior instances of conduct may be used to prove or rebut character where character or a trait of character operates as an essential element of a charge, claim or defense, *i.e.*, where character is "in issue."[25] Where character is in issue, all methods of proving character or character trait are available.

Specific instances of conduct may be established through a character witness or through the testimony of any person who has the requisite first-hand knowledge of the relevant specific acts of the person characterized.[26]

fied he had known defendant for over 20 years to be asked if he had heard of 1950 conviction and arrests occurring more than 10 years prior to trial; court expressly refused to apply 10 year limitation of Rule 609); Harbin v. Interlake S. S. Co., 570 F.2d 99, 106 (6th Cir. 1978).

[23] Government of Virgin Islands v. Roldan, 612 F.2d 775, 778 (3d Cir. 1979). *See also* United States v. Tempesta, 587 F.2d 931, 936 (8th Cir. 1978) (where there was no indication that trial court did not weigh the probative value against prejudice, no error in allowing inquiry about 1958 burglary).

[24] United States v. Polsinell, 649 F.2d 793, 795-96 (10th Cir. 1981); United States v. Hewitt, 663 F.2d 1381, 1391 (11th Cir. 1983); United States v. Davis, 546 F.2d 583, 592 (5th Cir. 1977), *cert. denied*, 431 U.S. 906, 97 S.Ct. 1701, 52 L.Ed.2d 391 (1977) (rarely and only upon a clear showing of prejudicial abuse will appellate courts disturb the rulings of trial courts in the admissibility of character evidence).

[25] *See, e.g.*, Crumpton v. Confederation Life Ins. Co., 672 F.2d 1248, 1252 (5th Cir. 1982); Christy v. United States, 68 F.R.D. 375, 377 (N.D. Tex. 1975), United States v. Dennis, 625 F.2d 782, 800 (8th Cir. 1980).

[26] *See, e.g.*, United States v. Oliver, 492 F.2d 943, 945-47 (8th Cir. 1974); United States v. Parker, 447 F.2d 826, 831 (7th Cir. 1971). *See also* § 405.2 of this Chapter.

The proponent of the character evidence offers the specific acts, and this method of proof should be distinguished from the use of specific acts for the purpose of cross-examining and testing the credibility of a character witness.[27]

---

[27] *See* § 405.5 of this Chapter.

Chapter 406

RULE 406. HABIT; ROUTINE PRACTICE

SECTION
406.1   Habit evidence—In general
406.2   Definition of habit evidence
406.3   Application of habit evidence
406.4   Proof of the existence of a habit

Rule 406 reads as follows:

> Evidence of the habit of a person or of the routine practice of an organization, whether corroborated or not and regardless of the presence of eyewitnesses, is relevant to prove that the conduct of the person or organization on a particular occasion was in conformity with the habit or routine practice.

§ 406.1   Habit Evidence—In General.

Rule 406 governs the admissibility of the habit of a natural person and the routine practice of a business or organization.[1] Habits of persons and the routine practices of businesses are equivalent in concept for the operation of Rule 406.

Rule 406 essentially serves two functions. First, the Rule confirms the relevancy of habit or routine practice when used to establish conduct which conforms with the habit or routine practice. In this regard, Rule 406 is dissimilar from most other evidentiary Rules. It is essentially a rule of admissibility rather than inadmissibility. Its function is declaratory in light of any confusion that might have been engendered by pre-Rule case

---

[1] *See, generally*, McCORMICK, § 195; 2 WEINSTEIN, ¶¶ 406[01]-[04]; 2 LOUISELL & MUELLER, §§ 155-59; 1 WIGMORE, §§ 92-97. *See also* Green, *Relevancy and Its Limits*, 1969 LAW & THE SOCIAL ORDER, 533, 549-50 (1969); Lewan, *Rationale of Habit Evi-* *dence*, 16 SYRACUSE L. REV. 39 (1964); Slough, *Relevancy Unraveled*, 5 KAN. L. REV. 404, 444-51 (1957); Note, *Relevancy and its Limits in the Proposed Rules of Evidence*, 16 WAYNE L. REV. 167, 179-182 (1969).

law. The second function of Rule 406 is to confirm that the relevancy of habit or routine practice is not eliminated by the absence of eyewitnesses or corroboration. Again, the Rule is declaratory.

§ 406.2　　Definition of Habit Evidence.

McCormick has defined habit evidence:

"Habit" . . . describes one's regular response to a repeated specific situation. If we speak of character for care, we think of the person's tendency to act prudently in all the varying situations of life, in business, in family life, in handling automobiles and walking across the street. A habit on the other hand is the person's regular practice of meeting a particular kind of situation with a specific type of conduct, such as the habit of going down a particular stairway two stairs at a time, or of giving the hand signal for a left turn, or alighting from railway cars while they are moving. The doing of the habitual acts may become semiautomatic.[2]

Much of the analytic imprecision surrounding the admission of habit evidence results from a failure to adhere to a consistently applied definition of habit. In everyday parlance, the word "habit" is used in varying ways. What are called "habitual acts" by laymen will only infrequently rise to the dignity of a habit as recognized by Rule 406.[3]

In order to establish the existence of a habit for the purpose of Rule 406, it must be shown that a person meets a certain situation with a response that approaches invariability. It is critical that a specific stimulus and a resulting response can be identified. Accordingly, "intemperate habits" may not be shown in order to establish inebriation on a particular occasion. The fact that a person "habitually" drinks is insufficiently specific to satisfy the concept of habit embraced by Rule 406, because no stimulus can be identified which is connected with a semiautomatic response.

§ 406.3　　Application of Habit Evidence.

The relevancy of habit evidence has been traditionally recognized. As discussed by McCormick:

Character may be thought of as the sum of one's habits though doubtless it is more than this. But unquestionably the uniformity of one's

---

[2] McCormick, § 195, at 574-75.　　　　[3] McCormick, § 195, at 575-76.

response to habit is far greater than the consistency with which one's conduct conforms to character or disposition. Even though character comes in only exceptionally as evidence of an act, surely any sensible man investigating whether X did a particular act would be greatly helped in his inquiry by evidence as to whether he was in the habit of doing it.[4]

Habit evidence usually falls into the format of the proponent seeking to establish that a habitual response occurred on a particular occasion. In order to establish such a conclusion, the proponent of the habit evidence must first establish that the habit in fact exists.[5] After establishing the habit, the proponent of the evidence submits evidence which would prove that the stimulus for the habitual response occurred on a particular occasion. Habit evidence being relevant and admissible, the habitual response is circumstantially indicated. The stimulus for the habitual response may be established through any witness possessing firsthand knowledge as required by Rule 602.

By its express terms, Rule 406 does not indicate that habit evidence will be admissible in every instance in which it is offered. Most fundamentally, the Rule merely affirms the *relevancy*, and implicitly the admissibility, of habit evidence.[6] In essence the Rule provides that habit evidence satisfies the definition of relevancy contained in Rule 401. Nevertheless, habit evidence may be inadmissible by virtue of an express exclusionary rule. For example, Rule 403 may operate to exclude habit evidence where its probative value is outweighed by such counterweights as unfair prejudice or confusion of the issues.[7]

§ 406.4   Proof of the Existence of a Habit.

In order to capitalize upon habit evidence, the proponent of the evidence must establish the existence of the habit of the person in question or

---

[4] McCORMICK, § 195, at 575.

[5] *See* United States v. Sampol, 636 F.2d 621, 656 (1980); Reyes v. Missouri Pacific Railroad Co., 589 F.2d 791, 795 (5th Cir. 1979). *See also* Reyes v. Missouri Pacific Railroad Co., 589 F.2d 791, 794 (5th Cir. 1979) (four prior convictions for public intoxication spanning a three and one-half year period was of insufficient regularity to rise to the level of "habit" evidence).

[6] United States v. Holman, 680 F.2d 1340, 1350-52 (11th Cir. 1982).

[7] Utility Control Corp. v. Prince William Construction Co., Inc., 558 F.2d 716, 721 (4th Cir. 1977) (fact that individual defendant had previously acted as a guarantor did not mean that a habit had been established pursuant to Rule 406 from which it could be concluded that defendant had guaranteed contract in question, which did not describe capacity in which he joined; relevancy was so slight that evidence should have been excluded).

the routine practice of the organization or business.[8] In establishing the existence of the habit or routine practice, the proponent may utilize opinion testimony, or in the alternative, he may establish the habit or routine practice through proof of specific instances of conduct sufficient in number to warrant a conclusion that the habit exists.[9] Proof of the existence of a habit is normally effected through the testimony of a person who has first-hand knowledge of the individual or business whose habit or custom is sought to be established,[10] Generally, the trial judge has broad discretion to determine whether the foundation for the existence of the habit or routine practice is sufficient to warrant the inference of conforming conduct.

[8] Karme v. Commissioner, 673 F.2d 1062, 1064 (9th Cir. 1982). *See also* United States v. General Foods Corp., 446 F. Supp. 740, 752 (D.C. N.Y. 1978), *aff'd. mem.*, 591 F.2d 1332 (1978) (to rebut allegations of a violation of Federal Food, Drug, & Cosmetic Act, defendant may introduce evidence of routine customs, or business habits, involving established cleanup, sanitation, and maintenance procedures, if they fall within Rule 406).

[9] Wells Fargo Business Credit v. Ben Kozloff Inc., 695 F.2d 940, 944 (5th Cir. 1983), *cert. denied*, 104 S.Ct. 77 (1983).

[10] *See* Rule 602.

Chapter 407

RULE 407. SUBSEQUENT REMEDIAL MEASURES

Rule 407 reads as follows:

> When, after an event, measures are taken which, if taken previously, would have made the event less likely to occur, evidence of the subsequent measures is not admissible to prove negligence or culpable conduct in connection with the event. This rule does not require the exclusion of evidence of subsequent measures when offered for another purpose, such as proving ownership, control, or feasibility of precautionary measures, if controverted, or impeachment.

§ 407.1   Subsequent Remedial Measures—In General.

Rule 407 provides that evidence of remedial action taken after an alleged negligent act or omission will not be admissible to show negligence at the time the injury occurred.[1] The Rule excludes evidence of the subsequent

---

[1] See, generally, MCCORMICK, § 275, at 815-18; 2 LOUISELL & MUELLER, §§ 163-66; 2 WEINSTEIN, ¶¶ 407[01]-[07]; 2 WIGMORE, § 283. See also Fincham, Federal Rule of Evidence 407 and Its State Variations: The Courts Perform Some Subsequent Remedial Measures of Their Own in Products Liability Cases, 49 UMKC L. REV. 388 (1981); Twerski, Post-Accident Design Modification Evidence in Manufacturing Defect Setting: Strict Liability and Beyond, 4 J. PROD. LIAB. 143 (1981); Kaminsky, Post Transaction Evidence in Securities Litigation, 19 B.C.L. REV. 617 (1978); Comment, Chart v. General Motors Corp: Did It Chart the Way for Admission of Evidence of Subsequent Remedial Measures in Products Liability Actions?, 41 OHIO ST. L.J. 211 (1980).

remedial actions to prove negligence or any type of culpable conduct in connection with the event which caused injury.[2]

§ 407.2   Scope of Rule 407.

Virtually any kind of subsequent remedial action is within the purview of Rule 407, and the Rule is not directed simply to the repair of a mechanical device after the mechanical device causes personal injury. For example, the Rule is sufficiently broad to apply to the discharge of an employee subsequent to an accident where it appeared to the employer that the employee was responsible for the accident.[3] Likewise, the Rule includes within its scope a change in company operating procedures after an accident.[4] As a basic principle the rule will apply to any measure which, if taken prior to the accident, would have made the injury less likely to occur.

§ 407.3   Policy of Rule 407.

Rule 407 is supported by two underpinnings. First, evidence of subsequent remedial actions is thought to have low or nonexistent probative value in establishing negligence, *i.e.*, subsequent remedial actions need not be admissions of culpability. Wigmore has analyzed the concept:

> If machines, bridges, sidewalks, or other objects never caused corporal injury except through negligence of their owner, then his act of improving their condition, after the happening of an injury thereat, would indicate a belief on his part that the injury was caused by negligence. But the assumption is plainly faulty; injuries may be and constantly are caused by reason of the inevitable accident, and also by reason of contributory negligence of the injured person.[5]

Wigmore's views notwithstanding, subsequent remedial actions may have some degree of probative value under a standard as liberal as Rule 401,[6]

[2] The Rule is largely declaratory of pre-existing law. New York, L.E. § W.R.R. v. Madison, 123 U.S. 524, 526, 8 S.Ct. 246, 247, 31 L.Ed. 258, 260 (1887); Columbia and P.S. R.R. v. Hawthorne, 144 U.S. 202, 206-08, 12 S.Ct. 591, 593, 36 L.Ed. 405, 406-07 (1892).

[3] *See* 2 WEINSTEIN, ¶ 407[01], at 407-6; 2 LOUISELL & MUELLER, § 163, AT 235. *See, e.g.*, Robbins v. Farmers Union Grain Terminal Association, 552 F.2d 788, 790 (5th Cir. 1977).

[4] *See* 2 WEINSTEIN, ¶ 407[01], at 407-6; 2 LOUISELL & MUELLER, 1 163, at 235. *See*

also Hall v. American Steamship Co., 688 F.2d 1062, 1067 (6th Cir. 1982). *See e.g.*, Steele v. Wiedeman Co., 280 F.2d 380, 382-83 (3d Cir. 1960) (defendant permitted to show in rebuttal that one month after the accident, employer ordered a new safety lever of the original type; evidence was relevant since it suggested a plausible inference that the original part was worn or missing at the time of the accident).

[5] 2 WIGMORE, § 283, at 174.

[6] *See* § 401.3 of Chapter 401.

and a justification for excluding remedial actions solely on the basis of probative value is unimpressive. Unquestionably, remedial action does alter the probabilities of negligence or culpability in certain cases even in light of the non-culpable motivations which might compel a remedial action.

The second justification for Rule 407 is based upon the extrinsic social policy of encouraging remedial action, and under this policy, truth-seeking through the evidentiary system is subordinated to the higher social value of encouraging remedial action.[7] The justification is not without its critics. As Judge Weinstein has stated:

> Nevertheless, Rule 407 has only a marginal justification. Its underlying assumption is that a person will not take remedial measures because his corrective actions might be used in evidence at a future trial. Such an assumption seems absurd. Not every defendant will be aware of the possibility that subsequent remedial measures might constitute an admission. Of those who would know of the Rule, any responsible insured defendant that will not be likely to refrain deliberately from taking action to prevent the recurrence of subsequent serious injuries. In any subsequent case, evidence of the earlier accident would be admissible to show that defendant knew of a dangerous condition.[8]

Consistent with Judge Weinstein's evaluation, it should be appreciated that the basic evidentiary principle embodied in Rule 407 was developed primarily to apply to industrial accidents.[9] The litigation of such accidents now is generally governed and limited by workers' compensation where negligence is largely irrelevant.[10] Today, the Rule more frequently applies in the context of manufacturers' liability actions, and the justification for the exclusion of evidence in this area is considerably less impressive.[11]

§ 407.4 Admissible Remedial Actions.

As the second sentence of Rule 407 indicates, exclusion of the evidence of subsequent remedial actions is only required where the evidence is offered

---

[7] See Rule 407, Advisory Committee's Note.

[8] 2 WEINSTEIN, ¶ 407[02], at 407-10.

[9] See 2 WEINSTEIN, ¶ 407[01], at 407-5. See also General Motors Corp. v. Holler, 150 F.2d 297, 300 (8th Cir. 1945) (glass booth installed to protect employees from noxious fumes; reversal required); Antietam

Paper Co. v. Womble, 294 F. 795, 797 (5th Cir. 1923) (machine redesigned).

[10] See 2 WEINSTEIN, ¶ 407[01], at 407-5; 2 LOUISELL & MUELLER, § 163, at 235.

[11] See, supra. § 407.5. See also 2 WEINSTEIN, ¶ 407[01], at 407-5; Vander Missen v. Kellogg Citizens National Bank of Green Bay, 481 F. Supp. 742, 747 (E.D. Wis. 1979).

to establish negligence or culpable conduct. A specific inferential pattern is prohibited,[12] and evidence of the subsequent remedial action may be offered to establish other relevant issues within a case such as ownership, control, or feasibility of precautionary measures.[13] For remedial actions to be admissible, such issues must be controverted in the case, and, of course, the remedial action must be probative of the controverted consequential facts.[14] Also, a subsequent remedial measure may be offered to contradict and impeach the credibility of a witness where the witness has testified as to the condition of the instrumentality of the injury.[15]

As one commentator has indicated, ingenuity of trial counsel may well account for the admissibility of subsequent remedial actions in virtually any case:

> Opportunities for circumventing the purpose of the Rule are legion, and it is quite evident that admission or exclusion will be judged on the basis of subtle trial maneuvers. By the process of exaggeration in placing undue emphasis upon the importance of physical details, the plaintiff may force the defendant to dispute his contentions, thus paving the way for admission of proof of subsequent repair.[16]

The problems created by admitting remedial action for reasons other than to show negligence or culpable conduct may be tempered by judicious application of Rule 403.[17] Where the subsequent remedial action is only minimally probative of an issue other than negligence or culpability, the

---

[12] The inferential pattern may be diagrammed as:

Remedial Measure $\longrightarrow$ Negligence or Culpability

[13] See, e.g., Rimkus v. Northwest Colorado Ski Corp., 706 F.2d 1060, 1066 (10th Cir. 1983); Anderson v. Malloy, 700 F.2d 1208, 1212-14 (8th Cir. 1983); Rozier v. Ford Motor Co., 573 F.2d 1332, 1343 (5th Cir. 1978) (document prepared by defendant in anticipation of a revised safety standard to be required by National Highway Traffic Safety Administration did not meet exclusion rationale of Rule 407).

[14] Grenada Steel Industries, Inc. v. Alabama Oxygen Co., 695 F.2d 883, 888-89 (5th Cir. 1983); Haynes v. American Motors Corp., 691 F.2d 1268, 1272-73 (8th Cir. 1982); Hall v. American SS. Co., 688 F.2d 1062, 1067 (6th Cir. 1982). See also Falknor, Extrinsic Policies Affecting Admissibility, 10 RUTGERS L. REV. 574, 591 (1956).

[15] Bickerstaff v. South Central Bell Telephone Co., 676 F.2d 163, 166 (5th Cir. 1982). See also Dollar v. Long Mfg., N.C., Inc., 561 F.2d 613, 618 (5th Cir. 1977), cert. denied, 435 U.S. 996, 98 S.Ct. 1648, 56 L.Ed.2d 85 (1978) (reversible error for trial judge not to have permitted plaintiffs to impeach defendant's design engineer in products liability case by asking him about letter he had sent to dealers warning them of "death dealing propensities" of product when used in the fashion employed in instant case).

[16] Slough, Relevancy Unraveled — Art. III: Remote and Prejudicial Evidence, 5 KAN. L. REV. 675, 707-08 (1956).

[17] See Chapter 403 of this Treatise. As stated in one commentary: ". . . the principal impact of Rule 407 is not so much in keeping evidence out altogether as it is in limiting the use to which the evidence may be put. Unless outweighted, by the 'danger' or 'considerations' described in Rule 403, the proof usually gets in." 2 LOUISELL & MUELLER, § 163, at 236. See also, id., 165 at 249.

trial judge possesses discretion to exclude the evidence of the remedial action on the basis of prejudice, confusion of the issues, or misleading the jury.[18] At the very least, the trial judge should provide a limiting instruction pursuant to Rule 105 where evidence of remedial action is admitted on a theory of relevancy outside the inferential pattern prohibited in the first sentence of Rule 407.[19]

§ 407.5   Application of Rule 407 in Products Liability Actions.

There is tension and interesting debate between the circuits as to whether Rule 407 should apply to products liability actions. The Advisory Committee's Note does not address this issue.

The advocates of admitting evidence of a subsequent remedial measure argue that an action based upon strict product liability does not require the plaintiff to prove that the manufacturer was negligent in its design, manufacture or marketing of a product. The plaintiff need only prove the product was in a defective condition and unreasonably dangerous when it left the possession of the manufacturer.[20] Logically, because the plaintiff need not prove manufacturer negligence, evidence of subsequent remedial measures should be admissible to prove the defect in the product that injured the plaintiff. Application of Rule 407 to products liability actions in this context would be as inappropriate as applying Rule 407 to bar the use of evidence of a subsequent remedial measure when it is used to impeach a witness. Neither purpose is barred by a literal application of Rule 407.

The issue, however, is not necessarily resolved by focusing upon a literal reading of the text of the rule. Some courts and commentators would rather look to whether the policies that underlie Rule 407 are furthered by admitting this type of evidence. Proponents of admitting evidence of subsequent remedial measures in products liability actions argue that it is absurd to believe that a manufacturer would forgo repairs in a product's design or manufacture in order to avoid the admission at trial of evidence of its subsequent changes in the product. A rational business does not risk millions of dollars in liability that may result from further injuries in order to avoid creating evidence of subsequent remedial measures.[21] This argument is strengthened when one considers the additional liability in puni-

---

[18] *See* Gardner v. Chevron U.S.A., Inc., 675 F.2d 658, 660 (5th Cir. 1982).

[19] *See* Chapter 105 of this Treatise. *See also* Bauman v. Volkswagenwerk Aktiengesellshaft, 621 F.2d 230, 232-33 (6th Cir. 1980).

[20] *See* the RESTATEMENT OF TORTS, Rule 402(a).

[21] *See, e.g.*, Haynes v. American Motors Corp., 691 F.2d 1268, 1272-73, n.5 (8th Cir. 1982); Unterburger v. Snow Inc., 630 F.2d 599, 601 (8th Cir. 1980).

tive damages that may result from leaving a known dangerous condition remain unremedied.

Courts and commentators that oppose admission of evidence of subsequent remedial measures in products liability actions do not refute the position that it is unlikely manufacturers will cease to repair or redesign their products if this type of evidence is admitted. Instead they espouse the traditional Wigmore view that this type of evidence is irrelevant in determining liability and that it is, at least potentially, highly prejudicial.[22] The opponents of admissibility also fear that by receiving evidence of subsequent remedial measures, the defendant will be effectively required to prove his own due care in order to lessen the adverse impact caused by admitting the evidence.[23] The defendant, of course, does not properly carry the burden of persuasion in this context.

Some courts suggest that Rule 403 be utilized exclusively in products liability actions instead of Rule 407.[24] This flexible, discretionary approach would allow for the admission of relevant evidence when it is not at the expense of unfairly prejudicing the defendant.

[22] *See, e.g.,* Grenada Steel Industries Inc. v. Alabama Oxygen Company, Inc., 695 F.2d 883, 885-87 (5th Cir. 1983); Hall v. American Steamship Co., 688 F.2d 1062, 1066-67 (6th Cir. 1982); Werner v. Upjohn Co., Inc., 628 F.2d 848, 856-58 (4th Cir. 1980), *cert. denied,* 449 U.S. 1080, 101 S.Ct. 861, 66 L.Ed.2d 804 (1981). *See also* Knight v. Otis Elevator Co., 596 F.2d 84, 91 (3d Cir. 1979) (evidence of placing guards around elevator buttons subsequent to accident properly excluded).

[23] Birnbaum, *Growing Trend to Deny Admission of Post-Accident Remedial Measures,* Nat'l. L.J. 18 (July 23, 1979).

[24] *See* Grenada Steel Industries, 695 F.2d 883, 889 (5th Cir. 1983); Lindsay v. Ortho Pharmaceutical Corp., 637 F.2d 87, 90-91 (2d Cir. 1980). *See also* 2 Weinstein, ¶ 407[03], at 407-14 (endorsing this position).

Chapter 408

RULE 408. COMPROMISE AND OFFERS TO COMPROMISE

Rule 408 reads as follows:

Evidence of (1) furnishing or offering or promising to furnish or (2) accepting or offering or promising to accept, a valuable consideration in compromising or attempting to compromise a claim which was disputed as to either validity or amount, is not admissible to prove liability for or invalidity of the claim or its amount. Evidence of conduct or statements made in compromise negotiations is likewise not admissible. This rule does not require the exclusion of any evidence otherwise discoverable merely because it is presented in the course of compromise negotiations. This rule also does not require exclusion when the evidence is offered for another purpose, such as proving bias or prejudice of a witness, negativing a contention of undue delay, or proving an effort to obstruct a criminal investigation or prosecution.

§ 408.1   Compromise and Offers to Compromise—In General.

The primary purpose of Rule 408 is to provide for the inadmissibility of evidence relating to an offer of compromise or to a completed compromise.[1] Rule 408 also precludes the admissibility of evidence of conduct or

---

[1] *See, generally,* McCORMICK, § 274; 2 WEINSTEIN, ¶¶ 408[01]-[07]; 2 LOUISELL & MUELLER, §§ 170-74; 4 WIGMORE, § 1061. *See also* Note, *Rule 408 and Erie: The Latent Conflict,* 12 GA. L. REV. 275 (1978); Note, *The Admission in Evidence Pleading Under the Codes and Under Federal Rules* *of Civil Procedure,* 106 U. PA. L. REV. 98 (1957); Slough, *Relevancy Unraveled—Part III: Remote and Prejudicial Evidence,* 5 KAN. L. REV. 657 (1957); Falknor, *Extrinsic Policies Affecting Admissibility,* 10 RUTGERS L. REV. 574 (1956).

statements made during the course of compromise negotiation. The Rule is designed to promote free and open discussion in the course of settlement negotiations with the ultimate objective of encouraging settlements,[2] and it represents an extension of generally recognized law concerning the admissibility of settlement negotiations.[3]

§ 408.2   Policy of Rule 408.

Two alternate policies have been advanced supporting the exclusionary principle of Rule 408. First, it has been suggested that evidence of an offer of settlement has little or no probative value because the offer may be an indication of a desire for resolution rather than an admission of culpability or weakness of position. As Wigmore has stated:

> The true reason for excluding an offer of compromise is that it does not ordinarily proceed from and imply a specific belief that the adversary claim is well founded, but rather the belief that the further prosecution of that claim, well founded or not, would in any event cause such annoyance as is preferably avoided by the sum offered. In short, the offer implies merely a desire for peace, not a concession of wrong done.[4]

McCormick, however has more correctly analyzed the relevancy of an offer of settlement as varying in probative value:

> The relevancy of the offer will vary according to the circumstances, with a very small offer of payment to settle a very large claim being much more readily construed as a desire for peace rather than an admission of weakness of position. Relevancy would increase, however, as the amount of the offer approached the amount claimed.[5]

Under the liberal standard of relevancy contained in Rule 401, it is difficult to argue that offers of settlement have no probative value whatsoever, and a theory of inadmissibility based solely on irrelevancy is unimpressive.

[2] *See* 2 WEINSTEIN, ¶ 408[01], at 408-9. *See also* Ward v. Allegheny Ludlum Steel Corp., 560 F.2d 579, 581 (3d Cir. 1979) (employee charged that labor union and employer had failed to accommodate his religious beliefs; evidence that employee had offered to reimburse company for expenses it would incur in hiring substitutes should not be admitted). *See, e.g.*, Thomas v. Resort Health Related Facility, 539 F. Supp. 630, 637-38 (E.D. N.Y. 1982).

[3] West v. Smith, 101 U.S. 263, 272-73, 25 L.Ed. 809, 813 (1879); Home Insurance Company v. Balitmore Warehouse Co., 93 U.S. 527, 548, 23 L.Ed. 868, 871 (1876). *See also* Insurance Companies v. Weides, 81 U.S. (14 Wall.) 375, 381, 20 L.Ed. 894, 895 (1872) (a compromise, proposed or accepted, is not evidence of an admission of the amount of the debt).

[4] 4 WIGMORE, § 1061, at 36.

[5] McCORMICK, § 247, at 663.

The alternate justification advanced for the inadmissibility of settlement negotiations is the extrinsic social policy of promoting the settlement of disputes and resolving conflicts, and this latter policy predominates in supporting Rule 408.[6]

§ 408.3   Scope of Rule 408.

Rule 408 provides for the exclusion of settlement offers and acceptances. Rule 408 also comprehends "collateral admissions" within its exclusionary scope, and it may be invoked to exclude collateral conduct and statements made during compromise negotiations.[7] The policy for including factual statements made in the course of negotiations within the exclusionary scope of Rule 408 is summarized by McCormick:

> This generally accepted doctrine of denying the protection of the exclusionary rule to statements of fact has serious drawbacks, however. It tends to discourage freedom of communication, in attempting compromise, and, taken with its exceptions, it invokes difficulties of application.[8]

The inadmissibility of collateral admissions alters pre-Rule case law,[9] under which collateral admissions were not insulated from admissibility unless they were stated hypothetically, *i.e.*, "admitted without prejudice" or "admitted for the sake of compromise discussions only."[10] The Advisory Committee rejected this approach as overly formalistic, excessively oppressive and otherwise unsound.[11]

---

[6] *See* Rule 408 Advisory Committee's Note.

[7] *See* American Insurance Co. v. North American Co., etc., 697 F.2d 79, 82 (2d Cir. 1982); United States v. Contra Costa County Water District, 678 F.2d 90, 93 (9th Cir. 1982); Ramada Development Co. v. Rauch, 644 F.2d 1097, 1106 (5th Cir. 1981). As to whether Rule 408 applies to plea bargaining, *see* 2 LOUISELL & MUELLER, § 170, at 273. *See also* United States v. Verdoorn, 528 F.2d 103, 107 (8th Cir. 1976).

[8] McCORMICK, § 274, at 664.

[9] *E.g.*, Factor v. Commissioner, 281 F.2d 100, 125-27 (9th Cir. 1960), *cert. denied*, 364 U.S. 933, 81 S.Ct. 380, 5 L.Ed.2d 365 (1961) (taxpayer's statements at settlement meetings admissible, since offer of payment was not accompanied by denial of liability); Cooper v. Brown, 126 F.2d 874, 878 (3d Cir. 1942) (income statements submit-

ted by defendant during negotiations for compromise of partnership accounting). *Accord*, Albert Hanson Lumber Co. v. United States, 261 U.S. 581, 588-89, 43 S.Ct. 442, 445, 67 L.Ed. 809, 814 (1923); Nebraska Driller, Inc. v. Westchester Fire Ins. Co., 123 F. Supp. 678, 682 (D. Col. 1954).

[10] *E.g.*, In re Evansville Television, Inc., 286 F.2d 65, 70 (7th Cir. 1961), *cert. denied sub nom.*, Schepp v. Producers, Inc., 366 U.S. 903, 81 S.Ct. 1048, 6 L.Ed.2d 204 (1961) (counsel conducted negotiations contingent upon their being inadmissible); Nebraska Drillers, Inc. v. Westchester Fire Insurance, 123 F. Supp. 678, 682 (D. Col. 1954) (collected cases). *See, generally*, 2 LOUISELL & MUELLER, § 171, at 283.

[11] *See* Rule 408 Advisory Committee's Note. *See also* 2 LOUISELL & MUELLER, § 170, at 273.

Rule 408 expressly provides: "This rule does not require the exclusion of any evidence otherwise discoverable merely because it is presented in the course of compromise negotiations." Obviously, without this express restriction, abuse of the Rule would be possible by the mere recitation of discoverable evidence during the course of settlement negotiations.[12] The Rule expressly provides that such factual statements, which are otherwise discoverable, are not insulated merely by their presentation in conjunction with inadmissible statements.

While Rule 408 expands upon pre-existing law, the limitations of the scope of the Rule should be appreciated. The exclusionary principle is inapplicable where a dispute does not exist as to liability or the amount of the claim.[13] The Rule cannot be invoked where settlement discussions relate to an amount that is admittedly due.[14] The amount of the claim must be in dispute, or alternatively, liability for the claim must be contested in order for the exclusionary principle to apply.[15] As stated by McCormick:

> An offer to pay an admitted claim is not privileged. There is no policy of encouraging compromises of undisputed claims. They should be paid in full. If the validity of the claim and the amount due are undisputed, an offer to pay a lesser sum in settlement or to pay in installments would accordingly be admissible.[16]

§ 408.4   Admissible Statements of Compromise—In General.

The final sentence of Rule 408 emphasizes that the Rule excludes evidence of compromise negotiations only where such evidence is offered to establish liability for, or invalidity of, a claim or its amount. The principle of exclusion does not operate when compromise-related evidence is used to establish some other fact of consequence in the litigation. For example, evidence of statements during the course of settlement negotiations are not rendered inadmissible by Rule 408 where the statements are offered to establish bias or prejudice of a witness,[17] or where offered to show an effort to obstruct a criminal investigation or prosecution.[18] The examples pro-

---

[12] 2 WEINSTEIN, ¶ 408[02], at 408-14.

[13] *See* Deere & Co. v. International Harvester Co., 710 F.2d 1151, 1156-57 (Fed. Cir. 1983); United States v. Meadows, 598 F.2d 984, 989 (5th Cir. 1979).

[14] *See, e.g.,* United States v. Meadows, 598 F.2d 984, 989 (5th Cir. 1979) (remark made by defendant that he knew checks were issued by mistake was in no sense offer to compromise claim; although testimony

that defendant agreed to repayment schedule might have been barred by Rule 408, defendant's counsel brought this out on cross-examination). *See also* Perzinski v. Chevron Chemical Co., 503 F.2d 654, 658 (7th Cir. 1974).

[15] *See* 2 WEINSTEIN, ¶ 408[01], at 408-10.

[16] McCORMICK, § 274, at 663.

[17] *See* 2 WEINSTEIN, ¶ 408[05], at 408-25.

[18] McCORMICK, § 274, at 813.

vided by the last sentence of Rule 408 are not exhaustive, and any theory of relevancy is permissible providing the evidence is not offered to establish liability for, or invalidity of, the claim or its amount. It should be noted, however, that in any case in which compromise-related evidence is offered on theory of relevancy not presented by Rule 408, Rule 403 may operate to exclude the evidence where the probative value is low and the risk of prejudice or confusion is substantial.[19]

§ 408.5 Admissible Statements of Compromise to Show Bias.

Most frequently, statements derived from settlement negotiations will be admissible where they are utilized to demonstrate the bias of a witness who has compromised his claim with one of the parties. While the right to a good faith cross-examination of such a witness is recognized as superior to the public policy underpinning the exclusionary principle of Rule 408, pursuant to the balancing principle of Rule 403, the trial judge may restrict the inquiry on cross-examination in order to preserve the integrity of the fact-finding process.[20] Where the witness sought to be impeached is a party to the litigation, the danger for prejudice is substantial, and limitation of the cross-examination under Rule 403 may be particularly warranted.[21] Critical in determining whether settlement negotiations should be excluded under Rule 403 is the consideration of whether the settlement was one made in good faith, or rather, one designed to invite favorable testimony.[22] The court's rulings under Rule 408 in this context will be overturned only where the trial court has abused its discretion in admitting evidence.[23] Counsel, of course, may waive certain errors by failing to object in a timely manner.[24]

§ 408.6 Applicability of Rule 408 in Multiparty Litigation and Subsequent Actions.

It is common for a party to have potential liability to more than one claimant, or for a single plaintiff to seek damages from more than one

[19] *See e.g.*, United States v. Peed, 714 F.2d 7, 9-10 (4th Cir. 1983); Ramada Development Co. v. Rauch, 644 F.2d 1097, 1106-07 (5th Cir. 1981); Estate of Spinosa, 621 F.2d 1154, 1158 (1st Cir. 1980).

[20] *See also* Rule 611(a).

[21] *See, generally,* 2 WEINSTEIN, ¶ 408[06], at 408-29; McCORMICK, § 274, at 665.

[22] Urico v. Parnell Oil Co., 708 F.2d 852, 854-55 (1st Cir. 1983).

[23] Medelovitz v. Adolph Coors Company, 693 F.2d 570, 580 n.23 (5th Cir. 1982); MCI Communications v. American Telephone & Telegraph Co., 708 F.2d 1081, 1083 (7th Cir. 1983).

[24] Madding v. Louisville's N.R.R., 168 F.2d 880, 882 (7th Cir. 1948).

defendant. This type of lawsuit requires settlement negotiations to occur on more than one front.[25] Rule 408 furthers settlement in this context by providing the necessary protection from the use of the settlement negotiations between the original parties in a lawsuit, as well as in subsequent litigation, to prove the liability, invalidity, or amount of any claim of a party to the original lawsuit against a new opponent.[26]

[25] 2 LOUISELL & MUELLER, § 171, at 289.

[26] *See e.g.*, McHann v. Firestone Tire and Rubber Co., 713 F.2d 161, 166-67 (5th Cir. 1983); American Ins. Co. v. North American Co. for Property & Casualty Ins., 697 F.2d 79, 82 (2d Cir. 1982); United States v. Contra Costa County Water Dist., 678 F.2d 90, 92 (9th Cir. 1982).

Chapter 409

RULE 409. PAYMENT OF MEDICAL AND SIMILAR EXPENSES

Rule 409 reads as follows:

> Evidence of furnishing or offering or promising to pay medical, hospital, or similar expenses occasioned by an injury is not admissible to prove liability for the injury.

§ 409.1   Payment of Medical Expenses—In General.

Rule 409 renders inadmissible evidence of the furnishing, or the offering, or the promising to pay medical, hospital, or similar expenses occasioned by an injury where such evidence is offered to establish liability for the injury or harm.[1]

§ 409.2   Policy of Rule 409.

Rule 409 is supported by essentially the same rationale which underpins Rule 408, "Compromise and Offers to Compromise." Rule 409 is designed to encourage humane impulses regarding expenses occasioned by an injury.[2] Likewise, in many situations, an offer to pay medical or similar expenses has little probative value as an admission of liability.[3] Professors

---

[1] *See, generally*, McCormick, § 275, at 815-19; 2 Weinstein, ¶¶ 409[01]-[03], at 409-1-6; 2 Louisell & Mueller, §§ 177-80, at 305-14; 2 Wigmore, § 283(a), at 159-60.

[2] 2 Weinstein, ¶ 409[01], at 409-3; 2 Louisell & Mueller, § 177, at 307.

[3] *See* Advisory Committee's Note to Rule 409. *See also* 2 Louisell & Mueller, § 178, at 309.

Louisell and Mueller contend that the Rule is particularly significant in the context of advance payments by insurers to persons injured in accidents, pointing out that the importance of encouraging such payments is obvious.[4]

§ 409.3   Scope of Rule 409.

Unlike Rule 408 which pertains to compromises, Rule 409 does not render inadmissible conduct or statements which are part of the act of furnishing, offering, or promising to pay expenses. As stated in the Advisory Committee's Note to Rule 409:

> This difference in treatment arises from fundamental differences in nature. Communication is essential if compromises are to be effected, and consequently broad protection [under Rule 408] of statements is needed. This is not so in cases of payments or offers or promises to pay medical expenses [under Rule 409], where factual statements may be expected to be incidental in nature.

Whenever an express admission of liability arises in conjunction with an offer to pay medical expenses, the trial judge should make an effort to sever any aspect of the statement related to the payment of medical expenses. The express admission of liability is admissible, but to the extent practicable, any offers to pay medical expenses should be insulated from admissibility. Where severance is impossible, the admission should be submitted to the jury with proper instructions,[5] unless excessive prejudice or confusion would justify exclusion under Rule 403.[6] The balancing principle of Rule 403 may ultimately exclude even an express admission of liability in this context where the probative value of such admission is extremely low (perhaps because of its cumulative nature), and where it is inseparable from an offer to pay medical expenses.

§ 409.4   Admissible Evidence Relating to the Payment of Medical Statements.

Unlike Rule 408, relating to compromises and offers to compromise, Rule 409 does not expressly address the issue of whether evidence relating to the payment of medical expenses is admissible to establish issues other

---

[4] 2 LOUISELL & MUELLER, § 177, at 306.

[5] *See* Rule 104, discussed in § 104.1 of Chapter 104.

[6] *See* Rule 403, discussed in § 403.1 of Chapter 403.

than proof of liability. Nevertheless, it is abundantly apparent that Rule 409 only limits admissibility where the evidence of payment or offer of payment is directed to liability.[7] Other consequential facts may be established by such evidence, *e.g.* control, identity, responsibility, etc.[8] Before admitting evidence relating to medical payments on a theory of relevancy outside the prohibition of Rule 409, however, the trial judge should apply the balancing principle of Rule 403. If the probative value of such evidence is substantially outweighed by a designated adverse effect, the evidence may be excluded. Where evidence of the payment of medical or like expenses is received on a relevancy theory outside the proscription of Rule 409, a limiting instruction under Rule 105 should accompany the evidence.

[7] Advisory Committee's Note to Rule 409; 2 WEINSTEIN, ¶ 409[02], at 409-4. *See* Savoie v. Otto Candies, Inc., 692 F.2d 363, 370 (5th Cir. 1982).

[8] 2 WEINSTEIN, ¶ 409[02], at 409-4.

Chapter 410

RULE 410. INADMISSIBILITY OF PLEAS, PLEA DISCUSSIONS, AND RELATED STATEMENTS

Rule 410 reads as follows:

Except as otherwise provided in this rule, evidence of the following is not, in any civil or criminal proceeding, admissible against the defendant who made the plea or was a participant in the plea discussions:

(1) a plea of guilty which was later withdrawn;

(2) a plea of nolo condendere;

(3) any statement made in the course of any proceedings under Rule 11 of the Federal Rules of Criminal Procedure or comparable state procedure regarding either of the foregoing pleas; or

(4) any statement made in the course of plea discussions with an attorney for the prosecuting authority which do not result in a plea of guilty or which result in a plea of guilty later withdrawn.

However, such a statement is admissible (i) in any proceeding wherein another statement made in the course of the same plea or plea discussions has been introduced and the statement ought in fairness be considered contemporaneously with it, or (ii) in a criminal proceeding for perjury or false statement if the statement was made by the defendant under oath, on the record and in the presence of counsel.

§ 410.1   Inadmissibility of Pleas, Plea Discussions, and Related Statements—In General.

Rule 410 insulates from admissibility certain pleas and certain statements made in conjunction with plea bargaining.[1] It is the criminal counterpart to Rule 408 which relates to the inadmissibility of statements made in conjunction with compromise negotiations in civil actions.[2]

Subject only to the second sentence of Rule 410, the pleas or statements identified in the Rule are inadmissible regardless of the issues sought to be established. Unlike Rules 408 and 409, which render certain statements inadmissible only when offered for a specified purpose, Rule 410 comprehensively prohibits the admission of the identified statements, offers and pleas.

The Rule as enacted and subsequently amended, prohibits the use of statements made in connection with plea bargaining for impeachment purposes. The Senate version of Rule 410 would have allowed use of the defendant's statements for this purpose and[3] would have paralleled the

[1] See, generally, McCORMICK, § 265; 2 LOUISELL & MUELLER, §§ 184-88; 2 WEINSTEIN, ¶¶ 410[01]-[08]; 4 WIGMORE, §§ 1066-67. See also, When is statement of accused made in connection with plea bargain negotiations so as to render statement inadmissible under Rule 11(e) of the Federal Rules of Criminal Procedure, 60 A.L.R. FED. 854 (1982); Note, The Oath in Rule 11 Proceedings, 46 FORDHAM L. REV. 1242 (1978); Evidence—Guilty Plea Not Admissible in Subsequent Civil Suit Based Upon the Same Occurrences, 24 KAN. L. REV. 193 (1975).

[2] See Chapter 408 of this Treatise. See also, United States v. Arroyo-Angulo, 580 F.2d 1137, 1148 (2d Cir. 1978) ("the purpose of Rule 410 is to encourage frank discussion in plea bargaining negotiations . . . since plea agreements are essential to the disposition of bulk of cases in our criminal system"); United States v. Herman, 544 F.2d 791, 797 (5th Cir. 1977) (a defendant who knows full well that an agent had no authority to plea bargain is not protected by the rule, no matter whether the defendant offers to plead guilty or makes statements that would otherwise fall within the rule).

[3] The Supreme Court submitted to the Congress a proposed Rule 410 identical to the first sentence of the Rule as finally enacted in 1975. The House version of Rule 410 was substantially similar to the Supreme Court's proposal. The Senate version, however, provided for the use of plea bargaining testimony to impeach the defendant at trial. At the time the Senate passed its version of Rule 410, the Congress had before it Rule 11(e)(6). Rule 11(e)(6) as proposed was identical to the Supreme Court's version of Rule 410. The conference committee proposed that Congress adopt the Senate version of Rule 410, but provided that its effective date be deferred, and that any change in the criminal rules of procedure would supersede Rule 410. Rule 11(e)(6) was enacted one day after the Senate version of 410 went into effect. Rule 410 was then amended to make it identical with Rule 11(e)(6). Rule 410, as amended, and Rule 11(e)(6) prohibit the use of plea bargain evidence to impeach the defendant at trial. The Rule was further amended in 1980. The text of the 1975 rule was rewritten to clarify its meaning. The Rule was also altered to assure that it would not be applicable to conversations between the accused and law enforcement personnel. The congressional intention of the 1975 version of Rule 410 to prohibit the impeachment of the defendant by his prior inconsistent plea bargaining statements survived the 1980 amendment of Rule 410. Rule 11(e)(6) of the Rules of Criminal Procedure reads as follows:

(6) **Inadmissibility of Pleas, Plea Discussions, and Related Statements.** Except as otherwise provided in this

Supreme Court's holding in *Harris v. N.Y.*,[4] *i.e.*, statements obtained by the defendant in violation of *Miranda v. Arizona*,[5] though inadmissible in the prosecution's case in chief, may still be used for impeachment purposes. The Court in *Harris* reasoned that such statements obtained from the defendant should not be excluded when the defendant takes the stand and testifies inconsistently at trial.[6] The Senate thought that this type of protection was sufficient for plea bargaining related statements.[7] Congress, however, ultimately rejected such an approach in Rule 11 of the Rules of Criminal Procedure and the subsequent amendment of Rule 410.[8] By eliminating impeachment use of plea bargaining statements, Rule 410 is designed to further the goal of encouraging guilty pleas and plea bargaining discussions.[9]

§ 410.2   Withdrawn Pleas of Guilty.

The policy for insulating withdrawn guilty pleas from admissibility is discussed by McCormick:

> If the leave to withdraw is granted because of denial of assistance of counsel, lack of ratification by the accused, involuntariness, or similar reason, it is evident that a manifest injustice is sought to be corrected. If the withdrawn plea is nevertheless allowed into evidence, the effectiveness of the corrective measure is greatly impaired.[10]

paragraph, evidence of the following is not, in any civil or criminal proceeding, admissible against the defendant who made the plea or was a participant in the plea discussions:

    (A) a plea of guilty which was later withdrawn;

    (B) a plea of nolo contendere;

    (C) any statement made in the course of any proceedings under this rule regarding either of the foregoing pleas; or

    (D) any statement made in the course of plea discussions with an attorney for the government which do not result in a plea of guilty later withdrawn.

However, such a statement is admissible (i) in any proceeding wherein another statement made in the course of the same plea or plea discussions has been introduced and the statement ought in fairness be considered contemporaneously with it, or (ii) in a criminal proceeding for perjury or false statement if the statement was made by the defendant under oath, on the record, and in the presence of counsel.

[4] 401 U.S. 222, 226, 91 S.Ct. 643, 646, 28 L.Ed.2d 1, 4 (1971).

[5] 384 U.S. 436, 498, 86 S.Ct. 1602, 1640, 16 L.Ed.2d 694, 736 (1966).

[6] Harris v. N.Y., 401 U.S. 222, 223, 91 S.Ct. 643, 644, 28 L.Ed.2d 1, 2 (1971).

[7] Report of the Senate Committee on the Judiciary, 93rd Cong., 2d Sess., Oct. 18, 1974, 93-1277 at 11.

[8] Report of Comm. on Judiciary, House of Representatives, 94th Cong., 1st Sess., No. 94-247, May 29, 1975 at 7.

[9] Advisory Committee's Note to Rule 410 as amended in 1980.

[10] McCORMICK, § 265, at 782.

As analyzed by the United States Supreme Court in *Kercheval v. United States*,[11] to admit the withdrawn plea would in practical effect render meaningless the permission to withdraw the plea in the first instance. However, as Judge Weinstein notes, the Supreme Court's reasoning in *Kercheval* was based upon an assumption that when the Court allows the withdrawal of a guilty plea, it is because the Court has found that the plea was not voluntarily or knowingly entered by the defendant.[12] This assumption does not coincide with the practice of the federal courts of allowing the withdrawal of a guilty plea at almost any time until sentencing.[13]

Judge Weinstein believes a better rationale for denying the prosecution's use of the withdrawn guilty plea is that to allow the use of this type of evidence would make the granting of the trial a meaningless gesture. Allowing the admission of evidence in the prosecution's case that a guilty plea was withdrawn would be irreparably damaging to the defense.[14] This reasoning is consistent with the general practice of ordering a new trial where evidence in violation of Rule 410 is inappropriately elicited from the accused.[15]

A guilty plea which is not withdrawn may be admissible in subsequent litigation as an admission of the person who entered the plea.[16] Unwithdrawn guilty pleas in prior criminal cases are admissible in subsequent civil litigation under exceptions to the hearsay rules, such as an admission of a party or declaration against interest.[17] Likewise, a conviction may be admissible under certain circumstances, *e.g.*, impeachment of a witness under Rule 609.[18] In regard to guilty pleas, Rule 410 only addresses the admissibility of pleas of guilty which are subsequently withdrawn.

§ 410.3   Pleas of Nolo Contendere.

Rule 410 protects a party from the use of a nolo contendere plea in litigation subsequent to the case in which the plea is entered. Similarly,

---

[11] 274 U.S. 220, 222, 47 S.Ct. 582, 584, 71 L.Ed. 1009, 1011 (1927) ("both sides gave evidence as to matters considered by the court in setting aside the conviction").

[12] 2 WEINSTEIN, ¶ 410[03], at 410-28.

[13] *Id* at 410-29. *See also* United States v. Abano, 414 F. Supp. 67, 69 (S.D. N.Y. 1976) (statements made in connection with withdrawn plea may not be used in later proceeding).

[14] 2 WEINSTEIN, ¶ 410[03], at 410-29.

[15] Kercheval v. United States, 274 U.S. 220, 221, 47 S.Ct. 582, 583, 71 L.Ed. 1009, 1011 (1927); United States v. Long, 323 F.2d 468, 472 (6th Cir. 1963); Oliver v. United States, 202 F.2d 521, 523 (6th Cir. 1953).

[16] *See* Rule 801(d)(2).

[17] *See* Rain v. Pavkov, 357 F.2d 506, 510 (3d Cir. 1966) (admissible despite state statute declaring guilty plea in traffic offenses inadmissible); Interstate Securities Co. v. United States, 151 F.2d 224, 226 (10th Cir. 1945) (suit for forfeiture of car; owner's guilty plea admissible against chattel mortgagee). *See* 2 WEINSTEIN, ¶ 410[06].

[18] *See* Rule 803(21). *See also* Rules 608 and 609 regarding impeachment.

Criminal Procedure Rule 11(e)(6) also provides that a nolo contendere plea may not be used against the defendant in subsequent civil or criminal proceedings.[19]

Policy dictates that the protection offered the party who pleads nolo condendere is greater than the protection afforded his counterpart who pleads guilty: The party who pleads guilty is not protected from the use against him of his entered guilty plea in any subsequent litigation whereas the party who pleads nolo condendere is so protected. This distinction rests on a premise that in some instances the government has a duty to truncate litigation by accepting a plea of nolo condendere at the expense of requiring some other party to relitigate the issue of liability against the defendant at a subsequent hearing.[20] Criminal Procedure Rule 11(b) grants the trial court the discretion to accept pleas of nolo condendere when it determines in the interest of justice that such a plea should be entered.

The policy supporting Rule 410 is that of encouraging the entering of nolo condendere pleas. The Rule also gives weight to the traditional policy supporting a plea of nolo condendere, *i.e.*, the defendant may avoid the issue of guilt at the expense of accepting punishment.[21] The Rule recognizes that the nature of such pleas is one of compromise, and that the making of such a plea is not a sufficiently sound indicator of guilt to enable a subsequent litigant to be relieved of its burden of proving the issue of liability.[22]

§ 410.4   Statements Attending Pleas and Offers to Plead.

Within the exclusionary scope of Rule 410 are statements made in connection with, and relevant to, the specified pleas or offers to plead. Such statements are inadmissible except as provided in the final sentence of the Rule.[23] Under the Rule, a statement may only be admitted for the purpose

[19] Dalweld Co. v. Westinghouse Electric Corp., 252 F. Supp. 939, 941-42 (S.D. N.Y. 1966).

[20] *See* Advisory Committee's Note to Rule 410.

[21] *Id.*

[22] *Id.*

[23] Where a bargain to plead guilty has been reached pursuant to Criminal Procedure Rule 11 and the defendant has agreed to testify for the government before the grand jury and at trial, if the defendant later dishonors the agreement after providing grand jury testimony, the statements made by him before the grand jury are not protected by Rule 410. *See* United States v. Stirling, 571 F.2d 708, 731-32, 736-37 (2d Cir. 1978). The policy underlying Rule 410 is to encourage plea bargaining discussions that result in guilty pleas. In the situation where the defendant violates the bargain and pleads not guilty, protection of the testimony that was covered by the agreement would not promote plea bargaining. *See* United States v. Davis, 617 F.2d 677, 686 (D.C. Cir. 1979). It should be noted that both of these cases involve statements made before the grand jury, not statements made in the course of plea bargaining. Consequently, it may be more appropriate to view these cases as outside of the scope of Rule 410, instead of as an exception to its application.

of either clarifying a plea bargaining statement that the accused offers into evidence, or to substantiate a perjury charge subsequently brought against the accused.

The prosecution is afforded the right to present other statements made in a plea bargaining session, after the accused has entered into evidence a statement otherwise protected, in order to ensure the evidence of the defense is viewed in the proper context by the trier of fact. When the accused is charged with perjury, plea bargaining statements may also be admitted but only if several procedural prerequisites are met. In accordance with Criminal Procedure Rule 11, such statements may only be used where made by the accused on the record, under oath and in the presence of his attorney. In these two situations, the operative policy of Rule 410 to encourage fluid and open discussion during plea bargaining is outweighed by the risk that the truth-finding function of the trial would be impaired if the evidence was not admitted.

§ 410.5   Co-Offender Pleas.

Rule 410 and Criminal Rule 11(e)(6) do not address the question of the admissibility of a co-offender's guilty plea against the defendant. The prejudice to the defendant is extreme if the jury believes that because one party is guilty, all others engaged in the same criminal transaction must also be guilty by association. Traditional rules of hearsay may preclude the use of a co-offender's plea against the defendant; the guilty plea of the co-offender is clearly an out-of-court statement offered for its truth and, as such, is hearsay.[24]

If a co-offender appears as a witness, it may be appropriate to admit evidence of the guilty plea to impeach his credibility.[25] A limiting instruction should be issued by the court to ensure that the evidence is not impermissibly used by the jury.[26] It may also be necessary to instruct the jury not

---

[24] See Chapter 801 of this Treatise.

[25] Smith v. United States, 331 F.2d 265, 275-76 (8th Cir. 1964), cert. denied, 379 U.S. 824, 84 S.Ct. 49, 13 L.Ed.2d 34 (1964), rehearing denied, 379 US. 940, 85 S.Ct. 321, 13 L.Ed.2d 350 (1964) (no prejudice where codefendant available for cross-examination and careful admonition). See also Walker v. United States, 93 F.2d 383, 395 (8th Cir. 1937), cert. denied, 303 U.S. 644, 58 S.Ct. 642, 82 L.Ed. 1103 (1937), rehearing denied, 303 U.S. 668, 58 S.Ct. 755, 82 L.Ed. 1124 (1938) (reception of pleas of nolo condendere before jury; code-

fendants became witnesses and testified fully).

[26] See United States v. Light, 394 F.2d 908, 910 (2d Cir. 1968). See also 2 WEINSTEIN, ¶ 410[07] AT 410-43. But see Bruton v. United States, 391 U.S. 123, 135-36, 88 S.Ct. 1620, 1627-28, 20 L.Ed.2d 476, 484-85 (1968) (even though a limiting instruction was submitted to the jury, the Supreme Court set aside the conviction of a defendant at a joint trial in which a co-defendant's confession implicating the accused was admitted into evidence). See also the discussion of this case in 2 WEINSTEIN, ¶ 410[07], at 410-45.

to speculate into the motivation of a co-offender who does not testify. The instruction is necessary to avoid a jury from correctly surmising that the co-offender has pleaded guilty to the charge, and then incorrectly using this speculation as evidence of the defendant's guilt.[27]

[27] *See* WEINSTEIN, ¶ 410[07], at 410-44.

Chapter 411

RULE 411. LIABILITY INSURANCE

SECTION
411.1   Liability insurance evidence—In general
411.2   Policy of Rule 411
411.3   Scope of Rule 411
411.4   Admissible evidence relating to liability insurance

Rule 411 reads as follows:

> Evidence that a person was or was not insured against liability is not admissible upon the issue whether he acted negligently or otherwise wrongfully. This rule does not require the exclusion of evidence of insurance against liability when offered for another purpose, such as proof of agency, ownership, or control, or bias or prejudice of a witness.

§ 411.1   Liability Insurance Evidence—In General.

Rule 411 codifies the exclusionary rule regarding liability insurance.[1] According to Rule 411, the fact that a person was or was not insured against liability is not admissible in order to establish negligent or wrongful conduct by the individual. This principle of exclusion, however, does not prohibit the admission of evidence of insurance coverage where a consequential fact, other than negligence or wrongful conduct, is the object of proof.

[1] See, generally, McCORMICK, § 201; 2 WEINSTEIN, ¶¶ 411[01]-411[12]; 2 LOUISELL & MUELLER, §§ 192-96; 2 WIGMORE, § 282. See also Fannin, Disclosure of Insurance in Negligence Trials — The Arizona Rule, 5 ARIZ. L. REV. 83 (1963); Fournier, Pre-Trial Discovery of Insurance Coverage and Limits, 28 FORDHAM L. REV. 215 (1959); Jenkins, Discovery of Automobile Liability Insurance Limits: Quillets of the Law, 14 KAN. L. REV. 59 (1965); Laverci, Disclosure of Insurance Policy Limits, 1957 INS. L.J. 505 (1957); McCurn, Battleground: Liability Insurance and the Rules of Discovery, 1 FORUM, Jan. 1966, at 3; Slough, Relevancy Unraveled, Part III — Remote and Prejudicial Evidence, 5 KAN. L. REV. 675, 710-18 (1957); Stopher, Should a Change be Made in Discovery Rules to Permit Inquiry as to Limits of Liability Insurance?, 35 INS. COUNSEL J. 53 (1968); Vetter, Voir Dire III: Liability Insurance, 29 MO. L. REV. 305 (1964). See Eichel v. New York Central R. R. Co., 375 U.S. 253, 255, 84 S.Ct. 316, 317, 11 L.Ed.2d 307, 309 (1963) (per curiam) (dictum). Rule 411 is in accord with pre-Rule law.

Accordingly, the second sentence of Rule 411 sets forth illustrations of the use of evidence of insurance coverage which are not prohibited by the first sentence of the Rule.[2]

§ 411.2   Policy of Rule 411.

Rule 411 is designed to minimize unfair prejudice relating to the consideration of liability insurance. On one hand, the probative value of liability insurance is exceedingly low regarding issues of liability, while on the other hand, the risks of prejudice are extremely high.[3] As stated by McCormick:

> The financial protection [of liability insurance] may somewhat diminish the normal incentive to be careful, but this is of slight effect since the motive of regard for personal safety is usually present and is a much stronger incentive, and in any event it is overborne by the counter-arguments that the fact of insurance marks the defendant as one of the insured class, who may be assumed to be the more prudent and careful group as compared to the uninsured class.[4]

Consequently, with the probative value of insurance at best equivocal on the issue of negligence or fault, the policy for exclusion is ultimately grounded in the prejudicial risk that awareness by the fact finder of insurance invites a finding based on ability or inability to absorb the loss.[5]

---

[2] *See, e.g.*, Posttape Associates v. Eastman Kodak Co., 537 F.2d 751, 758 (3d Cir. 1976) ("generally, evidence of liability coverage is not admissible when a party is accused of acting wrongfully, because of the likelihood for spillover between insurance and inference of fault; knowledge that a party is insured may also affect a verdict if the jury knows that some of the loss has been paid by insurance or that it would satisfy a judgment against a defendant"). *See, e.g.*, Brown v. Walter, 62 F.2d 798, 800 (2d Cir. 1933) ("there can be no rational excuse for mentioning insurance, except the flimsy one that a man is more likely to be careless if insured; that is at most the merest guess, much more than outweighed by the probability that the real issues will be obscured"). *See, generally*, 2 WEINSTEIN, ¶ 411[01], at 411-4.

[3] *See, e.g.*, Posttape Associates v. Eastman Kodak Co., 537 F.2d 751, 758 (3rd Cir. 1976) (suit claiming damages for increased costs and lost profits because of defective film; Kodak attempted to show that limitation of damages to replacement of film was a custom and usage of trade of which plaintiff had knowledge; error for trial judge to have excluded evidence of plaintiff's insurance coverage indemnifying it against defective film; the proferred evidence was relevant, and it is doubtful there would be any prejudice, because the parties were both commercial entities, the injury was not likely to stir emotions, and the existence of such coverage might have been so unusual that the purchase itself would have significance in the circumstances; the exclusion of this relevant evidence was far more prejudicial to the defense than its admission would have been to the plaintiffs). *See generally*, 2 WEINSTEIN, ¶ 411[02], at 411-5.

[4] McCORMICK, § 201, at 479.

[5] *See* 2 LOUISELL & MUELLER, § 193, at 365.

Accordingly, knowledge by the trier of fact of insurance coverage possesses the prejudicial risk of inflating damage awards.[6]

§ 411.3 Scope of Rule 411.

The exclusionary principle of Rule 411 applies by its terms both to the fault of a defendant and to the contributory negligence or other fault of a plaintiff. It should also be noted that Rule 411 specifically excludes evidence of not only the existence, but also the non-existence of insurance where such evidence is offered to establish negligence or wrongful conduct.[7]

Rule 411 does not address the issue of whether liability insurance is subject to pretrial discovery; the issue is beyond the scope of the Rule.[8] Likewise, Rule 411 is not intended to resolve the issue of whether it is proper to question a prospective juror as to possible interest or bias in connection with an insurance carrier.[9] Rule 411 only addresses the question of whether

---

[6] *See id. See also* Ouachita National Bank v. Tosco Corp., 686 F.2d 1291, 1299 (8th Cir. 1982); Posttape Associates v. Eastman Kodak Co., 537 F.2d 751, 758 (3d Cir. 1976). The text and the foregoing authority reflect conventional wisdom on the issue of the admissibility of insurance coverage, a position which is not, however, invulnerable to criticism. *See* 2 Louisell & Mueller, § 193, at 367-8. *See also* McCormick, § 201, at 482. *See, e.g.*, Scheveling v. Johnson, 122 F. Supp. 85, 89 (D. Conn. 1953), *aff'd on opinion below*, 213 F.2d 959 (2d Cir. 1954) ("justice does not require that law suits shall be torn from their context and tried in an artificially produced vacuum").

[7] Stephenson v. Steinhauer, 188 F.2d 432, 438 (8th Cir. 1951). *See, generally*, 2 Weinstein, ¶ 411[01], at 411-4; McCormick, § 201, at 596.

[8] *See* Civil Procedure Rule 26(b)(2), which provides:

 Insurance Agreements. A party may obtain discovery of the existence and contents of any insurance agreement under which any person carrying on an insurance business may be liable to satisfy part or all of a judgment which may be entered in the action or to indemnify or reimburse

for payments made to satisfy the judgment. Information concerning the insurance agreement is not by reason of disclosure admissible in evidence at trial. For purposes of this paragraph, an application for insurance shall not be treated as part of an insurance agreement.

[9] As stated by McCormick:

 In some jurisdictions the trial judge may allow or disallow the questioning, as he sees fit, and in general, many refinements and variations exist as to consultation with the court in advance and as to the questions that may be asked. It is usually said that the questions must be propounded in good faith. Such "good faith" involves establishing that the party is in fact insured, that prospective jurors may be associated with a liability carrier or otherwise unusually concerned with insurance policies or premiums.

§ 201 at 596, n.20. *See, generally*, Langley v. Turner's Exp. Inc., 375 F.2d 296 (4th Cir. 1967); Kiernan v. Van Schaik, 347 F.2d 775 (3d Cir. 1965). *See also* Kaab, *Insurance Questions on Voir Dire*, 17 Cleveland Mar. L. Rev. 504 (1968).

liability insurance is admissible in evidence in order to establish negligence or wrongful conduct.

As McCormick notes, "Witnesses have been known to make unexpected and unresponsive references to insurance."[10] The curative measure is usually a limiting instruction and not a mistrial[11] unless bad faith abuse by trial counsel is evident.[12]

§ 411.4　Admissible Evidence Relating to Liability Insurance.

The exclusionary principle of Rule 411 applies only where liability insurance is offered to establish negligence or wrongful conduct. Where liability insurance is offered to establish other consequential controverted issues, the exclusionary principle of Rule 411 will not foreclose the admissibility of the evidence. As the second sentence to Rule 411 confirms, evidence of liability insurance is not excluded under Rule 411 where offered to prove agency, ownership or control, or to establish the bias or prejudice of a witness. The list of alternate issues, of course, is illustrative and not exhaustive.[13] While Rule 411 does not on its face require that the alternate issue must be controverted, it is clear that if the issue is not contested, exclusion under the balance of Rule 403 will be justified.

Accordingly, where an issue of agency is contested, evidence that the alleged principal carried liability insurance covering the alleged agent is probative of, and not excluded under Rule 411 as to the existence of the relationship.[14] Likewise, where control is contested, the fact that a particular person carried insurance against risks involving the instrumentality of the injury is probative of, and not inadmissible under Rule 411 as to control by the insured person.[15]

---

[10] McCORMICK, § 201, at 595. *See, generally,* 2 LOUISELL & MUELLER, § 193, at 369; 2 WEINSTEIN, ¶ 411[01], at 411-16.

[11] McCORMICK, § 201, at 595. *But see* Pickwick Stage Lines, Inc. v. Edwards, 64 F.2d 758, 761-62 (10th Cir. 1933) (bad faith abuse by trial counsel).

[12] McCORMICK, § 201, at 595.

[13] Hunziker v. Scheidemantle, 543 F.2d 489, 495-96 (3rd Cir. 1976). *See, generally,* 3 WEINSTEIN, ¶411[01], at 411-4.

[14] *E.g.,* Eldridge v. McGeorge, 99 F.2d 835, 841 (8th Cir. 1938) (in suit against contractor for injuries sustained when plaintiff was run over by truck owned by Callan, where contractor claimed Callan was an independent contractor, and Callan testified that he controlled the operation of the truck, it was error to disallow plaintiff from asking Callan whether he carried liability insurance on the truck, since a negative answer would tend circumstantially to indicate that Callan did not control the truck, or at least not solely). *See also* McCoy v. Universal Carloading & Distrib. Co., 82 F.2d 342, 344 (6th Cir. 1936). *See, generally,* 2 WEINSTEIN, ¶ 411[03], at 411-8.

[15] *E.g.,* Dobbins v. Crain Brothers, Inc., 432 F. Supp. 1060, 1069 (W.D. Pa. 1976), *modified on other grounds,* 567 F.2d 559 (3d Cir. 1977) (ownership; limiting instructions given).

Liability insurance may be permissibly revealed to the trier of fact in the course of an impeachment involving a statement taken from the witness by an insurance adjuster.[16] Likewise, cross-examination as to interest or bias may permissibly reveal sympathies with an insurance company.[17]

In all situations in which liability insurance is offered to establish a consequential issue other than negligence or wrongful conduct, the balancing principle of Rule 403 may be invoked in an effort to exclude the evidence from consideration.[18] Likewise, a limiting instruction is appropriate where evidence of liability insurance is admitted to establish a consequential fact other than wrongful conduct.[19]

[16] *E.g.*, Varlack v. S.W.C. Caribbean, Inc., 550 F.2d 171, 176-77 (3rd Cir. 1977) (references to insurance were made in course of arguing that the criteria of Rule 15(c) for amending complaint by adding an additional party had been met, since proposed defendant knew of suit because he had provided insurance carrier with information and would not be prejudiced, because carrier was real party in interest; also not error to mention insurance when identifying statement for impeachment use as prior inconsistent statement).

[17] *E.g.*, Charter v. Chleborad, 551 F.2d 246, 249 (8th Cir. 1977), *cert. denied*, 434 U.S. 856, 98 S.Ct. 176, 54 L.Ed.2d 128. *See e.g.*, Majestic v. Louisville & N.R.R. Co., 147 F.2d 621, 627 (6th Cir. 1945). *See, generally*, 2 WEINSTEIN, ¶ 411[04], at 411-10.

[18] Charter v. Chleborad, 551 F.2d 246, 249 (8th Cir. 1977) (finding balance in favor of admissibility).

[19] *See* § 104.1 of this Treatise. *See also* Majestic v. Louisville & N.R.R. Co., 147 F.2d 621, 627 (6th Cir. 1945).

Chapter 412

RULE 412. RAPE CASES; RELEVANCE OF VICTIM'S PAST BEHAVIOR

Rule 412 reads as follows:

(a) Notwithstanding any other provision of law, in a criminal case in which a person is accused of rape or of assault with intent to commit rape, reputation or opinion evidence of the past sexual behavior of an alleged victim of such rape or assault is not admissible.

(b) Notwithstanding any other provision of law, in a criminal case in which a person is accused of rape or of assault with intent to commit rape, evidence of a victim's past sexual behavior other than reputation or opinion evidence is also not admissible, unless such evidence other than reputation or opinion evidence is:

(1) admitted in accordance with subdivisions (c)(1) and (c)(2) and is constitutionally required to be admitted; or

(2) admitted in accordance with subdivision (c) and is evidence of:

(A) past sexual behavior with persons other than the accused, offered by the accused upon the issue of whether the accused was or was not, with respect to the alleged victim, the source of semen or injury; or

(B) past sexual behavior with the accused and is offered by the accused upon the issue of whether the alleged victim consented to the sexual behavior with respect to which rape or assault is alleged.

(c)(1) If the person accused of committing rape or assault with intent to commit rape intends to offer under subdivision (b) evidence of specific instances of the alleged victim's past sexual behavior, the accused shall make a written motion to offer such evidence not later than fifteen days before the date on which the trial in which such evidence is to be offered is scheduled to begin, except that the court may allow the motion to be made at a later date, including during trial, if the court determines either that the evidence is newly discovered and could not have been obtained earlier through the exercise of due diligence or that the issue to which such evidence relates has newly arisen in the case. Any motion made under this paragraph shall be served on all other parties and on the alleged victim.

(2) The motion described in paragraph (1) shall be accompanied by a written offer of proof. If the court determines that the offer of proof contains evidence described in subdivision (b), the court shall order a hearing in chambers to determine if such evidence is admissible. At such hearing the parties may call witnesses, including the alleged victim, and offer relevant evidence. Notwithstanding subdivision (b) of Rule 104, if the relevancy of the evidence which the accused seeks to offer in the trial depends upon the fulfillment of a condition of fact, the court, at the hearing in chambers or at a subsequent hearing in chambers scheduled for such purpose, shall accept evidence on the issue of whether such condition of fact is fulfilled and shall determine such issue.

(3) If the court determines on the basis of the hearing described in paragraph (2) that the evidence which the accused seeks to offer is relevant and that the probative value of such evidence outweighs the danger of unfair prejudice, such evidence shall be admissible in the trial to the extent an order made by the court specifies evidence which may be offered and areas with respect to which the alleged victim may be examined or cross-examined.

(d) For purposes of this rule, the term "past sexual behavior" means sexual behavior other than the sexual behavior with respect to which rape or assault with intent to commit rape is alleged.

§ 412.1 Rule 412—Legislative History.

Legislation entitled "The Privacy Protection for Rape Victims Act of 1978," was signed into law by President Carter on October 28, 1978, and became effective as Federal Evidence Rule 412 with respect to trials which commenced after November 28, 1978.[1] The Rule has a unique legislative

---

[1] Pub. L. No. 95-540 [H.R. 4727], 92 Stat. 2046 (1978). *See, generally,* 2 WEINSTEIN, ¶ 412[01]; 2 LOUISELL & MUELLER, §§ 197-99 (Supp.); McCORMICK, § 193; 3A WIGMORE, § 942a. *See also* Boyce & McCloskey, *Legal Application of Standard Laboratory Test for the Identification of* *Seminal Fluid,* 7 J. CONTEMP. L. 1 (1982); Tanford & Bocchino, *Rape Victim Shield Laws and the Sixth Amendment,* 128 U. PA. L. REV. 244 (1980); Comment, *Federal Rule of Evidence 412: Was the Change an Improvement?* 49 U. CIN. L. REV. 244 (1980).

history. Unlike the original Federal Rules of Evidence, Rule 412 was not promulgated by the Supreme Court. Instead, it was initiated in the Congress as a separate piece of legislation to protect rape victims from the admission of certain types of prejudicial evidence.[2]

The Rule was designed to change prior federal practice in several respects. Most significantly, it reflects the conclusion of the Congress that evidence of a rape victim's past sexual behavior is in most instances irrelevant to a determination of the ultimate issue of the trial, *i.e.*, whether a rape has occurred.[3] Congress, therefore, thought it was desirable to alter the prior practice of the federal courts which admitted evidence of a rape victim's past sexual behavior under Rule 404(a)(2).[4] This practice was thought to have the undesirable effects of shifting the focus of the trial away from the guilt or innocence of the accused to a determination of the morality of the victim's sexual behavior.[5] This practice also had the effect of humiliating the victim without measurably furthering the truth finding function of the jury. Consequently, it expended valuable judicial resources on a collateral matter.[6] Additionally, a destructive result of this practice from a societal standpoint, was a determent of the prosecution of rapists by victims who wished to avoid public exposure of their past sexual behavior.[7] Federal case law did not provide clear guidance in this area. Consequently, arbitrariness further exacerbated undesirable results.[8]

Congress also intended to establish a detailed set of procedures defense counsel must follow when it wishes to introduce evidence of the rape victim's sexual behavior under Rule 412. Congress was particularly concerned that evidence proffered under the Rule not be exposed to the jury until it was first reviewed and evaluated in chambers by the judge.[9] The Rule so provides. Congress also intended to acknowledge that in some instances the

---

[2] 124 Cong. Rec. H11944-45 (daily ed. Oct. 10, 1978).

[3] 124 Cong. Rec. S18580 (daily ed. Oct. 12, 1978). *See also,* United States v. Kasto, 584 F.2d 268, 271 (8th Cir. 1978).

[4] 124 Cong. Rec. H11944 (daily ed. Oct. 10, 1978).

[5] *See* 124 Cong. Rec. H11944-45 (daily ed. Oct. 10, 1978). *See also* McClean v. United States, 377 A.2d 74, 77-79 (D.C. Cir. 1977) (supports trial judge's discretion in excluding testimony concerning a rape victim's sexual contacts on prior occasions with persons other than the defendants).

[6] McClean v. United States, 377 A.2d 74, 77-79 (D.C. Cir. 1977) (refusing to permit evidence of prior sexual reputation; citing Rule 404). *See also* State ex rel. Pope v. Superior Court of County of Mohave, 113

Ariz. 22, 29, 545 P.2d 946, 953 (1976); United States v. Driver, 581 F.2d 80, 81 (4th Cir. 1978).

[7] *See* Lovely v. United States, 175 F.2d 312, 314 (4th Cir. 1949), *cert. denied,* 338 U.S. 834, 70 S.Ct. 38, 94 L.Ed. 508 (1949). (an example of prior practice). *See also* 124 Cong. Rec. H11944-11945. *See, e.g.,* Gish v. Wisner, 288 F. 562, 563 (5th Cir. 1923); Packineau v. United States, 202 F.2d 681, 685 (8th Cir. 1953); People v. Rincon-Pineda, 14 Cal.3d 864, 865, 123 Cal. Rptr. 119, 120, 538 P.2d 247, 258 ("rape in particular has been shown by repeated studies to be grossly under-reported").

[8] *See* 3 WEINSTEIN, ¶ 412[01], at 412-10; 3 LOUISELL & MUELLER, § 197, at 310-11.

[9] 124 Cong. Rec. H11944 (daily ed. Oct. 10, 1978).

Constitution may require the admissibility of evidence.[10] In this situation, the exclusionary effect of the Rule, by its own language, is inapplicable.

§ 412.2 Rule 412—Scope.

Rule 412(a) absolutely prohibits the accused from offering reputation or opinion evidence concerning a victim's past sexual behavior in a prosecution for rape or attempted rape. Thus, reputation or opinion evidence of the victim's sexual behavior is inadmissible as to the issue of whether a rape has occurred and whether the victim consented to the sexual act.[11] There are no exceptions to this provision of the Rule. Under Rule 412(b) evidence of a victim's prior sexual behavior is likewise inadmissible except in three situations:

(1) when the Constitution requires the evidence be admitted [Rule 412(b)(1)],

(2) when the accused is attempting to prove that someone else was the source of the victim's injury or the semen found on or near the victim [Rule 412(b)(2)(A)], and

(3) if the accused is attempting to show the alleged rape victim consented to sexual contact with the defendant [Rule 412(b)(2)(B)].

The Constitution will require evidence of the specific acts of the alleged rape victim be admitted when the due process or confrontation clauses would be violated by refusing the proffered evidence.[12] The remaining exceptions to Rule 412 are properly invoked when the accused wishes to show that he did not commit the resulting injury to the victim, or alternately, that the alleged rape victim consented to his sexual advances. Evidence is admissible under these exceptions because the past sexual behavior of the victim is thought to be specifically relevant to the crime with which the accused is charged.[13]

Rule 412 also contains several procedural prerequisites to the admissibility of any evidence within its structure. Rule 412(c) requires the accused to

[10] 124 Cong. Rec. H11945 (daily ed. Oct. 10, 1978).

[11] Doe v. United States, 666 F.2d 43, 47-48 (4th Cir. 1981); United States v. Kasto, 584 F.2d 268, 271-72 (8th Cir. 1978).

[12] See, e.g., Doe v. United States, 666 F.2d 43, 47-48 (4th Cir. 1981) (alleged rape; reviewing court reverses ruling by trial judge which would have permitted introduction at trial of certain evidence of complainant's reputation, habit, and sexual conduct, all characterized here as "essentially opinion or reputation evidence;" this evidence was barred by Rule 412(a)). Cf. United States v. Holy Bear, 624 F.2d 853, 855-56 (8th Cir. 1980) (defendant indicted for alleged rape of his half-sister and incest; court rejected defense claim of error in ruling by trial judge directing defendant not to offer evidence concerning complainant's reputation for unchastity or her specific acts of sexual intercourse with men other than defendant).

[13] 124 Cong. Rec. H11944 (daily ed. Oct. 10, 1978).

make a pretrial motion and a written offer of proof when counsel intends to introduce evidence that would be admissible under one of the exceptions in Rule 412(b).[14]

If the court finds that the offer of proof fairly indicates that evidence would be admissible under Rule 412(b), then it should proceed to hold an evidentiary hearing in chambers. It should be noted, however, that even if evidence is facially admissible under Rule 412(c), the court has the discretion under Rule 412(c)(3) to refuse to admit evidence where probative value is outweighed by the danger of unfair prejudice.[15] Where evidence of a victim's past sexual behavior is admissible because it is constitutionally required, the procedures of Rule 412(c)(1) and (2) are still applicable. The court, however, may not balance the probative value of the evidence against its potential for prejudice under 412(c)(3) before admitting the evidence.

Rule 412, by its strict terms, is not applicable to prosecutions of crimes other than rape or attempted rape, e.g., statutory rape, other sex crimes, etc. However, the policies underlying the rule of avoiding either digression into irrelevant issues at trial or humiliating the victim of a crime should ensure the Rule provides at least guidance in this area.[16] For example, in a case of statutory rape, the underlying policies of Rule 412 apply. Reputation or opinion evidence of the victim's sexual conduct should not be admitted. The procedural constraints of Rule 412 are also likely to be followed because of the high degree of prejudice this type of evidence could cause to the prosecution if the admissibility of the evidence were argued in front of the jury. Additionally, Rule 403 serves the same purpose in the context of statutory rape as Rule 412(c)(3) by excluding otherwise admissible, but highly prejudicial, evidence.

§ 412.3   Rule 412(a).

Rule 412(a) prohibits the accused from offering reputation or opinion evidence concerning a victim's past sexual behavior in a prosecution for rape or attempted rape. Consequently, reputation or opinion evidence of

---

[14] United States v. Nez, 661 F.2d 1203, 1205-06 (10th Cir. 1981) (alleged assault with intent to commit rape; trial court disallowed defense cross-examination about two previous unreported rapes; reviewing court upholds trial court's ruling).

[15] Cf. United States v. Kasto, 584 F.2d 268, 271-72 (8th Cir. 1978) (pre-Rule 412 application of 403 balancing).

[16] Government of Virgin Islands v. Scuito, 623 F.2d 869, 874-76 (3d Cir. 1980) (where trial court excluded evidence under the spirit of Rule 412, reviewing court holds that trial court properly exercised its discretion, since purpose of Rule 412 is to protect against embarrassing disclosure).

the victim's sexual behavior is inadmissible as to the issue of whether a rape has occurred notwithstanding the general defense right to introduce opinion or reputation evidence concerning the character of the victim of a crime under Rule 404(a)(2). When the complainant testifies as a witness at the trial, opinion or reputation evidence of past sexual behavior is also not admissible to impeach a testifying witness under Rule 608(a). This type of evidence has no bearing on the truthful disposition of the complainant and is consequently inadmissible under that Rule.[17]

The Rule itself contains no explicit exception to its operation. However, to the extent that evidence would be admissible because it is constitutionally required, Rule 412(a) clearly cannot be read to limit the type of evidence the accused may admit at trial. Opinion or reputation evidence of the victim's past sexual behavior would be admissible for this purpose where constitutionally mandated.[18]

§ 412.4   Rule 412(b)(1).

Rule 412(b) precludes the admission of evidence of a victim's past sexual conduct unless the proffer falls within one of the exceptions to the Rule. Rule 412(b)(1) authorizes the defendant to introduce evidence of specific acts of a victim's past sexual behavior when the constitution requires the evidence be admitted.

It is obvious this provision is superfluous because the Rules of evidence cannot limit the admissibility of evidence which is constitutionally compelled. Nor can the Rule limit constitutionally compelled admissibility to one form of evidence.

Rule 412(b)(1) refers to the constitutionally compelled admissibility of evidence of "sexual behavior." The term is ambiguous. However, any definition of the term should encompass the physical as well as emotional aspects of a sexual relationship. This would include the psychological and emotional disturbances the victim may have within the context of a sexual relationship.

The circumstances under which evidence of a victim's past sexual behavior is constitutionally compelled are at best only capable of a rough assessment. This provision clearly does not authorize a general inquiry into the victim's past sexual behavior. At minimum, the defendant must establish the relevance of the proffered evidence before the victim will be subject to

---

[17] See the discussion of Rule 608 in this Treatise.

[18] See 3 WEINSTEIN, ¶ 412[01], at 412-11; 3 LOUISELL & MUELLER, § 198[13], at 319.

exposure of her past sexual behavior,[19] and the evidence must do more than indicate the general likelihood of the victim's consent to a specific sexual act.[20] Evidence that would tend to show the victim was biased, prejudiced or had an ulterior motive for blaming the defendant are likely to be admissible because constitutionally compelled.[21] For example, if a friend of the defendant states at trial that, "The defendant told me that he forced the victim to have intercourse with him." Any relationship, sexual or otherwise, between the witness and the victim is probative of the witness' bias in the provision of testimony on behalf of the prosecution against the defendant. The witness may be simultaneously sympathetic to the prosecution in the hope that the victim's position will be vindicated, and antagonistic toward the defendant because he has interfered with the witness' relationship with the victim. Consequently, the witness' sexual relationship with the victim may be admissible. Exposing bias of a witness is traditionally a fundamental method of impeaching a witness, and the right to expose the bias of a witness may be constitutionally required under the confrontation clause. Evidence that is constitutionally compelled will be admissible under Rule 412(b)(1) and not subject to the constraint of Rule 608(a) or (b).[22]

§ 412.5   Rule 412(b)(2)(A).

The second exception to Rule 412 allows the admission of evidence of a victim's past sexual behavior when the accused is attempting to prove that someone else was the source of the victim's injury or the semen found on or near the victim. The relevance of this type of evidence is apparent. The only ambiguity to the operation of this exception is the scope of the term "injury." The term should be interpreted in a broad sense to include cuts, scratches, bruises or other evidence of physical abuse or physical indications of intercourse.[23] Professors Louisell and Mueller also suggest the term extends to the victim's pregnancy, because in a real sense, a pregnancy

---

[19] Bell v. Harrison, 670 F.2d 656, 658-59 (6th Cir. 1982) (court finds statute constitutional on its face and as applied; statute required defendant to establish relevance before subjecting complainant to embarrassing and humiliating exposure of sexual history or social life); Doe v. United States, 666 F.2d 43, 47 (4th Cir. 1981) (court reversed ruling allowing evidence of complainant's reputation, habits, and sexual behavior, all characterized as opinion or reputation evidence).

[20] Bell v. Harrison, 670 F.2d 656, 658-59 (6th Cir. 1982).

[21] See, generally, Davis v. Alaska, 415 U.S. 308, 39 L.Ed.2d 347, 94 S.Ct. 1105 (1974). See also State v. Jalo, 27 Ore. App. 845, 848, 557 P.2d 1359, 1362 (1976); United States v. Nez, 661 F.2d 1203, 1205-06 (10th Cir. 1981).

[22] See the discussion in Chapter 608 of this Treatise.

[23] United States v. Kasto, 584 F.2d 268, 272 (8th Cir. 1978).

following a rape is an injury to the woman.[24] However, they suggest that to extend this concept to non-physical injuries could undermine the purpose of the Rule. If this type of evidence were admissible, the defense may argue that the defendant was not responsible for the mental injury of the victim, instead, blaming the past sexual behavior of the victim for that specific type of injury. This would have the affect of presenting to the jury evidence of a nature otherwise inadmissible under Rule 412.[25]

When evidence is admissible under either this exception or Rule 412(b)(2)(B), the trial court may in its discretion refuse to admit evidence the probative value of which is outweighed by the danger of unfair prejudice. Evidence, the probative value of which is approximately equal to its prejudicial value, will not be admitted under Rule 412. Rule 412(c), unlike Rule 403, is balanced in favor of excluding evidence.[26] Under Rule 403 evidence will only be excluded if its prejudical affect *substantially* outweighs its probative value.[27] Rule 412 employs a simple balance of probity versus prejudice.

Prejudice under Rule 412 is defined in a broad sense to include such concerns as the potential of the evidence for harassment of the victim of the crime, and the societal cost of the impact of admitting evidence of this nature on the future reporting of rapes.[28]

§ 412.6   Rule 412(b)(2)(B).

The third exception to Rule 412 allows the accused to introduce evidence of the past sexual behavior of the victim with the accused to prove the victim consented to intercourse and, consequently, was not raped. Evidence admitted under this exception is relevant in one of two ways. First, if the victim has consented before, there is an alteration of the probabilities that she has consented in connection with the operative facts. This theory of relevancy would seem to violate the forbidden inference of Rule 404(b). Consequently, if Rule 412 is construed to permit such a theory, it must be seen as an exception to the first sentence of Rule 404(b). Alternately, past consents alter the probabilities as to the reasonableness of the accused perception or interpretation of the victim's action in connection with the operative facts.

---

[24] *See* 3 Louisell & Mueller, § 198[13], at 319; 3 Weinstein, ¶ 412[01], at 412-12. *See also,* McClean v. United States, 377 A.2d 74, 78 n.6 (1977).

[25] 3 Louisell & Mueller, § 198[13], at 320; 3 Weinstein, ¶ 412[01], at 412-11.

[26] *See* 3 Louisell & Mueller, § 198[13], at 323.

[27] See Rule 403 discussed *infra*.

[28] See United States v. Kasto, 584 F.2d 268, 271-72 (8th Cir. 1978); State v. Greer, 13 Wash. App. 71, 73, 533 P.2d 389, 391 (1975).

It should be noted that this exception to the Rule only allows the admission of evidence of past sexual behavior with the accused. Evidence of past sexual behavior with persons other than the accused falls within the general prohibition of Rule 412 and may be admitted only through other exceptions to Rule 412. Evidence of past sexual conduct not admitted under this rule will also be inadmissible under Rule 608(b). Impeachment under Rule 608(b) is allowed through evidence of prior inconsistent conduct only when the conduct proffered is probative of truthfulness, and evidence of past sexual behavior generally does not meet this test.[29]

Consistent with the procedure followed under the exception contained in Rule 412(b)(2)(A), before evidence is admitted pursuant to this exception, its probative value will be weighed against its potential for prejudice under Rule 412(c).

§ 412.7   Procedural Requirements of Rule 412.

When the defendant wishes to introduce evidence under Rule 412, several procedural steps must be followed. Rule 412(c) requires the accused to make a pretrial motion and a written offer of proof where counsel intends to introduce evidence under one of the exceptions in Rule 412(b).[30] If the defendant could not with due diligence have made a timely pretrial motion, the court may entertain a motion made during trial. The court should determine if a continuance is necessary to insure fairness to the defendant and the prosecution.[31]

If the court finds that the offer of proof fairly indicates that evidence would be admissible under Rule 412(b), then it should proceed to hold an evidentiary hearing in chambers. At the hearing both parties will be allowed to introduce evidence and call witnesses. The purpose of the in chambers hearing is to protect the victim's right to privacy.[32] The drafters of Rule 412 felt this hearing was not part of the public trial afforded as a constitutional right to the accused. Consequently, reporters and court room observers may be barred from the proceeding.[33] A public proceeding would be inconsistent with the interests the Rule attempts to protect.[34] There are, however, competing interests of both the accused and the public

---

[29] See the discussion of Rule 608 *infra*.

[30] United States v. Nez, 661 F.2d 1203, 1205-06 (10th Cir. 1981).

[31] *See* 3 Louisell & Mueller, § 199, at 329; 3 Weinstein, ¶ 412[01], at 412-12.

[32] *See* Rule 412(c). *See also* 3 Louisell & Mueller, § 199, at 330.

[33] *Id. See also* 3 Louisell & Mueller, § 199, at 329; 3 Weinstein, ¶412[01], at 412-12.

[34] 3 Louisell & Mueller, § 199 at 329; 3 Weinstein, ¶ 412[01], at 412-12.

in the institution of a public trial, and the constitutionality of the procedure dictated by Rule 412 has yet to be resolved.[35]

Even if evidence is facially admissible under Rule 412(c), the court has the discretion under Rule 412(c)(3) to refuse to admit evidence where its probative value is outweighed by the danger of unfair prejudice.[36] If the trial judge decides to admit the proffered evidence, he must formulate an order that specifies exception to the Rule under which he is admitting the evidence, the purpose for admitting the evidence, and the form in which the evidence may be admitted (on direct or cross-examination of the accused, a witness, or the victim).[37] This procedure need not be followed where the evidence to be admitted is constitutionally compelled.[38] Finally, if the trial court allows the introduction of evidence of the victim's past sexual behavior, the victim may take an interlocutory appeal from this ruling.[39]

---

[35] *See, generally,* Gannett Co., Inc. v. De Pasquale, 443 U.S. 368, 99 S.Ct. 2898, 61 L.Ed.2d 608 (1979); Oklahoma Publishing Co. v. District Court, 430 U.S. 308, 97 S.Ct. 1045, 51 L.Ed.2d 355 (1977); Nebraska Press Association v. Stuart, 427 U.S. 539, 96 S.Ct. 2791, 49 L.Ed.2d 683 (1976); Cox Broadcasting Corp. v. Cohn, 420 U.S. 469, 95 S.Ct. 1029, 43 L.Ed.2d 328 (1975). *See also* United States v. Cianfrani, 573 F.2d 835, 837 (3rd Cir. 1978).

[36] *See* United States v. Kasto, 584 F.2d 268, 271-72 (8th Cir. 1978); State v. Greer, 13 Wash. App. 71, 73, 533 P.2d 389, 391 (1975).

[37] *See* Rule 412(c). *See also,* 3 LOUISELL & MUELLER, § 199, at 330; 3 WEINSTEIN, ¶ 412[01], at 412-11.

[38] *See* 3 LOUISELL & MUELLER, § 199, at 330; 3 WEINSTEIN, ¶ 412[01], at 412-11.

[39] Doe v. United States, 666 F.2d 43, 47-48 (4th Cir. 1981).

V
PRIVILEGES

Chapter 501

RULE 501. PRIVILEGES

Rule 501 reads as follows:

Except as otherwise required by the Constitution of the United States or provided by Act of Congress or in rules prescribed by the Supreme Court pursuant to statutory authority, the privilege of a witness, person, government, State, or political subdivision thereof shall be governed by the principles of the common law as they may be interpreted by the courts of the United States in the light of reason and experience. However, in civil actions and proceedings, with respect to an element of a claim or defense as to which State law supplies the rule of decision, the privilege of a witness, person, government, State or political subdivision thereof shall be determined in accordance with State law.

§ 501.1   The Rule as to Privileges—In General.

Rule 501 reserves the matter of privileges to the common law and statutes for determination, interpretation and development. Rule 501 in essence provides that privileges are to be governed either by common law principles as interpreted by the federal courts, or in those civil actions in which state law supplies the rule of decision as to an element of a claim or defense, by principles of state law.[1]

[1] *See, generally*, McCormick, §§ 72-76.1 at 171-82; 2 Weinstein, ¶¶ 501[01]-[06]; 2 Louisell & Mueller, §§ 200-39; 8 Wigmore, §§ 2201-2396. *See also* Weissenberger, *Toward Precision in the Attorney-Client Privilege for Corporations*, 65 Iowa

In adopting Rule 501, Congress rejected the Supreme Court's proposed Article V which contained thirteen Rules relating to privilege. The proposed Rules set forth nine substantive areas of privileged communications as well as four procedural provisions. Congress chose, however, to reject this attempt at specification, which attempt also included several modifications of common law privileges.[2] It instead promulgated a single Rule which left the law of privilege in *status quo*.[3]

Rule 501 is significant in three respects. First, it acknowledges that privileges are applicable not only to witnesses, but also to any person, state or political subdivision. This expansive treatment is necessary in view of the broad applicability of the protection traditionally accorded to privileged communications.[4] Thus, while evidentiary rules in general apply only to courtroom proceedings, privileges ". . . apply at all stages of all actions, cases and proceedings conducted under these rules," as provided by Rule 1101(c).[5] For example, a privilege may be invoked during the early stages of a lawsuit in order to justify the refusal of a party to comply with a discovery request. Moreover, Rule 501 contemplates that a witness may be precluded from testifying as to matters that are privileged when the holder of the privilege is a person other than the witness. For example, while the physician-patient privilege may function to shield the patient as witness from testifying as to confidential communications made within a specific relational framework, it also functions to protect the patient when the physician is the witness.

Second, the Rule specifies the sources from which the substantive law governing privileges are to be drawn. As noted above, where state law does not apply, it is necessary to look to Acts of Congress, rules promulgated by the Supreme Court, and to federal common law principles in order to determine whether the cloak of privilege is properly available. Implicit in the Rule is the common law concept that, absent statutory or common law authority, there is no privilege to withhold information in the face of the judicial process, or to force another to withhold such information.[6] The

L. REV. 899 (1980); *The Rights of Criminal Defendants and the Subpoena Duces Tecum: The Aftermath of Fisher v. United States*, 95 HARV. L. REV. 683 (1982); Comment, *The Spousal Testimonial Privilege After Trammel v. United States*, 58 DEN. L.J. 357 (1981); Fregant, *Confidentiality of Personnel Files in the Private Sector*, U.C.D. L. REV. 473 (1981); Hill, *Testimonial Privileges and Fair Trial*, 80 COLUM. L. REV. 1173 (1980).

[2] Federal Rule 501, Report of Senate Committee on the Judiciary. There was

some concern in Congress and elsewhere that disregard of state privileges might be unconstitutional or, at the least, contrary to the concept of federalism. See 2 WEINSTEIN, ¶ 501[01], at 501-14.

[3] Federal Rule 501, House Comm. on the Judiciary, 93rd Cong., 1st Sess., Report on Article V (Comm. Print 1950).

[4] *See, e.g.*, Rules 101 and 104(a).

[5] *See* § 1101.1 *et seq.* of this Treatise.

[6] *See, generally*, 2 LOUISELL & MUELLER, § 201.

various privileges available under federal law are discussed in subsequent sections of this Chapter.

Third, the Rule specifies the manner in which federal common law principles respecting privilege are to be interpreted by the courts, that is, "in the light of reason and experience." The language is derived from the Federal Rules of Criminal Procedure.[7] In this regard, the Rule contemplates a continuing development in the area of privileges, whether by expansion or contraction of the traditional theories of privileges. Under Rule 501, federal courts must develop the federal common law of privileges on a case-by-case basis:

> In performing this task, 'reason and experience' dictate balancing the public's need for the full development of relevant facts in federal litigation against the countervailing demand for confidentiality in order to achieve the objective underlying the privilege in issue.[8]

§ 501.2   Other Rules of Evidence that Relate to Privilege.

Rules 1101 and 104 relate to procedural aspects of the application of privilege laws. Rule 1101 sets forth the broad applicability of privilege law and it provides in subsection (c) that: "The rule with respect to privileges applies at all stages of all actions, cases, and proceedings." Reading Rule 1101 in its entirety, it is clear that privilege rules apply even to proceedings not conducted under the Rules of Evidence.

Rule 104 provides that the question as to whether privilege exists in a given situation is a preliminary question to be determined by the court. In making this determination, as well as the determination as to all preliminary questions of admissibility, the court remains bound by rules with respect to privilege even though it is not bound at this stage by other evidentiary rules, *e.g.*, rules on admissibility.[9] In this regard, Rule 104 serves to emphasize the Rules' overriding concern with maintaining the protection of privileged communications.

In operation, Rule 104(a) requires the judge to make all preliminary determinations without invading the area of privileged communications. In deciding, for example, whether a privilege exists, the court will consider whether the necessary facts exist supportive of a privilege (*e.g.*, whether a statutorily or judicially recognized confidential relationship has been shown, whether the relevant communication was made in confidence,

---

[7] Fed. R. Crim. P. 26. *See also* Rule 501, House Comm. on the Judiciary, 93rd Cong., 1st Sess., Report on Article V (Comm. Print 1950).

[8] 2 WEINSTEIN, ¶ 501[03], at 501-31.
[9] Rule 104(a).

etc.)[10] without, however, exposing the substance of the allegedly privileged subject matter. The communication itself remains protected unless there is either an insufficient showing of the prerequisites for invoking a privilege, or, in the alternative, a showing that a party claiming privilege has in some manner waived the privilege.

§ 501.3　The Theory and the Parameters of Privilege Law.

Considering privilege within the ambit of the Rules of Evidence is somewhat anomalous; while evidentiary rules are in large part designed to promote the ascertainment of the truth, privileges may be seen as rules which operate to suppress relevant, otherwise helpful evidence. Inadmissibility is an incidental derivative of privilege rules which seek to preserve the confidentiality of certain private communications. Privilege law, then, is anchored in considerations of policy that exist independently of the usual evidentiary concerns with accuracy and reliability of evidence.[11]

As discussed in the preceding section, rules of privilege function beyond the arena of a trial and may be invoked at any stage of any proceeding. A privilege may involve a refusal to testify, a refusal to disclose a matter during the discovery stage, a refusal to produce real proof, or the right to prevent other people from doing any of the foregoing. A privilege allows a person to resist any governmental process aimed at eliciting protected information. As such, it relieves a person from the duty of revealing facts in response to governmental process and from the corollary risks of contempt for failure to do so. However, recent decisions by the Supreme Court indicate that privileges may be limited by constitutional considerations in criminal cases.[12] A claim of privilege may be overcome, for example, where

---

[10] See discussion at § 501.3, infra.

[11] See McCORMICK, § 72, at 170, in which the author critically compares the general exclusionary rules of evidence which seek "the elucidation of the truth, a purpose which these rules seek to effect by operating to exclude evidence which is unreliable or which is calculated to prejudice or mislead," with rules of privilege which "do not aid the ascertainment of truth" but rather protect "interests and relationships which, rightly or wrongly, are regarded as of sufficient social importance to justify some incidental sacrifice of availability of evidence relevant to the administration of justice."

[12] Nixon v. United States, 418 U.S. 683, 713, 94 S.Ct. 3090, 4016, 41 L.Ed.2d 1039,

1063 (1974) (claim of absolute privilege for presidential communications "must yield to the demonstrated, specific need for evidence in a pending criminal trial."); Davis v. Alaska, 415 U.S. 308, 314, 94 S.Ct. 1105, 1118, 39 L.Ed.2d 347, 353 (1974) (confrontation clause was violated by state privilege protecting juvenile records where privilege deprived defendant of the opportunity to impeach the prosecution's chief witness); Washington v. Texas, 388 U.S. 14, 19, 87 S.Ct. 1920, 1925, 18 L.Ed.2d 1019, 1023 (1967), on remand 417 S.W.2d 278 (Tex. Cr. App.) (compulsory process clause was violated by Texas statute which provided that persons charged or convicted as joint participants in the same crime were incompetent to testify for one another).

a criminal defendant asserts: (1) a need to use the privileged matter as exculpatory, or (2) a need to use the privileged matter to impeach testimony introduced against him.[13]

The rationale behind most non-constitutional testimonial privileges is the protection of certain confidential relationships.[14] Wigmore analyzed the operation of privileges as a guarded exception to the obligation to give testimony which would apply under four prerequisite conditions:

(1) The communications must originate in a *confidence* that they will not be discussed;

(2) This element of *confidentiality must be essential* to the full and satisfactory maintenance of the relation between the parties;

(3) The *relation* must be one which in the opinion of the community ought to be sedulously fostered;

(4) The *injury* that would inure to the relation by the disclosure of the communications must be *greater than the benefit* thereby gained for the correct disposal of litigation.[15]

Wigmore concluded that these prerequisites serve as justifications for the widely recognized attorney-client, spousal and clergyman-parishioner privileges.[16] Under Wigmore's analysis, no justification could be found for a physician-patient privilege,[17] although many contemporary commentators would disagree.[18] A more recent rationale for privileges is the protection of the privacy interests of the parties, regardless of whether the existence of a privilege affects the behavior of the persons involved in the relationship.[19] Under Federal law, privileges which protect confidential relationships attach, for example, to communications between husband and wife,[20] attorney and client,[21] clergyman and parishioner,[22] and physician and patient.[23] The goal of protecting and reinforcing the relationship is sought to be achieved by protecting certain communications made within its confines. In this regard, facts incident to the existence of the relationship itself are not within the privilege. For example, one who invokes the attorney-client privilege may properly refuse to testify concerning the substance of certain communications made to or by the attorney, but must

---

[13] McCORMICK, § 74.2, at 179 (3d ed. 1984).

[14] *See* McCORMICK, § 72, at 171.

[15] 8 WIGMORE, § 2285.

[16] *Id.*

[17] 8 WIGMORE, § 2380(a).

[18] *See* 2 LOUISELL & MUELLER, § 201, at 417; McCORMICK, § 99, at 247. *See also* Louisell, *Confidentiality, Conformity and Confusion; Privileges in Federal Court Today*, 31 TUL. L. REV. 101 (1956).

[19] McCORMICK, § 72, at 172 (3d ed. 1984).

[20] *See, generally*, 8 WIGMORE, § 2332; 2 LOUISELL & MUELLER, § 217.

[21] *See, generally*, 8 WIGMORE, § 2291; 2 LOUISELL & MUELLER, § 207.

[22] *See, generally*, 8 WIGMORE, § 2396; 2 LOUISELL & MUELLER, § 214

[23] *See, generally*, 8 WIGMORE, § 2380(a); 2 LOUISELL & MUELLER, § 215.

respond to questions, if otherwise relevant, concerning the name of the attorney, the time frame of the attorney-client relationship, etc.[24]

Certain principles are common to all privileges. Initially, it must be noted that not all confidential relationships are privileged. Rather, rights incident to privilege law are available only in connection with relationships that are defined and recognized as privileged by legislative enactment or judicial ruling. Privileges will be generally confined to their express limits. For example, although a patient's communications with a licensed psychologist or licensed school psychologist may be accorded a privilege,[25] this privilege does not by its terms extend to psychological therapy received from any other kind of therapist or counselor.[26] The only privileged relationship among family members is that of husband and wife, and such privilege is not extended by implication.[27]

A second common dimension of privilege law is that rights incident to privilege apply only to privileged *communications*.[28] In this regard, the protected status applies to oral or written communications, although it may also extend in certain instances to nonverbal acts[29] and to knowledge gained by means of observation.[30] The protection generally extends to communications made both by and to the holder of the privilege. For example, in the attorney-client relationship, the privilege protects not only statements made by the holder of the privilege, *i.e.*, the client, to the attorney, but also advisory statements made by the attorney to the client.[31] As previously mentioned, the protection accorded privileged communications does not extend to objective facts regarding the relationship.

---

[24] *See* United States v. Clemons, 676 F.2d 124, 126 (5th Cir. 1982) (attorney's message regarding date of trial not privileged); NLRB v. Harvey, 349 F.2d 900, 904 (4th Cir. 1965) (identity of client not privileged).

[25] *See, generally,* 2 LOUISELL & MUELLER, § 216, at 608.

[26] *Id. See also* Advisory Committee's Note to the proposed-but-rejected Rule 504.

[27] The privilege was intended for preservation of marital harmony and tranquility and may only be asserted in a valid marriage. *See* United States v. Lustig, 555 F.2d 737, 739 (9th Cir. 1977); United States v. Neeley, 475 F.2d 1136, 1139 (4th Cir. 1973).

[28] *See, e.g.,* Olender v. United States, 210 F.2d 795, 800 (9th Cir. 1954).

[29] Pereira v. United States, 347 U.S. 1, 6, 74 S.Ct. 358, 362, 98 L.Ed. 435, 439 (1954) (any communication between spouses in the absence of a third party is presumptively privileged). *See also* United States v. Lus-

tig, 555 F.2d 737, 747 (9th Cir. 1977) (even if privilege applied to common-law marriage, it would not apply where relationship had been terminated with no chance of reconciliation).

[30] *See, generally,* McCORMICK, § 89, at 212; 8 WIGMORE, § 2306.

[31] Schwimmer v. United States, 232 F.2d 855, 863 (8th Cir. 1956), *cert. denied,* 355 U.S. 833, 77 S.Ct. 48, 1 L.Ed.2d 52 (1956) (attorney has duty to make assertion of privilege upon any attempt to require him to produce documents or testify as a matter of professional responsibility). *Cf.* United States v. Silverman, 430 F.2d 106, 122 (2d Cir. 1970), *modified,* 439 F.2d 1198 (2d Cir. 1970), *cert. denied,* 402 U.S. 953, 91 S.Ct. 1619, 29 L.Ed.2d 123 (1970), *reh'g denied,* 403 U.S. 924, 91 S.Ct. 2227, 29 L.Ed.2d 704 (1970) (statements made by attorney should not be privileged unless they reveal confidential statements made by client).

A further common consideration is that privilege attaches only to communications made in confidence. In this regard, one seeking to invoke the husband-wife privilege, for example, is aided by a presumption that communications made within the marital relationship are in fact confidential; in other privilege situations confidentiality is not presumed but must be shown.[32] Confidentiality may be negated by a showing that the communication was made in the presence of a third person whose presence was not essential to the transaction. However, a third person's presence will not preclude a finding of confidentiality, where that person is essential to the transaction (*e.g.*, an interpreter or a nurse), where that person is an agent of one of the principals, or where the relationship with the third person is itself privileged (*e.g.*, where a wife is present during her husband's consultation with his physician). The second manner in which confidentiality is negated is where the communication is carelessly made, that is, with little or no concern for maintaining confidentiality. For example, a conversation between an attorney and his client in the midst of a social gathering would generally not be considered privileged. At common law, confidentiality also could be destroyed through application of the "eavesdropper" rule. Under this doctrine, a person who inadvertently overheard a privileged communication could testify as to the communication even though no carelessness of the holder could be shown.[33] For example, if a telephone operator overheard a telephone conversation between an attorney and her client, the operator could testify as to the contents of the communication even though the attorney would be prohibited from so testifying. The eavesdropper rule has been abrogated by statute in most jurisdictions.

Another common incident of privileges is that only the owner, *i.e.*, the holder, of the privilege may assert a privilege in order to suppress relevant evidence. The holders in the testimonial privileges are both husband and wife in the marital privilege, the client in the attorney-client privilege, the patient in the physician-patient privilege, and the parishioner in the clergyman-parishioner privilege.[34] If the holder does not assert the privilege, the otherwise privileged matter may be revealed. In this regard, it should be noted that the holder of a privilege need not be a party to a suit in order to assert the right. He may authorize another person to assert the privilege on his behalf. Or, he may depend in some instances upon the party with whom he maintains the privileged relationship to assert the privilege on his behalf. For example, a lawyer is ethically bound to assert the privilege on

[32] *See* McCORMICK, § 80, at 194 as to assumed confidentiality in the husband-wife situation. *See, e.g.*, Pereira v. United States, 347 U.S. 1, 6, 74 S.Ct. 358, 362, 98 L.Ed. 435, 439 (1954).

[33] McCORMICK, § 89, at 212-14.
[34] McCORMICK, § 75, at 181.

behalf of his client,[35] and he is presumed to have the authority to do so. It may also occur in a given situation that a judge will in effect assert the privilege for an absent holder. In this instance, although the judge has no explicit authorization, he functions to protect society's interest by maintaining the *status quo* until the holder of the privilege can be contacted to assert it on his own behalf.

Only the holder of a privilege may waive the right to the protection of the privilege. A waiver may come about in one of two ways: it may result from an express consent by the holder to testimony of a person who would otherwise be bound by the privilege,[36] or it may result from the voluntary disclosure of a substantial portion of the privileged communication by the holder.[37] The disclosure may be made in court or it may be made entirely in the absence of judicial or governmental process. The disclosure, however, must be voluntary, and if a holder is erroneously compelled to reveal privileged information at one proceeding, he may reassert the privilege at a subsequent proceeding.[38]

In addition to the foregoing incidents of privilege, most privileges have recognized exceptions where they do not apply. The exceptions generally arise due to a special need for disclosure in certain situations. Generally, for example, in an action between the holder and the confidant, the privilege does not apply. Accordingly, if an attorney sues her client for the payment of fees, or a patient sues her physician for alleged malpractice, the privilege ceases to function.[39] The need for confidentiality no longer exists in such situations, or, at the very least, it has been abrogated or superseded by the need for disclosure of information in order to prosecute the cause of action.

[35] Code of Professional Responsibility, Canon 4. Ethical Consideration 4-4 provides in part that "A lawyer owes an obligation to advise the client of the attorney-client privilege and timely to assert the privilege unless it is waived by the client."

[36] United States v. Blackburn, 446 F.2d 1089, 1091 (5th Cir. 1971), *cert. denied*, 404 U.S. 1017, 92 S.Ct. 679, 30 L.Ed.2d 665 (1971) (communications between client and attorney in presence of third party were not privileged). *See also* United States v. Crouthers, 669 F.2d 635, 637 (10th Cir. 1982); United States v. Gordon-Nikkar, 518 F.2d 972, 975 (5th Cir. 1975).

[37] United States v. Bump, 605 F.2d 548, 550-51 (10th Cir. 1979); United States v. Lilley, 581 F.2d 182, 187 (8th Cir. 1978).

[38] *See* 2 LOUISELL & MUELLER, § 238, at 405 (1983 Supp.). *See also* McCORMICK, § 92, at 222, where the author contends that the privilege should be considered waived where a client testifies on cross-examination concerning communications with his lawyer without asserting the claim of privilege.

[39] Tasby v. United States, 504 F.2d 332, 336 (8th Cir. 1974), *cert. denied*, 419 U.S. 1125, 95 S.Ct. 811, 42 L.Ed.2d 826 (1974). *See also* Hunt v. Blackburn, 128 U.S. 464, 470, 9 S.Ct. 125, 129, 32 L.Ed. 488, 490 (1888) (client waived right to object to testimony when she entered upon that line of defense); Haymes v. Smith, 73 F.R.D. 572, 577 (D.C. N.Y. 1976) (attorney-client privilege waived if client injects privileged communication as an issue in the case).

§ 501.4   Ascertaining Applicable Privilege Law in Federal Courts.

The two separate sentences of Rule 501 clearly establish that applicable privilege law will vary in federal courts depending upon the surrounding circumstances and the type of action or proceeding. This result reflects the position taken in the House Report that "federal law should not supersede that of the States in substantive areas such as privilege absent a compelling reason."[40]

The Advisory Committee presented two arguments against federal recognition of state-created privileges. First, privileges are in essence exclusionary rules. Even though privileges suppress evidence to preserve a relationship, the Committee noted that when the relationship itself is an issue in a case, exceptions to state-created privileges often apply and therefore:

> [t]he appearance of privilege in the case is quite by accident, and its effect is to block off the tribunal from a source of information. Thus its real impact is on the method of proof in the case, and in comparison any substantive aspect appears tenuous.[41]

The second argument countered the recognition of state-created privileges by the fact that they are not applicable in federal criminal prosecutions. The Committee believed that in light of its absence in criminal cases, a state-created privilege becomes "illusory as a significant aspect of the relationship out of which it arises."[42] The prevailing Congressional position, however, was that deference should be given to state-created privileges.[43]

By giving deference to state-created privileges, the second sentence of Rule 501 serves the purpose of insuring that all aspects of substantive state law will apply in a claim or defense based on or having a background relation to state law. The expansive interpretation of Rule 501 requiring application of state privilege law to all aspects of a claim or defense controlled by state law is grounded in the legislative history of Rule 501.[44] The Report of the House/Senate Conferees directs a liberal interpretation of what constitutes an element of a claim or defense based on state law:

> If an item of proof tends to support or defeat a claim or defense, or an element of a claim or defense, and if state law supplies the rule of decision for that claim or defense, then state privilege law applies to that item of proof.[45]

[40] H. R. Rep. No. 93-650, 93d Cong., 1st Sess. 8-9 (1973).

[41] See Rule 501, Advisory Committee's Note. See also 2 LOUISELL & MUELLER, § 204, at 478.

[42] Rule 501, Advisory Committee's Note.

[43] See § 501.3, supra.

[44] 2 LOUISELL & MUELLER, § 204, at 462.

[45] H.R. Conf. Rep. No. 93-1597, 93d Cong., 2d Sess. 7 (1974).

This interpretation, which varied somewhat from the Senate proposal, was in accord with case law authority prior to the adoption of the Rules.[46] Moreover, the liberal interpretation intended by Congress is currently being followed in federal courts.[47]

Rule 501 attempts to reconcile privilege law with the *Erie* doctrine[48] by simply offering a directive that in civil cases principles of federal common law will be applied in federal question litigation and in diversity actions where an element of a claim is not based on state law. In a civil action where state law supplies the rule of decision, the state-created privilege law must be applied.

Rule 501 leaves unanswered the question of which of several state's laws to apply, once it has been determined that a state's law concerning a privilege should govern. In resolving this issue, the Federal Courts have largely continued to apply the rule established by the Supreme Court in *Klaxon Co. v. Stentor Electric Manufacturing Co.*[49] Consequently, a claim of privilege that is made at trial is governed by the state law of the forum in which the federal court sits.[50] When a claim of privilege arises in the course of a deposition taken in a forum other than the one in which the federal court is sitting, that state's law governing privileges will be applied.[51]

§ 501.5　　Attorney-Client Privilege

The privilege for confidential communications between clients and their attorneys had its source in English law centuries ago.[52] As the oldest privilege for confidential communications, it has served as a model for other privileges. The purpose and intent behind the attorney-client privilege is to "promote freedom of consultation of legal advisors by clients."[53] In order to

[46] Massachusetts Mut. Life Ins. Co. v. Brei, 311 F.2d 463, 466 (2d Cir. 1962); Pritchard v. Insurance Co. of North America, 61 F.R.D. 104, 109 (D.C. Miss. 1973); Dixon v. 80 Pine Street Corp., 516 F.2d 1278, 1280-81 (2d Cir. 1975) (data obtained not privileged since "societal interest in uncovering the facts which underlie wrongful death claim" was paramount).

[47] 2 LOUISELL & MUELLER, § 203, at 463.

[48] 2 WEINSTEIN, ¶ 501[02], at 501-21.

[49] 313 U.S. 487, 61 S.Ct. 1070, 85 L.Ed.2d 1477 (1941).

[50] Miller v. Trans American Press Inc., 621 F.2d 721, 723 (5th Cir. 1980), *cert. denied*, 450 U.S. 1040, 101 S.Ct. 1759, 68 L.Ed.2d 238 (1981); Samuelson v. Susen, 576 F.2d 546, 551 (3d Cir. 1978) (neurosurgeon brought diversity action based upon

defamation; plaintiff then sought to depose physicians, who in return sought protective orders; district court properly applied state law in granting the protective orders).

[51] *See In re* Westinghouse Electric Corp. Uranium Contracts Litigation, 76 F.R.D. 47, 49 (W.D. Va. 1977) (multidistrict litigation; court applied conflict of law rule of the forum rather than the privilege law of the state whose substantive law would apply). *See also* Palmer v. Fisher, 228 F.2d 603, 606 (7th Cir. 1955), *cert. denied sub nom.*, Fisher v. Pierce, 351 U.S. 965, 76 S.Ct. 1029, 100 L.Ed.2d 1485 (1956). *But cf.* Wm. T. Thompson Co. v. General Nutrition Corp., Inc., 671 F.2d 100, 104 (3d Cir. 1980).

[52] 8 WIGMORE, § 2290, at 542.

[53] 8 WIGMORE, § 2201, at 550.

accomplish this goal, "the apprehension of compelled disclosure by the legal advisors must be removed; and hence the law must prohibit such disclosure except on the client's consent."[54]

Elements of the Privilege.

The privilege may be summarized as follows: "A client holds a privilege to prevent testimonial disclosure of communications made in confidence between himself and his lawyer during the course of a professional lawyer-client relationship."[55] The client need not be an individual, but may be any type of public or private entity, including a corporation, government or governmental agency.[56] It is the client who actually holds the privilege and who may object to the disclosure of confidential communications. The client need not be a party to the action to assert the privilege.[57] The attorney may claim the privilege on his client's behalf[58] and the code of professional ethics obliges him to do so.[59]

In order for the privilege to vest, the client must be represented by a lawyer or by a person whom the client reasonably believes to be an attorney, even if the belief is mistaken.[60] The attorney need not be a member of the bar in the jurisdiction in which the communication takes place but need only be authorized to practice law in some jurisdiction.[61] However, a privilege does not apply to communications between the client and a practitioner such as a patent representative who is not licensed by any bar, even though the identical communication would be privileged if the practitioner were an attorney.[62]

---

[54] *Id.*

[55] 2 LOUISELL & MUELLER, § 209, at 578.

[56] *Id.* at 578-19.

[57] 2 WEINSTEIN, ¶ 503(c)[01], at 503-66.

[58] Fisher v. United States, 425 U.S. 391, 402, 96 S.Ct. 1569, 1573, 48 L.Ed.2d 39, 51 (1976) (it is universally accepted that the attorney-client privilege may be raised by the attorney).

[59] Schwimmer v. United States, 232 F.2d 855, 863 (8th Cir. 1956), *cert. denied*, 352 U.S. 833, 77 S.Ct. 48, 1 L.Ed.2d 52 (1956) (attorney-client privilege exists for the benefit of the client and not the attorney); Baldwin v. Commission, 125 F.2d 812, 814 (9th Cir. 1942) (privilege is that of client rather than of attorney). *See also* American Bar Association, Canon of Professional Ethics, Canon 37.

[60] 2 LOUISELL & MUELLER, § 209, at 520-21 (citing People v. Barker, 60 Mich. 277, 27 N.W. 539 (1886)).

[61] Paper Converting Co. v. FMC Corp., 215 F. Supp. 249, 251 (E.D. Wis. 1963) (privilege applied with respect to correspondence from patent counsel, who was a member of Ohio bar, but not the bar of California, where he was located and employed); Georgia-Pacific Plywood Co. v. United States Plywood Corp., 18 F.R.D. 463, 466 (S.D. N.Y. 1956) (privilege applied in regard to house counsel who belonged to District of Columbia bar, but not to bar of New York, in which was pending litigation in which the lawyer was taking active part). *See also* Zenith Radio Corp. v. Radio Corp. of America, 121 F. Supp. 792, 794 (D.C. Del. 1954).

[62] United States v. United Shoe Machinery Corp., 89 F. Supp. 357, 360 (D.C. Mass. 1958). *But cf.* Renfield Corp. v. E. Remy Martin Co., S.A., 98 F.R.D. 442, 445 (D. Del. 1982) (court found it irrelevant that French in-house attorneys were not

To assert the privilege successfully, the claimant has the burden of proving that the requisite professional relationship existed.[63] The privilege protects a prospective client's preliminary consultation with an attorney concerning possible representation, even if the client does not pay or ultimately retains another lawyer.[64] The consultation need not be related to litigation.[65] However, the relationship must be that of attorney and client; the privilege does not apply when the attorney is consulted as a business advisor,[66] accountant,[67] friend[68] or in some other capacity.[69]

As one commentator has stated, "Only the communication is privileged; the client's knowledge is not."[70] The client cannot immunize a fact from discovery or compelled testimony by communicating it to his attorney. However, if the privilege applies, it protects not only the client's communications to the attorney but also statements by the attorney which would tend to reveal what the client had said.[71] Acts or gestures by the client which are intended to be communicative also are within the privilege.[72] An

members of any bar since they were competent and lawfully able to give legal advice; therefore communications between the attorneys and corporate personnel were within the attorney-client privilege).

[63] United States v. Kelly, 569 F.2d 928, 938 (5th Cir. 1978); In re Bonanno, 344 F.2d 830, 833 (2d Cir. 1965); United States v. Blackburn, 538 F. Supp. 1376, 1382 (M.D. Fla. 1982).

[64] Westinghouse Electric Corp. v. Kerr-McGee Corp., 580 F.2d 1311, 1317-18 (7th Cir. 1978) (where law firm represented American Petroleum Institute, which requested its members to provide law firm with confidential information, attorney-client relationship arose even though none of the members had requested the firm to act as its attorney orally or in writing and the firm did not accept such employment orally or in writing). See also Note, Nature of the Professional Relationship Required Under Privileged Communication Rule, 24 IOWA L. REV. 538, 542 (1939). See, e.g., Kearns v. Fred Lavery/Porsche Audi Co., 573 F. Supp. 91, 94-95 (E.D. Mich. 1983).

[65] 2 WEINSTEIN, ¶ 503(a)(1)[01], at 503-19.

[66] Colton v. United States, 306 F.2d 633, 637 (2d Cir. 1962), cert. denied, 371 U.S. 951, 83 S.Ct. 505, 9 L.Ed.2d 499 (1962) (attorney had to supply information concerning the times and general nature of services performed for client, as well as turn over documents given to him by his client which had not been prepared specifi-

cally for purpose of communicating with attorney). See also Computer Network Corp. v. Spohler, 95 F.R.D. 500, 502 (D.D.C. 1982).

[67] United States v. Jurtner, 474 F.2d 297, 298-99 (9th Cir. 1973); In re Fisher, 51 F.2d 424, 425 (S.D. N.Y. 1931); In re Shapiro, 381 F. Supp. 21, 23 (D.C. Ill. 1974). See also Couch v. United States, 409 U.S. 322, 335, 558 S.Ct. 611, 620, 34 L.Ed.2d 548, 558 (1973) (no federal accountant-client privilege).

[68] Modern Woodmen of America v. Watkins, 132 F.2d 352, 354 (5th Cir. 1942).

[69] In re Grand Jury Proceedings of Browning Arms Co., 528 F.2d 1301, 1303 (8th Cir. 1976) (privilege inapplicable where attorney served as member of board of directors); Harris v. United States, 413 F.2d 316, 319-20 (9th Cir. 1969) (privilege inapplicable where attorney performed clerical services related to trust fund); Banks v. United States, 204 F.2d 666, 670 (8th Cir. 1963) (privilege inapplicable where attorney served as agent in IRS negotiations).

[70] 2 WEINSTEIN, ¶ 503(b)[03], at 503-37.

[71] Mead Data Central, Inc. v. United States Dept't of Air Force, 566 F.2d 242, 254 (D.C. Cir. 1977); Matter of Fischel, 557 F.2d 209, 212 (9th Cir. 1977); Natta v. Hogan, 392 F.2d 686, 693 (10th Cir. 1968); Schwimmer v. United States, 232 F.2d 855, 863 (8th Cir. 1965).

[72] McCORMICK, EVIDENCE, § 89(a).

unresolved issue is whether observations by the attorney about the client, such as his dress, demeanor or mental condition, are privileged. The weight of authority denies privileged status if the observations could be made by anyone.[73] Generally, the privilege is inapplicable to basic facts such as the client's identity, the fact that he has consulted an attorney, the fees paid and the nature of the services to be rendered.[74] An exception is recognized, however, when the substance of the communication already has been revealed and revelation of the client's identity consequently would amount to disclosure of the communication.[75] The client's identity also is within the privilege when its revelation would implicate the client in the crime for which he sought legal advice.[76] Although the privilege protects

---

[73] *In re* Walsh, 623 F.2d 489, 492-93 (7th Cir. 1980); United States v. Pipkins, 528 F.2d 559, 561 (5th Cir. 1976), *cert. denied*, 426 U.S. 952, 96 S.Ct. 3177, 49 L.Ed.2d 1191 (1976) (handwriting samples given to handwriting expert retained by defense were not confidential communications within the realm of the attorney-client privilege); United States v. Kendrick, 331 F.2d 110, 113 (4th Cir. 1964).

[74] United States v. Clemons, 676 F.2d 124, 124 (5th Cir. 1982); *In re* Grand Jury Proceedings in Matter of Fine, 641 F.2d 199, 204 (5th Cir. 1981); United States v. Strahl, 590 F.2d 10, 11-12 (1st Cir. 1978); United States v. Haddad, 527 F.2d 537, 538-39 (6th Cir. 1975).

[75] In re Grand Jury Proceedings, 600 F.2d 215, 217 (9th Cir. 1979) (attorney entitled to assert attorney-client privilege even though individuals had not paid their fees, in refusing to divulge to the grand jury names of clients who had paid fees for two individuals arrested in connection with narcotics conspiracy); In re Grand Jury Proceedings, 517 F.2d 666, 674 (5th Cir. 1975) (court held names of unidentified persons who arranged for bonds and legal fees on behalf of known clients to be privileged, since the names would be directly relevant to supplementing already existent incriminating information about persons suspected of income tax evasion). *See also* United States v. Tratner, 511 F.2d 248, 251 (7th Cir. 1975) (taxpayer-attorney claimed privilege when government sought information regarding $10,000 check deposited in his escrow account; appellate court found attorney had not sustained burden of proving that transaction was part of relationship and remanded to give attorney op-

portunity to include in record on appeal any other evidence which would indicate existence of privilege); NLRB v. Harvey, 349 F.2d 900, 903 (4th Cir. 1965), *on remand*, 264 F. Supp. 770 (W.D. Va. 1966) (unfair labor practice charging that employer fired persons visited by union organizer and that company had put organizer under detective surveillance; attorney refused to divulge identity of client but indicated it was not employer involved in NLRB proceeding; appellate court remanded to district court to ascertain whether hiring of detective was in connection with rendition of legal services; district court found that it was and sustained privilege; client was trying to find out if his plant was being organized so that he would know what he could legally do).

[76] United States v. Hodge & Zweig, 548 F.2d 1347, 1354 (9th Cir. 1977) (disclosure of facts concerning actions of known person in obtaining legal services for another known person would be required, even though the former made a prima facie showing that he would be implicated by the disclosure in activity for which he had sought legal advice, but only because government made a prima facie showing that the attorney was retained to continue criminal or fraudulent activity). *See also* United States v. Liddy, 509 F.2d 428, 430 (D.C. Cir. 1974), *cert. denied*, 420 U.S. 911, 95 S.Ct. 833, 42 L.Ed.2d 842 (1974) (error, but harmless, to instruct jury that it might draw an appropriate inference from the fact that defendant sought counsel in the small hours of the morning shortly after the break-in forming the subject matter of the prosecution had occurred); United States ex rel. Macon v. Yeager, 476 F.2d 613, 615 (3d

the existence and terms of a document drawn up by the attorney for the client, documents which already existed or which are intended to be disclosed are not within the privilege.[77]

The attorney-client privilege also is subject to a requirement of confidentiality. In determining whether a communication is confidential, the client's intent is controlling. The circumstances surrounding the communication often are indicative of the client's intent.[78] For example, if a disinterested third party is present, the client probably did not intend for his statements to the attorney to remain confidential and thus the privilege is inapplicable.[79] On the other hand, if the transaction requires a third person, such as an interpreter, confidentiality is not destroyed by his presence during the communication.[80] Although at common law an eavesdropper could testify to otherwise privileged communications, in this day of sophisticated listening devices, an eavesdropper's testimony is barred by the privilege provided the client has taken reasonable precautions to insure confidentiality.[81] Communications which are intended to be disclosed to another person or which the client actually discloses are not privileged.[82]

Corporate Clients.

Application of the attorney-client privilege becomes complicated where the client is a corporation. As McCormick explained, "The difficulty is basically one of extrapolating the essential operating conditions of the privilege from the paradigm case of the traditional individual client who both

Cir. 1973), *cert. denied*, 414 U.S. 855, 94 S.Ct. 154, 38 L.Ed.2d 104 (1973) (reversible error under Sixth Amendment to allow prosecutor to comment to jury that defendant consulted attorney shortly after the murder with which defendant was subsequently charged).

[77] Fisher v. United States, 425 U.S. 391, 402, 96 S.Ct. 1569, 1576, 48 L.Ed.2d 39, 51 (1976) (questions of attorney-client privilege in tax investigation are controlled by common law principles); United States v. Panetta, 436 F. Supp. 114, 125 (E.D. Pa. 1977), *aff'd without opinion*, 568 F.2d 771 (3d Cir. 1978) (rules of privilege applied in criminal case). *See also* McCormick, *Evidence*, § 89, at 214 ("[I]f a document would be subject to an order for production if it were in the hands of the client it will be equally subject to such an order if it is in the hands of his attorney.").

[78] 2 WEINSTEIN, ¶ 503(a)(4)[01], at 503-29. *See also* United States v. Bigos, 459 F.2d

639, 643 (1st Cir. 1972), *cert. denied*, 409 U.S. 847, 93 S.Ct. 53, 34 L.Ed.2d 88 (1972) ("While we agree that the presence of a third party commonly destroys the privilege, it does so only insofar as it is indicative of the intent of the parties that their communication not be confidential").

[79] United States v. Flores, 628 F.2d 521, 523 (9th Cir. 1980); United States v. Cochran, 546 F.2d 27, 29 (5th Cir. 1977); Johnson v. United States, 542 F.2d 941, 942 (5th Cir. 1976).

[80] United States v. Landof, 591 F.2d 36, 38-39 (9th Cir. 1978); Himmelfarb v. United States, 175 F.2d 924, 931-32 (9th Cir. 1949).

[81] 2 WEINSTEIN, ¶ 503(b)[02], at 503-37.

[82] United States v. Bump, 605 F.2d 548, 550 (10th Cir. 1979); Esposito v. United States, 436 F.2d 603, 605 (9th Cir. 1970); United States v. Tellier, 255 F.2d 441, 442 (2d Cir. 1958).

supplies information to, and receives counsel from, the attorney."[83] In the corporate context these functions typically are divided between several different individuals of varying rank. While extending the privilege to communications by any officer or employee of the corporation has been acknowledged as unduly broad,[84] the precise parameters of the privilege remain unclear. In 1962 a district court in Pennsylvania formulated the "control group" test which limited the privilege to communications by corporate personnel in a position to control or even to take a substantial part in a decision about any action which the corporation may take upon the advice of the attorney.[85] Although the control group test was widely followed,[86] the Supreme Court expressly rejected it in its 1981 decision in *Upjohn Co. v. United States.*[87] The Court concluded that the control group test "cannot . . . govern the development of the law in this area"[88] because it "overlooks the fact that the privilege exists to protect not only the giving of professional advice to those who can act on it but also the giving of information to the lawyer to enable him to give sound and informed advice."[89] The Court declined to establish an alternative to the control group test, choosing instead to decide only the case before it. However, the Court's opinion indicates that information communicated to an attorney should be privileged if it is treated as confidential within the corporation, it is communicated to the attorney for the purpose of receiving legal advice and it is closely related to the duties of the corporate employer who conveys it to the attorney.[90]

Another issue in the corporate context is whether otherwise privileged information must be disclosed in suits by the shareholders against the corporation. The leading federal case, *Garner v. Wolfinbarger,* held that the privilege may be overcome by a showing of good cause, at least where the

---

[83] McCORMICK, EVIDENCE, § 87, at 207. *See also* Weissenberger, *Toward Precision in the Attorney-Client Privilege for Corporations,* 65 IOWA L. REV. 899 (1980).

[84] *See, e.g.,* Philadelphia v. Westinghouse Electric Corp., 210 F. Supp. 483, 485 (E.D. Pa. 1962), *mandamus and prohibition denied sub nom.* General Electric Co. v. Kirkpatrick, 312 F.2d 742 (3d Cir. 1962), *cert. denied,* 372 U.S. 943, 83 S.Ct. 937, 9 L.Ed.2d 969 (1936).

[85] *Id.* at 485.

[86] Many, but not all courts adopted the control group test. In 1970, the Seventh Circuit propounded the subject matter test under which corporate communications with an attorney are privileged if the employee "makes the communication at the direction of his superiors in the corporation," even though the employee is not in a position of control, and the subject matter of the communication "is the performance by the employee of the duties of his employment." Harper and Row Publishers, Inc. v. Decker, 423 F.2d 487, 491-92 (7th Cir. 1970), *aff'd mem. by equally divided court,* 400 U.S. 955, 91 S.Ct. 479, 27 L.Ed.2d 433, *rehearing denied,* 401 U.S. 950, 91 S.Ct. 917, 28 L.Ed.2d 234 (1971).

[87] 449 U.S. 383, 397, 101 S.Ct. 677, 685, 66 L.Ed.2d 584, 594 (1981).

[88] *Id.* at 402.

[89] *Id.* at 390.

[90] *Id* at 394.

shareholders charge the corporation with "acting inimically to stockholder interests."[91]

Multiple Clients.

When two or more persons consult an attorney about a common matter, each client retains the right to assert the attorney-client privilege against a third party. However, in a dispute between the joint clients the privilege is inapplicable since joint consultation indicates the clients did not intend for their communications to be confidential.[92] Where several clients, each with separate counsel, meet to plan a joint defense or course of action for the common good, the situation usually is treated as if the clients jointly consulted one attorney.[93] If there is no common interest among the various clients and they meet on a purely adversary basis, however, the privilege does not apply.[94]

Work Product Doctrine Distinguished.

Although the attorney-client privilege and the work product doctrine often are confused, the two doctrines are distinct. A complete discussion of the work product doctrine is beyond the scope of this Treatise, but the major differences between the attorney-client privilege and the work product doctrine are briefly summarized here: (1) While the purpose of the attorney-client privilege is to encourage full disclosure by the client, the work product doctrine is designed to protect the attorney's privacy by preserving the confidentiality of his research and analysis.[95] (2) Unlike the

[91] 430 F.2d 1093, 1103 (5th Cir. 1970), *cert. denied*, 401 U.S. 974, 91 S.Ct. 1191, 28 L.Ed.2d 323 (1971). *See also* Van Dusen, *The Responsibility of Lawyers Advising Management Under the ABA Code of Professional Responsibility*, N.Y.S. Bar J. 565 (Dec. 1974). *But cf.*, Brennan's Inc. v. Brennan's Restaurants, Inc., 590 F.2d 168, 170 (5th Cir. 1979).

[92] Simpson v. Motorists Mut. Inc. Co., 494 F.2d 850, 855 (7th Cir. 1974), *cert. denied*, 419 U.S. 901, 95 S.Ct. 184, 42 L.Ed.2d 147 (1974), (when one attorney represents two parties having a common interest, communications of each party with attorney are privileged from third party but not between the two original parties); Baldwin v. Commissioner, 125 F.2d 812, 815 (9th Cir. 1942) (when two or more parties address lawyer as their common agent, their communications are privileged as against strangers, but not among themselves); Grand Trunk Western R. Co. v. H.W. Nelson Co., 116 F.2d 823, 835 (6th Cir. 1941), *reh. denied*, 118 F.2d 252 (6th Cir. 1941) ("when two persons employ an attorney as their common agent, their communications to him as to strangers will be privileged, but as to themselves, they stand on the same footing as to the attorney, and either can compel him to testify against the other as to their negotiations in any litigation between them, when the subject of the conversation is competent").

[93] United States v. McPartlin, 595 F.2d 1321, 1323 (7th Cir. 1979); Hunydee v. United States, 355 F.2d 183, 186 (9th Cir. 1965).

[94] United States v. Cariello, 536 F. Supp. 698, 701 (D.N.J. 1982); Magnaleasing, Inc. v. Staten Island Mall, 76 F.R.D. 559, 561 (D.C. N.Y. 1977).

[95] 2 LOUISELL & MUELLER, § 211, at 549-50.

attorney-client privilege, the work product doctrine is limited to documents and tangible items prepared in anticipation of litigation.[96] (3) When the privilege is applicable its protection is absolute, while the work product doctrine can be overcome by a showing of substantial need.[97]

Waiver.

The attorney-client privilege is recognized to protect the client and therefore only the client may waive the privilege.[98] Waiver may occur by voluntary disclosure of the communication,[99] waiver at a former trial or earlier proceeding, waiver by a trustee of a corporation in bankruptcy[100] or waiver by the representative of a deceased client.[101] The client's failure to object to the disclosure of privileged information when he had the opportunity to do so also operates as a waiver.[102] Since the privilege protects confidential communications rather than facts, the client can testify about the facts which were the subject of his consultation with the attorney without waiving the privilege.[103]

Exceptions.

The privilege is subject to several exceptions. When the client consults the attorney in the furtherance of a continuing or future crime or fraud, the privilege does not apply. The exception bars the privilege only if the client is aware of the illegality of his conduct and is inapplicable when the client consults the attorney about a crime or fraudulent act he committed in the past.[104] Although the privilege survives the death of the client and

[96] *Id.* at 550.

[97] *Id.* at 551.

[98] 8 WIGMORE, § 2327, at 635.

[99] United States v. McCambridge, 551 F.2d 865, 867 (1st Cir. 1977); United States v. Pauldino, 487 F.2d 127, 129 (10th Cir. 1973). *See also* Howell v. United States, 442 F.2d 265, 268-69 (7th Cir. 1971) (lawyer permitted to testify that his client was competent to stand trial; testimony amounted to nonconfidential matters).

[100] 8 WIGMORE, § 2327, at 638.

[101] 8 WIGMORE, § 2329, at 639; *See* CFTC v. Weintraub, #84-261 (SupCt., Apr. 29, 1985) (trustee of a coporation in bankruptcy has the power to waive the debtor corporation's attorney-client privilege with respect to communications that took place before the filing of the petition in bankruptcy; the trustee plays the role most closely analogous to that of a solvent corporation's management.)

[102] Steen v. First National Bank, 298 F. 36, 41 (6th Cir. 1924).

[103] *In re* Ampicillin, Antitrust Litigation, 81 F.R.D. 377, 380 (D.C. D.C. 1977); Magida v. Continental Can Co., 12 F.R.D. 74, 78 (1951).

[104] *In re* Grand Jury Proceedings, 604 F.2d 798, 801 (3d Cir. 1979); United States v. Calvert, 523 F.2d 895, 909 (8th Cir. 1975), *cert. denied*, 424 U.S. 911, 96 S.Ct. 1106, 47 L.Ed.2d 314 (1975) ("[I]t is the client's purpose which is controlling, and it matters not that the attorney was ignorant of the client's purpose in making the statements."); United States v. Aldridge, 484 F.2d 655, 658 (7th Cir. 1973), *cert. denied*, 415 U.S. 921, 94 S.Ct. 1423, 39 L.Ed.2d 477 (1973) (same). *See also* United States v. Friedman, 445 F.2d 1076, 1086 (9th Cir. 1971), *cert. denied*, 404 U.S. 958, 92 S.Ct. 326, 30 L.Ed.2d 275 (1971).

may be asserted by his representative, an exception to the privilege arises when there is a dispute between persons who claim a right to property or money through the decedent. In this situation it is unclear which person is entitled to claim the privilege and therefore neither is permitted to assert it.[105] Another exception is recognized when the attorney acts as an attesting witness to a document executed by the client. The privilege does not apply to communications between the client and attorney which are relevant to an issue concerning the document because the attorney-client privilege does not protect communications to the attorney in the role of attesting witness.[106] The attorney-client privilege is inapplicable in the event of a breach of duty by either the client or the attorney. When the client fails to pay his fees, or charges the attorney with malpractice, the attorney may reveal otherwise privileged communications to the extent necessary to recover his fee or to protect his reputation.[107]

§ 501.6   Spousal Privileges.

Federal courts recognize a privilege against adverse spousal testimony and a privilege for confidential marital communications. Both are discussed below.

Privilege Against Adverse Spousal Testimony.

At common law the spouse of a party was considered incompetent to testify either for or against the party. This practice resulted from the combination of the common law rule which disqualified a party from testifying in his own behalf and the legal fiction, inspired by Judeo-Christian tradition, that husband and wife were one.[108] In federal courts the disqualification of spouses to testify *for* one another was abolished by the Supreme Court in 1933.[109]

The rule excluding adverse testimony by a spouse evolved into a privilege and was justified as a means to preserve marital harmony and tranquility.

---

[105] 2 LOUISELL & MUELLER, § 213, at 583.

[106] *Id*. at 585-86.

[107] Johnson v. United States, 542 F.2d 941, 942 (5th Cir. 1976); Tasby v. United States, 504 F.2d 332, 336 (8th Cir. 1974), *cert. denied*, 419 U.S. 1125, 95 S.Ct. 811, 42 L.Ed.2d 826 (1974); Laughner v. United States, 373 F.2d 326, 327 (5th Cir. 1967); Housler v. First Nat'l Bank of East Islip, 484 F. Supp. 1321, 1323-24 (E.D. N.Y. 1980). *See also* United States v. Woodall, 438 F.2d 1317, 1324 (5th Cir. 1970), *cert.*

denied, 403 U.S. 933, 91 S.Ct. 2262, 29 L.Ed.2d 712 (1970); United States v. Wiggins, 184 F. Supp. 673, 677-78 (D.C. Cir. 1960).

[108] 2 LOUISELL & MUELLER, § 217, at 618-19.

[109] Funk v. United States, 290 U.S. 371, 380-81, 54 S.Ct. 212, 217-18, 78 L.Ed. 369, 374-75 (1933). *See also* United States v. Graham, 87 F. Supp. 237, 240-41 (D.C. Mich. 1949).

It was believed that adverse testimony by a spouse would destroy a marriage. In *Hawkins v. United States*, the Supreme Court endorsed this rationale and established that both spouses held the privilege to bar adverse testimony.[110] However, in its 1980 decision in *Trammel v. United States*, the Court sharply cut the broad privilege approved in *Hawkins* by ruling that the privilege to exclude adverse spousal testimony is held solely by the witness spouse; the party spouse cannot object if the witness spouse freely elects to testify.[111] The Court noted that privileges may impede the search for truth by suppressing evidence, and thus must be strictly construed. In the light of reason and experience, the Court found that the goal of preserving marital harmony no longer justified so sweeping a privilege. The Court observed that the willingness of one spouse to testify against the other suggested the marriage already was beyond saving.[112]

The privilege against adverse spousal testimony applies in federal criminal proceedings. Its role in civil litigation in federal courts remains unclear. Although Rule 501 seems to indicate the privilege should apply in civil cases in which state law does not provide the rule of decision, at least one federal court has held the privilege inapplicable in civil cases.[113]

Unlike the privilege for marital communications, the testimonial privilege is not limited to confidential statements; it covers testimony on all subjects, including matters which occurred before and during the marriage.[114] To claim the privilege, the party and the witness must have a valid marriage at the time of trial, as determined by the law of the domiciliary state.[115] A sham or fraudulent marriage will not support the privilege. In the event of divorce, annulment or death the privilege ends.[116]

[110] 358 U.S. 74, 78, 79 S.Ct. 136, 138, 3 L.Ed.2d 125, 128 (1958) ("adverse testimony, given by a spouse in criminal proceedings would, we think, be likely to destroy almost any marriage").

[111] 445 U.S. 40, 53, 100 S.Ct. 906, 918, 63 L.Ed.2d 186, 199 (1980).

[112] *Id.* at 52.

[113] Ryan v. Commissioner, 568 F.2d 531, 542-44 (7th Cir. 1977).

[114] United States v. Apodaca, 522 F.2d 568, 570 (10th Cir. 1975) (noting that spousal testimonial privilege would apply as to matters occurring prior to the marriage, but affirming denial of the privilege upon ground that marriage was fraudulent). *See also* United States v. Van Drunen, 501 F.2d 1393, 1397 (9th Cir. 1974), *cert. denied*, 419 U.S. 1091, 95 S.Ct. 684, 42 L.Ed.2d 684 (1974).

[115] United States v. Snyder, 707 F.2d 139, 141 (5th Cir. 1983); United States v.

McElrath, 377 F.2d 508, 510 (6th Cir 1967); *In re* Grand Jury Proceedings Witness Ms. X, 562 F. Supp. 486, 488 (N.D. Cal. 1983).

[116] Pereira v. United States, 347 U.S. 1, 6, 74 S.Ct. 358, 363, 98 L.Ed. 435, 440 (1954) (spouses' divorce ends "any bar of incompetency"); Lutwak v. United States, 344 U.S. 604, 614-15, 73 S.Ct. 726, 736-37, 97 L.Ed. 1352, 1362-63 (1953), *reh. denied*, 345 U.S. 919, 73 S.Ct. 726, 97 L.Ed 1352 (1953) (marriage entered into to obtain the illegal entry into the United States of aliens was a sham and therefore did not support the marital privilege); Yaldo v. Immigration & Naturalization Service, 424 F.2d 501, 504 (6th Cir. 1970) (annulment ends the marital privilege); United States v. Gonella, 103 F.2d 123, 125 (3d Cir. 1939) (death of the spouse ends the privilege).

Generally, the privilege only applies in situations where the witness spouse's testimony will have a direct effect upon the marriage. The majority of courts agree that one of the spouses must be a party to the proceedings. Even though the witness's testimony may be damaging to his or her spouse and thus pose a threat to marital harmony, unless the spouse is a party he does not have the requisite direction stake in the outcome of the litigation which justifies the privilege.[117] Similarly, although the privilege applies at grand jury proceedings pursuant to Federal Evidence Rule 1101(d)(2), in cases in which the spouse is not the focus of the grand jury's inquiry, the witness spouse normally may not refuse to testify regardless of the testimony's negative reflection on his or her spouse.[118]

To ensure the effectiveness of the privilege, the witness spouse must be permitted to claim the privilege outside the presence of the jury. The prosecution may not call the witness spouse with the knowledge that the spouse does not wish to testify and force the spouse to claim the privilege in open court.[119] Once the privilege is asserted, most courts prohibit the prosecution from commenting upon its exercise to the jury.[120]

The exceptions to the privilege against adverse spousal testimony were designed to prevent the injustice which would result if the party could prevent his or her spouse from testifying in certain cases. After *Trammel* removed the party's ability to bar adverse testimony by his or her spouse, the exceptions have less significance. The privilege does not apply where one spouse is charged with committing a crime against the other.[121] Recent

[117] United States v. Burks, 470 F.2d 432, 435-36 (D.C. Cir. 1972) (murder prosecution; privilege inapplicable where interests of spouse of witness "were in no way at stake"); Halback v. Hill, 261 F. 1007, 1009 (D.C. Cir. 1919) (father's petition to obtain custody of child from child's grandmother where father had remarried; proper to require him to authenticate letters written by his new wife, offered by grandmother to demonstrate unfitness of this wife to have custody of child). *Contra*, United States v. Hoffa, 349 F.2d 20, 23 (6th Cir. 1965), *aff'd*, 385 U.S. 293, 87 S.Ct. 408, 17 L.Ed.2d 374, *reh. denied*, 386 U.S. 940, 87 S.Ct. 970, 17 L.Ed.2d 880 (1965) (prosecution for jury tampering; testimony of wife privileged as to whether defendant's encounters with the law and domestic troubles were associated with drug addiction and his association with other women).

[118] *In re* Snoonian, 502 F.2d 110, 112 (1st Cir. 1974) (husband could not invoke spousal testimonial privilege where government had stated that wife was not target of grand jury investigation). *See also* United States v. George, 444 F.2d 310, 313 (6th Cir. 1971).

[119] 2 WEINSTEIN, ¶ 505[03], at 505-14.

[120] United States v. Pariente, 558 F.2d 1186, 1189 (5th Cir. 1977); United States v. Tapia-Lopez, 521 F.2d 582, 584 (9th Cir. 1975). *See also* Courtney v. United States, 390 F.2d 521, 523 (9th Cir. 1968), *cert. denied*, 393 U.S. 857, 89 S.Ct. 98, 21 L.Ed.2d 126 (1968), *reh. denied*, 393 U.S. 892, 89 S.Ct. 440, 21 L.Ed.2d 456 (1968) (plain error to allow prosecutor to comment upon defendant's failure to call his wife, whom he had married between the first and second trial, to testify, where defendant had properly claimed his privilege not to have her testify against him).

[121] Wyatt v. United States, 362 U.S. 525, 532, 80 S.Ct. 901, 905, 4 L.Ed.2d 931, 935 (1960); United States v. Smith, 533 F.2d 1077, 1079 (8th Cir. 1976).

cases have extended this exception to include crimes against a child of either spouse.[122] An exception also arises in cases in which the spouse is one of several victims of a crime committed by the other spouse.[123]

Privilege for Confidential Marital Communications.

In addition to the privilege against adverse spousal testimony the federal common law has long recognized a privilege for confidential communications between spouses. The privilege is justified as a means to preserve marital harmony and provide a "safe harbour of intimacy where spouses can confide in each other freely without any fear that what they say will be published under compulsion."[124] Critics contend that the privilege has virtually no effect on the behavior of spouses because most are unaware of its existence.[125] Proposed Federal Evidence Rule 505 sought to change the existing federal practice by eliminating the privilege, but the Rule was rejected by Congress. Lower federal court decisions and dictum in the Supreme Court's opinion in *Trammel* indicate that private communications between spouses remain privileged under Rule 501.[126]

The privilege for confidential communications applies in both federal criminal cases and civil cases in which state law does not provide the rule of decision.[127] Both spouses hold the privilege and both may assert it to bar disclosure of statements made in confidence by either spouse. The privilege does not cover statements made before or after the marriage but confidences disclosed during the marriage are protected forever. Death, divorce or annulment do not end the privilege for communications made during the marriage.[128] Oral and written statements are protected by the privilege, as are gestures or other acts which are intended to communicate.[129] How-

[122] United States v. Lilley, 581 F.2d 182, 184 (8th Cir. 1978); United States v. Allery, 526 F.2d 1362, 1365 (8th Cir. 1975).

[123] Wilkerson v. United States, 342 F.2d 807, 809 (8th Cir. 1965).

[124] 2 WEINSTEIN, ¶ 505[02], at 505-12.

[125] See, e.g., Hutchins and Slesinger, *Some Observations on the Law of Evidence: Family Relations*, 13 Minn. L. Rev. 675, 682 (1929) ("[m]arital harmony among lawyers who know about privileged communications is not vastly superior to that of other professional groups.")

[126] Trammel v. United States, 445 U.S. 40, 45 n.5, 100 S.Ct. 906, 911-12, n.9, 63 L.Ed.2d 186, 193-94, n.9 (1980) ("[T]his Court recognized just such a confidential communications privilege in *Wolfle v. United States*, 291 U.S. 7, 54 S.Ct. 279, 284, 78 L.Ed. 617 (1934), and in *Blau v.*

United States, 340 U.S. 332, 71 S.Ct. 301, 95 L.Ed. 306 (1951) . . . The privilege as to confidential marital communications is not at issue in the instant case; accordingly, our holding today does not disturb *Wolfle* and *Blau*."); United States v. Tsinnijinnie, 601 F.2d 1035, 1038 (9th Cir. 1979); United States v. Mendoza, 574 F.2d 1373, 1375, reh. denied, 579 F.2d 644 (5th Cir. 1978).

[127] 2 LOUISELL & MUELLER, § 219, at 637.

[128] Pereira v. United States, 347 U.S. 1, 6, 74 S.Ct. 358, 362, 98 L.Ed. 435, 439 (1954); United States v. Lilley, 581 F.2d 182, 184 (8th Cir. 1978); United States v. Burks, 470 F.2d 432, 435 (D.C. Cir. 1972).

[129] Pereira v. United States, 347 U.S. 1, 6, 74 S.Ct. 358, 362, 98 L.Ed. 435, 439 (1954); United States v. Smith, 533 F.2d 1077, 1079 (8th Cir. 1976).

ever, federal courts generally do not permit the privilege to be invoked to prevent disclosure of the circumstances and events of the marriage or acts which are not solely communicative.[130]

The privilege is subject to the requirement of a valid marriage. Federal courts have refused to extend the privilege to other relationships which claim to be the functional equivalent of marriage.[131] To invoke the privilege the spouses also must meet the requirement of confidentiality. In this respect they are aided by a presumption that any statements made in the absence of a third person were intended to be confidential. If a third person is present, however, the statements are presumed not to be confidential.[132] Most courts find that communications in the presence of a child who is old enough to understand are not confidential.[133] Disclosure by one spouse destroys confidentiality, as does the expectation that the communication will be related to a third person.[134]

Exceptions to the privilege for confidential communications include interspousal suits and the prosecution of one spouse for a crime committed against the other.[135] Another commonly recognized exception arises where one spouse is charged with a crime and wishes to introduce into evidence confidential statements made to the other to help in the defense.[136]

§ 501.7   Clergyman-Parishioner Privilege.

As a matter of federal common law, a privilege for confidential communications to religious officials for spiritual advice or personal counseling

---

[130] United States v. Thomann, 609 F.2d 560, 564 (1st Cir. 1979); United States v. Moore, 604 F.2d 1228, 1232 (9th Cir. 1979); United States v. Long, 468 F.2d 755, 756-57 (8th Cir. 1972); United States v. Harper, 450 F.2d 1032, 1046 (5th Cir. 1971).

[131] United States v. Lustig, 555 F.2d 737, 748-49 (9th Cir. 1977) ("[B]oth privileges depend upon the existence of a valid marriage, as determined by state law; since defendant claimed only a common-law marriage to the witness, and since such a marriage is not valid under Alaska law, neither privilege could apply in this case"); United States v. Neeley, 475 F.2d 1136, 1137-38 (4th Cir. 1973) (defendant could not rely upon state spousal testimonial privilege to exclude testimony by another woman, since he had never divorced his wife, and the privilege operates only where there is a valid marriage). *See also* United

States v. Boatright, 446 F.2d 913, 915 (5th Cir. 1971).

[132] Pereira v. United States, 347 U.S. 1, 6, 74 S.Ct. 358, 362, 98 L.Ed. 435, 439 (1954); Wolfle v. United States, 291 U.S. 7, 13, 54 S.Ct. 279, 284, 78 L.Ed. 617, 621 (1934).

[133] Wolfle v. United States, 291 U.S. 7, 13, 54 S.Ct. 279, 284, 78 L.Ed. 617, 621 (1934); United States v. Penn, 647 F.2d 876, 879 (9th Cir. 1980); *In re* Kinoy, 326 F. Supp 400, 402 (D.C. N.Y. 1970).

[134] Wolfle v. United States, 291 U.S. 7, 13, 54 S.Ct. 279, 284, 78 L.Ed. 617, 621 (1934); Grulkey v. United States, 394 F.2d 244, 248 (8th Cir. 1968); United States v. Mitchell, 137 F.2d 1006, 1009 (1943).

[135] McCORMICK, EVIDENCE, § 84, at 199-200.

[136] *Id.* at 200.

is recognized under Rule 501.[137] The privilege also is widely recognized by the states.[138] The rationale underlying the privilege was described by Judge Fahy in his concurring opinion in *Mullen v. United States:*

> Sound policy—reason and experience—concedes to religious liberty a rule of evidence that a clergyman shall not disclose on a trial the secrets of a penitent's confidential confession to him, at least absent the penitent's consent. Knowledge so acquired in the performance of a spiritual function . . . is not to be transformed into evidence to be given to the whole world. As Wigmore points out, such a confidential communication meets all the requirements that have rendered communications between husband and wife and attorney and client privileged and incompetent. The benefit of preserving these confidences inviolate overbalances the possible benefit of permitting litigation to prosper at the expense of the tranquility of the home, the integrity of the professional relationship, and the spiritual rehabilitation of a penitent. The rules of evidence have always been concerned not only with truth but with the manner of its ascertainment.[139]

Because the clergyman-parishioner privilege is so widely and uniformly recognized it has posed very few problems in litigation. The only problems arise in establishing the outer limits of the privilege; specifically, in establishing standards for the class of religious officials as to whom communications are privileged and for the types of communications which are privileged. Proposed-but-rejected Rule 506 defined a clergyman as "a minister, priest, rabbi, or other similar functionary of a religious organization, or an individual reasonably believed so to be by the person consulting him."[140]

[137] Totten v. United States, 92 U.S. 105, 108, 23 L.Ed. 605, 608 (1876) ("[I]t may be stated that public policy forbids the maintenance of any suit in a court of justice, the trial of which would inevitably lead to the disclosure of matters which the law itself regards as confidential, and respecting which it will not allow the confidence to be violated; on this principle, suits cannot be maintained which would require a disclosure of the confidences of the confessional, or those between husband and wife, or of communications by a client to his counsel for professional advice, or of a patient to his physician for a similar purpose"). *See also* Mullen v. United States, 263 F.2d 275, 276-80 (D.C. Cir. 1958); McMann v. Securities and Exchange Comm'n, 87 F.2d 377, 378 (2d Cir. 1937), *cert. denied*, 301 U.S.

684, 57 S.Ct. 785, 81 L.Ed. 1342 (1937). *But cf.* United States v. Webb, 615 F.2d 828, 830 (9th Cir. 1980) (court declined to discuss whether clergyman-parishioner privilege was applicable in federal courts under Rule 501). Traditionally, the privilege was referred to as the priest-penitent privilege, but in modern times the privilege encompasses communications made to a broader group of religions than the traditional name indicates. 2 LOUISELL & MUELLER, § 214, at 587.

[138] *See* Kuhlmann, *Communications to Clergyman-When Are They Privileged?* 2 VAL. U.L. REV. 265 (1968).

[139] 263 F.2d 275, 280 (D.C. Cir. 1958) (concurring opinion).

[140] Supreme Court Standard 506(a)(1).

Although this definition is broader than the definition recognized in many states, the Advisory Committee's Note indicates it was not intended to be "so broad as to include all self-denominated 'ministers'."[141] To come within the definition the religious official must "be regularly engaged in activities conforming at least in a general way with those of a Catholic priest, Jewish rabbi, or minister of an established Protestant denomination, though not necessarily on a full-time basis."[142] Proposed-but-rejected Rule 506 also expanded the type of communications which fall within the privilege. Protected communications are not limited to confessions but include any type of personal counseling.[143]

Like the attorney-client privilege, the parishioner must intend for the communication to remain confidential in order for the clergyman-parishioner privilege to apply.[144] The privilege is not limited to oral or written communications but also protects observations made by the clergyman.[145] The privilege is held by the parishioner but, in the absence of evidence to the contrary, the clergyman may claim it on behalf of the parishioner.[146]

§ 501.8   Physician-Patient Privilege.

Unlike the attorney-client, spousal and clergyman-parishioner privileges, at common law there was no privilege for communications between a physician and his patient.[147] Following the lead of New York and California,[148] the majority of states passed statutes establishing a physician-patient privilege. Although there was no corresponding federal privilege, prior to the enactment of the Federal Rules of Evidence federal courts sitting in diversity cases often applied state-created physician-patient privileges. In

---

[141] Supreme Court Standard 506 Advisory Committee Note.

[142] Id. See also 2 WEINSTEIN, ¶ 506[02], at 506-7.

[143] 2 LOUISELL & MUELLER, § 214, at 590-91. See also United States v. Gordon, 493 F. Supp. 822, 824 (N.D. N.Y. 1980), aff'd 655 F.2d 478 (2d Cir. 1981) (privilege inapplicable where communication pertained to business).

[144] United States v. Webb, 615 F.2d 828, 830 (9th Cir. 1980). See also United States v. Wells, 446 F.2d 2, 4 (2d Cir. 1971) (priest-penitent privilege did not cover letter from defendant to priest requesting priest to ask an FBI agent to see the defendant, since the letter contained no hint that its contents were to be kept secret or that its purpose

was to obtain religious or other counsel or advice).

[145] 2 LOUISELL & MUELLER, § 214, at 592.

[146] 2 WEINSTEIN, ¶ 506[03], at 506-12.

[147] McCORMICK, EVIDENCE, § 98, at 243.

[148] In 1828 New York passed the following statute and became the first state to recognize a physician-patient privilege: "No person authorized to practice physic or surgery shall be allowed to disclose any information which he may have acquired in attending any patient, in a professional character, and which information was necessary to enable him to prescribe for such patient as a physician, or to do any act for him as a surgeon." N.Y. REV. STATS. 1829, vol. II, part III, c. 7. tit. 3, art. eight, § 73. In 1872, California passed a similar statute. CAL. CIV. PROC. CODE § 1881 par. 4 (1872).

addition, federal courts sometimes applied the privilege in federal question and federal criminal cases. While Rule 501 on its face now prohibits the application of state privileges in these cases, it authorizes federal courts to recognize a federal physician-patient privilege as the federal common law evolves "in the light of reason and experience."[149] A number of federal courts also have acknowledged that an alternative source of protection for the physician-patient relationship may be the patient's constitutional right to privacy in receiving medical treatment.[150]

The physician-patient privilege is justified as a means to promote quality medical care by encouraging the patient to disclose all information which would help the physician in diagnosing and treating illness and injury.[151] Some scholars have observed that the privilege also may serve to protect the privacy interests of the patient.[152] The privilege has been criticized as not fulfilling the goal of effective medical care because "[t]he ordinary citizen who contemplates consulting a physician not only has no thought of a lawsuit, but he is entirely ignorant of the rules of evidence. He has no idea whether a communication to a physician is or is not privileged."[153] Despite this criticism, an increasing number of states have enacted physician-patient privileges.[154] Another trend is toward recognition of a privilege for the patients of psychiatrists and psychologists due to their special need for confidentiality:

[149] 2 Louisell & Mueller, § 215, at 594-95.

[150] Caesar v. Mountanos, 542 F.2d 1064, 1067 (9th Cir. 1976), cert. denied, 430 U.S. 954, 97 S.Ct. 1598, 51 L.Ed.2d 804 (1976); Hawaii Psychiatric Society v. Ariyoshi, 481 F. Supp. 1028, 1030 (D. Hawaii 1979). See also United States ex rel. Edney v. Smith, 425 F. Supp. 1038, 1044 (E.D. N.Y. 1976), aff'd sub nom. Edney v. Smith, 556 F.2d 556 (E.D. N.Y. 1977) (petitioner sought habeas corpus review of state conviction on the ground that the prosecution had called a psychiatric expert who had examined the defendant at his attorney's request and who had testified that defendant knew his conduct was wrong at the trial, where sanity was the only significant issue; petitioner argued that the physician-patient privilege is constitutionally compelled; court, after discussing the arguments for and against affording constitutional protection to the privilege, found that even were there a constitutional basis, the privilege could not be supported in the instant case "when the issue as to which the physician has knowl-

edge is placed in question by the party relying on the privilege — typically in negligence cases, but in criminal proceedings as well — the privilege is deemed waived); Robinson v. Magovern, 83 F.R.D. 79, 81 (W.D. Pa. 1979) (even assuming that there is a constitutional right of privacy protecting the general doctor-patient relationship, this right must be balanced against competing interests).

[151] McCormick, Evidence, § 98, at 244.

[152] See 2 Louisell & Mueller, § 215, at 602 (1978) ("[P]ersonal illness often involves matters which patients reasonably prefer to keep confidential, and the privilege may serve a valid social purpose in this regard.")

[153] Morgan, Forward to Model Code of Evidence 28 (1942). See also Lora v. Board of Education, 74 F.R.D. 565, 567 (E.D. N.Y. 1977) (material not protected because it is unlikely that there was an expectation of privacy by students or families since third parties had access to the data).

[154] McCormick, Evidence, § 98, at 244 and n.5 (fewer than 10 states do not recognize a physician-patient privilege).

Among physicians, the psychiatrist has a special need to maintain confidentiality. His capacity to help his patients is completely dependent upon their willingness and ability to talk freely. This makes it difficult if not impossible for him to function without being able to assure his patients of confidentiality and, indeed, privileged communication.[155]

As proposed, Article V of the Federal Rules of Evidence contained a psychotherapist-patient privilege but no general physician-patient privilege.[156]

The physician-patient privilege commonly includes the following elements: The privilege is available only where the patient consults the doctor for treatment or diagnosis looking toward treatment.[157] It is not available where the patient is examined by a physician in some other context, such as where a plaintiff in the course of personal injury litigation is examined by doctors hired either by the plaintiff's or defendant's attorney in order to determine the extent of injury.[158] As with privileges in general, the physician-patient privilege protects only communications made in confidence. Confidentiality is not destroyed, however, by the presence of a third person who is necessary for the patient's diagnosis or treatment or who is a close family member.[159] According to the better view, the privilege covers both verbal and nonverbal communications, such as the exhibition of body parts to the physician, and also covers observations made by the doctor.[160] However, the privilege does not prohibit a physician from testifying to facts incidental to the relationship, e.g., that he was consulted in a professional capacity by a person on a given date.[161] The privilege is held by the patient but the physician is ethically bound to assert it on the patient's behalf.[162]

The privilege is inapplicable in a variety of situations. If the patient consults the physician for an unlawful purpose the privilege does not apply.[163] The patient is considered to have waived the privilege if he puts his mental or physical condition in issue.[164] The privilege does not operate to relieve the physician of the duty to report certain diseases or injuries, such

---

[155] Report No. 45, Group for the Advancement of Psychiatry 92 (1960).

[156] The Advisory Committee explained that no general physician-patient privilege was proposed because "the exceptions which have been found necessary in order to obtain information required by the public interest or to avoid fraud are so numerous as to leave little if any basis for the privilege." Supreme Court Standard 504 Advisory Committee Note.

[157] MCCORMICK, EVIDENCE, § 99, at 246.

[158] See Catol v. United States, 131 F.2d 16, 18 (D.C. Cir. 1942).

[159] 2 LOUISELL & MUELLER, § 215, at 597.

[160] Id at 598-99.

[161] Padovani v. Liggett & Myers Tobacco Co., 23 F.R.D. 255, 257 (E.D. N.Y. 1959).

[162] 2 LOUISELL & MUELLER, § 215, at 597.

[163] MCCORMICK, § 99, at 247-48.

[164] O'Brien v. General Acc., Fire & Life Assur. Corp., 42 F.2d 53, 54 (8th Cir. 1930); Lind v. Canada Dry Corp., 283 F. Supp. 861, 864 (D.C. Minn. 1968); Burlage v. Handenshield, 42 F.R.D. 397, 399 (D.C. Iowa 1967); Awtry v. United States, 27 F.R.D. 399, 402 (D.C. N.Y. 1961).

as venereal diseases or gunshot wounds, which affect public health and safety. Laws requiring physicians to report these conditions generally have been upheld against constitutional challenges and claims that they violate the privilege.[165]

[165] McCORMICK, § 101, at 251.

VI
WITNESSES

Chapter 601

RULE 601. GENERAL RULE
OF COMPETENCY

Rule 601 reads as follows:

Every person is competent to be a witness except as otherwise provided in
these rules. However, in civil actions and proceedings, with respect to an
element of a claim or defense as to which State law supplies the rule of
decision, the competency of a witness shall be determined in accordance
with State law.

§ 601.1   Competency of Witnesses—In General.

Federal Rule 601 declares that all witnesses are competent to testify in
federal matters, except where other specified Federal Evidence Rules render a potential witness incompetent.[1] Where the witness is to provide testimony which pertains to claims or defenses as to which state law provides
the rule of decision, witness competency is controlled by state law. In the
latter category, the statutory or common law of the applicable state law
controls the competency of witnesses.[2]

[1] See, generally, McCORMICK, §§ 61-67, at 155-64; 3 WEINSTEIN, ¶¶ 601[01]-[05]; 3 LOUISELL & MUELLER, §§ 250-55; WIGMORE, §§ 483-721. See also Melton, Children's Competency to Testify, 5 LAW & HUMAN BEHAVIOR, 73 (1981); Brooks, Treatment of Witnesses in the Proposed Federal Rules of Evidence for the United States District Courts, Article VI, 25 REC. 632 (1970); Comment, The Uniformity-Conformity,

Dilemma Facing Draftsmen of Federal Rules of Evidence, 69 COLUM. L. REV. 353 (1969). See also Rock v Arkansas, ____ U.S. ____, 55 L.W. 4925 (March 23, 1987), holding that Arkansas' per se rule excluding all hypnotically refreshed testimony infringes impermissibly on a criminal defendant's right to testify on his or her own behalf.

[2] The Supreme Court's proposed Rule

The purpose of Rule 601 is to create a broad presumption of competency except where other Rules explicitly render a party incompetent or where governing state law disqualifies the witness. Rule 601 abolishes any remnants of federal common law grounds for incompetency including: religious belief; conviction of a crime; insanity; infancy; and interest in the litigation, *e.g.*, as a party or as a spouse of a party.[3] The Rule also renders inapplicable any so-called Dead Man's Statutes in cases where state law does not control.[4] Rule 601 effectively shifts the focus from the witness's competency to his credibility in cases where federal principles apply. An alleged infirmity often held to be a threshold question of competency at common law is now frequently considered an issue of credibility for the trier of fact.[5]

§ 601.2   The Court's Power to Exclude Testimony Contained in the Rules of Evidence: The Interplay between Rule 601 and Rules 104 and 403.

Since Rule 601 establishes a general presumption of competency, there is no requirement for a preliminary examination to determine competency under Rule 104.[6] While such a preliminary examination is not mandated, it is advisable in any case in which the trial judge has reason to believe that the witness's testimony might be impaired by infancy, counter-probative mental or psychological conditions or chemical influence.[7]

601 did not contain the second sentence of the Rule as enacted. This language was added by the House in order to protect strong state policies, such as the so-called Dead Man's Statutes, in cases where the federal court was constitutionally required under the *Erie* doctrine to apply state law to an issue or defense. *See* Courtland v. Watson & Co., Inc., 340 F. Supp. 1076 (S.D. N.Y. 1972), which the House Judiciary Committee cited in its Report to the House of Representatives.

[3] *See* 3 WEINSTEIN, ¶ 601[02], at 601-11.

[4] *See* Advisory Committee's Note, Rule 601. *See also* Sunstrand Corp. v. Sun Chemical Corp., 553 F.2d 1033, 1051 (7th Cir. 1977), *cert. denied*, 434 U.S. 875, 98 S.Ct. 225, 54 L.Ed.2d 155 (1977) (Illinois Dead Man's Act was not applied in action charging violations of securities laws); Donaldson v. Hovanec, 473 F. Supp. 602, 610 (E.D. Pa. 1979) (in civil rights action, Pennsylvania Dead Man's Act does not apply); United States v. Diehl, 460 F. Supp. 1282, 1289 (S.D. Tex. 1978) (Dead Man's Act does not apply in federal question case).

[5] *See, generally,* MCCORMICK, §§ 61-62, 71.

[6] United States v. Roach, 590 F.2d 181, 186 (5th Cir. 1979) (court found there no longer to be an occasion for judicially-ordered psychiatric examinations or competency hearings of witnesses).

[7] *See, e.g.,* United States v. Strahl, 590 F.2d 10, 12 (1st Cir. 1978), *cert. denied*, 440 U.S. 918, 99 S.Ct. 1237, 59 L.Ed.2d 468 (1979) (defendant claimed that testimony of prosecution witness should have been struck because his memory faded and he had drunk heavily at time of events in question; appellate court found that objections were suitably treated as questions concerning the credibility of the witness rather than his competency); United States v. Narciso, 446 F. Supp. 252, 277-84 (E.D. Mich. 1977) (court on motion in limine to suppress identification testimony of witness held that witness could testify even though he made his identification after a hypnotic interrogation). *See also* United States v. Raineri, 91 F.R.D. 159, 161 (W.D. Wis. 1980).

Despite the strong preference for witness competency embodied in Rule 601, a trial judge is not without inherent and express authority to prevent a witness from testifying. The trial judge, of course, retains the power to exclude irrevelant testimony under Rule 401, or to determine that offered evidence is inherently incredible and insufficient to sustain a verdict when asked to rule on a motion for acquittal, a directed verdict, or a motion for a judgment notwithstanding the verdict. Control of witness's testimony is also authorized under Rule 403 which may be invoked where the testimony is relevant but where its probative value is substantially outweighed by the dangers of unfair prejudice, confusion, delay, or when it results in the needless presentation of cumulative evidence.[8] A judge may apply Rule 403 to exclude testimony in a manner effectively similar to a finding of the incompetency of a witness where the judge determines the jury will be misled by the witness due to the jury's inability to assess accurately the credibility of the witness's testimony.[9] While there is a divergence of view as to the restraint that should be exercised in foreclosing a witness's testimony under Rule 403, no question exists that the trial judge has such authority.[10] Application of Rule 403 in this context requires an appreciation of the analytic balance of Rule 403 as well as the preference expressed in Rule 601 for competency. The result should be to permit the jury to consider the witness's testimony in most cases.

As an alternative to preventing a witness from testifying altogether, a trial judge should consider available means of assisting the trier of fact in its role of assessing witness credibility. Appropriate instructions may be given. Also, under Rule 614(b) the court may interrogate witnesses in an impartial manner in order to identify limitations in the probity of the witness' testimony. Other pertinent authority is provided in Rule 611(a)

---

[8] *See, e.g.,* WRIGHT & MILLER, FEDERAL PRACTICE AND PROCEDURE (CIVIL) § 2527 (1971); United States v. Hyson, 721 F.2d 856, 863-64 (1st Cir. 1983).

[9] United States v. Banks, 520 F.2d 627, 630 (7th Cir. 1979) (line of inquiry involved taking of drugs, including methadone, during the trial; court ruled it was error to preclude this inquiry, since it prevented the jury from assessing credibility). *See also* Commonwealth v. Whitehead, 400 N.E.2d 821, 834 (1980) (in prosecution for rape, armed robbery, armed assault with intent to murder, and assault and battery by means of a dangerous weapon, where defendant moved to strike victim's testimony as incompetent on the grounds of inconsistencies and her limited intelligence, no er-

ror in trial judge's decision to allow victim to testify).

[10] Professors Louisell & Mueller state:

Only in extreme cases — imaginable, but unlikely to be encountered often — should a trial judge exclude a witness altogether upon the grounds described above [Rule 403]. Neither immaturity nor mental or psychological disability, nor even the use of drugs or alcohol, will ordinarily signify that a witness cannot provide relevant evidence, or will inject in a case in undue degree the concerns of Rule 403 . . .

3 LOUISELL & MUELLER, § 252, at 18. *Compare* WEINSTEIN, ¶ 601[04], at 601-29. *See* Rock v. Arkansas, n.1 *supra.*

which provides the judge with authority over the mode and order of the interrogation of witnesses and in Rule 103(b) which provides:

> The court may add any other or further statement which shows the character of the evidence, the form in which it was offered, the objection made, and rulings thereon. . . .

§ 601.3   Infancy and Psychological and Mental Impairment.

It is imperative that the trial judge ascertain any intrinsic limitations on a witness's ability to testify.[11] Rule 611 commands the court to control the presentation of witness's testimony, and discharge of this mandate compels the trial judge to assess inherent limitations in potential testimony and undertake any appropriate corrective measures described in the previous section of this chapter. If the jury cannot make this determination, Rule 403 should be used to exclude the offered testimony.

On voir dire of the witness as authorized by Rule 104(c), the court should determine the witness's ability to state correctly matters which have come within his perception;[12] whether the witness can communicate to the jury;[13] the witness's ability to tell the difference between truth and falsity;[14] and the likelihood that the witness will subject to effective cross-examination.[15] The court may also inquire into extrinsic sources to determine the wisdom of excluding the witness's testimony.[16]

When the limitation is one of infancy, the possibility of substantial influence on the witness by others should be considered in determining the reliability of the witness' testimony.[17] Further, when mental or psychological impairment is evident, there is no requirement that the judge order a

---

[11] *See, e.g.,* United States v. Gutman, 725 F.2d 417, 420 (7th Cir. 1984); United States v. Lightly, 677 F.2d 1027, 1028 (4th Cir. 1982).

[12] United States v. Benn, 476 F.2d 1127, 1129-30 (D.C. Cir. 1973).

[13] United States v. Roach, 590 F.2d 181, 186 (5th Cir. 1979). *See also* United States v. Van Meerbeke, 548 F.2d 415, 418-19 (2d Cir. 1976), *cert. denied,* 430 U.S. 974, 97 S.Ct. 1663, 52 L.Ed.2d 368 (1977) (witness who may have taken drug while on stand could testify where jury observed his actions); United States v. Callahan, 442 F. Supp. 1213, 1221 (D. Minn. 1978) (court held competency hearing to determine whether witness' drug use negated minimum level of required competency; found

that witness could testify in a clear and lucid manner).

[14] United States v. Perez, 526 F.2d 859, 865 (5th Cir. 1976), *cert. denied,* 429 U.S. 846, 97 S.Ct. 129, 50 L.Ed.2d 118 (1976) (finding that judge had not erred in proceeding without a voir dire or in permitting minors to testify). *See also* Note, *The Child As A Witness,* 37 WASH. L. REV. 303 (1962).

[15] United States v. Benn, 476 F.2d 1127, 1129 (D.C. Cir. 1973).

[16] *Id.,* at 1129.

[17] Hollaris v. Jankowski, 315 Ill.App. 154, 159-60, 42 N.E.2d 859, 861 (1942) (aphasia due to accident; cross-examination emphasized disability). *See also* 3 WEINSTEIN, ¶ 601[04], at 601-29.

psychiatric examination of a witness before the witness testifies. Authority exists, however, for the court to order such an examination where it deems such an evaluation necessary.[18]

Under Rule 601, a witness who is under the influence of alcohol or drugs at the time of testifying is not presumptively incompetent because of his condition.[19] This condition will, however, be a basis for impeachment, either to cast doubt on the witness's ability to narrate accurately his testimony, or to prove his ability to accurately remember the event in question has been impaired.[20] Drug or alcohol use may also have the effect of exaggerating the witness's emotional response to what was said resulting in a bias against a party.[21] The court may order a physical examination of the witness to determine the extent to which the witness's ability to testify accurately has been impaired.[22] In cases where a real threat to the accuracy of the witness's testimony exists because of the witness' drug or alcohol use, the court should issue an instruction to the jury cautioning it on this potential defect in the witness's testimony.[23] As discussed above, Rule 403 may be applied to exclude the testimony in extreme cases.

§ 601.4   Rule 601—Other Provisions in the Rules.

Rule 601 provides that exceptions to the declaration of general competency in the first sentence of the Rule are contained in other provisions of the Rules of Evidence. Accordingly, Rule 602 sets forth the familiar rule requiring firsthand knowledge for the testimony of lay witnesses. Judges

---

[18] United States v. Jackson, 576 F.2d 46, 50 (5th Cir. 1978) (narcotics use goes to credibility not competency).

[19] See, e.g., United States v. Jackson, 576 F.2d 46, 48-49 (5th Cir. 1978). See also United States v. Killian, 524 F.2d 1268, 1275 (5th Cir.), cert. denied, 425 U.S. 935, 96 S.Ct. 1667, 48 L.Ed.2d 177 (1975) (no error to refuse to strike testimony of prosecution witness who was drug user, where he had not used drugs for several days prior to testifying); United States v. Davis, 486 F.2d 725, 726 (7th Cir. 1973), cert. denied, 415 U.S. 979, 94 S.Ct. 1569, 39 L.Ed.2d 876 (1973) (no error in failing to inquire into competency of witness where he was not under influence of narcotics while testifying, his testimony was corroborated, and his condition at the time about which he was testifying was developed on cross-examination).

[20] See, e.g., United States v. Hyson, 721 F.2d 856, 863-64 (1st Cir. 1983); United States v. Banks, 520 F.2d 627, 630-31 (7th Cir. 1975).

[21] See 3 LOUISELL & MUELLER, § 252, at 24.

[22] See, e.g., United States v. Raineri, 670 F.2d 702, 709 (7th Cir. 1981), United States v. Riley, 657 F.2d 1377, 1387 (8th Cir. 1981); United States v. Martino, 648 F.2d 367, 384-85 (5th Cir. 1981).

[23] See United States v. Benn, 476 F.2d 1127, 1130-31 (D.C. Cir. 1972) (in sex offense prosecution, no error for trial judge to decline to order psychological examination of mentally retarded 18-year old victim, since he provided a comprehensible narrative which was substantially corroborated). See also 3 LOUISELL & MUELLER, § 252, at 27.

are not competent to testify in trials at which they preside under Rule 605, and jurors are not competent to testify in trials for which they sit as jurors under Rule 606(a) or to impeach their verdicts under Rule 606(b).

§ 601.5   The Role of the Judge and Jury.

Rule 601 is the culmination of a process of restructuring the roles of the judge and jury in trial proceedings.[24] Except in cases where state law must be applied by federal courts, the jury has the prerogative of weighing the credibility of all testimony.[25] Testimonial defects that would have rendered the witness incompetent under the common law now must be brought to the jury's attention through impeachment of the witness.

The trial court retains some power to control the jury and analyze the credibility of a witness by directing a verdict for a civil party, commenting on the evidence, or setting aside a verdict because it is not supported by the weight of the evidence.[26]

§ 601.6   Application of State Law.

The second sentence of Rule 601 states that ". . . [i]n civil actions and proceedings, with respect to an element of a claim or defense as to which state law supplies the rule of decision, the competency of a witness shall be determined in accordance with state law." This provision will be utilized when the *Erie* doctrine requires the federal courts to apply state law as a rule of decision to a particular issue or defense.[27] This provision will not be applied in cases where state law is used as a rule of decision but is not applicable by its own force, *e.g.*, when state law is incorporated by a judge in creating federal common law.[28]

[24] *See* United States v. Jones, 482 F.2d 747, 751-52 (D.C. Cir. 1973). *See also* 3 WEINSTEIN, ¶ 601[05], at 601-37.

[25] United States v. Hyson, 721 F.2d 856, 863-64 (1st Cir. 1983). *See also* United States v. Jones, 482 F.2d 747, 751-52 (D.C. Cir. 1973) (it has become the modern trend to limit even the trial court's power to exclude testimony because of incompetency and to make the pivotal question one of credibility, for the jury); United States v. Zeiler, 470 F.2d 717, 720 (3d Cir. 1972) (the practice of disqualifying witnesses because of presumed bias has been abandoned; bias is examined through cross-examination and juries are free to disregard it).

[26] *See* 3 WEINSTEIN, ¶ 601[05], at 601-38.

[27] *See, generally,* Erie v. Tompkins, 304 U.S. 64, 58 S.Ct. 817, 82 L.Ed. 1188 (1938); Hanna v. Plumer, 380 U.S. 460, 85 S.Ct. 1136, 14 L.Ed.2d 8 (1965); Byrd v. Blue Ridge Rural Electric Co-operative Inc., 356 U.S. 325, 78 S.Ct. 893, 2 L.Ed.2d 953 (1958). *See also* Higgenbottom v. Noreen, 586 F.2d 719, 722 (9th Cir. 1978).

[28] *See* the discussion of Rule 501 in the Conference Report. See H.R. REP. No. 93-1597, 93d Cong., 2d Sess. 7 (1974). *See also* 3 LOUISELL & MUELLER, § 253, at 29.

Chapter 602

RULE 602. LACK OF PERSONAL KNOWLEDGE

Rule 602 reads as follows:

A witness may not testify to a matter unless evidence is introduced sufficient to support a finding that he has personal knowledge of the matter. Evidence to prove personal knowledge may, but need not, consist of the testimony of the witness himself. This rule is subject to the provisions of Rule 703, relating to opinion testimony by expert witnesses.

§ 602.1   General Requirement of Personal Knowledge.

Federal Rule 602 requires a witness to testify from firsthand, or personal, knowledge of the subject matter.[1] The subject of a witness's testimony must have been perceived through one or more of the senses of the witness. Traditionally, as well as under Rule 602, the firsthand knowledge requirement is treated as a matter of competency, *i.e.*, a witness is "incompetent" to testify to any fact unless she possesses firsthand knowledge (direct perception) of that fact. Accordingly, the requirement of the Rule exemplifies the common law insistence upon the most reliable sources of information.[2] This philosophy is also evident in the treatment by the Rules of opinion testimony, hearsay and non-original documents.

---

[1] *See, generally*, McCormick, § 69, at 167; 3 Weinstein, ¶¶ 602[01]-[03]; 3 Louisell & Mueller, §§ 259-61; 2 Wigmore, §§ 650-70. *See also* Note, *Lay Opinion in Civil Cases—Speed of Motor Vehicles*, 4 Vill. L. Rev. 245 (1959).

[2] Elizarraras v. Bank of El Paso, 631 F.2d 366, 373-74 (5th Cir. 1980) (reversible error to admit plaintiff's testimony where he had no personal knowledge and hearsay rule barred his relating what he had been told); United States v. Brown, 548 F.2d 1194,

§ 602.2   Foundation as to Personal Knowledge.

The party offering the witness must establish the requisite personal knowledge through foundation evidence. Rule 602 expressly provides that extrinsic foundation evidence is not necessary, and the witness's own preliminary testimony may establish that the witness was in a position to see or otherwise perceive the matters to which he will testify. Also, this foundation for personal knowledge may be supplied by other witnesses or documentary evidence. This determination of competency is within the discretion of the trial court, and unless it is clearly apparent that the witness had no personal knowledge of the subject matter, a reviewing court will not disturb the finding.[3]

According to Rule 104(b) the proponent of the witness must establish a foundation "sufficient to support a finding" that the witness possesses first-hand knowledge of the facts to which he will testify. The standard, and the appropriate procedure, is discussed in conjunction with Rule 104(b) in Chapter 104.

§ 602.3   Competency Versus Weight.

Assessment of the accuracy, as opposed to the existence, of a witness's perception is a question of credibility for the trier of fact. The fact-finder bears the responsibility of considering the adequacy of the witness's opportunity for knowing or observing the facts as to which testimony is provided. Accordingly, once the court determines that the foundation as to

---

1204-05 (5th Cir. 1977) (I.R.S. agent could not testify that over 90% of the returns which had been prepared by defendant contained overstated deductions where she was testifying on the basis of out-of-court statements made to her by taxpayers she had interviewed, rather than on the basis of her personal knowledge). *See also* United States v. Pastore, 537 F.2d 675, 678 (2d Cir. 1976) (testimony unobjectionable where basis of witness's knowledge was made clear before he left the stand); United States v. Larry, 536 F.2d 1149, 1155 (6th Cir. 1976), *cert. denied*, 429 U.S. 984, 97 S.Ct. 502, 50 L.Ed.2d 595 (where testimony was not based on personal knowledge, proper to exclude testimony as to witness's belief about activities of another). *See, generally,* 3 WEINSTEIN, ¶ 602[01]; 3 LOUISELL & MUELLER, § 260; MCCORMICK, § 10; 2 WIGMORE, §§ 650-70.

[3] *E.g.,* United States v. Thompson, 559 F.2d 552, 553-54 (9th Cir. 1977), *cert. denied*, 434 U.S. 973, 98 S.Ct. 528, 54 L.Ed.2d 464 (1977) (bank robbery prosecution; where defendant claimed he had been at certain restaurant on day of robbery, restaurant manager could testify that receipt produced by defendant's father was not the type which was normally issued to customers, even though he did not become manager until three months after robbery; manager had ample personal knowledge to testify about normal company procedures). *See also* United States v. Larry, 536 F.2d 1149, 1151 (6th Cir. 1976), *cert. denied*, 429 U.S. 984, 97 S.Ct. 502, 50 L.Ed.2d 595 (1976). *See, generally,* 3 WEINSTEIN, ¶ 602 [2]; 3 LOUISELL & MUELLER § 260; MCCORMICK, § 10 at 21; 2 WIGMORE, § 654.

personal knowledge is sufficient to admit the testimony of the witness, any defects in testimony resulting from faulty perception should govern the weight to be accorded the offered testimony or the credibility of the witness.[4]

§ 602.4   Rule 602 and Other Rules.

Rule 602, of course, in itself does not prevent an individual from relating statements constituting hearsay. Provided that the witness has personal knowledge of the making of the statement, he is competent to testify that a particular statement was made. Whether the out-of-court statement is admissible is a matter within the purview of Article VIII of the Rules.[5] In similar fashion, Rule 602 is expressly made subject to the provisions of Article VII concerning the testimony of expert witnesses. Experts may render opinions which are not based upon firsthand observation or perception. Rule 703 specifically addresses the permissible bases of expert opinion.[6] Finally, Rule 602 reinforces Rule 701 which provides:

> If a witness is not testifying as an expert, his testimony in the form of opinions and inferences is limited to those opinions or inferences which are (a) rationally based on the perception of the witness and (b) helpful to a clear understanding of his testimony of the determination of a fact in issue.

[4] United States v. Evans, 484 F.2d 1178, 1181-1182 (2d Cir. 1973) (in bank robbery three eyewitnesses properly permitted to testify over defendant's objection that identification rested not upon their personal familiarity with robber's appearance, but upon their recollection of surveillance film); Auberbach v. United States, 136 F.2d 882, 885 (6th Cir. 1943) (criminal prosecution for concealing liquor; defendant's principal competitor permitted to testify that he overheard a conversation while he was in a telephone booth between two persons he never saw, and that one of them was the voice of defendant). *See also* Rule 104(b) and § 104.2 of this Treatise.

[5] United States v. Beasley, 545 F.2d 403, 405 (5th Cir. 1977) (witness was asked whether he told IRS agents that two pro-

moters had to pay off; witness affirmed statement); Cities Service Oil Co. v. Coleman Oil Co. Inc., 470 F.2d 925, 932 (1st Cir. 1972), *cert. denied,* 411 U.S. 967, 93 S.Ct. 2150, 36 L.Ed.2d 688 (1972) (witness could testify to the contents of records kept in the regular course of business without having personal knowledge of the facts therein reported).

[6] *See* §§ 703.1 *et seq.* of this Treatise. Rule 703, entitled "Bases of Opinion Testimony by Experts," provides:

> The facts or data in the particular case upon which an expert bases an opinion or inference may be those perceived by him or admitted in evidence at the hearing.

Chapter 603

RULE 603. OATH OR AFFIRMATION

Rule 603 reads as follows:

> Before testifying, every witness shall be required to declare that he will testify truthfully, by oath or affirmation administered in a form calculated to awaken his conscience and impress his mind with his duty to do so.

§ 603.1 Oath or Affirmation.

Rule 603 fundamentally requires that before testifying a witness must declare his intention to relate the subject matter of his testimony truthfully.[1] The declaration of intent may be by oath or affirmation.

The oath or affirmation serves the dual purposes of arousing the witness's conscience to speak the truth and exposing the witness to punishment for perjury should he purposely testify falsely.[2] The Rule is consistent with the common law in authorizing any mode or declaration the witness subjectively believes to be binding on his conscience and in discarding the operative distinction between oaths and affirmations.

---

[1] *See, generally,* McCormick, § 63, at 157; 3 Weinstein, ¶ 603[01]; 3 Louisell & Mueller, §§ 265-66; 6 Wigmore, §§ 1815-29. *See also* Note, *A Reconsideration of the Sworn Testimony Requirement: Securing Trust in the Twentieth Century,* 75 Mich. L. Rev. 1681 (1977).

[2] Wilcoxon v. United States, 231 F.2d 384, 387 (10th Cir. 1956), *cert. denied,* 351 U.S. 943, 76 S.Ct. 834, 100 L.Ed. 1469 (1956) (court stated the twofold purpose of the oath as binding the conscience of the witness and making him amenable to prosecution if he gives perjured testimony). *See, generally,* 3 Weinstein, ¶ 603[1]; 3 Louisell & Mueller, § 265; McCormick, § 245, at 582; 6 Wigmore, § 1827.

§ 603.2 Operation of the Oath or Affirmation Requirement.

Regardless of the form of the oath or affirmation, it must be administered in the presence of an officer authorized to administer it, and it must be an unequivocal act by which the witness consciously undertakes the burden to testify truthfully. The Rule clearly requires the court to focus on the witness's beliefs and to administer an oath or affirmation designed to affect whatever peculiarities or idiosyncrasies of conscience are presented.[3] Moreover, the Rule applies to all witnesses, including children, mentally impaired persons, and interpreters.[4] Witnesses who refuse to be sworn or to make an affirmation may be held in contempt.[5]

§ 603.3   Testimony in the Absence of Oath or Affirmation.

The requirement of an oath may be waived by competent parties either expressly or impliedly, e.g., when an adverse party goes forward without inquiry or objection.[6] Where no objection to unsworn testimony is interposed, and the party adversely affected is aware of the receipt of the unsworn testimony, the irregularity is waived. No constitutional provision is violated when unsworn testimony is received, and any objection to the sufficiency of the oath administered to a witness must be made prior to the rendition of a verdict.[7]

The failure to swear a witness may be cured by withdrawing the testimony of the witness, and then resubmitting the testimony after administering the oath or affirmation. Alternately, the witness may, after oath or affirmation, adopt her prior unsworn testimony.

[3] *See, e.g.*, United States v. Looper, 419 F.2d 1405, 1407 (4th Cir. 1969) (reversible error not to allow defendant to testify where he refused a form of affirmation which made a reference to God); United States v. Moore, 217 F.2d 428, 431-32 (7th Cir. 1954), *rev'd*, 348 U.S. 966, 75 S.Ct. 530, 99 L.Ed. 753 (1955) (conscientious objector who had refused to submit to induction into armed forces because he refused to use the word "solemnly" on religious grounds; trial court refused to allow him to testify; court of appeals affirmed; Supreme Court reversed and remanded, finding per curiam that there was no requirement that the word "solemnly" be used).

[4] United States v. Fowler, 605 F.2d 181, 185 (5th Cir. 1979) (court properly refused to allow defendant to testify after he refused to swear or affirm to tell the truth); United States v. Fiore, 443 F.2d 112, 115 (2d Cir. 1971), *cert. denied*, 410 U.S. 984, 93 S.Ct. 1510, 36 L.Ed.2d 181 (1973) (error to question witness before grand jury who refused to take oath).

[5] United States v. Wilson, 421 U.S. 309, 316, 95 S.Ct. 1802, 1807, 44 L.Ed.2d 186, 193 (1975); United States v. Brannon, 546 F.2d 1242, 1247 (5th Cir. 1977).

[6] United States v. Perez, 651 F.2d 268, 272-73 (5th Cir. 1981).

[7] Jackson v. Garrity, 250 F. Supp. 1, 2 (Md. 1965).

Chapter 604

RULE 604. INTERPRETERS

SECTION
604.1 Interpreters—In general
604.2 Function of the trial judge
604.3 Credibility of the interpreter; function of the trier of fact

Rule 604 reads as follows:

> An interpreter is subject to the provisions of these rules relating to qualification as an expert and the administration of an oath or affirmation that he will make a true translation.

§ 604.1   Interpreters—In General.

Federal Rule 604 subjects an interpreter to the qualifications and requirements of other expert witnesses under Article VII.[1] The purpose of Rule 604 is to identify the evidentiary function of an interpreter, and it does not provide authority governing the appropriateness or necessity of using an interpreter.

Where a witness is unable to speak or understand the English language, the court may in its discretion receive the witness's testimony through an interpreter, provided the interpreter takes an oath or affirmation declaring that he will render a true and literal translation.[2] The court's discretion, however, is more circumscribed in a criminal proceeding. If the accused or a witness on his behalf cannot adequately understand English, the court is required to appoint an interpreter in order to protect the defendant's fundamental rights.[3]

---

[1] See, generally, 3 WEINSTEIN, ¶ 604[01]; 3 LOUISELL & MUELLER, §§ 270-72; 6 WIGMORE, § 1824. See also Chang and Araujo, Interpreters for the Defense: Due Process for the Non-English-Speaking Defendant, 63 CALIF. L. REV. 801 (1975); Note, The Right to An Interpreter, 25 RUTGERS L. REV. 145 (1970).

[2] Court Interpreters Act, 25 U.S.C. § 1827 (1978). See, generally, 3 WEINSTEIN, ¶ 604[1]; 3 LOUISELL & MUELLER, § 272; 3 WIGMORE, § 811.

[3] United States v. Carrion, 488 F.2d 12, 14 (1st Cir. 1973), cert. denied, 416 U.S. 907, 94 S.Ct. 1613, 40 L.Ed.2d 112 (1973) (indigent has right to interpreter when he has obvious difficulty with the language); United States v. Sanchez, 483 F.2d 1052, 1056 (2d Cir. 1973), cert. denied, 415 U.S. 991, 94 S.Ct. 1590, 39 L.Ed.2d 888 (1973)

The court also fixes the reasonable compensation of the interpreter in civil litigation[4] and criminal proceedings.[5] Additionally, the court determines who will pay for the interpreter's services.[6]

§ 604.2   Function of the Trial Judge.

The determination of an interpreter's qualifications is an issue peculiarly within the discretion of the trial court as provided in Article VII of the Rules, and close relatives or friends of the witness are not precluded from serving as interpreters where such relatives qualify as experts.[7] Interpreters should be admonished by the court not to embellish or rearrange the words of the witness.[8]

The Rule permitting interpreters is itself a relaxation of the general proscription against testimony from sources lacking firsthand knowledge, and it remains within the discretion of the trial judge whether to apply strictly other Rules, such as those regarding leading questions, cross-examination, impeachment and the like.

§ 604.3   Credibility of the Interpreter; Function of the Trier of Fact.

There are situations in which an interpreter's accuracy may become subject to attack. As in the case of other experts, interpreters possess varying

(interpreter must be provided when necessary); United States ex rel. Negron v. New York, 434 F.2d 386, 389 (2d Cir. 1970) (affirming issuance of writ of habeas corpus in connection with state murder conviction). *But see,* Fairbanks v. Cowan, 551 F.2d 97, 99 (6th Cir. 1977) (appointment of interpreter does not reach constitutional proportions); Cervantes v. Cox, 350 F.2d 855, (10th Cir. 1965) (no constitutional right to court appointed interpreter).

[4] *See* Civil Procedure Rule 43(f) which provides:

> The court may appoint an interpreter of its own selection and may fix his reasonable compensation. The compensation shall be paid out of funds provided by law or by one or more of the parties as the court may direct, and may be taxed ultimately as costs, in the discretion of the court.

[5] *See* Criminal Procedure Rule 28 which provides:

> The Court may appoint an interpreter of its own selection and may fix the reasonable compensation of such interpreter. Such compensation shall be paid out of funds provided by law or by the government, as the court may direct.

[6] *See* Civil Procedure Rule 43(f); Criminal Procedure Rule 28.

[7] United States v. Addonizio, 451 F.2d 49, 68 (3d Cir. 1971), *cert. denied*, 405 U.S. 936, 92 S.Ct. 949, 30 L.Ed.2d 812 (1971); Fairbanks v. Cowan, 551 F.2d 97, 99 (5th Cir. 1977); Chee v. United States, 449 F.2d 747, 748 (9th Cir. 1971), *disapproved on other grounds,* Davis v. United States, 411 U.S. 233, 93 S.Ct. 1577, 36 L.Ed.2d 216 (1971).

[8] Court Interpreters Act, § 1827 (1978).

degrees of ability and competence, and whether this ability will affect the accuracy of the translation becomes an issue for the trier of fact.[9] In such cases, the credibility of the interpreter, and his competence to translate, become issues properly for the jury.

[9] Rule 702, entitled "Testimony by Experts," provides:

If scientific, technical, or other specialized knowledge will assist the trier of fact to understand the evidence or to determine a fact in issue, a witness qualified as an expert by knowledge, skill, experience, training, or education, may testify thereto in the form of an opinion or otherwise.

Chapter 605

RULE 605. COMPETENCY OF JUDGE AS WITNESS

SECTION
605.1   Competency of trial judge—In general
605.2   When a judge is called on or testifies in a civil proceeding
605.3   When a judge is called on or testifies in a criminal proceeding
605.4   When the judge implicitly testifies in violation of Rule 605

Rule 605 reads as follows:

> The judge presiding at the trial may not testify in that trial as a witness. No objection need be made in order to preserve the point.

§ 605.1   Competency of Trial Judge—In General.

Federal Rule 605 provides simply and without reservation that the judge presiding at the trial may not testify in that trial as a witness, and, further, that no objection need be interposed at trial to preserve the error on appeal.[1]

The application of the Rule does not render the testimony incompetent because it is of an unreliable nature, but rather incompetency is based upon practical reasons for rejecting this type of evidence. For example, if the judge may testify at the trial, "Who rules on objections? Who compels him to answer? Can he rule impartially on the weight and admissibility of his own testimony?, etc."[2]

The Rule does not prevent a judge from testifying in a subsequent trial about matters or incidents occurring in the original trial, e.g., where a

---

[1] See, generally, MCCORMICK, § 68; 3 WEINSTEIN, ¶¶ 605[01]-[04]; 3 LOUISELL & MUELLER, §§ 276-80; 6 WIGMORE, § 1909. See also Saltzburg, The Unnecessarily Expanding Role of the American Trial Judge, 64 VA. L. REV. 39 (1978); Field, Double Jeopardy in Federal Criminal Cases, 3 CA-

LIF. W.L. REV. 76 (1967); Hart, Testimony By a Judge or Juror, 44 MARQ. L. REV. 183 (1960); Field, Disability of the Judge in Federal Criminal Procedure, 6 ST. LOUIS U.L.J. 150 (1960).

[2] Advisory Committee's Note, Rule 605.

trial judge is called as a witness in a hearing on a petition for post-conviction relief from a previous judgment.[3]

Rule 605 does not address the question of whether a judge who does not testify at trial because of Rule 605, but has been sought as a witness by one party, should disqualify himself. This question is answered in Title 28 § 455 U.S.C. which provides a judge should disqualify himself in a proceeding in which his impartiality may be reasonably questioned. A judge should withdraw from the case when faced with this situation.[4]

§ 605.2   When a Judge is Called on or Testifies in a Civil Proceeding.

In a civil case, if the judge has not disqualified himself before trial and is called to testify by a party, he may either excuse himself or continue the trial. If the judge excuses himself, he must declare a mistrial and enter an order for a new trial.[5] If, however, the judge continues the trial and testifies to a material fact, the appellate court should reverse the judgment. In this situation prejudice will be presumed.[6]

If the judge is called to testify and does not testify at the trial, the appellate court must determine if his failure to testify was prejudicial to the appellant. If found to be prejudicial, a new trial should be ordered.[7] It should be noted that a party need not object to a violation of Rule 605 in order to preserve review of the issue. However, a violation of Rule 605 may be waived by both parties and the judge's testimony admitted.[8]

§ 605.3   When a Judge is Called on or Testifies in a Criminal Proceeding.

Similar to his civil counterpart, the judge who presides in a criminal trial who has not disqualified herself before trial and is called to testify by a party may either excuse herself or continue the trial. If the judge disqualifies herself, Rule 25(a) of the Federal Rules of Criminal Procedure allows

---

[3] Nipp v. United States, 422 F.2d 509, 513 (10th Cir. 1969), *cert. denied*, 399 U.S. 913, 91 S.Ct. 1198, 28 L.Ed.2d 334 (1970); United States v. Cross, 516 F. Supp. 700, 708 (M.D. Ga. 1981). *But see*, Washington v. Strickland, 673 F.2d 879, 902-906 (5th Cir. 1982). *See, generally*, 3 WEINSTEIN, ¶ 605; 3 LOUISELL & MUELLER, § 277; MCCORMICK, § 68; 6 WIGMORE, § 1909.

[4] *See* 3 WEINSTEIN, ¶ 605[01], at 605-4.

[5] *See, e.g.*, Stoltzfus v. United States, 264 F. Supp. 824, 826 (E.D. Pa. 1967), *cert.*

denied, 393 U.S. 1020, 89 S.Ct. 627, 21 L.Ed.2d 565 (1969); In re Schoenfield, 608 F.2d 930, 932-33 (2d Cir. 1979). *Cf.*, United States v. Schipani, 293 F. Supp. 156, 157 (E.D.N.Y. 1968), *aff'd*, 414 F.2d 1262 (2d Cir. 1969), *cert. denied*, 397 U.S. 922, 90 S.Ct. 902, 25 L.Ed.2d 102 (1970) (retrial on transcript of trial before another judge).

[6] *See* 3 WEINSTEIN, ¶ 605[02], at 605-8.

[7] *Id.*

[8] *See* 3 WEINSTEIN, ¶ 605[02], at 605-9.

for the substitution of a new judge in the event of the disability of the original trial judge.[9] Doubt, however, has been cast on the constitutional applicability of this rule in the context of a judge who must disqualify herself under Rule 605.[10] If the substitution is consensual on the part of the defendant and the prosecution, a due process problem does not arise.[11] If, however, the defendant does not agree to the substitution, the due process question again becomes an issue. Consequently, wise practice would lead the trial judge to order a mistrial where she must disqualify herself under Rule 605.[12]

If the mistrial is ordered, the problem becomes whether the defendant may be retried consistent with protections against double jeopardy. Retrial is permissible in cases where the judge is disabled and must withdraw during a trial. In the present context, however, neither party has caused the disability; the disability envisioned by Rule 605 is caused because a party has called the judge as a witness.[13] Judge Weinstein suggests retrial is permissible unless the prosecution has deliberately sought to invite a mistrial by calling the presiding judge.[14] The reviewing court should also consider whether the trial judge knew she would be called as a witness or was attempting to help the prosecution[15] or whether the prosecution called the trial judge in response to an unanticipated defense that was raised by the accused.[16] Additionally, the court should consider whether the testimony sought to be admitted concerned a material issue.[17] If the defendant calls the judge as a witness, she should be presumed to know that a mistrial will result by applications of Rule 605 and consequently to have acquiesced to a retrial.[18]

If the judge is called to testify but does not, the appellate court will determine if a reversible error has occurred. If it has, a new trial will be

[9] *See* Rule 25(a) of the Federal Rules of Criminal Procedure.

[10] 2 Wright, Federal Practice and Procedure—Criminal, § 392, at 56 (1969).

[11] *Cf.* Randel v. Beto, 354 F.2d 496, 500-501 (5th Cir. 1965), *cert. denied*, 387 U.S. 935, 87 S.Ct. 2058, 18 L.Ed.2d 996 (1967) (habeas corpus attack on state court conviction where judge had been substituted at trial; court indicated that substitution might violate right to jury trial); Freeman v. United States, 227 F. 732, 734 (2d Cir. 1915) (did not permit substitution of judges as violation of right to jury trial). But *c.f.*, ABA Project on Minimum Standards for Criminal Justice, Trial by Jury, § 4.3 (Tent. Dr. 1968) (assumes substitution of judges would be constitutionally permissible).

[12] Freeman v. United States, 237 F. 815 (2d Cir. 1916).

[13] 3 Weinstein, ¶ 605[03], at 605-11.

[14] Carsey v. United States, 392 F.2d 810, 812 (D.C. Cir. 1967). *See also* 3 Weinstein, ¶ 605[03], at 605-11.

[15] *Cf.* Downum v. United States, 372 U.S. 734, 736, 83 S.Ct. 1033, 1035, 10 L.Ed.2d 100, 102 (1963).

[16] Wright v. Boles, 275 F. Supp. 571, 575 (N.D. W.Va. 1967) (defendant not placed in double jeopardy where court had declared mistrial on defendant's motion in first prosecution, since state had called defendant's wife as witness without defendant's consent).

[17] 3 Weinstein, ¶ 605[03], at 605-13.

[18] *Id.*

ordered.[19] No objection is necessary to preserve appellate review of this issue.[20]

§ 605.4   When the Judge Implicitly Testifies in Violation of Rule 605.

The judge may implicitly testify in a trial without formally taking the stand. When this occurs, Rule 605 has been violated and the appellate court should examine the record for reversible error.[21] A special problem may arise when the court makes an impermissible comment on the facts under the pretext of judicial notice.[22] The court may also consider taking judicial notice of prior proceedings which are not substantiated by the record.[23] The materiality of the judge's comments is a crucial element in determining whether a reversible error has occurred in these contexts.[24]

[19] *Id.*

[20] *See* the Advisory Committee's Note to Rule 605.

[21] Pierce Brothers Co. v. Philadelphia Gear Corp., 629 F.2d 444, 446 (6th Cir. 1980) (sending trial judge's law clerk to gather evidence in a non-jury trial would be destructive of the appearance of impartiality required).

[22] Furtado v. Bishop, 604 F.2d 80, 90 (1st Cir. 1979), *cert. denied*, 444 U.S. 1035, 100 S.Ct. 710, 62 L.Ed.2d 672 (1980) (trial judge admitted affidavit of dead lawyer after determining its trustworthiness based on personal knowledge of the deceased).

[23] Tyler v. Swenson, 427 F.2d 412, 414-15 (8th Cir. 1970) (same judge may not consider his own crucial testimony and recollection rebutting petitioner's claim and simultaneously pass upon the credibility of all witnesses in weighing the evidence; a party should be permitted to test a judge's recollection as a witness upon cross-examination). *Cf.*, Coley v. Star & Herald Co., 390 F.2d 364, 369 (5th Cir. 1968) (litigants should have opportunity to challenge even a judge's recollections). *See* 3 WEINSTEIN, ¶ 605[04], at 605-16.

[24] *See* 3 WEINSTEIN, ¶ 605[04], at 605-16.

Chapter 606

RULE 606. COMPETENCY OF JUROR AS WITNESS

Rule 606 reads as follows:

(a) **At the Trial.** A member of the jury may not testify as a witness before that jury in the trial of the case in which he is sitting as a juror. If he is called so to testify, the opposing party shall be afforded an opportunity to object outside the presence of the jury.

(b) **Inquiry into Validity of Verdict or Indictment.** Upon an inquiry into the validity of a verdict or indictment, a juror may not testify as to any matter or statement occurring during the course of the jury's deliberations or the effect of anything upon his or any other juror's mind or emotions as influencing him to assent to or dissent from the verdict or indictment or concerning his mental processes in connection therewith, nor may his affidavit or evidence of any statement by him concerning a matter about which he would be precluded from testifying be received, but a juror may testify on the questions whether extraneous prejudicial information was improperly brought to the jury's attention or whether any outside influence was improperly brought to bear upon any juror.

§ 606.1   Rule 606(a)—Competency of Juror at Trial as Witness— In General.

Rule 606(a) declares incompetent any witness who is a member of the jury impaneled to hear the case in question.[1] The rationale for disqualifying a juror under Rule 606 is similar to that underlying the disqualification of judges under Rule 605. First, counsel may be inhibited in cross-examining a juror, in fear of invoking a disfavorable reaction by the juror. Second, the juror may be unable to weigh objectively the credibility of his own testimony when it is contradicted by an adverse witness. Third, the juror may overidentify with one party and become biased. Fourth, the panel of jurors may more favorably weigh the testimony of a fellow juror.[2]

While the Rule does not provide that it is plain error for a witness to serve as a juror, Rule 606(a) does expressly permit the adverse party to object out of the presence of the jury. A reversal by a reviewing court nevertheless should be predicated upon some cognizable prejudice flowing from the error, as well as a proper preservation of the error in the trial court record.[3]

§ 606.2   Rule 606(b)—Competency of Juror to Testify at a Subsequent Proceeding Concerning Original Verdict or Indictment; Matters Internal to the Deliberative Process.

Rule 606(b) reflects the common law tradition of protecting and preserving the integrity of the jury room by declaring jurors generally incompetent to testify as to any matter purely internal to the jury's deliberations.[4] The Rule pertains to a jury's collective discussions and exchanges as well as individual jurors' mental and emotional deliberative processes. The Rule is

[1] See, generally, McCormick, § 65; 3 Weinstein, ¶¶ 606[01]-[07]; 3 Louisell & Mueller, §§ 284-92; 6 Wigmore, § 1910. See also Comment, Juror Privilege: The Answer to the Impeachment Puzzle, 3 Wes. New Eng. L. Rev. 446 (1981); Broeder, The Impact of the Vicinage Requirement: An Empirical Look, 45 Neb. L. Rev. 99 (1966); Carlson & Sunberg, Attacking Jury Verdicts: Paradigms for Rule Revision, 1977 Ariz. St. L.J. 247 (1977).

[2] 3 Louisell & Mueller, § 285, at 107.

[3] Compare this procedure to Rule 605, pertaining to the competency of a judge as a witness, where the party adversely affected need not preserve the error by objection. See also, Rule 103 and § 103.1 of this Treatise regarding the preservation of error.

[4] United States v. Campbell, 684 F.2d 141, 151-52 (D.C. Cir. 1982). See also United States v. MacQueen, 596 F.2d 76, 82 (2d Cir. 1979) (statements in affidavits of jurors as to mental processes of their deliberations could not be admitted). See, e.g., Vaise v. Delavel, 1 Term Rep. 11, 99 Eng. Rep. 944 (K.B. 1785). See, generally, 3 Weinstein, ¶ 606[03]; 3 Louisell & Mueller, § 286; McCormick, § 68; 8 Wigmore, § 2348. See also Comment, Impeachment of Verdicts by Jurors — Rule of Evidence 606(b), 4 Wm. Mitch. L. Rev. 417 (1978); Comment, Judgment by Your Peers? The Impeachment of Jury Verdicts and the Case of the Insane Juror, 21 N.Y.U.F. 57 (1975); Note, Impeachment of Jury Verdicts, 53 Marq. L. Rev. 258 (1970).

designed to ensure the finality of verdicts and to protect jurors from being unceasingly harassed by defeated parties. In the absence of such protection, the confidentiality and candor of the jury room would become the constant subject of public investigation. Consequently, the Rule is designed to foster the time-honored and highly valued freedom of conference critical to the entire scheme of trial by jury,[5] and it erects a barrier to the introduction of evidence from a juror concerning matters which are purely internal to the jury's deliberations.[6]

The restrictions of Rule 606(b) apply only to inquiry after the verdict or indictment has been reached and recorded. Such restrictions, however, do not prevent a court from questioning members of a panel that returns with an ambiguous or inconsistent verdict.[7] The dangers of continual uncertainty and tampering with jurors, sought to be prevented by the Rule, are absent where the inquiry into the jury process is conducted by the court before the jurors are discharged and separated.[8]

By its express terms, Rule 606(b) includes within its proscription evidence tending to support as well as impeach verdicts. Likewise, it prohibits evidence from third parties concerning statements made by jurors.[9]

§ 606.3 Juror Competency as to Extraneous Prejudicial Information or Outside Influence.

Rule 606(b) recognizes limited situations in which a juror is competent to impeach a verdict or indictment after it has been rendered. According to the Rule, a juror may testify to whether extraneous information was brought to the jury's attention in an improper manner, or whether any juror's deliberation was improperly affected by an outside influence.

It will not always be apparent whether the testimony offered falls within this exception.[10] While Rule 606(b) does not explicitly define "extraneous

---

[5] McDonald v. Pless, 238 U.S. 264, 267-68, 35 S.Ct. 783, 784, 59 L.Ed. 1300, 1302 (1915) (affidavit as to quotient verdict excluded); Mattox v. United States, 146 U.S. 140, 13 S.Ct. 50, 36 L.Ed. 917 (1892) (affidavits of jurors admitted that they read newspaper clippings about case during deliberation). See also Jorgensen v. York Ice Machinery Corp., 160 F.2d 432, 435 (2d Cir. 1947), cert. denied, 332 U.S. 764, 68 S.Ct. 69, 92 L.Ed. 349 (1947).

[6] See Rule 606(b), Advisory Committee's Note.

[7] 3 WEINSTEIN, ¶ 606[04], at 606-25. See also United States v. Robinson, 645 F.2d

616, 618 (8th Cir. 1981); United States v. Williams, 568 F.2d 464, 470 (5th Cir. 1978).

[8] See, generally, 3 WEINSTEIN, ¶ 606[04]; 3 LOUISELL & MUELLER, § 290; 8 WIGMORE, § 2350, at 691.

[9] 3 WEINSTEIN, ¶ 606[04], at 606-25.

[10] E.g., Gault v. Poor Sisters of St. Francis Seraph of Perpetual Adoration, Inc., 375 F.2d 539, 551 (6th Cir. 1967) (affidavits of jurors stated that they discussed amount of income tax plaintiff would have to pay and amount attorney would get; court affirmed trial judge's denial of new trial).

prejudicial information" or improper "outside influence," admissibility should depend upon an initial finding that the substance of the juror's testimony is of a type concerning impermissible outside influence or information, and not merely evidence of the juror's individual or collective predisposition, mental state or knowledge. Moreover, it should be noted that the Rule only addresses the circumstances under which a juror is competent to provide evidence on the validity of a verdict, and it does not govern standards pertaining to the degree or substance of evidence necessary to set aside a verdict or indictment.[11]

Rule 606 will allow a juror to testify to misconduct such as intoxication,[12] drug use,[13] acceptance of bribes,[14] or threats made against a juror.[15] Testimony may be admitted to prove a juror was influenced by knowledge he improperly obtained through extrinsic evidence such as books[16] or the news media.[17] Unauthorized views,[18] investigations,[19] or experiments[20] may

[11] Rule 606, Advisory Committee's Note.

[12] Jorgensen v. York Ice Machinery Corp., 160 F.2d 432, 435 (2d Cir. 1947), cert. denied, 332 U.S. 764, 68 S.Ct. 69, 92 L.Ed. 349 (1947); Annot., Use of Intoxicating Liquors by Jurors, 7 A.L.R. 3d 1040 (1966).

[13] United States v. Provenzano, 620 F.2d 985, 997 (3d Cir. 1980), cert. denied, 449 U.S. 899, 101 S.Ct. 267, 66 L.Ed.2d 129 (1980) (smoking marijuana).

[14] E.g., Remmer v. United States, 347 U.S. 227, 229, 74 S.Ct. 450, 452, 98 L.Ed. 654, 656 (1954) ("any private communication, contact, or tampering, directly or indirectly" is presumptively prejudicial).

[15] E.g., Stimack v. Texas, 548 F.2d 588, 589 (5th Cir. 1977) (jurors received phone calls from someone identifying himself as defense counsel and stating that jurors would be killed by Mafia if guilty verdict returned; grant of habeas corpus relief affirmed). See also; Miller v. United States, 403 F.2d 77, 83 n.11 (2d Cir. 1977) (dictum). But cf., Government of Virgin Islands v. Gereau, 523 F.2d 140, 149 (3d Cir. 1975), cert. denied, 424 U.S. 917, 96 S.Ct. 1119, 47 L.Ed.2d 323 (1975) (rumors of other killings and of FBI investigation would not constitute coercive force).

[16] United States v. Vasquez, 597 F.2d 192, 193 (9th Cir. 1979).

[17] Marshal v. United States, 360 U.S. 310, 314, 79 S.Ct. 1171, 1174, 3 L.Ed. 1250, 1254 (1959); United States v. Bruscino, 662 F.2d 450, 452 (7th Cir. 1981), rev'd on other grounds, 687 F.2d 938 (7th Cir. 1982), cert. denied, 103 S.Ct. 1205 (1983); Bulger v. McClay, 575 F.2d 407, 411 (2d Cir. 1978) (where specific facts enter without appropriate safeguards, the constitutional role of jury is undermined).

[18] United States ex rel. De Lucia v. McMann, 373 F.2d 759, 762 (2d Cir. 1967); Kilgore v. Greyhound Corp., Southern Greyhound Lines, 30 F.R.D. 385, 387 (E.D. Tenn. 1962) (court held hearing to determine whether juror had visited scene of accident while trial was in progress; no prejudice since foreman stopped him from relating his experience to other jurors).

[19] Gafford v. Warden, U.S. Penitentiary, 434 F.2d 318, 320 (10th Cir. 1970) (affidavit by one juror, to effect that one or more others had checked the time a late show ended, and that a juror went to a gas station to determine whether it was open at a time stated by a witness, established grounds for a hearing to determine whether conviction of defendant violated Sixth Amendment rights to an impartial jury and to confront witnesses).

[20] United States v. Beach, 296 F.2d 153, 156-57 (4th Cir. 1961) (appellate court remanded and ordered trial court to inquire whether jury had conducted experiments in jury room concerning conflict in testimony as to audibility of adding machines). See also United States v. Castello, 526 F. Supp. 847, 849 (W.D. Tex. 1981); Simon v. Kuhlman, 488 F. Supp. 59, 63 (S.D.N.Y. 1979).

be disclosed through juror testimony. Prejudicial conversations with parties,[21] witnesses,[22] or officers of the court[23] are also admissible. Evidence of a juror's insanity, though rare, is admissible.[24]

If the jurors agree that, through clerical error or mistake in calculation, the verdict announced is not that upon which the jury agreed, this information will be admitted.[25] There is conflict in the circuits whether evidence of a quotient verdict, one obtained through drawing lots, or by prior agreement to support the majority vote, is admissible.[26]

§ 606.4　Procedure in Determining Juror Misconduct.

While Rule 606(b) does not expressly establish a minimum showing of sufficiency that must be established before a judge will investigate a claim of jury misconduct, it is clear that the moving party must demonstrate that the tendered testimony is admissible under 606(b).[27] Once this is established, the court should investigate the claim however insufficient this evidence may be standing alone.[28]

During the proceeding in which the judge hears the evidence of alleged misconduct, the judge should not ask the juror the extent to which he was affected by the misconduct. Such an inquiry would be contrary to the express provisions to Rule 606(b) pertaining to the privacy of jurors' mental

[21] Leger v. Westinghouse Electric Corp , 483 F.2d 428, 430 (5th Cir. 1973) (where representative of defendant had deliberate conversations with juror, jury verdict set aside); Washington Gas Light Co. v. Connolly, 214 F.2d 254, 257-58 (D.C. Cir. 1954) (appellate court ordered judge to decide issue of prejudice where juror called defendant gas company and sought advice as to functioning of furnace).

[22] E.g., United States v. Pittman, 449 F.2d 1284, 1285 (9th Cir. 1971).

[23] United States v. United States Gypsum Co., 438 U.S. 422, 462, 98 S.Ct. 2864, 2898, 57 L.Ed.2d 854, 887 (1978); United States v. Greer, 620 F.2d 1383, 1385-86 (10th Cir. 1980).

[24] Peter v. Kiff, 407 U.S. 493, 501, 92 S.Ct. 2163, 2170, 33 L.Ed.2d 83, 89 (1972); United States v. Perry, 643 F.2d 38, 51-52 (2d Cir. 1981), cert. denied, 102 S.Ct. 138 (1982).

[25] United States v. Love, 597 F.2d 81, 85 (6th Cir. 1979); Mount Airy Lodge, Inc. v. Upjohn Co., 96 F.R.D. 378, 380 (E.D. Pa. 1982).

[26] Jorgensen v. York Ice Machinery Corp., 160 F.2d 432, 435 (2d Cir. 1947), cert. denied, 322 U.S. 764, 68 S.Ct. 69, 92 L.Ed. 349 (1947) (jury agreed to abide majority vote so that jury foreman could go home, since his son had been killed in military action; this did not justify new trial); Domeracki v. Humble Oil and Refining Co., 443 F.2d 1245, 1247-48 (3d Cir. 1971), cert. denied, 404 U.S. 883, 92 S.Ct. 212, 30 L.Ed.2d 165 (1971) (scratch paper attached to verdict indicating that jury may not have followed judge's instructions, could not be considered to impeach verdict). See, generally, 3 WEINSTEIN, ¶ 606[04], at 38; 8 WIGMORE, § 2354, at 711-12.

[27] See, generally, 3 WEINSTEIN, ¶ 606[05]; 3 LOUISELL & MUELLER, § 290.

[28] Sullivan v. Fogg, 613 F.2d 465, 467 (2d Cir. 1980); Tobias v. Smith, 468 F. Supp. 1287, 1289 (W.D. N.Y. 1979); United States v. Parker, 549 F.2d 999, 1002 (5th Cir. 1977); United States v. Doe, 513 F.2d 709, 711 (1st Cir. 1975).

and emotional processes. The judge is limited to determining whether the misconduct occurred and the number of jurors affected by the misconduct.[29] Based on these facts, the court should apply an objective evaluation to infer whether a prejudicial effect has occurred.[30] The moving party may be entitled to a rebuttable presumption of prejudice upon a showing of certain, but not all, types of misconduct.[31] Also, counsel should have at least a limited right to interrogate the jury panel to discover the grounds for a showing of jury misconduct.[32]

§ 606.5   Affidavits and Other Evidence of Juror's Statements Competent Only to the Extent Testimony is Competent.

Where a juror's testimony would be inadmissible for inquiry into a verdict, his affidavit or evidence from a third person are likewise inadmissible. For example, where a party makes a Civil Rule 59(A)(2) motion for a new trial alleging juror misconduct, and attaches an affidavit of a juror in support of this motion, the court may not consider the substance of this affidavit unless the tendered affidavit is of a type admissible under Rule 602(b). Similarly, the affidavit or testimony of a third person, such as a friend or spouse, concerning a juror's out-of-court statements may not be considered, unless this third person has firsthand knowledge of the offending conduct.

[29] 3 LOUISELL & MUELLER, § 291, at 160; United States v. Greer, 620 F.2d 1383, 1385 (10th Cir. 1980); United States v. Howard, 506 F.2d 865, 869 (5th Cir. 1975). *But see* 3 WEINSTEIN, ¶ 606[05], at 606-41, discussing pre-Rule law under Remmer v. United States, 350 U.S. 377; 76 S.Ct. 425, 100 L.Ed. 435 (1955).

[30] 3 WEINSTEIN, ¶ 606[05], at 606-41.

[31] Krause v. Rhodes, 570 F.2d 563, 569-70 (6th Cir. 1977), *cert. denied*, 435 U.S. 924, 98 S.Ct. 1488, 55 L.Ed.2d 517 (1977) (threats on life of juror and his family and physical assault upon juror were presumptively prejudicial); Stiles v. Lawrie, 211 F.2d 188, 189-90 (6th Cir. 1954) (when juror's affidavit or testimony indicates that the jury received improper information, the law presumes that prejudice has resulted); Paramount Film Distributing Corp. v. Ap-

plebaum, 217 F.2d 101, 105-106 (5th Cir. 1954), *cert. denied*, 349 U.S. 961, 75 S.Ct. 892, 99 L.Ed. 1284 (1954) (in deciding whether outside influence affected verdict, solution involves a determination that it was made reasonably certain that they were not influenced).

[32] *See*, United States v. Moten, 582 F.2d 654, 667 (2d Cir. 1978) (protection of jury from harassment by the defeated party and protection of the finality of verdicts are reasons for rule). *But see*, King v. United States, 576 F.2d 432, 438 (2d Cir. 1978), *cert. denied*, 439 U.S. 850, 99 S.Ct. 155, 58 L.Ed.2d 154 (1978) (summarizing point that jurors should not be subjected to harassment). *See also* Smith v. Cupp, 457 F.2d 1098-1100 (9th Cir. 1972), *cert. denied*, 409 U.S. 880, 93 S.Ct. 208, 34 L.Ed.2d 135 (1972).

Chapter 607

RULE 607. WHO MAY IMPEACH

Rule 607 reads as follows:

> The credibility of a witness may be attacked by any party, including the party calling him.

§ 607.1 Impeachment—In General.

Rule 607 provides that any party may attack the credibility of a witness, including the party who called the witness to testify.[1] Rule 607 departs from the common law tradition, sometimes known as the "voucher rule," which prevented a party from impeaching its own witness.[2]

Rule 607 does not limit or identify the techniques by which a party may impeach a witness. Its primary purpose, rather, is to abandon all pre-existing constraints imposed upon a party in regard to impeaching a wit-

---

[1] See, generally, McCORMICK, §§ 45-47; 3 WEINSTEIN, ¶¶ 607[02]-607[07]; 3 LOUISELL & MUELLER, §§ 296-98; WIGMORE, §§ 896-918. See also Moss, The Sweeping-Claims Exception to the Federal Rules of Evidence, 1982 DUKE L.J. 61 (1982); Note, The Fifth Amendment and a Defendant's Pre-Arrest Failure to Come Forward: The Sounds of Silence, 46 ALB. L. REV. 546 (1982); Comment, Impeachment of Cross-Examination Response with Suppressed Evidence: United States v. Havens, 48 TENN. L. REV. 721 (1981); Diamond, Inherent Problems in the Use of Pretrial Hypnosis on a Prospective Witness, 68 CALIF. L. REV. 313 (1980).

[2] See Advisory Committee's Note, Rule 607.

ness which that party has called to testify.[3] It should be noted that the voucher rule had previously been the subject of reform and erosion, and in certain recognized contexts, pre-Rule law permitted a party to impeach its own witness.[4] The most commonly encountered situation under pre-Rule practice where a party was permitted to attack the credibility of its own witness was under the so-called "surprise" principle.[5] Under the surprise exception, a party was permitted to impeach its own witness where the witness's testimony was authentically unanticipated and simultaneously affirmatively damaging to the party's case.[6] Other exceptions to the voucher rule also developed.[7]

The Federal Rules of Evidence do not treat impeachment with a comprehensive constellation of rules, and much of the law governing impeachment in federal courts is in the nature of federal common law.[8] Rules governing certain aspects of impeachment include: Rules 608 and 609 pertaining to the character, prior acts and convictions of witnesses; Rule 610 pertaining to impeachment evidence relating to religious belief; and Rule 613 pertaining to limited aspects of prior inconsistent statement impeachment (also known as "self-contradiction"). Consequently, many impeachment principles, such as those governing the exposure of witnesses' bias or interest, are left uncodified.

Traditionally, the law of evidence has recognized several specific techniques which might be used to diminish the credibility of witnesses: prior inconsistent statement impeachment (self-contradiction); contradiction; prior acts and convictions; character impeachment (propensity for lack of

---

[3] United States v. DeLillo, 620 F.2d 939, 946-47 (2d Cir. 1980), *cert. denied*, 449 U.S. 835, 101 S.Ct. 107, 66 L.Ed.2d 41 (1980) (government entitled to question and impeach witness when testimony conflicts with other prosecution witness's account). *See also* United States v. Dennis, 625 F.2d 782, 795, n.6 (8th Cir. 1980) ("surprise is no longer a prerequisite").

[4] *See* the Advisory Committee's Note, Rule 607. *See also*, 3 Wigmore, §§ 896-918.

[5] *See, e.g.*, United States v. Jiordano, 521 F.2d 695, 697 (2d Cir. 1975) ("surprise, if a necessary element for impeachment at the time of trial, was a very modest element and was not to be construed as synonymous with amazement"); Ewing v. United States, 386 F.2d 10, 15 (9th Cir. 1967), *cert. denied*, 390 U.S. 991, 88 S.Ct. 1192, 19 L.Ed.2d 1299 (1968) (impeachment allowed). *See also* United States v. Budge, 359 F.2d 732, 735 (7th Cir. 1966); Goings v.

United States, 377 F.2d 753, 762 (8th Cir. 1967); United States v. Hicks, 420 F.2d 814, 817 (5th Cir. 1970).

[6] *See, e.g.*, United States v. Budge, 359 F.2d 732, 735 (7th Cir. 1966); Goings v. United States, 377 F.2d 753, 762 (8th Cir. 1967).

[7] *See, e.g.*, United States v. Browne, 313 F.2d 197, 199 (2d Cir. 1963), *cert. denied*, 374 U.S. 814, 83 S.Ct. 1707, 10 L.Ed.2d 1037 (1963) (judge, not counsel, calls the witness); Stevens v. United States, 256 F.2d 619, 622-23 (9th Cir. 1958) (impeachment of a compulsory witness); Gaines v. United States, 349 F.2d 190, 192 (D.C. Cir. 1965) (impeachment through the guise of refreshing the recollection of the witness). For additional examples, *see, generally*, 3 Weinstein, ¶ 607[04], at 607-8-10; 3A Wigmore, §§ 907-08.

[8] *See* 3 Weinstein, ¶ 607[02], at 607-21.

veracity); exposing bias (subsuming interest in the outcome); exposing perceptual incapacity; and exposing mental incapacity.[9] Some additional techniques, such as encouraging a witness to recant on cross-examination, defy specific categorization but are unquestionably permissible. All means of impeachment are essentially designed to accomplish the same fundamental objective of diminishing the credibility or believeability of the witness. Nevertheless, the diminution in credibility is not exclusively directed to suggesting or demonstrating that the witness is purposefully deceitful. Other defects in the testimony may diminish accuracy and devalue the credibility of the witness. Accordingly, the law of evidence has traditionally recognized that in addition to exposing the insincerity of a witness, impeachment may also operate to show less purposeful flaws in the testimony, *i.e.*, defects in narration (the witness misspoke), defects in perception (the witness misperceived), and defects in memory (the witness forgot).[10] In light of Rule 402 governing relevancy, any technique not prohibited by the Rules or federal common law, which rationally operates to expose one of these testimonial defects (sincerity, narration, perception and memory), may be used to impeach a witness.

Certain impeachment techniques are discussed in conjunction with the specific rules which pertain to them.[11] Others, in regard to which there is no codification, are discussed later in this chapter.

§ 607.2   Policy of Rule 607 in Rejecting the Voucher Rule.

At common law, the voucher rule was predicated upon the theory that by offering a witness, a party would thereby guarantee his trustworthiness; consequently, such party logically could not be permitted to challenge the witness's testimony or credibility.[12] Even at common law, however, several exceptions to the blanket proscription against impeaching one's own witness had developed.[13] Courts generally came to recognize that the implacable impediment erected by the voucher rule too often served to frustrate the search for the truth rather than aid it.[14] Courts increasingly recognized that the voucher rule was based upon invalid assumptions concerning the

---

[9] *See* McCORMICK, § 33, at 72-73.

[10] United States v. Lindstrom, 698 F.2d 1154, 1162 (11th Cir. 1983). *See also,* McCORMICK, § 45, at 104.

[11] *See* Chapters 608, 609, 610, and 613 of this Treatise.

[12] *See, generally,* 3 WEINSTEIN, ¶ 607[01]; 3 LOUISELL & MUELLER, § 297; 3A WIGMORE, §§ 896-918. "Except in a few in-

stances such as character witnesses or expert witnesses, the party has little or no choice of witnesses." McCORMICK, § 38, at 82.

[13] *See* n.7 *infra.*

[14] 3 WEINSTEIN, ¶ 607[01], nn.5-13; 3 LOUISELL & MUELLER, § 297; McCORMICK, § 38; 3A WIGMORE, § 899.

relationships between parties and their witnesses. The fact that a party calls a witness does not mean that the party has exercised complete freedom in selecting the witness to testify.[15] Except in regard to such witnesses as experts or character witnesses, the party's choice of witnesses is dictated almost entirely by the particular facts in dispute, and the party usually has no choice but the call to the stand those witnesses with personal knowledge of the relevant facts.[16] Accordingly, Rule 607 is the culmination of a well-reasoned trend to jettison the voucher rule.[17]

Some commentators have justifiably admonished, however, that abandonment of the voucher rule may have undesirable effects specifically in the context of prior inconsistent impeachment.[18] As the Federal Rules were originally proposed by the Supreme Court's Advisory Committee, all prior inconsistent statements of a witness were contemplated as admissible substantive evidence under Rule 801(d)(1)(A), a constituent rule of the hearsay scheme.[19] Nevertheless, Congress amended Rule 801(d)(1)(A) to provide that only prior inconsistent statements given under oath at a hearing, deposition, or formal proceeding could be considered as substantive evidence, i.e, considered for the truth of their contents.[20] When Rule 607 was originally fashioned, it was contemplated that all prior inconsistent statements would be substantially admitted for their truth, and no abuse by a party

---

[15] See McCORMICK, § 38, at 82.

[16] Id.

[17] See, generally, 3 WEINSTEIN, ¶ 607[01]; 3 LOUISELL & MUELLER, § 297; McCORMICK, § 38; See also, Chambers v. Mississippi, 410 U.S. 284, 93 S.Ct. 1038, 35 L.Ed.2d 297 (1973) (Supreme Court held that the voucher system as applied interfered with the defendant's constitutional rights under the confrontation clause; in that case, Chambers was the defendant in a murder case; another man had made several oral and one written confession to the crime which he repudiated in a preliminary hearing; Chambers' motion to cross-examine the witness as a hostile witness was denied; the court held that the voucher system interfered with his constitutional right to defend himself, because he was prevented from cross-examining the witness and was also restrained in his direct examination of the witness, because he would have been bound by any damaging statements made on direct examination).

[18] See 3 WEINSTEIN, ¶ 607[01], at 607-15; 3 LOUISELL & MUELLER, § 299, at 197. Most of the criticism is centered around the admission of prior inconsistent statements in cases similar to United States v. Morlang, 531 F.2d 183, 186 (4th Cir. 1975). In that

case the defendant was indicted for bribery and attempted bribery. The government called as a witness a co-defendant who had entered a guilty plea to the charge. The government knew that the witness would not implicate the defendant with his direct testimony. On direct, the witness denied having had any conversations with a fellow prisoner which implicated the defendant in the crime charged. The government then called the prisoner to impeach the witness. The prisoner's testimony implicated the defendant. The appellate court reversed finding that the limiting instruction to use the prisoner's testimony only for the purpose of impeaching the witness was ineffective, and held that it was impermissible to call a witness a party knows will not testify to his advantage and then impeach the witness. The commentators agree with the appellate court's reversal of the conviction but not with its rationale. The question they raise is what is the outcome in cases where it is unclear if the party knew the witness would testify adversely. Professor Weinstein suggests Rule 403 be utilized to limit impeachment in this context.

[19] See the Discussion of Rule 801 in this Treatise.

[20] See Rule 801.

impeaching his own witness could occur in the context of using a prior inconsistent statement to contradict the witness's testimony. Under the originally proposed version, all such statements would have been substantively admissible, and a party could not call a witness merely as a device for exposing to the jury a self-contradictory statement that was substantively inadmissible.[21] Under the adopted version of Rule 801(d)(1)(A), however, this kind of abuse is conceivable if Rule 607 is applied indiscriminately. The abuse, to be fully understood, should be considered in conjunction with the description of prior inconsistent impeachment in the latter portion of this Treatise.[22] The problem specifically lies in the function of a limiting instruction which must accompany a witness's prior contradictory statement which, because it is otherwise inadmissible hearsay, must be limited to impeachment purposes.[23] In essence, the jury is instructed that it may not consider such a statement for its truth, but rather that it must consider the statement only for the purpose of evaluating the credibility of the witness who, because of conflicting versions of the same facts, cannot recount consistently.[24] For obvious reasons, the jury may decline to, or may not be able to follow the instruction. Consequently, where some prior inconsistent statements may, and some may not, be considered substantively for their truth, impeaching one's own witness may be used as an artifice for exposing non-substantive prior inconsistent statements to the jury.

Control of this potential abuse is obviously reposed in the trial judge. Most fundamentally, when a party seeks not to impeach, but rather to expose the jury to facts which it might misuse despite a limiting instruction, the latitude provided by Rule 607 is not apposite. Rule 607 pertains to "impeachment," and such misuse of prior inconsistent statements is not part of the process of "impeaching" one's own witness. Alternately stated, the trial judge traditionally, as well as under the Rules, possesses inherent power to control any abuse of the principles of evidence. Such inherent authority is reflected in Rules 102, 403 and 611. In the section that follows, case law is analyzed which applies the inherent authority of the trial judge to avoid abuse of Rule 607 in the context of prior inconsistent statements.

§ 607.3 The Court's Power to Prohibit a Party from Impeaching His Own Witness.

Whenever an out-of-court inconsistent statement is offered solely for impeachment purposes and not as substantive evidence, there is a risk the jury

---

[21] *See* Advisory Committee's Note, Rule 607.

[22] *See* Chapter 613 of this Treatise.

[23] *See* Rule 105.

[24] *See* Chapters 105 and 613 of this Treatise.

will consider the statement for its truth even when it is accompanied by a limiting instruction from the trial judge. As discussed in the previous section, the problem is particularly acute in the context of a party impeaching his own witness. Reinforced by Rule 102 and 611, Rule 403 is properly applied in this situation to determine whether the use of the prior inconsistent statement to impeach the witness's credibility is substantially outweighed by the prejudicial impact that would result from the jury's potential improper use of the evidence.

When the court is asked to disallow a party's impeachment of witness under Rule 403, the court will consider the reliability and relevancy of the offered evidence and to some degree the motivation of the party in impeaching his witness.[25] The reliability of the offered testimony will depend upon whether the witness has admitted making the prior inconsistent statement[26] as well as the likelihood that the opponent of the witness will be able effectively to cross-examine the witness.[27]

The relevancy of the impeachment evidence should be assessed in two ways: (1) the extent to which the evidence is probative of the witness's credibility, and (2) the probity of the evidence if used prejudicially as substantive evidence.[28] The court should also consider the effectiveness of a limiting instruction in avoiding improper use of the impeachment evidence.[29] If the relevancy of the credibility evidence is low, and its potential prejudicial impact high, the court is justified in disallowing the impeachment of the witness.

Whether the party wishing to impeach her witness was surprised or damaged by the direct testimony may be considered in a Rule 403 balancing.[30] Surprise is an indication that the impeachment request is not merely

[25] United States v. MacDonald, 688 F.2d 224, 234 (4th Cir. 1982), cert. denied, 451 U.S. 1016, 103 S.Ct. 726 (1983); United States v. DeLillo, 620 F.2d 939, 947 (2d Cir. 1980).

[26] See United States v. DeLillo, 620 F.2d 939, 947 (2d Cir. 1980), cert. denied, 449 U.S. 835, 101 S.Ct. 107, 66 L.Ed.2d 41, (1980); United States v. Long Soldier, 562 F.2d 601, 605 (8th Cir. 1977).

[27] See United States v. Leslie, 542 F.2d 288, 290 (5th Cir. 1976) (statement could be used even though it did not qualify as a prior inconsistent statement pursuant to Rule 801(d)(1), provided it satisfied the residual hearsay exception of Rule 803(24)).

[28] United States v. Rogers, 549 F.2d 490, 492 (8th Cir. 1976), cert. denied, 431 U.S. 918, 97 S.Ct. 2182, 53 L.Ed.2d 229 (1977) (proper to allow government to cross-examine its own witness concerning his prior

statement that defendant had admitted guilt, even though witness denied that defendant had made any such admission). See also United States v. Robinson, 530 F.2d 1076, 1081 (D.C. Cir. 1976) (rebuttal testimony of witness shows that he was engaged in a criminal enterprise; must confront problem and weigh both prejudice and probative worth of impeachment in the spirit of balancing stressed in the Federal Rules).

[29] See United States v. DeLillo, 620 F.2d 939, 948 (2d Cir. 1980), cert. denied, 449 U.S. 835, 101 S.Ct. 107, 66 L.Ed.2d 41 (1980). Cf., Commonwealth v. Gee, 467 Pa. 123, 125, 354 A.2d 875, 878 (1976).

[30] See Ordover, Surprise! That Damaging Turncoat Witness Is Still With Us: An Analysis of Federal Rules of Evidence, 607, 801(d)(1)(A) and 403, 5 HOFSTRA. L. REV. 65, 67-73 (1976). Cf., Parker v. United

a device to allow the jury to consider a hearsay statement that is not substantively admissible under Rule 801. A finding by the court that the proponent of the impeachment has an improper motive may result in a denial of the impeachment.[31]

§ 607.4   Impeachment by Exposure of Bias or Interest.

The Federal Rules of Evidence do not specifically address when or how a party may impeach a witness by exposing a bias or interest of the witness. Consequently, case law continues to define the parameters of this type of impeachment. When a party attempts to demonstrate a witness is biased or interested, it is relying on a theory of relevancy premised on a theory that certain types of relationships may affect the witness's testimony, and consequently, the accuracy of the truthfinding process.[32] The exposure of potential bias or interest has always been considered highly relevant, and courts have been reluctant to hamper counsel's use of this impeachment technique.[33]

Bias or interest may be proven by conduct or words of a witness.[34] Additionally, almost all types of relationships will facially establish some potential bias or interest. As Wigmore states, "The range of external circumstances from which bias may be inferred is infinite."[35]

States, 363 A.2d 975, 978 (D.C. App. 1976) (under D.C. Code surprise still required).

[31] E.g., United States v. Miller, 664 F.2d 94, 97 (5th Cir. 1981), cert. denied, 459 U.S. 854, 103 S.Ct. 121, 74 L.Ed.2d 106 (1982); Whitehurst v. Wright, 592 F.2d 834, 839-40 (5th Cir. 1979); United States v. Morlang, 531 F.2d 183, 190 (4th Cir. 1975).

[32] See McCORMICK, § 40, at 85. "Case law recognizes the slanting effect upon human testimony of the emotions or feelings of the witness toward the parties or the self-interest of the witness in the outcome of the case or in matters somehow related to the case." See also, 3 WEINSTEIN, ¶ 607[03], at 607-23.

[33] See United States v. Abel, 469 U.S. 45, 105 S.Ct. 465, 83 L.Ed.2d 450 (1984) (extrinsic evidence testimony revealing witness's membership in organization having tenet to "commit perjury" admitted to show bias; court rejected defense argument, this testimony barred by Rule 608(b) as extrinsic evidence of witness's past conduct); United States v. Rios Ruiz, 579 F.2d 670, 673 (1st Cir. 1978); Dick v. Watonwan County, 562 F. Supp. 1083, 1085 (D. Minn. 1983). See also Wilmington Trust Co. v. Mfgrs. Life Ins. Co., 624 F.2d 707, 709 (5th

Cir. 1980); United States v. James, 609 F.2d 36, 46 (2d Cir. 1979), cert. denied, 445 U.S. 905, 100 S.Ct. 1082, 63 L.Ed.2d 321 (1980).

[34] See, e.g., United States v. Willis, 647 F.2d 54, 56 (9th Cir. 1981). See also United States v. Nuccio, 373 F.2d 168, 171 (2d Cir. 1967), cert. denied, 387 U.S. 906, 87 S.Ct. 1688, 18 L.Ed.2d 623, reh. denied, 389 U.S. 889, 88 S.Ct. 16, 19 L.Ed.2d 199 (1967) (wrong to permit cross-examination on homosexuality merely to discredit, but not so as far as interrogation concerning repulsed homosexual advances to one of the defendants, since it went to witness's bias and motive). See, e.g., United States v. Diecidue, 603 F.2d 535, 538 (5th Cir. 1979), cert. denied, 445 U.S. 946, 100 S.Ct. 1345, 63 L.Ed.2d 781 (1980); United States v. Wright, 489 F.2d 1181, 1186 (D.C. Cir. 1973); Tinker v. United States, 417 F.2d 542, 544 (D.C. Cir. 1969), cert. denied, 396 U.S. 864, 90 S.Ct. 141, 24 L.Ed.2d 118 (1969).

[35] See, e.g., United States v. Abel, 469 U.S. 45, 105 S.Ct. 465, 83 L.Ed.2d 450 (1984); United States v. Lawson, 683 F.2d 688, 693-94 (2d Cir. 1982); Clay v. United States, 542 F.2d 1283, 1285 (7th Cir. 1977),

The Rules of Evidence do not indicate whether there are foundation requirements that must be fulfilled before "extrinsic evidence" will be admitted to prove a witness bias or interest. Extrinsic evidence is evidence offered to impeach the witness, offered after the witness sought to be impeached leaves the stand. For example, if a party wishes to prove a witness is the brother of the other party, he may choose to introduce other witnesses who will testify to the relationship. If instead counsel puts the witness on the stand, asks him about the relationship under question, and the witness concedes the relationship, the bias has been established by a means other than extrinsic proof. As the first example indicates, extrinsic proof uses substantial trial time to prove issues that may be objectively indisputable. Logic would dictate that some foundation should be required before allowing a party to impeach the witness through extrinsic evidence. Pre-Rule practice followed Wigmore's formula, that before a witness is impeached by extrinsic evidence of a prior statement indicating bias or interest, he should be asked the question and given the opportunity to confirm or deny the statement.[36] Wigmore did not feel the same foundation was required if bias was to be proven by objective evidence of conduct.[37] Under the Wigmore formula a foundation was only necessary where impeachment was proven by a prior statement of the witness.

Rule 613(b) applies to the requirement of affording a witness the opportunity to explain or deny where "extrinsic evidence of a prior inconsistent statement by a witness" is admitted.[38] The Rule by its terms does not extend to impeachment by bias or interest, but the policy of the Rule, however, is in agreement with the Wigmore model. Consequently, prior practice should be followed when impeachment is sought by showing bias or interest.[39] The Advisory Committee's Note to Rule 613 indicates that when

cert. denied, 430 U.S. 934, 97 S.Ct. 1558, 51 L.Ed.2d 779 (1977); WIGMORE, § 948. ("Among the common sorts of circumstances [indicating bias] are all those involving some *intimate family* relationship to one of the parties . . . or some such relationship to a person, *other than a party*, who is involved on one . . . side of the litigation, or is otherwise prejudiced for or against one of the parties").

[36] WIGMORE, § 953, at 512 ("the same reasons of fairness that require a witness to be given an opportunity of denying or explaining away a supposed self contradictory utterance require him also to have a similar opportunity to deny or explain away a supposed utterance indicating bias"). *See* United States v. Hayutin, 398 F.2d 944, 953 (2d Cir. 1968), *cert. denied*, 393 U.S. 961,

89 S.Ct. 400, 21 L.Ed.2d 374 (1968), *reh. denied*, 393 U.S. 1045, 89 S.Ct. 615, 21 L.Ed.2d 597, 394 U.S. 939, 89 S.Ct. 1178, 22 L.Ed.2d 475 (1969); Commer v. Pennsylvania R.R. Co., 323 F.2d 863, 866 (2d Cir. 1963).

[37] WIGMORE, § 953, at 514, n.2. It would be "erroneous to extend this rule to require prior inquiry as to an objective circumstance from which bias may be inferred."

[38] *See* Rule 613.

[39] *See, e.g.*, United States v. DiNapoli, 557 F.2d 962, 965 (2d Cir. 1977), *cert. denied*, 434 U.S. 858, 98 S.Ct. 181, 54 L.Ed.2d 130 (1977) (trial judge did not err in refusing to allow wife of government witness to testify about her husband's bias against defendant, where defense which had cross-examined husband for almost en-

extrinsic evidence takes the form of biased conduct, the Rule is inapplicable.[40] This approach is consistent with the Wigmore rationale as well as prior practice.[41] The post-Rule practice should remain unchanged.

§ 607.5 Impeachment by Contradiction.

An initial distinction must be made between impeachment by contradiction and impeachment through self-contradiction considered in conjunction with Rule 613. A simple illustration is helpful. A witness, X, testifies at trial that the truck that hit plaintiff was yellow. If opposing counsel wishes to establish X was wrong, he may proceed to contradict X in one of two ways. Counsel may either have another witness testify that he also saw the car and it was green or, alternately, counsel may choose to contradict X by introducing his deposition or statement (written or oral) in which he stated the car was green. When the new witness testifies the car was green, X has been "contradicted." When X's deposition or other statement is introduced, this is "self-contradiction" governed by Rule 613.

Impeachment by contradiction rests on a theory of relevancy bottomed on the inference that a witness whose testimony can be contradicted on specific issues is not to be believed as a whole.[42] The degree to which this impeachment technique will be effective depends upon the significance of the issue that is contradicted. Obviously, contradiction on a minor point will not have the same effect on the jury's presumption of the witness's credibility as would contradiction on a major issue.[43]

Impeachment by contradiction through extrinsic evidence can be time consuming or appear of exaggerated importance to the trier of fact.[44] Consequently, there has long been recognized a limitation on a party's right to contradict a witness by extrinsic evidence. Called the "collateral matter doctrine," this doctrine provides that a party may not present extrinsic

---

tire day failed to lay a foundation for the introduction of wife's evidence by bringing the alleged hostility to the witness' attention); United States v. Marzano, 537 F.2d 257, 265 (7th Cir. 1976), *cert. denied*, 429 U.S. 1038, 97 S.Ct. 734, 50 L.Ed.2d 749 (1977) (prejudice outweighed probative value of proffered impeaching testimony). *See also* 3 WEINSTEIN, ¶ 607[03], at 607-43.

[40] *See* Advisory Committee's Note, Rule 613.

[41] *See* 3 WEINSTEIN, ¶ 607[03], at 607-43.

[42] *See* McCORMICK, § 47, at 110.

[43] *See* United States v. Robinson, 544 F.2d 110, 114 (2d Cir. 1976), *cert. denied*,

435 U.S. 905, 98 S.Ct. 901, 54 L.Ed.2d 803 (1978) (prosecution could properly attempt to impeach witness by proving that he had not received a check on the date that alibi witness claimed that he had picked up check while with defendant).

[44] *See, e.g.*, United States v. Harris, 542 F.2d 1283, 1302 (7th Cir. 1976), *cert. denied sub nom.*, Clay v. United States, 430 U.S. 934, 97 S.Ct. 1558, 51 L.Ed.2d 779 (1977) (no error to exclude evidence of prior sexual relationship where there was no indication how the witness's prior conduct would create bias). *See also* United States v. Jaqua, 485 F.2d 193, 195 (5th Cir. 1973).

evidence to contradict a witness on a so-called collateral matter.[45] This concept is sometimes expressed in the statement that where a witness testifies on cross-examination to a collateral matter, the questioner must "take the witness's answer," *i.e.*, he may not disprove it by extrinsic evidence.[46] McCormick defines a collateral matter in the negative, "facts which would have been provable regardless of the contradictions are not 'collateral'."[47] Substantive issues in the case are clear examples of issues that are not collateral; they are relevant to impeach a witness and are also admissible as substantive proof. Another category of non-collateral issues are facts which are offered to impeach the witness on an independent impeachment purpose which permits the use of extrinsic evidence, such as bias or interest, or defective perception,[48] or defective mental capacity.[49]

Professor Weinstein advocates the rejection of the collateral matter doctrine and suggests the trial courts should exclude extrinsic evidence where appropriate under Rule 403.[50] This change in analysis, however, should not frequently alter the ultimate admissibility or inadmissibility of evidence in a given situation. The avoidance of jury confusion and needless delay are both policies that underlie the collateral matter doctrine and issues to be considered in a balancing under Rule 403.

§ 607.6   Impeachment by Demonstrating Defects in Mental Capacity or Perception.

A witness may be mistaken in his perception of an event. Alternately, later at trial he may be unable to testify accurately to, or recall the event. In these situations, counsel may wish to impeach the witness by demonstrating a defect in the witness's narration or perception of the event. This type of impeachment is based upon the need to present accurate information to the jury,[51] and this same policy is reflected in Rule 602 which requires that every witness have firsthand knowledge of any event to which he testifies.[52]

---

[45] Klein v. Keresey, 307 Mass. 51, 53, 29 N.E.2d 703, 705 (1940).

[46] *See* McCormick, § 47, at 110.

[47] *See* McCormick, § 47, at 111. *See also* United States v. Lambert, 463 F.2d 552, 556-57 (7th Cir. 1972) (not collateral to impeach defendant's denial where evidence could have been introduced during case).

[48] *See* McCormick, § 47, at 111.

[49] *Id.*

[50] 3 Weinstein, ¶ 607[05], at 607-62.

[51] United States v. Partin, 493 F.2d 750, 762 (5th Cir. 1974) ("[I]t is just as reasonable that a jury be informed of a witness's mental incapacity at a time about which he proposes to testify as it would be for the jury to know that he then suffered an impairment of sight or hearing; it all goes to the ability to comprehend, know, and correctly relate the truth").

[52] *See* Rule 602.

When a party impeaches a witness and demonstrates a defect in the witness's ability to perceive or narrate an event, the party is not necessarily asserting the witness lacks firsthand knowledge of the event. The party is instead asserting that, for some reason, the witness testifying either did not interpret what he saw correctly or is unable now to remember or testify accurately. Both Rules 602 and 607 attempt to ensure that only accurate information is presented to the jury.

Some types of perceptional defects may be demonstrated effectively through cross-examination or in-court experiments.[53] For example, the witness's memory may be tested by questioning him concerning circumstances connected or unconnected to the trial.[54] Additionally, in the trial judge's discretion, eyesight or hearing are easy to test by simple experiments in the courtroom. The extent to which extrinsic evidence will be admitted to prove a defect in narration or perception will be governed by the trial court's application of Rule 403.

When the testimonial defect arises because the witness was mentally incapable of perceiving the event, either because of mental disease or because it was self-induced through the use of drugs or alcohol, different problems arise. The jury may not be able to assess accurately without the help of expert witnesses the effect a certain drug may have had on the ability of the witness to either accurately perceive the event in question or convey the information at trial.[55] Additionally, admitting evidence of drug/alcohol use by a witness may unfairly prejudice a party, particularly if the drug or alcohol use could not in fact have influenced the witness's perception on the occasion in question.[56]

Most courts will admit evidence that the witness in question was intoxicated or drinking at the time she perceived the event.[57] Evidence of chronic alcoholism generally is not admitted.[58] Judge Weinstein believes that excluding evidence of chronic alcoholism is incorrect because it ignores the

---

[53] *See, e.g.*, Battle v. United States, 345 F.2d 438, 440 (D.C. Cir. 1955) (serious error in denying defense counsel the opportunity to cross-examine the witness respecting her eyesight, where identification of a man at night was the principle issue).

[54] *See*, United States v. Hoffman, 415 F.2d 14, 20-21 (7th Cir. 1969), *cert. denied*, 396 U.S. 958, 90 S.Ct. 431, 24 L.Ed.2d 423 (1969) (cross-examination permitted for testing witness's memory on solvency).

[55] 3 WEINSTEIN, ¶ 607[04], at 607-47.

[56] *Id.*

[57] *See* Rheaume v. Patterson, 289 F.2d 611, 614 (2d Cir. 1961) (testimony that wit-

ness had been drinking during the morning and afternoon hours preceding the accident was relevant to witness's credibility). *See also* Dick v. Watonwon County, 562 F. Supp. 1083, 1086 (D. Minn. 1983); Order of United Commercial Travelers v. Tripp, 63 F.2d 37, 41 (10th Cir. 1933).

[58] Poppell v. United States, 418 F.2d 214, 215 (5th Cir. 1969) (excluded testimony of a general reputation for intemperance was wholly unrelated to the ability of the witness to testify, and had no bearing on witness's veracity).

long term physical effects the disease may have on the mental capacity of the alcoholic.[59] Additionally, evidence of chronic alcoholism may tend to establish whether the witness was intoxicated at the time he saw the event to which he is testifying. However, this later inference may be impermissible under Rule 404.[60]

There is no consistent rule under federal practice whether evidence of drug use will be admitted to impeach a witness. Some jurisdictions routinely allow evidence of drug use to be admitted without requiring a demonstration that the use of the drugs adversely affects the ability of the witness to testify.[61] The rationale of the court's following this practice is that drug use, like stealing, is indicative of dishonesty. This theory underlies impeachment pursuant to Rule 608. Another group of cases requires the party wishing to admit the evidence to prove that the drug use impaired the witness's perception.[62] Some courts will admit the evidence assuming the jury can accurately assess the impact of the evidence of drug use as credibility.[63] This may, however, be a faulty conclusion given the fact that even experts cannot always agree on the impact of some drugs on the ability of the witness to perceive an event.[64]

When counsel wishes to introduce evidence of the use of a drug where there is no consensus on the impact of the drug on a witness's ability to perceive events, the court should take care to ascertain whether the conflicting expert testimony may be useful to the jury or result in a time-consuming digression. Rule 403 provides a vehicle to exclude evidence of questionable validity and possible prejudice to a party.[65] To enhance his position, counsel should be able to demonstrate the relevancy of the drug use on the witness's ability to perceive or narrate the event. The court should be advised of the dosage of drugs ingested, the impact of the drugs

---

[59] 3 WEINSTEIN, ¶ 607[04], at 607-74.

[60] See Chapter 404 of this Treatise.

[61] United States v. Hoppe, 645 F.2d 620, 623 (8th Cir. 1981); People of Territory of Guam v. Dela Rosa, 644 F.2d 1257, 1261 (9th Cir. 1981).

[62] See, e.g., Kelly v. Maryland Casualty Co., 45 F.2d 782, 788 (W.D. Va. 1938).

[63] See, e.g., United States v. Jackson, 576 F.2d 46, 49 (5th Cir. 1978) (court properly denied defense request for physical and mental examinations of witnesses, since it would infringe witness's privacy). See also United States v. Banks, 520 F.2d 627, 629 (7th Cir. 1975); Gurleski v. United States, 405 F.2d 253, 267 (5th Cir. 1968), cert. denied, 395 U.S. 981, 89 S.Ct. 2140, 23 L.Ed.2d 769 (1969); United States v. Hicks, 389 F.2d 49, 50 (3d Cir. 1968), cert. denied,

391 U.S. 970, 88 S.Ct. 1046, 20 L.Ed.2d 885 (1968). Cf., United States v. Cook, 608 F.2d 1175, 1182 (9th Cir. 1979), cert. denied, 444 U.S. 1034, 100 S.Ct. 706, 62 L.Ed.2d 670 (1980).

[64] 3 WEINSTEIN, ¶ 607[04], at 607-49.

[65] See, e.g., United States v. Holman, 680 F.2d 1340, 1352-53 (11th Cir. 1982). See also United States v. Sampol, 636 F.2d 621, 667 (D.C. Cir. 1980) (proffer that witness was under influence of drugs at time he witnessed events, but must be made outside hearing of jury where there was dubious basis for counsel's proffer). Cf., United States v. James, 576 F.2d 1121, 1123 (5th Cir. 1978), cert. denied, 99 S.Ct. 2836 (1979); United States v. Kizer, 569 F.2d 504 (9th Cir. 1978), cert. denied, 435 U.S. 976, 98 S.Ct. 1626 (1978).

on the individual witness, the witness's past habit for ingesting drugs, and the time at which the witness took the drug in relation to his perception of the occurrence to which he is testifying.[66]

When a party wishes to establish the witness was mentally ill at the time he perceived the event, the question becomes whether psychiatric testimony may be admitted on the issue and whether a court can order the examination of the witness. The courts are reluctant to admit psychiatric evidence or order mental examinations because of the fear of testimony that is nonconclusive, confusing to the jury, and results merely in a digression at trial.[67] Whether the evidence will be admitted or the examination ordered will depend upon the preliminary work of counsel in making a showing to the trial court. Counsel should demonstrate the type of mental illness suffered by the witness, the illnesses affecting the testimony or perception of the witness and any prior history of mental illness, such as periods of prior commitment.[68] The court, of course, has discretion under Rule 403 to exclude the evidence if it is highly prejudicial, confusing or needlessly time consuming.[69]

[66] See 3 WEINSTEIN, ¶ 607[04], at 607-50.

[67] See, e.g., United States v. Provenzano, 688 F.2d 194, 204 (3d Cir. 1982), cert. denied, 103 S.Ct. 492 (1982); United States v. Riley, 657 F.2d 1377, 1387 (8th Cir. 1981), cert denied, 103 S.Ct. 742 (1983).

[68] See 3 WEINSTEIN, ¶ 607[04], at 607-58.

[69] See, e.g., United States v. Jackson, 576 F.2d 46, 48 (5th Cir. 1978); United States v. Hughes, 411 F.2d 461 (2d Cir. 1969), cert. denied, 396 U.S. 867, 90 S.Ct. 145, 24 L.Ed.2d 120 (1969).

Chapter 608

RULE 608. EVIDENCE OF CHARACTER AND CONDUCT OF WITNESS

Rule 608 reads as follows:

(a) **Opinion and Reputation Evidence of Character.** The credibility of a witness may be attacked or supported by evidence in the form of opinion or reputation, but subject to these limitations: (1) the evidence may refer only to character for truthfulness or untruthfulness, and (2) evidence of truthful character is admissible only after the character of the witness for truthfulness has been attacked by opinion or reputation evidence or otherwise.

(b) **Specific Instances of Conduct.** Specific instances of the conduct of a witness, for the purpose of attacking or supporting his credibility, other than

219

conviction of crime as provided in Rule 609, may not be proved by extrinsic evidence. They may, however, in the discretion of the court, if probative of truthfulness or untruthfulness, be inquired into on cross-examination of the witness (1) concerning his character for truthfulness or untruthfulness, or (2) concerning the character for truthfulness or untruthfulness of another witness as to which character the witness being cross-examined has testified.

The giving of testimony, whether by an accused or by any other witness, does not operate as a waiver of his privilege against self-incrimination when examined with respect to matters which related only to credibility.

§ 608.1   Evidence of Character and Conduct of Witness—In General.

Rule 404(a), considered earlier in this Treatise, contains the general prohibition relating to the use of character evidence as a means of proving conforming conduct. Three exceptions, however, are set forth in Rule 404(a) which authorize the use of the character-conforming conduct inference in limited situations. Two of these exceptions are available in criminal cases, and Rule 404(a)(1) and Rule 404(a)(2) pertain, respectively, to the character of the accused and the character of the victim. The third exception, Rule 404(a)(3), pertains to the character of a witness who takes the stand to testify, and this exception authorizes the use of the otherwise forbidden inferential pattern in regard to any witness who testifies in any suit, criminal or civil. Specifically, Rule 404(a)(3) authorizes the use of the character-conforming conduct inference as prescribed by Rules 607, 608 and 609.[1]

For reasons discussed in conjunction with Rule 404(a), character evidence has a tendency to arouse the emotions and prejudices of the trier of fact, and the use of character evidence is consequently attended by a substantial risk of a distortion of the accuracy of the fact-finding process. Accordingly, the use of character or propensity evidence as an inferential

---

[1] See, generally, McCORMICK, § 41; 3 WEINSTEIN, ¶¶ 608[01]-[10]; 3 LOUISELL & MUELLER, §§ 303-10; 3 WIGMORE, §§ 977-88; 4 WIGMORE, §§ 1100-44; 8 WIGMORE, § 2276. See also Hale, Specific Acts and Related Matters as Affecting Credibility. 1 HASTINGS L.J. 89 (1950); Ladd, Techniques and Theory of Character Testimony, 24 IOWA L. REV. 498 (1939); Noonan, Inferenced from the Invocation of the Privilege Against Self-Incrimination, 41 VA. L. REV. 311 (1955); Note, Expanding Double Jeopardy: Collateral Estoppel and the Evidentiary Use of Prior Crimes of Which the Defendant Has Been Acquitted, 2 FLA. ST. U.L. REV. 511 (1974); Note, Witnesses Under Rule VI of the Proposed Federal Rules of Evidence, 15 WAYNE L. REV. 1236 (1969); Comment, Procedural Protections of the Criminal Defendant — a Reevaluation of the Privilege Against Self-Incrimination and the Rule Excluding Evidence of Propensity to Commit Crime, 78 HARV. L. REV. 426 (1964); Comment, Use of Bad Character and Prior Convictions to Impeach a Defendant Witness, 34 FORDHAM L. REV. 107 (1965).

basis for establishing conduct consistent with the character trait or propensity is restricted to those situations delineated in the exceptions to Rule 404(a). Each exception reflects special policy considerations supporting the use of the otherwise prohibited inferential pattern.

The vast majority of evidence at most trials is admitted through the testimony of witnesses. Witnesses play a pivotal role in the fact-finding process of a trial, and, consequently, it is critical to the fact-finding process for litigants to be able to present impeachment or rehabilitation evidence regarding a witness's propensity to testify falsely or truthfully. Alternately stated, there is a special need for evidence relating to a witness's character trait of veracity.

Rule 608 governs the use of character and conduct evidence for the purpose of impeaching the credibility of a witness. The Rule applies to any witness, party or nonparty, and it applies in both civil and criminal cases. The Rule also governs the use of reputation and opinion evidence for rehabilitating the credibility of a witness whose character for veracity has been impeached.

§ 608.2   Rule 608(a)(1)—Impeachment Through Opinion and Reputation Evidence of Character—In General.

Any witness who testifies in any lawsuit is subject to impeachment by reputation and opinion evidence relating to his character.[2] This type of impeachment is presented through the testimony of a character witness who has firsthand knowledge of the principal witness's reputation for truth and veracity in the community where he lives or, in an appropriate case, the business community in which he operates.[3] Rule 608(a) also allows the character witness to testify in the form of personal opinion which, consistent with Rule 701, must be based on firsthand knowledge.[4] The qualifica-

---

[2] *E.g.*, United States v. Bruscino, 662 F.2d 450, 463 (7th Cir. 1981); United States v. Rios, 611 F.2d 1335, 1350 (10th Cir. 1979); United States v. Mandel, 591 F.2d 1347, 1370 (4th Cir. 1979). *See, generally*, 3 WEINSTEIN, ¶ 608[05]; 3 LOUISELL & MUELLER, § 304; McCORMICK, § 44, at 90-91; 3A WIGMORE, §§ 920-30.

[3] *E.g.*, United States v. Watson, 669 F.2d 1374, 1381-82 (11th Cir. 1982). *See also* United States v. Salazar, 425 F.2d 1284, 1286 (9th Cir. 1970) (where witness knew defendant "only through two months of occasional business dealings," this was insufficient foundation evidence to qualify him to

testify to defendant's reputation for honesty and veracity); United States v. Augello, 452 F.2d 1135, 1139-40 (2d Cir. 1971), *cert. denied*, 406 U.S. 922, 92 S.Ct. 1787, 32 L.Ed.2d 122 (1972) (where it was unclear that witness was a member of the communities in which defendant lived or worked, error to have admitted it as reputation testimony). *But cf.*, United States v. Oliver, 492 F.2d 943, 946 (8th Cir. 1973).

[4] *See, generally*, 3 WEINSTEIN, ¶ 608[04], at 608-19; 3 LOUISELL & MUELLER, § 304; McCORMICK, § 44, at 90-91; 7 WIGMORE, §§ 1981-86. *See also* Chapter 701 of this Treatise.

tions for an impeachment character witness are essentially the same as those for character witnesses under Rule 405.[5]

The character witness is called by the party seeking to impeach the primary witness, and the timing of the testimony of the character witness is determined by the impeaching party's next opportunity to call witnesses.[6] Consequently, a witness called by the plaintiff during its case-in-chief may be impeached by the defendant through a character witness called by the defendant during the case-in-defense. A witness called by defendant may be impeached by the plaintiff through a character witness called by the plaintiff during its case in rebuttal.

§ 608.3   Rule 608(a)(1)—Foundation as to Impeachment Character Witness's Knowledge.

Prior to the character witness's testimony, a foundation must be elicited from the character witness which establishes the basis for his opinion or reputation testimony.[7] The foundation must demonstrate the character witness's familiarity with the primary witness's reputation, or in the alternative, where the character witness is to render an opinion as to the primary witness's veracity, the character witness's firsthand knowledge of the primary witness must be established. The familiarity with reputation, or knowledge of the person to be characterized, must pertain to a time period reasonably proximate to the trial testimony.[8]

---

[5] *See, e.g.,* Michelson v. United States, 335 U.S. 469, 477-87, 69 S.Ct. 213, 93 L.Ed. 168 (1948); United States v. Salazar, 425 F.2d 1284, 1286 (9th Cir. 1970). *See also* United States v. Augello, 452 F.2d 1135, 1139-40 (2d Cir. 1971), *cert. denied,* 406 U.S. 922, 92 S.Ct. 1787, 32 L.Ed.2d 122 (1972) (witness's qualifications for knowing defendant had not been adequately established).

[6] *See* United States v. Cylkovski, 556 F.2d 799, 802 (6th Cir. 1977) (proper to rule that character witness could only testify after defendant testified and his truthfulness became an issue). *See also* United States v. Nace, 561 F.2d 763, 771 (9th Cir. 1977) (where character witnesses lived in same community as principal witness for eight and 21 years respectively, both were adequate to testify as to reputation for truth and veracity of the principal witness).

[7] *E.g.,* United States v. Oliver, 492 F.2d 943, 945-47 (8th Cir. 1973), *later app.,* 525 F.2d 731 (8th Cir. 1973), *cert. denied,* 424 U.S. 973, 96 S.Ct. 1477, 47 L.Ed.2d 743 (1974) (where character witnesses had been dormitory roommates of the complainant in rape case and had known her for seven weeks, error to exclude their testimony, since they were qualified to testify as to her truth and veracity). *See also* United States v. Salazar, 325 F.2d 1284, 1286 (9th Cir. 1970).

[8] United States v. Watson, 669 F.2d 1374, 1382 n.5 (11th Cir. 1982); United States v. Oliver, 492 F.2d 943, 947 (8th Cir. 1973), *cert. denied,* 424 U.S. 973, 96 S.Ct. 1477, 47 L.Ed.2d 743 (1974); United States v. Null, 415 F.2d 1178, 1180 (4th Cir. 1969).

§ 608.4   Rule 608(a)(1)—Substance of Impeachment Character Witness's Testimony.

Rule 608 limits impeachment by character evidence to testimony regarding the principal witness's truth and veracity. The impeachment may not extend to an exploration of the primary witness's general character, and in this respect Rule 608 is generally consistent with pre-Rule law.[9] Rule 608 extends prior law, however, by permitting the use of opinion as well as reputation evidence in order to prove character, and consequently, Rule 608 is parallel to Rule 405.[10]

Rules 403 and 611 provide the trial judge with the inherent discretion to limit impeachment attacks through character evidence, and where the issue presented is whether the character witness is prepared to testify to the sufficiently distinct character trait of veracity, the trial judge properly exercises his discretion when he excludes overly broad testimony as to general reputation for moral conduct.[11] The trial judge must ensure that the character witness is properly qualified to address the distinct character trait of veracity, *i.e.*, the propensity to tell the truth or to lie.

Under the Rule, character witnesses may not on direct examination testify to specific instances of conduct of the principal witness (the witness sought to be impeached). The testimony is restricted to the character witness's knowledge of the reputation, or his opinion of the veracity, of the principal witness.[12] Consistent with Rule 608(b)(2), however, the impeachment character witness may be cross-examined concerning specific in-

---

[9] *See, e.g.*, United States v. Walker, 313 F.2d 236, 238 (6th Cir. 1963), *cert. denied*, 374 U.S. 807, 83 S.Ct. 1695, 10 L.Ed.2d 1031 (1963) (impeachment of defendant who takes the stand is not limited to cross-examination). *See also* Salgado v. United States, 278 F.2d 830, 831-32 (1st Cir. 1960).

[10] United States v. Greer, 643 F.2d 280, 282 (5th Cir. 1981), *cert. denied*, 454 U.S. 854, 102 S.Ct. 300, 70 L.Ed.2d 147 (1981); United States v. Walker, 313 F.2d 236, 239 (6th Cir. 1963), *cert. denied*, 374 U.S. 807, 83 S.Ct. 1695, 10 L.Ed.2d 1031 (1963). *See, generally*, 3 WEINSTEIN, ¶ 608[03], at 608-17; 3 LOUISELL & MUELLER, § 304; McCORMICK, § 44, at 101. *See also* §§ 405.1 *et seq.* of this Treatise.

[11] *See* United States v. Herzberg, 558 F.2d 1219, 1223 (5th Cir. 1977), *cert. denied*, 434 U.S. 930, 98 S.Ct. 417, 54 L.Ed.2d 290 (1977) (trial court limited in-quiry of defendant-witness to his reputation for "truthfulness" rather than "honesty and fair dealing"); Carbo v. United States, 314 F.2d 718, 743-44 (9th Cir. 1963), *cert. denied*, 377 U.S. 953, 84 S.Ct. 1625-27, 12 L.Ed.2d 498, *reh. denied*, 377 U.S. 1010, 84 S.Ct. 1902, 12 L.Ed.2d 1058 (proper on redirect to establish that witness had been threatened, to make it clear that his motive for leaving county was fear, not corruption).

[12] United States v. Mangiameli, 668 F.2d 1172, 1175-76 (10th Cir. 1982), *cert. denied*, 456 U.S. 918, 102 S.Ct. 1776, 72 L.Ed.2d 179 (1982); United States v. Hoskins, 628 F.2d 295, 298 (5th Cir. 1980), *cert. denied*, 449 U.S. 987, 101 S.Ct. 406, 66 L.Ed.2d 249 (1980) (no error to refuse to allow witness to give specific examples about why he doubted prosecution witness' honesty).

stances of conduct of the primary witness.[13] Such specific instances must be probative of veracity and may be the subject of inquiry only after the judge has exercised discretion and authorized the examination.[14] While Rule 608(b)(2) is designed primarily to regulate the cross-examination of *rehabilitation* character witnesses, it simultaneously operates to authorize inquiry into acts reflective of truth-telling, *i.e.*, good acts probative of veracity where such acts are the subject of inquiry on cross-examination of an impeachment character witness. Accordingly, subject to the express limitations in Rule 608(b)(2) discussed in § 608.7 of this Treatise, an impeachment character witness may be asked on cross-examination whether he considered certain exemplary acts of the primary witness when he formulated his direct testimony as to opinion and reputation.[15] From a tactical perspective, however, this inquiry should be undertaken with extreme caution because once the witness has been cross-examined about the basis of his direct examination testimony, further explanation may be authorized by the trial judge on redirect examination.

§ 608.5 Rule 608(a)(2)—Bolstering the Credibility of a Witness with Reputation and Opinion Evidence—When Authorized.

Rule 608(a)(2) provides that reputation and opinion evidence tending to establish the truthful propensity of any witness may be admitted only after the principal witness's *character* has in fact been attacked by opinion or reputation evidence or by other impeachment evidence which represents an attack on character.[16] The underlying theory provides that all witnesses under oath are presumed to be telling the truth and that the issue of a witness's truthfulness or credibility is collateral to the principal issues in the case.[17] While every witness's credibility is an issue for the trier of fact,[18] this does not, in the absence of an attack on character, authorize a party to bolster any witness through use of a character witness. The condition precedent for the use of a rehabilitation character witness is an attack on the *character* of the primary witness, and mere impeachment of the primary witness is insufficient to authorize the calling of a positive character witness.

[13] *See, generally,* 3 WEINSTEIN, ¶ 608[06], at 608-37; 3 LOUISELL & MUELLER, § 304.

[14] *See, generally,* 3 WEINSTEIN, ¶ 608[07], at 608-43; 3 LOUISELL & MUELLER, § 310.

[15] *Id.*

[16] United States v. Mack, 643 F.2d 1119, 1124 (5th Cir. 1981); United States v. Solomon, 686 F.2d 863, 873-74 (11th Cir. 1982). *See* Advisory Committee's Note to Federal Rule 608.

[17] United States v. Danehy, 680 F.2d 1311, 1314 (11th Cir. 1982); Osborne v. United States, 542 F.2d 1015, 1019 (8th Cir. 1976).

[18] *See* United States v. Augelini, 678 F.2d 380, 382 (1st Cir. 1982).

A witness merely discredited by evidence of bias not involving corruption has not been subjected to *character* impeachment.[19] Also, where a prior inconsistent statement of a witness is introduced, where a witness is simply confused, or where a witness merely provides conflicting testimony, the witness's credibility may not be bolstered through a character witness attesting to the primary witness's good character for veracity.[20] By comparison, however, where impeachment is effected by a negative character witness pursuant to Rule 608(a), by interrogation as to prior acts probative of untruthful character under Rule 608(b), or by evidence of a criminal conviction under Rule 609, the *character* of the primary witness is, in fact, attacked and, therefore, may be rehabilitated with a positive character witness.[21] Beyond these presumptive attacks on character expressly addressed in the Rules, the careful discretion of the trial judge must be exercised on a case-by-case basis to determine whether the form of impeachment employed effectively operates as an attack on character.[22]

§ 608.6   Rule 608(a)(2)—Substance of Testimony from Rehabilitation Character Witness.

Rehabilitation is accomplished by calling a character witness to testify to the truthful character of the impeached witness. The rehabilitation character witness is subject to the same rules governing impeachment character

---

[19] *See, generally,* 3 WEINSTEIN, ¶ 608[08], at 608-47; 3 LOUISELL & MUELLER, § 308; 4 WIGMORE, § 1107.

[20] Stokes v. Delacambre, 710 F.2d 1120, 1122 (5th Cir. 1983). *See also* Homan v. United States, 279 F.2d 767, 772 (8th Cir. 1960), *cert. denied*, 364 U.S. 866, 81 S.Ct. 110, 5 L.Ed.2d 88 (1960) (no right to introduce testimony in support of truthfulness unless it is an issue). *See, e.g.,* Osborne v. United States, 542 F.2d 1015, 1019 (8th Cir. 1976).

[21] *See, generally,* 3 WEINSTEIN, ¶ 608[08], at 608-46; McCORMICK, § 49.

[22] McCormick advocates a case-by-case evaluation of the trial court:

> Attempts to support the witness by showing his good character for truth have resulted in contradictory conclusions when the witness has been impeached by evidence of an inconsistent statement, or has been met by the adversary's evidence denying the facts to which the witness has so testified. If the witness has been impeached by the introduction of an inconsistent statement, the greater number of courts permit a showing of his good character for truth, but if the adversary has merely introduced evidence denying the facts to which the witness testified, the greater number of courts will not permit a showing of the witness's good character for truth. Convenient as automatic answers to these seemingly minor trial questions may be, surely it is unrealistic to handle them in this mechanical fashion. A more sensible view is the notion that the judge should consider in each case whether the particular impeachment for inconsistency and the conflict in testimony, or either of them, amounts in net effect to an attack on character for truth and should exercise his discretion accordingly to admit or exclude the character-support.

witnesses. A foundation as to the basis for his testimony must be established, and the subject of testimony is limited to reputation and opinion.
On cross-examination, the rehabilitation character witness may be interrogated concerning specific acts of conduct of the principal witness, and the
procedure directly parallels that used in conjunction with Rule 405.[23]
Whether a particular instance of conduct may be the subject of cross-
examination is a matter treated in Rule 608(b) and discussed in § 608.9 of
this Treatise.

§ 608.7   Rule 608(b)—Specific Instances of Prior Conduct of the Princi-pal Witness—In General.

Rule 608(b) governs the use of prior acts of the primary witness where
such specific instances of conduct are used to impeach his credibility. Pro-
cedurally, Rule 608(b) operates in two distinct contexts. Rule 608(b)(1)
governs the procedure of cross-examining the primary witness concerning
prior untruthful acts. Rule 608(b)(2) also governs the interrogation of a
character witness concerning specific instances of untruthful conduct of
the primary witness. As discussed previously in this Chapter, the latter
procedure usually arises in the context of cross-examination of a rehabilitation character witness who is offered to bolster the credibility of an impeached principal witness. Regardless of which procedure is employed, the
standards governing admissibility are the same.

In applying the Rule, it is important to recognize that Rule 608(b) governs prior acts of the principal witness which are not subject to, or which
have not resulted in, conviction. Where impeachment is sought through
exposing a prior conviction of the witness, Rule 609 is applicable.[24]

§ 608.8   Rule 608(b)—Restriction on Extrinsic Evidence; Exercise of Dis-cretion by the Trial Judge.

The expressly mandated exercise of discretion of Rule 608(b) contemplates that the trial judge must evaluate the net probative value of the act
before authorizing inquiry on cross-examination. The exercise of discretion
entails balancing the probative value of the evidence against such counter-

---

[23] United States v. Jackson, 696 F.2d 578, 594 (8th Cir. 1982), *cert. denied*, 460 U.S. 1073, 103 S.Ct. 1531 (1983); United States v. Bright, 588 F.2d 504, 511-12 (5th Cir. 1979); United States v. Nace, 561 F.2d 763, 772 (9th Cir. 1977). *See also* Chapter 405 of this Treatise.

[24] *See, generally*, 3 Weinstein, ¶ 608[05]; 3 Louisell & Mueller, § 307.

weights as unfair prejudice, remoteness and confusion.[25] Of course, prejudice is more likely in the case of party witnesses.[26] Rule 608 is essentially a rule of limitation which prohibits proof of specific instances of conduct by evidence extrinsic to the cross-examination of the principal witness or of the character witness.[27] "Extrinsic evidence" as used in this Rule (as well as in other Rules such as Rule 613) pertains to evidence received after the witness steps down from testifying. Such instances of conduct may be the subject of interrogation only on cross-examination of the principal witness or on cross-examination of the character witness where the inquiry is probative of the principal witness's character for truthfulness.

In prohibiting extrinsic evidence of the prior acts of the principal witness, Rule 608(b) operates as a device to curtail digressions. The party conducting a cross-examination is given broad latitude in pressing for an admission of a prior untruthful act as long as she proceeds in good faith.[28] If, however, the witness denies the act, the cross-examiner has no other recourse in the matter. She is said to be "stuck with the answer," and the act may not be proven after the witness steps down. The prohibition of extrinsic evidence in such situations is designed to prevent the trier of fact from being side-tracked by collateral issues.[29]

§ 608.9   Rule 608(b)—Types of Specific Instances of Conduct Appropriate for Inquiry.

In requiring the trial judge to weigh the probative value of impeachment evidence against its potential misuse by the jury, it is clear that Rule 608(b) contemplates authorization by the trial judge of inquiry into a limited class of acts committed by the principal witness. Only certain acts are rationally probative of truthfulness or untruthfulness, and all types of antisocial conduct will not qualify. Specific instances of conduct which might qualify include acts of cheating, acts of embezzlement, acts of fraud and

---

[25] United States v. Abel, 469 U.S. 45, 105 S.Ct. 465, 83 L.Ed.2d 450 (1984); United States v. Fortes, 619 F.2d 108, 118 (1st Cir. 1980); United States v. Whitehead, 618 F.2d 523, 529 (4th Cir. 1980); United States v. Cole, 617 F.2d 151, 154 (5th Cir. 1980).

[26] United States v. Pintar, 630 F.2d 1270, 1285-86 (8th Cir. 1980). *See, generally,* 3 WEINSTEIN, ¶ 608[05], at 608-35; 3 LOUISELL & MUELLER, § 305.

[27] *See, e.g.,* United States v. Bosley, 615 F.2d 1274, 1276-77 (9th Cir. 1980); United States v. Ling, 581 F.2d 1118, 1120-21 (4th Cir. 1978).

[28] Carter v. Hewitt, 617 F.2d 961, 969 (3d Cir. 1980). *See, generally,* 3 WEINSTEIN, ¶ 608[05], at 608-22-23; 3 LOUISELL & MUELLER, § 306; McCORMICK, § 42, at 92.

[29] *See, generally,* 3 WEINSTEIN, ¶ 608[05], at 608-21; 3 LOUISELL & MUELLER, § 306; 3A WIGMORE, § 979.

acts of evidence destruction.[30] Acts of violence, however, generally do not qualify no matter how antisocial such acts might be.[31] Falling within the gray area is an act such as narcotics trafficking and certain crimes involving the theft of property.[32]

§ 608.10   Right of Witness to Foreclose Inquiry Unrelated to Credibility.

The final sentence of Rule 608(b) provides that by taking the stand to testify, a witness does not waive his right against self-incrimination with respect to matters relating solely to his credibility.[33] This provision, which applies to a criminal defendant as well as any other witness at any trial, is designed to encourage reluctant witnesses affording them protection against disclosure of past incriminating misconduct. The restriction on waiver applies as long as the inquiry into any misconduct is for the sole purpose of testing the witness's credibility and is not related to a consequential issue in the case.[34]

While this provision serves as notice that a witness does not waive his constitutional privilege against self-incrimination merely by taking the stand to testify, its practical effect is functionally limited. The Rule does not preclude interrogation about a past conviction since such inquiry is no longer incriminating.[35] For the same reason, the Rule does not prevent

[30] See Carter v. Hewitt, 617 F.2d 961, 969-73 (3d Cir. 1980) (quoting paragraph in Treatise). See also United States v. Leake, 642 F.2d 715, 718-19 (4th Cir. 1981); Williams v. Warren Bros. Const. Co., 412 A.2d 334, 336 (Del. Super. 1980). See, generally, 3 WEINSTEIN, ¶ 608[05], at 608-32-33; 3 LOUISELL & MUELLER, § 305; McCORMICK, § 42; 3A WIGMORE, § 982.

[31] United States v. Hill, 550 F. Supp. 983, 990 (C.D. Pa. 1982), aff'd, 716 F.2d 893 (3d Cir. 1983), cert. denied, 104 S.Ct. 699 (1984); United States v. Bynum, 566 F.2d 914, 923 (5th Cir. 1978), cert. denied sub nom.; Becker v. United States, 439 U.S. 840, 99 S.Ct. 129, 58 L.Ed.2d 138 (1978). See, generally, 3 WEINSTEIN, ¶ 608[05], at 608-33; 3 LOUISELL & MUELLER, § 305; Mc-CORMICK, § 42; 3A WIGMORE, § 982.

[32] United States v. Mehrmanesh, 682 F.2d 1301, 1303 (9th Cir. 1982). See, generally, 3 WEINSTEIN, ¶ 608[05], at 608-32-33; 3 LOUISELL & MUELLER, § 305; McCOR-MICK, § 42, at 82; 3A WIGMORE, §§ 981-87.

[33] E.g., United States v. Burch, 490 F.2d 1300, 1302 (8th Cir. 1974), cert. denied, 416 U.S. 990, 94 S.Ct. 2400, 40 L.Ed.2d 769 (1974) (proper to prevent defense cross-ex-

amination of prosecution witness in regard to past misconduct, since witness was facing state criminal charge and U.S. Attorney could not offer immunity). See also United States v. Newman, 490 F.2d 139, 144-45 (3d Cir. 1974); United States v. Varelli, 407 F.2d 735, 751 (7th Cir. 1969), later app., 452 F.2d 193 (7th Cir. 1969), cert. denied, 405 U.S. 1040, 92 S.Ct. 1311, 31 L.Ed.2d 581; United States v. Hudson, 422 F. Supp. 395, 399 (D.C. Pa. 1976), aff'd without op., 556 F.2d 566 (3d Cir. 1976), cert. denied, 431 U.S. 922, 97 S.Ct. 2194, 53 L.Ed.2d 236 (1976).

[34] See, generally, 3 WEINSTEIN, ¶ 608[07]; 3 LOUISELL & MUELLER, § 310; Mc-CORMICK, § 131; 8 WIGMORE, § 2276. See also Rule 104(d) and related discussion, supra.

[35] In re Liddy, 506 F.2d 1293, 1300 (D.C. Cir. 1974); Park v. Huff, 506 F.2d 849, 864 n.1 (5th Cir.), cert. denied, 423 U.S. 824, 96 S.Ct. 38, 46 L.Ed.2d 40 (1975); United States v. Skolek, 474 F.2d 582, 585 (10th Cir. 1973). See, generally, 3 WEINSTEIN, ¶ 608[07], at 608-42; 3 LOUISELL & MUELLER, § 310; McCORMICK, § 135, at 284.

inquiry into misconduct which can no longer be prosecuted due to the expiration of the statute of limitations.[36] And, most notably, it does not curtail evidence of prior misconduct that is relevant to some issue other than credibility.[37] Accordingly, the Rule provides a relatively narrow exception to the general rule that all witnesses are subject to cross-examination for purposes of testing credibility.

[36] *See, generally,* 3 WEINSTEIN, ¶ 608[07], at 608-42-43; 3 LOUISELL & MUELLER, § 310; 8 WIGMORE, § 2279.

[37] *See, generally,* 3 WEINSTEIN, ¶ 608[07], at 608-43; 3 LOUISELL & MUELLER, § 310.

Chapter 609

RULE 609. IMPEACHMENT BY EVIDENCE OF CONVICTION OF CRIME

Rule 609 reads as follows:

(a) **General Rule.** For the purpose of attacking the credibility of a witness, evidence that he has been convicted of a crime shall be admitted if elicited from him or established by public record during cross-examination but only if the crime (1) was punishable by death or imprisonment in excess of one year under the law under which he was convicted, and the court determines that the probative value of admitting this evidence outweighs its prejudicial effect to the defendant, or (2) involved dishonesty or false statement, regardless of the punishment.

231

(b) Time Limit. Evidence of a conviction under this rule is not admissible if a period of more than ten years has elapsed since the date of the conviction or of the release of the witness from the confinement imposed for that conviction, whichever is the later date, unless the court determines, in the interests of justice, that the probative value of the conviction supported by specific facts and circumstances substantially outweighs its prejudicial effect. However, evidence of a conviction more than 10 years old as calculated herein, is not admissible unless the proponent gives to the adverse party sufficient advance written notice of intent to use such evidence to provide the adverse party with a fair opportunity to contest the use of such evidence.

(c) Effect of Pardon, Annulment, or Certificate of Rehabilitation. Evidence of a conviction is not admissible under this rule if (1) the conviction has been the subject of a pardon, annulment, certificate of rehabilitation, or other equivalent procedure based on a finding of the rehabilitation of the person convicted, and that person has not been convicted of a subsequent crime which was punishable by death or imprisonment in excess of one year, or (2) the conviction has been the subject of a pardon, annulment or other equivalent procedure based on a finding of innocence.

(d) Juvenile Adjudication. Evidence of juvenile adjudications is generally not admissible under this rule. The court may, however, in a criminal case allow evidence of a juvenile adjudication of a witness other than the accused if conviction of the offense would be admissible to attack the credibility of an adult and the court is satisfied that admission in evidence is necessary for a fair determination of the issue of guilt or innocence.

(e) Pendency of Appeal. The pendency of an appeal therefrom does not render evidence of a conviction inadmissible. Evidence of the pendency of an appeal is admissible.

§ 609.1   Rule 609(a)—Impeachment by Evidence of Conviction of Crime—In General.

Rule 609 governs the impeachment of a witness by evidence of prior criminal convictions of the witness.[1] Where a conviction is authorized by

---

[1] *See, generally*, McCormick, § 43; 3 Weinstein, ¶¶ 609[01]-[13]; 3 Louisell & Mueller, §§ 314-24; 3A Wigmore, §§ 980-88; 4 Wigmore, §§ 1106, 1116. *See also* Chestnut, *Problems, Policies and Objectives of the Oklahoma Pardon and Parole Board*, 32 Okla. B.A.J. 795 (1961); Friendly, *Is Innocence Irrelevant? Collateral Attack on Criminal Judgments*, 38 U. Chi. L. Rev. 142 (1970); Griswold, *The Long View*, 51 A.B.A.J. 1017 (1965); Ketcham, *Guidelines From Gault: Revolutionary Requirements and Reappraisal*, 53 Va. L. Rev. 1700 (1967); Schwartz, *Proposed Federal Rules of Evidence: An Introduction and Critique*, 38 U. Cin. L. Rev. 449 (1969); Weihofen, *Pardon: An Extraordinary Remedy*, 12 Rocky Mtn. L. Rev. 112 (1939).

Rule 609 as appropriate for impeachment, it may be proven through an acknowledgment by the witness on cross-examination or by documentation from a public record.[2] It is critical to note that evidence admitted under Rule 609 is directed to the limited purpose of impeaching the witness's credibility, and at least in theory, the Rule does not operate to contradict the general prohibition of certain forms of character evidence contained in Rule 404(b).[3]

Rule 609 has roots in traditional common law practice which generally rendered incompetent as a witness any person who had previously been convicted of treason, a felony or crimen falsi. Under modern practice, this blanket disqualification has been universally abandoned, and instead, the matter of past convictions has been transformed to issues of credibility and impeachment. Modern practice rests upon the assumption that certain prior convictions of a witness are probative of lack of credibility, or as courts have suggested, that a witness's demonstrated willingness to engage in antisocial conduct in one instance is probative of his willingness to give false testimony.[4]

Impeachment by evidence of a conviction frequently risks prejudice and confusion, and application of prior conviction impeachment may be particularly harsh where, for example, an accused who takes the stand suffers revelations of past criminal conduct. Despite limiting instructions, impeachment through conviction evidence operates in this situation as an invitation to the jury to draw an inference from past conduct concerning the propensity of the accused to commit the crime charged rather than an inference regarding his present propensity to tell the truth or lie on the witness stand. Nevertheless, the theory persists that the past criminal conduct resulting in conviction is indicative of an individual's present proclivity for untruthfulness in the provision of testimony.[5]

Rule 609(a) recognizes that in certain contexts evidence of a past conviction of a witness may result in excessive prejudice when compared to the benefit obtained in assisting the jury to assess credibility. Consequently,

[2] *See* United States v. Nevitt, 563 F.2d 406, 409 (9th Cir. 1977) (defense required to produce a public record of conviction to lay foundation for cross-examination of government witness). *See also* United States v. Scott, 592 F.2d 1139, 1141 (10th Cir. 1979).

[3] *See, generally,* 3 WEINSTEIN, ¶ 609[02]; 3 LOUISELL & MUELLER, § 319.

[4] *See, e.g.,* Blakney v. United States, 397 F.2d 648, 649-50 (D.C. Cir. 1968) ("as its language indicates, that law [D.C. Statute allowing impeachment by record of conviction] was put on the books almost 70 years ago for the primary purpose of removing the ancient common law disqualification of persons with criminal records from testifying in either civil or criminal cases. There is apparently no relevant legislative history, so we can only speculate as to why the attainder continued to some degree in the form of persuasive employment of the past conviction to impeach credibility").

[5] *See* United States v. Lipscomb, 702 F.2d 1049, 1058 n.36 (D.C. Cir. 1983) (en banc) United States v. Bailey, 426 F.2d 1236, 1243 (1970).

Rule 609(a) creates a special exercise of discretion which must be under-taken before certain types of convictions may be utilized by the prosecution in criminal cases. Also, consistent with the common law and pre-existing practice, certain convictions are rendered unavailable for impeachment because of minimal probity as to credibility. Reading subsections (a)(1) and (a)(2) of Rule 609 together, convictions which are wholly unavailable for impeachment are those which do not involve dishonesty or false statement and which are not punishable by death or imprisonment for an excess of one year. Accordingly, it should be noted that under the substance of Rule 609(a), impeachment through evidence of past convictions is appropriate in regard to all witnesses, parties and non-parties, in all cases, civil and criminal. Nevertheless, certain convictions are not available in regard to any witnesses (*i.e.*, petty crimes not involving dishonesty or false state-ment), and certain witnesses may only be impeached with certain convic-tions after an exercise of special judicial discretion (*i.e.*, defense witness in criminal cases in regard to convictions for crimes, otherwise permissible, which do not involve dishonesty and false statement). To summarize, for the purposes of affecting the credibility of a witness under Rule 609(a), convictions may be introduced by public documentation or by admission on cross-examination pertaining to: (1) crimes punishable by death or im-prisonment of more than one year, (a) for all witnesses in all civil proceed-ings, or (b) in criminal proceedings for all prosecution witnesses, or (c) when the prosecution seeks to impeach the criminal accused or witnesses testifying on his behalf and the court in its discretion allows the impeach-ment (subsection (a)(1); or (2)) crimes involving dishonesty or false state-ment regardless of the applicable sentence in all proceedings in regard to all witnesses (subsection (a)(2)).[6] The Rule authorizes the admission of evi-dence of convictions within these categories subject to the limitations ex-pressed in subsections (b) through (d). In any case, the evidence so admit-ted is for the limited purpose of evaluating a witness's credibility, and because danger exists that the trier of fact may misuse the information, a limiting instruction from the court is appropriate.[7]

§ 609.2   Operation of Discretionary Balancing Under Rule 609(a)(1)— Impeachment by Evidence of Capital Offenses and Crimes Punishable by Imprisonment in Excess of One Year.

Rule 609(a)(1) regulates the use of convictions for impeachment where the crime underlying the conviction is punishable by death or imprison-

---

[6] *See* 3 WEINSTEIN, ¶ 609[02].

[7] *See, generally*, 3 LOUISELL & MUELLER, § 315.

ment for in excess of one year. Also, Rule 609(a)(1) conditions the introduction of evidence of the convictions specified in the subsection upon the exercise of the court's determination that the conviction's probative value in assessing the credibility of the witness ". . . outweighs its prejudicial effect to the [criminal] defendant." The express language in Rule 609(a)(1) is admittedly confusing. Subsection (a)(1) refers unqualifiedly to "prejudicial effect to the defendant," and it is unclear from the face of the Rule that "defendant" was intended only to refer to a criminal defendant, *i.e.*, an "accused."[8] Moreover, even if it is understood that "defendant" refers to a criminal accused, subsection (a)(1) seems to suggest that it only authorizes impeachment for the convictions in its scope in regard to witnesses offered by the accused. Such an interpretation is clearly contrary to the intended application of subsection (a)(1). Rule 609(a)(1) applies in both civil[9] and criminal[10] cases, and it applies to all witnesses, parties and non-parties, in authorizing the impeachment use of convictions for crimes punishable by death or imprisonment in excess of one year.[11] The language pertaining to the "defendant" simply provides that for the crimes within the scope of subsection (a)(1), special discretion is to be exercised before defense witnesses in a criminal case are impeached pursuant to this technique.[12] (Of course, for convictions identified in subsection (a)(2), this special discretion is not applicable.) All other witnesses in both civil and criminal cases may be impeached with convictions where the crime underlying the conviction was punishable by death or imprisonment in excess of one year.[13] (Additionally, of course, such witnesses may also be impeached by convictions within the scope of subsection (a)(2).) Accordingly, in criminal cases a special buffer of judicial discretion is provided for defense witnesses in regard to the use of convictions identified in subsection (a)(1). Before permitting the impeachment in this context, the trial judge must balance probative value and prejudice as prescribed in the Rule.

Under the literal terms of Rule 609(a), the balancing required under subsection (a)(1) applies when the accused himself wishes to testify or when the accused calls a witness on his own behalf. Only in rare instances, however, will impeachment by prior conviction of a defense witness other

---

[8] *See, generally,* 3 Louisell & Mueller, § 316, at 324-25.

[9] *Id.*

[10] *Id.*

[11] *Id.*

[12] 3 Louisell & Mueller, (1984 Supplement), § 316, at 120.

[13] *See* United States v. Nevitt, 563 F.2d 406, 408-09 (9th Cir. 1977). *See also* United States v. Mahone, 537 F.2d 922, 928 (7th Cir. 1976), *cert. denied,* 429 U.S. 1025, 97 S.Ct. 646, 50 L.Ed.2d 627 (1976) (robbery within Rule 609(a)(1)); United States v. Wilson, 536 F.2d 883, 885 (9th Cir. 1976), *cert. denied,* 429 U.S. 982, 97 S.Ct. 497, 50 L.Ed.2d 592 (1976) (receiving stolen property within Rule 609(a)(1)); United States v. McMillan, 535 F.2d 1035, 1039 (8th Cir. 1976), *cert. denied,* 434 U.S. 1074, 98 S.Ct. 1262, 55 L.Ed.2d 779 (1976) (robbery within Rule 609(a)(1)). *See, e.g.,* McCormick, § 43, at 94.

than the accused himself impermissibly prejudice the accused.[14] For instance, if the crime committed by the defense witness is similar to the one with which the defendant is charged, the accused arguably may be prejudiced. Likewise, where a close family member of the accused testifies for the defense, convictions of such a witness may arguably result in "spillover" prejudice to the accused. These possibilities of prejudice to the accused resulting from impeachment of defense witnesses other than the accused himself are remote, and it is clear that the primary intent of Rule 609(a)(1) is to provide a buffer of discretion when the accused himself elects to testify.

Rule 609(a)(1) does not require the court to balance probative value and prejudice in permitting conviction impeachment of witnesses in a civil proceeding or in a criminal proceeding when prosecution witnesses testify.[15] Consequently, in these contexts eligible convictions should be admitted without a preliminary showing. Case law is unclear, however, whether impeachment otherwise available under Rule 609(a)(1) may be preempted by invoking Rule 403.[16]

Where balancing is required under Rule 609(a)(1) (i.e., on behalf of a criminal accused), a court must consider the type of prior crime committed by the witness.[17] Crimes that do not bear on credibility directly, such as murder or assault, are less probative of the witness's credibility than do crimes such as shoplifting or robbery which, by their elements, imply some

---

[14] United States v. Rosales, 680 F.2d 1304, 1306 (10th Cir. 1982). Cf. United States v. Edwards, 549 F.2d 362, 365 (5th Cir. 1977), cert. denied, 434 U.S. 828, 98 S.Ct. 107, 54 L.Ed.2d 87 (1978) (impeachment of codefendant by prior crimes not too prejudicial). See also United States v. Lewis, 626 F.2d 940, 950 (D.C. Cir. 1980); United States v. Barnes, 622 F.2d 107, 109 (5th Cir. 1980); United States v. Cohen, 544 F.2d 781, 785 (5th Cir. 1977), cert. denied, 431 U.S. 914, 97 S.Ct. 2175, 53 L.Ed.2d 224 (1977). See, generally, 3 WEINSTEIN, ¶ 609[05]; 3 LOUISELL & MUELLER, § 315.

[15] See United States v. Ortega, 561 F.2d 803, 806 (9th Cir. 1977); N.L.R.B. v. Jacob E. Decker and Sons, 569 F.2d 357, 362-63 (5th Cir. 1978).

[16] See Czajka v. Hickman, 703 F.2d 317, 319 (8th Cir. 1983); Shows v. M/V Red Eagle, 695 F.2d 114, 119 (5th Cir. 1983); United States v. Beahm, 664 F.2d 414, 417-18 (4th Cir. 1981); United States v. Martin, 563 F.2d 673, 680-81 n.16 (D.C. Cir. 1977).

See also United States v. Toney, 615 F.2d 277, 280 (5th Cir. 1980), cert. denied, 449 U.S. 985, 101 S.Ct. 403, 66 L.Ed.2d 248 (1980).

[17] Gordon v. United States, 383 F.2d 936, 939 (D.C. Cir. 1967), cert. denied, 390 U.S. 1029, 88 S.Ct. 1421, 20 L.Ed.2d 287 (1968) ("[L]uck also contemplated that it was for the defendant to present to the trial court sufficient reasons for withholding past convictions from the jury in the face of a statute which makes such convictions admissible; the underlying assumption was that prior convictions would ordinarily be admissible unless this burden is met"). See also United States v. Hayes, 553 F.2d 824, 828 (2d Cir. 1977), cert. denied, 434 U.S. 867, 98 S.Ct. 204, 54 L.Ed.2d 142 (1977); United States v. Smith, 551 F.2d 348, 359-60 (D.C. Cir. 1976). Cf., United States v. Preston, 608 F.2d 626, 638 n.14 (5th Cir. 1979); United States v. Vanderbosch, 610 F.2d 95, 98 (2d Cir. 1979).

dishonesty.[18] (Crimes directly involving dishonesty or false statement, such as perjury or fraud will be admissible to impeach a witness under Rule 609(a)(2) discussed in § 609.3 of this Treatise.) However, under Rule 609(a)(1), even a crime with little bearing upon credibility may be admitted for impeachment purposes, if it is not outweighed by the prejudicial impact to the defendant.[19]

In determining the probative value of the prior conviction, the past conviction history of the witness may be considered.[20] The length of time which has elapsed since the witness's conviction or release from prison is an objective manifestation of the witness's break with his criminal past.[21] A conviction that is excessively stale may also be rendered inadmissible to impeach a witness under Rule 609(b).

Whether the impeachment by the prior conviction will be allowed may also depend upon the importance of assessing the credibility of the witness to be impeached.[22] The similarity between the prior crime committed by the accused and the crime with which he is charged will affect the likelihood of unfair prejudice to the accused if the prior crime is admitted for impeachment.[23] If the prior crime and the charged crime are similar, it is more likely the jury will ignore the judge's limiting instruction to consider the conviction only on the issue of credibility, and consider the past conviction as evidence of the accused's propensity to commit the charged crime. Such an application of the conviction is an impermissible inference under Rule 404 and severally prejudicial to the accused.

The tactical need for the accused to testify in her own behalf may militate against use of his prior convictions. If it is apparent to the trial court

[18] United States v. Halbert, 668 F.2d 489, 495 (10th Cir. 1982), *cert. denied*, 456 U.S. 934, 102 S.Ct. 1989, 72 L.Ed. 453 (1928) (mail fraud, false pretenses, aggravated robbery). *See also* United States v. Crawford, 613 F.2d 1045, 1052 (D.C. Cir. 1979).

[19] United States v. Fountain, 642 F.2d 1083, 1091-92 (7th Cir. 1981), *cert. denied*, 451 U.S. 993, 101 S.Ct. 2335, 68 L.Ed.2d 854 (1982) (premeditated murder; acknowledged general rule that a court should "err on the side of excluding a challenged prior conviction," but trial court could have concluded that the probative value of the conviction did outweigh its prejudicial effect).

[20] *E.g.,* United States v. Jones, 647 F.2d 696, 700 (6th Cir.), *cert. denied*, 454 U.S. 898, 102 S.Ct. 399, 70 L.Ed.2d 214 (1981).

[21] *E.g.,* United States v. Field, 625 F.2d 862, 872 (9th Cir. 1980).

[22] United States v. Rosales, 680 F.2d 1304, 1306 (10th Cir. 1982) (probative value present, since witnesses were inmates whose testimony directly contradicted that of the guards; also inmates were serving substantial terms, giving them some motivation to testify falsely in a dispute with prison guards, diminishing prejudice); United States v. Bogers, 635 F.2d 749, 750 (8th Cir. 1980) (cross-examination of defendant concerning state felony conviction permitted, because of the conflict in testimony between government and defense witnesses and the consequent importance of credibility issues). *See also* United States v. Jackson, 627 F.2d 1198, 1208-10 (D.C. App. 1980); United States v. Barnes, 622 F.2d 107, 109 (5th Cir. 1980).

[23] *See* United States v. Fay, 668 F.2d 345, 379 (8th Cir. 1981); United States v. Beahm, 664 F.2d 414, 419 (4th Cir. 1981).

that the accused must testify to refute strong prosecution evidence, then the court should consider whether by permitting conviction impeachment, the court in effect prevents the accused from testifying in his own behalf.[24]

The court's ruling under Rule 609(a)(1) should properly be decided prior to trial[25] and its rationale fully articulated on the record.[26] The prosecution has the burden of persuading the court that impeachment should be allowed under this subdivision.[27] The United States Supreme Court has ruled, however, that the trial court's *in limine* ruling under Rule 609(a)(1) is preserved and available for review only if the accused testifies at trial.[28] The precise nature of the defendant's testimony is necessary on review to weigh the prior conviction's probative value against its prejudicial effect as required under Rule 609(a)(1).[29] The absence of the defendant's testimony would force a reviewing court to speculate whether the District Court would have actually allowed the prior conviction as impeachment evidence since the initial *in limine* rulings are subject to change during the trial.[30] Furthermore, the court would be forced to speculate whether the government would have actually used the prior convictions to impeach the defendant, especially where the defendant is subject to impeachment by other means.[31] In addition, the reviewing court cannot assume that the trial court's adverse ruling was the sole reason for the defendant's decision not to testify.[32] Finally, an *in limine* ruling under Rule 609(a), reviewable even when the defendant did not testify, would almost always result in an automatic reversal because the error that presumptively kept the defendant from testifying would not be considered "harmless."[33] Consequently, the

[24] United States v. Mehrmanesh, 682 F.2d 1303, 1309 (9th Cir. 1982); United States v. Jackson, 627 F.2d 1198, 1208-10 (D.C. Cir. 1980).

[25] *See* United States v. Burkhead, 646 F.2d 1283, 1285-86 (8th Cir. 1981), *cert. denied*, 454 U.S. 898, 102 S.Ct. 399, 70 L.Ed.2d 214 (1981); United States v. Cook, 608 F.2d 1178, 1186-89 (9th Cir. 1979). *See also* United States v. Oakes, 565 F.2d 170, 172 (1st Cir. 1977) (explicit statements by District Court on the record revealing its knowledge of Rule 609(a) and basis for its resolution of the balancing problem "are most helpful to this court in carrying out our review").

[26] United States v. Preston, 608 F.2d 626, 639 (5th Cir. 1979); United States v. Seamaster, 568 F.2d 188, 191 (10th Cir. 1978); United States v. Mahone, 537 F.2d 922, 929 (7th Cir.), *cert. denied*, 429 U.S. 1025, 97 S.Ct. 646, 50 L.Ed.2d 627 (1976).

[27] *E.g.*, Government of Virgin Islands v. Bedford, 671 F.2d 758, 761 (3d Cir. 1982) (trial court's permitting impeachment of defendant by cross-examination concerning his prior conviction for possession of a switchblade knife was error, but harmless; felony conviction is not automatically admissible); United States v. Hendershot, 614 F.2d 648, 651-53 (9th Cir. 1980) (ruling that prior bank robbery conviction would be usable to impeach defendant was reversible error; trial judge did not balance probative worth against prejudicial impact as he should have under Rule 609(a)(1)).

[28] Luce v. United States, 469 U.S. 38, 83 L.Ed.2d 443, 105 S.Ct. 460, 461 (1984).

[29] *Id*. at 448.

[30] *Id*.

[31] *Id*.

[32] *Id*.

[33] *Id*.

defendant's testimony is necessary to determine the impact of any erroneous impeachment in light of the record as a whole.[34] The testimony also discourages motions to exclude impeachment evidence made solely to "plant" reversible error in the event of a conviction.[35]

§ 609.3   Rule 609(a)(1)—Convictions Appropriate for Impeachment Under Subsection (a)(1) of Rule 609.

Rule 609(a)(1) applies to those convictions which are punishable by death or imprisonment for more than one year under the relevant state or federal law. (Convictions for crimes involving dishonesty or false statement, regardless of punishment, are admissible under Rule 609(a)(2).) Accordingly, in regard to crimes which do not involve dishonesty or false statement, Rule 609(a) looks to the maximum possible punishment accompanying the conviction, and it is notable that the Rule is cast in terms of the possible maximum sentence for a conviction in the jurisdiction in which the conviction was sustained.[36] Operation of the Rule does not depend upon the sentence that was actually imposed.[37] For example, a witness convicted of a drug-related offense punishable by imprisonment in excess of one year who received a suspended sentence may be impeached by evidence of the conviction. The crime was punishable by a term of incarceration within the scope of the Rule.

§ 609.4   Operation of Rule 609(a)(2)—Offenses in the Nature of Crimen Falsi: Interplay with Rule 403.

Under Rule 609(a)(2), all convictions for crimes involving dishonesty or false statement, regardless of the possible punishment, are admissible for the purpose of impeaching witnesses.[38] Thus, read together, Rule 609(a)(1) and (a)(2) provide that the only convictions never available for impeachment are those convictions which are punishable by imprisonment for one year or less and which do not involve dishonesty or false statement.

---

[34] *Id.* at 448-449.

[35] *Id.* at 449.

[36] *See* United States v. McLister, 608 F.2d 785, 789 n.4 (9th Cir. 1979). *See, generally,* 3 LOUISELL & MUELLER, § 316.

[37] United States v. Hall, 588 F.2d 613, 615 n.4 (8th Cir. 1978) (narcotics prosecution; no error to permit cross-examination of defendant concerning two prior felony convictions for distribution and possession of heroin, even though accused received suspended sentence for the conviction). *See, generally,* 3 LOUISELL & MUELLER, § 316.

[38] H.R. CONF. REP. No. 93-1597, 93d Cong., 2d Sess. 9 (1974).

If the conviction is of a type admissible to impeach a witness under 609(a)(2), the question remains whether the court can exclude the impeachment evidence by applying Rule 403 and finding the value of allowing impeachment by prior conviction is substantially outweighed by potential prejudice to a party. The essence of the conflict appears between the view that Rule 403 supersedes all the evidentiary rules[39] and the alternate position that since Congress debated Rule 609 extensively, the Rule should be considered the final authority on impeachment by prior conviction.[40] While the issue is not finally settled, the majority of the circuits will not allow exclusion of evidence under Rule 403.[41]

The debate may have more academic than practical importance. Because of the high probative value of convictions involving dishonesty or false statement, Rule 403 would be invoked successfully in the context of Rule 609(a)(2) convictions only on rare occasions. Nevertheless, Rule 403 represents the embodiment of longstanding inherent authority reposed in the trial judge to protect the integrity of the fact-finding process. Its abrogation in any context should not be lightly considered.

§ 609.5   Rule 609(a)(2)—Convictions Available for Impeachment Without Regard to Possible Penalty.

Rule 609(a)(2) does not attempt to delineate precisely which offenses may be characterized as supporting convictions involving "dishonesty or

[39] *See* United States v. Lipscomb, 702 F.2d 1049, 1057 n.28 (where defendant testified in his trial for possession of heroin with intent to distribute, he could be impeached by eight-year old robbery conviction, since he was a repeat offender and had been released from prison only a year-and-a-half ago); United States v. Provenzano, 620 F.2d 985, 1003 n.23 (3d Cir. 1980), *cert. denied*, 449 U.S. 899, 101 S.Ct. 267, 66 L.Ed.2d 129 (1980) (in prosecution for alleged labor racketeering, proper to admit convictions for extortion and conspiracy involving kickbacks if defendant testified); United States v. Hayes, 553 F.2d 824, 827 n.4 (2d Cir. 1977), *cert. denied*, 434 U.S. 867, 98 S.Ct. 204, 54 L.Ed.2d 143 (1977).

[40] United States v. Wong, 703 F.2d 65, 68 (3d Cir. 1983), *cert. denied*, 104 S.Ct. 140 (1983); United States v. Kiendra, 663 F.2d 349, 351 (1st Cir. 1981); United States v. Cunningham, 638 F.2d 696, 698 (4th Cir. 1981) (no error to curtail attack, since burden is upon proponent of establishing prior

conviction that such conviction was punishable by death or imprisonment in excess of one year); United States v. Leyva, 659 F.2d 118, 121 (9th Cir. 1981), *cert. denied*, 454 U.S. 1156, 102 S.Ct. 1030, 71 L.Ed.2d 315 (1982); United States v. Coats, 652 F.2d 1002, 1003 (D.C. Cir. 1981); United States v. Toney, 615 F.2d 277, 280 (5th Cir. 1980), *cert. denied*, 449 U.S. 985, 101 S.Ct. 403, 66 L.Ed.2d 248 (1980), (mail fraud is a crime involving dishonesty, to which 609(a)(2) applies); United States v. Mucci, 630 F.2d 737, 743-44 (10th Cir. 1980).

[41] United States v. Wong, 703 F.2d 65, 67-68 (3d Cir. 1983); United States v. Kiendra, 663 F.2d 343, 353-55 (1st Cir. 1981); United States v. Leyva, 659 F.2d 118, 121-22 (9th Cir. 1981); United States v. Coats, 652 F.2d 1002, 1003 (D.C. Cir. 1981); United States v. Williams, 642 F.2d 136, 140 (5th Cir. 1981); United States v. Cunningham, 633 F.2d 696, 698 (4th Cir. 1981); United States v. Toney, 615 F.2d 277, 279-80 (5th Cir. 1980).

false statement." Consequently, it is unclear on the face of the Rule whether the Rule is strictly co-extensive with the common law identification of crimen falsi convictions or whether it encompasses a broader class of crimes. It would logically appear that since admissibility of such evidence is generally predicated upon a conviction for specific conduct, the statutory definition of the crime should not control its availability for impeachment. Rather, the trial court should look to the underlying facts of the conviction to decide whether the conviction is supported by conduct that logically involves deceit, false statement or dishonesty.[42]

Consequently, the approach which is consistent with the modern justification for permitting such impeachment would hold that in applying Rule 609(a)(2) courts should analyze the conduct supporting the conviction for the specific purpose of determining the legitimacy of any adverse inferences as to a witness's credibility. While there is no question that a rather mechanical approach of focusing on the statutory elements of a conviction provides a rule of convenience in a somewhat confusing area of the law, the fact remains that such an approach too often manifests itself in the introduction of impeachment evidence of little or no probative value. If impeachment of witnesses is truly collateral to the main issues in any trial, impeachment under Rule 609(a)(2) should not be permitted absent a clear nexus between the offending conduct and the witness's propensity for untruthfulness. To apply Rule 609(a)(2) otherwise would be to permit the mere fact of conviction to override the fundamental purpose of such impeachment evidence, namely, to expose a defect in the witness's credibility.

Case law is instructive in determining whether the type of criminal activity resulting in conviction may be characterized as involving dishonesty or false statement. There is no question, for instance, that convictions for criminal activity such as perjury, subornation of perjury, bribery, false statement, criminal fraud, embezzlement, false pretense or concealment fall within the scope of the Rule,[43] while crimes solely involving force, assault, disorderly conduct, criminal damaging, public intoxication or driving under the influence do not.[44]

[42] E.g., United States v. Grandmont, 680 F.2d 867, 870-72 (1st Cir. 1982); United States v. Glenn, 667 F.2d 1269, 1273 (9th Cir. 1982). But see 3 WEINSTEIN, ¶ 609[04] (commentator adopts position taken by court in United States v. Lewis, 626 F.2d 940 (D.C. Cir. 1980), asserting that admissibility of a conviction depends on whether the crime involved "dishonesty or false statement" as an element of the statutory offense).

[43] United States v. Wong, 703 F.2d 65, 67 (3d Cir. 1983); United States v. Cunningham, 638 F.2d 696, 698-99 (4th Cir. 1981). See, generally, 3 WEINSTEIN, ¶ 609[04], at 609-71; 3 LOUISELL & MUELLER, § 317.

[44] See, generally, 3 WEINSTEIN, ¶ 609[04]; 3 LOUISELL & MUELLER, § 317; McCORMICK, §43; 2 WIGMORE, § 520. See also United States v. Cook, 608 F.2d 1175, 1186-89 (9th Cir. 1979) (en banc); United States v. Cavender, 578 F.2d 528, 530-31 and n.5 (4th Cir. 1978); United States v. Oakes, 565 F.2d 170, 172 (1st Cir. 1977).

More difficult problems, however, surround criminal activity involving the taking of another's property, such as robbery, burglary, theft, larceny and shoplifting.[45] Likewise, such crimes as possession or sale of narcotics, procuring, soliciting and prostitution lie within this uncharted area. If the scope of the phrase "dishonesty or false statement" is held to be coextensive with the historical concept of crimen falsi (*i.e.*, offenses characterized by an element of deceit of deliberate interference with the ascertainment of truth by a court or other official investigatory body), convictions for such crimes as theft and narcotics possession would be inadmissible under subsection (a)(2), although, depending on possible penalty, they may be admissible under Rule 609(a)(1). If, however, Rule 609(a)(2) is held to encompass more than the traditional notion of crimen falsi, such criminal conduct as theft and sale of narcotics may fall within the scope of the Rule. It remains doubtful, however, that possessory crimes, such as receiving stolen property or possession of a small amount of marijuana, would be admissible for impeachment purposes under subsection (a)(2).

§ 609.6   What Constitutes "Conviction" Under Rule 609.

By expressly providing that impeachment of witnesses may be effected through the introduction of certain convictions, Rule 609(a) does not authorize the use of prior arrests or indictments. The Rule, however, does not preclude use of a pending indictment against a witness for an impeachment purpose other than that regulated by Rule 609. For example, a pending indictment or arrest may be probative in showing bias, prejudice, interest or coercion.[46] Accordingly, where a witness has been jointly indicted with the accused but awarded a separate trial, the witness's credibility may be impaired due to his interest in securing a favorable outcome at his own trial. For example, a witness indicted for receiving stolen property from the accused has an interest in the outcome of the action against the accused for theft. In this situation, the evidence of the witness's pending indictment may be admitted, not to impeach his general character for truthfulness under Rule 609, but to show that his or her testimony may be biased or prejudiced.[47]

[45] United States v. Lipscomb, 702 F.2d 1049, 1071 (D.C. Cir. 1983); United States v. Grandmont, 680 F.2d 867, 870-71 (1st Cir. 1982); United States v. Del Toro Soto, 676 F.2d 13, 18 (1st Cir. 1982); United States v. Glenn, 667 F.2d 1269, 1272-73 (9th Cir. 1982). *See, generally,* 3 Weinstein, ¶ 609[04], at 609-72-73; 3 Louisell & Mueller, § 317.

[46] *See,* 3A Wigmore, at 949; 3 Louisell & Mueller, § 319.

[47] United States v. Martinez, 555 F.2d 1273, 1276 (5th Cir. 1977) (prosecution for conspiracy to distribute cocaine; reversible error to allow cross-examination of defendant concerning conviction for aiding and abetting in the commission of the same offense).

Generally, arrests or indictments not leading to convictions and not pending at the time of testifying are inadmissible.[48] Similarly, convictions which have been reversed on appeal prior to the witness's taking the stand are not available for impeachment use under the Rule, since the reversal vitiates the conviction.[49] This result obtains whether the reversal was occasioned by a finding in the appellate court that the guilty verdict was against the manifest weight of the evidence or that prejudicial procedural error attended the trial. In either event, whether the accused is discharged or the cause remanded for retrial, the conviction is erased as the fundament for Rule 609 impeachment.

Under Rule 609 a confession or a plea of nolo contendere with a subsequent finding of guilty is equivalent to a conviction.[50]

§ 609.7   Introduction of the Conviction.

Impeachment through prior convictions may be effected through an acknowledgment of the conviction by the witness sought to be impeached or by the introduction of a public record of the conviction during the course of the cross-examination.[51] Regardless of whether an acknowledgment of the conviction or the introduction of a public record is utilized, the impeachment must be effected while the witness is on the stand. Because a certified public record is generally self-authenticating under Rule 902, no special foundation is necessary for the introduction of the certified public record.[52]

When the cross-examination seeks to obtain an admission from the witness sought to be impeached that he has suffered a conviction, specific information about the conviction should be elicited. The date and place of the conviction should be established. Likewise, the witness may be asked about any sentence that was imposed. Generally, in order to minimize the prejudicial effect, impeachment may not inquire into exact details concerning the conviction.[53] Whenever a prior conviction is utilized for the purposes of impeaching the credibility of a witness, the proponent of the

---

[48] *E.g.*, United States v. Werbrouck, 589 F.2d 273, 277 (7th Cir. 1978), *cert. denied*, 440 U.S. 962, 99 S.Ct. 1507, 59 L.Ed.2d 776 (1978) (police officer planting marijuana on certain person, which led to discharge of officer from police department, did not amount to conviction admissible to impeach under Rule 609). *See also* United States v. Ling, 581 F.2d 1118, 1121 (4th Cir. 1978).

[49] United States v. Williams, 484 F.2d 428, 430-31 (8th Cir. 1973). *See, generally,* 3 LOUISELL & MUELLER, § 323.

[50] United States v. Williams, 642 F.2d 136, 138-40 (5th Cir. 1981).

[51] *E.g.*, United States v. Bovain, 708 F.2d 606, 613-14 (11th Cir. 1983).

[52] *See* 5 WEINSTEIN, ¶ 902(4)[01]; 5 LOUISELL & MUELLER, § 532, at 192.

[53] *E.g.*, United States v. Boyer, 150 F.2d 595, 596 (D.C. Cir. 1945).

witness impeached should request a limiting instruction under Rule 105 to minimize the prejudicial impact of the conviction and to insure that the jury will use the conviction only for the purposes of evaluating the credibility of the witness.

As a rehabilitative device, nothing in the Rule prohibits an "explanation" by the witness of extenuating circumstances of the conviction. Some courts permit "brief protestations" of innocence or testimony of extenuating circumstances to explain away the implications of a conviction. No collateral evidence of such extenuating circumstances, however, should be permitted in rehabilitation efforts.[54]

§ 609.8　Rule 609(b)—Time Limit.

Under Rule 609(b), if more than ten years has elapsed since the date of conviction or the termination of confinement, whichever is later, the conviction is not admissible unless the court finds that the probative value of such evidence substantially outweighs its prejudicial effect. The applicable period should be measured up to the date upon which the witness testifies, since the trier of fact must evaluate credibility at that moment.[55]

Where a party seeks to introduce evidence of a conviction that predates the ten-year limitation, the proponent must provide the adverse party with sufficient advance notice in writing of its intent to employ such evidence in order to provide ample opportunity to contest the use of the conviction. The burden is on the proponent of such evidence to persuade the court that the probative value substantially outweighs its unfair prejudicial effect, and in ruling on such matters, the court should make an on-the-record finding supported by articulated facts and circumstances justifying the introduction.[56]

§ 609.9　Rule 609(c)—Effect of Pardon, Annulment or Certification of Rehabilitation.

Rule 609(c) provides that evidence of a conviction is not admissible for the purpose of impeachment where a pardon, annulment, certificate of

[54] United States v. Canniff, 521 F.2d 565, 569 (2d Cir. 1975), *cert. denied*, 423 U.S. 1059, 96 S.Ct. 796, 46 L.Ed.2d 650 (1976); Fagerstrom v. United States, 311 F.2d 717, 720 (8th Cir. 1963); Thomas v. United States, 121 F.2d 905, 907-909 (D.C. Cir. 1941).

[55] United States v. Cathey, 591 F.2d 268, 274 n.13, 278 n.2 (5th Cir. 1979) (majority suggested correct point from which to measure is the date one testified rather than the date when the trial commenced). *See, generally*, 3 WEINSTEIN, ¶ 609[07], at 609-91.

[56] United States v. Cavender, 578 F.2d 528, 531-32 (4th Cir. 1978).

rehabilitation or other equivalent procedure is based either (i) upon a finding of innocence, or (ii) upon a required showing of rehabilitation and where the witness has not subsequently been convicted of a felony.

The Rule rests upon the theory that since a conviction is legally reflective of the witness's untrustworthiness, the effect on credibility may not be abated by a pardon based upon a finding other than that of innocence. Where the reasons for extending a pardon or annulment are not related to innocence, such as where a pardon is granted due to political influence or overcrowded jail conditions, the conviction is still probative of credibility.[57] By comparison, a pardon based upon a subsequent finding of innocence negates the presumption of untrustworthiness flowing from the conviction and, consequently, it abrogates the attendant negative effect on credibility.

While not negating the original damage to credibility, a finding of rehabilitation is believed to serve as sufficient evidence that the witness is now credible, *i.e.*, he should not suffer the stigma of untrustworthiness associated with a past conviction.[58]

The burden of proving that a witness's prior conviction is inadmissible under Rule 609(c) rests with the party who opposes the use of the conviction, and it must be demonstrated that the pardon, annulment or equivalent procedure bars introduction of an otherwise admissible conviction.[59]

§ 609.10   Rule 609(d)—Juvenile Adjudications.

Rule 609(d) establishes a general principle that evidence of the juvenile adjudication of a witness is not admissible for the purpose of impeaching his testimony. The principle is predicated upon the dual concept that juvenile adjudications of delinquency are not probative of the witness's propensity to tell the truth as an adult and that since the purpose of the juvenile proceeding is not to punish the individual, it is undesirable to allow the juvenile offense to be treated as a criminal conviction that bears on the witness's credibility.[60]

Evidence of a juvenile adjudication is admissible under Rule 609(d) to impeach the witness in a limited situation, *i.e.*, when the judge determines

---

[57] *See* 3 WEINSTEIN, ¶ 609[08].

[58] *See, generally*, 3 WEINSTEIN, ¶ 609[08]; 3 LOUISELL & MUELLER, § 321.

[59] United States v. Wiggins, 566 F.2d 944, 946 (5th Cir. 1978), *cert. denied*, 436 U.S. 950, 98 S.Ct. 2859, 56 L.Ed.2d 793 (1978) (fact that defendant was released from a Halfway House, where he had been placed as a condition of his probation on a drug offense did not make the conviction usable where neither the program and objectives of the institution nor the qualification required for release were demonstrated).

[60] *See* United States v. Ashley, 569 F.2d 975, 978 (5th Cir.), *cert. denied*, 439 U.S. 854, 99 S.Ct. 163, 58 L.Ed.2d 159 (1978).

in a criminal proceeding that admission of the evidence is necessary for a fair determination of the defendant's guilt or innocence. This exception to the general rule prohibiting impeachment by juvenile adjudication is inapplicable in civil proceedings or where the witness to be impeached is the criminal defendant.

The Rule does not preclude impeachment of a witness by inquiring into conduct for which the witness, although a juvenile at the time, was tried, convicted and sentenced as an adult where a distinct basis for admissibility is present.[61] The Rule also allows a party to use a juvenile record to impeach a witness by contradiction, since Rule 609 does not regulate contradiction as an impeachment device.[62] Nor may the Rule operate so as to deny a constitutional right of a litigant, such as where an expunged juvenile record must be disclosed to enable the accused to present relevant evidence regarding a material aspect of his defense.[63]

§ 609.11   Rule 609(e)—Effect of Pendency of Appeal.

Since the Rule is cast in terms of convictions, the final provision of Rule 609 permits the introduction of prior convictions for the purpose of impeachment despite the fact that an appeal is pending on the conviction used for impeachment.[64] The Rule provides, however, that where a witness is questioned about a prior conviction which has since been appealed, the fact that the appeal is pending is admissible. Thus, the matter of the appeal is left to the trier of fact in weighing the conviction in regard to the issue of credibility, and the pendency of the appeal is appropriate for comment during closing argument.

[61] United States v. Canniff, 521 F.2d 565, 569 (2d Cir. 1975), *cert. denied*, 423 U.S. 1059, 96 S.Ct. 796, 46 L.Ed.2d 650 (1975).

[62] Davis v. Alaska, 415 U.S. 308, 319, 94 S.Ct. 1105, 1112, 39 L.Ed.2d 347, 355 (1974) (right of confrontation is paramount to the state's policy of protecting a juvenile offender).

[63] *Id.*

[64] United States v. Klayer, 707 F.2d 892, 895 (6th Cir.), *cert. denied*, 104 S.Ct. 180 (1983); United States v. De La Torre, 639 F.2d 245, 248-49 (5th Cir. 1981).

Chapter 610

RULE 610. RELIGIOUS BELIEFS
OR OPINIONS

SECTION

610.1 Religious beliefs or opinions as affecting credibility of witness—
In general

610.2 Admissible evidence of religious beliefs

Rule 610 reads as follows:

Evidence of the beliefs or opinions of a witness on matters of religion is not admissible for the purpose of showing that by reason of their nature his credibility is impaired or enhanced.

§ 610.1 Religious Beliefs or Opinions as Affecting Credibility of Witness—In General.

Rule 610 generally proscribes the introduction of evidence as to religious beliefs or opinions for the purpose of impeaching or bolstering a witness's credibility.[1] The Rule is in harmony with prior federal practice, which has for a number of years forbidden inquiry into the religious beliefs of a party for the purpose of impeaching his credibility.[2]

The principle of inadmissibility contained in Rule 610 rests upon grounds of unfair prejudice and minimal probative value,[3] and it is likely derived, at least obliquely, from the federal constitutional guarantees of

[1] See, generally, 3 WEINSTEIN, ¶ 610[01]; 3 LOUISELL & MUELLER, § 329; McCORMICK, § 48; 3 WIGMORE, § 936. See also Swancara, Impeachment of Non-Religious Witness, 13 ROCKY MTN. L. REV. 336 (1941); Non-Religious Witness, 8 WIS. L. REV. 49 (1932); Note, Evidence — Impeaching Witness by Showing Religious Belief, 9 N.C. L. REV. 77 (1930).

[2] See 3 WEINSTEIN, ¶ 610[01], at 610-4; 3 LOUISELL & MUELLER, § 329, at 388.

[3] United States v. Sampol, 636 F.2d 621, 666 (D.C. Cir. 1980); Government of Virgin Islands v. Petersen, 553 F.2d 324, 327 (3d Cir. 1977). Cf., La Rocca v. Lane, 37 N.Y.2d 575, 583, 376 N.Y.S.2d 93, 101, 338 N.E.2d 606, 614 (1975), cert. denied, 424 U.S. 968, 96 S.Ct. 1464, 47 L.Ed.2d 734 (1976).

the free exercise of religion.[4] Accordingly, the Rule prohibits inquiries on cross-examination into the religious beliefs, or lack thereof, of a witness for the purpose of testing the witness's ability to tell the truth.

It should be noted that although Rule 603 still requires a witness to swear or affirm before testifying that he will do so truthfully, the option of an affirmation allows the witness to avoid basing the declaration on any religious conviction.

§ 610.2   Admissible Evidence of Religious Belief.

Since the impeachment process is limited by the concepts of relevancy and unfair prejudice, the Rule restricts the introduction of evidence related to religious beliefs. The Rule does not, however, foreclose the admission of evidence of religious beliefs where such evidence is relevant in a manner other than to show that the witness's trustworthiness is enhanced or diminished by virtue of religious convictions. Accordingly, the Rule does not exclude evidence tending to demonstrate bias or interest on the part of a witness, such as where the witness is affiliated with a church that is a party to the action. Under these circumstances, the probative value of the evidence is focused on a permissible target of inquiry, *e.g.*, bias or interest, rather than on the witness's inclination toward credibility as indicated by the nature of his religious beliefs or opinions.[5]

---

[4] *See, generally*, 3 Weinstein, ¶ 610[01]; 3 Louisell & Mueller, § 329; McCormick, § 48, at 104; 2 Wigmore, §§ 518, 936, 2213.

[5] *See, generally*, 3 Weinstein, ¶ 610[01]; 3 Louisell & Mueller, § 329; McCormick, § 48, at 104 n.68; 2 Wigmore, § 936.

Chapter 611

RULE 611. MODE AND ORDER OF INTERROGATION AND PRESENTATION

Rule 611 reads as follows:

(a) **Control by Court.** The Court shall exercise reasonable control over the mode and order of interrogating witnesses and presenting evidence so as to (1) make the interrogation and presentation effective for the ascertainment of the truth, (2) avoid needless consumption of time and, (3) protect witnesses from harassment or undue embarrassment.

(b) **Scope of Cross-Examination.** Cross-examination should be limited to the subject matter of the direct examination and matters affecting the credibility of the witness. The court may, in the exercise of discretion, permit inquiry into additional matters as if on direct examination.

(c) **Leading Questions.** Leading questions should not be used on the direct examination of a witness except as may be necessary to develop his testimony. Ordinarily leading questions should be permitted on cross-examination. When a party calls a hostile witness, an adverse party, or a witness identified with an adverse party, interrogation may be by leading questions.

§ 611.1 Rule 611—Background and Purpose.

Rule 611 addresses the trial court's control over the mode and order of interrogating witnesses and presenting evidence, the scope of cross-examination and the use of leading questions.[1] Essentially, the Rule embodies general principles enunciated elsewhere throughout the Rules, e.g., Rules 102 and 403, and it specifically applies those principles to witnesses. It is designed to encourage flexibility in the reception of evidence by promoting the efficient determination of the truth without unnecessary abuse of the dignity of witnesses.[2]

Rule 611(a) gives the trial court authority to control the interrogation of witnesses and the presentation of evidence. In the exercise of its discretion, the trial court is guided by three generalized principles, any or all of which may serve as the basis for the court's decision: (i) efficient ascertainment of truth;[3] (ii) avoidance of needless consumption of time;[4] and (iii) protection of witnesses from harassment or undue embarrassment.[5]

[1] See, generally, McCORMICK, §§ 5, 6, 19-31; 3 WEINSTEIN, ¶¶ 611[01]-[06]; 3 LOUISELL & MUELLER, §§ 333-43; 3 WIGMORE, §§ 768-80; 5 WIGMORE, §§ 1390-94; 6 WIGMORE, §§ 1884-94; 8 WIGMORE, § 2276. See also Bergman, A Practical Approach to Cross-Examination: Safety First, 25 U.C.L.A. L. REV. 547 (1978); Carlson, Scope of Cross-Examination and the Proposed Federal Rules, 32 FED. B.J. 244 (1973); Carlson, Cross-Examination of the Accused, 52 CORNELL L.Q. 705 (1967); Cleary, Evidence As a Problem in Communicating, 5 VAND. L. REV. 277 (1952); Degnan Non-Rules Evidence Law: Cross-Examination, 6 UTAH L. REV. 323 (1959); Denbeaux and Risinger, Questioning Questions: Objections to Form in the Interrogation of Witnesses, 33 ARK. L. REV. 439 (1980); Denroche, Leading Questions, 6 CRIM. L. Q. 21 (1963); Friendly, The Fifth Amendment Tomorrow: The Case for Constitutional Change, 37 U. CIN. L. REV. 671 (1968); Lawson, Order of Presentation as a Factor in Jury Persuasion, 56 KY. L.J. 523 (1968); Marshall, Marquis and Oskamp, Effects of Kind of Questions and Atmosphere of Interrogation on Accuracy and Completeness of Testimony, 84 HARV. L. REV. 1620 (1971); Westen, Order of Proof: An Accused's Right to Control the Timing and Sequence of Evidence in His Defense, 66 CALIF. L. REV. 935 (1978).

[2] See, e.g., United States v. Kizer, 569 F.2d 504, 505 (9th Cir. 1978), cert. denied, 435 U.S. 976, 98 S.Ct. 1626, 56 L.Ed.2d 71 (1978) (defense counsel properly prevented from asking prosecution witness about prior drug use and hospitalization for drug ad-

diction; sixth amendment interest outweighed by danger of harassing witness). See also Goings v. United States, 377 F.2d 753, 762-63 (9th Cir. 1967), later app., 393 F.2d 884 (8th Cir. 1967), cert. denied, 393 U.S. 883, 89 S.Ct. 191, 21 L.Ed.2d 158 (1967); Teti v. Firestone Tire and Rubber Co., 392 F.2d 294, 296 (6th Cir. 1968).

[3] E.g., United States v. Clark, 613 F.2d 391, 406-08 (2d Cir. 1979); Beard v. Mitchell, 604 F.2d 485, 488 (7th Cir. 1979); United States v. Cooper, 596 F.2d 327, 330 (8th Cir. 1979).

[4] See United States v. Coven, 662 F.2d 162, 170 (2d Cir. 1981). See also United States v. Anthony, 565 F.2d 533, 536 (8th Cir. 1977), cert. denied, 434 U.S. 1079, 98 S.Ct. 1274, 55 L.Ed.2d 787 (1978) (defendants allowed to cross-examine witnesses on both appearances, even though some witnesses were called twice). See, e.g., Beard v. Mitchell, 604 F.2d 485, 487 (7th Cir. 1979); United States v. Jackson, 549 F.2d 517, 519 (8th Cir. 1977), cert. denied sub nom., Muhammed v. United States, 430 U.S. 985, 97 S.Ct. 1682, 52 L.Ed.2d 379 (1977); United States v. Hathaway, 534 F.2d 386, 401 (1st Cir. 1976), cert. denied, 429 U.S. 819, 97 S.Ct. 64, 50 L.Ed.2d 79 (1976).

[5] See United States v. Sampol, 636 F.2d 621, 667 (D.C. Cir. 1980). See also United States v. Singh, 628 F.2d 758, 763-64 (2d Cir. 1980), cert. denied, 449 U.S. 1034, 101 S.Ct. 609, 66 L.Ed.2d 496 (1980) (in alleged exploitation of illegal aliens in violation of immigration laws, many government witnesses testified that they worked without pay at restaurant operated by de-

As submitted to Congress by the Supreme Court,[6] Rule 611(b) provided that a witness could be cross-examined on any relevant issue, including credibility, subject to the trial court's discretion to limit inquiry into matters not the subject of testimony on direct examination.[7] Although the "wide open rule" received much favorable comment during congressional consideration, Congress ultimately chose to return to the traditional, more restrictive version of the rule on the grounds that it "facilitates orderly presentation by each party at trial"[8] and that "the factors of insuring an orderly and predictable development of the evidence weigh in favor of the narrower rule, especially when discretion is given to the trial judge to permit inquiry into additional matters."[9]

The first two sentences of Rule 611(c) provide that on direct examination leading questions generally should not be used except as necessary to develop the witness's testimony, but on cross-examination leading questions usually should be permitted.[10] This portion of the rule remained unchanged by Congress. In the Advisory Committee's draft, as approved by the Supreme Court and submitted to Congress, the final sentence read, "In civil cases, a party is entitled to call an adverse party or witness identified with him and interrogate by leading questions."[11] Congress expanded the Rule to include criminal cases and specified that hostile witnesses could be interrogated by leading questions. The Senate Judiciary Committee noted "it may be difficult in criminal cases to determine when a witness is 'identified with an adverse party,' and thus the rule should be applied with caution."[12] The Committee also questioned whether the specific inclusion of hostile witnesses was necessary since the first sentence of Rule 611(c) already authorized the use of leading questions when necessary to develop the witness's testimony. Nevertheless, the Committee approved the amendment, finding "it was not intended to affect the meaning of the first sentence of the subsection and was intended solely to clarify the fact that leading questions are permissible in the interrogation of a witness, who is hostile in fact."[13]

---

fendants making only tips; no abuse by trial court in refusing to permit defense to establish that witness traveled to and from Bangladesh with another, since it was a collateral matter with little, if any, probative value).

[6] 3 LOUISELL & MUELLER, § 333, at 399.

[7] The Supreme Court's version of Rule 611(b) read: "A witness may be cross-examined on any matter relevant to any issue in the case, including credibility. In the interests of justice, the judge may limit cross-examination with respect to matters not testified to on direct examination." Draft of November, 1972, 56 F.R.D. 183, 273 (1972).

[8] H.R. REP. No. 93-650, 93d Cong., 1st Sess. 12 (1973).

[9] S. REP. No. 93-1277, 93d Cong., 2d Sess. 25 (1974).

[10] Fed. R. Evid. 611(c).

[11] Draft of November, 1972, 56 F.R.D. 183, 273 (1972).

[12] S. REP. No. 93-1277, 93d Cong., 2d Sess. 25-26 (1974).

[13] Id.

§ 611.2   Rule 611(a)—Mode and Order of Proof Within Discretion of Court.

Rather than attempt to formulate specific rules governing the mode and order of proof in all conceivable situations, Rule 611(a) leaves decisions on these issues to the trial court's discretion.[14] In exercising its discretion, the trial court should seek to attain the objectives of effective ascertainment of the truth, avoidance of needless consumption of time and prevention of undue embarrassment or harassment of witnesses. Since determinations on the mode and order of interrogating witnesses and presenting evidence depend on particular circumstances at trial which will not be apparent to the reviewing court from the record, the trial court's decision will not serve as the basis for reversal on appeal absent a clear showing of abuse of discretion and abridgment of a substantive right.[15]

Rule 611(a) seeks to effectuate goals similar to those underlying Rules 102 and 403 and recognizes that the manner in which evidence is presented may have a substantial impact on these objectives, independent of the substance of the evidence. Although the parties normally determine the order in which evidence is introduced and witnesses testify, Rule 611 empowers the trial court to make this decision. At times the court's decision on the order of proof may affect admissibility of the evidence under Rule 104(a) or conditional relevancy under Rule 104(b).[16] By setting the order of proof, the trial court also may be able to postpone its decision on whether to admit probative but prejudicial evidence.[17]

The trial court has discretionary power over decisions such as whether and to what extent to allow redirect and re-cross-examination,[18] whether a witness can be recalled,[19] and whether a party may reopen its case.[20]

---

[14] Fed. R. Evid. 611(a) Advisory Committee Note.

[15] United States v. Leon, 679 F.2d 534, 536 (5th Cir. 1982); Oberlin v. Marlin American Corp., 596 F.2d 1322, 1329 (7th Cir. 1979).

[16] 3 LOUISELL & MUELLER, § 334, at 408-10.

[17] United States v. Brunson, 549 F.2d 348, 361 n.20 (5th Cir. 1977), *reh. denied*, 552 F.2d 369 (5th Cir. 1977), *cert. denied*, 434 U.S. 842, 98 S.Ct. 140, 54 L.Ed.2d 107 (1977), *reh. denied*, 434 U.S. 961, 98 S.Ct. 495, 54 L.Ed.2d 322 (1977) (robbery prosecution; proof of defendant's involvement in another robbery permitted to be introduced at end of government's case-in-chief on question of intent, since it was clear that intent would be an issue).

[18] United States v. Marler, 614 F.2d 47,

49 (5th Cir. 1980); United States v. Taylor, 599 F.2d 832, 838-39 (8th Cir. 1979); United States v. Hyde, 574 F.2d 856, 872 (5th Cir. 1978) (denial of re-cross-examination is discretionary and reviewable only for abuse).

[19] United States v. Jensen, 608 F.2d 1349, 1356 (10th Cir. 1979). *See also* United States v. Heath, 580 F.2d 1011, 1025 (10th Cir. 1978) (no error to permit recall); United States v. Rucker, 557 F.2d 1046, 1049 (4th Cir. 1977) (recall properly allowed).

[20] United States v. Clark, 617 F.2d 180, 187 (9th Cir. 1980); United States v. Alderete, 614 F.2d 726, 727 (10th Cir. 1980); United States v. McDonough, 603 F.2d 19, 22 (7th Cir. 1979); Skehan v. Board of Trustees, 590 F.2d 470, 480 (3d Cir. 1978), *cert. denied*, 444 U.S. 832, 100 S.Ct. 61, 62 L.Ed.2d 41 (1978).

Where evidence could have been introduced during a party's case-in-chief but was not, it is within the court's discretion to allow or disallow its introduction on rebuttal.[21] Impeachment by cross-examination about prior bad acts under Rule 608(b) may be limited under Rule 611(a) where the questions are aimed solely at embarrassing or harassing the witness.[22] The trial court also can curtail cross-examination if it finds that the probative value of the witness's testimony is outweighed by the Rule 403 factors of prejudice, confusion of the issues or time consumption.[23]

The trial court may prevent attempts by trial counsel to intimidate witnesses physically or psychologically. Since cross-examination necessarily entails confrontation of the witness, a certain degree of intimidation may be required to expose bias, untruthfulness or uncertainty, but Rule 611(a) authorizes the trial court to disallow "*unnecessary* discomfort, caused by the excesses of over-zealous trial counsel."[24] The trial court's power over the mode of interrogation enables it to exclude abusive, misleading or unfair questions, such as argumentative, repetitious or ambiguous questions or questions which assume facts which are not in evidence. When a question is objected to on one of these grounds, the court often will permit counsel to rephrase the question and continue.[25]

Rule 611(a) allows for innovative approaches to the reception of evidence, such as the "free narrative," where the witness is asked simply to relate her story without intermittent questions. As long as the manner of interrogation does not have a prejudicial effect on a witness or a party, the method chosen is within the court's discretion.[26]

[21] Page v. Barko Hydraulics, 673 F.2d 134, 136 (5th Cir. 1982); United States v. Wilford, 710 F.2d 439, 448 (8th Cir. 1983), *cert. denied*, ___ U.S. ___, 104 S.Ct. 701 (1984); United States v. Glass, 709 F.2d 669, 671 (11th Cir. 1983); Smith v. Conley, 584 F.2d 844, 846 (8th Cir. 1978).

[22] United States v. Singh, 628 F.2d 758, 763-64 (2d Cir. 1980), *cert. denied*, 449 U.S. 1034, 101 S.Ct. 609, 66 L.Ed.2d 496 (1980); United States v. Colyer, 571 F.2d 941, 946 n.7 (5th Cir. 1978), *reh. denied*, 576 F.2d 1249 (5th Cir. 1978); United States v. Provoo, 215 F.2d 531, 534-37 (2d Cir. 1954).

[23] United States v. 10.48 Acres of Land, 621 F.2d 338, 340 (9th Cir. 1980). *See also* United States v. Gleason, 616 F.2d 110, 113 (2d Cir. 1979), *cert. denied*, 444 U.S. 1082, 100 S.Ct. 1037, 62 L.Ed.2d 767 (1980) (cross-examination not permitted where it was beyond scope of direct and could have opened up a flood of evidence regarding a possibly confusing collateral issue); United

States v. Walker, 613 F.2d 1349, 1351 (5th Cir. 1980), *cert. denied*, 446 U.S. 944, 100 S.Ct. 2172, 64 L.Ed.2d 800 (1980) (where door opened by defense that witness was a prostitute, no error for government to bring out that she was turning earnings over to defendant on re-direct). *See, e.g.*, United States v. Summers, 598 F.2d 450, 452 (5th Cir. 1979); United States v. Ellison, 557 F.2d 128, 131 (7th Cir. 1977), *cert. denied*, 434 U.S. 965, 98 S.Ct. 504, 54 L.Ed.2d 450 (1977).

[24] 3 LOUISELL & MUELLER, § 334, at 414.

[25] 3 WIGMORE, EVIDENCE §§ 780, 782. *See, e.g.*, United States v. Weiner, 578 F.2d 757, 766 (9th Cir. 1978); United States v. Arlt, 567 F.2d 1295, 1298 (5th Cir. 1978), *reh. denied*, 570 F.2d 949 (5th Cir. 1978), *cert. denied*, 436 U.S. 911, 98 S.Ct. 2250, 56 L.Ed.2d 412 (1978); United States v. Cash, 499 F.2d 26, 29 (9th Cir. 1974).

[26] 3 LOUISELL & MUELLER, § 334, at 407-08.

§ 611.3   Rule 611(b)—Scope of Cross-Examination.

Rule 611(b) restricts the scope of cross-examination of a witness to matters which bear on his credibility or which are within the subject matter of the direct examination. Inquiry into areas not authorized explicitly by the Rule is permissible only if authorized by the trial court in the exercise of its discretion.

Rule 611(b) as adopted is consistent with prior federal practice in the sense that the Rule rejects a "wide open" approach to cross-examination in favor of a narrower rule which limits the scope of cross-examination. Under the wide open rule, which is followed in England and a significant minority of states,[27] the witness may, subject to the court's control, be asked about any relevant fact on cross-examination, including matters not addressed on direct examination.[28] The wide-open rule is preferred by leading scholars, including McCormick and Wigmore, who contend that it advances the search for truth by providing an opportunity for the witness to divulge all he knows, in contrast to the scope-of-direct rule which permits the proponent of the witness to limit disclosure by carefully restricting the questions asked on direct.[29] As Dean McCormick stated:

> [I]n many instances a mere postponement of the questions will not necessarily be the result of a ruling excluding a cross-question as not in the scope of the direct. Unless the question is vital and he is fairly confident of a favorable answer, the cross-examiner will at the least take considerable risk if he calls the adversary's witness at a later stage as his own, and will often be motivated to abandon the inquiry. Getting concessions from the opponent's witness while his story is fresh is worth trying for. To call the perhaps unfriendly witness later when his first testimony is stale is usually a much less effective expedient.[30]

Dean Wigmore argued that in practice, the scope-of-direct rule is difficult to apply and it "increases the opportunities for securing a retrial on trifling errors of ruling which do not affect the merits of the cause or the truth of the facts."[31] An overabundance of technical appeals results from the imprecision in the definition of the scope-of-direct examination. Professor Degnan found the rule susceptible of six different interpretations:

> [Cross-examination is limited] to (1) any issue properly a part of the case of the party who called the witness, as opposed to establishing the defenses or points of the cross-examiner, or (2) any issue properly a

---

[27] McCORMICK, § 21, at 51.
[28] See 3 WEINSTEIN, ¶ 611[02], at 611-25.
[29] 3 LOUISELL & MUELLER, § 336, at 429.

[30] McCORMICK, § 23, at 54-55.
[31] 6 WIGMORE, EVIDENCE, § 1888.

part of his case in chief, or (3) any issue or inference raised by testimony already received in the case, by whatever witness, or (4) any issue or inference raised by the testimony given by the witness presently being cross-examined, or (5) any transaction or occurrence testified to by that witness, even if those aspects of it were not mentioned by him, or (6) only those precise matters testified to by the witness upon direct examination.[32]

The better-reasoned cases find that cross-examination "may embrace any matter germane to the direct examination, qualifying or destroying it, or tending to elucidate, modify, explain, contradict, or rebut testimony given in chief by the witness."[33]

The rationale of restricted cross-examination is that the Rule preserves order in the presentation of evidence. The approach taken by Rule 611(b) allows each party to present its entire case without interruption from its opponent who, under the wide open approach, could present counter-evidence through the process of cross-examining the witness.[34] Other arguments in favor of a narrow scope of cross-examination generally have been rejected by the commentators.[35]

Rule 611(b) alleviates to some degree the problem of excessive appeals contending cross-examination went beyond the scope of direct, by granting the court discretion to allow inquiry on cross-examination in the manner that would be permitted on direct examination of the witness. In other words, if the court authorizes a broad cross-examination, in probing matters not addressed on direct, the examiner will be restricted from asking the witness leading questions, i.e., a right he does not normally have on

---

[32] Degnan, *Non-Rules Evidence Law: Cross-Examination*, 6 UTAH L. REV. 323, 330-31 (1959).

[33] Leeper v. United States, 446 F.2d 281, 288 (10th Cir. 1971), *cert. denied*, 404 U.S. 1021, 92 S.Ct. 695, 30 L.Ed.2d 671 (1971); *see also* Roberts v. Hollocher, 664 F.2d 200, 203 (8th Cir. 1981); United States v. Dickens, 417 F.2d 958, 962 (8th Cir. 1969).

[34] *See, e.g.*, Wills v. Russell, 100 U.S. (10 Otto) 621, 626, 25 L.Ed. 607 (1879); United States v. Ellison, 557 F.2d 128, 135 (7th Cir. 1977), *cert. denied*, 434 U.S. 965, 98 S.Ct. 504, 54 L.Ed.2d 450 (1977); United States v. Furr, 528 F.2d 578, 579 (5th Cir. 1976).

[35] One argument supporting restricted cross-examination was that the calling party vouched for his witness only to the extent of direct examination and therefore should not be bound by his testimony on

cross-examination with no opportunity to impeach him. This argument is foreclosed by Rule 607's abandonment of the voucher principle. 3 WEINSTEIN, ¶ 611[02], at 611-27 to 28. Another argument was that by permitting unrestricted cross-examination, a party could make his case by leading questions. Dean Wigmore rejected this argument on the following grounds:

> [T]he rule as to leading questions concerns the partisan disposition of the individual witness, and depends on the supposed willingness of a partisan witness to assist his party. . . . Its criterion is solely the individual witness' state of mind, —not the kind of fact that is to be asked, nor the stage of asking.

6 WIGMORE, EVIDENCE, § 1887, at 538.

direct examination.[36] Leading questions also are disallowed on cross-examination in two other situations. If the party calling the witness is permitted to ask leading questions on direct examination because, for example, the witness is hostile to the calling party, on cross-examination leading questions usually will be disallowed.[37] Also, in a civil case where a party calls his opponent as a witness, leading questions are permitted on direct examination but prohibited on cross-examination.[38]

It is within the court's discretion to allow a broad or narrow cross-examination and the court may limit cross-examination of a witness normally allowed under Rule 611(b) by invoking Rule 403 or Rule 611(a). The court will be overruled on appeal only upon showing an abuse of discretion.[39] However, in a criminal case, excessively restrictive limits on the defendant's cross-examination of prosecution witnesses may amount to a violation of his constitutional right of confrontation.[40]

§ 611.4 Rule 611(b)—Cross-Examination Relating to the Credibility of the Witness.

Rule 611(b) authorizes cross-examination as to matters affecting the credibility of the witness. Consequently, regardless of the factual substance of a witness's direct examination testimony, the witness's veracity may be

[36] Lis v. Robert Packer Hospital, 579 F.2d 819, 823 (3d Cir. 1978) (medical malpractice case; plaintiffs called physician to testify; after defense cross-examination was completed, trial judge permitted defendants to qualify the physician as its witness). *See, generally,* 3 LOUISELL & MUELLER, § 336, at 434.

[37] Morvant v. Construction Aggregates Corp., 570 F.2d 626, 635 n.12 (6th Cir. 1978) (right to leading questions is not absolute; court may forbid use of leading questions on cross-examination); United States v. Bensinger Co., 430 F.2d 584, 591-92 (8th Cir. 1970) (after permission secured to lead person as a hostile witness, proper thereafter to limit defense on cross-examination of witness to non-leading questions). Leading questions may be permitted on both direct and cross-examination if the witness is hostile to both parties or if leading questions are needed to develop the witness's testimony. 3 LOUISELL & MUELLER, § 336, at 434-35.

[38] Oberlin v. Marlin American Corp., 596 F.2d 1322, 1328 (7th Cir. 1979); J. & B.

Motors v. Margolis, 75 Ariz. 392, 394, 257 P.2d 588, 590 (1953).

[39] *E.g.,* Alford v. United States, 282 U.S. 687, 694 (1931); United States v. Diaz, 662 F.2d 713, 718 (11th Cir. 1981); United States v. Young, 655 F.2d 624, 626 (5th Cir. 1981); United States v. Praetorious, 622 F.2d 1054, 1056 (2d Cir. 1979), *cert. denied,* 449 U.S. 860, 101 S.Ct. 162, 66 L.Ed.2d 76 (1980).

[40] *See, e.g.,* Davis v. Alaska, 415 U.S. 308, 316, 94 S.Ct. 1105, 1113, 39 L.Ed.2d 347, 353 (1974) (where defense was precluded from asking prosecution witness about his status as juvenile offender defendant's right of confrontation was violated); Smith v. Illinois, 390 U.S. 129, 134, 88 S.Ct. 733, 737, 19 L.Ed.2d 936, 941 (1968) (failure to permit defense to ask chief prosecution witness his correct name and address violated right of confrontation); United States v. Crumley, 565 F.2d 945, 949 (5th Cir. 1978) (denial of right of confrontation resulted where defense was not permitted to ask prosecution witness if he had been charged with crime); *see also infra* § 611.5.

the subject of inquiry on cross-examination. Accordingly, consistent with the specific rules regarding discrediting a witness, the impeachment of a witness is always appropriate on cross-examination regardless of the subject matter of his testimony. Under Rule 608(b) a witness does not, by testifying, waive his privilege against self-incrimination as to matters which are related only to credibility.

§ 611.5 Rule 611(b)—Impact of Privilege Against Self-Incrimination.

Rule 611(b) controls the scope of cross-examination to effectuate the orderly presentation of evidence at trial. Although it is true that a witness who takes the stand subjects himself to reasonable cross-examination, difficult issues may arise regarding constitutional privileges which may be invoked to limit the extent and subject matter of cross-examination. An individual does not necessarily waive his constitutional rights merely by taking the stand.[41] To so hold would permit a principle of evidence, *i.e.*, a procedural device designed to govern the introduction of evidence at trial, to determine the scope of a witness's constitutional rights.

In the case of a criminal defendant who voluntarily testifies in his own behalf but then on cross-examination seeks to assert the privilege against self-incrimination, Rule 611(b) must give way to constitutional considerations in determining the scope of cross-examination. In comparison with other witnesses, the permissible scope of cross-examination of the accused takes on added significance because, unlike other witnesses, the prosecution cannot call the defendant to testify in its case-in-chief.[42] Rule 611(b) grants the trial court discretion to allow cross-examination beyond the scope of direct but does not address the extent to which the accused's privilege against self-incrimination operates as an independent limit upon cross-examination.[43] It is clear that the defendant's choice to testify at least subjects him to cross-examination on his direct testimony:

> He cannot reasonably claim that the Fifth Amendment gives him not only this choice [whether or not to testify] but, if he elects to testify, an immunity from cross-examination on the matters he has himself put in dispute. It would make of the Fifth Amendment not only a humane safeguard against judicially coerced self-disclosure but a positive invitation to mutilate the truth a party offers to tell.[44]

[41] *See* Fed. R. Evid. 611 Advisory Committee Note.

[42] *See* 3 WEINSTEIN, ¶ 611[03], at 611-39.

[43] *See* Fed. R. Evid. 611 Advisory Committee Note.

[44] Brown v. United States, 356 U.S. 148, 155-56, *reh. denied*, 356 U.S. 948 (1958).

However, the precise extent to which the accused's choice to testify constitutes a waiver of the privilege remains unclear.

Two major theories have been advanced. The first theory contends the privilege is waived on all relevant facts, with the exception of matters which relate only to credibility.[45] Wigmore and McCormick both support this approach.[46] Although the complete waiver approach is justified as providing the fact finder with more information, critics contend it may have the opposite effect because the accused may be less likely to testify in his behalf if he can be cross-examined on any relevant matter.[47] Under the second theory the accused waives his privilege against self-incrimination only as to those matters addressed on direct because "if there is a good reason why a defendant should not be compelled to be a witness against himself, there is an equally good reason why he should not be compelled to testify against his will respecting matters untouched by his direct testimony."[48] Of course, some evidence may be irretrievably lost since the accused cannot be called to testify by the prosecution. Nevertheless, many federal courts follow this approach because it "provides adequate insurance that [the accused] cannot distort the fact-finding process by telling only one side of the story, for he may be thoroughly cross-examined upon matters reasonably related to what he says."[49] If the accused does not discuss certain matters on direct and thereby forecloses cross-examination, "any tendency in this tactic to distort the truth will be offset by the common-sense unavoidable tendency of the jury to assume that his silence on certain matters means that he has something to hide."[50]

The issue remains essentially unresolved. The difficulty lies in reconciling the defendant's right not to be compelled to be a witness against himself with the need for complete disclosure of evidence. In many cases the court simply equates the permissible scope of cross-examination with the scope of the privilege without considering the different policies which underlie each.[51]

[45] See 3 WEINSTEIN, ¶ 611[03], at 611-37. Rule 608(b) explicitly provides that the giving of testimony does not constitute a waiver of the privilege against self-incrimination as to matters which only affect credibility.

[46] 8 WIGMORE, EVIDENCE, § 2276; McCORMICK, EVIDENCE, § 131.

[47] 3 LOUISELL & MUELLER, § 337, at 440.

[48] Carlson, Cross-Examination of the Accused, 52 CORNELL L.J. 705, 722 (1967).

[49] 3 LOUISELL & MUELLER, § 337, at 446. See, e.g., United States v. Miranda-Uriarte, 649 F.2d 1345, 1353-54 (9th Cir. 1981); United States v. Hernandez, 646 F.2d 970, 978-79 (5th Cir. 1981); United States v.

Lutz, 621 F.2d 940, 944-45 (9th Cir.), cert. denied, 449 U.S. 859, 101 S.Ct. 160, 66 L.Ed.2d 75 (1980).

[50] 3 LOUISELL & MUELLER, § 337, at 446.

[51] E.g., Hankins v. Civiletti, 614 F.2d 953, 954-55 (5th Cir. 1980) (taxpayer incarcerated for contempt in refusing to answer questions on cross-examination; petitioner waived his Fifth Amendment privilege with regard to matters relevant to his direct testimony; questions propounded were clearly proper). See also United States v. Brannon, 546 F.2d 1242, 1246 (5th Cir. 1957) (once defendant testified, only issue is whether questions were within scope of permissible cross-examination).

In summary, cross-examination of a criminal defendant is *not* governed solely by Rule 611(b); rather, it is additionally circumscribed by distinct constitutional considerations. Consequently, where the accused takes the stand in his own defense, he remains possessed of the constitutional guarantee against self-incrimination, and any waiver of that right must be grounded upon constitutional considerations and not upon strict application of Rule 611(b).

Where the accused testifies on his own behalf but refuses to answer questions on cross-examination based on an unjustified claim of privilege, the court may enforce appropriate sanctions such as allowing the prosecution to comment to the jury on the defendant's failure to answer or striking the defendant's direct testimony.[52]

Unlike the accused, other witnesses in both civil and criminal trials do not have a choice whether to testify. Although a witness does not automatically waive the privilege against self-incrimination merely by testifying, he cannot invoke the privilege whenever he chooses after testifying to only a portion of his story.[53] There is no definitive answer as to when the witness's testimony will be deemed a waiver of the privilege, but federal courts generally find that "[w]aiver occurs when the witness has admitted any incriminating fact and extends to all subsequent questions rendered innocuous as a result of the admission."[54]

Where a witness for the prosecution successfully asserts the privilege against self-incrimination on cross-examination, the defendant's sixth amendment right of confrontation may require that the witness's direct testimony be stricken if questioning was curtailed before the defense could challenge the substance of the witness's testimony.[55] In civil cases, a party who invokes the privilege to avoid testifying is subject to sanctions, including dismissal of the claim in some cases.[56]

---

[52] *See* United States v. Panza, 612 F.2d 432, 437-39 (9th Cir. 1979) ("by testifying on his own behalf, Panza waived his Fifth Amendment privilege against self-incrimination with respect to all relevant matters covered by his direct testimony"). *See also* United States v. Hearst, 563 F.2d 1331, 1344 (9th Cir. 1977), *reh. denied*, 573 F.2d 579 (9th Cir. 1977), *cert. denied*, 435 U.S. 1000, 98 S.Ct. 1656, 56 L.Ed.2d 90 (1977) ("when a defendant voluntarily becomes a witness in his own behalf, he subjects himself to cross-examination and impeachment to the same extent as any other witness in the same situation").

[53] Hoffman v. United States, 341 U.S. 479, 486, 71 S.Ct. 814, 820, 95 L.Ed. 1118, 1124 (1951); Blau v. United States, 340 U.S. 159, 161, 71 S.Ct. 223, 95 L.Ed. 170 (1950); McCarthy v. Arndstein, 262 U.S. 355, 359 (1923), *aff'd on reh.*, 266 U.S. 34 (1924).

[54] Note, *Waiver of the Privilege Against Self-Incrimination*, 14 STAN. L. REV. 811, 815 (1962).

[55] *See* Smith v. Illinois, 390 U.S. 129, 134, 88 S.Ct. 748, 753, 19 L.Ed.2d 956, 961 (1968) (defense attorney prevented from asking prosecution's chief witness his correct name and where he lived; this was a denial of right of confrontation guaranteed by Sixth and Fourteenth Amendments). *See also* Douglas v. Alabama, 380 U.S. 415, 421, 85 S.Ct. 1074, 1079, 13 L.Ed.2d 934, 939 (1965).

[56] Bramble v. Kleindienst, 357 F. Supp. 1028, 1036 (D.C. Colo. 1973), *aff'd* 498

§ 611.6 Rule 611(c)—Leading Questions.

Rule 611(c) provides the court with discretion to control the use of leading questions. The authorized judicial control applies to both direct and cross-examination. The court's discretion is guided by the principle that leading questions generally are permissible on cross-examination but not on direct examination.[57] On direct examination where the witness favors the calling party's case, leading questions are disapproved because the witness may acquiesce in the version of events stated in the examiner's question rather than describe the occurrence as he actually remembers it.[58] Also, leading questions pose the dangers of providing a "false memory"[59] for the witness or of focusing his testimony solely on those aspects of the case favorable to the calling party.[60] On cross-examination where the witness is biased in favor of the opposing party, leading questions are permissible because the witness is less susceptible to their suggestiveness.[61]

A leading question is one which suggests the particular response desired by the examiner.[62] Many factors influence whether a question is leading. The form of a question may cause it to be leading. For example, a question which begins "Isn't it a fact . . ." is usually leading.[63] More often, however, whether or not a question is leading must be determined on a case-by-case basis. The examiner's tone of voice, gestures or other non-verbal conduct may render an otherwise unobjectionable question leading.[64] Another factor is the context in which the question is asked.[65] Frequently, the degree of specificity determines whether a question is leading. Where the examiner

---

F.2d 968 (10th Cir. 1973), *cert. denied*, 419 U.S. 1069, 95 S.Ct. 656, 42 L.Ed.2d 665 (1973) (dismissal was appropriate sanction where plaintiff invoked Fifth Amendment privilege in course of discovery); Kisting v. Westchester Fire Ins. Co., 290 F. Supp. 141, 149 (W.D. Wis. 1968), *aff'd*, 416 F.2d 967 (7th Cir. 1969) (less harsh sanctions often in order).

[57] *E.g.*, United States v. Orand, 491 F.2d 1173, 1176 (9th Cir. 1973), *cert. denied*, 414 U.S. 1006, 94 S.Ct. 365, 38 L.Ed.2d 243 (1973); United States v. Lewis, 406 F.2d 486, 493 (7th Cir. 1969), *cert. denied*, 394 U.S. 1013, 89 S.Ct. 1630, 23 L.Ed.2d 39 (1969); Ewing v. United States, 77 App. D.C. 14, 16, 135 F.2d 633, 635, *cert. denied*, 318 U.S. 776, 63 S.Ct. 829, 87 L.Ed. 1145, *reh. denied*, 318 U.S. 803, 63 S.Ct. 991, 87 L.Ed. 1167 (1942).

[58] 3 LOUISELL & MUELLER, § 339, at 460.

[59] United States v. Cooper, 606 F.2d 96, 98 (5th Cir. 1979); United States v.

McGovern, 499 F.2d 1140, 1142 (1st Cir. 1974); United States v. Johnson, 495 F.2d 1097, 1101 (5th Cir. 1974). *See, e.g.*, United States v. Durham, 319 F.2d 590, 592 (4th Cir. 1973) ("[T]he essential test of a leading question is whether it so suggests to the witness the specific tenor of the reply desired by counsel that such a reply is likely to be given irrespective of an actual memory; the evil to be avoided is that of supplying a false memory for the witness).

[60] Denroche, *Leading Questions*, 6 CRIM. L.Q. 21, 22 (1963).

[61] McCORMICK, § 6, at 12.

[62] 3 LOUISELL & MUELLER, § 339, at 459; McCORMICK, § 6, at 11.

[63] 3 LOUISELL & MUELLER, § 339, at 461-62; McCORMICK, § 6, at 11.

[64] 3 WEINSTEIN, ¶ 611[05], at 611-58.

[65] *See, e.g.*, 3 LOUISELL & MUELLER, § 339, at 462.

describes an event in great detail and then asks the witness whether the event occurred, his question suggests the correct response is "yes" and thus the question is leading.[66] Similarly, if the examiner phrases a question in the alternative, with one choice described in detail while the other is stated vaguely ("Did he say he would call you at six o'clock, or what?"), it is clear that he is seeking the detailed response.[67]

Where an objection that the questioner is leading the witness is sustained, the examiner generally is permitted to cure the objection by rephrasing the question or restating it without the objectionable gesture or tone of voice.[68] It is within the court's discretion to foreclose further inquiry on the subject, but this power is rarely exercised. As one commentator noted, "The harm done is usually not very significant, and continued use of leading questions in some circumstances will soon draw sharp criticism from the court and embarrass the examiner before the jury. . . . The jury soon realizes that it is the lawyer and not the witness who is testifying."[69]

Leading questions should be allowed on direct examination only when necessary to develop testimony or when used to elicit preliminary undisputed matters.[70] For example, exceptions may be made where the witness is a reticent child,[71] or where the witness has temporarily forgotten events on which he is being called to testify.[72] Rule 611(c) expressly authorizes leading questions when a party calls a hostile witness, an adverse party or a witness

---

[66] MCCORMICK, § 6, at 11.

[67] *Id.*

[68] People v. Campbell, 233 Cal. App. 2d 38, 44, 43 Cal. Rptr. 237, 241 (1965) (district attorney withdrew his question and properly reframed it after an objection for leading the witness); Georgetown v. Groff, 136 Ky. 662, 664, 124 S.W. 888, 890 (1910) (where questions were leading, the court "should have required counsel to so frame his questions so as not to suggest the answers desired). *See also* Allen v. Hartford Life Ins. Co., 72 Conn. 693, 695, 45 A. 955, 956 (1900).

[69] Enfield, *Direct Examination of Witnesses*, 15 ARK. L. REV. 32, 36 (1960).

[70] McClard v. United States, 386 F.2d 495, 501 (8th Cir. 1967), *cert. denied sub nom.* Usery v. United States, 393 U.S. 886, 89 S.Ct. 149, 21 L.Ed.2d 134 (1968), *reh. denied*, 393 U.S. 1045, 89 S.Ct. 638, 21 L.Ed.2d 598 (1969) ("oftentimes leading questions are asked on preliminary and collateral matters to expedite the trial; in any

event, the control of leading questions is a matter left to the discretion of the trial judge"). *See also* 3 WEINSTEIN, ¶ 611[05]; 3 WIGMORE, § 775, at 165; MCCORMICK, § 6, at 12-13.

[71] United States v. Iron Shell, 633 F.2d 77, 92 (8th Cir. 1980); United States v. Littlewind, 551 F.2d 244, 245 (8th Cir. 1977); Rotolo v. United States, 404 F.2d 316, 317 (5th Cir. 1968); Antelope v. United States, 185 F.2d 174, 175 (10th Cir. 1950).

[72] United States v. McGovern, 499 F.2d 1140, 1142 (1st Cir. 1974); Green v. United States, 121 App. D.C. 111, 113, 348 F.2d 340, 342, *cert. denied*, 382 U.S. 930, 86 S.Ct. 321, 15 L.Ed.2d 342 (1965); Robertson v. United States, 249 F.2d 737, 742 (5th Cir. 1957), *cert. denied*, 356 U.S. 919, 78 S.Ct. 704, 2 L.Ed.2d 715 (1958) (district attorney was permitted to ask leading questions to refresh the memory of the witness, based on statements from the transcript of the witness at the previous trial).

Identified with an adverse party.[73] The court's discretion with regard to this use of leading questions appears limited to the determination of whether a witness is indeed hostile or identifiable with an adverse party.[74] A hostile witness is one who is so evasive or uncooperative on examination that his testimony is impeded. The Advisory Committee intended the term "witness identified with an adverse party" to be more expansive than former Rule 43(b) of the Federal Rules of Civil Procedure, which limited the witnesses automatically treated as hostile to "an adversary or an officer, director, or managing agent of a public or private corporation or of a partnership or association which is an adverse party."[75] Under Rule 611(c), a witness may be "identified with an adverse party" due to employment by the party or mere sympathy with the party's cause.[76] For example, a party may examine an employee of his opponent by leading questions.[77] In a criminal case, the defense may put leading questions to a government informer called on direct examination.[78]

Rule 611(c) embodies the general policy that leading questions in certain instances represent excessive intervention by trial counsel. Consequently, leading questions are appropriate only when necessary or when the adverse or hostile quality of the witness counter-balances counsel's effectiveness in leading the witness. The Rule is a more specific application of the court's general authority to control the mode and order of proof to insure the orderly and efficient determination of the truth.[79] Since the use of leading questions generally lies within the discretion of the court, a determination as to the propriety of their use will not serve as the basis for reversal on appeal absent a clear showing that the adverse party has been unfairly prejudiced by an abuse of discretion.[80]

---

[73] United States v. Shursen, 649 F.2d 1250, 1254 (8th Cir. 1981). *See also* United States v. Brown, 603 F.2d 1022, 1026 (1st Cir. 1979) (no abuse of discretion in allowing witness to be examined by leading questions where witness had apparent lapses of memory and conveyed general confusion). *See, e.g.*, United States v. Karnes, 531 F.2d 214, 217 (4th Cir. 1976).

[74] United States v. Diaz, 662 F.2d 713, 718 (11th Cir. 1981); United States v. Tsui, 646 F.2d 365, 368-69 (9th Cir. 1981); United States v. Brown, 603 F.2d 1022, 1025-26 (1st Cir. 1979).

[75] Fed. R. Evid. 611(c) Advisory Committee Note. *See also* 3 WEINSTEIN, ¶ 611[05], at 611-61.

[76] 3 WEINSTEIN, ¶ 611[05], at 611-62.

[77] *E.g.*, Perkins v. Volkswagen of America, Inc., 596 F.2d 681, 683 (5th Cir. 1979)

(error in ruling that employee of defendant would be plaintiff's own witness if called by plaintiff).

[78] *E.g.*, United States v. Bryant, 461 F.2d 912, 918-19 (6th Cir. 1972) (defense is permitted to ask leading questions of a Government witness such as an agent, who is closely identified with the interests of the Government, since such a witness will not be predisposed to accept suggestions offered by defense counsel's questions).

[79] *See supra* § 611.2.

[80] United States v. De Fiore, 720 F.2d 757, 764 (2d Cir. 1983), *cert. denied*, 467 U.S. 1241, 104 S.Ct. 3511 (1984); Ellis v. City of Chicago, 667 F.2d 606, 613 (7th Cir. 1981); United States v. Tsui, 646 F.2d 365, 368 (9th Cir. 1981).

Chapter 612

RULE 612. WRITING USED TO REFRESH MEMORY

Rule 612 reads as follows:

Except as otherwise provided in criminal proceedings by section 3500 of title 18, United States Code, if a witness uses a writing to refresh his memory for the purpose of testifying either:

(1) while testifying, or

(2) before testifying, if the court in its discretion determines it is necessary in the interests of justice, an adverse party is entitled to have the writing produced at the hearing, to inspect it, to cross-examine the witness thereon, and to introduce in evidence those portions which relate to the testimony of the witness. If it is claimed that the writing contains matters not related to the subject matter of the testimony the court shall examine the writing in camera, excise any portions not so related, and order delivery of the remainder to the party entitled thereto. Any portion withheld over objections shall be preserved and made available to the appellate court in the event of an appeal. If a writing is not produced or delivered pursuant to order under this rule, the court shall make any order justice requires, except that in criminal cases when the prosecution elects not to comply, the order shall be one striking the testimony or, if the court in its discretion determines that the interests of justice so require, declaring a mistrial.

§ 612.1　Refreshing Recollection—In General.

When a witness at a trial is unable or seems disinclined to relate the totality of facts within his knowledge, a party is afforded the opportunity to prompt testimony or correct omissions by "refreshing" the witness's recollection through the use of an object or writing.[1] Federal Rule 612 pertains to one aspect of the process of refreshing a witness's recollection. Specifically, the Rule governs the production of writings used to revive a witness's memory, and it pertains to writings which are used *at* trial or *before* trial to refresh a witness's recollection.[2] Other aspects of the procedure are governed by case law and custom.

The process of refreshing a witness's recollection may involve any of a number of recognized techniques. It may assume the form of using a leading question where appropriate under the guidelines of Rule 611(c).[3] It may involve playing an audio or even a video recording for the witness.[4] Usually, however, the process involves showing the witness a writing, a picture or a photograph in an effort to prompt the witness's recollection of a fact or event of which he has firsthand knowledge. After the witness has been exposed to the memory jogging device, he then—at least in theory—testifies independently of the device as to the facts being offered into evidence. After being used to revive the recollection, the device is devoid of evidentiary status,[5] and it effectively becomes inconsequential in the case unless

---

[1] *See, generally,* 3 Weinstein, ¶ 612[01]; 3 Louisell & Mueller, § 348; McCormick, § 9; 3 Wigmore, §§ 758-65. *See, e.g.,* Bankers Trust Co. v. Publicker Industries, Inc., 641 F.2d 1361, 1363 (2d Cir. 1981). *See also* Carter, *Suppression of Evidence Favorable to an Accused,* 34 F.R.D. 87 (1964); Everett, *Discovery in Criminal Cases—In Search of a Standard,* 1964 Duke L.J. 477; Kalo, *Refreshing Recollection: Problems with Laying a Foundation,* 10 Rutgers-Cam. L.J. 233 (1979); Maguire & Quick, *Testimony: Memory and Memoranda,* 3 How. L.J. 1 (1957); Orfield, *Discovery During Trial in Federal Criminal Cases: The Jencks Act,* 18 Sw. L.J. 212 (1964); Note, *Constitutionality of Conditional Mutual Discovery under Federal Rule 16,* 19 Okla. L. Rev. 417 (1969); Note, *The Prosecutor's Constitutional Duty to Reveal Evidence to the Defendant,* 74 Yale L.J. 136 (1964); Note, *The Constitutional Limits of Discovery,* 35 Ind. L.J. 337 (1960); Comment, *The Aftermath of the Jencks Case,* 11 Stan. L. Rev. 297 (1959).

[2] *See* Spivey v. Zant, 683 F.2d 881, 883 (5th Cir. 1982); Marcus v. United States, 422 F.2d 752, 754 (5th Cir. 1970).

[3] *See, generally,* 3 Louisell & Mueller, § 348, at 515.

[4] *See, generally,* 3 Weinstein, ¶ 612[01], at 612-10. *See also* United States v. Faulkner, 538 F.2d 724, 727 (6th Cir. 1976), *cert. denied,* 429 U.S. 1023, 97 S.Ct. 640, 50 L.Ed.2d 624 (1976) (tape recordings could be used to refresh recollection, even though they could not be introduced in evidence because they were partly unintelligible).

[5] *See* United States v. Scott, 701 F.2d 1340, 1346 (11th Cir. 1983), *reh. denied,* 707 F.2d 529 (11th Cir. 1983), *cert. denied,* 104 S.Ct. 175 (1983); United States v. Davis, 551 F.2d 233, 235 (8th Cir. 1977), *cert. denied,* 431 U.S. 923, 97 S.Ct. 2197, 53 L.Ed.2d 237 (1977) (no reversal required where statement used to refresh recollection was not materially different from other evidence properly received). *See, e.g.,* United States v. Smith, 521 F.2d 957, 969 (D.C. Cir. 1975).

the opposing party exercises the express options identified in Rule 612.[6] As stated in Rule 612, the memory jogging device may be subject to production under certain circumstances, and if produced, inspected, and used for cross-examination and introduced for consideration by the trier of fact.

It is obvious that the process of refreshing recollection invites a compliant witness to embrace as testimony anything he sees or reads in the document, picture, recording, etc. The risk has long been acknowledged but nevertheless accepted. Ultimately, control of the process is reposed in the trial judge who must ensure that the technique is not used to introduce out-of-court statements in the memory jogging device.[7] Additionally, the adversary process, aided by the opposing party's rights identified in Rule 612, is presumed to operate to expose such abuse through cross-examination.[8]

§ 612.2   Past Recollection Recorded Distinguished.

The technique of refreshing a witness's recollection must be distinguished from the hearsay exception, "past recollection recorded," the subject of Rule 803(5). Under the technique of refreshing recollection the witness reviews the writing to revive his memory of the material event and then proceeds to testify on the basis of present, personal knowledge. The writing itself is not offered as evidence. It merely serves as a memory jogging device, and compliance with the hearsay rule, the authentication rule or the so-called "best evidence rule" is not required. In contrast, under the "past recollection recorded" exception to the general proscription against hearsay, the document itself is offered as the evidence.[9] Rule 803(5) may operate to admit written hearsay in certain instances where the witness's

---

[6] United States v. Smith, 521 F.2d 957, 969 (D.C. Cir. 1975). *See also* Borel v. Fibreboard, 493 F.2d 1076, 1102-1103 (5th Cir. 1973), *cert. denied*, 419 U.S. 869, 95 S.Ct. 127, 42 L.Ed.2d 107 (1973) (trial court may permit jury to inspect the writing on its own motion). *See, e.g.*, United States v. Booz, 451 F.2d 719, 724-25 (3d Cir. 1971).

[7] 3 WEINSTEIN, ¶ 612[01], at 612-12-13; 3 LOUISELL & MUELLER, § 348, at 518. *See also* United States v. Socony-Vacuum Oil, 310 U.S. 150, 233, 60 S.Ct. 811, 863, 84 L.Ed. 1129, 1173, *reh. denied*, 310 U.S. 658, 60 S.Ct. 1091, 84 L.Ed. 1421 (1940) (antitrust prosecution; prior grand jury testimony by government witnesses used by government to refresh their recollection).

See, e.g., United States v. Conley, 503 F.2d 520, 522 (8th Cir. 1974); Esperti v. United States, 406 F.2d 148, 150-51 (5th Cir. 1969), *cert. denied*, 395 U.S. 938, 89 S.Ct. 2005, 23 L.Ed.2d 454 (1969).

[8] *See, generally*, 3 WEINSTEIN, ¶ 612[01], at 612-13-15.

[9] *See* United States v. Riccardi, 174 F.2d 883, 889 (3d Cir. 1949), *cert. denied*, 337 U.S. 941, 69 S.Ct. 1519, 93 L.Ed.2d 1746 (1949). *See, e.g.*, Imperial Meat Company v. United States, 316 F.2d 435, 437-38 (10th Cir. 1963), *cert. denied*, 375 U.S. 820, 84 S.Ct. 57, 11 L.Ed.2d 54 (1963) (judge conducted extensive examination to determine whether witness needed to refresh memory). *See also*, the discussion of Rule 803(5) in § 803.23 of this Treatise.

present recollection remains absent or incomplete and cannot be refreshed by the writing. Under Rule 803(5) the witness's trial testimony establishes the foundational fact that recollection was complete at the time of writing and that the facts were accurately recorded in the document. Obviously, where a writing is offered into evidence, it must comply with all the rules regarding the admissibility of documentary evidence, one of which is the hearsay rule. Where a writing is offered, one of the hearsay exceptions available to admit the out-of-court statement is Rule 803(5). Of course, other exceptions might be available as well.

§ 612.3   Prior Inconsistent Statement Distinguished.

Refreshing a witness's recollection with a document must be distinguished from using a writing prepared by the witness for the purpose of "prior inconsistent statement" impeachment. Frequently, trial counsel will show a witness a document containing a prior statement in a mildly confrontational effort to encourage the witness to change some aspect of his testimony. Providing the usual practices attending "refreshing recollection" are followed, no real abuse occurs. In fact, the deviation from the written statement articulated in the testimony may be the product of a passing memory failure which is legitimately corrected by showing the witness his prior statement. As long as the prior statement is not read aloud to the witness, and merely shown to the witness, the process is legitimately an effort to refresh recollection.

Where the prior statement of a witness is exposed to the trier of fact in an effort to discredit the witness by demonstrating his inability to keep his story consistent, the process assumes the status of impeachment.[10] Self-contradiction or prior inconsistent impeachment is governed by principles which are distinguishable from those applicable to refreshing recollection, and these principles are discussed in conjunction with Rule 613.[11]

§ 612.4   Refreshing Recollection During the Course of Testimony.

Before a witness may be shown a writing to refresh his recollection and aid his testimony, the court must be satisfied that the witness lacks a present recollection of the relevant events.[12] This lack of present recollec-

[10] See, generally, 3 LOUISELL & MUELLER, § 348, at 516.

[11] Id. See Chapter 613 of this Treatise.

[12] E.g., United States v. Morlang, 531 F.2d 183, 191 (4th Cir. 1975); United States v. Lewis, 406 F.2d 486, 493 (7th Cir. 1969), cert. denied, 394 U.S. 1013, 89 S.Ct. 1630, 23 L.Ed.2d 39 (1969).

tion may be express, such as where a witness cannot recall the events inquired into, or it may be apparent from the course of testimony, such as where the substance of a witness's testimony is vague or incomplete.[13]

While the form of the questioning is largely within the discretion of the trial court,[14] the usual procedure is for trial counsel to elicit testimony first that the witness's unaided recollection is exhausted. The witness is then handed a writing and asked to read the document silently to refresh his recollection.[15] In order to avoid inviting the jury to accord the writing evidentiary status, the writing should not be read aloud. If after reading the document, the witness's recollection has been revived, she then proceeds to provide testimony as to the relevant facts.

It is well-established that the type of "writing" authorized under the refreshed recollection doctrine includes not only books, documents or other papers, but recordings and photographs as well.[16] Since the object of the technique is to awaken the memory of a witness, any allusion to previous events which fulfills that purpose may be used. The "writing," further, need not be an original document or recording. Nor must it be a writing executed or previously adopted by the witness. Since the question is limited to whether the writing is calculated to refresh the witness's memory, the ultimate question of the writing's admissibility is inapposite.[17] Consequently, Articles VIII, IX and X of the Rules are inapplicable to the writ-

---

[13] See United States v. Boyd, 605 F.2d 792, 794 (8th Cir. 1979) (no abuse of discretion where witness assured court of need to refer to report summarizing his previous statements to FBI); Goings v. United States, 377 F.2d 753, 761 (8th Cir. 1967), later app., 393 F.2d 884 (8th Cir. 1967), cert. denied, 393 U.S. 883, 89 S.Ct. 191, 21 L.Ed.2d 158 (1967) (discretion allows witness a chance to review statements given to a third person and then independently testify). Cf., Morgan, Basic Problems of Evidence 62 (1962).

[14] E.g., United States v. Conley, 503 F.2d 520, 522 (8th Cir. 1974); Esperti v. United States, 406 F.2d 148, 150-51, (5th Cir. 1969), cert. denied, 395 U.S. 938, 89 S.Ct. 2005, 23 L.Ed.2d 454 (1969).

[15] E.g., United States v. Shoupe, 548 F.2d 636, 639 (6th Cir. 1977). See also Johnston v. Earle, 313 F.2d 686, 688 (9th Cir. 1962), cert. denied, 373 U.S. 910, 83 S.Ct. 1300, 10 L.Ed.2d 412 (1963) (witness looked at copies of original notes prepared by another to refresh his memory). Cf., Thompson v. United States, 342 F.2d 137, 140 (5th Cir. 1965), cert. denied, 381 U.S.

926, 85 S.Ct. 1560, 14 L.Ed.2d 685 (1965); Williams v. United States, 365 F.2d 21, 22 (7th Cir. 1966), cert. denied, 385 U.S. 981, 87 S.Ct. 530, 17 L.Ed.2d 443 (1966).

[16] See United States v. Faulkner, 538 F.2d 724, 727 (6th Cir. 1976), cert. denied, 429 U.S. 1023, 97 S.Ct. 640, 50 L.Ed.2d 624 (1976) (tape recordings); Williams v. United States, 365 F.2d 21, 22 (7th Cir.), cert. denied, 385 U.S. 981, 87 S.Ct. 530, 17 L.Ed.2d 879 (1966) (memorandum of conversation); United States v. Rappy, 157 F.2d 964, 967 (2d Cir. 1947), cert. denied, 329 U.S. 806, 67 S.Ct. 501, 91 L.Ed.2d 688 (1947) (songs, photographs).

[17] See United States v. Scott, 701 F.2d 1340, 1346 (11th Cir. 1983). See also United States v. Ricco, 566 F.2d 433, 436 (2d Cir. 1977), cert. denied, 436 U.S. 926, 98 S.Ct. 2819, 56 L.Ed.2d 768 (1978) (illegal wiretaps may be used before trial to refresh witness's recollection of his own conversations). Cf., United States v. Baretta, 397 F.2d 215, 222 (2d Cir. 1968), cert. denied, 393 U.S. 939, 89 S.Ct. 293, 21 L.Ed.2d 276 (1968), reh. denied, 393 U.S. 1045, 89 S.Ct. 613, 21 L.Ed.2d 597 (1969).

ing. In this regard, however, the witness's recollection must be genuinely revived after she inspects the writing so that his testimony is based upon present recollection and not a mere recitation of the contents of the writing.[18] Ultimately, it is incumbent upon the trial judge to insure that the technique is not abused.

Where the witness testifies that a document fails to revive her memory of the material event or facts at issue, but testifies that the writing was prepared or adopted by the witness when the subject matter was fresh in her memory, an adequate foundation may exist for the introduction of the writing itself under Rule 803(5). Alternately, some other hearsay exception may be applicable. Accordingly, if the witness's memory is not revived, the writing itself may be admitted for the truth of its contents only if it meets the requirements of a hearsay exception.[19] Likewise, other considerations for the admissibility of documentary evidence, *e.g.*, authentication, "best evidence," etc., must be satisfied.

§ 612.5   Production of the Writing Used to Refresh Recollection.

The primary focus of Rule 612 is upon the procedural requirements governing the production of a document used to revive the recollection of the witness. When a document is used *at trial* to refresh a witness's memory, the Rule provides that the adverse party is entitled, as of right, to inspect the writing, to cross-examine the witness concerning the document and to introduce those portions of the writing pertinent to the trial testimony.[20] When a document is used *prior to trial* to refresh the recollection of the witness, Rule 612 provides the trial judge with discretion to order the pro-

---

[18] *See, e.g.*, United States v. Cheyenne, 558 F.2d 902, 904-06 (8th Cir. 1977), *cert. denied*, 434 U.S. 957, 98 S.Ct. 486, 54 L.Ed.2d 316 (1977) (where FBI agent refreshed his recollection of defendant's confession by reading FBI report at suppression hearing and testified at trial without reference to the report, there was no error; no merit to defendant's argument that agent had no independent recollection, since defendant had a copy of the report and had full opportunity to probe agent on cross-examination); NLRB v. Federal Dairy Co., 297 F.2d 487, 488-89 (1st Cir. 1962) ("the witness, unless opposing counsel waives it, should not refresh his recollection unless he has been examined without leading, if it is

direct examination, and has testified that his recollection is exhausted"). *But cf.*, United States v. Jiminez, 613 F.2d 1373, 1377 (5th Cir. 1980) (no showing of need necessary).

[19] *See*, 3 Weinstein, ¶ 612[01], at 612-11-14; 3 Louisell & Mueller, § 348; McCormick, § 9, at 18; 3 Wigmore, §§ 762-64. *See also* cases cited in Chapter 804 of this Treatise.

[20] *See, e.g.*, Spivey v. Zant, 683 F.2d 881, 885 n.5; United States v. Howtan, 688 F.2d 272, 276 (5th Cir. 1982); United States v. Costner, 684 F.2d 370, 372-73 (6th Cir. 1982).

duction of the writing.[21] Accordingly, a writing used prior to the trial or hearing to prepare a witness's testimony is subject to production at the trial or hearing if the trial judge determines that such document should be, "in the interests of justice," inspected by the adverse party. A trial judge may properly refuse inspection when the documents contain sensitive material or contain information not closely related to the witness's testimony.[22]

The existence of a document used to refresh recollection frequently emerges during cross-examination, and a recess may be requested and granted where the document is not readily available for production. Once produced, the document may be used in conjunction with the cross-examination of the witness, and it may be submitted to the jury to the extent that it relates to the testimony.

It should be noted that when a document used to refresh a witness's recollection is submitted to the jury pursuant to Rule 612, the document is not being offered as substantive evidence. Rather, the document is offered as a basis for evaluating the testimony of the witness, and unless the document has an independent basis for admissibility as substantive evidence, the trial judge should instruct the jury to consider the document only for the limited purpose of assessing the credibility of the witness.[23]

§ 612.6   Limitations On the Production of Writings Used to Refresh Recollection.

By its express terms, Rule 612 is limited by Section 3500 of Title 18 of the United States Code, the so-called "Jencks Act." Accordingly, the discretion of the trial judge to order production of a writing used prior to trial to refresh a witness's recollection may not exceed the authority of the court to order production under this Act.[24]

The Jencks Act, now incorporated into Rule 26.2 of the Rules of Criminal Procedure, requires the government to deliver to a criminal defendant

---

[21] *See* United States v. Howtan, 688 F.2d 272, 276 (5th Cir. 1982); Tillman v. United States, 268 F.2d 422, 424 (5th Cir. 1959); McGill v. United States, 270 F.2d 239, 241 (D.C. Cir. 1959), *cert. denied*, 362 U.S. 905, 80 S.Ct. 615, 4 L.Ed.2d 555 (1960); McCORMICK, § 9, at 17; 3 WIGMORE, §762, at 140.

[22] *See* United States v. Howtan, 688 F.2d 272, 276 (5th Cir. 1982).

[23] See Rule 105 and §§ 105.1 *et seq.* of this Treatise.

[24] *Contra* United States v. Algle, 503 F. Supp. 783, 791 (E.D. Ky. 1980), *rev'd*, 667 F.2d 569 (6th Cir. 1982). *But see*, Brady v. Maryland, 373 U.S. 83, 89, 83 S.Ct. 1194, 1199, 10 L.Ed.2d 215, 219 (1963) ("[S]uppression by the prosecution of evidence favorable to an accused upon request violates due process where the evidence is material either to guilt or punishment irrespective of the good faith or bad faith of the prosecutor." It should be noted that in a criminal proceeding the limitations of the Jencks Act may be superseded by the Brady doctrine).

any statement[25] in its possession made by a government witness.[26] This right is triggered only after the witness has testified on direct examination.[27] Therefore, the defendant is entitled to receive the statements before his cross-examination of the witnesses.

The statements available to the defendant are those that relate to the subject matter concerning which the government witness has testified on direct.[28] There is no additional requirement that production under the Act is conditioned upon the witness having referred to the statement before or while testifying. In this sense the Jencks Act is broader than Rule 612. The Jencks Act, however, limits the application of Rule 612 in certain instances. Under Rule 612 a statement which is properly authenticated by the testifying witness in accordance with the Act and which is reviewed by the witness before testifying may, at the court's discretion, be inspected and used by the accused during cross-examination of the witness and otherwise. Under the Jencks Act and Criminal Rule 26.2, however, the accused has an express right to inspect and use such a statement during cross-examination or otherwise.[29] Thus, the Act preempts the operation of the discretionary power created by clause (2) of Rule 612.[30]

Similarly, the discretionary power of Rule 612 is inoperative when a statement which is not authenticated in accordance with the Act by the testifying witness is reviewed by the witness prior to testifying.[31] In this situation the Rule on its face would otherwise permit the court, at its discretion, to grant inspection by the accused, but such an inspection is precluded under the Act and the accused will not be allowed to inspect or use the writing if the government objects.[32] Likewise, when a witness reviews a writing by some other government witness prior to trial, the Jencks Act denies inspection by the accused.[33] Once again, the Act preempts the discretionary power of Rule 612.

---

[25] United States v. Sotto, 711 F.2d 1558, 1561-62 (11th Cir. 1983); United States v. Vella, 562 F.2d 275, 276 (3d Cir. 1977). *See, e.g.*, United States v. Parker, 549 F.2d 1217, 1224 (9th Cir. 1977), *cert. denied*, 430 U.S. 971, 97 S.Ct. 1659, 52 L.Ed.2d 365 (1977) (notes made by FBI agents in connection with interviews with defendant and eyewitnesses may have constituted statements within Jencks Act; but since court could not make this determination since notes had been destroyed, court properly prohibited government from introducing reports compiled from notes). *See also* 18 U.S.C., § 3500(c).

[26] *See* United States v. Wright, 480 F.2d 1181, 1191 (D.C. Cir. 1973) (even if witness used investigative report to refresh his recollection, only those parts of the report relating to his testimony on direct need to be turned over to opponent).

[27] *See* 18 U.S.C., § 3500.

[28] *See* 18 U.S.C., § 3500(b).

[29] 3 Louisell & Mueller, § 349, at 528.

[30] *Id.*

[31] *Id.*

[32] *Id.*

[33] First Kleindienst Letter, 117 Cong. Rec. 33648, 33657 (Sept. 28, 1971). *See, generally*, 3 Louisell & Mueller, § 349.

An issue left unresolved by Rule 612 is the extent to which a witness may justifiably refuse to produce a writing used to revive recollection prior to trial under an assertion of privilege or under a work product doctrine. Rule 501 acknowledges the legitimacy of these doctrines, and should govern their application to Rule 612.[34]

The attorney-client privilege, generally considered an absolute privilege, should bar inspection of privileged documents used to refresh recollection. Case law, however, is divided.[35] Under a waiver theory, utilization of a privileged document to refresh recollection renders the document discoverable.[36] Conversely, in some cases the mere use of privileged documents to refresh recollection is an inadequate reason to conclude that the privilege is destroyed.[37]

Unlike the attorney-client privilege, the work product doctrine is not an absolute privilege since a showing of "substantial need" may overcome the protection.[38] Courts, however, have denied inspection when work product documents are used to refresh recollection.[39]

§ 612.7   Failure to Produce A Writing Pursuant To Court Order Under Rule 612; Unrelated Matters in Document Used to Refresh Recollection.

Where a claim is made that the writing used to refresh recollection contains matters which are unrelated to the litigation and which have not affected the witness's testimony, the court has the duty to inspect the writing *in camera* to excise any unrelated portions. The remainder is delivered to the adverse party, preserving the portions excised in the record for purposes of appellate review.

---

[34] 3 Weinstein, ¶ 612[04]; 3 Louisell & Mueller, § 351.

[35] *Compare* Leucadia, Inc. v. Reliance Ins. Co., 101 F.R.D. 674 (1983) *with* Wheeling Pittsburgh Steel Corp. v. Underwriters Laboratories, Inc., 81 F.R.D. 8 (1978).

[36] Wheeling Pittsburgh Steel Corp. v. Underwriters Laboratories, Inc., 81 F.R.D. 8, 10 (1978) (witness at deposition who was ex-employee of plaintiff, refreshed his recollection prior to deposition with file containing communications between representatives of the plaintiff; court granted defendant access to the files noting that access is limited only to those writings which may have fairly been said to have an impact upon the testimony of the witness).

[37] *See, generally,* Leucadia, Inc. v. Reliance Ins. Co., 101 F.R.D. 674 (1983); Jos. Schlitz Brewing Co. v. Muller & Phipps, Ltd., 85 F.R.D. 118 (1980). *See also* Sporck v. Peil, 759 F.2d 312, 318-19 (3d Cir. 1985).

[38] Federal Rule of Civil Procedure, 26(b)(3).

[39] Carter-Wallace, Inc. v. Hartz Mountain Industries, Inc., 553 F. Supp. 45, 50 (1982); Al-Rowarshan Establishment Universal Trading & Agencies Ltd. v. Beatrice Foods Co., 92 F.R.D. 779, 782 (1982).

Where a party fails to produce documents in compliance with the trial court's order, the court may make any further order necessitated by the ends of justice, including in criminal cases, ordering a mistrial where the prosecution fails to comply.[40]

[40] The Advisory Committee Note to Federal Rule 612 provides:

The consequences of nonproduction by the government in a criminal case are those of the Jencks statute, striking the testimony or in exceptional cases a mistrial. 18 U.S.C. § 3500(d). In other cases these alternatives are unduly limited, and such possibilities as contempt, dismissal, finding issues against the offender, and the like are available.

It should be noted that as of December 1, 1980, the Jencks Act was incorporated into the Federal Rules of Criminal Procedure, Rule 26.2.

Chapter 613

RULE 613. PRIOR STATEMENTS OF WITNESSES

Rule 613 reads as follows:

(a) **Examining Witness Concerning Prior Statement.** In examining a witness concerning a prior statement made by him, whether written or not, the statement need not be shown or disclosed to opposing counsel.

(b) **Extrinsic Evidence of Prior Inconsistent Statement of Witness.** Extrinsic evidence of a prior inconsistent statement by a witness is not admissible unless the witness is afforded an opportunity to explain or deny the same and the opposite party is afforded an opportunity to interrogate him thereon, or the interests of justice otherwise require. This provision does not apply to admissions of a party-opponent as defined in Rule 801(d)(2).

§ 613.1 Prior Statements of Witnesses—In General.

Rule 613 generally governs certain procedures which attend the process of impeaching a witness with a prior inconsistent statement.[1] Through the

---

[1] *See, generally,* 3 WEINSTEIN, ¶ 613[01]-[04]; 3 LOUISELL & MUELLER, §§ 355-59; McCORMICK, §§ 34-39; 3A WIGMORE, §§ 1017-46. *See also* Hale, *Impeachment of Witnesses by Prior Inconsistent Statements,* 10 S. CAL. L. REV. 135 (1937); Ladd, *Some Observations on Credibility: Impeachment* of *Witnesses,* 52 CORNELL L.Q. 239 (1967); Slough, *Impeachment of Witnesses, Common Law Principles and Modern Trends,* 34 IND. L.J. 1 (1958); Note, *Modification of the Foundational Requirement for Impeaching Witnesses: California Evidence Code Section 770,* 18 HASTINGS L.J. 210

impeachment device of "self-contradiction," a witness may be interrogated about a statement made prior to trial which is inconsistent with his trial testimony.[2] The statement may be introduced during cross-examination, and in certain situations evidence of the contents of the prior statement may be introduced after the witness has concluded his testimony.

The prior contradictory statement may be written or it may be oral.[3] Where the statement is written, it may be used in conjunction with the cross-examination of the witness sought to be impeached. In certain cases, it may be authenticated by a distinct witness and introduced after the primary witness (*i.e.*, the witness sought to be impeached) has concluded his testimony. Likewise, where the statement is oral, it may be the subject of inquiry or cross-examination, and, in certain instances, the statement may be the subject of testimony of a distinct witness who has firsthand knowledge of the primary witness's contradictory out-of-court statement.

The purpose of self-contradiction is to demonstrate that the witness is the type of person who makes conflicting statements regarding the same set of facts. The suggestion to the trier of fact is that the witness is untrustworthy because of intentional false statements or because of a defect of memory.[4]

It should be noted that Rule 613 does not govern the issue of whether the prior statement may be considered by the trier of fact as substantive evidence, *i.e.*, for the truth of its contents. This issue, which involves hearsay considerations, is discussed at length in §§ 801.8 and 801.20 of this Treatise. Fundamentally, if the prior inconsistent statement is not admissible hearsay, its only function is to aid the trier of fact in assessing the credibility of the witness. A limiting instruction from the trial judge should direct the jury to consider the prior statement not for its truth, but rather for the restricted purpose of assessing the trustworthiness of the witness. Where the prior statement is admissible hearsay, however, it serves a dual purpose. The statement operates to impeach the witness, and it may be considered

(1966); Comment, *Hearsay Under the Proposed Federal Rules: A Discretionary Approach*, 15 Wayne L. Rev. 1077 (1969); Comment, *Prior Inconsistent Statements as an Exception to the Hearsay Rule: An Analysis of People v. Johnson*, 6 San Diego L. Rev. 92 (1969).

[2] United States v. Hale, 422 U.S. 171, 176, 95 S.Ct. 2133, 2137, 45 L.Ed.2d 99, 104 (1975); United States v. Porter, 544 F.2d 936, 938 n.2 (8th Cir. 1976); United States v. Sisto, 534 F.2d 616, 622 (5th Cir. 1976);

United States v. MaiZumi, 526 F.2d 848, 850 (5th Cir. 1976); United States v. Jordano, 521 F.2d 695, 697-98 (2d Cir. 1975).

[3] *See, e.g.,* United States v. Simmons, 567 F.2d 314, 320-21 (7th Cir. 1977); United States v. Rogers, 549 F.2d 490, 496 (8th Cir. 1976); *cert. denied,* 431 U.S. 918, 97 S.Ct. 2182, 53 L.Ed.2d 229 (1976).

[4] *See* 3 Louisell & Mueller, § 355, at 541-42; 3 Weinstein, ¶ 613[02], at 613-7. *See also,* 4 Wigmore, § 1263, at 518.

as substantive evidence in the case. Generally, where the statement is substantively admissible pursuant to the hearsay system, no limiting instruction is necessary.

Rule 613 does not identify the circumstances under which self-contradiction impeachment is authorized. Rather, its primary function is to prescribe the procedure to be used in disclosing the statement to the witness and to his counsel. It also governs the procedure to be applied to "extrinsic evidence" of a prior inconsistent statement. Extrinsic evidence of an inconsistent statement is evidence that is offered after the witness sought to be impeached has concluded his testimony. Alternately stated, extrinsic evidence is evidence which is offered through the testimony of a distinct witness, or written evidence authenticated by a distinct witness.

§613.2   Rule 613(a)—Interrogation on Prior Statement—In General.

In essence, Rule 613(a) permits inquiry regarding a prior statement, whether written or oral, without requiring the witness to be apprised of its contents before questioning.[5] The prior practice in some Federal courts was to follow the rule established in *Queen Caroline's* case.[6] Under this rule, the cross-examiner was required to reveal the statement to the witness prior to questioning. This procedure was founded on the interest of protecting the witness from unfair surprise.[7] Rule 613, however, dispenses with the *Queen's* Rule in favor of a procedure which is designed to enhance the effective use of cross-examination.[8]

To protect a party from any unfair advantage that might be gained by his adversary's inquiry concerning a prior statement, Rule 613(a) provides that on request the statement must be shown or disclosed to opposing counsel. Through this procedure, the party offering the witness may protect him from unfair insinuations or misleading questions by making appropri-

---

[5] *E.g.*, Wood v. Stibl Inc., 705 F.2d 1101, 1103 (9th Cir. 1983); United States v. Williams, 668 F.2d 1064, 1068 n.9 (9th Cir. 1981).

[6] 129 Eng. Rep. 976 (1820). *See, generally*, 3A WIGMORE, § 1019, at 691.

[7] *See* Robertson v. M/S Sanyo Maru, 374 F.2d 463, 465 (5th Cir. 1967), *on remand*, 239 F. Supp. 931, *aff'd in part and remanded in part*, 424 F.2d 520 (5th Cir. 1967), *cert. denied*, 400 U.S. 854, 91 S.Ct. 59, 27 L.Ed.2d 91 (1967) (error to have ad-

mitted statement which witness denied without proving authenticity or showing excuse for not producing original); Brooks v. United States, 304 F.2d 580, 582 (10th Cir. 1962) (necessary for prior statements to be called to attention of witness and that he be given opportunity to admit, deny, or explain them in order to lay foundation for their admission).

[8] *See* Advisory Committee's Note to F.R.E. 613.

ate objections.[9] Moreover, redirect examination is available for the elicitation of an explanation as to the inconsistency.

The notable impact of Rule 613(a) is to give enhanced emphasis to the element of surprise, rather than disclosure, as a means of achieving accurate trial results.

§ 613.3   Rule 613(b)—Extrinsic Evidence of Prior Inconsistent Statements.

Rule 613(b) governs the admissibility of "extrinsic evidence" of a prior inconsistent statement of a witness where such statement is used pursuant to the impeachment device of self-contradiction. Extrinsic evidence is evidence as to the contents of the prior statement which is introduced after the witness sought to be impeached has stepped down from testifying. Consequently, extrinsic evidence may assume the form of testimony from another witness, or it may be a document containing the inconsistent statement. Accordingly, extrinsic evidence is evidence introduced other than through the testimony of the witness who is the subject of the impeachment.

Rule 613(b) requires only that the primary witness be given an opportunity at some point in the trial to explain or deny the inconsistent statement, and in contrast to the prior Federal approach, the explanation by the witness and interrogation by opposing counsel need not precede the introduction of extrinsic evidence.[10] This Rule, therefore, dispenses with the necessity of laying a foundation as a prerequisite to the introduction of extrinsic evidence. Prior practice generally required a foundation *prior to* the introduction of the inconsistent statement. The witness had to be interrogated concerning the substance of the statement, the time, place and circumstances of the making of the statement as well as an identification of persons present to hear the statement if it was oral.[11] Rule 613 dispenses with this foundation requirement in favor of the opportunity of the witness to explain any inconsistency between his trial testimony and prior statement.

[9] United States v. Lawson, 683 F.2d 688, 694 (2d Cir. 1982). *See also* United States v. Rogers, 459 F.2d 490, 495-502 (8th Cir. 1976), *cert. denied*, 431 U.S. 918, 97 S.Ct. 2182, 53 L.Ed.2d 229 (1977) (full discussion of evidentiary standards for use of extrinsic proof of prior inconsistent testimony for impeachment purposes).

[10] United States v. McLaughlin, 663 F.2d 949, 951 (9th Cir. 1981). *See also* United States v. Praetorius, 622 F.2d 1054, 1056 (2d Cir. 1979) (trial court misinterpreted rule in requiring witness to be confronted with prior inconsistent statement immediately); United States v. Harvey, 547 F.2d 720, 722 (2d Cir. 1976) (Rule 613 satisfied where witness was afforded an opportunity to explain or deny circumstances suggesting prejudice three times and reference was made to person with whom conversation was held so as to obviate any surprise).

[11] *See* McCORMICK, § 37, at 79 n.2.

§ 613.4 Discretion to Dispense with the Explanation Requirement.

Rule 613(b) affords the trial judge discretion to permit the introduction of extrinsic evidence in the absence of an opportunity for an explanation from the witness where "the interests of justice . . . require." Occasion for the exercise of this discretion would arise, for example, where the witness has testified but has become unavailable before opposing counsel learns of a prior inconsistent statement.[12] In general, whether the trial judge will admit evidence under this rubric will depend upon several factors: the practicability of recalling the witness, the materiality of the issue to which the statement relates, the probable impact on the trial by not allowing introduction of the statement, and the effectiveness of a jury instruction in restricting the consideration of the statement by the jury.[13]

§ 613.5 Collateral Matter Doctrine.

A basic common law doctrine provides that a prior inconsistent statement relating to a "collateral matter" may not be proved by extrinsic evidence. It may, however, be the subject of inquiry while the witness is on the stand. The adoption of Rule 613 leaves this doctrine undisturbed.[14] If counsel questions a witness about a prior statement concerning a collateral matter, he must accept the witness's answer because extrinsic evidence is not available to prove a prior statement embracing a collateral matter. Counsel may not produce other witnesses or documentary evidence to prove the factual nature of the statement as to the collateral matter.

The question of whether a matter is collateral is essentially a question of fact. McCormick defines a non-collateral matter as one involving: "(1) facts relevant to the issues in the cause, or (2) facts which are themselves provable by extrinsic evidence to discredit the witness."[15] A matter is not collateral if the fact inquired into could have been proved by either party as part of its case-in-chief, if it reveals a bias or interest on the part of the

---

[12] United States v. International Business Machines Corp., 432 F. Supp 138, 140 (S.D. N.Y. 1977) ("[T]he use of multi-page documents for impeachment purposes without providing specific references to the purported inconsistencies contained therein does not afford the witness an opportunity to explain or deny, or the opposing party an opportunity to interrogate him thereon. To the extent that the documents are also used as impeachment material, the witness and

the adversary are entitled to specific notice of this intended use as well as the portions of the document and the witness' testimony which IBM alleges are contradictory or inconsistent").

[13] See 3 WEINSTEIN, ¶ 613[04], at 613-23.

[14] See Rule 102 and ¶ 102.1 of this Treatise.

[15] See McCORMICK, § 36, at 77.

witness or if it reveals a perceptual defect of the witness. Although not codified, the collateral matter doctrine remains a part of Federal law.[16]

§ 613.6   Necessity of Denial.

Where a witness is impeached with extrinsic evidence of a prior inconsistent statement, he must at some point in the trial be given an opportunity to first deny making the statement. Where the witness admits that he uttered the prior inconsistent statement, extrinsic evidence as to the statement serves no useful purpose. The impeachment is effectively accomplished upon the witness's acknowledgment that his version of the fact has not remained consistent.[17] Therefore, if the witness admits making the prior statement, there is no necessity to provide further proof that it was made.[18]

While McCormick notes that the court certainly has the power to disallow the introduction of extrinsic evidence when the witness has admitted making the statement, he does not think that this result is necessarily mandated by Rule 613. He proposes that the liberal nature of this Rule allows the judge to admit extrinsic evidence even if the witness has verified making the statement in question.

§ 613.7   Rule 613—The Degree of Inconsistency Required for Impeachment.

When a prior statement is introduced to impeach a party, the impeaching party is relying upon an inference that the statement introduced will cast doubt on the credibility of the witness. The negative effect on the credibility of the witness will depend upon the degree of inconsistency between the prior statement and the witness's statement on the stand. McCormick suggests that a direct contradiction need not be found between the prior statement and the in-court testimony, and that "any material variance between the testimony and the previous statement will suffice."[19] Inconsistency will exist when a former statement does not mention a mate-

---

[16] *Id.* at 78. *See* United States v. Nace, 561 F.2d 763, 771 (9th Cir. 1977) (refusal to allow defendant to use prior sworn statement by prosecution witness to impeach was on a collateral matter and therefore not erroneous). *See also* Note, *The Prejudice Rule in Evidence*, 49 S. Cal. L. Rev. 220 (1976).

[17] *E.g.*, United States v. Jones, 578 F.2d 1332, 1340 (10th Cir. 1978); United States v. Cline, 570 F.2d 731, 735 (8th Cir. 1978) (dictum).

[18] *See* McCormick, § 34, at 80.

[19] *Id.* § 34, at 74.

rial fact to which the witness has presently testified which is so important that he would naturally have mentioned it in his prior statement.[20] Also, if the witness testified to facts at trial that in his prior statement he said he could not remember, impeachment should be allowed.[21]

Rule 613 does not contain a test that determines when a statement is inconsistent, and the degree of necessary inconsistency will be governed by prior case law. A general test endorsed by McCormick is set forth in *United States v. Barrett*,[22] in which the court stated that, "It is enough if the proffered testimony, taken as a whole, either by what it says or by what it omits to say, affords some indication that the fact was different from the testimony of the witness whom it sought to contradict."[23]

§ 613.8   Admissions of a Party-Opponent.

The opportunity for explanation requirement of Rule 613(b) does not apply to out-of-court statements of a party-opponent admissible as substantive evidence under Rule 801(d)(2). Trial counsel, therefore, may prove that a party-witness made an inconsistent statement without affording the party an opportunity to explain or deny the statement.

Out-of-court statements of a party, offered against the party, have an independent basis for admissibility under Rule 801(d)(2). Consistent with the estoppel theory supporting the admissibility of such statements under Rule 801(d)(2),[24] there is no "opportunity for explanation requirement" for the introduction of extrinsic evidence of out-of-court statements of a party-witness. Providing they are offered against the party at trial, statements qualify for admission regardless of whether the party testifies as a witness.[25]

---

[20] *Id.* § 34, at 44. *See also* United States v. Standard Oil Co., 316 F.2d 884, 891-92 (7th Cir. 1963) (error to disallow defense cross-examination concerning prior statement by witness which omitted matters to which witness testified at trial). *See, e.g.,* Chicago, M. & St. P. R. Co. v. Harrellson, 14 F.2d 893, 896-97 (8th Cir. 1926).

[21] *See* McCormick, § 34, at 75.

[22] 539 F.2d 244 (1st Cir. 1976) *cited in* McCormick, § 34, at 75 n.18.

[23] United States v. Barrett, 539 F.2d 244, 254 (1st Cir. 1976).

[24] *See* United States v. Kenny, 645 F.2d 1323, 1340 (9th Cir. 1981), *cert. denied,* 454 U.S. 828, 102 S.Ct. 121, 70 L.Ed.2d 104 (1982). *See, generally,* 3 Weinstein, ¶ 613[02]; 3 Louisell & Mueller, § 358; 4 Wigmore, § 1051.

[25] *See* §§ 801.23 *et seq.* of this Treatise. *See also* 4 Wigmore, § 1051.

Chapter 614

RULE 614. CALLING AND INTERROGATION OF WITNESSES BY COURT

Rule 614 reads as follows:

(a) **Calling by Court.** The court may, on its own motion or at the suggestion of a party, call witnesses, and all parties are entitled to cross-examine witnesses thus called.

(b) **Interrogation by Court.** The court may interrogate witnesses, whether called by itself or by a party.

(c) **Objections.** Objections to the calling of witnesses by the court or to interrogation by it may be made at the time or at the next available opportunity when the jury is not present.

§ 614.1 Calling and Interrogation of Witnesses by Court—In General.

Rule 614 permits trial judges to call and interrogate witnesses in civil and criminal cases.[1] The Rule is predicated upon the theory that the trial judge bears the ultimate duty of ensuring that the truth emerges from the

---

[1] *See, generally,* 3 WEINSTEIN, ¶ 614[01]-[04]; 3 LOUISELL & MUELLER, §§ 363-66; McCORMICK, § 8, at 12-14; 3 WIGMORE, § 784; 9 WIGMORE, § 2484. *See also* Close, *The Right and Duty of a Trial Court to Call Witnesses in Civil Actions,* 25 INS. COUNS. J. 278 (1958); Gitelson & Gitelson, *A Trial Judge's Credo Must Include His Affirmative Duty to Be An Instrumentality of Justice,* 7 SANTA CLARA LAWYER 7 (1966); Newark & Samuels, *Let the Judge Call the Witness,* 1969 CRIM. L. REV. 399; Comment, *Evidence — Impeachment of Witness Called by Court,* 20 WAYNE L. REV. 1385 (1974); Note, *The Power of a Trial Judge to Call a Witness — A Tool to Mend Defects,* 21 S.C.L. REV. 224 (1969); Note, *The Trial Judge's Use of His Power to Call Witnesses — An Aid to Adversary Presentation,* 51 N.W. U.L. REV. 761 (1957).

proceedings before him.[2] Since, as Wigmore explains, the power to adjudicate involves the power to investigate, the authority to summon and question witnesses is an implied authority of judges.[3]

The power to call witnesses, however, may not be wielded indiscriminately by the trial judge, and where the trial court engages in excessive intervention, amounting to an abridgment of a party's right of an impartial arbiter or the jury's obligation to determine the facts, the resulting prejudice to the affected party may be a reversible abuse of discretion.[4] There is often a fine line between helpful clarification and unwarranted intervention, and reviewing courts have cautioned that trial courts should exercise utmost care in calling witnesses.[5]

§ 614.2   Rule 614(a)—Calling by Court.

Rule 614(a) follows prior Federal practice in permitting the court to call witnesses on its own initiative or at the urging of counsel. Should the court elect to call a witness, all parties are allowed to cross-examine that witness. This procedure affords the trial judge flexibility in obtaining information he deems essential to a fair determination of the dispute but which the parties have failed to provide.[6]

As a practical matter courts will approach the exercise of the right to call witnesses with some degree of circumspection since merely presenting a person as the court's witness may clothe that witness with an enhanced measure of dignity and prestige. The result may be an unwarranted invasion of the adversarial system and the parties' interest in controlling the presentation of evidence in a dispute.[7]

[2] *See, e.g.*, United States v. Leslie, 542 F.2d 285, 288 (5th Cir. 1976); United States v. Wilson, 361 F.2d 134, 136 (7th Cir. 1966).

[3] 9 WIGMORE, § 2484, at 267; 3 WEINSTEIN, ¶ 614[01].

[4] *See* United States v. Herring, 602 F.2d 1220, 1226 (5th Cir. 1979) (no abuse of discretion, considering collateral nature of testimony, where court refused to call witness so that defendant could cross-examine him). *See also* United States v. Karnes, 531 F.2d 214, 216-17 (4th Cir. 1976). *See, e.g.*, Smith v. United States, 331 F.2d 265, 273 (8th Cir. 1964); United States v. Lutwak, 195 F.2d 748, 754 (7th Cir. 1952), *aff'd*, 344 U.S. 60, 73 S.Ct. 481, 97 L.Ed. 593 (1953).

[5] *See, e.g.*, United States v. Meding-Verdugo, 637 F.2d 649, 653 (9th Cir. 1980);

United States v. Gunter, 631 F.2d 583, 587-88 (8th Cir. 1980); United States v. Price, 623 F.2d 587, 592-93 (9th Cir. 1980), *cert. denied*, 449 U.S. 1016, 101 S.Ct. 577, 66 L.Ed.2d 475 (1981).

[6] *See* Johnson v. United States, 333 U.S. 46, 54, 68 S.Ct. 391, 395, 92 L.Ed. 468, 475 (1948) (dissenting opinion discusses right and duty of judge to call witnesses); United States v. Nelson, 570 F.2d 258, 262 (8th Cir. 1978) ("a federal district judge is more than a moderator and has an active duty to see that any trial, including a criminal one, is fairly conducted and the issues clearly presented").

[7] Close, *The Right and Duty of a Trial Court to Call Witnesses in Civil Actions*, 25 INS. COUNS. J. 278, 287 (1958), *cited in*, 3 WEINSTEIN, ¶ 614[02], at 614-6.

§ 614.3   Rule 614(b)—Interrogation by Court.

The power of the trial court to interrogate witnesses brought before it existed at common law and was recognized long before its codification in formal rules of evidence. This power, of course, is subject always to the restriction that the judge must maintain her status as an impartial arbiter.[8] Accordingly, it would be an abuse of discretion for the trial judge, through his interrogation, to convey to the jury his personal appraisal of the credibility of the witness or the merits of the case.[9] To do so would be to invade the province of the trier of fact in determining factual issues. However, the trial judge is permitted to comment on the evidence, providing of course, such commentary does not evince advocacy or bias.[10]

In reviewing any alleged prejudicial errors resulting from the court's independent interrogation of witnesses, a reviewing court will examine the questioning in light of the entire record and, based upon the totality of the circumstances, determine whether there has been a manifest abuse of discretion.[11]

§ 614.4   Rule 614(c)—Objections.

The final provision of Rule 614 permits trial counsel to make objections to either the court's calling of its own witness or the court's manner of questioning of any witness. Moreover, Rule 614(c) provides that such objection is timely if it is made at the earliest opportunity out of the hearing of the jury. The Rule seeks an accommodation between the attorney's responsibility of timely objection to evidentiary matters and the protection from possible embarrassment or prejudice resulting from objecting to conduct from the bench in front of the jury. Under Rule 614(c), a party may assess the prejudice to his case before interposing an objection since he does not

---

[8] *See, e.g.*, United States v. Moore, 627 F.2d 830, 832 (7th Cir. 1980); Rogers v. United States, 609 F.2d 1315, 1318 (9th Cir. 1979).

[9] *See* United States v. Welliver, 601 F.2d 203, 208-09 (5th Cir. 1979); United States v. Hickman, 592 F.2d 931, 933 (6th Cir. 1979). *See also*, Advisory Committee's Note, Rule 614.

[10] *See* Union Carbide and Carbon Corp. v. Nisley, 300 F.2d 561, 586 (10th Cir. 1961), *dismissed sub. nom.*, Wade v. Union Carbide and Carbon Corp., 371 U.S. 801, 83 S.Ct. 13, 9 L.Ed.2d 46 (1962) ("a judge

presiding over a federal court is not a mere umpire; he has both the responsibility of assuring the proper conduct of the trial and the power to bring out the facts of the case"). *See also* United States v. Guglielmini, 384 F.2d 602, 605 (2d Cir. 1967); United States v. Barbour, 420 F.2d 1319, 1321 (D.C. Cir. 1969).

[11] *See* United States v. Parodi, 703 F.2d 768, 775-78 (4th Cir. 1983); Moore v. United States, 598 F.2d 439, 442-43 (5th Cir. 1979); United States v. Cooper, 596 F.2d 327, 330 (8th Cir. 1979).

forfeit his right to object by failing to object when the court first asks the question or calls the witness.

It must be noted that Rule 614(c) does not entirely relieve the litigant of his duty to object in order to preserve the exception on appeal. Where a party fails to object in timely fashion, *i.e.*, at the next available time when the jury is not present, objection to the alleged error will be deemed waived unless it constitutes plain error.[12] The Rule implicitly recognizes the duty of counsel to preserve his objection to the improper introduction of any evidence, despite its solicitation by the bench.

[12] *See* United States v. Vega, 589 F.2d 1147, 1152-53 (2d Cir. 1978) (waiver); United States v. Hickman, 592 F.2d 931, 936 (6th Cir. 1979) (plain error standard). *See also* Rule 103 and Chapter 103 of this Treatise.

Chapter 615

RULE 615. EXCLUSION OF WITNESSES

Rule 615 reads as follows:

At the request of a party the court shall order witnesses excluded so that they cannot hear the testimony of other witnesses, and it may make the order of its own motion. This rule does not authorize exclusion of (1) a party who is a natural person, or (2) an officer or employee of a party which is not a natural person designated as its representative by its attorney, or (3) a person whose presence is shown by a party to be essential to the presentation of his cause.

§ 615.1   Rule 615—Exclusion of Witnesses—In General.

Rule 615 provides that a party has a right to the separation of witnesses upon a timely request.[1] Where the request is made, the trial judge lacks the discretion to deny the request except in regard to certain necessary witnesses identified in the Rule. As the Advisory Committee's Note reflects, the use of the term "shall" in the Rule is intended to convey the absence of discretion of the trial judge in response to a separation request. The present rule adopts the position of Wigmore that:

[The sequestration of a witness] seems properly to be demandable as of right, precisely as in cross-examination. In the first place, it is

---

[1] *See, generally,* 3 WEINSTEIN, ¶¶ 615[01]-[03]; 3 LOUISELL & MUELLER, §§ 370-71; 6 WIGMORE, §§ 1837-41. *See also* Comment, *Witnesses Under Article VI of the Proposed Federal Rules of Evidence,* 15 WAYNE L. REV. 1236, 1247-49; Note, *Witnesses — Enforcing a Sequestration Order to Exclude Witnesses — Barring the Witness from Testifying,* 11 KAN. L. REV. 410 (1963).

simple and feasible. In the next place, it is so powerful and practical a weapon of defense that no contingency can justify its denial as being a mere formality or an empty sentimentality. In the third place, in the case when it is most useful (namely, a combination to perjure), it is almost the only hope of an innocent opponent.[2] . . . [Furthermore, to require counsel] to show some probable need to the judge, and to leave to the latter the estimation of the need, is to misunderstand the whole virtue of the expedient, and to deny it in perhaps that very situation of forlorn hope and desperate extreme when it is most valuable and most demandable.[3]

The Rule is predicated upon the well-established practice of separating witnesses in order to facilitate the exposure of inconsistencies in their testimony. Likewise, the Rule is designed to prevent the possibility of a witness shaping his testimony to conform with that of another.[4]

§ 615.2   Persons Not Subject to Exclusion.

While the Rule mandates that witnesses must be separated at the request of a party, and further permits the court on its own motion to effect the same result, certain persons may not be excluded or separated under any circumstances.

Subsection (1) prohibits the separation of a party who is a natural person.[5] Subsection (2) prohibits exclusion of the designated representative of a party which is not a natural person, *e.g.*, a corporate director, officer or employee, or a government agent or police officer responsible for the investigation of the case.[6] Subsection (3) prohibits separation or exclusion of a witness whose presence is shown by the party to be essential to the presentation of his cause.[7] One example of a witness whose presence at trial

---

[2] 6 WIGMORE, § 1839, at 357.

[3] *Id.* at 358.

[4] United States v. Juarez, 573 F.2d 267, 281 (5th Cir. 1978), *cert. denied*, 439 U.S. 915, 99 S.Ct. 289, 58 L.Ed.2d 263 (1978) (proper to exclude witnesses during closing arguments which often restate witnesses' testimony, since the trial judge could fear that if witnesses learned the testimony of other witnesses, the fairness of a second trial might be jeopardized). *See also* United States v. Leggett, 326 F.2d 613, 615 (4th Cir. 1964), *cert. denied*, 377 U.S. 955, 84 S.Ct. 1633, 12 L.Ed.2d 499 (1964).

[5] Varlack v. SWC Caribbean, Inc., 550 F.2d 171, 173 (3d Cir. 1977) (sequestering person until he was formally made a party, where court refused to rule on whether it would permit complaint to be amended to add the additional party until some of the most important testimony in the case had been given, was reversible error).

[6] United States v. Jones, 687 F.2d 1265, 1268 (8th Cir. 1982); United States v. Parodi, 703 F.2d 768, 773-75 (4th Cir. 1983).

[7] United States v. Burgess, 691 F.2d 1146, 1157 (4th Cir. 1982). *See also* Morvant v. Construction Aggregates Corp., 570 F.2d 626, 629-30 (6th Cir. 1978), *cert. dismissed*, 439 U.S. 801, 99 S.Ct. 44, 58 L.Ed.2d 94 (1978) (not automatic basis for exemption

would be mandated under this subsection, is an expert witness who will testify from facts or data he acquires at trial.[8] If the expert plans to testify at trial and will base his testimony on the facts or data contained in the testimony of other witnesses, the court may not separate this witness.[9] Under subsection (3), the court has discretion in determining whether the witness's presence is essential, and the burden of demonstrating the necessity is upon the proponent of the witness.[10]

§ 615.3   Violation of a Separation Order.

Where the exclusion or separation order is violated by a witness or party, the court possesses the customary discretion in taking corrective measures.[11] Remedial measures include citing the witness for contempt, refusing to permit him to testify, striking his testimony, or permitting the transgression to reflect upon the witness's credibility.[12] Unfortunately, no remedy is "wholly satisfactory." A contempt citation has the effect of punishing the witness involved and may deter others,[13] but it "does nothing to extinguish any false testimony which the witness may have fabricated by listening to other witnesses."[14] Commenting on the witness's noncompliance is undesirable because it may cause a jury to wrongfully diminish the weight of truthful testimony which was untainted by the witness's violation of the sequestration order.[15] Finally, forbidding the witness to testify at the trial is the severest sanction, and may have the effect of removing relevant evi-

---

from sequestration that expert witness may be assisted by being present in courtroom to hear testimony upon which he is expected to base his expert testimony; the decision whether to permit the expert witness to remain is within the discretion of the trial judge and should not normally be disturbed on appeal). *Cf.*, N.L.R.B. v. Pope Maintenance Corp., 573 F.2d 898, 906-07 (5th Cir. 1978).

[8] *See* Rule 703 *infra*.

[9] United States v. Burgess, 691 F.2d 1146, 1157 (4th Cir. 1982); Morvant v. Construction Aggregates Corp., 570 F.2d 626, 630 (6th Cir. 1978).

[10] *See* Marathon Pipe Line Co. v. Drilling Rig Rowan/Odessa, 699 F.2d 240, 241-42 (5th Cir. 1983), *cert. denied*, 104 S.Ct. 82 (1983); Government of Virgin Islands v. Edinborough, 625 F.2d 472, 475 (3d Cir. 1980); United States v. Causey, 609 F.2d 777, 778 (5th Cir. 1980). *See also* Curlee Clothing Corp. v. N.L.R.B., 607 F.2d 1213,

1215 (7th Cir. 1979); Sturgiss Newport Business Forms, Inc. v. N.L.R.B., 563 F.2d 1252, 1255 (5th Cir. 1977).

[11] *See, e.g.*, United States v. Nash, 649 F.2d 369, 371 (5th Cir. 1981). *See also* Reeves v. International Tel. & Tel. Corp., 616 F.2d 1342, 1344 (5th Cir. 1980), *cert. denied*, 449 U.S. 1078, 101 S.Ct. 857, 66 L.Ed.2d 800 (1981) (court refused to overturn district court's order prohibiting any testimony from witnesses with whom counsel for defendant met with and discussed the case in preparation for testimony, in flagrant violation of previously entered sequestration and separation order).

[12] *See* 3 WEINSTEIN, ¶ 615[03], at 615-14.

[13] *Id.*

[14] Note, *Witnesses - Enforcing a Sequestration Order to Exclude Witnesses - Barring the Witness from Testifying*, 11 KAN. L. REV. 410, 411 (1963), *cited in*, 3 WEINSTEIN, ¶ 615[03], at 615-15.

[15] *See* 3 WEINSTEIN, ¶ 615[03], at 615-15.

dence entirely from the jury's consideration.[16] Generally, the court may be reversed only for an abuse of discretion in taking such measures.[17]

[16] *See* United States v. Nash, 649 F.2d 369, 371 (5th Cir. 1981); Reeves v. I.T. & T. Corp., 616 F.2d 1342, 1344 (5th Cir. 1980), *cert. denied*, 449 U.S. 1078, 101 S.Ct. 857, 66 L.Ed.2d 800 (1981). *See* Holder v. United States, 150 U.S. 91, 95, 14 S.Ct. 10, 14, 37 L.Ed. 1010, 1012 (1893) (the Supreme Court endorsed the proposition that a trial court may not routinely disqualify the testimony of a witness who violates a sequestration order without first finding that some particular factual issue exists which justifies such a drastic remedy).

[17] *See, e.g.*, United States v. Gibson, 675 F.2d 825, 835-36 (6th Cir. 1982), *cert. denied*, 459 U.S. 972, 103 S.Ct. 305, 74 L.Ed.2d 285 (1982); United States *ex rel.* Clark v. Fike, 538 F.2d 750, 757 (7th Cir. 1976), *cert. denied*, 429 U.S. 1064, 97 S.Ct. 791, 59 L.Ed.2d 781 (1976) (court has discretion to allow witness who has disobeyed sequestration order to testify).

VII

OPINIONS AND EXPERT TESTIMONY

Chapter 701

RULE 701. OPINION TESTIMONY BY LAY WITNESSES

Rule 701 reads as follows:

> If the witness is not testifying as an expert, his testimony in the form of opinions or inferences is limited to those opinions or inferences which are (a) rationally based on the perception of the witness and (b) helpful to a clear understanding of his testimony or the determination of a fact in issue.

§ 701.1 Lay Opinion Testimony—In General.

Traditionally, courts have required lay witnesses to testify to facts rather than opinions. The line between fact and opinion often proved nearly impossible to draw, and Rule 701 obviates the necessity for such compartmentalization by permitting lay witnesses to render opinions when the criteria for admissibility contained in the Rule are satisfied.[1]

---

[1] See, generally, McCORMICK, § 11; 3 WEINSTEIN, ¶¶ 701[01]-[04]; 3 LOUISELL & MUELLER, §§ 375-79; 7 WIGMORE, §§ 1917-29. See also Ladd, Expert Testimony, 5 VAND. L. REV. 414 (1952); Manning & Mewitt, Psychiatric Evidence, 18 CRIM. L.Q. 325 (1976); McCormick, Opinion Evidence in Iowa, 19 DRAKE L. REV. 245 (1970); Martin, The Uncertain Rules of Certainty: An Analysis and Proposal for a Federal Evidence Rule, 20 WAYNE L. REV. 781 (1974); Spector & Foster, Admissibility of Hypnotic Statements: Is the Law of Evidence Susceptible?, 38 OHIO L. REV. 567 (1977); Spies, Opinion Evidence, 15 ARK. L. REV. 105 (1960); Slovenko, The Opinion Rule and Wittgenstein's Tractatus, 14 MIAMI L. REV. 1 (1959); Tyree, The Opinion Rule, 10 RUTGERS L. REV. 601 (1956); Williams, Law and Practice in the Identification of Controlled Drugs by Lay Testimony, 11 CRIM. L. BULL. 814 (1975).

§ 701.2 History of the Rule Prohibiting Lay Opinion Testimony.

Even prior to the adoption of the Federal Rules of Evidence, federal courts have deviated from a strict interpretation of the general proposition that witnesses may testify only to facts and not to inferences or opinions predicated upon facts.[2] This general rule of exclusion was based largely on the misapprehension that opinions from witnesses would invade the province of the jury.[3] Exceptions to the general prohibition of opinion testimony developed, and at an early date, opinion testimony by experts was removed from the proscription of the general rule.[4] The "collective facts" or "shorthand rendition" exception developed after federal courts recognized that some lay testimony containing a composite of fact and opinion should be admitted when the witness cannot adequately convey his point through strictly factual descriptions. For example, the witness may testify to his conclusion or impression that someone was nervous rather than describing the various details which led him to reach his conclusion. On cross-examination, the party opposing the evidence can question the witness about the specific facts upon which he based his conclusion.[5]

The creation of the "collective facts" exception reveals a limited recognition of the invalidity of the fact/opinion dichotomy which underpins the general prohibition of opinion testimony. The now-obsolete exclusionary rule rested on the notion that a distinction always can be made between

---

[2] *See, e.g.*, Panger v. Duluth, Winnipeg & Pacific Railway Co., 490 F.2d 1112, 1114 (8th Cir. 1974) (railway employees allowed to express opinions as to the safety of certain business practices); Fullerton v. Sauer, 337 F.2d 474, 478 (8th Cir. 1964) (plaintiff allowed to express opinion on whether he could have avoided the auto accident when the car with which he collided suddenly came into view).

[3] McCormick, § 12, at 30 (3d ed. 1984). The history of the rule against opinions by lay witnesses indicates that it may have developed due to a misunderstanding of the meaning of the word "opinion." Before the 1800's, "opinion" referred to a notion unsupported by definite knowledge. Therefore, the rule against opinions was another way of stating the requirement that witnesses must have personal knowledge of the facts. In reference to the firsthand knowledge rule, English text writers used the shorthand expression that witnesses must testify to facts, not opinions. In the Ameri-

can courts, "[t]his statement of the rule led to more than a hundred years of confusion." King & Pillinger, Opinion Evidence in Illinois 7 (1942).

[4] *See* 7 Wigmore, § 1917, at 13.

[5] 3 Louisell & Mueller, § 376, at 622. *See, e.g.*, Kerry Coal Co. v. United Mine Workers, 637 F.2d 957, 967 (3d Cir. 1981), *cert. denied*, 454 U.S. 823, 102 S.Ct. 109, 70 L.Ed.2d 95 (1981) (witness's testimony that employees were nervous and afraid was a shorthand report of his observations); United States v. McClintic, 570 F.2d 685, 689-90 (8th Cir. 1978) (prosecution witness permitted to testify that in his opinion defendant knew the goods were obtained by fraud); United States v. Freeman, 514 F.2d 1184, 1191 (10th Cir. 1975) (prosecution for interstate fraud scheme; bank officer properly permitted to testify that there was no doubt in his mind that appellant was selling all of his equipment; he was merely giving rendition of his knowledge).

"fact" and "opinion." McCormick's condemnation of this concept is pertinent:

> There is no conceivable statement however specific, detailed and "factual," that is not in some measure the product of inference and reflection as well as observation and memory. The difference between the statement, "He was driving on the left-hand side of the road" which would be classed as fact under the rule, and "He was driving carelessly" which would be called "opinion" is merely a difference between a more concrete and specific form of descriptive statement and a less specific and concrete form. The difference between the so-called "fact," then, and "opinion," is not a difference between opposites or contrasting absolutes, but a mere difference in degree with no recognizable line to mark the boundary.[6]

In a particular case, the distinction between fact and opinion depends upon whether the lay witness's testimony relates to a critical issue or to a peripheral matter: "In the outer circle of collateral facts, near the rim of relevancy, evidence in general terms will be received with relative freedom, but as we come closer to the hub of the issue, the courts have been more careful to call for details instead of inferences."[7]

§ 701.3 Standards of Admissibility—Opinions Rationally Based on the Perception of a Witness.

Rule 701 permits the rendering of lay opinion testimony only when each of the Rule's standards for admissibility are satisfied. The first standard articulated by the Rule, which requires that the opinion or inference of a lay witness be rationally based on the perceptions of the witness, is in actuality two distinct limitations. The first limitation is the principle prescribed by Rule 602 which requires that the witness have firsthand knowledge of the subject of his testimony. The second limitation, termed the "rational connection" test, requires that the opinion or inference advanced by the witness must be one that a rational person would form on the basis of the observed facts.[8] Strained or contrived inferences do not satisfy the standard. Likewise, mere speculations are not rendered admissible by the Rule. However, the fact that the witness qualifies his testimony with statements such as "I think" or "to the best of my recollection" does not transform the testimony into an inadmissible opinion under Rule 701.[9]

[6] McCormick, § 11, at 27.
[7] Id., § 12, at 30.

[8] 3 Weinstein, ¶ 701[02], at 701-11.
[9] Id. at 701-17.

§ 701.4   Standards of Admissibility—Helpfulness to the Jury; Judicial Discretion.

The second standard of admissibility articulated by Rule 701 is the requirement that the lay opinion testimony must be "helpful" to the trier of fact in understanding the testimony of the witness or in determining a fact in issue.[10] Under the "helpfulness" test, opinion evidence should be admitted in a wide range of situations. The witness should be able to testify in the form of opinion if necessary to avoid misleading the jury, *i.e.*, the witness cannot "accurately, adequately and with reasonable facility describe the fundamental facts upon which the opinion is erected."[11]

The witness should also be allowed to testify in the form of an opinion to conclusions or observations that he draws through his senses, such as "the appearance of persons or things, identity, the manner of conduct, competency of a person, feeling degrees of light or darkness, sound, size, weight, distance and an endless number of things that cannot be described factually in words apart from inferences."[12] If the personal knowledge and helpfulness requirements of Rule 701 are satisfied, lay witnesses should be permitted to testify to the "unspoken knowledge, intent, understanding or feelings of another."[13]

It is important to note that lay opinions are not "helpful" under the Rule whenever the jury can readily draw the necessary inferences and conclusions without the aid of the opinion. In this regard Wigmore notes that the true theory underlying the exclusion of lay opinion testimony is that such opinions are superfluous when the jury, unaided by opinion, can draw the necessary inferences as effectively as the witness.[14] Accordingly, the Rule vests considerable discretion in the trial court and mandates care in determining whether the jury will be aided by lay opinion testimony in reaching

---

[10] *See, e.g.*, United States v. Jackson, 569 F.2d 1003, 1011 (7th Cir. 1978), *cert. denied*, 437 U.S. 907, 98 S.Ct. 3096, 57 L.Ed.2d 1137 (trial judge properly refused to allow lay witness to testify why her husband was depressed). *See also* United States v. Thompson, 708 F.2d 1294, 1296 (8th Cir. 1983); Kroeger v. State Farm Mutual Automobile Ins. Co., 707 F.2d 312, 315 (8th Cir. 1983); United States v. Goodheim, 686 F.2d 776, 778 (9th Cir. 1982).

[11] MORGAN, BASIC PROBLEMS OF EVIDENCE, § 217 (1962).

[12] Ladd, *Expert testimony*, 5 VAND. L. REV. 414, 417 (1952). *See, e.g.*, Singletary v.

Secretary of Health, Education and Welfare, 623 F.2d 217, 219 (2d Cir. 1980) (drunkenness); Young v. Illinois C.G.R. Co., 618 F.2d 332, 337 (5th Cir. 1980) (poor condition of grade crossing); United States v. Arrasmith, 557 F.2d 1093, 1094 (5th Cir. 1977) (odor of marijuana). *See also* United States v. Murray, 523 F.2d 489, 491, n.1 (8th Cir. 1975); United States v. Mastberg, 503 F.2d 465, 467 (9th Cir. 1974); Wood v. United States, 361 F.2d 802, 805 (8th Cir. 1966).

[13] 3 LOUISELL & MUELLER, § 376, at 626 (1979).

[14] 7 WIGMORE, §§ 1917-18, at 10-11.

a just result.[15] Furthermore, in a proper case, lay opinion testimony otherwise admissible may be excluded by the trial court if the probative value of the testimony is sufficiently outweighed by the considerations set forth in Rule 403.

---

[15] *See* 3 WEINSTEIN, ¶ 701[02], at 701-17; 3 LOUISELL & MUELLER, § 376, at 627.

Chapter 702

RULE 702. TESTIMONY BY EXPERTS

Rule 702 reads as follows:

> If scientific, technical, or other specialized knowledge will assist the trier of fact to understand the evidence or to determine a fact in issue, a witness qualified as an expert by knowledge, skill, experience, training, or education, may testify thereto in the form of an opinion or otherwise.

§ 702.1 Testimony by Experts—In General.

Rule 702, which governs the admissibility of the testimony by experts, performs four distinct functions.[1] First, it serves as an authorization for the use of expert testimony. Second, the Rule articulates standards to be ap-

---

[1] *See, generally,* McCormick, § 13; 3 Weinstein, ¶¶ 702[01]-[05]; 3 Louisell & Mueller, §§ 380-83. *See also* Addison, *Expert Testimony on Eyewitness Perception,* 82 Dickinson L. Rev. 465 (1978); Decker & Handler, *Voiceprint Identification - Out of the Frye Pan and Into Admissibility,* 26 Am. U.L. Rev. 314 (1977); Diamond & Louisell, *The Psychiatrist as an Expert Witness: Some Ruminations and Speculations,* 63 Mich. L. Rev. 1335 (1965); Donaher, Piehler, Twerski, & Weinstein, *The Technological Expert in Products Liability Litigation,* 52 Tex. L. Rev. 1303 (1974); Finkelstein, *A Statistical Analysis of Guilty Plea Practice in the Federal Court,* 89 Harv. L. Rev. 293 (1975); Frank, *Obscenity: Some Problems of Values and the Use of Experts,* 41 Wash. L. Rev. 631 (1966); Giannelli, *The Admissibility of Novel Scientific Evidence: Frye v. United States, a Half Century Later,* 80 Colum. L. Rev. 1197 (1980); Hale, *The Admissibility of Bite Mark Evidence,* 51 S. Cal. L. Rev. 309 (1978); Lewin, *Psychiatric Evidence in Criminal Cases for Purposes Other Than the Defense of Insanity,* 26 Syracuse L. Rev. 1051 (1975); O'Connor, *That's the Man: A Sobering Study of Eyewitness Identification and the Polygraph,* 49 St. John's L. Rev. 1 (1974); Richards & Kidner, *Judicial Attitudes Towards Actuarial Evidence,* 124 New L.J. 105 (1974); Wolfgang, *The Social Scientist in Court,* 65 J. Crim. L. 239 (1974).

plied in determining whether expert testimony should be admitted in a particular case. Third, the Rule provides criteria to be applied in determining whether an individual tendered as an expert witness should be accorded expert status by the trial court. Finally, the Rule expands the form the expert testimony may assume.

§ 702.2   Rationale and Purpose of Rule 702.

Expert testimony has traditionally been considered an exception to the general rule requiring witnesses to testify to facts rather than opinions.[2] By reason of his expertise in a particular area, the expert is qualified to draw inferences from facts that a jury would be unable to draw. Because the expert's value to the litigation process lies in his special inferential skills, the expert is not required to have firsthand knowledge of the particular set of facts supporting his opinion or inference as is required of a lay witness under Rules 602 and 701.

§ 702.3   Subjects Regarding Which Expert Testimony is Proper.

Expert testimony is used to enable the jury to draw the proper inferences from the facts in certain situations. Under prior practice, the subject matter of the expertise of the witness had to relate to some area of specialization beyond the experience of average laymen.[3] Rule 702 is more expansive in providing that testimony may extend to all types of "specialized knowledge," including, specifically, scientific and technical matters. Federal courts may admit expert testimony on subjects within the knowledge of the average juror. The ultimate standard is whether the expert brings a helpful quality to the litigation which otherwise would be lacking.[4]

While the test for the use of expert testimony requires that the trier of fact be aided by the testimony,[5] the standard is a relative one which de-

[2] See § 701.2, supra.

[3] Bridger v. Union Railway Co., 355 F.2d 382, 387 (6th Cir. 1966). See also United States v. Scavo, 593 F.2d 837, 844 (8th Cir. 1979); United States v. Johnson, 575 F.2d 1347, 1360-61 (5th Cir. 1978), cert. denied, 440 U.S. 907, 99 S.Ct. 1214, 59 L.Ed.2d 454 (1979).

[4] United States v. Sickles, 524 F. Supp. 506, 511-12 (D.Del. 1981), aff'd, 688 F.2d 827 (3d Cir. 1982). See also Zenith Radio Corp. v. Matsushita Electric Industrial Co.,

Inc., 505 F. Supp. 1313, 1330 (E.D. Pa. 1980) ("[a]s defined by the Advisory Committee, the helpfulness inquiry is whether the untrained layman would be qualified to determine intelligently and to the best possible degree the particular issue without enlightenment from those having a specialized understanding of the subject involved in the dispute").

[5] See Advisory Committee's Note to Federal Rule 702.

pends upon the particular subject or the particular witness. Wigmore articulated the test as, "[o]n *this subject* can a jury receive from *this person* appreciable help?"[6] By necessity, the trial court must be afforded a substantial degree of discretion in determining whether to permit expert testimony in a particular case. Expert testimony may be excluded when it is more prejudicial that probative, confusing to the jury or unduly time-consumptive.[7]

The trial court's discretion also should extend to the determination of whether the state of the art in a particular discipline permits a rational and reliable opinion to be asserted by an expert. In 1923, the court in *Frye v. United States* held that novel scientific evidence should not be admitted until it "gained general acceptance in the particular field in which it belongs."[8] The *Frye* test was widely followed prior to the adoption of the Federal Rules of Evidence, although critics contended that "general acceptance" was a more appropriate standard for judicial notice of new techniques than for the admissibility of evidence.[9] Rule 702 appears to have abandoned the *Frye* doctrine in favor of the broader test of whether evidence based on a new technique or principle is "sufficiently reliable so that it will aid the jury in reaching accurate results."[10] Doubts as to the usefulness of an expert's opinion should be resolved in favor of admissibility unless the helpfulness of the opinion is outweighed by such dangers as misleading the jury with an aura of infallibility which surrounds the evidence, waste of time or surprise.[11]

The admission of expert testimony usually is discretionary. However, in some cases, such as medical malpractice actions, the substantive law may require the plaintiff to produce expert evidence.[12] Conversely, expert testi-

---

[6] 7 WIGMORE, § 1923, at 21 (emphasis in original).

[7] United States v. Purham, 725 F.2d 450, 454 (8th Cir. 1984); United States v. Rohrer, 708 F.2d 429, 431 (9th Cir. 1983); Zenith Radio Corp. v. Matsushita Electric Industrial Co., 505 F. Supp. 1313, 1330 (E.D. Pa. 1980).

[8] 293 F. 1013, 1014 (D.C. Cir. 1923).

[9] *See* McCORMICK, EVIDENCE, § 203, at 608.

[10] 3 WEINSTEIN, ¶ 702[03], at 702-15. *See, e.g.,* United States v. Black, 684 F.2d 481, 484 (7th Cir. 1982), *cert. denied,* 459 U.S. 1043, 103 S.Ct. 463 (court has discretion to admit or exclude polygraph evidence); Garwood v. International Paper Co., 666 F.2d 217, 223 (5th Cir. 1982)

(court has discretion to exclude human factors engineering expert); Seese v. Volkswagenwerk A.G., 648 F.2d 833, 844-45 (3d Cir.), *cert. denied,* 454 U.S. 867, 102 S.CT. 330, 70 L.Ed.2d 168 (1981) (court has discretion to admit accident reconstruction expert).

[11] 3 WEINSTEIN, ¶ 702[03], at 702-19 to 20 (1982).

[12] Int'l Brotherhood of Teamsters v. United States, 431 U.S. 324, 339, 97 S.Ct. 1843, 1851, 52 L.Ed.2d 396, 407 (1977); Randolph v. Collectramatic, Inc., 590 F.2d 844, 848 (10th Cir. 1979); Huddell v. Levin, 537 F.2d 726, 736 (3d Cir. 1976). *See also* Comment, *Medical Malpractice—Expert Testimony,* 60 Nw. L. REV. 834 (1966).

mony on American law is inadmissible although experts are permitted to testify on issues involving foreign law.[13]

§ 702.4   Qualifications of Expert Witness; Function of Trial Judge.

Rule 702 addresses the qualifications necessary to accord a witness expert status. Under the Rule, special education or certification is not required; a witness may qualify as an expert by reason of his knowledge, skill, experience, training or education. It is important to note that any one of these characteristics may qualify an individual as an expert, although in the usual case more than one of these factors will be present. The individual offered as an expert need not have complete knowledge of the field in question as long as the knowledge he does possess will aid the trier in performing its function.[14] Expert testimony is not rendered inadmissible because the witness is not absolutely certain[15] or is not unbiased.[16] Relative weaknesses in the expert's body of expertise may be exposed on cross-examination to affect the weight of the testimony.

The determination of whether an individual qualifies as an expert is for the court pursuant to Rule 104(a). This determination is addressed to the discretion of the trial court and will not be reversed on appeal absent clear abuse.[17]

---

[13] Marx & Co. v. Diner's Club, Inc., 550 F.2d 505, 509-11 (2d Cir. 1977), *cert. denied*, 434 U.S. 861, 98 S.Ct. 188, 54 L.Ed.2d 134 (1977) (prejudicial to allow expert to testify to the customary practices of the industry, as well as the "legal standards" which apply in securities fraud case; it is for the judge to explain the applicable principles of law rather than the witness). *Cf.*, Capri Jewelry, Inc. v. Hattie Carnegie Jewelry Enterprises, Ltd., 539 F.2d 846, 849 (2d Cir. 1976).

[14] *See, e.g.*, Carlson Equipment Co. v. International Harvester, 710 F.2d 481, 484 (8th Cir. 1983); United States v. Carroll, 710 F.2d 164, 167-68 (4th Cir. 1983); LaCombe v. A.T.O. Inc., 679 F.2d 431, 434 (5th Cir. 1982).

[15] United States v. Johnson, 575 F.2d 1347, 1361-62 (5th Cir. 1978), *cert. denied*,

440 U.S. 907, 99 S.Ct. 1214, 59 L.Ed.2d 454 (1979) (witness qualified as expert to testify about marijuana and where it had come from, since he had smoked it more than a thousand times, and correctly identified it more than one hundred times and knew more about it than was within the knowledge of an average juror). *See also* United States v. Oaxaca, 569 F.2d 518, 526 (9th Cir. 1978), *cert. denied*, 439 U.S. 926, 99 S.Ct. 310, 58 L.Ed.2d 319 (1978).

[16] *Cf.* United States v. Masson, 582 F.2d 961, 963 (5th Cir. 1978).

[17] Grindstaff v. Coleman, 681 F.2d 740, 743 (11th Cir. 1982); Dunn v. Sears, Roebuck and Co., 639 F.2d 1171, 1174 (5th Cir. 1981), *modified on other grounds*, 645 F.2d 511 (5th Cir. 1981).

§ 702.5   Forms of Expert Testimony.

Traditionally, the primary purpose for qualifying a witness as an expert has been to enable that individual to express his opinion on the matter in issue. Rule 702 authorizes expert testimony in the form of opinion "or otherwise." Allowing an expert to testify in other than opinion form introduces a measure of flexibility into Federal practice. The "or otherwise" language of Rule 702 is designed to permit an expert to provide an exposition of relevant scientific, professional, technical or other principles as a basis for the trier of fact to apply those principles to the relevant issues. Thus, if the jury can draw the needed inferences itself after a technical foundation has been laid by the expert, counsel is free to forego asking the expert's opinion on the ultimate issue.[18]

[18] *See* Advisory Committee's Note to Federal Rule 702.

Chapter 703

RULE 703. BASES OF OPINION TESTIMONY BY EXPERTS

Rule 703 reads as follows:

The facts or data in the particular case upon which an expert bases an opinion or inference may be those perceived by or made known to him at or before the hearing. If of a type reasonably relied upon by experts in the particular field in forming opinions or inferences upon the subject, the facts or data need not be admissible in evidence.

§ 703.1   Bases of Opinion Testimony by Experts—In General.

Rule 703 identifies three permissible sources of facts or data upon which the expert may base his opinion or inference. Two of these sources of expert testimony traditionally have been recognized by the court: the expert may predicate his testimony on firsthand perceptions, or in the alternative, the expert may draw upon facts or information admitted in the hearing at which he is called to testify. Rule 703 departs from prior practice by recognizing a third permissible source of facts or data, *i.e.*, information "made known to" the expert before the hearing. The Rule further provides that if the facts or data are reasonably relied upon by experts in the same field in reaching conclusions, the facts and data constitute a permissible source of information even if they would not be admissible in evidence.

§ 703.2   Policy of Rule 703.

Under Rule 703, the permissible bases for expert opinion include facts "made known to" the expert before the hearing.[1] If of a kind reasonably relied upon, the data itself need not be admissible in evidence. Under previous practice, expert opinions based on evidence not admitted at trial normally were disallowed due to the rule against hearsay, although exceptions were recognized for certain experts, such as physicians[2] and real estate appraisers.[3] In defense of this innovation in the Rule, the Advisory Committee conceded that most of the facts or data upon which an expert would rely in forming an opinion would be admissible in evidence, but only after the expenditure of substantial time in producing and examining various authenticating witnesses.[4] Rule 703 was designed to avoid this needless waste of trial time.

The Rule also seeks to bring judicial procedure in line with the custom and practice of most experts. The usual critical nature of the expert's deter-

---

[1] See, generally, McCormick, § 15; 3 Weinstein, ¶¶ 703[01]-[06]; 3 Louisell & Mueller, §§ 387-90; 3 Wigmore, § 687. See also Dession, Trial of Economic and Technical Issues of Fact: II, 58 Yale L.J. 1242 (1949); Diamond & Louisell, The Psychiatrist As An Expert Witness: Some Ruminations and Speculations, 63 Mich. L. Rev. 1335 (1965); Dieden and Gasparich, Psychiatric Evidence and Full Disclosure in the Criminal Trial, 52 Cal. L. Rev. 543 (1964); Maguire & Hahesy, Requisite Proof of Bases for Expert Opinion, 5 Vand. L. Rev. 432 (1952); Martin, The Uncertain Rule of Certainty: An Analysis and Proposal for a Federal Evidence Rule, 20 Wayne L. Rev. 781 (1974); Rheingold, The Basis of Medical Testimony, 15 Vand. L. Rev. 473 (1962); Romero, The Admissibility of Scientific Evidence Under the New Mexico and Federal Rules of Evidence, 6 N.M. L. Rev. 187, 209-11 (1976); Note, Hearsay Bases of Psychiatric Opinion Testimony: A Critique of Federal Rule of Evidence 703, 51 S. Cal. L. Rev. 129 (1977).

[2] 3 Weinstein, ¶ 703[02], at 703-10 ("The rationale for exempting a physician's opinion from the strict application of the hearsay rule is that reliance on hearsay facts is often necessary, and that the use to which the facts are put guarantees their reliability."). See, e.g., Padgett v. Southern Rail-

way Co., 396 F.2d 303, 308 (6th Cir. 1968) (statements made to a physician for treatment are reliable, but statements made to a physician to qualify him to testify are not; Rule 803(4) rejects this distinction, and statements made for purposes of diagnosis could be the basis for opinions); Birdsell v. United States, 346 F.3d 775, 780 (5th Cir. 1965), cert. denied, 382 U.S. 963, 86 S.Ct. 449, 15 L.Ed.2d 366 (1965), reh, denied, 383 U.S. 923, 86 S.Ct. 900, 15 L.Ed.2d 680, 384 U.S. 914, 86 S.Ct. 1347, 16 L.Ed.2d 368 (1966) (history given by patient, results of tests, recorded objective observations by others). See also Kilbert v. Peyton, 383 F.2d 566, 570 (4th Cir. 1967); Brown v. United States, 375 F.2d 310, 318 (D.C. Cir. 1966), cert. denied, 388 U.S. 915, 87 S.Ct. 2133, 18 L.Ed.2d 1359 (1967); Peterson v. Gaughan, 285 F. Supp. 377, 379 (D. Mass.), aff'd, 404 F.2d 1375 (1st Cir. 1968).

[3] 3 Weinstein, ¶ 703[02], at 703-12 (appraisers were exempted from hearsay rule due to necessity). See, e.g., United States v. 1129.75 Acres of Land, 473 F.2d 996, 998 (8th Cir. 1973); District of Columbia Redevelopment Land Agency v. 61 Parcels of Land, 235 F.2d 864, 866-67 (D.C. Cir. 1956).

[4] See Advisory Committee's Note to Rule 703.

minations, according to Federal theory, guarantees the trustworthiness of the information upon which he relies.[5] McCormick notes that under Rule 703, the jury is asked to accept the expert witness's inference where it is based upon a hearsay assertion of fact which is, presumably, unsupported by any evidence at trial.[6] He responds to this criticism by noting that, "an expert in a science is competent to judge the reliability of statements made to him by other investigators or technicians. He is just as competent indeed to do this as a judge and jury are to pass upon the credibility of an ordinary witness on the stand."[7] The Advisory Committee adopted this reasoning in drafting Rule 703.

§ 703.3   Bases of Expert Testimony—Firsthand Knowledge.

The Rule provides that a basis for expert testimony may be facts or data perceived by the expert through personal observations, examinations or tests. When an expert has personal knowledge of the facts or data underlying his opinion, the personal knowledge is a permissible predicate for his testimony. For example, an attending physician who treated an injured plaintiff would have firsthand knowledge of the facts which could permissibly support his expert opinion testimony as to the permanence of plaintiff's disability. In this instance the expert is aware of the supporting data by reason of his firsthand experience.

Where an expert has firsthand knowledge, it is unnecessary for him to assume any particular state of facts.[8] The testimony of an expert with firsthand knowledge is likely to be credible and convincing, especially if not elicited by means of a protracted hypothetical question.[9] Under Rule 705 the expert need not disclose the facts or data underlying his opinion or inference prior to giving that opinion or inference, and no hypothetical question is required.

The witness is of course subject to attacks on his ability to observe the event in question.[10] His testimony must also be relevant under Rule 401.[11]

[5] *Id.*

[6] McCormick, § 15, at 39-40.

[7] *Id* at 40.

[8] *See* 2 Wigmore, § 675, at 937; McCormick, § 14, at 31.

[9] 3 Weinstein, ¶ 703[02], at 703-7. *See also* Rheingold, *The Basis of Medical Testimony*, 15 Vand. L. Rev. 473, 489 (1962).

[10] *See* the discussion of Rule 602, *infra*.

[11] *See, e.g.*, United States v. Busic, 592 F.2d 13, 15 (2d Cir. 1978) (expert psychiatric testimony properly excluded where only a showing of general criminal intent was required; "questions of intent and motivation are for the jury and not expert witnesses"). *See also* Horton v. W. T. Grant Co., 537 F.2d 1215, 1217 (4th Cir. 1976). *Cf.*, Nolan v. Greene, 383 F.2d 814, 817 (6th Cir. 1967).

§ 703.4   Bases of Expert Testimony—Evidence Admitted at the Hearing.

Where the expert lacks firsthand knowledge of the facts supporting his opinion, the expert may base his opinion on a particular item of evidence if that item has been previously admitted. Of course, Rule 703 does not specify that an expert cannot be informed of pertinent facts prior to trial in order to prepare his testimony. Unquestionably, proper use of the expert witness contemplates application of the expert's special skill in planning the presentation of evidence which serves as a foundation for the expert's testimony.

It should be noted that Rule 705 does not require that the expert designate the specific facts supporting his opinion "in response to a hypothetical question or otherwise" prior to rendering an opinion. Consequently, the expert may be apprised of the necessary data by means of a hypothetical question; he may simply sit at trial and hear the testimony and view the exhibits introduced; or he may be advised by counsel of the facts which have been admitted. As long as the data or facts have been admitted into evidence, they may serve as a basis for an expert opinion or inference under this provision of Rule 703.

§ 703.5   Bases of Expert Testimony—Evidence Not Admitted at the Hearing.

When the expert lacks personal knowledge of the operative facts and they are not made known to him at trial, the expert may still, within the court's discretion, rely upon hearsay evidence in forming his opinion on the question in controversy. Rule 703 recognizes that the customary restrictions on hearsay do not apply to expert witnesses.[12] The expert who is capable of assessing the accuracy of a given set of data need not be protected from forming an opinion based on hearsay evidence; however, a juror or judge who lacks scientific expertise should be protected by the hearsay rules due to their inability to assess accurately the reliability of the evidence without the procedural safeguards of a trial. Thus, the breadth of admissibility under this provision of Rule 703 will depend upon the trial court's assessment of the expert witness's ability to filter hearsay evidence and present the trier of fact with accurate testimony from which it can render a verdict. An expert, however, cannot be used as a means to introduce inadmissible evidence by merely summarizing or repeating the information in court.[13]

---

[12] *See* 3 Weinstein, ¶ 703[01], at 703-5.
[13] United States v. Swaim, 642 F.2d 726,

728 (4th Cir. 1981); United States v. Brown, 548 F.2d 1194, 1206 (5th Cir. 1977).

The degree to which the trial judge allows an expert to rely upon hearsay evidence for his testimony will depend upon a finding under Rule 104(a) that it was reasonable for the expert witness to rely on the hearsay evidence in forming his opinion.[14] One factor the court will consider is the established nature of the source of the expert witness's data,[15] *i.e.*, appraisal of real estate is more highly established than accidentology. Intangible factors may also play key roles in the judge's decision to permit the testimony. The trial judge's belief in the professional stature and ethics of the group to which the expert witness belongs could bear heavily on the latitude given the testifying witness in forming his opinion.[16] Because Rule 703 is concerned with the reliability of expert opinions, to show that it is reasonable for the expert witness to rely on hearsay evidence in forming his opinion, the proponent of the testifying witness should present evidence that other experts in his field rely on the same type of evidence in making decisions in their work.[17]

In a criminal case, the defendant's constitutional right to confront the witnesses against him may entitle him to an opportunity to cross-examine the persons who provided the information upon which the expert relied.[18]

As discussed in regard to Rule 701, the trial judge has extensive discretion to admit or exclude expert testimony under Rule 703. Her ruling will be overturned only upon a showing of an abuse of this discretion.[19]

---

[14] *E.g.*, Lima v. United States, 708 F.2d 502, 505 (10th Cir. 1983); United States v. Cox, 696 F.2d 1294, 1296 (11th Cir. 1983), *cert. denied*, 104 S.Ct. 99 (1983); Barris v. Bob's Drag Chutes and Equipment, Inc., 685 F.2d 94, 101 n.10 (3d Cir. 1982).

[15] *See* 3 WEINSTEIN, ¶ 703[01], at 703-4. *See also* Carlson, *Policing the Bases of Modern Expert Testimony*, 39 VAND. L. REV. 577 (1986).

[16] *See* 3 WEINSTEIN, ¶ 703[01], at 703-5.

[17] *E.g.*, In re Air crash in Bali, Indonesia on April 22, 1974, 684 F.2d 1301, 1314-15 (9th Cir. 1982); United States v. Arias, 678 F.2d 1202, 1206 (4th Cir. 1982), *cert. denied*, 103 S.Ct. 218 (1982); United States v. Jones, 687 F.2d 1265, 1268 (8th Cir. 1982).

[18] *See, generally,* 3 WEINSTEIN, ¶ 703[04].

[19] *See e.g.*, United States v. Tranowski, 659 F.2d 750, 755 (7th Cir. 1981).

Chapter 704

RULE 704. OPINION ON ULTIMATE ISSUE

Rule 704 reads as follows:

(a) Except as provided in subdivision (b), testimony in the form of an opinion or inference otherwise admissible is not objectionable because it embraces an ultimate issue to be decided by the trier of fact.

(b) No expert witness testifying with respect to the mental state or condition of a defendant in a criminal case may state an opinion or inference as to whether the defendant did or did not have the mental state or condition constituting an element of the crime charged or of a defense thereto. Such ultimate issues are matters for the trier of fact alone.

§ 704.1   Opinion on Ultimate Issue—In General.

Rule 704 provides that testimony in the form of an opinion generally is not excludable *per se* because it addresses the ultimate issue in the case.[1] In criminal cases, however, expert witnesses are precluded from giving their opinion on the ultimate issue of whether the accused possessed the requisite mental state or condition.

---

[1] *See, generally,* McCoRMICK, § 12; 3 WEINSTEIN, ¶¶ 704[01]-[04]; 3 LOUISELL & MUELLER, §§ 394-95; 7 WIGMORE, §§ 1920-21. *See also,* Ladd, *Expert Testimony,* 5 VAND. L. REV. 414 (1952); Norvell, *Invasion of the Province of the Jury,* 31 TEX. L. REV. 731 (1953); Slough, *Testimonial Capacity, Evidentiary Aspects,* 36 TEX. L. REV. 1 (1957); Stoebuck, *Opinions on Ultimate Facts: Status, Trends, and a Note of Caution,* 41 Den. L.C.J. 226 (1964); Note, *Evidence-Expert Testimony-The Ultimate-Issue Rule,* 40 CHI.-KENT L. REV. 147 (1963); Note, *Opinion Testimony "Invading the Province of the Jury,"* 20 U. CIN. L. REV. 484 (1951); Note, *Expert Testimony as an Invasion of the Province of the Jury,* 26 IOWA L. REV. 819 (1941).

Although subsection (b) of Rule 704 was added by amendment as part of the Insanity Defense Reform Act of 1984,[2] the legislative history shows that the scope of subsection (b) reaches not only the insanity defense but also "all such 'ultimate' issues, *e.g.*, premeditation in a homicide case, or lack of predisposition in entrapment."[3] It should be noted that the Rule as amended does not totally bar expert testimony on the criminal defendant's mental state, but instead, merely prohibits an expert from expressing his views on the ultimate issue which the trier of fact is to determine. For example, an expert may testify as to the diagnosis of the accused's mental condition but may not state an opinion on whether the defendant was legally insane.[4] The amendment does not otherwise change previous practice under Rule 704.

§ 704.2   Rationale.

Case law once provided that a question to any witness was objectionable if it called for his opinion on the precise issue the jury was sworn to determine.[5] Courts sustaining the basic prohibition reasoned that allowing the witness to testify to one of the ultimate issues in the case would invade the province of the jury. The jury, it was feared, would abdicate its duty to determine the facts and instead, merely adopt the opinion of the witness.[6]

[2] 18 U.S.C. § 20 (1984). The Act provides that insanity is an affirmative defense which the defendant must prove by clear and convincing evidence:

(a) **Affirmative Defense.** It is an affirmative defense to a prosecution under any Federal statute that, at the time of the commission of the acts constituting the offense, the defendant, as a result of a severe mental disease or defect, was unable to appreciate the nature and quality or the wrongfulness of his acts. Mental disease or defect does not otherwise constitute a defense.

(b) **Burden of Proof.** The defendant has the burden of proving the defense of insanity by clear and convincing evidence.

Id.

[3] H. REP. No. 98-1030, 98th Cong., 2d Sess. 224, 233, U.S. CODE CONG. & AD. NEWS 1984, p.1.

[4] *See, e.g.*, United States v. Prickett, 604 F. Supp. 407, 409 (S.D. Ohio 1985).

[5] *See, e.g.*, United States v. Spaulding, 293 U.S. 498, 506, 55 S.Ct. 273, 278, 79 L.Ed. 617, 623 (1935) (in an action on war risk insurance policy, the medical opinions were without weight, since it was the ultimate issue to be decided by the jury; the experts should not have been allowed to state their conclusions on the whole case). *See also* Stoebuck, *"Opinions on Ultimate Facts: Status, Trends, and a Note of Caution,"* 41 DEN. L.C.J. 226, 227 (1964); Slough, *"Testamentary Capacity — Evidentiary Aspects,"* 36 TEX. L. REV. 1, 14 (1957).

[6] United States v. Ragano, 476 F.2d 410, 416-17 (5th Cir. 1973), *app. after remand*, 520 F.2d 1191 (5th Cr. 1973), *reh. denied*, 526 F.2d 815 (5th Cir. 1973), *cert. denied*, 427 U.S. 905, 96 S.Ct. 3192, 49 L.Ed.2d 1199 (1973) (court erred in refusing to strike testimony by government witness in prosecution for filing false return, since the testimony invaded the province of the jury, despite the "modern trend" to abandon the ultimate issue objection). *See also* Kentucky Trust Co. v. Glenn, 217 F.2d 462, 467 (1954).

A witness could not testify to "ultimate facts," but could testify only to "evidentiary facts," *i.e.*, those subsidiary facts introduced to prove ultimate facts.[7] Later cases carved out an exception to the prohibition which allowed experts to render opinions on the ultimate issue.[8]

As originally adopted, Rule 704 reflected the modern trend to abolish the ultimate issue prohibition. In practice, the distinction between an ultimate fact and an evidentiary fact proved too tenuous to be consistently applied.[9] McCormick concluded that the prohibition was "pregnant with close questions of application and the possibility of misapplication, and often unfairly obstructive to the presentation of a party's case."[10]

Despite these criticisms, Rule 704(b) partially reinstates the prohibition against ultimate issue testimony. The amendment to Rule 704 reflects a legislative judgment that expert opinions on the ultimate issue of a criminal defendant's mental state are more misleading than helpful to the jury. Rule 704 was amended as part of an effort to clarify and improve federal law concerning the insanity defense and the procedures applicable to other offenders with mental diseases or defects. To illustrate the problems raised by the insanity defense, the Department of Justice offered the following description of a typical trial where the defense is raised:

> Since the experts themselves are in disagreement about both the meaning of the terms used to define the defendant's mental state and the effect of a particular state on the defendant's actions—but still freely allowed to state their opinion to the jury on the ultimate question of the defendant's sanity—it is small wonder that trials involving an insanity defense are arduous, expensive, and worst of all, thoroughly confusing to the jury. Indeed the disagreement of the experts is so basic that it makes rational deliberation by the jury virtually impossible.[11]

The amendment to Rule 704 is designed:

> . . . to eliminate the confusing spectacle of competing expert witnesses testifying to directly contradictory conclusions as to the ultimate legal issue to be found by the trier of fact. Under this proposal, expert psychiatric testimony would be limited to presenting and explaining their diagnoses, such as whether the defendant had a severe mental

---

[7] *See, generally*, Note, *Opinion Testimony and Ultimate Issues — Incompatible?* 51 KY. L.J. 540 (1963). *See also* Note, *Opinion Testimony "Invading the Province of the Jury"* 20 U. CIN. L. REV. 484 (1951).

[8] Transportation Line v. Hope, 95 U.S. 297, 24 L.Ed. 477 (1877).

[9] 3 WEINSTEIN, ¶ 704[01], at 704-4.

[10] McCORMICK, § 12, at 27-28.

[11] H. REP. No. 98-1030, 98th Cong., 2d Sess. 224, 225.

disease or defect and what the characteristics of such a disease or defect, if any, may have been.[12]

§ 704.3   Admissibility of Ultimate Issue Opinions.

Rule 704(a) provides that ultimate issue testimony "otherwise admissible" is not *per se* excludable. Consequently, in addition to escaping the prohibition contained in subsection (b), the testimony at issue must also minimally satisfy the requirements of all Rules of Evidence. For example, Rule 701 governs opinions offered by a lay witness. The ultimate issue testimony of a layman must be rationally based on facts perceived by the witness. Moreover, under Rule 701 the opinion or inference is not admissible if it is not helpful to the trier of fact in the determination of a factual issue.[13] When the jury can easily draw the inference from a simple recitation of facts by the witness, the witness's opinion on the ultimate issue might be excludable under Rule 701.

Where proffered testimony does not fall within the prohibition of Rule 704(b), courts should be reluctant to exclude the ultimate issue testimony of an expert under the standards set forth in Rule 702. Under Rule 702, which governs the admissibility of expert testimony, the trial court must determine that the subject matter of the testimony presented is helpful to the jury. To confer expert status on the witness, the expert's specialized body of knowledge must assist the trier of fact in determining a fact in issue or in understanding the evidence. It is the inability of the unaided jury to reach the ultimate opinion that renders the expert's opinion valuable. For this reason, an ultimate issue opinion by a properly qualified expert should not be excluded except in the extreme case where the expert's opinion is inherently misleading or unfairly prejudicial.[14]

---

[12] H. Rep. No. 98-1030, 98th Cong., 2d Sess. 224, 232.

[13] United States v. Baskes, 649 F.2d 471, 479 (7th Cir. 1980). *See also* United States v. Kelley, 617 F.2d 378, 381 (5th Cir. 1980) (bank officers permitted to testify that documents had the capacity to influence the bank in prosecution for conspiracy to make false statements on applications for credit cards, loans, etc.; statements were helpful to jury); Bauman v. Centex Corp., 611 F.2d 1115, 1120 (5th Cir. 1980) (test is not whether evidence invades province of jury, but whether it is helpful in complex case involving issues of corporate management).

[14] United States v. Milton, 555 F.2d 1198, 1203 (5th Cir. 1977) (in prosecution for illegal gambling government experts permitted to testify that lay off bets were being placed and to give their opinions as to the role each defendant played; no invasion of province of jury). *See also* Shatkin v. McDonnell Douglas Corp., 565 F. Supp. 93, 96 (S.D. N.Y. 1983).

§ 704.4   Discretion of the Trial Court.

Rule 704(a)'s relaxation of the ultimate issue prohibition necessarily implies that the trial court must be vested with substantial discretion in its rulings as to the admissibility of ultimate issue testimony. Primarily, the trial court should be concerned with whether the jury can itself reach a correct conclusion unaided by the opinion of the witness. The Advisory Committee's Note to Rule 704 concludes that the trial court has a secondary vehicle for excluding ultimate issue opinion under Rule 403.

In applying Rule 704(b), the trial court must determine not only whether the expert's testimony constitutes fact or opinion but also, if it is found to be opinion, whether it embraces an ultimate issue. Testimony by psychiatric experts must be "limited to presenting and explaining their diagnoses, such as whether the defendant had a severe mental disease or defect and what the characteristics of such a disease or defect, if any, may have been."[15]

---

[15] H. REP. No. 98-1030, 98th Cong., 2d Sess. 224, 232.

Chapter 705

RULE 705. DISCLOSURE OF FACTS OR DATA UNDERLYING EXPERT OPINION

Rule 705 reads as follows:

> The expert may testify in terms of opinion or inference and give his reasons therefor without prior discussion of the underlying facts or data, unless the court requires otherwise. The expert may in any event be required to disclose the underlying facts or data on cross-examination.

§ 705.1 Disclosure of Facts or Data Underlying Expert Opinion— In General.

Rule 705 sets forth the procedure governing the disclosure of the facts or data used by an expert in formulating his opinion.[1] The Rule departs from prior practice by removing a foundational requirement compelling the expert witness to identify the facts or data underpinning his opinion prior to rendering the opinion. Rule 705, however, grants the trial court the right to

---

[1] *See, generally,* McCormick, § 14; 3 Weinstein, ¶¶ 705[01]-[03]; 3 Louisell & Mueller, §§ 399-400; 2 Wigmore, §§ 672-86. *See also* Conason, *Medical Cross-Examination—Refusal to Recognize Medical Authorities,* 10 Trial Law. Q. 29 (1974); Friedenthal, *Discovery and Use of Adverse Party's Expert Information,* 14 Stan. L. Rev. 455 (1962); Ladd, *Expert Testimony,* 5 Vand. L. Rev. 414, 426-27 (1952); Moller, *Cross-Examining the Plaintiff's Medical Expert,* 42 Ins. Counsel J. 198 (1975); Note, *A Reconsideration of the Admissibility of Computerized Evidence,* 126 U. Pa. L. Rev. 425 (1977); Comment, *The Physician's Testimony—Hearsay Evidence or Expert Opinion—A Question of Professional Competence,* 55 Tex. L. Rev. 296 (1975); Note, *Expert Witness and Hypothetical Questions,* 13 W. Res. L. Rev. 755 (1962).

order the preliminary disclosure of the facts underlying the expert witness's opinion. In any event, the factual basis of the opinion may be further explored on cross-examination of the witness.

The Rule also dispenses with any remnant of the requirement that expert witnesses render their opinions in response to hypothetical questions. Under Rule 705 counsel may still ask hypothetical questions, but the Rule no longer mandates this testifying technique.

§ 705.2   Use of Hypothetical Questions Under Rule 705.

In making the use of the hypothetical question optional, Rule 705 bows toward the weight of modern commentary which assails the hypothetical question as an anachronism. Wigmore concluded:

> The hypothetical question, misused by the clumsy and abused by the clever, has in practice led to intolerable obstruction of truth. In the first place, it has artificially clamped the mouth of the expert witness, so that his answer to a complex question may not express his actual opinion on the actual case. This is because the question may be so built up and contrived by counsel as to represent only a partisan conclusion. In the second place, it has tended to mislead the jury as to the purport of actual expert opinion. This is due to the same reason. In the third place, it has tended to confuse the jury, so that its employment becomes a mere waste of time and a futile obstruction.[2]

The Advisory Committee adopted the position espoused by Wigmore that the use of a hypothetical question be purely elective.[3] Consequently, under Rule 705 the trial judge lacks the discretion to order trial counsel to use a hypothetical question.

Liberating attorneys from the mandatory use of the hypothetical question marks a significant advancement in Federal practice. Nevertheless, attorneys comfortable with the use of hypothetical questions will undoubtedly continue to use them whenever a tactical advantage may be attained. An attorney may, for example, wish to enlighten the jury as to the relative absence of controverted facts in a case by asking the expert to assume as a hypothesis the facts advanced by his opponent. Likewise, the significance of a controverted fact may be emphasized by the use of comparative hypothetical questions proposed to the expert. When an attorney asks a confus-

[2] *See* 2 WIGMORE, § 686, at 962-63.
[3] *See* Advisory Committee's Note to Rule 705.

ing hypothetical question, a court has the power to exclude such a question pursuant to Rule 403.[4]

§ 705.3   Disclosure of Supporting Facts Under Rule 705.

Rule 705 abolishes the pre-Rule position that required counsel to lay a factual foundation for an expert witness's testimony before the expert testified. The present Rule does not require a testimonial foundation unless the court in its discretion orders it.

The pre-Rule position has some merit. It is both sensible and logical to require the expert witness to disclose the facts that underlie his position. If these facts are not disclosed to the jury, the expert's opinion might be irrelevant and misleading if grounded on facts ultimately discounted by the trier of fact.[5] The trier of fact could not adequately assess the validity of the expert testimony without knowing the particular facts which support the expert opinion. The pre-Rule position was designed to aid the trier of fact in his assessment of the validity of the expert's opinion.

The Advisory Committee rejected the orthodox position because of the ineffective nature of the usual means of informing the witness of the underlying basis for the expert witness's testimony, *i.e.*, the hypothetical question discussed, *supra* in § 705.2. Also, by allowing the trial judge the discretion to order the disclosure of the facts that underlie the expert's testimony, the Rule provides a mechanism by which the court can ensure the jury is made aware of facts that are necessary to a clear understanding of the expert's testimony.[6] It should also be noted that when the facts or data that underlie the witness's testimony are disputed, they may be disclosed to the jury through cross-examination of the expert witness.[7] The

---

[4] 3 WEINSTEIN, ¶ 705[01], at 705-7.

[5] *See, e.g.*, Daniels v. Mathews, 566 F.2d 845, 847 (8th Cir. 1977) (administrative law judge asked expert a question about claimant's capacity to do certain jobs without informing the expert of the underlying factual premise; this was error); Grand Island Grain Co. v. Roush Mobile Home Sales, Inc., 391 F.2d 35, 37 (8th Cir. 1968) (objections to hypothetical questions sustained on the basis of insufficient proof). *Cf.*, Haufman v. Edelstein, 539 F.2d 811, 821 (2d Cir. 1976). *See also* 3 WEINSTEIN, ¶ 705[01], at 705-5.

[6] 2 WIGMORE, § 686, at 813.

[7] *See, e.g.*, Vermont Food Industries, Inc. v. Ralston Purina Co., 514 F.2d 456,

463 (2d Cir. 1975) ("[i]n asking a hypothetical question, the examiner may seek the witness's opinion on any combination of the facts within the tendency of the evidence"); United States v. Taylor, 510 F.2d 1283, 1291 (D.C. Cir. 1975), *reh denied*, 516 F.2d 1243 (D.C. Cir. 1975) (defense psychiatric testimony, based in part upon examination of paintings, indicated that the accused was schizophrenic; on retrial of the insanity issue, it was improper to permit prosecutor to exhibit reproductions of paintings by Picasso, El Greco, Braque, Gaugin, Nolde, and Klee, and to ask whether witness would say that those artists suffered from mental illness).

approach of Rule 705 places a "premium not only upon cross-examination, but also upon the kind of pretrial discovery which may be necessary to prepare the cross-examiner for the attack."[8] When an expert's testimony is preceded by little or no foundation, the trial judge should permit great freedom in cross-examination in order to expose any deficiencies in the expert's opinion.

Pragmatic trial concerns will in most cases result in disclosure of the facts that underlie an expert witness's testimony. For example, an expert witness who has firsthand knowledge of the facts in a dispute may be asked to disclose the foundation for his testimony because the facts themselves must appear in the record in order to satisfy the proponent's burden of proof.[9] Likewise, the need for counsel to advance a coherent presentation to the jury may require the disclosure of some relevant facts to the jury prior to hearing the expert testimony.[10] Rule 702 may also require that the witness exhibit some acquaintance with the underlying facts of the case in order to qualify as an expert witness.[11] Due to the limited scope of discovery in criminal cases, the trial court may require counsel in a criminal case to reveal the basis upon which the expert's opinion rests.

§ 705.4   Disclosure of Supporting Facts: Relation to Rule 703.

By allowing the expert to give his opinion in response to a hypothetical question or in any other manner, Rule 705 invites the attorney simply to ask the expert to render his opinion. It is his opponent's responsibility to develop any factual defects in the expert's testimony on cross-examination of the witness.

Rule 705 interfaces with Rule 703 which requires that the facts or data underlying the expert's opinion be facts directly perceived by the expert, facts already "admitted into evidence," or, in the alternative, hearsay facts which were reasonably relied upon by the expert witness in forming his opinion. Where the expert lacks firsthand knowledge of the pertinent facts, Rule 705 places no restriction on the way in which the witness learns of the specific facts admitted into evidence. If the expert has the time and patience, he may sit at trial and hear the evidence as it is adduced. If he does not have such a flexible schedule, the data may be related to him in the form of a hypothetical question, or he may simply be informed of the relevant data by counsel.

---

[8] 3 LOUISELL & MUELLER, § 400, at 708.
[9] 3 WEINSTEIN, ¶ 705[01], at 705-7.
[10] *Id.*
[11] *Id.*

§ 705.5   Explaining the Expert Opinion.

Consistent with prior Federal Law, Rule 705 provides that after the opinion of the expert is elicited, he may "give his reasons therefor." A trial court errs if it excludes the testimony of an expert which provides an explanation of his opinion. The ability of the expert to explain his answer is vital to the jury's appreciation of the weight to be accorded expert opinions, and such explanation should not be limited except under extraordinary circumstances.

Chapter 706

RULE 706. COURT APPOINTED EXPERTS

Rule 706 reads as follows:

(a) **Appointment.** The court may on its own motion or on the motion of any party enter an order to show cause why expert witnesses should not be appointed, and may request the parties to submit nominations. The court may appoint any expert witnesses agreed upon by the parties, and may appoint expert witnesses of its own selection. An expert witness shall not be appointed by the court unless he consents to act. A witness so appointed shall be informed of his duties by the court in writing, a copy of which shall be filed with the clerk, or at a conference in which the parties shall have opportunity to participate. A witness so appointed shall advise the parties of his findings, if any; his deposition may be taken by any party; and he may be called to testify by the court or any party. He shall be subject to cross-examination by each party, including a party calling him as a witness.

(b) **Compensation.** Expert witnesses so appointed are entitled to reasonable compensation in whatever sum the court may allow. The compensation thus fixed is payable from funds which may be provided by law in criminal cases and civil actions and proceedings involving just compensation under the fifth amendment. In other civil actions and proceedings the compensation shall be paid by the parties in such proportion and at such time as the court directs, and thereafter charged in like manner as other costs.

(c) **Disclosure of appointment.** In the exercise of its discretion, the court may authorize disclosure to the jury of the fact that the court appointed the expert witness.

(d) **Parties' experts of own selection.** Nothing in this rule limits the parties in calling expert witnesses of their own selection.

§ 706.1   Court Appointed Experts—Scope and Rationale.

Rule 706 empowers the court, on its own motion, to appoint and select an expert witness to testify in a given lawsuit.[1] Although federal judges had inherent authority to appoint experts prior to the enactment of Rule 706, the power rarely was exercised.[2] The Rule was enacted to cure a variety of problems that surround the use of expert testimony authorized under Rule 702. Under the liberal standards qualifying expert witnesses, it is not uncommon for the trier of fact to be expected to determine which of two diametrically opposing views is the more valid assessment of an issue in controversy. In this situation the trier of fact may be forced to choose between two conflicting interpretations of an event based upon the knowledge of two opposing experts, who look to the fringes of their disciplines for intellectual support of their respective positions. Rule 706 authorizes the trial court to appoint an expert witness who will restore some impartiality to the litigation,[3] and who will present the jury with an interpretation of the event in controversy which is based upon theory more generally supported in the given field.[4]

The Advisory Committee also concluded that by enacting Rule 706, trial counsel would be deterred from presenting partisan experts who were capable of being discredited by a court-appointed expert.[5] This, it was

---

[1] See, generally, McCormick, § 17; 3 Weinstein, ¶¶ 706[01]-[05]; 3 Louisell & Mueller, §§ 404-406; 2 Wigmore, § 563. See also DeParq, Law, Science, and the Expert Witness, 24 Tenn. L. Rev. 166 (1956); Diamond, The Fallacy of the Impartial Expert, 3 Archives of Crim. Psychodynamics 221 (1959); Griffin, Impartial Medical Testimony: A Trial Lawyer in Favor, 34 Temp. L.Q. 402 (1961); Levy, Impartial Medical Testimony-Revisited, 34 Temp. L.Q. 416 (1961); Myers, The Battle of the Experts: A New Approach to an Old Problem in Medical Testimony, 44 Neb. L. Rev. 539 (1965); Morgan, Suggested Remedy for Obstruction to Expert Testimony by Rule of Evidence, 10 U. Chi. L. Rev. 285 (1943); Sink, The Unused Power of a Federal Judge to Call His Own Expert Witness, 29 S. Cal. L. Rev. 195 (1956); Travis, Impartial Expert Testimony Under the Federal Rules of Evidence: A French Perspective, 8 Int'l Law 492 (1974); Van Dusen, The Impartial Medical Expert System: The Judicial Point of View, 34 Temp. L.Q. 386 (1961); Wick & Kightlinger, Impartial Medical Testimony Under the Federal Civil Rules: A Tale of

Three Doctors, 34 Ins. Counsel L.J. 115 (1967); Comment, Compelling Experts to Testify: A Proposal, 44 U. Chi. L. Rev. 851 (1977).

[2] 3 Louisell & Mueller, § 404, at 720. The power of federal judges to call expert witnesses in criminal cases was codified by Rule 28 of the Federal Rules of Criminal Procedure, but the rule was used infrequently. 2 Wright, Federal Practice and Procedure, § 452, at 230 (1969).

[3] See United States v. Faison, 564 F. Supp. 514, 517 (D. N.J. 1983).

[4] Sink, The Unused Power of a Federal Judge to Call His Own Expert Witness, 29 S. Cal. L. Rev. 195, 197 (1956). See also 3 Weinstein, ¶ 706[01], at 706-7.

[5] Eastern Air Lines Inc. v. McDonnell Douglas Corp., 532 F.2d 957, 1000 (5th Cir. 1976) (experts differed by $24.5 million in their estimates of plaintiff's losses; court on retrial should consider calling an expert witness on its own who could provide an objective insight into the difference in the opinion of the experts). See Rule 706, Advisory Committee's Note.

hoped, would have the desired effect of forcing weak cases into settlement and increasing the general caliber of the experts testifying under Rule 702.[6]

Several arguments were advanced against the use of court-appointed experts, including: (1) the appointment of experts interferes with the adversary system's tradition of placing responsibility for presenting evidence on the parties;[7] (2) the jury may be overly impressed by the fact that the expert was selected by the court to render an unbiased opinion and consequently may rely too heavily on his opinion in reaching its decision;[8] (3) where the experts called by the parties give conflicting opinions due to a division in theory or philosophy within their field, it may be impossible to find a neutral witness because the expert will indorse one viewpoint or the other;[9] and (4) the use of court-appointed experts raises procedural uncertainties, such as the method of compensation and the availability of discovery by the parties.[10] The flexible approach taken by Rule 706 resolves many of these problems.[11]

§ 706.2   Procedure for Enacting Rule 706.

Before appointing an expert witness the trial court is required to allow the parties to show cause why an expert witness should not be appointed by the court. Despite this procedure, trial counsel is unlikely to prevail on this issue because the arguments that a party would present to dissuade the trial court of its intention to appoint an expert witness are largely based upon factors which the court is more capable of assessing. For example, a party may argue that the appointed expert's testimony will be repetitious, or alternatively, that it will be misleading and prejudicial because the jury may unfairly assign a greater weight to the testimony of an expert appointed by the judge, than it will to the expert testimony for a given party.[12] The court will respond that it has the discretion under Rule 403 to determine the extent of any prejudice resulting to a party from admitting evidence. Further, by refusing to inform the jury that the court appointed the witness under Rule 706(c), the expert's testimony will not be misleading.[13] As under other Rules granting discretion to the court, the judge's

---

[6] *See* Report of the New Jersey Supreme Court Committee on Evidence 116 (1963). *See, generally,* 3 WEINSTEIN, ¶ 706[01]; 3 LOUISELL & MUELLER, § 404; 2 WIGMORE, § 563; McCORMICK, § 17.

[7] De Parq, *Law, Science and the Expert Witness,* 24 TENN. L. REV. 166, 171 (1956).

[8] Levy, *Impartial Medical Testimony— Revisited,* 34 TEMP. L.Q. 416, 424-25 (1961).

[9] 3 WEINSTEIN, ¶ 706[01], at 706-10.

[10] 3 LOUISELL & MUELLER, § 404, at 723.

[11] *See infra* § 706.2.

[12] Levy, *Impartial Medical Testimony— Revisited,* 34 TEMP. L.Q. 416, 424-25 (1961).

[13] *See* 3 WEINSTEIN, ¶ 706[02], at 706-12.

decision to appoint an expert witness should be overturned only upon finding an abuse of his discretion.[14]

The court is granted the option under Rule 706(a) of selecting the expert it wishes to appoint, or it may request that counsel submit nominations of potential expert witnesses. The court in its discretion may either appoint the experts upon which the parties agree, or it may select someone of its own choosing. The potential expert witness must agree to submit to appointment under Rule 706. The witness's qualifications will then be assessed under Rule 702.

Once the witness agrees to testify, he is to be informed of his duties in writing by the court. The court then files a copy of this report with the clerk or submits a copy to a conference in which the parties, the appointed expert and the judge participate. As Wigmore suggests, this type of conference may help to limit the scope of the conflict between the experts who will testify, thus avoiding confusion or waste of time at trial.[15] The Advisory Committee, however, thought that to require this conference would be expensive and time consuming, and consequently, Rule 706 authorizes a discretionary, rather than a mandatory conference.[16]

Rule 706 grants the parties the right to be informed of the expert witness's findings. Such apprisal may take many forms, but the parties have a right to depose the expert witness. Trial counsel is also authorized by the Rule to call the expert witness in his own case and to cross-examine the appointed expert.

Rule 706 does not establish the point in the trial at which the court may appoint an expert witness. However, because the court must have time to: (1) hear motions against appointing the expert witness; (2) receive consent to appointment by the expert; (3) notify counsel and the expert of his duties through writing or the discretionary conference; (4) allow the expert time to make findings of fact; and (5) present the findings to trial counsel within reasonable time to prepare a cross-examination at trial,[17] it would appear the court should determine whether it wishes to appoint an expert witness at the pretrial stage. Liberal discovery should enable the court to determine at an early stage whether it will need to appoint an expert witness.[18]

---

[14] *E.g.*, Georgia-Pacific Corp. v. United States, 640 F.2d 328, 334 (Ct. Cl. 1980).

[15] The Committee on Expert Testimony of the American Bar Association Section of Judicial Administration, Report (Jan. 1970), *cited in*, 3 Weinstein, ¶ 706[02], at 706-15.

[16] Rule 706, Advisory Committee Note.

[17] United States v. Weathers, 618 F.2d 663, 664 (10th Cir. 1980), *cert. denied*, 446 U.S. 956, 100 S.Ct. 2927, 64 L.Ed.2d 814 (1980) (doubtful whether post-trial employment of psychiatric expert comported with Rule, yet only harmless error).

[18] 3 Weinstein, ¶ 706[02], at 706-12.

§ 706.3   Compensation of Appointed Expert Witnesses Under Rule 706(b).

Rule 706(b) applies to both criminal and civil proceedings, and it requires that compensation of appointed experts be reasonable. The Rule also delineates the source of the payment to the expert witness. In general the Rule charges compensation from a source, "provided by law." Consequently, in a criminal case the Department of Justice will pay for the cost of the expert witness.[19] The Justice Department will also pay for the cost of the expert witness in a civil condemnation case under the just compensation clause of the Fifth Amendment.[20]

In civil actions not involving just compensation, the trial judge may charge each party with the expert witness's costs, to an extent he determines is fair. In assessing the expert's costs, the court will consider such factors as the nature of the case, the reason the court had to appoint an expert witness, the financial status of the parties, and the outcome of the litigation.[21]

---

[19] Decision of the Comptroller General B-139703 (March 21, 1980).

[20] *Id.*

[21] 3 Weinstein, ¶ 706[03], at 706-22.

VIII
HEARSAY

Chapter 801

RULE 801. DEFINITIONS

Rule 801(a)–(c)   "Statement"; "Declarant"; "Hearsay"

Rule 801(a)–(c) reads as follows:

The following definitions apply under this article: **(a) Statement.** A "statement" is (1) an oral or written assertion or (2) non-verbal conduct of a person, if it is intended by him as an assertion. **(b) Declarant.** A "declarant" is a person who makes a statement. **(c) Hearsay.** "Hearsay" is a statement, other than one made by the declarant while testifying at the trial or hearing, offered in evidence to prove the truth of the matter asserted.

§ 801.1   The Hearsay System—An Overview.

The hearsay system governs the admissibility of "out-of-court statements," *i.e.*, statements that are made by a person other than while testifying at the trial at which the statement is offered.[1]

In understanding the structure of the hearsay system, it is important to appreciate that the trial of a law suit customarily relies on three fundamental devices to maximize the accuracy of testimony submitted to the trier of fact:

[1] *See, generally*, McCORMICK, §§ 250, 246, 248-49; 4 WEINSTEIN ¶¶ 801(a)[01]-[02]; 801(c)[01], 801(a)-(c)[02]-[03]; 4 LOUISELL & MUELLER, §§ 410-18; 2 WIGMORE, § 267; 5 WIGMORE, § 1361; 6 WIGMORE, § 1766. *See also* Blakely, *You Can Say That If You Want - The Redefinition of Hearsay in Rule 801 of the Proposed Federal Rules of Evidence*, 35 OHIO ST. L.J. 601 (1974); Booker & Morton, *The Hearsay Rule, the St. George Plays and the Road to the Year Twenty-Fifty*, 44 NOTRE DAME L. REV. 7 (1968); Donnelly, *The Hearsay Rule and Its Exceptions*, 40 MINN. L. REV. 455 (1956); Falknor, *The "Hear-say" Rule as a "See-Do" Rule: Evidence of Conduct*, 33 ROCKY MTN. L. REV. 133 (1961); Falknor, *"Indirect" Hearsay*, 31 TUL. L. REV. 3 (1956); Falknor, *Silence as Hearsay*, 89 U. PA. L. REV. 192 (1940); Finman, *Implied Assertions as Hearsay: Some Criticism of the Uniform Rules of Evidence*, 14 STAN. L. REV. 682 (1962); Graham, *"Stickperson Hearsay": A Simplified Approach to Understanding the Rule Against Hearsay*, 4 U. ILL. L. REV. 887 (1982); McCormick, *The Borderland of Hearsay*, 39 YALE L.J. 489 (1930); Maguire, *The Hearsay System: Around and Through the Thicket*, 14 VAND. L. REV. 741 (1961); Morgan, *Hearsay*, 25 MISS. L.J. 1 (1953); Morgan, *A Suggested System of Utterances Admissible as Res Gestae*, 31 YALE L.J. 229 (1922); Morgan, *Hearsay Dangers and the Application of the Hearsay Concept*, 62 HARV. L. REV. 177 (1948); Park, *McCormick on Evidence and the Concept of Hearsay: A Critical Analysis Followed by Suggestions to Law Teachers*, 65 MINN. L. REV. 423 (1981); Rucker, *The Twilight Zone of Hearsay*, 9 VAND. L. REV. 453 (1956); Seligman, *An Exception to the Hearsay Rule*, 26 HARV. L. REV. 146 (1912); Tribe, *Triangulating Hearsay*, 87 HARV. L. REV. 957 (1974); Wellborn, *The Definition of Hearsay in the Federal Rules of Evidence*, 61 TEX. L. REV. 49 (1982).

1. The first safeguard, and the most important, is the device of prompt (*i.e.*, "fresh") cross-examination of witnesses testifying at trial.[2]
2. The second device is the oath administered to a witness before he or she takes the stand to testify at trial.[3]
3. The third safeguard is the opportunity of the trier of fact to observe the demeanor of the witness while he or she is testifying.

The law of evidence surrounding hearsay has developed a system of exclusion which rejects the admission of much evidence that fails to satisfy these three safeguards.[4] Accordingly, many out-of-court statements are rendered inadmissible by the hearsay system because of their inherent unreliability.

The general hearsay rule of exclusion is codified in Rule 802. It must be recognized that Rule 802, "Hearsay Rule," operates to exclude much evidence that satisfies the basic definition of relevancy set forth in Rule 401. Consequently, the hearsay system excludes much relevant evidence because it is inherently untrustworthy in such a way that the trier of fact is incapable of attributing weight to the evidence.[5]

As a first step in applying the hearsay system, it is necessary to determine whether the evidence in question is hearsay. To resolve this issue, the definition of hearsay in Rule 801(c) must be consulted. If the evidence is not hearsay, the hearsay exclusionary rule will not operate to exclude the evidence. Nevertheless, if the evidence is hearsay as defined in Rule 801(c), the evidence is presumptively inadmissible and may only be received in accordance with one of the bases for admission expressly identified in Rule 801(d) or Rule 802.[6]

As a second step in applying the hearsay system, it is necessary to determine whether an exception to the basic definition of hearsay will operate

---

[2] California v. Green, 399 U.S. 149, 158, 90 S.Ct. 1930, 1936, 26 L.Ed.2d 489, 494 (1970), *on remand*, 3 Cal. 3d 981, 92 Cal. Rptr. 494, 479 P.2d 998 (1970), *cert. dismissed*, 404 U.S. 801, 92 S.Ct. 20, 30 L.Ed.2d 34; Pointer v. Texas, 380 U.S. 400, 404, 85 S.Ct. 1065, 1069, 13 L.Ed.2d 923, 926 (1965); *See also* 5 WIGMORE, § 1362, at 3 (absence of cross-examination is the exclusive reason for rejecting hearsay).

[3] Bridges v. Wixon, 326 U.S. 135, 153, 65 S.Ct. 1443, 1461, 89 L.Ed. 2103, 2118 (1945) (written statement under oath and signed "would have afforded protection against mistakes in hearing, mistakes in memory, mistakes in transcription"). *But cf.* United States v. DeSisto, 329 F.2d 929, 933 (2d Cir. 1964), *cert. denied*, 377 U.S. 979, 84 S.Ct. 1885, 12 L.Ed.2d 747 (1964).

[4] California v. Green, 399 U.S. 149, 155, 90 S.Ct. 1930, 1935, 26 L.Ed.2d 489, 494 (1970); Bridges v. Wixon, 326 U.S. 135, 153, 65 S.Ct. 1443, 1461, 89 L.Ed. 2103, 2108 (1945).

[5] Ladd, *The Hearsay We Admit*, 5 OKLA. L. REV. 271 (1952).

[6] *See* Rule 802, *infra*.

to admit the hearsay. All such exceptions to the basic definition are contained in Rule 801(d). Technically, such exceptions denominate the identified out-of-court statements as "not hearsay" or "non-hearsay." Functionally, however, such exceptions to the definition operate identically to exceptions to the exclusionary rule in circumscribing admissible classes of out-of-court statements, offered for their truth. Rule 801(d)(1) identifies certain prior statements of a witness which are admissible despite the fact that these statements fall within the basic definition of hearsay contained in Rule 801(c). Rule 801(d)(2) renders admissible certain prior statements of a party where the statements are encompassed by the definition of hearsay contained in Rule 801(c).

As a third step in applying the hearsay system, it should be considered whether a statement determined to be hearsay under the basic definition in Rule 801(c) is nevertheless admissible pursuant to an exception to the exclusionary rule. These exceptions are codified in Rules 803 and 804. In applying Rule 803 the availability of the out-of-court declarant is immaterial. In order to invoke an exception codified in Rule 804, however, the out-of-court declarant must be unavailable to testify at trial as provided in Rule 804(a).[7] It should be noted that in regard to the exceptions set forth in Rule 804, the hearsay system operates as a rule of preference. The system prefers the declarant's testimony if it is available. Nevertheless, if the declarant is unavailable as defined in Rule 804(a), a hearsay statement of such individual may be offered if such hearsay is available, and if it satisfies one of the exceptions circumscribed in Rule 804(b).

Where hearsay is received pursuant to a Rule 803 or Rule 804 exception to the exclusionary rule, the receipt customarily will be based upon the policy that the class of hearsay in question is more reliable than hearsay generally. Accordingly, as a general principle, a class of hearsay evidence is identified as an exception because the risk of one of the recognized testimonial defects is diminished. The potential testimonial defects, which are normally exposed through cross-examination, are: (1) the risk of insincerity; (2) the risk of impaired perception; (3) the risk of a defect in memory; and (4) the risk of a defect in narration. Cross-examination usually can be utilized to attempt to expose one of these risks where a defect may occur at the time a witness testifies at trial. Because hearsay involves out-of-court statements, fresh cross-examination is not available to test the accuracy of the statement. The hearsay system, however, circumscribes certain classes of admissible hearsay in regard to which at least one of the testimonial risks is minimized.

[7] *See* Rule 804(a), *infra.*

As the fourth step in applying the hearsay system, it should be determined whether a statement which is hearsay as defined by Rule 801(c) is nevertheless admissible pursuant to a statute or a rule of procedure identified in Rule 802.

Finally, if offered in a criminal case, a criminal defendant may have a constitutional right to the admission of the evidence despite the fact that the evidence falls within the basic definition of hearsay and despite the fact that no recognized exceptions will admit the hearsay.[8] Likewise, hearsay evidence admissible through one of the recognized exceptions may be subject to exclusion on constitutional grounds where the evidence is offered by the prosecution against the accused in a criminal case, *i.e,* where its admission would deprive the accused of a fundamental right.[9]

§ 801.2   Definition of a Statement.

Rule 801(a) provides the definition of a "statement." Because the definition of hearsay in Rule 801(c) comprehends out-of-court "statements," evidence not meeting the definition of a statement cannot be hearsay. Rule 801(a) defines a statement for hearsay purposes as either an oral or written assertion, or conduct of a person which is intended to be an assertion.

Any oral statement made outside the courtroom, reported by a witness on the stand, is a statement satisfying the definition of Rule 801. Likewise, documentary evidence contains out-of-court statements. It should be noted, however, that not all oral or written out-of-court statements are inadmissible. Whether an out-of-court statement is hearsay and presumptively inadmissible is determined by application of Rule 801(c). Also, where an out-of-court statement does fall within the definition of Rule 801(c), it may nevertheless be admissible pursuant to an exception to either the basic definition or the exclusionary rule or pursuant to other bases identified in Rule 802.

According to Rule 801(a), certain nonverbal conduct may be a statement. Many nonverbal signals are obviously the equivalent of words for

---

[8] *See* Chambers v. Mississippi, 410 U.S. 284, 93 S.Ct. 1038, 35 L.Ed.2d 297 (1973). At defendant's trial for the murder of a police officer, the *Chambers* trial court ruled that the testimony of three witnesses of another man's confession to the murder was inadmissible hearsay. The Supreme Court reversed, holding that the testimony was admissible, even though it did not fall within a recognized hearsay exception. Because the evidence bore sufficient indicia of reliability, and because its exclusion would deny defendant's right to due process by preventing him from presenting witnesses in his defense, the admission of the evidence was held to be constitutionally compelled.

[9] *See* § 402.3, *supra.* Constitutional limitations to the various hearsay exceptions, where applicable, are discussed in conjunction with each hearsay exception, *infra.*

purposes of communication. Nodding, pointing, and the sign language of the hearing impaired are plainly assertive conduct which are the equivalent of spoken words. Such conduct may be hearsay if Rule 801(c) is satisfied.[10] The same result was reached under federal case law prior to the adoption of the federal rules.[11]

Other types of cognitive nonverbal conduct are more difficult to characterize as statements. The conduct of a person may reflect his belief, and in certain situations a person's belief, circumstantially established by his conduct, might be relevant in a particular case. Early case law often found conduct, relevant in circumstantially reflecting belief, to be hearsay. The classic case of *Wright v. Doe d'Tatham*,[12] held that whenever conduct is relevant in reflecting belief, hearsay communications are presented because the belief should be subjected to the safeguards of cross-examination, oath and opportunity for observation of demeanor.[13] In *Tatham*, the proponent sought to establish the testator's competence by introducing into evidence

---

[10] *See* McCORMICK, § 250, at 736 *et seq.* *See also* United States v. Caro, 569 F.2d 411, 416-17 (5th Cir. 1978) (pointing to car as source of heroin is assertive conduct and constitutes inadmissible hearsay); United States *ex rel.* Carter Equipment Co. v. H.R. Morgan, Inc., 544 F.2d 1271, 1273-74 (5th Cir. 1977), *rev'd on other grounds*, 554 F.2d 164 (5th Cir. 1977) (initialing invoices is nonverbal assertion by person signing that he owed money).

[11] United States v. Nakalodski, 481 F.2d 289, 300 (5th Cir. 1983), *cert. denied*, 414 U.S. 1064, 94 S.Ct. 570, 38 L.Ed.2d 469 (1973), (can be inferred from court's comments that defendant's smile coupled with silence amounted to an assertion; silence and smile were admissible as a party admission); United States v. Ross, 321 F.2d 61, 69 (2d Cir. 1963), *cert. denied*, 375 U.S. 894, 84 S.Ct. 170, 11 L.Ed.2d 123 (1963) (pointing to a list of identifying numbers was a communication; error in admitting hearsay not prejudicial in context of case).

[12] 112 Eng. R. 488 (1837).

[13] *See discussion* in § 801.1. *See, generally*, McCORMICK, § 250, at 736 *et seq. See also* United States v. Groce, 682 F.2d 1359, 1363-64 (11th Cir. 1982) (markings on map which supposedly showed course of a shrimping vessel allegedly used in conspiracy to smuggle marijuana into the United States were not intended as assertions and thus did not constitute inadmissible hearsay); United States v. Ariza-Ibarra, 605

F.2d 1216, 1223-24 (1st Cir. 1979) (in prosecution for conspiracy to possess and distribute cocaine, district court committed reversible error in admitting evidence that informant, whose tip led to the arrest of defendants, previously had provided information leading to successful prosecution of drug offenders; evidence of informant's past ability to identify drug offenders was tantamount to hearsay statement that he believed defendants were guilty); United States v. Zenni, 492 F.Supp. 464, 469 (E.D. Ky 1980) (in prosecution for illegal bookmaking activities, statement of unknown persons telephoning their bets to defendant's establishment were admissible as implied assertions of caller's belief that bets could be placed at the premise's telephone; statements were not inadmissible hearsay because callers did not intend to make an assertion about the fact sought to be proved). In the *Zeni* decision, Judge Bertelsman provides a particularly helpful analysis of the contemporary application of the *Wright v. Doe d'Tatham* doctrine. As illustrated by Judge Bertelsman's analysis, the definition of hearsay under Rule 801 renders all "implied assertions" to be non-hearsay even where such "implied assertions" are verbal. Accordingly, no statement is offered for its truth where the declarant does not intend to assert conclusions or beliefs merely implied by his out-of-court statement.

several letters written to the testator by persons deceased at the time of trial, on the theory that the matters discussed in the letters and their general tone demonstrated the writers' belief that the testator was sane.[14] The House of Lords found that the letters contained inadmissible hearsay because the writers' implied assertions that the testator was mentally competent should be treated the same as an express declaration of the testator's sanity.[15] In the course of the opinion, several other examples of implied assertions barred by the hearsay rule were given, including: (1) proof that underwriters paid the amount of the policy as evidence of loss of the ship; (2) proof that a person was elected to office as evidence of his sanity; (3) proof that a wager was paid as evidence that the event which was the subject of the bet occurred; (4) as evidence of seaworthiness, proof that the deceased captain embarked in a ship with his family after conducting an inspection of it.[16]

Early cases generally followed the reasoning in *Tatham*, providing the court even recognized the hearsay issue.[17] However, the modern trend, in accord with the views of most commentators, is to find a statement in conduct only when the actor subjectively intended to make an assertion.[18] As McCormick observed, in the examples set forth in *Tatham* as well as the facts of the case itself, the actor did not intend to make an assertion by his conduct, and therefore the hearsay risk of insincerity is minimized.[19] Although the risks of errors in perception, memory and narration still exist, they are reduced in the case of nonverbal conduct as compared to verbal assertions. The Advisory Committee endorsed this rationale in promulgating Rule 801(a), which treats nonverbal conduct as a statement only in those situations where the actor subjectively intends his or her conduct to be an assertion:

> Admittedly, evidence of this character is untested with respect to the perception, memory, and narration (or their equivalents) of the actor,

[14] 112 Eng. R. 488, 490-94 (1837).

[15] *Id*. at 506.

[16] *Id*. at 515-17.

[17] *See, e.g.*, Hanson v. State, 160 Ark. 329, 331, 254 S.W. 691, 693 (1923); Powell v. State, 88 Tex. Cr. R. 367, 369, 227 S.W. 188, 190 (1921). *See, generally*, Falknor, *The "Hear-Say" Rule as a "See-Do" Rule: Evidence of Conduct*, 33 ROCKY MTN. L. REV. 133, 135 (1961).

[18] *See* United States v. Singer, 687 F.2d 1135, 1147 (8th Cir. 1982). *See also* United States v. May, 622 F.2d 1000, 1007 (9th Cir.), *cert. denied*, 449 U.S. 984, 101 S.Ct. 402, 66 L.Ed.2d 247 (1980) (trial court's ruling that photographs were not hearsay

affirmed, since they were not assertions); United States v. Moskowitz, 581 F.2d 14, 16 (2d Cir. 1978), *cert. denied*, 439 U.S. 871, 99 S.Ct. 204, 58 L.Ed.2d 184 (1978) (police artist's sketch is not hearsay under Rule 801).

[19] McCORMICK, EVIDENCE, § 250, at 739. *See also* Falknor, The *"Hear-Say" Rule as a "See-Do" Rule: Evidence of Conduct*, 33 ROCKY MTN. L. REV. 133, 136 (1961) ("[if] in doing what he does a man has no intention of asserting the existence or non-existence of a fact, it would appear that the trustworthiness of evidence of this conduct is the same whether he is an egregious liar or a paragon of veracity.")

but the Advisory Committee is of the view that these dangers are minimal in the absence of an intent to assert and do not justify the loss of the evidence on hearsay grounds. No class of evidence is free of the possibility of fabrication, but the likelihood is less with nonverbal than with assertive verbal conduct.[20]

Under Rule 801, evidence must be characterized as a statement before the hearsay definition may attach.

In many cases, the actor may make verbal assertions which accompany his conduct. For example, in a raid of a suspected bookmaker where the police answer the phone and the caller places a bet, the prosecution may seek to introduce evidence of the call to prove the nature of the premises by showing the caller believed he was reaching a bookmaking joint. This evidence is not barred as hearsay under Rule 801 because the actor's conduct does not qualify as a statement, and his verbal assertions, *i.e.*, placing the bet, are not offered to prove the truth of the matter asserted.[21] Rather, the relevance of the evidence lies in the actor's implied assertion that he is calling a bookmaker. Where statements are involved, the hearsay risk of insincerity is reintroduced to a certain extent because the actor intended to make an assertion, but it still remains slight since the actor did not intend to assert the fact at issue.[22] Accordingly, Rule 801(c) excludes such assertions from the definition of hearsay.

Under Rule 801, the question of whether conduct may be a statement is resolved exclusively on the determination of whether the actor subjectively intended to make a communicative assertion.[23] Where evidence of conduct is offered on the theory that it is not intended by the actor as an assertion, and consequently not excludable under the hearsay system, the burden of showing that an assertion is intended should logically fall on the party objecting to the admission of the evidence on hearsay grounds.

---

[20] Fed. R. Evid. 801(a) Advisory Committee Note.

[21] *E.g.*, United States v. Southard, 700 F.2d 1, 13 (1st Cir. 1983), *cert. denied*, 464 U.S. 1051, 104 S.Ct. 89, 78 L.Ed.2d 97 (1983) (records and tapes of telephone conversations in prosecution for aiding and abetting gambling, which requires proof that substantive crime had been committed, were verbal acts offered only to prove that bets had been recorded and betting conversations had taken place); United States v. Pasha, 332 F.2d 193, 196-97 (7th Cir. 1964), *cert. denied*, 379 U.S. 839, 85 S.Ct. 75, 13 L.Ed.2d 45 (1964) (incoming calls received from persons seeking to place bets was properly received in a bookmaking operation prosecution as circumstantial evidence of the type of operation that was being conducted); Billeci v. United States, 184 F.2d 394, 396-97 (D.C. Cir. 1950) (in prosecution for operating a lottery, marshalls answering calls from people placing bets was properly received to show the nature and scope of activities conducted on the premises).

[22] *See* McCORMICK, § 250, at 740.

[23] *See* 4 WEINSTEIN, ¶ 801(a)[01], at 801-51.

§ 801.3   Definition of Declarant.

Rule 801(b) defines "declarant" as a person who makes a statement. Accordingly, a declarant is a person who makes an oral or written statement or who engages in intentionally assertive conduct. Under the definition of hearsay in Rule 801(c), the declarant is the person who makes the out-of-court statement which is reported or otherwise introduced at trial through a witness or a document.[24]

Of significance in the definition of declarant, is the use of the word "person." Under the hearsay system only a person may make a statement. As a result, machine or animal statements cannot be hearsay. The trail of a bloodhound, consequently, cannot be hearsay, and likewise, the meter reading on a radar machine cannot be hearsay. Accordingly, such animal or machine statements are not subject to exclusion under the hearsay system.[25]

§ 801.4   Definition of Hearsay.

Rule 801(c) codifies the generally accepted definition of hearsay. Hearsay is defined as a statement, other than one made by the declarant while testifying at the trial or hearing, offered in evidence to prove the truth of the matter asserted.[26] Two key components must be identified in order to apply the definition of hearsay. The first component of the hearsay definition relates to out-of-court statements. Hearsay potentially involves any statement made outside of the courtroom by any person, even a prior statement made by a witness who later testifies. In applying this element of the definition, it is necessary to determine when and where the statement was made. If the statement was made off the witness stand, prior to the provision of the testimony or the offering of the exhibit embracing the statement, then the statement qualifies as an "out-of-court statement."

The second element of the hearsay definition provides that the out-of-court statement must be "offered in evidence to prove the truth of the matter asserted." The application of this element of the definition requires an examination of whether the statement is offered to prove the substance

---

[24] Grimes v. Employers Mut. Liab. Ins. Co., 73 F.R.D. 607, 610 (D. Alaska 1977).

[25] *See* R. Lᴇᴍᴘᴇʀᴛ & S. Sᴀʟᴛᴢʙᴜʀɢ, A Mᴏᴅᴇʀɴ Aᴘᴘʀᴏᴀᴄʜ ᴛᴏ Eᴠɪᴅᴇɴᴄᴇ, 370-71 (1982).

[26] United States v. Bagaric, 706 F.2d 42, 64-65 (2d Cir. 1983) (in racketeering prosecution pursuant to RICO statute alleging international extortion scheme, defendant was not denied a chance to rebut the evidence linking him to planned attack on a certain victim where his testimony constituted excludable hearsay). *See also* Winans v. Rockwell Intern. Corp., 705 F.2d 1449, 1457 (5th Cir. 1983).

of its contents. If the statement is offered for its truth, then the second element of the hearsay definition is satisfied, *i.e.*, the out-of-court statement is hearsay. Where an out-of-court statement is offered for its truth and determined to be hearsay, the evidence is presumptively inadmissible, and admissibility may only be achieved through the vehicle of an exception to the basic definition, an exception to the exclusionary rule or some other basis identified in Rule 802.[27]

Not all out-of-court statements are relevant in a law suit in a manner that relies upon their truthfulness. When an out-of-court statement is relevant in a manner that does not depend upon the truth of the statement, the out-of-court statement is not hearsay under the definition, and consequently, the exclusionary rule does not operate to bar the out-of-court statement. To determine whether an out-of-court statement is offered for its truth, it is necessary to consider first the substance of the statement, and second, the relevant purpose for which the statement is offered.[28] Generally, when the facts sought to be proven and the substance of the out-of-court statement coincide, it may be assumed that the statement is offered for its truth.

The immediately following sections contain analyses of traditionally recognized classes of non-hearsay out-of-court statements. There is no requirement to fit a particular out-of-court statement within one of these classes to qualify it as admissible non-hearsay. Nevertheless, these traditionally recognized categories are helpful in determining whether a statement should be classified as non-hearsay.

§ 801.5   Non-Hearsay, Out-of-Court Statements; Statements Offered for Effect on a Particular Listener or Reader.

As a digression, it should be initially noted that if a witness testifies that D, an out-of-court declarant, made the statement "A murdered B," and the proponent of the witness is seeking to establish the relevant proposition that A, in fact, murdered B, the substance of the statement coincides with the matter sought to be proved, and consequently, the out-of-court statement is hearsay and would only be admissible pursuant to one of the bases identified in Rule 802. If the purpose for which the out-of-court statement

---

[27] *See* discussion in § 801.1, *supra*.

[28] Of course, the purpose in offering the evidence must be relevant according to the substantive law in the particular lawsuit. *See* § 401.1 *et seq.*

     See, e.g., Tennessee v. Street, 471 U.S. ____, 105 S.Ct. 2078, 85 L.Ed.2d 425 (1985) (a codefendant's confession was admitted to rebut the defendant's defense his confession was a coerced imitation; codefendant's confession was not admitted to prove the truth of matter asserted in confession but to demonstrate defendant's confession was not imitation).

is offered is altered, however, a non-hearsay use of the out-of-court statement may result. Accordingly, where a statement is relevant under the facts and circumstances of a case to show its impact or effect on a particular listener, the statement may be relevant without regard to its truth.

To illustrate, where the relevant purpose for offering the out-of-court statement, "A murdered B," is to show emotional injury inflicted upon a particular listener, *e.g.*, B's spouse, the statement is not offered for its truth. A qualified witness may testify to the fact that the statement was made in the presence of B's spouse in order to substantiate the emotional trauma caused by the out-of-court declarant. Under these facts, the immediate emotional trauma inflicted upon B's spouse is identical regardless of whether the out-of-court declarant is truthful or deceitful in his assertion. Operative to establishing the issue is the fact that the statement was made in the presence of B's spouse. Accordingly, such out-of-court statement is not hearsay and is not affected by the exclusionary rule.

Statements communicating warnings and notices,[29] and threats to the accused to show reasonable apprehension of danger, may fall within this category of non-hearsay, out-of-court statements.[30]

§ 801.6   Non-Hearsay, Out-of-Court Statements; Verbal Acts or Operative Facts.

In cases in which words have independent legal consequences, the words are relevant without regard to their truth, and such statements are not hearsay.[31] These types of statements are customarily known as "verbal acts" or "operative facts." For example, if an out-of-court statement made by D, "A murdered B," is offered by A to establish that D slandered A by accusing him of a crime, relevancy attaches to the making of the statement rather

---

[29] *See, e.g.*, United States v. Freeman, 619 F.2d 1112, 1121 (5th Cir. 1980), *cert. denied*, 450 U.S. 910, 101 S.Ct. 1348, 67 L.Ed.2d 334 (1981) (mail fraud prosecution stemming from sale of oil leases which defendant never even owned; letter of complaint by investors was properly used to cross-examine a defendant concerning his good faith defense; it was not hearsay since it was not offered to prove truth of contents). *See also* United States v. Sheehan, 428 F.2d 67, 70-74 (8th Cir. 1970), *cert. denied*, 400 U.S. 853, 91 S.Ct. 66, 27 L.Ed.2d 90 (1970); United States v. Press, 336 F.2d 1003, 1011 (2d Cir. 1964), *cert. denied*, 379 U.S. 965, 85 S.Ct. 658, 13 L.Ed.2d 559 (1965).

[30] *See* McCORMICK, § 249, at 733-34; 6 WIGMORE, § 1789, at 235 *et seq.*; United States v. Herrera, 600 F.2d 502, 504 (5th Cir. 1979). *See also*, Park v. Huff, 493 F.2d 923, 927-28 (5th Cir. 1974), *cert. denied*, 423 U.S. 824, 96 S.Ct. 38, 46 L.Ed.2d 40 (1975).

[31] *See, e.g.*, United States v. Southard, 700 F.2d 1, 13 (1st Cir. 1983), *cert. denied*, 464 U.S. 1051, 104 S.Ct. 89, 78 L.Ed.2d 97 (1983); Yarborough v. City of Warren, 383 F.Supp. 676, 682 (E.D. Mich. 1974).

than the truth of the statement.[32] The out-of-court statement is not offered for its truth, and consequently, it is not hearsay. Another example of "verbal acts" or "operative facts" would be statements which are the terms of an oral or written contract or statements which show that an agreement was made.[33] The law imposes certain consequences in regard to such statements regardless of the truth, and accordingly, such out-of-court statements are not hearsay. Statements also may constitute operative facts in cases involving fraud,[34] entrapment,[35] conspiracy[36] or extortion.[37] Likewise, statements forming the basis for a claim of solicitation under a criminal statute fall within the category of verbal acts or operative facts.[38]

§ 801.7   Non-Hearsay, Out-of-Court Statements; Verbal Parts of Acts.

Where the legal significance of an act, considered in isolation, is ambiguous, contemporaneous statements made by the actors may be admissible as verbal parts of the act to clarify the nature of the transaction. For example, the delivery of money may constitute a loan, gift, bribe or some other transaction. Utterances by the parties which explain the character of their conduct are not barred by the hearsay rule where the substantive law is

[32] If the truth of the statement becomes relevant in the case discussed in the text, it would be by virtue of the assertion of an affirmative defense presumably supportive of D's case. The proponent of the evidence discussed in the text would be merely seeking to establish that the operative words were spoken; the truthfulness of the words is not sought to be established by the proponent.

[33] NLRB v. H. Koch & Sons, 578 F.2d 1287, 1290-91 (9th Cir. 1978).

[34] Itel Capitol Corp. v. Cups Coal Co., 707 F.2d 1253, 1259-60 (11th Cir. 1983); United States v. Gibson, 690 F.2d 697, 700-702 (9th Cir. 1982).

[35] Crispo v. United States, 443 F.2d 13, 14 (4th Cir. 1971) (statements of informer hearing on defendant's entrapment defense should have been admitted).

[36] United States v. Saavedra, 684 F.2d 1293, 1297-99 (9th Cir. 1982). See also United States v. Alvarez-Porras, 643 F.2d 54, 58 (2d Cir. 1981), cert. denied, 454 U.S. 839, 20 S.Ct. 146, 70 L.Ed.2d 121 (1981) (statements were admissible to show defendants' involvement in the conspiracy, where they indicated that she had brought stuff from Columbia and was going to ac-

company principal in narcotics ring the following morning, since it constituted significant verbal acts made regardless of their truth); United States v. Wolfson, 634 F.2d 1217, 1219 (9th Cir. 1980) ("[w]hen a witness is present at a meeting between a group of conspirators, and they orally, in his presence, agree upon the conspiracy, its objectives, and its modus operandi, the witness's testimony about what each of them said is not hearsay; it is not offered to prove that what the conspirators said is true, but to prove their verbal acts in saying it"). See, e.g., United States v. Mazyak, 650 F.2d 788, 792 (5th Cir. 1981), cert. denied, 455 U.S. 922, 102 S.Ct. 1281, 71 L.Ed.2d 464 (1982).

[37] United States v. De Vincent, 632 F.2d 147, 151 (1st Cir. 1980), cert. denied, 449 U.S. 986, 101 S.Ct. 405, 66 L.Ed.2d 249 (1980) (in prosecution for making extortionate extension of credit, statement that defendant had been jailed for loansharking and was "pretty bad" was admissible). See also United States v. Lynn, 608 F.2d 132, 135 (5th Cir. 1979).

[38] See, generally, 6 Wigmore, § 1766, at 177 et seq.

concerned only with the objective conduct rather than the state of mind or intent of the actors.[39] The statements are not hearsay because they are not offered for the truth of the matter asserted. The truth or falsity of such statements is inconsequential. For instance, if a person uses words indicating that he intends to make a gift as he delivers money, he cannot later demand repayment of the money as a loan even if that was his true intention at the time of the transfer.[40]

To qualify as non-hearsay, the statement must not be offered for its truth. If a contemporaneous statement regarding an act "makes an assertion about some previous act, condition, or event, it is hearsay to the extent that it tends to prove what it asserts."[41]

§ 801.8   Non-Hearsay, Out-of-Court Statements; State of Mind.

Where the state of mind of the declarant is relevant in a lawsuit, the out-of-court statements of the declarant which do not directly assert the state of mind are not offered for their truth.

To illustrate, if a child makes the out-of-court statement, "My father, A, murdered B," this out-of-court statement may be relevant in a particular case in a manner that does not rely upon the truth of the matter asserted, *i.e.*, the fact of the purported murder.[42] Rather it might be reported by a witness on the stand in order to demonstrate the state of mind of the child where this state of mind is relevant, *e.g.*, in a custody proceeding. Where such fear or antipathy is relevant, the proponent of the out-of-court statement may be seeking to establish antipathy to, or the fear of the father by the child, circumstantially reflected in the child's statement. Consequently, the out-of-court statement would not be offered for its truth, and it would be admissible as a non-hearsay out-of-court statement.[43]

---

[39] National Bank of the Metropolis v. Kennedy, 84 U.S. (17 Wall.) 19, 21 L.Ed. 611 (1873). *See also* United States v. Romano, 684 F.2d 1057, 1066 (2d Cir. 1982), *cert. denied*, 459 U.S. 1016, 103 S.Ct. 375, 74 L.Ed.2d 509 (1982) (requests to give money to the "boys in the union" was evidence admissible as utterances contemporaneous with independently admissible non-verbal act of picking up the money); United States v. Jackson, 588 F.2d 1046, 1049 (5th Cir. 1979), *cert. denied*, 442 U.S. 941, 99 S.Ct. 2882, 61 L.Ed.2d 310 (1979) (witness permitted to testify, since court classified statements made as non-hearsay statements under 801(c) - utterances made contemporaneously with a non-verbal act for the purpose of throwing light on it). *Cf.*, United States v. Abascal, 564 F.2d 821, 829-30 (9th Cir. 1977), *cert. denied*, 435 U.S. 942, 98 S.Ct. 1521, 55 L.Ed.2d 538, 435 U.S. 953, 98 S.Ct. 1583, 55 L.Ed.2d 804 (1978).

[40] Morgan, *A Suggested Classification of Utterances Admissible as Res Gestae*, 31 Yale L.J. 229, 232 (1922).

[41] 4 Louisell & Mueller, § 417, at 107.

[42] *See* Betts v. Betts, 3 Wash. App. 53, 55, 473 P.2d 403, 406 (1970).

[43] *See* United States v. West, 666 F.2d 16, 20 (2d Cir. 1981).

Similarly, statements of an out-of-court declarant which manifest the declarant's insanity are not offered for their truth and are consequently not hearsay. Accordingly, in the classic example, if the out-of-court declarant states that he is Napoleon Bonaparte, such statement is not offered to establish the truth of the assertion, *i.e*, that the declarant is Napoleon. Rather, the out-of-court, non-hearsay statement is offered as a manifestation of the declarant's deranged mental state.[44]

§ 801.9   Non-Hearsay, Out-of-Court Statements; Prior Inconsistent Statements Used for Impeachment Purposes.

Prior inconsistent statements offered only for impeachment pursuant to the technique of self-contradiction are operatively not hearsay because of the limiting instructions which accompany such statements.[45] Such statements are admissible for the limited purpose of affecting the credibility of the witness sought to be impeached. Accordingly, if a witness testifies at trial that "X murdered B," he may be impeached by his prior written or oral out-of-court contradictory statement, "A murdered B." Specific rules govern this impeachment procedure.[46]

Where used for the purpose of impeachment, the contrived but traditionally recognized theory is that the prior inconsistent statement of the witness is not offered to establish the truth of its substance, but rather only to show that the witness is the type of person who makes conflicting statements regarding the same set of facts. Where an out-of-court statement of a witness is offered solely for the purpose of impeachment, a limiting instruction from the trial judge must direct the trier of fact to consider the prior statement not for its truth, but rather only for the purpose of assessing the credibility of the witness.[47] It is the limiting instruction which operates to afford the statement its non-hearsay character and function.

Prior statements of a witness which satisfy an exception which would admit hearsay may be considered for their substantive value, *i.e*, they may

---

[44] *See* 4 WEINSTEIN, ¶ 801(c)[01], at 801-70; McCORMICK, § 249, at 734. It should be noted that where the out-of-court declarant directly asserts the emotion, *e.g.*, "I am afraid," the statement is usually admissible pursuant to Rule 803(3).

[45] *See* ROTHSTEIN, FEDERAL RULES OF EVIDENCE, 240 (2d ed. 1979).

[46] *See* Rule 613 and § 613.1 *et seq.* of this Treatise.

[47] *See, generally,* McCORMICK, § 251, at 744 n.3 ("[T]he opposite party is, of course, entitled to a jury instruction as to the limited use of the evidence. . . . Failure to give the instruction even though not requested, has been held plain error.") *See also* United States v. Lipscomb, 425 F.2d 226, 227 (6th Cir. 1970). The impeachment technique of self-contradiction is governed by Rule 613 and is discussed at § 613.1 of this Treatise.

be considered for their truth. Certain prior statements of a witness identified in Rule 801(d)(1)(A) are designated as admissible substantive evidence,
and this exception particularly should be consulted.[48] Any exception may,
however, be utilized to render the statement admissible for substantive evidence as well as for impeachment purposes. Of course, where the inconsistent statement is admissible for its substantive value as well as for impeachment, no limiting instruction is required or appropriate.

§ 801.10   Hearsay and Relevancy.

Whether an out-of-court statement is offered for its truth depends upon
the statement's relevancy in regard to the substantive issues of the particular case. Accordingly, the proponent of an out-of-court statement may not
appropriately argue, for example, that the statement is offered to demonstrate effect on the listener where notice to the listener or impact on the
listener is not a relevant issue in the case under Rule 401. Likewise, an out-
of-court statement cannot be offered to demonstrate the state of mind of
the declarant, unless the declarant's state of mind is properly a relevant
issue in the case. The application of the definition of hearsay inevitably
involves the consideration of the definition of relevancy which must take
cognizance of the substantive issues of the case.[49]

Rule 801(d)(1)   Statements Which are not Hearsay—
Prior Statement by Witness

Rule 801(d)(1) reads as follows:

(d) **Statements which are not hearsay.** A statement is not hearsay if—(1)
Prior statement by witness. The declarant testifies at the trial or hearing and
is subject to cross-examination concerning the statement, and the statement
is (A) inconsistent with his testimony, and was given under oath subject to
the penalty of perjury at a trial, hearing, or other proceeding, or in a deposition, or (B) consistent with his testimony and is offered to rebut an express or
implied charge against him of recent fabrication or improper influence or
motive, or (C) one of identification of a person made after perceiving him;
or. . . .

[48] *See § 801.19, infra.*
[49] *See § 401.1 et seq.*

§ 801.11　Statements Identified in Rule 801(d)—In General.

Under Rule 801(d) certain out-of-court statements of witnesses and parties are excepted from the definition of hearsay.[50] These designated out-of-court statements which are offered for their truth, and which fall within the basic definition of hearsay, are nevertheless considered to be "non-hearsay" by virtue of this exception to the basic definition. Because such statements are designated non-hearsay, they are not rendered inadmissible by the hearsay system. Under the more traditional approach, admissions of a party are designated as hearsay but admissible through an exception to the basic exclusionary rule. Also under the traditional approach, prior statements of a witness are admissible only under limited circumstances.[51]

Rule 801(d)(1) contains vehicles for the admission of prior out-of-court statements of witnesses. The term "witness" indicates that the out-of-court declarant must be present to testify at the trial at which his statement is offered such that the declarant is subject to delayed cross-examination concerning his out-of-court statement.

Rule 801(d)(2), considered in a subsequent chapter, contains vehicles for the admission of out-of-court statements of parties. The term "parties" refers to parties to the litigation.

---

[50] See, generally, McCORMICK, § 251; 4 WEINSTEIN, ¶¶ 801(d)(1)[01], 801(d)(1)(A)[01]-[10], 801(d)(1)(B)[01]-[03], 801 (d)(1)(C)[01]-[03]; 4 LOUISELL & MUELLER, §§ 419-422; 5 WIGMORE, § 1361; 6 WIGMORE, § 1766. See also Bein, Prior Inconsistent Statements: The Hearsay Rule, 801(d)(1)(A) and 803(24), 26 U.C.LA. L. REV. 967 (1979); Blakely Substantive Use of Prior Inconsistent Statements Under the Federal Rules of Evidence, 64 KY L.J. 3 (1976); Graham, Prior Inconsistent Statements: Rule 801(d)(1)(B) of the Federal Rules of Evidence, Critique and Proposal, 30 HASTINGS L.J. 575 (1979); Graham, Employing Inconsistent Statements for Impeachment and as Substantive Evidence: A Critical Review and Proposed Amendment of Federal Rules of Evidence 801(d)(1)(A), 613 and 607, 75 MICH. L. REV. 1565 (1977); Gooderson, Previous Consistent Statements, 26 CAMBRIDGE L.J. 64 (1968); Mavet, Prior Identification in Criminal Cases: Hearsay and Confrontation Issues, 24 ARIZ. L. REV. 29 (1982); McCormick, The Turncoat Witness: Previous Statements as Substantive Evidence, 25 TEX. L. REV. 573 (1947); Morgan, Hearsay Dangers and the Application of the Hearsay Concept, 62 HARV. L. REV. 177 (1948); Reutlinger, Prior Inconsistent Statements: Presently Inconsistent Doctrine, 26 HASTINGS L.J. 361 (1974); Silbert, Federal Rule of Evidence 801(d)(1)(A), 49 TEMP. L.Q. 880 (1976); Weinstein, Book Review of Eyewitness Testimony by Elizabeth F. Lotus, 81 COLUM. L. REV. 441 (1981).

[51] Pre-Rule federal law followed the traditional approach. A witness's own statements were considered hearsay and, unless they fell within one of the very few exceptions to the hearsay rule, were inadmissible. See, e.g., United States v. Gregory, 472 F.2d 484, 488 (5th Cir. 1973); United States v. Cunningham, 446 F.2d 194, 197 (2d Cir. 1971), 76cert. denied, 404 U.S. 950, 92 S.Ct. 302, 30 L.Ed.2d 226 (1971); State of Mississippi v. Durham, 444 F.2d 152, 156 (5th Cir. 1971). Cf., United States v. Hill, 481 F.2d 929, 932 (5th Cir. 1973), cert. denied, 414 U.S. 1115, 94 S.Ct. 847, 38 L.Ed.2d 742 (1973).

§ 801.12   Prior Inconsistent Statements.

Rule 801(d)(1)(A) pertains exclusively to prior inconsistent statements of a witness used in conjunction with the impeachment technique of self-contradiction.[52] Where the out-of-court statement is inconsistent with the declarant's trial testimony and was given under the penalty of perjury at a deposition, trial, hearing, or like proceeding, the prior statement may be received for its truth. Although the Rule does not offer a definition of inconsistency, federal courts have found statements to be inconsistent where a "reasonable . . . person could infer on comparing the whole effect of the two statements that they had been produced by inconsistent beliefs."[53] The statement may be considered as substantive evidence, and the jury may predicate its verdict upon the statement. Such statements are admissible because of procedural guarantees of trustworthiness. The prior inconsistent statement was made under oath and the declarant is subject to *delayed* cross-examination and evaluation of demeanor at the trial at which the statement is offered for the purpose of impeachment. Also, since the prior statement was nearer in time to the event at issue, it is arguably more trustworthy than the declarant's trial testimony because "memory hinges on recency."[54]

It is important to note that the substantive use of statements under Rule 801(d)(1)(A) is not restricted to situations where the party against whom the statement is offered had an opportunity to cross-examine the witness at the proceeding at which the statement was originally made.[55] For example, the prosecutor in a criminal case may wish to offer into evidence the grand jury testimony as a prior inconsistent statement. Under Rule 801(d)(1)(A), such grand jury testimony might be available as substantive evidence where offered in conjunction with the impeachment of the witness who had earlier testified at the grand jury hearing.[56] Generally, the use of prior

---

[52] *See* Rule 613 and § 613.1 *et seq.* of this Treatise.

[53] 4 WEINSTEIN, ¶ 801(d)(1)(A)[01], at 801-110 (1982). *See, e.g.*, United States v. Morgan, 555 F.2d 238, 242-43 (9th Cir. 1977) (there was inconsistency between trial testimony and grand jury testimony, making the latter permissible pursuant to Rule 801(d)(1)(A).

[54] McCORMICK, EVIDENCE, § 251, at 745.

[55] *See* Rule 801, Advisory Committee's Note.

[56] *See, e.g.*, United States v. Coran, 589 F.2d 70, 75-76 (1st Cir. 1978); United States v. Marchand, 564 F.2d 983, 999 (2d Cir. 1977), *cert. denied*, 434 U.S. 1015, 98 S.Ct. 732, 54 L.Ed.2d 760 (1977) (witness's grand jury testimony that defendant was marijuana supplier admissible at trial as substantive evidence after witness claimed he could not identify defendant as supplier); United States v. Long Soldier, 562 F.2d 601, 605 (8th Cir. 1977) (where witness made statement before grand jury relating statements made to him by defendant concerning a crime and then denied at trial that conversation took place, grand jury testimony was admissible as substantive evidence).

inconsistent statements as substantive evidence against the accused is not in violation of the confrontation clause of the constitution.[57]

Under pre-Rule federal law, a prior inconsistent statement of a witness, whether or not rendered under oath, was admissible only for impeachment purposes.[58] It could not be considered for its substantive value. Accordingly, under pre-Rule practice, where an out-of-court statement was offered to impeach the credibility of a witness, the jury could only consider the prior statement as a basis for assessing the credibility of the witness. A limiting instruction was required to restrict the jury's consideration to the proper purpose.[59]

It should be noted that prior inconsistent statements not conforming to Rule 801(d)(1)(A) are available for impeachment use. Where prior inconsistent statements do not conform with Rule 801(d)(1)(A), such statements are available for contradiction purposes only and the jury must be so instructed.[60] Where the prior inconsistent statement conforms with the requirements of Rule 801(d)(1)(A), the prior statement serves a dual function. It serves to impeach the witness, and it operates as substantive evidence.

§ 801.13   Prior Consistent Statements.

Rule 801(d)(1)(B) applies to prior statements of a witness used to rehabilitate the witness where such statements are consistent with the trial testimony of the witness. Under pre-Rule federal law, such evidence was admissible to bolster the credibility of a witness whose credibility had been attacked, but it could not be used as substantive evidence.[61]

Under Rule 801(d)(1)(B), a prior consistent statement of a witness is admissible without regard to whether an oath or cross-examination attended the prior statement. No oath or cross-examination is necessary for the prior consistent statement to be considered as substantive evidence.[62]

[57] See California v. Green, 399 U.S. 149, 168-69, 90 S.Ct. 1930, 1940, 26 L.Ed.2d 489, 503 (1970) (on remand, California Supreme Court concluded that the statement in question could be used substantively since the confrontation clause had been satisfied). But see Ohio v. Roberts, 448 U.S. 56, 100 S.Ct. 2531, 65 L.Ed.2d 597 (1980) (in which the Court declined to decide whether the mere opportunity to cross-examine is itself determinative of the confrontation analysis).

[58] See, e.g., United States v. Allsup, 485 F.2d 287, 290-91 (8th Cir. 1973); United States v. Rainwater, 283 F.2d 386, 390 (8th Cir. 1960).

[59] See Rule 105.

[60] See § 801.8, supra. Of course, where offered only for the purpose of impeachment, the statement is subject to a limiting instruction. See Rule 105.

[61] See United States v. Scholle, 553 F.2d 1109, 1119-20 (8th Cir. 1977), cert. denied, 434 U.S. 940, 98 S.Ct. 432, 54 L.Ed.2d 300 (1977); Comment, Hearsay Under the Proposed Federal Rules: A Discretionary Approach, 15 WAYNE L. REV. 1077, 1092-93 (1969).

[62] See 4 WEINSTEIN, ¶ 801(d)(1)(B)[01], at 801-116. Compare Rule 801(d)(1)(A).

However, the witness must be subject to cross-examination at the proceeding at which the prior consistent statement is offered regarding both his trial testimony and the earlier statement.[63] Some courts continue to impose the traditional requirement that the party offering the prior consistent statement must show that it was made before a motive to fabricate existed or improper influence was exercised over the declarant,[64] but other courts do not read such a requirement into Rule 801(d)(1)(B).[65]

It should be noted that this subdivision has a narrow application. The exception is only triggered where there has been an express or implied inference of recent fabrication, fraud or improper motive of such a nature that a prior consistent statement would be probative to negate such impeachment. In this respect, therefore, the admissibility of prior consistent statements of a witness is dependent upon whether the opponent opens the door by attempting to impeach the witness.[66] The wording of Rule 801(d)(1)(B) indicates that impeachment of the witness must suggest that he intentionally changed his version of the events before prior consistent statements are admissible as substantive evidence.[67] Attempts to impeach

[63] United States v. West, 670 F.2d 675, 686-87 (7th Cir. 1982), *cert. denied*, 457 U.S. 1124, 102 S.Ct. 2944, 73 L.Ed.2d 1340, *cert. denied*, 457 U.S. 1139, 102 S.Ct. 2972, 73 L.Ed.2d 1359 (1982) (error to permit government witness to adduce rebuttal testimony describing prior consistent statement by one of its witnesses, since defense never had an opportunity to cross-examine the witness regarding the statement).

[64] *E.g.*, United States v. Henderson, 717 F.2d 135, 138 (4th Cir. 1983), *cert. denied*, 104 S.Ct. 1006, 79 L.Ed.2d 238 (1983) (indicating acceptance of the gloss on Rule 801(d)(1)(B) that a prior consistent statement is admissible under the rule only if the statement was made prior to the time the supposed motive to falsify arose); United States v. Feldman, 711 F.2d 758, 766-67 (7th Cir. 1983), *cert. denied*, 104 S.Ct. 352, 78 L.Ed.2d 317 (1983) ("a prior consistent statement would be relevant to rebut a charge of recent fabrication only if the statement were made prior to the time the alleged motive to falsify arose"); United States v. Rohrer, 708 F.2d 429, 433 (9th Cir. 1983) (court admitted prior consistent statement; reviewing court concludes it was inadmissible because it "did not precede his motive to fabricate"). *See also* United States v. Sampol, 636 F.2d 621, 673 (D.C. Cir. 1980); United States v. Shulman, 624 F.2d 384, 393 (2d Cir. 1980).

[65] *E.g.*, United States v. Hamilton, 689 F.2d 1262, 1273-74 (6th Cir. 1982), *cert. denied*, 459 U.S. 1117, 103 S.Ct. 754 (1983) (statement to government agents by alleged coconspirator who entered a plea and cooperated with government was properly received); United States v. Parry, 649 F.2d 292, 295-96 (5th Cir. 1981) (court here noted that the rule requiring the prior inconsistent statement to have been made before the motive to falsify came into play has been rejected); United States v. Rios, 611 F.2d 1335, 1349 (10th Cir. 1979) ("it is necessary for a witness's consistent statements to have been made prior to the statements which have been used to impeach him").

[66] Fed. R. Evid. 801(d)(1)(B) Advisory Committee Note.

[67] *See* United States v. Rinn, 586 F.2d 113, 119-20 (9th Cir. 1978), *cert. denied*, 441 U.S. 931, 99 S.Ct. 2051, 60 L.Ed.2d 659 (1978) (defense question to police officer whether the officer had prepared a report indicating a government witness named Neuberger had said that he was able to obtain large quantities of cocaine paved the way for government to establish on cross-examination of the police officer that Neuberger had said he was able to purchase this cocaine from the defendants). *See also* United States v. Herring, 582 F.2d 535, 541 (10th Cir. 1978); United States v. Consolidated Packaging Corp. 575 F.2d 117, 130

the witness by showing a flaw in memory or narration do not charge him with "recent fabrication or improper influence or motive," and therefore should not open the door to the substantive use of prior consistent statements. The trial court has discretion to exclude prior consistent statements which constitute essentially cumulative evidence.[68]

§ 801.14   Statements of Identification.

Rule 801(d)(1)(C) provides for the admissibility of an out-of-court statement of identification made by a declarant after perceiving the person identified, where the declarant is a witness at the trial at which the statement of identification is offered. Rule 801(d)(1)(C) does not operate in the context of impeachment or rehabilitation as do Rules 801(d)(1)(A) and (B). Rather, its application is limited to the situation in which a witness is present at trial, and a prior out-of-court identification made by that witness is offered into evidence. Rule 801(d)(1)(C) operates independently of subdivisions (d)(1)(A) and (d)(1)(B) and therefore a prior statement of identification may be admissible even though it does not meet the requirements for a prior inconsistent or prior consistent statement.

Rule 801(d)(1)(C) extends the pre-Rule trend of admitting as substantive proof a prior communication made by a witness who is subject to cross-examination of trial[69] provided constitutional demands are satisfied.[70] Rule 801(d)(1)(C) will apply to an out-of-court statement identifying an individual in a line-up, a street identification or even a photographic array identification.[71] The Rule reflects a recognition that identification in the courtroom is frequently less reliable than a prior identification which is more proximate in time to the operative facts of the case. Courtroom identification has low probative value in light of the inherent suggestibility of the

(7th Cir. 1978); United States v. Navarro-Varelas, 541 F.2d 1311, 1344 (9th Cir. 1976), cert. denied, 429 U.S. 1045, 97 S.Ct. 751, 50 L.Ed.2d 759 (1977).

[68] 4 WEINSTEIN, ¶ 801(d)(1)(B)[01], at 801-150. See, e.g., United States v. Mock, 640 F.2d 629, 632 (2d Cir. 1981).

[69] See Gilbert v. California, 388 U.S. 263, 272, 87 S.Ct. 1951, 1960, 18 L.Ed.2d 1178, 1186 (1967). See also Clemons v. United States, 408 F.2d 1230, 1243 (D.C. Cir. 1968), cert. denied, 394 U.S. 964, 89 S.Ct. 1318, 22 L.Ed.2d 567 (1969) (identification at preliminary hearings).

[70] See United States v. Crews, 445 U.S. 463, 472 n.16, 100 S.Ct. 1244, 1252, 63 L.Ed.2d 537, 545 (1980); Manson v. Brathwaite, 432 U.S. 98, 104, 97 S.Ct. 2243, 2249, 53 L.Ed.2d 140, 147 (1977); Styers v. Smith, 659 F.2d 293, 297 (2d Cir. 1981).

[71] See United States v. Cueto, 611 F.2d 1056, 1063 (5th Cir. 1980); United States v. Fosher, 568 F.2d 207, 210 (1st Cir. 1978); United States v. Moore, 550 F.2d 180, 182 (4th Cir. 1976); United States v. Mills, 535 F.2d 1325, 1328 (D.C. Cir. 1976).

process, and accordingly, where the person who made the prior identification is available as a witness to testify, his or her earlier identification is admissible as substantive evidence.[72]

Rule 801(d)(1)(C) addresses only the question of whether the hearsay hurdle may be overcome regarding statements of prior identification. The Rule does not purport to address constitutional bases for exclusion that might result from an identification conducted in a manner which would jeopardize constitutional rights.[73]

Rule 801(d)(2)   Statements Which are not Hearsay— Admission by Party-Opponent

Rule 801(d)(2) reads as follows:

> **(d) Statements which are not hearsay.** A statement is not hearsay if—
> . . . **(2) Admission by party-opponent.** The statement is offered against a party and is (A) his own statement, in either his individual or a representative capacity or (B) a statement of which he has manifested his adoption or belief in its truth, or (C) a statement by a person authorized by him to make a statement concerning the subject, or (D) a statement by his agent or servant concerning a matter within the scope of his agency or employment, made during the existence of the relationship, or (E) a statement by a coconspirator of a party during the course and in furtherance of the conspiracy.

§ 801.15   Party Admissions—In General.

Rule 801(d)(2) governs out-of-court statements by a party or by other persons where the statements of such persons may be legally attributed to a

---

[72] See United States v. Barbati, 284 F.Supp. 409, 413 (E.D.N.Y. 1968). See also McCormick, § 251, at 747-48 ("Admissibility of the prior identification [where the person who made the identification is in court and available for cross-examination] has the support of substantial authority in the cases. . . . Justification is found in the unsatisfactory nature of courtroom identification and the safeguards which now surround staged out-of-court identifications.").

[73] See, e.g., Kirby v. Illinois, 406 U.S. 682, 689, 92 S.Ct. 1877, 1884, 32 L.Ed.2d 411, 417 (1972) (petitioner did not have constitutional right to counsel at police station showup which took place after arrest but before formal charges were made, therefore robbery victim's testimony describing his prior identification of petitioner at showup was admissible); United States v. Wade, 388 U.S. 218, 226, 87 S.Ct. 1926, 1933, 18 L.Ed.2d 1149, 1155 (1967) (where defendant was deprived of aid of counsel at post-indictment lineup, his conviction was vacated pending hearing to determine whether courtroom identification was tainted by earlier illegal identification, thereby necessitating a new trial).

party to the lawsuit.[74] Pre-Rule federal law characterized an admission of a party as either an exception to the hearsay rule,[75] non-hearsay,[76] or as a statement not within the purpose of the hearsay rule.[77] While under the codification of the Federal Rules of Evidence, prior statements of a party and statements legally attributable to a party are considered to be exceptions to the basic definition of hearsay, this codification does not affect a substantive change in federal law even in courts that espoused a different pre-Rule rationale for admissibility. The functional result is the same: The out-of-court statement of the party offered for its truth will be admissible at trial providing it conforms to one of the stated exceptions in Rule 801(d)(2).

§ 801.16 Party's Own Statement.

Rule 801(d)(2)(A) provides for the admissibility of statements by a party in his individual or representative capacity. An out-of-court statement of a party, offered against the party by the opposing party, is admissible pursuant to Rule 801(d)(2)(A).[78]

[74] See, generally, McCormick, § 262, 269-75, 263-266, 267; 4 Weinstein, ¶¶ 801(d)(2)[01], 801(d)(2)(A)[01], 801(d)(2)(B)[01], 801(d)(2)(C)[01], 801(d)(2)(D)[01], 801(d)(2)(E)[01]; 4 Louisell & Mueller, §§ 423-428; 4 Wigmore, §§ 1048, 1063-67, 1069-75, 1078, 1079; 9 Wigmore, §§ 2588-94. See also Boyce, Rule 63(9)(a) of Uniform Rules of Evidence - A Vector Analysis, 5 Utah L. Rev. 311 (1957); Dow, KLM v. Tuller: A New Approach to Admissibility of Prior Statements of a Witness, 41 Neb. L. Rev. 598 (1962); Falknor, Hearsay, 1969 Law & Soc. Ord. 591; Falknor, Vicarious Admissions and the Uniform Rules, 14 Vand. L. Rev. 855 (1961); Gamble, The Tacit Admission Rule: Unreliable and Unconstitutional Doctrine Ripe for Abandonment, 14 Ga. L. Rev. 27 (1979); Griffin, Admissions: A Time for Change, 20 How. L.J. 128 (1977); Heller, Admission by Acquiescence, 15 U. Miami L. Rev. 161 (1960); Hetland, Admissions in the Uniform Rules: Are They Necessary?, 46 Iowa L. Rev. 307 (1961); Lev, The Law of Vicarious Admissions - An Estoppel, 26 U. Cin. L. Rev. 17 (1957); Morgan, Admissions as an Exception to the Hearsay Rule, 30 Yale L.J. 355 (1921); Morgan, Rationale of Vicarious Admissions, 42 Harv. L. Rev. 461 (1929); Strahorn, A Reconsideration of the Hearsay Rule and Admissions, 85 U. Pa. L. Rev. 564 (1937).

[75] See, e.g., Dutton v. Evans, 400 U.S. 74, 80-81, 91 S.Ct. 210, 215-16, 27 L.Ed.2d 213, 22-23 (1970); Sablan v. People of Territory of Guam, 434 F.2d 837, 840 (9th Cir. 1970). See also Morgan, Admission as an Exception to the Hearsay Rule, 30 Yale L.J. 355 (1921).

[76] See, e.g., United States v. Rosenstein, 474 F.2d 705, 711 n.2 (2d Cir. 1973) ("[W]e note that the new Federal Rules of Evidence do not classify admissions or coconspirators' declarations as exceptions to the hearsay rule, but rather as statements which are not hearsay"). See also Wigmore, § 1048, at 3.

[77] See, e.g., United States v. United Shoe Machinery Corp., 89 F.Supp 349, 352 (D.C. Mass. 1950) ("an extrajudicial admission of a party is receivable against him not as an exception to the hearsay rule, but as not being within the purpose of the hearsay rule"). See also United States v. Puco, 475 F.2d 1099, 1102 n.3 (2d Cir. 1973), cert. denied, 414 U.S. 825, 94 S.Ct. 127, 38 L.Ed.2d 58 (1973).

[78] See United States v. Ramirez, 710 F.2d 535, 537 (9th Cir. 1983). See also Coughlin v. Capitol Cement Co., 571 F.2d 290, 306 (5th Cir. 1978) (admissions must be offered

The term "admission" is often misleading. While the term "admission" appears to imply that the out-of-court statement must be a confession or statement against interest, in actuality, any prior statement of a party is admissible providing it is offered against the party at trial. The statement need not be against interest when it was made as long as the opposing party is offering the out-of-court statement at trial for a purpose that is appropriate in the lawsuit pursuant to the rules of relevancy.[79] There is no requirement that the party had first-hand knowledge of the subject of his statement.[80] The party's admission may be express, or it may be inferred from his conduct where he intended to make an assertion.[81]

As a general principle, a party may not introduce his own out-of-court statement as an admission.[82] While other exceptions might be utilized to admit a proponent's own hearsay statement, the admissions exception is not available because such evidence is not offered *against* the party who made the out-of-court statement.

Admissions of a party are admissible not because they are inherently more reliable as a class than hearsay generally. Rather, admissions of a party are admissible by virtue of the nature of adversary process. When a prior out-of-court statement is offered against a party, that party will not be heard to object that he is unable to cross-examine the declarant, or observe the declarant's demeanor, or put the declarant under oath. Obviously, the declarant is the party who would object to the admissibility of the statement; such party will not be heard to complain that the safeguards normally attendant to testimonial evidence are unavailable in regard to his own statement. In essence, admissions are predicated on an estoppel theory.[83]

against, not for, party); United States v. Porter, 554 F.2d 936, 938 (8th Cir. 1976) (distinguishing between statements admissible as substantive and admissible only to impeach).

[79] See § 401.1 et seq.

[80] Mahlandt v. Wild Canid Survival & Research Center, Inc., 588 F.2d 626, 629-30 (8th Cir. 1978); Ross v. Salminen, 191 F. 504, 505 (1st Cir. 1911).

[81] United States v. Myers, 550 F.2d 1036, 1049 (5th Cir. 1977), *cert. denied*, 439 U.S. 847, 99 S.Ct. 147, 58 L.Ed.2d 149 (1978), Harrington v. Shariff, 305 F.2d 333, 338 (2d Cir. 1962). Where the actor did not intend to make an assertion, his conduct does not qualify as a statement under Rule 801(a) and therefore is not barred by the hearsay rule. See *supra* § 801.2.

[82] See Rule 801(d)(2)(A) n.5 (Chapter 801) of this Treatise.

[83] See, *generally*, McCORMICK, § 262, at 774 (quoting MORGAN, BASIC PROBLEMS OF EVIDENCE 266 (1962)):

> The admissibility of an admission made by the party himself rests not upon any notion that the circumstances in which it was made furnish the trier means of evaluating it fairly, but upon the adversary theory of litigation. A party can hardly object that he had no opportunity to cross-examine himself or that he is unworthy of credence save when speaking under sanction of an oath.

Id. at 628-29. See also Lev, *The Law of Vicarious Admissions - An Estoppel*, 26 U. CIN. L. REV. 17, 29-30 (1957).

§ 801.17 Adoptive Admissions.

Rule 801(d)(2)(B) provides for adoptive admissions of a party. Pursuant to this subdivision, an out-of-court statement by a person who is not a party is attributable to a party through express or implied adoption.[84] For the exception to apply, the statement must be offered against the adopting party, and it must be shown that a declarant made an out-of-court statement of which the party was apprised or had knowledge.[85] The party must have comprehended the statement[86] and either expressly acknowledged the truth of the statement or remained silent where a reasonable person would have denied the statement.[87] Whether a reasonable person would deny a statement will vary greatly with the circumstances under which the statement is made.[88] Nevertheless, the federal courts have been reluctant to

[84] United States v. Handy, 668 F.2d 407, 408 (8th Cir. 1982) (coconspirators were discussing an attempt at killing victim, which ended up resulting in their retreat when a dog attacked; appellant interjected, "Yes, we did;" held to be an adoptive admission); United States v. Murray, 618 F.2d 892, 900 (2d Cir. 1980) (no violation of confrontation in admitting tape of conversation between defendant and unavailable informant; jury was instructed not to consider statements for their truth except to the extent that appellant adopted them); United States v. Giese, 569 F.2d 527, 544 (9th Cir. 1978), cert. denied, 439 U.S. 876, 99 S.Ct. 214, 58 L.Ed.2d 190 (1978), cert. denied, 439 U.S. 876, 99 S.Ct. 214, 58 L.Ed.2d 190 (1978) ("[n]either due process, fundamental fairness, nor any more explicit right contained in the constitution is violated by the admission of the silence of a person, not in custody or under indictment, in the face of accusations of criminal behavior"); United States v. DiGiovanni, 544 F.2d 642, 645 (2d Cir. 1976) (direct admissions and adoptive admissions were satisfied by the testimony of cellmate of two defendants in which he related a three-way conversation of defendants describing the bank robbery).

[85] Cedeck v. Hamiltonian Savings & Loan Association, 551 F.2d 1136, 1139 (8th Cir. 1977).

[86] United States v. Sears, 663 F.2d 896, 904 (9th Cir. 1981), cert. denied, 445 U.S. 1027, 102 S.Ct. 1731, 72 L.Ed.2d 148 (1982) ("[T]he District Court should not submit the evidence of an admission by silence to the jury unless it first finds that

sufficient foundational facts have been introduced for the jury reasonably to conclude that the defendant did actually hear, understand, and accede to the statement"). See also McCormick, § 269, at 797-99.

[87] Southern Stone Co., Inc. v. Singer, 665 F.2d 698, 702-03 (5th Cir. 1982) (letter written by plaintiff's counsel to individual defendant which purported to relate several statements made by recipient to writer concerning activities of the defendants should not have been admitted, since the circumstances surrounding the letter do not support a reasonable expectation of a response); United States v. Shulman, 624 F.2d 384, 390 (2d Cir. 1980) (in the case of silence courts will consider the incriminatory content of the statement in order to determine whether the defendant actually has adopted the statement by his silence); United States v. Agee, 597 F.2d 350, 369 (3d Cir. 1979) (en banc), cert. denied, 442 U.S. 944, 99 S.Ct. 2889, 61 L.Ed.2d 315 (1979) (defendant did not remain silent, but made statements to the police which he knew to be false and which he hoped would prevent them from discovering an ongoing crime).

[88] See, generally, McCormick, § 161, at 430 for a comparative discussion of statements made during judicial proceeding, statements made during custodial interrogation, and statements made in contexts totally devoid of state influence or authority.

[89] See Note, Silence as Incrimination in Federal Courts, 40 Minn. L. Rev. 598 (1956). See also Note, Tacit Criminal Admission, 112 U. Pa. L. Rev. 210 (1963).

utilize their discretion to endorse the liberal use of a party's silence as an adoptive admission.[89] As McCormick writes: "[T]he courts have evolved a variety of safeguarding requirements against misuse [of a party's silence as an adoptive admission] of which the following are illustrative. (1) The statement must have been heard by the party claimed to have acquiesced. (2) It must have been understood by him. (3) The subject matter must have been within his knowledge."[90] Absent these determinations, a statement of a third party will not be admitted as an adoptive admission by a party. Of course, there are situations in which a person has a constitutional right to remain silent. Under these circumstances, silence is inadmissible for constitutional reasons, and the question of an adoptive admission is not reached.[91] In any situation in which an adoptive admission is advanced, the burden is on the proponent of such evidence to demonstrate that the adoption was intended.[92]

The admission by acquiescence or adoption is a restricted doctrine applicable only where the statement made by another is reasonably attributable to the party against whom the statement is offered. Foundational requirements should be strictly applied to assure the existence of conditions which establish that the statement of another person is unequivocally attributable to a party. In some jurisdictions this very limited principle has been misapplied and enlarged to create a specious doctrine which provides for the indiscriminate admission of any statement which is merely made in the presence of a party. Such application of the doctrine of admission by acquiescence is totally misplaced, and any misconception concerning adoptive admissions under pre-Rule practice is clarified and rectified by the express provisions of Rule 801(d)(2)(B).[93]

§ 801.18   Vicarious Admissions.

Vicarious admissions are recognized under Rule 801(d)(2)(C) and Rule 801(d)(2)(D). Under Rule 801(d)(2)(C), a statement which is authorized by a party may be imputed to that party and considered to be an admission for the purpose of the hearsay system.[94] Foundational evidence must estab-

---

[90] McCORMICK, § 270, at 800-01.

[91] See, e.g., Doyle v. Ohio, 426 U.S. 610, 96 S.Ct. 2240, 49 L.Ed.2d 91 (1976) (the Supreme Court held unconstitutional the use of a criminal defendant's silence after receiving Miranda warnings for impeachment purposes). See also United States v. Hale, 422 U.S. 171, 95 S.Ct. 2133, 45 L.Ed.2d 99 (1975). Cf., Moore v. Cowan, 560 F.2d 1298, 1301 (6th Cir. 1977), cert.

denied, 435 U.S. 929, 98 S.Ct. 1500, 55 L.Ed.2d 525, 436 U.S. 960, 98 S.Ct. 3079, 57 L.Ed.2d 1127 (1978).

[92] See Rules 104(a) and (b).

[93] See 4 WEINSTEIN, ¶ 801(d)(2)(B)[01], at 801-205.

[94] See, e.g., Astra Pharmaceutical Products, Inc. v. Occupational Safety and Health Review Commission, 681 F.2d 69, 73 n.8 (1st Cir. 1972); B-W Acceptance

lish that the declarant who made the out-of-court statement had express or implied "speaking authority" to make the declarations on behalf of the party opponent.[95] The substantive law of agency governs whether or not the declarant had speaking authority.[96]

Rule 801(d)(2)(D) authorizes the admission of a statement by a party's agent or servant concerning a matter within the scope of the agency or employment where the statement is offered against the party-principal or the party-employer. The proponent of the vicarious admission must establish a foundation which demonstrates that the declarant at the time of the making of the statement was an employee or an agent of the party against whom the statement is offered. Statements made after the employment or agency has concluded do not qualify as vicarious admissions. Also, under Rule 801(d)(2)(D) the statement of the agent or employee need only "concern" a matter within the scope of the agency or employment. Unlike pre-Rule law, no express or implied speaking authority need be established on behalf of the agent or employee as is required under Rule 801(d)(2)(C).[97]

Rule 801(d)(2)(D) is the product of a conceptual refinement of older case law which treated the admissibility of an agent's statement under the principle of *res gestae*.[98] While the resulting admissibility may be essentially the same under pre-Rule and post-Rule practice, the conceptual underpinnings of the *res gestae* doctrine are totally different from those which support Rule 801(d)(2)(D). Where an agent's statement has been admitted on a *res gestae* theory, the agent's statement must be made at the time of some act then being performed in the scope of the agent's duty.[99] Moreover, the act must be the central, operative fact of the case. Rule 801(d)(2)(D) provides

Corp. v. Porter, 568 F.2d 1179, 1182 (5th Cir. 1978); Securities and Exchange Commission v. American Realty Trust, 429 F.Supp. 1148, 1178 (E.D. Va. 1977).

[95] *See* 4 WEINSTEIN, ¶ 801(d)(2)(C)[01], at 801-210.

[96] *See* Baughman v. Cooper-Jarret, Inc., 530 F.2d 529, 532 (3d Cir. 1976), *cert. denied sub nom;* Wilson Freight Forwarding Co. v. Baughman, 429 U.S. 825, 97 S.Ct. 78, 50 L.Ed.2d 87, and *on remand* 79 FRD 520 (W.D. Pa.), *rev'd on other grounds,* 583 F.2d 1208 (1976) (employee had express or implied authority to speak about why employer was rejecting plaintiff's job application). *See also* United States v. Iaconetti, 406 F.Supp. 554, 557 (E.D.N.Y.), *aff'd,* 540 F.2d 574 (2d Cir. 1976), *cert. denied,* 429 U.S. 1041, 97 S.Ct. 739, 51 L.Ed.2d 589 (1977).

[97] Nekolny v. Painter, 653 F.2d 1164, 1171-72 (7th Cir. 1981), *cert. denied,* 455

U.S. 1021, 102 S.Ct. 1719, 72 L.Ed.2d 139 (1982); Town of East Troy v. Soo Line R. Co., 653 F.2d 1123, 1133 (7th Cir. 1980), *cert. denied,* 450 U.S. 922, 101 S.Ct. 1373, 67 L.Ed.2d 351 (1981); United States v. Summers, 598 F.2d 450, 459-60 (5th Cir. 1979).

[98] Fairlie v. Hastings, 10 Ves. Jr. 123, 32 Eng. Rep. 792 (Ch., 1804); Vicksburg & Meridian Railroad v. O'Brien, 119 U.S. 99, 7 S.Ct. 118, 30 L.Ed. 299 (1886).

[99] *See, generally,* McCORMICK, § 267, at 787 ("The early texts and cases . . . formulated the inadequate theory that the agent's statements could be received against the principal only when made at the time, and in relation to, some act then being performed in the scope of the agent's duty.") Under the Rules of Evidence *res gestae* has been replaced by specific hearsay exceptions. *See* discussion of Rules 803(1), (2), (3) and (4) in this Treatise, *infra.*

for the admissibility of an agent's statement regardless of whether the agent makes the statement in conjunction with an act he is obligated to perform on behalf of the principal. The statement need only concern a matter within the scope of the agency or employment, and as long as the statement is made while the agency or employment continues, the agent's statement is admissible against the principal.

Unresolved by Rule 801(d)(2)(C) and Rule 801(d)(2)(D) is the issue of whether the agent's or employee's own out-of-court statement may be utilized to establish the foundational fact of the agency or employment. On one hand, Rule 104(a) would seem to indicate that an agent's out-of-court statement, though hearsay, may be used to establish the foundation for the application of Rules 801(d)(2)(C) and (D).[1] On the other hand, many courts and scholars find that independent, admissible proof of the existence of the agency or the employment must be offered as a foundation. Such requirements are considered to be matters of the substantive law of agency, rather than a matter of evidence.[2] Federal courts ultimately will be required to resolve this issue when interpreting Rules 801(d)(2)(C) and (D).

Rules 801(d)(2)(C) and (D) should be interpreted as treating as admissions statements made by the agent to his principal as well as statements made to third persons.[3]

§ 801.19 Coconspirator's Statements—In General.

Rule 801(d)(2)(E) provides that the statement of a coconspirator of a party is admissible as substantive evidence if the coconspirator's statement

[1] *See* Rule 104(a) discussed *supra*. Rule 104(a) provides that the trial judge is not bound by the Rules of Evidence in evaluating foundational facts.

[2] *See* 4 WEINSTEIN, ¶ 801(d)(2)(C)[01], at 801-211; 4 LOUISELL & MUELLER, § 425, at 299. *See also* United States v. Portsmouth Paving Corp., 694 F.2d 312, 321 (4th Cir. 1982); City of New York v. Pullman, Inc., 662 F.2d 910, 915 (2d Cir. 1981), *cert. denied*, 454 U.S. 1164, 102 S.Ct. 1038, 71 L.Ed.2d 320 (1982) (federal government's funding for subway cars through the Urban Mass Transportation Act was not sufficient to create an agency relationship); Lubbock Feed Lots, Inc. v. Iowa Beef Processors, Inc., 630 F.2d 250, 262 (5th Cir. 1980), *reh. denied*, 634 F.2d 1355 (1980); Oberlin v. Marlin American Corp., 596 F.2d 1322, 1328 (7th Cir. 1979); Federal Deposit Ins.

Co. v. Glickman, 450 F.2d 416, 418 (9th Cir. 1971).

[3] *See, e.g.*, Reid Brothers Logging Co. v. Ketchian Pulp Co., 699 F.2d 1292, 1306-07 (9th Cir. 1983) (anti-trust action; report prepared by employee of company which was shareholder of defendant's parent company, and at the request of defendant's chairman of the board, and presented at a meeting attended by defendant's executives and circulated to offices and mangers was properly admitted); B-W Acceptance Corp. v. Porter, 568 F.2d 1179, 1182 (5th Cir. 1978) (corporate plaintiff had authorized its branch manager to testify at first trial; when this testimony was introduced by defendant at second trial it constituted an admission); Kingsley v. Baker/Beech-Nut Corp., 546 F.2d 1136, 1139 (5th Cir. 1977) (statements by agent to his principal covered by Rule 801(d)(2)(C)).

is offered against that party and the statement was made during the course of and in furtherance of the conspiracy. In *Bourjaily v. United States*[4] the Supreme Court held that a trial court may consider the offered hearsay statement itself in making the preliminary factual determinations of whether the conspiracy existed and whether the statement was made in the furtherance of the conspiracy. In reaching this conclusion, the Court discarded the so-called "boot-strapping rule" which previously prevented the use of the statement itself to support its own admission.[5] The Court also confirmed that the offering party must establish foundational facts pertinent to Rule 801(d)(2)(E) by a preponderance of the evidence. Finally, the Court held that the adoption of the Federal Rules did not alter the status of the coconspirator exception as a "firmly rooted hearsay exception." Consequently, the Sixth Amendment's confrontation clause does not require an independent inquiry as to the reliability of the hearsay statement.

§ 801.20   Coconspirator's Statements—Foundation—Degree of Proof.

While the Rule is silent as to the standard of proof necessary to satisfy this foundational requirement, the Supreme Court has recently held in this context that the existence of the conspiracy is sufficiently established when, as a foundation for use of the exception, the proponent of the statement has made a preponderant case of conspiracy.[6] Nevertheless, this relatively low threshold of proof has been criticized by commentators[7] as lacking sufficient protection for criminal defendants.[8]

---

[4] ___ U.S. ___, 55 L.W. 4962 (June 23, 1987).

[5] Glasser v. United States, 315 U.S. 60 (1942) announced the now obsolete bootstrapping doctrine which was later revisited in United States v. Nixon, 418 U.S. 683 (1974). The *Bourjaily* Court held that these cases were superceded by the adoption of the Federal Rules of Evidence, particularly Rule 104(a) which provides that the trial judge determines preliminary issues of admissibility and that the judge in making such determination is not bound by the rules of evidence, except those relating to privilege. *See* § 104.1 of this Treatise.

[6] Bourjaily v. United States, ___ U.S. ___, 55 L.W. 4962 (June 23, 1987); *see also* United States v. Clark, 613 F.2d 391, 402-04 (2d Cir. 1979), *cert. denied*, 449 U.S. 820, 101 S.Ct. 78, 66 L.Ed.2d 22 (1980) (acquittal on conspiracy count does not destroy admissibility of the declarations

of the coconspirators on the substantive charge, since different standards govern the two determinations); United States v. Cravero, 545 F.2d 406, 419 (5th Cir. 1976), *cert. denied*, 430 U.S. 983, 97 S.Ct. 1679, 52 L.Ed.2d 377 (1977) ("[e]arlier acquittal signifies that the government failed to prove the declarant a participant in the conspiracy beyond a reasonable doubt; this circumstance in no way forecloses the government, in a subsequent case, from establishing by slight or even preponderant evidence the declarant's participation"); United States v. Blackshire, 538 F.2d 569, 571 (4th Cir. 1976), *cert. denied*, 429 U.S. 840, 97 S.Ct. 113, 50 L.Ed.2d 108 (1976) (subsequent acquittal of declarant does not render evidence admitted under coconspirator's exception admissible).

[7] 4 WEINSTEIN, ¶ 801(d)(2)(E)[01], at 801-258.

[8] *But see* n.6 *supra*.

Application of Rule 801(d)(2)(E) requires consideration of whether concealment efforts exhibit the continuance of a conspiracy such that statements made during the concealment are within the scope of the exception. It can be argued that one of the self-evident goals of any conspiracy is to avoid detection, and that consequently, any statement made by a coconspirator in the concealment context is admissible against a party who is a member of the conspiracy. In *Krulewitch v. United States*,[9] however, the Supreme Court rejected this argument and restricted the federal coconspirator hearsay exception to the duration of the conspiracy's "main aim." The Court reasoned that otherwise the conspiracy would never end. Nevertheless, McCormick has concluded that extending the duration of the conspiracy beyond commission of the principal crime to include "concomitant and closely connected disposition of its fruits or concealment of its traces" is justified in some situations.[10] This latter interpretation of the duration of the conspiracy has been rejected by the federal courts.[11] Even if the conspirator's statement is not admissible under the restrictive approach adopted by Rule 801(d)(2)(E), other exceptions in Article VIII may be used as vehicles for admission of the statement.[12]

§ 801.21 Coconspirator's Statements—When Statement is Made.

Application of Rule 801(d)(2)(E) requires consideration of the status of coconspirators' statements made before the party has joined the conspiracy or after he has severed his connection with the conspiracy. It has long been held that statements of coconspirators made before a party joins a conspiracy are admissible against her.[13] Nevertheless, it has also been traditionally recognized that once the party terminates her relationship with the conspiracy, or the conspiracy ends, subsequent statements of coconspirators are not admissible against the party.[14] Judge Weinstein sees no logic in the distinction and advocates that only statements made by coconspirators while the party is a member of the conspiracy should be admissible against the party.[15]

[9] 336 U.S. 440, 443-44, 69 S.Ct. 716, 718, 93 L.Ed. 790, 794 (1949).

[10] MCCORMICK, § 267, at 793.

[11] Krulewitch v. United States, 336 U.S. 440, 443, 69 S.Ct. 716, 718, 93 L.Ed. 790, 794 (1949); Dutton v. Evans, 400 U.S. 74, 81, 91 S.Ct. 210, 215, 27 L.Ed.2d 213, 222 (1970). *But cf.* Mares v. United States, 383 F.2d 805, 810 (10th Cir. 1967), *cert. denied,* 394 U.S. 963, 89 S.Ct. 1314, 22 L.Ed.2d 564 (1969).

[12] *See* Rules 801(d)(2)(B), 801(c), 801(d)(1)(A) and 804(b)(3). *See also* 4 WEINSTEIN, ¶ 801(d)(2)(E)[01], at 801-243.

[13] United States v. Trombrello, 668 F.2d 485, 490-91 (11th Cir. 1982); United States v. Heater, 689 F.2d 783, 786 (8th Cir. 1982); United States v. Torres, 685 F.2d 921, 926 (5th Cir. 1982).

[14] United States v. Gibbs, 703 F.2d 683, 689 (3d Cir. 1983); United States v. Smith, 578 F.2d 1227, 1233 (8th Cir. 1978).

[15] 4 WEINSTEIN, ¶ 801(d)(2)(E)[01], at 801-248-249.

§ 801.22   Coconspirator's Statements—In Furtherance Requirement.

In addition to showing the existence of a conspiracy and the party's membership in that conspiracy, the proponent of a coconspirator's statement must also show that the statement was made in furtherance of the objectives of the conspiracy in order to satisfy Rule 801(d)(2)(E). This requirement reflects prior case law.[16] While consideration of whether a statement is made in furtherance of a conspiracy depends on the context in which it is made,[17] the requirement is clearly not met by statements of a coconspirator which are merely narrative of past events[18] or which are disclosed to those known to be government agents.[19] A statement not made in furtherance of a conspiracy may be admissible as non-hearsay or under an exception to the hearsay exclusionary rule.[20]

The "in furtherance" requirement is designed "to strike a balance between the great need for conspirators' statements in combatting undesirable criminal activity which is inherently secretive and difficult of proof, and the need to protect the accused against idle chatter of criminal partners as well as inadvertently misreported and deliberately fabricated evidence,"[21] and the requirement should be applied accordingly.

---

[16] *See* Dutton v. Evans, 400 U.S. 74, 81, 91 S.Ct. 210, 215, 27 L.Ed.2d 213, 222 (1970); Wong v. United States, 371 U.S. 471, 490, 83 S.Ct. 407, 421, 9 L.Ed.2d 441, 453 (1963); Krulewitch v. United States, 336 U.S. 440, 443, 69 S.Ct. 716, 718, 93 L.Ed. 790, 794 (1949). *See also* United States v. Harris, 546 F.2d 234, 237 (8th Cir. 1976).

[17] *See* 4 Weinstein, ¶ 801(d)(2)(E)[01], at 801-241. *See also* United States v. Gibbs, 703 F.2d 683, 690 (3d Cir. 1983). *See, e.g.,* United States v. Handy, 668 F.2d 407, 408 (8th Cir. 1982) (court may consider not only the nature of the statements, but take into account the time and circumstances under which they were made in determining whether they were intended to further the scheme's ultimate objective); United States v. Regilio, 669 F.2d 1169, 1176 (7th Cir. 1981), *cert. denied,* 457 U.S. 1133, 102 S.Ct. 2959, 73 L.Ed.2d 1350 (1982) (statements made in furtherance of inducing buyer of cocaine not to leave).

[18] United States v. Means, 695 F.2d 811, 817-18 (5th Cir. 1983); United States v. Sandoval-Villalvazo, 620 F.2d 744, 747 (9th Cir. 1980); United States v. Goodman, 605 F.2d 870, 877-78 (5th Cir. 1979).

[19] Battle v. Lubrizol Corp., 673 F.2d 984, 990 (8th Cir. 1982) (private antitrust action; in furtherance requirement not satisfied); United States v. Miller, 664 F.2d 94, 98 (5th Cir. 1981), *cert. denied,* 103 S.Ct. 121, 74 L.Ed.2d 106 (1982) ("[p]uffing, boasts, and other conversations are admissible when used by the declarant to obtain the confidence of one involved in the conspiracy or to allay suspicions"); United States v. Castillo, 615 F.2d 878, 880 (9th Cir. 1980) (casual admission by conspirator to another of objective did not further the conspiracy).

[20] *See* United States v. Liberman, 637 F.2d 95, 102-03 (2d Cir. 1980) (declarant, the foreman of a moving company, and defendant, the manager, were charged with conspiring to distribute marijuana by sending a truck filled with marijuana from the company's Florida offices to New York, where it was intercepted); United States v. Hacket, 638 F.2d 1179, 1186 (9th Cir. 1980), *cert. denied,* 450 U.S. 1001, 101 S.Ct. 1709, 68 L.Ed.2d 203 (1981) (false statement of coconspirator admissible as non-hearsay and could be admitted against other conspirators).

[21] 4 Weinstein, ¶ 801(d)(2)(E)[01], at 801-235.

§ 801.23 Coconspirator's Statements—Other Considerations—Unavailability.

It should be noted that even if the statements of a coconspirator are not admissible against a party under Rule 801(d)(2)(E) because one of the foundational requirements for admissibility is lacking, such statements may be admissible under another Rule. Accordingly, statements of coconspirators not offered for their truth may be admissible as non-hearsay under Rule 801(c).[22] Failure to deny a statement made outside the conspiracy but in the party's presence may qualify for admission pursuant to Rule 801(d)(2)(B).[23] Or a post-conspiracy declaration against interest may meet the test of Rule 804(b)(3).[24]

It should also be noted that as a general rule, the coconspirator exception has been traditionally applicable in both criminal and civil cases.[25] Further, courts have generally held that there is no need to show that the party has been indicted for conspiracy for the exception to apply.[26] These general rules would appear to be preserved on the face of the federal Rule, with Rule 801(d)(2)(B) using the term "party" as opposed to "accused." Throughout the Rules, the latter term is reserved only for the criminal defendant.

Finally, it should be noted the Supreme Court has recently settled the confusion as to whether the confrontation clause requires a showing the coconspirator is unavailable before his out of court statements may be admitted. In *U.S. v. Inadi*,[27] the Supreme Court held the Confrontation Clause does not require a showing of unavailability as a condition to admission of the out of court statements of a non-testifying coconspirator. Provided those statements otherwise satisfy the requirements of Rule 801(d)(2)(E), unavailability of the declarant need not be demonstrated.

§ 801.24 Unique Doctrines Applicable to Admissions.

Admissions are unique forms of hearsay evidence. Because the underlying theory of an admission is essentially an estoppel doctrine, peculiar rules apply to parties' out-of-court statements. For example, the first-hand knowledge requirement of Rule 602 is relaxed in regard to statements of a

---

[22] *See* § 801.4, *supra.*

[23] *See* § 801.17, *supra.*

[24] *See* § 804.1 *et seq., infra.*

[25] *See* 4 Weinstein, ¶ 801(d)(2)(E)[01], at 801-229 ("[Rule 801(d)(2)(E)] applies in both civil and criminal cases, though it is most frequently involved in criminal litigation.")

[26] *Id.;* United States v. Monaco, 702 F.2d 860, 880 n.35 (11th Cir. 1983); United States v. Kiefer, 694 F.2d 1109, 1112 (8th Cir. 1982); United States v. Scavo, 593 F.2d 837, 845 and n.4 (8th Cir. 1979).

[27] 475 U.S. ___, 106 S.Ct. 1121, 89 L.Ed.2d 390 (1986). *See also* Bourjaily v. United States, ___ U.S. ___, 55 L.W. 4962 (June 23, 1987).

party.[28] Also, as a general rule, an admission of a party will not be excluded because it expresses an opinion or a conclusion.[29] While lay opinions are generally admissible where Rule 701 is satisfied,[30] an even lower threshold will apply to opinions embraced by an admission of a party.

Because an admission is substantive evidence, its admissibility does not depend upon whether the party has testified as a witness. In this respect the exceptions contained in Rule 801(d)(2) are distinguishable from those set forth in 801(d)(1). Where a party has testified, a pre-trial admission may, however, be used for the purposes of impeachment under the device of prior inconsistent statement.[31] Where a prior statement of a party is used for purposes of impeachment, it serves a dual function. On one hand the evidence affects the credibility of the party-witness, and on the other hand, the pre-trial statement is admissible as substantive evidence pursuant to Rule 801(d)(2).

§ 801.25   Admissions and Statements Against Interest Distinguished.

Admissions of a party are often confused with statements against interest codified in Rule 804(b)(3). The statement against interest exception is based upon a different theory than that supporting the admission of a party. The statement against interest exception depends upon the statement being against interest at the time the declarant utters the out-of-court statement. The statement is inherently more reliable than hearsay generally because, presumably, people do not carelessly make statements which are against their interest. Also, the statement against interest exception applies only when the out-of-court declarant is unavailable as the concept is defined in Rule 804(a). An admission of a party, by comparison, only applies to an out-of-court statement of a *party*, and it is immaterial whether the statement was against interest when the party made the statement. Unavailability is not a consideration in applying the party admission exceptions.

[28] *See* Mahlandt v. Wild Canid Survival & Research Center, Inc., 588 F.2d 626, 631 (8th Cir. 1978); Russell v. United Parcel Service, Inc., 666 F.2d 1188, 1190-91 (8th Cir. 1981). *See also* McCORMICK, § 263, at 778-79.

[29] Russell v. United Parcel Service, Inc., 666 F.2d 1188, 1190 (8th Cir. 1981); Cox v. Esso Shipping Co., 247 F.2d 629, 632-33 (5th Cir. 1957); Pekelis v. Transcontinental & Western Air, Inc., 187 F.2d 122, 128-29 (2d Cir. 1951). *See also* McCORMICK, § 264, at 779.

[30] *See* § 701.1 *et seq.* of this Treatise.

[31] *See* § 613.1 *et seq.* of this Treatise.

Chapter 802

RULE 802. HEARSAY RULE

Rule 802 reads as follows:

> Hearsay is not admissible except as provided by these rules or by other rules prescribed by the Supreme Court pursuant to statutory authority or by Act of Congress.

§ 802.1 Hearsay Rule—Function.

Rule 802 is the general rule of exclusion for statements falling within the definition of hearsay codified in Rule 801(c). Rule 802 provides that evidence which is hearsay is presumptively inadmissible unless the proponent of the evidence can properly invoke an exception to the basic definition or an exception to the exclusionary rule contained in either Rule 803 or 804. The Rule also permits legislative regulation of hearsay by specific reference to statutes which may also provide for the admissibility of hearsay to the extent not otherwise provided or prescribed by the Rules of Evidence.[1]

The Advisory Committee Note refers to several examples of rules or statutes which operate to admit hearsay evidence.[2] Among these include several references to the Federal Rules of Civil Procedure: Rule 4(g): proof of service by affidavit; Rule 43(e): concerning the admissibility of affidavits when a motion is based on facts that do no appear on the record; Rule 56: the use of affidavits in summary judgment proceeding; Rule 65(b): use of affidavits to support a petition for a temporary rehearing order.

References to the Federal Rules of Criminal Procedure include: Rule 4(a): which authorizes affidavits to be used to establish probable cause to issue a search warrant and Rule 12(b)(4): which allows affidavits to be used to determine issues of fact in connection with motions to the court.

Several acts of Congress also have the effect of authorizing the use of affidavits or depositions. For example, in a N.L.R.B. proceeding proof of

---

[1] See, generally, 4 WEINSTEIN, ¶ 802[01]-[04]; 4 LOUISELL & MUELLER, §§ 432-33. See also, Consideration, in Determining Facts, of Inadmissible Hearsay Evidence Introduced Without Objection, 79 A.L.R.2d 890; Written Recitals or Statements as Within Rule Excluding Hearsay, 10 A.L.R.2d 1035.

[2] See the Advisory Committee's Note to Rule 802.

service may be established through the use of affidavits.[3] In the area of foreign trade, affidavits may be used to establish the foreign value of exports.[4] Depositions are used in extradition proceedings[5] or in proceedings before the Customs Court when the value of merchandise is to be established.[6]

Finally, there are also Congressional statutes that do not proport to admit hearsay evidence, but that by their operation have this effect. These include statements that provide what documents are used to establish title to a res,[7] or statutes that make findings of government articles prima facie evidence of the facts found.[8]

[3] 29 U.S.C. § 161(4).

[4] 19 U.S.C. § 1402(b).

[5] 18 U.S.C. § 3190.

[6] 28 U.S.C. § 2635. *See also* 4 Weinstein, ¶ 802[02], at 802-4 for a more exhaustive list of statutes that authorize the admissibility of hearsay evidence.

[7] *See, e.g.*, 26 U.S.C. § 6340(b) (record of tax sale is conclusive on facts asserted).

[8] *See, e.g.*, 18 U.S.C. § 4245 (director of prison's certification that the prisoner was mentally incompetent at the time of trial). 7 U.S.C. § 499(g)(b) (the Secretary of Agriculture's order under the Perishable Agricultural Commodities Act is evidence of the facts found).

Chapter 803

RULE 803. HEARSAY EXCEPTIONS; AVAILABILITY OF DECLARANT IMMATERIAL

Rule 803(1)　Present Sense Impression

Rule 803(1) reads as follows:

> The following are not excluded by the hearsay rule, even though the declarant is available as a witness: **(1) Present sense impression.** A statement describing or explaining an event or condition made while the declarant was perceiving the event or condition, or immediately thereafter.

§ 803.1　Present Sense Impression—In General.

Rule 803(1), which provides a hearsay exception for statements of present sense impressions, is relatively new to the law of evidence.[1] Prior to the enactment of Rule 803(1), few federal cases recognized an exception for "present sense impressions." The federal courts, largely influenced by Wigmore, emphasized the necessity of the excitement of some stimulus as ensuring the trustworthiness of a spontaneous declaration, *i.e.*, the basis for the excited utterance exception of Rule 803(2).[2] Consequently, most courts required the statement to be uttered under the stress of some nervous shock,[3] or, in the alternative, resorted to the historically ambiguous concept of *res gestae* as a basis for admission.[4] Nevertheless, while the present

---

[1] *See, generally,* McCormick, § 298; 4 Weinstein, ¶¶ 803[01]-[03]; 4 Louisell & Mueller, §§ 437-38. *See also,* Falknor, *The Hearsay Rule and Its Exceptions,* 2 U.C.L.A. L. Rev. 43, 60-62 (1954); Foster, *Present Sense Impressions: An Analysis and a Proposal,* 10 Loyola U. L.J. 299 (1979); Hutchins & Slesinger, *Some Observations on the Law of Evidence: Spontaneous Exclamations,* 46 Colum. L. Rev. 432 (1946); Morgan, *Res Gestae,* 12 Wash. L. Rev. 91 (1937); Morgan, *A Suggested Classification of Utterances Admissible as Res Gestae,* 31 Yale L.J. 229 (1922); Quick, *Hearsay, Excitement, Necessity, and the Uniform Rules: A Reappraisal of Rule 63(4),* 6 Wayne L. Rev. 204 (1960); Slough, *Res Gestae,* 2 U. Kan. L. Rev. 246 (1954);

Slough, *Spontaneous Statements and State of Mind,* 46 Iowa L. Rev. 224 (1961); Thayer, *Bedingfield's Case - Declarations as a Part of the Res Gestae,* 15 Am. L. Rev. 71 (1881); Waltz, *The Present Sense Impression Exception to the Rule Against Hearsay: Origins and Attitudes,* 66 Iowa L. Rev. 869 (1981).

[2] *See, generally,* McCormick, § 298.

[3] *See, e.g.,* Griffin v. Ensign, 234 F.2d 307, 315 (3d Cir. 1956); Roth v. Swanson, 145 F.2d 262, 269 (8th Cir. 1944); Kornicke v. Calmar S.S. Corp., 460 F.2d 1134, 1138 (3d Cir. 1972). *See, generally,* 6 Wigmore, § 1747, at 135.

[4] *See* definition and discussion at n.6 of §803.1 of this Treatise.

sense impression was not recognized as an exception in pre-Rule case law, the underlying principle was sometimes endorsed.[5]

Rule 803(1) provides a vehicle for the admission of out-of-court statements concerning an event or condition where the statement describes or explains the event. The statement must be uttered contemporaneously with the event or condition or "immediately thereafter."[6] The exception to the hearsay rule embodied in Rule 803(1) is distinguishable from that contained in Rule 803(2) concerning excited utterances in that Rule 803(1) does not require the presence of a startling event as a stimulus for the utterance. Rule 803(1) merely requires a contemporaneous report of sense impressions. For example, where X and Y are standing at an intersection and X blurts out to Y, "Look at that blue truck, it's running the red light," Y may testify at trial as to X's statement under Rule 803(1). The statement is inadmissible under Rule 803(2), however, since presumably the event is not sufficiently startling.

§ 803.2   Policy Supporting Rule 803(1).

The hearsay exception for present sense impressions can be traced to the traditional common law concept of *res gestae*,[7] a term historically denoting

[5] *E.g.*, Emens v. Lehigh Valley R. Co., 223 F. 810, 823-26 (N.D.N.Y. 1915), *cert. denied*, 242 U.S. 627, 37 S.Ct. 14, 61 L.Ed. 535 (1916) (where witness testified that immediately prior to grade crossing accident his wife said, "Do you suppose the people in that automobile see the train?" and "Why don't the train whistle?," these statements were properly admitted; court noted that the remarks were spontaneous and voluntary). *See also* Picker X-Ray Corp. v. Frerker, 405 F.2d 916, 922 (8th Cir. 1969).

[6] *E.g.*, United States v. Kehoe, 562 F.2d 65, 70 (1st Cir. 1977) (reporter's notation that defendant had been sworn in prosecution for perjury arising out of testimony given by defendant before grand jury, the notation was properly admitted since it was made shortly after the event). *See also* Wolfson v. Mutual Life Ins. Co. of New York, 455 F.Supp. 82, 86-87 (M.D. Pa. 1978), *aff'd*, 588 F.2d 825 (3d Cir. 1978); Hilyer v. Howat Concrete Co., 578 F.2d 422, 425-26 (D.C. Cir. 1978); Nuttall v. Reading Co., 235 F.2d 546, 551-52 (3d Cir. 1956). *See, generally*, McCORMICK, § 273; WEINSTEIN, ¶ 803(1)[01]; 4 LOUISELL & MUELLER, § 438; Note, *Spontaneous Exclamations in the Absence of a Startling*

Event, 46 COLUM. L. REV. 430 (1946); Comment, *Hearsay Under the Proposed Federal Rules: A Discretionary Approach*, 15 WAYNE L. REV. 1077 (1969).

[7] Literally, Latin for "things done." At common law, the term was broadly defined and applied to include evidence of any matter incidental to the main fact and explicative of it, including words and acts so intertwined with it as to constitute part of the transaction or occurrence. In essence, while these matters are incident of the act and not the act itself, they were considered admissible for their illustrative or explanatory value. U.S. v. King, 34 F. 302, 314 (1888) (principle of *res gestae* admits "declarations of an individual made at the moment of a particular occurrence, when the circumstances are such that we may assume that his mind is controlled by the event. . . ." It must have been "made at a time when it was forced out as an utterance of truth, forced out against his will or without his will, and at a period of time so closely connected with the transaction that there has been no opportunity for subsequent reflection or determination as to what it might or might not be wise for him to say.").

words or statements which accompany the principal litigated fact. The phrase, literally and in practice, is so vague and imprecise that it has served as a convenient means of escaping the hearsay proscription. Moreover, it has often been indiscriminately applied to several evidentiary principles, although some are not related to the hearsay rule.[8] Under the Rules of Evidence, evidence traditionally admitted by resort to the *res gestae* doctrine is categorized into four distinct exceptions to the hearsay rule: (i) present sense impressions (Rule 803(1)); (ii) excited utterances (Rule 803(2)); (iii) statements describing mental or physical condition (Rule 803(3)); and (iv) statements for purposes of medical treatment or diagnosis (Rule 803(4)). In related fashion, statements constituting verbal acts or verbal parts of acts, traditionally honored as *res gestae*, have been excluded from the threshold definition of hearsay under Rule 801(c). Thus, while courts may still make reference to the *res gestae* concept as reason for admitting certain evidence, it is clear that the increased sophistication of the hearsay rule has largely rendered the term obsolete as an expression of an evidentiary doctrine.[9]

---

[8] *See, e.g.,* 6 WIGMORE, § 1767, at 180-82.

The phrase *res gestae* has long been not only entirely useless, but even positively harmful. It is useless, because every rule of evidence to which it has ever been applied exists as a part of some other well-established principle and can be explained in the terms of that principle. It is harmful, because by its ambiguity it invites the confusion of one rule with another and thus creates uncertainty as to the limitations of both. It ought therefore wholly to be repudiated as a vicious element in our legal phraseology. No rule of evidence can be created or applied by the mere muttering of a shibboleth. There are words enough to describe the rules of evidence. Even if there were no accepted name for one or another doctrine, any name would be preferable to an empty phrase so encouraging to looseness of thinking and uncertainty of decision.

See also, Thayer, *Bedingfield's Case—Declarations as Part of Res Gestae,* 15 AMER. L. REP. 1 (1881); Morgan, *A Suggestive Classification of Utterances Admissible as Res Gestae,* 31 YALE L.J. 229 (1923). While Commentators have for some time attacked the *res gestae* doctrine as not founded upon reliable principles of law or as an unwieldly "catch-all" phrase of convenience, courts have been reluctant to discard the doctrine in favor of more detailed examinations of evidence. *E.g.,* U.S. v. Leonard, 494 F.2d 955, 968 (D.C. Cir. 1974).

[9] McCormick explains the doctrine's obsolescence:

Commentators and, less frequently, courts, have criticized use of the phrase *res gestae.* Its vagueness and imprecision are, of course, apparent. Moreover, traditional limitations on the doctrine, such as the requirement that it be used only in regard to the principal litigated fact and the frequent insistence of concurrence (or at least a close relationship in time) between the words and the act or situation, have restricted its usefulness as a tool for avoiding unjustified application of the hearsay rule. Historically, however, the phrase served its purpose well. Its very vagueness made it easier for courts to broaden it and thus provide for the admissibility of certain declarations in new fields. But it seems clear that the law has now reached a stage at which this desirable policy of widening admissibility will be best served by other means. The ancient

The principle underlying the hearsay exception contained in Rule 803(1) is the assumption that statements of perception, describing the event and uttered in close temporal proximity to the event, bear a high degree of trustworthiness. Due to the statement's contemporaneous nature, there is little danger of a lapse in memory. Also, there is little time for calculated misstatement, and the usual circumstance of other persons being present at the time serves as a check on any misstatement.[10] Consequently, the testimonial defects in memory and sincerity, normally attendant to other forms of hearsay, are largely absent where spontaneity is present and where the declarant's statement is free from distortion often resulting from impending events. Further, where the declarant herself is available for cross-examination, her credibility and narration of the event will be subject to verification before the trier of fact.[11]

§ 803.3　　Requirement of Temporal Proximity.

Admissibility of a hearsay statement under Rule 803(1) is conditioned on the statement being uttered either while the event or condition is being perceived by the declarant or "immediately thereafter." This time requirement should be strictly applied, because it is the element of contemporaneity which serves as the basis for trustworthiness of this hearsay exception. Generally, the Rule will be employed to admit statements uttered during the course of the event or transaction or seconds after the event or transaction. The phrase "immediately thereafter" is intended to accommodate the pragmatic realization that an event may be so fleeting in time as to preclude simultaneous comment, and it consequently permits flexibility in admitting statements made moments after the event where a slight lapse in

phrase can well be jettisoned, with due acknowledgment that it has served well its era in the evolution of evidence law.

McCORMICK, § 288, at 687. *See also,* Wabisky v. D.C. Transit Systems, Inc., 309 F.2d 317, 318 (D.C. Cir. 1962) (per Berger, J.) (identifying these various categories of *res gestae*, although not mentioning those statements not defined as hearsay).

[10] WEINSTEIN, ¶ 803(1)[01]. The notable exception to those scholars supporting the recognition and usefulness of the present sense impression is Wigmore, who prefers to include such statements under the excited utterance exception. 6 WIGMORE, §§ 1745-56. Since Wigmore stresses that trust-

worthiness is predicated more upon the nervous excitement produced by the declarant's exposure to a startling event than upon the contemporaneity of the utterance with the event, Wigmore advocates the presence of a startling event as a condition precedent to admission. Compare 6 WIGMORE, § 1757, with Morgan, *Res Gestae,* 12 WASH. L. REV. 91 (1937), and Thayer, *Bedingfield's Case—Declarations as Part of Res Gestae,* 15 AMER. L. REP. 1 (1881). *See also* Hutchins & Slesinger, *Some Observations on the Law of Evidence: Spontaneous Exclamations,* 28 COLUM. L. REV. 432, 437-40 (1928).

[11] *See* McCORMICK, § 298, at 709-10; 4 LOUISELL & MUELLER, § 438, at 483-85.

time appears natural under the circumstances. The time elapsed between the statement and event must be sufficiently short to indicate a lack of reflection on the event perceived—a fact which would detract from the trustworthiness of the utterance.[12] Accordingly, the "immediately thereafter" language of Rule 803(1) should be strictly construed and narrowly applied such that operation of the Rule does not result in the admission of statements which do not satisfy the underlying rationale.[13]

§ 803.4   Requirement of "Perception" by Declarant.

Rule 803(1) further requires that the declarant actually perceive the transaction or event described in the hearsay statement.[14] While "perceiving" most assuredly means, in the greater number of instances, "seeing,"[15] it may also include any other type of sensory perception, including hearing.[16] The Rule does not require that the declarant actually participate in the

---

[12] See Advisory Committee's Note to Rule 803(1): "Exception (1) recognizes that in many, if not most, instances precise contemporaneity is not possible, and hence a slight lapse is allowable."

[13] See, generally, Quick, Hearsay, Excitement, Necessity and the Uniform Rules: A Reappraisal of Rule 63(4), 6 WAYNE L. REV. 204, 210 (1960) ("Even the argument that . . . spontaneity . . . is a reasonable guaranty of sincerity has been questioned because psychological studies indicate that the time interval required to assure lack of conscious or unconscious falsification is measured in stopwatch time intervals rather than in minutes."). See also United States v. Cain, 587 F.2d 678, 681-82 (5th Cir. 1979), cert. denied, 440 U.S. 975, 99 S.Ct. 1543, 59 L.Ed.2d 793 (1979); United States v. Narciso, 446 F. Supp. 252, 284-88 (E.D. Mich. 1977).

[14] Cf. United States v. Bell, 351 F.2d 868, 870 (6th Cir. 1965), cert. denied, 383 U.S. 947, 86 S.Ct. 1203, 16 L.Ed.2d 210 (1966) (hearsay statement admitted under Federal Rule 803(1), although uttered after significant time lapse to person lacking firsthand knowledge of the event). See also United States v. Blakely, 607 F.2d 779, 785-86 (7th Cir. 1979) ("[T]he underlying rationale of the present sense impression exception is that substantial contemporaneity

of event and statement minimizes unreliability due to defective recollection or conscious fabrication.").

[15] 4 LOUISELL & MUELLER, § 438, at 490. See Houston Oxygen Co. v. Davis, 139 Tex. 1, 3-4, 161 S.W.2d 274, 276-77 (1942) (as one car was being passed by another, comment of driver that "they must have been drunk; we could find them somewhere on the road wrecked if they kept up that rate of speed."). See also Anderson v. State, 454 S.W.2d 740, 741 (Tex. Crim. 1970) (at the very time the event was occurring the comment was made, "Seems like there is a car being stripped down the street there.").

[16] E.g., Nuttall v. Reading Co., 235 F.2d 546, 551-53 (3d Cir. 1956) (reversible error to exclude testimony by decedent's widow which were characterizations made at the time the event was perceived, and free from the possibility of lapse of memory on the part of the declarant; this contemporaneousness lessens the likelihood of conscious misrepresentation). See also MCA, Inc. v. Wilson, 425 F.Supp. 443, 450-51 (S.D.N.Y. 1976) (court admitted spontaneous reactions of cast and audience to the playing of an allegedly copied copyrighted song without authorization, as "sense impressions of weight . . . their spontaneity provides their reliability and cures any hearsay infirmities.").

event, but the more removed the declarant from the relevant event, the more questionable it is that he did perceive it.[17]

Although the Rule does not predicate admission of hearsay under this exception upon the declarant being available to testify, a greater suspicion of untrustworthiness arises where the declarant does not appear.[18] Absent some foundational evidence from the declarant or other witness showing that the declarant actually perceived the event or transaction, the trustworthiness attendant to such hearsay statements is not present, and application of Rule 803(1) is inappropriate.

§ 803.5   Subject Matter Requirement.

The express language of Rule 803(1) requires that the hearsay statement be one "describing or explaining" the condition or event perceived. Accordingly, a statement prompted by an event, but not descriptive or explanatory of it, is inadmissible under this exception. Where a statement is contemporaneous with an event and asserts the existence of the condition or the occurrence of the event perceived, it is "descriptive" within the language of Rule 803(1). If the statement tends to interpret, assess or evaluate the condition perceived, it is "explanatory" under the Rule.[19] While the "describing or explaining" elements should not be so narrowly applied as to exclude statements which moderately expand upon the declarant's perceptions, Rule 803(1) should not be used to admit statements which embrace a risk of a defect in memory. For example, if the declarant makes the out-of-court statement, "Look at that blue truck run the light; I saw that truck at the service station yesterday getting its brakes repaired," the latter statement should not be admitted under Rule 803(1). The statement as to an occurrence on the previous day unavoidably involves a possible defect in memory, and it is not a contemporaneous report of present sense impressions.

---

[17] WEINSTEIN, ¶ 803(1)[01], at 803-74. See, e.g., McClure v. Price, 300 F.2d 538, 545 (4th Cir. 1962). See Advisory Committee's Note to Rule 803(1) (suggesting that declarant's statement via CB radio was inadmissible since the event was not "perceived" by the witness). Cf., United States v. Portsmouth Paving Corp., 694 F.2d 312, 323 (4th Cir. 1982) (finding that witness had "perceived" a telephone call where he had heard words and saw the declarant hang up; court noted that the declarant was not an unidentified bystander so that his capacity to observe could be substantiated).

[18] See, generally, 4 WEINSTEIN, ¶ 803(1) [02].

[19] Compare MCA, Inc. v. Wilson, 425 F.Supp. 443, 451 (S.D.N.Y. 1976) (statement admitted as explanatory of event) with Elek v. Boyce, 308 F. Supp. 26, 28-29 (D.S.C.) (hearsay statement inadmissible since neither descriptive nor explanatory). See, generally, 4 WEINSTEIN, ¶ 803(1)[02].

Rule 803(2)   Excited Utterance

Rule 803(2) reads as follows:

> The following are not excluded by the hearsay rule, even though the declarant is available as a witness. . . **(2) Excited utterance.** A statement relating to a startling event or condition made while the declarant was under the stress of excitement caused by the event or condition.

§ 803.6   Excited Utterances—In General.

It has long been the law in the federal system that statements provoked by, and uttered contemporaneously with, startling events are admissible pursuant to an exception to the hearsay rule. Rule 803(2) merely codifies the traditional federal practice.[20]

Under the Rule, a declarant's hearsay statement in reaction to a startling external stimulus is admissible for the truth of the substance contained in the statement where the statement relates to the external event and is uttered under the stress of excitement occasioned by the event.[21] While the exceptions identified in Rule 803(1) and Rule 803(2) are frequently confused, their respective applications are distinct. Rule 803(2) requires the declaration to be in response to some startling occurrence, whereas Rule

[20] *E.g.,* Travelers' Ins. Co. v. Miller, 62 F.2d 910, 912 (7th Cir. 1933), Wicker v. Scott, 29 F.2d 807, 809 (6th Cir. 1928); Travelers' Protective Ass'n of America v. West, 102 F. 226, 228-29 (7th Cir. 1900); National Masonic Accident Ass'n v. Shyrock, 73 F. 774, 780-81 (8th Cir. 1896); Cross Lake Logging Co. v. Joyce, 83 F. 989, 990-91 (8th Cir. 1897). *See, generally,* 4 LOUISELL & MUELLER, § 439; 4 WEINSTEIN, ¶ 802(2)[01]; McCORMICK § 297; 6 WIGMORE, §§ 1745-64. *See also* Hutchins & Slesinger, *Some Observations on the Law of Evidence: Spontaneous Exclamations,* 28 COLUM. L. REV. 432 (1928); Quick, *Hearsay, Excitement, Necessity, and the Uniform Rules: A Reappraisal of Rule 63(4),* 6 WAYNE L. REV. 204, (1960); Slough, *Res Gestae,* 2 U. KAN. L. REV. 246 (1954); Slough, *Spontaneous Statements and State of Mind,* 46 IOWA L. REV. 224 (1961); Stewart, *Perception, Memory, and Hearsay: A Criticism of Present Law and the Proposed*

Federal Rules of Evidence, 1970 UTAH L. REV. 1, 25-36; Comment, *Hearsay Under the Proposed Federal Rules: A Discretionary Approach,* 15 WAYNE L. REV. 1077, 1114-15 (1969).

[21] *E.g.,* United States v. Bowdach, 414 F.Supp. 1346, 1348 (5th Cir. 1976), *aff'd,* 561 F.2d 1160, *reh'g denied,* 562 F.2d 163 (5th Cir. 1976) (statement excluded as not sufficiently relevant to fact sought to be proven); Zibelman v. Gibbs, 252 F.Supp. 360, 361-62 (E.D. Pa. 1966) (even though made "reasonably close" to time of accident the statement was excluded because a routine rear-end collision is not particularly violent); Kornicki v. Calmar S.S. Corp., 460 F.2d 1134, 1138 (3d Cir. 1972) (court excluded utterance on the ground that it lacked spontaneity but noted that the statement was also a "matter of opinion rather than sensory perception."). *See, generally,* WEINSTEIN, ¶ 803(2)[01]; McCORMICK, § 297, at 704-05.

803(1) does not. Rule 803(2) also differs from Rule 803(1) in not restricting the subject matter of the declaration to descriptive or explanatory statements of the event perceived.[22] Under Rule 803(2) that statement need only "relate" to the startling event. Accordingly, where the statement is in response to a startling event in satisfaction of Rule 803(2), the scope of the subject matter standard is considerably broader than that under Rule 803(1). Like Rule 803(1), however, Rule 803(2) represents a condensed and more refined facet of the common law doctrine of *res gestae*,[23] and like Rule 803(1), Rule 803(2) does not require that the declarant be a participant in the startling event or condition.[24]

§ 803.7　Theory Supporting Rule 803(2).

The admissibility of hearsay statements classified as "excited utterances" is predicated upon the theory that a spontaneous statement by the declarant in response to an external startling stimulus indicates a sufficient degree of trustworthiness to warrant admission of the hearsay.[25] Statements

[22] *See* § 803.1 *et seq.* of this Treatise.

[23] Courts have recently referred to this exception as well as to others related to it, by the generic term *res gestae. E.g.,* United States v. Brady, 579 F.2d 1121, 1130-31 (9th Cir. 1978), *cert. denied,* 439 U.S. 1074, 99 S.Ct. 849, 59 L.Ed.2d 41 (1978); United States v. Gutierrez, 576 F.2d 269, 273 (10th Cir. 1978), *cert. denied,* 439 U.S. 954, 99 S.Ct. 351, 58 L.Ed.2d 345 (1978); United States v. Smith, 520 F.2d 1245, 1247-48 (8th Cir. 1975), *aff'd,* 533 F.2d 1077 (1975); Wetherbee v. Safety Casualty Co., 219 F.2d 274, 275-76 (5th Cir. 1955).

[24] *E.g.,* United States v. Boyd, 620 F.2d 129, 132 (6th Cir. 1980), *cert. denied,* 449 U.S. 855, 101 S.Ct. 151, 66 L.Ed.2d 69 (1980). *See also* McLaughlin v. Vinzant, 522 F.2d 448, 451 (1st Cir. 1975), *cert. denied,* 423 U.S. 1037, 96 S.Ct. 573, 46 L.Ed.2d 412 (1975) (court found it permissible to draw an inference from the force of statement, even though declarant witness did not witness the event, since she was accompanying defendant, and was somewhere in the immediate vicinity of the fatal event, and therefore possessed firsthand knowledge).

[25] Dutton v. Evans, 400 U.S. 74, 89, 91 S.Ct. 210, 223, 27 L.Ed. 213, 227 (1970), *on remand,* 441 F.2d 657 (5th Cir. 1970) (declarant did not misrepresent defendant's involvement in the crime, since the statement was spontaneous). *See also* United States v. Glenn, 473 F.2d 191, 194 (D.C. Cir. 1972) (declarations of victims of violent crime "are sometimes admitted in evidence as exceptions to the hearsay rule, upon the theory that the shock of the injury and the excitement of the moment have produced an utterance that is spontaneous and sincere as distinguished from one engendered by deliberation and design"); McCurdy v. Greyhound Corp., 346 F.2d 224, 224 (3d Cir. 1965) (res gestae exception since participant was incapable of reasoned reflection about the occurrence). *See, generally,* 6 Wigmore, § 1747; Weinstein, ¶ 803(2)[01]. McCormick describes the rationale as well as the basis for much of its criticism, in these succinct terms:

> The rationale for the exception lies in the special reliability which is regarded as furnished by the excitement suspending the declarant's powers of reflection and fabrication. This factor also serves to justify dispensing with any requirement that the declarant be unavailable, because it suggests that his testimony on the stand, given at a time when his powers of reflection and fabrication are operative, is less reliable than his out-of-court declaration. The entire

made in reaction to a startling stimulus are considered more trustworthy than hearsay generally on the dual grounds that, first, the stimulus renders the declarant incapable of fabrication and, second, the impression on the declarant's memory at the time of the statement is still fresh and intense. Accordingly, Rule 803(2) assumes that excited utterances are less susceptible to lapses of memory or dangers of insincerity than ordinary hearsay.[26] Of course, this reasoning also lends itself to a contradictory conclusion as to reliability, namely, that spontaneous reaction to a startling event increases the possibility of problems in narration or perception.[27] Such arguable untrustworthiness, however, has not been considered sufficient to set aside the time-honored exception codified in Rule 803(2), and it is assumed that the critical characteristic of the exception is that the startling occurrence draws the declarant's complete attention to the perceived event so that other counterweights become negligible.

§ 803.8 Elements for Application of Rule 803(2).

In general, qualification of any hearsay statement as an "excited utterance" under Rule 803(2) depends upon the proponent of such evidence demonstrating three essential elements to the trial court's satisfaction: (i) that the statement was in reaction to a truly startling event; (ii) that the

---

basis for the exception is, of course, subject to question. While psychologists would probably concede that excitement minimized the possibility of reflective self-interest influencing the declarant's statements, they would likely question whether this might be outweighed by the distorting effect of shock and excitement upon the declarant's observation and judgment. Despite this doubt concerning its justification, however, the exception is well established.

McCORMICK, EVIDENCE, § 297, at 855 (3d ed. 1984).

[26] E.g., Murphy Auto Parts Co. v. Ball, 249 F.2d 508, 510 (D.C. Cir. 1957), cert. denied, 355 U.S. 932, 78 S.Ct. 413, 2 L.Ed.2d 415 (1957) ("the prompt, spontaneous character of the utterance under the impact and stress of the exciting event which stills the reflective process provides the circumstances which, experience shows us, make for reliability."). See also United States v. Knife, 592 F.2d 472, 481 (8th Cir. 1979). Cf., United States v. Moss, 544 F.2d

954, 958 (8th Cir. 1976), cert. denied, 429 U.S. 1077, 97 S.Ct. 822, 50 L.Ed.2d 797 (1977) (time factor coupled with subject matter of statement demonstrated that statement was not excited utterance within the exception).

[27] See, generally, Stewart, Perception, Memory, and Hearsay: A Criticism of Present Law and The Proposed Federal Rules of Evidence, 1970 UTAH L. REV. 1; Hutchins & Slessinger, Some Observations on the Law of Evidence, 28 COLUM. L. REV. 432 (1928); Gardner, The Perception and Memory of Witnesses, 18 CORNELL L.Q. 391 (1933) ("[S]hock . . . draws attention to the causes of the emotion and thus divides the attention as to the incident itself and the details immediately following it. . . ." Memory before the startling event is keen while memory accompanying or following the event is less reliable). Id. at 395 (relying on Stratton, Retroactive Hyperamnesia, 26 Psych. Rev. 474 (1919)). Cf., McLaughlin v. Vinzant, 552 F.2d 448, 451 (1st Cir. 1975), cert. denied, 423 U.S. 1037, 96 S.Ct. 573, 46 L.Ed.2d 412 (1975).

statement was made under the stress of excitement caused by that event; and (iii) that the statement relates to the event. Where any of these elements is wanting in foundational proof, the statement must be viewed more as a reflective narrative of the past event, and it does not qualify as an excited utterance under Rule 803(2).[28]

In applying the foundational elements, the Rule contemplates that the foundation should be judged on a subjective, rather than objective, standard. The critical feature is that the declarant in question was excited by, and moved to comment on, the occasion. That another person similarly situated would not react as emotionally is not the critical issue in determining admissibility under Rule 803(2).[29]

§ 803.9   Nature of the Stimulus—Requirement that Event or Condition be Startling.

Rule 803(2) conditions admissibility of statements within its scope on the existence of a "startling event or condition." In this regard, such events as an automobile crash, an assault, a murder or other catastrophe might readily qualify as "startling" events. Other less traumatic experiences, however, do not so readily admit of inclusion. Whether or not an event is sufficiently startling depends upon its impact upon the declarant, and the subjective standard necessarily dictates an *ad hoc* approach in the application of this element.[30] Factors critical to this determination may include

---

[28] United States v. Cain, 587 F.2d 678, 680-81 (5th Cir. 1979), *cert. denied*, 440 U.S. 974, 99 S.Ct. 1543, 59 L. Ed.2d 787 (1979); United States v. Phelps, 572 F. Supp. 262m 265 (E.D. Ky. 1983); Zibelman v. Gibbs, 252 F. Supp. 360, 361-62 (E.D. Pa. 1966) (utterance was not excited, since accident was a routine rear-end collision, which was by no means spectacular, bloody, violent, etc., which in itself would lead inescapably to the inference that the utterances were shock-induced).

[29] United States v. Lawrence, 699 F.2d 697, 703-04 (5th Cir. 1983), *cert. denied*, 461 U.S. 935, 103 S.Ct. 2103, 77 L.Ed.2d 309 (1983) (at trial for assault on post office truck driver with intent to rob, no abuse of discretion for trial judge to view statement as spontaneous or excited, that immediately after defendant had been arrested, truck driver asked arresting officer if he had heard defendant tell him that (the truck driver) was a dead man); United States v. Golden, 671 F.2d 369, 371 (10th Cir. 1982),

cert. denied, 456 U.S. 919, 102 S.Ct. 1777, 72 L.Ed.2d 179 (1982) (statement of victim made to his mother after he drove to her house from scene at approximately 120 miles per hour, was properly admitted; statement occurred within 15 minutes of startling event); United States v. Napier, 518 F.2d 316, 317-18 (9th Cir. 1975), *cert. denied*, 423 U.S. 895, 96 S.Ct. 196, 46 L.Ed.2d 128 (1975) (courts look to the effect of the event upon declarant; if the event caused excitement to that person, courts are satisfied).

[30] *E.g.*, United States v. Boyd, 620 F.2d 129, 132 (6th Cir. 1980), *cert. denied*, 449 U.S. 855, 101 S.Ct. 151, 66 L.Ed.2d 69 (1980); Lampe v. U.S., 229 F.2d 43, 45-46 (D.C. Cir. 1956), *cert. denied*, 359 U.S. 929, 79 S.Ct. 612, 2 L.Ed.2d 820 (1956). *See also* Wheeler v. United States, 211 F.2d 19, 23-24 (D.C. Cir. 1953), *cert. denied*, 347 U.S. 1019, 74 S.Ct. 876, 98 L.Ed. 1140 (1953), *reh. denied*, 348 U.S. 852, 75 S.Ct. 21, 99 L.Ed. 671 (1953) (in prosecution for

such considerations as the nature of the event, the appearance, behavior or condition of the declarant, the content of the statement, the declarant's age and profession, his physical proximity to, or psychological perspective of, the event, and whether the statement was unsolicited or in response to a question.

In the majority of cases, the occurrence of the startling event is established by evidence independent of the declarant's statement, such as the testimony of other witnesses or circumstantial evidence showing an unusual event occurred.[31] There is nothing in the Rule or its underlying rationale, however, which would prevent proof of the existence of the startling event by the declarant's statement itself.[32] Consequently, where an individual suffers injury from a solitary mishap, his excited utterance made shortly after the accident should be received as proof that the event occurred. While arguably circular, this approach is particularly sound in actions where a firsthand account of the startling occurrence from a source other than the declarant may be unavailable.[33] Nevertheless, in any case in which the court is satisfied that the declarant was under the stress of excitement when the statement was made, the indicium of reliability is present, and the statement should be received even absent extrinsic foundation. Rule 104(a) expressly provides that the court is not bound by the Rules of Evidence, except those respecting privileges, in considering preliminary, foundational questions as to admissibility.[34]

carnal abuse of 10-year-old, girl's statement to grandmother naming defendant was properly received, since her statement was made within one hour of the event and she was highly distraught and in tears at the time).

[31] E.g., McCurdy v. Greyhound Corp., 346 F.2d 224, 226 (3d Cir. 1965) ("[w]hen the police arrived, McCurdy was still noticeably nervous and shaken up. In view of this, there is little danger that he had either the time to reflect or sufficient use of his reason to fabricate and manufacture an account of the accident"); Cole v. United State, 327 F.2d 360, 316 (9th Cir. 1961); Wetherbee v. Safety Casualty Co., 219 F.2d 274, 278 (5th Cir. 1955) ("pain and suffering prolonged the influence of the event itself").

[32] See Insurance Co. v. Mosley, 75 U.S. (1 Wall) 397, 19 L.Ed. 437 (1869) (insurance policy case which turned on whether deceased had died from injuries incurred in an accidental fall down stairs or from natural causes; widow testified that he left his bed during the night and upon his return

reported that he had fallen and hit the back of his head; widow's testimony that his voice was trembling was some evidence other than his declaration that a startling event had occurred). See, e.g., Stewart v. Baltimore & Ohio R. Co., 137 F.2d 527, 529 (2d Cir. 1943). See also McCORMICK, § 297, at 705; Slough, Res Gestae, 12 WASH. L. REV. 91 (1937). But see Comment, A Study Relating to the Hearsay Evidence Article of the Uniform Rules of Evidence, 4 CAL. L. REV. 468 (1962) ("The judge would reason in a circle if, being bound by the hearsay rule, he nevertheless considered the statement for the purpose of establishing the very fact which is the condition precedent to his original consideration of that statement. He would, to use the hackneyed but respected figure, permit X's declaration to lift itself into evidence by its own bootstraps.").

[33] Wetherbee v. Safety Casualty Co., 219 F.2d 274, 275-76 (5th Cir. 1955); Stewart v. Baltimore & O.R. Co., 137 F.2d 527, 528-29 (2d Cir. 1943).

[34] See Chapter 104 of this Treatise.

§ 803.10   Requirement that Declarant Be Under Stress of Excitement Caused by Startling Event When Statement is Uttered.

To qualify as an "excited utterance," the hearsay statement must have been made while the declarant was under the nervous stress occasioned by the startling incident. This element is critical because the Rule is predicated upon the theory that excited utterances are more trustworthy than hearsay generally because the declarant has little or no capability of fabricating while under extreme stress. This requirement is essentially one of time, *i.e.*, in order to qualify under the exception, the declarant must have made the statement while still under the nervous strain resulting from the event.[35]

There is no set rule as to how much time must pass after the startling event before a statement is no longer an excited utterance, because the exception is primarily founded upon the declarant's inability to fabricate and not on the lack of time to do so.[36] While each set of facts must receive individual treatment, the trial court must focus on the declarant's state of mind at the time the statement was made, and the shock of the event must be present at that time in order for the exception to apply.[37] Factors con-

---

[35] United States v. Iron Shell, 633 F.2d 77, 85-87 (8th Cir. 1980), *cert. denied*, 450 U.S. 1001, 101 S.Ct. 1709, 68 L.Ed.2d 203 (1981) (no abuse of discretion to admit statement made to police officer by 9-year-old victim of assault with intent to rape 45 minutes after the event; court took into consideration age of victim, testimony that she had struggled, that defendant had pulled down her jeans, and that officer asked only "what happened" to which victim replied in short bursts rather than detailed narrative); United States v. Lawrence, 699 F.2d 697, 703-04 (5th Cir. 1983), *cert. denied*, 461 U.S. 935, 103 S.Ct. 2103, 77 L.Ed.2d 309 (1983) (no abuse of discretion for trial judge to view statement made by victim to arresting officer as spontaneous or excited, that defendant told victim he was a dead man); United States v. Golden, 671 F.2d 369, 371 (10th Cir. 1982), *cert. denied*, 456 U.S. 919, 102 S.Ct. 1777, 72 L.Ed.2d 179 (1982) (statement made 15 minutes after startling event immediately after a high-speed flight admitted as spontaneous or excited).

[36] *See, generally,* WEINSTEIN ¶ 803(2)[01]; 6 WIGMORE, §§ 1750, at 1757-59; United States v. Napier, 518 F.2d 316, 317-18 (9th Cir. 1975), *cert. denied*, 423 U.S. 895, 96 S.Ct. 196, 46 L.Ed.2d 128

(1975) (courts look at the effect of the event upon the declarant as primary, and are satisfied as long as the event caused excitement to that person); United States v. Barnes, 464 F.2d 828, 831 (D.C. Cir. 1972), *cert. denied*, 410 U.S. 986, 93 S.Ct. 1514, 36 L.Ed.2d 183 (1972), (spontaneous, excited utterance where victim was allegedly burned to death by a fire set by defendant in the kitchen by means of gasoline poured on the floor, upholding receipt of testimony that victim said to defendant, "you had no call to do that to me" as she was being removed from the house to the hospital); United States v. Kearney, 420 F.2d 170, 175 (D.C. Cir. 1969) ("what must be taken into account is not only the length of the intervening time period, but also an assessment of the declarant's activities and attitudes in the meanwhile.").

[37] McCormick provides this characteristically cogent analysis:

> Probably the most important of the many factors entering into this determination is the time factor. If the statement occurs while the exciting event is still in progress, courts have little difficulty finding that the excitement prompted the statement. But as the time between the event and the statement increases, so does

tributing to this determination include consideration of physical characteristics such as the presence of shock or trauma, the age and maturity of the declarant, periods of unconsciousness or pain, as well as the circumstances surrounding the statement, such as the nature of the startling event.[38] The tenor of the statement itself may also be considered.

Accordingly, trustworthiness is not determined solely by the lapse of time between the event and the hearsay exclamation, although the time elapsed may be probative in determining whether the declarant was still under stress when the statement was uttered.

§ 803.11   Subject Matter of Excited Utterance—Requirement That Statement "Relate" to the Startling Event.

In contrast to the requisite element of a present sense impression statement under Rule 803(1), where the substance of the hearsay statement must "describe or explain" the event or condition,[39] Rule 803(2) requires only that the hearsay statement "relate" to the startling event or condition. A statement embracing facts which are distinct from the startling event or

the reluctance to find the statement an excited utterance. . . . Perhaps an accurate rule of thumb might be that where the time interval between the event and the statement is long enough to permit reflective thought, the statement will be excluded in the absence of some proof that the declarant did not in fact engage in a reflective thought process. Testimony that the declarant still appeared "nervous" or "distraught" and that there was a reasonable basis for continuing emotional upset will often suffice. The nature of the exciting event and the declarant's concern with it are relevant, of course. . . . Other factors may indicate the opposite conclusion. Evidence that the statement was self-serving or made in response to an inquiry, while not justification for automatic exclusion, is an indication that the statement was the result of reflective thought, and where the time interval permitted such thought these factors might swing the balance in favor of exclusion. Proof that between the event and the statement the declarant performed tasks requiring relatively careful thought, of course, is strong evidence that the effect of the exciting event had subsided.

McCormick, § 297, at 706. See Garcia v. Williams, 605 F.2d 1297, 1299 (10th Cir. 1979) (statement of ten-year-old boy made more than one hour after car accident in which his father was killed could properly be excluded by trial court where boy's statement could have been prompted by loss of loved one rather than the accident); United States v. Mountain State Fabricating Co., 282 F.2d 263, 265-66 (4th Cir. 1960) (under all the circumstances, the statement was excluded although it related to a startling event and was made shortly thereafter); Chestnut v. Ford Motor Co., 445 F.2d 967, 972-73 (4th Cir. 1971) (remanded to trial court to reconsider exclusion of plaintiff's statement to doctor 20 hours after the accident where the plaintiff may still have been in nervous shock).

[38] E.g., Haggins v. Warden, Fort Pillow State Farm, 715 F.2d 1050, 1057-58, (6th Cir. 1983); United States v. Iron Shell, 633 F.2d 77, 85-87 (8th Cir. 1980), cert. denied, 450 U.S. 1001, 101 S.Ct. 1709, 68 L.Ed.2d 203 (1981); United States v. Nick, 604 F.2d 1199, 1202 (9th Cir. 1979); McCurdy v. Greyhound Corp., 346 F.2d 224, 226 (3d Cir. 1965).

[39] See § 803.3 of this Treatise.

condition may be admissible under Rule 803(2) where the statement in some rational manner relates to the event.[40]

While the fact that the statement neither describes nor explains the exciting condition or event may be an indication that the utterance is not truly spontaneous, the Rule only requires that the statement relate to the startling event.[41] Consequently, statements containing beliefs about past facts may be admissible where such remembered facts relate to the startling event which provoked the out-of-court statement. Consequently, if a declarant makes an out-of-court statement in response to a sufficiently startling event, "Look at that blue truck smash into that car; I saw that truck at the service station yesterday getting its brakes serviced," the entire declaration may be admissible under Rule 803(2). The latter statement regarding a past event at a service station rationally *relates* to the startling event even though it does not actually describe it.[42]

Rule 803(3)   Then Existing, Mental, Emotional, or Physical Condition

Rule 803(3) reads as follows:

The following are not excluded by the hearsay rule, even though the declarant is available as a witness: . . . (3) **Then existing, mental, emotional, or physical condition.** Statement of the declarant's then existing state of mind, emotion, sensation, or physical condition (such as intent, plan, mo-

---

[40] Rule 803(2) does not admit statements made during or immediately after the event which bear no relation to it, however. This analysis of the Rule is in accord with Wigmore, who provides this simple example as illustrative of an inadmissible statement:

Suppose, for example, an injured passenger in a railway collision, thinking of his family's condition, exclaims "I hope that my insurance premium, which I mailed yesterday, has reached the company," referring to premium-money alleged by the insurance-company not to have been received.

6 Wigmore, § 1754, at 159. *See also* Murphy Auto Parts Co. v. Ball, 249 F.2d 508, 510 (D.C. Cir. 1957), *cert. denied*, 355 U.S. 932, 78 S.Ct. 413, 2 L.Ed.2d 415 (1958). (Berger, J.) ("[A] careful analysis of the entire subject demonstrates that the third element, mechanically and narrowly construed, is a spurious element, and that reliability of the utterance is not inflexible, dependent upon the subject matter of the utterance."). *See, generally,* Weinstein, ¶ 802(2)[01]; McCormick, § 297, at 707.

[41] *E.g.,* United States v. Napier, 518 F.2d 316, 317-18 (9th Cir. 1975), *cert. denied*, 423 U.S. 895, 96 S.Ct. 196, 46 L.Ed.2d 128 (1975); Harrison v. United States, 200 F. 662, 674 (6th Cir. 1912). *See also* United States v. Flecha, 539 F.2d 874, 876 (2d Cir. 1976) (in narcotics prosecution, error to receive evidence by codefendant made after arrest, "why so much excitement? If we are caught, we are caught;" statement indicated a lack of excitement). *See, generally,* 4 Louisell & Mueller, § 439, at 513-16.

[42] *Compare* discussion of Rule 803(1) at § 803.5 of this Treatise.

tive, design, mental feeling, pain, and bodily health), but not including a statement of memory or belief to prove the fact remembered or believed unless it relates to the execution, revocation, identification, or terms of declarant's will.

§ 803.12   Then Existing, Mental, Emotional, or Physical Condition.

Rule 803(3) codifies[43] a hearsay exception traditionally comprehended in part by the common-law phrase *res gestae*,[44] and it operates to admit hearsay statements offered in the context of four different situations: (i) statements as to then existing physical condition; (ii) statements as to then existing mental or emotional condition; (iii) certain statements probative of subsequent conduct; and (iv) statements of beliefs and intent concerning the declarant's will.[45] The Rule combines two common-law exceptions, *i.e.*, the relatively simple and less troublesome exception pertaining to statements concerning then existing physical conditions and the complicated and more intractable exception pertaining to statements concerning mental or emotional conditions.[46]

The underlying rationale for this hearsay exception is that statements concerning the declarant's then existing physical or mental condition are

[43] *See, generally*, McCORMICK, §§ 291, 294-96; 4 WEINSTEIN, ¶ 803(3)[01]-[06]; 4 LOUISELL & MUELLER, §§ 440-443; 6 WIGMORE, §§ 1718-1740. *See also* Hinton, *States of Mind and the Hearsay Rule*, 1 U. CHI. L. REV. 394 (1934); Hutchins & Slesinger, *Some Observations on the Law of Evidence - State of Mind to Prove an Act*, 38 YALE L.J. 283 (1929); McBaine, *Admissibility in California of Declarations of Physical or Mental Condition*, 19 CALIF. L. REV. 231 (1931); Maguire, *The Hillmon Case - Thirty-Three Years After*, 38 HARV. L. REV. 709 (1925); Morgan, *Hearsay Dangers and the Application of the Hearsay Concept*, 62 HARV. L. REV. 177 (1948); Payne, *The Hillmon Case — An Old Problem Revisited*, 41 VA. L. REV. 1011 (1955); Rice, *The State of Mind Exception to the Hearsay Rule: A Response to "Secondary" Relevance*, 14 DUQ. L. REV. 219 (1975-76); Seidelson, *State of Mind Exception to the Hearsay Rule*, 13 DUQ. L. REV. 251 (1974); Seligman, *An Exception to the Hearsay Rule*, 26 HARV. L. REV. 146 (1912); Slough, *Res Gestae*, 2 KAN. L. REV. 121 (1953); Slough, *Spontaneous Statements and State of Mind*, 46 IOWA L. REV. 224 (1961); Comment, *Hearsay Under the Proposed Federal Rules: A Discretionary Approach*, 15 WAYNE L. REV. 1077, 1120-1130 (1969).

[44] The exception contained in Rule 803(3) springs from the dual common law exceptions which permitted the admission of hearsay statements demonstrating bodily pain and hearsay statements asserting emotions. Both exceptions rely upon an identical justification, *i.e.*, enhanced trustworthiness due to spontaneity. *See, generally*, Slough, *Res Gestae*, 2 KAN. L. REV. 121, 126-27 (1953) ("The basic policy justifying this hearsay exception [for state of mind] parallels the policy . . . in relation to declarations of physical condition. Except for the fact that the physical condition exception found acceptance at an earlier date, the general principles underlying both exceptions are identical."). *See also* Wabisky v. D.C. Transit System, Inc., 309 F.2d 317, 318 (D.C. Cir. 1962) (Burger, J.).

[45] 4 LOUISELL & MUELLER, § 440, at 518 (1979).

[46] *See, generally*, WEINSTEIN, ¶ 803 (3)[01].

trustworthy because their spontaneity makes them at least as, if not more, reliable than testimony at trial on the same subject. Subsequent testimony concerning a prior condition at the very least would present a risk as to a defect in memory.[47] Moreover, the element of spontaneity attending statements of then existing conditions renders the risk of fabrication almost negligible since, as one commentator has noted, every person is "the world's foremost authority" on his contemporaneous internal states.[48] Of course, statements comprehended by Rule 803(3) are not conclusively trustworthy since such declarations, even though sincerely uttered, may nevertheless be misleading because the declarant may have miscalculated his own motives, feelings or physical sensations. Nevertheless, these risks are thought to be insufficient to preclude introduction of statements embraced by Rule 803(3), especially where the risk of a memory defect is so minimal. In this sense, the Rule 803(3) exception is parallel to the present sense impression exception formulated in Rule 803(1).

Whether the statement concerns a physical condition or a mental or emotional state, Rule 803(3) requires that the declaration be directed at a present condition, *i.e.*, a "then existing" condition. Only where the subject matter of the statement is a present condition are the testimonial defects in memory and sincerity reduced. Where the statement concerns a past condition, the potential defects in memory and sincerity are present and the hearsay statement is not within this exception. Where the statement does not pertain to a "then existing" condition, it must be viewed as a narrative of a past event formulated after time for reflection, and it is not admissible under Rule 803(3).[49]

---

[47] This reduced chance of fabrication is reinforced by the genuine need for such evidence. *See, generally*, Wigmore, § 1714. As McCormick explains:

Special reliability is considered to be furnished by the spontaneous quality of the declarations, assured by the requirement that the declarations purport to describe a condition presently existing at the time of the declaration. This assurance of reliability is almost certainly not always effective, however, since some statements describing present symptoms or the like are probably not spontaneous but rather calculated misstatements. Nevertheless, a sufficiently large percentage are probably spontaneous to justify the exception. The strong likelihood of spontaneity is also the basis for the special need for receiving the declarations. Being spontaneous, they are considered of greater probative value than the present testimony of the declarant, and consequently are admissible despite the availability of the declarant at the time of trial.

McCORMICK, § 291, at 689.

[48] Seidelson, *The State of Mind Exception to the Hearsay Rule*, 13 DUQ. L. REV. 251, 253 (1974). *But see* 4 LOUISELL & MUELLER, § 440, at 519 n.41 (even though statements admitted under this exception will often be uttered spontaneously in response to an external stimulus, the rule does not require it; hence, there is no assurance of candor.)

[49] *Compare, e.g.*, Mabry v. Travelers Ins. Co., 193 F.2d 497, 498 (5th Cir. 1952) (contemporaneous expression of pain and suffering admissible), *with* Huff v. White Motor Corp., 609 F.2d 286, 291-92 (7th Cir. 1979) (in wrongful death action, dece-

Finally, Rule 803(3) should be compared with Rule 803(4) which pertains to statements made in aid of medical treatment or diagnosis. Rule 803(3) does not require that the statement be directed to, or made in the presence of medical personnel. Any person who had an opportunity to hear it may testify to the declaration, including friends, family, and unrelated bystanders.[50] While the respective scopes of Rule 803(3) and Rule 803(4) overlap, the applications of these hearsay exceptions are distinct.

§ 803.13 Declarations of Bodily Feelings, Symptoms, Condition.

Rule 803(3) authorizes the introduction of a declarant's statement concerning his present internal physical condition. Accordingly, Rule 803(3) operates as a vehicle for the admission of such statements as "I am ill," "I am tired," "I have a pain in my chest," and "I feel dizzy." Self-diagnostic statements or statements as to the external source of an internal condition are not, however, admissible under Rule 803(3) although they may be admissible under Rule 803(4). Accordingly, Rule 803(3) does not authorize admission of such statements as "X broke my arm," "I am in pain because I swallowed poison," or "That food made me ill."

A requisite element for qualification under this exception is that the expression must be contemporaneous with the physical sensation or condition and consequently, descriptions of past conditions (*i.e.*, past sensations, pains or physical symptoms) or descriptions of a past event are not admissible under Rule 803(3).[51] Accordingly, the statement "I felt ill yesterday" would not be admissible pursuant to this exception.

While the Rule is predicated upon the characteristic element of the contemporaneousness of the statement and the physical condition,[52] there is no

dent's description of how accident occurred given to friend in hospital room properly excluded).

[50] *E.g.*, Insurance Co. v. Mosley, 75 U.S. 397, 404-05, 19 L.Ed. 437, 443 (1869) (wife); Northern Pacific R. Co. v. Urlin, 158 U.S. 271, 274, 39 L.Ed. 977, 981 (1895) (made to "any other person," dictum, citing 1 Greenleaf, Evidence). *See also* Baltimore & Ohio R. Co. v. Rambo, 59 F. 75, 82 (8th Cir. 1893). *See, generally*, 6 Wigmore, § 1719.

[51] *E.g.*, Hartford Accident & Indemnity Co. v. Carter, 110 F.2d 355, 356 (5th Cir. 1940) (statement to treating physician that claimant had received a blow to the head was improperly received; it was the relation of a past event, not an exclamation of

present pain or suffering). *See also* Wolf v. Procter & Gamble Co., 555 F. Supp. 613, 615 (D.N.J. 1982); D'Angelo v. U.S., 456 F. Supp. 127, 130-31, *aff'd*, 605 F.2d 1194 (1978) (employee's statement that he expected a promotion when he completed his training and obtained his license could not be considered as evidence that declarant's employer planned such a promotion).

[52] *See, generally*, Weinstein, ¶ 803(3)[01], at 803-105, *citing* Northern Pacific R. Co. v. Urlin, 158 U.S. 271, 274, 15 S.Ct. 840, 844, 39 L.Ed. 977, 980-81 (1895) ("[E]veryone knows that when injuries are internal and not obvious to visual inspection, the surgeon has to largely depend upon the responses and exclamations of the patient when subjected to examination.").

requirement that the statement be made contemporaneously with an external stimulus that produced the condition.[53] For example, where an individual is injured on Monday and still feels pain on Wednesday, his declaration on Wednesday concerning his then existing pain is admissible under Rule 803(3).

§ 803.14   State of Mind in Issue.

A certain state of mind of a person may be a relevant factual issue,[54] and, while circumstantial evidence may be admitted to prove mental state, the most probative evidence of a person's mental state is usually the contemporaneous declarations of the person whose state of mind is at issue. Where the statements are *indirect* assertions of the mental state, the out-of-court statements are not hearsay. This type of admissible evidence of state of mind is discussed in § 801.7 of this Treatise. Where, however, the statements are direct assertions of the then existing mental or emotional condition, the statements are hearsay but nevertheless admissible pursuant to Rule 803(3).

Accordingly, where relevant, Rule 803(3) would operate as a vehicle for the admission of such statements as "I am depressed," "I am happy," "I am fond of X," and "I am afraid of X." Rule 803(3) will frequently be applied in criminal cases concerning bribery, extortion, or intimidation where the hearsay is probative of the victim's mental state.[55] The exception also arises

[53] *E.g.*, Casualty Insurance Co. v. Salinas, 160 Tex. 445, 452-53, 333 S.W.2d 109, 116-18 (1960) (reversible error to exclude testimony that plaintiff complained of present pain various times after his injury.).

[54] *E.g.*, United States v. Partyka, 561 F.2d 118, 125 (8th Cir. 1977), *cert. denied*, 434 U.S. 1037, 98 S.Ct. 773, 54 L.Ed.2d 785 (1977) (out-of-court declarations of defendant admissible in criminal action in support of entrapment defense); Monroe v. Board of Education, 65 F.R.D. 641, 649-50 (D.C. Conn. 1975) (in action by high school student for wrongful suspension, defense affidavits filed in opposition to motion for summary judgment admissible to show motive or reason for the suspension). McCormick explains the particular rationale for this exception:

> This special assurance of reliability for declarations of present state of mind rests, as in the case with declarations of bodily condition, upon

their spontaneity and probable sincerity. This is assured by the requirements that the declarations must purport to relate to a condition of mind or emotion existing at the time of the statement and must have been made under circumstances indicating apparent sincerity. The special need for use of the declarations does not rest on the unavailability of the declarant—this is not required—but upon the ground that if the declarant were called to testify "his own memory of his state of mind at a former time is no more likely to be clear and true than a bystander's recollection of what he then said."

McCormick, § 294, at 695. *See also* Slough, *Spontaneous Statements of State of Mind*, 46 Iowa L. Rev. 224 (1961). *See, generally*, Weinstein, ¶ 803(3)[03].

[55] Hydrolevel Corp. v. American Society of Mechanical Engineers, Inc., 635 F.2d 118, 128-29 (2d Cir. 1980), *aff'd*, 456 U.S.

with some frequency in civil cases where the statement is offered to show mental suffering, ill will or malice.[56] In any case, Rule 803(3) may be appropriately applied wherever the declarant's mental state is relevant.

§ 803.15   State of Mind to Demonstrate Subsequent Acts.

Rule 803(3) not only admits a declarant's statement where his state of mind is relevant; it also operates to admit statements concerning mental or emotional conditions where such mental states are probative of subsequent conduct.[57] In 1892, the Supreme Court in the landmark case of *Mutual Life Insurance Co. v. Hillmon*,[58] endorsed the use of statements of plan or intent to show that the planned or intended act was undertaken. In a widow's action to collect the proceeds of insurance policies on the life of her husband, the main factual issue was whether the body of a man found shot at Crooked Creek was that of the insured, Hillmon. The defense argued that the body belonged to a man named Walters and sought to introduce in evidence letters from Walters to his sister and fiancee in which he stated that he planned to leave Wichita in early March with Hillmon.[59] The Supreme Court found that the letters should have been admitted:

> The letters in question were competent, not as narratives of facts communicated to the writer by others, nor yet as proof that he actually went away from Wichita, but as evidence that, shortly before the time when other evidence tended to show that he went away, he had the intention of going, and of going with Hillmon, which made it more probable both that he did go and that he went with Hillmon, than if there had been no proof of such intention.[60]

556, 102 S.Ct. 1935, 72 L.Ed.2d 330, *cert. denied*, 456 U.S. 989, 102 S.Ct. 2267, 73 L.Ed.2d 1283 (1982). *See also* Morris v. General Electric Credit Corp., 714 F.2d 32, 34-35 (5th Cir. 1983) (in action by jewelry store against collection agency alleging loss of goodwill, hearsay letters and statements of jewelry store customers admitted which indicated customers' anger about the way the collection agency was handling accounts).

[56] McCORMICK, § 294, at 695. *See, generally*, WEINSTEIN, ¶ 803(3)[03]; 6 WIGMORE, § 1732.

[57] *See, generally*, 4 WEINSTEIN, ¶ 803(3)[04]; McCORMICK, § 295.

[58] 145 U.S. 285, 12 S.Ct. 909, 36 L.Ed. 706 (1892). *Hillmon* was tried six times and

the litigation continued over twenty years. For commentaries on the *Hillmon* decision and the concepts engendered thereby, see Payne, *The Hillmon Case—An Old Problem Revisited*, 41 VA. L. REV. 1011 (1955); Hutchins & Slesinger, *Some Observations on the Law of Evidence—State of Mind to Prove an Act*, 38 YALE L.J. 283 (1929); Seligman, *An Exception to the Hearsay Rule*, 26 HARV. L. REV. 146 (1912).

[59] The man who claimed he had accidentally shot Hillmon identified the body, but the defense contended that as part of a scheme to defraud the insurance companies, Hillmon killed Walters and then had his companion attempt to pass the body off as Hillmon. *Id*. at 288.

[60] *Id*. at 295-96.

In accord with *Hillmon*, Rule 803(3) embraces declarations of plan or intent to show subsequent conforming conduct. For example, the declarant's statement, "I plan to go to work tomorrow" is admissible as relevant evidence of the proposition that the declarant went to work on the day after the out-of-court statement. Likewise, statements such as "I plan to murder X," and "I don't intend to fulfill my obligations under the contract," are admissible under Rule 803(3) as probative evidence of the occurrence of the subsequent relevant conduct. In sum, a plan or intent is a mental state expressly comprehended by Rule 803(3).

Arguably, the special reliability usually attending Rule 803(3) hearsay statements is absent where declarations of intent are offered to prove subsequent conduct since it is less likely that a declared intention will be executed than it is that a declared state of mind is actually held. Further, there would appear to be no special need for this type of evidence where the declarant's conduct is an objective fact capable of proof in other ways.[61] Nevertheless, out-of-court statements of a declarant's plan, design, or intention are admissible to prove that the plan, design, or intention was executed by the declarant. Such statements comprehend then existing mental states, and as such, they do not suffer from possible defects in memory. Moreover, as relating to purely internal conditions, statements of intent, plan or design are free of risks of defects in perception. Finally, while not conclusive proof of subsequent actions, statements of intent, plan, or design unquestionably alter the probabilities of subsequent conduct and are, consequently, relevant under Rule 401 as to whether the subsequent conduct occurred.

---

[61] McCormick posits the peculiar problem as follows, placing special emphasis upon factors involving relevancy:

. . .[I]t is arguable that there is less special need for the use of declarations of state of mind to prove conduct than there is for use of such declarations to prove state of mind as an end in itself. State of mind is a matter inherently difficult of proof; where it is at issue, the usual absence of other evidence reliably tending to prove it arguably justifies relaxing normal exclusionary rules in order to bring in the declarations of the person best able to know the state of mind. On the other hand , this special difficulty of proof does not exist generally in regard to conduct, so arguably there is less justification for relaxation where it is at issue.

Despite the failure until recently to recognize the potential value of declarations of state of mind to prove subsequent conduct, it is now clear that out-of-court statements which tend to prove a plan, design, or intention of the declarant are admissible, subject to the usual limitations as to remoteness in time and apparent sincerity common to all declarations of mental state, to prove the plan, design, or intention of the declarant was carried out by the declarant.

McCORMICK, § 295, at 697. *See also* 4 WEINSTEIN, ¶ 803(3)[04] (questioning relevancy of such evidence on the basis that the theory that an intent to perform an act is generally carried out questionable on psychological grounds).

Accordingly, Rule 803(3) admits statements of intent as evidence of the declarant's subsequent conduct since at least a modicum of relevancy is presented. Because the issue is really one of relevancy, admission of evidence of state of mind offered to prove subsequent conduct is peculiarly subject to the general exclusionary principles of Rule 403. Obviously where the statement of intent and the subsequent event are separated by substantial time, the probative value of the out-of-court declaration of intent is relatively low. Likewise, certain tentative assertions of intent have marginal probative value of subsequent conduct. In such situations the risk that the trier of fact may use this evidence improperly may substantially outweigh its probative value, and Rule 403 may operate to preclude admission of the evidence.

The reliability of a declaration of intent as proof of subsequent conduct is further reduced where the cooperation of another person in addition to the declarant is necessary to successfully carry out the act.[62] Arguably, *Hillmon* itself presented this type of joint action issue, because Walters' expressed intention to leave Wichita with Hillmon depended upon Hillmon's continued willingness to travel with Walters. The post-Rules force of *Hillmon* with respect to joint action is unclear. While the Advisory Committee stated that Rule 803(3) was not intended to disturb *Hillmon*,[63] the House Judiciary Committee disagreed:

> [T]he Committee intends that the Rule be construed to limit the doctrine of [Hillmon], so as to render statements of intent by a declarant admissible only to prove his future conduct, not the future conduct of another person.[64]

Federal courts have been reluctant to permit statements of intent to be used to prove subsequent conduct of someone other than the declarant.[65] Never-

---

[62] *See* 4 LOUISELL & MUELLER, § 442, at 560; 4 WEINSTEIN, ¶ 803(3)[04], at 803-118; McCORMICK, § 295, at 848.

[63] Fed. R. Evid. 803(3) Advisory Committee Note.

[64] H.R. Rep. No. 93-650, 93d Cong., 1st Sess. 13-14 (1973).

[65] Gual-Morales v. Hernandez Vega, 579 F.2d 677, 680 (1st Cir. 1978), *on remand,* 461 F.Supp. 656 (D.C.P.R.) (plaintiff sought to prove that defendant was part of conspiracy against him and wanted court to consider affidavit that claimed employer's lawyer sought to get to defendant; court concluded, "statements that this lawyer is claimed to have made concerning his intention of seeing defendant would not be admissible against [defendant]"); United

States v. Jenkins, 579 F.2d 840, 842-44 (4th Cir. 1978), *cert. denied,* 439 U.S. 931, 99 S.Ct. 320, 58 L.Ed.2d 324 (1978) (statements of intent by a declarant are admissible only to prove the declarant's future conduct); United States v. Mangan, 575 F.2d 32, 43 n.12 (2d Cir. 1978), *cert. denied,* 439 U.S. 931, 99 S.Ct. 320, 58 L.Ed. 2d 324 (1978) (in prosecution for fraud against the government and related conspiracy, court noted government's argument and concluded that defendant's statements "might be admissible"); United States v. Stanchich, 550 F.2d 1294, 1297 n.1 (2d Cir. 1977) (under the *Hillmon* doctrine a statement of intent may be received, even where the jury will infer a previous fact; statements admissible).

theless, some federal authority has approved statements of intent to show joint action of the declarant and others, particularly where other corroborating evidence of the conduct is presented.[66]

§ 803.16   State of Mind to Demonstrate Previous Conduct.

While Rule 803(3) permits introduction of hearsay statements tending to demonstrate subsequent conduct by the declarant, a statement of belief is not admissible for the purpose of proving an act or conduct alleged to have been performed prior to the making of the statement.[67] Accordingly, Rule 803(3) excludes from the exception mental state declarations that are "a statement of memory or belief to prove the fact remembered or believed." Obviously, if the exception for statements of then existing mental condition included the mental states of memory or belief offered to prove facts external to the declarant, this exception would swallow the entire hearsay rule.[68] In the absence of this disqualification of statements of memory or belief, all hearsay statements could be construed as admissible declarations of mental state thereby emasculating the entire hearsay system.[69]

[66] United States v. Sperling, 726 F.2d 69, 73-74 (2d Cir. 1984). *See also* United States v. Astorga-Torres, 682 F.2d 1331, 1335-36 (9th Cir. 1982), *cert. denied*, 459 U.S. 1040, 103 S.Ct. 455, 74 L.Ed.2d 608 (1982) (co-defendant's statements properly admitted as evidence of his intent, from which jury could properly draw inferences); United States v. Cicale, 691 F.2d 95, 103-04 (2d Cir. 1982), *cert. denied*, 460 U.S. 1082, 103 S.Ct. 1771, 76 L.Ed.2d 344 (statements by declarant to undercover agent that he was going to meet his source in order to make arrangements to obtain heroin were admissible to show defendant's participation in conspiracy, where on each occasion declarant was seen soon afterward with defendant or arriving at defendant's address, thus supported by a "ring of reliability"). *See, e.g.*, United States v. Moore, 571 F.2d 76, 81-82 (2d Cir. 1978).

[67] *See, e.g.*, Shepard v. United States, 290 U.S. 96, 54 S.Ct. 22, 78 L.Ed. 196 (1933) (statement of deceased made to nurse two days after the incident that "Dr. Shepard has poisoned me" inadmissible to prove she was poisoned); Marshall v. Commonwealth Aquarium, 611 F.2d 1, 3 (1st Cir. 1979) (testimony by witness of declarant's recollection of telephone conversation

inadmissible to prove contents of conversation). *See, generally*, Payne, *The Hillmon Case—An Old Problem Revisited*, 41 VA. L. REV. 1011 (1955). Facts external to the declarant occurring contemporaneously with the out-of-court statement may be admissible under Rule 803(1) or (2).

[68] McCORMICK, § 296, at 701; 4 WEINSTEIN, ¶ 803(3)[05]; 4 LOUISELL & MUELLER, § 442, at 570-571. *See, e.g.*, United States v. Murray, 297 F.2d 812, 814 (2d Cir. 1962), *cert. denied*, 369 U.S. 828, 82 S.Ct. 845, 8 L.Ed.2d 508 (1962); United States v. Margiotta, 688 F.2d 108, 136 (3d Cir. 1982); Prather v. Prather, 650 F.2d 88, 90-91 (5th Cir. 1981). *See, generally*, Seligman, *An Exception to the Hearsay Rule*, 26 HARV. L. REV. 146 (1912).

[69] The clearest expression against this type of evidence is contained in Shepard v. United States, 290 U.S. 96, 105-06, 54 S.Ct. 22, 33, 78 L.Ed. 196, 203 (1933) (Cardozo, J.) ("[D]eclarations of intention, casting light upon the future, have been sharply distinguished from declarations of memory, pointing backwards to the past. There would be an end, or nearly that, to the rule against hearsay if the distinction were ignored."). *See also* McCORMICK, § 295, at 701.

Any statement which looks back to a prior event external to the declarant inevitably presents risks of defects in sincerity, perception, narration and memory, and as a consequence, there is no justification for the admission of such hearsay statements. Statements tending to prove past conduct or facts are more appropriately termed "present memory" of a past event and are not admissible pursuant to Rule 803(3), except in certain situations occurring in will cases discussed in the next section.

§ 803.17   State of Body or Mind to Demonstrate Past Conduct Concerning Declarant's Last Will and Testament.

While Rule 803(3) does not generally operate to admit statements of memory or belief to prove the fact remembered or believed, such statements of memory or belief are admissible where they relate to the execution, revocation, identification or terms of the declarant's will. In this regard, Rule 803(3) is in accord with the prevailing view.[70]

The rationale for this exception to the general inadmissibility of statements of past events is grounded on the special need for such evidence. The testator, who is the person best in a position to know the facts, and sometimes the only person in possession of such facts, is obviously unavailable at the time his will is in need of interpretation.[71] In almost every dispute over a will, the state of mind of the testator assumes paramount importance, and the testator's own statements are likely to be the most probative evidence of the import of his own will. This need for the testator's statement is often coupled with the recognition that a testator's statements bear peculiar reliability due to the fact that a will is a serious matter. Consequently, it is reasonably assumed that in the absence of suspicious circumstances, the testator spoke from firsthand knowledge and with due regard for the seriousness and candor required of the occasion.[72]

---

[70] *See, generally,* McCormick, § 296, at 702.

[71] *E.g.,* Savoy v. Savoy, 220 F.2d 364, 366-67 (D.C. Cir. 1954) (reversible error to exclude evidence that several months after tearing up a will which had been torn in two pieces and then taped together, the testator had made statements indicating that he had disposed of his property in the manner which the torn will provided). *See also* Lingham v. Harmon, 502 F. Supp. 302, 306-07 (D. Md. 1980); Rhode Island Hospital Trust Co. v. U.S., 241 F.Supp. 586, 589 (D.C.R.I. 1965), *vacated,* Wolfson v. Mutual Life Ins. Co. of New York, 455 F.Supp.

83, *aff'd,* 588 F.2d 825 (D.C. Pa. 1978). *See, generally,* 6 WIGMORE, § 1736; McCormick, § 296; Slough, *Res Gestae,* 2 KAN. L. REV. 121 (1953); Fed. R. Evid. 803(3) Advisory Committee Note.

[72] Under the pre-code decision of Throckmorton v. Holt, 180 U.S. 552, 580, 21 S.Ct. 474, 498, 45 L.Ed. 663, 685 (1901), declarations of this type were often inadmissible unless they were near enough in time to the execution of the will to be considered part of the *res gestae,* whether they were made before or after the execution of the will. *Id.* Regarding the decision, Wigmore says that it "is only a quicksand

Under Rule 803(3) statements offered for the purpose of proving that the testator was of sound mind, that he or she harbored certain emotions or feelings toward those whom he or she either included or failed to mention, or that he or she was or was not under the sort of personal pressure amounting to "undue influence" are all admissible. Also admissible are statements indicating his or her intent to execute, revoke or modify a will when offered to prove subsequent conforming conduct. The Rule, however, does not permit the introduction of a testator's hearsay statements of believed past facts to prove any facts which do not relate to the execution, revocation, identification or terms of the declarant's will.[73]

Rule 803(4)   Statement For Purposes of Medical Diagnosis or Treatment

Rule 803(4) reads as follows:

The following are not excluded by the hearsay rule, even though the declarant is available as a witness: . . . **(4) Statements for purposes of medical diagnosis or treatment.** Statements made for purposes of medical diagnosis or treatment and describing medical history, or past or present symptoms, pain, or sensations, or the inception or general character of the cause or external source thereof insofar as reasonably pertinent to diagnosis or treatment.

§ 803.18   Statements for Purposes of Medical Diagnosis or Treatment— In General.

Rule 803(4), which governs the standards for admissibility of hearsay declarations made for the purpose of securing medical treatment or diagnosis, represents both a continuance and an extension of prior federal law.[74]

for those who seek guidance on the subject." § 1736, at 108. Under Rule 803(3) all relevant statements of the testator made either before or after execution of the will are admissible. *See* WEINSTEIN, ¶ 803(3)[05].

[73] *Compare* Yarborough v. Prudential Insurance Co. of America, 100 F.2d 547, 548 (5th Cir. 1939) (error to admit wife's testimony that deceased had handed over insurance policy assuring her that it was paid as part of *res gestae*) *with* Krimlofski v. United States, 190 F.Supp. 734, 746-47 (D. Iowa 1961)) (general rule of construction admitting statements of testator regarding will

especially is applicable in cases where designated beneficiary is not clear).

[74] *See, generally,* McCORMIC, §§ 292-93; 4 WEINSTEIN, ¶¶ 803(4)[01]-[03]; 4 LOUISELL & MUELLER, § 444; 6 WIGMORE, §§ 1719-20. *See also* Seidel & Gingrich, *Hearsay Objections to Expert Psychiatric Opinion Testimony and the Proposed Federal Rules of Evidence,* 39 U.M.K.C. REV. 141 (1970); Slough, *Res Gestae,* 2 KAN. L. REV. 41 (1953); Slough, *Spontaneous Statements and State of Mind,* 46 IOWA L. REV. 224 (1961); Comment, *Hearsay Under the Proposed Federal Rules: A Discretionary*

Rule 803(4) codifies the last of four hearsay exceptions known under the common law as *res gestae*. Along with present sense impressions (Rule 803(1)), excited utterances (Rule 803(2)), and then existing mental, emotional or physical conditions (Rule 803(3)), Rule 803(4) represents the modern application of the now obsolete *res gestae* concept.[75] Under Rule 803(4) hearsay statements made by a declarant regarding present and past physical conditions are admissible where they are made in subjective contemplation of obtaining treatment or diagnosis. Prior to the adoption of the Rule, many of the federal courts restricted the exception to allow only statements of present symptoms.[76] Likewise, pre-Rule cases limited the exception to include statements made in contemplation of treatment alone but not those merely seeking diagnosis or assessment.[77] Rule 803(4) admits declarations without regard to the purpose of the examination or the need for the patient's medical history. Statements made in anticipation of diagnosis which are in preparation of the expert trial testimony are admissible, and consequently, Rule 803(4) avoids the necessity of making artificial distinctions between diagnoses made for treatment and those made for purposes of trial preparation.[78] Finally, it should be noted that Rule 803(4) does not permit

Approach, 15 WAYNE L. REV. 1077, 1134-35 (1969); Note, *Medical Testimony and the Hearsay Rule*, 1964 WASH. U.L.Q. 192; Note, *Evidence - Admissibility of Expressions of Pain and Suffering*, 51 MICH. L. REV. 902 (1953).

[75] *See* § 803.2 of this Treatise for a discussion of the common-law *res gestae* concept.

[76] *Compare* Meaney v. United States, 112 F.2d 538, 539-40 (2d Cir. 1940) (reversible error to exclude physician's testimony of patient's "declarations as to the time of the onset of his disease and its immediate severity") *with* Felice v. Long Island R. Co., 426 F.2d 192, 196-97 (2d Cir. 1970), *cert. denied*, 400 U.S. 820, 91 S.Ct. 37, 27 L.Ed.2d 47 (1970) (reversible error to permit plaintiff to introduce medical reports prepared by treating physician indicating patient's description of circumstances of the accident causing his injury).

[77] *E.g.*, Nutt v. Black Hills Stage Lines, Inc., 452 F.2d 480, 482 (8th Cir. 1971). *See also* Chicago & N.W.R. Co. v. Garwood, 167 F.2d 848, 859 (8th Cir. 1948) (medical history of claimant in FELA action, which was given to physician only to qualify him as a favorable witness, and not for purposes of "effecting a cure" was inadmissible); Nashville, C. & St. L. R. Co. v. York, 127 F.2d 606, 611 (6th Cir. 1942) (statements

made to physician in order to qualify him as an expert witness inadmissible). *But cf.*, Atlantic C.L.R. Co. v. Dixon, 207 F.2d 899, 903-04 (5th Cir. 1953); Chicago R. Co. v. Kramer, 234 F. 245, 251-52 (7th Cir. 1916).

[78] McCormick explains:

　　The dubious propriety of these restrictions is probably at least partially responsible for the restrictive view taken by the courts as to what constitutes consultation solely for purposes of obtaining testimony from the physician consulted. The ultimate issue is whether there was any significant treatment motive; if this existed, any additional motive of obtained testimony is ignored. For example, a physician's testimony is not within these restrictions despite the fact that he was consulted after the declarant retained an attorney or even at the attorney's recommendation. The fact that no treatment was actually given is not controlling, but subsequent reliance upon advice of a treatment nature given by the physician is strong evidence of a treatment motive for the final consultation.

McCORMICK, § 293, at 693. *But see* 4 LOUISELL & MUELLER, § 444, at 594-95.

the introduction of out-of-court statements by physicians as to the treatment prescribed or the diagnosis reached. The hearsay exception in Rule 803(4) reaches only statements of persons seeking the treatment or diagnosis.

One rationale underpinning the exception for statements made for purposes of obtaining treatment and diagnosis is that the declarant's subjective motive generally guarantees trustworthiness; the declarant has a motive to tell the truth because his treatment or diagnosis will depend upon what he says.[79] Also, there is a special need for such evidence in light of the scarcity of evidence concerning subjective symptoms.[80]

Where the out-of-court statement is made to a physician consulted as a prospective expert witness, however, the exception rests more upon considerations of practicality than enhanced trustworthiness. Under pre-Rule practice such statements were inadmissible as substantive evidence since it was thought the declarant had a motive to make self-serving statements to the prospective expert witness. Such out-of-court statements could be introduced not for the truth of the contents, but to disclose the underlying basis for a physician's in-court opinion testimony.[81] As a practical matter, however, juries tended not to accord the distinction much deference despite an appropriate limiting instruction.[82] Consequently, Rule 803(4) admits state-

---

[79] Roberts v. Hollocher, 664 F.2d 200, 204 (8th Cir. 1981). See, e.g., United States v. Narciso, 446 F. Supp. 252, 289 (E.D. Mich. 1977) ("[T]he rationale of [FRE 803(4)] is that statements made to physicians for purposes of diagnosis and treatment are exceptionally trustworthy since the declarant has a strong motive to tell the truth in order to receive proper care. Moreover, no other way of determining subjective symptoms has yet been devised."). See also McCORMICK, § 292, at 690 ("[A]lthough statements to physicians are not likely to be spontaneous, since they are usually made in response to questions, their reliability is assured by the likelihood that the patient believes that the effectiveness of the treatment he receives may depend largely upon the accuracy of the information he provides the physician.").

[80] WEINSTEIN, ¶ 803(4)[01], at 802-144 and n.9. This is in accord with a rationale supporting the exception contained in Rule 803(3) for present sense impressions because a patient's description of a present physical sensation may well be from the best source of information. See § 803.13 of this Treatise.

[81] See, generally, Aetna Life Ins. Co. v. Quinley, 87 F.2d 732, 733-34 (8th Cir. 1937) (expressing concern that if such statements were admitted for their truth, an injured person could be examined by a physician, relate his version of the facts, and then call the physician as a witness to recite the patient's account of what occurred).

[82] Advisory Committee's Note to Rule 803(4) states:

Conventional doctrine has excluded from the hearsay exception, as not within its guarantee of truthfulness, statements to a physician consulted only for the purpose of enabling him to testify. While these statements were not admissible as substantive evidence, the expert was allowed to state the basis of his opinion, including statements of this kind. The distinction thus called for was one most unlikely to be made by juries. The rule accordingly rejects the limitation.

See also O'Gee v. Dobbs Houses, Inc., 470 F.2d 1084, 1088-89 (2d Cir. 1978) (recognizing the futility of asking the jury to

ments made for the purpose of obtaining a diagnosis where the statement reveals data upon which the physician as an expert witness would be justified in relying in rendering his opinion.

The pre-Rule distinction between physicians called upon to treat a patient and those called upon in anticipation of testifying at trial resulted in the exclusion of out-of-court statements of present pain or symptoms as substantive proof of their existence because the declarant's motive to falsify or exaggerate was thought to vitiate reliability generally attending statements to treating physicians. Prior practice also limited the use of statements as to medical history to demonstrating the basis for the physician's diagnosis and treatment and they were not admitted for the truth of *past* illness, symptoms, or injury.[83] Since the underlying rationale for each of these restrictions has been superseded by modern medical and legal practices, Rule 803(4) casts aside these limitations.

§ 803.19   "Reasonably Pertinent" Requirement.

Rule 803(4) bases admissibility of statements made for purposes of obtaining medical treatment or diagnosis upon the objective standard that such hearsay declarations must be "reasonably pertinent" to the treatment or diagnosis sought. The exception consequently may operate as a vehicle for the admission of statements of medical history, past and present symptoms and conditions, past and present pain or sensations, the inception or cause of the medical condition or illness and the external causal source, if any, of the medical condition, injury or illness.

Although the "reasonably pertinent to diagnosis or treatment" standard imparts a degree of objectivity, it should be read broadly in order to give meaning to the policy supporting the exception. Generally, the physician's conclusion as to pertinency should be decisive, despite the fact that on a conceptual level it is the declarant's subjective motives which control whether or not he is truthful. In practice, the doctor's analysis assumes greater importance since the physician usually directs the course of the examination through the questions asked. Consequently, the physician's

perform the mental gymnastics required under the common law doctrine). *See, generally,* WEINSTEIN, ¶ 803(4)[01]; McCOR- MICK, § 294, at 694.

[83] Padgett v. Southern Ry. Co. 396 F.2d 303, 308 (6th Cir. 1968) (approving receipt of expert testimony by examining physician where plaintiff relied upon the advice in obtaining treatment). *See* WEINSTEIN, ¶ 803(4)[01] (Procedural rules ensure the reliability of medical testimony by giving the parties access to medical reports before trial and empowering the judge to compel a party to undergo a mental or physician examination).

solicitation of certain information indicates that the statement is reasonably pertinent to diagnosis or treatment.[84]

While statements concerning past injuries or conditions may be admitted pursuant to Rule 803(4), the pertinency standard generally operates to preclude expansion of the Rule beyond its underlying rationale by excluding statements which are clearly self-serving narrations of past events.[85] Nevertheless, the Rule should not be read as excluding details which the declarant includes as he apprises the physician of the necessary data, such as statements describing the general nature of the physical injury, the object causing the injury,[86] and the time of its occurrence.[87] Where a physi-

[84] *See* WEINSTEIN, ¶ 803(4)[01]; McCORMICK, § 292.

[85] This facet of the Rule is an expansion of pre-Rule federal law. Under prior law, such statements were restricted to present sensations of pain and did not embrace statements concerning medical history. *E.g.*, Aetna Life Ins. Co. v. Quinley, 87 F.2d 732, 733-34 (8th Cir. 1937) (if statements to a physician relating the circumstances attending an accident were admissible, "then an injured person might have himself examined by a physician called for treatment, relate to him the alleged facts with reference to the circumstances under which he received his injuries, [and] might [then] place this physician on the witness stand to narrate his version of the facts and circumstances under which he received his injuries, and not himself take the witness stand at all, and by so doing deprive the defendant of the right to cross-examination, and if he perchance employed a number of physicians, his testimony might be multiplied with impunity as far as cross-examination is concerned."). *Cf.* Petrocelli v. Gallison, 679 F.2d 286, 291 (1st Cir. 1982) (Rule 803(4) provides a basis for admitting patient statements regarding medical history or prior treatment). McCormick provides the basis for extension of the rationale supporting present physical condition to statements of past conditions:

This strong assurance of reliability has caused some courts to expand the exception to include statements made by a patient to a physician concerning past symptoms. This seems appropriate, as patients are likely to recognize the importance to their treatment of accurate statements as to past, as well as, present symptoms. Wider acceptance of this expansion might well be expected, although at present more courts would probably admit the testimony for the limited purpose of explaining the basis for the physician's conclusion than would admit it to prove the fact of the prior symptoms.

McCORMICK, § 292, at 691. *See also* Advisory Committee's Note to Rule 803(4) ("The same guarantee of trustworthiness extends to statements of past conditions and medical history, made for purposes of diagnosis or treatment.")

[86] United States v. Iron Thunder, 714 F.2d 765, 772 (8th Cir. 1983). *See also* United States v. Iron Shell, 633 F.2d 77, 81-85 (8th Cir. 1980), *cert. denied*, 450 U.S. 1001, 101 S.Ct. 1709, 68 L.Ed.2d 203 (1981) (statements made to physician who examined nine-year-old female victim of the alleged assault with intent to rape on the night of the assault, repeated by doctor at trial properly received because of the patient's strong motive to tell the truth). *Cf.* Brown v. Seaboard A. R. Co., 434 F.2d 1101, 1104 (5th Cir. 1970) (directed verdict in favor of defendant affirmed in personal injury case where only indication of defendant's negligence was in portion of medical report recorded by intern indicating that plaintiff had told the doctor that he was walking beside the train when a projection from the train struck him, causing him to fall under the train).

[87] *See* Gaussen v. United Fruit Co., 412 F.2d 72, 74 (2d Cir. 1969). *See also* Britt v. Corporation Peruana De Vapores, 506 F.2d 927, 930-31 (5th Cir. 1975) (in slip-and-fall accident, defendant introduced medical record in which plaintiff was said to have attributed his back problem to the fact that he had been pitching flour, and receipt of this record was proper; "statements made

cian is consulted about an illness, the reasonably pertinent standard usually is satisfied by declarations of the believed cause, such as exposure, consumption of certain foods or inhaling noxious fumes, and the type of symptoms, such as pain, aches, fever, nausea or dizziness.[88] Permitting the jury to hear details which the declarant naturally recites in obtaining medical treatment or diagnosis does not violate the purpose of the hearsay rule by exposing them to unreliable evidence.

Rule 803(4) does not open the door to all statements made to a physician, however. Statements concerning fault or guilt usually are not reasonably pertinent to diagnosis or treatment.[89] A declarant's statements that his injury resulted, for example, from the defendant's negligent driving, refusing to provide a safe work environment, or maintaining an unreasonably dangerous condition, are immaterial to the diagnosis and treatment of an injury, and consequently, fall outside the scope of the exception. Similarly, assertions charging that the injury was knowingly and maliciously perpetrated by the defendant are inadmissible under the Rule.[90]

for purposes of medical diagnosis or treatment which describe medical history or the general cause of an ailment are not excluded by the hearsay rule"); Pagano v. Magic Chef, Inc., 181 F. Supp. 146, 148-49 (E.D. Pa. 1960) (proper for doctor to testify that he took defendant's statement as to fainting into consideration in rendering opinion and diagnosis). McCormick provides the rationale for this extension:

The exception might be taken one step further to encompass statements made to a physician concerning the cause or the external source of the condition to be treated. In some cases the special assurance of the reliability—the patient's belief that accuracy is essential to effective treatment— also applies to statements concerning the cause, and a physician who views this as related to diagnosis and treatment might reasonably be expected to communicate this to the patient and perhaps take other steps to assure a reliable response. . . . On the other hand, when statements as to causation enter the realm of fixing fault it is unlikely that the patient of the physician regarded them as related to diagnosis or treatment. In such cases, the statements lack any assurance of reliability and would properly be excluded.

McCormick, § 292, at 691.

[88] McCormick, § 292, at 691-92. See, generally, 4 Louisell & Mueller § 444.

[89] Roberts v. Hollocher, 664 F.2d 200, 204-05 (8th Cir. 1981) (in civil rights action against police officers for damages arising out of incident which led to his requiring hospital treatment after arrest, district court properly excluded entry in hospital record which read, "multiple contusions and hematoma, consistent with excessive force;" statement was conclusion going to fault rather than the cause of the condition); United States v. Narciso, 446 F. Supp. 252, 289 (E.D. Mich. 1977) ("[FRE 803(4)] has never been held to apply to accusations of personal fault either in a civil or criminal context. Thus . . . it is stated that a statement by a patient that he was shot would be admissible, but a statement that he was shot by a white man would not." [court cites example given in Advisory Committee's Note to Rule 803(04): "[A] patient's statements that he was struck by an automobile would qualify but not his statement that the car was driven through a red light."].

[90] Compare United States v. Iron Shell, 633 F.2d 77, 83-85 (8th Cir. 1980), cert. denied, 450 U.S. 1001, 101 S.Ct. 1709, 68 L.Ed.2d 203 (1981) (admitted statements of nine-year-old female victim of alleged assault with intent to rape made in response to physician's questions concerning the cause of her injuries) with Roberts v. Hollo-

§ 803.20   By and To Whom.

Although a hearsay declaration offered under Rule 803(4) typically will have been made to the physician by the person seeking medical treatment or diagnosis, the Rule also encompasses statements made by persons who bring the patient to the hospital or doctor's office, as long as the third person's statements are made in subjective contemplation of treatment or diagnosis. This result obtains, for example, where a parent brings a child to a doctor for treatment. The admission of statements in such circumstances rests on the assumption that the declarant's action in seeking medical assistance for the patient shows concern which in turn is evidence of the sincerity of any statements made to the physician where the physician is prepared to rely upon the word of another who speaks for a patient who, for whatever reason, does not speak for himself, trustworthiness is indicated.[91] Rule 803(4) does not support admission, however, where it appears that the declarant does not have firsthand knowledge of the facts surrounding the injury and is basing his statement on pure speculation. Generally, where the relationship between the declarant and the patient is remote, the trustworthiness is less probable, not only due to the diminished incentive to tell the truth but also because a stranger may not be able to identify a patient's subjective symptoms as reliably as one who has greater familiarity with the patient.

Much the same analysis attends statements made to persons other than the treating or diagnosing physician. Rule 803(4) requires that the declarant make the statement in subjective contemplation that the statement will ultimately be relayed to a physician who will provide diagnosis or treatment. Consequently, Rule 803(4) may operate to admit hearsay declarations made to such persons as nurses, nurses' aides, interns, administrative assistants, paramedics, and ambulance drivers.[92] Likewise, where there is contemplation of medical treatment or diagnosis, the statement may be made to family members and friends, firemen, policemen, etc. Moreover, the Rule operates to admit declarations where information is passed along from one individual to another, thus raising multiple hearsay issues.[93] For

---

cher, 664 F.2d 200, 204-205 (8th Cir. 1981) (trial court properly excluded physician's diagnosis in medical record indicating patient's injuries were "consistent with excessive force;" *Iron Shell* was distinguished because in that case, there was no improper motive behind the declarations, the age of the declarant assured trustworthiness and the statements aided the doctor in limiting his examination).

[91] *See* Advisory Committee's Note to Federal Rule 803(4). *See, generally,* 4 LOUISELL & MUELLER, § 444.

[92] *See, generally,* WEINSTEIN, ¶ 803(4)[01]; Fed. R. Evid. 803(4) Advisory Committee Note.

[93] *E.g.,* O'Gee v. Dobbs Houses, Inc., 570 F.2d 1084, 1088-89 (2d Cir. 1978) (treating physician permitted to testify about not only what patient told him about her injuries, but what other doctors had told her about her injuries). *See* Fed. R. Evid. 803(4) Advisory Committee Note.

example, where the patient is found at the scene of an automobile accident and states to the attending paramedic that his jaw is in pain as a result of colliding with the steering wheel, and where this fact is passed along to the intern at the entrance of the hospital by the paramedic and then to the attending physician in the emergency room by the intern, the physician may testify to the statement at trial since the statement by the patient was made in contemplation of obtaining medical treatment and each person in the chain possessed the same purpose. Since the Rule does not limit the scope of the exception by reference to either the speaker or the listener, each statement in the chain may satisfy the exception.[94]

§ 803.21   Psychiatrists.

Difficult problems may emerge where the out-of-court statement is made in order to obtain medical aid for a mental problem. Since Rule 803(4) does not require that a statement be relevant to the declarant's physical condition, a statement directed to, for example, a psychiatrist may be within the scope of the exception. The patient's narrative ability, memory, perception or truthfulness may be impaired by his mental condition, however, and therefore considerable discretion is required.[95]

Where psychiatric treatment or diagnosis is sought, questions of relevancy and reliability may overshadow other issues arising under Rule 803(4). The trial judge has inherent discretion under Rule 403 to admit such statements only as proof of the condition complained of and not as proof of the occurrence of the related events. For example, statements made to a physician which exhibit hallucination, detachment or incoherence may be admitted as proof of the condition but may be excluded as proof of facts indicating the cause of such symptoms.

Additionally, the psychiatrist should not be permitted to become a "surrogate witness" by testifying to a party's out-of-court statements as evidence on substantive issues, particularly where the party is a criminal defendant and elects not to testify.[96] In any event, where the reliability of such a statement appears minimal, and its probative value is substantially outweighed by its unfair prejudicial impact, or its tendency to confuse or mislead the jury, the statement is subject to exclusion under Rule 403.

---

[94] *See* Rule 805 and § 805.1 of this Treatise.

[95] *See, generally* Weinstein, ¶ 803(4)[01]; McCormick, § 292, at 690 n.28.

[96] 4 Louisell & Mueller, § 444, at 612. *See* Drayton v. Jiffee Chemical Corp., 591 F.2d 352, 367 (6th Cir. 1978) (in modifying damage award to small child who was accidentally doused with and disfigured by liquid drain cleaner, court assigned a very minimal value to the psychiatric testimony, since he was consulted for trial testimony and not treatment, but did not reject the testimony altogether).

Rule 803(5)　Recorded Recollection

Rule 803(5) reads as follows:

The following are not excluded by the hearsay rule, even though the declarant is available as a witness: . . . **(5) Recorded recollection.** A memorandum or record concerning a matter about which a witness once had knowledge but now has insufficient recollection to enable him to testify fully and accurately, shown to have been made or adopted when the matter was fresh in his memory and to reflect that knowledge correctly. If admitted the memorandum or record may be read into evidence but may not itself be received as an exhibit unless offered by an adverse party.

§ 803.22　Recollection Recorded—In General.

Rule 803(5) authorizes the introduction of past recorded hearsay statements where the witness at trial no longer adequately remembers the substance of the writing.[97] The Rule is a codification of pre-existing federal law.[98] The exception, commonly referred to as "past recollection recorded," has long been recognized under the common law,[99] and its development has

---

[97] See, generally, McCormick, §§ 299-303; 4 Weinstein, ¶¶ 803(5)[01]-[03]; 4 Louisell & Mueller, §445; 3 Wigmore, §§ 735-755. See also Hutchins & Slesinger, Memory, 41 Harv. L. Rev. 860 (1928); Morgan, The Relation Between Hearsay and Preserved Memory, 40 Harv. L. Rev. 712 (1927); Note, Past Recollection Recorded: The "Forward Looking" Federal Rules of Evidence Lean Backwards, 50 Notre Dame L. Rev. 737 (1975); Comment, Hearsay Under the Proposed Federal Rules: A Discretionary Approach, 15 Wayne L. Rev. 1077, 1138-1139 (1969); Note, Past Recollection Recorded, 28 Iowa L. Rev. 530 (1943).

[98] See United States v. Kelly, 349 F.2d 720, 770 (2d Cir. 1965).

[99] McCormick briefly outlines this development in the common law:

By the middle 1600's it had become customary to permit a witness to refresh his memory by looking at a written memorandum and to testify from this then-revived memory. It often happened, however, that, although examining the writing did not bring the facts recorded back to the witness's memory, he was able to recognize the writing as one prepared by him and was willing to testify on the basis of the writing that the facts recited in it were true. By the 1700's this also was accepted as proper, although the theoretical difficulty of justifying the result was often swept under the rug by referring to it by the old term of "refreshing recollection," which clearly did not fit it. Beginning with the early 1800's, the courts came to distinguish between the two situations, and to recognize that the use of past recollection recorded was a far different matter from permitting the witness to testify from a memory refreshed by examining a writing.

McCormick, § 299, at 712. See, generally, Morgan, The Relation Between Hearsay and Preserved Memory, 40 Harv. L. Rev. 712 (1927); Note, Past Recollection Recorded: The "Forward Looking" Federal Rules of Evidence Lean Backwards, 50 Notre Dame Law, 737 (1975).

been closely linked with the evolution of the related doctrine, "refreshing recollection," now codified in part in Rule 612.

The distinction between "past recollection recorded" and "present recollection refreshed" is critical. As discussed in Chapter 612 of this Treatise,[1] the technique of refreshing recollection permits a trial witness who is unable or unwilling to recall an event to be prompted by resort to extrinsic aids, including documents, which might revive his memory. Where the memory of the witness is thereby adequately jogged, the witness proceeds to testify. Because the evidence is the trial testimony, there is no hearsay problem, and the document is not accorded evidentiary status when used pursuant to the refreshing recollection technique. Under the hearsay exception for "recorded recollection," however, the writing itself assumes evidentiary status. Where the witness is unable or disinclined to testify in conformity with an earlier recording which was made while the event was fresh in his mind, the recording itself may be introduced into evidence for the truth of the matters asserted in the writing. Consequently, under Rule 803(5) it is not the testimony of the witness, but the recorded recollection itself, which is submitted as evidence to the trier of fact.

At common law, two alternate theories existed to support the admissibility of extrajudicial statements contained in recorded recollections. Some courts treated the evidence, when offered for its truth, as hearsay but nevertheless forged the instant exception because of inherent trustworthiness. Alternatively, some courts deemed the recording to be adopted and incorporated into the present testimony of the witness, thereby eliminating the hearsay issue.[2] With either approach, however, the underlying rationales for the admission of the recorded recollection are identical, and statements of past recorded recollection traditionally have been viewed as reasonably trustworthy for three reasons: (i) while the declarant may not be cross-examined and his memory may not be tested on the precise substance of the recording (*i.e.*, because his memory is exhausted on the subject), he is otherwise available for cross-examination and a limited opportunity to test his sincerity and to uncover factors bearing upon his perceptive or narrative ability; (ii) the requirement that the recording be made while the matter was "fresh" in the mind of the declarant reduces the danger of

[1] *See* § 612.1 *et seq.* of this Treatise.

[2] Treating the statement as adopted by the witness and therefore not constituting hearsay received general acceptance in the federal system under pre-Rule practice. *See, e.g.*, Ettelson v. Metropolitan Life Ins. Co., 164 F.2d 660, 667 (3rd Cir. 1947) ("[T]his record, which he verified and adopted, thus became . . . a present evidentiary statement."); Leuders v. United States, 210 F. 419, 425 (9th Cir. 1914) ("[T]he rule is that if the witness, at or about the time the memorandum was made, knew its contents and knew them to be true, this legalizes and lets in both the testimony of the witness and the memorandum.").

failed or faulty memory at the time the statement was recorded; and, to a lesser extent, (iii) the requirement that the recording "correctly" state the facts of the matter asserted reduces to some degree the risk of ambiguity. A more pragmatic theory rests in the recognition that a contemporary, accurate record of a relevant event is inherently more trustworthy than a present recollection offered through trial testimony because the recorded recollection is more proximate in time to the event.[3] In recognition of all of the foregoing reliability factors, Rule 803(5) provides that a memorandum of recorded recollection is hearsay, but may be admissible under certain conditions stated in the Rule.

To qualify for admission under Rule 803(5), a memorandum or recorded recollection must satisfy four requirements, each of which shall be addressed separately in the following sections of this Chapter: (i) the witness-declarant must lack a present recollection of the matter recorded; (ii) the recording of the witness's recollection must "correctly" reflect the prior "knowledge" of the declarant; (iii) the recorded recollection must have been made or adopted by the witness; and (iv) the recorded recollection must have been prepared or adopted at a time when the matter in question was "fresh" in the memory of the declarant.[4] Where any of these requirements is wanting, the recording or memorandum may not be admitted under Rule 803(5), although depending upon the surrounding circumstances, the hearsay declaration may be admitted under other exceptions, *e.g.*, as a prior inconsistent statement under Rule 801(d)(1)(A), as an admission under Rule 801(d)(2), or as a business record under Rule 803(6).

§ 803.23   Requirement that Witness Lack a Present Recollection of Matter Contained in Memorandum.

Under Rule 803(5), at the time of his trial testimony, the witness must lack memory or present knowledge of the matter recorded. The requirement reflects a preference for live testimony over recorded evidence whenever the former is available. This rationale is particularly compelling where the prior statements are prepared in anticipation of litigation, and absent this requirement, lengthy argumentative documents could be pre-

---

[3] Insurance Cos. v. Weide, 81 U.S. 375, 379, 20 L.Ed. 894, 898 (1872). *See, generally*, Weinstein, ¶ 803(5)[01]; McCormick, § 299; 3 Wigmore, §§ 735-55. *See also* Advisory Committee's Note to Rule 803(5).

[4] Wolcher v. United States, 200 F.2d 493, 495 (9th Cir. 1952). *See, generally*, 4 Louisell & Mueller, § 445.

pared prior to trial which would be merely adopted by the witness as part of his testimony.[5]

Accordingly, Rule 803(5) envisions a preliminary attempt by the party presenting the evidence to refresh the witness's recollection pursuant to the provisions of Rule 612. Only if this attempt is unsuccessful may the party resort to Rule 803(5). The requirement that the witness make some demonstration of impaired memory to show that he "now has insufficient recollection to enable him to testify fully and accurately" is in part designed to discourage the indiscriminate use of self-serving statements, and consistent with this policy, the trial court must make a careful factual determination that the witness's memory is genuinely incomplete or exhausted before admitting the writing.

Since the Rule is based, at least in part, upon the assumption that a contemporary, accurate recording is likely to be more trustworthy (or suffer from fewer risks of faulty memory) than a present recollection at trial, hearsay declarations constituting recorded recollections may be admitted even if the witness still retains some knowledge of the facts. Accordingly, where the witness recalls the event in general terms but cannot describe it in detail, the Rule is sufficiently satisfied. In such cases, these details may be admitted to establish specific points that "tie up" the witness's testimony. To impose a blanket proscription against the admission of any recorded recollection in the absence of a complete failure of memory would be supported by neither the theoretical nor the pragmatic underpinnings of the exception. Where the witness recalls the matter in question in fragmented, general terms, this recollection serves to enhance the degree of

---

[5] McCormick, § 302, at 714-15, explains:

The traditional formulation of the rule, still adhered to by most courts, requires that before a past recollection recorded could be received in evidence the witness who made or recognized it as correct must testify that he lacks present memory of the events and therefore is unable to testify concerning them. If examining the writing refreshes the recollection of the witness, under this approach the writing is thus rendered inadmissible and the witness must testify from his newly refreshed recollection.

See also United States v. Felix-Jerez, 667 F.2d 1297, 1302 (9th Cir. 1982) (defendant who could speak no English was interrogated by marshal, whose questions were translated by prison guard; marshal made notes of his questions and defendant's answers as translated by guard; marshal then wrote statement from his notes; error to admit statement since there was no showing that marshal had insufficient recollection to testify); United States v. Judon, 567 F.2d 1289, 1293 (5th Cir. 1978) (admission of memorandum as an exhibit was error). *See,* *e.g.,* Baker v. Elcona Homes Corp., 588 F.2d 551, 553 (6th Cir. 1978), *cert. denied,* 441 U.S. 933, 99 S.Ct. 2054, 60 L.Ed.2d 661 (1979).

reliability in the recorded statement, not detract from it.[6] Incomplete recollection should operate to affect the weight of the evidence, not its admissibility.

Where Rule 803(5) is invoked in the context of an adverse or hostile witness, special consideration should be accorded the requirement of insufficient memory. Where the claimed lack of memory is thought to be disingenuous or evasive, application of Rule 803(5) is proper as long as the trial judge in his discretion determines from the witness's demeanor and testimony that he is not testifying "fully and accurately."[7] Where the court is satisfied that the proponent has made a good faith effort to secure live testimony and that the witness's recalcitrance is not the product of collusion with the proponent, receipt of the declaration under Rule 803(5) may be proper. Where the witness repudiates certain parts of the statement, but not others, the Rules do not direct exclusion of the entire memorandum, and the discrepancy should operate to affect credibility and weight.

§ 803.24   Requirement that Memorandum Correctly Reflect Prior Knowledge of Matter Contained Therein.

The requirement of Rule 803(5) that the writing "reflect [the witness-declarant's] . . . knowledge correctly," actually embodies two requirements, *i.e.*, prior firsthand knowledge and accuracy. In essence, the firsthand knowledge requirement dictates that the individual must have had personal knowledge of the underlying events as required by Rule 602.[8] The firsthand knowledge requirement thus aids in establishing the reliability of the statement.

The complementary requirement of Rule 803(5) that the recorded recollection accurately state the prior knowledge of the witness is obviously satisfied where the witness can currently remember making the statement (though not the underlying facts) and can testify that he carefully insured the accuracy of the recorded statement. Problems may arise in establishing accuracy, however, where the witness fails to recall not only the underlying facts or events, but also the specific occasion of the recording. Where the

[6] *E.g.*, United States v. Senak, 527 F.2d 129, 142-43 (7th Cir. 1975) (requirement satisfied where witness recalls part of conversation but cannot remember the remainder). *See also* United States v. Riley, 657 F.2d 1377, 1385-86 (8th Cir. 1981); United States v. Marcantoni, 590 F.2d 1324, 1330-31 (5th Cir. 1979). *See, generally,* WEINSTEIN, ¶ 803(5)[01].

[7] *E.g.*, United States v. Williams, 571 F.2d 344, 348 (6th Cir. 1978), *cert. denied*, 439 U.S. 841, 99 S.Ct. 131, 58 L.Ed.2d 139 (1978) (witness exercising "selective memory" and therefore court admitted portions of statement asserted as not within present recollection).

[8] *See, generally,* § 602.1 *et seq.* of this Treatise.

preparation of the writing does not involve a unique occasion, but is prepared in the routine course of personal bookkeeping or in conjunction with a business or profession and the witness can testify to the routine method of preparation, the accuracy requirement should be satisfied. A different situation is presented, however, where the witness cannot recall the preparation of the record and can testify only that he would not have signed or prepared the memorandum had he not believed it to be a true and accurate account of the event in question. In this situation, most commentators advocate admitting the statement, despite the fact that the foundation is nothing more than a general declaration of honesty which reveals little about the accuracy of the statement at issue.[9] Consequently, where the witness can attest to the statement's accuracy only by such a nominal endorsement, the trial court should approach such a statement with considerable caution in exercising its discretion.

Finally, contradiction of a declaration contained in a memorandum of recorded recollection by another witness does not preclude admission under Rule 803(5) as long as the court finds that the memorandum accurately sets forth prior personal knowledge. Such contradiction presents an issue of credibility or weight to be assessed by the trier of fact, and it does not affect the threshold question of admissibility.

§ 803.25 Requirement that Memorandum be Made or Adopted by Witness.

The third requirement under Rule 803(5), that the statement be made or adopted by the witness, is relatively uncomplicated. Where the witness has written and signed the memorandum, Rule 803(5) is unarguably satisfied. Nevertheless, this requirement mandates no specific or particular formality since the requirement is intended only to implement the fundamental concern that accuracy be assured. More specifically, this requirement of Rule 803(5) in essence corroborates the witness's assertion at trial that the account is accurate. Consequently, where the witness signed a document prepared by another or recorded the event without signing it, the instant requirement of Rule 803(5) should be satisfied. Only where the witness did

---

[9] *E.g.*, United States v. Patterson, 678 F.2d 774, 779-80 (9th Cir. 1982), *cert. denied*, 459 U.S. 911, 103 S.Ct. 219, 74 L.Ed.2d 174 (1982); Washington v. Washington, Virginia & Maryland Coach Co., 250 F.Supp. 888, 890 (D.D.C. 1966) (accident report admitted where supervisor of preparer, although having no present recollection, testified that he had read it and would have caused it to be corrected if it had misstated the facts). *See also* McCORMICK, § 303, at 71. *See, generally*, 3 WIGMORE, § 747.

not participate in preparing the prior statement in any way should it be excluded.[10]

Special problems may arise where there is joint authorship of the memorandum, *i.e.*, where one person observes the event in question and relates it to another who, in turn, records what he has been told. Under such circumstances, the resultant recording may nevertheless be admissible under Rule 803(5), where each person in the chain satisfies each requirement of the Rule. The person who observed the matter must testify that he perceived the matter and accurately related the information to another while the person who actually prepared the writing must testify that he listened and understood the statement and accurately recorded it.[11] Where, however, a person in the chain fails to testify, the issue becomes one of multiple hearsay under Rule 805, and each out-of-court statement must either be classified as non-hearsay or satisfy an exception to the hearsay exclusionary rule.[12]

§ 803.26   Requirement that Memorandum be Prepared or Adopted When "Fresh" in Declarant's Memory.

The final element in Rule 803(5) provides that the memorandum containing past recorded recollection must have been prepared or adopted when the matter contained in the writing was "fresh" in the memory of the witness.[13] The requirement of "freshness" is intended to be liberally con-

---

[10] McCORMICK, § 303, at 716. *See also* Felice v. Long Island R. Co., 426 F.2d 192, 195-96 (2d Cir. 1970), *cert. denied*, 400 U.S. 820, 91 S.Ct. 37, 27 L.Ed.2d 47 (1970) ("no adequate foundation was, or apparently could have been, laid for qualifying the note as a record of past recollection"). *See, e.g.*, Curtis v. Bradley, 65 Conn. 99, 101, 31 A. 591, 593 (1894).

[11] *See* Rule 805 and § 805.1 of this Treatise.

[12] *See, e.g.*, United States v. Williams, 571 F.2d 344, 348 (6th Cir. 1978), *cert. denied*, 439 U.S. 841, 99 S.Ct. 131, 58 L.Ed.2d 139 (1978) (rejecting contention that accused's statement prepared by government agent, then signed and sworn by accused, was not the accused's statement under Federal Rule 803(5): "By signing and swearing to the statement [the witness] adopted it.").

[13] *Compare* Maxwell's Ex'rs v. Wilkinson, 113 U.S. 656, 649, 5 S.Ct. 691, 694, 28 L.Ed. 1037, 1039 (1885) (rejecting memo-

randum prepared some twenty months after event where witness relied on his habit never to sign something false) *with* United States v. Williams, 571 F.2d 344, 347 (6th Cir.), *cert. denied*, 439 U.S. 841, 99 S.Ct. 131, 58 L.Ed.2d 139 (1978) (although statement was recorded six months after event, witness testified unequivocally that the event was still "fresh" in his memory). McCormick provides a succinct statement of the rationale underlying this requirement:

The writing must have been prepared or recognized as correct at a time close to the event. Some opinions use the older strict formulation that requires the writing to have been made or recognized as correct "at or near the time" of the events recorded. This finds some support in psychological research suggesting that a rapid rate of forgetting occurs within the first two or three days following the observation of the event. But the tendency seems to be towards accept-

strued, and it should be construed as less restrictive than either the "imme-diacy" requirement for present sense impressions under Rule 803(1) or the "spontaneity" requirement for excited utterances under Rule 803(2). The fact that the declarant has had time for reflection before recording the facts of the event does not disqualify the writing under Rule 803(5). While absolute contemporaneousness between the event recorded and the writing is not required, it may be said generally that the lesser the lapse of time between the event and the recording, the greater the degree of reliability.[14]

Courts should focus on the circumstances surrounding the event and the recording as well as the lapse of time between the two in an effort to ascertain whether the resultant memorandum is reasonably reliable. In considering "freshness" and "accuracy," a court may justifiably consider whether the event in question was so significant to the declarant that his memory probably is unaffected by the time lapse, whether the memoran-dum was prepared by the declarant himself or at his personal direction, whether it was cursorily reviewed and casually signed, and whether the recording was prepared in anticipation of litigation.[15]

§ 803.27 Procedure for Admission.

Rule 803(5) provides that a memorandum or recording of a past recollec-tion ". . . may be read into evidence but may not itself be received as an exhibit unless offered by an adverse party." The purpose of this provision is presumably to prevent the trier of fact from granting excessive weight to the writing or recording, because it generally is inextricably interwoven with and dependent upon the testimony of witnesses.[16] If the record is an electronic recording, the tape may be played to the jury during trial and transcribed in the record at that time.

ance of the formulation favored by Wigmore which would require only that the writing be made or recog-nized at a time when the events were fairly fresh in the mind of the wit-ness. No precise formula can be ap-plied to determine whether this test has been met; perhaps the best rule of thumb is that the requirement is not met if the time lapse is such, un-der the circumstances, as to suggest that the writing is not likely to be ac-curate.

McCormick, § 301, at 714.

[14] 3 WIGMORE, § 745. See Comment, Hearsay Under the Proposed Federal Rules: A Discretionary Approach, 15 WAYNE L.

REV. 1077 (1969). But see Hutchins & Sle-singer, Some Observations on the Law of Evidence: Memory, 41 HARV. L. REV. 860 (1928); Gardner, Perception and Memory of Witnesses, 18 CORNELL L.Q. 391 (1933) (suggesting passage of a few days seriously enhances risk of error).

[15] See McCormick, § 301, at 714.

[16] WEINSTEIN, ¶ 803(5)[01]; Fed. R. Evid. 803(5) Advisory Committee Note. See also Baker v. Elcona Homes Corp., 588 F.2d 551, 556 (6th Cir. 1978) (if accident report was admitted into evidence, it could not have been done so under Rule 803(5)); United States v. Judon, 567 F.2d 1289, 1294 (5th Cir. 1978). See, generally, Comment, Hearsay Under the Proposed Federal Rules:

While the writing or recording should be marked as an exhibit and lodged with the clerk to maintain a full record for appellate review, the exhibit should not be permitted in the jury room unless the adverse party so requests. Nevertheless, the Rule does not preclude re-reading portions of the transcript containing the past recorded recollection upon proper request from the jury.

Rule 803(6)   Records of Regularly Conducted Activity

Rule 803(6) reads as follows:

The following are not excluded by the hearsay rule, even though the declarant is available as a witness: . . . **(6) Records of regularly conducted activity.** A memorandum, report, record, or data compilation, in any form, of acts, events, or conditions, opinions, or diagnoses made at or near the time by, or from information transmitted by, a person with knowledge, if kept in the course of a regularly conducted business activity, and if it was the regular practice of that business activity to make the memorandum, report, record, or data compilation, all as shown by the testimony of the custodian or other qualified witness, unless the source of information or the method or circumstances of preparation indicate lack of trustworthiness. The term 'business' as used in this paragraph includes business, institution, association, profession, occupation, and calling of every kind, whether or not conducted for profit.

§ 803.28   Records of Regularly Conducted Activity—In General.

The hearsay exception embodied in Rule 803(6)[17] replaces a similar pro-

A Discretionary Approach, 15 WAYNE L. REV. 1077 (1969). This procedure received considerable criticism as not being in conformity with the principles supporting the Rule. See McCORMICK, § 299, at 712; 3 WIGMORE, § 754, at 114.

[17] See, generally, McCORMICK, §§ 304-314; 4 WEINSTEIN, ¶¶ 803(6)[01]-[09]; 4 LOUISELL & MUELLER, §§ 446-52; 3 WIGMORE, §§ 735-55; 5 WIGMORE, §§ 1517-61. See also Delroy, Flight Recordings as Evidence in Civil Litigation, 9 VAL. U.L. REV. 321 (1975); Green, The Model and Uniform Statutes Relating to Business Entries as Evidence, 31 TUL. L. REV. 49 (1956); Hale, Hospital Records as Evi-

dence, 14 S. CAL. L. REV. 99 (1941); Laughlin, Business Entries and the Like, 46 IOWA L. REV. 276 (1961); Powell, Admissibility of Hospital Records Into Evidence, 21 MD. L. REV. 22 (1961); Ray, Business Records - A Proposed Rule of Admissibility, 5 SW. L.J. 33 (1951); Comment, A Reconsideration of the Admissibility of Computer-Generated Evidence, 126 U. PA. L. REV. 425 (1977); Note, Admissibility of Computer-Kept Records, 55 CORNELL L.Q. 1033 (1970); Note, Business Records Rule, Repeated Target of Legal Reform, 36 BROOKLYN L. REV. 250 (1970); Comment, Computer Print-Outs of Business Records and Their Admissibility in New York, 31 ALB.

vision contained in the Federal Business Records Act.[18] The last phrase of the Rule, which allows an otherwise admissible record to be excluded if "the source of information or the method or circumstances of preparation indicate lack of trustworthiness" codifies pre-Rule practice but is a departure from the actual wording of the Act.[19]

The so-called "business record" exception can be traced to the common-law doctrine known as the "shop-book" rule,[20] under which the books of account of merchants, retailers, professionals and other entrepreneurs were admissible in evidence in certain limited situations. Originally, the shop-book rule applied only to merchants who kept their own books and who could prove the existence of debts only by their ledgers. Under the now obsolete common-law competency rules, there was a special need for such evidence because parties were disqualified as witnesses.[21] A distinct branch of the shop-book doctrine subsequently evolved, however, which admitted entries in a ledger recorded by a clerk who was deceased at the time of trial.[22] This later doctrine, known as the "regular entries" rule, focused more on the regularity of the entries than on the recorder. Where the books of account represented ledgers of the routine recording of transactions, purchases, sales, services, or labor, and contained original entries recorded contemporaneously with the transactions in the usual course of business, the book was admissible for the truth of its contents. Subsequent developments provided that anyone who contributed to the preparation of the document had to be produced or his absence justified.[23]

Although the common-law "regular entries" exception was appropriate for the relatively simple bookkeeping methods prevailing in a small business economy, it became increasingly unwieldy and incompatible with the

L. REV. 61 (1967); Note, *Revised Business Entry Statutes: Theory and Practice*, 48 COLUM. L. REV. 920 (1948).

[18] 28 U.S.C.S. § 1732(a)(1936). This provision was repealed when the Rules were enacted. For discussions of Rule 803(6), see 4 LOUISELL & MUELLER, §§ 446-52; 4 WEINSTEIN, ¶¶ 803(6)[01]-803(6)[07].

[19] *See, e.g.,* Palmer v. Hoffman, 318 U.S. 109, 113, 63 S.Ct. 477, 481, 87 L.Ed. 645, 649 (1943), *reh'g denied,* 318 U.S. 800, 63 S.Ct. 757, 87 L.Ed. 1163 (1943) (accident report excluded even though meeting the technical requirements of the act where it was "dripping with motivations to misrepresent"). *Cf.* Tupman Thurlow Co. v. S.S. Cap Castillo, 490 F.2d 302, 309-10 (2d Cir. 1974) (report which was normally made by defendant business should have been received where there was no indication that it

was prepared with litigation in mind); Diamond Shamrock Corp. v. Lumbermans Mutual Casualty Co., 466 F.2d 722, 727 (7th Cir. 1982) (error to exclude report of defendant where such reports were routinely prepared and there was no indication it was made to protect the party in later litigation).

[20] The genesis of the "business records" exception to the hearsay rule and its evolution to modern times in Anglo-American jurisprudence is traced in McCORMICK, § 305, at 717-19, and 5 WIGMORE, §§ 1518, 1538-44. *See also* 4 WEINSTEIN, ¶ 803(6)[01].

[21] *See, generally,* § 601.1 *et seq.* of this Treatise.

[22] McCORMICK, § 305, at 718; 5 WIGMORE, § 1518, at 153.

[23] 4 WEINSTEIN, ¶ 803(6)[01], at 803-148.

ever-expanding and changing circles of business and finance, and there emerged a host of petty rules and exceptions founded more upon expediency than upon any adherence to common-law foundational doctrines. In the context of the larger corporate forms with complex data gathering systems, it proved impracticable to account for all the persons who had participated in gathering, transmitting and entering the information contained in the records as an evidentiary means for proving a business transaction. Consequently, several efforts were made to codify a business records exception which would accommodate the diverse nature of modern business enterprises while preserving the guarantees of trustworthiness underlying the old "shop-book" rule.[24] Some of these efforts, such as the Commonwealth Fund Act and the Uniform Act concentrated primarily on relaxing common-law requirements that every participant in the gathering, transmitting and recording processes be produced or accounted for.[25]

Rule 803(6) represents the most recent effort to reformulate, modernize and codify the old shop-book rule while retaining the advantages of the prior formulations. It differs from previous formulations in that it operates to admit records of businesses not conducted for profit.[26] It expands pre-Rule law in that it is not limited to any particular type or form of record or subject of information. Accordingly, the Rule encompasses any "memorandum, report, record or data compilation," and the current exception has operated to admit a wide diversity of documents.[27]

To qualify for admission under Rule 803(6), a business record must satisfy four essential elements: (i) the record must be one regularly recorded in a regularly conducted activity; (ii) it must have been entered by a person

---

[24] E.g., The Commonwealth Fund Act, 28 U.S.C. § 1732 (1936); Uniform Business Records as Evidence Act, 9A U.L.A. 506 (1965); Model Code Rule 514. See, generally, MORGAN, ET AL., THE LAW OF EVIDENCE, SOME PROPOSALS FOR ITS REFORM, at 63 (1927); Note, Business Records Rule: Repeated Target of Legal Reform, 36 BROOKLYN L. REV. 241 (1970).

[25] 4 WEINSTEIN, ¶803(6)[01], at 803-148 through 803-157. See also Fed. R. Evid. 803(6) Advisory Committee Note.

[26] See Pittsburgh Press Club v. United States, 536 F.2d 572, 575-76 (3d Cir.), on remand, 426 F.Supp. 553 (W.D. Pa.), rev'd on other grounds, 579 F.2d 751 (3d Cir.), on remand, 462 F. Supp. 322 (W.D. Pa. 1976) (in suit by private club where issue was club's tax exempt status, court refers to club's articles of incorporation, by-laws and receipts, although making no mention of

business records exception). See, generally, 4 LOUISELL & MUELLER, § 446, at 650.

[27] See, e.g., Royal China, Inc. v. Travelers Indemnity Co., 497 F.2d 989, 992 (6th Cir. 1974) (ledger cards); United States v. Cincotta, 689 F.2d 238, 243 (1st Cir. 1982), cert. denied, 459 U.S. 991, 103 S.Ct. 347, 74 L.Ed.2d 387 (1982) (truck driver's notebook in which he recorded deliveries); United States v. Shepard, 688 F.2d 952, 953 (5th Cir. 1982) (freight bills containing handwritten notations to the effect that some of the shipment was missing); Re Aircrash in Bali, Indonesia, 684 F.2d 1301, 1315 (9th Cir. 1982) (flight training records, as proof that airline had notice of pilot's inadequacies). See, generally, 4 WEINSTEIN, ¶ 803(6)[05]; Note, Admissibility of Computer - Kept Records, 55 CORNELL L.Q. 1033 (1970).

with knowledge of the act, event or condition; (iii) it must have been recorded at or near the time of the transaction; and (iv) a foundation must be laid by the "custodian" of the record or by some "other qualified witness." Reflected in these elements is the recognition that the Rule places less emphasis on the repetitiveness and routineness of the record keeping function, emphasizing instead the fact that the record was made in conjunction with a routine of established operation or activity.

§ 803.29   Rationale.

While the original "shop-book" rule was predicated more upon necessity than upon accuracy, the later evolution of the "regular entries" exception was derived more from the policy of reliability. Under the earlier formulations of the exception, these two principles, necessity and reliability, evolved into the underlying rationale pertaining to the necessity of obtaining relevant and reliable information without the undue inconvenience of producing all the participants in the record's creation.[28] Throughout the later evolution of this doctrine, the element essential to any exception to the hearsay rule—the guarantee of trustworthiness or reliability—was presumed to be present for a variety of reasons: (i) such records are regularly checked for accuracy; (ii) the regularity and continuity of such records instill habits of precision in the preparer and custodian of the records; (iii) businesses can function only if they have accurate records and consequently businesses promote environments which ensure accuracy; and (iv) employees are generally required to prepare and maintain accurate records as part of their jobs, and they face possible embarrassment, censure or termination if they err.[29]

---

[28] *See, generally*, WEINSTEIN, ¶ 803 (6)[01].

[29] McCormick explains:

The exception is justified on grounds analogous to those underlying other exceptions to the hearsay rule. Unusual reliability is regarded as furnished by the fact that in practice regular entries have a comparatively high degree of accuracy (as compared to other memoranda) because such books and records are customarily checked as to correctness by systematic balance-striking, because the very regularity and continuity of the records is calculated to train the record-keeper in habits of precision, and because in actual experience the entire business of the nation and many other activities constantly function in reliance upon entries of this kind. The necessity for resort to these hearsay statements was manifested at common law by the requirements that the entries be used only upon a showing that the person or persons who made the entry and upon whose knowledge it was based were unavailable as witnesses because of death, insanity, disappearance or other reason. Today, the inconvenience of calling those with firsthand knowledge and the unlikelihood of their remembering accurately the details of spe-

Accordingly, Rule 803(6), like the common-law doctrines from which it evolved, rests upon the dual rationales of necessity and reliability. The Rule implicitly recognizes that modern business transactions are frequently dependent upon recorded data. This information is usually in the form of written documents or ledgers, but increasingly it is found in the memory of computers and retrievable only by means of tapes, printouts, screen displays and the like. The reliability element is especially reinforced by current commercial pressures for accuracy.

Additionally, since a business record often consists of information derived from a variety of sources, its admission pursuant to Rule 803(6) averts the need for calling all persons involved in preparing the record. As a practical matter, the Rule recognizes that if the participants in modern business transactions were called to testify, they often would be unable to do more than state matters which could be observed from the record itself due to their involvement in a large number of such transactions.

Despite the fact that some degree of "self-interest" necessarily and naturally affects any business record offered under Rule 803(6), this risk is not deemed substantial enough to disqualify it as evidence except in certain limited situations discussed in § 803.35 of this Chapter.

§ 803.30   Medical Opinions and Diagnoses.

Under pre-Rule practice, the federal courts were often reluctant to admit opinions or diagnoses contained in business records. The admission of business records was limited to those which represented an "act, transaction, occurrence, event or condition."[30] The more rigorous standard was based upon the historical suspicion of any record which might be prepared with an eye to litigation. Rule 803(6) specifically embraces opinions and diagnoses in order to make admissible those which are "incident to or part of factual reports of contemporaneous events or transactions."[31] Federal

cific transactions convincingly demonstrate the need for recourse to their written records, without regard to physical unavailability.

McCORMICK, § 306, at 720.

[30] The Model Act provided only for records of an "act, transaction, occurrence or event." 28 U.S.C.S. § 1732(a). The Uniform Act dropped "transaction and occurrence" and added "condition." 9A U.L.A. 506. See New York Life Insurance Co. v. Taylor, 147 F.2d 297, 299 (D.C. Cir. 1945) (applying the Federal Business Records Act [Model

Act]); Standard Oil Company of California v. Moore, 251 F.2d 188, 213-214 (9th Cir. 1957), cert. denied, 356 U.S. 975, 78 S.Ct. 1139, 2 L.Ed.2d 1148 (1958) ("[T]he context of § 1732, read as a whole, also indicate[s] that a writing cannot ordinarily be considered a 'memorandum or record' of an 'act, transaction, occurrence or event,' unless the recitals in such writings are factual in nature.")

[31] Forward Communication Corp. v. United States, 608 F.2d 485, 509-11 (Ct. Cl. 1979) (action for recovery of federal taxes;

courts have remained reluctant to admit records containing opinions or diagnoses which concern unusual physical conditions or psychiatric disorders.[32] Due to the subjective nature of opinions and diagnoses in these cases, physicians may reach different conclusions and therefore the trustworthiness of the records may be reduced unless the physician is in court to explain his findings and to be cross-examined.

Reports which are prepared to state or support expert opinions may be admissible provided the requirements of Rules 701-706 regarding expert testimony are met. Although such reports will not be relied upon in treating patients and therefore lack one indication of reliability, the professional standards of the expert supply an alternative guarantee of trustworthiness.[33] Moreover, the trial court retains discretion to require the preparer of the record to appear in court to testify as to his qualifications as an expert and to be cross-examined on the substance of his testimony.[34]

It should be noted that the express language of Rule 803(6) accords the trial court discretion to exclude business records which reflect untrustworthiness in preparation, a matter specifically addressed in § 803.35 of this Chapter.

---

plaintiff sought to prove valuation by proffering report by appraiser; court held that report could not be admitted where record failed to disclose qualifications or identity of appraiser, and the opinions were not incident to or part of factual reports of contemporaneous events or transactions). See also United States v. Licavoli, 604 F.2d 613, 622-23 (9th Cir. 1979), cert. denied, 446 U.S. 935, 100 S.Ct. 2151, 64 L.Ed.2d 787 (1980); Velsicol Chemical Corp. v. Monsanto Co., 579 F.2d 1038, 1048 (7th Cir. 1978).

[32] E.g., Phillips v. Neil, 452 F.2d 337, 340-49 (6th Cir. 1971), cert. denied, 409 U.S. 884, 93 S.Ct. 96, 34 L.Ed.2d 141 (1971) (receipt of hospital records offered by prosecution in rebuttal of insanity defense violated defendant's rights under the confrontation clause, since the records contained opinions and conclusions and the accused had no opportunity to confront the authors of the reports); United States v. Bohle, 445 F.2d 54, 60-66 (7th Cir. 1971), later app., 475 F.2d 872 (2d Cir. 1971) (in criminal prosecution, proper for trial judge to admit hospital records offered by defendant in support of insanity defense, since he advised the jury that they could be used only as a basis for expert opinion testimony

with respect to diagnosis of defendant's medical condition). See also Skogen v. Dow Chemical Co., 375 F.2d 692, 704-705 (8th Cir. 1967); Mullican v. United States, 252 F.2d 398, 400 (5th Cir. 1958); Lyles v. United States, 254 F.2d 725, 731 (D.C. Cir. 1957), cert. denied, 362 U.S. 943, 80 S.Ct. 809, 4 L.Ed.2d 771, and cert. denied, 368 U.S. 992, 82 S.Ct. 610, 7 L.Ed.2d 529, overruled on other grounds, United States v. Brawner, 471 F.2d 969 (D.C. Cir. 1957).

[33] See, e.g., Terrasi v. South Atlantic Lines, Inc., 226 F.2d 823, 825 (2d Cir. 1955), cert. denied, 350 U.S. 988, 76 S.Ct. 475, 100 L.Ed. 855 (1956). See also 4 Weinstein, ¶ 803(6)[06], at 803-202.

[34] Richardson v. Perales, 402 U.S. 389, 402, 91 S.Ct. 1420, 1431, 28 L.Ed.2d 842, 853 (1971) (routine, standard, unbiased medical reports by physician specialists constituted substantial evidence; claimant should have taken advantage of the opportunity afforded him under applicable regulations to request subpoenas for the physicians). See also Petrocelli v. Gallison, 679 F.2d 286, 289 (1st Cir. 1982). See § 803.35 infra for discussion of trial court's power to exclude otherwise admissible records due to untrustworthiness.

§ 803.31   Necessity that Record be Regularly Prepared and Maintained in Course of Regularly Conducted Business Activity—Scope of Business.

The first element for application of Rule 803(6) amounts to a dual condition embodying the modern concepts of a regular business-type activity and the regularity of record keeping.

In the first instance, the term "regularly conducted business activity" includes all types of commercial operations, including profit as well as non-profit institutions, *e.g.*, health, charitable, religious, and educational institutions.[35] Also included within this term would be fraternal groups, political parties, lobbying organizations, labor unions, trade and professional associations, and every variety of club or organization, as long as the routine of such bodies is characterized by the type of formality which guarantees the requisite degree of reliability. Additionally, where all other elements of the Rule are satisfied, the records of illegal enterprises are equally admissible, since the mere fact of illegality lessens neither the necessity for, nor reliability of, such records.[36] Further, while reference to a "business activity" usually suggests a venture involving more than one person, the Rule does not so provide. The Rule extends to the records of a sole proprietorship and the records of an individual who operates as an independent contractor.[37]

Records prepared and maintained by an individual concerning purely personal matters are not within the scope of the instant exception.[38] The rationale for Rule 803(6) is not satisfied in the absence of some special

[35] *See, e.g.*, United States v. Reese, 568 F.2d 1246, 1252 (6th Cir. 1977) (hospital scrapbook of newspaper clippings introduced to prove visiting hours); United States v. Sackett, 598 F.2d 739, 742-43 (2d Cir. 1979) (hospital records reflecting patient's history properly received); Stone v. Morris, 546 F.2d 730, 738-39 (7th Cir. 1976) (state prison records). *See, generally,* WEINSTEIN, ¶ 803(6)[03]; MCCORMICK, § 308, at 722.

[36] *E.g.*, United States v. Hedman, 630 F.2d 1184, 1192 (7th Cir. 1980) (notebook kept by employee of lumber company recording illegal payoffs to city building inspectors); United States v. McPartlin, 595 F.2d 1321, 1347-48 (7th Cir. 1979) (desk calendar appointment diaries kept in connection with illegal bribery scheme); United States v. Baxter, 492 F.2d 150, 164 (9th Cir. 1973), *cert. dismissed,* 414 U.S. 801, 94 S.Ct. 16, 38 L.Ed.2d 38, and *cert. denied,* 416 U.S. 940, 94 S.Ct. 1945, 40 L.Ed.2d 292 (1974) (customer book, notebook, mis-

cellaneous papers and notes kept in connection with alleged drug importing conspiracy admitted under Federal Business Records Act).

[37] *E.g.*, United States v. McPartlin, 595 F.2d 1321, 1347-48 (7th Cir. 1979) (rejecting argument that records prepared by a person for his own benefit are for that reason outside Rule 803(6); United States v. Goins, 593 F.2d 88, 91-92 (8th Cir. 1979) (memorandum made by tavern operator listing payments made to "silent or concealed partner").

[38] *See, e.g.*, Clark v. City of Los Angeles, 650 F.2d 1033, 1037 (9th Cir. 1981), *cert. denied*, 456 U.S. 927, 102 S.Ct. 1974, 72 L.Ed.2d 443 (1982) (properly excluded). *But see* United States v. Hedman, 630 F.2d 1184, 1194 (7th Cir. 1980), *cert. denied*, 450 U.S. 965, 101 S.Ct. 1481, 67 L.Ed.2d 614 (1981) (diary of employee recording payoffs made to city officials was properly admitted where such entries were made with regularity and recorder kept diary because

indicia of reliability, such as periodic checking, reliance on the records by others, or some cognizable duty to keep reliable records. Accordingly, memoranda such as those contained in diaries, shopping lists, reminder notes, phone messages, checking or savings accounts, mileage records regarding an automobile for personal use, or inventories for a hobby ordinarily do not qualify.[39] Where, however, business and personal purposes are combined in one record, receipt of the business entries under Rule 803(6) may be proper. Accordingly, a checking account containing the financial record of one self-employed is admissible to the extent those entries reflect the individual business. The same analysis would apply to cars, boats or planes used for both personal and business purposes.

In order to be admissible under Rule 803(6) the record must be one which is regularly maintained in the business. In addition, it must be shown that the record is prepared and maintained as part of the regular practice of the business.[40] This requirement is supportive of trustworthiness, and its practical impact is to exclude records prepared solely in anticipation of potential or pending litigation. This issue is more fully discussed in § 803.35 of this Treatise.

§ 803.32 Necessity of Personal Knowledge—Multiple Hearsay Problems.

The second element that must be satisfied under Rule 803(6) is that the information be provided by "a person with knowledge." This condition is rather easily satisfied; it is parallel to the firsthand knowledge requirement for testifying witnesses under Rule 602.[41] This requirement rests upon the obvious reasoning that no business record may be more reliable than its source of information.[42] The Rule's insistence that the memorandum be

he felt he might have to account for the payments); Aluminum Co. of America v. Sperry Products, Inc., 285 F.2d 911, 916 (6th Cir. 1960), *cert. denied*, 368 U.S. 890, 82 S.Ct. 139, 7 L.Ed.2d 87 (1961) (notebook of inventor admitted in patent infringement case). *See, generally*, Green, *The Model and Uniform Statutes Relating to Business Entries as Evidence*, 31 TUL. L. REV. 49, 57 (1956).

[39] 4 LOUISELL & MUELLER, § 446, at 652.

[40] *See* United States v. Davis, 571 F.2d 1354, 1359 (5th Cir. 1978) (reversible error to receive in federal evidence a federal form filled out by custodian of records of arms manufacturer Colt indicating that a certain gun had been made by Colt and shipped by it to Georgia, since there was no indication that it was the regular practice of Colt to

make such a record); Hiram Ricker & Sons v. Students Int'l Meditation Soc'y, 501 F.2d 550, 554 (1st Cir. 1974) (applying Federal Business Records Act to find that the room-check made by plaintiff's maintenance employees "was hardly the kind of regular, systematic, business activity which is encompassed by the exception").

[41] *See* discussion at § 602.1 of this Treatise.

[42] *See, e.g.*, Chaffee & Co. v. United States, 85 U.S. 516, 520, 21 L.Ed. 908, 912 (1874). *See also* United States v. Reese, 568 F.2d 1246, 1252 (6th Cir. 1977) (upholding receipt of scrapbook prepared by public relations department of hospital and containing Xerox copies of newspaper articles purporting to show visiting hours of hospital).

"made . . . by, or from information transmitted by, a person with knowledge" should, however, be liberally construed and applied. Where the actual name of the source is unknown, the record is not barred by the Rule as long as it is the regular practice of the business activity to procure the information from such employee or agent.[43]

While the source of the information must have personal knowledge, others participating in the chain of transmission of that record, including the person who ultimately causes the record to be made, need not have such knowledge. Essentially, this is a question of multiple hearsay, and where each participant in the chain of transmission is acting in the course of his regularly conducted activity, the requirement is satisfied.[44] Consequently, where the initial source of the business data has personal knowledge and each person in the chain of transmission is performing his routine function for the business concern, the record is admissible. In essence, Rule 803(6) creates a hearsay exception for each person in the chain, and the Rule requires only that the first person have personal knowledge of the facts or

---

[43] *E.g.*, United States v. Reese, 568 F.2d 1246, 1252 (6th Cir. 1977) (court rejected contention that authenticating witness was not the supervisor who oversaw the preparation of the scrapbook, since the rule embraces records made on the basis of information transmitted by a person with knowledge, and the hospital itself would qualify as such a person). *See, generally*, 4 LOUISELL & MUELLER, § 446, at 659-60.

[44] United States v. Ahrens, 530 F.2d 781, 784 (8th Cir. 1976) (personal knowledge on the part of the maker of the record is not a condition precedent to its admission under Federal Rule 803(6)); Lewis v. Baker, 526 F.2d 470, 474 (2d Cir. 1975) (fact that employee had prepared the report on basis of information given to him by fellow employee did not make report inadmissible under the Federal Business Records Act; [although the language of this exception under the Act was different from that under Rule 803(6), the opinion makes it clear the same result would obtain under the Rule.]). McCormick explains the rationale:

> Thus a business record containing an assertion by someone other than the maker should be admitted to prove the truth of that assertion only if the assertion itself comes within an exception to the hearsay rule. In most cases this involves essentially a double

application of the business records exception. First, the entry is admissible to prove the truth of what the maker knew of his own knowledge, *i.e.*, that he was told something of an informant, if the entry was made in the course of business by the maker. Second, the entry is admissible to prove the truth of what the informant told the maker only if the informant's action in reporting this was within the regular course of business, *i.e*, if the informant was a part of the business organization with a duty to make such reports. If, however, the informant's statement comes within another exception, this double application of the business entry exception is unnecessary. For example, a police report of an accident might contain an assertion made by one driver soon after the accident. The driver's statement might be an excited utterance, and the police report a business record. The police report would therefore be admissible to prove the truth of the driver's spontaneous utterance, despite the fact that the driver had no business duty to made the statement.

McCORMICK, § 310, at 725-26. *See also* 4 WEINSTEIN, ¶ 803(6)[04].

data recorded. It is critical to note, however, that each person in the chain must be an employee or agent of the business which retains the records in the regular course of its activity, *i.e.*, each person in the chain must have a business duty to report accurately to the business keeping the record. A duty to some other entity or a "civic duty" will not qualify.

Where the supplier of the information is not acting within the course of the business which retains the record, such as where a non-employee volunteers information to an employee-investigator, the multiple hearsay analysis requires a different result. In this situation, the volunteer's statement either must be defined as non-hearsay under Rule 801, or it must meet the tests of some other hearsay exception in order to admit the entire record under Rule 803(6). Rule 805 specifically admits hearsay contained within hearsay only where each statement is independently admissible. For example, a business record qualifying under Rule 803(6) might contain a statement of a volunteer embraced by Rule 803(2) which authorizes the admission of excited utterances. Here the entire document would be admissible despite the fact that the declarant of the excited utterance has no business duty to report to the business which keeps the record. Obviously, where a record prepared by one business is transmitted to another business, both records may qualify under Rule 803(6). Similarly, where the outsider's statement is defined as nonhearsay, *e.g.*, where it is offered for its impact on the listener (Rule 801(c)) or as an admission (Rule 801(d)), the source's statement is admissible where the record containing the statement was prepared in the ordinary course of business under Rule 803(6). Where the outsider's statement is not independently admissible, however, it must be excised from the record, and it is not admissible under Rule 803(6). This analysis is further amplified in Chapter 805 of this Treatise.

§ 803.33   Necessity that Record be Made Contemporaneously with Act, Event or Condition.

Rule 803(6) further requires that the transaction in question be recorded "at or near the time" of its occurrence. This element of contemporaneity, or "freshness," was required at common law, and it is intended to enhance accuracy. Like the contemporaneity requirement for past recollection recorded under Rule 803(5), the contemporaneity required here is not as strict as the "immediacy" test for present sense impressions under Rule 803(1) or the "spontaneity" test for excited utterances under Rule 803(2). Thus, entries should be admitted if they are of the type that businesses would ordinarily regard as current entries, *i.e.*, those recorded while the

matter is still fresh and reasonably verified by the memories of the participants.[45]

§ 803.34   Foundational Requirements: Custodian or Some Other Qualified Person—Rule 901(b)(1).

The final requirement of Rule 803(6) is that where a business record is offered, a foundation must first be established by the testimony of either the custodian or some other qualified person. Alternately, the foundation may be established consistent with Rule 901(b)(10), *i.e.*, pursuant to statutory means of authentication. This foundational provision requires not only that the record be identified and authenticated in accordance with Article IX of the Rules, but also that the other requirements of regular business activity, personal knowledge and contemporaneity, be shown as well.[46] Generally, the essential testimony is that of the custodian or other qualified person who can explain the record keeping practices of the organization. The phrase "other qualified person" should be broadly construed. For example, a certified public accountant or a purchasing agent who is not an employee of the entity, but understands the system used by the entity, should be qualified to testify to the foundation if he possesses firsthand knowledge of the facts supporting the requirements of Rule 803(6).[47]

[45] A substantial factor in the reliability of any system of records is the promptness with which transactions are recorded. Accordingly, all formulations of the exception for regularly kept records require that the entry be made either at the time of the transaction or within a reasonable time thereafter. Whether an entry made subsequent to the transaction has been made within a sufficient time to render it within the exception depends upon whether the time span between the transaction and the entry was so great as to suggest a danger of inaccuracy by lapse of memory. Only if such a danger appears from the circumstances of the case should the entry be held to have been made beyond the time limitation. McCormick, § 309, at 724. *See, e.g.,* United States v. Kim, 595 F.2d 755, 760 (D.C. Cir. 1979) (telex from a bank stating that defendant had deposited funds to his account was properly excluded as hearsay, since it reported deposits that took place in 1975 but was not prepared until 1977; timeliness requirement could not be waived).

See also United States v. Davis, 571 F.2d 1354, 1360 (5th Cir. 1978); Missouri Pacific Railroad Co. v. Austin, 292 F.2d 415, 419 (5th Cir. 1961). *See, e.g.,* Williams v. Humble Oil and Refining Co., 53 F.R.D. 694, 698 (E.D. La. 1971).

[46] *See, e.g.,* Norwood v. Great American Indem. Co., 146 F.2d 797, 800 (3d Cir. 1944) (hospital record admitted under Federal Business Records Act). *See also,* Stengel v. Belcher, 522 F.2d 438, 440 (6th Cir. 1975). *See, generally,* 4 Weinstein, ¶ 803(6)[02]; McCormick, § 312; 5 Wigmore, § 1530.

[47] *E.g.,* Matador Drilling Co. v. Post, 662 F.2d 1190, 1192 (5th Cir. 1981). *See also* United States v. Grossman, 614 F.2d 295, 297 (1st Cir. 1980) (retail catalogue properly received where purchasing agent testified as to "the preparation, uses, and issuance of the catalogue"); United States v. Veytia-Bravo, 603 F.2d 1187, 1191-92 (5th Cir. 1979), *reh. denied,* 607 F.2d 1006 (5th Cir. 1979), *cert. denied,* 444 U.S. 1024, 100 S.Ct. 686, 62 L.Ed.2d 658 (1979) (records prepared by arms dealer in compliance with federal regulations properly received, where agent of Bureau of Alcohol, Tobacco,

The witness providing the foundation need not have firsthand knowledge of the transaction. Rather, it must be demonstrated that the witness is sufficiently familiar with the operation of the business and with the circumstances of the record's preparation, maintenance and retrieval, that he can reasonably testify on the basis of this knowledge that the record is what it purports to be, and that it was made in the ordinary course of business consistent with the elements of Rule 803(6).[48] Where the witness fails to demonstrate this elemental knowledge, the evidence should not be admitted under Rule 803(6).[49]

§ 803.35   Exclusion Where Lack of Trustworthiness is Indicated.

Where a business record facially satisfies all the requirements of Rule 803(6), it may nevertheless be excluded on objection from the opponent where the trial court, in its discretion, determines that the source of the information or the method of its preparation indicates that the resultant record is untrustworthy.[50]

Special principles attend the admissibility of business records prepared in anticipation of litigation,[51] and courts are especially careful to scrutinize

---

and Firearms testified that the dealer had prepared the records and that they were currently in custody of the ATF).

[48] *E.g.*, Pacific Service Stations Co. v. Mobile, 689 F.2d 1055, 1058 (Em. Ct. App. 1982). *See also* United States v. Colyer, 571 F.2d 941, 943 (5th Cir. 1978), *cert. denied*, 439 U.S. 933, 99 S.Ct. 325, 58 L.Ed.2d 328 (1978) (where the witness testified that records were made and kept in regular course of business and that he was custodian of records and knowledgeable as to how they were handled, there was no violation of defendant's right to confrontation, even though person who made record did not testify); United States v. Reese, 568 F.2d 1246 (5th Cir. 1977) (no requirement that custodian had personal knowledge of the particular evidence contained in the record). *See, e.g.*, United States v. Rose, 562 F.2d 409, 411 (7th Cir. 1977); Fernandez v. Ohio Shipping Co., Ltd., 542 F.2d 145, 154 (2d Cir. 1976); United States v. Pfeiffer, 539 F.2d 668, 671 (8th Cir. 1976).

[49] *E.g.*, Karne v. Commissioner, 673 F.2d 1062, 1064 (9th Cir. 1982) (records of bank introduced by IRS agent outside Rule 803(6) since agent was not custodian and could not testify as to preparation); Calhoun v. Baylor, 646 F.2d 1158, 1162 (6th

Cir. 1981) (no error to exclude records sent to defendants where the defendant's attorney as the authenticating witness "played no role in the creation or compilation of the records and was therefore in no position to attest to their reliability"); Campbell v. Nordco Products, 629 F.2d 1258, 1264-65 (7th Cir. 1980) (accident report excluded where authenticating witness indicated that the preparer was not acting within the ordinary course of business).

[50] *See, e.g.*, Meder v. Everest & Jennings, Inc., 637 F.2d 1182, 1187 (8th Cir. 1981). *See also* Pan-Islamic Trade Corp. v. Exxon Corp., 632 F.2d 539, 541 (5th Cir. 1980), *reh'g denied*, 642 F.2d 1210 (5th Cir.) and *cert. denied*, 454 U.S. 927, 102 S.Ct. 427, 70 L.Ed.2d 236 (1980) (court did not determine if memorandum satisfied requirements of Rule 806(6) but excluded the memorandum nonetheless "because the circumstances of its preparation indicate a lack of trustworthiness"). *Cf.*, Aluminum Co. of America v. Sperry Products, Inc., 285 F.2d 911, 922-23 (6th Cir. 1960).

[51] *See, e.g.*, Mitchell v. American Export Isbrandtsen Lines, Inc., 430 F.2d 1023, 1028-29 (2d Cir. 1970) (in personal injury suit, no error to admit illness report prepared by defendant's physician who exam-

such records as accident reports because these records have proven peculiarly subject to distortion and self-interest.[52] An employee preparing an accident report to be kept by his own employer presents the most vivid illustration. Where a document generally satisfies the elements of Rule 803(6), but nevertheless was prepared in anticipation of possible use in litigation, the underlying rationale of trustworthiness is undercut.[53] In this situation the business duty to report accurately, which predominates in supporting the admissibility of business records, is feared to be, and often is, supplanted by a natural motivation of the preparer to color facts in favor of the business entity. In any case in which a subjective motivation to make self-serving statements in a business record is evident, the trial court is expressly accorded discretion under Rule 803(6) to exclude the document despite the fact that all requirements for the business record exception have been otherwise satisfied. Specifically, the Rule provides that a record satisfying the requisites of the exception is nevertheless inadmissible where "the source of information or the method or circumstances of preparation indicate lack of trustworthiness." The burden is upon the opponent of the document to show that it is sufficiently untrustworthy to warrant its exclusion.[54]

§ 803.36 Exclusion in Criminal Cases Under the Constitutional Guarantee of Confrontation.

The discretion invested in the trial court under Rule 803(6) to exclude evidence qualified as a business record which is nevertheless deemed to be

ined plaintiff where there is no motive to falsify or where surrounding circumstances negate such a motive; here, the entries were made during the course of a physician-patient relationship, and the preparing physician was testifying in court and subject to cross-examination); Lindheimer v. United Fruit Co., 418 F.2d 606, 607-08 (2d Cir. 1969) (no error to admit report prepared by defendant's Safety Committee; the test in such a case is not simply the presence of a motive to falsify, but whether the motive is checked by other factors such as purpose and practice). *See, generally,* 4 LOUISELL & MUELLER, § 447.

[52] *See, e.g.,* Koppinger v. Cullen-Schiltz & Associates, 573 F.2d 901, 907 (8th Cir. 1975) (accident report excluded in wrongful death action); Bracey v. Herringa, 466 F.2d 702, 703-05 (7th Cir. 1972) (in civil rights action by prisoner against prison guards, "conduct reports" prepared by defendants

which contained self-serving statements by defendants should be excluded; legal accountability of the guards may have affected the reports). *See also* § 803.34 of this Treatise.

[53] The leading case which is the genesis of the doctrine is Palmer v. Hoffman, 129 F.2d 976, 979 (2d Cir. 1942), *aff'd,* 318 U.S. 109, 63 S.Ct. 477, 87 L.Ed. 645 (1943). The Second Circuit opinion, Hoffman v. Palmer, 129 F.2d 976, 979 (2d Cir. 1942), is generally regarded as presenting the pertinent reasoning. *See* MCCORMICK, § 287, at 604; 4 WEINSTEIN, ¶ 803(6)[7], at 803-173-75. *See also* United States v. Smith, 521 F.2d 957, 967 (D.C. Cir. 1975) (discretion exercised; constitutional issue as to Sixth Amendment avoided).

[54] *See* Fed. R. Evid. 803(6) Advisory Committee Note. *See, generally,* 4 WEINSTEIN, ¶ 803(6)[07], at 803-204 *et seq.*

"untrustworthy" in either its preparation or maintenance is particularly required in criminal proceedings where the modern trend toward liberalizing the admissibility of hearsay evidence may not be in perfect harmony with the accused's constitutional guarantees.[55]

It must be noted that the Rules of Evidence merely provide a system for the orderly presentation of evidence at trial and, though generally applicable in criminal as well as civil proceedings, the Rules are not designed to delineate the constitutional rights of litigants. Moreover, it is clear that constitutional issues are more acute in criminal proceedings where the liberty interests of the accused are at stake and where the onus of criminal conviction is substantial. Accordingly, in the context of Rule 803(6), the trial court must remain especially cognizant that the scope of the accused's constitutional right to confront adverse witnesses is not necessarily delineated with precision by the language of the Rule, and while the Rule provides a convenient mechanism for an evidentiary scheme, it does not in itself determine the extent of the accused's right to exclude evidence based upon the right of confrontation. Consequently, evidence facially admissible under the express terms of Rule 803(6) may still be inadmissible under the Sixth Amendment.

Broad generalizations are inappropriate as to constitutional inadmissibility and, accordingly, a case-by-case scrutiny has been exercised by the courts interpreting the Sixth Amendment right of confrontation.[56] While the full scope of the constitutional restriction on use of hearsay evidence against a criminal defendant is still unclear, the key factors upon which courts will generally focus include: (i) the availability of the declarant as a witness; (ii) the extent to which the fact sought to be proven is central or peripheral to the case; (iii) whether the declarant is available and testifies, and extent to which he is subject to effective delayed cross-examination concerning his out-of-court statement; and (iv) the extent to which circum-

[55] *Compare* McDaniel v. United States, 343 F.2d 785, 789 (5th Cir. 1965) (excluding report on Constitutional grounds) *with* United States v. Peden, 556 F.2d 278, 281 (5th Cir. 1977), *cert. denied*, 434 U.S. 871, 98 S.Ct. 216, 54 L.Ed.2d 150 (1977) (while not holding that all business records do not offend confrontational rights, court finds that under the circumstances, the defendant's rights were not violated by admission of business records).

[56] *See, e.g.*, United States v. Oates, 560 F.2d 45, 79 (2d Cir. 1977) ("[C]ongress has expressed a firm intention that, if there are plausible doubts that evidence fitting within the literal terms of the hearsay exception could survive confrontational analysis, the hearsay exception should be construed with considerable flexibility so that the court can, if possible, avoid deciding this constitutional question."); United States v. Snow, 521 F.2d 730, 734 (9th Cir. 1975), *cert. denied*, 423 U.S. 1089, 96 S.Ct. 881, 47 L.Ed.2d 99 (1976) (whether evidence admissible under a co-conspirator exception must be determined on a case-by-case basis). *See also* Park v. Huff, 493 F.2d 923, 926 (5th Cir. 1974), *cert. denied*, 423 U.S. 824, 96 S.Ct. 38, 46 L.Ed.2d 40 (1975).

stantial guarantees of trustworthiness operate as an effective substitute for cross-examination.[57]

Finally, it should be noted that while the right of confrontation is vested in the accused, the prosecution may properly seek to exclude evidence otherwise qualifying under Rule 803(6) where the evidence is inherently untrustworthy.[58]

Rule 803(7)   Absence of Entry in Record Kept in Accordance With the Provisions of Paragraph (6)

Rule 803(7) reads as follows:

The following are not excluded by the hearsay rule, even though the declarant is available as a witness: . . . (7) **Absence of entry in record kept in accordance with the provisions of paragraph (6).** Evidence that a matter is not included in the memoranda, reports, records, or data compilations, in any form, kept in accordance with the provisions of paragraph (6) to prove nonoccurrence or nonexistence of the matter, if the matter was of a kind of which a memorandum, report, record, or data compilation was regularly made and preserved, unless the sources of information or other circumstances indicate lack of trustworthiness.

§ 803.37   Absence of Entry in Records of Regularly Conducted Activity— In General.

Rule 803(7) admits evidence of the absence of an entry in a record of a regularly conducted business activity.[59] It serves the simple purpose of per-

[57] *See, e.g.,* Ohio v. Roberts, 448 U.S. 56, 61, 100 S.Ct. 2531, 2536, 65 L.Ed.2d 597, 601 (1980) (admission of preliminary hearing testimony did not violate confrontation clause where declarant was unavailable at trial and preliminary hearing testimony was subjected to equivalent of cross-examination); California v. Green, 399 U.S. 149, 154, 90 S.Ct. 1930, 1936, 26 L.Ed.2d 489, 494 (1970) (if declarant is present at trial, under oath, and subject to effective cross-examination, confrontation clause is satisfied); United States v. White, 553 F.2d 310, 313 (2d Cir. 1977), *cert. denied,* 431 U.S. 972, 97 S.Ct. 2937, 53 L.Ed.2d 1070 (1977) (no violation of con-

frontation clause where declarant is dead and unavailable to both sides and statements have adequate indicia of reliability); United States v. Wigerman, 549 F.2d 1192, 1194 (5th Cir. 1977) (business records did not violate right to confrontation where they were inherently reliable, unambiguous and were used to corroborate direct evidence). *See, generally,* 4 WEINSTEIN, ¶ 803(6)[07].

[58] 4 WEINSTEIN, ¶ 803(6)[07].

[59] *See, generally,* MCCORMICK, § 307; 4 WEINSTEIN, ¶ 803(7)[01]; 4 LOUISELL & MUELLER, § 453; 5 WIGMORE, § 1531. *See also* 30 AM. JUR. 2d, *Evidence,* § 959; Uniform Rules of Evidence, Rule 63(14).

mitting a fact to be proved by the absence of an entry in the same manner and under the same conditions as Rule 803(6) permits a fact to be proved by the existence of an entry.[60] Of course, where an entry is absent, evidence to that effect may not represent hearsay at all, since the preparer of the record (*i.e.*, the declarant) may intend to make no assertion about matters not mentioned.[61] Where no assertion is subjectively intended, there can be no out-of-court statement as defined by Rule 801(a), and in the absence of a statement, no hearsay is presented.[62] Nevertheless, the subject has been addressed as an exception to the hearsay rule in order to remove any doubt and to eliminate the possibility that such evidence may be excluded.[63]

The rationale for this exception obviously mirrors the rationale supporting Rule 803(6), and the probative value of such evidence derives from similar factors.[64] The habits of precision of employees which render positive statements in such a record reliable also make the failure to mention trustworthy. In a regularly conducted business activity where a person with personal knowledge systematically prepares and maintains records at a time proximate to the occurrence of the event or transaction recorded, comprehensiveness and accuracy may be assumed. Consequently, lack of a record concerning the event is persuasive evidence of its nonoccurrence or nonexistence.

[60] *See, e.g.*, United States v. Lanier, 578 F.2d 1246, 1254-55 (8th Cir. 1978), *cert. denied*, 439 U.S. 856, 99 S.Ct. 169, 58 L.Ed.2d 163 (1978) (testimony by auditor of failure to find deposits in Federal Reserve Bank admitted); Veneri v. Draper, 22 F.2d 33, 37 (4th Cir. 1927), *cert. denied*, 276 U.S. 633, 48 S.Ct. 339, 72 L.Ed.2d 742 (1928) (bank ledger sheets admitted to show checks in question had not been charged against the account); Keith v. United States, 250 F.2d 355, 356 (5th Cir. 1957) (to show that liquor dealer had made false entries reporting sales to fictitious customers, court permitted evidence that agent was unable to locate the customers). Commentators uniformly support the introduction of such evidence. Wigmore succinctly states the rationale:

When a book purports to contain all items transacted within the scope of the book's subject, the absence of an entry of transaction of a specific purport is in plain implication, a statement by the maker of the book that no such transaction was had. The psychology of it is the same as that of testimony on the stand by a person who denies that a sound took place in

his presence because he heard no such sound. . . . The practical reliability of it is shown by every day's practice in every business house. All industry and commerce is daily conducted on the negative as well as on the affirmative showings of the regular books of entry.

5 WIGMORE, § 1531, at 463. *See also* McCORMICK, § 307, at 722.

[61] *See* Fed. R. Evid. 803(7) Advisory Committee Note.

[62] *See* § 801.2 of this Treatise.

[63] 4 WEINSTEIN, ¶ 803(7)[01], at 227-28; United States v. Lee, 589 F.2d 980, 982 (9th Cir. 1979).

[64] United States v. De Georgia, 420 F.2d 889, 893 (9th Cir. 1969) ("[R]egularly maintained business records are admissible in evidence as an exception to the hearsay rule because the circumstance that they are regularly-maintained records upon which the company relies in conducting its business assures accuracy not likely to be enhanced by introducing into evidence the original documents upon which the records are based"). *See, generally*, WEINSTEIN, ¶ 803(7)[01]; 5 WIGMORE, § 1531, at 462-63.

The final sentence of Rule 803(7) is identical to that of Rule 803(6) and should be interpreted and treated the same.[65] Where the motivation and qualification of the record keeper and the manner of recording indicate untrustworthiness, the evidence of the absence of an entry in such a record may be excluded.

§ 803.38   Foundational Requirements.

The foundational requirements for Rule 803(7) parallel those for Rule 803(6). The proponent of evidence of the absence of an entry must demonstrate that the business regularly maintained records of events or transactions like the one which was not recorded. The proponent also must demonstrate that the event or transaction not recorded was of such a nature that, had it occurred, it would have alerted the record keeper and would have been recorded immediately.

The foundations under Rule 803(6) and Rule 803(7) may differ in two significant ways. First, where Rule 803(6) expressly requires that business records be introduced by the testimony of "the custodian or other qualified witness," such language is notably omitted from Rule 803(7). Nevertheless, the custodian or another qualified witness may need to testify to satisfy the requirements of the Rule.[66] The omission probably results from the fact that, as a practical matter, the foundational requirements may be relaxed where proof of a transaction's nonoccurrence is by way of the absence of an entry in a record. Second, where proof under Rule 803(6) generally takes the form of real evidence (*e.g.*, ledgers, notebooks, etc.), proof under Rule 803(7) may take the form exclusively of testimony to the effect that an examination of the relevant records revealed no mention of the event or transaction in question. Despite this distinction, the proponent of such evidence should be prepared to produce the relevant record at trial, especially where the absence of a record is the sole means of proving the nonexistence or nonoccurrence of a fact or an event.[67]

---

[65] *See* § 803.35 of this Treatise.

[66] *E.g.*, United States v. Rich, 580 F.2d 929, 937-39 (9th Cir. 1978), *cert. denied*, 439 U.S. 935, 99 S.Ct. 330, 58 L.Ed.2d 331 (1978) ("[R]ule 803(7), which governs admission of evidence of the absence of entries in business records, does not specifically require the testimony of a custodian or another qualified witness; for the purpose of our opinion here, we assume, without deciding, that such a foundation is a necessary predicate to the admission of evidence of the entries, and that this requirement was not met").

[67] *See, generally,* 4 LOUISELL & MUELLER, § 453, at 713-16.

Rule 803(8)   Public Records and Reports

Rule 803(8) reads as follows:

> The following are not excluded by the hearsay rule, even though the declarant is available as a witness: . . . **(8) Public records and reports.** Records, reports, statements, or data compilations, in any form, of public offices or agencies, setting forth (A) the activities of the office or agency, or (B) matters observed pursuant to duty imposed by law as to which matters there was a duty to report, excluding, however, in criminal cases matters observed by police officers and other law enforcement personnel, or (C) in civil actions and proceedings and against the government in criminal cases, factual findings resulting from an investigation made pursuant to authority granted by law, unless the sources of information or other circumstances indicate lack of trustworthiness.

§ 803.39   Public Records and Reports—In General.

Rule 803(8) contains an exception to the hearsay rule applicable to records and reports prepared and maintained by public offices and agencies.[68] The Rule reflects well-settled common law[69] and legislative efforts to codify the exception,[70] although some of the Rule's provisions represent somewhat of an expansion of pre-Rule law and remain the subject of some

---

[68] *See, generally,* McCORMICK, §§ 315-17; 4 WEINSTEIN, ¶¶ 803(8)[01]-[06]; 4 LOUISELL & MUELLER, §§ 454-56; 5 WIGMORE, §§ 1630-84. *See also* Alexander, *Hearsay Exception for Public Records in Federal Criminal Trials,* 47 ALB. L. REV. 699 (1983); McCormick, *Can the Courts Make Wider Use of Reports of Official Investigations?,* 42 IOWA L. REV. 256 (1961); Note, *The Trustworthiness of Government Evaluative Reports Under Federal Rule of Evidence 803(8)(C),* 96 HARV. L. REV. 492 (1982); Note, *Scope of Federal Rule of Evidence 803(8)(C),* 59 TEX. L. REV. 155 (1980); Comment, *Admissibility of Evaluative Reports Under Federal Rule of Evidence 803(8),* 68 KY. L.J. 197 (1979); Comment, *The Admissibility of Police Reports Under the Federal Rules of Evidence,* 71

Nw. U.L. REV. 691 (1976); Comment, *Hearsay Under the Proposed Federal Rules: A Discretionary Approach,* 15 WAYNE L. REV. 1076, 1156-62 (1969); Comment, *Evaluative Reports By Public Officials — Admissible as Official Statements?,* 30 TEX. L. REV. 112 (1951).

[69] 5 WIGMORE, § 1638a, at 651 n.1. *See also* Chesapeake & Delaware Canal Co. v. United States, 240 F. 903, 907 (3d Cir. 1917), *aff'd,* 250 U.S. 193, 39 S. Ct. 407, 63 L.Ed. 889 (1919) (records of Treasury offered to prove receipts and disbursements of that Department).

[70] *E.g.,* Model Code of Evidence, Rule 516 (1942); Unif. R. Evid. 63 (16) (1953); Official Records Act, 28 U.S.C., § 1733 (1949).

dispute.[71] Under common law, investigative reports, prepared by government agencies now admitted under subdivision (C) were often rejected on the basis of the rule against opinions. Rule 803(8)(C) represents a determination by the Advisory Committee and Congress that such reports possess sufficient indicia of reliability to be presumptively admissible. Nevertheless, the Rule provides an escape provision which allows exclusion if the trial judge determines that "the sources of information or other circumstances indicate a lack of trustworthiness."[72]

The admissibility of public records was governed by the Official Records Act[73] prior to the adoption of the federal rules, except where some other specific statute applied.[74] This codification proved inadequate for two reasons. First, the statute admitted only records and reports of federal departments or agencies, and therefore severely restricted the scope of the exception. Rule 803(8) makes no distinction between federal and non-federal agencies but simply requires that the record is that of a public body.[75] Second, the statute was so narrowly worded that courts often resorted to the Federal Business Records Act exception to admit public records.[76] Consequently, even though public records are more reliable than business records, the proponent of the former had to satisfy the most foundational requirements for business records.[77] Rule 803(8) recognizes the inherent reliability of public records and so omits most foundational requirements found in Rule 803(6).

At the outset, it should be emphasized that the Rule's use of the descriptive term "public" when referring to the records embraced by the exception is actually a misnomer. The term "public" can connote simply that a record is "open to all" or "capable of being known or observed by all," as well as "made or done by a[n] officer of the government." Although each of these definitions has different connotations, the third definition indicates the general import of the Rule. A more accurate term, and one which

[71] See §§ 803.44 and 803.45 of this Chapter.

[72] See WEINSTEIN, ¶ 803(8)[01], at 803-236.

[73] 28 U.S.C., § 1733 (a) (1949). The statute provides: "Books or records of account or minutes of proceedings of any department or agency of the United States shall be admissible to prove the act, transaction or occurrence as a memorandum of which the same were made or kept." This section, by its own amendment, has been superseded by the Rules of Evidence when they apply.

[74] By virtue of Rule 802, specific statutes will continue to apply. See discussion of Rule 802 of this Treatise.

[75] See Fed. R. Evid. 803(8) Advisory Committee Note.

[76] 28 U.S.C. § 1732 (1949). See, e.g., Blanchard v. United States, 360 F.2d 318, 320 (5th Cir. 1966) (certificate of Drugs Disposal Committee of Federal Bureau of Narcotics); La Porte v. United States, 300 F.2d 878, 880 (9th Cir. 1962) (selective service file); Kay v. United States, 225 F.2d 476, 480 (4th Cir. 1958), cert. denied, 358 U.S. 825, 79 S.Ct. 42, 3 L.Ed.2d 65 (1958) (certificate of blood alcohol test prepared by state medical examiner).

[77] See § 803.34 of this Treatise.

should be engrafted into the Rule's provisions, is "official records." This term should be applied in order to avoid the uncertainty of the Rule's confusing terminology and to insure that only records of governmental instrumentalities or officers are admitted. Moreover, such a reading reflects the common law genesis of the hearsay exception codified in Rule 803(8).[78]

§ 803.40   Rationale.

The rationale underlying the exception for official reports contained in Rule 803(8) rests upon the dual grounds of necessity and reliability. The necessity principle is twofold. First, there is a high likelihood that a public official may not have independent memory respecting his action in regard to entries that are frequently little more than mechanical; consequently, proof of the fact through the record may be necessary.[79] Second, the exception avoids the inconvenience of calling to the witness stand officials who have made written hearsay statements concerning events or transactions occurring within their jurisdictions.[80] Accordingly, Rule 803(8) does not require the testimony of the custodian of the official record to testify for foundational purposes.

The further basis for this exception lies in the circumstantial guarantee of trustworthiness accorded official records. This principle is twofold as well. In the first instance, the Rule presumes that public servants are impartial and free from corruption and that they perform their official tasks carefully and promptly. Further, the Rule is predicated on the theory that an official record is necessarily subject to public scrutiny, thus exposing

[78] *See* 5 WIGMORE, § 1631, at 617. *See also* McCormick, § 315, at 735-36.

[79] *See* Wong Wing Foo v. McGrath, 196 F.2d 120, 123 (9th Cir. 1952) ("[T]he reasons for this codified exception to the hearsay rule are principally two: There is a practical necessity for the use of such records to which is attached the presumption of a proper performance of official duty; and there is a great likelihood that a public official would have no memory at all respecting his action in hundreds of entries that are little more than mechanical. A further necessity lies in the inconvenience of calling to the witness stand all over the county government officers who have made in the course of their duties thousands of similar written hearsay statements concerning events coming within their jurisdictions").

[80] McCormick explains:

A special need for this category of hearsay is found in the inconvenience of requiring public officials to appear in court and testify concerning the subject matter of their statements. Not only would this disrupt the administration of public affairs, but it almost certainly would create a class of official witnesses. Moreover, given the volume of business in public officers [offices], the official written statement will usually be more reliable than the official's present memory. For these same reasons, there is no requirement that the declarant be shown to be unavailable as a witness.

McCormick, § 315, at 736. *See also* WEINSTEIN, ¶ 803(8)[01]. *See, generally,* 5 WIGMORE, § 1631.

error in such records to prompt correction. Public scrutiny arguably supplies a further measure of reliability, since it prospectively operates as a stimulus to care and accuracy on the part of officials.[81] Also, it is likely that the routine underlying the preparation and maintenance of most official records reduces the risk of error.[82] Unlike this feature's reflection with regard to Rule 803(6) concerning business records, the concept of routine preparation has never been a foundation requirement of the official records exception. The fact remains, however, that for the vast majority of records introduced under Rule 803(8), this feature is present.

§ 803.41　Foundational Requirements—In General.

The foundational conditions for evidence introduced pursuant to Rule 803(8) are minimal. Unlike the business records exception of Rule 803(6), the official records exception does not require the testimony of the custo-

[81] The thought here is a composite one and is closely related to that which is recognized as a reason for the exception for regular entries. Where an official record is one necessarily subject to public inspection, the facility and certainty with which errors would be exposed and corrected furnishes a special and additional guarantee of accuracy. Not only would the periodic inspection by members of the public tend to produce correction of errors actually perpetrated but, chiefly, the knowledge that the record is to be open to public inspection would subjectively act in advance as a stimulus to care and sincerity on the part of the official. 5 WIGMORE, § 1632, at 620. *See* Evanston v. Gunn, 99 U.S. 660, 662, 25 L.Ed. 306, 307 (1879); United States v. Hardin, 710 F.2d 1231, 1233 (7th Cir. 1983). *See also* McCORMICK, § 315, at 735-36. Both commentators emphasize, however, that while this circumstance of "publicity" serves to insure reliability in many official records, and finds support in the common law, particularly in England, it is neither the only nor the most important basis for this hearsay exception. Were the fact of publicity most critical, a great many public records could be excluded upon a party's demonstration that, although the statement in question was "officially" recorded, it was never adequately subjected to public scrutiny. 5 WIGMORE, § 1632; McCORMICK, § 315, at 736.

[82] Wigmore provides the most cogent statement of this element:

The first reason is related in its thought to the presumption that public officers do their duty. When it is a part of the *duty of a public officer* to make a statement as to a fact coming within his official cognizance, the great probability is that he does his duty and makes a correct statement. The consideration that regularity of habit, a chief basis for the exception for regular entries, will tend to this end is not here an essential one; for casual statements, such as certificates, may be admissible, as well as a regular series of entries in a registry. The fundamental circumstance is that an official duty exists to make an accurate statement, and that this special and weighty duty will usually suffice as a motive to incite the officer to its fulfillment. The duty may or may not be one for whose violation a penalty is expressly prescribed. The officer may or may not be one from whom in advance an express oath of office is required. No stress seems to be laid judicially on either of these considerations; nor need they be emphasized. It is the influence of the official duty, broadly considered, which is taken as the sufficient element of trustworthiness, justifying the acceptance of the hearsay statement.

5 WIGMORE, § 1632, at 618 (emphasis in original). *See also* McCORMICK, § 315, at 736; 4 LOUISELL & MUELLER, § 454.

dian or other qualified witness as a pre-condition to admissibility.[83] Official records frequently are admissible without a foundation witness because the self-authentication provisions of Rule 902 obviate the need for live foundational testimony.[84] Similarly, in contrast to the exception for business records, Rule 803(8) does not require that the record be created contemporaneously with the event or transaction in question. Also, subdivisions (A) and (C) have no requirement that the record be routinely maintained. Subdivision (B) does not expressly require routine recordkeeping, but it is limited to matters observed and reported in accordance with a legal duty, and therefore it usually is successfully invoked only with respect to regularly kept records.

Under pre-Rule practice the official, *i.e.*, the declarant, must have possessed firsthand knowledge of the underlying event or transaction, although it was generally deemed sufficient if the record was based upon information received from a subordinate with personal knowledge.[85] Rule 803(8) is conspicuously silent in this regard, although nothing in Rules 803 and 804 should be construed to dispense with the requirement of personal knowledge by the declarant absent an express contrary indication. Accordingly, courts should construe Rule 803(8) in accordance with the fundamental purpose of the hearsay rule in excluding untrustworthy evidence.[86]

[83] *See* § 803.28 *et seq.* of this Treatise. *But see* Givens v. Lederle, 556 F.2d 1341, 1346 (5th Cir. 1977) (where documents offered were of questionable reliability, editor identified reports and was subject to cross-examination).

[84] *See* §§ 902.1 *et seq.* of this Treatise. *See, e.g.,* United States v. Taxe, 540 F.2d 961, 966 (9th Cir. 1976), *cert. denied,* 429 U.S. 1040, 97 S.Ct. 737, 50 L.Ed.2d 751 (1976), *reh. denied,* 429 U.S. 1124, 97 S.Ct. 1163, 51 L.Ed.2d 575 (1976) (certificate by Registrar of Copyrights admissible to prove date when sound recordings were first "fixed" and when they first became copyrightable). *See also* United States v. Harris, 446 F.2d 129, 131 (7th Cir. 1971), *cert. denied,* 404 U.S. 994, 92 S.Ct. 533, 30 L.Ed.2d 546 (1971); American Airlines, Inc. v. United States, 418 F.2d 180, 186 (5th Cir. 1969); United States v. Van Hook, 284 F.2d 489, 492-94 (7th Cir. 1961), *remanded for resentencing,* 365 U.S. 609, 81 S.Ct. 823, 5 L.Ed.2d 821 (1961), *motion denied,* 366 U.S. 915, 81 S.Ct. 1092, 6 L.Ed.2d 240.

[85] McCORMICK, § 291, at 689; Comment, *Hearsay Under the Proposed Federal Rules: A Discretionary Approach,* 15 WAYNE L. REV. 1076 (1969). At common law, the requirement of firsthand knowledge by pub-

lic officers was generally applied by reference to the scope of the officer's duty. Where the circumstances under which an official recorded a statement fell outside the scope of his lawful duty, or that of his subordinates, it was excluded. Where, on the other hand, it was clearly an official's duty to investigate and record or report irrespective of personal knowledge, the resulting statement was admitted. *See* La Porte v. United States, 300 F.2d 878, 881-82 (9th Cir. 1962) (in prosecution for failure to perform civilian duties required by Selective Service Act, form prepared by Department of Charities stating that defendant did not report for work was properly received under Official Records Act); Olender v. United States, 210 F.2d 795, 801 (9th Cir. 1954), *cert. denied,* 352 U.S. 982, 77 S.Ct. 382, 1 L.Ed.2d 365 (1957) ("the facts stated in the document must have been within the personal knowledge and observation of the recording official or his subordinates"). *See, generally,* WEINSTEIN, ¶ 803(8)[02]; 5 WIGMORE, §§ 1635-38.

[86] *See, generally,* 4 LOUISELL & MUELLER, § 455. Wigmore suggests that with respect to records of an agency's internal activities (Rule 803(8)(A)) and facts observed pursuant to a legal duty (Rule 803(8)(B)),

With respect to subdivision (C), a more flexible requirement of personal knowledge may be warranted. Reports introduced under subdivision (C), such as police accident reports and investigative field reports, will, more often than under subdivisions (A) and (B), contain conclusions based upon facts of which the investigating official has no firsthand knowledge. Investigative reports are often a necessity prepared partially on the basis of interviews after the transaction in question has occurred.[87] Although there is arguably some danger that such reports will be based in part upon unreliable or inaccurate statements made by outsiders to the government, it is assumed that the report will reflect the expertise of the agency and that the reporting official will have based his findings upon the most trustworthy information available to him.[88] In addition, it should be noted that Rule 803(8) contains an express provision which allows the trial judge to exclude reports where lack of trustworthiness is indicated.[89]

§ 803.42   Activities of Office or Agency, Rule 803(8)(A).

Subdivision (A) of Rule 803(8) admits records of a public office or agency to prove its activities. Foundational requirements for this exception are minimal, and where the record is authenticated in accordance with Article IX, it is presumed that dependable employees, acting in the course

personal knowledge of the official (or his subordinate) should be required because the official cannot fulfill his duty to carry out or supervise the transaction except so far as it is done by or before him, and thus the correlative duty to record, certify, or return involves necessarily a personal knowledge of the transaction. 5 WIGMORE, § 1635, at 633-34.

[87] See, e.g., Smith v. Ithaca Corp., 612 F.2d 215, 220-23 (5th Cir. 1980) (investigative report of Coast Guard regarding marine disaster); Moran v. Pittsburgh-Des Moines Steel Co., 183 F.2d 467, 470-71 (3d Cir. 1950) (Bureau of Mines Report on gas tank explosion). See LOUISELL & MUELLER, § 455, at 729-30; McCORMICK, § 317, at 737-38.

[88] E.g., Smith v. Ithaca Corp., 612 F.2d 215, 220-23 (5th Cir. 1980) (court admitted investigative report as trustworthy relying on "experience and expertise" of Coast Guard in investigating accidents, the timeliness of the investigation, and the impartiality of the Coast Guard); Baker v. Elcona Homes Corp., 588 F.2d 551, 559 (6th Cir.

1978), cert. denied, 441 U.S. 933, 99 S.Ct. 2054, 60 L.Ed.2d 661 (1978) (police accident report of matters observed by the officer and his factual findings; report held admissible under 803(8)(C) even though it contained findings based upon "disputed evidence," including an interview with one of the drivers involved, since that fact "no doubt had a bearing" upon the officer's conclusion). See also Robbins v. Whelan, 635 F.2d 47, 50 (1st Cir. 1981), cert. denied, 454 U.S. 1123, 102 S.Ct. 972, 71 L.Ed.2d 110 (1981).

[89] See, e.g., Dallas & Mavis Forwarding Co., Inc. v. Stegall, 659 F.2d 721, 723 (6th Cir. 1981) (not error to exclude state trooper's accident report based solely on story of biased eyewitness); Denny v. Hutchinson Sales Corp., 649 F.2d 816, 821 (10th Cir. 1981) (findings based upon ex parte hearing of Colorado Civil Rights Commission properly excluded as untrustworthy; "The lack of formal procedures and an opportunity to cross-examine witnesses are proper factors in determining the trustworthiness of the finding.").

of their official duties, prepared and maintained accurate records on the basis of trustworthy information. Further, records offered under this subdivision are not subject to any use restrictions, *i.e.*, they may be offered as proof of the matter stated in the record against either party, in both civil and criminal cases.[90]

The admission of records containing simple assertions of fact regarding the function of the official agency under subdivision (A) is the most accepted application of the doctrine. Examples of evidence admissible as proof of the activities of official agencies include: accounting records of governmental agencies;[91] dockets and journal entries of courts, legislative bodies and administrative tribunals;[92] certificates of title;[93] registry, death and birth; records of licensing agencies;[94] and records of deeds and conveyances.[95] Often, records of this sort are arguably also within the scope of subdivision (B). Nevertheless, because these records are uncomplicated and concern factual matters involving the *internal* function of the particular agency, they are likely to be accurate and thus they qualify for admission under subdivision (A). This qualification avoids the restrictions of subdivision (B) which operate in criminal proceedings.

A caveat to this generalized description of records qualifying under subdivision (A) must, however, be noted. Where the focus of the particular record is more *external* to the functioning of the agency, in that it largely concerns the activities and conduct of certain citizens, or events or transac-

---

[90] *E.g.*, United States v. Union Nacional de Trabajadores, 576 F.2d 388, 390-91 (1st Cir. 1978) (in criminal contempt prosecution, certified copy of marshal's return admitted as proof of service pursuant to Rule 803(8)(B); [However, it is clear that reliance upon (A) would have been equally appropriate]). In a criminal case where the prosecution offers official records under Rule 803(8)(A) against the accused, the defendant's Sixth Amendment right to confrontation may be violated. *See infra* note 29 and accompanying text.

[91] *E.g.*, Chesapeake & Delaware Canal Co. v. United States, 250 U.S. 193, 39 S.Ct. 407, 63 L.Ed. 889 (1919) (accounting records of Treasury Department); Howard v. Perrin, 200 U.S. 71, 75, 26 S.Ct. 195, 199, 50 L.Ed. 374, 379 (1906) (records of General Land Office); Southern Glass and Builders Supply Co., 298 F.2d 109, 111 (5th Cir. 1968) (records of Small Business Administration).

[92] *E.g.*, Debs v. United States, 249 U.S. 211, 215, 39 S.Ct. 252, 257, 63 L.Ed. 566,

569 (1919) (records of convictions); Carver v. Jackson, 29 U.S. (4 Pet.) (1830) (journals of legislature).

[93] *E.g.*, United States v. King, 590 F.2d 253, 255 (8th Cir. 1978), *cert. denied*, 440 U.S. 973, 99 S.Ct. 1538, 59 L.Ed.2d 790 (1978) (certificates of ownership of motor vehicle).

[94] *E.g.*, Seese v. Volkswagenwerk A.G., Inc. 648 F.2d 833, 845-46 (3d Cir. 1981) (motor vehicle standard of federal safety agency admitted as a "public record"); Van Bokkelen Rohr, S.A. v. Grumman Aerospace Corp., 432 F. Supp. 329, 331 (E.D.N.Y. 1977) (minutes of meeting at which licenses denied admitted under Rule 803(8) generally).

[95] *E.g.*, Coan v. Flagg, 123 U.S. 117, 123, 8 S.Ct. 47, 53, 31 L.Ed. 107, 111 (1887) (land office records); Galt v. Galloway, 29 U.S. (4 Pet.) 332, 7 L.Ed. 876 (1830) (land office); Knaggs v. Cleveland-Cliffs Iron Co., 287 F. 314, 316 (6th Cir. 1923) (deed).

tions outside the operation of the agency or office, it should not be admitted under subsection (A).[96] It is more properly to be regarded as a record reflecting a matter observed under a legal duty, and it is consequently subject to the limiting aspects of subsection (B) which obviate certain constitutional confrontation problems in criminal cases by making specified official records inadmissible against the accused.

A final caveat to the application of subdivision (A) relates to the confrontation rights of the accused in criminal cases. While the admission of records of internal governmental functions has been held not to violate the confrontation rights of the accused,[97] it is clear that a procedural rule of evidence may not supersede the Constitution. Where confrontation rights are at issue, sweeping generalizations are impossible and inappropriate, and the confrontation rights of the accused are subject to evaluation on a case-by-case basis.[98] It is thus conceivable that an official record which meets the express conditions of Rule 803(8)(A) is nevertheless inadmissible under the constitutional guarantees of confrontation. Section 803.36 of this Treatise should be consulted for a more detailed discussion of the accused's right to exclude documentary evidence under the Sixth Amendment. The discussion in § 803.36 as to business records is equally pertinent to public records.

§ 803.43   Matters Observable Under Legal Duty, Rule 803(8)(B).

Records of events or transactions within the scope of subdivision (B), which concern matters observed under a legal duty, are admissible as proof of matters external to the agency or public office.

In general, subdivision (B) is designed to embrace primarily factual records in a variety of forms, and Rule 803(8)(B) may be used as a vehicle for

---

[96] *E.g.*, Minnehaha County v. Kelley, 150 F.2d 356, 361 (8th Cir. 1945) (records of Weather Bureau containing rainfall data); La Porte v. United States, 300 F.2d 878, 880 (in prosecution for failure to perform civilian duties required by the Selective Service Act, report prepared by federal agency stating that defendant failed to report to work received under Official Records Act). *See* 4 LOUISELL & MUELLER, § 455, at 726-27.

[97] *See* Kay v. United States, 255 F.2d 476, 480-81 (4th Cir. 1958), *cert. denied*, 358 U.S. 825, 79 S.Ct. 42, 3 L.Ed.2d 65 (1958) (commenting that the Sixth Amendment to the United States Constitution and the applicable provision in the Virginia Constitution were "intended to prevent the

trial of criminal cases upon affidavits, not to serve as a rigid and inflexible barrier against the orderly development of reasonable and necessary exceptions to the hearsay rule").

[98] Chambers v. Mississippi, 410 U.S. 284, 295, 93 S.Ct. 1038, 1049, 35 L.Ed.2d 297, 309 (1973) (commenting that the right to confront and cross-examine witnesses in appropriate cases may "bow to accomodate other legitimate interests in the criminal trial process"). *See also* Dowdell v. United States, 221 U.S. 325, 334, 31 S.Ct. 590, 599, 55 L.Ed. 753, 762 (1911); Mattox v. United States, 156 U.S. 237, 243, 15 S.Ct. 337, 342, 39 L.Ed. 409, 415 (1895).

the admission of records reflecting events, transactions and conditions of almost any sort. For example, the Rule encompasses records of the United States agencies or armed forces,[99] and records of state agencies, bureaus and administrative bodies,[1] including police report and hospital records. Some of these records (or portions thereof) may qualify as well under subdivision (A). Where, however, the clear focus of the report is on facts and circumstances *external* to the agency, qualification under either Rule 803(8)(B) or Rule 803(8)(C) is required for its admission. Although Rule 803(8)(B) operates to admit factual information contained in an accident report, such as a description of the scene and the degree of damage, subdivision (C) controls to the extent that the report contains evaluations of causation or fault or other statements requiring interpretation of data.[2]

Three foundational requirements are imposed for admission of official records pursuant to Rule 803(8)(B). First, the governmental employee or agent who supplies the information must have firsthand knowledge of the event or condition described in the report.[3] Second, the source must be under a legal duty to report the information.[4] And third, the official agency must have a legal obligation to prepare and maintain the record, as

---

[99] *E.g.*, Evanston v. Gunn, 99 U.S. 660, 662, 57 S.Ct. 791, 25 L.Ed. 306, 307 (1978) (meteorological observations of U.S. Signal Service); Minnehaha County v. Kelley, 150 F.2d 356, 361 (8th Cir. 1945) (U.S. Weather Bureau rainfall data); United States v. Van Hook, 284 F.2d 489, 491 (7th Cir. 1960), *remanded for resentencing*, 365 U.S. 609, 81 S.Ct. 823, 6 L.Ed.2d 240 (1960) (letter from induction officer to District Attorney, pursuant to army regulations stating refusal to be inducted); United States v. Meyer, 113 F.2d 387, 389 (7th Cir. 1940), *cert. denied*, 311 U.S. 706, 61 S.Ct. 174, 59 L.Ed. 129 (1940) (map of government engineer based upon information supplied by those working under his supervision).

[1] *See* De Pinto v. Provident Security Life Insurance Co., 374 F.2d 37, 40 (9th Cir. 1967) (report of state insurance examiner of Arizona admitted under Federal Business Records).

[2] *See, e.g.*, Baker v. Elcona Homes Corp., 588 F.2d 551, 559 (6th Cir. 1978), *cert. denied*, 441 U.S. 933, 99 S.Ct. 2054, 60 L.Ed.2d 661 (1979) (automobile collision report by police officer); Fraley v. Rockwell International Corp., 470 F. Supp. 1264, 1266 (S.D. Ohio 1979) (naval office's report on air crash); Colvin v. United States, 479 F.2d 998, 1002 (9th Cir. 1973)

(report of criminal investigator of Bureau of Indian Affairs describing scene of accident admitted under Official Records Act).

[3] *Cf.* United States v. Perlmutter, 693 F.2d 1290, 1292 (9th Cir. 1982) (reversible error to admit exhibit listing alleged convictions where there was no indication that person who signed the exhibit had firsthand knowledge of conviction or was under any legal duty to record convictions). *But see* United States v. Hudson, 479 F.2d 251, 253-56 (9th Cir. 1972), *cert. denied*, 414 U.S. 1012, 94 S.Ct. 377, 38 L.Ed.2d 250 (1973) (rule requiring firsthand knowledge does not apply where subordinate with firsthand knowledge reports to the recorder).

[4] *Cf.* Wetherill v. University of Chicago, 518 F. Supp. 1387, 1390 (N.D. Ill. 1981) (government report excluded where it was based on several non-official sources who had "no duty imposed by law" to report). Under pre-Rule law, reports made by private persons pursuant to a statutory duty were sometimes admissible, *e.g.*, Sternberg Dredging Co. v. Moran Towing and Transport Co., Inc., 196 F.2d 1002, 1004 (2d Cir. 1952). However, the status and scope of this "exception" to the requirement is unclear. *See* MORGAN, BASIC PROBLEMS OF EVIDENCE, 318 (1962); WEINSTEIN, ¶ 803(8)[02], at 803-239 to 803-242.

the term "duty" implies. The second and third requirements should not be construed so as to require that an express duty be imposed by statute or regulation, but only that the nature of the agency's responsibilities be such that the record in question is of the type routinely or regularly prepared.[5] On the other hand, the personal knowledge requirement should be more carefully applied, especially where persons from outside the agency may contribute critical information, a situation raising problems of multiple hearsay.[6] The admissibility of investigatory reports is addressed in detail in § 803.44 of this Chapter.

§ 803.44   Special Problem: Admissibility of Investigative Reports.

Rule 803(8)(C) provides an exception for reports containing "factual findings resulting from an investigation made pursuant to authority granted by law." While subdivisions (A) and (B) have ample support in pre-Rule law, subdivision (C) has been the subject of considerable controversy. Two problems have arisen regarding the admissibility of "evaluative" reports: 1) whether the preparer must have possessed personal knowledge of the underlying facts, and 2) what determinations constitute "factual findings." The former problem is discussed in connection with foundational requirements in § 803.41 of this Chapter. To re-emphasize an earlier point, the fact that the findings contained in the report are based in part on hearsay should not in itself render the findings so untrustworthy as to be inadmissible.[7] In interpreting subdivision (C), it should be recognized that the intent of the drafters was to assume admissibility in the first instance

[5] See White v. United States, 164 U.S. 100, 107, 17 S.Ct. 38, 44, 41 L.Ed. 365, 371 (1896) (record of county jailer properly received to prove that certain prisoner was there on a particular day; court notes that the requirement that the agency be legally required to keep the record does not demand that the duty be required by statutes; it is sufficient if the duty was required of the maker by his superior officer if it is necessary to the proper functioning of the office).

[6] See, Colvin v. United States, 479 F.2d 998, 1003 (9th Cir. 1973) (Official Records Act does not embrace records containing statements that are not within the personal knowledge of the recording official or his subordinates).

[7] See Hodge v. Seiler, 558 F.2d 284, 288 (5th Cir. 1977) (in housing discrimination suit, "Final Investigation Report" of HUD property received against defense contention that it was hearsay; court noted that Rule 803(8)(C) makes such reports admissible.); Zenith Radio Corp. v. Matsushita Electric Industrial Co., 505 F. Supp. 1125, 1147-48 (E.D. Pa. 1980) (in determining trustworthiness of administrative agency's evaluative report, court stated that "[t]he fact that the findings were based in part on hearsay or on confidential sources . . . does not ipso facto render the findings so untrustworthy as to be inadmissible," yet the court concluded that "when hearsay dominates, the report may be excluded."); United States v. Amer. Tel. & Tel. Co., 498 F. Supp 353, 364 (D.D.C. 1980) ("[T]he multiple hearsay issue is reducible to one of the trustworthiness of the factual findings.")

but provide an escape provision for cases in which the court determines that the report is not sufficiently reliable.[8] Judge Weinstein suggests that "[i]f the trial judge finds that the particular expert in question would not have relied upon facts not directly observed by him, unless he, in the light of his experience, knew them to be trustworthy, the report should not be rejected on the ground of lack of personal knowledge."[9]

While the conclusions of a report based on hearsay are generally admissible under Rule 803(8)(C), the hearsay statements themselves, to the extent they appear in the report, are not admissible pursuant to this exception.[10] This seemingly inconsistent treatment is explained by the reliance of subdivision (C) on the skill of agency officials in sorting reliable from unreliable statements as they prepare public reports. Of course, where the hearsay statements which form the basis of an official report independently satisfy a distinct hearsay exception, the statements are admissible for their truth under a multiple hearsay theory.[11]

Whether "factual findings" indicate only facts rather than conclusions or opinions is a matter of some dispute. The House Judiciary Committee, in approving the Rule added the caveat that the phrase should be "strictly construed and that evaluations or opinions contained in public reports shall not be admissible under this Rule."[12] However, the Senate Judiciary Committee strongly dissented from this narrow interpretation for two reasons. First, several statutes, preserved by Rule 802, admit evaluative reports of various kinds, thus indicating congressional support for the admission of evaluative reports. Second, the Advisory Committee found "evaluative" reports sufficiently reliable to be included within the provision, providing ample safeguards if they appear unreliable.[13]

---

[8] *See* Fed. R. Evid. 803(8) Advisory Committee Note.

[9] 4 Weinstein, ¶ 803(8)[03], at 803-249.

[10] *See* McKinnon v. Skil Corp., 638 F.2d 270, 278 (1st Cir. 1981). *See also* John McShain, Inc. v. Cessna Aircraft Co., 563 F.2d 632, 635-36 (3d Cir. 1977) (accident reports submitted to the National Transportation Safety Board were properly excluded as hearsay because Rule 803(8) exempts from the rule only reports by officials, and the government investigator's reports often contained statements by witnesses "which would make such memoranda encompass double hearsay"; elimination of these hearsay statements from the reports would have led to unwarranted delay and waste of time).

[11] Federal Aviation Admin. v. Landy, 705 F.2d 624, 632-33 (2d Cir.), *cert. denied*, 104 S.Ct. 243 (1983) (in action to impose civil penalties for violation of FAA regulations, telex by German government to FAA was properly admitted as incorporated in the FAA's factual findings resulting from an investigation made pursuant to authority granted by law). *See also* Baker v. Elcona Homes Corp., 588 F.2d 551, 559 (6th Cir. 1978), *cert. denied*, 441 U.S. 933, 99 S.Ct. 2054, 60 L.Ed.2d 661 (1978).

[12] H.R. Rep. No. 93-650, 93d Cong., 1st Sess. 14 (1973).

[13] S. Rep. No. 93-1277, 93d Cong., 2d Sess. 18 (1974).

In addition, as discussed in connection with Rule 701, it is impossible to draw a clear line between fact and opinion.[14] Moreover, it was not the intent of the drafters to contract the scope of reports admitted prior to the Rule under the business records exception.[15] Consequently, it seems relatively clear that reliable reports falling within subdivision (C), although containing conclusions or opinions, should normally be admissible, and the weight of authority so holds.[16]

§ 803.45   Use Restrictions on Public Records and Reports in Criminal Cases, Rule 803(8)(B) and Rule 803(8)(C).

Rule 803(8)(B), in contrast to Rule 803(8)(A), imposes a restriction in criminal cases upon the use of records or reports from "police officers or other law enforcement personnel" containing matters observed pursuant to official duty. Although the wording of Rule 803(8)(B) suggests such reports cannot be used by either the prosecution or defense, it is clear from the legislative history of the clause that Congress was only concerned with protecting the right of the accused to confront and cross-examine witnesses.[17] Under a broad definition of "law enforcement personnel," reports

[14] See, e.g., American Airlines, Inc. v. United States, 418 F.2d 180, 196 (5th Cir. 1969) (in affirming the lower court's admission of an investigating committee's report, the court noted that the report, while based upon factual information, contained a "sophisticated evaluation of the data"; however, the court disapproved of Fidelity and Casualty Co. of New York v. Frank, 222 F. Supp. 948 (D.C. Conn. 1964) which distinguished "between 'factual' testimony by investigators and 'evaluation, opinion or conclusion evidence' that is objectionable . . . . Because of the uncertainty which the Frank rule would introduce in sorting fact from opinion, it would be better to exclude opinion testimony only when it embraces the probable cause of the accident or the negligence of the defendant.") See also 4 WEINSTEIN, ¶ 803(8)[03], at 803-250 to 803-251.

[15] See, generally, 4 WEINSTEIN, ¶ 803(8)[01].

[16] E.g., Melville v. American Home Assur. Co., 443 F. Supp. 1064, 1112-15 (E.D. Pa. 1977), reversed on other grounds, 584 F.2d 1306 (3d Cir. 1978) (trial court admitted Federal Aviation Administration's Airworthiness Directives, which impinged mechanical safety of model of plane involved in lawsuit); Lloyd v. American Export Lines, Inc., 580 F.2d 1179, 1183 (3d Cir. 1978), cert. denied, 439 U.S. 969, 99 S.Ct. 461, 58 L.Ed.2d 428 (1978) (decision and order of Coast Guard hearing examiner finding should have been admitted); United States v. School Dist., 577 F.2d 1339, 1341 (6th Cir. 1979), on remand, 460 F.Supp. 352 (E.D. Mich. 1978) (findings of HEW Hearing Examiner were factual findings and should have been admitted); Miller v. New York Produce Exchange, 550 F.2d 762, 769 (2d Cir. 1977), cert. denied, 434 U.S. 823, 98 S.Ct. 68, 54 L.Ed.2d 80 (1977) (trial court did not err in admitting official document concerning cottonseed oil transactions, which also contained some conclusive statements about prices and a commodity squeeze); United States v. Smith, 521 F.2d 957, 964-65 (D.C. Cir. 1975) (error to exclude police report offered by defendant to prove a statement made by the victim, who testified at trial). See also 4 LOUISELL & MUELLER, § 455, at 740-41.

[17] See discussion of legislative history contained in United States v. Oates, 560 F.2d 45, 67-72 (2d Cir. 1977), on remand, 445 F. Supp. 351, aff'd without opinion, 591 F.2d 1332 (2d Cir. 1977). See 4 WEINSTEIN, ¶ 803(8)[04], at 803-258.

such as ballistics analyses, blood-alcohol tests and analyses of purported illegal substances could be excluded under this restriction, and at least one court has so construed the provision.[18] In *United States v. Oates*, the court defined "law enforcement personnel" to include "at the least, any officer or employee of a governmental agency which has law enforcement responsibilities."[19] In *Oates*, the Court concluded that the full-time chemists of the United States Customs Service clearly fall within that definition and therefore, the chemist's report and worksheet prepared in connection with the analysis of a substance alleged to be heroin could be excluded under the 803(8)(B) restriction.[20]

Other courts, however, have concluded that the restrictive language of subsection (B) is not an absolute bar to all public records offered by the government against the accused in criminal cases. In one line of cases, the courts have found that the Rule's restriction pertaining to "police officers" and "law enforcement personnel" does not encompass the entire group of public officials who perform investigatory work and who prepare and maintain official records.[21] Even though many government employees may, to a limited extent, have some indirect law enforcement responsibilities, the restriction should not be construed so broadly as to include records only remotely concerned with police and law enforcement operations. This exception to the restriction of subdivision (B) rests upon the theory that, "[i]n adopting this exception, Congress was concerned about prosecutors attempting to prove their case in chief simply by putting into evidence police officers' reports of their contemporaneous observations of crime."[22]

A related "exception" to the restriction of 803(B) has operated to admit reports found to be of routine and non-adversarial nature.[23] In *United*

---

[18] *E.g.*, United States v. Oates, 560 F.2d 45, 75 (2d Cir. 1977); *on remand*, 445 F. Supp. 351 (E.D.N.Y. 1978), *aff'd without opinion*, 591 F.2d 1332 (2d Cir. 1978).

[19] *Id.* at 68.

[20] *Id.*

[21] *E.g.*, United States v. Hansen, 583 F.2d 325, 327 (7th Cir. 1978), *cert. denied*, 439 U.S. 912, 99 S.Ct. 283, 58 L.Ed.2d 259 (1978). *See also* United States v. Union Nacional de Trabajadores, 576 F.2d 388, 390 (1st Cir. 1978) (United States marshal's return stating that he had served injunction was admissible under Rule 803(8), since sheriffs' returns were admissible at common law and there was no indication of Congressional intent to overrule the common law rule); United States v. Arias, 575 F.2d 253, 254-55 (9th Cir. 1978), *cert. denied*, 439 U.S. 868, 99 S.Ct. 196, 58 L.Ed.2d 179 (1978) (in perjury prosecution, transcript

from proceedings in which defendant had allegedly perjured himself was admitted in evidence, through testimony by court reporter who prepared it). *But see* United States v. Ruffin, 575 F.2d 346, 355-56 (2d Cir. 1978) (computer print-out of an IRS record is inadmissible against a criminal defendant).

[22] United States v. Grady, 544 F.2d 598, 604 (2d Cir. 1976). *See, generally*, 4 WEINSTEIN, ¶ 803(8)[04]; 4 LOUISELL & MUELLER, § 455, at 756-57.

[23] *E.g.*, United States v. Hernandez-Rojas, 617 F.2d 533, 535 (9th Cir. 1980), *cert. denied*, 449 U.S. 864, 101 S.Ct. 170, 66 L.Ed.2d 81 (1980) (no error in admitting warrant of deportation, which contained notation of previous deportation; "this court has looked to the purpose of the law enforcement exception in determining admissibility"); United States v. King, 590

States v. Orozco,[24] the court concluded that Congress intended the restriction to exclude such reports only where the circumstances surrounding the official's observation were of such an adversarial nature as to indicate unreliability. Although the court concluded that a customs inspector was an official within the meaning of subdivision (B), the court found the "simple recordation of license numbers of all vehicles which pass his station is not of the adversarial confrontation nature which might cloud his perception."[25] When the matter observed, however, is non-routine or adversarial in nature, the record containing the matter may not be used against the accused at trial under the express terms of subdivision (B).

Subdivision (C) prohibits the use of evaluative reports against the accused under any circumstances. Unlike subdivision (B), the operation of subdivision (C) is not affected by who made the report, and it excludes even routine or non-adversarial reports. This exclusion is predicated on the recognition that admission in such cases would almost necessarily involve a collision with the confrontation rights of the accused.[26] Conversely, subdivision (C) expressly allows the introduction of investigative reports in civil cases and against the government in criminal cases.

It should be noted that the exclusion pertaining to reports of police officers and law enforcement personnel under subdivision (B) does not contain language expressly permitting the introduction of such reports against the government by the accused. However, subdivision (B) has been read to authorize admission at the request of the defendant.[27]

The potential overlap between subdivisions (B) and (C) should be apparent. To the extent that a report offered against an accused is characterized as one containing "matters observed" under subdivision (B), it may nevertheless be admitted by some courts under the theory that either the preparer does not fall within the class of "other law enforcement personnel" or that the report was of a routine and non-adversarial nature. However, a report characterized as purely evaluative under subdivision (C) will be excluded pursuant to the absolute use restriction contained therein. This problem of classification becomes particularly acute in the case of official laboratory reports such as ballistics analyses, blood-alcohol tests and analyses of suspected drugs. While such reports have traditionally been admissi-

F.2d 253, 255 (8th Cir. 1978), *cert. denied*, 440 U.S. 973, 99 S.Ct. 1538, 59 L.Ed.2d 790 (1979) (certified documents of Missouri Department of Revenue showing that defendant was owner of car were admissible). *See also* United States v. Grady, 544 F.2d 598, 601 (2d Cir. 1976).

[24] 590 F.2d 789, 793 (9th Cir. 1979).
[25] *Id.* at 793.
[26] *See* Fed. R. Evid. 803(8) Advisory Committee Note.
[27] United States v. Smith, 521 F.2d 957, 968 (D.C. Cir. 1975) (Rule 803(8) "appears to overlap rather than diminish 803(6)").

ble,[28] some post-Rule authority interpreting Rule 803(8) has concluded that official laboratory reports fall within subdivision (C) and are, therefore, absolutely inadmissible against the accused in a criminal case.[29] This position of inadmissibility is arguably supported by the construction of the Rule as well as policy considerations. Laboratory reports will, in the great majority of cases, contain more information of an evaluative nature than information merely reflecting "matters observed." Furthermore, there is ample support for the proposition that laboratory reports are susceptible of considerable error which will often not be evident from the face of the document.[30]

Arguments in favor of admitting certain evaluative reports have stressed three points: first, the existence of an improper motive on the part of the preparers of such reports is unlikely since they will ordinarily be scientists and technicians unconcerned with the impact of the report in a particular case; second, obtaining live testimony would involve considerable cost; and third, little would be gained from live testimony since it would most likely rest upon the reports rather than present memory.[31]

It is yet unclear whether the decisions will come to a consensus on the proper analysis of laboratory reports under Rule 803(B) and (C). A proposal set forth by Professor Imwinkelried in his study of the constitutional limitations of admitting laboratory reports may be helpful in interpreting Rule 803(8): Where the accused can establish "that more likely than not the conclusion expressed in the report is so evaluative that it could be the subject of varying expert opinion," the report should be inadmissible "as direct evidence of an essential element of the crime" charged against the accused.[32] Such an analysis would save the government the cost and inconvenience of calling the expert preparer in every instance while enabling the accused to exclude the report where the conclusion of the report is disputed.

As a caveat it should be emphasized once again that the Rules of Evidence are not necessary determinants of constitutional rights, and the limiting aspects of subdivisions (B) and (C) may not be a complete delineation

---

[28] *See, e.g.,* United States v. Stern, 519 F.2d 521, 523 (9th Cir. 1975), *cert. denied,* 423 U.S. 1033, 96 S.Ct. 565, 46 L.Ed.2d 407 (1975); United States v. Fratini, 501 F.2d 1234, 1237 (2d Cir. 1974); Sanchez v. United States, 293 F.2d 260, 263 (8th Cir. 1961); Kay v. United States, 255 F.2d 476, 479 (4th Cir. 1958). *See also* Imwinkelried, *The Constitutionality of Introducing Evaluative Laboratory Reports Against Criminal Defendants,* 30 HAST. L.J. 621, 623 (1979).

[29] *See* United States v. Oates, 560 F.2d 45, 75 (2d Cir. 1977), *on remand,* 445 F. Supp. 351 (E.D.N.Y. 1978), *aff'd without opinion,* 591 F.2d 1332 (2d Cir. 1978).

[30] Imwinkelried, *supra* note 59, at 637.

[31] 4 LOUISELL & MUELLER, § 455, at 754.

[32] Imwinkelried, *supra* note 59, at 647.

of those official records which are inadmissible against the accused under the Sixth Amendment. In certain situations the Constitution may demand a broader exclusion.[33] This issue is more fully discussed in § 803.36 of this Treatise, and the analysis in § 803.36 as to business records is equally pertinent to public records.

Finally, it should be noted that the limiting aspects of Rules 803(8) may not be circumvented by introducing a public record under Rule 803(6) which pertains to records of regularly conducted activity.[34] Such circumvention would obviously result in a perversion of the intent and policy of the Rules.

§ 803.46   Trustworthiness.

Rule 803(8) contains a "trustworthiness" clause identical to that of the Rule 803(6) under which the trial court may exclude an official record or report which otherwise satisfies the requirements of the Rule on the ground that the circumstances surrounding the source of the information or the manner of its recording indicate an unusual degree of unreliability.

It is uncertain, however, whether the qualifying phrase refers only to subdivision (C), as its syntax might suggest, or whether it also qualifies those records offered under subdivisions (A) and (B). The Advisory Committee's Note strongly suggests that the special consideration of trustworthiness applies only to subdivision (C).[35] Nevertheless, the better approach would view all official records as subject to this qualification in the same fashion as are business records under Rule 803(6)[36] because it is unreasonable to assume that records offered under subsections (A) and (B) are inherently free from problems of untrustworthiness.[37] In any event, the oppo-

---

[33] See, e.g., Dutton v. Evans, 400 U.S. 74, 89, 91 S.Ct. 210, 223, 27 L.Ed.2d 213, 228 (1970) (suggesting a "reliability" requirement for hearsay exceptions); Barber v. Page, 390 U.S. 719, 723-24, 88 S.Ct. 1318, 1322-23, 20 L.Ed.2d 255, 258-59 (1968) (suggesting that the confrontation clause requires the proponent to demonstrate the unavailability of the declarant). See, generally, Dow, Criminal Hearsay Rules: Constitutional Issues, 53 Neb. L. Rev. 425 (1974).

[34] See United States v. Orozco, 590 F.2d 789, 793 (9th Cir. 1975), cert. denied, 442 U.S. 920, 99 S.Ct. 2845, 61 L.Ed.2d 288 (1979) ("while governmental functions would be included within the broad defini-

tion of 'business' in Rule 803(6), such a result is obviated by Rule 803(8), which is the 'business records' exception for public records such as those in issue here").

[35] See Fed. R. Evid. 803(8) Advisory Committee Note.

[36] See § 803.28 et seq. of this Treatise.

[37] See 4 Louisell & Mueller, § 456. See, e.g., United States v. Orozco, 590 F.2d 789, 793 (9th Cir. 1979), cert. denied, 442 U.S. 920, 99 S.Ct. 2845, 61 L.Ed.2d 288 (1977) (although admitting receipt of customs records under Rule 803(8)(B), court suggests that records could be excluded if circumstances indicate lack of trustworthiness).

nent of such evidence bears the burden of proving the untrustworthiness of the record once its proponent meets the foundational requirements.[38]

The Advisory Committee's Note to Rule 803(8) sets forth four considerations which may be helpful in determining the trustworthiness of records offered under the Rule: (1) the timeliness of the investigation,[39] (2) the special skill or experience of the official,[40] (3) whether a hearing was held and the level at which it was conducted,[41] and (4) possible motivational problems such as those suggested by *Palmer v. Hoffman.*[42] As the Advisory Committee's Note suggests, the list is not exhaustive of the factors which may bear upon the trustworthiness of a particular record and the courts have appropriately undertaken a case-by-case analysis of trustworthiness.[43] Accordingly, even where one or more of the above factors has suggested

---

[38] *See* Melville v. American Home Assur. Co., 443 F. Supp. 1064, 1112-15 (E.D. Pa. 1978), *reversed on other grounds*, 584 F.2d 1306 (3d Cir. 1978); United States v. Taxe, 540 F.2d 961, 966 (9th Cir. 1976), *cert. denied*, 429 U.S. 1040, 97 S.Ct. 737, 50 L.Ed.2d 751 (1976), *reh. denied*, 429 U.S. 1124, 97 S.Ct. 1163, 51 L.Ed.2d 575 (1976); Securities & Exchange Comm. v. General Refractories Co., 400 F. Supp. 1248, 1250 (D.D.C. 1975).

[39] *See, e.g.*, Smith v. Ithaca Corp., 612 F.2d 215, 220-23 (5th Cir. 1980); Baker v. Elcona Homes Corp., 588 F.2d 551, 559 (6th Cir. 1978), *cert. denied*, 441 U.S. 933, 99 S.Ct. 2054, 60 L.Ed.2d 661 (1978). *See also* McCormick, *Can the Courts Make Wider Use of Reports of Official Investigations?*, 42 IOWA L. REV. 363 (1957).

[40] *See, e.g.*, Baker v. Elcona Homes Corp., 588 F.2d 551, 559 (6th Cir. 1978), *cert. denied*, 441 U.S. 933, 99 S.Ct. 2054, 60 L.Ed.2d 661 (1978); Walker v. Fairchild Industries, 554 F. Supp. 530, 532 (D. Nev. 1982); Fraley v. Rockwell International Corp., 470 F. Supp. 1264, 1266 (S.D. Ohio 1979). *Cf.* Sage v. Rockwell International Corp., 477 F. Supp. 1205, 1206-07 (D.N.H. 1979) (lack of experience of investigator goes only to weight, not admissibility).

[41] *See, e.g.*, United States v. Corr, 543 F.2d 1042, 1050-51 (2d Cir. 1976) (erroneously suggesting that SEC document lies outside Rule 803(8)(C); court found document to have but "minimal" relevance). *See also* Franklin v. Skelly Oil Co., 141 F.2d 568, 570 (10th Cir. 1944).

[42] See discussion of Palmer v. Hoffman, 318 U.S. 109, 63 S.Ct. 477, 87 L.Ed.2d 645 (1943), *reh'g denied*, 318 U.S. 800, 63 S.Ct. 757, 87 L.Ed.2d 1163 (1943) at § 803(6).1 n.2 of this Treatise. *See also* Abdel v. United States, 670 F.2d 73, 76 (7th Cir. 1982); Dallas & Mavis Forwarding Co. v. Stegall, 659 F.2d 721, 723 (6th Cir. 1981); Robbins v. Whelan, 653 F.2d 47, 50 (1st Cir. 1981), *cert. denied*, 454 U.S. 1123, 102 S.Ct. 972, 71 L.Ed.2d 110 (1981); United States v. Stone, 604 F.2d 922, 925-26 (5th Cir. 1979).

[43] Re Complaint of Paducah Towing Co., 692 F.2d 412, 420-21 (6th Cir. 1982) (findings resting largely on hearsay could be excluded; court finds, however, that objecting party did not show untrustworthiness); Meder v. Everest & Jannings, Inc., 637 F.2d 1182, 1187-88 (8th Cir. 1981) (reversible error to receive police accident report where testifying officer could not recall the source of his information, parties could not recall the source of his information, parties could not otherwise test the reliability of the report, and the substance of the report was contradicted by eye witness testimony); United States v. Orozco, 590 F.2d 789, 793 (9th Cir. 1979), *cert. denied*, 439 U.S. 1049, 99 S.Ct. 728, 58 L.Ed.2d 709, *and cert. denied*, 442 U.S. 920, 99 S.Ct. 2845, 61 L.Ed.2d 288 (1979) (receipt of computer records showing license numbers of cars crossing Mexican-American border proper where the recording procedure was simple and the recording officer had opportunity to correct mistakes as the numbers were entered).

inadmissibility in a particular case, the record has nevertheless been admitted where special guarantees of trustworthiness have been present.[44]

As indicated by the discussion of subdivision (C) contained in §§ 803.44 and 803.45, special problems of admissibility may attend evaluative reports offered under the Rule. In *Zenith Radio Corp. v. Matsushita Electric Industrial Co.*,[45] the district court examined three additional factors which may be particularly relevant to the trustworthiness of evaluative reports: (1) the finality of the findings, (2) the extent to which the report is based upon hearsay or confidential sources, and (3) the possibility that the report reflects the agency's desire to further preconceived policy objectives, thus tainting the objectivity of the findings.[46]

Rule 803(9)   Records of Vital Statistics

Rule 803(9) reads as follows:

The following are not excluded by the hearsay rule, even though the declarant is available as a witness: . . . **(9) Records of vital statistics.** Records or data compilations, in any form, of births, fetal deaths, deaths, or marriages, if the report thereof was made to a public office pursuant to requirements of law.

§ 803.47   Records of Vital Statistics—In Conjunction with Statute and Other Rules.

Rule 803(9) creates a hearsay exception for public records relating to births, fetal deaths, deaths, and marriages.[47] It allows the contents of such records to be introduced as substantive evidence, thereby facilitating the proof of a wide variety of information, such as the date, time, place of birth, and identity of parents; date, time, and cause of death; date and place of marriage and the parties thereto.

[44] *E.g.,* United States v. School Dist., 577 F.2d 1339, 1341 (6th Cir. 1979), *on remand*, 460 F. Supp. 352 (E.D. Mich. 1978) (error to exclude administrative findings of HEW in school desegregation suit despite contention that school district lacked subpoena power at hearings and there was no evidence that hearing examiner possessed any special expertise; court found these to be suitable considerations but found that circumstances indicated overall trustworthiness of the proceedings).

[45] 505 F. Supp. 1125 (E.D. Pa. 1980).

[46] *Id.* at 1147-49.

[47] *See, generally,* McCormick, §§ 319-20; 4 Weinstein, ¶¶ 803(9)[01]-[02]; 4 Louisell & Mueller, § 457; 5 Wigmore, §§ 1674-1684. *See also* Comment, *Hearsay Under the Proposed Federal Rules: A Discretionary Approach*, 15 Wayne L. Rev. 1077, 1162-65 (1969).

The proponent of the record must establish that the report was made to a public office pursuant to requirements of law, and in this respect, the Rule relies heavily on existing state statutory reporting requirements.[48] Accordingly, Rule 803(9) should be read in conjunction with the applicable state statute as well as with Rule 902(4) and Rule 1005. Such records are self-authenticating if the certification is in accordance with the requirements set forth in Rule 902(4).[49] Alternatively, such records may be authenticated by a method provided in Rule 901, for example, by a witness who has compared the copy with the original and testifies that the record is what it is claimed to be. The two methods of authentication are acknowledged by Rule 1005 which permits certified copies of public records to be introduced in lieu of the original in order to prove the contents.[50] By virtue of the foregoing provisions, the foundational requirement of Rule 803(9) (*i.e.*, that the report was made to a public office pursuant to requirement of law) may be met, for example, by introducing the copy of a record made pursuant to the provisions of a state statute and certified in compliance with Rule 902(4).

Two problems may arise in fulfilling the requirements that the report be made pursuant to requirements of law. First, a state law may not have a requirement that the matter be reported. Second, the pertinent statute may even require that the matter involved be excluded from the report or that certain reported matters be excluded from evidence at trial.[51]

Regarding matters that are not required to be reported, the court should determine whether the exempted matter is related so closely to the required matters that it fulfills the purpose of the exception. In situations where the omitted facts would logically be mentioned in the report, their exclusion from the statute should be given little weight.[52]

Matters which the state statute requires to be excluded from the report or from evidence at trial are more problematic. Such matters may only involve a legislative judgment as to the proper scope of the hearsay exception, in which case, the judgment may be considered by the court in determining the matter's reliability, but should not be taken as binding on the

---

[48] State statutes relating to this requirement are collected in 5 WIGMORE, § 1644.

[49] Under Rule 902(4), copies of public records are certified in accordance with provisions (1), (2) or (3) of Rule 902 or "any Act of Congress or rule prescribed by the Supreme Court pursuant to statutory authority." *See* Fed. R. Evid. 902(4) Advisory Committee Note and Chapter 902 of this Treatise.

[50] Fed. R. Evid. 1005 and Advisory Committee Note.

[51] *E.g.*, Woodward v. United States, 167 F.2d 774, 779 (8th Cir. 1948) (under Missouri law physician had a duty *not* to record information regarding paternity if birth was illegitimate); Pollack v. Metropolitan Life Ins. Co., 138 F.2d 123, 127-28 (3d Cir. 1943) (birth certificate admitted to show age of parents even though state law did not require this to be recorded).

[52] 4 LOUISELL & MUELLER, § 457, at 786.

court any more than any other state hearsay rule which differs from the pertinent Federal Rule.[53] However, the exclusion by the state statute may reflect a legislative judgment regarding some substantive policy. In this situation, exclusion of the matter in deference to the state statute and its limits may well be justified.

An example of a statutory provision reflecting a substantive legislative judgment is a statute which forbids the recording of information about the paternity of an illegitimate child.[54] Such a prohibition may represent a legislative judgment as to the reliability of the matter as well as reflecting a worthy social policy. In cases where the statute and the Rule appear to be at variance, the court should determine the purpose sought to be achieved by the law and, unless the law merely represents an attempt to regulate the receipt of hearsay, the court should give the state statute considerable weight in determining admissibility.

§ 803.48   Rationale.

The rationale underlying the exception for records of vital statistics rests upon the familiar factors of necessity and reliability. The necessity principle is twofold. First, vital statistics regarding events such as births and marriages may become significant only in litigation occurring long after the event, and locating those who witnessed the event may be difficult. Further, those witnesses who are found will not likely have even traces of memory. Second, requiring direct testimony about such events would significantly inconvenience those called as witnesses without any corresponding benefit to the integrity of the fact-finding process.[55]

The trustworthiness principle is satisfied for four reasons: First, vital statistics are recorded by professionals in the performance of both their public and professional duty. Second, such statistics normally involve relatively uncomplicated facts, and their recording is ordinarily substantially contemporaneous with the event, thus minimizing the risks of faulty perception and memory. Third, since these events are fairly important to those who report them, it may safely be assumed that those involved will make

---

[53] See Pollack v. Metropolitan Life Ins. Co., 138 F.2d 123, 127-28 (3d Cir. 1943) (described in note 5, supra).

[54] E.g., Woodward v. United States, 167 F.2d 774, 779-80 (8th Cir. 1948) (statute prohibited any information in birth certificate relating to paternity if the birth was illegitimate).

[55] See 4 LOUISELL & MUELLER, § 457, at 777-78. See, generally, 5 WIGMORE, § 1631; McCORMICK, § 315; 4 WEINSTEIN, ¶ 803(9)[01]. See, e.g., Charleston Nat'l Bank v. Hennessy, 404 F.2d 539, 540 (5th Cir. 1968) ("use of the certificate is a convenience . . . to require the official to be called from his public duties to testify may be inconvenient to him, the court, and the public").

an effort to be truthful. Finally, vital statistics will often be prepared before litigation is contemplated, and therefore the prospect of intentional misstatement by the reporter is reduced.[56]

§ 803.49 Foundation.

As previously discussed in § 803.47 of this Chapter, records of vital statistics will often be self-authenticating, and accordingly, Rule 803(9) requires no foundational testimony of the custodian or other qualified witness as a pre-condition to admissibility. The Rule requires only that the report be made to a public office pursuant to requirements of law.[57]

Likewise, Rule 803(9) should not be interpreted as requiring firsthand knowledge by the recording official on every point contained in the report.[58] In some instances, the certifying officer will have personal knowledge of the event recorded or certified, such as where a notary acknowledges that the signatory has personally appeared before him, or where a certificate of marriage is prepared by the person performing the ceremony.[59] However, where certificates require information such as the age, identity or address of the person involved, the certifying officer will ordinarily lack firsthand knowledge of those matters and should be allowed to rely on hearsay declarations of those present and concerned. As a practical consideration, requiring firsthand knowledge of the recording official on such matters would virtually destroy the utility of the exception.[60]

§ 803.50 Application.

Federal case law illustrates the manner in which public records may be used to establish a variety of facts. For example, court records may be used

---

[56] *See, generally,* 4 LOUISELL & MUELLER, § 457, at 777-78.

[57] See 4 WEINSTEIN, ¶ 803(9)[01], at 803-280.

[58] *Id.* at 220. The author concludes that in accordance with pre-Rule federal case law, Rule 803(9) should not be limited to statements based on firsthand knowledge, even though the general notes to Rule 803 state that the Rule does not dispense with such a requirement.

[59] Charleston Nat'l Bank v. Hennessy, 404 F.2d 539, 540 (5th Cir. 1968) ("written official statements, which include certificates officially required to be made, are to some extent recognized as exceptions to the rules prohibiting hearsay assertions. There is a tendency to trustworthiness because the certificate is made by a public officer while carrying out his required duty and because the document is available for public inspection.").

[60] 5 WIGMORE, § 1646 ("If we are to insist with pedantic strictness upon the entrant's personal knowledge, it will be found that the registers [of birth, marriage and death] will cease to be of much practical service for any purpose.").

to establish the date or place of marriage.[61] A birth certificate may be offered as proof of the fact of birth, the date of birth,[62] and the identity of the parents.[63] Likewise, a death certificate may be introduced to prove the fact, date, time and place of death.[64] Death certificates may also be introduced to prove the cause of death or the duration of an illness.[65]

However, in the latter two instances, special consideration should be given to the character of the contents of the report and the qualifications of the person making the report. For instance, where it is disputed whether the decedent died as the consequence of a fall or from a brain tumor, as listed on his death certificate, the certificate should be admitted only where the maker possessed the necessary expertise to make such a distinction.[66] Likewise, where the onset of the decedent's fatal illness is in dispute, statements contained in the certificate as to the probable duration of the illness should be admitted only if made by a qualified physician.[67]

Frequently, a death certificate will state not only the physical or medical cause of death but will also state facts which may be relevant to determinations of fault or criminal liability. For instance, statements that the decedent committed suicide, or that he died as a result of an accident or homicide may be contained in the certificate. While coroners and physicians are

[61] E.g., Williams v. Butterfield, 145 F. Supp. 567, 568 (E.D. Mich. 1956), aff'd, 250 F.2d 127 (6th Cir.), reh'g denied, 253 F.2d 709 (1957), and cert. denied, 356 U.S. 946, 78 S.Ct. 793, 2 L.Ed.2d 821 (1957), reh'd denied, 356 U.S. 970, 78 S.Ct. 1009, 2 L.Ed.2d 1076 (1957) (court approved receipt of record of marriage of plaintiff, asserting that plaintiff had been born in Pennsylvania, to set aside deportation order).

[62] E.g., United States v. Austrew, 202 F. Supp. 816, 822 (D. Md. 1962), aff'd per curiam, 317 F.2d 926 (4th Cir. 1962) (birth certificate used to prove that girl was under eighteen).

[63] E.g., Williams v. Butterfield, 145 F. Supp. 567, 568 (E.D. Mich. 1956), aff'd, 250 F.2d 127 (6th Cir.), reh'g denied, 253 F.2d 707 (1957), cert. denied, 356 U.S. 946, 78 S.Ct. 793, 2 L.Ed.2d 821 (1957), reh'g denied, 356 U.S. 970, 78 S.Ct. 1009, 2 L.Ed.2d 1076 (1957) (court approved receipt of marriage license indicating that plaintiff's parents were married in Great Britain).

[64] E.g., Aetna Life Ins. Co. v. Mitchell, 180 F. Supp 674, 678 (D. Pa. 1960) (court received certified copies of coroner's report indicating time that husband and wife were

shot; certificate was admissible, even though it was open to contradiction and not binding upon the jury).

[65] E.g., Minyen v. American Home Assurance Co., 443 F.2d 788, 791 (10th Cir. 1971) (court upheld the introduction of a death certificate, which stated that death was caused by a brain tumor); Meth v. United Ben. Life Ins. Co., 198 F.2d 446, 447 (3d Cir. 1952) (no error to receive death certificate prepared by attending physician which stated that "the interval from the onset of illness to the date of death was two years"); Hunter v. Derby Foods, Inc., 110 F.2d 970, 972-73 (2d Cir. 1940) (proper to receive death certificate prepared by coroner on basis of autopsy, listing as the cause of death "accident - eating canned meat - enteritis with an acute nephritis"). See also Weiner v. Metropolitan Life Ins. Co., 416 F. Supp. 551, 557-58 (E.D. Pa. 1976); Cropper v. Titanium Pigment Co., 47 F.2d 1038, 1044-45 (8th Cir. 1931).

[66] See 4 LOUISELL & MUELLER, § 457, at 780-82.

[67] See Meth v. United Ben. Life Ins. Co., 198 F.2d 446, 447 (3d Cir. 1952) (death certificate as evidence of onset of illness). See also 5 WIGMORE, § 1671, at 804.

ordinarily not qualified to draw such conclusions, this may be required as part of the official's duties. Most courts have approved receipt of statements of this nature in appropriate circumstances.[68]

Although death certificates containing statements regarding fault may be admitted under Rule 803(9), such a report may also fall under Rule 803(8)(C).[69] Where the report is offered as evidence against the accused in a criminal prosecution, it will be inadmissible under 803(8)(C). In other contexts, a report falling within both exceptions should be excluded if "sources of information or other circumstances indicate lack of trustworthiness." When the record sought to be admitted speaks in terms of legal conclusions of the sort described above, and it was not prepared by a public official to bring it within the purview of Rule 803(8), the terms of Rule 803(9) would appear to determine admissibility. While Rule 803(9) does not contain a provision for discretionary exclusion if lack of trustworthiness is indicated, as does 803(8)(C), there is authority for the proposition that in the latter situation, the court should nonetheless consider whether circumstantial guarantees of trustworthiness are lacking in ruling on admissibility.[70]

Finally, it should be emphasized that the Rules of Evidence cannot operate as determinants of constitutional rights, and in criminal matters, introduction of a record pursuant to Rule 803(9) could operate to deny rights of confrontation. The accused's confrontation rights are more fully discussed in this Treatise in conjunction with Rules 803(6) and 803(8).

Rule 803(10)　Absence of Public Record or Entry

Rule 803(10) reads as follows:

The following are not excluded by the hearsay rule, even though the declarant is available as a witness: . . . **(10) Absence of public record or entry.**

---

[68] See, e.g., Shell v. Parrish, 448 F.2d 528, 530-31 (6th Cir. 1971) (error for trial court to delete language in death certificate that "victim fell in open ditch"); Metropolitan Life Ins. Co. v. Butte, 333 F.2d 82, 83-84 (10th Cir. 1964) (error to exclude city physician's statement in death certificate that decedent "died a suicide as the result of carbon monoxide poisoning"); Thomas v. Conemaugh & B.L.R. Co., 234 F.2d 429, 433-34 (3d Cir. 1956) (no error to receive coroner's death certificate as proof of cause of death).

[69] See § 803.45 of this Treatise.

[70] See, Charleston Nat'l. Bank v. Hennessy, 404 F.2d 539, 540 (5th Cir. 1968) (in personal injury suit, dispute over whether decedent died of a heart attack prior to being injured in an automobile accident; no abuse of discretion for trial court to delete from death certificate the statement that decedent "apparently had a heart attack"; the coroner was a layman without medical training and there was no evidence showing him to be qualified as an expert on causes of death). See also 4 Louisell & Mueller, § 457, at 782-83.

To prove the absence of a record, report, statement, or data compilation, in any form, or the nonoccurrence or nonexistence of a matter of which a record, report, statement, or data compilation, in any form, was regularly made and preserved by a public office or agency, evidence in the form of a certification in accordance with Rule 902, or testimony, that diligent search failed to disclose the record, report, statement, or data compilation, or entry.

§ 803.51   Absence of Public Record or Entry—In General.

Rule 803(10) admits evidence of the absence of a public record or entry in order to prove either the absence of certain documents or the nonexistence or nonoccurrence of a matter regarding which there would normally be a public record.[71] The Rule is similar in effect to the provisions of Rule 803(7), which governs proof of the absence of an entry in the records of a regularly conducted business activity. The discussion of Rule 803(7) at § 803.37 *et seq.* of this Treatise should be consulted for further pertinent analysis.

Under pre-Rule law, evidence to prove the absence of a public record,[72] the nonexistence,[73] or the nonoccurrence[74] of a matter normally recorded by a public official was similarly admissible. In continuation of this practice, Rule 803(10) operates, for example, to allow proof that a person

---

[71] *See, generally*, McCormick, §§ 319-320; 4 Weinstein, ¶ 803(10)[01]; 4 Louisell & Mueller, § 458; 5 Wigmore, § 1633. Wigmore explains the rationale underlying this exception:

Since the assumption of the fulfillment of duty is the foundation of the exception, it would seem to follow that if a duty exists to record certain matters when they occur, and if no record of such matters is found, then the *absence of any entry* about them is evidence that they did not occur; or, to put it another way, the record, taken as a whole, is evidence that the matters recorded, and those only, occurred.

5 Wigmore, § 1633, at 624 (emphasis in original).

[72] *See* United States v. Sussman, 37 F. Supp. 294, 296 (D.C. Pa. 1941) (proof of the absence of registration certificate in SEC files).

[73] *See* United States v. Rich, 580 F.2d 929, 937-38 (9th Cir. 1978), *cert. denied*, 439 U.S. 935, 99 S.Ct. 330, 58 L.Ed.2d 331 (1978) (in prosecution for bank robbery, defendant alleged that on the day in question, he had loaned his car, which had been seen at the bank, to a certain individual; court properly allowed testimony by FBI official that he had searched various official records and had found no trace of the alleged borrower; [although the trial court erred in admitting the testimony because of foundation inadequacy, court affirms, noting that the defendant failed to object to the foundation]).

[74] Jackson v. United States, 250 F.2d 897, 900-01 (5th Cir. 1958) (in prosecution for filing false claim for benefits as serviceman's widow, FBI official permitted to testify that a search of public records of defendant's county revealed no record that defendant and deceased had ever been divorced).

claiming to be a personal envoy of the president was, in fact, never employed as a personal representative of the president.[75]

§ 803.52   Foundation and Authentication Requirements.

Rule 803(10) requires that in order to utilize the negative inference arising from the absence of a public record, a proponent of the evidence must establish that a diligent search failed to disclose the public record or entry.[76] This may be shown either by testimony or by introduction of a certification prepared in accordance with Rule 902.[77]

Under pre-Rule law, testimony of the custodian of the records,[78] as well as testimony of a private citizen,[79] was admissible. However, at common law proof of the absence of an entry in a record was not permitted by the introduction of the certification of the custodian.[80] Rule 803(10) admits

---

[75] See T'Kach v. United States, 242 F.2d 937, 938 (5th Cir. 1957) (in prosecution for falsely representing oneself to be an officer and employee of the United States, affidavit of personnel officer and custodian of records for White House admitted to prove defendant was never employed in such a capacity). See also Fed. R. Civ. P. 44(b) which provides that:

> (b) **Lack of Record.** A written statement that after diligent search no record or entry of a specified tenor is found to exist in the records designated by the statement, authenticated as provided in subdivision (a)(1) of this rule in the case of a domestic record, or complying with the requirements of subdivision (a)(2) of this rule for a summary in the case of a foreign record, is admissible as evidence that the records contain no such record or entry.

Fed. R. Crim. P. 27 makes Rule 44(b) applicable to criminal proceedings.

[76] See 4 Louisell & Mueller, § 458, at 796-97:

> It is hard to imagine an excuse for not using the word "diligent" in any certificate or testimony proffered under Rule 803(10), but there should be no magic attached to the term, and failure to use it should not be fatal if in fact the proponent makes a showing that a diligent search was made.

Conversely, use of the term should not be conclusive if it appears that in fact the search was sloppy or half-hearted.

See also United States v. Yakobov, 712 F.2d 20, 24 (2d Cir. 1983) (despite the certificate's recitation that "a diligent search" had been undertaken, error to admit certificate to show that defendant had not been licensed to deal in firearms where officer had searched only under defendant's name as misspelled: "The diligence requirement is one of substance, not form. It is not satisfied merely by a ritual incantation that the certificate results from a 'diligent' search").

[77] See § 803.41 of this Treatise.

[78] See, e.g., T'Kach v. United States, 242 F.2d 937, 938 (5th Cir. 1957) (testimony of custodian of records).

[79] See, e.g., Moerman v. Zipco, Inc., 302 F. Supp. 429, 448-49 (E.D. N.Y. 1969), aff'd, 422 F.2d 871 (2d Cir. 1969), adhered to, 430 F.2d 362 (2d Cir. 1969) (testimony of attorney to the effect that search of records failed to reveal defendant's registration required by Connecticut Blue Sky Law properly admitted).

[80] Federal Rule of Civil Procedure 44(6), in contrast to the common law, permitted proof in the form of a certification by the custodian to show the nonexistence of a record. See supra note 5. See, generally, 4 Weinstein, ¶ 803(10)[01], at 803-288; 5 Wigmore, § 1678; McCormick, § 320, at 742.

evidence in the form of a certification, provided that the authentication requirements of Rule 902 are met.

Rule 803(11)   Records of Religious Organizations

Rule 803(11) reads as follows:

> The following are not excluded by the hearsay rule, even though the declarant is available as a witness: . . . **(11) Records or religious organizations.** Statements of births, marriages, divorces, deaths, legitimacy, ancestry, relationship by blood or marriage, or other similar facts of personal or family history, contained in a regularly kept record of a religious organization.

§ 803.53   Records of Religious Organizations—In General.

Rule 803(11) creates a hearsay exception for statements of personal or family history contained in a regularly kept record of a religious organization.[81] The principle incorporated into Rule 803(11) is generally in accord with pre-Rule law.[82]

Traditionally, church records were admitted under the business records exception.[83] Such a categorization, however, required proof of the foundational facts necessary to invoke the business record exception, for example, through the testimony of the custodian of the records. Moreover, such records could be used only to prove the fact that an activity, such as a baptism, had occurred and not to prove underlying facts of personal history, such as age of the child, which would not be within the personal knowledge of the recorder.[84] Rule 803(11), by way of contrast, does not require firsthand knowledge of the person preparing the entry.[85] Consequently, information on the enumerated subjects, *i.e.*, statements of births, marriages, divorces, deaths, and the like, are admissible if they meet the criteria of the Rule, without any inquiry into the source of the information. The only criteria which must be established relate to proof that the state-

---

[81] *See, generally,* 4 WEINSTEIN, ¶¶ 803(11)[01]-[03]; 4 LOUISELL & MUELLER, § 459; 5 WIGMORE, § 1633(b). *See also* 4 AM. JUR. *Proof of Facts, Death, Proof 3* (church record); 29 AM. JUR. 2d, *Evidence,* §§ 508, 875; 30 AM. JUR. 2d, *Evidence,* § 928.

[82] *See* Lewis v. Marshall, 30 U.S. (1 Pet.) 470, 476, 8 L.Ed. 195, 197 (1831) (register of burials in church).

[83] 5 WIGMORE, § 1523, at 444.

[84] 4 WEINSTEIN, ¶ 803(11)[01], at 803-294.

[85] *See* Fed. R. Evid 803(11) Advisory Committee Note.

ments are contained in the records of a religious organization and that such records are those that are regularly kept by that organization.

§ 803.54   Rationale for the Exception.

The hearsay exception for familial or personal history statements contained in the records of religious organizations is based on the circumstantial guarantees of trustworthiness of such records. The statements are generally made in connection with ceremonies such as a baptism, wedding or funeral where there exists a lack of motivation to fabricate in regard to the type of information required on such occasions.[86] Furthermore, there is an opportunity for scrutiny of the information contained in such records by persons who would be in a position to verify or dispute the recorded data. The requirement that the record be "regularly kept" is a further safeguard as to reliability.

§ 803.55   Practical Considerations.

The foundational evidence necessary to invoke the religious record hearsay exception is directed to the court. Such evidence includes proof as to the record itself, the regularity with which it is kept, and the nature of the organization from which the record emanates. Questions as to the bona fide status of a group as a religious organization must be decided by the court as a preliminary determination under Rule 104(a).[87]

In order to admit records of the type described by Rule 803(11), the proponent must properly authenticate the records in accordance with Article IX.

Rule 803(12)   Marriage, Baptismal, and Similar Certificates

Rule 803(12) reads as follows:

The following are not excluded by the hearsay rule, even though the declarant is available as a witness: . . . **(12) Marriage, baptismal, and similar certificates.** Statements of fact contained in a certificate that the maker per-

---

[86] 4 Weinstein, ¶ 803(11)[01], at 803-294.

[87] *Id.*

formed a marriage or other ceremony or administered a sacrament, made by a clergyman, public official, or other person authorized by the rules or practices of a religious organization or by law to perform the act certified, and purporting to have been issued at the time of the act or within a reasonable time thereafter.

§ 803.56　Ceremonial Certificates—In General.

Rule 803(12) provides for the admission of factual statements contained in a certificate of marriage, baptism, or other ceremony or sacrament.[88] The type of information that may be proved by such certificates is similar to that which may be proved under Rule 803(11).[89] Nevertheless, the events for which a certificate is issued are fewer in number than events or statements that may be kept in the records of a religious organization.

In some situations the scope of Rule 803(12) also overlaps with that of Rule 803(9). Accordingly, if the information is contained in a report made to a public office pursuant to a requirement of law, the statement may be proved either by the report under Rule 803(9) or by a certificate that complies with Rule 803(12). The former Rule may not be utilized, however, in connection with acts that are not required or authorized by law to be recorded. For example, baptisms are not required or authorized to be recorded, and proof regarding this sacrament must consequently be made either by certificate or by a Rule 803(11) or a Rule 803(13) record.

The rationale of the exception for marriage, baptismal and other similar certificates is identical to that underlying Rule 803(11), namely, that a guarantee as to trustworthiness exists due to the unlikelihood that anyone would fabricate the type of information contained in such certificates.[90]

---

[88] *E.g.*, Blackburn v. Crawford, 70 U.S. (1 Pet.) 175, 182-83, 18 L.Ed. 186, 192-93 (1865) (baptismal certificate required by church usage to be kept); Young Ti v. United States, 246 F.110, 111-12 (3d Cir. 1917) (birth certificates from Chicago vital statistics department). *See, generally*, McCormick, § 319; 4 Weinstein, ¶ 803(12)[01]; 4 Louisell & Mueller, § 460; 5 Wigmore, § 1674. *See also* Comment, *Hearsay Under the Proposed Federal Rules: A Discretionary Approach*, 15 Wayne L. Rev. 1077, 1169 (1969).

[89] *But see* Martinez v. Ribicoff, 200 F. Supp. 191, 192 (D.P.R. 1961) (baptismal certificate inadmissible to prove parentage); United States v. Bukis, 17 F. Supp. 77, 78 (E.D. Pa. 1936) (baptismal certificate from Lithuanian church excluded to show alien was native of that country; "[the certificate] was merely a church record of baptism and it was not admissible to prove the date or place of birth, even though it contained recitals of those facts.").

[90] *See, generally*, 5 Wigmore, § 1645, at 702-3; 4 Louisell & Mueller, § 460.

§ 803.57 Methodology.

In order to invoke the exception as to certificates, the proponent must establish as a preliminary matter that the maker of the certificate, that is, a clergyman, public official, or other such person, was authorized to perform the act certified, either by law or by the precepts or practices of a religious organization. There must additionally be proof to satisfy the second criterion of the Rule, *i.e.*, that the certificate purports to have been issued at the time of the act in question or within a reasonable time thereafter. The requirement is met by a showing that the certificate bears a date of issuance which coincides with, or bears a reasonable correspondence with, the date of the act certified.[91] Finally, it should be noted that the certificate must be authenticated in accordance with Article IX of the Rules.

Rule 803(13) Family Records

Rule 803(13) reads as follows:

The following are not excluded by the hearsay rule, even though the declarant is available as a witness: . . . **(13) Family records.** Statements of fact concerning personal or family history contained in family Bibles, genealogies, charts, engravings on rings, inscriptions on family portraits, engravings on urns, crypts, or tombstones, or the like.

§ 803.58 Family Records—In General.

Rule 803(13) creates a hearsay exception for statements concerning personal or family history contained in family Bibles, genealogies, charts, engravings on rings, inscriptions on family portraits, engravings on urns, crypts or tombstones, and the like.[92] The types of facts contemplated by the Rule are those identified in Rule 803(11), namely, statements of births,

---

[91] 4 Weinstein, ¶ 803(12)[01], at 803-297.

[92] *See, generally,* McCormick, § 322; 4 Weinstein, ¶¶ 803(13)[01]-[03]; 4 Louisell & Mueller, § 461; 5 Wigmore, §§ 1495-1496. *See also,* Hale, *Proof of Facts of Family History,* 2 Hastings L.J. (1950); Comment, *Admissibility of Hearsay Evidence on Matters of Family History,* 5 Ark. L. Rev. 58 (1951).

marriages, divorces, deaths, legitimacy, ancestry, relationship by blood or marriage, or similar facts.[93] Rule 803(13) is consistent with pre-Rule practice.[94]

A common theme is apparent in Rules 803(11), (12), and (13), both as to types of information deemed admissible and as to rationale. The specific rationale of Rule 803(13) is "the unlikelihood that members of a family would allow an untruthful inscription or entry to be made, or to remain without protest."[95] This guarantee of trustworthiness obviates any need to show that the entry was made by a family member or by someone with personal knowledge. It should be noted that similar matters of personal or family history may be proved by reputation evidence pursuant to Rule 803(18).

The items enumerated in this Rule would generally be offered as proof of the contents of the writing contained therein or inscribed thereon. Accordingly, there must also be some consideration of the "best evidence rule" set forth in Article X in determining whether the inscribed object must be used to prove the contents of the writing. This matter is specifically addressed in Chapter 1002 of this Treatise. Also, any writing offered must be authenticated in accordance with Article IX.

Rule 803(14)   Records of Documents Affecting an Interest in Property

Rule 803(14) reads as follows:

> The following are not excluded by the hearsay rule, even though the declarant is available as a witness: . . . **(14) Records of documents affecting an interest in property.** The record of a document purporting to establish or affect an interest in property, as proof of the content of the original recorded document and its execution and delivery by each person by whom it purports to have been executed, if the record is a record of a public office and an applicable statute authorizes the recording of documents of that kind in that office.

---

[93] 4 WEINSTEIN, ¶ 803(13)[01], at 803-299, citing House Judiciary Committee Report approving the adoption of Rule 803(13).

[94] E.g., Lewis v. Marshall, 30 U.S. (1 Pet.) 470, 476, 8 L.Ed. 195, 197 (1831) (entry in family Bible admitted to prove date of death); Miami County National Bank of Paolo, Kan. v. Bancroft, 121 F.2d 921, 924 (10th Cir. 1941) (evidence in the form of ge-

nealogy and history of family admitted). See also Comment, Admissibility of Hearsay Evidence in Matters of Family History, 5 ARK. L. REV. 58 (1951); Annot., 29 A.L.R. 372 (1924). See, generally, McCORMICK, § 322.

[95] 4 WEINSTEIN, ¶ 803(13)[01], at 803-300. See also 4 LOUISELL & MUELLER, § 461, at 804.

§ 803.59   Records of Documents Affecting an Interest in Property— In General.

Rule 803(14) permits the record of a document purporting to establish or affect an interest in property, such as a deed, to be admitted as proof of the content of the original recorded document and as proof of its execution and delivery.[96]

In order to utilize Rule 803(14), the proponent of the record must first establish that the record is that of a public office and that an applicable state statute authorizes the recording of documents of that kind in that office. Upon such a foundation, the record of a deed may be used as proof, for example, that at the time of execution, the grantor was an unmarried person where such fact can be derived from the record. Based on the grantor's signature, the record would also be admissible to prove that the grantor executed and delivered the deed.[97]

Contents of a title record may be proved without resort to this Rule, for example, pursuant to the public record exception or possibly the business record exception.[98] These other Rules would not necessarily, however, provide an exception as to proof of proper execution and delivery of the title or document.

Rule 803(14) is in accordance with the common law[99] and it functions, in essence, to render the hearsay prohibition inapplicable to records of instruments relating to real property properly recorded as evidence of the facts set forth in the original.[1]

§ 803.60   Rationale.

The hearsay exception for records of title documents is supported by two

[96] See, generally, McCORMICK, § 323; 4 WEINSTEIN, ¶¶ 803(14)[01]-[03]; 4 LOUISELL & MUELLER, § 462; 5 WIGMORE, §§ 1647-1651. See also Comment, Hearsay Under the Proposed Federal Rules: A Discretionary Approach, 15 WAYNE L. REV. 1077, 1172-1173 (1969).

[97] See Collins v. Streitz, 95 F.2d 430, 434-35 (9th Cir. 1938) ("[I]f the acknowledgment is made by the officers of a corporation, the certificate shall show that such persons as such officers [naming the office of each person] acknowledged the execution of the instrument as the free act and deed of such corporation, by each of them voluntarily executed"). See, generally, 4 WEINSTEIN, ¶ 803(14)[01], at 803-302; 5 WIGMORE, § 1651; 4 LOUISELL & MUELLER, § 462.

[98] 4 WEINSTEIN, ¶ 803(14)[01], at 803-302.

[99] See, e.g., Carpenter v. Dexter, 75 U.S. (8 Wall.) 513, 526, 19 L.Ed. 426, 437 (1869); M'Keen v. Delancy, 9 U.S. (5 Cr.) 22, 26, 3 L.Ed. 25, 29 (1809). See, generally, 5 WIGMORE, § 1651.

[1] See, e.g., Connecticut Light & Power Co. v. Federal Power Comm., 557 F.2d 349, 354-56 (2d Cir. 1977) (administrative law judge relied upon historical material, to grant the right to use and benefit of the Housatonic River; "evidence contained in recorded deeds affecting interest in real property . . . are exceptions to the hearsay rule"). See also Fed. R. Evid. 803(14) Advisory Committee Note.

rationales. First, necessity justifies the exception where the recorded document is of such an age that witnesses and declarants would in all likelihood be unavailable. Even in cases where such parties might be available, the exception dispenses with the inconvenience of locating and utilizing such witnesses. Second, the exception is justified by the circumstantial guarantees of trustworthiness that attend recorded documents of this nature.

§ 803.61   Relation to Other Rules and Statutes.

Analysis of the practical application of the hearsay rule regarding recorded title documents should include a consideration of the principles relating to authentication. In order to be offered into evidence as a hearsay exception, the record must be authenticated under Article IX. For example, it might be authenticated as an ancient document under Rule 901(b)(8) or as a public record under Rule 902(2) (domestic documents not under seal), or Rule 902(4) (certified copies of public records).

In addition, note should be taken of rule 1005, the provisions of which allow contents of an official record to be proved by a copy certified or attested to be correct. In concert with Rule 1005, Rule 803(14) applies to the official record of a document and not to the original itself, the rationale being the trustworthiness that attends the recording process.

Rule 803(14) should be considered in conjunction with statutory provisions respecting the use of certified copies of deeds as evidence of the existence of the instrument and the record thereof, and in actions to cure title defects, as evidence of the existence and execution of the instrument.[2]

*Rule 803(15)   Statements In Documents Affecting
an Interest in Property*

Rule 803(15) reads as follows:

> The following are not excluded by the hearsay rule, even though the declarant is available as a witness: . . . **(15) Statements in documents affecting an interest in property.** A statement contained in a document purporting to establish or affect an interest in property if the matter stated was relevant to

[2] *E.g.*, Amoco Production Co. v. United States, 455 F. Supp. 46, 49-50 (D.C. Utah 1977) (since the original deed and all executed copies thereof were apparently lost or destroyed, other evidence was admissible to establish the contents of the deed; certified copy of the deed as recorded in the County Recorder's office was admissible and highly probative evidence of the contents of the deed).

the purpose of the document, unless dealings with the property since the document was made have been inconsistent with the truth of the statement or the purport of the document.

§ 803.62   Statements in Documents Affecting an Interest in Property—In General.

Rule 803(15) admits into evidence recitals of fact contained in a document purporting to establish or affect an interest in property, where the matter stated is relevant to the purpose of the document.[3] The document may be excluded, however, upon a showing that dealings with the property since the document was made have been inconsistent with the truth of the statement or the purport of the document.

The Rule does not require the document to have been recorded or to be recordable. Also, documents affecting personalty as well as realty are within the scope of the Rule, *e.g.*, contracts, bills of sale, security agreements, wills, estate inventories, and other documents that establish or affect an interest in property.[4] Rule 803(15) is essentially consistent with pre-Rule law.[5]

It should be noted that when the existence or occurrence of a particular transaction is at issue or the terms of a particular dispositive agreement are sought to be proven, the out-of-court statements constituting the agreement or dispositive document are not offered for their truth. In such case the statements are "verbal acts" or "operative facts," and as discussed in § 801.6 of this Treatise, a hearsay exception is not needed to admit the document in such a situation because of the non-hearsay nature of the statements. By comparison, Rule 803(15) applies where a party seeks to offer evidence on a factual matter that is the subject of a recital or a description in a dispositive document. For example, Rule 803(15) might be invoked to offer probative evidence as to the existence of an improvement on certain land where such fact is recited in an unrecorded deed. Likewise, the exception might be utilized to offer evidence that certain parties to a transaction

---

[3] *See, generally,* McCORMICK, § 323; 4 WEINSTEIN, ¶¶ 803(15)[01]-[03]; 4 LOUISELL & MUELLER, § 463; 5 WIGMORE, §§ 1573-1574. *See also* Comment, *Hearsay Under the Proposed Federal Rules: A Discretionary Approach,* 15 WAYNE L. REV. 1077, 1174-1175 (1969).

[4] *See* 4 WEINSTEIN, ¶ 803(15)[01], at 803-307; McCORMICK, § 323; 5 WIGMORE, §§ 1573-74.

[5] Although pre-Rule codifications generally recognized a similar exception to the hearsay rule, pre-Rule common law often admitted only statements contained in "ancient" documents. *See* 4 LOUISELL & MUELLER, § 463, at 817. Rule 803(15) makes the age of the document insignificant, although, as a practical matter, the document will often be an ancient one. *See* Fed. R. Evid. 803(15) Advisory Committee Note.

were married where the document designates the parties as husband and wife or as tenants by the entirety.

§ 803.63   Conditions and Rationale.

Rule 803(15) imposes two conditions to admissibility. First, there must be a showing that the statement sought to be introduced is relevant to the dispositive purpose of the document. The requirement provides some guarantee as to trustworthiness because a protest would be expected concerning any false information that is intrinsic to the transaction.[6] Second, the Rule provides that the hearsay exception is not available if dealings subsequent to the making of the document in question have been inconsistent with the statement or the purport of the document. In practical terms, where authentication is satisfied, the document should be admissible upon proof satisfying the first element unless the opponent offers to the court sufficient evidence of subsequent inconsistent dealings.

In addition to the two criteria specified in the Rule, other indicia of trustworthiness justify this exception. These include the circumstances under which dispositive instruments are made and the financial interests at stake that promote reliability, as well as the fact that the risk of errors in the transmission of statements is minimized because the statements are in writing.[7]

The Rule also rests in many instances on the basis of necessity, especially where litigation arises at a time when declarants or witnesses to the transaction may not be available. In such a case, although there is no requirement that the document under Rule 803(15) be of any given age, the instrument in question may well qualify as an ancient document under Rule 803(16).

[6] 4 WEINSTEIN, ¶ 803(15)[01], at 803-307; 4 LOUISELL & MUELLER, § 463, at 814 to 815.

[7] 4 WEINSTEIN, ¶ 803(15)[01], at 803-307. *See* United States v. 478.34 Acres of Land, 578 F.2d 156, 159 (6th Cir. 1978) (in condemnation proceeding "statistical survey" made by government engineer improperly admitted to prove the true prices paid for other land in the county; the survey was not relevant to prove the value of the defendant's land because the government failed to show that the other properties covered by the survey were comparable; moreover, the government made no effort to verify or authenticate the data and there was no way for the landowner to test the reliability or the accuracy of the data).

Rule 803(16)   Statements in Ancient Documents

Rule 803(16) reads as follows:

> The following are not excluded by the hearsay rule, even though the declarant is available as a witness: . . . **(16) Statements in ancient documents.** Statements in a document in existence twenty years or more the authenticity of which is established.

§ 803.64   Statements in Ancient Documents—Relationship to Common Law.

Rule 803(16) permits written statements in a document to be offered for their truth upon a preliminary showing that the document is authentic and that it is at least twenty years old.[8]

Originally, the common law doctrine of "ancient documents" pertained only to authenticity,[9] but many American courts admitted the authenticated writing to prove the truth of statements made in the document.[10] The

---

[8] See, generally, McCORMICK, § 323; 4 WEINSTEIN, ¶¶ 803(16)[01]-[03]; 4 LOUISELL & MUELLER, § 464; 5 WIGMORE, §§ 1573-1574; 7 WIGMORE, § 2145. See also Wickes, Ancient Documents and Hearsay, 8 TEX. L. REV. 451 (1930); Note, Recitals in Ancient Documents, 46 IOWA L. REV. 448 (1961); Note, The Effect of the Ancient Document Rule on the Hearsay Rule, 83 U. PA. L. REV. 247 (1934); Comment, Ancient Documents as an Exception to the Hearsay Rule, 33 YALE L.J. 412 (1924).

[9] McCORMICK, § 323, at 747. See Ninety Six v. Southern Railway Co., 267 F.2d 579, 583 (4th Cir. 1959) (stating that the exception for ancient documents "deals only with the authentication of the document sought to be proved, and not with its competency or admissibility"); King v. Watkins, 98 F. 913, 917 (4th Cir. 1899), rev'd on other grounds, 118 F. 524 (4th Cir. 1902) ("[T]he doctrine of admitting ancient documents in evidence, without proof of their genuine-

ness, is based on the ground that they prove themselves, the witness being presumed to be dead. The doctrine goes no further than this. The questions of its relevancy and admissibility as evidence cannot be affected by the fact that it is an ancient document. It is no more admissible on that ground than if it were a newly-executed instrument"). See, generally, 5 WIGMORE, §§ 1573-74; 4 WEINSTEIN, ¶ 803(16)[01], at 803-310; 4 LOUISELL & MUELLER, § 464.

[10] See, e.g., Stewart Oil Co. v. Sohio Petroleum Co., 202 F. Supp. 952, 957-58 (E.D. Ill. 1962), aff'd, 315 F.2d 759 (7th Cir. 1963), cert. denied, 375 U.S. 828, 84 S.Ct. 71, 11 L.Ed.2d 60 (1963) (recognizing hearsay exception for ancient documents but finding particular document inadmissible on basis of untrustworthiness); Burns v. United States, 160 F. 631, 633 (2d Cir. 1908) (maps). Cf., Lee Pong Tai v. Acheson, 104 F. Supp. 503, 506 (E.D. Pa. 1952).

common law tradition required the document in question to be in existence for at least *thirty years*, and in respect to age Rule 803(16) represents a modification of pre-Rule law.[11]

§ 803.65   Application.

The ancient document hearsay exception applies only to writings, but it contains no restriction as to the type of writing that may qualify under its terms. Thus, Rule 803(16) may be invoked in connection with documents of a formal nature, such as wills and deeds, as well as any other types of writing, such as letters, leases, powers of attorney, receipts, maps and public surveys.[12]

The Rule contains an express requirement that the authenticity of the document must be established in order for the hearsay exception to apply. Inclusion of such a requirement within the hearsay rule is redundant inasmuch as establishment of authenticity of documents is always a prerequisite to the admissibility of a writing. Nevertheless, the provision serves to emphasize that the Rule must be read in conjunction with Rule 901(b)(8), "Ancient documents or data compilation." Under the latter Rule, authentication requires proof not only that the document is at least twenty years old, but also that the document's condition is such that it creates no suspicion as to authenticity, and that the document was found in a place where, if authentic, it would likely be.[13] Pre-Rule cases required a similar showing, with the exception of the longer age requirement.[14] Accordingly, compliance with the authentication requirements of Rule 901(b)(8) will simultaneously satisfy the hearsay requirements of Rule 803(16).

§ 803.66   Rationale.

The hearsay exception for ancient documents has been criticized mainly on the basis that age alone does not assure reliability.[15] Nevertheless, propo-

[11] For a recital of common law decisions, see Comment, *Ancient Documents as an Exception to the Hearsay Rule*, 33 YALE L.J. 412, 413 n.8 (1924).

[12] *See* Fed. R. Evid. 803(16) Advisory Committee Note; 4 Weinstein, ¶ 803(16)[01], at 803-310. *See, e.g.*, Bell v. Combined Registry Co., 536 F.2d 164, 166-67 (7th Cir. 1976), *cert. denied*, 429 U.S. 1001, 97 S.Ct. 530, 50 L.Ed.2d 612 (1976) (letters and magazine articles); Dallas County v. Commercial Union Assurance

Co., 286 F.2d 388, 396 (5th Cir. 1961) (newspaper story).

[13] *See* Rule 901(b)(8) and the related discussion in this Treatise as to conditions creating suspicion and the likely sources of authentic documents.

[14] *E.g.*, McGuire v. Blount, 199 U.S. 142, 145, 26 S.Ct. 1, 4, 50 L.Ed. 125, 128 (1905); Fulkerson v. Holmes, 117 U.S. 389, 398, 6 S.Ct. 780, 788, 29 L.Ed. 915, 923 (1886).

[15] *See* 4 WEINSTEIN, ¶ 803(16)[01], at 803-312; McCORMICK, § 323, at 747.

nents of the exception have pointed to the special necessity of admitting such evidence due to the passage of twenty or more years.[16] The Rule accepts the latter argument and attempts to infuse an element of trustworthiness through authentication procedures, namely, by requiring the absence of suspicious condition of the document and by requiring a showing that the document was found in a logical place for a document of its nature. Other guarantees of trustworthiness are supplied: (i) by the fact that the document is in writing, thereby minimizing any errors in transmission; (ii) by the age itself which provides that the document was likely generated prior to the present controversy and consequently was not influenced by any partisanship or motive to falsify; and finally, (iii) by imposing the usual qualifications as to out-of-court declarants, *i.e.*, that the declarant be required to have firsthand knowledge of the facts asserted.[17] While strict compliance with the firsthand knowledge requirement may not be feasible with regard to ancient documents, courts may nonetheless require a showing that the declarant was in a position to have had the requisite knowledge.[18]

In sum, the need for the exception outweighs the possible risks of admitting unreliable evidence. If circumstances are shown which suggest unreliability, for example, where the document was written at a time when a motive for misrepresentation already existed, the judge may exclude the document pursuant to Rule 403 on the basis that the possibility of prejudice or confusion outweighs the probative value of such evidence.[19]

Rule 803(17)   Market Reports, Commercial Publications

Rule 803(17) reads as follows:

> The following are not excluded by the hearsay rule, even though the declarant is available as a witness: . . . **(17) Market reports, commercial publications.** Market quotations, tabulations, lists, directories, or other published compilations, generally used and relied upon by the public or by persons in particular occupations.

---

[16] *Id. See also* Wickes, *Ancient Documents and Hearsay*, 8 TEX. L. REV. 451, 461-62 (1930); 4 LOUISELL & MUELLER, § 464, at 822-23.

[17] *See* 4 WEINSTEIN, ¶ 803(16)[01], at 803-312; McCORMICK, § 323, at 747. *See also* Fed. R. Evid. 803 Advisory Committee Note, which states: "In a hearsay situation, the declarant is, of course, a witness, and

neither this rule nor Rule 804 dispenses with requirement of firsthand knowledge. It may appear from his statement or be inferable from the circumstances. See Rule 602."

[18] 4 WEINSTEIN, ¶ 803(16)[01], at 803-313.

[19] *Id.*

§ 803.67   Market Reports and Commercial Publications—In General.

Rule 803(17) authorizes the admission of certain commercial publications and reports as substantive proof of the information contained in such sources, including market quotations, tabulations, lists, directories, or other published compilations.[20] These reports and publications are admissible where the proponent shows by way of foundation that the publication sought to be introduced is one that is both generally used and generally relied upon either by the public or by persons in particular occupations. Rule 803(17) is in accord with pre-Rule law.[21]

§ 803.68   Scope and Rationale of the Exception.

Numerous types of publications are encompassed by the exception for market reports and commercial publications. In fact, as one commentator has noted, "The only difficulty with the exception is determining how narrowly it should be interpreted."[22] In determining the type of publication to which the exception properly applies, implementation of the rationale for the exception should be sought. While the exception is supported by necessity (i.e., because of the near impossibility of obtaining testimony from each person who contributed to the publication), it is most fundamentally justified by the trustworthiness which attends reports prepared with the knowledge that the public and persons in particular trades will rely upon them and will continue to rely upon them only if they are in fact trustworthy.[23]

The exception is appropriately invoked for reports and publications that contain objective facts as opposed to statements of opinion. Accordingly, such items as stock market quotations,[24] reports of prices listed in trade

[20] See, generally, MCCORMICK, § 321; 4 WEINSTEIN, ¶¶ 803(17)[01]-[03]; 4 LOUISELL & MUELLER, § 465; 6 WIGMORE, §§ 1702-1706. See also McElroy, Public Surveys—The Latest Exception to the Hearsay Rule, 28 BAYLOR L. REV. 59 (1976); Sorenson & Sorenson, The Admissibility and Use of Opinion Research Evidence, 28 N.Y.U. L. REV. 1213 (1953); Note, Commercial Lists, 46 IOWA L. REV. 455 (1961); Note, Mercantile Credit Reports as Evidence, 44 MINN. L. REV. 719 (1960); Note, Public Opinion Surveys as Evidence: The Pollsters Go to Court, 66 HARV. L. REV. 498 (1953).

[21] See Fed. R. Evid. 803(17) Advisory Committee Note.

[22] 4 WEINSTEIN, ¶ 803(17)[01], at 803-316.

[23] Id. See also 4 LOUISELL & MUELLER, § 465, at 827; MCCORMICK, § 321; 6 WIGMORE, §§ 1702-06.

[24] See Virginia v. West Virginia, 238 U.S. 202, 212, 35 S.Ct. 795, 800, 59 L.Ed. 1272, 1279 (1915) ("[I]t is unquestioned that in proving the fact of market value, accredited price-current lists and market reports, including those published in trade journals or newspapers which are accepted as trustworthy, are admissible in evidence"); G.E. Employees Secur. Corp. v. Manning, 137 F.2d 637, 641 (3d Cir. 1943) (since "a free and ready market existed" at the necessary times, "the value of the stock may be established by the market quotations"). See also United States v. Anderson, 532 F.2d 1218, 1225 (9th Cir. 1976), cert. denied, 429 U.S.

journals[25] and newspapers,[26] city directories,[27] mortality and annuity tables[28] have been recognized as within the exception. In addition, the Rule has been found to embrace annual books published by a car manufacturer reflecting a car's estimated value[29] and "industrial statistics" reflecting annual or quarterly corporate income as published by the Internal Revenue Service or similar government agency.[30]

§ 803.69   Utilization of the Exception.

Proper considerations in determining the admissibility of a publication under this exception may include the manner in which it was prepared and the extent to which it is consulted by members of a trade or by the public.[31]

839, 97 S.Ct. 111, 50 L.Ed.2d 107 (1976); Coplin v. United States, 88 F.2d 652, 669 (9th Cir. 1937), *cert. denied*, 301 U.S. 703, 57 S.Ct. 929, 81 L.Ed. 1357 (1937).

[25] *See* Cliquot's Champagne, 70 U.S. 114, 141, 18 L.Ed. 116, 120 (1866) (trial court properly received Price-current prepared by Parisian wine dealer indicating wholesale prices of wine); Wolcher v. United States, 200 F.2d 493, 498-99 (9th Cir. 1952), *later app'd*, 218 F.2d 505 (9th Cir. 1952), *cert. denied*, 350 U.S. 905, 76 S.Ct. 48, 100 L.Ed.2d 734 (1952), *reh. denied*, 350 U.S. 905, 76 S.Ct. 175, 100 L.Ed. 794 (1952), and *later app.*, 233 F.2d 748 (9th Cir. 1952), and *cert. denied*, 352 U.S. 839, 77 S.Ct. 61, 1 L.Ed.2d 56 (1953) (error to exclude evidence of weekly issues of the "Billboard" for the year in question, since it was a national publication and a trade paper specializing in the sort of information in issue; conviction for tax evasion reversed). *See also* United States v. Grossman, 614 F.2d 295, 297-98 (1st Cir. 1980); Fraser-Smith Co. v. Chicago R.I. & P.R. Co., 435 F.2d 1396, 1402 (8th Cir. 1971).

[26] *See* Virginia v. West Virginia, 238 U.S. 202, 212, 35 S.Ct. 795, 800, 59 L.Ed. 1272, 1279 (1915) (proper to accredit stock market quotations published in a newspaper of high reputation); United States v. Anderson, 532 F.2d 1218, 1225 (9th Cir. 1976), *cert. denied*, 429 U.S. 839, 97 S.Ct. 111, 50 L.Ed.2d 107 (1976) (value of stock proved by evidence of the over-the-counter price as published in the Wall Street Journal).

[27] *See* Williams v. Campbell Soup Co., 80 F. Supp. 865, 868 (D.C. Mo. 1948) (proper to use city directory to find address of business in order to determine if business is doing business in the forum state; "the directory of a city is continually used for business purposes and experience has shown that the data contained therein is dependable").

[28] *See* Roberts v. United States, 316 F.2d 489, 497 (3d Cir. 1963) (mortality tables). *See also* Kanelos v. Kettler, 406 F.2d 951, 956, n.30 (D.C. App. 1968); Kershaw v. Sterling Drug, Inc., 415 F.2d 1009, 1012 (5th Cir. 1969).

[29] *See* United States v. Johnson, 515 F.2d 730, 732, n.4 (7th Cir. 1975) (disagreed with on other grounds, United States v. Levine, 569 F.2d 1175 (1st Cir. 1975)), *cert. denied*, 436 U.S. 928, 98 S.Ct. 2824, 56 L.Ed.2d 771 (1975) (testimony as to "Red Book" value of stolen Cadillacs was properly received, since published by National Market Reports for more than 64 years)

[30] *See* Aero Spacelines, Inc. v. United States, 530 F.2d 324, 351, n.26 (Ct. Cl. 1976) (statistics published by IRS and FTC with SEC).

[31] *See, e.g.*, United States v. Martin, 167 F. Supp. 301, 302-03 (D.C. Ill. 1958) (Dunn & Bradstreet credit reports not admissible since they "are not prepared or made under the supervision or control of any employer or officer of the creditor companies, and therefore are not records whose trustworthiness can be established by the testimony of any person who systematically kept or supervised the records of these companies"). *See, e.g.*, Phillip Van Huesen, Inc. v. Korn, 204 Kan. 172, 174, 460 P.2d 549, 552 ("[T]he general rule is that a credit report

It has been suggested that courts should determine whether the publication in question meets the requisite standard of trustworthiness entitling it to hearsay exemption. If not, the court should exclude such a report or require that the offer thereof be made pursuant to another exception, for example, as a business record, which requires a more extensive foundation as a prerequisite to admissibility.[32]

Reports or publications offered pursuant to Rule 803(17) must be authenticated and must be relevant to an issue in the action. Many of the writings falling within this exception will be self-authenticating under Rule 902(5) (official publications), Rule 902(6) (newspapers and periodicals) or Rule 902(7) (trade inscriptions and the like). Others may be easily authenticated under Rule 901(b)(7) (public records or reports) or Rule 901(b)(8) (ancient documents or data compilation).

Rule 803(18)　　Learned Treatises

Rule 803(18) reads as follows:

> The following are not excluded by the hearsay rule, even though the declarant is available as a witness: . . . (18) **Learned Treatises.** To the extent called to the attention of an expert witness upon cross-examination or relied upon by him in direct examination, statements contained in published treatises, periodicals or pamphlets on a subject of history, medicine, or other science or art, established as a reliable authority by the testimony or admission of the witness or by other expert testimony or by judicial notice. If admitted, the statements may be read into evidence but may not be received as exhibits.

§ 803.70　　Learned Treatises—In General.

Rule 803(18) creates a hearsay exception for statements contained in published treatises, periodicals or pamphlets on a subject of history, medi-

---

of a commercial or credit reporting company such as Dunn & Bradstreet is not admissible in evidence").

[32] 4 WEINSTEIN, ¶ 803(17)[01], at 803-317 through 803-321. Judge Weinstein argues that Rule 803(17) should not be utilized to admit mercantile credit reports, for example, which may not be based on firsthand knowledge and which may include "the kind of gossip against which the hearsay rule is designed to protect—opinions of neighbors, ex-spouses, and disgruntled former employees." The author suggests that such a report should be admitted, if at all, "only when the proponent can show that the information was obtained and compiled in a manner indicative of trustworthiness." *Id.* at 803-318, 319. *See also* 4 LOUISELL & MUELLER, § 465, at 832-36.

cine or other science or art established as a reliable authority to the extent that such statements are called to the attention of an expert witness upon cross-examination or relied upon by him in direct examination. The reliability of the authority may be established by the testimony or admission of the witness, by other expert testimony, or by judicial notice. Once the authority is established as reliable, statements contained in treatises and the like which are addressed on direct or cross-examination may be considered as substantive evidence.[33]

At common law, the only permissible use of learned treatises was to show the basis for the expert's opinion on direct examination, or for impeachment on cross-examination.[34] Courts differed on the proper use of treatises for impeachment purposes, however:

> Most courts have permitted this use where the expert has relied upon the specific material in forming the opinion to which he testified on direct, some of these courts have extended the rule to situations in which the witness admits to having relied upon some general authorities although not that particular material sought to be used to impeach him. Other courts have required only that the witness himself acknowledge that the material sought to be used to impeach him is a recognized authority in his field; if he does so, the material may be used although the witness himself may not have relied upon it. Finally, some courts have permitted this use without regard to the witness's having relied upon or acknowledged the authority of the source if the cross-examiner establishes the general authority of the material by any proof or judicial notice.[35]

[33] *See, generally,* McCormick, § 321; 4 Weinstein, ¶¶ 803(18)[01]-[04]; 4 Louisell & Mueller, § 466; 6 Wigmore, §§ 1690-92. *See also* Goldman, *The Use of Learned Treatises in Canadian and United States Litigation,* 24 U. Toronto L. Rev. 423 (1974); Comment, *Learned Treatises in Illinois: Are We Witnessing the Birth of a New Hearsay Exception?,* 9 Loy. U. Chi. L.J. 193 (1977); Comment, *Substantive Admissibility of Learned Treatises and the Medical Malpractice Plaintiff,* 71 Nw. U.L. Rev. 678 (1976); Note, *Evidence—Products Liability—Federal Rule of Evidence 803(18)—Federal Rule of Admitting Evidence May Be of Significant Litigational Importance, Especially in Products Liability Suits,* 27 S.C.L. Rev. 766 (1976); Note, *Learned Treatises and Rule 803(b)(18) of the Proposed Federal Rules of Evidence,* 5 Val. U.L. Rev. 126 (1970); Comment, *Learned*

Treatises as Direct Evidence: The Alabama Experience, 1967 Duke L.J. 1157; Comment, *Medical Malpractice—Expert Testimony,* 60 Nw. U.L. Rev. 834 (1966); Note, *Learned Treatises,* 46 Iowa L. Rev. 463 (1961); Note, *Medical Treatises as Evidence—Helpful But Too Strictly Limited,* 29 U. Cin. L. Rev. 255 (1960).

[34] *E.g.,* Brown v. United States, 419 F.2d 337, 341 (8th Cir. 1969) ("medical treatises, recognized by the expert witness as authoritative, may be used in cross-examination, but are not admissible to prove the probative facts of opinions in the treatises, since they are subject to the hearsay rule"). *See, generally,* 6 Wigmore, §§ 1690-1708; 4 Weinstein, ¶ 803(18)[02], at 803-327; 4 Louisell & Mueller, § 466, at 838; McCormick, § 321, at 743.

[35] McCormick, § 321, at 900 (3d ed. 1984).

In drafting Rule 803(18), the Advisory Committee extended the last approach described above by permitting statements contained in learned treatises to be offered to prove the truth of the matter asserted due to the inherent reliability of such works. To prevent the possibility of misuse of the evidence by the jury, however, statements contained in books and articles may not be offered as substantive evidence independent of expert testimony.[36]

§ 803.71   Rationale.

The common law's failure to recognize a hearsay exception for learned treatises rested upon four principal objections: First, the trier of fact may be confused by scholarly works of a technical nature and may be misled into according material undue weight. A second concern is that there exists a potential for the proponent of the evidence to present it out of context or in a distorted form. Third, live testimony by an expert has been considered a better means to resolve technical issues than consulting written works. Finally, it is argued that information and skills in the fields of art, science and history change so rapidly that learned treatises and the like become quickly outdated, thus presenting the opportunity for the proponent of the material to present obsolete information to the trier of fact.[37]

The drafters of Rule 803(18), in accord with the position advanced by most legal writers, found that the concerns underlying the hearsay objection are not significant.[38] The Rule's requirement that the admission of the Treatise accompany the examination and cross-examination is believed to obviate the problems of misunderstanding and misapplication. Moreover, the prohibition against receiving the publication as an exhibit contained in the last sentence of the Rule provides an additional safeguard against the misuse of such evidence.[39]

The second argument that passages from publications may be presented out of context is clearly applicable as well to expert testimony by virtue of what the expert witness chooses to disclose or not disclose. The Rule recognizes that the adversarial process provides a sufficient safeguard to this type of abuse in the latter instance and should likewise be sufficient where learned treatises are presented.[40]

[36] See 4 WEINSTEIN, ¶ 803(19)[02], at 803-328.

[37] 6 WIGMORE, § 1690 (Chadbourn rev. 1976).

[38] See 4 WEINSTEIN, ¶ 803(18)[01], at 803-326; McCORMICK, § 321, at 745; Note, Learned Treatises, 46 IOWA L. REV. 463 (1961).

[39] See Fed. R. Evid. 803(18) Advisory Committee Note. See also 4 LOUISELL & MUELLER, § 466, at 845.

[40] See 4 WEINSTEIN, ¶ 803(18)[01], at 803-325; Comment, Learned Treatises as Direct Evidence: The Alabama Experience, DUKE L.J. 1157 (1967).

The objection that written material is inferior to live testimony is likewise without merit. There is no reason to assume that a testifying expert will possess a requisite degree of knowledge and experience and that authors of books and articles will lack it. Moreover, any deficiency presented by publications will largely be compensated by the testimony of the expert required under the Rule.[41] Finally, there is as much likelihood that the knowledge underlying the opinion of an expert witness will be outdated as there is that information contained in publications will be. Just as the proponent of expert testimony must demonstrate the qualifications of the expert before he is permitted to testify, the proponent of a learned publication must demonstrate that the material is reliable before it can be offered into evidence. Furthermore, the availability of cross-examination provides an additional safeguard against the danger that obsolete information will be presented.[42]

Learned treatises also satisfy the criteria of trustworthiness and necessity which traditionally underlie hearsay exceptions. Authors of publications have a strong incentive to be truthful and accurate since their works will be subject to the scrutiny of other professionals in their field. Related to this guarantee of trustworthiness is the fact that the authors of books and articles do not have a motive to misrepresent or distort information because such materials will not be prepared in anticipation of litigation.[43]

There is a special need for the exception since it is unlikely that the party seeking to prove a matter will be able "to produce all or even the best experts in any given case, and excluding written works by experts whose live testimony is beyond reach results only in depriving the trier of fact of useful information."[44]

§ 803.72   Foundation.

Rule 803(18) provides that the party offering a publication must establish it as a "reliable authority." This requirement may be met by the testimony or admission of the expert witness or by other expert testimony that the expertise of the author is recognized in the field and that the particular

[41] 4 LOUISELL & MUELLER, § 466, at 846.

[42] See 4 LOUISELL & MUELLER, § 466, at 846. See also 6 WIGMORE, § 1690, at 3.

[43] See Fed. R. Evid. 803(18) Advisory Committee Note.

[44] 4 LOUISELL & MUELLER, § 466, at 847. See, e.g., Johnson v. William C. Ellis & Sons Iron Works, Inc., 609 F.2d 820, 822 (5th Cir. 1980) (exclusion of safety codes was reversible error, since they are prepared by organizations for the chief purpose of promoting safety and are inherently trustworthy); Bair v. American Motors Corp., 473 F.2d 740, 744 (3d Cir. 1973) (reversible error to exclude statistical surveys prepared by Automotive Crash Injury Research of Cornell University).

publication is regarded as accurate by other professionals.[45] Alternatively, the requirement may be satisfied by judicial notice of the reliability of the treatise. Widely accepted publications such as the Merck Index, The Encyclopedia Britannica and the Physician's Desk Reference are examples of the types of materials admissible through judicial notice.[46] It should be noted that judicial notice under Rule 803(18) does not assign probative value to the evidence. Rather, judicial notice under the Rule operates only to qualify the work as a reliable source, and, accordingly, the question of the material's weight should be left to the jury.[47]

In order to use a treatise as substantive evidence, the proponent also must demonstrate either that the expert relied upon the work on direct examination or that the work was called to the attention of the expert on cross-examination. This requirement is "designed to ensure that the materials are used only under the chaperonage of an expert to assist and explain in applying them."[48] To this end, admission of a treatise is proper only when an expert is given an opportunity to rebut or explain the material, give his reaction to the work and the basis for his reaction.[49] Where the proponent's expert proves to be a hostile witness, the proponent should be

---

[45] See Burgess v. Premier Corp., 727 F.2d 826, 834 (9th Cir. 1984); Weise v. United States, 724 F.2d 587, 590 (7th Cir. 1984). See also Dawson v. Chrysler Corp., 630 F.2d 950, 961 (3d Cir. 1980), cert. denied, 450 U.S. 959, 101 S.Ct. 1418, 67 L.Ed.2d 383 (1981) (no error in admitting reports prepared for United States Department of Transportation, since authoritativeness of reports was inferentially conceded and defendant failed to object to use of the reports); Maggipinto v. Reichman, 481 F. Supp. 547, 548-50 (E.D. Pa. 1979) (treatise was used solely for impeachment; court must decide whether authority is reliable before it can admit treatise).

[46] E.g., Baenitz v. Ladd, 363 F.2d 969, 970 (D.C. App. 1966) (court approves judicial notice of facts contained in chemistry treatise where information was also published in the Encyclopedia Britannica); Application of Hartop, 311 F.2d 249, 253-55, 50 Cust. & Pat. App. 780, 783 (1962) (in patent litigation court approves judicial notice of information from "The Merck Index of Chemicals and Drugs"). See also Wise v. George C. Rothwell, Inc., 382 F. Supp.

563, 568 (D.C. Del. 1974), aff'd without op., 513 F.2d 627 (3rd Cir. 1974) (judicial notice of average perception reaction and stopping distance for passenger vehicles traveling at 40 miles per hour); Azoplate Corp. v. Silverlith, Inc., 367 F. Supp. 711, 731 (D.C. Del. 1973), aff'd without op., 506 F.2d 1050 (3rd Cir. 1973), cert. denied, 421 U.S. 914, 95 S.Ct. 1572, 43 L.Ed.2d 780 (1973) (judicial notice of certain chemical dictionaries).

[47] See 4 WEINSTEIN, ¶ 803(18)[02], at 803-332.

[48] McCORMICK, § 321, at 901 (3d ed. 1984).

[49] See Tart v. McGann, 697 F.2d 75, 78 (2d Cir. 1982). See also Generella v. Weinberger, 388 F. Supp. 1086, 1089-90 (E.D. Pa. 1974) (error for administrative law judge to rely upon four medical publications, since the cited publications are not recognized as standard authority by the medical field, and no experts were called). See, e.g., Foster v. McKeesport Hospital, 394 A.2d 1031, 1034 (Pa. Super. 1978); Kansas City v. Dugan, 524 S.W. 2d 194, 197 (Mo. App. 1975).

permitted to call the witness's attention to the publication through the use of leading questions pursuant to Rule 611.[50]

§ 803.73   Scope of the Exception.

Although Rule 803(18) expressly mentions, "published treatises, periodicals or pamphlets," the scope of the exception extends to any scholarly work, regardless of its form, where a proper foundation is laid. For example, charts extracted from a learned treatise,[51] almanacs, interest tables, astronomical calculations,[52] and government publications[53] may be admitted under the Rule.

While publications offered under Rule 803(18) will often be of a medical nature, the Rule is not restricted to medical treatises. Rather, it operates to admit works "on the subject of history, medicine or other science or art."[54]

The final sentence of Rule 803(18) contains the restriction that evidence offered under the Rule may not be "received as exhibits." As previously discussed in § 803.71, this restriction is designed to prevent the trier of fact from misunderstanding or misapplying the evidence as a result of its examination in the jury room.[55] However, this restriction should not be read so

---

[50] *See* Rule 611(c) and accompanying discussion. *Cf.* Stottlemire v. Cawood, 215 F. Supp. 266, 267-68 (D.D.C. 1963) (pre-Rules medical malpractice case; physician called by plaintiff did not answer questions as expected; plaintiff not permitted to contradict witness with treatise because such works were not admissible as substantive evidence and party not permitted to impeach his own witness; this result would be different under Rules 607 and 803(18)).

[51] United States v. Mangan, 575 F.2d 32, 48 (2d Cir. 1978), *cert. denied*, 439 U.S. 931, 99 S.Ct. 320, 58 L.Ed.2d 324 (1978) (proper to admit into evidence chart from a learned treatise, since its significance had been fully explored with the expert). *See also* Jamison v. Kline, 454 F.2d 1256, 1257-58 (3rd Cir. 1972).

[52] Bain v. American Motors Corp., 473 F.2d 740, 743 (3d Cir. 1973) (learned treatises include "annuity tables, weather reports, and tables of the rise and fall of the tide, all of which have been admitted in evidence").

[53] Dawson v. Chrysler Corp., 630 F.2d 950, 961 (3d Cir. 1980); Garbincius v. Boston Edison Co., 621 F.2d 1171, 1175 (1st Cir. 1980).

[54] *E.g.*, Connecticut Light & Power Co. v. Federal Power Comm. 557 F.2d 349, 354-56 (2d Cir. 1977) (historical teatises); United States v. Erdos, 474 F.2d 157, 161-62 (4th Cir. 1973), *cert. denied*, 414 U.S. 876, 94 S.Ct. 42, 38 L.Ed.2d 122 (1973) (psychiatric treatise); George v. Morgan Construction Co., 389 F. Supp. 253, 262-64 (E.D. Pa. 1975) (industry safety standard published by International Labour Organization).

[55] *See* Fed. R. Evid. 803(18) Advisory Committee Note. 4 WEINSTEIN, ¶ 803(18)[02], at 803-330. *See, e.g.*, United States v. Mangan, 575 F.2d 32, 48 (2d Cir. 1978), *cert. denied*, 439 U.S. 931, 99 S.Ct. 320, 58 L.Ed.2d 324 (1978) (court refuses to fault trial judge for not permitting handwriting charts to be taken to the jury room, although noting that it may be difficult to "read" charts into evidence).

broadly as to preclude the proponent from presenting the evidence to the jury in the form of a visual presentation where the presentation aids the trier of fact in evaluating and understanding the material.[56]

Rule 803(19)   Reputation Concerning Personal or Family History

Rule 803(19) reads as follows:

The following are not excluded by the hearsay rule, even though the declarant is available as a witness: . . . **(19) Reputation concerning personal or family history.** Reputation among members of his family by blood, adoption, or marriage or among his associates, or in the community, concerning a person's birth, adoption, marriage, divorce, death, legitimacy, relationship by blood, adoption or marriage, ancestry, or other similar fact of his personal or family history.

§ 803.74   Reputation Concerning Personal or Family History— In General.

Rule 803(19) authorizes the admission of reputation evidence when offered to prove a fact of personal or family history.[57] The reputation evidence may be drawn from three sources, namely: (i) from among members of a person's family; (ii) from his associates; or (iii) from someone in the community. The facts sought to be proven may include reputation as to those matters specified in the Rule, *i.e.*, a person's birth, adoption, marriage, divorce, death, legitimacy, relationship by blood, adoption or marriage, ancestry, or any other similar fact concerning personal or family history.

Several other hearsay exceptions pertain to related matters. The Rule covers the same subject matter as that which may be proved by records of religious organizations under Rule 803(11), by family records under Rule 803(13), or, where the declarant is unavailable, by statements of personal or family history under Rule 804(b)(5). Also, Rule 803(22) authorizes proof

---

[56] 4 LOUISELL & MUELLER, § 466, at 863. *See, e.g.,* United States v. Mangan, 575 F.2d 32, 48 (2d Cir. 1978), *cert. denied,* 439 U.S. 931, 99 S.Ct. 320, 58 L.Ed.2d 324 (1978).

[57] *See, generally,* McCORMICK, § 324; 4 WEINSTEIN, ¶¶ 803(19)[01]-[03]; 4 LOUISELL & MUELLER, § 467; 5 WIGMORE, §§ 1580, 1602-1605. *See also* Hale, *Proof of Facts of Family History,* 2 HASTINGS L.J. 1 (1950); Comment, *Hearsay Under the Proposed Federal Rules: A Discretionary Approach,* 15 WAYNE L. REV. 1077, 1189 (1969); Note, *Reputation,* 46 IOWA L. REV. 426 (1961).

by judgments of personal or family history matters where they would be provable by reputation evidence.

The Rule is generally in accord with prior law.[58] Its justification lies in the special need for this type of evidence due to the difficulty in obtaining other evidence of family matters and in the circumstantial guarantee of trustworthiness afforded by the likelihood "that these matters have been sufficiently inquired about and discussed with persons having personal knowledge so that a trustworthy consensus has been reached."[59]

§ 803.75 Application of the Rule.

Rule 803(19) is confined to reputation evidence as to personal or family history matters and not to direct statements of such matters. Reputation in this regard refers to the composite of a large number of out-of-court declarations evincing belief in a particular fact or set of facts. As a prerequisite to offering reputation testimony, the proponent must establish that the witness belongs to one of the three groups specified in the Rule and that he accordingly has sufficient familiarity with the subject matter, i.e., the reputation as to personal or family history of the person in question. If it appears that sufficient familiarity is lacking, the judge may exclude the testimony.[60]

The Rule does not establish any preference among the three groups of witnesses, i.e., family, associates or community.[61] Nor is there any requirement as to when the reputation must have been formulated. While not affecting admissibility, these considerations may affect the weight to be accorded the evidence by the trier of fact. For example, the trier might well accord more weight to reputation testimony offered by a close family member than to that offered by a business associate. Likewise, more weight might be attributed to reputation evidence that appears to be long

---

[58] See, generally, 5 WIGMORE, §§ 1602-1606; McCORMICK, § 322, at 745.

[59] 4 WEINSTEIN, ¶ 803(19)[01], 803-339. See also 4 LOUISELL & MUELLER, § 467, at 867; Fed. R. Evid. 803(19), (20) and (21) Advisory Committee Note.

[60] See Young Ah Chor v. Dulles, 270 F.2d 338, 343-45 (9th Cir. 1959) (reversible error to receive testimony concerning genealogy where witness "was not in any sense an intimate acquaintance" of the family).

[61] Cf. United States v. Mid-Continent Petroleum Corp. 67 F.2d 37, 45 (10th Cir.

1933), cert. denied sub nom, Hosey v. Mid-Continent Petroleum Corp., 290 U.S. 702, 54 S.Ct. 346, 78 L.Ed. 603 (1933) (stating that, in general, proof of reputation and tradition should ordinarily be accepted only from the family in question; however, in exeptional circumstances, proof of reputation among friends, acquaintances or the neighborhood is admissible). See also State v. Axilrod, 248 Minn. 204, 209, 79 N.W. 2d 677, 682 (1956), cert. denied, 353 U.S. 938, 77 S.Ct. 815, 1 L.Ed.2d 760 (1956).

standing than to that which is shown to have developed after the instant controversy arose.[62] If, however, sufficient indications of unreliability exist which outweigh the probative value of the evidence, the testimony is subject to exclusion pursuant to Rule 403.

Rule 803(20)　　Reputation Concerning Boundaries or General History

Rule 803(20) reads as follows:

The following are not excluded by the hearsay rule, even though the declarant is available as a witness: . . . **(20) Reputation concerning boundaries or general history.** Reputation in a community, arising before the controversy, as to boundaries of or customs affecting lands in the community, and reputation as to events of general history important to the community or state or nation in which located.

§ 803.76　　Reputation Concerning Boundaries or Customs—In General.

Rule 803(20) creates a hearsay exception for two categories of reputation evidence: (i) that relating to boundaries of or customs affecting land; and (ii) that relating to important events of general history.[63]

The use of reputation evidence to prove the location of public and private boundaries and customs affecting land was well established at common law.[64] While the exception is justified by the general lack of other reliable sources of information, it is more fundamentally supported by the trustworthiness that attends general reputation concerning facts of community interest.[65] Traditionally, however, the reputation had to be "ancient," that is, it had to derive from a past generation.[66] The Rule elimi-

---

[62] *See* 4 WEINSTEIN, ¶ 803(19)[01], at 803-339; 4 LOUISELL & MUELLER, § 467, at 869-70.

[63] *See, generally,* McCORMICK, § 324; 4 WEINSTEIN, ¶¶ 803(20)[01]-[03]; 4 LOUISELL & MUELLER, § 468; 5 WIGMORE, §§ 1582-1595. *See also* Note, *Reputation,* 46 IOWA L. REV. 426 (1961).

[64] 5 WIGMORE, §§ 1586-87.

[65] *See* 4 WEINSTEIN, ¶ 803(20)[01], at 803-344, citing *Walley v. United States,* 148 Ct. Cl. 371, 373 (Ct. Cl. 1960). *See also* McCORMICK, § 324, at 749, which explains the underpinnings of the reputation exceptions as follows:

A general lack of other reliable sources of information provides the necessity. A high probability of reliability is provided by restricting the use of reputation to those subjects in regard to which persons with personal knowledge are likely to have disclosed facts which have been the subject of general inquiry; thus the community's conclusion is likely to be accurate.

See also 4 LOUISELL & MUELLER, § 468, at 873-74.

[66] 5 WIGMORE, § 1582; McCORMICK, § 324, at 749.

nates any requirement concerning antiquity while retaining the common law requirement that the reputation as to boundaries or customs must antedate the present controversy.[67] It should be noted that boundaries may also be proved by judgments under Rule 803(22).

§ 803.77   Reputation Concerning General History—In General.

Rule 803(20) also encompasses a hearsay exception for reputation concerning events of general history. While there is no requirement under this portion of the Rule that the reputation antedate the instant controversy, the event must be one that is important to the community, state or nation in which it occurred, "so that it can accurately be said that there is a high probability that the matter underwent general scrutiny as the community reputation was formed."[68] Here again, the Rule dispenses with any requirement that the matter in question be an ancient one, although some commentators suggest that use of the term "history" suggests some requirement of age.[69] This suggestion may be an unnecessary concession to an outdated common law requirement, however, since certain events of recent occurrence may well be of general historical value to a community or nation.

Reputation evidence utilized to prove events or facts of general history will often consist of a written record[70] which may also be admissible under the exception for ancient documents or business records, or be appropriate for judicial notice.[71]

Rule 803(21)   Reputations as to Character

Rule 803(21) reads as follows:

The following are not excluded by the hearsay rule, even though the de-

---

[67] *See* Fed. R. Evid. 803(20) Advisory Committee Note. *See, generally,* 5 WIGMORE, § 1592.

[68] McCORMICK, § 324, at 750.

[69] *Id. See also* 4 LOUISELL & MUELLER, § 468, at 878; 4 WEINSTEIN, ¶ 803(20)[01], at 803-344; Pan American World Airways, Inc. v. Aetna Casualty & Surety Co., 368 F. Supp. 1098, 1104 (S.D.N.Y. 1973), *aff'd,* 505 F.2d 989 (2d Cir. 1973) (membership of foreign paramilitary or terrorist groups, as well as the facts of even small battles or guerrilla attacks cannot be "reported" in court). *Cf.* Morris v. Lessee of Harmer's

Heirs, 32 U.S. 554, 558-59, 8 L.Ed. 781, 783 (1833) (no error in receipt of book of author who was within the reach of the process of the court, since the party objecting to the proof had himself called the author to testify, making the book admissible to explain or qualify his testimony).

[70] *See, e.g.,* Connecticut Light & Power Co. v. Federal Power Comm., 557 F.2d 349, 354-56 (2d Cir. 1977) (historical writing). *See, generally,* 4 WEINSTEIN, ¶ 803(20)[01], at 803-345; 5 WIGMORE, § 1597.

[71] *Id.*

clarant is available as a witness: . . . **(21) Reputation as to character.** Reputation of a person's character among his associates or in the community.

§ 803.78 Reputation as to Character—In General.

Rule 803(21) provides that evidence in the form of reputation is admissible for its truth.[72] The reputation may be that which a person enjoys "among his associates or in the community."

While reputation evidence was traditionally limited to that derived from the neighborhood in which a person lived,[73] Rule 803(21) expands the groups from which character evidence may be derived in acknowledgment of the highly mobile nature of modern society. The term "associates" may refer to a variety of settings such as business, church, or social groups, and the only prerequisite to utilization of the exception is a showing that the person characterized is sufficiently known in the group in question to have permitted others to have become acquainted with him such that a reputation has developed. These prerequisites are established through the qualification of a reputation witness who must have sufficient familiarity with the reputation of the person in question to offer probative testimony on the subject.

Rule 803(21) effects a result which is consistent with pre-Rule law.[74]

§ 803.79 Purpose and Extent of the Exception.

Rule 803(21) serves to reinforce other Rules which allow the introduction of reputation testimony in specific situations. For example, under Rule 404(a)(1), an accused in a criminal trial may offer evidence of his character, and if he does so, the prosecution may offer character evidence to rebut that which the accused has offered. Additionally, under Rule 404(a)(2), the accused and the prosecution may under certain circumstances offer evidence relating to the character of the victim. In these instances, and also in situations where character itself is "in issue" in the case, Rule 405 permits

[72] See, generally, McCORMICK, § 324; 4 WEINSTEIN, ¶¶ 803(21)[01]-[03]; 4 LOUISELL & MUELLER, § 469; 5 WIGMORE, §§ 1608-1621. See also 82 A.L.R.2d 525, Admissibility of Testimony as to General Reputation at Place of Employment.

[73] 5 WIGMORE, § 1615.

[74] See Michaelson v. United States, 335 U.S. 469, 477, 69 S.Ct. 213, 219, 93 L.Ed.

168, 174 (1948) (the hearsay exception allows a witness "to summarize what he has heard in the community, although much of it may have been said by persons less qualified to judge than himself"). See, generally, McCORMICK, § 324, at 749; 4 LOUISELL & MUELLER, § 469.

proof of character to be established by testimony as to reputation. Reputation testimony as to the truthfulness of a witness may also be offered pursuant to Rule 608.[75] Rule 803(21) ensures that where reputation evidence is admissible, it may be received for the truth of the matter asserted. The exception is necessary because reputation "consists of a summary of uncross-examined views expressed outside the courtroom offered to prove the truth of the matter asserted."[76]

Rule 803(21) does not attempt to specify the situations in which character evidence is admissible. Nor does it address the specific type of character trait that may be proved by means of reputation evidence. The Rule merely provides that such evidence will not be excluded because of hearsay considerations. The admissibility of character evidence and the permissible focus of such evidence depend upon considerations of relevancy as well as the criteria set forth in the Rules identified above. Moreover, such evidence, even though admissible, may be excluded pursuant to Rule 403 if the prejudicial effect is deemed substantially to outweigh its probative value.

Rule 803(22)   Judgment of Previous Conviction

Rule 803(22) reads as follows:

> The following are not excluded by the hearsay rule, even though the declarant is available as a witness: . . . (22) **Judgment of previous conviction.** Evidence of a final judgment, entered after a trial or upon a plea of guilty (but not upon a plea of nolo contendere), adjudging a person guilty of a crime punishable by death or imprisonment in excess of one year, to prove any fact essential to sustain the judgment, but not including, when offered by the Government in a criminal prosecution for purposes other than impeachment, judgments against persons other than the accused. The pendency of an appeal may be shown but does not affect admissibility.

---

[75] See, e.g., United States v. Prevatt, 526 F.2d 400, 404 (5th Cir. 1976), reh'g denied, 531 F.2d 575 (5th Cir. 1976), and overruled on other grounds, United States v. Smyth, 556 F.2d 1179 (5th Cir. 1976), reh'g denied, 557 F.2d 823 (5th Cir. 1976), cert. denied, 434 U.S. 862, 98 S.Ct. 190, 54 L.Ed.2d 135 (1976) ("character witnesses may testify as to a defendant's reputation in the community under a common exception of the hearsay rule"); United States v. Oliver, 492 F.2d 943, 946 (8th Cir. 1974), later app'd, 492 F.2d 731 (8th Cir. 1974), cert. denied, 424 U.S. 973, 96 S.Ct. 1477, 47 L.Ed.2d 743 (1974) (noting that Rule 803(21) admits evidence of reputation as to the truth and veracity of a witness).

[76] 4 WEINSTEIN, ¶ 803(21)[01], at 803-347. See Moore v. United States, 123 F.2d 207, 209-10 (5th Cir. 1941) (noting that "[m]ere rumors are not reputation but reputation involves a notion of the general estimate of a person by the community as a whole").

§ 803.80 Judgment of Previous Conviction—In General.

Subject to specified restrictions, Rule 803(22) authorizes the admission into evidence of felony convictions in subsequent civil and criminal actions in order to prove any fact essential to the previous criminal judgment.[77] The evidence offered pursuant to this exception must be that of a final judgment, entered after a trial or upon a guilty plea, but not upon a plea of nolo contendere. Additional limitations imposed by the Rule provide that the previous conviction must relate to a crime punishable by death or imprisonment in excess of one year and that, in a criminal prosecution, the Government may not utilize the prior conviction of persons other than the accused for a purpose other than impeachment. It should be emphasized that evidence offered pursuant to Rule 803(22) is merely probative, rather than conclusive, of the fact sought to be proved.

While Rule 803(22) is in conflict with the common law practice of most state jurisdictions,[78] it is in accord with prior federal law and policy.[79]

§ 803.81 Rationale of the Rule.

A hearsay exception is necessary in order to admit evidence of a previous conviction because, "[a]nalytically, such a judgment of conviction is hear-

---

[77] See, generally, McCORMICK, § 318; 4 WEINSTEIN, ¶¶ 803(22)[01]-[03]; 4 LOUISELL & MUELLER, § 470; 4 WIGMORE, § 1346; 5 WIGMORE, § 1671. See also Bush, Criminal Convictions as Evidence in Civil Proceedings, 29 MISS. L.J. 276 (1959); Cowen, The Admissibility of Criminal Convictions in Subsequent Civil Proceedings, 40 CALIF. L. REV. 225 (1952); Hinton, Judgment of Conviction—Effect on a Civil Case as Res Judicata or as Evidence, 27 ILL. L. REV. 195 (1932); Comment, Hearsay Under the Proposed Federal Rules: A Discretionary Approach, 15 WAYNE L. REV. 1077, 1194 (1969); Note, Use of Record of Criminal Conviction in Subsequent Civil Action Arising From the Same Facts as the Prosecution, 64 MICH. L. REV. 702 (1966); Note, Judgments as Evidence, 46 IOWA L. REV. 400 (1961); Note, Admissibility and Weight of a Criminal Conviction in a Subsequent Civil Action, 39 VA. L. REV. 995 (1953); Note, Evidence: Judgments: Admissibility in Evidence in a Civil Action of Party's Conviction of Traffic Infraction, 35 CORNELL L.Q. 872 (1950); Note, Admissibility of Traffic Conviction as Proof of Facts in Subsequent Civil Action, 50 COLUM. L.

REV. 529 (1950); Note, Evidence—Traffic Infraction—Admissibility as Proof of Underlying Fact, 16 Bklyn. L. Rev. 286 (1950); Note, Effect of a Criminal Conviction in Subsequent Civil Suits, 50 YALE L.J. 499 (1941).

[78] See Comment, Hearsay Under the Proposed Federal Rules: A Discretionary Approach, 15 WAYNE L. REV. 1077, 1194 (1969); 5 WIGMORE, § 1671(a), at 806.

[79] See, e.g., United States v. Fabric Garment Co., 366 F.2d 530, 533-34 (2d Cir. 1966) ("[U]nder federal law, a prior criminal conviction will work an estoppel in favor of the government in a subsequent civil proceeding with respect to questions distinctly put in issue and directly determined in the criminal prosecution."); Connecticut Fire Ins. Co. v. Ferrara, 277 F.2d 388, 392 (8th Cir. 1960), cert. denied, 364 U.S. 903, 81 S.Ct. 231, 5 L.Ed.2d 195 (1960) (arson conviction admitted in suit on fire insurance policy); United States Fidelity & Guaranty Co. v. Moore, 306 F. Supp. 1088, 1095 (N.D. Miss. 1969) (prior criminal conviction given conclusive effect in subsequent civil action). See, generally, McCORMICK, § 318, at 739-41.

say, since it is based on the opinion of twelve persons who have not been cross-examined and have no personal knowledge of the underlying facts."[80]

The principal rationale for a hearsay exception for prior convictions is that of reliability.[81] The exception reflects faith in the criminal justice system and in the capacity of jurors to arrive at a just determination.[82] Reliability is also assured by the high burden of proof in criminal cases and by the defendant's motivation to defend fully in the face of a serious criminal charge.[83]

§ 803.82 Scope of the Rule.

Rule 803(22) limits the use of previous judgments in several respects. Notably, the exception operates to admit criminal judgments only, and civil judgments are admissible only to the extent provided by other Rules or by the non-evidentiary doctrines of res judicata and collateral estoppel. Also, evidence of final criminal judgments is limited to convictions resulting from a trial or a guilty plea. These requirements assure reliability by providing either that a full trial will have preceded the conviction or that the defendant will have admitted his guilt in accordance with procedures which assure that such a plea is made knowingly, voluntarily, and with full appreciation of the consequences.[84] By way of contrast, a plea of nolo contendere is not admissible. The result is in accordance with Rule 410 and with previous practice.[85]

The Rule is limited by its terms to convictions, and it does not accord hearsay exemption to judgments of acquittal. The latter are excluded because they show, at most, that the prosecution did not prove each element of the case beyond a reasonable doubt. Since a judgment of acquittal does not prove innocence, it is excluded due to minimal or nonexistent relevancy.[86] As a further limitation, the exception applies only to convictions

---

[80] 4 WEINSTEIN, ¶ 803(22)[01], at 803-350.

[81] Id. at 803-352. See also 4 LOUISELL & MUELLER, § 470, at 888.

[82] See 5 WIGMORE, § 1671a, at 808. But see Hinton, Judgment of Conviction—Effect in a Civil Case as Res Judicata or as Evidence, 27 Ill. L. Rev. 195, 198 (1932).

[83] McCORMICK, § 328, at 739.

[84] See Fed. R. Crim. P. 11(c) and (d).

[85] See Fed. R. Evid. 803(22) Advisory Committee Note and Chapter 410 of this Treatise. See, e.g., Greenberg v. Cutler-Hammer, Inc., 403 F. Supp. 1231, 1234 (E.D. Wis. 1975) (citing Treatise to find

that Rule 803(22) "makes clear that evidence of a final judgment based upon a plea of nolo contendere cannot be used to prove any fact essential to sustain the judgment").

[86] 4 Weinstein, ¶ 803(22)[01], at 803-354; McCormick, § 318, at 740-41. But cf. Bush, Criminal Convictions as Evidence in Civil Proceedings, 29 MISS. L.J. 276, 278 (1959), (the author suggests that judgments of acquittal should be admitted "since the failure of the state to prove guilt to the required degree may have some tendency to show that the accused was not in fact guilty.").

for crimes punishable by death or imprisonment in excess of one year. Again, the rationale for the limitation is reliability, *i.e.*, the motivation to defend fully is significantly less where the charge involves a misdemeanor.[87]

Admissibility of convictions meeting the foregoing restrictions is further limited when evidence of the conviction is offered against the accused in a criminal trial. In this context the rule provides that the Government may not use the prior conviction of any person other than the accused for a purpose other than impeachment. Consequently, while the government may utilize a third person's previous conviction in order to impeach that person as a witness under Rule 609,[88] it may not use a conviction of a third person against the accused as proof of any fact essential to the prior determination. The limitation has a constitutional derivation, namely, that of the accused's right to confront witnesses against him.[89] As discussed in the following section, the Government may, however, utilize the previous conviction of the accused as long as it is not prevented from doing so by the prohibition of Rule 404(b) or by constitutional considerations.[90]

§ 803.83   Application of the Rule.

Subject to the limitations discussed in the foregoing section, the Rule admits evidence of previous convictions in criminal and civil actions as proof of any fact essential to sustain the conviction. Consequently, the proponent must establish not only the conviction itself through, for example, introduction of a certified record, but he must also establish that the

[87] 4 WEINSTEIN, ¶ 803(22)[01], at 803-354. *See also* Rule 410 which provides, *inter alia*, that a plea of guilty in a violations bureau is not admissible in any civil or criminal proceeding against the person who made the plea. Judge Weinstein suggests that the policy of admitting only judgments of felonies should be extended such that guilty pleas in non-felony cases would not be allowed as admissions or as statements against interest, notwitstanding case law to the contrary. ¶ 803(22)[01], at 355. It might be argued in response that evidence of a guilty plea may not be as persuasive to a jury as a judgment, and that a party against whom a guilty plea has been admitted may always explain the circumstances surrounding the plea and advance reasons limiting its weight.

[88] Although a previous conviction utilized for impeachment purposes under Rule 609 presumably requires a hearsay exception, it may be more appropriate to invoke Rule 803(8) rather than Rule 803(22) in this context since the conviction itself is the focus of proof rather than the facts underlying the conviction. The point is academic, however, since convictions are an acknowledged method of impeachment and a hearsay objection would be frivolously made.

[89] *See* Kirby v. United States, 174 U.S. 47, 54, 19 S.Ct. 574, 582, 43 L.Ed. 890, 893 (1899) (in prosecution for possession of stolen postage stamps, conviction reversed where the only evidence that the stamps were stolen was the record of the conviction of the thieves). *Cf.* Roe v. United States, 316 F.2d 617, 622-23 (5th Cir. 1963) (record of conviction of third person admissible to show defendant's state of mind). Also distinguished should be the situation in which the conviction of a third person is an element of the crime. *See* Fed. R. Evid. 803(22) Advisory Committee Note.

[90] *See* § 404.21 *et seq.* of this Treatise.

fact sought to be proved was essential to sustain the prior judgment. The judge must determine that issue as a preliminary matter, based, if necessary, upon "an examination of the record, including the pleadings, the evidence submitted, the instructions under which the jury arrived at its verdict, and any opinions of the court."[91]

Admissibility of a prior conviction to prove a fact essential to that determination also depends on its relevancy to, and admissibility in, the action in which it is offered as evidence. In this regard, the proponent may not run afoul of the forbidden inference of Rule 404(b), that is, by utilizing the previously established fact as evidence of character in order to prove that a person acted in conformity therewith. The evidence may, on the other hand, be offered for other purposes such as those expressly authorized in Rule 404(b), that is, to prove motive, opportunity, intent, preparation, plan, knowledge, identity, or absence of mistake or accident.[92]

Evidence offered pursuant to Rule 803(22) is not conclusive of the fact sought to be proved, and the opponent may explain the prior conviction and may offer any evidence rebutting the fact sought to be proved by the proponent. Nevertheless, convictions may be excessively persuasive and, if such evidence would be unfairly prejudicial, exclusion pursuant to Rule 403 may be indicated.

Pendency of an appeal of the prior conviction does not affect admissibility, although it may be offered to affect weight. The opponent may accordingly show that an appeal is pending in order to limit the persuasiveness of the conviction evidence. The Rule is thus parallel to Rule 609(e).

Rule 803(23) Judgment as to Personal, Family, or General History, or Boundaries

Rule 803(23) reads as follows:

The following are not excluded by the hearsay rule, even though the declarant is available as a witness: . . . (23) **Judgment as to personal, family, or**

---

[91] Emich Motors Corp. v. General Motors Corp., 340 U.S. 558, 569-71, 71 S.Ct. 408, 417, 95 L.Ed. 534, 544-45 (1951), reh. denied, 341 U.S. 906, 71 S.Ct. 610, 95 L.Ed. 1345 (1952) (plaintiff auto dealer properly allowed to introduce evidence of a prior antitrust conviction of General Motors as "prima facie evidence of the general conspiracy for the purpose of monopolizing the financing of General Motors cars, and also of its effectuation by coercing General Motors dealers to use GMAC"); 4 WEINSTEIN, ¶ 803(22)[01], at 803-358.

[92] It should be noted that Rule 404(b) is broader than Rule 803(22) in that it covers any evidence of other crimes, wrongs or acts. Use of a prior conviction under 803(22) is, accordingly, an expedient method of proving the prior crime when evidence thereof is adminisible under Rule 404(b). Where prior act evidence is admissible consistent with Rule 404(b), however, any admissible evidence may be used to prove the occurrence of the act. A conviction is but one means of proving the act.

general history, or boundaries. Judgments as proof of matters of personal, family, or general history, or boundaries, essential to the judgment, if the same would be provable by evidence of reputation.

§ 803.84　Judgment as to Personal, Family, or General History, or Boundaries—In General.

Rule 803(23) authorizes admissibility of a judgment as substantive proof of certain matters in a subsequent action.[93] The matters which may be proved by this method are limited to those of personal, family or general history, or boundaries. The exception is further circumscribed by the requirements that the fact sought to be proved must have been essential to the prior judgment and that the matter must be one which would be provable by reputation evidence. The exception is consequently of limited application.

The subject matter overlap between Rule 803(23) and the hearsay exceptions for reputation testimony, *i.e.*, Rules 803(19) and (20), is apparent, and the connection between the two concepts—judgments and reputation—is historically based. The hearsay exception as to judgments was justified at early common law because judgments were considered to be evidence of reputation, that is, a jury verdict was thought to be based upon the individual knowledge of the jurors. Consequently, it represented the reputation in the neighborhood.[94] Although the historical underpinnings no longer exist, a separate exception for the admissibility of judgments has persisted. The exception is justified by the assumed reliability of the judicial process reinforced by the belief that, at the least, judgments are as reliable as reputation.[95] The Rule, accordingly, maintains the link between the two concepts, and in what is perhaps a cautious approach, limits the use of judgments to those matters provable by reputation. Any restrictions

---

[93] *See, generally,* McCormick, § 325; 4 Weinstein, ¶¶ 803(23)[01]-[03]; 4 Louisell & Mueller, § 471; 5 Wigmore, § 1593. *See also* Comment, *Hearsay Under the Proposed Federal Rules: A Discretionary Approach,* 15 Wayne L. Rev. 1077, 1199-1201 (1969).

[94] 4 Weinstein, ¶ 803(23)[01], at 803-365; 5 Wigmore, § 1593, at 559-60; Fed. R. Evid. 803(23) Advisory Committee Note. *See, e.g.,* Patterson v. Gaines, 47 U.S. (6 How.) 550, 559, 2 L.Ed. 553, 598 (1840) ("[T]he general rule certainly is, that a person cannot be affected, much less con-

cluded, by any evidence, decree, or judgment, to which he was not actually, or in consideration of law, privy. But the general rule has been departed from so far that wherever reputation would be admissible evidence, there a verdict between strangers, in a former action, is evidence also; such as in cases of manorial rights, public rights of way, immemorial custom, disputed boundaries, and pedigrees.").

[95] 4 Weinstein, ¶ 803(23)[01], at 803-366. *See also* 4 Louisell & Mueller, § 471, at 916 to 917.

on the use of reputation evidence are consequently applicable to the use of judgments under this Rule.[96]

§ 803.85   Res Judicata and Collateral Estoppel Distinguished.

Two judicial doctrines, res judicata and collateral estoppel, must be distinguished from the concept reflected in Rule 803(23). Rule 803(23) permits the use of judgments as *evidence*. Such evidence is not conclusive, however, and may be rebutted in the same fashion as any other item of evidence.[97] This use of a judgment is distinct from the concept of res judicata in which a judgment operates as a bar to further litigation between the same parties concerning the same subject matter. It is also distinct from the concept of collateral estoppel which operates as a bar to relitigation of facts previously litigated between the same parties. A judgment offered under Rule 803(23), then, is merely probative of the fact to which it is relevant. It is not conclusive of the matter.

§ 803.86   Scope of the Exception.

Unlike Rule 803(22), Rule 803(23) does not limit the types of judgments that may be utilized as evidence, *i.e.*, civil or criminal. It is unclear whether a civil judgment properly qualified may be utilized in a subsequent criminal action as proof of one of the specified topics, even though a higher burden of proof is required in criminal trials.[98] Arguably, although

---

[96] *See* 4 Weinstein, ¶ 803(23)[01], at 803-366. *See also* § 803.81 *et seq.* and § 803.86 *et seq.* of this Treatise.

[97] *See* Jung Yen Loy v. Cahill, 81 F.2d 809, 813 (9th Cir. 1936) (evidence of prior determination by immigration officers affirming citizenship of appellant's father was admitted, but rebutted and overcome by appellant's positive testimony); United States v. Mid-Continent Petroleum Corp., 67 F.2d 37, 43-46 (10th Cir. 1933), *cert. denied*, 290 U.S. 702, 54 S.Ct. 346, 78 L.Ed. 603 (1933) (findings by Dawes Commission as to age, sex, and alias were admissible, but not conclusive).

[98] *See* 4 Weinstein, ¶ 803.(23)[01], at 803-367 in which the author raises this question and notes that while such evidence is as reliable as reputation evidence which may be introduced in a criminal action,

there is a risk that a jury may be far more impressed with a judgment than with reputation testimony. The author suggests that a judge must consequently weigh the probative value of such evidence against the danger of prejudice in determining its admissibility. *See also* Comment, *Hearsay Under the Proposed Federal Rule: A Discretionary Approach*, 15 Wayne L. Rev. 1077, 1200 (1969) ("The civil judgment is at least as trustworthy as the reputation evidence which may be introduced in the criminal action."). Pre-Rule law recognized the essence of this exception in Grant Bros. Construction Co. v. United States, 232 U.S. 647, 662-63, 34 S.Ct. 452, 463, 58 L.Ed. 776, 785 (1914). In that case the Supreme Court held that the finding of an administrative board that certain persons were aliens was properly admitted in a subsequent action

the prosecution must prove every element of the crime beyond a reasonable doubt but does not need to establish every piece of evidence to that standard in order to obtain admissibility of such evidence, a civil judgment offered pursuant to Rule 803(23) should be admitted in criminal cases with an understanding that such admission does not in any manner alter the prosecution's burden of proof on any element of the crime. The differential burdens of proof reflect on the weight to be accorded the evidence. Nevertheless, if any risk of undue prejudice is presented by the admission of such evidence, it may be excluded pursuant to Rule 403.

§ 803.87 Application of the Exception.

The proponent who seeks to offer a judgment as proof of a matter specified in Rule 803(23) must first establish the judgment itself, for example, through the use of a certified copy of the court record. The proponent must further establish that the matter sought to be introduced was "essential" to the prior judgment. The court must determine as a preliminary matter whether a sufficient showing of "essentiality" has been made to justify admission of the judgment. The proponent must also show that the matter sought to be introduced through this vehicle would be provable by evidence of reputation, for example, facts of personal or family history such as those specified in Rule 803(19). If proof of a matter would require evidence other than reputation, Rule 803(23) may not be utilized.

Rule 803(24)   Other Exceptions

§ 803.88 In General.

Because all pertinent principles contained in Rule 803(24) are identical to those in Rule 804(b)(5), please refer to Chapter 804.

by the government to recover penalties against a third party for violations of the Alien Contract Labor Act. Although the court commented that the action under the Act was technically civil in form, "it is in fact in the nature of a criminal proceeding in that it seeks to recover a penalty for the commission of a crime." *Id.* at 653.

Chapter 804

RULE 804. HEARSAY EXCEPTIONS; DECLARANT UNAVAILABLE

481

Rule 804(a)   Definition of Unavailability

Rule 804(a) reads as follows:

(a) **Definition of Unavailability.** "Unavailability as a witness" includes situations in which the declarant—

(1) is exempted by ruling of the court on the ground of privilege from testifying concerning the subject matter of his statement; or

(2) persists in refusing to testify concerning the subject matter of his statement despite an order of the court to do so; or

(3) testifies to a lack of memory of the subject matter of his statement; or

(4) is unable to be present or to testify at the hearing because of death or then existing physical or mental illness or infirmity; or

(5) is absent from the hearing and the proponent of his statement has been unable to procure his attendance (or in the case of a hearsay exception under subdivision (b)(2), (3), or (4), his attendance or testimony) by process or other reasonable means. A declarant is not unavailable as a witness if his exemption, refusal, claim of lack of memory, inability, or absence is due to the procurement or wrongdoing of the proponent of his statement for the purpose of preventing the witness from attending or testifying.

§ 804.1   Admissible Hearsay When Declarant Unavailable.

Rule 804 establishes a rule of preference for the admissibility of certain types of hearsay:[1] "The preference is for in-court testimony over hearsay, and hearsay, if of a certain quality, over a complete loss of evidence."[2] In contrast to the Rule 803 exceptions to the hearsay rule, the admissibility of Rule 804(b) exceptions is dependent upon laying a foundation satisfactory to the court[3] that the declarant is unavailable as a witness.[4]

The availability-unavailability distinction of Rules 803 and 804 is a product of historical development, with the criterion of unavailability developing in conjunction with particular hearsay exceptions.[5] While there remains substantial dispute among commentators as to which exceptions should be conditioned upon the showing of the declarant's unavailability,[6] designated classes of hearsay are admitted under Rule 804 on the assumption that it is better to admit Rule 804 hearsay than receive no evidence at all.[7]

Subsection (a) of Rule 804 defines situations in which a declarant is considered unavailable, and subsection (b) sets forth five hearsay excep-

[1] See, generally, McCORMICK, § 253; 4 WEINSTEIN, ¶¶ 804(a)[01]-[02]; 4 LOUISELL & MUELLER, § 486; 5 WIGMORE, §§ 1401-14, 1456. See also Stewart, Perception, Memory, and Hearsay: A Criticism of Present Laws and the Proposed Federal Rules of Evidence, 1970 UTAH L. REV. 1; Comment, Evidence—Hearsay Exception—Requirements for Unavailability of Witness in Criminal Case Under the Federal Law of Evidence, 29 RUTGERS L. REV. 133 (1975); Comment, Evidence: The Unavailability Requirement of Declaration Against Interest Hearsay, 55 IOWA L. REV. 477 (1969); Comment, Hearsay Under the Proposed Federal Rules: A Discretionary Approach, 15 WAYNE L. REV. 1079, 1101-1106 (1969).

[2] Comment, Evidence: The Unavailability Requirement of Declaration Against Interest Hearsay, 55 IOWA L. REV. 477, 484 (1969). See Fed. R. Evid. 804 Advisory Committee Note.

[3] See Fed. R. Evid. 804 Advisory Committee Note. See also Rule 104(a) and § 104.1 of this Treatise.

[4] Fed. R. Evid. 804 Advisory Committee Note.

[5] Id. See also 4 WEINSTEIN, ¶ 804(a)[01], at 804-32 to 804-33.

[6] 4 WEINSTEIN, ¶ 804(a)[01], at 804-33.

[7] Id. at 804-32.

tions which are conditional on the unavailability of the declarant. One substantial change in pre-Rule law effected by Rule 804 is that the Rule makes the standard of unavailability uniform for each exception.[8]

§ 804.2   Unavailability—An Overview.

Rule 804(a) identifies five types of situations in which a declarant is "unavailable as a witness" and in which the condition to the utilization of the Rule 804(b) exceptions is satisfied: (1) where the declarant's testimony is exempt due to privilege; (2) where the declarant refuses to testify; (3) where the declarant testifies to a lack of memory; (4) where the declarant is unable to testify due to death, illness or infirmity; and (5) where the declarant is absent and the proponent of the declarant's statement has been unable to obtain the testimony by process or reasonable means.[9]

Although the wording of Rule 804(a) emphasizes the unavailability of the declarant, the crucial issue is whether the declarant's *testimony* is unavailable. In each of the first three types of situations identified in Rule 804(a), the declarant may be present in the courtroom, but hearsay is admissible because his testimony is unavailable.[10] Rule 804(a) treats "unavailability" in a uniform fashion. Consequently, if any of the identified situations arise, the witness is unavailable regardless of which of the Rule 804(b) exceptions is invoked to admit the hearsay.

Rule 804(a) also provides that if the proponent of the hearsay statement procured the unavailability of the declarant, the declarant is not considered unavailable. Consequently, the hearsay statement would be inadmissible under Rule 804(b). The obvious justification for this principle is that a proponent of hearsay should not be permitted to evade the Rule or benefit from evidence made admissible by his own wrongdoing.[11]

Rule 804 continues the traditional practice of placing the burden of establishing the unavailability of a declarant on the proponent of the hearsay.[12] The court must determine whether the declarant is unavailable as a

---

[8] Fed. R. Evid. 804 Advisory Committee Note.

[9] *See id*. For a discussion of unavailability, *see, generally*, 4 LOUISELL & MUELLER, § 486; MCCORMICK, § 253; 4 WEINSTEIN, ¶ 804(a)[01]; 5 WIGMORE, §§ 1401-18.

[10] *Cf*. MCCORMICK, § 253, at 608 ("the critical factor is the unavailability of [the witness'] testimony."); 4 WEINSTEIN, ¶ 804(a)[01] at 804-33. *E.g.*, Mason v. United States, 408 F.2d 903, 906 (10th Cir. 1969), *cert. denied*, 400 U.S. 993, 91 S.Ct. 462, 27 L.Ed.2d 441 (1971) ("the important ele-

ment is whether the testimony of the witness is sought and is available, not whether the witness's body is available").

[11] *See, e.g.*, Reynolds v. United States, 98 U.S. 145, 159, 25 L.Ed. 244, 255 (1878) ("[T]he rule has its foundation in the maxim that no one shall be permitted to take advantage of his own wrong.").

[12] 4 LOUISELL & MUELLER, § 486, at 1026. *See, e.g.*, United States v. Fernandez-Roque, 703 F.2d 808, 812-13 (5th Cir. 1983); United States v. Pelton, 578 F.2d 701, 709 (8th Cir. 1978), *cert. denied*, 439 U.S.

witness, and it has considerable discretion in making its determination.[13] Under Rule 104(a) the court is not bound by the Rules of Evidence, except in regard to privileges, in considering the foundational evidence as to unavailability.

Rule 804 not only treats all types of unavailability uniformly, it also treats civil and criminal cases alike.[14] Consistent with the Sixth Amendment, however, courts have required a more stringent application of the unavailability standard in criminal cases where the evidence is offered against the accused.[15]

§ 804.3   Unavailability—Privilege.

Rule 804(a)(1) provides that a witness's valid claim of privilege, exempting him from testifying, satisfies the unavailability requirement of Rule 804.[16] The witness's bare assertion of the privilege, however, is insuffient to make the witness unavailable. Instead, the court must rule that assertion of the privilege is justified.[17]

Unavailability due to a justified assertion of privilege occurs most frequently because of a claim of spousal privilege[18] or the privilege against self-incrimination.[19] Federal courts do not generally require a grant of immunity to a witness who has invoked the privilege against self-incrimination. By obtaining immunity, the witness would not qualify under the

---

964, 99 S.Ct. 451, 58 L.Ed.2d 422 (1978) (unavailability not established where attorney simply stated that declarant would exercise her privilege against self-incrimination; the possibility that she "might decide to choose to exercise her privilege amounted to a wholly inadequate showing of unavailability under Rule 804(a)(1)").

[13] 4 LOUISELL & MUELLER, § 486, at 1026.

[14] *See* 4 WEINSTEIN, ¶ 804(a)[01], at 804-34.

[15] *Id. See also* 4 LOUISELL & MUELLER, § 486, at 1026; § 804.7 of this Treatise.

[16] The Rule is consistent with previous practice in the federal courts. *See, e.g.,* United States v. Elmore, 423 F.2d 775, 778 (4th Cir. 1970), *cert. denied,* 400 U.S. 825, 91 S.Ct. 49, 27 L.Ed.2d 54 (1970) ("[T]he requirement that the declarant be unavailable to testify is satisfied by the fact that West successfully asserted his fifth amendment privilege against self-incrimination and declined to answer any questions about

the matter"). *See also* United States v. Allen, 409 F.2d 611, 613 (10th Cir. 1969).

[17] 4 LOUISELL & MUELLER, § 486, at 1028; 4 WEINSTEIN, ¶ 804(a)[01], at 804-35.

[18] United States v. Lilley, 581 F.2d 182, 187-88 (8th Cir. 1978). *See also* United States v. Mathis, 559 F.2d 294, 298 (5th Cir. 1977) (extra-judicial statements made by wife could not be admitted, since witness was not unavailable where trial judge found that marriage was a sham and witness would testify against her husband if ordered to do so). *See* United States v. Trammel, 445 U.S. 40, 100 S.Ct. 906, 63 L.Ed.2d 186 (1980) (holding that only the witness spouse holds a testimonial privilege, so that the defendant spouse cannot prevent the witness spouse from testifying).

[19] United States v. Rodriquez, 706 F.2d 31, 40 (2d Cir. 1983); United States v. Gibbs, 703 F.2d 683, 692 (3d Cir. 1983); United States v. Zappola, 646 F.2d 48, 54 (2d Cir. 1981), *cert. denied,* 459 U.S. 866, 103 S.Ct. 145, 74 L.Ed.2d 122 (1982).

unavailability requirement of Rule 804, and consequently, his preferable live testimony would be presented.[20]

§ 804.4   Unavailability—Refusal to Testify.

Rule 804(a)(2) conforms to the pre-existing majority practice which recognizes that "[i]f a witness simply refuses to testify, despite the bringing to bear upon him of all appropriate judicial pressures, the conclusion that as a practical matter he is unavailable can scarcely be avoided."[21]

The Rule requires that the proponent of the hearsay show more than an indication by the potential witness of an unwillingness to testify. The witness must disobey a court order to testify,[22] and this disobedience by the witness in the face of a court order distinguishes a refusal to testify from an assertion of a privilege. Without the requirement of disobedience of a court order, the *mistaken* assertion of a privilege not to testify would satisfy the requirement of unavailability.[23]

§ 804.5   Unavailability—Lack of Memory.

Rule 804(a)(3) extends prior case law by providing that a hearsay declarant is unavailable if he testifies to a lack of memory as to the content of the out-of-court declaration.[24] Rule 804(a)(3) rejects the argument that an assertion of lack of memory in this context invites perjury from witnesses who seek to avoid being impeached or cross-examined as to the subject

[20] *See, e.g.,* United States v. Lang, 589 F.2d 92, 95-96 (2d Cir. 1978) (government's refusal to grant immunity to witness who claimed privilege against self-incrimination did not prevent the witness from testifying). *See, generally,* Westen, *Confrontation and Compulsory Process: A Unified Theory of Evidence for Criminal Cases,* 91 HARV. L. REV. 567, 582-86 (1978).

[21] McCORMICK, § 253, at 612.

[22] United States v. Bizzard, 674 F.2d 1382, 1387 (11th Cir. 1982), *cert. denied,* 459 U.S. 973, 103 S.Ct. 305, 74 L.Ed.2d 286 (1982). *See also* United States v. Bailey, 581 F.2d 341, 344-47 & 347 n.10 (3d Cir. 1978) (declarant was brought before trial judge and stated that he would not testify; court then told him he was being ordered to testify, whereupon he still refused to testify); United States v. Garner, 574 F.2d 1141, 1143 (4th Cir. 1978), *cert. denied,* 439 U.S. 936, 99 S.Ct. 333, 58 L.Ed.2d 333

(1978) (grand jury witness refused to testify, persisting in his refusal even after court granted him immunity and threatened him with contempt); United States v. Gonzalez, 559 F.2d 1271, 1272-73 (5th Cir. 1977) (government witness refused to testify at trial, even though he had already been convicted, was granted immunity, and was ultimately found in contempt). *Cf.* United States v. Pelton, 578 F.2d 701, 709-10 (8th Cir. 1978), *cert. denied,* 439 U.S. 964, 99 S.Ct. 451, 58 L.Ed.2d 422 (1978) (court held witness's attorney's statement that witness would refuse to testify as inadequate foundation to establish unavailability of witness).

[23] *See* 4 WEINSTEIN, ¶ 804(a)[01], at 804-35 (arguing that silence due to an ill-founded claim of privilege may constitute unavailability due to refusal to testify).

[24] Fed. R. Evid. 804 Advisory Committee Note.

matter.[25] Instead, the Rule adopts the modern position that the value of admission of the hearsay statements outweighs the danger arising from the potential for perjury.[26] Moreover, the potential for perjury can be addressed in several ways. The court can determine that the testimony as to forgetfulness is made in bad faith and refuse to find that the unavailability condition is satisfied.[27] The hearsay, however, still might be admissible under Rule 804(a)(2) as a refusal to testify unless the claim of forgetfulness was procured by the proponent of the hearsay.[28] Alternatively, if the hearsay statement is former testimony subject to cross-examination, the court can treat the in-court claim of lack of memory as a denial of the prior testimony which is then admissible for its truth as a prior inconsistent statement under Rule 801(d)(1)(A).[29] The declarant would still be subject "to cross-examination on his motives and memory" by the opposing party.[30] Finally, the prior testimony might be admissible under Rule 803(5) as recorded recollection,[31] particularly where the opponent of the witness seeks admission of the hearsay.[32]

It has been held that a criminal defendant's right of confrontation is not violated when a witness's prior hearsay statement is admitted upon a finding of unavailability because of a failure of memory.[33] The issue of a right of confrontation may arise where a government witness claims a failure of memory and the accused cannot fully cross-examine the witness concerning a statement which the witness does not remember.[34]

§ 804.6　Unavailability—Death and Infirmity.

Rule 804(a)(4) follows a long established tradition in treating a declarant of Rule 804(b) hearsay as unavailable when the declarant is determined to

[25] See, e.g., Turner v. Missouri-Kansas-Texas Ry. Co., 346 Mo. 28, 35-36, 142 S.W.2d 455, 463-64 (1940). See, generally, Annot., 129 A.L.R. 843.

[26] McCormick, § 253, at 611; 5 Wigmore, § 1408, at 223-24.

[27] See 4 Weinstein, ¶ 804(a)[01], at 804-37 ("Cross-examination about the making of the statement [alleging lack of memory] and his present recollection gives the trial judge a good opportunity for assessing the witness's credibility.").

[28] See § 804.8 of this Treatise.

[29] 4 Louisell & Mueller, § 486, at 1039; 4 Weinstein, ¶ 804(a)[01], at 804-37.

[30] McCormick, § 253, at 611. Accord 5 Wigmore, § 1408, at 224 n.6 ("the witness must be called in order that [his lack of memory] may appear, so that in practical

application there would be no dispensation of his presence.").

[31] See 5 Wigmore, § 1408, at 224 n.6.

[32] See § 803.10 of this Treatise.

[33] United States v. Davis, 551 F.2d 233, 235 (8th Cir. 1977), cert. denied, 431 U.S. 923, 97 S.Ct. 2197, 53 L.Ed.2d 237 (1977) (no confrontation problem where lack of memory was basis for introduction of prior testimony, since declarant had been fully cross-examined at the prior proceeding).

[34] California v. Green, 399 U.S. 149, 168-70, 90 S.Ct. 1930, 1942, 26 L.Ed.2d 489, 502-03 (1970), on remand, 3 Cal. 3d 981, 92 Cal. Rptr. 494, 479 P.2d 998 (1970), cert. dismissed, 404 U.S. 801, 92 S.Ct. 20, 30 L.Ed.2d 34 (1970) (Supreme Court noted this issue but did not resolve it). See 4 Louisell & Mueller, § 486, at 1038-39.

be dead.[35] Rule 804(a)(4) also incorporates traditional practice that a declarant is unavailable where he is subject to mental or physical infirmity.[36]

The infirmity condition was early viewed as an extension of the rule that death constituted unavailability.[37] One obvious difference is that infirmity, unlike death, may not be permanent. If an infirmity is temporary, the trial can be continued until the witness is available,[38] and continuance may be necessary to satisfy the criminal defendant's constitutional right to confrontation in certain situations.[39] Rather than continuing the trial, the court may make other arrangements because of an infirm witness, such as obtaining testimony at the bedside of the witness. The trial judge must be given discretion to decide what is most appropriate based upon the facts of each case.[40] One difficulty with temporary infirmity is that mental infirmity may not be clearly temporary, and consistent with the right of confrontation, a case of transitory incompacity may be of such uncertain duration as to constitute a "permanent" unavailability justifying admission of hearsay.[41]

In the case of mental infirmity, the judge must decide, based on the opinions of medical experts, whether the witness will sufficiently improve to sustain the rigors of a trial and to offer useful testimony. The judge may order a continuance if there is a strong probability of recovery.[42] The question before the judge is not one of legal insanity because, according to Rule 601, insanity need not disqualify a person from being a witness.[43] If a person is competent to testify, but will be traumatized by testifying at trial or will offer useless testimony, then the witness is effectively unavailable.[44] McCormick has suggested that the question of the unavailability of the witness should be decided by determining whether the prior hearsay is

[35] McCormick, § 253, at 609.

[36] Fed. R. Evid. 804 Advisory Committee Note. See 4 Weinstein, ¶ 804(a)[01], at 804-39 ("Unavailability exists if the trial judge finds that the declarant is suffering from a physical condition which is not expected to improve and which renders him unable to testify within a reasonable time.").

[37] See, generally, McCormick, § 253, at 610.

[38] E.g., Parrott v. Wilson, 707 F.2d 1262, 1268-69 (11th Cir. 1983), cert. denied, 104 S.Ct. 344 (1983); United States v. Faison, 679 F.2d 292, 297 (3d Cir. 1982). See also Peterson v. United States, 344 F.2d 419, 422-25 (5th Cir. 1965) (former testimony of pregnant declarant admitted after her doctor testified that she was not able to travel to trial; therefore, conviction reversed).

[39] See Barber v. Page, 390 U.S. 719, 723-25, 88 S.Ct. 1318, 1321-22, 20 L.Ed.2d 255, 259 (1968) (requiring good-faith effort by State to procure unavailable State hearsay declarant); see also Ohio v. Roberts, 448 U.S. 56, 100 S.Ct. 2531, 65 L.Ed.2d 597 (1980) (construing Barber).

[40] 4 Louisell & Mueller, § 486, at 1043-44; 4 Weinstein, ¶ 804(a)[01], at 804-39.

[41] 4 Weinstein, ¶ 804(a)[01], at 804-40. E.g., Parrott v. Wilson, 707 F.2d 1262, 1268-69 (11th Cir. 1983), cert. denied, 104 S.Ct. 344 (1983).

[42] See 4 Louisell & Mueller, § 486, at 1044.

[43] Fed. R. Evid. 601 Advisory Committee Note.

[44] 4 Louisell & Mueller, § 486, at 1044.

more reliable than the present testimony of the mentally infirm witness,[45] but the judge's determination can be further complicated by the fact that the witness may have been mentally or emotionally impaired at the time the prior statement was made.[46]

§ 804.7   Unavailability—Absence.

Rule 804(a)(5) provides that if a person and his testimony cannot be procured, the witness is unavailable. The Rule requires that not only must the declarant be unavailable, but his *testimony*, which in many cases includes a deposition, must be unavailable. Congress included the requirement in the Rule that an attempt be made to depose the witness before the witness is found unavailable and his hearsay statements are admitted under Rule 804(b)(2), (3), or (4).[47]

Although the question of whether absence makes a person unavailable may seem obvious,[48] several issues may be presented. First, the position that the permanent or indefinite absence of a person from a jurisdiction is a sufficient basis for finding the person unavailable as a witness has been limited in criminal cases.[49] In *Barber v. Page*,[50] the United States Supreme Court held that admission of hearsay upon a simple showing that a prosecution witness was absent from the state may be insufficient to satisfy the defendant's right of confrontation. Therefore, in federal criminal trials the government must subpoena the witness,[51] as well as search for the witness or attempt in other ways to enforce the subpoena.[52] Additionally, the government must use "reasonable means" to secure the witness's appearance, such as keeping track of or restraining the witness.[53] According to the

---

[45] McCORMICK, § 253, at 611.

[46] 4 WEINSTEIN, ¶ 804(a)[01], at 804-40.

[47] Fed. R. Evid. 804 Advisory Committee Note.

[48] McCORMICK, § 253, at 609 ("If a witness cannot be found, he obviously is unavailable.").

[49] 4 WEINSTEIN, ¶ 804(a)[01], at 804-41. *See, generally*, McCORMICK, § 253, at 609; 5 WIGMORE, § 1404, at 205-10.

[50] 390 U.S. 719, 723-25, 88 S.Ct. 1318, 1321-22, 20 L.Ed.2d 255, 259 (1968).

[51] 4 LOUISELL & MUELLER, § 486, at 1048-50.

[52] *Id.* at 1051. *See* Ohio v. Roberts, 448 U.S. 56, 100 S.Ct. 2531, 65 L.Ed.2d 597 (1980) (confrontation clause was not violated by admission of preliminary hearing testimony of witness who was unavailable

at trial where prosecution unsuccessfully tried to serve subpoenas five times at witness' last known residence and questioned witness's mother, who stated she did not know her daughter's whereabouts). *See also* United States v. Lynch, 499 F.2d 1011, 1022-24 (D.C. Cir. 1974).

[53] United States v. Thomas, 705 F.2d 709, 711-12 (4th Cir.), *cert. denied*, 462 U.S. 1108, 104 S.Ct. 232, 78 L.Ed.2d 225 (1983); United States v. Puckett, 692 F.2d 663, 670 (10th Cir. 1982), *cert. denied*, 459 U.S. 1091, 103 S.Ct. 579, 74 L.Ed.2d 939 (1982), *cert. denied, sub. nom.* Krown v. United States, 460 U.S. 1024, 103 S.Ct. 1276, 75 L.Ed.2d 497 (1983); Perricone v. Kansas City Southern Ry. Co., 630 F.2d 317, 321 (5th Cir. 1980); Creamer v. Gen'l Teamsters Local Union 326, 560 F. Supp.

United States Supreme Court decision in *Ohio v. Roberts*,[54] the "reasonable means" principle does not require the government to engage in futile acts in an attempt to procure the testimony of a witness.

Second, in civil cases the proponent's obtaining the issuance of a subpoena for the witness generally suffices as a reasonable effort to procure the witness.[55]

Third, at least for purposes of Rules 804(b)(2), (3) and (4), using "reasonable means" to secure a witness's availability includes attempting to take the witness's deposition when the witness cannot appear at the trial.[56]

§ 804.8   Hearsay Proponent Procurement of Unavailability of Declarant.

According to the last sentence of Rule 804(a), where the proponent of the hearsay procures the unavailability of the declarant, hearsay will be inadmissible pursuant to the Rule 804(b) exceptions. Federal courts have held that "purposefulness" is essential to precluding a finding of unavailability.[57] This result appears to be in accord with the intent of the unavailability requirement, *vis.*, setting a minimum threshold of necessity without compromising reliability. Only if the proponent of the hearsay purposefully procures the unavailability of the declarant is the reliability of the hearsay compromised.

In criminal cases, the government can grant immunity to a witness in order to avoid a claim of privilege against self-incrimination from a critical witness. Courts have held that the government's failure to immunize a witness who asserts the privilege not to testify is not "procurement or

495, 499 (D. Del. 1983). *See, generally,* 4 LOUISELL & MUELLER, § 486, at 1066-68 (discussing reasonableness standard).

[54] 448 U.S. 56, 100 S.Ct. 2531, 65 L.Ed.2d 597 (1980).

[55] McCORMICK, § 253; United States v. Squella-Avendano, 478 F.2d 433, 439 (5th Cir. 1973) (deponent's unavailability was sufficiently established by virtue of the absence of an extradition treaty with Chile). *See also* McIntyre v. Reynolds Metal Company, 468 F.2d 1098, 1098 n.2 (5th Cir. 1972); Trade Development Bank v. Continental Insurance Co., 469 F.2d 35, 42 (2d Cir. 1972); Zenith Radio Corp. v. Matsushita Electric Industrial Co., Ltd., 505 F. Supp. 1190, 1249 (E.D. Pa. 1980).

[56] 4 WEINSTEIN, ¶ 804(a)[01], at 804-47 to 804-48 ("Congress has . . . expressed a

strong policy in favor of depositions rather than these hearsay exceptions.").

[57] *See* United States v. Seijo, 595 F.2d 116, 119-20 (2d Cir. 1979) (trial judge in illegal harboring case in holding that government had procured absence of declarants for the purpose of preventing them from testifying, since Rule 804(a) requires a "purpose" to prevent witnesses from attending or testifying); United States v. Mathis, 550 F.2d 180, 181-82 (4th Cir. 1976), *cert. denied, sub. nom.;* Moore v. United States, 429 U.S. 1107, 97 S.Ct. 1140, 51 L.Ed.2d 560 (1977) (trial court properly admitted testimony by prosecution witness given at prior trial on same charged, since the disappearance of the witness was due to inadvertence, not reckless disregard of an obligation by prison officials to produce her).

wrongdoing" under Rule 804(a).[58] However, where the government denies immunity, as well as threatens prosecution, resulting in the witness's intimidation and claim of privilege, some courts find that the government has procured the unavailability of the declarant.[59] Thus, in this context there is a basis for preventing the government from taking advantage of the exceptions contained in Rule 804(b).[60]

Rule 804(b)(1)   Hearsay Exceptions—Former Testimony

Rule 804(b)(1) reads as follows:

(b) **Hearsay Exceptions.** The following are not excluded by the hearsay rule if the declarant is unavailable as a witness:

(1) Former testimony. Testimony given as a witness at another hearing of the same or a different proceeding, or in a deposition taken in compliance with law in the course of the same or another proceeding, if the party against whom the testimony is now offered, or, in a civil action or proceeding, a predecessor in interest, had an opportunity and similar motive to develop the testimony by direct, cross, or redirect examination.

§ 804.9   Former Testimony—In General.

Rule 804(b)(1) creates a hearsay exception[61] for former testimony[62] by an

---

[58] United States v. Lang, 589 F.2d 92, 95-96 (2d Cir. 1978) ("the law appears to be well settled that the power of the Executive Branch to grant immunity to a witness is discretionary and no obligation exists on the part of the United States Attorney to seek such immunity").

[59] United States v. Morrison, 535 F.2d 223, 225-29 (3d Cir. 1976) (prosecutor's repeated warnings to 18-year-old defense witness, which culminated in a highly intimidating personal interview in the presence of the three law enforcement agents whose testimony she was supposed to refute, was completely unnecessary; due process demanded that the Government request use immunity for this witness).

[60] 4 LOUISELL & MUELLER, § 486, at 1070-73.

[61] *See, generally,* MCCORMICK, §§ 254-61; 4 WEINSTEIN, ¶¶ 804(b)(1)[01]-[06]; 4 LOUISELL & MUELLER, § 487; 5 WIGMORE, §§ 1370, 1371, 1386-89, 1402-15, 1660-69; 7 WIGMORE, §§ 2098-99, 2103. *See also* Falknor, *Former Testimony and the Uniform Rules: A Comment,* 38 N.Y.U. L. REV. 651 (1963); Comment, *Hearsay Under the Proposed Federal Rules: A Discretionary Approach,* 15 Wayne L. Rev. 1077, 1201-1209 (1969); Note, *Affidavits, Depositions, and Prior Testimony,* 46 IOWA L. REV. 356 (1961).

[62] Wigmore classified such statements contained in former testimony as nonhearsay, in light of the fact that they are, by definition, given under oath with adequate opportunity for cross-examination. 5 WIGMORE, § 1370, at 55:

unavailable declarant[63] where the declarant made the statement under oath while testifying "as a witness" in a "proceeding" and the party against whom the statement is offered (or in civil cases "a predecessor in interest") had an "opportunity" and "similar motive" to "develop" the declarant's testimony by direct, redirect or cross-examination at the former proceeding.

Since Rule 804(b)(1) is concerned solely with the hearsay issue, it does not affect an objection to the prior testimony evidence predicated upon some other basis which would render in person testimony with the same content objectionable.[64] Accordingly, although the prior testimony may qualify under Rule 804(b)(1), it may nevertheless be excluded because it is irrelevant or, if relevant, because of the operation of any other exclusionary rule or doctrine. This principle clearly applies where the objecting party was effectively denied an opportunity to object to the former testimony at the time of its taking. For example, former opinion testimony of a non-expert declarant, adduced at an administrative hearing where the Rules of Evidence do not apply, may be subject to objection at a subsequent trial despite the prior failure to object, *i.e.*, where it would have been out of order and futile for the objecting party to interpose an objection before the

When, therefore, a statement has already been subjected to cross-examination and is hence admitted—as in the case of a deposition or testimony at a former trial—it comes in because the rule is satisfied, not because an exception to the rule is allowed. The statement may have been made before the present trial, but if it has already been subjected to proper cross-examination, it has satisfied the rule and needs no exception in its favor.

This position reflects Wigmore's characteristic emphasis upon the value of cross-examination in insuring reliability. Most courts and commentators, however, adopt the position taken by Rule 804(b)(1) that such statements are hearsay and thus require a specific exception for their introduction as substantive evidence at trial. *See, e.g.*, United States v. Maturo, 536 F.2d 427, 429 (D.C. Cir. 1976) (deposition in civil case admitted in criminal trial as a recognized exception to the hearsay rule); Morgan, Basic Problems of Evidence 255 (1962). For a discussion of the former testimony exception, *see, generally*, 4 LOUISELL & MUELLER, § 487; McCORMICK, §§ 254-61; 4 Weinstein, ¶¶ 804(b)(1)[01]-[05]; 5 WIGMORE, §§ 1370,

1371, 1386-89 (requirements of adequate opportunity to cross-examine); §§ 1402-15 (unavailability of witness); §§ 1660-69 (proof by official notes, records, reports, etc.); 7 id. §§ 2098, 2099, 2103 (proof of entire testimony).

[63] For a discussion of the requirement of unavailability, see §§ 804.1 *et seq.* of this Treatise.

[64] United States v. Cervantes, 542 F.2d 773, 778 (9th Cir. 1976) (no abuse of discretion where trial judge excluded prior testimony of informant in unrelated case, since there had been extensive testimony as to informant's activities and criminal past); Hackley v. Roudebush, 520 F.2d 108, 156 n.195 (D.C. Cir. 1975) (since testimony before hearing examiner in VA case is admissible in administrative proceedings it may pose a double hearsay problem, thus the parties should be able to object to the admissibility of particular portions of the administrative record on specific grounds); Scotti v. National Airlines, Inc., 15 F.R.D. 502, 502-03 (D.C.N.Y. 1954) (depositions from prior actions against airline in personal injury action and another defendant arising out of the same accident would be admissible against the airline).

administrative tribunal. In this situation, the objecting party did not have an "opportunity" to object under the evidentiary rules governing the administrative hearing and may, therefore, properly object at a subsequent judicial trial or hearing. It must be noted, however, that this principle may be inapplicable where the objecting party (or his successor in civil cases) had an opportunity to object to the form of the question or the testimony at the prior proceeding and failed to do so. Consequently, an objection to the form of the question or the unresponsive nature of the answer should not operate to exclude the statement under the Rule absent a prior assertion of the objection at the former proceeding. In this situation, the party empowered to object in the former proceeding may be estopped from doing so in the latter proceeding for his failure to avail himself of the opportunity.[65] This principle applies to depositions in civil actions under Civil Procedure Rule 32(d)(3) and should have like force under the Rule.

It should be noted that Rule 804(b)(1) is not the only vehicle for the admission of former testimony. For example, a transcript may be used for impeachment purposes under Rule 801(d)(1)(A).[66] Also, its receipt into evidence may be justified by resort to some other exception to the hearsay doctrine, such as a statement against interest under Rule 804(b)(3) or an admission under Rule 801(d)(2).[67] Alternately, testimony of a witness at a former hearing may be used at trial, not as proof of the matter asserted therein, but instead to refresh the witness's present recollection under Rule 612. The fact that a statement is contained in former testimony does not preclude application of other Rules for its use or admission at subsequent trials.

While official transcripts generally are used to prove former testimony, Rule 804(b)(1) does not mandate this type of proof. Admission of former testimony through a recorded transcript involves, by necessity, two levels of hearsay—the declarant and the reporter. In this context, the official transcript is usually admissible through the public records' exception of Rule

---

[65] McCormick, § 259, at 623 ("[O]bjections which go merely to the form of the testimony, as on the grounds of leading questions, unresponsiveness, or opinion, must be made at the original hearing, when they can be corrected, but objections which go to the relevancy or the competence of the evidence may be asserted for the first time when the former testimony is offered at the present trial.").

[66] See discussion of this Rule in § 801.12 of this Treatise.

[67] See, e.g., B-W Acceptance Corp. v. Porter, 568 F.2d 1179, 1183 (5th Cir. 1978)

(defendant properly permitted to elicit from witness the substance of testimony given at prior trial by plaintiff's branch manager); United States v. Vecchiarello, 569 F.2d 656, 663-65 (D.C. Cir. 1977) (previous depositions of defendants for prosecution for wire and mail fraud in civil action properly admitted in instant criminal action); Rule v. International Ass'n of Bridge, etc., 568 F.2d 558, 568-69 (8th Cir. 1977) (depositions taken in previous government action admissible in instant class action regardless whether deponents were available to testify).

803(8), thus resolving the double hearsay problem.[68] But neither Rule 804(b)(1) nor the best evidence doctrine requires use of an official transcript, and, consequently, the proponent of former testimony may offer proof of the testimony in several other ways:[69] (i) through the testimony of a person who has firsthand knowledge of the former proceedings who remembers the general thrust of the testimony though perhaps not the exact language;[70] (ii) through the testimony of a firsthand observer whose recollection was refreshed by resort to a memorandum, such as a recording or stenographer's notes;[71] or (iii) through the notes of a firsthand observer if this evidence satisfies the requirements under Rule 803(5) for recorded recollection or under Rule 803(8) for public records.[72] Since it is arguable that at least one modern rationale for this exception is the unusual degree of reliability provided by official transcripts, where any other form of proof is offered, courts should be especially cautious in receiving evidence of former testimony.

Finally, where the proponent offers only part of the former testimony or deposition, the adverse party is entitled under Rule 106 to require her to introduce any other part which should in fairness be considered by the trier of fact.[73]

[68] Mattox v. United States, 156 U.S. 237, 244, 15 S.Ct. 337, 340, 39 L.Ed. 409, 411 (1895) (copy of stenographic report of former testimony supported by oath of stenographer and testimony of deceased witness is competent evidence); United States v. Arias, 575 F.2d 253, 254-55 (9th Cir. 1975), cert. denied, 439 U.S. 868, 99 S.Ct. 196, 58 L.Ed.2d 179 (1978) (transcript of allegedly perjured testimony introduced against defendant); Hackley v. Roudebush, 520 F.2d 108, 110 (D.C. Cir. 1975) (transcript of hearing forming basis of arbitrator's decision in discrimination proceedings admissible).

[69] 4 WEINSTEIN, ¶ 804(b)(1)[01], at 804-56.

[70] Id. See Meyers v. United States, 171 F.2d 800, 812-13 (D.C. Cir. 1948), cert. denied, 336 U.S. 912, 69 S.Ct. 602, 93 L.Ed. 1076 (1949) (former testimony could be proved by oral testimony of one present at former trial, even though transcript was available).

[71] 4 WEINSTEIN, ¶ 804(b)(1)[01], at 804-56. See §§ 612.1 et seq. of this Treatise; Mc-

CORMICK, § 260, at 624-25. See also Mulcahey v. Lake Erie & W. R. Co., 69 F. 172, 173 (6th Cir. 1895) (Congressional act does not admit former testimony found in stenographer's notes, although some state statutes do).

[72] 4 WEINSTEIN, ¶ 804(b)(1)[01], at 804-56. See §§ 803.22 et seq. and §§ 803.39 et seq. of this Treatise; McCORMICK, § 260, at 625. See also United States v. Arias, 575 F.2d 253, 255 (9th Cir. 1978), cert. denied, 439 U.S. 868, 99 S.Ct. 196, 58 L.Ed.2d 179 (1978).

[73] See § 106.1 of this Treatise. See also McCORMICK, § 260, at 624 ("When only a portion of the former testimony of a witness is introduced by the proponent, the result may be a distorted and inaccurate impression. Hence the adversary is entitled to the introduction of such other parts as fairness requires, and to have them introduced at that time, rather than waiting until the presentation of his own case."); 4 WEINSTEIN, ¶ 804(b)(1)[01], at 804-57.

§ 804.10   Former Testimony—Rationale.

The common law exception to the hearsay rule codified in Rule 804(b)(1) is justified by the traditional policies of necessity and trustworthiness.[74] The necessity lies in the simple fact that the declarant, once available as a witness in a former proceeding, is unavailable at trial in accordance with Rule 804(a). Trustworthiness is present because, by definition, the declarant was under oath and subject to examination and cross-examination as a means of developing the testimonial evidence at the former proceeding. Where the declarant served as a witness under penalty of perjury, there exists a high degree of reliability that the substance of his prior testimony is accurate and complete, thus justifying its admission.[75]

It is somewhat anomalous, however, that hearsay statements taken under oath and subject to cross-examination do not qualify for admission absent an affirmative demonstration of unavailability of the declarant. The only explanation for this requirement seems to be traceable to the historical treatment of such evidence, coupled with the traditional suspicion of deciding cases without the benefit of live testimony. Where a transcript is presented to the trier of fact, an opportunity to evaluate a witness's demeanor is lacking.[76] In deference to this common law approach, the exception for former testimony requires as a condition precedent the unavailability of the declarant.[77]

§ 804.11   "Testimony" Adduced in a "Proceeding."

Rule 804(b)(1) restricts use of a declarant's testimonial statements to those made in a duly authorized deposition or hearing of a "proceeding."

[74] See 4 Louisell & Mueller, § 487, at 1075.

[75] See Ohio v. Roberts, 448 U.S. 56, 69, 100 S.Ct. 2531, 2542, 65 L.Ed.2d 597, 612 (1980) (upheld receipt of testimony by witness who had been subjected to what the court considered the functional equivalent of cross-examination); Mancusi v. Stubbs, 408 U.S. 204, 216, 92 S.Ct. 2308, 2318, 33 L.Ed.2d 293, 303 (1972) (upheld receipt of testimony given in prior trial, since it was reliable and provided an adequate basis for evaluating its truth).

[76] Broadcast Music v. Havana Madrid Restaurant Corp., 175 F.2d 77, 80 (2d Cir. 1949) ("[T]he liar's story may seem uncontradicted to one who merely reads it, yet it may be 'contradicted' in the trial court by his manner, his intonations, his grimaces, his gestures and the like—all matters which 'cold print does not preserve' and which constitute 'lost evidence' so far as an upper court is concerned.").

[77] See Fed. R. Evid. 804(b)(1) Advisory Committee Note:

However, opportunity to observe demeanor is what in large measure confers depth and meaning upon oath and cross-examination. Thus in cases under Rule 803 demeanor lacks the

The term "proceeding" should, absent any statutory definition, be broadly interpreted to encompass any form of official inquiry conducted in accordance with law, including judicial, administrative, or legislative forums.[78] Conversely, however, the term "testimony" should be restricted to only recorded statements which are made under oath and subject to prosecution for perjury.[79] Accordingly, Rule 804(b)(1) clearly encompasses testimony adduced at a former trial, a deposition, a grand jury proceeding, and an administrative hearing. Equally clear, the Rule does not include statements contained in affidavits, statements made to police during investigations, or other witness statements. Essentially, if the general requirements of an oath, adequate opportunity to examine or cross-examine and present unavailability are satisfied, then the character of the tribunal and the precise form of the proceedings should not be determinative.

§ 804.12　Opportunity to Develop Testimony—Cross-Examination.

Historically, the cross-examination attending prior testimony has been considered the foremost guarantee of reliability justifying this hearsay exception.[80] Where the opportunity for cross-examination was lacking in the prior tribunal, the formal testimony traditionally has been excluded. Even where the prior tribunal lacked jurisdiction to compel the testimony, the admission of testimonial evidence at a subsequent trial has been considered justified where "the sworn statements of the witness, now dead or unavailable, about the facts of which he had knowledge, were made under such circumstances of opportunity and motive for cross-examination as to make them sufficiently trustworthy to be used in the effort to ascertain the truth."[81]

Under the Rule, *actual* cross-examination is not a condition precedent to admission of former testimony, but merely, as Wigmore has asserted, "an *opportunity to exercise the right to cross-examine if desired.*"[82] (Moreover,

significance which it possesses with respect to testimony. In any event, the tradition, founded in experience, uniformly favors production of the witness if he is available. The exception indicates continuation of the policy.

[78] *See* 4 Louisell & Mueller, § 487, at 1082 to 1085; McCormick, § 258, at 622-23.

[79] *See* United States v. Callahan, 442 F. Supp. 1213, 1222 (D.C. Minn. 1978), *later proceeding*, 455 F.Supp. 524 (D.C. Minn. 1978), *rev'd on other grounds*, 596 F.2d 759 (8th Cir. 1978) (transcript of the plea bar-

gain made by a third person, who was unavailable not admissible, since declarant had not been sworn in and cross-examined).

[80] *See, e.g.*, Ohio v. Roberts, 448 U.S. 56, 69, 100 S.Ct. 2531, 2542, 65 L.Ed.2d 597, 612 (1980). *See also* 4 Weinstein, ¶ 804(b)(1)[02], at 804-57.

[81] McCormick, § 258, at 623. *See also* 4 Weinstein, ¶ 804(b)(1)[02], at 804-58.

[82] 5 Wigmore, § 1371, at 55 (emphasis in original). *See also* Ohio v. Roberts, 448 U.S. 56, 69, 100 S.Ct. 2531, 2542, 65 L.Ed.2d 597, 612 (1980).

as discussed in the next section of this Chapter, an opportunity to develop testimony at the former proceeding by direct or redirect examination may also satisfy the Rule.) The rationale for this aspect of the Rule rests primarily upon estoppel principles. Wherever a party (or his predecessor in a civil case) fails or refuses to avail himself of the opportunity to test the testimony of a witness, it is presumed to have been because he believes that the testimony could not or need not be disputed.[83] Where the party foregoes cross-examination, it is not unfair to make him suffer the consequences.[84] Of course, in some cases an opportunity for cross-examination is presented, but special circumstances hamper efforts to test the credibility of the witness or the reliability of the testimony. Accordingly, in order to satisfy the opportunity requirement of Rule 804(b)(1), "[t]he opportunity must have been such as to render the conduct of the cross-examination or the decision not to cross-examine meaningful in the light of the circumstances which prevail when the former testimony is offered."[85]

Factors affecting the opportunity requirement with regard to testimonial evidence include: (i) the nature of the former tribunal or hearing, *i.e.*, whether the rules of the forum or the scope of the inquiry furnished adequate opportunity to cross-examine; (ii) notice to the opponent as affecting the opportunity to prepare for any cross-examination; and (iii) the course of the cross-examination itself, and whether it furnished only an incomplete opportunity to test the witness's sincerity, narrative ability, perceptive ability and memory.[86] This analysis obtains whether the evidence is in the form of trial or deposition testimony.

§ 804.13   Former Testimony—Direct or Indirect Examination.

Rule 804(b)(1) permits testimony offered by a party at a prior proceeding to be used against him where the party or, in a civil case, his predecessor in interest, had an opportunity to develop the testimony "by direct . . . or indirect examination." While this practice is in consonance with the historical common law, it creates different issues which do not arise where the evidence is offered *against the same party* in both proceedings. Where

[83] McCormick, § 255, at 616 to 617; 5 Wigmore, § 1371. *See, generally*, 4 Weinstein, ¶ 804(b)(1)[02].

[84] 4 Weinstein, ¶ 804(b)(1)[02], at 804-58; *In re* Related Asbestos Cases, 543 F. Supp. 1142, 1148 (N.D. Cal. 1982).

[85] McCormick, § 255, at 761-62. *See also* United States v. Monaco, 702 F.2d 860, 864-72 (11th Cir. 1983); United States v. Franklin, 235 F. Supp. 338, 341 (D.D.C. 1964).

Courts have excluded prior testimony when the opportunity requirement of Rule 804(b)(1) has not been met. *See, e.g.,* Whetherill v. University of Chicago, 565 F. Supp. 1553, 1564-65 (N.D. Ill. 1983); *In re* Shangri-La Nursing Center, Inc., 31 B.R. 367, 370 (E.D.N.Y. 1983); Matter of Sterling Navigation Co., Ltd., 444 F. Supp. 1043, 1046 (S.D.N.Y. 1977).

[86] McCormick, § 255, at 616-17.

testimony adduced on direct examination by a party at a former proceeding is offered against that party at a subsequent proceeding, questions may fairly arise as to whether the direct examination at the former trial is the functional equivalent of adequate cross-examination. Commentators generally assert that direct examination should be considered the equivalent of cross-examination for the purposes of satisfying the prior testimony exception.[87] Because the opportunity for cross-examination is intended to protect a party against the evidence of an *adverse* witness, the party has no particular need to use such a device for a witness he had offered at the prior trial. This common law concept, coupled with the right to impeach a party's own witness under Rule 607, diminishes the problem to a significant degree. Accordingly, where the testimony of a witness at a prior trial is offered against the party who called the witness at the prior proceeding (or a successor in interest in a civil case), the "opportunity" requirements of Rule 804(b) may be satisfied.

The question may arise as to whether the opportunity requirement is satisfied where cross-examination testimony from a former proceeding is offered against the party who called the witness at the prior trial, hearing or deposition. In this context the issue focuses upon whether the party had an adequate opportunity to conduct a meaningful *redirect* examination of the witness as to the pertinent factual matter. As to the opportunity to conduct a redirect examination, the issues are essentially the same as those presented in the context of the opportunity to conduct a cross-examination, and the immediately preceding section of this Chapter sets forth the applicable analysis.

§ 804.14   "Identity of Issues;" "Identity of Parties"—Successor in Interest in Civil Cases.

The former testimony exception at common law focused on whether the examination of the witness at the prior proceeding was substantially similar to that which would have occurred at the current proceeding if the

---

[87] *See, e.g.*, McCormick, § 255; 4 Weinstein, ¶ 804(b)(1)[03], at 804-62; Falknor, *Former Testimony and the Uniform Rules: A Comment*, 38 N.Y.U. L. Rev. 651, n.1 (1963). Wigmore aptly explains:

[T]he whole notion of cross-examination refers to one's right to probe the statements of an opponent's witness, not one's own witness; thus, if A has taken X's deposition or called X to the stand, and B has cross-examined, it is not for A to object that he has not had the benefit of cross-examination: that benefit was not intended for him nor needed by him; it was intended only to protect against an opponent's witness, who would be otherwise unexamined by A; and if A has had the benefit of examinating a witness called on his own behalf, he has had all that he needs, and the right to probe by cross-examination is B's, not A's.

5 Wigmore, § 1389, at 121.

witness had testified.[88] Consequently, the common law exception developed two related—though distinct—requirements: identity of parties and identity of issues.[89] These now obsolete requirements essentially represent an overly formalistic approach to fulfilling the goal of ensuring adequate development of the appropriate facts by the party against whom the testimony is now offered.[90] Rule 804(b)(1) abandons the strict common law approach as to identity of issues in favor of the more critical consideration of ensuring that similar interests in developing facts are at stake in both proceedings. Consequently, Rule 804(b)(1) provides that former testimony may be admitted ". . . if the party against whom the testimony is now offered, or, in a civil action or proceeding, a predecessor in interest, had an opportunity and similar motive to develop the testimony by direct, cross, or redirect examination." As such, the Rule expands the common law restrictions without abandoning the essential fairness policy supporting the common law approach by focusing on the party against whom the hearsay is offered.

Rule 804(b)(1) reflects the historical concern "that it is generally unfair to impose upon the party against whom the hearsay evidence is being offered responsibility for the manner in which the witness was previously handled by another party"[91] except where, in a civil case, that other party was a predecessor in interest with a similar motive for interrogation. Consistent with this policy grounded in fairness, the relationship between the proponent of the prior testimony and any party in the prior proceeding is not significant in applying the Rule. Rather, it is the hearsay opponent's connection with the prior proceeding that is critical. The party against whom the hearsay is offered must have had an opportunity and similar motive to develop the testimony at the former proceeding, or in a civil case, his or her predecessor in interest must have had an opportunity and similar motive to develop the testimony.

The exact purport of the "predecessor in interest" language in the Rule is less than clear. The phrase could be narrowly construed as requiring privity between the opponent of the evidence and the party who had an opportunity to develop the testimony at the prior proceeding, as in the relationships of donor and donee, executor and testator, or principal and surety.[92]

---

[88] 4 WEINSTEIN, ¶ 804(b)(1)[04], at 804-65.

[89] Id.

[90] See, generally, McCORMICK, §§ 256-57; 4 WEINSTEIN, ¶ 804(b)(1)[04]; Fed. R. Evid. 804(b)(1) Advisory Committee Note.

[91] Report of Committee on the Judiciary, House of Representatives, 93d Cong., 1st

Sess., Federal Rules of Evidence, No. 93-650, p. 15 (1973).

[92] See, e.g., Federal Deposit Ins. Corp. v. Glickman, 450 F.2d 416, 418 (9th Cir. 1971) (in action by FDIC as bank receiver against obligor on promissory notes in favor of bank, proper to exclude testimony offered by government in prior criminal prosecu-

Conversely, the phrase could be read to require simply that the party to the prior proceeding, *i.e.* the predecessor, had a similar motive and "interest" as the present opponent. While such an expansive reading of this language would appear to reduce the opportunity requirement to a nullity, some federal courts interpreting the Rule, nevertheless, have read the language broadly to include virtually anyone who would satisfy the similar motive requirement.[93] While perhaps reliability and fairness are not sacrificed by the broader interpretation of the predecessor in interest requirement, the stricter reading more logically comports with the customary meaning of the term "predecessor in interest," and moreover, it preserves the obvious intent of the Rule to require more than simply a similarity in motive as between the party developing the testimony at the prior proceeding and the party against whom it is offered in the instant proceeding.[94]

It should be noted that the flexibility in the Rule with respect to predecessors in interest expressly applies only in civil proceedings. Where the former testimony is offered against the accused in a criminal case, identity of parties is a strict requirement, a topic further discussed in § 804.16 of this Chapter.

§ 804.15 Similar Motive Requirement.

The "similar motive" element of Rule 804(b)(1) is more expansive than the common law identity of issues doctrine.[95] Different causes of action, additional issues, or a shift in theory are of no substantive consequence under the Rule and should not defeat admissibility.[96] At most what is required under Rule 804(b)(1) is that the *factual* issue upon which the testimony was offered in the prior proceeding must be the same as the *factual* issue upon which it is offered in the instant cause. Even this statement of

tion of bank president and another agent, offered in instant case by defendant to prove that another was agent). *See also* Metropolitan St. Ry. Co. v. Gumby, 99 F. 192, 198 (2d Cir. 1900).

[93] Lloyd v. American Export Lines, Inc., 580 F.2d 1179, 1185 (3d Cir. 1978), *cert. denied*, 439 U.S. 969, 99 S.Ct. 461, 58 L.Ed.2d 428 (1978) (court found error in exclusion of testimony, preferring a "realistically generous" interpretation of the term "predecessor in interest" over "one that is formalistically grudging"). *See also* Clay v. Johns-Manville Sales Corp., 772 F.2d 1289, 1294-95 (6th Cir. 1983); Matter of Johns-Manville/Asbestosis Cases, 93 F.R.D. 853, 854-56 (N.D. Ill. 1982); Zenith Radio Corp.

v. Matsushita Electric Industrial Co., Ltd., 505 F. Supp. 1190, 1288-91 (E.D. Pa. 1980); In re Master Key Antitrust Litigation, 72 F.R.D. 108, 109 (D. Conn. 1976), *aff'd per curiam*, 551 F.2d 300 (2d Cir. 1976).

[94] *See* In re IBM Peripheral EDP Devices Antitrust Litig. v. IBM Corp., 444 F. Supp. 110, 112-13 (N.D. Cal. 1978) (refusing to find parties in other cases predecessors in interest of party in instant case).

[95] 4 Weinstein, ¶ 804(b)(1)[04], at 804-65 to 804-66.

[96] *Id*. at 804-66 ("A shift in the theory of the case does not defeat admissibility when the underlying liability remains the same thereby guaranteeing cross-examination with the same purpose . . . .").

the requirement of the Rule may be too restrictive in certain cases, and the similar motive requirement may be satisfied even in the absence of precise identity of *factual* issues. The Rule requires only a *similar* motive, not an *identical* motive, to develop or limit the testimony. The intent of the Rule is not to bind anyone to a position formerly adopted, as may be the theory in res judicata or collateral estoppel, but rather to salvage the testimonial evidence of a person now unavailable for its apparent worth. Consequently, the common law identity of issue requirement is relaxed to provide that the issue in the prior proceeding (hence, the purpose for which the testimony was offered) must have been such that the present opponent had an adequate motive to test and further develop the prior testimony now offered.[97] The Rule seeks to achieve fairness by imposing factual testimony on a party only where he (or his predecessor in a civil case) had a motive to develop or, alternatively, to limit the weight of the testimony at the former proceeding.[98] Accordingly, the similar motive requirement should be read to mean "motive to develop *facts*" or "motive to *limit* the weight to be accorded the prior testimony."

The Rule treats former testimony and depositions equally,[99] despite the fact that a party may have a lessened or different motive to interrogate a deponent as opposed to a witness at trial. It is at least arguable that since the deposition is essentially a discovery technique, the motive to interrogate at a deposition is sufficiently distinct to preclude admissibility of statements of declarants taken during depositions. This argument, however, is grounded on faulty or obsolete premises and should not, *in itself*, lead to different treatment for depositions. Deponents may not be, and often are not expected to be, present at the trial or subsequent proceeding. Consequently, a party can rarely afford to forego an opportunity to cross-examine and impeach the deponent, and any decision to defer interrogation

---

[97] *See* McCORMICK, § 257; 4 WEINSTEIN, ¶ 804(b)(1)[04].

[98] Some courts have recognized the fairness policy of Rule 804(b)(1) when interpreting the rule. *See, e.g.,* DeLuryea v. Winthrop, 697 F.2d 222, 226-27 (8th Cir. 1983); Complaint of Paducah Towing Co., Inc., 692 F.2d 412, 418-19 (6th Cir. 1982); Lloyd v. American Export Lines, Inc., 580 F.2d 1179, 1190-1193 (3d Cir. 1978) (Stern, J., concurring), *cert. denied sub nom.* Alvarez v. American Export Lines, Inc., 439 U.S. 969, 99 S.Ct. 461, 58 L.Ed.2d 428 (1978); In the Matter of Johns-Manville Asbestosis Cases, 93 F.R.D. 853, 854-56 (N.D. Ill. 1982); Zenith Radio Corp. v. Matsushita Elec. Indus. Co., Ltd., 505 F. Supp. 1190, 1288-91 (E.D. Penn. 1980); In re Master Key Antitrust Litig., 72 F.R.D. 108, 109 (D. Conn. 1976), *aff'd per curiam,* 551 F.2d 300 (2d Cir. 1976).

[99] *See* Oberlin v. Marlin American Corp., 596 F.2d 1322, 1329 (7th Cir. 1979); Rutledge v. Electric Hose & Rubber Co., 327 F. Supp. 1267, 1271 (C.D. Cal.), *aff'd,* 511 F.2d 668 (9th Cir. 1971); Hertz v. Graham, 23 F.R.D. 17, 22-23 (D.C.N.Y. 1958); First National Bank v. National Airlines, Inc., 22 F.R.D. 46, 47-49 (D.C.N.Y. 1958); Scotti v. National Airlines, Inc., 15 F.R.D. 502, 502-03 (D.C.N.Y. 1954); Wolf v. United Air Lines, Inc., 12 F.R.D. 1, 3-4 (D.C. Pa. 1951).

should be seen as assuming the risk.[1] Even where the deposition is offered in a different proceeding than the one for which it was taken, if the opportunity and the similar motive requirements are satisfied, the hearsay generally should be admissible. The critical issue raised by Rule 804(b)(1) is whether to admit the evidence or completely sacrifice the testimony of the deponent, and, consequently, only genuinely dissimilar motives should result in exclusion.[2]

§ 804.16   Similar Motive—Criminal Proceedings—Constitutional Considerations

Rule 804(b)(1) is expressly applicable in criminal as well as civil proceedings, and should be construed and applied in consonance with Federal Criminal Procedure Rule 15(e) governing the use of depositions in criminal trials.[3] As is true with any hearsay offered in criminal cases, however, special problems are presented by the accused's sixth amendment right to confront witnesses against him.[4]

As a general constitutional principle, the government bears the burden in criminal cases of presenting live testimony, and failure to do so diligently and in good faith prevents use of the former testimony exception.[5] Where

---

[1] Cf. Wright Root Beer Co. v. Dr. Pepper Co., 414 F.2d 887, 889-91 (5th Cir. 1969) (discovery depositions should be "fully admissible").

[2] 4 WEINSTEIN, ¶ 804(b)(1)[04].

[3] Criminal Procedure Rule 15(e) provides:

At the trial or upon any hearing, a part or all of a deposition, so far as otherwise admissible under the rules of evidence, may be used as substantive evidence if the witness is unavailable, as defined in Rule 804(a) of the Federal Rules of Evidence, or the witness gives testimony at the trial or hearing inconsistent with his deposition. Any deposition may also be used by any party for the purpose of contradicting or impeaching the testimony of the deponent as a witness. If only a part of a deposition is offered in evidence by a party, an adverse party may require him to offer all of it which is relevant to the part offered and any party may offer other parts.

Fed. R. Crim. P. 15(e).

[4] 4 WEINSTEIN, ¶ 804(b)(1)[05]; see §§ 804.1 et seq. of this Treatise. See also Ohio v. Roberts, 448 U.S. 56, 69, 100 S.Ct. 2531, 2542, 65 L.Ed.2d 597, 612 (1980) (court upheld use of preliminary hearing testimony, since the witness had been subjected to the functional equivalent of defense cross-examination); Barber v. Page, 390 U.S. 719, 725-26, 88 S.Ct. 1318, 1323, 20 L.Ed.2d 255, 260-61 (1968) ("[W]hile there may be some justification for holding that the opportunity for cross-examination of a witness at a preliminary hearing satisfies the demands of the confrontation clause where the witness is shown to be actually unavailable, this is not, as we have pointed out, such a case"). See, generally, 4 LOUISELL & MUELLER, § 487, at 1111-14.

[5] 4 WEINSTEIN, ¶ 804(b)(1)[05]. See Mancusi v. Stubbs, 408 U.S. 204, 209, 92 S.Ct. 2308, 2312, 33 L.Ed.2d 293, 298 (1972) (upholding testimony by principal prosecution witness given in earlier trial, since witnesses had moved to Sweden in the meantime); Mattox v. United States, 156 U.S. 237, 242-44, 15 S.Ct. 337, 342, 39 L.Ed. 409, 411 (1895) (upholding testimony of prosecution witness given in earlier trial, since witness had died in the meantime); Thomas v. Cardwell, 626 F.2d 1375, 1384-

the government is unable through diligent efforts to produce the declarant at trial, however, the testimony of the declarant may be introduced against the accused under the former testimony exception where the testimony was adduced at a distinct trial of the accused[6] and the earlier trial did not suffer from prejudicial constitutional infirmities.[7]

More difficult problems, however, surround the use of testimony adduced at an accused's preliminary hearing on the charged offense. In this situation, it is at least arguable that, while an opportunity to cross-examine adverse witnesses at the preliminary hearing was presented, the "similar motive" to develop testimony does not exist. The interrogation at the preliminary hearing generally represents a "less searching exploration into the merits" of the government's case because the issue under consideration is not the ultimate guilt or innocence of the accused but merely the existence of probable cause to believe that the accused committed the charged offense.[8] However, the United States Supreme Court in Ohio v. Roberts,[9] has upheld the use against the accused of preliminary hearing testimony by a prosecution witness who was unavailable at trial.

In *Roberts,* the accused was charged with forgery and possession of stolen credit cards. At the preliminary hearing the defendant called the witness in the hope that she would testify that she had given the accused forged checks and credit cards without informing him of her lack of authority to use them. On the stand at the preliminary hearing, however, the witness refused to provide the anticipated testimony and actually repudiated the expected version of the facts. Defense counsel did not request to have her declared a hostile witness or to cross-examine her. The State did not interrogate. In concluding that the testimony was sufficiently reliable to be offered against the accused at his trial, the United States Supreme Court did not find it necessary to evaluate whether the "mere opportunity" to cross-examine the witness at the preliminary hearing satisfied the sixth amendment because defense counsel was permitted to use leading questions and impeach the witness on direct examination and therefore subjected her testimony to the "equivalent of significant cross-examination."[10]

---

86 (9th Cir. 1980); United States v. Davis, 551 F.2d 233, 235 (8th Cir. 1977), *cert. denied* 431 U.S. 923, 97 S.Ct. 2197, 53 L.Ed.2d 237 (1977) (upholding testimony given for government in previous prosecution of same defendant for another robbery); United States v. Amaya, 533 F.2d 188, 190-91 (5th Cir. 1976), *reh'd denied,* 540 F.2d 1086 (5th Cir. 1976), *cert. denied,* 429 U.S. 1101, 97 S.Ct. 1125, 51 L.Ed.2d 551 (1976) (upholding testimony on retrial that was used at original trial in action for conspiracy to distribute heroin).

[6] 4 LOUISELL & MUELLER, § 487, at 1111-14; 4 WEINSTEIN, ¶ 804(b)(1)[05].

[7] 4 LOUISELL & MUELLER, § 487, at 1111-14.

[8] Barber v. Page, 390 U.S. 719, 725, 88 S.Ct. 1318, 1323, 20 L.Ed.2d 255, 260 (1968).

[9] 448 U.S. 56, 100 S.Ct. 2531, 65 L.Ed.2d 597 (1980).

[10] *Id.* at 488 U.S. 56, 70, 100 S.Ct. 2531, 2543, 65 L.Ed.2d 597, 609 (1980).

Thus, the testimony was sufficiently reliable to warrant admission under the former testimony exception to the hearsay rule.

The ruling in *Roberts* relied substantially upon *California v. Green*,[11] in which the Court upheld use of preliminary hearing testimony against the accused at trial where the witness was actually called at trial by the prosecution. At trial the witness became uncooperative and evasive, and the prior testimony was offered both for impeachment of the witness and as substantive evidence. In *Green*, unlike *Roberts*, the Court focused on the "opportunity" for cross-examination, asserting that where the opportunity existed and counsel availed himself of the opportunity to cross-examine, the evidence bears sufficient indicia of trustworthiness to afford the trier of fact a satisfactory basis for evaluating the truth of the prior statement. Moreover, in *Green*, the declarant, *i.e.*, the witness at the preliminary hearing, was present as a witness at the trial at which his preliminary hearing testimony was offered. He was consequently available for *delayed* cross-examination as to his former testimony.[12]

While the holding in *Roberts* indicates that preliminary hearing testimony is not always inadmissible against the accused, the converse does not hold. The decisions in *Roberts* and *Green* should not be read to provide that testimony adduced at a preliminary hearing is, as a matter of universal principle, admissible against the accused in every case where the declarant is unavailable. It is clear that somewhat peculiar factual circumstances attended the original testimony in each case. In *Roberts*, the witness was actually called by the defendant, who, even after ascertaining the adverse nature of the testimony, failed to avail himself of the chance to discredit the substance of the testimony adduced. To similar effect, in *Green* the declarant was not only available at trial but was subjected to extensive examination at the preliminary hearing. Thus, despite the apparent broad holding of *Roberts* and *Green*, the testimony from a preliminary hearing must be tested by the same standards as any other form of former testimony for use in a criminal trial.[13] In light of the grave consequences flowing from criminal convictions, the trial court must remain especially cautious in exercising its discretion under the Rule and the complementary provisions of Rule 403 to exclude hearsay evidence where probative value is substantially outweighed by the danger of unfair prejudice or by its tendency to confuse or mislead the trier of fact. In this case-by-case determination, the contention that neither sufficient opportunity nor similar mo-

---

[11] 399 U.S. 149, 165-68, 90 S.Ct. 1930, 1942, 26 L.Ed.2d 489, 501-02 (1970), *on remand*, 3 Cal. 3d 981, 92 Cal. Rptr. 494, 479 P.2d 998 (1970), *cert. dismissed*, 404 U.S. 801, 92 S.Ct. 20, 30 L.Ed.2d 34 (1970).

[12] *Id.* at 399 U.S. 149, 165, 90 S.Ct. 1930, 1942, 26 L.Ed.2d 489, 501 (1970).

[13] *See, generally*, 4 LOUISELL & MUELLER, § 487, at 1111-14; 4 Weinstein, ¶ 804(b)(1)[05].

tive to develop testimony attended the preliminary hearing remains a viable argument which may operate to exclude former testimony adduced at a preliminary hearing under certain circumstances.

Finally, it should be noted that where the accused wishes to introduce former testimony qualifying under Rule 804(b)(1), the special constitutional problems under the confrontation clause are, of course, inapplicable, and in fact, due process may require admission of the testimony against the United States even though a state may have prosecuted the prior case.[14]

Rule 804(b)(2) Hearsay Exceptions—
Statement Under Belief of Impending Death

Rule 804(b)(2) reads as follows:

(b) **Hearsay Exceptions.** The following are not excluded by the hearsay rule if the declarant is unavailable as a witness: . . .

(2) *Statement under belief of impending death.* In a prosecution for homicide or in a civil action or proceeding, a statement made by a declarant while believing that his death was imminent, concerning the cause or circumstances of what he believed to be his impending death.

§ 804.17   Statement Under Belief of Impending Death—In General— Rationale.

The exception to the hearsay rule contained in Rule 804(b)(2) for statements traditionally known as "dying declarations" is a modern codification of the common law doctrine.[15] It has been described by McCormick as ". . . the most mystical in its theory and traditionally the most arbitrary in its limitations."[16] The exception for deathbed statements, which developed

---

[14] *See* Chambers v. Mississippi, 410 U.S. 284, 299, 93 S.Ct. 1038, 1049, 35 L.Ed.2d 397, 311 (1973). *Cf.* United States v. Lanci, 669 F.2d 391, 394-95 (6th Cir.), *cert. denied*, 457 U.S. 1134, 102 S.Ct. 2960, 73 L.Ed.2d 1350 (1982) (court denied defendant's request to introduce testimony given in state criminal trial because state did not have "similar motive to develop facts concerning the bribery of an FBI employee").

[15] *See, generally,* McCORMICK, §§ 281-87; 4 WEINSTEIN, ¶¶ 804(b)(2)[01]-[02]; 4

LOUISELL & MUELLER, § 488; 5 WIGMORE, §§ 1430-52. *See also* Quick, *Some Reflections on Dying Declarations,* 6 How. L.J. 109 (1960); Comment, *The Admissibility of Dying Declarations,* 38 FORDHAM L. REV. 509 (1970); Note, *Dying Declarations,* 46 IOWA L. REV. 375 (1961).

[16] McCORMICK, § 281, at 680. *See also* Quick, *Some Reflections on Dying Declarations,* 6 How. L.J. 109 (1960). *See, generally,* 5 WIGMORE, § 143. Notably, special reverence for the sincerity and veracity of

in the common law well before the development of the general rule prohibiting hearsay, originally derived its assumed guarantee of trustworthiness from the religious belief that no person would meet his maker with a lie on his lips.[17] In the more secular world, however, this rationale for the exception has largely been supplanted by the theory that the powerful psychological forces bearing on the declarant at the moment of death engender a compulsion to speak truthfully.[18] In any case, dying declarations are considered trustworthy because, given the restrictions on their use at trial, they are unlikely to be affected by problems in memory, although psychological stress and physical pain may as readily cause flaws in perception and narration.[19] It is for this reason that courts are, and should be, espe-

---

deathbed statements was not lost upon the Bard, who expressed the doctrine long before it was accepted by judicial process. *E.g.*, *Hamlet*, V, ii, 328-31 (1601) (Laertes: "[T]he foul practice / Hath turn'd itself on me; lo, here I lie, / Never to rise again: thy mother's poison'd: / I can no more: the king, the king's to blame."); *Henry IV, Part II*, IV, v, 182-88 (1598) (King Henry: "Come Hither, Harry, sit thou by my bed; / And hear, I think, the very latest counsel / That ever I shall breathe. God knows, my son, / By what by-paths and indirect crook'd ways / I met this crown; and I myself know well / How troublesome it sat upon my head."); *King John*, V, iv, 22-29 (1596) (Melun: "Have I not hideous death within my view, / Retaining but a quantity of life, / Which bleeds away, even as a form of wax / Resolveth from his figure 'gainst the fire? / What in the world should make me now deceive, / Since I must lose the use of all deceit? / Why should I then be false, since it is true / That I must die here and live hence by truth?").

[17] *See, generally*, 4 LOUISELL & MUELLER, § 488; McCORMICK, § 281; 4 WEINSTEIN, ¶ 804(b)(2)[01]; 5 WIGMORE, § 1438.

[18] Fed. R. Evid. 804(b)(2) Advisory Committee Note. Some commentators have looked askance at this exception's reliance upon modern psychological concepts for its primary justification. *See, e.g.*, Quick, *Some Reflections on Dying Declarations*, 6 How L.J. 109, 112 (1960) ("Indeed, in many instances the declarant is either suffering from an appreciable amount of pain or anxiety which may itself cloud his perception and ability to communicate, or his perception and consciousness have been dulled by pain-depressant drugs."); Note, *Dying Declarations*, 46 IOWA L. REV. 357, 376 (1961) (observing that experience indicates that desires for revenge or self-exoneration or to protect one's loved ones may continue until the moment of death).

[19] One of the most notable and vociferous attacks against the dying declaration exception to the hearsay rule may be found in Kidd v. State, 258 S.2d 423, 429-30 (Miss. 1972) (Smith, J., concurring):

[C]an it be said that a man who has been wounded and feels that he is dying, is by those circumstances alone, automatically stripped of all human malice, anger, and desire for revenge and is transformed *ipso facto* into a devout believer in life after death and in divine punishment? I cannot think so. Certainly the accused should not be deprived of his constitutional right to confrontation by the witnesses against him on a theory that meets neither the test of reason nor the facts of common knowledge and human experience. This harmful effect of the admission of this type of hearsay is enhanced by a recital of dramatic circumstances under which the statement is alleged to have been made, and the law having in effect declared this type of hearsay sacrosanct, there is no effective way to challenge its truth and it is more than just likely that the jury will attach undue importance to it and give it undue weight in arriving at a verdict.

Id. See generally, McCORMICK, § 286; 4 WEINSTEIN, ¶ 804(b)(2)[01].

cially cautious in scrutinizing the admissibility of statements offered under this exception. The exception contained in Rule 804(b)(2) also rests in part upon the necessity principle.[20] The Rule does not require that the declarant be dead, but only unavailable as defined in Rule 804(a).[21] In the usual case the words of the declarant are offered to prove that the accused was his murderer, and in this situation, necessity assumes special importance in justifying the exception.

Rule 804(b)(2) admits hearsay statements of declarants who are under the belief that death is imminent, where the statement concerns the cause or circumstances of what the declarant believed to be his impending death. Under the Rule the exception may be used in homicide cases, against or on behalf of the accused, as well as in any civil case. Accordingly, the Rule adopts the position of commentators that the reliability of the statement and its admissibility should not depend upon the character of the litigation in which it is offered.[22] If such statements are reliable against the accused in a homicide case, their reliability should not be diminished in, for example, a wrongful death action. Dying declarations remain, however, inadmissible in any criminal cases other than homicides.[23]

[20] *See* Carver v. United States, 164 U.S. 694, 697, 17 S.Ct. 228, 230, 41 L.Ed. 602, 603 (1897) (dying declarations "are received from the necessitations of the case and to prevent an entire failure of justice, as it frequently happens that no other witnesses to the homicide are present."); Mattox v. United States, 146 U.S. 140, 152, 13 S.Ct. 50, 61, 36 L.Ed.2d 917, 922 (1892) (mentioning "necessity" as reason for dying declaration exception and resolving the confrontation issue); United States Auto. Ass'n. v. Wharton, 237 F. Supp. 255, 258 (W.D. N.C. 1965) (court reasoned that untested testimony in this case is better than no testimony at all.)

See, generally, 5 WIGMORE, § 1436.

[21] *See* Fed. R. Evid. 804(b)(2) Advisory Committee's Note ("unavailability is not limited to death."). Accordingly, where the subjective contemplation of death is present, an out-of-court statement may satisfy the exception where an unexpected recovery occurs and the declarant becomes unavailable for a reason identified in Rule 804(a) other than death.

[22] Wigmore condemned the limitation of the use of this Rule to certain types of cases:

[I]t is as much consequence to the cause of justice that robberies and rapes be punished and torts and

breaches of trust be redressed as that murders be detected; the notion that a crime is more worthy the attention of Courts than a civil wrong is a traditional relic of the days when civil justice was administered in the royal courts as a purchased favor, and criminal prosecutions in the King's name were zealously encouraged because of the fines which they added to the royal revenues. . . . The sanction of a dying declaration is equally efficacious whether it speaks of a murder or a robbery or a fraudulent will; and the necessity being the same, the admissibility should be the same. . . . [The] limitations are heresies of the last century, which have not even the sanction of antiquity.

5 WIGMORE, § 1436. *See also* McCORMICK, § 283, at 681 ("The subsequent history of the rule is an object lesson in the dangers of the use by the judges of our system of precedents to preserve and fossilize judicial mistakes of an earlier generation.") *See, generally,* 4 WEINSTEIN, ¶ 804(b)(2)[01]; Quick, *Some Reflections on Dying Declarations,* 6 How L.J. 109, 115 n.26 (1960).

[23] 4 WEINSTEIN, ¶ 804(b)(2)[01].

Additionally, Rule 804(b)(2) discards the common law requirement that dying declarations be "voluntary" and uttered "in good faith." Commonly, these requirements were imposed to exclude statements made in response to questioning by bystanders, relatives, police officers, or investigators, and these requirements were especially designed to address questionable techniques of prodding answers out of a dying person.[24] In discarding these arbitrary restrictions, the Rule tacitly recognizes that the "good faith" element is satisfied by the declarant's belief in the imminence of death. Moreover, the "voluntariness" of any statement, as determined by the circumstances surrounding its making may be evaluated by the trial court under Rule 403.

Although Rule 804(b)(2) does not expressly so provide, the firsthand knowledge requirement of Rule 602 is applicable to the out-of-court statement of the declarant. Foundational evidence must be presented to permit the inference "that there was knowledge or the opportunity for knowledge as to the acts that are declared."[25]

§ 804.18   Requirement that Declarant Possess Subjective Belief in Certainty of Death—Spontaneity.

Rule 804(b)(2) expressly provides that before a dying declaration may be admitted, foundational evidence must establish that the declarant possessed a subjective belief in the certainty of his death. In theory, it is subjective consciousness of the death which critically reduces the motivation for fabrication. There is no standard rule of thumb here, and the requisite consciousness may be gleaned from many sources, including: the declarant's own words, the opinions of his attending physicians, the nature and extent of his wounds or illness, the fact that he received last rites, the statements made to the declarant about his condition, and similar circumstantial facts.[26] Moreover, the standard is subjective, and not what a "reasonable person" under similar conditions would believe regarding the im-

---

[24] See discussion in § 804.18 of this Treatise.

[25] See Shepard v. United States, 290 U.S. 96, 101, 54 S.Ct. 22, 26, 78 L.Ed. 196, 200 (1933). See also MCCORMICK, § 285, at 683 ("If it appears that the declarant did not have adequate opportunity to observe the facts recounted, the declaration will be rejected for want of the knowledge qualification.") (citing Mattox v. United States, 146 U.S. 140, 13 S.Ct. 50, 36 L.Ed. 917 (1892)).

See, generally, 5 WIGMORE, § 1445(2) and cases cited therein.

[26] See, e.g., United States v. Barnes, 464 F.2d 828, 831 (D.C. Cir. 1972), cert. denied, 410 U.S. 986, 93 S.Ct. 1514, 36 L.Ed.2d 183 (1972) (belief in impending death proved by declarant's statements and extent of injuries); United States v. Mobley, 421 F.2d 345, 347-48 (5th Cir. 1970) (by what declarant has been told about illness or injuries and by physicians' opinions).

minence of his demise.[27] As long as the declarant subjectively believes in the certainty of his death, or as Justice Cardozo cogently notes, "a settled hopeless expectation that death is near at hand,"[28] the statement concerning its cause or surrounding circumstances satisfies the instant requirement.

It must be noted that the exception for dying declarations presumes that the declarant's statements possess a degree of spontaneity, thus resembling the underlying characteristics of the exceptions for present sense impressions under Rule 803(1) and excited utterances under Rule 803(2). This element is reflected in the Rule's use of the word "imminent." This spontaneity element, however, should not be viewed as imposing a particular time limit on the amount of time that may elapse between the making of the statement and the expected moment of death of the declarant. No doubt, since the Rule requires the expectancy of death to be *imminent*, knowledge of a terminally ill or fatally wounded declarant that death is likely to arrive in a matter of years, months, weeks or, in some cases, days should not suffice. Although it may generally be said that as more time passes between the utterance of the statement and the death of the declarant, it becomes less probable that he believed his death to be imminent,[29] the primary focus of the trial court should be on the presence of physical and psychological forces tending to ensure reliability in the substance of the statement.[30]

In this regard the fact that the statement was solicited does not, *per se*, preclude use of the instant exception. Often, a person in the throes of death

---

[27] 4 LOUISELL & MUELLER, § 488, at 1120-23.

[28] Shepard v. United States, 290 U.S. 96, 99, 54 S.Ct. 22, 25, 78 L.Ed. 196, 199 (1933). *See also* 5 WIGMORE, § 1440, at 292-93 ("It follows from the general principle that the belief must be, not merely of the possibility of death, nor even of its probability, but of its *certainty*. A less stringent rule might with safety have been adopted; but this is the accepted one.") (emphasis in original).

[29] *See, e.g.,* United States v. Tovar, 687 F.2d 1210, 1212 (8th Cir. 1982); United States v. Etheridge, 424 F.2d 951, 959 (6th Cir. 1970), *cert. granted,* 400 U.S. 991, 91 S.Ct. 462, 27 L.Ed.2d 438 (1970), *cert. dismissed,* 402 U.S. 547, 91 S.Ct. 2174, 29 L.Ed.2d 102 (1970), *reh. denied,* 404 U.S. 875, 92 S.Ct. 32, 30 L.Ed.2d 122 (1970), *cert. denied,* 400 U.S. 993, 91 S.Ct. 463, 27

L.Ed.2d 442 (1970), *cert. denied,* 400 U.S. 1000, 91 S.Ct. 464, 27 L.Ed.2d 452 (1970), *reh. denied,* 401 U.S. 926, 91 S.Ct. 885, 27 L.Ed.2d 830 (1970) (approving receipt of statement by victim for dying declaration where he had been shot five times in the head and his own statements indicated that he contemplated death, notwithstanding the fact that declarant asked for an ambulance, since he did die shortly after making the declaration of naming his assailant).

[30] 4 LOUISELL & MUELLER, § 488; 4 WEINSTEIN, ¶ 804(b)(2)[01]. *E.g.,* Shepard v. United States, 290 U.S. 96, 99, 54 S.Ct. 22, 25, 78 L.Ed. 196, 199 (1933) ("[W]hat is decisive is the state of mind. Even so, the state of mind must be exhibited in the evidence, and not left to conjecture. The patient must have spoken with the consciousness of a swift and certain doom.").

may quite understandably be disposed "more toward silence than conversation, and the stimulus of a question may be essential" in eliciting information.[31] In fact, rational answers to pertinent inquiries may demonstrate the unlikelihood of misperception or a mistake in narration, thereby enhancing trustworthiness. Where it appears, however, that the interrogative technique was unduly burdensome or leading, so as to raise reasonable suspicions about the statement's accuracy, the trial court should exclude the statement under Rule 403.

§ 804.19   Requirement that Subject Pertain to "Cause or Circumstances" of Death.

In conformity with the traditional common law requirements, Rule 804(b)(2) requires that the statement concern "the cause or circumstances" of what declarant "believed to be his impending death."[32] Some commentators have criticized the rule as too vague or too susceptible of narrow application.[33]

The limitation presents little problem in its application where a victim identifies his murderer and characterizes the attack as unprovoked. Similarly, the statement qualifies if it describes the accident or occurrence causing the declarant mortal injury.[34] More difficult problems, however, arise

[31] 4 LOUISELL & MUELLER, § 488, at 1124. Statements made under the belief of impending death may be solicited. *See* United States v. Barnes, 464 F.2d 828, 831 (D.C. Cir.), *cert. denied*, 410 U.S. 986, 93 S.Ct. 1514, 36 L.Ed.2d 183 (1972); United States v. Etheridge, 424 F.2d 951, 959, 965-67 (6th Cir. 1970), *cert. denied*, 400 U.S. 991, 91 S.Ct. 462, 27 L.Ed.2d 438 (1970), *cert. dismissed*, 402 U.S. 547, 91 S.Ct. 2174, 29 L.Ed.2d 102 (1970), *reh. denied*, 404 U.S. 875, 92 S.Ct. 32, 30 L.Ed.2d 122 (1970), *cert. denied*, 400 U.S. 993, 91 S.Ct. 463, 27 L.Ed.2d 442 (1970), *cert. denied*, 400 U.S. 1000, 91 S.Ct. 464, 27 L.Ed.2d 452 (1970), *reh. denied*, 401 U.S. 926, 91 S.Ct. 885, 27 L.Ed.2d 830 (1970).

[32] 5 WIGMORE, § 1434, at 282 ("It must concern the facts leading up to or causing or attending the injurious act which has resulted in the declarant's death; for it is only to such facts that the supposed necessity for the statements can exist."). *See, generally*, 4 LOUISELL & MUELLER, § 488, at 1116-20; 4 WEINSTEIN, ¶ 804(b)(2)[01].

[33] *See* 5 WIGMORE, § 1434, at 284 (doctrine provides "opportunity for prolific quibbling"); McCORMICK, § 283, at 683; Quick, *Some Reflections on Dying Declarations*, 6 How L.J. 109, 116 (1960).

[34] United States v. Barnes, 464 F.2d 828, 831 (D.C. Cir.), *cert. denied*, 410 U.S. 986, 93 S.Ct. 1514, 36 L.Ed.2d 183 (1972); United States v. Etheridge, 424 F.2d 951, 965-67 (6th Cir. 1970), *cert. denied*, 400 U.S. 991, 91 S.Ct. 462, 27 L.Ed.2d 438 (1970), *cert. dismissed*, 402 U.S. 547, 91 S.Ct. 2174, 29 L.Ed.2d 102 (1970), *reh. denied*, 404 U.S. 875, 92 S.Ct. 32, 30 L.Ed.2d 122 (1970), *cert. denied*, 400 U.S. 993, 91 S.Ct. 463, 27 L.Ed.2d 442 (1970), *cert. denied*, 400 U.S. 1000, 91 S.Ct. 464, 27 L.Ed.2d 452 (1970), *reh. denied*, 401 U.S. 926, 91 S.Ct. 885, 27 L.Ed.2d 830 (1970). *See also* United States v. Mobley, 421 F.2d 345, 346-48 (5th Cir. 1970) (statement by bank president, who had been beaten and shot in course of robbery, was a dying declaration, since declarant knew he was dying and had been told "that he would be able to see his family, his minister, and bank officials"); United States Auto. Ass'n. v. Wharton, 237 F. Supp. 255, 257-60 (W.D.N.C. 1965) (statement made by driver just prior

where the statement relates not to direct causes, but to "circumstances" spatially or temporally removed from the declarant's expected death. Assertions concerning a previous threat or an earlier argument between the parties, or even those describing past physical pain or substances ingested or injected are illustrative. While a broad reading of the Rule would permit introduction of such statements, the trial court must nevertheless focus on the nexus between the time and circumstances of the event and the expected death in an effort to determine whether the declarant's subjective purpose is to describe the cause or circumstances of his expected death.[35] The determinant of admissibility here is, simply, whether the evidence will aid the trier of fact in ascertaining the truth, *i.e.*, whether it is sufficiently trustworthy and relevant to withstand the exclusionary provision of Rule 403.[36]

Rule 701's test of "helpfulness" should also resolve objections to the form of the statement where the declaration is phrased in terms of an opinion.[37] Where the requirements of firsthand knowledge and belief of imminent death are satisfied, a statement in opinion form should be admitted if it will help the fact-finding process, a contingency generally satisfied in light of the declarant's unavailability.

Rule 804(b)(3)   Hearsay Exceptions—Statement Against Interest

Rule 804(b)(3) reads as follows:

(b) **Hearsay Exceptions.** The following are not excluded by the hearsay rule if the declarant is unavailable as a witness: . . .

(3) *Statement against interest.* A statement which was at the time of its making so far contrary to the declarant's pecuniary or proprietary interest,

to accident to the passenger [his wife] that "we will go to eternity together" as he put the accelerator on the floorboard and turned the car deliberately head-on into the tractor trailer, and further that he "did it on purpose" clearly qualifies as a dying declaration, even though the end anticipated by the declarant did not befall him).

[35] *See, e.g.*, Carver v. United States, 160 U.S. 553, 556, 16 S.Ct. 388, 391, 40 L.Ed. 532, 535 (1896), *later appeal*, 164 U.S. 694, 17 S.Ct. 228, 41 L.Ed. 602 (1896) (endorses receipt of statement by murder victim as dying declaration; victim was shot on March 25, her statement was made on March 27, and she died on May 19); Mattox v. United States, 146 U.S. 140, 151-52, 13 S.Ct. 50, 59, 36 L.Ed. 917, 921-22 (1892), *later appeal*, 156 U.S. 237, 15 S.Ct. 337, 39 L.Ed. 409 (1892) ("[T]he length of time elapsing between the making of the declaration and the death is one of the elements to be considered, although . . . it is the impression of almost immediate dissolution, and not the rapid succession of death, in point of fact, that renders the testimony admissible").

[36] *See, generally*, 4 WEINSTEIN, ¶ 804(b)(2)[01].

[37] *See* 5 WIGMORE, § 1447, at 308:

The theory of [the opinion rule] is that, wherever the witness can state specifically the detailed facts ob-

or so far tended to subject him to civil or criminal liability, or to render invalid a claim by him against another, that a reasonable man in his position would not have made the statement unless he believed it to be true. A statement tending to expose the declarant to criminal liability and offered to exculpate the accused, is not admissible unless corroborating circumstances clearly indicate the trustworthiness of the statement.

§ 804.20   Statement Against Interest—In General—Foundational Requirements.

Rule 804(b)(3) codifies the common law exception to the hearsay rule for statements against interest.[38] The Rule embraces the traditional exception for statements against the financial or proprietary interests of the declarant and statements which tend to subject the declarant to civil liability.[39] It significantly expands the traditional pre-Rule doctrine, however, to include statements which tend to subject the declarant to criminal punishment— statements against "penal" interest.[40] Insofar as the statement is against the

served by him, the inferences to be drawn from them can equally well be drawn by the jury, so that the witness' inferences become superfluous. Now, since the declarant is here deceased, it is no longer possible to obtain from him by questions any more detailed data than his statement may contain, and hence his inferences are not in this instance superfluous.

Id.

[38] *See, generally*, McCORMICK, §§ 276-80; 4 WEINSTEIN, ¶¶ 804(b)(3)[01]-[04]; 4 LOUISELL & MUELLER, § 489; 5 WIGMORE, §§ 1455-77. *See also* Donelan, *An Increase in Interest*, FBI Law Enforcement Bulletin, May-July, 1974, 27; Fine, *Declarations Against Penal Interest in New York: Carte Blanche?*, 21 Syr. L. Rev. 1095 (1970); Jefferson, *Declarations Against Interest: An Exception to the Hearsay Rule*, 58 HARV. L. REV. 1 (1944); Morgan, *Declarations Against Interest*, 5 VAND. L. REV. 451 (1952); Reimer, *Admissibility of Third Party Declarations Against a Surety Under Fidelity Covers*, INSURANCE COUNCIL JOURNAL, April, 1973, 306; Note, *Declaration Against Penal Interest Recognized as an Exception to the Hearsay Rule*, 1977 WASH. U.L.Q. 349; Note, *Declaration Against Penal Interest: What Must be Corroborated Under the Newly Enacted Federal Rules of*

Evidence, Rule 804(b)(3)?, 9 VAL. U.L. REV. 421 (1975); Comment, *Evidence—The Unavailability Requirement of Declaration Against Interest Hearsay*, 55 IOWA L. REV. 477 (1969); Note, *Declarations Against Interest: A Critical Review of the Unavailability Requirement*, 52 CORNELL L.Q. 301 (1967).

[39] *See, generally*, McCORMICK, § 276; 5 WIGMORE, §§ 1458-67.

[40] Wigmore, as well as other eminent scholars, long assailed the limitation against statements tending to subject the declarant to criminal liability, characterizing it as a "barbarous doctrine," noting:

[I]t cannot be justified on grounds of policy. The only plausible reason of policy that has ever been advanced for such a limitation is the policy of procuring fabricated testimony to such an admission if oral. This is the ancient rusty weapon that has always been brandished to oppose any reform in the rules of evidence, *viz.*, the argument of danger of abuse. This would be a good argument against admitting any witnesses at all, for it is notorious that some witnesses will lie and that it is difficult to avoid being deceived by their lies. The truth is that any rule which ham-

declarant's penal interest, the Rule imposes the safeguard that the statement be "corroborated" in order to assure reliability.[41]

While Rule 804(b)(3) generally requires the trier of fact to evaluate statements against interest, Rule 403 nevertheless enables the trial judge to exclude statements otherwise qualifying under the exception where surrounding circumstances indicate that the probative value is substantially outweighed by the danger of its unfair prejudicial effect or tendency to confuse or mislead the trier of fact.[42]

At the outset, it must be noted that Rule 804(b)(3) does not include within its scope statements which would be against the "social" interest of the declarant, *i.e.*, those tending to make the declarant "an object of hatred, ridicule, or disgrace" in his community.[43] Where only "social" inter-

---

pers an honest man in exonerating himself is a bad rule, even if it also hampers a villain in falsely passing for an innocent.

5 Wigmore, § 1477, at 358-59. *See also* McCORMICK, § 278, at 674 ("[T]he argument of the danger of perjury is a dubious one since the danger is one that attends all human testimony."); Jefferson, *Declarations Against Interest: An Exception to the Hearsay Rule*, 58 HARV. L. REV. 1, 39 (1944) ("[P]enal interest is certainly as important to a person as pecuniary or proprietary interest."); Morgan, *Declarations Against Interest*, 5 VAND. L. REV. 451, 475 (1952) ("set tled foolish rule"). Justice Holmes, dissenting in *Donnelly v. United States*, 228 U.S. 243, 277, 33 S.Ct. 449, 478, 57 L.Ed. 820, 851 (1913), *reh. denied*, 228 U.S. 708, 33 S.Ct. 1024, 57 L.Ed. 1035, was no less vehement in his protest of the historical restriction:

> [T]he exception to the hearsay rule in the case of declarations against interest is well known; no other statement is so much against interest as a confession of murder; it is far more calculated to convince than dying declarations, which would be let in to hang a man; and when we surround the accused with so many safeguards, some of which seem to me excessive, I think we ought to give him the benefit of a fact that, if proved, commonly would have such weight.

Id. Rule 804(b)(3) recognizes this criticism and expands the common law to include statements against penal interest, if corroborated.

[41] This corroboration requirement was advanced by Justice Holmes, dissenting in Donnelly v. United States, 228 U.S. 243, 278, 33 S.Ct. 449, 479, 57 L.Ed. 820, 852 (1913) (arguing for admission of a declaration against penal interest, when "coupled with circumstances pointing to its truth," noting that one such factor would be that there existed no connection between the declarant and the accused). *See also* McCORMICK, § 278; 4 WEINSTEIN, ¶ 804(b)(3)[03].

[42] 4 WEINSTEIN, ¶ 804(b)(3)[03], at 804-92. *E.g.*, United States v. Love, 592 F.2d 1022, 1024 (8th Cir. 1979) (prior grand jury testimony offered by government properly excluded, since witness had formally been granted immunity prior to her grand jury testimony).

[43] As proposed by the Supreme Court, Rule 804(b)(3) included statements against these social interests, but Congress deleted the provision. *See* H.R. Rep. No. 93-650, 93d Cong., 1st Sess., pp. 15-16 (1973). The restriction against statements contrary to so-called "social interest," although in conformity with the common law, has been attacked by a number of commentators. *See, e.g.*, McCORMICK, § 278, at 674-75 ("Declarations against social interests, such as acknowledgements of facts which would subject the declarant to ridicule or disgrace, or facts calculated to arouse in the declarant a sense of shame or remorse, seem adequately buttressed in trustworthiness and should be received under the present principle."); Jefferson, *Declarations Against Interest: An Exception to the Hearsay Rule*, 58 HARV. L. REV. 1, 39 (1944) ("[O]ne [is not] likely to concede the existence of facts which would

ests are concerned, the requisite guarantees of trustworthiness are not thought sufficiently high to outweigh the danger that, in a world of rapidly changing moral attitudes, the statement may not have been against the declarant's interest as he perceived it.

The foundational requirements for statements against interest under Rule 804(b)(3) are: (i) the declarant must be unavailable as defined in Rule 804(a); (ii) the declarant must have firsthand knowledge as contemplated by Rule 602; (iii) the nature of the statement must be such that a reasonable person would not have uttered it unless he believed it to be true; and (iv) the statement must be contrary to a pecuniary, proprietary or penal interest at the time of its utterance.[44] In addition, where the statement is one against penal interest, which exculpates the accused in a criminal trial, there must be corroboration tending to guarantee the statement's trustworthiness.[45] The trial court must determine whether these foundational requirements are met pursuant to Rule 104(a). Since the requirements are derived from the rationale underlying the Rule, where any one is wanting, the statement may not be admitted under the aegis of Rule 804(b)(3). Nothing, however, would preclude the statement's admission pursuant to some other hearsay exception, such as that for business records, Rule 803(6),[46] or public records, Rule 803(8).[47]

§ 804.21   Admission of a Party-Opponent Distinguished.

It is critical to appreciate the distinction between declarations constituting statements against interest, as identified in Rule 804(b)(3), and those which are admissions of a party-opponent, as defined in Rule 801(d)(2). While it often happens that an admission will be contrary to some interest of a party to the litigation, none of the foundational requirements of Rule 804(b)(3) is required to be satisfied prior to the introduction of admissions.[48] Admissions of a party-opponent are excluded from the definition of

make him an object of social disapproval in the community unless the facts are true."); Morgan, *Declarations Against Interest*, 5 VAND. L. REV. 451, 475 (1952) ("[I]t requires no argument to convince that the realization of such a consequence is generally a much more powerful influence upon conduct, than the realization of legal responsibility for a sum of money.").

[44] *See, generally,* McCORMICK, § 276; 4 WEINSTEIN, ¶ 804(b)(3)[02]; 5 WIGMORE, § 1471.

[45] *See, e.g.,* United States v. Toney, 599 F.2d 787, 789-90 (6th Cir. 1979) (reversible error to exclude statement that was against interest because it "revealed his illicit gambling activities" and disclosed that he had "been gambling with a large sum of money a few hours after the bank robbery"). *See also* 4 WEINSTEIN, ¶ 804(b)(3)[03], at 804-103 to 804-109.

[46] *See* § 803.28 *et seq.* of this Treatise.

[47] *See* § 803.39 *et seq.* of this Treatise.

[48] *See* McCORMICK, § 276, at 820. *See also* 5 WIGMORE, § 1475.

hearsay under the Rules' evidentiary scheme,[49] and admissions may be introduced without regard to whether the declarant is unavailable, whether the statement was against any particular interest when made, whether the party had any firsthand knowledge of the underlying events, or whether any sort of "reasonable man" test is satisfied.

Since the underlying theory of admissions by a party-opponent essentially rests upon principles of estoppel, rather than upon circumstantial guarantees of trustworthiness, the prerequisites to the introduction of statements against interest are not applicable to admissions of a party-opponent. The critical distinction rests in the requirement that an admission be adverse to a party's case *at the time of introduction at trial*. A statement admitted under Rule 804(b)(3) must have had apparent adverse consequences for the declarant *at the time of its utterance*. The estoppel nature of admissions is reflected in the principle that an admission may only be introduced *against* the party-declarant who uttered the out-of-court statement, whereas a statement against interest may be introduced for or against any party as long as the declaration was against a recognized interest at the time of its utterance.

Finally, and perhaps most critically, an admission must be a statement of a party or a statement attributable to a party to the litigation. A statement against interest involves an assertion by any out-of-court declarant.

§ 804.22 Rationale.

Like the other hearsay exceptions contained in Rules 803 and 804, the exception for statements against interest is predicated upon the dual grounds of necessity and trustworthiness. The necessity principle is reflected by the requirement that the declarant be unavailable. Where unavailability is demonstrated, there exists a genuine need to accept the declarant's out-of-court statement since obtaining evidence from the same source is otherwise impossible.[50]

The guarantee of trustworthiness is traditionally presumed to be present for statements against interest because human experience indicates that a statement asserting a fact distinctly against the declarant's interest is unlikely to be deliberately false or heedlessly incorrect. Consequently, state-

---

[49] *See* § 801.15 *et seq.* of this Treatise.

[50] *See* 5 WIGMORE, § 1456, at 326. ("The necessity principle, . . . as here applied, signifies the impossibility of obtaining other evidence from the same source, the declarant being unavailable in person on the stand. Whenever the witness is practically unavailable, his statements should be received.") A discussion of the principles and requirements of unavailability is contained in § 804.1 *et seq.* of this Treatise.

ments conforming to Rule 804(b)(3) are admissible despite the fact that oath and cross-examination are wanting.[51] Accordingly, assertions adverse to a declarant's proprietary (*i.e.*, concerning interests in real or personal property), pecuniary (*i.e.*, concerning financial interests or acquisitions), or penal (*i.e.*, concerning one's liberty) interests, are admitted on the theory that the sanctions of a judicial oath and cross-examination are justifiably supplanted by the powerful sanction of self-interest, a human characteristic which induces most people to be peculiarly cautious in saying anything against themselves.

The generalized psychological theory supporting the admissibility of statements against interest may be superficially appealing, but the fact remains that common experience also teaches that individuals will fabricate or tell half-truths despite the personal consequences in order to protect friends or family members or to incriminate enemies.[52] Moreover, a person may inadvertently make a statement adverse to his or her personal interest, or may make an ambiguous statement which can be construed in different ways.[53] It is judicial cognizance of these facets of human nature which underlies the time-honored requirement that the need for the statement be supported by the unavailability of the declarant.[54]

§ 804.23　Admission of "Statement" of "Fact Asserted" Therein— "Reasonable Man" Test.

The underlying rationale of Rule 804(b)(3) implicitly raises the problem of whether the statement itself or only the fact asserted in the statement must be adverse to the declarant's interest. While Rule 804(b)(3) provides that any "*statement . . .* contrary to . . . interest" is admissible, commenta-

---

[51] *See, generally,* 4 Weinstein, ¶ 804(b)(3)[01]; 4 Louisell & Mueller, § 489; 5 Wigmore, §§ 1457-64; McCormick, § 276; Jefferson, *Declarations Against Interest: An Exception to the Hearsay Rule,* 58 Harv. L. Rev. 1 (1944); Morgan, *Declarations Against Interest,* 5 Vand. L. Rev. 451 (1952); Comment, *Hearsay Under the Proposed Federal Rules: A Discretionary Approach,* 15 Wayne L. Rev. 1079 (1969).

[52] 4 Weinstein, ¶ 804(b)(3)[01], at 804-90.

[53] *Id.*

[54] *See, e.g.,* United States v. Matlock, 415 U.S. 164, 176, 94 S.Ct. 988, 998, 39 L.Ed.2d 242, 252 (1974) (statements by woman cohabitating with defendant were against her penal interest and carried their own indicia of reliability; statements would be admissible only if declarant were unavailable); Dutton v. Evans, 400 U.S. 74, 89, 91 S.Ct. 210, 223, 27 L.Ed.2d 213, 227 (1970), *on remand,* 441 F.2d 657 (5th Cir. 1970) (receipt of statement did not violate defense confrontation rights; making the statement was "against his penal interest"); Donnelly v. United States, 228 U.S. 243, 277-78, 33 S.Ct. 449, 462, 57 L.Ed. 820, 834-35 (1913), *reh. denied,* 228 U.S. 708, 33 S.Ct. 1024, 57 L.Ed. 1035 (1913) (Holmes' dissenting opinion noting that "no other statement is so much against interest as a confession of murder").

tors like Wigmore,[55] Morgan,[56] and to a more circumspect degree, McCormick,[57] have maintained that the *fact* must be contrary to a declarant's interest. These commentators have asserted generally that it is only because the fact is against interest that the overt and purposeful mention of it is likely to be true.

For the most part, this distinction will prove to be little more than academic quibbling because both the fact and the statement are likely to be against the declarant's interest. However, in some situations the distinction may be important. For example, in some cases the fact may be against the declarant's interest but the statement is not because it is made to the declarant's attorney or spouse and therefore is subject to a privilege. In this situation, if one focuses on the *fact asserted*, the historical guarantee of trustworthiness is present; but, if one focuses on the *statement* and the situation in which the declarant communicated, the indicia of reliability are not present. Under these facts, a too restrictive application of the Rule would preclude admission of the statement if the privilege should be waived or avoided after the making of the statement.

In other cases, it may be unclear whether the fact asserted is against the declarant's interest. For example, consider the statement, "We were drunk, we ran the red light, but I wasn't driving." In this situation, the fact asserted may be considered an assertion against penal interest exposing the declarant to criminal liability for public drunkenness, but the statement may equally be construed to relieve the declarant of criminal liability for drunken driving, a far more serious crime. In this case, the matter becomes clear if one focuses on the statement as opposed to the fact. If it was made to a bystander, whom the declarant had no reason to trust, it is likely to be against his interest, and hence reliable and admissible under Rule 804(b)(3). If, however, the statement is made to the prosecution in the hope of receiving more lenient treatment in exchange for his testimony

---

[55] 5 WIGMORE, § 1462, at 337.

It must be remembered that it is not merely the statement that must be against interest, but the fact *stated*. It is because the fact is against interest that the open and deliberate mention of it is likely to be true. Hence the question whether the *statement* of the fact could create liability is beside the mark.

(emphasis in original).

[56] Morgan, *Basic Problems of Evidence*, 291-92 (1963) (a ". . . declarant's subjective stimulus to tell the truth lies in the disserving quality of the fact declared.").

[57] *See* McCORMICK, § 276, at 819 ("[T]he declaration must state facts which are against the pecuniary or proprietary interest of the declarant, or the making of the declaration itself must create evidence which would endanger his pocketbook if the statement were true.") *See also* Jefferson, *Declarations Against Interest: An Exception to the Hearsay Rule*, 58 HARV. L. REV. 1, 60 (1944) ("The probability of trustworthiness comes from the facts asserted being disserving in character."). *See, generally*, 4 WEINSTEIN, ¶ 804(b)(3)[02]; 4 LOUISELL & MUELLER, § 489.

against the driver, the statement is clearly self-serving, even though it admits some criminal conduct.

Accordingly, in determining whether a declaration satisfies the "against interest" requirement, the term "statement" as used in the Rule should be interpreted to include the fact asserted as well as the statement. Where the surrounding circumstances indicate that the statement is self-serving, however, the against interest requirement is not met despite the adverse character of the fact asserted. In addition, where a statement includes self-serving and disserving facts, the trial court should attempt to sever the statement, admitting only that portion which is supported by the underlying rationale, *i.e.*, that against interest.[58]

The appropriateness of focusing on the circumstances surrounding the making of the statement in determining satisfaction of the "against interest" requirement is further reinforced by, and not entirely distinct from, the "reasonable man" test of the Rule. In determining whether a statement is self-serving or disserving under the traditional statement against interest exception, the declarant must have been apparently *aware* that his statement was contrary to some personal interest. Since the exception may only be invoked where the declarant is unavailable, however, the question of personal awareness usually may be resolved only by resort to objective circumstantial evidence.[59] Since it is impossible to read a person's mind, Rule 804(b)(3) states the requirement that the declarant knew and understood the ramifications of his statement as an *objective* test: Would a "reasonable

---

[58] Most commentators support the concept of severance. *E.g.*, McCORMICK, § 279(d), at 677:

> When a declaration contains statements of facts in favor of interest, and in addition statements of facts against interest, three methods of handling the evidence under this exception have been advocated. First, admit the entire declaration because part is disserving and hence by a kind of contagion of truthfulness, all will be trustworthy. Second, compare the strength of the self-serving interest and the disserving interest in making the statement as a whole, and admit it all if the disserving interest preponderates, and exclude it all if the self-serving interest is greater. Third, admit the disserving parts of the declaration, and exclude the self-serving parts. The third solution seems the most re-

alistic method of adjusting admissibility to trustworthiness, where the serving and disserving parts can be severed.

See also 4 LOUISELL & MUELLER, § 489; 4 WEINSTEIN, ¶ 804(b)(3)[02]; 5 WIGMORE, § 1464; Morgan, *Declarations Against Interest*, 5 VAND. L. REV. 451 (1952). A more cautious approach is advocated by Professor Jefferson. *See Declarations Against Interest: An Exception to the Hearsay Rule*, 58 HARV. L. REV. 1, 60 (1944) ("[I]t would seem, therefore, that the courts are not justified in admitting self-serving statements merely because they accompany disserving statements, and a neutral collateral statement should serve no better.").

[59] *See* Jefferson, *Declarations Against Interest: An Exception to the Hearsay Rule*, 58 HARV. L. REV. 1, 22 (1944). *See also* 5 WIGMORE, § 1456.

man *in his position*" have made the statement if it were untrue?[60] The "in his position" language clearly reflects an intent to include the surrounding circumstances and factual context of the statement in the evaluation of whether the statement is contrary to the declarant's interest.

The trial court may consider surrounding circumstances in determining whether the declarant knew his statement was against interest. Since the Rule is cast in terms of an objective standard, however, the trial court generally should assume that the declarant acted as a reasonable person would in similar circumstances.[61] Subjective psychological factors indicating a lack of trustworthiness and detracting from reliability may be addressed by the trial court under Rule 403.

§ 804.24 Foundational Requirements—Unavailability and Personal Knowledge.

The traditional requirement that the declarant be unavailable has been retained as a prerequisite to the admission of a statement against interest, although, consistent with pre-Rule authority, the definition of "unavailability" has been expanded beyond the common law limitation of death.[62]

Consistent with Rule 602, Rule 804(b)(3) maintains the common law requirement that the declarant have personal knowledge.[63] Though un-

---

[60] *E.g.*, McCormick, § 276, at 820 ("[T]he declarant, as in the case of hearsay exceptions generally, must, so far as appears, have had the opportunity to observe the facts, as witnesses must have."); 5 Wigmore, § 1471, at 346-47:

> The qualifications of the declarant . . . with reference to testimonial *knowledge of the fact* stated are those of the ordinary witness . . . It has once or twice loosely been said that the declarant must have "peculiar knowledge"; but so far as this may mean a knowledge better than that ordinarily required of witnesses, *i.e.*, the usual knowledge by personal observation, . . . it is not the law.

(emphasis in original).

[61] 4 Weinstein, ¶ 804(b)(3)[02], at 804-98 and 804-99. *E.g.*, United States v. MacDonald, 688 F.2d 224, 232 (4th Cir. 1982), *cert. denied*, 459 U.S. 1103, 103 S.Ct. 726, 74 L.Ed.2d 951 (1983).

[62] *See, e.g.*, Oscar Gruss & Son v. Lumbermen's Mutual Casualty Co., 422 F.2d 1278, 1282-83 (2d Cir. 1970) (declarant apparently outside reach of process); Gichner v. Antonio Troiano Tile & Marble Co., 410 F.2d 238, 242-43 (D.C. Cir. 1969) (in finding that statement made to police was against the interest of the declarant, court stated: "it is not necessary for the statement to include every aspect of negligence; it is enough if the statement could reasonably provide an important link in a chain of evidence which is the basis for civil liability;" case was remanded to determine whether declarant was unavailable).

[63] *E.g.*, United States v. Lanci, 669 F.2d 391, 394-95 (6th Cir. 1982), *cert. denied*, 457 U.S. 1134, 102 S.Ct. 2960, 73 L.Ed.2d 1351 (1982). *See also* United States v. Toney, 599 F.2d 787, 789-90 (6th Cir. 1979) (reversible error to exclude statement made by individual after he was arrested for robbery that both he and defendant had won a great deal of money, since this statement was

stated, this requirement is implicit in the concept of statements against interest.[64]

§ 804.25   Foundational Requirements—Contrary to Interest—"Pecuniary or Proprietary" Interest—"Penal" Interest.

Traditionally, the statement against interest exception admitted only those declarations which, *at the time of their making*, could be characterized as contrary to the pecuniary or proprietary interest of the declarant. Common examples of statements affecting proprietary interests are acknowledgments that the declarant does not own particular property, or that he has conveyed or encumbered it in some manner.[65] Similarly, statements concerning boundary lines and easements, or acknowledgments that one's ownership is something less than fee simple, have traditionally been embraced within the exception for proprietary interest.[66]

The traditional exception for pecuniary interest is best illustrated by such statements as acknowledgments of a debt on the thoery that to owe a debt is contrary to one's financial interest.[67] Somewhat less obvious, but also included, are statements acknowledging the receipt of money in payment of a debt owing to the declarant or statements that certain money is being held in trust.[68] These traditional limitations to the subjects of money and property have been expanded to include adverse statements concerning liability for unliquidated damages for a tort claim or a seeming breach of contract, or, conversely, waiver of a defense to any such action.[69] Rule 804(b)(3) is sufficiently broad to encompass all the traditionally admitted subjects, and it should be construed even more expansively in a contemporary age when the majority of people are aware of the possibility and consequences of civil litigation.

Under the Rule, however, a statement of an employee of a business entity is not within the scope of the exception simply because it tends to subject

against his interest, both because it revealed his illicit gambling activities and because it disclosed that he had been gambling with a large sum of money a few hours after the bank robbery); Sucher Packing Co. v. Manufacturer's Cas. Ins. Co., 245 F.2d 513, 521-22 (6th Cir. 1957), *cert. denied*, 355 U.S. 956, 78 S.Ct. 541, 2 L.Ed.2d 531 (1958) (rule excluding declarations against interest may no longer hold, but exclusion under circumstances of case harmless).

[64] Comment, *Declarations Against Interest - Rules of Admissibility*, 62 Nw. U.L. REV. 934 (1968).

[65] McCORMICK, § 277, at 821.

[66] *Id. See, generally*, MORGAN, *Basic Problems of Evidence*, 261-63 (1963); 4 WEINSTEIN, ¶ 804(b)(3)[01]; 4 LOUISELL & MUELLER, § 489.

[67] McCORMICK, § 277, at 821.

[68] *Id.*

[69] *Id.*

the entity to some obligation, although the declaration may nevertheless qualify as an admission in an action where the entity is a party.[70] The statement may be adverse to the declarant's interest in the sense that his employer may disapprove and reprimand him, but this is more analogous to the social interests, discussed earlier, which are not embraced by Rule 804(b)(3). To satisfy the against interest requirement, the statement must *directly* affect the pecuniary interest of the declarant, as where the declarant is a partner with a personal stake in the earnings of the entity, or where the declarant faces demotion or termination due to the statement. Here, the pecuniary interest is patent, and the statement satisfies the condition of being contrary to an interest within the scope of Rule 804(b)(3).

A major expansion of the historical common law limitations on hearsay statements against interest is effected by the inclusion in Rule 804(b)(3) of statements adversely affecting the declarant's "penal" interest, or in the language of the Rule, those which tend to "subject him to . . . criminal liability." This expansion of the Rule, supported by most commentators,[71] is a recognition that restriction of the exception to material interests ignores other equally compelling human motives. A statement against penal interest, however, must be carefully scrutinized to insure that the declaration was contrary to the declarant's interest at the time of its utterance. Where the statement is offered to incriminate the accused, the against interest requirement is strictly construed because "the consequent denial or diminution of so essential and fundamental a confrontation value as the opportunity to cross-examine demands that the competing interest to which that value yields be 'closely examined.' "[72] Moreover, in certain situations discussed in the following section of this Chapter, corroboration is a condition to the admissibility of statements against penal interests.

As to third party confessions exculpating the accused which qualify under the Rule, the "against interest" requirement should ordinarily be satisfied where the substance of the declaration admits culpability for the crime of which the accused stands charged or incriminates both the declarant and the accused in some other crime, thus presenting an alibi or similar affirmative defense to the charged offense.[73] In these situations, corroboration is expressly required.

---

[70] *See, generally,* MORGAN, *Basic Problems of Evidence*, 260 (1963); Jones, *Evidence* § 9:10, at 209 (rev. ed. 1972); 4 LOUISELL & MUELLER, § 489.

[71] *See* nn. 40-41 *supra* and accompanying text.

[72] United States v. Sarmiento-Perez, 633 F.2d 1092, 1100-1101 (5th Cir. 1980) (citing Chambers v. Mississippi, 410 U.S. 284, 93 S.Ct. 1038, 35 L.Ed.2d 297 (1973)).

[73] 4 WEINSTEIN, ¶ 804(b)(3)[03]; 4 LOUISELL & MUELLER, § 489.

§ 804.26 Statements Against Penal Interest—Requirement of "Corroborating Circumstances"—In General

Under Rule 804(b)(3), statements against the declarant's penal interest offered to exculpate the accused must be "corroborated" prior to their admission. At the outset, it should be noted that this corroboration requirement should not be confused with the corroboration rule for substantive crimes such as treason.[74] The Rule pertains to the introduction of discrete items of evidence, not the substantive elements of an offense.

To the extent that an out-of-court statement exculpates the accused by embodying an admission to the perpetration of the crime with which the accused is charged, the corroboration requirement is derived from a long-standing recognition that third-party out-of-court confessions are inherently subject to fabrication and abuse. A variety of factors, such as a grant of immunity by the prosecution or personal ties with the accused, may motivate the declarant to concoct a third-party confession or to make an out-of-court statement which is beneficial to the accused by creating a reasonable doubt as to the accused's guilt. Moreover, the unavailability of the declarant, required by Rule 804, hinders attempts to attack the credibility of the witness and protects the witness from possible prosecution for perjury. Third-party confessions may possess a high degree of probative value, however, and the accused's need for such evidence is obvious. Consequently, the Rule reaches a compromise by enabling the accused to offer the expulpatory statement of an unavailable third party but gives the prosecution the opportunity to exclude such evidence where corroboration is lacking.

Just what constitutes sufficient "corroborating circumstances" must be determined on a case-by-case basis. Where the facts contained in the declarant's statement are supported by proof outside of the statement itself, the corroboration requirement should be satisfied. For example, if a third party confesses to committing the crime charged against the accused, the declarant's revelation of facts about the crime which only the perpetrator could know should be sufficient corroboration. However, the defense should not be required to produce independent evidence confirming the substance of the declarant's statement. Rather, evidence amounting to corroborating circumstances clearly indicating trustworthiness is satisfactory, such as proof that the statement was made to a law enforcement officer who would respond officially. In general, the corroboration requirement

[74] 4 WEINSTEIN, ¶ 804(b)(3)[03], at 804-104.

should be satisfied if the evidence allows "a reasonable man to believe that the statement might have been made in good faith and that it could be true."[75] The trial court should consider the entire context in which the declaration was made in an effort to determine whether sufficient corroboration as to the trustworthiness of the statement has been established.[76]

Although the express language of the Rule requires that corroboration be directed toward the trustworthiness, *i.e.*, the accuracy, of the out-of-court statement, some courts have excluded evidence as not meeting the corroboration requirement where the credibility of the witness recounting the out-of-court statement was questionable.[77] However, the witness's credibility can be evaluated by the trier of fact because his testimony is given under oath and is subject to cross-examination and observation of demeanor. Consequently, it is the out-of-court *declarant's* veracity, not the *witness's* veracity, which should be corroborated.[78] Nevertheless, in many, if not in most cases, corroboration of the declarant's trustworthiness will functionally coincide with corroboration of the veracity of the witness on the stand who transmits the out-of-court statement against interest.

[75] 4 WEINSTEIN, ¶ 804(b)(3)[03], at 804-104. *E.g.*, United States v. Zappola, 704 F.2d 23, 26-27 (1st Cir. 1983), *cert. denied*, 104 S.Ct. 87, 74 L.Ed.2d 122 (1983); United States v. Rodriquez, 706 F.2d 31, 40 (2d Cir. 1983).

[76] 4 WEINSTEIN, ¶ 804(b)(3)[03], at 804-105. *E.g.*, United States v. MacDonald, 688 F.2d 224, 230-32 (4th Cir. 1982), *cert. denied*, 459 U.S. 1103, 103 S.Ct. 726, 74 L.Ed.2d 951 (1983). *See also* United States v. Garris, 616 F.2d 626, 629-33 (2d Cir. 1979), *cert. denied*, 447 U.S. 926, 100 S.Ct. 3021, 65 L.Ed.2d 1119 (1980) ("it suffices . . . that a remark which is itself neutral as to the declarant's interest be integral to a larger statement which is against the declarant's interest;" here the sister's repetition of defendant's admission, even putting aside its weight against her as an accessory after the fact in the Banker's Trust robbery, was integral to her admission of complicity in the Manufacturers Hanover Trust robbery, since it explained her motive to aid her brother's escape after the Bankers Trust robbery).

[77] United States v. Rodriquez, 706 F.2d 31, 40-41 (2d Cir. 1983); United States v. Poland, 659 F.2d 884, 894-895 (9th Cir. 1981); United States v. Annese, 631 F.2d 1041,

1044-1045 (1st Cir. 1980); United States v. Bagley, 537 F.2d 162, 167-168 (5th Cir. 1976), *cert. denied*, 429 U.S. 1075, 975 S.Ct. 816, 50 L.Ed.2d 794 (1977).

[78] United States v. Katsougrakis, 715 F.2d 769, 777 (2d Cir. 1983), *cert. denied*, 104 S.Ct. 704 (1984); United States v. Brainard, 690 F.2d 1117, 1124-25 (4th Cir. 1982). *See also* United States v. Satterfield, 572 F.2d 687, 691-93 (9th Cir. 1978), *cert. denied*, 439 U.S. 840, 99 S.Ct. 128, 58 L.Ed.2d 138 (1978) (defendant sought to offer statement by codefendant, who was unavailable because he refused to testify, exculpating defendant, which was allegedly made during course of an argument while both were inmates in penitentiary two years after bank robbery in question; court found that even assuming declarant made the statement, there were insufficient corroborating circumstances as to trustworthiness of statement because it was not really against penal interest, a substantial length of time had elapsed between statement and robbery, and because a substantial portion of the statement which lent it credibility was not integral part of statement and not against interest; corroborating circumstances "must clearly" indicate the trustworthiness of the statement).

§ 804.27   Corroboration—Standards Applicable to Declarations Tending to Exculpate the Accused.

In regard to statements against penal interest tending to exculpate the accused, a strict standard for corroboration has been particularly discouraged by the United States Supreme Court in *Chambers v. Mississippi*.[79] In *Chambers* the Court reversed the conviction of the accused on due process grounds where the state court prevented extensive cross-examination of a witness who had admitted on a number of occasions that he had committed the crime with which the accused stood charged. The witness later repudiated these statements and offered an alibi, but the accused proved the alibi to be concocted and showed that the witness was near the scene. The accused was denied the opportunity to cross-examine the witness due to the jurisdiction's "voucher rule." Likewise, he was prevented from calling witnesses who overheard the repeated out-of-court statements admitting to the crime. While Rule 804(b)(3) would probably be inapplicable in light of the witness's presence in court, the *Chambers* court, in *dicta*, indicated that due process requires the trial court to permit proof that the hearsay statements in question represented admissible declarations against penal interest:

Few rights are more fundamental than that of an accused to present witnesses in his own defense. . . . In the exercise of this right, the accused, as is required of the State, must comply with established rules of procedure and evidence designed to assure both fairness and reliability in the ascertainment of guilt and innocence. Although perhaps no rule of evidence has been more respected or more frequently applied in jury trials than that applicable to the exclusion of hearsay, exceptions tailored to allow the introduction of evidence which in fact is likely to be trustworthy have long existed. The testimony rejected by the trial court here bore persuasive assurances of trustworthiness and thus was well within the basic rationale of the exception for declarations against interest. That testimony also was critical to Chambers' defense. In these circumstances, where constitutional rights directly affecting the ascertainment of guilt are implicated, the hearsay rule may not be applied mechanistically to defeat the ends of justice . . . .

. . . [We] hold quite simply that under the facts and circumstances of this case the rulings of the trial court deprived Chambers of a fair trial.[80]

---

[79] 410 U.S. 284, 93 S.Ct. 1038, 35 L.Ed.2d 297 (1973). *See, generally*, 4 WEINSTEIN, ¶ 804(b)(3)[03].

[80] Chambers v. Mississippi, 410 U.S. 284, 300-303, 93 S.Ct. 1038, 1051, 35 L.Ed.2d 297, 311 (1973).

The pertinency of *Chambers* to the developing law of "corroboration" under Rule 804(b)(3) is unclear in light of unique facts of the case, *i.e.*, the witness's availability, the application of the state's "voucher" rule, and the fact that error was found in the truncated cross-examination after damaging evidence had already been admitted. Still, the emphasis of the *Chambers* court upon the reliability factor of the third-party confession, finding support for trustworthiness in scant attendant circumstances, lends weight to the assertion that where the third-party confession tends to exculpate the accused, an overly restrictive construction of the corroboration requirement may raise questions of constitutional significance.[81]

§ 804.28 Corroboration—Standards Applicable to Declarations Tending to Inculpate the Accused.

While Rule 804 does not expressly require corroboration of statements inculpating the accused as a precondition to admissibility of the statement on behalf of the prosecution, many courts have imposed this requirement.[82] The question of the admissibility of statements against interest inculpating the accused will almost inevitably raise issues under the Sixth Amendment, and while the precise commands of the confrontation clause in this context are not crystalline,[83] it is clear that evidentiary doctrines may be invoked and applied by the trial court in obviation of the constitutional issues. In this regard Rule 403's exclusion of evidence where the danger of prejudice

---

[81] 4 WEINSTEIN, ¶ 804(b)(3)[03], at 804-106. *See also* Green v. Georgia, 442 U.S. 95, 99 S.Ct. 2150, 60 L.Ed.2d 738 (1979) (citing *Chambers;* death sentence vacated where accused was prohibited from introducing at sentencing trial the confession of the codefendant for the actual murderous act upon victim; holding grounded in due process since Georgia law does not recognize statements against penal interest as exception to hearsay rule). *See, e.g.,* United States v. MacDonald, 688 F.2d 224, 232 and n.13 (4th Cir. 1982). *See also* United States v. Benveniste, 564 F.2d 335, 341-42 (9th Cir. 1977) (reversible error to exclude statements by co-offender, since defendant did not "play a significant role" and statements had been offered in support of entrapment defense).

[82] United States v. Katsougrakis, 715 F.2d 769, 775 (2d Cir. 1983), *cert. denied,* 104 S.Ct. 704 (1983); United States v. Riley, 657 F.2d 1377, 1382-83 (8th Cir. 1981); United States v. Sarmiento-Perez, 633 F.2d 1092, 1098-1101 (5th Cir. 1980). *See also* United States v. Alvarez, 584 F.2d 694, 701 (5th Cir. 1978) (corroboration required for statements against penal interest implicating the accused). *But see* United States v. Layton, 720 F.2d 548, 559 (9th Cir. 1983) (declining to decide whether corroboration was required for statements inculpating accused).

[83] *See* 4 WEINSTEIN, ¶ 804(b)(3)[03], at 804-110 to 804-111 (discussing Dutton v. Evans, 400 U.S. 74, 91 S.Ct. 210, 27 L.Ed.2d 213 (1970); Bruton v. United States, 391 U.S. 123, 88 S.Ct. 1620, 20 L.Ed.2d 476 (1968); Douglas v. Alabama, 380 U.S. 415, 85 S.Ct. 1074, 13 L.Ed.2d 934 (1965).

substantially outweighs probative value is significant in a criminal matter. In determining whether a statement inculpating the accused is admissible, Judge Weinstein takes the position that the trial court must consider the circumstances surrounding the making of the statement to assess its reliability and probative value and then must weigh these factors against the risk of prejudice to the accused, which is influenced by the need for the evidence. He concludes that prejudice generally preponderates and therefore "exclusion should almost always result when a statement against penal interest is offered *against* an accused."[84] The Fifth Circuit's decision in *United States v. Sarmiento-Perez* lends support to this approach by finding that a statement which inculpates the accused must satisfy a more restrictive interpretation of the against interest requirement than an exculpatory statement.[85] Such strict analysis may not, however, be required when the declaration does not expressly implicate the accused in the substantive crime confessed by the declarant, such as where the declarant's confession of a theft offense is introduced at the accused's trial for receiving stolen property.[86]

Rule 804(b)(4)   Hearsay Exceptions— Statement of Personal or Family History

Rule 804(b)(4) reads as follows:

(b) **Hearsay Exceptions.** The following are not excluded by the hearsay rule if the declarant is unavailable as a witness: . . .

(4) Statement of personal or family history. (A) A statement concerning the declarant's own birth, adoption, marriage, divorce, legitimacy, relation-

---

[84] 4 WEINSTEIN, ¶ 804(b)(3)[04], at 804-113. *See also* Parker v. Randolph, 442 U.S. 62, 87, 99 S.Ct. 2132, 2151, 60 L.Ed.2d 713, 732 (1979) (Stevens, J., dissenting):

If relevant at all in the present context, the factors relied on by the plurality support a proposition no one has even remotely advocated in this case—that the corroborated evidence used in this case was so trustworthy that it should have been fully admissible against all of the defendants, and the jury instructed as much. Conceivably, corroborating or other circumstances surrounding otherwise inadmissible hearsay may so enhance its reliability that its admission in evidence is justified in some situations. But before allowing such a rule to defeat a defendant's fundamental right to confront his accusers, this Court surely should insist upon a strong showing not only of the reliability of the hearsay in the particular case but also of the impossibility, or at least difficulty, of making the accusers available for cross-examination.

[85] 633 F.2d 1092 (5th Cir. 1980), *cert. denied*, 459 U.S. 834, 103 S.Ct. 77, 74 L.Ed.2d 75 (1982).

[86] 4 WEINSTEIN, ¶ 803(b)(3)[04], at 804-113 to 804-114.

ship by blood, adoption, or marriage, ancestry, or other similar fact of personal or family history, even though declarant had no means of acquiring personal knowledge of the matter stated; or (B) a statement concerning the foregoing matters, and death also, of another person, if the declarant was related to the other by blood, adoption, or marriage or was so intimately associated with the other's family as to be likely to have accurate information concerning the matter declared.

§ 804.29 Statement of Personal or Family History—In General— Rationale.

Rule 804(b)(4) codifies one of the oldest exceptions to the hearsay rule and, in several ways, significantly expands its scope. Rule 804(b)(4)(A) admits statements concerning an unavailable declarant's own personal or family history, embracing such topics as "birth, adoption, marriage, divorce, legitimacy, relationship by blood." Rule 804(b)(4)(B) admits declarations concerning these subjects pertaining to another person if the declarant was related by blood, adoption, or marriage, or ". . . was so intimately associated with the other's family as to be likely to have accurate information concerning the matter declared."[87] The exception was originally termed at common law the "pedigree exception," since it generally applied only to matters of genealogy, *i.e.*, questions of lineage, descent and succession, and it usually operated only in inheritance cases where pedigree was an issue.[88] The Rule, in accordance with the modern trend, has expanded the historical exception to encompass the whole area of family history—an enlargement designated by the Rule's title.

The Rule departs from the common law restriction against declarations concerning the family history of another person. Traditionally, it was believed that only members of the family could be presumed to have accurate knowledge of pedigree facts which are acquired by the normal interest in family affairs.[89] Rule 804(b)(4)(B), in conformity with the view espoused

---

[87] *See, generally*, McCormick, § 322; 4 Weinstein, ¶¶ 804(b)(4)[01]-[02]; 4 Louisell & Mueller, § 490; 5 Wigmore, §§ 1480-1503. *See also* Hale, *Proof of Facts of Family History*, 2 Hastings L.J.1 (1950); Note, *Pedigree*, 46 Iowa L. Rev. 414 (1962); Comment, *Admissibility of Hearsay Evidence on Matters of Family History*, 5 Ark. L. Rev. 58 (1951).

[88] *E.g.*, Flora v. Anderson, 75 F. 217, 220-21 (6th Cir. 1896). *See, generally*, 4 Weinstein, ¶ 804(b)(4)[01]; McCormick, § 322; 5 Wigmore, § 1480; 4 Louisell & Mueller, § 490.

[89] *See, generally*, 4 Weinstein, ¶ 804(b)(4)[01]; Note, *Pedigree*, 46 Iowa L. Rev. 414 (1961); Comment, *Hearsay Under the Proposed Federal Rules: A Discretionary Approach*, 15 Wayne L. Rev. 1077 (1969); Comment, *Admissibility of Hearsay Evidence on Matters of Family History*, 5 Ark. L. Rev. 58 (1951).

by Wigmore,[90] extends the common law restriction to include declarants "intimately associated" with the family, *e.g.*, family physicians, lawyers, clergymen, nurses and domestic servants, or intimate friends and neighbors, where circumstances indicate trustworthiness in an extended, close relationship with the family in question.[91] Even where this degree of intimacy cannot be sufficiently demonstrated, however, such facts may nevertheless be admissible under Rule 803(18) as the general reputation in the community, whether or not the declarant is available.[92]

Similarly, if the hearsay facts are contained in a writing, they may be admissible, regardless of the declarant's availability, under such exceptions as those governing regularly conducted activity (Rule 803(6)), public records or reports (Rule 803(8)), records of vital statistics (Rule 803(9)), records of marriage, baptismal or similar certificates (Rule 803(12)), family records (Rule 803(13)), or ancient documents (Rule 803(16)).

§ 804.30   Foundational Requirements

The conditions precedent to the admission of statements of personal or family history are threefold: (i) unavailability of the declarant as defined in Rule 804(a) must be established,[93] (ii) the statement must be restricted to the subject matters described in the Rule; and (iii) an appropriate relation to, or association with the family in question must be shown. Each of these foundational requirements represents the modern expansion of the common law tradition, and the Rule presents little complexity or difficulty in construction or application.

What is notable about Rule 804(b)(4), as it relates to other hearsay rules and its antecedent common law restrictions, is what is *not* required as a

---

[90] "[I]t seems too much to say that only those who have this immediate property-interest in learning the family history [because of the possibility of inheritance] can possibly have adequate information; for family physicians and chaplains, old servants, and intimate friends may in cases be equally and sufficiently informed." 5 Wigmore, § 1487, at 382. *See also* McCormick, § 322.

[91] *See* Fed. R. Evid. 804(b)(4) Advisory Committee Note. *See also* 5 Wigmore, § 1487, at 382 ("[I]t is not necessary to maintain that the statements of *any friend* are always admissible; but it is desirable to disavow any limitation which would exclude the statements of one whose intimacy with the family could leave no doubt as to his sufficient knowledge, equally with the family members, of the facts of family history."). *See, generally,* 4 Weinstein, ¶ 804(b)(4)[01]; 4 Louisell & Mueller, § 490.

[92] *See* §§ 803.70 *et seq.* of this Treatise. *See also* 4 Weinstein, ¶ 804(b)(4)[01]; McCormick, § 322; 5 Wigmore, § 1605.

[93] In so providing, the Rule expands the concept of "unavailability" beyond the common law requirement of death, and thus supersedes decisional law to the contrary. *See, e.g.,* Flora v. Anderson, 75 F. 217, 220-21 (6th Cir. 1896) (declarant must be dead).

condition to admissibility under the exception contained therein. In the first instance, the Rule continues in force the common law requirement that, in lieu of personal knowledge as that term is defined in Rule 602, the declarant must appear to have familiarity, or fair opportunity for acquiring familiarity, with the subject matter asserted in the declaration. Strict adherence to the general rule of personal observation, however, was not required at common law and is not required under the Rule.[94] Consequently, while statements about other persons must be predicated upon some familiarity with the family, statements concerning the declarant's *own* age, descent, or similar family history, are admissible despite the fact that the declarant could not possibly have personally perceived and remembered the event. The personal knowledge requirement, therefore, applies only to statements about others, and moreover, it is not as strict as that imposed by Rule 602.

Second, and most significant, the Rule does not restrict admissibility to declarations made *ante litem motam, i.e.,* prior in time to the commencement of the controversy. This restriction was imposed at common law in light of the historical reliance upon the rationale that prior to the controversy, the declarant would have no apparent motive, bias or interest in giving false information concerning his pedigree,[95] but might well have a motive to falsify such information once the controversy had begun. Elimination of this restriction is justified on the grounds that it is increasingly difficult to establish with any reasonable certainty the point at which a controversy arises. Moreover, the applicability of the exclusionary provisions of Rule 403 to the instant Rule enables the trial court to exclude untrustworthy or misleading evidence.[96] Thus, the exception for statements

---

[94] *E.g.,* 5 WIGMORE, § 1486, at 378:

It is of course *not* to be expected that *personal observation* shall be demanded, *i.e.,* that only from those who were present at birth, wedding, or death, shall hearsay statements be received; this would be to misconceive the theory of the exception. That theory is that the constant (though casual) mention and discussion of important family affairs, whether of the present or of past generations, puts it in the power of members of the family circle to be fully acquainted with the original personal knowledge and the consequent tradition on the subject, and that those members will therefore know, as well as anyone can be expected to know,

the facts of the matter. It is not that they have, each and all, a knowledge by personal observation, but that they at least know the fact as accepted by family understanding and tradition, and that this understanding, based as it was originally on observation, is prima facie trustworthy.

Id. See also Pollack v. Metropolitan Life Ins. Co., 138 F.2d 123, 146 (3d Cir. 1943) (reversible error to exclude evidence offered by defendant that statement made by decedent indicating his age was within the family history exception in beneficiary's action against life insurance company).

[95] *See* MCCORMICK, § 322; 5 WIGMORE, § 1483.

[96] 5 WIGMORE, § 1484.

concerning family history no longer requires a demonstration that the statement was uttered at a time when no bias or interest could affect its content.

§ 804.31   Rationale.

At common law, the exception for declarations concerning personal or family history rested upon the usual principles of necessity and trustworthiness. The necessity principle was derived from the general difficulty of obtaining any other evidence in matters of family history.[97] As enunciated by Justice Story, "In cases of pedigree, [hearsay] is admitted upon the ground of necessity, or the great difficulty and sometimes the impossibility of proving remote facts of this sort by living witnesses, . . . there being no 'lis mota' or other interest to affect the credit of the statement."[98]

The circumstantial guarantee of trustworthiness was supplied at common law by the notion that the declarations of family affairs are trustworthy and deserving of consideration by judges and juries in the same fashion as they are in the ordinary affairs of life.[99] This rationale presumes that in common human experience pronouncements of this sort are likely to rest upon accurate knowledge with due regard for the truth of the matter asserted, at least in the absence of circumstantial indicia to the contrary.

Application of the common law rule, however, was expressly conditioned upon a showing that the declarant had no motive to fabricate or distort the facts, and, accordingly, it imposed the requirement that the statement must have been made *ante litem motam, i.e.,* before the controversy which led to the litigation in which the declaration is offered. Rule 804(b)(4) eliminates this historical condition. Consequently, while the common law rationale holds true for statements which qualify as *ante litem motam,* those declarations made after the controversy arises must rest upon an alternate rationale, namely, that a statement concerning a fact within the

---

[97] *See, generally,* 5 Wigmore, §§ 1480-82; Note, *Pedigree,* 46 Iowa L. Rev. 414 (1961); Comment, *Admissibility of Hearsay on Matters of Family History,* 5 Ark. L. Rev. 58 (1951).

[98] Ellicott v. Pearl, 35 U.S. 412, 434, 9 L.Ed. 475, 496 (10 Pet). *See also* Fulkerson v. Holmes, 117 U.S. 389, 393, 6 S.Ct. 780, 783, 29 L.Ed. 915, 918 (1886) ("[T]his exception has been recognized on the ground of necessity; for as, in inquiries respecting relationship or descent, facts must often be proved which occurred many years before the trial and were known to but few persons, it is obvious that the strict enforcement in such cases of the rule against hearsay evidence would frequently occasion failure of justice.").

[99] *See, generally,* McCormick, § 322; 5 Wigmore, § 1482. *E.g.,* Rassano v. Immigration and Naturalization Service, 377 F.2d 971, 973 (7th Cir. 1966) ("[T]he family history exception is based in part upon the inherent trustworthiness of declarations by a family member regarding matters of family history and the usual unavailability of other evidence on these matter").

Rule will not be uttered unless it is reliable, regardless of the presence of bias, interest or passion. In this regard, the Rule is peculiarly subject to the exclusionary provisions of Rule 403, and where the court in its discretion finds that the statement was made under suspicious circumstances, indicating low probative value, it may exclude it totally. Alternately, the court may admit the statement and permit the fact that the statement was made after the controversy to affect the weight of the evidence.[1]

Rule 804(b)(5)   Hearsay Exceptions—Other Exceptions

Rule 804(b)(5) reads as follows:

(b) **Hearsay Exceptions.** The following are not excluded by the hearsay rule if the declarant is unavailable as a witness: . . .

(5) *Other exceptions.* A statement not specifically covered by any of the foregoing exceptions but having equivalent circumstantial guarantees of trustworthiness, if the court determines that (A) the statement is offered as evidence of a material fact; (B) the statement is more probative on the point for which it is offered than any other evidence which the proponent can procure through reasonable efforts; and (C) the general purposes of these rules and the interest of justice will best be served by admisssion of the statement into evidence. However, a statement may not be admitted under this exception unless the proponent of it makes known to the adverse party sufficiently in advance of the trial or hearing to provide the adverse party with a fair opportunity to prepare to meet it, his intention to offer the statement and the particulars of it, including the name and address of the declarant.

§ 804.32   Other Exceptions—In General—Rationale.

Rule 803(24) and Rule 804(b)(5) contain identical exceptions for hearsay statements which do not fall within a specific exception but have "equivalent circumstantial guarantees of trustworthiness," provided the statements satisfy certain additional requirements.[2] While Rule 804(b)(5) may be uti-

---

[1] *See* Rassano v. Immigration and Naturalization Service, 377 F.2d 971, 973 (7th Cir. 1966); McClaskey v. Barr, 54 F. 781, 783 (6th Cir. 1893). *See also* 4 Weinstein, ¶ 804(b)(4)[01], at 804-117 to 804-118.

[2] *See, generally,* McCormick, §§ 325-27; 4 Weinstein, ¶¶ 804(b)(5)[01]-[04]; 4

Louisell & Mueller, § 472, 491. *See also* Weinstein, *Probative Force of Hearsay,* 46 Iowa L. Rev. 331 (1961); Chadbourn, *Bentham and the Hearsay Rule—A Benthamite View of Rule 63(4)(c) of the Uniform Rules of Evidence,* 75 Harv. L. Rev. 932 (1962); Quick, *Hearsay, Excitement, Necessity and*

lized only where the declarant is unavailable to testify at trial, Rule 803(24) does not impose this restriction. The necessity for both exceptions, as opposed to Rule 803(24) alone, remains somewhat mysterious and has never been adequately explained.

The residual exceptions provide a vehicle for admitting hearsay "in situations unanticipated by the other exceptions, but involving equal guarantees of trustworthiness."[3] The legislative history illustrates that the exceptions represent a compromise between the competing goals of allowing flexibility in the development of the hearsay system on one hand and ensuring some degree of certainty for trial preparation on the other. Although the Supreme Court approved the Advisory Committee's draft, the House Judiciary Committee deleted the residual exceptions from Rule 803 and Rule 804 as "injecting too much uncertainty into the law of evidence and impairing the ability of practitioners to prepare for trial."[4] The Committee believed that "if additional hearsay exceptions are to be created, they should be by amendments to the Rules, not on a case-by-case basis."[5] The Senate Judiciary Committee reinstated the residual exceptions, but added several restrictions to narrow their scope. While the Senate's draft was intended to provide room for growth in the hearsay rules, the Committee nevertheless cautioned that "[i]t is intended that the residual hearsay exceptions will be used very rarely, and only in exceptional circumstances."[6] The Conference Committee approved the Senate's version of the Rules but added a requirement that the proponent of evidence offered under one of the residual exceptions must give his opponent sufficient notice before trial to enable him to prepare to meet the evidence.[7] As enacted, Rule 803(24) and Rule 804(b)(5) adopt the approach taken by some pre-Rules decisions which evaluated the trustworthiness and need for a particular hearsay statement rather than the strict applicability of a specific exception.[8]

the Uniform Rules: A Reappraisal of Rule 63(4), 6 WAYNE L. REV. 204 (1960).

[3] Weissenberger, The Admissibility of Grand Jury Transcripts: Avoiding the Constitutional Issue, 59 TUL. L. REV. 335, 340 (1984). See also Fed. R. Evid. 803(24) Advisory Committee's Note.

[4] H. R. Rep. No. 93-650, 93d Cong., 1st Sess. 5-6 (1973).

[5] Id.

[6] S. Rep. No. 93-1277, 93d Cong., 2d Sess. 18-20 (1974).

[7] H. R. Conf. Rep. No. 93-1597, 93d Cong., 2d Sess. 3 (1974).

[8] See, e.g., Chestnut v. Ford Motor Company, 445 F.2d 967, 972 n.5 (4th Cir. 1971) (noting modern trend to consider need and trustworthiness rather than formal labels);

United States v. Kearney, 420 F.2d 170, 174-75 (D.C. Cir. 1969) (admitting statement made by police officer one day prior to his death as "in the penumbra of both the spontaneous utterance and dying declaration exceptions to the hearsay rule."); Dallas County v. Commercial Union Assurance Co., 286 F.2d 388, 397-98 (5th Cir. 1961) (in action to determine insurance coverage where plaintiffs claimed courthouse tower had been struck by lighting, court permitted defendant to introduce 1901 newspaper article which reported a fire in the tower while the courthouse was being built; court declined to categorize the hearsay in one of the recognized exceptions, finding it was admissible "because it is necessary and trustworthy, relevant and material . . .").

§ 804.33   Application.

Hearsay offered under Rule 803(24) or Rule 804(b)(5) must satisfy five requirements to be admissible. First, the statement must possess "circumstantial guarantees of trustworthiness" which are "equivalent" to those supporting the specific hearsay exceptions. In assessing the reliability of proffered evidence, courts consider a variety of factors. Some courts infer reliability from the absence of the traditional hearsay dangers, *i.e.*, problems in perception, narration, memory and sincerity.[9] Other decisions find that the factors which support the specific hearsay exceptions, such as spontaneous statements or dying declarations, are indicative of reliability.[10] The existence of corroborating evidence and, in cases applying Rule 803(24), the declarant's availability to testify and to be cross-examined concerning the statement, are also important considerations.[11]

Second, the statement must be "offered as evidence of a material fact." In essence, this amounts to a restatement of the requirement of relevancy already imposed by Rule 401 and 402.[12]

Third, the hearsay statement must be "more probative on the point for which it is offered than any other evidence which the proponent can procure through reasonable efforts." This requirement imposes a duty of diligence on the proponent in seeking better evidence than the proffered hearsay. In determining what constitutes "reasonable efforts," the court should

[9] *E.g.*, United States v. White, 611 F.2d 531, 537-38 (5th Cir. 1980) (evidence of claim form properly received as trustworthy because it was executed only three months after the check should have arrived, and "length of time between an event and the declarant's statement concerning it is a significant indicator of reliability"). *See also* United States v. Smith, 571 F.2d 370, 373-74 (7th Cir. 1978); Grimes v. Employers Mutual Liability Ins. Co. of Wisconsin, 73 F.R.D. 607, 609 (D. Alaska 1977).

[10] *E.g.*, Herdman v. Smith, 707 F.2d 839, 841-42 (5th Cir. 1983). *See also* United States v. McPartlin, 595 F.2d 1321, 1350 (7th Cir. 1979), *cert. denied*, 444 U.S. 833, 100 S.Ct. 65, 62 L.Ed. 43 (1979) (entries made in desk calendar appointment diary kept by government witness were admissible within Rule 803(24) since they were regularly made, and his need to rely on the entries).

[11] United States v. Hitsman, 604 F.2d 443, 447 (5th Cir. 1979) (college transcript properly received as reliable, since corroborated by government witness); United States v. Barnes, 586 F.2d 1052, 1054-56 (5th Cir.

1978) (previous confession by defense witness); United States v. Williams, 573 F.2d 284, 288-89 (5th Cir. 1978) (pre-trial affidavit by prosecution witness). *See also* Sherrell Perfumers, Inc. v. Revlon, Inc., 524 F. Supp. 302, 303 (S.D.N.Y. 1980).

[12] United States v. Boulahanis, 677 F.2d 586, 588-89 (7th Cir. 1982), *cert. denied*, 459 U.S. 1016, 103 S.Ct. 375, 74 L.Ed.2d 509 (1982). *See also* DeMars v. Equitable Life Assur. Soc., 610 F.2d 55, 61 (1st Cir. 1979) (error to permit plaintiff to introduce letter from deceased physician, since plaintiff did not satisfy the diligence/probativity requirement; any other physician could have been obtained to render an opinion on fairly short notice); Huff v. White Motor Corp., 609 F.2d 286, 294 (7th Cir. 1979) (statement made by plaintiff satisfied the materiality requirement of the catchall exception); United States v. Friedman, 593 F.2d 109, 119 (9th Cir. 1979) (receipt of Chilean travel documents satisfied materiality requirement, since they showed appellant's entrance into and exit from Chile at relevant times).

weigh the importance of the evidence, the financial resources available to the proponent and the amount at stake in the action.[13] Taking these factors into consideration, the court must find that the hearsay statement is more probative than other available evidence in order to render the statement admissible.[14]

Fourth, the proponent of the statement must show that its admission would serve "the general purposes of these rules and the interests of justice." This requirement is based on the same principles as Rule 102 and in practice has not engendered much discussion.[15]

Finally, the statement is not admissible unless the proponent notifies the opponent of his intention to offer it "sufficiently in advance of the trial or hearing to provide the adverse party with a fair opportunity to prepare to meet it." The proponent of the statement must also inform his adversary of "the particulars of it, including the name and address of the declarant." While notice generally should be given at the pre-trial conference or earlier, in some cases courts have excused the proponent's failure to give advance notice where his conduct was reasonable in view of the circumstances.[16] In such cases the court may grant a continuance to enable the adversary to prepare to meet the statement. Other courts, however, have construed this requirement inflexibly and have found that the failure to give notice prior to trial acts as a complete bar to the admission of the statement.[17]

The proponent of evidence offered under the residual exceptions bears the burden of proving that the five requirements have been satisfied. Admissibility of the statement is determined by the trial court pursuant to Rule 104(a). Where all the requirements are met, the court nevertheless

[13] Byrd v. Hunt Tool Shipyard, 650 F.2d 44, 46-47 (5th Cir. 1981); United States v. American Cyanamid Co., 427 F. Supp. 859, 865-66 (S.D.N.Y. 1977).

[14] Huff v. White Motor Corp., 609 F.2d 286, 291-92 (7th Cir. 1979) (court had "little choice except to attempt to replicate the exercise of discretion that would be made by a trial judge in making the ruling"); United States v. Leslie, 542 F.2d 285, 289-91 (5th Cir. 1976), reh. denied, 545 F.2d 168 (5th Cir. 1976) (court finds that the statements could properly be used as substantive evidence, thus adequacy of the instruction did not matter).

[15] United States v. Friedman, 593 F.2d 109, 119 (9th Cir. 1979) (upholding receipt of Chilean travel documents, noting that appellants received sufficient advance notice); United States v. Mathis, 559 F.2d 294,

299 (5th Cir. 1977) ("tight reins must be held to insure that this provision does not emasculate our well developed body of law and the notions underlying our evidentiary rules").

[16] Piva v. Xerox Corp., 654 F.2d 591, 593 (9th Cir. 1981). See also United States v. Bailey, 581 F.2d 341, 348 (3d Cir. 1978) (reversible error to receive statement by alleged co-offender, because of its questionable reliability and devastating impact). See, e.g., State Farm Mut. Auto Ins. Co. v. Gudmunson, 495 F. Supp. 794, 797 (D. Mont. 1980).

[17] United States v. Cowley, 720 F.2d 1037, 1044-45 (9th Cir. 1983); Elizarraras v. Bank of El Paso, 631 F.2d 366, 373-74 (5th Cir. 1980); United States v. Ruffin, 575 F.2d 346, 357 (2d Cir. 1978); United States v. Oates, 560 F.2d 45, 78-80 (2d Cir. 1977).

retains discretion to exclude the statement pursuant to Rule 403 to prevent unfair prejudice, confusion of the issues or undue delay.[18]

§ 804.34   Application: Admissibility of Grand Jury Transcripts.

There is a growing conflict in the circuits over whether the testimony of a witness before the grand jury may be admitted against the accused under Rule 804(b)(5) when the witness is unavailable to testify at trial. Since grand jury transcripts fail to satisfy the requirements of any of the specific hearsay exceptions, this issue "may have wide ramifications in the criminal justice system."[19] The former testimony exception contained in Rule 804(b)(1) is inapplicable because grand jury proceedings are essentially *ex parte* and do not afford the defendant an opportunity to "develop the testimony by direct, cross, or redirect examination."[20] In addition to the hearsay problem, admission of grand jury testimony against an accused where the declarant does not testify at trial and thus is unavailable for cross-examination also may violate the confrontation clause.

Several decisions have admitted grand jury testimony under Rule 804(b)(5) despite the hearsay and constitutional concerns. In *United States v. Carlson*,[21] the Eighth Circuit utilized Rule 804(b)(5) to admit the grand jury testimony of a witness who refused to testify at trial because of fear of reprisal from the defendant. The court held that the following factors were strong indicators of reliability in the witness's grand jury testimony: the witness was testifying under oath, thus subjecting himself to indictment for perjury if he misrepresented the truth in his testimony before the grand jury; the witness participated in the transaction to which he testified and thus had firsthand knowledge of the events comprising his testimony; the witness never recanted his grand jury testimony but merely expressed fear of testifying; there was a need for the testimony; the witness stated at the time of trial his testimony before the grand jury was accurate and true.[22] The court dismissed the defendant's argument against admissibility based upon the confrontation clause by asserting that the defendant had waived

---

[18] *E.g.*, United States v. Kim, 193 App. D.C. 370, 595 F.2d 755, 764-66 (1979) (telex summarizing banking transactions properly excluded, since it did not have circumstantial guarantees of trustworthiness, because it was not sent for business purposes and was not relied upon by the business). *See, generally*, 4 WEINSTEIN, ¶ 803(24)[01], at 803-383.

[19] United States v. Carlson, 547 F.2d 1346, 1357 (8th Cir. 1976), *cert. denied*, 431

U.S. 914, 97 S.Ct. 2174, 53 L.Ed.2d 224 (1976) (prior grand jury testimony by unavailable government witness implicating defendant in previous transaction satisfied diligence/probativity requirement).

[20] Fed. R. Evid. 804(b)(1).

[21] 547 F.2d 1346, 1357 (8th Cir. 1976), *cert. denied*, 431 U.S. 914, 97 S.Ct. 2174, 53 L.Ed.2d 224 (1976).

[22] *Id.* at 1354.

his right to confront the witness by intimidating the witness. The fact that there had been no formal pre-trial notification to the defendant was excused under the circumstances.[23]

In *United States v. West*,[24] the witness who testified before the grand jury was murdered before he could testify at trial. The court found the required indicia of reliability in the fact that the witness was debriefed after each encounter with the defendant and signed a statement of what transpired at the meeting. Additionally, the witness's grand jury testimony was corroborated by evidence of tapes from a body transmitter the witness wore and surveillance photographs of the defendant making the heroin buys. The court noted that though the witness was unavailable for cross-examination, the FBI agents who corroborated the witness's testimony were subject to cross-examination and the witness was subject to impeachment concerning his prior criminal record even though he did not testify at the trial.[25]

In *United States v. Garner*,[26] the court admitted testimony of a witness who testified before the grand jury and who later denied the truth of his grand jury testimony at trial. The court found the required indicia of reliability in the fact that an unindicated coconspirator confirmed the testimony of the reluctant witness.[27]

While these decisions justified the admission of grand jury transcripts on the basis of enhanced reliability, a careful examination of the legislative history of the residual exceptions and the former testimony exception shows that the use of Rule 804(b)(5) for this purpose is improper. The residual exceptions were intended to cover situations unanticipated when the specific hearsay exceptions were drafted where the proffered hearsay possessed equivalent indications of reliability.[28] In many cases the residual exceptions may properly be used to admit hearsay statements which are reliable but fail to satisfy the precise requirements of one of the specific exceptions. However, the residual exceptions should not be used to circumvent the policies underlying the hearsay rule or the specific exceptions: "[I]f the admission of the hearsay under the residual exception runs afoul of some other Federal Rule, the other rule should control to exclude the hearsay. Where Congress has specifically addressed an issue in another rule, the more general language of the residual exceptions must give way."[29]

[23] *See* 4 WEINSTEIN, ¶ 804(b)(5)[01], at 804-126 n.9.

[24] 574 F.2d 1131, 1134 (4th Cir. 1978).

[25] *Id.* at 1136.

[26] 574 F.2d 1141, 1144-46 (4th Cir. 1978), *cert. denied*, 439 U.S. 936, 99 S.Ct. 333, 58 L.Ed.2d 333 (1978).

[27] *Id.* at 1144.

[28] *See supra* § 804.32.

[29] Sonenshein, *The Residual Exceptions to the Federal Hearsay Rule: Two Exceptions in Search of a Rule*, 57 N.Y.U. L. REV. 867, 900-901 (1982). *See, e.g.,* United States v. Metz, 608 F.2d 147, 157 (5th Cir. 1979), *cert. denied*, 449 U.S. 821, 101 S.Ct. 80, 66 L.Ed.2d 24 (1980) (statement inad-

The admission of grand jury transcripts pursuant to Rule 804(b)(5) is contrary to the policy underlying the former testimony exception of Rule 804(b)(1) and therefore should not be permitted. In addition to the bases of trustworthiness and need which traditionally support hearsay exceptions, Rule 804(b)(1) is also based on a policy of fairness to the party against whom the evidence is offered. The legislative history of the exception shows that Congress found it "generally unfair" to admit former testimony against a party who did not have an "opportunity and similar motive to develop the testimony by direct, cross, or redirect examination."[30] Since the accused does not have the opportunity to develop the testimony of a witness before the grand jury, such testimony is clearly inadmissible under the former testimony exception because its use would be unfair. Grand jury testimony is equally inadmissible under Rule 804(b)(5), regardless of its enhanced reliability, because its admission would circumvent the fairness policy underlying Rule 804(b)(1).

Because the Federal Rules of Evidence render grand jury testimony inadmissible where the witness does not testify at trial, courts do not need to reach the constitutional issue of whether the use of this evidence violates the accused's right of confrontation unless the hearsay objection is waived.[31]

missible under Rule 804(b)(3) also inadmissible under Rule 804(b)(5)); United States v. Kim, 595 F.2d 755, 763-66 (D.C. Cir. 1979) (telex inadmissible under Rule 803(6) inadmissible under Rule 803(24)).

[30] H. R. Rep. No. 650, 93d Cong., 1st Sess. (1973), *reprinted in* 1974 U.S. Code Cong. & Ad. News 7075, 7088. In civil cases, former testimony is admissible if a party or his predecessor in interest had an opportunity to develop the witness' testimony. In criminal cases, however, the accused himself must have had this opportunity at the former proceeding; the "predecessor in interest" provision does not apply.

[31] Weissenberger, *The Admissibility of Grand Jury Transcripts: Avoiding the Constitutional Issue*, 59 TUL. L. REV. 335, 351 (1984). *See, generally*, Spector Motor Co. v. McLaughlin, 323 U.S. 101, 105, 65 S.Ct. 152, 155, 89 L.Ed. 101, 104 (1944) ("[I]f there is one doctrine more deeply rooted than any other in the process of constitutional adjudication, it is that we ought not to pass on questions of constitutionality . . . unless such adjudication is unavoidable."); United States v. Gonzalez, 559 F.2d 1271, 1274 (5th Cir. 1977) (court declined to address sixth amendment issue because it found grand jury transcripts inadmissible under rules of evidence).

Chapter 805

RULE 805. HEARSAY WITHIN HEARSAY

Rule 805 reads as follows:

Hearsay included within hearsay is not excluded under the hearsay rule if each part of the combined statements conforms with an exception to the hearsay rule provided in these rules.

§ 805.1 Hearsay Within Hearsay.

Rule 805 *expressly* authorizes the admission of multiple hearsay where each element or level of hearsay conforms to an exception to the hearsay rule.[1] While not explicitly set forth in the express language of the Rule, Rule 805 *implicitly* authorizes the admission of multiple levels of out-of-court statements offered for their truth where each level conforms to *either* a hearsay exception (*i.e.*, the exceptions set forth in Rules 803 and 804), *or* to an exception to the *definition* of hearsay. These latter exceptions are set forth in Rule 801(d)(1) and Rule 801(d)(2). For example, where an admission of a party admissible under Rule 801(d)(2) is contained within a business record admissible under Rule 803(6), the entire document is admissible. Likewise, where an out-of-court statement, not offered for its truth, is contained within an admissible hearsay statement, Rule 805 implicitly provides that both levels of out-of-court statements are admissible. For example, where a witness's prior inconsistent statement, not under oath, offered

---

[1] *See, generally*, McCormick, § 313; 4 Weinstein, ¶ 805[01]-[02]; 4 Louisell & Mueller, §§ 495-96; 5 Wigmore, § 1361-63. *See also* Jelsema, Murphy, Nichols, and Tannenbaum, *Hearsay Under the Proposed Federal Rules: A Discretionary Approach*, 15 Wayne L. Rev. 1077, 1231 (1969). *See also* §§ 801.8 and 801.20 of this Treatise.

only for its impeachment value is contained within a public record admissible under Rule 803(8), both levels of out-of-court statements may be received.[2] The converse of the latter example, however, does not obtain, and where a hearsay statement, admissible under an exception, is embraced within an out-of-court statement not offered for its truth, neither level is rendered admissible by Rule 805. The first level of hearsay must be admissible for its truth (*i.e.*, via an exception to the definition or the exclusionary rule) in order to establish that the embraced hearsay statement was actually uttered or otherwise made. All of the foregoing analysis, while not explicit on the face of Rule 805, is implicitly indicated by the Rule and the theory of the hearsay system.[3]

Examples of multiple hearsay exist in federal law. A witness's testimony concerning an out-of-court statement made by him to an FBI agent constitutes hearsay where the statement is offered for its truth; the testimony constitutes double hearsay where the statement of the witness describes statements made by others to him which are also offered for their truth.[4] A document offered for the truth of its contents is hearsay because it was prepared out-of-court; where the document is based upon data derived from other sources which is also offered for its truth, it is double hearsay.[5] When a witness testifies that an informer has made an out-of-court statement to him, it is hearsay when the testimony is offered for its truth; where the substance of the informer's statement is offered for its truth to prove what the co-conspirator told the informer, it is double hearsay.[6]

Rule 805 provides that hearsay within hearsay is not excluded under the hearsay rule where each component of the multiple hearsay is admissible under an exception to the hearsay rule. For example, when a medical record containing a patient's statement of the manner in which he was injured is offered to prove the cause of the injury, Rule 805 would require that both the record and the patient's statement qualify for admission under an exception to the hearsay rule. The record might be admissible if it satisfies Rule 803(6), "Records of regularly conducted activity." The statement made by the patient might be admissible as a statement against inter-

---

[2] *E.g.*, United States v. Smith, 521 F.2d 957, 964-65 (D.C. Cir. 1975) (hearsay recorded by police officer in Form 251 admissible if it was on admission, spontaneous exclamation, dying declaration, or declaration against interest).

[3] *See* Weinstein, ¶ 805[01], at 805-2 (The...result [of Rule 805] could be achieved in the absence of a rule. . .").

[4] United States v. Beasley, 545 F.2d 403, 405-06 (5th Cir. 1977).

[5] Hunters International Manufacturing Corp. v. Christiana Metals Corp., 561 F.Supp. 614, 617 (E.D. Mich. 1982) (invoices and testimony of non-expert layperson introduced en masse by plaintiff are without foundation).

[6] United States v. Abrahamson, 568 F.2d 604, 606-07 (8th Cir. 1978) (statement made by unidentified informant to agent was hearsay and should have been excluded).

est under Rule 804(b)(3) if the patient is unavailable, or as a statement made for the purpose of medical diagnosis under Rule 803(4). In such a situation, the report would be admissible without any deletion of the patient's statement.[7]

A special problem of double hearsay lies in establishing a proper foundation to show that the internal hearsay actually satisfies an exception to the hearsay rule. Failure to lay a proper foundation may require exclusion of the evidence or excision of the internal hearsay statements from the otherwise admissible hearsay evidence.[8]

§ 805.2   Multiple Hearsay Exceeding Two Levels.

Rule 805 does not limit admissibility to double, *i.e.*, two-level, hearsay; rather, multiple hearsay exceeding two levels of out-of-court statements is admissible as long as each level of out-of-court statement possesses a basis for admission. One difficulty with multiple hearsay is that the reliability of the evidence is diminished by each additional layer of hearsay.[9] Rule 403 authorizes the court to exclude multiple hearsay when it determines that the reliability of the evidence has been diminished to an unacceptable degree.[10] Undoubtedly, in a particular case where reliability has been excessively undermined, Rule 403 might justify exclusion of double hearsay as well.[11] The principal question is whether the reliability arising from satisfaction of exceptions to the hearsay rule is counterbalanced by the increased unreliability inherent in each additional trier of hearsay.[12]

---

[7] *See* text note 1 *supra*.

[8] *See* United States v. Lang, 589 F.2d 92, 99 (2d Cir. 1978).

[9] Comment, *Hearsay Under the Proposed Federal Rules: A Discretionary Approach*, 15 WAYNE L. REV. 1077, 1231-32 (1969).

[10] *Id.* at 1232 (suggesting that after a number of repetitions the evidence is merely rumor).

[11] *See* § 403.1 *et seq.* of this Treatise.

[12] WEINSTEIN ¶ 805[01], at 805-5, *citing*, Naples v. United States, 334 F.2d 508, 511 (D.C. Cir. 1964).

Chapter 806

RULE 806. ATTACKING AND SUPPORTING CREDIBILITY OF DECLARANT

SECTION

806.1   Attacking and supporting the credibility of hearsay declarants—
        An overview
806.2   The procedure
806.3   Inconsistent statements attacking the hearsay declarant's credibility
806.4   Cross-examination of a hearsay declarant

Rule 806 reads as follows:

> When a hearsay statement, or a statement defined in Rule 801(d)(2), (C), (D), or (E), has been admitted in evidence, the credibility of the declarant may be attacked, and if attacked may be supported, by any evidence which would be admissible for those purposes if declarant had testified as a witness. Evidence of a statement or conduct by the declarant at any time, inconsistent with his hearsay statement, is not subject to any requirement that he may have been afforded an opportunity to deny or explain. If the party against whom a hearsay statement has been admitted calls the declarant as a witness, the party is entitled to examine him on the statement as if under cross-examination.

§ 806.1   Attacking and Supporting the Credibility of Hearsay Declarants —An Overview.

Rule 806 delineates the procedure for attacking and, if attacked, supporting the credibility of declarants of hearsay statements admitted at trial.[1] Acknowledging that admissions by authorized spokespersons, agents

---

[1] *See, generally,* McCORMICK, § 37; 4 WEINSTEIN, ¶ 806 [01]-[02]; 4 LOUISELL & MUELLER, §§ 500-501; 3A WIGMORE, § 1025- 39. *See also* Hale, *Inconsistent Statements,* 10 S. CAL. L. REV. 135 (1937).

or co-conspirators are technically not hearsay under Rule 801(d)(2)(C), (D), and (E), Rule 806 treats such admissions as hearsay for the purpose of impeaching or rehabilitating the declarant.[2] Rule 806 authorizes the admissibility of any evidence that would be admissible to impeach or rehabilitate a declarant of hearsay if the declarant had testified as a witness,[3] and in so doing, the Rule reflects the position that justice is best served by presentation of all evidence relevant to the reliability of statements made out-of-court.[4]

Rule 806 has three principal effects. First, Rule 806 provides that the credibility of a hearsay declarant may be attacked by any evidence that would be admissible to attack the credibility of the declarant if the declarant had testified as a witness.[5] The most frequently encountered practical effect of the Rule is to permit a hearsay declarant to be impeached by inconsistent statements.[6] Of course, other means of impeachment provided by Article VI may also be used. Additionally, the credibility of a hearsay declarant may be rehabilitated once it has been attacked.[7] Second, Rule 806 eliminates, with respect to hearsay declarants, the Rule 613[8] requirement that the declarant must be afforded an opportunity to explain or deny the statements.[9] Third, Rule 806 allows a party to call as a witness the declarant of hearsay offered against that party and to question the declarant concerning the hearsay as if under cross-examination.[10]

§ 806.2   The Procedure.

Rule 806 provides that a party may attack or support the credibility of a hearsay declarant by any evidence that would be admissible if the declarant had testified in court. For example, just as a party pursuant to Rule 608 may attack a *witness's* credibility by opinion or reputation evidence, so also may a party attack or support a hearsay *declarant's* credibility by opinion or reputation evidence concerning the declarant's character for

[2] *See* § 801.19 of this Treatise.

[3] *See* Rule 806, Advisory Committee's Note.

[4] *See* M<small>c</small>C<small>ORMICK</small>, § 37. *Cf.* 3A W<small>IG-</small>M<small>ORE</small>, § 1033 at 1037-38.

[5] *See* § 806.2 of this Treatise. *See also* Rules 608 and 609. Credibility also may be attacked in other ways, *e.g.*, by showing the bias of a hearsay declarant. *Cf.* United States v. Check, 582 F.2d 668, 684 n. 44 (2d Cir. 1978) (impeachment technique employed by defense counsel of use of witness to get at complete testimony of confidential undercover informant without calling him was entirely proper).

[6] *See* Rule 806, Advisory Committee's Note.

[7] *Cf.* Rule 608(a)(2).

[8] *See* 613.1 *et seq.* of this Treatise.

[9] *See* § 806.3 of this Treatise.

[10] *See* § 806.4 of this Treatise.

truthfulness or untruthfulness.[11] Rule 806 continues the policy of Rule 608 that rehabilitative evidence of truthfulness is inadmissible until the declarant's character for truthfulness is attacked.

Pursuant to Rule 609, the credibility of the declarant may be attacked by evidence of conviction of specified crimes.[12] Additionally, the credibility of a declarant of hearsay may be attacked by demonstrating the declarant's biases and prejudices.[13] Finally, Rule 806 provides that the credibility of a hearsay declarant may be attacked by an inconsistent statement in the manner analyzed in the next section.[14]

§ 806.3   Inconsistent Statements Attacking the Hearsay Declarant's Credibility.

Rule 806 adopts the majority position that impeachment of a hearsay statement may be effected by introduction of inconsistent statements without the requirement of affording the declarant an opportunity to explain or deny the inconsistent statement.[15] Rule 806 does not, however, adopt Wigmore's suggestion that a foundation should be required where the declarant *could* have been afforded an opportunity to explain or deny the inconsistency, *i.e.*, as in the case of prior testimony at a hearing or deposition. Wigmore would dispense with the foundation only where the declarant could not reasonably be afforded the opportunity to explain or deny the contradictory statement.[16] Contrary to Wigmore's position, Rule 806 applies broadly and uniformly and does not distinguish, for example, dying declarations from prior testimony.[17]

Because hearsay, by its nature, occurs prior to trial, Rule 806 does not limit, as does Rule 613, attack of a hearsay declarant to impeachment by *prior* inconsistent statements.[18] Instead, evidence of an inconsistent state-

---

[11] United States v. Lechoco, 542 F.2d 84, 89 (D.C. Cir. 1976) (government's closing argument evidences the extent to which defendant's honesty was in issue).

[12] *See* United States v. Lawson, 608 F.2d 1129, 1130 (6th Cir. 1979) (by putting hearsay statements before jury, his counsel made Lawson's credibility an issue the same as if Lawson had made the statements from the witness stand).

[13] *See* United States v. Check, 582 F.2d 668, 684 n. 44 (2d Cir. 1978).

[14] *See* § 806.3 of this Treatise.

[15] *See* Carver v. United States, 164 U.S. 694, 696, 17 S.Ct. 228, 232, 41 L.Ed. 602,

606 (1897); Trade Development Bank v. Continental Ins. Co., 469 F.2d 35, 43 (2d Cir. 1972); McConney v. United States, 421 F.2d 248, 251 (9th Cir. 1969). *But see*, Mattox v. United States, 156 U.S. 237, 244-50, 15 S.Ct. 337, 343, 39 L.Ed. 409, 415 (1895). *See also* McCORMICK, § 37; 3A WIGMORE, § 1033; 4 LOUISELL & MUELLER, 501.

[16] 3A WIGMORE, §§ 1030-35.

[17] *See* McCORMICK, § 37, at 81.

[18] *See* Rule 806, Advisory Committee's Note.

ment made at any time either before or after the hearsay declaration is admissible to impeach the hearsay declarant.[19]

Where an inconsistent statement is introduced to contradict and impeach a hearsay declarant, the inconsistent statement should be introduced during the case of the party who is offering the statement to impeach the hearsay declarant. The case of the proponent of the hearsay statement should not be interrupted for the purpose of receiving the inconsistent statement offered for impeachment.

§ 806.4   Cross-Examination of a Hearsay Declarant.

Where a party calls as a witness the declarant of hearsay admitted against him, Rule 806 provides that the party may examine the declarant on the hearsay as if on cross-examination.[20] In so providing, Rule 806 complements Rule 611(c), which provides for cross-examination of hostile and adverse witnesses by the proponent of the witness,[21] and Rule 607, which, subject to certain express limitations, allows a party to impeach his own witness.[22]

[19] *Id.*
[20] *Id.*

[21] *See* § 611.1 *et seq.* of this Treatise.
[22] *See* § 607.1 *et seq.* of this Treatise.

IX
AUTHENTICATION AND IDENTIFICATION

Chapter 901

RULE 901. REQUIREMENT OF AUTHENTICATION OR IDENTIFICATION

Rule 901(a)   General Provision

Rule 901(a) reads as follows:

(a) **General Provision.** The requirement of authentication or identification as a condition precedent to admissibility is satisfied by evidence sufficient to support a finding that the matter in question is what its proponent claims.

§ 901.1   Authentication or Identification—In General.

Authentication and identification are terms which apply to the process of laying a foundation for the admission of such nontestimonial evidence as documents and objects.[1] These terms may also refer to the foundational evidence which identifies a person's voice on a tape recording or in a telephone conversation.[2] Conceptually, the function of authentication or identification is to establish, by way of preliminary evidence, a connection between the evidence offered and the relevant facts of the case. The connection is necessary in order to establish the relevancy of the particular object or item, since an object or item is of no relevance if it is not attributed to, or connected with a particular person, place or issue in a case. For example, a writing purportedly signed by a party to an action is of no relevance and hence of no significance to the case unless evidence is offered that it was actually authored or signed by that person.[3] The Rules pertinent to authentication may consequently be viewed as specialized rules of relevance.[4] Article IX provides the methodology by which to establish "connective relevancy," and it defines the standard by which the determination as to admissibility will be made.

Accordingly, Rule 901(a) provides that authentication or identification is a prerequisite to admissibility. Additionally, it sets forth the standard by which the initial determination of admissibility shall be governed, i.e., the "sufficient to support a finding" standard. Rule 901(b) sets forth various

---

[1] See, generally, McCormick, § 218; 5 Weinstein, ¶ 901(a)[01]-[02]; 5 Louisell & Mueller, §§ 505-506; 7 Wigmore, §§ 2128-35. See also Alexander and Bickel, The Authentication of Documents Requirements: Barrier to Falsehood or to Truth, 10 San Diego L. Rev. 266 (1973); Brown, Authentication and Contents of Writings, 1969 Law and the Social Order 611 (1969); Eisenberg and Fenstel, Pretrial Identification, 58 Marq. L. Rev. 659 (1975); Michael and Adler, Real Proof: I, 5 Vand. L. Rev. 344 (1952); Strong, Liberalizing the Authentication of Private Writings, 52 Cornell L. Rev. 284 (1967); Levin, Authentication and the Content of Writings, 10 Rutgers L. Rev. 632 (1956).

[2] The examples set forth in Rule 901(b) for establishing authenticity also demonstrate the type of evidence subject to this requirement. The illustrations cover documentary evidence, other tangible real proof, i.e., objects of any sort, as well as conversations, and processes or systems.

[3] As theorized by Wigmore, authentication or identification is "an inherent logical necessity." 7 Wigmore, § 2129, at 564. Dean Wigmore explains that, "[i]n short, when a claim or offer involves impliedly or expressly any element of personal connection with a corporal object, that connection must be made to appear, like the other elements, or else the whole fails in effort." Id. See Advisory Committee's Note to Rule 901, Subdivision(a). See also McCormick, § 218, at 543.

[4] 5 Weinstein, ¶ 901(a)[02], at 901-21. Weinstein notes that in a theoretical sense, the rules as to authentication are redundant of relevancy requirements implicit in Rules 401 and 402. He concludes, however, that the traditional justifications for erecting a preliminary condition of fact for admission of writings—possibility of fraud, mistaken attribution, and jury credulity—still militate in favor of explicitly recognizing the special problems of authentication and identification. See also 5 Louisell & Mueller, § 506, at 18-19.

methodologies, in a non-exhaustive listing of ten examples, by which items of evidence may be authenticated or identified in order to meet the threshold standard of Rule 901(a). Rule 902, governing self-authentication, provides that certain types of written evidence are deemed authenticated without the necessity of any foundational testimony.

In addition to establishing authenticity pursuant to Rules 901 or 902, parties may utilize a variety of pretrial procedures that obviate the necessity of authenticating or identifying evidence at trial.[5] For example, a party may submit to the opponent a request for an admission as to the genuineness of any document. Alternatively, a party may seek to establish authenticity of certain evidence through pleadings, interrogatories or depositions. Likewise, a party may elicit a stipulation as to authenticity during a pretrial conference.[6]

It should be kept in mind that authentication is merely one prerequisite to the admissibility of evidence. In addition to establishing connective relevancy through authentication, a proponent of evidence may need to satisfy requirements as to hearsay, best evidence, and general relevancy principles in order to achieve admissibility of the evidence in question.

§ 901.2   Threshold Standard of Authentication Evidence.

Rule 901(a) sets forth a standard of authentication that effectively operates to screen out certain evidence which cannot meet a minimal threshold test of connective relevancy. The Rule accordingly provides that "[t]he requirement of authentication or identification as a condition precedent to admissibility is satisfied by evidence sufficient to support a finding that the matter in question is what its proponent claims." The "sufficient to support a finding" standard merely means that foundational evidence must be sufficient to constitute a rational basis for a jury decision that the primary evidence is what its proponent claims it to be. Alternately stated, the proponent need not offer conclusive evidence as a foundation but must merely offer sufficient evidence to allow the question as to authenticity or genuineness to reach the jury. The threshold standard consequently reflects the principle that both the judge and the jury participate in the determination as to authenticity, as discussed in § 901.3 *infra*. The standard itself is not rigorous, and its low threshold reflects an orientation of the Rules toward favoring the admission of evidence.[7]

---

[5] *Id. See also* Advisory Committee's Note to Rule 901, Subdivision (a).

[6] For a more detailed discussion as to alternative methods of establishing authenticity, *see* Rule 901(b)(10) and § 901.1 *et. seq.* of this Treatise.

[7] 5 WEINSTEIN, ¶ 901(a)[01], at 901-19; 5 LOUISELL & MUELLER, § 506 at 22-23.

§ 901.3 Function of the Court and the Jury in Authentication.

While both the judge and the jury participate in determinations as to authenticity, only the judge makes determinations as to admissibility. The judge must make an initial determination that the foundational evidence has met the threshold standard of admissiblity, i.e., that the foundational testimony is sufficient to support a rational jury finding as to authenticity. In this regard, the judge is governed by Rule 104(b) which defines the court's role in making decisions as to admissibility when the relevancy of evidence depends upon the fulfillment of a condition of fact. When the issue is one of authentication or identification, the condition of fact relates to the genuineness of the item in question. Inasmuch as the ultimate determination as to genuineness is a jury question, the court must, under Rule 104(b), admit the evidence upon the introduction of foundational evidence sufficient to support a finding as to authenticity.[8]

If a proper foundation is offered, the judge may not exclude the evidence merely because she does not believe it to be genuine. The ultimate question of authenticity is within the province of the jury.[9] The preliminary determination as to whether a party has met the threshold standard of Rule 901(a) is, however, within the court's discretion. Additionally, a judge may exclude evidence pursuant to Rule 403 if there exists a danger of unfair prejudice, confusion of the issues, or misleading the jury. Exclusion pursuant to Rule 403 may occur more frequently in connection with real proof than with testimonial proof due to the impact that such evidence is likely to have upon jurors.[10]

If the judge admits evidence upon a sufficient showing as to authenticity, the jury considers the evidence. In this regard, it should be noted that an opponent of evidence is never precluded from contesting the genuine-

---

[8] See Rules 104(a) and (b) and accompanying sections of this Treatise for a discussion as to the limitation on the court's role in making preliminary admissibility determinations. *See also* Rule 1008 which similarly limits the court's role in determining the admissibility of other evidence of contents of writings and the like, and hence excusal of using an original, when certain questions are raised in connection with the writing.

[9] *See* McCormick, § 227, at 555:

It must be noticed, however, that authenticity is not to be classed as one of those preliminary questions of fact conditioning admissibility under technical evidentiary rules of competency or privilege. As to these latter,

the trial judge will permit the adversary to introduce controverting proof on the preliminary issue in support of his objection, and the judge will decide this issue, without submission to the jury, as a basis for his ruling on admissibility. On the other hand, the authenticity of a writing or statement is not a question of the application of a technical rule of evidence. It goes to genuineness and conditional relevance, as the jury can readily understand. Thus, if a prima facie showing is made, the writing or statement comes in, and the ultimate question of authenticity is left to the jury.

[10] 6 Weinstein, ¶ 901(a)[01], at 901-19. *See also* McCormick, § 212, at 525.

ness of any item, even after it has been admitted upon a preliminary show-ing as to authenticity.[11] Even in the absence of contradictory testimony, however, the jury need not accept the foundational evidence as truthful. It need not believe that the evidence is in any way connected to the facts of the case. The jury may, accordingly, reject the authenticity of the evidence and accord it no weight in its deliberations.[12]

In view of the jury's role with regard to authentication, the proponent of evidence requiring authentication may offer foundational evidence that exceeds that which is required to satisfy the threshold standard of Rule 901(a). The proponent may offer evidence under any one or more of the ten examples listed in Rule 901(b) not only to establish admissibility of the particular item of proof but also to persuade the trier of fact, consistent with the proponent's burden of proof, as to the genuineness of such item. It must be emphasized that the standard as to admissibilty for authenticating evidence is the low threshold, "sufficient to support a finding." This stand-ard is considerably less demanding than such burdens of proof as "a pre-ponderance of the evidence" or "beyond a reasonable doubt."

Rule 901(b)(1)   Illustrations—Testimony of Witness With Knowledge

Rule 901(b)(1) reads as follows:

(b) Illustrations. By way of illustration only, and not by way of limitation, the following are examples of authentication or identification conforming with the requirements of this rule: . . .

(1) Testimony of witness with knowledge. Testimony that a matter is what it is claimed to be.

§ 901.4   Testimony of a Witness with Knowledge—In General.

Rule 901(b) provides illustrations of authentication and identification which may be used to meet the threshold standard provided in Rule 901(a). As specified in the introduction of Rule 901(b), the ten examples are pre-

---

[11] 5 Weinstein, ¶ 901(a)[02], at 901-23; 5 Louisell & Mueller, § 506, at 23-24.

[12] 5 Weinstein, ¶ 901(a)[01], at 901-16 through 901-17: Once the evidence is admit-ted the question becomes one of credibility and probative force and the trier may ulti-mately disbelieve the proponent's proof and entirely disregard or substantially discount the persuasive impact of the evidence ad-mitted. *See also* 5 Louisell & Mueller, § 506, at 25. *Cf.* United States v. Carriger, 592 F.2d 312, 316-17 (6th Cir. 1979) (finding reversible error in exclusion of promissory note, which was authenticated by hand-writing testimony).

sented by way of illustration only and not by way of limitation. Moreover, the illustrative methods are not mutually exclusive, and two or more may be utilized in combination in order to authenticate or identify a particular item of evidence.[13]

Rule 901(b)(1) provides that any competent witness who has knowledge that a matter is what its proponent claims may testify to such pertinent facts, thereby establishing, in whole or in part, the foundation for authentication.[14] The witness may be either a lay or expert witness, and his knowledge may be either direct or circumstantial.[15] Moreover, the witness is not required to provide conclusive evidence as to authenticity. Rather, the testimony must merely be relevant to the issue of authenticity or identification, and it must be, either of itself or in combination with other testimony or evidence, sufficient to support a jury finding that the matter is what its proponent claims.[16]

Testimony of a witness with knowledge may be utilized to authenticate documentary evidence of all types. It may also be used in connection with other types of evidence, such as tangible objects, photographs, films, recordings and the like. It should be noted that in many instances, Rule 901(b)(1) may be used in conjunction with one or more of the other examples listed in the Rule. For example, a police witness might identify an object as being the same as that involved in a crime, based on the fact that he recovered the item from the scene of the crime and on the fact that the item possesses distinctive characteristics sufficient to justify it pursuant to Rule 901(b)(4).

The knowledge of a witness testifying pursuant to Rule 901(b)(1) may be derived from a variety of sources. For example, a witness may have participated in or observed an event or transaction, or he may have heard a pertinent conversation.[17] Knowledge may also be acquired through a per-

[13] See, generally, McCORMICK, § 220, 5 WEINSTEIN, ¶901(b)(1)[01]; 5 LOUISELL & MUELLER, § 507; 2 WIGMORE, § 666. See also Evans, The Competency of Testamentary Witnesses, 25 MICH. L. REV. 238 (1927); C.J.S. 693, "Wills" § 392 and "Witnesses" § 53.

[14] Cf. Rule 602, providing that a witness may not testify to a matter unless evidence is introduced sufficient to support a finding that he has personal knowledge of the matter.

[15] See 5 WEINSTEIN, 901(b)[01], at 901-25: "A witness can give relevant testimony with respect to events which occur outside his presence where he has some circumstantial knowledge of these events based on his own

observations or perceptions." See also United States v. McNair, 439 F.Supp. 103, 105 (E.D. Pa. 1977), aff'd, 571 F.2d 573 (3d Cir. 1978), cert. denied, 435 U.S. 976, 98 S.Ct. 1624, 56 L.Ed.2d 87 (1978).

[16] 5 WEINSTEIN, ¶ 901(b)(1)[01], at 901-21 through 901-22. See also 5 LOUISELL & MUELLER, § 507, at 26. It should be noted, however, that the less precisely one testifies, the more likely the proponent will fail in his attempt to admit the evidence.

[17] 5 WEINSTEIN ¶ 901(b)(1)[01], at 901-25: "Relevant testimony concerning knowledge obtained by way of the five senses is ordinarily admissible." See Fox v. Order of United Commercial Travelers of America, 192 F.2d 844, 846 (5th Cir. 1951).

son's position or experience. For example, the manager of a bookkeeping department should have sufficient firsthand knowledge to authenticate bookkeeping entries made under his supervision.[18] An expert witness, who has knowledge of the nature of the evidence in question based on his skill or experience, may offer testimony which circumstantially authenticates the item.[19]

Authentication of evidence is merely one prerequisite to admissibility, and satisfaction of Article IX does not guarantee that an item will be admitted. Other evidentiary doctrines, such as hearsay, best evidence, and general relevancy must be considered and satisfied if pertinent to admissibility in a given case. Additionally, admission of an authenticated item of evidence is not conclusive proof: the trier of fact is free to accord it whatever weight it deems appropriate. In this regard, the opponent of any evidence authenticated by testimony of a witness with knowledge may attack the issue of genuineness by cross-examination of the authenticating witness or by offering conflicting rebuttal evidence.[20]

§ 901.5 Authentication of Documentary Evidence.

A writing may be authenticated under Rule 901(b)(1) by testimony of a witness who has firsthand knowledge of the execution, preparation or custody of the writing. For example, where connective relevancy involves attributing authorship or execution to a particular individual, a person who was present at the signing of the document may testify that the document offered at trial is the same one he saw executed by a particular individual.[21] Additionally, a witness may authenticate a writing based on his familiarity with the writing, acquired by having read, typed, or prepared it,[22] or by having supervised its preparation or having had custody of the document.[23]

---

[18] 5 WEINSTEIN, ¶ 901(b)(1)[01], at 901-25. *See also* 5 LOUISELL & MUELLER, § 507, at 30.

[19] *See* 5 WEINSTEIN, ¶ 901(b)(1)[01], at 901-27.

[20] Zenith Radio Corp. v. Matsushita Electric Industrial Co., Ltd., 723 F.2d 238, 285 (3d Cir. 1983) (prima facie showing of genuineness is subject to opposing party offering evidence to dispute authenticity).

[21] *See* 5 WEINSTEIN, ¶ 901(b)(1)[01], at 901-24; McCORMICK, § 219, at 545; 5 LOUISELL & MUELLER, § 507, at 28.

[22] 5 WEINSTEIN, ¶ 901(b)(1)[01], at 901-24; 5 LOUISELL & MUELLER, § 507, at 28. *See also* United States v. Moskowitz, 581 F.2d 14, 21 (2d Cir. 1978), *cert. denied*, 439

U.S. 871, 99 S. Ct. 204, 58 L. Ed. 2d 184 (1978) (bank robbery prosecution; sketch by police artist was properly received on basis of testimony by eyewitness "that they had previously said the sketch looked like the robber," this satisfied the authentication requirements of Rule 901, and testimony by the artist was unnecessary); United States v. Levine, 546 F.2d 658, 668 (5th Cir. 1977), *reh. denied*, 551 F.2d 687 (5th Cir. 1977) (obscenity prosecution; testimony by film producer that release print of movie viewed during trial "was substantially the same as the work print he shipped" on occasion in question provided sufficient authentication).

[23] *See also* McCORMICK, § 219, at 545.

With regard to business records, for example, authenticating testimony might be offered by a witness who prepared the record, or by one who supervised the preparation of such record.[24] Any firsthand knowledge of a writing, however acquired, is an appropriate basis for testimony on the issue of authentication where the testimony logically connects the document with the issues of the case.[25]

§ 901.6   Identification of Real Proof.

The testimony of a witness with knowledge will often be used to authenticate or identify items of real proof. Foundational testimony must establish a connection between the physical evidence offered at trial and the relevant transaction, incident, person or place in question. In other words, the witness must identify the item in a way that ties it to an element in the case.[26]

Authentication of real proof under Rule 901(b)(1) involves offering testimony of a witness with firsthand knowledge which is sufficient to support a finding that the object offered at trial is the same object as that connected to the operative relevant facts of the case, and that the condition of the object is substantially unchanged.[27] (Alternately, as explained below, any change in the object may be subject to explanation thereby satisfying the authentication process.) In order to establish this foundation, testimony may be offered as to unique characteristics, such as a serial number, an identification tag or a distinct appearance.[28] Where the item does not possess unique characteristics, it may be identified by the person or persons who had custody of the item from the time it was found in connection with the relevant fact of the case until the time it is offered into evidence. If more than one person has had custody, identification may involve establishing a "chain of custody." Pursuant to this technique, testimony is provided by each person who had custody of the item from the time it was taken from its relevant setting in the operative facts of the case until the time it is offered at trial. The "chain of custody" procedure for identifying

[24] United States v. Atchley, 699 F.2d 1055, 1058-59 (11th Cir. 1983) (not essential that authenticating witness be the one who actually prepared the records).

[25] Clifford v. Transouth Financial Corp., 566 F.2d 1023, 1025 (5th Cir. 1978) (security deed without notorial seal admissible in light of notary's testimony as to its execution).

[26] United States v. Fortes, 619 F.2d 108, 118 (1st Cir. 1980).

[27] McCORMICK, § 212, at 527. See United States v. S. B. Penick & Co., 136 F.2d 413, 415 (2d Cir. 1943) (evidence must remain unchanged in important respects). See also Rule 901(a), which establishes the threshold standard for authentication and identification.

[28] Walker v. Firestone Tire & Rubber Co., 412 F.2d 60, 62 (2d Cir. 1969).

real proof was utilized prior to the adoption of the Rules and is illustrated by the pre-Rule cases.[29] In applying the "chain of custody" technique at trial, a possible break in the chain of custody does not render the evidence inadmissible, but raises a question of weight of the evidence for the jury.[30] Establishing such a chain of custody authenticates an item by showing the improbability "that the original item has either been exchanged with another or been contaminated or tampered with."[31]

Change that occurs in an item of real proof between the time it was connected with the operative facts of the case and the time of trial does not necessarily render the item inadmissible. It may still be properly authenticated as long as the proponent offers testimony that fully describes or explains the change.[32] Any change in evidence, however, must not be so great as to render the evidence irrelevant or misleading, and, in this regard, the judge may reject any evidence where its changed condition warrants application of the exclusionary provision of Rule 403. Change may be manifested, for example, whenever the evidence offered at trial is a sample drawn from a larger mass. Such evidence should be admissible where the authenticating evidence indicates that the sample is accurately representative of the mass and that it has undergone no changes which would affect its relevance.[33]

The adoption of the Rules of Evidence emphasizes through the express language of Rule 901(a) and Rule 901(b) that there is no singularly prescribed method of authentication for a particular item of real proof. Any foundational evidence satisfying the threshold standard set forth in Rule 901(a) is sufficient to meet the authentication requirement. It must be remembered, however, that because the trier of fact is required to ascribe weight to the genuineness of any item of real proof, the foundation of preference in a given case may often involve more than an effort to satisfy the minimal test of Rule 901(a). Accordingly, in an effort to convince the trier of fact of a particular element of its case beyond a reasonable doubt, the prosecution might establish a meticulous foundation under the chain of custody technique where a less exacting foundation would satisfy Rule 901(a).

---

[29] Gallego v. United States, 276 F.2d 914, 917 (9th Cir. 1960) (tracing chain of custody sufficient in narcotics case). *See also* United States v. S. B. Penick & Co., 136 F.2d 413, 415 (2d Cir. 1943).

[30] United States v. White, 569 F.2d 263, 266 (5th Cir. 1978), *cert. denied*, 439 U.S. 848, 99 S. Ct. 148, 58 L.Ed.2d 149 (1978); Harmon v. Anderson, 495 F.Supp. 341, 347 (E.D. Mich. 1980).

[31] McCORMICK, § 212, at 528.

[32] United States v. Lambert, 580 F.2d 740, 745 (5th Cir. 1978) (physical condition of vehicle identification number plates altered substantially by time of trial admissible because officers who seized plates were thoroughly cross-examined about original condition).

[33] *See* McCORMICK, § 212, at 528.

§ 901.7   Authentication of Other Types of Demonstrative Evidence.

Identification or authentication is also required with other types of demonstrative evidence such as photographs, x-rays, video films and the like.[34] Identification of photographs, for example, under Rule 901(b)(1) requires testimony that the authenticating witness has firsthand knowledge of the person, place or object depicted.[35] It is not necessary that the witness was the actual photographer or even that the witness saw the photograph being taken.[36] The witness must testify that the photograph fairly and accurately represents the person, place or object which it purports to portray,[37] or, alternatively, he must testify as to any differences between the portrayal and the item sought to be portrayed.[38]

Rule 901(b)(2)   Illustrations—Nonexpert Opinion on Handwriting

Rule 901(b)(2) reads as follows:

(b) Illustrations. By way of illustration only, and not by way of limitation, the following are examples of authentication or identification conforming with the requirements of this rule: . . .

(2) Nonexpert opinion on handwriting. Nonexpert opinion as to the genuineness of handwriting, based upon familiarity not acquired for purposes of the litigation.

§ 901.8   Nonexpert Opinion on Handwriting—In General.

Rule 901(b)(2) governs the authentication of documentary evidence by testimony of a nonexpert who is familiar with the handwriting of the au-

---

[34] United States v. Blackwell, 694 F.2d 1325, 1329 (D.C. Cir. 1982) (tangible evidence such as photographs must be authenticated or identified); United States v. Pageau, 526 F. Supp. 1221, 1224 (N.D.N.Y. 1981) (videotape depicting alleged crime must be authenticated, but no separate authentication required for sound portion of the same videotape).

[35] United States v. Brannon, 616 F.2d 413, 417 (9th Cir. 1980), *cert. denied*, 447 U.S. 908, 100 S.Ct. 2992, 64 L.Ed.2d 857 (1980) (testimony by bank tellers that defendant was the person depicted in surveillance photo was approved by the court).

[36] United States v. Clayton, 643 F.2d 1071, 1074 (5th Cir. 1981).

[37] United States v. Richardson, 562 F.2d 476, 479 (7th Cir. 1977), *cert. denied*, 434 U.S. 1021, 98 S. Ct. 745, 54 L. Ed. 2d 768 (1978) (bank surveillance photographs authenticated by testimony that they fairly and accurately depicted the robbery).

[38] Photographs, movies, x-rays and similar evidence may, of course, be authenticated by other means. *See, e.g.*, Rule 901(b)(9), "Process or System," and § 901.38 *et seq.* of this Treatise.

thor or signatory of a document that is handwritten or signed. Consistent with the conceptual basis of authentication, this type of authentication is probative of the attribution of authorship or execution where these issues are relevant in the case.

Conceptually and mechanically, the method of authentication provided by this provision is among the simplest of the Rule 901(b) techniques. Essentially, the authenticating witness is asked whether he is familiar with the handwriting of the author or signatory and, if so, whether the document or signature in question is in the handwriting of that person. An affirmative response to the latter question provides sufficient authentication to warrant admission of the document into evidence.[39] As discussed in the following section, there may be additional inquiry, either on direct or cross-examination, concerning the basis of the witness's familiarity with the handwriting in question. The latter inquiry, however, is directed more to the weight to be accorded such lay testimony than to the admissibility of the document.[40]

§ 901.9   Bases of Familiarity.

A witness may be familiar with the handwriting of another person through any one of a number of means.[41] The only explicit limitation imposed by the Rule is that the witness's familiarity must not have been acquired for purposes of the litigation in which he is testifying. Sufficient familiarity may be acquired through a special relationship with the author, e.g., a familial or business relationship, that allows the witness to testify concerning the genuineness of a document. For example, a husband may testify that a document bears his wife's signature, or an employee may testify similarly as to a document written or signed by his superior.[42] In

---

[39] See, generally, McCormick, § 221; 5 Weinstein, ¶ 901(b)(2)[01]; 5 Louisell & Mueller, § 509; 2 Wigmore, §§ 570, 694-97. See also Annot.: Knowledge derived from family correspondence as qualifying one to testify to handwriting, 7 A.L.R. 261 (1920).

[40] Holmes v. Goldsmith, 147 U.S. 150, 163, 13 S. Ct. 288, 292, 37 L. Ed. 118, 123 (1893) (questions on cross-examination permitted to show the strength and value of witness's opinion).

[41] United States v. Carriger, 592 F.2d 312, 316 (6th Cir. 1979) (general familiarity by observing signers write their names); Throckmorton v. Holt, 180 U.S. 552, 563-65, 21 S. Ct. 474, 477, 45 L. Ed. 663, 670-

71 (1901) (familiarity acquired by having engaged in correspondence for several years); United States v. Dreitzler, 577 F.2d 539, 551 (9th Cir. 1978) (former secretary permitted to testify as to handwriting of employer); Ryan v. United States, 384 F.2d 379, 380 (1st Cir. 1967) (assistant treasurer familiar with signature of bank clerk).

[42] 5 Weinstein, ¶ 901(b)(2)[01], at 901-33; 5 Louisell & Mueller, § 508, at 33. See also United States v. Dreitzler, 577 F.2d 539, 553 (9th Cir. 1978), cert. denied, 440 U.S. 921, 59 L. Ed. 2d 473, 99 S. Ct. 1246 (1978) (former secretary of defendant was qualified as nonexpert to testify as to whether certain handwriting was that of defendant); Ryan v. United States, 384 F.2d

these examples familiarity is acquired by virtue of an extended relationship with repeated exposure to the person's handwriting rather than by a single instance of viewing the handwriting. Pre-Rule law has held, however, that a witness who has merely seen the person write on one or more occasions may offer testimony sufficient to authenticate a document.[43] Additionally, it has been held that testimony may be offered by one who has "seen writings purporting to be those of the person in question under circumstances indicating their genuineness,"[44] even though the witness has never actually seen the person write anything or sign his name. For example, requisite familiarity may be acquired through an exchange of correspondence with the person in question.[45] Notably, then, the standard for assessing the qualification of a witness under this Rule is quite liberal, and the personal knowledge requirement of Rule 602 is satisfied by a minimal showing.[46]

§ 901.10   Admissibility Versus Weight of Nonexpert Opinion.

As noted above, a document may be authenticated under this Rule on rather scant testimony pertaining to the issue of familiarity with a person's handwriting. Inquiry into the extent of familiarity goes to the weight to be accorded nonexpert testimony.[47] Accordingly, a jury may be persuaded to accord little weight to the testimony of a witness who has viewed the handwriting of a person on one or two occasions as compared with a witness who has been in a position to view the handwriting on numerous occasions. Likewise, the testimony of a nonexpert on the issue of genuineness may be outweighed by other factors, such as the witness's "lack of credibility, by the contradictory testimony of an expert, or by the jury's own comparison [Rule 901(b)(3)], or by inconsistency with other evidence."[48]

379, 380 (1967) (on question whether check was forged, assistant treasurer familiar with signature of defendant bank clerk was properly permitted to testify that the latter had signed the check).

[43] Rogers v. Ritter, 79 U.S. 317, 322, 20 L.Ed. 417, 421 (1871) (clerk in recorder's office, custodian of archives, and secretary for Board of Land Commissioners all permitted to testify because the circumstances of observing signatures in question enabled them to judge genuineness with a degree of certainty).

[44] McCormick, § 221, at 547.

[45] Id. McCormick provides further illustration of this type of familiarity, such as where the witness "has seen writings which the person has asserted are his own, or has been present in an office or other place where genuine writings of a particular person in the ordinary course of business would naturally be seen."

[46] Id. See also Strong, Liberalizing the Authentication of Private Writings, 52 Cornell L.Q. 284 (1967).

[47] See Holmes v. Goldsmith, n. 2, infra. See also Throckmorton v. Holt, n. 3, infra.

[48] 5 Weinstein, ¶ 901(b)(2)[01], at 901-33. The author suggests that the witness may also be tested by asking him to identify a genuine specimen among false copies, or by asking the witness whether he would rely on the signatures he identified in an ordinary business transaction. See also 5 Louisell & Mueller, § 508, at 37.

§ 901.11　Utility of Nonexpert Testimony.

Opinion testimony of a nonexpert on the issue of genuineness of hand-writing is admissible by virtue of Rule 701. Rule 701 authorizes testimony in the form of opinion by a lay witness where the opinion is rationally based on the perception of the witness and where it is helpful to the determination of a fact in issue, i.e., in this case, genuineness.[49] The permissive standard of Rule 901(b)(2) as to a witness's qualification to testify on this issue, however, has compelled McCormick to question the utility of such testimony.[50] He notes that nonexpert testimony on the issue of genuineness is "essentially meaningless in cases where the authenticity is actually disputed," inasmuch as "[i]f a writing is in fact questioned no person not trained in the science and art of document examination is truly competent to distinguish a skilled forgery from a genuine writing."[51] The author similarly questions the utility of this methodology in cases of undisputed authenticity where courts might just as easily establish a presumption as to authenticity in the absence of challenge.[52] In response it might be noted that the Rule provides a measure of reliability by requiring the testimony of a witness who has acquired at least passing familiarity with the hand-writing of the author or signatory of a document being offered into evidence.

Rule 901(b)(3)　Illustrations—Comparison by Trier or Expert Witness

Rule 901(b)(3) reads as follows:

(b) Illustrations. By way of illustration only, and not by way of limitation, the following are examples of authentication or identification conforming with the requirements of this rule: . . .

(3) **Comparison by trier or expert witness.** Comparison by the trier of fact or by expert witness with specimens which have been authenticated.

§ 901.12　Authentication by Comparison—In General.

Rule 901(b)(3) provides for authentication or identification by comparison of the item in question with a specimen. The comparison may be made either by the trier of fact in situations in which a layman would be competent to make such a comparison, or by a witness who has been qualified as an expert pursuant to Article VII of the Rules. If the item is authenticated

---

[49] See Throckmorton v. Holt, n. 41, supra.
[50] McCormick, § 221, at 548.
[51] Id.
[52] Id.

by expert testimony sufficient to support a finding that the matter in question is what its proponent claims it to be, it will be admitted. However, as in the case of all forms of authentication, the ultimate question as to authenticity or genuineness remains a question of fact for the jury. Where Rule 901(b)(3) is utilized and expert testimony is not offered, the trier of fact makes both the initial and ultimate decision as to authenticity, subject to some control by the court as discussed in § 901.3 of this Chapter.[53]

The technique of comparison with a specimen may be utilized in a variety of situations to authenticate or identify such items as handwriting, typewriting, bullets, tire tread marks, shoe prints, fingerprints, voiceprints, hair, blood, fabric fibers and the like.[54] In each instance, the goal of the comparison is to establish relevancy by connecting the item in question with an incident, person or place where, for example, authorship, use of a gun by an individual, or presence at a particular location is a relevant fact of the case. Establishment of authenticity by means of this technique "depends upon a statistical demonstration or assumption that the markings or other identifying characteristics are so rare (alone or in combination) that it is likely that they had the same source."[55] Authentication by comparison was authorized by Congress in 1913.[56] The comparison of an unidentified writing with a genuine specimen has long been recognized as a valid authentication technique,[57] although as discussed in the next section, the Rule is less restrictive than prior law with respect to the evidence necessary to authenticate a specimen.[58]

[53] *See, generally,* McCORMICK, §§ 205, 221; 5 WEINSTEIN, ¶¶ 901(b)(3)[01]-[05]; 5 LOUISELL & MUELLER, §§ 509-11; 2 WIGMORE, § 570; 7 WIGMORE, §§ 1997-2015. *See also* Hilton, *The Detection of Forgery,* 30 J. CRIM. L. & CRIMINOLOGY, 568 (1939); Inbau, *Toy Witness Identification of Handwriting (an Experiment),* 34 ILL. L. REV. 433 (1939); Strong, *Liberalizing the Authentication of Private Writings,* 52 CORNELL L.Q. 284 (1967); Note, 41 OR. L. REV. 154 (1962); *Modern Educational Aids for Simplified Explanations of Handwriting Comparisons,* 13 J. OF FORENSIC SCIENCES 509 (1968).

[54] *See* 5 WEINSTEIN, ¶ 901(b)(3)[01], at 901-34; 5 LOUISELL & MUELLER, § 509, at 39.

[55] 5 WEINSTEIN, ¶ 901(b)(3)[01], at 901-34.

[56] Act of 1913, Ch. 79, 37 Stat. 683 (1913).

[57] *See* Rule 901, Advisory Committee's Note, Subdivision (b). *See also* Brandon v.

Collins, 267 F.2d 731, 733 (2d Cir. 1959) (comparing signature with "concededly authentic signature"); United States v. Ortiz, 176 U.S. 422, 429, 20 S. Ct. 466, 469, 44 L. Ed. 529, 531 (1900).

[58] 5 WEINSTEIN, ¶ 901(b)(3)[02], at 901-35; 5 LOUISELL & MUELLER, § 510, at 51. *See also* United States v. Stembridge, 477 F.2d 874, 875-877 (5th Cir. 1973) (on basis of exemplars and job application form, government expert testified that the accused wrote a certain note used in the alleged bank robbery; during "rigorous cross-examination" by defense counsel, the expert admitted that he could not identify the note as being defendant's handwriting on the basis of the exemplars alone; on redirect, government was properly permitted to bring out the opinion of the expert that the accused had disguised or distorted the exemplars, but that the printing on the exemplars and the application form were produced by the same person; "it is not improper for the prosecution to show that the defendant at-

§ 901.13   Authentication of the Specimen.

Use of the comparison technique to establish authenticity actually involves two levels of authentication, i.e., authentication of the specimen and authentication of the offered exhibit. In order to establish the requisite connective relevancy, the item or document in question must be compared with an item the authenticity of which has been demonstrated. Authenticity of the specimen, then, is a logical prerequisite to the procedure. With regard to the specimen, the Rule requires only that it be authenticated to the same degree of proof as any other item, that is, by evidence sufficient to support a finding that the specimen is genuine. In theory, then, if not in practice, the Rule modifies prior law at least with respect to writings. Courts previously required that genuineness of the specimen be established by clear and convincing proof or, in some cases, by proof beyond a reasonable doubt.[59] Despite the apparently less rigorous standard required by the Rule, there is a logical justification for requiring a more compelling showing of the specimen's genuineness where the authenticity of the item in question depends entirely upon the authenticity of the specimen. Where appropriate, the trial judge is justified in excluding the specimen pursuant to Rule 403 in order to avoid unnecessary confusion.[60]

Establishing authenticity of a specimen should ideally be accomplished by means of a stipulation obtained prior to trial. It may also be established through pretrial discovery procedures such as a request for admission.[61] Otherwise, the proponent may demonstrate that the specimen is self-authenticating under Rule 902, or, alternately, establish its authenticity by a technique provided by Rule 901(b).[62] A specimen or exemplar may be received into evidence as such even though its substance is not itself relevant to any issue in the case.[63]

Appropriate specimens may be obtained from a variety of sources including writings already in evidence for some other purpose, documents

tempted to avoid providing a valid handwriting sample by intentionally distorting his handwriting"). *See, e.g.*, Fredricksen v. Fullmer, 74 Idaho 164, 168, 258 P.2d 1155, 1158 (1953) (single word goes to weight and not admissibility).

[59] 41 A.L.R. 2d 575 (1955). *See also* Rule 901(b)(3), Advisory Committee's Note.

[60] 5 WEINSTEIN, ¶ 901(b)(3)[02], at 901-35; 5 LOUISELL & MUELLER, § 509, at 44. *See also* Citizen's Bank & Trust Co. of Middlesboro, Ky. v. Allen, 43 F.2d 549, 550 (4th Cir. 1930), *cert. denied*, 284 U.S. 662, 52 S. Ct. 37, 76 L. Ed. 561 (1931) (trial judge must be satisfied of genuineness of sample). *See, e.g.*, United States v. Tur-

quitt, 557 F.2d 464, 468-70 (5th Cir. 1977).

[61] Fuston v. United States, 22 F.2d 66, 67 (9th Cir. 1927) (defendant's signature on answer in attorney's office and testimony of attorney identifying client is sufficient).

[62] United States v. Minker, 197 F.Supp. 295, 298 (E.D. Pa. 1961), *aff'd*, 312 F.2d 632 (3d Cir. 1962), *cert. denied*, 372 U.S. 953, 83 S. Ct. 952, 10 L.Ed.2d 127 (1963) (public accountant who had done work for defendant for some years and had seen him write "a dozen or more times" was found to be able to form an opinion with respect to defendant's handwriting).

[63] 5 WEINSTEIN, ¶ 901 (b)(3)[02], *et seq.*

contained in the official case file, business records, or private writings.[64] A handwriting specimen, for example, might be obtained in a civil case through interrogatories or a pretrial request for production, or by an in-court request made during cross-examination.[65] A handwriting or voice specimen of a defendant in a criminal case, or other type of specimen, may also be obtained by compulsion without violating the defendant's Fifth or Sixth Amendment rights.[66]

§ 901.14   Comparison by Expert or by Trier of Fact.

Given an authenticated specimen, Rule 901(b)(3) requires that a comparison of the item in question be made by the trier of fact or by an expert witness. In either case, unlike Rule 901(b)(2), there need be no prior familiarity with the specimen or the handwriting.

Comparison by the trier of fact is appropriate in those instances where a layman's knowledge is sufficient to compare the specimen and the item sought to be authenticated. In other instances, where meaningful comparison requires some specialized skill or knowledge, an expert witness should provide the authentication testimony.

Where an expert is used to establish authenticity under Rule 901(b)(2), the expert witness preliminarily must be qualified under the provisions of Rule 702, and the proponent must lay a sufficient foundation demonstrating that the witness possesses the requisite knowledge, skill, experience, training, or education to be qualified as an expert in the area of, e.g., handwriting or ballistics analysis. An expert need not be such by profession in order to testify on a particular subject; rather, he must be "better qualified to express opinions on that subject than other men usually are."[67]

---

[64] 5 Weinstein, ¶ 901 (b)(3)[02], at 901-36 through 901-37; 5 Louisell & Mueller, § 509, at 39. *See also* Reining v. United States, 167 F.2d 362, 365 (5th Cir. 1948), *cert. denied*, 335 U.S. 830, 69 S. Ct. 48, 93 L. Ed. 383 (1948) (allowing comparison to signature on pleading filed in a state court action); Moore v. United States, 91 U.S. 270, 274, 23 L.Ed. 346, 349 (1875) (use of paper giving power of attorney as specimen).

[65] *See, e.g.,* Stokes v. United States, 157 U.S. 187, 194, 15 S. Ct. 617, 620-21, 39 L. Ed. 667, 670 (1895) (simple concession at trial as to genuineness of specimen).

[66] *See, e.g.,* Gilbert v. California, 388 U.S. 263, 266, 87 S. Ct. 1951, 1953, 18 L. Ed. 2d 1178, 1180 (1967) (handwriting exemplars obtained from defendant by compulsion held to be non-testimonial and consequently not violative of defendant's Fifth Amendment right against self-incrimination). *See also* Schmerber v. California, 384 U.S. 757, 761, 86 S. Ct. 1826, 1830-31, 16 L. Ed. 2d 908, 911 (1965) (blood samples); United States v. Williams, 704 F.2d 315, 320 (6th Cir. 1983) (required to read a neutral passage from *Time* magazine for the purpose of voice identification).

[67] 5 Weinstein, ¶ 901 (b)(3)[03], at 901-40; 5 Louisell & Mueller, § 510, at 52; 7 Wigmore, § 2004.

An explanation of the expert's conclusion is desirable in order to persuade the trier of fact to accord significant weight to the testimony.[68] Explication of the underlying reasons is furthermore appropriate since the jury must ultimately reach its own conclusion as to authenticity, utilizing the expert's testimony only as an aid.[69] Accordingly, an unsupported conclusion will be of little probative value on the issue of authenticity. At a minimum, Rule 705 provides that the expert must disclose the facts or data underlying his opinion prior to rendering his opinion.

An expert is subject to cross-examination both as to his qualifications as an expert and as to the basis of his opinion on authenticity.[70] With regard to the latter, it is permissible to test the expert's skill by an in-court demonstration. For example, a handwriting expert may be tested by having him attempt to identify genuine signatures from among a group of genuine and false signatures.[71] While any reasonable test of skill should be allowed, the court should exclude as unreasonable or unfair tests of skill which would properly require specialized equipment or chemicals unavailable to the expert in a courtroom setting.[72]

§ 901.15   Comparison with Specimen—Application.

The most common application of the comparison technique of authentication traditionally has been in the area of expert testimony on handwriting.[73] More recently , the technique has been used increasingly to identify a person's voice and thus to authenticate conversations.[74] As noted previously,

[68] *See* Rules 703 and 705, § 703.1 *et seq.* and § 705.1 *et seq.* of this Treatise.

[69] 5 WEINSTEIN, ¶ 901(b)(3)[03], at 901-41; 5 LOUISELL & MUELLER, § 510 at 52. The jury is free to accept or reject the opinions and comparison results of an expert. *See, e.g.,* Strauss v. United States, 311 F.2d 926, 928 (5th Cir. 1963), *cert. denied,* 373 U.S. 910, 83 S. Ct. 1299, 10 L.Ed.2d 412 (1963).

[70] Lemmons v. United States, 62 F.2d 608, 611 (10th Cir. 1932) (expert witness used to substantiate handwriting on packages; jurors permitted to examine and compare the writings and form a judgment for themselves that the opinion of the expert was well founded in fact).

[71] 5 WEINSTEIN, ¶ 901(b)(3)[03], at 901-43; 5 LOUISELL & MUELLER, § 510, at 52.

[72] 5 WEINSTEIN, ¶ 901(b)(3)[03], at 901-44; 5 LOUISELL & MUELLER, § 510, at 51.

[73] *See, e.g.,* United States v. Stembridge, 477 F.2d 874, 876 (5th Cir. 1973) (job application form used for comparison; such proof was expressly stated to be an "illustration of evidence sufficient to support a finding that the matter in question was what its proponent claimed").

[74] *See, e.g.,* United States v. Bayncs, 687 F.2d 659, 666 (3d Cir. 1982); United States v. Williams, 583 F.2d 1194, 1198 (2d Cir. 1978) (voice analysis held to have reached a level of reliability sufficient to warrant its use in a courtroom for identification purposes). *See also* Cederbaums, *Voiceprint Identification: A Scientific and Legal Dilemma,* 5 CRIM. L. BULL. 323 (1969); Jones, *Danger - Voiceprints Ahead,* 11 AM. CRIM. L. REV. 549 (1973). The process involves spectrographic analysis in which a voice exemplar is run through a spectrograph. The expert then determines whether the sound wave patterns from the exemplar match those produced by the voice on the tape recording sought to be authenticated. Weinstein discusses this method of authentication and identification under Federal Rule

however, the technique provides a means for authenticating a wide variety of items.[75] For example, an experiment might identify a typewritten sheet by analyzing marks peculiar to a given typewriter and also by noting any unique characteristics of the typist where the specimen and the offered document have allegedly been typed by the same person.[76] Another frequent use of the comparison technique is in the science of ballistics where the proponent seeks to establish, for example, that a victim was killed by a bullet from the accused's gun.[77] In such a case, the prosecution may seek to establish through expert testimony that bullets found in the possession of the defendant bear markings similar to those of identified bullets taken from the victim or from the scene of the killing.[78] In each case of authentication by comparison, the proponent is establishing connective relevancy in a somewhat indirect manner as compared with the other Rule 901(b) illustrations, i.e., by using an identified specimen to complete the connection.

§ 901.16   Role of Judge, Witness and Jury.

As discussed in the foregoing sections, the comparison required by Rule 901(b)(3) may be made either by the trier of fact or by an expert witness. In the former case, the jury is presented with the item in question in order to compare it with the authenticated specimen. Both the offered exhibit and the specimen for comparison are taken into the jury room for examination. To be admitted to the jury for consideration, however, the specimen must meet the threshold "sufficient to support a finding" standard for authentication. If expert testimony is utilized, the preliminary decision as to admissibility is made by the court; that is, the judge determines first whether the specimen, and then whether the exhibit, satisfies the minimal finding as to authenticity. Ultimately, however, authenticity or genuine-

---

901(b)(5). See WEINSTEIN ¶ 901(b)(5)[01], at 901-61 and 901-67 et seq. In this sense, voice identification by an expert through spectrographic analysis and comparison, rather than by the opinion of a lay person who is familiar with the voice of the person sought to be identified, may be seen as a specialized application of Rule 901(b)(3). It should be noted in this regard that the illustrations provided in Rule 901(b) are not necessarily mutually exclusive, and, in some situations, the terms of two or more illustrations may be pertinent to the authentication of a particular item.

[75] Pyle and Mockbee, *Authentication and Identification*, 49 MISS. L.J. 151, 165 (1978).

[76] See 5 WEINSTEIN, ¶ 901(b)(3)[04], at 901-46; 5 LOUISELL & MUELLER, § 510, at 53.

[77] See 5 WEINSTEIN, ¶ 901(b)(3)[04], at 901-46; 5 LOUISELL & MUELLER, § 510, at 53. See also Laney v. United States, 294 F. 412, 416 (D.C. Cir. 1923) (expert testimony that the bullet extracted from decedent's head was shot from the pistol found in defendant's possession was competent, especially where defendant admitted firing a number of shots at a crowd).

[78] See also Medley v. United States, 155 F.2d 857, 859-60 (D.C. Cir. 1946), *cert. denied*, 328 U.S. 873, 66 S.Ct. 1377, 90 L.Ed. 1642 (1946), *reh. denied*, 329 U.S. 822, 67 S. Ct. 35, 91 L. Ed. 699 (1946).

ness, both of the specimen and of the item to be identified, is a question for the jury in attributing weight.[79] Accordingly, any demonstrative evidence utilized by the expert witness to explain his opinion, such as photographs, diagrams and the like, should be available to the jury for their consideration.[80]

Whether the comparison as to authenticity is made by the trier of fact or by an expert, the judge retains control over the procedure. In either case, the judge must make a preliminary determination as to authenticity of the specimen and, if necessary to avoid confusion, may exclude it under Rule 403 if there is a substantial risk of misleading the trier of fact.[81] Where expert testimony is utilized, the judge must also determine whether the expert witness has been sufficiently qualified and, as previously noted, must determine whether the expert's testimony constitutes evidence sufficient to support a finding as to authenticity of the item in question. The court must also determine the admissibility of any evidence utilized by the expert to justify or explain his conclusion.

Rule 901(b)(4)　　Illustrations—Distinctive Characteristics and the Like

Rule 901(b)(4) reads as follows:

(b) **Illustrations.** By way of illustration only, and not by way of limitation, the following are examples of authentication or identification conforming with the requirements of this rule: . . .

(4) **Distinctive characteristics and the like.** Appearance, contents, substance, internal patterns, or other distinctive characteristics, taken in conjunction with circumstances.

§ 901.17　　Distinctive Characteristics—In General.

Rule 901(b)(4) provides for authentication by reference to distinctive identifying characteristics of an item. Such characteristics may relate to

---

[79] 5 Weinstein ¶ 901 (b)(3)[03], at 901-41; 5 Louisell & Mueller, § 510, at 52. See n. 17 *infra* and accompanying text.

[80] *See, e.g.,* Weinstein, ¶ 901(b)(3)[03], at 901-41. (Jury should be allowed to take handwriting specimen into the jury room to compare it with the writing to be identified) and ¶ 901(b)(3)[05], at 901-47, where

the issue concerns identification of bullets, "[t]he jury should be allowed to make its own comparison of the bullets, and it should be allowed to use the expert's photographs or microscope for the comparison if these aids are offered.")

[81] *See* n. 8, *infra* and accompanying text.

appearance, contents, substance, internal patterns or the like, and, when taken in conjunction with surrounding circumstances, proof of unique qualities may provide foundational evidence sufficient to authenticate an item. Authentication in this situation is used to connect the item in question with a particular person or place where that connection is relevant to an issue in the case.

The methodology of Rule 901(b)(4) establishes connective relevancy by means of circumstantial evidence rather than by direct proof.[82] Unique characteristics, as discussed in the following sections, may be utilized to authenticate items such as letters, other written documents, telegrams, and voices over the telephone. Rule 901(b)(4) represents no significant departure from prior law.[83]

§ 901.18   Authentication by Proof of Contents or Substance—In General.

Foundational evidence as to distinctive contents or substances of an item may operate to authenticate it. One mode of circumstantial proof illustrative of this application of the Rule is a showing of the unlikelihood that anyone but the purported writer or speaker would be familiar with the contents of the document or statements in question.[84] The probative value of such evidence depends upon the relative obscurity of the subject matter since familiarity with a topic of common knowledge would not advance the task of identifying the author or speaker. Accordingly, a proponent seeking to establish authenticity of an item pursuant to this method must offer foundational evidence as to the subject matter of the item in question, the degree to which such subject matter is known, and the purported author or speaker's familiarity with the unique subject matter. Where the

[82] See, generally, McCormick, § 225; 5 Weinstein, ¶¶ 901(b)(4)[01]-[05]; 5 Louisell & Mueller, §§ 512-15; 7 Wigmore, §§ 2148-54. See also Annots.: Proof of Authenticity or Genuineness of Letter Other than by Proof of Handwriting or Typewriting, 9 A.L.R. 984 (1920); Proof of Authorship or Identity of Sender of Telegram as Prerequisite of its Admission in Evidence, 5 A.L.R. 3d 1018 (1966).

[83] Rule 901(b)(4), Advisory Committee's Note.

[84] See Rule 901(b)(4), Advisory Committee's Note; McCormick, § 225, at 552; 5 Weinstein, ¶ 901(b)(4)[01], at 901-49; 5 Louisell & Mueller, § 514, at 70. See also Zenith Radio Corp. v. Matsushita Electric

Industrial Co., Ltd., 505 F. Supp. 1190, 1225 (E.D. Penn. 1980); Chaplin v. Sullivan, 67 Cal. App. 2d 728, 731, 155 P.2d 368, 371-72 (1945) (quiet title action in which issue was whether certain moneys had been paid on installment contract; letters from administrator of estate acknowledging receipt of installment payments were properly received; parties conceded that installment payments had been paid currently through time indicated on letters, and court here notes that circumstantial evidence may authenticate: "Among other things upon which reliance may be placed is that a letter states facts which could only be known to or relate to the purported writer").

subject matter is not generally known and the purported author or speaker is shown to have had knowledge of its substance, there exists foundational evidence sufficient to support a finding that that person is the source of the item.[85]

The inference may be strengthened by proof of consistent surrounding circumstances such as, for example, evidence that a document was one of a series of consistent transactions in which the purported author was a known participant.[86] Of course, even though a preliminary finding of authenticity is made sufficient to admit the evidence, an opponent may seek to diminish its weight by offering evidence to the contrary.[87] As with all forms of authentication, authenticity may be challenged by the opponent and disbelieved by the trier of fact.

§ 901.19　Authentication by Proof of Contents—Reply Technique.

One specific application of authentication by proof of contents is known as the reply technique or the reply doctrine.[88] If it can be shown, for exam-

[85] It need not be shown that the purported author was the only person who could have known the pertinent details contained in a document. This idea, espoused by Wigmore, 7 Wigmore, § 2148, at 604-06 is not carried over into the Rules. See 5 Weinstein, ¶ 901(b)(4)[01], at 901-47. Weinstein recognizes that the force of the inference decreases as the number of people who know of the details and who might have written the document increases. See also 5 Louisell & Mueller, § 514, at 74. See, e.g., United States v. Wilson, 532 F.2d 641, 644-45 (8th Cir. 1976) (provides a helpful discussion of other circumstantial evidence, along with the contents, that may be probative on the issue of authenticity).

[86] See 5 Weinstein, ¶ 901(b)(4)[01], at 901-49 et seq. See also 5 Louisell & Mueller, § 514, at 72. See, e.g., United States v. Luschen, 614 F.2d 1164, 1174 (1980), cert. denied, 446 U.S. 939, 100 S. Ct. 2161, 64 L. Ed. 2d 793 (1981) (drug prosecution; notebook found in defendant's bedroom in the handwriting of a single person apparently describing drug transactions and interpreted for the trier of fact by an expert was properly received; contents of a writing may be used in determining identity of author: "who wrote the notebook was established by the correspondence of the dates and prices to those involved in the case;"

extrinsic evidence linked defendant to various drug transactions at least circumstantially).

[87] See 5 Weinstein, ¶ 901(b)(4)[01], at 901-49 in which the author notes, for example, that:

> if there is a serious question of forgery, the inference is subject to being rebutted by the possibility that the [distinctive] details were added by someone to give an air of verity to the document rather than by the purported author who obtained the information in the usual way.

See also, United States v. Wilson, 532 F.2d 641, 644-45 (8th Cir. 1976), cert. denied, 429 U.S. 846, 97 S. Ct. 128, 50 L.Ed.2d 117 (1976) (court admitted contents of two notebooks found in house, which according to informer was being used in narcotics operation; informer further testified that drug transactions were recorded in these notebooks; author of notebooks was unknown, but court found that contents, containing nicknames of defendants and code terms referring to heroin, sufficed to make a prima facie showing of authenticity, which had not been countered by any evidence from the defendants).

[88] McCormick, § 225, at 552; 5 Weinstein, ¶ 901(b)(4)[05], at 901-62; 5 Louisell & Mueller, § 514, at 74 to 76.

ple, that a letter was written to a particular person, and that the letter being offered into evidence is purported to be written by another person in timely response to the communication of the first person, the second letter's authenticity may be established by virtue of its unique contents.[89] Authentication in this instance rests upon the theory that the reply document reflects the respondent's knowledge of details derived from the first communication that are not generally known.[90]

In order to utilize the reply technique, the proponent of the purported reply must establish that the first letter was actually sent to the person whose reply communication is sought to be authenticated. This may be established by testimony by the first letter itself or by a copy.[91] Proof of other corroborating circumstances may also be made, such as the fact that the reply letter bears the address of the purported writer on a letterhead or personalized stationery.[92]

The reply or knowledge technique may be utilized to authenticate evidence such as a telegram[93] or a telephone conversation.[94] For example, a speaker in a telephone conversation may be identified circumstantially

---

[89] See McCormick, § 225, at 552-53. See also Winel v. United States, 365 F.2d 646, 648 (8th Cir. 1966) (authenticity of letter established where it can be shown that the letter was sent in reply to a previous communication).

[90] McCormick, § 225, at 553 notes other corroborating inferences as follows:

In view of the regularity of the mails the first letter would almost invariably come exclusively into the hands of X, or those authorized to act for him, who would alone know of the terms of the letter. It is supported also by the fact that in common experience we know that reply letters do come from the person addressed in the first letter.

[91] As noted by McCormick, the requirements of Article X may have to be satisfied where the reply letter merely refers to or responds to the terms of the first letter. If the first letter is in the hands of the party opponent, a notice to produce may be required prior to any attempt to prove the contents by means of a copy. See Rule 1004 and McCormick, § 225, at 553. See also Levinson v. United States, 5 F.2d 567, 569 (6th Cir. 1925), cert. denied, 269 U.S. 564, 46 S. Ct. 23, 70 L. Ed. 414 (certain letters

were properly authenticated; as to one, court notes that it "was a response to a request addressed to the furniture company at Cincinnati only two days before;" letters in question were on company letterhead and seemingly sent from its place of business in Cincinnati).

[92] 5 Weinstein, ¶ 901(b)(4)[05], at 901-62; 5 Louisell & Mueller, § 514, at 74. See also National Acci. Soc. v. Spiro, 78 F. 774, 777 (6th Cir. 1897), cert. denied, 168 U.S. 708, 18 S. Ct. 941, 42 L. Ed. 1211 (letter was properly identified, despite fact that signature was affixed by rubber stamp, and seal was lacking, because it was one received in reply to one addressed to defendant at its home office in New York; it came from New York and was a communication from defendant, and was accepted since it was written on the business letterhead of the corporation).

[93] See also McCormick, § 225, at 553, noting that some courts are reluctant to authenticate telegrams pursuant to this theory.

[94] Van Riper v. United States, 13 F.2d 961, 968 (2d Cir. 1926), cert. denied, 273 U.S. 702, 47 S. Ct. 97, 71 L. Ed. 848 (1927) (Judge Learned Hand applied the reply letter doctrine to telephone conversation).

where he subsequently took some action that was prompted by the discussion held during the telephone call in question.[95]

§ 901.20   Authentication by Proof of Distinctive Characteristics of Appearance.

In addition to proof relating to a unique knowledge of contents, authenticity may be established by proof concerning distinctive characteristics of appearance or physical attributes of an item. For example, a letter's "physical appearance, postmark, return address, contents, and letterhead may in combination sufficiently authenticate the writing."[96] Another example of unique physical appearance is that of a signature affixed by a rubber stamp, where it can be shown that it was the purported writer's custom to use such a stamp.[97]

§ 901.21   Authentication by Proof of Internal Patterns.

A writing may be authenticated pursuant to Rule 901(b)(4) by internal linguistic patterns or characteristics that connect a particular person to the writing in question.[98] The formalized science dealing with this area is known as psycholinguistics, that is, "the study of the relationship between messages and characteristics of the persons sending messages."[99] Proof of

[95] See 5 Weinstein, ¶ 901(b)(6)[02], at 901-90 and 5 Louisell & Mueller, § 514, at 75. Authentication of telephone conversations under Rule 901(b)(4) may be indicated where the witness cannot identify the caller or recipient's voice so as to satisfy Rule 901(b)(5), or where the requirements of Rule 901(b)(6), relating particularly to authentication of outgoing telephone calls, cannot be met. See also Malouff v. Pope, 9 F.2d 254, 254-55 (8th Cir. 1925).

[96] 5 Weinstein, ¶ 901(b)(4)[02], at 901-55. The author concludes that by such proof, the appearance of the letter, in essence, "speaks for itself and makes the document self-authenticating." Technically, Judge Weinstein's statements may be overly broad if taken literally because prior foundational evidence must generally establish the connection between such indicia of authenticity and the facts of the case. For example, if a postmark is probative of authenticity, some evidence must establish the connective relevancy of the mark, e.g. that the writer resided in the location indicated by the postmark. See also 5 Louisell & Mueller, § 512, at 54.

[97] 5 Weinstein, ¶ 901(b)(4)[02], at 901-55 through 901-56; 5 Louisell & Mueller, § 512, at 54.

[98] See Rule 901(b)(4), Advisory Committee's Note; 5 Weinstein, ¶ 901(b)(4)[03], at 901-54 et seq.; 5 Louisell & Mueller, § 512, at 54 et seq.

[99] 5 Weinstein, ¶ 901(b)(4)[03], at 901-58; 5 Louisell & Mueller, § 513, at 61-70. A comprehensive treatment of this topic is provided in Arens and Meadows, Psycholinguistics and the Confession Dilemma, 56 Colum. L. Rev. 19 (1956). More explicitly, the psycholinguist explores such things as the "length, type, and distribution of sentences, relative frequency of imagery, word length and extent of vocabulary" to provide "some evidence of idiosyncratic characteristics of writers," Id. at 25. See also Comment, Stylistics Evidence in the Trial of Patricia Hearst, 1977 Ariz. St. L. J. 387, 393-97 (useful general discussion of evidence of stylistics and psycholinguistics).

pertinent linguistic traits may be offered by a psycholinguist, although expert testimony is not necessarily required. Judge Weinstein notes, for example, that linguistic comparison has long been utilized by courts without the aid of experts:

> One of the standard arguments of attorneys is that this witness, whom the jury observed speaking on the witness stand, could not possibly have used the language and style attributed to him in a writing.[1]

Expert testimony may be utilized, of course, to bolster such an argument, although such supporting evidence would go to weight rather than admissibility.[2] It should be noted that where an expert testifies by comparing the linguistic patterns of a document sought to be authenticated with a writing specimen, there exists a theoretical and functional overlap with the authentication technique provided by Rule 901(b)(3). The duplication, however, poses no practical problems in authenticating the document.

§ 901.22　Authentication by Proof of External Circumstances.

Circumstantial proof relating to external circumstances, such as custody of an item, for example, may be utilized in conjunction with appearance, contents, substance, and the like, to authenticate an item. In this regard, proof that a document was found in the possession of the purported writer, or that it came from a corporate defendant's files, is strong circumstantial evidence of authenticity.[3] While testimony by one who has had custody of an item may be offered pursuant to Rule 901(b)(1), a witness who has not actually had custody might testify pursuant to this Rule that he recognizes the document offered at trial as one which was removed from the business's files by virtue of its distinctive characteristics or contents.

Other external circumstances which may support a finding of authenticity include the integration of the document in question within a continuum of correspondence or a series of consistent transactions.[4] It may also be shown that the document contains references to an independently established event or to particular relationships or places with which the purported writer was integrally connected.[5]

See, e.g., Throckmorton v. Holt, 180 U.S. 552, 568-70, 21 S. Ct. 474, 478, 45 L. Ed. 663, 670-71 (testimony about legal attainments and composition and style allowed to remain in case).

[1] 5 WEINSTEIN, ¶ 901(b)(4)[03], at 901-58; 5 LOUISELL & MUELLER, § 513, at 69.

[2] 5 WEINSTEIN, ¶ 901(b)(4)[03], at 901-58; 5 LOUISELL & MUELLER, § 513, at 69.

[3] See McCORMICK, § 224, at 552. Compare Rule 901(b)(7) concerning custodial evidence pertaining to public records or reports.

[4] 5 WEINSTEIN, ¶ 901(b)(4)[04], at 901-61; 5 LOUISELL & MUELLER, § 515, at 77.

[5] 5 WEINSTEIN, ¶ 901(b)(4)[04], at 901-61; 5 LOUISELL & MUELLER, § 515, at 77.

Rule 901(b)(5) Illustrations—Voice Identification

Rule 901(b)(5) reads as follows:

(b) Illustrations. By way of illustration only, and not by way of limitation, the following are examples of authentication or identification conforming with the requirements of this rule: . . .

(5) Voice Identification. Identification of a voice, whether heard firsthand or through mechanical or electronic transmission or recording, by opinion based upon hearing the voice at any time under circumstances connecting it with the alleged speaker.

§ 901.23 Voice Identification—In General.

Rule 901(b)(5) governs the identification of a particular voice by anyone who has familiarity with the alleged speaker's voice. Such testimony provides the requisite connection between a voice, heard either directly or otherwise, and the alleged speaker where the speaker's identity is relevant to an issue in the case.

Voice identification is established by opinion evidence, that is, by testimony of a witness that, based upon his familiarity with a speaker's voice, it is his belief that the voice sought to be identified or authenticated is that of the specific speaker. The technique may be utilized to authenticate, for example, a telephone call received by the witness, or a tape recording that is being offered into evidence. The opinion may be offered by a lay person or by an expert witness.

§ 901.24 Subject Matter of the Identification.

The voice that is the subject of the identification may have been heard by the witness either directly or indirectly.[6] Direct, firsthand exposure to a

---

[6] McCORMICK, § 226; 5 WEINSTEIN, ¶¶ 901(b)(5)[01]-[03]; 5 LOUISELL & MUELLER, § 516; 2 WIGMORE, §§ 658, 660. *See also* Decker & Handler, *Voiceprint Identification Evidence - Out of the Frye Pan and into Admissibility,* 26 AM. U.L.REV. 314 (1977); Greene, *Voiceprint Identification: The Case in Favor of Admissibility,* 13 AM. CRIM. L. REV. 171 (1975); Kamine, *The Voiceprint Technique: Its Structure and Reliability,* 6 SAN DIEGO L. REV. 213 (1969); Kersta, *Speaker Recognition and Identification by Voiceprints,* 40 CONN. BAR JOURNAL 586 (1966); O'Neill, *The Reliability of the Identification of the Human Voice,* 33 J. OF AMER. INST. OF CRIM. LAW and CRIMINOLOGY 487 (1943); Thomas, *Voiceprint—Myth or Miracle (The Eyes Have It),* 3 U. of SAN FERNANDO L. REV. 15 (1974); Weintraub, *Voice Identification, Writing Exemplars and the Privilege Against Self-Incrimination,* 10 VAND. L. REV. 485 (1967); WEISS-

voice might occur where the witness heard someone talking in the next room but did not see the speaker. Similarly, the witness may have heard a conversation in the dark, or may have been exposed to a conversation while otherwise unable to see the speaker.[7] In these cases, identification of the speaker by means of voice familiarity is required inasmuch as a visual identification of the speaker's person is not possible.

Indirect exposure to a voice may, according to the Rule, be through mechanical or electronic transmission or by means of a recording. Accordingly, voice identification may be pertinent to authenticating a voice heard over a telephone, a public address system, a radio broadcast, or an audio recording.[8] Regardless of the manner in which a witness has experienced a particular voice, he may identify that voice if he has the requisite familiarity with the alleged speaker's voice.

§ 901.25 Voice Identification by Lay or Expert Witness.

It is clear from the provisions of Rule 901(b)(5) that anyone who has heard the voice of the alleged speaker, at anytime, may offer opinion testimony sufficient to identify the voice. Such a witness need not offer conclusive proof on the issue of identity but must merely offer testimony sufficient to establish a rational jury finding of identity.[9] Accordingly, a lay witness who has heard the alleged speaker on but one occasion may, within the

MAN, *Voiceprints and the Defense*, 10 N. ENG. L. REV. 25 (1974); Symposium, Trial Magazine, Jan. Feb. 1973, p. 44. Note, *A Foundational Standard for the Admission of Sound Recordings into Evidence in Criminal Trials*, 4 S. CAL. L. REV. 1273 (1979); Comment, *Voiceprints: The Determination of Admissibility*, 2 U. DAYTON L. REV. 73 (1977).

[7] United States v. Wilkes, 451 F.2d 938, 940-41 (2d Cir. 1971) (narcotics agent overheard conversation while outside defendant's apartment); Auerbach v. United States, 136 F.2d 882, 885 (6th Cir. 1943) (witness overheard conversation while in a phone booth).

[8] United States v. Thomas, 586 F.2d 123, 133 (9th Cir. 1978) (identification of tape conversation); United States v. Albergo, 539 F.2d 860, 864 (2d Cir. 1976) (tape of intercepted telephone call).

[9] 5 WEINSTEIN, ¶ 901(b)(5)[01], at 901-66; 5 LOUISELL & MUELLER, § 516, at 93. *See also* Auerbach v. United States, 136 F.2d 882, 885 (6th Cir. 1943) (testimony was

properly received despite the fact that witness did not even see the two men, one of whom he identified by the conversation he overheard while he was in a telephone booth in the lobby of a hotel; although it was possible that the witness could be mistaken, as well as the lack of certainty involved, this testimony was used to identify the defendant's voice). *See, e.g.*, Pilcher v. United States, 113 F. 248, 249 (5th Cir. 1902) (in a prosecution for the illegal removal of whiskey a revenue officer testified that he had crawled under defendant's house one night and overheard some men discussing the removal of whiskey from a warehouse, and "it was his impression that one of the voices he heard talking was that of the defendant, with whom he was acquainted, but of this he was not certain, and he could not say it was the defendant's voice because he did not see him"; the witness' uncertainty did not preclude his testimony, but the conviction was reversed for allowing the witness to testify to irrelevant and prejudicial matters).

court's discretion, give an opinion as to the identity of the voice in question.[10] Although such testimony may be sufficient to support admissibility, the circumstances surrounding the identification may be considered by the jury in assessing the weight to be accorded such an identification. Consequently, the jury may consider information, elicited on direct or cross-examination concerning, for example:

[t]he opportunity a witness had to become familiar with the speaker's voice, its peculiarities, the time between hearing and identification, acuteness of the witness' hearing and the witness' state of awareness and proximity to the speaker at the time the voice was heard.[11]

Rule 901(b)(5) contemplates that voice identification by a lay witness will be in the form of an opinion, apparently in recognition of the obvious fact that testimony of this nature cannot be conclusive. In this regard, the Rule is analogous to Rule 901(b)(2) which provides for authentication of handwriting by opinion testimony of a lay witness who is familiar with the alleged author's handwriting. The two provisions differ, however, with respect to the foundation required for such testimony. In order to testify as to the genuineness of handwriting, familiarity of the authenticating witness with the alleged author's handwriting must pre-exist the litigation. Rule 901(b)(5) contains no similar time requirement regarding the witness's familiarity with the alleged speaker's voice. As discussed in the following section, the familiarity as to voice may be acquired at any time and presumably may be acquired specifically for purposes of the litigation in which the voice identification is offered.

Rule 901(b)(5) does not specify the type of witness who may give opinion testimony as to voice identification, and such testimony may be given by a

---

[10] 5 WEINSTEIN, ¶ 901(b)(5)[01], at 901-67. Judge Weinstein notes that a witness may testify, pursuant to Rule 602, if "evidence is introduced sufficient to support a finding that he has personal knowledge of the matter." The threshold is consequently low and in Judge Weinstein's view, the court should give a voice identification witness the benefit of every doubt. *See also* 5 LOUISELL & MUELLER, § 516, at 94-95. *See also* United States v. Axselle, 604 F.2d 1330, 1338 (10th Cir. 1979) (witness heard defendant's voice once at a hearing 30 days after telephone conversation to be identified; this exposure to defendant's voice sufficed). *See, e.g.,* United States v. Washington, 253 F.2d 913, 917 (7th Cir. 1958) (Duffy's dissent) ("the conversation con-

sisted of not more than thirty-five words, which ordinarily could consume about twelve seconds of time. It is the unbelievable testimony of the agents that as Mrs. Kernick was telephoning, each agent got his head close enough to Mrs. Kernick's head so that he not only heard the voice on the other end, but heard it clearly and distinctly enough so that on the following day he was able to recognize the voice he had heard . . . as belonging to Fred Washington").

[11] *See, e.g.,* United States v. Moia, 251 F.2d 255, 257 (2d Cir. 1958) (a government agent had twelve telephone conversations with an unidentified person whose voice he recognized during a face to face conversation the day after the last call).

lay or expert witness.[12] Expert testimony may involve the use of voice prints and the spectrographic comparison of, for example, the tape recorded voice of a known speaker with that of a speaker whose identity is sought to be established.[13] Voice identification by an expert witness may be viewed as a specialized application of Rule 901(b)(3), because the expert testifies on the basis of comparing a given voice with a specimen of known origin. Familiarity based upon "hearing" the voice of the alleged speaker as provided by Rule 901(b)(5) should be construed broadly enough to include familiarity based upon voice print analysis.[14] In view of studies which indicate the relative unreliability of voice recognition by most laymen, voice print authentication is particularly warranted.[15]

§ 901.26   Foundational Requirements for Voice Identification Testimony.

The proponent of voice identification testimony must establish by way of foundation that the witness has some familiarity with the alleged speaker's voice. According to the Rule, this may be established by showing that the witness has heard the voice sought to be identified "at any time under circumstances connecting it with the alleged speaker." Consequently, the requisite familiarity may arise from exposure to the alleged speaker's voice prior to or subsequent to the conversation or communication in question.

In the typical situation a witness offering an opinion on voice identification will do so based on his *prior* familiarity with the voice in question. For example, a witness may authenticate a telephone conversation by testifying that he received a telephone call from a person whom he was able to

---

[12] *Cf.* Rule 901(b)(5), Advisory Committee's Note, noting that aural voice identification is not a subject of expert testimony. For an implicit rejection of this view, *see* 5 WEINSTEIN, ¶ 901(b)(5)[01], at 901-65 *et seq.*; 5 LOUISELL & MUELLER, § 516, at 94. *See also* United States v. Hughes, 658 F.2d 317, 319 (5th Cir. 1981), *cert. denied*, 455 U.S. 922, 102 S. Ct. 1280, 71 L. Ed.2d 463 (1982) (past conversations); United States v. Cuesta, 597 F.2d 903, 915 (5th Cir. 1979), *cert. denied*, 444 U.S. 964, 100 S. Ct. 451, 452, 62 L. Ed. 2d 377 (1979), ("[R]ule 901(b)(5) merely requires that the witness have some familiarity with the voice he identifies"); United States v. Vitale, 549 F.2d 71 (8th Cir. 1977), *cert. denied*, 431 U.S. 907, 97 S. Ct. 1704, 52 L. Ed. 2d 393 (1977) (testimony of witness that he had

spoken twice to defendant and recognized his voice on telephone as sufficient foundation); United States v. McCartney, 264 F.2d 628, 631 (7th Cir. 1959) (agent heard three calls by putting his ear near receiver and recognized voice as defendant's when he met him a few hours later).

[13] *See* 5 WEINSTEIN, ¶ 901(b)(5)[01], at 901-65 *et seq.*; 5 LOUISELL & MUELLER, § 516, at 94 *et seq.*

[14] *See* 5 WEINSTEIN , ¶ 901(b)(5)[01], at 901-71; 5 LOUISELL & MUELLER, § 516, at 101. *See also* Kamine, *The Voiceprint Technique: Its Structure and Reliability*, 6 SAN DIEGO L. REV. 213, 224 (1969).

[15] *See also* O'Neill, *The Reliability of the Identification of the Human Voice*, 3 J. CRIM. L. AND CRIMINOLOGY 487 (1942).

identify because he was familiar with that person's voice from previous communications.[16]

The pertinent identification to which the witness is testifying need not, however, occur simultaneously with the witness's exposure to the voice the identity of which is in question. Thus, for example, a witness might have been exposed to an unfamiliar voice which he is able to identify at a later point in time based on subsequently acquired familiarity.[17] It should be pointed out that in this situation the witness is not so much identifying or remembering the prior voice as he is identifying the present voice, of known origin, as being the same as that which he previously experienced. Subsequent identification might occur, for example, where the witness was a victim or a robber who, although masked, had spoken several sentences in the victim's (witness's) presence. Assuming the robber was previously unknown to the victim, voice identification would occur, if at all, based on the witness's subsequent exposure to a known suspect's voice. The foundation in this instance would consist of testimony by the witness that he became familiar with the accused's voice through a subsequent encounter during which the accused spoke. Such subsequent exposure might be voluntary on the part of the accused, or it might involve a compulsory elicitation of his voice on a recording or during a line-up.[18] In this latter regard, courts have held that the prosecution may compel an accused to give a voice exemplar without violating the accused's constitutional rights.[19]

[16] See Rule 901(b)(5), Advisory Committee's Note: "The requisite familiarity may be acquired either before or after the particular speaking which is the subject of the identification."

[17] Id. See, e.g., State v. Dick, 27 Ohio St. 2d 162, 166-67, 271 N.E.2d 797, 800 (1971) (victim who heard perpetrator's voice during an attempted rape was able to make a subsequent identification based upon seeing suspect in a line-up and hearing him speak). See also United States v. DiMuro, 540 F.2d 503, 504 (1st Cir. 1976), cert. denied, 429 U.S. 1038, 97 S. Ct. 733, 50 L. Ed. 2d 749 (1977) (agent properly allowed to identify defendant's voice in June telephone conversations on basis of "a personal confrontation" in August).

[18] See 5 WEINSTEIN, ¶ 901(b)(5)[03], at 901-81; 5 LOUISELL & MUELLER, § 516, at 99. See also United States v. Chibbaro, 361 F.2d 365, 374-76 (3rd Cir. 1966) (defendant and other suspects were observed and listened to from behind a one-way mirror); United States v. Wade, 388 U.S. 218, 221, 87 S. Ct. 1926, 1929, 18 L. Ed. 2d 1149, 1154

(1967) (compelled voice exemplar does not infringe Fifth Amendment right against self-incrimination); Meggs v. Fair, 621 F.2d 460, 462 (1st Cir. 1980) (voice identification testimony based upon hearing defendant speak did not violate Fifth Amendment privilege against self-incrimination, despite fact that defendant did not know he was being listened to at the police station, where there was no showing that his statements were used for any other purpose than to identify him).

[19] Compulsory voice exemplars are categorized, along with blood samples, visual display of one's person and the like, as real or physical evidence rather than testimonial communication, and as such they do not violate the accused's privilege against self-incrimination. See, e.g., United States v. Williams, 704 F.2d 315, 320 (6th Cir. 1983) (defendant compelled to read a neutral passage from Time magazine for purposes of voice identification); see 5 WEINSTEIN, ¶ 901(b)(5)[03], at 901-80; 5 LOUISELL & MUELLER, § 516, at 98-99. Cf. Weintraub, Voice Identification, Writing Exemplars

A voice exemplar might also consist of a tape recording of a person whose identity is known. Conversely, the voice sought to be identified may be a recorded voice. In either case, the proponent should offer foundational testimony to the effect that the recording is an accurate reproduction of the voice in question or that the recording equipment is of such a quality as to assure accurate reproduction.[20]

§ 901.27   Evidence Establishing Voice Identification.

Voice identification pursuant to Rule 901(b)(5) may be offered into evidence in one of several forms. A witness may testify as to his opinion that a voice he heard on a particular occasion was that of a given person. Alternatively, the evidence may consist of a tape recording that is played in the courtroom, accompanied by testimony of a witness who identifies the voice on the recording.[21] In some cases, a transcript of a tape may be admissible where a transcript would aid authentication in, e.g., revealing speech patterns.[22] It should be noted that evidence of this type, as well as any testimony as to contents, is being offered to prove identity of a speaker and not

and the Privilege Against Self-Incrimination, 10 VAND. L. REV. 485 (1967). Judge Weinstein points out, however, that the constitutional propriety of obtaining a voice exemplar may depend upon the manner in which a voice identification is conducted and the words a suspect is asked to repeat. 5 WEINSTEIN, ¶ 901(b)(5)[03], at 901-83.

[20] See 5 WEINSTEIN, ¶ 901(b)(5)[02], at 901-75; 5 LOUISELL & MUELLER, § 516, at 101. See also 58 A.L.R.2d 1024 (1958).

[21] See 5 WEINSTEIN, ¶ 901(b)(5)[02], at 901-74 and 5 LOUISELL & MUELLER, § 516, at 102. Where the evidence itself consists of sound recordings, Judge Herlands, of the Southern District of New York, suggests several elements which should be established by foundation testimony. These include the following:

(1) That the recording device was capable of taking the conversation now offered in evidence.
(2) That the operator of the device was competent to operate the device.
(3) That the recording is authentic and correct.
(4) That changes, additions or deletions have not been made in the recording.

(5) That the recording has been preserved in a manner that is shown to the court.
(6) That the speakers are identified.
(7) That the conversation elicited was made voluntarily and in good faith, without any kind of inducement.

The elements are derived from the pre-Rule case of United States v. McKeever, 169 F.Supp. 426, 430 (S.D.N.Y. 1958), rev'd on other grounds, 271 F.2d 669 (2d Cir. 1959). Since the enactment of Rule 901, the McKeever test is no longer rigidly followed but serves only as a guideline.

[22] 5 WEINSTEIN, ¶ 901(b)(5)[02], at 901-80; 5 LOUISELL & MUELLER, § 516, at 107. See also United States v. MacMillan, 508 F.2d 101, 105-06 (8th Cir. 1974), cert. denied, 421 U.S. 916, 95 S. Ct. 1577, 43 L. Ed.2d 782 (1975) (found to be appropriate, in the sound discretion of the trial judge, to furnish the jurors with copies of a transcript to assist them in listening to the tapes); United States v. Rochan, 563 F.2d 1246, 1251 (5th Cir. 1977) (stenographers who typed transcript need not testify if one of the parties to the taped conversation testifies that it is correct).

as proof of the contents of what was said.[23] It should also be kept in mind that admissibility of a tape recording or transcript thereof is within the discretion of the trial judge. The former might be rejected, for example, where the recordings were of poor quality or where, for some other reason, it would not be helpful to the jury.[24]

Evidence concerning voice identification may be buttressed by circumstantial evidence, some of which may properly fall within one of the other Rule 901(b) illustrations. For example, the witness's identification of a voice may be based partially on distinctive characteristics of a speaker's voice, such as a lisp or speech impediment. In such a case, the identification is based on Rule 901(b)(4) as well as 901(b)(5). Other circumstantial evidence may affect the weight of the identification testimony. For example, a witness's voice identification may be reinforced by evidence that the alleged speaker was present at the particular place and at the time where the witness claims to have heard that person's voice.

Rule 901(b)(6)   Illustrations—Telephone Conversations

Rule 901(b)(6) reads as follows:

(b) **Illustrations.** By way of illustration only, and not by way of limitation, the following are examples of authentication or identification conforming with the requirements of this rule: . . .

(6) **Telephone conversations.** Telephone conversations, by evidence that a call was made to the number assigned at the time by the telephone company to a particular person or business, if (A) in the case of a person, circumstances, including self-identification, show the person answering to be the one called, or (B) in the case of a business, the call was made to a place of business and the conversation related to business reasonably transacted over the telephone.

---

[23] The same evidence may be utilized to prove contents if the same are not rendered inadmissible because of the hearsay exclusionary rules or because of noncompliance with the best evidence provisions of Article X.

[24] 5 WEINSTEIN, ¶ 901(b)(5)[02], at 901-80; 5 LOUISELL & MUELLER, § 516, at 107.

See also United States v. Watson, 594 F.2d 1330, 1336 (10th Cir. 1979), *cert. denied*, 444 U.S. 840, 62 L. Ed. 2d 51, 100 S. Ct. 78 (1979) (upholding use of transcripts of taped conversations since proponent offered proof of the accuracy of the transcripts at a pretrial hearing).

§ 901.28 Telephone Conversations—In General.

Rule 901(b)(6) provides for the authentication of telephone conversations.[25] More particularly, the Rule is designed to apply specifically to calls initiated by the person who offers the foundational testimony, i.e., the person initiating an outgoing call.[26] The Rule is applicable in the case of telephone calls both to individuals and business establishments, with a slightly different foundational requirement indicated for each. The Rule provides a method for attributing oral statements to a particular speaker or to a person who speaks for a particular business establishment where the identity of the speaker is relevant to an issue in the case. Establishing identity by means of Rule 901(b)(6) largely involves the use of circumstantial rather than direct proof.

The standard for authenticating telephone calls is liberal.[27] Initially, there must be evidence that a call was placed to a number assigned at the time by the telephone company to a particular person or business. Such evidence may consist of testimony or other proof such as, for example, telephone company records.[28] The additional specific requirements for au-

---

[25] See, generally, McCormick, § 226; 5 Weinstein, ¶ 901(b)(6)[01]-[03]; 5 Louisell & Mueller, §§ 517-19; 7 Wigmore, § 2155. See also Comment, Authentication and the Best Evidence Rule Under the Federal Rules of Evidence, 16 Wayne L. Rev. 195 (1969); Annot.: Admissibility of Telephone Conversations in Evidence, 71 A.L.R. 5 (1927), 105 A.L.R. 326 (1936).

[26] See Rule 901(b)(6), Advisory Committee's Note. For a discussion as to authentication of incoming telephone calls, see Rule 901(b)(4) and Rule 901(b)(5) and accompanying discussion at § 901.53 et seq. As to analogous authentication of amateur radio transmissions, see the discussion in 5 Weinstein, ¶ 901(b)(6)[03], at 901-96. See, e.g., United States v. Sansone, 231 F.2d 887, 890 (2d Cir. 1956), cert. denied, 351 U.S. 987, 76 S. Ct. 1055, 100 L. Ed. 1500 (1956) (conversation heard over portable transmitting and receiving set); United States v. Johnson, 314 F.2d 49, 50 (6th Cir. 1963) (witness may testify that radio transmitter produced distinct reproduction of sound and that witness was able to identify speaker heard over his receiver). Judge Weinstein also discusses authentication of telephone calls, both in-

coming and outgoing, by a variety of techniques other than specified by Rule 901(b)(6), in a discussion which is perhaps more pertinent to Rules 901(b)(4) and 901(b)(5). See 5 Weinstein, ¶ 901(b)(6)[02], at 901-86 et seq. See also 5 Louisell & Mueller, § 519, at 118.

[27] 5 Weinstein, ¶ 901(b)(6)[01], at 901-83; 5 Louisell & Mueller, § 517, at 109.

[28] 5 Weinstein, ¶ 901(b)(6)[01], at 901-83; 5 Louisell & Mueller, § 517, at 109. See also United States v. Sawyer, 607 F.2d 1190, 1192-93, cert. denied, 445 U.S. 943, 100 S.Ct. 1338, 63 L.Ed.2d 776 (1980) (call to defendant Sawyer placed by Revenue Agent was properly authenticated because it was "undisputed that the number listed in the agent's report was Sawyer's business number); Palos v. United States, 416 F.2d 438, 440 (1969), cert. denied, 397 U.S. 980, 90 S.Ct. 1107, 25 L.Ed.2d 391 (1970) (narcotics prosecution; government agent Villar properly authenticated phone call which he placed: "Villar dialed a number registered to the appellant. When the phone was answered, Villar asked 'Palitos?', a name under which appellant was known, and received a response 'Yes, this is he'").

thenticating calls to individuals and to business establishments are discussed in the following sections. It should be noted that if a sufficient foundation is established, testimony as to the contents of the telephone conversation is admissible as long as it is not otherwise excludable on such bases as general relevancy or hearsay.

The Rule is premised upon factors which are indicative of trustworthiness. These include the presumed accuracy of the telephone system, the probable absence of a motive to falsify on the part of the answering party, and the lack of opportunity for premeditated misrepresentation of fraud.[29] The Rule codifies the majority rule in the United States as to both personal and business telephone calls.[30]

Rule 901(b)(6) is not an exclusive method for authenticating outgoing telephone calls. As discussed in the Advisory Committee's Note to Rule 901(b)(6), the testifying witness may also identify the recipient of the call on the basis of voice recognition pursuant to Rule 901(b)(5) or on the basis that contents of the recipient's statements related to matters known only by the alleged speaker, as provided in Rule 901(b)(4).[31]

§ 901.29   Authenticating Telephone Calls to an Individual.

In order to authenticate a telephone call to an individual under Rule 901(b)(6), there must be testimony that a call was made to an assigned number. Additionally, there must be circumstantial evidence that identifies the person who answered the call as the one who was intended to be called.[32] This element may be satisfied by testimony that the recipient identified himself, or by other circumstances that are probative of identity. Self-identification is recognized as a reliable indicium of identity in the case of outgoing calls, because in such situations there is a probable ab-

---

[29] See McCORMICK, § 226, at 554. The Rule reflects what Wigmore calls "mercantile custom," which assumes in ordinary circumstances that: "the numbers in the telephone directory do correspond to the stated names and addresses, and the operators do call up the correct number, and the person does in fact answer." 7 WIGMORE, § 2155, cited in 5 WEINSTEIN, ¶ 901(b)(6)[01], at 901-84. See also O'Neal v. Morgan, 637 F.2d 846, 850 (2d Cir. 1980), cert. denied, 451 U.S. 972, 101 S.Ct. 2050, 68 L.Ed. 2d 351 (1981) ("[I]n this circuit, self-identification of the person called at a place where he reasonably could be expected to be has long been regarded as sufficient.").

[30] See Rule 901(b), Advisory Committee's Note.

[31] Id.

[32] See United States v. Benjamin, 328 F.2d 854, 860-61 (2d Cir. 1964) (self-identification and proper dialing establishes prima facie case for authenticity). Self-identification alone, without evidence that a number assigned in a telephone directory was called, is insufficient to authenticate a telephone conversation. See United States v. Ross, 321 F.2d 61, 69 (2d Cir. 1963) (fact that man who telephoned customer identified himself with defendant's name was not sufficient to permit jury to infer that defendant was caller).

sence of motive and opportunity to falsify.[33] The same guarantees are not necessarily present in connection with incoming calls, where self-identification is insufficient in itself to establish authenticity.[34]

In addition to self-identification, identity may be proved by a variety of circumstances. For example, a telephone call may produce results that are unlikely to have occurred in the absence of the call, such as where an action is requested of the recipient and that action is subsequently taken by the individual in question.[35] Alternatively, there might be testimony that a conversation played an intermediate and significant role in ongoing negotiations, or that the recipient's statements reflected familiarity with matters known only by the one to whom the call was made.[36]

§ 901.30 Authenticating Telephone Calls to a Business.

Authentication of telephone calls to a business establishment requires, in addition to evidence that a call was made to a number assigned by the telephone company, evidence that the call was made to a place of business and that the conversation related to business reasonably transacted over the telephone. In such a case, where the witness has spoken with someone purporting to speak for the business with respect to business matters, "it is presumed that the speaker was authorized to speak for the employer."[37] The

---

[33] McCORMICK, § 226, at 554.

[34] See United States v. Benjamin, 328 F.2d 854, 860-61 (2d Cir. 1964). Incoming telephone calls must be authenticated pursuant to Rule 901(b)(4) or Rule 901(b)(5). These Rules may also provide the methodology for authenticating outgoing telephone calls to a person at a number other than that assigned to him in a telephone directory. For example, in accordance with the provisions of Rule 901(b)(4), there might be testimony that a person told the witness to call him at a given number, and that the witness subsequently called that number. Self-identification in such an instance would operate as the distinctive contents required by Rule 901(b)(4), which, taken in conjunction with the alleged speaker's having given the witness a number to call, should be sufficient to authenticate the telephone conversation.

[35] See 5 WEINSTEIN, ¶ 901(b)(6)[02], at 901-90; 5 LOUISELL & MUELLER, § 517, at 111. See also Commercial Casualty Ins. Co. v. Lawhead, 62 F.2d 928, 930-31 (4th Cir. 1953) (correction and return of bond in ac-

cordance with telephone conversation sufficiently identifies the individual).

[36] See 5 WEINSTEIN, ¶ 901(b)(6)[02], at 901-85 through 901-90. See also 5 LOUISELL & MUELLER, § 517, at 111-112.

[37] McCORMICK, § 226, at 554-55; 5 WEINSTEIN, ¶ 901(b)(6)[01], at 901-85; 7 WIGMORE, § 2156, at 769; 5 LOUISELL & MUELLER, § 517, at 113. See also Lynn v. Farm Bureau Mut. Auto. Ins. Co., 264 F.2d 921, 924-26 (4th Cir. 1959) (in personal injury action against insurance carrier arising out of automobile accident; evidence showed that driver purchased car, and that on day of purchase he telephoned defendant and spoke with unidentified woman who told him that he had coverage on the new car; court rejects contention that defendant was not effectively bound by call, finding it unnecessary that the person to whom driver spoke be further identified, since it was an established place of business listed in the telephone directory). Judge Weinstein notes that a business must accept the consequences of having invited the public, by listing a business telephone number

Rule should apply to all types of business concerns, including public offices.[38]

If the answering person has purported to speak for the business, it is not necessary that his individual identity be established, as long as the conversation is circumstantially probative of the identity of the place of business.[39] In this regard, the Rule requires that the conversation relate to business "reasonably transacted" over the telephone. The requirement is somewhat nebulous, but should be interpreted liberally in view of the Rules' policy toward favoring the admissibility of evidence. In this regard, the recipient of the call "need only speak with apparent understanding of the matter put to him."[40]

§ 901.31　Witnesses Who May Testify as to Telephone Conversations.

In most situations, testimony pursuant to Rule 901(b)(6) will be offered by the person who made the telephone call which is sought to be authenticated. Under pre-Rule Federal law, and under the Rule, the witnesses competent to authenticate a telephone conversation are not limited to the participants.[41] A person who eavesdrops or otherwise overhears a telephone conversation may testify to the conversation she heard by satisfying the same requirements of authentication that apply to the participants.[42] The

---

in a directory, to transact business with the company by calling that number. In such a case, the business "cannot prevent the admission of testimony concerning a call placed to his business office by claiming that the person answering was not authorized to do so." 5 WEINSTEIN ¶ 901(b)(6)[01], at 901-85.

[38] 5 WEINSTEIN, ¶ 901(b)(6)[01], at 901-85; 5 LOUISELL & MUELLER, § 517, at 113. See also Zurich General Accident & Liability Co. v. Baum, 159 Va. 404, 411, 165 S.E. 518, 520 (1932) (listing a business telephone number in a directory is assumed to be an invitation to the public to transact business with the company by calling that number; presumption is that they authorize communications made over the telephone in ordinary business transactions).

[39] 5 WEINSTEIN, ¶ 901(b)(6)[01], at 901-84; 5 LOUISELL & MUELLER, § 517, at 113.

[40] 5 WEINSTEIN, ¶ 901(b)(6)[01], at 901-86; 5 LOUISELL & MUELLER, § 517, at 113. See, e.g., Ley v. Home Ins. Co. of New York, 64 N.D. 200, 205-06, 251 N.W. 137,

139 (1933). See also Rice v. Fidelity & Casualty Co. of New York, 250 Mich. 398, 401, 230 N.W. 181, 182 (1930) ("the call for Mr. Upington at his business telephone number, together with the claimed relevant reply . . . furnished prima facie proof of identity").

[41] See United States v. Bucur, 194 F.2d 297, 303-04 (7th Cir. 1952) (same rules of authentication apply to bystander or nonparticipant). See also 5 WEINSTEIN, ¶ 901(b)(6)[02], at 901-93 through 901-95; 5 LOUISELL & MUELLER, § 518, at 113-114. See, e.g., United States v. Scully, 546 F.2d 255, 270 (9th Cir. 1976), vacated and remanded on other grounds sub. nom., United States v. Cabral, 430 U.S. 902, 97 S.Ct. 1168, 51 L.Ed. 2d 578 (1977) (authentication by circumstantial evidence).

[42] 5 WEINSTEIN, ¶ 901(b)(6)[02], at 901-95; 5 LOUISELL & MUELLER, § 519, at 117. See also United States v. Savage, 564 F.2d 728, 731-32 (5th Cir. 1977). See, e.g., Rathbun v. United States, 236 F.2d 514, 516-17 (10th Cir. 1956) (wiretapper).

role which a witness played in a call to which she testifies is not determinative of the admissibility of her testimony.[43]

Rule 901(b)(7)   Illustrations—Public Records or Reports

Rule 901(b)(7) reads as follows:

(b) **Illustrations.** By way of illustration only, and not by way of limitation, the following are examples of authentication or identification conforming with the requirements of this rule: . . .

(7) **Public records or reports.** Evidence that a writing authorized by law to be recorded or filed and in fact recorded or filed in a public office, or a purported public record, report, statement, or data compilation, in any form, is from the public office where items of this nature are kept.

§ 901.32 Public Records or Reports—In General.

Rule 901(b)(7) provides for authentication of public records based upon a prima facie showing that the records are from a public office where records of that type are kept.[44] Accordingly, a party may authenticate public records by foundational evidence that, prior to the trial, such records were in the custody of an appropriate public office. By its terms, the Rule applies to writings that are authorized by law to be recorded or filed in a public office and that are in fact so recorded or filed.[45] Additionally, the Rule applies to any purported public record, report, statement, or data compilation, in any form, that is kept in a public office.

---

[43] 5 WEINSTEIN, ¶ 901(b)(6)[02], at 901-93; 5 LOUISELL & MUELLER, § 519, at 117. Questions as to whether a person actually heard the conversation in question, as well as the accuracy of his interpretation, are questions of fact which affect weight.

[44] *See, generally,* McCORMICK, § 224; 5 WEINSTEIN, ¶ 901(b)(7)[01]; 5 LOUISELL & MUELLER, § 520; 7 WIGMORE, §§ 2158, 2159. *See also* Annots.: *Federal Civil Procedure Rule 44 and Federal Criminal Procedure Rule 27, Relating to Proof of Official Records,* 70 A.L.R. 2d 1227 (1960); *What are Official Records within the Purview of 28 U.S.C. § 1733, Making Such Records or Books Admissible in Evidence,* 50 A.L.R. 2d 1197 (1956); *Mutilations, Alterations,*

and Deletions as Affecting Admissibility in Evidence of Public Records, 28 A.L.R. 2d 1143 (1953); *Authentication or Verification of Photographs as Basis for Introduction in Evidence,* 9 A.L.R. 2d 899 (§ 11 "Photographs of or Constituting Part of, Public Record") (1950); *Compelling Production or Authentication for use as Evidence of Court Records or Writings or Object in Custody of Court or Officer Thereof,* 170 A.L.R. 334 (1947).

[45] *See* Rule 901(b)(7), Advisory Committee's Note; 5 WEINSTEIN, ¶ 901(b)(7)[01], at 901-99; 5 LOUISELL & MUELLER, § 520, at 127-28. *See* Rule 901(a) as to the standard for authentication.

The policy justification for such a rule is based upon the circumstantial guarantees of trustworthiness that attend recorded or filed documents. Such guarantees arise from the duty imposed upon public officials to accept only purportedly genuine writings for recording or filing.[46]

Authentication of public records pursuant to Rule 901(b)(7) contemplates that the record itself will be offered into evidence. Frequently, however, due to the inconvenience or impossibility of producing the original public record in court, the proponent will seek to introduce a copy of the record. If the copy is certified, it may be authenticated pursuant to Civil Rule 44 or Criminal Rule 27,[47] or pursuant to Rule 902(4).[48] If the copy is uncertified, it may also be offered into evidence and authenticated pursuant to Rule 901(b)(7). In such a case, however, the proponent must also satisfy the best evidence requirements set forth in Rule 1005 which governs the admissibility of copies as proof of the contents of public records. A copy may be utilized if it is certified or, alternatively, if it is authenticated by a witness who has compared it with the original. Accordingly, where the proponent offers an uncertified copy of a public record, he must elicit testimony from a witness that satisfies the requirements of Rule 1004 or Rule 1005 and he must establish, through testimony of that witness or otherwise, the foundational requirements of Rule 901(b)(7). The latter are discussed in § 901.34 of this Chapter.

Authenticity of public records is merely one prerequisite to admissibility. In addition to establishing genuineness, the proponent must consider any other pertinent evidentiary requirements such as those relating to the best

---

[46] *See* McCORMICK, § 224, at 694:

If a writing purports to be an official report or record and is proved to have come from the proper public office where such official papers are kept, it is generally agreed that this authenticates the offered document as genuine. This result is founded on the probability that the officers in custody of such records will carry out their public duty to receive or record only genuine official papers and reports. Similarly, where a public office is the depository for private papers, such as wills, conveyances, or income tax returns, the proof that such a purporting deed, bill of sale, tax return or the like has come from the proper custody is usually accepted as sufficient authentication. This again can

be sustained on the same principle if it appears that the official custodian had a public duty to verify the genuineness of the papers offered for record or deposit and to accept only the genuine.

See also United States v. City of New York, 132 F.Supp. 779, 782 (E.D.N.Y. 1955) (there is a presumption of regularity that attaches to the administration of governmental affairs).

[47] Civil Rule 44 and Criminal Rule 27 provide that foreign or domestic records, or entries therein, if otherwise admissible, may be evidenced by an official publication of the record or by a certified copy.

[48] Rule 902(4) provides that certified copies of certain public records are self-authenticating. *See* Rule 902(4) and § 902.09 *et seq.* of this Treatise.

evidence rules, as discussed above, or to general relevancy and hearsay rules.[49]

§ 901.33   Types of Evidence Admissible as a Public Record or Report.

Rule 901(b)(7) applies expressly to two categories of evidence. The first includes any writing that is authorized by law to be recorded or filed and in fact recorded or filed in a public office. The definition includes writings of both a public and private nature, as long as they are authorized to be recorded or filed in a public office and are so recorded or filed. The range of pertinent writings may include, for example, judicial records,[50] legislative records,[51] records of administrative agencies,[52] records of correctional institutions and law enforcement agencies,[53] coroner's records and reports,[54] tax returns,[55] selective service files, weather reports, patent office records, military records, and any other official records from an office of any level of government, domestic as well as foreign.[56]

[49] *See* McCORMICK, § 224, at 551:

As is true with ancient documents, the question of the authenticity of official records should not be confused with the ultimate admissibility of such records. It is quite possible for a public record to be perfectly genuine, and yet remain inadmissible for some distinguishable reason, *e.g.*, that it is excludable hearsay.

See Rule 803(8) and accompanying discussion at § 803.39 *et seq.*

[50] Maroon v. Immigration & Naturalization Service, 364 F.2d 982, 984 (8th Cir. 1966) (judicial notice of the fact that the clerk is the legal custodian of the records of his office).

[51] United States v. Aluminum Co. of America, 1 F.R.D. 71, 73 (S.D.N.Y. 1939) (Senate document containing letter by Special Assistant to the Attorney General, two memoranda by Special Assistant to the Attorney General, and a report, all concerning alleged violations of court decree by Alcoa).

[52] Wausau Sulphate Fiber Co. v. Commissioner, 61 F.2d 879, 880 (7th Cir. 1932) (testimony of counsel that certain waivers were from the files of the Bureau of Internal Revenue); *Cf.* Concrete Engineering Co. v. Commissioner, 58 F.2d 567, 568 (8th Cir.

1932) (containing signature of Commissioner).

[53] United States v. Locke, 425 F.2d 313, 315 (5th Cir. 1970) (statement signed by prisoner).

[54] Morrow v. Wyrick, 646 F.2d 1229, 1232-33 (8th Cir. 1980) (introduction of preliminary hearing testimony of unavailable witness was constitutionally permissible).

[55] Desimone v. United States, 227 F.2d 864, 867-68 (9th Cir. 1955) (tax returns produced from file in offices of the federal government were official records).

[56] United States v. Ward, 173 F.2d 628, 629-30 (2d Cir. 1949) (selective service files); Pardo v. United States, 369 F.2d 922, 925 (5th Cir. 1966) (selective service files); Lowe v. United States, 389 F.2d 51, 52 (5th Cir. 1968) (Sec. 1606.35(a) of the Code of Federal Regulations provides that "any officer or employee of the Selective Service System who produces the records of a registrant in court shall be considered the custodian"); Morgan v. United States, 149 F.2d 185, 187-88 (5th Cir. 1945), *cert. denied*, 326 U.S. 731, 66 S.Ct. 39, 90 L.Ed. 435 (1945) (price memorandum apparently filed with local War Price and Rationing Board by company operated by defendant; document was properly authenticated, in part by the showing that it was taken from

The second category of evidence included within Rule 901(b)(7) is composed of any purported public record, report, statement, or data compilation, in any form that is kept in a public office. The category includes, for example, reports of investigations by public officials, such as a geology and water resources report published by a water conservation board.[57] The Rule refers to data compilations in any form. Consequently, public records or reports may consist of writings, as well as video tapes, public recordings, computer printouts and the like.[58]

§ 901.34   Foundation as to Custody of Public Records and Reports.

In addition to establishing that an exhibit is a public record or report within the limit of Rule 901(b)(7), the proponent must show that the exhibit is from the public office where items of its type are kept. The requisite foundation of appropriate custody may be established in one of several ways. Accordingly, custody may be shown by pertinent testimony of a person from the office where the particular record was kept, by a certification from the appropriate office, by testimony of any person with knowledge, or by judicial notice.[59] It must appear from the foundational evidence that the custodial public office was an appropriate, i.e., authorized, depository for the record or report in question.[60] The foundational witness, however, need not be the actual custodian of the record, nor need he have any particular knowledge of the contents of the record.[61] He must merely be

the official file of the Board). See 5 WEINSTEIN, ¶ 901(b)(7)[01], at 901-98 through 901-99; 5 LOUISELL & MUELLER, § 520, at 123-25.

[57] 5 WEINSTEIN, ¶ 901(b)(7)[01], at 901-100; 5 LOUISELL & MUELLER, § 520, at 126. See also Williamson v. Union Oil Co., 125 F. Supp. 570, 573 (D. Colo. 1954) (authentication was properly conceded; the issue before the court related solely to a hearsay objection).

[58] See 5 WEINSTEIN, ¶ 901(b)(7)[01], at 901-100 through 901-101; 5 LOUISELL & MUELLER, § 520, at 127. See also Halloran, Judicial Data Centers, 52 Judicature 156 (1958) (computerized data compilations are presently maintained by several judicial districts, and the use of computers is likely to increase as more public offices seek to reduce the paperwork involved in keeping records of such matters as traffic violations, jury management, docketing, calendaring accounting, criminal records, and post-trial treatment of convicts). Cf. Sunset Motor

Lines, Inc. v. Lu-Tex Packing Co., 256 F.2d 495, 499 (5th Cir. 1958) (punch card for an IBM machine kept by the United States Department of Agriculture excluded as heresay and because it was not certified as required by Fed. R. Civ. P. 44(a)).

[59] 5 WEINSTEIN, ¶ 8901(b)(7)[01], at 901-101; 5 LOUISELL & MUELLER, § 520, at 127-28. See also United States v. Ortiz, 176 U.S. 422, 429, 20 S. Ct. 466, 472, 44 L.Ed. 529, 535 (1900); United States v. Locke, 425 F.2d 313, 315 (5th Cir. 1970) (statement signed by prisoner); Pardo v. United States, 369 F.2d 922, 925-26 (5th Cir. 1966); Maroon v. Immigration & Naturalization Service, 364 F.2d 982, 984-85 (8th Cir. 1966).

[60] See, e.g., Bank of United States v. White, WRIGHT 51 (1832) (clerk of court certifying matters outside of his duties and powers).

[61] 5 WEINSTEIN, ¶ 901(b)(7)[01], at 901-102; 5 LOUISELL & MUELLER, § 520, at 128-29. See also Woods v. Turk, 171 F.2d 244, 245 (5th Cir. 1948) (order by area Rent Di-

589   AUTHENTICATION AND IDENTIFICATION   § 901.35

able to satisfy the threshold requirement that the record was in the custody of the appropriate public office.[62]

Rule 901(b)(8)   Illustrations—Ancient Documents or Data Compilation

Rule 901(b)(8) reads as follows:

(b) Illustrations. By way of illustration only, and not by way of limitation, the following are examples of authentication or identification conforming with the requirements of this rule: . . .

(8) Ancient documents or data compilation. Evidence that a document or data compilation, in any form, (A) is in such condition as to create no suspicion concerning its authenticity, (B) was in a place where it, if authentic, would likely be, and (C) has been in existence twenty years or more at the time it is offered.

§ 901.35   Authentication of Ancient Documents or Data Compilations— In General.

Rule 901(b)(8) provides a method for authenticating any document or data compilation on the combined bases of age and corroborating circumstances as to genuineness.[63] The threshold standard of admissibility may be satisfied by showing that a document is at least twenty years old, that its condition creates no suspicion as to its authenticity, and that it was kept or found in a place where, if authentic, it would likely be.

Rule 901(b)(8) represents a modification of prior law in two respects. First, the Rule includes data compilations as well as documents in recogni-

rector was properly proved by means of copy certified by Acting Area Rent Director and testimony by Area Rent Attorney; court here found no merit in view of trial judge that the order was insufficient evidence of the rent reduction because the Area Rent Director "did not personally appear and testify concerning the validity of the order;" his testimony was not essential to establish its authenticity, at least in absence of counterproof attacking its genuineness).

[62] 5 WEINSTEIN, ¶ 901(b)(7)[01], at 901-102; 5 LOUISELL & MUELLER, § 520, at 128. Proof of proper custody does not depend so much on the familiarity of office personnel with the material in question as with the authority of the office in which the material

is found. Persons who keep records in a public office need not be able to authenticate the material by their personal knowledge if proper custody is shown.

[63] *See, generally,* McCORMICK, § 223; 5 WEINSTEIN, ¶ 901(b)(8)[01]; 5 LOUISELL & MUELLER, § 521; 7 WIGMORE, §§ 2138-46. *See also* Annots.: *Dispensing with Proof of Proper Custody as Condition of Admission of Ancient Document,* 29 A.L.R. 630 (1924); *Questions of Evidence Involved in the Inspection and Examination of Type-written Documents and Typewriting Machines,* 406 A.L.R. 721 (1937); *Admissibility in Evidence of Ancient Maps and the Like,* 46 A.L.R. 2d 1320 (1956).

tion of modern methods of recording information.[64] Second, the Rule reduces to twenty years the common law age requirement of thirty years.[65] The age reduction from thirty years is justified because a twenty year period sufficiently guarantees that the document or data compilation was prepared prior to the inception of the controversy which forms the basis for the litigation.[66]

The rationale underlying the authentication of ancient documents focuses upon necessity and trustworthiness. First, the age of such evidence makes authentication by direct testimony difficult where the author, maker, or other witnesses with knowledge of the document have become unavailable due to the passage of time.[67] Second, the Rule admits evidence where the age requirements and the specified circumstantial evidence of authenticity indicate little likelihood of any motivation for false or fraudulent attribution.[68]

Authentication of an ancient document or data compilation under Rule 901(b)(8) simultaneously satisfies the hearsay requirements of Rule 803(16).[69] Nevertheless, the proponent may need to address best evidence considerations and must address general relevancy principles in order to insure admissibility of the document or data compilation.[70] As with all evidence, the court may exclude an ancient document pursuant to Rule 403 under appropriate circumstances.

---

[64] See 5 Weinstein, ¶ 901(b)(8)[01], at 901-102; 5 Louisell & Mueller, § 521, at 134.

[65] See Rule 902(b)(8), Advisory Committee's Note, for a thorough discussion of the reasons for the reduction.

[66] 5 Weinstein, ¶ 901(b)(8)[01], at 901-102; 5 Louisell & Mueller, § 521, at 134.

[67] McCormick, § 223, at 549. See also Wilson v. Snow, 228 U.S. 217, 220-21, 33 S.Ct. 487, 490-91, 57 L.Ed. 807, 810-11 (1913) (deed more than thirty years old proved itself; court notes underlying theory that witnesses are dead and that it is impossible in such cases to produce testimony as to signing, sealing, and delivery by grantor); Re Estate of Hall, 328 F. Supp. 1305, 1311 (D.D.C. 1971), aff'd, 466 F.2d 34 (D.C. Cir. 1971) (reason for ancient documents rule is the practical unavailability of testimony from those who actually witness the execution).

[68] 5 Weinstein, ¶ 901(b)(8)[01], at 901-103. Judge Weinstein contends that the Rule is based upon the improbability of fraud rather than upon the unavailability of attesting witnesses. See also 5 Louisell & Mueller, § 521, at 134. See, e.g., McGuire

v. Blount, 199 U.S. 142, 145, 26 S.Ct. 1, 2-3, 50 L.Ed. 125, 129 (1905) (in approving receipt of records of certain proceedings conducted during Spanish control of Florida, Court notes that there was no evidence that the originals were lost, nor "any evidence of a fraudulent substitution of a made-up record in the interest of parties to be benefitted thereby"). See, e.g., Commonwealth ex. rel. Ferguson v. Ball, 227 Pa. 301, 302, 121 A. 191, 192 (1923) (a book purporting to be the minute book of a turnpike company on the Lockawanna Trail was admitted as an ancient document where "the internal evidence of age and authenticity was so manifest that it might be said that the book proved itself").

[69] See Rule 803(16) and accompanying analysis at § 803.64 et seq.

[70] See, e.g., McCormick, § 223, at 550-51:

It should be borne in mind that, despite the utility of the rule here discussed, it is merely a rule of authentication, the satisfaction of which does not necessarily guarantee the admission of the writing authenticated. Thus, it is sometimes forgotten that a

§ 901.36　Types of Evidence to Which the Ancient Document Rule Applies.

Rule 901(b)(8) may be utilized to authenticate a variety of documentary evidence. By its terms the Rule applies to any "document or data compilation, in any form." "Data compilation" should be broadly interpreted, and according to at least one commentator, this term should include the items and processes listed in Rule 1001(1) and Rule 1001(2),[71] i.e., photostating, photography, magnetic impulse, mechanical or electronic recording, x-ray films, video tapes, motion pictures and the like. In any event, the Rule may be interpreted broadly in view of the illustrative rather than restrictive nature of Rule 901(b).[72]

Pre-Rule cases illustrate the types of documents which may be authenticated pursuant to the ancient document authentication doctrine. The technique has been utilized to establish the authenticity of such documents as receipts,[73] letters,[74] wills,[75] plats,[76] deeds,[77] and maps.[78] Other examples

writing may be proved perfectly genuine and yet remain inadmissible as being, e.g., hearsay or secondary evidence. This source of confusion is compounded by a partial overlap between the remnants of the present rule and those of the distinct doctrine which holds that recitals in certain types of ancient instruments may be received as evidence of the facts recited. The latter doctrine, however, constitutes an exception to the rule against hearsay and is quite distinct from the present rule concerning authentication.

Id. at 550.

[71] 5 WEINSTEIN, ¶ 901(b)(8)[01], at 901-102 *et seq.*; 5 LOUISELL & MUELLER, § 521, at 135-36. *See, e.g.*, Dallas County v. Commercial Union Assur. Co., 286 F.2d 388, 396-98 (5th Cir. 1961) (in approving receipt of 58-year-old newspaper article as against hearsay objections, court takes note of ancient documents rule, though it expressly declines to base its resolution of the hearsay problem upon that rule, relying instead upon the more general principles of trustworthiness and necessity).

[72] 5 WEINSTEIN, ¶ 901(b)(8)[01], at 901-102; 5 LOUISELL & MUELLER, § 521, at 135-36.

[73] *See, e.g.*, Bell v. Brewster, 44 Ohio St. 690, 695, 10 N.E. 679, 681 (1887) (stating that receipt if properly qualified can be an ancient document).

[74] Bell v. Combined Registry Co., 397 F.Supp. 1241, 1246-47 (N.D. Ill. 1975), *aff'd*, 536 F.2d 164 (7th Cir. 1975), *cert. denied*, 429 U.S. 1001, 97 S.Ct. 530, 50 L.Ed. 2d 612 (1975) (letters and newspaper articles from the 1930's and 1940's were admissible under "ancient documents" exception to hearsay rule).

[75] In Re Estate of Hall, 328 F.Supp. 1305, 1311 (D.D.C. 1971), *aff'd*, 466 F.2d 34 (D.C. Cir. 1971). *See also* Smythe v. New Orleans Canal & Bkg. Co., 93 F. 899, 914 (5th Cir. 1899) (considering the ancient character of the will, and the long line of possession of the property in question under it, it was properly admitted in evidence, having stood as a muniment of title to lands of great value for at least 100 years).

[76] *See, e.g.*, Steel v. Fowler, 111 Ind. App. 364, 377, 41 N.E. 2d 678, 683 (1942).

[77] Fulkerson v. Holmes, 117 U.S. 389, 396-97, 6 S.Ct. 780, 785, 29 L.Ed. 915, 919 (1886) (deed offered as proof that grantor was son of patentee of land in question was properly received under ancient documents rule; in discussing propriety of admitting deed, court noted that grantee had claimed title under the deed for more than sixty years). *See also* Wilson v. Snow, 228 U.S. 217, 220-21, 33 S.Ct. 487, 490-91, 57 L.Ed. 807, 810-11 (1913) (deed more than thirty years old proved itself where possession of the land in question had been consistent with its terms for more than forty years).

[78] Burns v. United States, 160 F. 631, 633 (2d Cir. 1909) (approving receipt of maps under ancient documents rule).

might include newspapers or other periodicals.[79] It should be noted, however, that resort to Rule 901(b)(8) may be unnecessary with regard to certain of these documents, inasmuch as they may be self-authenticating under Rule 902.[80]

§ 901.37   Requisite Foundation for Authenticating Ancient Documents.

The authentication of ancient documents is dependent upon foundational testimony relating to three considerations: age, condition and custody. Accordingly, there must be foundational evidence that the document or data compilation is at least twenty years old. Age may be established "by the testimony of a witness with knowledge, by expert testimony, by the physical appearance of the proffered evidence, or even by the contents of the material itself together with surrounding circumstances."[81] A witness who was familiar with the signature of a person deceased for twenty years or more, for example, might identify the signature on a document as being that of the decedent, thereby establishing circumstantially the age of the document.[82] An expert witness might be utilized to establish age by comparison testimony as to handwriting, or by identifying the age of the paper, ink or typewriting.[83] Information in the document itself may establish age, such as a written date, a postmark, certificate of recording or the like.[84] As

[79] Dallas County v. Commercial Union Assurance Co. 286 F.2d 388, 396-97 (5th Cir. 1961) (a newspaper article almost sixty years old was admitted to show that a fire had taken place; "It is inconceivable to us that a newspaper reporter in a small town would report there was a fire in the dome of the new courthouse - if there had been no fire; he is without motive to falsify"). See 5 WEINSTEIN, ¶ 901(b)(8)[01], at 901-107; 5 LOUISELL & MUELLER, § 521, at 134-35. For other examples of writings to which the Rule may apply, see McCORMICK, § 223, at 550.

[80] For example, under Rule 902(6), newspapers and periodicals are self-authenticating, as are acknowledged documents under Rule 902(8).

[81] 5 WEINSTEIN, ¶ 901(b)(8)[01], at 901-103. Judge Weinstein notes that these elements are not exclusive and that any facts supporting the inference that the document or data compilation has been in existence for twenty years or more should satisfy the age requirements for admission under the

Rule. Id. at 901-103. See also 5 LOUISELL & MUELLER, § 521, at 136-37.

[82] 5 WEINSTEIN, ¶ 901(b)(8)[01], at 901-104; 5 LOUISELL & MUELLER, § 521, at 136.

[83] 5 WEINSTEIN, ¶ 901(b)(8)[01], at 901-104; 5 LOUISELL & MUELLER, § 521, at 136.

[84] 5 WEINSTEIN, ¶ 901(b)(8)[01], at 901-105; 5 LOUISELL & MUELLER, § 521, at 136. The authors further note examples in which judicial notice may bear on the determination as to authenticity and age. See also Trustees of German Township v. Farmers & Citizens Savings Bank Co., 66 Ohio L. Abs., 332, 340, 113 N.E. 2d 409, 414 (C.P. 1953) (newspapers contained news items of public matters of local notoriety and historical importance from which the court could take judicial notice as to age). Cf. Rio Bravo Oil Co. v. Staley Oil Co., 138 Tex. 198, 199-200, 158 S.W.2d 293, 294-95 (1942) (contract for the sale of realty not admissible as an ancient document, since there was no evidence other than the date of the instrument showing that it was more than thirty years old).

illustrated by the foregoing examples, any reliable evidence may be utilized as long as it is probative of the age of the document in question.[85]

Consistent with the second express requirement of Rule 901(b)(8), the condition of an ancient document must be such that it raises no suspicion as to authenticity.[86] This requirement relates to the appearance or the contents of the document. Accordingly, questions of authenticity may be raised by evidence that the document has been altered or tampered with, such as by erasures or other changes. Suspicion may also be raised where statements in the document are inconsistent with historical fact.[87] Conversely, genuineness may be corroborated by proof of acts or transactions that are consistent with the contents of the documents or by attestation or recording.[88]

The third requirement of Rule 901(b)(8) provides that the proponent must show, through testimony or otherwise, that the document or data compilation was taken from a place where, if genuine, it would likely be. In other words, it must be shown that the evidence was in an appropriate custodial place or possession prior to its use at trial.[89] Appropriateness of

---

[85] Judge Weinstein argues that the twenty year figure should not be regarded as an absolute necessity, as long as the document appears to be authentic. ¶ 901(b)(8)[01], at 901-906. See also Smythe v. New Orleans Canal & Banking Co., 93 F. 899, 913 (5th Cir. 1899) (papers offered in evidence which bore signs of great age and of having been partially burned and doused with water admitted as ancient documents after court received evidence that office in which they were found had suffered a fire more than twenty years before trial).

[86] See, e.g., McGuire v. Blount, 199 U.S. 142, 145, 26 S.Ct. 1, 2-3, 50 L.Ed. 125, 129 (1905) (referring to the "ancient appearance" of the record offered, noted with respect to matters admitted under the ancient documents rule the necessity to "show that they are of the age of thirty years").

[87] 5 WEINSTEIN, ¶ 901(b)(8)[01], 901-106; 5 LOUISELL & MUELLER, § 521, at 138.

[88] See also Rule 902(8) as to self-authentication of acknowledged documents. See, e.g., Stewart Oil Co. v. Sohio Petroleum Co., 202 F. Supp. 952, 957-59 (E.D. Ill. 1962), aff'd, 315 F.2d 759 (7th Cir. 1962), cert. denied, 375 U.S. 828, 84 S.Ct. 71, 11 L.Ed. 2d 60 (1960) (court declined to admit photostatic copy of notice of acceptance of coal rights under option under ancient documents rule, finding on basis of comparison

of document with others executed at about the same time that the one in question was "substantially different in a number of details" from the others; court noted as well discrepancies in testimony by recorder and person who allegedly presented the original document for recording, and concluded that the copy would not be admitted "since in the opinion of the court it smacks of fraud"); Markiewicz v. Salt River Valley Water Users' Asso., 118 Ariz. 329, 338, 576 P.2d 517, 527-28 (1978) (graph purporting to show amounts of rainfall at various points in Salt River Valley did not qualify under ancient documents rule; it was found among defendant's records, but bore no date or identification of the sort normally found on defendant's records; hence, no one knew exactly when it was prepared, and because the author and purpose were unknown, it was difficult to say whether the document emerged from proper custody).

[89] 5 WEINSTEIN, ¶ 901(b)(8)[01], at 901-107. Weinstein notes that a chain of custody for the twenty year period need not be established in order to prove this element. Rather, the element will be satisfied "as long as all custodians or places of custody accounted for are consistent with the nature of the material." Id. See, e.g., Fulkerson v. Holmes, 117 U.S. 389, 396, 6 S.Ct. 780, 785, 29 L.Ed. 915, 919 (1886).

custody will depend primarily on the nature of the evidence. For example, a data compilation would likely be in the possession of the grantee named therein.[90] Conversely, for example, a deed would not normally be in the possession of the grantor or some third party to the instrument. Where the custodial requirement cannot be satisfied, authenticity must be established, if at all, through a means other than Rule 901(b)(8).

Rule 901(b)(9)   Illustrations—Process or System

Rule 901(b)(9) reads as follows:

(b) **Illustrations.** By way of illustration only, and not by way of limitation, the following are examples of authentication or identification conforming with the requirements of this rule: . . .

(9) **Process or system.** Evidence describing a process or system used to produce a result and showing that the process or system produces an accurate result.

§ 901.38   Process or System—In General.

Rule 901(b)(9) provides a method for authenticating the resulting product of a process or system. Authentication under Rule 901(b)(9) is established by foundational evidence which describes the process or system and which shows that the process or system produces an accurate result.[91] It

[90] 5 WEINSTEIN, ¶ 901(b)(8)[01], at 901-107 through 901-108; 5 LOUISELL & MUELLER, § 521, at 141. *See, e.g.,* McGuire v. Blount, 199 U.S. 142, 145, 26 S.Ct. 1, 2-3, 50 L.Ed. 125, 129 (1905) ("while testimony tends to show that these documents were subjected to various changes of possession during the transition of the government of Florida from Spain to the United States, and upon the evacuation of Pensacola during the Civil War, there is nothing to establish that they were even out of the hands of a proper custodian").

[91] *See, generally,* McCORMICK, § 228; 5 WEINSTEIN, ¶¶ 901(b)(9)[01]-[03]; 5 LOUISELL & MUELLER, § 522; 7 WIGMORE, §§ 2158-60. *See also* Bigelow, *Counseling the Computer User,* 52 A.B.A.J. 461 (1966); Brown, *Electronic Brains and the Legal Mind: Computing the Data Computer's Collision with the Law,* 71 YALE L.J. 239 (1961); Dessin, *The Trial of Economic and*

Technological Issues of Fact: II, 58 YALE L.J. 1242 (1949); Freed, *The Effect of Computer Technology on Legal Liability,* Proceedings of the Corporate Lawyers' Institute, Univ. of Wisc. 49 (1962); Freed, *A Lawyer's Guide Through the Computer Maze,* 6 PRAC. LAWYER 15 (1960); McCoid, *The Admissibility of Sample Data into a Court of Law: Some Further Thoughts,* 4 UCLA L.REV. 233 (1956); Roberts, *A Practitioner's Primer on Computer-Generated Evidence,* 41 U. CHI. L. REV. 254 (1974); Scott, *X-Ray Pictures as Evidence,* 44 MICH.L.REV. 173 (1946); Sherman & Kinnard, *The Development, Discovery, and Use of Computer Support Systems in Achieving Efficiency in Litigation,* 79 COLUM.L.REV. 267 (1979); Sigmon, *Rules of Evidence Before the I.C.C.,* 31 GEO.WASH.L.-REV. 258 (1962); Tapper, *Evidence From Computers,* 8 GA.L.REV. 562 (1974).

should be kept in mind that a preliminary showing of accuracy is merely one prerequisite to the admissibility of such results. As with all authenticated evidence, the exhibit must be relevant to an issue in the case and must satisfy any pertinent hearsay or best evidence requirements.

Rule 901(b)(9) may be utilized in a wide variety of situations which are discussed in the following section. Establishing authenticity pursuant to the method provided by this Rule is not new to federal law.[92]

§ 901.39 Illustrative Applications of Authentication of a Process or System.

The method of establishing authenticity provided by Rule 901(b)(9) may be utilized in connection with any process or system that produces results which a party desires to introduce into evidence. For example, Rule 901(b)(9) will frequently be used to authenticate computer results.[93] In view of the ever-increasing utilization of computers in all aspects of society, this application of the Rule will undoubtedly increase substantially.[94] There is no requirement under Rule 901(b)(9) that printouts have been produced in the regular course of business although this factor may be significant if Rule 803(6), "Records of regularly conducted activity," is used as a basis for satisfying the hearsay issue. Consequently, printouts produced either in the course of business or expressly for use at trial may be authenticated under Rule 901(b)(9).[95] Use of computer printouts is especially valuable in cases in which analyses and syntheses of massive data are involved.[96]

---

[92] Symposium, *Law and Computers in the Mix-Sixties*, ALI-ABA (1966); Scott, *Roentgenograms and their Chronological Legal Recognition*, 27 Ill.L.Rev. 674 (1930).

[93] *See generally*, 5 Weinstein, ¶ 901(b)(9)[02], at 901-110 *et seq.*, 5 Louisell & Mueller, § 522, at 142. *See also* Rule 901(b)(9), Advisory Committee's Note. *See*, *e.g.*, United States v. Scholle, 553 F.2d 1109, 1123-24 (8th Cir. 1977), *cert. denied*, 434 U.S. 940, 98 S.Ct. 432, 54 L.Ed. 2d 300 (1977) (computer analysis of physical characteristics of drugs seized and tested throughout the country); United States v. Liebert, 519 F.2d 542, 546-58 (3d Cir. 1975), *cert. denied*, 423 U.S. 985, 96 S.Ct. 392, 46 L.Ed. 2d 301 (1975) (computer-prepared list of nonfilers of income tax returns discoverable by defense in prosecution for failure to file return: court notes that computer output is admissible in criminal case under certain circumstances).

[94] For an early but leading case in the area of authenticating computer printouts, *see* Transport Indemnity Co. v. Seib, 178 Neb. 253, 132 N.W.2d 871 (1965). In this case, the Nebraska Supreme Court held that computer printouts produced from data stored on and retrieved from magnetic tapes were admissible in evidence under the Nebraska Business Records Act.

[95] 5 Weinstein, ¶ 901(b)(9)[02], at 901-111 through 901-112; 5 Louisell & Mueller, § 522, at 142.

[96] 5 Weinstein, ¶ 901(b)(9)[02], at 901-114:

Some computer outputs which can be authenticated by the accuracy of the process or system involved include translations, quality control or inspection systems, analyses of census data in reapportionment cases, and other instances where the mass of data involved is so great that use of an electronic computer is the only practical manner of gathering evidence.

Rule 901(b)(9) may be utilized to authenticate results from processes or systems other than computer systems. Such processes and systems may include, for example, x-ray films,[97] motion pictures, audio recordings,[98] medical tests such as electrocardiograms and electroencephalograms,[99] and certain out-of-court experiments,[1] polls and surveys.[2]

§ 901.40   Establishing Admissibility of Evidence as to Process or System Results—Foundation.

Rule 901(b)(9) sets forth two foundational requirements that govern the admissibility of results from a process or system. First, the process or system must be described. Second, there must be evidence that the process or system produces an accurate result. The requisite foundation may be established by testimony from a person with knowledge of the process or system in question. Description of computer functions may be provided either by the person who had control and direction of the computer system, or by someone who is familiar with the operation of the equipment that was used.[3]

See, e.g., Butterworth v. Dempsey, 237 F. Supp. 302, 313 (D. Conn. 1965); Bush v. Marin, 251 F. Supp. 484, 506 n.73 (S.D. Tex. 1966). See also Rule 1006 and § 1006.1 et seq. of this Treatise pertaining "Summaries."

[97] 5 WEINSTEIN, ¶ 901(b)(9)[01], at 901-108; 5 Louisell & Mueller, § 522, at 142. See also Scott, X-ray Pictures as Evidence, 44 MICH. L. REV. 773 (1946); Annot., X-Ray Reports-Admissibility, 6 A.L.R. 2d 406 (1949).

[98] 5 WEINSTEIN, ¶ 901(b)(9)[01], at 901-108; 5 LOUISELL & MUELLER, § 522, at 144. See also LeRoy v. Sabena Belgian World Airlines, 344 F.2d 266, 271-74 (2nd Cir. 1965), cert. denied, 382 U.S. 878, 86 S.Ct. 161, 15 L.Ed. 119 (1965) (transcript of inflight radio conversation between plane which ultimately crashed and ground control).

[99] 5 WEINSTEIN, ¶ 901(b)(9)[01], at 901-109; 5 LOUISELL & MUELLER, § 522, at 142. See Croll v. John Hancock Met. Life Ins. Co., 198 F.2d 562, 564-65 (3d Cir. 1952). See, generally, Annot., Admissibility in Civil Action of Electroencephalogram, Electrocardiogram, or Other Record Made by Instrument Used in Medical Test, or of Report Based upon Such a Test, 66 A.L.R. 2d 536 (1959).

[1] See, e.g., State v. Sheppard, 100 Ohio App. 399, 404, 128 N.E.2d 504, 513 (1955) (experiments must be performed with identical or substantially similar equipment and under conditions closely approximating those existing at the time of the occurrence in order for the result to be admissible).

[2] 5 WEINSTEIN, ¶ 901(b)(9)[01], at 901-109 and ¶ 901(b)(9)[03], at 901-105 et seq.; 5 LOUISELL & MUELLER, § 522, at 142. See also President & Trustees of Colby College v. Colby College-New Hampshire, 508 F.2d 804, 809-10 (1st Cir. 1975) (expert testimony based on survey); Union Carbide Corp. v. Ever-Ready, Inc., 531 F.2d 366, 381-88 (7th Cir. 1976), cert. denied, 429 U.S. 830, 97 S.Ct. 91, 50 L.Ed. 2d 94 (1976) (public opinion surveys offered on issue of public confusion); Stix Products, Inc. v. United Merchants & Mfgrs., Inc., 295 F. Supp. 479, 490-91 (1968) (survey evidence received to determine consumer understanding of word "contact"); Zippo Mfg. Co. v. Rogers Imports, Inc., 216 F. Supp. 670, 680-86 (1963) (survey evidence received to determine whether shape and design of cigarette lighters had acquired secondary meaning).

[3] See Rule 901(b)(9), Advisory Committee's Note and 5 WEINSTEIN, ¶ 901(b)(9)[02], at 901-113: "The witness should describe the computer's operation

The type of process or system involved dictates the type of foundation that should be established, and the admissibility of process or system results contemplated by Rule 901(b)(9) may frequently involve judicial notice, stipulations, or expert testimony. For example, a court might judicially notice the manner in which a computer performs mathematical operations.[4] Likewise, admissibility of survey results or opinion polls may require expert testimony that the poll or survey was conducted according to recognized scientific polling methods and that the persons polled represent an accurate sampling of the universe under consideration.[5]

In addition to determining whether the requisite foundation has been established under Rule 901(b)(9), the court may properly employ other judicial controls with regard to such evidence. In view of the complexity that is frequently involved in this area, the court may impose pretrial procedures to insure that the opposing party will have an adequate opportunity to review and rebut the evidence in question and to prepare a competent cross-examination of any authenticating witnesses.[6] Accordingly, a party intending to offer such evidence may be required in advance of trial to submit to opposing counsel the underlying data, the program method or other method of interpretation employed, and the conclusions or results that were reached.[7] The court may impose such conditions to admissibility in its discretion in order to insure fairness and economy.[8] The court may exercise further control with regard to admitting such evidence during the trial, pursuant to Rule 403, when considerations of undue delay, confusion and the like emerge.

---

with enough detail to support a finding that the result is accurate and reliable." *See also* 5 LOUISELL & MUELLER, § 522, at 144.

[4] *See* 5 WEINSTEIN, ¶ 901(b)(9)[02], at 901-112; 5 LOUISELL & MUELLER, § 522, at 144. *See also* Advisory Committee's Note to 901(b)(9), in which it is pointed out that the instant provision "does not, of course, foreclose taking judicial notice of the accuracy of the process or system."

[5] 5 WEINSTEIN, ¶ 901(b)(9)[03], at 901-119; 5 LOUISELL & MUELLER, § 522, at 146. *See also* Pyle and Mockbee, *Authentication and Identification*, 49 MISS. L.J. 151, 180 (1978).

[6] 5 WEINSTEIN, ¶ 901(b)(9)[01], at 901-110; 5 LOUISELL & MUELLER, § 522, at 144-45. *See also* United States v. Scholle, 553 F.2d 1109, 1125 (8th Cir. 1977), *cert. denied*, 434 U.S. 940, 98 S.Ct. 432, 54 L.Ed. 2d 300 (defense counsel should be advised before trial of the nature of computer evidence and the likelihood that it will be offered in evidence so that defense can prepare for cross-examination or rebuttal; if such warning has not been given, district court would be well advised, upon motion, to allow a continuance). *Cf.* United States v. Liebert, 519 F.2d 542, 547-51 (3rd Cir. 1975), *cert. denied*, 423 U.S. 985, 96 S.Ct. 392, 46 L.Ed. 2d 301 (government's offer of services of expert in connection with computerized I.R.S. data, along with relevant handbooks, procedures, and additional data, was enough to protect defense right to cross-examine the computer testimony confronting him by analyzing the reliability of the computer system in theory and checking the accuracy of the system in fact).

[7] 5 WEINSTEIN, ¶ 901(b)(9)[01], at 901-109 through 901-110; 5 LOUISELL & MUELLER, § 522, at 145.

[8] *See* Rule 102.

§ 901.41   Presentation at Trial of Evidence as to Results.

The manner of presenting evidence as to results from processes or systems will vary according to the type of evidence involved and the complexity of such results. In some instances, where the results are simple and straightforward, testimony alone may be presented. For example, a police officer may testify that his radar system indicated the defendant's speed. In other instances, presentation of results may involve the use of tangible proof, such as x-ray film, computer printouts, or electrocardiogram tapes. Additionally, a party may wish to clarify or simplify results by the use of charts, graphs, or written summaries, especially when the underlying data is voluminous. Because it is within the province of the trier of fact to assess the weight of any authenticated evidence, the proponent may well present foundational evidence that goes beyond that which is required to satisfy the threshold admissibility standard in order to convince the trier of fact of the accuracy and probative force of the results in question. For example, a person testifying as to the accuracy of computer printouts may, in addition to describing the system and its output, describe the controls utilized to detect human and machine errors.[9] The trier of fact may, of course, also consider any evidence either elicited on cross-examination of the proponent's own witnesses, which militates against the accuracy of the admitted results.

As previously emphasized, authentication is not tantamount to admissibility, and the proponent of process or system results must consider principles of hearsay, relevancy and best evidence in addition to authentication in attempting to introduce such evidence.

Rule 901(b)(10)   Illustrations—Methods Provided by Statute or Rule

Rule 901(b)(10) reads as follows:

(b) **Illustrations.** By way of illustration only, and not by way of limitation, the following are examples of authentication or identification conforming with the requirements of this rule: . . .

(10) **Methods provided by statute or rule.** Any method of authentication or identification provided by Act of Congress or by other rules prescribed by the Supreme Court pursuant to statutory authority.

---

[9] 5 WEINSTEIN, ¶ 901(b)(9)[02], at 901-112; 5 LOUISELL & MUELLER, § 522, at 146.

§ 901.42 Authentication Pursuant to Statue or Rule—In General.

Rule 901(b)(10) is in effect a clarifying provision.[10] The Rule preserves methodologies of authentication or identification provided by certain legislative provisions and by other rules promulgated by the Supreme Court. Rule 901(b)(10) reinforces the caveat expressed in the introductory sentence of the Rule, i.e., that the provisions of Rule 901(b) are by way of illustration only and not by way of limitation.[11]

§ 901.43 Illustrative Authentication Statutes and Rules

Alternative means of authentication or identification may be derived, for example, from Federal statutes, state statutes and from the Federal Rules of Civil Procedure and Criminal Procedure. For example, the Federal Business Records Act[12] provides a simplified method for authentication of numerous types of documents. The Act exempts certain public documents and private writings which were made in the regular course of business if the keeping of such records was in fact a regular procedure of that business.[13]

The Rules of Civil and Criminal Procedure contain several provisions pertinent to authentication or identification. For example, Civil Rule 10(c) permits a party to attach a written instrument to a pleading, thereby making it a part of the pleading for all purposes. Authenticity of the attached instrument may be established unless its genuineness is denied.[14] Of similar

---

[10] *See, generally,* McCormick, § 228; 5 Weinstein, ¶ 901(b)(10)[01]; 5 Louisell & Mueller, § 523; 5 Wigmore, § 1638(a), 1651, 1672, 1674, 1675, 1676, 1677, 1678, 1679, 1680, 1680(b), 1681, 1684; 7 Wigmore, § 2162, 2164, 2167. *See also* Cohn, *The New Federal Rules of Civil Procedure,* 54 Geo. L.J. 1204 (1966); Kaplan, *Continuing Work of the Civil Committee: 1966 Amendments of the Federal Rules of Civil Procedure(II),* 81 Harv. L. Rev. 591 (1968); Smit, *International Aspects of Federal Civil Procedure,* 61 Colum. L. Rev. 1031 (1961); *International Litigation Under the United States Code,* 65 Colum. L. Rev. 1015 (1965).

[11] *See* 5 Weinstein, ¶ 901(b)(10)[01], at 901-121; 5 Louisell & Mueller, § 523, at 148. *See also* Pyle and Mockbee, *Authentication and Identification,* 49 Miss. L.J. 151 (1978).

[12] 28 U.S.C. § 1732.

[13] 5 Weinstein, ¶ 901(b)(10)[01], at 901-124; 5 Louisell & Mueller, § 523, at 149. *See also* 18 U.S.C. § 3190. *But cf.* Van Cedarfield v. Laroche, 252 F.2d 817, 820 (1st Cir. 1958) (photostatic copy of an application for a title to a motor vehicle bore a certificate of authenticity from the Director of Revenue of the State of Colorado, but lacked a certificate from the secretary of state or other appropriate officer that the Revenue Director's attestation was in due form and by the proper officer; mere attestation by a State official that a record is genuine does not satisfy the authentication requirement).

[14] *See* 5 Weinstein, ¶ 901(b)(10)[01], at 901-125; 5 Louisell & Mueller, § 523, at 149.

effect is Rule 56(e) pertaining to evidence in support of, or in opposition to a motion for summary judgment. The Rule requires that a party submitting affidavits attach sworn or certified copies of all papers or parts thereof referred to in the affidavit. Unless a protest is made concerning such documentation, the court will consider it in making its determination as to whether there exists a genuine issue for trial.

Civil Rule 44(a) provides a method for authenticating foreign or domestic official records either by an official publication thereof or by a copy attested by a person designated in the Rules and certified in the manner specified. Such procedures also may be utilized in criminal proceedings by virtue of Criminal Rule 27. Depositions may be authenticated for use at trial by the procedure provided by Civil Rule 30(f) and 31(b).

The Rules of Civil Procedure contain other provisions which may be utilized in order to dispense with offering proof at trial as to authenticity. For example, a party may utilize Civil Rule 36, Requests for Admission, in order to elicit an admission as to the genuineness of any document described in the request. Unless the opposing party responds within the designated time period, the matter is admitted. Pursuant to Civil Rule 36b, any matter admitted is conclusively established unless the court permits withdrawal or amendment of the admission. Such a procedure might also be utilized to identify objects of real evidence other than documents.[15] Authentication or identification might also be established through the vehicle of interrogatories (Civil Rule 33) or depositions (Civil Rule 30 or 31), although in somewhat less effective fashion, since responses to interrogatories or deposition questions are subject to equivocation and are not necessarily conclusive on the issue of authenticity.[16]

Questions of authenticity may also be resolved through determinations at pretrial conferences in both civil and criminal cases. Accordingly, Civil

---

[15] *See* 5 WEINSTEIN, ¶ 901(b)(10)[01], at 901-125; 5 LOUISELL & MUELLER, § 523, at 149. *See, generally,* the discussion of this provision in 8 WRIGHT & MILLER, FEDERAL PRACTICE AND PROCEDURE (CIVIL), §§ 2151-265 (1970).

[16] 5 WEINSTEIN, ¶ 901(b)(10)[01], at 901-25 through 901-26. Judge Weinstein points out that authentication issues in criminal cases are less likely to be resolved through the use of pretrial or discovery procedures, inasmuch as depositions in criminal cases are granted only in exceptional circumstances, discovery is limited, and there is no provision analogous to the civil rules' request for admissions. *See also* 5 LOUISELL & MUELLER, § 523, at 150. *See, e.g.,* 28 U.S.C., § 1733(a), which provides that some writings of federal governmental agencies can be self-authenticated:

> Books or records of account or minutes of proceedings of any department or agency of the United States shall be admissible to prove the act, transaction, or occurrence as a memorandum of which the same were made or kept.

Rule 16 provides that a court may adopt pretrial procedural rules in order to accomplish various objectives, including the possibility of obtaining "[a]dmissions into evidence of documents and other exhibits which will avoid unnecessary proof."[17] Moreover, parties may, of course, stipulate to the genuineness or authenticity of any document or other object.

[17] Civil Rule 16(9)(b).

Chapter 902

RULE 902. SELF-AUTHENTICATION

Introduction

Rule 902 reads as follows:

> Extrinsic evidence of authenticity as a condition precedent to admissibility is not required with respect to the following: . . . .

§ 902.1   Self-Authentication—In General.

In contrast to Rule 901 which requires foundational evidence on the issue of authentication, Rule 902 eliminates the requirement of an extrinsic foundation for certain specified types of documents. Documents which fall within one of the ten categories identified within Rule 902 are considered self-authenticating. Consequently, the proponent of such a document need not offer any foundational evidence as to authenticity. If the document is otherwise admissible, it will be admitted without any testimony or other extrinsic evidence on the issue of genuineness.

§ 902.2   Theory of Self-Authentication.

The theory of self-authentication is that certain documents, by their very nature, are self-evidently genuine on their face.[1] Documents such as those under seal or those which bear a certification or acknowledgment contain sufficient indicia of genuineness to justify their admissibility without further extrinsic evidence on the issue. In such cases, where the risk of forgery is slight,[2] practical considerations of time, expense, and necessity dictate that foundational evidence be regarded as inessential.[3] Accordingly, the

[1] *See, generally,* MCCORMICK, § 218, 304-14; 5 WEINSTEIN, ¶ 902[01]; 5 LOUISELL & MUELLER, § 528; 7 WIGMORE, §§ 2130-69. *See also* Bigham, *Presumption, Burden of Proof, and the Uniform Commercial Code,* 21 VAND. L. REV. 184 (1968); Smit, *International Aspects of Federal Civil Procedure,* 61 COLUM. L. REV. 1031, 1061-72 (1961); Comment, *Judicial Notice and Presumptions Under the Proposed Federal Rules of Evidence,* 16 WAYNE L. REV. 209-16 (1969); Note, *The Law of Evidence in the Uniform Commercial Code,* 1 GA. L. REV. 44 (1966); *Evidence-Authentication-Necessity of Proof of Genuineness of Documents,* 29 TEMP. L.Q. 109 (1955); Note, *Evidence-Authentication of Documents-Proof of Publication,* 15 S. CAL. L. REV. 115 (1941); Comment, *Evidence-Authentication of Advertisement by Contents-Name Appearing in the Document,* 26 IOWA L. REV. 134 (1940).

[2] "Fortifying circumstances—difficulty, ease of detection and criminal sanctions—generally make the danger of forgery very slight in connection with this limited class of self-authenticating documents." 5 WEINSTEIN, ¶ 902[01], at 902-9. *See also* 7 WIGMORE, § 2161, at 784.

[3] *See* 5 WEINSTEIN, ¶ 902[01], at 902-9:

> "In the case of innumerable writings which almost invariably correctly show their origins on their face, the slight obstacle to fraud presented by authentication requirements is far

proponent of the document is relieved of the obligation of meeting the threshold test that the document is what he claims it to be. Rule 902 is applicable to various documents which experience has proved are generally reliable in showing their own authenticity.[4]

§ 902.3   Practical Significance of Self-Authentication.

The doctrine of self-authentication relieves the proponent of a document from establishing, by way of testimony or other evidence, that the document is what he claims it to be. The document is not, however, by virtue of this doctrine, deemed to be conclusively genuine. Although the preliminary barrier to admissibility is removed, the jury may still determine that the document is not genuine and accord it no weight in its deliberations. Similarly, the opponent of the evidence may dispute its authenticity and offer evidence that seeks to undermine a finding of genuineness.[5] In cases where authenticity is questioned or rebutted, the court may explain to the jury the background and theory of self-authentication.[6]

It must be kept in mind that the doctrine of self-authentication addresses only one of the preliminary questions as to admissibility of a document. In order to establish the admissibility of a self-authenticating document, the proponent must satisfy any pertinent evidentiary doctrines relating, e.g., to hearsay, best evidence and general relevancy. A self-authenticating document may also, under circumstances such as those set forth in Rule 403, be

---

outweighed by the time and expense of proving authenticity. The danger of injustice and delay is greater than the danger of forgery."

Id. at 902-9. *See also* McCormick, § 228, at 556; 7 Wigmore, § 2161, at 637. *See, e.g.,* The Atlanta, 82 F. Supp. 218, 236 (1948) (purportedly photostatic copy of official publication of Statutes of Republic of Panama held sufficiently authenticated; book was in Library of the New York Lawyer's Association and attorneys are "familiar with its high standing as a law library").

[4] 5 Weinstein, ¶ 902[01], at 902-9. *See also* 5 Louisell & Mueller, § 528, at 161.

[5] *See* Advisory Committee's Note to Rule 902 and 5 Weinstein, ¶ 902[01], at 902-9. *See also* McCormick, § 228, at 558; 5 Louisell & Mueller, § 528, at 167. *See, e.g.,* United States v. Giacalone, 408 F. Supp. 251, 253 (E.D. Mich. 1975), *rev'd on other grounds,* 541 F.2d 508 (6th Cir. 1976)

(defendant moved to dismiss indictment on ground that special United States attorney had no authority to conduct grand jury proceedings; certified copy of oath of office established authority where defendant "neither contradicted nor challenged the authenticity of this document"); Hedger v. Reynolds, 216 F.2d 202, 203 (2d Cir. 1954) (notary's certificate of acknowledgment admitted but held to be rebuttable evidence). *Cf.* United States v. Kaufman, 453 F.2d 306, 309 (2d Cir. 1971) (defendant convicted of falsely making affidavits, although evidence indicated the various notary publics never took his signature under oath).

[6] 5 Weinstein, § 902[01], at 902-8: "Should authenticity become an issue, the court may explain to the jury the background of reliability such as, for example, the sanctions against forgery of documents having government seals." *See also* 5 Louisell & Mueller, § 528, at 167.

excluded by the trial judge for reasons entirely apart from the genuineness of the document.

Rule 902(1)   Domestic Public Documents Under Seal

Rule 902(1) reads as follows:

> Extrinsic evidence of authenticity as a condition precedent to admissibility is not required with respect to the following:
>
> (1) **Domestic public documents under seal.** A document bearing a seal purporting to be that of the United States, or of any State, district, Commonwealth, territory, or insular possession thereof, or the Panama Canal Zone, or the Trust Territory of the Pacific Islands, or of a political subdivision, department, officer or agency thereof, and a signature purporting to be an attestation or execution.

§ 902.4   Domestic Public Documents Under Seal—In General.

Rule 902(1) applies the doctrine of self-authentication to domestic public documents that contain two indicia of genuineness.[7] The document must bear a seal that purports to be that of the United States, a State or other domestic political entity, subdivision, office or agency. Additionally, the document must bear a signature which purports to be an attestation or execution.

Rule 902(1) is justified by the practical consideration that forgery is a crime and that detection is fairly easy and certain.[8] The Rule is derived from various common law doctrines and statutory provisions that governed the admissibility of documents under seal.[9] Prior to the adoption of the Rules, state and federal statutes enacted in furtherance of the full faith and credit clause of the United States Constitution provided for the authentication and admissibility of the statutes, judicial records, public records, and

---

[7] *See, generally,* McCORMICK, § 218; 5 WEINSTEIN, ¶ 902(1)[01]; 5 LOUISELL & MUELLER, § 529; 7 WIGMORE, §§ 2161-65. *See also* Hunter, FEDERAL TRIAL HANDBOOK, § 58.6, "Authentication of domestic public documents under seal;" 30 AM. JUR. 2D, §§ 963, 966, 988, 991, 996.

[8] Advisory Committee's Note. The Rule may be theoretically based, in whole or in part, upon the doctrine of judicial notice. *See id. See also* 5 WEINSTEIN, ¶ 902(1)[01], at 902-12; 5 LOUISELL & MUELLER, § 529, at 174-75.

[9] 5 WEINSTEIN, ¶ 902(1)[01], at 902-10 *et seq. See also* 5 LOUISELL & MUELLER, § 529, at 174.

the like of other states and their political subdivisions.[10] Such statutes were generally more restrictive and more problematic than the provisions of Rule 902(1).[11]

§ 902.5   Documents Cognizable Under the Rule.

Rule 902(1) applies to any document bearing the purported seal of the United States, or of any state, district, Commonwealth, territory or insular possession thereof. It also includes possessions of the United States, specifically the Panama Canal Zone[12] and the Trust Territory of the Pacific Islands. The Rule further obviates problems that arose at common law by extending the doctrine to documents under the seal of any political subdivision, department, officer or agency of the entities named above. There is accordingly no limitation on the level of public authority to which the Rule applies. The Rule, however, retains the common law exclusion of documents under private seal.[13]

Rule 902(1) may be utilized as the basis for admitting a broad spectrum of documents including, for example, original documents bearing the seal of an executing officer or certified copies of public documents bearing the seal of a custodian on a certificate authenticating the copies.[14] The Rule may also be used in connection with a document that attests to the absence of specified documents within the records of the office the seal of which the document bears.[15]

---

[10] 5 WEINSTEIN, ¶ 902(1)[01], at 902-11; 5 LOUISELL & MUELLER, § 529, at 178. *See also* United States v. Amedy, 24 U.S. (11 Wheat) 392, 407, 6 L.Ed. 502, 504 (1826); United States v. Johns, 4 U.S. (4 Dall.) 412, 416, 1 L.Ed. 888, 890 (C.C.D. Pa. 1806).

[11] *See* 5 WEINSTEIN, ¶ 902(1)[01], at 902-13 to 902-14; 5 LOUISELL & MUELLER, § 529, at 178. *See also* United States v. Trotter, 538 F.2d 217, 218 (8th Cir. 1976), *cert. denied*, 429 U.S. 943, 97 S.Ct. 362, 50 L.Ed. 2d 313 (1976) (certificates by Commissioner of Bureau of Motor Vehicles and Governor of State of Indiana, duly signed and sealed, satisfied Federal Rule of Evidence 902(1)).

[12] Inasmuch as the Panama Canal is no longer under the control of the United States government, the references to documents under seal of the Panama Canal Zone appear to have no further pertinence.

[13] 5 WEINSTEIN, ¶ 902(1)[01], at 902-13. *See also* 7 WIGMORE, § 2169, at 816.

[14] 5 WEINSTEIN, ¶ 902(1)[01], at 902-14; 5 LOUISELL & MUELLER, § 529, at 180. *See also* United States v. Wingard, 522 F.2d 796, 797 (4th Cir. 1975), *cert. denied*, 423 U.S. 1058, 96 S.Ct. 792, 46 L.Ed. 2d 648 (1976) (holding FDIC certificate admissible without authentication by custodian; cites Rule 902, not then yet in effect, as indicative of rule generally followed in federal courts); United States v. Mackenzie, 601 F.2d 221, 222 (5th Cir. 1979), *cert. denied*, 444 U.S. 1018, 100 S.Ct. 673, 62 L.Ed. 2d 649 (1980) (order of Texas Board of Medical Examiners cancelling license to practice medicine); United States v. Moore, 555 F.2d 658, 659 (8th Cir. 1977) (certificate of United States Postal Service).

[15] Pyle and Mockbee, *Authentication and Identification*, 49 Miss. L.J. 151, 185 (1978). *See also* Rule 803(10) and United States v. Farris, 517 F.2d 226, 229 (7th Cir. 1975), *cert. denied*, 423 U.S. 892, 96 S.Ct. 189, 46

Rule 902(2). Domestic Public Documents Not Under Seal

Rule 902(2) reads as follows:

Extrinsic evidence of authenticity as a condition precedent to admissibility is not required with respect to the following: . . .

(2) **Domestic public documents not under seal.** A document purporting to bear the signature in his official capacity of an officer or employee of any entity included in paragraph (1) hereof, having no seal, if a public officer having a seal and having official duties in the district or political subdivision of the officer or employee certifies under seal that the signer has the official capacity and that the signature is genuine.

§ 902.6   Domestic Public Documents Not Under Seal—In General.

Rule 902(2) provides for self-authentication of domestic public documents that do not bear a seal.[16] In view of the fact that a signed public document not under seal poses a greater risk of forgery than that of a document under seal,[17] the Rule requires that two levels of authenticating indicia appear on the document. First, the document in question must purport to bear the signature, in his official capacity, of an officer or employee of any entity specified in Rule 902(1). This signature need not be under seal, and in most situations in which Rule 902(2) is utilized, the signing officer will lack an official seal. Second, the document must bear a certification, under seal, of a public officer having a seal, who has official duties in the political subdivision of the officer or employee. The certification must attest that the signing officer or employee has the requisite official capacity and that the signature is genuine.

The requirements of Rule 902(2) as to the certifying officer serve two purposes. First, the requirement that he have official duties in the same governmental entity as the signing officer insures that he will have sufficient knowledge of the other officer to be familiar with his signature and with his official capacity.[18] Second, the requirement that the certifying

---

L.Ed.2d 123 (computer data compilations officially certified under seal were self-authenticating and properly admitted in evidence for the purpose of showing that income tax returns had not been filed).

[16] *See, generally,* McCormick, § 218; 5 Weinstein, ¶ 902(2)[01]; 5 Louisell & Mueller, § 530; 7 Wigmore, § 2167. *See also* 30 Am. Jur.2d, §§ 963, 966, 988, 991, 996.

[17] *See* Advisory Committee's Note to Rule 902(2).

[18] 5 Weinstein ¶ 902(2)[01], at 902-15; 5 Louisell & Mueller, § 530, at 181. *See also* Morgan v. Curtenius, 17 F.Cas. 747, 4 McLean 366 (C.C.D. Ill. 1848), *aff'd,* 61 U.S. (20 How) 1 (1857) (signature of probate judge accepted without his seal since certificate of judge indicated his court, formerly one of record, no longer had a seal);

officer have a seal and make the requisite certification under seal insures that the document will bear the same guarantees against forgery, and hence of authenticity, as those documents admissible under Rule 902(1).

Where a document is offered pursuant to Rule 902(2), the signatures of both officers, accompanied by the seal of the certifying officer, are indicative in themselves that the requirements of the Rule have been satisfied.[19] Consequently, the document will be admitted without any preliminary showing of the underlying premises, for example, that the officer signing the document had no seal or that he signed in his official capacity.[20] The court may assume such facts by virtue of the theory of self-authentication, that is, that the document on its face is evidence of its genuineness.

Rule 902(2) rejects the notion that a document bearing an official signature and nothing more is self-evidently authentic.[21]

Rule 902(3)   Foreign Public Documents

Rule 902(3) reads as follows:

> Extrinsic evidence of authenticity as a condition precedent to admissibility is not required with respect to the following: . . .
>
> (3) **Foreign public documents.** A document purporting to be executed or attested in his official capacity by a person authorized by the laws of a foreign country to make the execution or attestation, and accompanied by a final certification as to the genuineness of the signature and official position (A) of the executing or attesting person, or (B) of any foreign official whose certificate of genuineness of signature and official position relates to the execution or attestation or is in a chain of certificates of genuineness of signature and official position relating to the execution or attestation. A final certification may be made by a secretary of embassy or legation, consul general, consul, vice consul, or consular agent of the United States, or a diplomatic or consular official of the foreign country assigned or accredited to the United States. If reasonable opportunity has been given to all parties

Hagen v. Porter, 156 F.2d 362, 365 (9th Cir. 1946), *cert. denied,* 329 U.S. 729, 67 S.Ct. 85, 91 L.Ed. 631 (1946) (relying on California statute permitting judicial notice of government officers).

[19] 5 Weinstein, ¶ 902(2)[01], at 902-15. *See also* 5 Louisell & Mueller, § 530, at 183.

[20] 5 Weinstein, ¶ 902(2)[01], at 902-15; 5 Louisell & Mueller, § 530, at 183-84. *See*

also Willink v. Miles, 30 F.Cas. 62, Pet C.C. 429 (C.C.D. Pa. 1817) (justice of peace assumed to have office he claims); Ruggles v. Buckner, 20 F.Cas. 1312, 1314, 1 Paine C.C. 358, 362 (C.C.S.D.N.Y. 1824) (officer taking deposition assumed to have powers).

[21] *See, generally,* 7 Wigmore, § 2167, at 806.

to investigate the authenticity and accuracy of official documents, the court may, for good cause shown, order that they be treated as presumptively authentic without final certification or permit them to be evidenced by an attested summary with or without final certification.

§ 902.7   Foreign Public Documents—In General.

Rule 902(3) applies the concepts of self-authentication to foreign public documents that bear two indicia of genuineness.[22] First, the document must purport to be executed or attested by a person, in his official capacity, who is authorized by the laws of a foreign country to make the execution or attestation. Second, there must be a certification that attests, directly or indirectly, to the genuineness of the signature and the official position of the executing or attesting person. In this regard, Rule 902(3) requires a final certification on foreign documents made by a United States official (a secretary of embassy or legation, consul general, consul, vice consul, or consular agent) or by a foreign official (a diplomatic or consular official) assigned or accredited to the United States.

Where the United States or foreign official is familiar with the person who has executed or attested the document in question, the final certification must attest to the genuineness of the signature and the official position of the executing or attesting person. Where there is no direct familiarity, the procedure of Rule 902(3) involves a chain of authentication, the last link of which consists of a certification by the appropriate United States or foreign official. In such a case, the final certification must attest to the genuineness of the signature and official position of any foreign official whose certificate of genuineness of signature and official position in turn corroborates the execution or attestation. Alternately, the final certification may result from a chain of certificates of genuineness that begins with a certificate corroborating the execution or attestation. The Rule, in essence, provides a procedure whereby the signature of a foreign official, certified as genuine, either directly or through a chain of certificates, by an appropriate United States or foreign official, is sufficient to render the document self-authenticating.

[22] *See, generally,* McCormick, § 218; 5 WEINSTEIN, ¶ 902(3)[01]-[02]; 5 LOUISELL & MUELLER, § 531; 7 WIGMORE, §§ 2161-62. *See also* Hunter, FEDERAL TRIAL HANDBOOK, § 58.8, "Authentication of Foreign Public Documents;" 30 AM. JUR. 2D, §§ 966-68, 970, 990; Smit, *International Aspects of Federal Civil Procedure,* 61 COLUM. L. REV. 1062 (1961).

§ 902.8   Scope and Effect of Rule 902(3).

Rule 902(3), which is derived from Civil Procedure Rule 44(a)(2), represents a far more liberal view toward the admissibility of foreign documents than that of the common law which accorded self-authenticating status only to foreign documents under seal of state.[23] Civil Rule 44(a)(2) and the correlative Criminal Rule 27 provide an authentication procedure for copies of foreign official records based upon an attestation and certification.[24] Rule 902(3) adopts the procedure set forth in the Civil Rule with slight modifications. Rule 902(3) applies to originals as well as copies and also expands the concept to embrace foreign public *documents* rather than the more limiting category of public *records*.[25] The structure of the Rule recognizes the practical problems associated with the authentication of foreign documents.[26]

---

[23] 5 Weinstein, ¶ 902(3)[01], at 902-15; 5 Louisell & Mueller, § 531, at 135. *See also* 7 Wigmore, § 2162, at 785. *See, e.g.,* United States v. Regner, 677 F.2d 754, 759 (9th Cir. 1982), *cert. denied*, 459 U.S. 911, 103 S.Ct. 220, 74 L.Ed. 2d 175 (1982) (court admitted certified records of state-run Hungarian taxicab company); United States v. Klissas, 218 F. Supp. 880, 882-83 (D.C. Md. 1963) (Greek birth certificate); New York Life Insurance Co. v. Aronson, 38 F. Supp. 687, 688 (D.C. Pa. 1941) (Polish birth certificate).

[24] *See* Advisory Committee's Note to Rule 902(3). Civil Rule 44(a)(2) which by the terms of Criminal Rule 27 is also applicable to criminal cases, provides as follows:

A foreign official record, or an entry therein, when admissible for any purpose, may be evidenced by an official publication thereof; or a copy thereof, attested by a person authorized to make the attestation, and accompanied by a final certification to the genuineness of the signature and official position (a) of the attesting person or (b) of any foreign official whose certificate of genuineness of signature and official position relates to the attestation or is in a chain of certificates of genuineness of signature and official position relating to the attestation. A final certification

may be made by a secretary of embassy or legation, consul general, consul, vice consul, or consular agent of the United States, or a diplomatic or consular official of the foreign country assigned or accredited to the United States. If reasonable opportunity has been given to all parties to investigate the authenticity and accuracy of the documents, the court may, for good cause shown, (a) admit an attested copy without final certification or (b) permit the foreign official record to be evidenced by an attested summary with or without a final certification.

[25] *See* Rule 902(3), Advisory Committee's Note and 5 Weinstein, ¶ 902(3)[01], at 902-17. *See also* 5 Louisell & Mueller, § 531, at 186. *See, e.g.,* United States v. Perlmuter, 693 F.2d 1290, 1292 (9th Cir. 1982) (allegedly official documents from Israel which purported to show criminal convictions and fingerprints of appellant admissible where there was neither evidence of attestation by authorized Israeli acting in official capacity nor final certification or good cause for lack of certification; "aura of authenticity" found by district court insufficient).

[26] Pyle and Mockbee, *Authentication and Identification*, 49 Miss. L.J. 151, 186 (1978).

Rule 902(3) follows Civil Rule 44(a)(2) in setting forth two other provisions that derive from practical considerations relating to litigation and the adversary system. Accordingly, if all parties have been given a reasonable opportunity to investigate the authenticity and accuracy of official documents, the court may upon a showing of good cause dispense with the requirement of final certification. Alternatively, the court may permit the documents to be evidence by an attested summary, with or without a final certification.[27]

Rule 902(4)   Certified Copies of Public Records

Rule 902(4) reads as follows:

> Extrinsic evidence of authenticity as a condition precedent to admissibility is not required with respect to the following: . . .
>
> (4) **Certified copies of public records.** A copy of an official record or report or entry therein, or of a document authorized by law to be recorded or filed and actually recorded or filed in a public office, including data compilations in any form, certified as correct by the custodian or other person authorized to make the certification, by certificate complying with paragraph (1), (2), or (3) of this rule or complying with any Act of Congress or rule prescribed by the Supreme Court pursuant to statutory authority.

§ 902.9   Certified Copies of Public Records—In General.

Rule 902(4) sets forth requirements under which copies of certain public records are admissible as self-authenticating documents.[28] The Rule applies to copies of official entries, records or reports. It also applies to any document authorized by law to be recorded or filed and actually recorded or filed in a public office, including data compilations in any form. The Rule does not apply to unrecorded documents.[29]

---

[27] See 5 WEINSTEIN, ¶ 902(3)[01], at 902-17; 5 LOUISELL & MUELLER, § 531, at 190.

[28] See, generally, McCORMICK, § 218; 5 WEINSTEIN, ¶ 902(4)[01]; 5 LOUISELL & MUELLER, § 532; 5 WIGMORE, §§ 1677, 1680. See also Smit, International Aspects of Federal Civil Procedure, 61 COLUM. L. REV. 1062, 1071 (1961); Hunter, FEDERAL TRIAL HANDBOOK, § 58.9; Authentication of Certified Copies of Public Records, 30 AM. JUR. 2D §§ 963, 988, 991, 996, 1006, 1011-1013, 1041.

[29] Advisory Committee's Note to Rule 902(4).

Rule 902(4) is premised upon necessity and convenience in view of the problems associated with producing original public documents at trial.[30] The Rule is further justified by the guarantees of trustworthiness that attend the certification process. The concept of utilizing certified copies as proof of public documents is not new to federal law,[31] although prior law generally required proof of additional facts and circumstances in order to authenticate the copy.

§ 902.10   Certification Requirements.

Rule 902(4) requires that a copy of a document offered pursuant to this Rule bear a certification by the custodian or other person authorized to make copies of such documents. The certification must attest to the correctness of the copy. Additionally, it must be made in compliance with the provisions of paragraph (1), (2) or (3) of Rule 902, or in compliance with any federal law or rule of the Supreme Court. The required content of the certificate consequently depends upon the type of document in question.[32] Accordingly, a foreign public document may be evidenced by a certified copy, the certification of which is made in compliance with Rule 902(3). Similarly, a copy of an official domestic or foreign record may be authenticated by the procedure set forth in Civil Rule 44 or Criminal Rule 27.[33]

---

[30] *See* 5 WEINSTEIN, ¶ 902(4)[01], at 902-24; 5 LOUISELL & MUELLER, § 532, at 192. *See also* United States v. Wilson, 690 F.2d 1267, 1275 (9th Cir. 1982) (copy of Judgment and Commitment Order, certified on both sides, adequately authenticated under Rule 902(4)); United States v. Simmons, 476 F.2d 33, 36 (9th Cir. 1973) (certified Selective Service file "prime example of self-authentication").

[31] *See, e.g.,* United States v. Percheman, 32 U.S. (7 Pet.) 51, 85, 8 L.Ed. 604, 636 (1833); United States v. Johns, 4 U.S. (4 Dall.) 412, 415, 1 L.Ed. 888, 891 (1806).

[32] *See* 5 WEINSTEIN, ¶ 902(4)[01], at 902-25 to 902-26; 5 LOUISELL & MUELLER, § 532, at 194-95. *See also* United States v. Beason, 690 F.2d 439, 444 (5th Cir. 1982) (Rule 902 does not require that actual custodian of official records secure certification of delegation of custodial authority from head of agency entrusted with custody of document; certification by actual custodian sat-

isfies Rule so that certificate by custodian of National Firearms Registration and Transfer Record that no registration in defendant's name existed sufficed without requiring certificate from Secretary of Treasury that custodian had been given custody); United States v. Stone, 604 F.2d 922, 924-25 (5th Cir. 1979) (photographic copy of "progress sheet" prepared by Regional Disbursing Center of Treasury was properly authenticated under 902(4) by attached affidavit of officer with legal custody and direct supervision of the progress sheets); United States v. Moore, 555 F.2d 658, 661 (8th Cir. 1977) (approving receipt of certified copy of certification of mailing; this exhibit bore a certification under formal seal of the United States Postal Service that said document constituted a true copy of the record retained in the official custody of the United States Postal Service).

[33] Rule 902(4), Advisory Committee's Note.

There exist a number of federal statutes under which a certified copy will be admissible under Rule 902(4).[34] Additionally, copies may be admitted pursuant to rules which in effect dispense with authentication requirements. For example, parties may stipulate to the genuineness of a document or copy thereof pursuant to Civil Rule 16(c)(3), or the proponent may elicit an admission of genuineness pursuant to Civil Rule 36(a).

Compliance with the certification requirements of Rule 902(4) simultaneously satisfied the best evidence requirements set forth in Rule 1005. Under the latter provision, contents of an official record or recorded document may be proved by a copy certified as correct in accordance with Rule 902, as long as the document is otherwise admissible.

Rule 902(5)   Official Publications

Rule 902(5) read as follows:

> Extrinsic evidence of authenticity as a condition precedent to admissibility is not required with respect to the following: . . .
>
> **(5) Official publications.** Books, pamphlets, or other publications purporting to be issued by public authority.

§ 902.11   Official Publications that are Self-Authenticating.

Rule 902(5) applies the doctrine of self-authentication to books, pamphlets and other publications that purport to be issued by public authority.[35] The Rule relieves the proponent from establishing by way of foundation that the publication was actually printed or issued by public authority. Documents purporting to be so issued are accordingly self-authenticating,

---

[34] *See* 5 WEINSTEIN, ¶ 902(4)[01] at 902-27 *et seq.*; 5 LOUISELL & MUELLER, § 532 at 199, n.49. *See, e.g.*, 28 U.S.C., § 1745 (copies of Patent Office documents can be authenticated); 25 U.S.C., § 6 (copies of public documents, records, maps, or papers kept by the office of the Commissioner of Indian Affairs can be authenticated); 31 U.S.C., § 46 (copies of any books, records, or other documents, and transcripts from the books and proceedings of the General Accounting Office can be certified by the Comptroller General or the Assistant Comptroller under its seal); 28 U.S.C., § 1740 (copies of all documents and papers and official entries can be authenticated by a consul or vice-consul); 38 U.S.C., § 202 (copies of public documents in files of Vet-eran's Administration can be authenticated by seal and certificate of Administrator or his delegate); 28 U.S.C., § 1736 (extracts from the Journals of the Senate and the House of Representatives and from the Executive Journal of the Senate can be authenticated by certification by the Secretary of the Senate or the clerk of the House of Representatives).

[35] *See, generally,* McCORMICK, § 218; 5 WEINSTEIN, ¶ 902(5)[01]; 5 LOUISELL & MUELLER, § 533; 5 WIGMORE, § 1684. *See also* Hunter, FEDERAL TRIAL HANDBOOK, § 58.10, "Authentication of official publications;" Smit, *International Aspects of Federal Civil Procedure*, 6 COLUM. L. REV. 1031 (1961); 30 AM. JUR. 2d, §§ 969, 971, 991, 1110.

although their admissibility may depend upon other considerations as well. Specifically, documents covered by Rule 902(5) are admissible as long as the proponent also satisfies any other pertinent requirements relating to such principles as hearsay, best evidence and general relevancy.

Rule 902(5) is most commonly applied in connection with statutes, court reports, rules and regulations,[36] although by its terms the Rule may apply to any publication that purports to be issued by public authority.[37] The Rule specifies no limitations as to the level of governmental authority which must authorize the publication, and accordingly, the Rule should be accorded a broad interpretation.[38]

The doctrine set forth in Rule 902(5) is generally in accordance with prior practice relating to the authentication of official publications.[39] Civil Rule 44 and Criminal Rule 27, which form the basis of Rule 902(5), provide that domestic[40] or foreign official records[41] may be evidenced by an official publication thereof.

Rule 902(6)   Newspapers and Periodicals

Rule 902(6) reads as follows:

> Extrinsic evidence of authenticity as a condition precedent to admissibility is not required with respect to the following: . . .
>
> **(6) Newspapers and periodicals.** Printed materials purporting to be newspapers or periodicals.

[36] Rule 902(5), Advisory Committee's Note.

[37] *See* 5 WEINSTEIN, ¶ 902(5)[01] at 902-30; 5 LOUISELL & MUELLER, § 533, at 207. *See, e.g.,* Watkins v. Holman, 41 U.S. (16 Pet.) 25, 55-56, 10 L.Ed. 873, 878 (1842) (American State Papers); Greg v. Forsythe, 65 U.S. (24 How.) 179, 184, 16 L.Ed. 731, 735 (1860) (American State Papers); Stewart v. United States, 211 F. 41, 45 (9th Cir. 1914) (map); United States v. Shafer, 132 F. Supp. 659, 665-66 (1955) (unsigned document in Federal Register).

[38] 5 WEINSTEIN, ¶ 902(5)[01], at 902-31; 5 LOUISELL & MUELLER, § 533, at 208. Recognition of locally published documents may theoretically be premised upon judicial notice of such publications. *See* Funk v. Commissioner, 163 F.2d 796, 800-801 (3d Cir. 1947). *See, e.g.,* Stewart v. United States, 211 F. 41, 45 (9th Cir. 1914) (territorial map showing boundaries of White Mountain Indian Reservation properly received without independent proof of au-

thenticity, where recitals on its face sufficiently evidence its character as a public document, indicating that it was issued from the General Land Office under the authority of the Secretary of the Interior); United States v. Shafer, 132 F. Supp. 659, 665 (D.C. Md. 1955), *aff'd,* 229 F.2d 124 (4th Cir. 1955), *cert. denied,* 351 U.S. 931, 76 S.Ct. 788, 100 L.Ed. 2d 1460 (regulations, proclamation, notice published in Federal Register are presumptively valid and correctly reproduced).

[39] Rule 902(5), Advisory Committee's Note. *See also* 5 WEINSTEIN, ¶ 902(5)[01], at 902-30; 5 LOUISELL & MUELLER, § 533, at 207.

[40] Federal, state, or local official publications can be self-authenticating. *See* Frates v. Eastman, 57 F.2d 522, 523 (10th Cir. 1932) (official publication of city ordinances self-authenticating).

[41] *See* Advisory Committee's Note to Rule 902(5); 5 WEINSTEIN, ¶ 902(5)[01], at

§ 902.12   Newspapers and Periodicals—In General.

Rule 902(6) makes the doctrine of self-authentication applicable to non-official printed materials purporting to be newspapers or periodicals.[42] The status of self-authentication is justified by the unlikelihood of forgery with regard to such documents.[43] Consequently, the documents identified in the Rule require no foundational evidence as to authenticity, although there may remain disputed issues regarding the authority and responsibility for items contained in such documents.[44]

Rule 902(6) makes no specific reference to notices and advertisements contained within newspapers and periodicals. The Rule merely states that there need be no extrinsic authentication evidence with regard to "[p]rinted materials purporting to be newspapers or periodicals." The Advisory Committee's Note to the Rule suggests that advertisements and notices are included within the grant of self-authenticating status.[45]

§ 902.13   Scope and Utility of Rule 902(6).

Rule 902(6) relaxes the common law requirements relating to the authentication of newspapers and periodicals.[46] Pursuant to the Rule, the types of printed material that are self-authenticating may range from newspapers of general circulation to specialized periodicals having a limited readership.[47]

902-29; 5 LOUISELL & MUELLER, § 533, at 209. *See also* Smit, *International Aspects of Federal Civil Procedure*, 62 COLUM. L. REV. 1031 (1961).

[42] *See, generally*, McCORMICK, § 218; 5 WEINSTEIN, ¶ 902(6)[01]; 5 LOUISELL & MUELLER, § 534; 4 WIGMORE, § 1234; 7 WIGMORE, § 2150. *See also* Note, *Evidence-Authentication of Documents-Proof of Publication*, 15 S. CAL. L. REV. 115, 117 (1941); Strong, *Liberalizing the Authentication of Private Writings*, 52 CORNELL L.Q. 284 (1967); 29 AM. JUR. 2d, § 885.

[43] Advisory Committee's Note to Rule 902(6); 5 WEINSTEIN, ¶ 902(6)[01], at 902-31; 5 LOUISELL & MUELLER, § 533, at 211.

[44] *See* 7 WIGMORE, § 2150, at 608-09; Advisory Committee's Note to Rule 902(6).

[45] *See* 5 WEINSTEIN, ¶ 902(6)[01], at 902-32; 5 LOUISELL & MUELLER, § 534, at 213. *See also* Mancari v. Frank P. Smith, Inc., 114 F.2d 834, 837-38 (D.C. Cir. 1902) (dissenting opinion by Rutledge); Canada Uniform Acts: Draft Act, § 42 (1938) ("the production of a printed copy of a newspaper shall be prima facie evidence that any notice or advertisement contained therein was inserted, advertised, and published in that newspaper by the person, by whom, or in whose behalf, the notice or advertisement purports or appears to be inserted, advertised, or published"). *Cf.* 39 U.S.C., § 4005(b) (1964) ("public advertisement . . . is prima facie evidence that the latter is the agent or representative of the advertisers"). *See, e.g.*, Comment, *Evidence-Authentication of Advertisement by Contents-Name Appearing in the Document*, 26 IOWA L. REV. 115, 134 (1940); Note, *Evidence-Authentication-Necessity of Proof of Genuineness of Documents*, 29 TEMP. L.Q. 109, 110 (1955).

[46] 5 WEINSTEIN, ¶ 902(6)[01], at 902-31; 5 LOUISELL & MUELLER, § 534, at 210.

[47] 5 WEINSTEIN, ¶ 902(6)[01], at 902-31; 5 LOUISELL & MUELLER, § 534, at 210.

Newspapers or periodicals may be utilized as proof of a variety of matters. For example, in a libel action, the publication containing the allegedly libelous material may be offered as evidence against the party whose authorship is claimed.[48] If authorization is disputed, the opponent may seek to convince the trier of fact that the advertisement was not properly authorized even though the publication and the advertisement have been admitted pursuant to the principle of self-authentication. Periodicals and newspapers may also be utilized as proof of collateral matters such as date and place of publication.[49]

Rule 902(7)　Trade Inscriptions and the Like

Rule 902(7) reads as follows:

> Extrinsic evidence of authenticity as a condition precedent to admissibility is not required with respect to the following: . . .
>
> **(7) Trade inscriptions and the like.** Inscriptions, signs, tags, or labels purporting to have been affixed in the course of business and indicating ownership, control, or origin.

§ 902.14　Trade Inscriptions and the Like—In General.

Rule 902(7) accords self-authenticating status to trade inscriptions, signs, tags or labels, as long as they purport to have been affixed in the course of business and are indicative of ownership, control or origin.[50] Such evidence

---

[48] Liberty Lobby, Inc. v. Anderson, 562 F. Supp. 201, 203 (D.D.C. 1983). *See also* 5 WEINSTEIN, ¶ 902(6)[01], at 902-31 through 902-32; 5 LOUISELL & MUELLER, § 534, at 213.

[49] 5 WEINSTEIN, ¶ 902(6)[01] at 902-31; 5 LOUISELL & MUELLER, § 534, at 211; Ellis v. Lyford, 270 Mass. 96, 98, 169 N.E. 800, 801 (1930) (newspaper which by its title page purports to be printed or published in such city, town, or county, and which has a circulation therein, shall be deemed to have been published therein).

[50] *See, generally,* McCORMICK, §§ 283, 308; 5 WEINSTEIN, ¶ 902(7)[01]; 5 LOUISELL & MUELLER, § 535; 7 WIGMORE, §§ 2129, 2150, 2152. *See also* Note, *Evidence-Authentication-Necessity of Proof of Genuineness of Documents,* 39 TEMP. L.Q. 109, 111 (1955); Hunter, FEDERAL TRIAL HANDBOOK, § 58.12, "Authentication of Trade Inscriptions and the Like;" Mueller, *Instructing the Jury Upon Presumptions in Civil Cases: Comparing Federal Rule 301 with Uniform Rule 301,* 12 AM. JUR. 2D, § 477; *Owning, Leasing, or Otherwise Engaging in Business of Furnishing Services for Taxicabs as Basis of Tort Liability for Acts of Taxi Driver Under Respondent Superior Doctrine,* 8 A.L.R. 3d 818.

will generally be introduced to prove ownership or control. For example, in a products liability action, the plaintiff may offer into evidence an item of real proof, such as a container for food, that is alleged to have caused injury. The defendant's distinctive label on the container is self-authenticating and consequently admissible as proof, for example, that the defendant processed the items in question. As with all authenticated evidence, the opponent is free to rebut the issue of authenticity.[51]

Rule 902(7) applies generally to commercial and mercantile tags or labels, and includes also such items as inscriptions on containers or vehicles, and signs of various types such as billboards. The Rule is justified because there is only a slight risk of forgery of such items due both to the difficulty of reproduction and because trademark infringement involves serious penalties. "Great efforts are devoted to inducing the public to buy in reliance on brand names, and substantial protection is given them. Hence, the fairness of this treatment finds recognition in the cases."[52]

The Rule requires that the inscription, label, or the like purport to have been affixed in the course of business. This phrase should be interpreted broadly to include any on-going enterprise or institution regardless of its commercial or non-commercial nature, including, for example, a private university or social organization that uses an identifying inscription or symbol.[53]

---

[51] See 5 WEINSTEIN, ¶ 902(7)[01], at 902-32; 5 LOUISELL & MUELLER, § 535, at 219. Rule 902(7) is especially helpful in the area of products liability where plaintiffs have sometimes encountered difficulty in attempting to link defendants to defective products. See, e.g., Weiner v. Mager & Throne, Inc., 167 Misc. 338, 340, 3 N.Y.S. 2d 918, 920 (1938) (plaintiff purchased an unwrapped loaf of bread from defendant B, to which was affixed the "trade label" of defendant M & T; finding worms embedded in a slice of bread from which he had eaten, and in the rest of the loaf, plaintiff allegedly became ill and nauseous; in the absence of counterproof that M & T did not manufacture the bread, court drew inference from trade label that M & T was the manufacturer); Swift & Co. v. Hawkins, 174 Miss. 253, 257, 164 So. 231, 236 (1935) (on basis of tradename "Brookfield" appearing on cheese wrappers, which name is exclusively used by Swift & Co., evidence sufficiently identified defendant as the manufacturer); Curtis Candy Co. v. Johnson, 163 Miss. 426, 434, 141 S. 762, 769 (1932) (plaintiff purchased candy bar in

package bearing label "Baby Ruth Candy, The Curtis Candy Company;" candy bar allegedly contained ground glass, from the ingestion of which plaintiff suffered injuries; jury was warranted in finding that this bar came from defendant's factory containing glass).

[52] Rule 902(7), Advisory Committee's Note.

[53] See 5 WEINSTEIN, ¶ 902(7)[01], at 902-34; 5 LOUISELL & MUELLER, § 535, at 218. In the absence of strong contrary proof, the court should assume that the mark was placed in the regular course of business if it is in a form that would ordinarily be used. See also United States v. Hitsman, 604 F.2d 443, 447 (5th Cir. 1979) (court found college transcript of defendant to be a self-authenticating document under Rules 901 and 902; court took judicial notice of the existence of the college and found it was normal for a college to make such a record in the course of its operations, and that the exhibit had the indicia of being an authentic copy since it bore a seal above the registrar's signature).

Rule 902(8)   Acknowledged Documents

Rule 902(8) reads as follows:

> Extrinsic evidence of authenticity as a condition precedent to admissibility is not required with respect to the following: . . .
>
> **(8) Acknowledged documents.** Documents accompanied by a certificate of acknowledgment executed in the manner provided by law by a notary public or other officer authorized by law to take acknowledgments.

§ 902.15   Acknowledged Documents—In General.

Rule 902(8) provides that documents accompanied by a certificate of acknowledgment are self-authenticating.[54] In such cases, the certificate of acknowledgment serves as sufficient evidence that the document is what it purports to be.[55] The Rule constitutes a significant expansion of the common law approach to the authentication of acknowledged documents.[56] The Rule does not specify the form which the acknowledgment must take. Nor, for example, does it require that the certificate be under seal unless the applicable acknowledgment law so requires.[57] The general rule with respect to acknowledgments requires a standard of only substantial compliance rather than strict compliance with the procedures of an acknowledgment statute.[58]

---

[54] *See, generally,* McCORMICK, § 218; 5 WEINSTEIN, ¶ 902(8)[01]; 5 LOUISELL & MUELLER, § 536; 7 WIGMORE, § 2165. *See also,* Hunter, FEDERAL TRIAL HANDBOOK, § 58.13, "Authentication of Acknowledged Documents;" 29 AM. JUR. 2d, §§ 853, 863; Annots., *Admissibility, in Action Against Notary Public, of Evidence as to Usual Business Practice of Notary Public of Identifying Person Seeking Certificate of Acknowledgement,* 59 A.L.R. 3d 1327 (1974); *Liability of Notary Public or his Bond for Negligence in Performance of Duties,* 44 A.L.R. 3d 555 (1972); *Liability of Notary Public or his Bond for Willful or Deliberate Misconduct in Performance of Duties,* 44 A.L.R. 3d 1243 (1972).

[55] Advisory Committee's Note to Rule 902(8). *See also* 7 WIGMORE, § 2165, at 801.

[56] 5 WEINSTEIN, ¶ 902(8)[01], at 902-34; 5 LOUISELL & MUELLER, § 536, at 229-30; 7 WIGMORE, § 2165.

[57] *Cf.* WEINSTEIN, ¶ 902(8)[01], at 902-29 and 902-31, in which the author implicitly suggests that such certificates must be under seal. Compare the Report of House Committee on the Judiciary Note to Federal Rule 902(8):

> Rule 902(8) as submitted by the Court referred to certificates of acknowledgment "under the hand and seal of" a notary public or other officer authorized by law to take acknowledgements. The Committee amended the Rule to eliminate the requirement, believed to be inconsistent with the law in some States, that a notary public must affix a seal to a document acknowledged before him.

[58] 5 WEINSTEIN, ¶ 902(8)[01], at 902-35; 5 LOUISELL & MUELLER, § 536, at 231.

As long as the basic requirements of the pertinent acknowledgment statute are met, the document should be admitted without any foundational evidence as to authenticity.[59] Where foreign acknowledgments are at issue, the provisions of Rule 902(3) may supersede those of Rule 902(8), thus requiring additional certifications in order for the document to be deemed self-authenticating.[60]

Rule 902(8) is justified by the guarantees of trustworthiness provided by acknowledgments:

> The duties of his office obligate a notary public to take reasonable steps to ascertain the true identity of a person who appears before him for the purpose of acknowledging execution of an instrument or swearing to a statement; those duties also include truthfully certifying to the underlying fact that the person acknowledged execution of the instrument or swore to the statement; and the certificate of the notary, usually sealed and bearing a stamped indication of commission and its expiration date, is easily recognized and likely itself to be genuine because forgery would be somewhat difficult and subject to stiff penalty.[61]

The risk of a false acknowledgment is slight in view of various statutory penalties that attend unauthorized acknowledgments.[62]

As with all self-authenticating documents, the principle is that an acknowledged document is admissible into evidence, as long as it is not otherwise excludable, in the absence of an extrinsic foundation. Self-authentication, however, is not conclusively determinative of the issue of authenticity. The opponent may offer rebuttal testimony in support of a contention that the document is not authentic. Such evidence goes to the weight to be given the acknowledged document rather than to the question of admissibility.[63]

[59] *Id.*

[60] 5 WEINSTEIN, ¶ 902(8)[01], at 902-35; 5 LOUISELL & MUELLER, § 536, at 231. The last sentence of Rule 902(8) allows the court to admit foreign documents under some circumstances even if the formalities have not been followed.

[61] 5 LOUISELL & MUELLER, § 536, at 229. *See also* 5 WEINSTEIN, ¶ 902(8)[01], at 902-35 through 902-36.

[62] 5 LOUISELL & MUELLER, § 536, at 229.

[63] *Id.*

See also Hedger v. Reynolds, 216 F.2d 202, 203 (2d Cir. 1954) (notary's certificate upon the document authorizing insured to change beneficiary in life insurance policy was rebuttable). *Cf.* United States v. Kaufman, 453 F.2d 306, 309 (2d Cir. 1971) (defendant claimed documents purporting to be affidavits were not, because notary had not taken his sworn statement before affixing signature; rejected).

Rule 902(9)   Commercial Paper and Related Documents

Rule 902(9) reads as follows:

> Extrinsic evidence of authenticity as a condition precedent to admissibility is not required with respect to the following: . . .
>
> **(9) Commercial paper and related documents.** Commercial paper, signatures thereon, and documents relating thereto to the extent provided by general commercial law.

§ 902.16   Commercial Paper and Related Documents—In General.

Rule 902(9) expressly adopts the tenets of general commercial law in applying the doctrine of self-authentication to commercial paper, signatures thereon, and documents relating thereto.[64] Reference must accordingly be made to the Uniform Commercial Code, which has been adopted in all states[65] in order to determine the extent to which such documents are self-authenticating.

While four provisions of the Uniform Commercial Code are pertinent to the issue of self-authentication, only one of these expressly addresses the issue of authenticity.[66] Section 1-202 expressly provides that certain commercial documents issued by a third party to a contract "shall be prima facie evidence of [their] own authenticity and genuineness and of the facts stated in the document by the third party." Such documents include those purporting to be a bill of lading, a policy or certificate of insurance, an official weigher's or inspector's certificate, a consular invoice or any other document authorized or required by the contract. As long as the document is "in due form" it is self-authenticating pursuant to Rule 902(9).[67]

---

[64] *See, generally,* McCormick, § 218; 5 Weinstein, ¶ 902(9)[01]-[02]; 5 Louisell & Mueller, § 537; 7 Wigmore, § 2130. *See also* Bigham, *Presumptions, Burden of Proof and the Uniform Commercial Code,* 21 Vand. L. Rev. 177, 195 (1968); Louisell, *Constructing Rule 301: Instructing the Jury on Presumptions in Civil Actions and Proceedings,* 63 Va. L. Rev. 281; Note, *Judicial Notice and Presumptions Under the Proposed Federal Rules of Evidence,* 16 Wayne L. Rev. 215, 216 (1969); Note, *The Law of* *Evidence in the Uniform Commercial Code,* 1 Ga. L. Rev. 44, 77 (1966).

[65] Louisiana adopted only articles 1, 3, 4 and 5; La. Rev. Stat. §§ 10:1-101 to 10:5-117 (1975).

[66] *See* 5 Weinstein, ¶ 902(9)[01], at 902-37; 5 Louisell & Mueller, § 537, at 236.

[67] U.C.C. § 1-202 (1977). *See also* 5 Weinstein, ¶ 902(9)[01], at 902-38; 5 Louisell & Mueller, § 537, at 236. *See also* United States v. Carriger, 592 F.2d 312, 316-17 (6th Cir. 1979) (in tax evasion prose-

Three other provisions of the Code that relate to the admissibility of commercial documents contain implied provisions as to self authentication. Section 3-307 accords a presumption of genuineness to signatures on negotiable instruments and, by implication, allows the introduction of signed instruments without any proof as to authenticity. Specifically, the statute provides that a signature on an instrument is admitted unless it is specifically denied in the pleadings.[68] If a denial is made, the burden is then upon the person claiming under the signature to establish its genuineness. However, the proponent is expressly aided in most circumstances by a statutorily imposed presumption that the signature is genuine or authorized, and consequently, the signature is admissible and is presumed authentic unless the opponent offers sufficient rebuttal evidence to support a finding that the signature is forged or unauthorized.[69] To the extent that the statute accords a *presumption* of authenticity to signed negotiable instruments, it goes beyond the doctrine of self-authentication.[70] In any event, the concept of self-authentication is inherent in the codified presumption of genuineness. Admissibility pursuant to Rule 902(9) is accordingly consistent with the effect of the code and with its apparent intent.[71]

Section 8-105 of the Uniform Commercial Code provides a similar format for the introduction and effect of signatures on securities. The code provides that securities are negotiable instruments, and consequently, that in an action on a security, a signature thereon is admitted unless specifically denied. Also, it is presumed genuine or authorized. The foregoing discussion concerning Section 3-307 is equally applicable to this section.

The fourth applicable Section is 3-510 which addresses the issue of evidence of dishonor and notice of dishonor. The code provides that certain documents are admissible in evidence, and it further creates a presumption of dishonor and of any notice of dishonor specified on the document. The types of evidence specified include a formal certificate of protest, the purported stamp by a drawee that payment was refused, or bank records which indicate dishonor.[72] The foregoing types of evidence are consequently self-authenticating, and, in the absence of contrary evidence suf-

---

cution, trial court erred in excluding promissory notes offered by defendant as evidence of his opening net worth on the ground that they had been insufficiently authenticated; mere production of a note is prima facie evidence of its validity, citing U.C.C., § 3-307 and Rule 902).

[68] U.C.C. § 3-307 (1977).

[69] *See* Rule 301 and the accompanying discussion in this Treatise relating to the effect of presumptions.

[70] In most instances of self-authentication, the document is admitted without foundational evidence but it is not *presumed* to be authentic, *i.e.*, it is merely *prima facie* authentic.

[71] *See* 5 WEINSTEIN, ¶ 902(9)[01], at 902-39; 5 LOUISELL & MUELLER, § 537, at 238-39.

[72] U.C.C. § 3-510 (1976). *See also* 5 WEINSTEIN, ¶ 902(9)[01], AT 902-40; 5 LOUISELL & MUELLER, § 537, at 237.

ficient to support a finding, the introduction of such evidence creates a presumption of dishonor and of notice of dishonor if the latter is indicated on the face of the document. If the opponent introduces sufficient evidence contrary to the presumption, the question of authenticity is left to the trier of fact.

§ 902.17　Rationale of Rule 902(9).

Self-authentication of commercial paper and related documents under Rule 902(9) is prompted by considerations of necessity and convenience. The Rule is further justified by guarantees of trustworthiness which are reflected by the reliance upon such documents by the business community and by society in general.[73] For example, the third party documents have traditionally been relied upon as trustworthy in commerce.[74] The Uniform Commercial Code, in recognition of this fact, eliminates the common law practice that required authentication of such documents by foundational evidence relating to the execution or preparation of the document.[75]

The status accorded to evidence of dishonor is also justified by the indicia of trustworthiness attending the modes of proof specific in Section 3-510. Accordingly, self-authentication of a formal certificate of protest is justified by the duties under which a notary operates.[76] As to the other modes of proof, "[i]t is improbable that bank records will show a dishonor that did not exist or that a holder will attempt to proceed on the basis of dishonor if he could have obtained payment."[77]

The rationale underlying self-authentication of signatures on commercial instruments is based mainly upon necessity. Negotiable instruments by their nature frequently pass through many hands, and accordingly, a recipient of such an instrument would likely have no knowledge of the circumstances surrounding its execution.[78] The lack of accessibility to evidence on this issue, combined with the general reliance upon negotiable instruments by the business community, justifies the application of the doctrine of self-authentication to such instruments.

---

[73] See 5 WEINSTEIN, ¶ 902(9)[02], at 902-39; 5 LOUISELL & MUELLER, § 537, at 244-45.

[74] 5 WEINSTEIN, ¶ 902(9)[02], at 902-40. Such documents are thought to be trustworthy, especially when introduced against one of the parties to the contract because they were given a preferred status by the parties when they required them, and because they are made by a third party who normally has no connection with any of the parties other than as the maker of one of these documents.

[75] 5 WEINSTEIN, ¶ 902(9)[02], at 902-40.

[76] Id.

[77] Id. at 902-40 through 902-41.

[78] 5 WEINSTEIN, ¶ 902(9)[02], at 902-40; 5 LOUISELL & MUELLER, § 537, at 236.

Rule 902(10)   Presumptions Under Acts of Congress

Rule 902(10) reads as follows:

Extrinsic evidence of authenticity as a condition precedent to admissibility is not required with respect to the following: . . .

(10) Presumptions under Acts of Congress. Any signature, document, or other matter declared by Act of Congress to be presumptively or prima facie genuine or authentic.

§ 902.18   Presumptions Created By Law—In General.

Rule 902(10) confers self-authenticating status to any signature, document or other matter that is declared to be authentic by any Act of Congress.[79] Specifically, the Rule incorporates any federal law which declares a matter to be "presumptively or prima facie genuine or authentic." The effect is twofold. First, the provisions of Rule 902(10) indicate that the examples of self-authentication set forth in Rule 902 are not exclusive.[80] Second, the Rule expressly acknowledges the continuing applicability of statutes that address the issue of self-authentication.

Rule 902(10) refers to statutes that declare a matter to be presumptively genuine as well as those that declare a matter to be prima facie genuine. Statutes which grant presumptive authenticity to a matter go beyond the doctrine of self-authentication in the sense that the trier of fact is bounded by the presumption in the absence of evidence sufficient to support a finding to the contrary.[81]

Rule 902(10) incorporates federal statutes pertinent to the issue of self-authentication.[82] Many of the applicable statutes deal with other evidentiary considerations as well as authentications.[83] The subject matter of such

---

[79] *See, generally,* MCCORMICK, § 218; 5 WEINSTEIN, ¶ 902(10)[01]; 5 LOUISELL & MUELLER, § 538. *See also* Hunter, FEDERAL TRIAL HANDBOOK, § 58.15, "Authentication of Documents, Presumed Under Acts of Congress to be Authentic."

[80] *See* Rule 902, Paragraph (10), Advisory Committee's Note.

[81] *See* Rule 902(9) and accompanying discussion in this Treatise regarding the dis-

tinction between presumptive and prima facie authenticity.

[82] For an example of pertinent federal statues which address self-authentication, *see* Rule 902(10), Advisory Committee's Note and 5 WEINSTEIN, ¶ 902(10)[01], at 902-41 through 902-42. *See also* 5 LOUISELL & MUELLER, § 538, at 248-49.

[83] 5 WEINSTEIN, ¶ 902(10)[01], at 902-41; 5 LOUISELL & MUELLER, § 538, at 249.

statutes includes the admissibility of, for example, notarized documents,[84] or documents bearing particular signatures, such as a tax return, S.E.C. registration, or negotiable instrument,[85] as well as official publications[86] and certain records and reports filed with government agencies.[87] There may frequently be an overlap between the statutes incorporated in Rule 902(10) and other illustrations regarding authentication and self-authentication. Rule 902(9), for example, which incorporates the self-authentication provisions of general commercial law, is actually redundant with reference to Rule 902(10) in that it represents a particularization of the latter Rule.

§ 902.19   Judicial Precedent Regarding Self-Authentication.

Although Rule 902(10) incorporates only legislative enactments, courts should arguably be open to setting judicial precedent on the subject of self-authentication. In view of the liberal standard of admissibility reflected by the authentication Rules, courts might adopt judicial rules to facilitate litigation and to obviate technical requirements in situations that do not warrant the time and expense associated with requirements of establishing authenticity of certain documents. For example, courts might well extend the doctrine of self-authentication to all documents produced during discovery or that have a connection with the party against whom they are offered unless there is a specific disclaimer of genuineness.[88]

---

[84] 5 WEINSTEIN, ¶ 902(10)[01], at 902-41; 5 LOUISELL & MUELLER, § 538, at 249. *See also* 10 U.S.C.A. § 936(d); 22 U.S.C.A. § 1203; 22 U.S.C.A. § 1195; 33 U.S.C.A. §§ 875, 876.

[85] *See, e.g.*, 26 U.S.C.A. §§ 6062, 6064; 15 U.S.C.A. § 77(a). *See also* 5 WEINSTEIN, ¶ 902(10)[01], at 902-42; 5 LOUISELL & MUELLER, § 538, at 249. *See, e.g.*, United States v. Mangan, 575 F.2d 32, 41-42 (2d Cir. 1978), *cert. denied*, 439 U.S. 931, 99 S.Ct. 320, 58 L.Ed. 2d 324 (1978) (in prosecution of IRS Agent for fraud, tax return and material from personnel file, all purporting to have been prepared and signed by defendant, were properly used as exemplars; presumption of genuineness of signature on tax return).

[86] *See, e.g.*, 44 U.S.C.A. §§ 1507, 1510(a) (Federal Register).

[87] *See, e.g.*, 47 U.S.C.A. § 412 (F.C.C.); 49 U.S.C.A. § 16(13) (I.C.C.).

[88] *See* McCORMICK, § 228, at 558: "The suggestion rests not only upon the proposition that the overwhelming majority of such writings will be genuine, but in addition on the superior position of the adversary to demonstrate through evidence that the purported connection of a writing with him is attributable to fraud or mistake." *See also* WEINSTEIN, ¶ 902[01], at 902-10, noting that in some cases, foundational facts as to authenticity are within the knowledge of the opponent of the evidence, thereby "making it unfair to require the proponent to present this evidence."

Chapter 903

RULE 903. SUBSCRIBING WITNESS' TESTIMONY UNNECESSARY

Rule 903 reads as follows:

> The testimony of a subscribing witness is not necessary to authenticate a writing unless required by the laws of the jurisdiction whose laws govern the validity of the writing.

§ 903.1   Subscribing Witness' Testimony—In General.

Rule 903 provides that authentication of a writing need not involve the testimony of a subscribing witness unless such testimony is ". . . required by the laws of the jurisdiction whose laws govern the validity of the writing." Accordingly, where there is no applicable statutory or common law provision requiring testimony of a subscribing witness, authentication of a document may be established, in some jurisdictions, pursuant to any of the provisions of Rule 901 or 902.[1] For example, there are pertinent statutory provisions concerning authentication of a will sought to be entered in probate.[2] Where the validity of a writing is governed by the laws of another jurisdiction, the laws of that jurisdiction must be consulted regarding authentication requirements. Wills are generally the only documents which states require to be authenticated by subscribing witnesses, and even this

[1] *See, generally,* McCORMICK, § 220; 5 WEINSTEIN, ¶ 903[01]-[05]; 5 LOUISELL & MUELLER, §§ 543-44; 4 WIGMORE, §§ 1287-1321. *See also* Comment, *Judicial Notice and Presumptions Under the Proposed Federal Rules of Evidence,* 16 WAYNE L. REV. 217 (1969); 20 Am. Jur. 2d, §§ 851-53, 923-29 (1967); Annots.: *Abrogation of Common Law Rule,* 65 A.L.R. 324 (1930); *Proof of Due Execution,* 79 A.L.R. 389 (1931).

[2] *See* Rule 903, Advisory Committee's Note and § 903.3 *infra.*

627

requirement is beginning to erode.[3] However, since wills are not probated in federal court, the state requirement of a subscribing witness will rarely affect Rule 903.[4]

§ 903.2 Common Law Practice as to Testimony of Subscribing Witnesses.

Traditionally at common law, when a document signed by subscribing witnesses was sought to be introduced into evidence, the proponent was required to first call an attesting witness, or, alternatively, to show that all attesters were unavailable before he could call any other witness to authenticate the document.[5] The rule applied even where the document was not required by law to be attested.[6] The origin of the common law rule was apparently rooted in early legal practices regarding the types of witnesses who could testify in court. It was also supported by questionable theories concerning an implicit agreement by the parties to the document to make the attester their witness to prove execution, as well as the attester's alleged preferential position to testify as to any fraud, duress or the like.[7] As the rule became more removed from its historical basis, the requirement of calling or accounting for particular persons was recognized by some courts as a burdensome and largely unjustifiable task. Consequently, various exceptions were formulated pertaining to ancient documents, writings collateral to the suit, and certified copies of recorded conveyances.[8] At an early date, federal courts modified the common law rule to permit authentication of a document by the party who executed it, without the necessity of first calling a subscribing witness.[9]

[3] 5 WEINSTEIN, ¶ 903[02], at 903-4.

[4] 5 LOUISELL & MUELLER, § 544, at 264.

[5] McCORMICK, § 220, at 545-46. *See also* 5 WEINSTEIN, ¶ 903[02], at 903-03; 4 WIGMORE, § 1287 *et seq. See, e.g.,* Jones v. Underwood, 28 Barb. 481, 482-83 (Sup. Ct. 1858) (setting forth the traditional common law requirements); Hollenbock v. Fleming, 6 Hill 303, 305 (N.Y. Sup. Ct. 1844) (even proof of confession or acknowledgement of the party not permitted to be received as a substitute for the testimony of the subscribing witness).

[6] *See* Advisory Committee's Note to Rule 903.

[7] *See* 5 WEINSTEIN, ¶ 903[02], at 903-4, and 4 WIGMORE § 1288, at 697-99, for a discussion of the faulty premises upon which the common law rule was apparently based.

[8] McCORMICK, § 220, at 546.

[9] *See, e.g.,* Drew v. Wodleigh, 7 Me. 94 (1930) (in action on promissory note, plaintiff was properly permitted to impeach defense witness by introducing a contract between plaintiff and the witness; contract tended to show that witness had acknowledged to be true certain facts in conflict with his testimony; since purpose of plaintiff was not to advance a claim on the contract, court here rejected defense contention that receipt of the contract was error because attesting witness was not called).

§ 903.3   Scope and Application of Rule 903.

Rule 903 dispenses with the requirement of testimony by subscribing witnesses unless the laws of the jurisdiction governing the validity of the writing require such testimony in order to authenticate the particular writing. As discussed in § 903.1 of this Chapter, wills are the most common subject for legislation in this area.

Testimony by subscribing witnesses, where mandated by applicable law, applies only where the validity of the document is in question, that is, where the party introducing it is seeking to prove "execution of the document by the person making it, *i.e.*, to authenticate its genuineness."[10] Such is the case, for example, where a will is offered into probate for the purpose of transferring property according to its terms. If, however, the proponent of the document is seeking to prove something other than the document's execution and validity, *e.g.*, delivery, proof of family history or the like, the requirement for subscribing witness testimony does not operate.[11]

---

[10] 4 Wigmore, § 1293, at 709. *See also* 5 Weinstein, ¶ 903[02], at 903-5.

[11] 4 Wigmore, § 1293, at 709.

X
CONTENTS OF WRITINGS, RECORDINGS, AND PHOTOGRAPHS

Chapter 1001

RULE 1001. DEFINITIONS

Rule 1001 reads as follows:

For purposes of this article the following definitions are applicable:

(1) Writings and recordings. "Writings" and "recordings" consist of letters, words, or numbers, or their equivalent, set down by handwriting, typewriting, printing, photostating, photographing, magnetic impulse, mechanical or electronic recording, or other forms of data compilation.

(2) Photographs. "Photographs" include still photographs, X-ray films, video tapes, and motion pictures.

(3) Original. An "original" of a writing or recording is the writing or recording itself or any counterpart intended to have the same effect by a person executing or issuing it. An "original" of a photograph includes the negative or any print therefrom. If data are stored in a computer or similar device, any printout or other output readable by sight, shown to reflect the data accurately, is an "original."

(4) Duplicate. A "duplicate" is a counterpart produced by the same impression as the original, or from the same matrix, or by means of photography, including enlargements and miniatures, or by mechanical or electronic re-recording, or by chemical reproduction, or by other equivalent techniques which accurately reproduces the original.

§ 1001.1   The Best Evidence Rule—An Overview.

The so-called "best evidence" rule is an ancillary rule of evidence having only a limited application. The essence of the best evidence rule is that in proving the contents of a writing, recording or photograph, the original is preferentially required; but if the original is unavailable through no fault of the proponent of the evidence, secondary evidence may be admitted.[1]

The best evidence rule does not apply to proving the contents of physical objects or things other than writings, recordings or photographs.[2] Accord-

[1] *See, generally,* 1 McCORMICK §§ 214, 229-31, 235; 5 WEINSTEIN, ¶¶ 1001(1)[1], 1001(2)[01]-[04], 1001(3)[01]-[04], 1001(4)-[01]-[07]; 5 LOUISELL & MUELLER, §§ 549-617; 3 WIGMORE, §§ 790, 792-98; 4 WIGMORE, §§ 1173-80, 1230, 1232-41. *See also,* Brown, *Authentication and the Contents of Writings,* 4 ARIZ. ST.L.J. 611 (1969); Byers, *Microfilming of Business Records,* 6 DRAKE L. REV. 74 (1957); Cleary & Strong, *The Best Evidence Rule: An Evaluation in Context,* 51 IOWA L. REV. 383 (1952); Cleary, *Evidence-Best Evidence Rule-Admissibility of a Carbon Copy as Primary Evidence,* 3 VILL. L. REV. 217 (1958); Gardner, *The Camera Goes to Court,* 24 N.C.L.R. 233 (1946); Gray, *Motion Pictures in Evidence,* 15 IND. L.J. 408 (1940); Jones, *Authentication and Contents of Writings,* 5 OKLA. L. REV. 383 (1952); Levin, *Authentication and the Contents of Writings,* 10 RUTGERS L. REV. 632 (1956); McMorrow, *Authentication and the Best Evidence Rule Under the Federal Rules of Evidence,* 16 WAYNE L. REV. 195 (1969); Mouser & Philbin, *Photographic Evidence-Is There a Recognized Basis for Admissibility?,* 8 HASTINGS L.J. 310 (1957); Parodis, *The Celluloid Witness,* 37 U. COLO. L. REV. 235 (1965); Portman, *Mechanical Testimony,* 17 CLEV.-MAR. L. REV. 519 (1968); Scott, *X-Ray Pictures as Evidence,* 44 MICH. L. REV. 773 (1946); Tracy, *The Introduction on Documentary Evidence,* 24 IOWA L. REV. 436 (1939); Wallace, *Computer Printouts of*

Business Records and Their Admissibility in New York, 31 ALB. L. REV. 61 (1967); Wharton, *Duplicate Originals and the Best Evidence Rule,* 19 OHIO ST. L.J. 520 (1958).

[2] *See, e.g.,* Burney v. United States, 339 F.2d 91, 92-94 (5th Cir. 1964) (prosecution for possession of non-tax-paid distilled spirits; government agents testified that they tasted and smelled the contents of the containers; court implicitly approved the position that the best evidence doctrine applies only to writings); Chandler v. United States, 318 F.2d 356, 357 (10th Cir. 1963) (alleged unlawful removal and transportation of non-tax-paid spirits; court here rejected defense best evidence objection to testimony by government agents that they seized containers of whiskey which did not bear revenue stamps; court held that best evidence Rule does not apply to situations like this, but is limited to cases where the question relates to the contents of written documents); Francis v. United States, 239 F.2d 560, 561-62 (10th Cir. 1956) (prosecution for possession of marijuana seeds, where government had to show that the seeds were capable of germinating; court here rejected defense best evidence objection to testimony by government chemist that he determined the seeds to be marijuana, and that he planted some and obtained sprouts within three and a half days).

ingly, there is no general requirement that the most probative evidence be used to prove a fact in every instance, and evidence need only be relevant under Rule 401 to satisfy the threshold qualification for admissibility. Nevertheless, there may be statutory requirements, independent of the Rules of Evidence which require a certain type of evidence as the "best evidence," e.g., postmark on petition to I.R.S. must be proven to establish timely filing.[3]

Because the application of the rule is limited to situations in which the contents of a writing, recording or photograph are to be proven,[4] the name, "best evidence rule," is a misnomer. More accurate would be "the original writing or document rule."[5] Even this name is misleading because Rule 1003 provides that a duplicate, as defined in Rule 1001(4), is admissible to the same extent as an original except where a question exists as to the authenticity of the original or where admission of the duplicate instead of the original would be unfair.[6]

While the best evidence rule generally requires use of the original to prove the contents of a writing, recording or photograph, Article X in Rules 1004, 1005, 1006 and 1007 sets forth exceptions in accordance with which secondary evidence may be admissible. Consequently, the best evidence rule is a rule of preference under which the original is preferred to secondary evidence. Secondary evidence may be admitted, however, where one of a number of conditions is shown to obtain.[7]

While Article X contains no express definition of "secondary evidence," it is clear that secondary evidence is any evidence which is probative of contents other than the original itself. For example, secondary evidence of the contents of a document could be testimony of a person with firsthand knowledge of the contents (i.e., a person who saw the document and remembers its substance), or it could be a hand transcribed copy. It should

[3] Shipley v. Commissioner, 572 F.2d 212, 214 (9th Cir. 1979) (tax court dismissed petition for redetermination of tax liability for lack of jurisdiction, holding that taxpayers had not met jurisdictional requirements for timely filing; court rejected argument of taxpayers that they should be allowed to show that they sent the petition by certified mail and that the postmark date on the receipt was within the time allowed).

[4] See, e.g., Sayen v. Rydzewski, 387 F.2d 815, 819 (7th Cir. 1967); Driggers v. United States, 384 F.2d 158, 159 (5th Cir. 1967).

[5] See McCormick, §§ 229, 230, at 703. McCormick notes that "the only actual role that the 'best evidence' phrase denotes today is the rule requiring the production of

the original writing." Id. See, e.g., Edwards v. Swilley, 196 Ark. 633, 635, 158 S.W.2d 584, 585 (1938).

[6] See Rule 1003. See also §§ 1003.2-3 of this Treatise.

[7] See Rules 1004, 1005, 1006 and 1007 discussed, infra. See also 5 Louisell & Mueller, § 550, at 290. See also United States v. Alexander, 326 F.2d 736, 738-43 (4th Cir. 1964) (reproduction of check failed to pick up the name and address of the payee, and these had been typed on the copy; absent an objection that the indictment was misleading, any testimony that the item in question was a treasury check payable to someone other than the accused should have sufficed to identify it).

be noted that, except in Rule 1005 regarding public records. Article X does *not* erect a hierarchy of secondary evidence such that, for example, a hand transcribed copy is preferred to oral testimony. Once an exception to the requirement for the original is satisfied, any secondary evidence may be used to prove contents. As stated in the Advisory Committee's Note to Federal Rule 1004:

> The rule recognizes no "degrees" of secondary evidence. While strict logic might call for extending the principle of preference beyond simply preferring the original, the formulation of a hierarchy of preferences and a procedure for making it effective is believed to involve unwarranted complexities. Most, if not all, that would be accomplished by an extended scheme of preferences will, in any event, be achieved through the normal motivation of a party to present the most convincing evidence possible and the arguments and procedures available to his opponent if he does not. Compare McCormick § 207.

Finally, it should be noted that the best evidence rule is triggered only when the *contents* of a writing, recording or photograph is the object of proof. Any other consequential fact sought to be proven will not invoke application of the rule.

§ 1001.2   Scope of Application of Best Evidence Rule.

As noted previously, Article X creates a preference for the "original evidence" only where a party seeks to prove the contents of writings, recordings and photographs.[8] By defining key terms, Rule 1001 effectively delineates the scope of the best evidence rule. Accordingly, Rule 1001(1) defines "writings and recordings." Rule 1001(2) defines "photographs." Rule 1001(3) defines an "original," providing separate definitions for "writings and recordings," for "photographs" and for "computer printouts." Rule 1001(4) defines a "duplicate" and implicitly distinguishes a duplicate from a copy.

§ 1001.3   Definition of Writings and Recordings.

Rule 1001(1) defines "writings and recordings" in their broadest sense. Any setting down of "letters, words, or numbers, or their equivalent" by virtually any means constitutes a writing or recording.[9] A writing or re-

---

[8] *See* Rule 1002, Advisory Committee's Note.

[9] *See* Rule 1001, Advisory Committee's Note (including computers, photographic systems, and other modern developments).

cording is not only a setting down of inscriptions of letters and numbers, but also any compilation or recording of data such as might be produced by a computer, modern electronic device or other newly developed machine or technique.[10] Thus, Rule 1001(1) allows the application of the best evidence rule to accommodate technological developments. Rule 1001(1) is also sufficiently broad to include within its purview the setting down of any symbols that have a verbal or numerical translation.

Recordings are not explicitly distinguished from writings in Rule 1001(1), and the ordinary definition of "recordings" could include most writings. The setting down of sounds or electronic impulses translatable into words or numbers would be a recording that is not simultaneously a writing.[11] Because application of the best evidence rule is identical for writings and recordings, however, the determination of whether a particular setting down of data is a writing or a recording is purely academic.

§ 1001.4   Application of Rule 1001(1).

The scope of the definition of terms "writing" and "recording" is not a question entirely free from dispute. A traditional problem involves the determination of whether an inscribed object, *e.g.*, a policeman's badge or a tombstone, is always a writing or recording subject to the best evidence rule.[12] Clearly, where the verbal or numerical contents of the inscribed object are not being proven, the best evidence rule is not triggered.[13] Commentators generally have maintained, however, that even where the contents of the inscribed object are to be proven, the object need not be produced, unless in the discretion of the court, factors are present which would justify requiring use of the original object.[14] There is little federal authority from which to predict whether a given court will require the production of an object simply because it is inscribed.[15] Factors which should be considered by the trial judge in deciding whether to require

---

[10] *Id.*

[11] *Cf.* United States v. Foley, 598 F.2d 1323, 1338 (4th Cir. 1979) (printouts treated as duplicates of machine readable diskettes).

[12] *See, generally,* McCORMICK, § 232, at 705; 5 WEINSTEIN, ¶ 1001(a)[01], at 1001-11; 5 LOUISELL & MUELLER, § 550, at 287; 4 WIGMORE, § 1182.

[13] *See* § 1002.1 *et seq.* of this Treatise.

[14] *See, generally,* McCORMICK, § 232, at 706; 5 WEINSTEIN, ¶ 1001(1)[01], at 1001-11; 5 LOUISELL & MUELLER, § 550, at 290; 4 WIGMORE, § 1182, at 421.

[15] *See* Watson v. United States, 224 F.2d 910, 911-12 (5th Cir. 1955) (conviction reversed where oral testimony was admitted to prove that whiskey bottles did not contain labels or tax stamps, instead of producing the bottles themselves). *Contra* Burney v. United States, 339 F.2d 91, 92-94 (5th Cir. 1964) (implicitly held that best evidence doctrine applies only to writings). *See also* Driggers v. United States, 384 F.2d 158, 159 (5th Cir. 1967); Chandler v. United States, 318 F.2d 356, 357 (10th Cir. 1963); Dicks v. United States, 253 F.2d 713, 715 (5th Cir. 1958).

proof by the original inscribed object include: (i) whether precise information is required; (ii) whether the original is feasibly subject to production; (iii) whether a view of the object is practical or appropriate; (iv) whether the inscribed data is central or peripheral to the litigation; and (v) whether secondary evidence (e.g., a photograph) is equally as probative as the original.

Where contents are the object of proof, federal courts have clearly held that writings within the scope of the best evidence rule include written contracts,[16] written statements or letters,[17] corporate records,[18] and public records.[19]

§ 1001.5   Definitions of Photographs—In General.

Rule 1002 extends the traditional best evidence rule by including photographs within its scope.[20] Rule 1001(2) defines photographs to include, "still photographs, X-ray films, video tapes, and motion pictures."

Offering photographs at trial will only invoke the best evidence rule when the contents of the photograph itself are at issue. For example, in the case of an allegedly obscene film, the film's contents must be proved in order to establish the alleged obscenity.[21] The best evidence rule would consequently operate to prefer use of the original film, and secondary evidence would only be appropriate where an exception to the best evidence rule could be satisfied. Where, however, a photograph of an item, itself not a writing, recording or photograph, is available to prove the appearance of the item, the best evidence rule does not operate to prefer the photograph over other evidence. Proof of the appearance of the object of the photograph is not subject to the best evidence rule.[22] For example, where the appearance of a person is sought to be proven, the best evidence rule is not involved. A photograph of the person in question is probative evidence of

---

[16] Vigano v. Wylain, Inc., 633 F.2d 522, 526 (8th Cir. 1980).

[17] Weeks v. Latter Day Saints Hospital, 418 F.2d 1035, 1040 (10th Cir. 1969).

[18] Farber v. Servan Land Co., Inc., 662 F.2d 371, 379 (5th Cir. 1981).

[19] See §§ 1005.1-2 of this Treatise.

[20] 4 WIGMORE, § 1183, at 423; 5 LOUISELL & MUELLER, § 552, at 294. See also McCORMICK, § 232 (1972): "since representations of objects generally cannot logically be said to exhibit less intricacy of detail than do objects, pictures and photographs seem to invite classification outside the Best Evidence Doctrine."

[21] United States v. Levine, 546 F.2d 658, 667-68 (5th Cir. 1977) (obscenity prosecution; court rejected defense Best Evidence objection to use in evidence of "release print" of allegedly obscene motion picture, finding that under Rule 1001(2), the workprint or cut negative as well as the answer prints and release prints were originals of the filmmaking process). See also Rule 1002, Advisory Committee's Note.

[22] HUGHES & CANTOR, PHOTOGRAPHS IN CIVIL LITIGATION, 61-69 (1973); 2 SCOTT, PHOTOGRAPHIC EVIDENCE, § 1003 (1969).

the person's appearance, but it is not preferred over any other method of proof. Other probative evidence of the person's appearance, *e.g.*, testimony of a person with first hand knowledge, would be equally admissible. This result is more fully discussed in Chapter 1002.

§ 1001.6 Still Photographs.

Still photographs do not invoke the best evidence rule unless a party is trying to prove the contents of the photographs.[23] For example, the contents of the photograph may be at issue where the photograph contains or reveals evidence to be derived uniquely from the photograph, a photograph produced by an automatically activated surveillance camera at a bank.[24] This use of a photograph to prove contents is relatively rare because usually a photograph is introduced merely to illustrate the testimony of a witness based on firsthand perceptions.[25] Accordingly, where used to illustrate the testimony of a witness with firsthand knowledge of the subject of the photograph, the best evidence rule is inapplicable because the object of proof is not the contents of the photograph itself, but the existence or nature of the subject of the photograph.

A photograph of a document that is itself subject to the best evidence rule may be inadmissible because the photograph of the documentary evidence is secondary evidence of the contents of the document. Thus, a photograph of a medical record cannot be admitted to prove the contents of the record unless one of the exceptions to Rule 1002 is shown to obtain, or a statute so provides.

§ 1001.7 Videotapes and Motion Pictures.

Videotapes and motion pictures have generally been admitted at trial without best evidence issues arising because usually when offered, videotapes and films are used to illustrate the testimony of a witness who has

---

[23] *See* McMorrow, D.W., *Authentication and the Best Evidence Rule Under the Federal Rules of Evidence*, 16 Wayne L. Rev. 195, 223 (1969).

[24] *See, e.g.*, Hill v. State, 142 S.E.2d 909, 912, 221 Ga. 65, 68 (1965) (defendant tried for robbery; state introduced evidence of photographs of art objects taken by defendant rather than the art works themselves; court rejected Best Evidence objection by defense since the Best Evidence rule applies only to the contents of a writing;

trial court did not err in admitting the photographs of the art objects over the objection that they were not the best evidence). *See also* United States v. Taylor, 530 F.2d 639, 641-42 (5th Cir. 1976), *cert. denied*, 429 U.S. 845, 97 S.Ct. 127, 50 L.Ed.2d 117 (1976) (bank surveillance camera; film properly received even though no teller saw the events).

[25] 5 Weinstein, ¶ 1001(2)[02], at 1001-18; 5 Louisell & Mueller, § 522, at 296.

firsthand knowledge of the subject depicted.[26] Nevertheless, situations involving libel, copyright infringement or invasion of privacy may raise best evidence questions because in these types of cases, the contents of the tape or film may be at issue.

The principal type of case involving best evidence questions has concerned obscenity.[27] Federal courts have readily admitted duplicates of films to prove that a particular film is obscene.[28] Frames of films have been admitted as still photographs, even though the whole film is excluded for reasons of prejudice, delay, repetition or confusion.[29] Nevertheless, there is the possibility of distortion where a film is edited prior to admission, either due to the absence of relevant or counterbalancing passages or due to the emphasis given particular items.[30]

§ 1001.8   X-rays.

X-rays and X-ray films may invoke the operation of the best evidence rule when offered at trial.[31] X-rays are frequently used at trial to corrobo-

---

[26] 5 Weinstein, ¶ 1001(2)[03], at 1001-21; 5 Louisell & Mueller, § 552, at 292. *See also* Barham v. Nowell, 243 Miss. 441, 443, 138 So.2d 493, 495 (1962) (plaintiff walking normally, and walking up and down stairs); Lambert v. Wolf's, Inc., 32 So.2d 522, 523 (La. Ct. App. 1961) (plaintiff bending over and lifting heavy objects); Wren v. St. Louis Pub. Serv. Co., 333 S.W.2d 92, 95 (Mo. 1960) (plaintiff working, lifting).

[27] United States v. Levine, 546 F.2d 658, 668 (5th Cir. 1977). *See also* Paradis, P.R., *The Celluloid Witness*, 37 U. Colo. L. Rev. 235, 250 (1965).

[28] 3 Scott, *Photographic Evidence*, § 1291 (1969); Paradis, 37 U. Colo. L. Rev. at 250. *See, e.g.*, United States v. One Reel of 35mm Color Motion Picture, 491 F.2d 956, 958 (2d Cir. 1974) (government need produce no more than film itself to show obscenity); People v. Byrnes, 33 N.Y.2d 343, 345, 352 N.Y.S.2d 913, 916 (1974) (photograph sufficiently corroborated fact of rape, sodomy, and incest).

[29] 3 Scott, at § 1295; *Motion Pictures as Evidence*, Am. Jur. 2d, 8 Proof of Facts, 153, 155 (1960). *See* Rule 403 and § 403.1 *et seq.* of this Treatise. *See also Motion Pictures as Evidence*, Am. Jur. 2d, 8 Proof of Facts, 153, 155 (1960).

[30] The spirit, although not the letter, of Rule 106 would appear to apply. Rule 106 provides: "When a writing or recorded statement or part thereof is introduced by a party, an adverse party may require him at that time to introduce any other part or any other writing or recorded statement which ought in fairness to be considered contemporaneously with it." In any event, Rule 403 is available as a basis for excluding misleading evidence.

[31] *See, generally*, Hughes & Cantor, at 68-69; Scott, § 1273. *See also* Chicago, R.I. & P.R. Co. v. Howell, 401 F.2d 752, 756 (10th Cir. 1968) (indictum agreeing that testimony based on an X-ray should not be received without the X-ray "because testimony alone would not be the best evidence"); Gay v. United States, 118 F.2d 160, 162 (7th Cir. 1941) (in suit on war risk insurance policy, it was error to admit testimony by physician interpreting chest X-ray without producing the X-ray plate, for the testimony was not the best evidence); Cellamare v. Third Ave. Transit Corp., 273 App. Div. 260, 262, 77 N.Y.S.2d 91, 92 (1948) (in personal injury action, prejudicial error to permit plaintiff's expert medical witness to testify over objection to matters shown on X-rays without producing the X-ray pictures and introducing them in evidence).

rate or illustrate the testimony of a medical expert regarding the physical condition of the person X-rayed. Where the object of proof is the physical condition of the person X-rayed (*e.g.*, a broken bone), the best evidence rule does not operate to prefer the X-ray over the testimony of the medical expert. The physical condition of the person in question is not a writing, recording or photograph, and, consequently, the best evidence rule is not triggered.[32] The X-ray and the testimony are equally admissible to prove facts that are not within the scope of the rule, and the testimony based on firsthand knowledge of the injury or condition is admissible in the absence of the X-ray. Where, however, the X-ray is offered to establish a fact which may be derived only from the contents of the X-ray (*e.g.*, a hairline bone fracture), the best evidence rule is invoked. While the ultimate fact to be proven is the physical condition of the person X-rayed, the only source of the information is the X-ray itself, and consequently its contents are sought to be proven.[33] The foregoing distinction is frequently overlooked, however, and, consequently, many courts have applied the best evidence rule in virtually any case in which X-rays are introduced into evidence.[34] Of course, the best evidence rule is unquestionably applicable where the contents of the X-rays are at issue, *e.g.*, where in proving malpractice it is claimed that the physician misread an X-ray.

[32] *See* § 1002.1 of this Treatise.

[33] Rules 602 and 703 reinforce the analysis. Testimony based on firsthand knowledge is impossible where the condition is only apparent through use of the X-ray. Thus, testimony as to the condition would be incompetent; testimony as to the contents of the X-ray would be secondary evidence. *See also* Sirico v. Cotto, 67 Misc. 2d 636, 639, 324 N.Y.S.2d 483, 485-87 (1971) (testimony by physician based upon examination of X-ray excluded on account of best evidence doctrine, where proponent did not offer the X-ray or account for its nonproduction; court acknowledged that physician was an expert in radiology and that the opinion of such a person is admissible in evidence to the extent that it will appreciably help the jury to analyze the proof, find the facts, and render a verdict); Patrick & Tillman v. Matkin, 154 Okla. 232, 233, 7 P.2d 414, 415-16 (1932) (in employee's suit to recover disability benefits, it was error to admit plaintiff's expert testimony as to what X-ray showed; court held X-rays to be within Best Evidence Doctrine, but also emphasized importance of expert testimony; Dr. Shaw as an expert was a competent witness to testify as to what the X-ray disclosed, but at the same time the petitioners were entitled to see and examine the picture for the purpose of cross-examination, and submit the same to other experts for interpretation); Welch v. Independent Coach Line, Inc., 198 N.C. 130, 132, 150 S.E. 717, 719 (1930) (in passenger's personal injury action against bus company arising out of accident, court rejected defense claim of error in receipt of expert testimony by dentist based upon X-ray pictures which dentist had first examined and then lost; court likened X-rays to demonstrative evidence and remarked that X-rays usually require an explanation by parol).

[34] 29 AM. JUR. 2d, *Evidence*, § 485 (1967). *See also* Fuller v. Lemmons, 434 P.2d 145, 147 (Okla. 1967) (court applied Best Evidence Rule to exclude expert testimony where the X-ray was in court but was not formally introduced into evidence); Neill v. Fidelity Mutual Life Ins. Co., 119 W.Va. 694, 696, 192 S.E. 860, 862 (1938) (opposing party had opportunity to examine the X-rays outside of court, through the discovery process).

§ 1001.9   Originals—An Overview.

Rule 1001(3) provides distinct definitions of "originals" for writings or recordings, photographs, and computer or electronic output. The definitions are not necessarily parallel, *e.g.*, although intent is essential to determining whether a writing is an original, intent is irrelevant to determining whether a photograph is an original.

"Original" as used in Chapter X is a term of art. What a layman would treat as an original may be treated as a duplicate or copy in court.[35] Moreover, what is an original for one action, may be a duplicate or copy for another action arising from the same operative facts.[36]

§ 1001.10   Original Writings or Recordings.

Rule 1001(3) provides that an original "writing or recording" is the writing or recording itself or any counterpart *intended* by the person executing or issuing it to be an original.[37] Thus, a contract which is signed by the parties is an original even though the parties may not have initially distinguished that writing for execution.[38]

Rule 1001(3) provides that the definition of an original includes a counterpart intended by the person issuing or executing it to be an original. It may be an original whether or not it was written before or after another, was copied from another, or was itself used to make copy.[39] Accordingly, a "duplicate original," *i.e.*, a counterpart of an original instrument intended by the parties to have the effect of an original,[40] is to be treated as an original.[41] Focusing upon the issuer's or executor's intention to determine

[35] *See* the discussion of Rule 1001(4) *infra*. *See also* 4 Wigmore, § 1232; Jones, Notes & Comments, *Authentication and Contents of Writings*, 5 Okla. L. Rev. 383, 388 (1952). *See, e.g.*, United States v. Rangel, 585 F.2d 344, 346 (8th Cir. 1978) (since defendant used altered photocopy of receipt in demanding unlawful payment, contents of photocopy and not of original receipt had to be proved).

[36] *See generally*, United States v. Taylor, 648 F.2d 565, 568 n.3 (9th Cir. 1981), *cert. denied*, 454 U.S. 866, 102 S.Ct. 329, 70 L.Ed.2d 168 (1981) (court noted, without deciding, that where letter was telecopied from San Diego to Houston, either telecopied letter or photocopy thereof may have been the document on which Texas bank relied, making it the legally operative original); McCormick, § 235, at 566-67; 5

Weinstein, ¶ 1001(3)[01]; 5 Louisell & Mueller, § 554; 4 Wigmore, § 1232.

[37] Jones, C.R., Notes & Comments, *Authentication and Contents of Writings*, 5 Okla. L. Rev. 383, 388 (1952).

[38] 4 Wigmore, § 1233.

[39] 5 Weinstein, ¶ 1001(3)[01], at 1001-44. *See also* 4 Wigmore, § 1232; Jones, Notes & Comments, *Authentication and Contents of Writings*, 5 Okla. L. Rev. 383, 388 (1952). *See, e.g.*, United States v. Rangel, 585 F.2d 344, 346 (8th Cir. 1978) (since defendant used altered photocopy of receipt in demanding unlawful payment, contents of photocopy and not of original receipt had to be proved, citing Treatise).

[40] McCormick, § 236, at 713.

[41] *See* Rule 1001, Advisory Committee's Note.

whether a counterpart of a writing is an original is far simpler than tests proposed by McCormick[42] and Wigmore.[43]

Finally, it should be noted that a "duplicate original" is a distinguishable concept from that of a "duplicate." Duplicates are discussed in § 1001.13 *et seq.* of this Treatise. The concept of a "duplicate original" or "multiple original" arises in the situation where, by virtue of intent, there is more than one original, *e.g.*, where parties to a bilateral contract intend that each should have an executed original. The concept of a "duplicate" arises in the situation where, under Rules 1001(4) and 1003, an accurate copy is introduced and treated as an original for purposes of the best evidence rule, *e.g.*, where a party offers a carbon copy or a thermofax copy of a document where the contents of the document are at issue.

§ 1001.11　Original Photographs.

Rule 1001(3) provides that an original of a photograph is either "the negative or any print therefrom." Accordingly, either the negative or the print made from the negative is equally admissible in evidence as an original.[44] The value of a print is that it is easily understandable and readable.[45] Negatives, however, are not only the ultimate source from which prints are made; they often indicate variations in shades or hues not reproduced in the prints.[46]

[42] McCormick, § 235, at 711 ("The question to be asked, then, is whether, under the substantive law, the creation, publication or other use of Y may be viewed as affecting the rights of the parties in a way material to the litigation.")

[43] 4 Wigmore, § 1232, at 548 ("Is this the very document whose contents are desired to be, and in the now state of the issues by the substantive law may be, proved?").

[44] *Cf.* Federal Rule 1001(3), Advisory Committee's Note (construing federal rule as including as originals prints as well as negatives, due to practicality and common usage).

[45] 5 Weinstein, ¶ 1001(3)[03], at 1001-58; 5 Louisell & Mueller, § 556, at 337. *See, e.g.*, United States v. Jacobs, 513 F.2d 564, 567 (9th Cir. 1974), *rev'd on other grounds*, 430 U.S. 188, 97 S.Ct. 990, 51 L.Ed.2d 260 (in connection with defense attack upon search warrant, court rejected contention that the allegedly obscene film which was seized was inadmissible absent a showing that it was the actual print received from interstate commerce on the date alleged in the indictment; government is permitted to establish that a print of the same film was received from interstate commerce as alleged, and may use any copy of the film to establish the obscenity of the film; question whether prints are identical must be a collateral subject for the jury's determination; International Union, United Auto., Aircraft & Agricultural Implement Workers v. Russell, 264 Ala. 456, 459, 88 So.2d 175, 186 (1956) *aff'd*, 356 U.S. 634, 78 S.Ct. 932, 2 L.Ed.2d 1030 (1956) (in litigation arising out of labor dispute, motion picture of behavior at picket line was properly received, despite fact that film was a copy and not the original film).

[46] 3 Scott, *Photographic Evidence*, at 1476 (1969). *See also* Beach v. Chollett, 31 Ohio App. 8, 9, 166 N.E. 145, 146 (1928) (where X-ray plates were introduced, no error to exclude two photographs or prints taken from two of these plates; proponent's witness testified that the prints were correct reproductions from the plates, but he fur-

Rule 1001(4) makes clear that enlargements or reductions made from a particular negative are not originals but duplicates. Treating enlargements and reductions as duplicates instead of originals provides the court with an element of discretion under Rule 1003 to determine whether admission of an enlargement or reduction instead of an original would be unfair to the adverse party.[47]

§ 1001.12   Original Computer Data.

Rule 1001(3) provides that "any printout or other output readable by sight" from a computer or electronic device is an original if the printout accurately reproduces the data that is stored. In addition to the printout, the computer data cards and magnetic tape should also be admissible as originals.[48] Two theories would justify such a view: (i) the data cards and magnetic tape are analogous to the negatives of a photograph, and (ii) the data cards and magnetic tape are recordings themselves which are originals. Of course, because magnetic tape generally is not readable by a juror, the tape itself may not possess probative value under Rule 401.

§ 1001.13   Duplicates—In General.

Rule 1001(4) provides a general definition of a duplicate that includes any counterpart that accurately reproduces the original. Accurate reproduction may be achieved by any of a variety of ways designated in the Rule: by the same impression, as in the case of a carbon copy; from the same matrix, as in the case of a published book; by means of photography, as in the case of photostats, enlargements, or reductions; by mechanical or electronic recordings as in the case of a tape recording; by chemical repro-

---

ther stated that they were not nearly so accurate as the plates, and did not show as much as the plates themselves, and that the prints were not reliable).

[47] See Chapter 1003 of this Treatise.

[48] Cf. United States v. Foley, 598 F.2d 1323, 1338 (4th Cir. 1979), cert. denied, 444 U.S. 1043, 100 S.Ct. 727, 62 L.Ed.2d 728 (1979) (alleged conspiracy on the part of certain realtors to fix real estate prices in violation of antitrust laws; defense objected to the receipt of a chart summarizing the percentage of houses sold by each defendant on the basis of purchase loans guaranteed by V.A. or F.H.A.; court found that chart was made from data contained in machine-readable diskettes; while diskettes were not made available, defendants did obtain a computer printout of the information they contained, and therefore the printouts qualified as duplicates of the diskettes within the meaning of Rule 1001(4)). See also, United States v. Russo, 480 F.2d 1228, 1239-40 (6th Cir. 1973), cert. denied, 414 U.S. 1157, 94 S.Ct. 915, 39 L.Ed.2d 109 (1973) (assuming that properly functioning computer equipment is used, once the reliability and trustworthiness of the information put into the computer has been established, the computer printouts should be received as evidence of the transactions covered by the input).

duction, as in the case of a thermofax copy; or by equivalent techniques. The last phrase of the Rule allows the definition of a duplicate to accommodate developments of new technology for recording and reproducing data and information.

Consistent with the policy underlying the best evidence rule which seeks to ensure the accurate presentation of the contents of the original, duplicates are generally admissible to prove contents to the same extent as originals.[49] Because an additional policy of the best evidence rule is the prevention of fraud, Rule 1003 provides the court with the discretion to require use of an original where introduction of a duplicate would be unfair or misleading.[50]

§ 1001.14   Carbon Copies.

Rule 1001 allows carbon copy duplicates of originals to be admissible to the same extent as originals unless special circumstances dictate otherwise.[51] Rule 1001(4) clearly provides that carbon copies are duplicates, regardless of the intention of their maker, *i.e.*, carbon copies are "produced by the same impression as the original," and consequently, are defined as duplicates.[52]

§ 1001.15   Duplicates from the Same Matrix by Means of Photography.

Consistent with Rules 1001(4) and 1003, courts have generally permitted the use of copies of books or newspapers to prove contents. Courts have

[49] *See* McCORMICK, § 236 at 714. *See also* United States v. Manton, 107 F.2d 834, 845 (2d Cir. 1938), *cert. denied,* 309 U.S. 664, 60 S.Ct. 590, 84 L.Ed. 1012 (1940) (the better rule is that the so-called original and carbon copies are duplicate originals); United States v. Gerhart, 538 F.2d 807, 810 (8th Cir. 1976) (photocopy could have been admitted as a duplicate instead of secondary evidence where the original was lost).

[50] *See* Rule 1003, Advisory Committee's Note. *See also* § 1003.3 *infra. See, e.g.,* Brown, *Authentication and Contents of Writings,* 4 ARIZ. ST. L.J. 613 (1969).

[51] *See* Rule 1001, Advisory Committee's Note. *See also* Rule 1003. *See, e.g.,* Stern Equipment Co. v. Portell, 116 A.2d 601, 602 (D.C. Mun. App. 1955) (although the contract in evidence was a carbon copy, it was a signed copy, and therefore a duplicate original rather than a mere copy); International Harvester Co. v. Elfstrom, 101 Minn.

203, 266, 112 N.W. 252, 253 (1907) (if the reproduction is complete, there is no practical reason why all the products of the single act of writing the contract and affixing a signature thereto should not be regarded as of equal and equivalent value; in this sense the same stroke of the pen produced both signatures).

[52] *See, e.g.,* CTS Corp. v. Piher International Corp., 527 F.2d 95, 104 n.29 (7th Cir. 1975), *cert. denied,* 424 U.S. 978, 96 S.Ct. 1485, 47 L.Ed.2d 748 (1976) (although there is no direct testimony describing the document as a carbon copy, in the absence of any evidence to the contrary, we draw this inference from the copy of the document which was offered for examination in light of the testimony of the witness); Liberty Chair v. Crawford, 193 N.C. 531, 533, 137 S.E. 577, 579 (1927) (no evidence that carbons were made at same time held not admissible).

viewed such evidence as highly reliable due to an assumption that fixed type or common plates are employed.[53]

Rule 1001(4) generally extends federal law, however, in providing that photographically produced copies are duplicates, and it should be noted that photographic copies which reduce or enlarge the original are considered to be duplicates under Rule 1001(4). Pre-Rule federal law treated such evidence as secondary.[54]

Additional methods of reproduction which satisfy Rule 1001(4) include the letterpress and thermofax machine. The letterpress provides for copies made by pressure or chemical reaction, while the thermofax process uses heat to reproduce the original. Copies produced by either means should be treated as duplicates under the Rule, despite Wigmore's concern that such copies are frequently not much better than secondary evidence due to their poor quality of reproduction.[55] The better view under Rule 1001(4) is that they are duplicates that can be excluded under Rule 1003 if the quality of reproduction is inadequate.

§ 1001.16   Electronic or Mechanical Re-recording.

Rule 1001(4) adopts a rule treating re-recordings as duplicates; subject to the limits set out in Rule 1003, it is as admissible as the original. This approach is contrary to the traditional general rule that such re-recordings are only secondary evidence.[56] Re-recordings of tapes or discs generally are used to provide a more durable copy than the original recording. Likewise, re-recording may produce a copy that is easier to hear or interpret. In the latter case, Rule 1003 provides the court with the discretion to require introduction of the original if the re-recording distorts the original recording in an unfair or misleading way.[57] Finally, it should be clear that a

---

[53] *See* McCormick, § 236, at 568 (1972): "There is warrant for believing that the courts would accept as primary evidence of the contents of a given book or a given issue of a newspaper any other book or newspaper printed from the same set of fixed type or the same plates or mats. A like result should be reached as to all copies run off from the same mat by the multigraph, lithoprint, or other duplicating process."

[54] *E.g.*, Toho Bussan Kaisha, Ltd. v. American President Lines, Ltd., 265 F.2d 418, 424 (2d Cir. 1959).

[55] 4 Wigmore, § 1234, at 551.

[56] *See* Rule 1001, Advisory Committee's Note.

[57] *See* Rule 1003, Advisory Committee's Note. *Cf.* United States v. Denton, 556 F.2d 811, 815-16 (6th Cir. 1977), *cert. denied*, 434 U.S. 892, 98 S.Ct. 269, 54 L.Ed.2d 178 (1978) (composite tape made from re-recording of original tape was properly received; use of composite tape saved the court much time and inconvenience); People v. Albert, 182 Cal. App.2d 729, 741, 6 Cal. Rptr. 473, 480 (1960) (re-recording of a recorded conversation and a transcript of the recording were submitted in evidence along with a police officer's testimony that the transcript and re-recording were accurate reproductions; the original wire recording was not produced due to its unavailability).

transcript of a recording produced by hand or type is not a duplicate because it would not be an electronic or mechanical re-recording that meets the accuracy requirements of Rule 1001(4).[58]

[58] *See* Rule 1003, Advisory Committee's Note.

Chapter 1002

RULE 1002. REQUIREMENT OF ORIGINAL

SECTION

1002.1 The best evidence rule defined

1002.2 Purpose of the best evidence rule

1002.3 Application of the best evidence rule; proving the contents of writings, recordings and photographs

1002.4 Exceptions to Rule 1002 in statutes and rules

Rule 1002 reads as follows:

> To prove the content of a writing, recording or photograph, the original writing, recording, or photograph is required, except as otherwise provided in these rules or by Act of Congress.

§ 1002.1 The Best Evidence Rule Defined.

Rule 1002 restates the traditional best evidence rule in modern and liberal terms.[1] The best evidence rule requires that in proving the contents of a writing, recording, or photograph, the original must be offered as evidence unless a foundation is laid to account for its nonproduction.[2] Additionally, Rule 1002 expressly provides that the Rule's application may be limited by statute and by other rules of evidence.[3]

[1] See, generally, 1 MCCORMICK §§ 229-33; 5 WEINSTEIN, ¶¶ 1002[01]-[06]; 5 LOUISELL & MUELLER, §§ 569-71; 4 WIGMORE, §§ 1171-83. See also Brown, Authentication and Contents of Writings, 4 ARIZ. ST. L.J. 611 (1969); Cleary & Strong, The Best Evidence Rule: An Evaluation in Context, 51 IOWA L. REV. 825 (1966); Levin, Authentication and Content of Writings, 10 RUTGERS L. REV. 632 (1956); Comment, Authentication and the Best Evidence Rule Under the Federal Rules of Evidence, 16 WAYNE L. REV. 195 (1969); Note, A Critical Appraisal of the Application of the Best Evidence Rule, 21 RUTGERS L. REV. 526 (1967).

[2] See MCCORMICK, § 230; 4 WIGMORE, §§ 1173, 1174. See also United States v. Alexander, 326 F.2d 736, 739 (4th Cir. 1964) ("it is now generally recognized that the 'best evidence' phrase denotes only the rule of evidence which requires that the contents of an available written document be proved by introduction of the document itself").

[3] See Rule 1002, Advisory Committee's Note.

The general scope of Rule 1002 is in part determined by Rule 1001, which defines the terms used in Rule 1002.[4] Rules 1001 and 1002 expand the traditional best evidence rule by making the rule applicable not only to writings but also to recordings, photographs and electronically recorded data.[5]

Article X, including Rule 1002, refrains from use of the term "best evidence rule," as does the Advisory Committee's Note to Rule 1002.[6] The reluctance of the drafters to use such a rubric is undoubtedly due to the recognition that the term is really a misnomer. The term "best evidence rule" is misleading because the rule has only a limited horizon, *i.e.*, there simply is no general requirement to produce the best evidence available to prove consequential facts.[7] Instead, the rule is applicable only when proving the contents of a writing, recording or photograph. As McCormick has noted, a better name would be "the original document rule."[8] Even this namem ay be misleading because Rule 1003 makes duplicates admissible in nearly all situations in which Rule 1002 requires that originals be offered.[9]

§ 1002.2   Purpose of the Best Evidence Rule.

Five related policies supporting the best evidence rule have been identified.[10] First, because words are so easily misunderstood and slight differences in words or terms have such a substantial effect on meaning, and ultimately on rights, the best evidence rule is said to be necessary to guarantee the accuracy of evidence introduced to prove the contents of writings, recordings, and some photographs.[11] Second, because secondary evidence is frequently a reproduction of the original, the possibility of error in

[4] *See* §§ 1001.3, 1001.14 of this Treatise.

[5] *See, generally,* 4 WIGMORE, § 1183.

[6] *See* Rule 1002, Advisory Committee's Note.

[7] *See, e.g.,* Herring v. Administrator, Federal Aviation Administration, 532 F.2d 1003, 1004 (5th Cir. 1976) (in connection with license suspension proceedings, rejected pilot's contention that judge should have looked at plane itself or its records to determine its condition, court found that there is no such requirement; best evidence has no meaning in the present context and applies only to the requirement that the terms of a writing be shown by production of the original document, unless the document is shown to be unavailable for reasons other than the serious fault of the propo-

nent). *See also* Rice v. United States, 411 F.2d 485, 486 (8th Cir. 1969); Wallin v. Greyhound Corporation, 341 F.2d 521, 523 (6th Cir. 1965).

[8] *See* McCORMICK, § 230, at 703.

[9] *See* Rule 1003, Advisory Committee's Note.

[10] *See, generally,* McCORMICK, § 231; 4 WIGMORE §§ 1179-80; Brown, *Authentication and Content of Writings,* 4 ARIZ. ST. L.J. 611 (1969); Cleary & Strong, *The Best Evidence Rule: An Evaluation in Context,* 51 IOWA L. REV. 825 (1966); Levin, *Authentication and Content of Writings,* 10 RUTGERS L. REV. 632 (1956).

[11] *See, e.g.,* E. MORGAN, BASIC PROBLEMS OF EVIDENCE, 385-87 (1962).

reproduction necessitates production of the original.[12] Because "duplicates" as defined in Rule 1001(4) provide such a high degree of accuracy in reproduction, Rule 1003 provides a sensible approach that avoids the harshness of a technical reading of the best evidence rule. Rule 1003 authorizes the use of duplicates unless exceptional conditions exist.[13] Third, requiring use of the original may provide information which copies cannot, *e.g.*, watermarks or indications of the ink type that may aid in the identification of a writing.[14] Rule 1003, which generally allows duplicates to be admitted instead of originals, is not inconsistent with this policy. Rule 1003 provides that the original may be required in lieu of a duplicate where a "genuine question is raised as to the authenticity of the original." Fourth, the prevention of fraud is fostered by the requirement of the original.[15] Although Wigmore contends that fraud is not always prevented by the application of the rule,[16] McCormick notes that prevention of fraud remains a significant justification:

> It has long been observed that the opportunity to inspect original writings may be of substantial importance in the detection of fraud. At least a few modern courts and commentators appear to regard the prevention of fraud as an ancillary justification of the rule. Unless this view is accepted it is difficult to explain the rule's frequent application to copies produced by modern techniques which virtually eliminate the possibility of unintentional mistransmission.[17]

Clearly then, prevention of fraud is at least an ancillary justification for the rule. The final reason suggests that the best evidence rule, in addition to guarding against the mistransmission of the contents of a writing, should also assure that portions of a text, though accurately transmitted, are not selectively removed from a document or a series of documents for use at trial. The best evidence rule, under this rationale, would assure that the jury receives a complete picture of the evidence before rendering its verdict.[18]

---

[12] *See, e.g.*, McCormick, § 231, at 704, 705; Brown, *Authentication and Content of Writings*, 4 Ariz. St. L.J. 611, 616 (1969).

[13] *See* § 1003.1 of this Treatise.

[14] *See, e.g.*, 4 Wigmore, § 1179, at 417 ("Moreover, the original may contain, and the copy will lack, such features of handwriting, paper, and the like, as may afford the opponent valuable means of learning legitimate objections to the significance of the document.")

[15] United States v. Manton, 107 F.2d 834, 835 (2d Cir. 1938); Rogers, *The Best Evidence Rule*, 20 Wis. L. Rev. 278 (1945).

[16] 4 Wigmore, § 1180, at 418.

[17] McCormick, § 231, at 704-705.

[18] Toho Bussan Kaisha, Ltd. v. American President's Lines, Ltd., 265 F.2d 418, 423 (2d Cir. 1959). *See also* McCormick, § 231, at 704.

§ 1002.3   Application of the Best Evidence Rule; Proving the Contents of Writings, Recordings and Photographs.

Rule 1002 is applicable only when two conditions concur: (1) the evidence involves a writing, recording, or photograph, and (2) the object of proof is the contents of that writing, recording or photograph.

The first condition indicates that Rule 1002 is inapplicable in proving the nature of uninscribed physical objects or a fact which is subsequently memorialized in a writing. Accordingly, the best evidence rule as codified in Rule 1002 does not require that a confiscated substance be introduced into evidence to prove the nature, identity or status of the substance.[19] Whether a writing is the object of proof may be unclear in particular relatively unusual cases, e.g., where the writing on an inscribed chattel such as a tombstone is sought to be proven.[20] Nevertheless, when the fact to be proven is independent of the contents of a writing, even though some writing may contain evidence of the fact, it is clear that the best evidence rule is inapplicable. Accordingly, the best evidence rule does not require exclusion of a wage earner's testimony as to his salary even though payroll records containing the same information are available.[21] Likewise, in the classic illustration, the best evidence rule does not require use of a receipt which memorializes a transaction where the fact of the transaction is the object of proof. In this illustration the transaction exists and is binding in the absence of the receipt. The receipt is merely one means of proof available to establish the transaction, and oral testimony to prove the transaction is equally admissible. In sum, the best evidence rule is not triggered simply because some act or transaction is subsequently recorded in a writing.

The second condition for invocation of the best evidence rule provides that the rule is applicable only where a party offering evidence seeks to prove the *contents* of the writing, recording, or photograph. A party seeks to prove the contents of a writing, recording or photograph only where the issue is what the writing or recording says or what the photograph depicts. Where the issue is the status, nature, or identity of the thing described in a

---

[19] *See, e.g.,* United States v. Marcantoni, 590 F.2d 1324, 1329-30 (5th Cir. 1979), *cert. denied,* 441 U.S. 937, 99 S.Ct. 861, 59 L.Ed.2d 49 (1979); Burney v. United States, 339 F.2d 91, 94 (5th Cir. 1964).

[20] *See* § 1001.4 of this Treatise.

[21] Sayen v. Rydzewski, 387 F.2d 815, 819 (7th Cir. 1967) (negligence action; plaintiff allowed to testify respecting his income; courts do not bar oral proof of a matter merely because it is also provable by a writing; question is one of admissibility, not weight). *See also* In re Ko-Ed Tavern, 129 F.2d 806, 810 (3d Cir. 1942) (testimony by witness as to who owned capital stock in corporation admitted over objection that books of corporation were best evidence). Herzig v. Swift & Co., 146 F.2d 444, 445-46 (2d Cir. 1945), *cert. denied,* 328 U.S. 849, 66 S.Ct. 1122, 90 L.Ed. 1622 (1946).

writing or recording, or depicted in the photograph, the best evidence rule is inapplicable.[22] Several examples may clarify the distinction.

Where the issue is whether a written contract obligates a party to perform in a certain way, the best evidence rule is applicable because the contract, being embodied in the writing, is established by proving the content of the writing.[23] Where the issue is whether a person committed perjury at a hearing, however, a transcript of the hearing is not the best evidence of what the person said. Other evidence such as the testimony of a witness who heard the alleged perjury is equally admissible.[24] The best evidence rule is not triggered, because the object of the proof is what was said at the hearing—not what is recorded in the transcript. The transcript is merely one means of proving the testimony at the hearing. Here, the spoken words form a basis for the perjury, and the perjury would exist even absent the preparation of the transcript. It should be noted, however, that a different analysis would obtain where, in order to prove the oral perjury, a witness is offered who bases his testimony entirely on a reading of the contents of the transcript. Here the witness lacks firsthand knowledge of the oral perjury. She possesses firsthand knowledge only of the contents of the transcript, and she is consequently offering testimony as to the contents of a writing. Under these facts Rule 602 and Rule 1002 intersect to provide that the original transcript is preferred to the secondary evidence, *i.e.*, the oral testimony offered to prove the contents of the transcript. Nevertheless, as between the transcript and a witness with firsthand knowledge of the oral perjury, there is no preference under Rule 1002, and each is equally appropriate. By comparison, however, if the alleged perjury occurred because of a purposeful misrepresentation of a fact set forth in a signed, sworn affidavit, the best evidence rule would apply to prefer the original affidavit. Here the perjury does not exist apart from the words embodied in the writing.

[22] *See* Rule 1002, Advisory Committee's Note.

[23] Harrington v. United States, 504 F.2d 1306, 1313-14 (1st Cir. 1974) (in tax refund suit, plaintiff sought to prove an alteration in a contract by evidence in the form of a copy of an agreement purporting to be a modification of the contract; court upheld exclusion of the copy). *See also* Weeks v. Latter-Day Saints Hospital, 418 F.2d 1035, 1039-40 (10th Cir. 1969) (suit for body burns sustained by two-year-old infant as a result of contact with a temperature-controlled mattress in hospital; evidence of hospital rules properly excluded; Best Evidence Doctrine barred oral testimony as to their contents).

[24] Meyers v. United States, 171 F.2d 800, 812-13 (D.C. Cir. 1948), *cert. denied*, 336 U.S. 912, 69 S.Ct. 602, 93 L.Ed. 1076 (1948) (businessman charged with perjury before a Senate Subcommittee looking into suspected waste and profiteering; Subcommittee's lawyer permitted to testify as to substance of testimony given by businessman during hearings; thereafter transcript of that testimony was also introduced; court upheld convictions, but Judge Prettyman wrote a strenuous and now-famous dissent, arguing that receipt of this testimony called for reversal).

Where a motion picture is offered to prove an external fact, such as the mobility of the plaintiff, the best evidence rule is not implicated because the contents of the film are not at issue, only the mobility of the plaintiff.[25] The best evidence rule is applicable, however, in an obscenity trial at which the film is claimed to be obscene. In such a case the best evidence rule is applicable because the object of proof is the content of the film, *i.e.*, the issue to be resolved is the content of the film.[26]

When proving the confession of a person, a taped recording of the confession would be the best evidence of the confession, only if the tape is itself viewed as the confession, much as a signed, written confession is the confession itself. Otherwise, the tape recording is merely a recording of the oral confession and the best evidence rule is not involved.[27]

§ 1002.4　　Exceptions to Rule 1002 in Statutes and Rules.

Rule 1002 provides that the originals must be used to prove the contents of writings, recordings, or photographs *except* as provided in the Federal Rules of Evidence or by Acts of Congress. Article X contains a number of such exceptions. Rule 1003 provides that duplicates are admissible to the same extent as originals unless there is a genuine question as to authenticity or where admission of the duplicate would be unfair. Rule 1004 provides four exceptions to the rule: (1) original is lost or destroyed; (2) original is not obtainable by judicial process; (3) original is in possession of adverse party; or (4) original pertains to collateral matter. Rule 1005 provides that copies of public records are admissible as originals if properly certified. Upon proper notice, Rule 1006 allows admission of charts, calculations or summaries based on originals if the originals are voluminous and cannot be conveniently introduced. Finally, Rule 1007 authorizes the use of certain admission by adverse parties in order to prove the contents of writings.

---

[25] Kortz v. Guardian Life Ins. Co. of America, 144 F.2d 676, 679 (10th Cir. 1944); Maryland Cas. Co. v. Coker, 118 F.2d 43, 44 (5th Cir. 1941).

[26] United States v. Levine, 546 F.2d 658, 668 (5th Cir. 1977) (alleged interstate shipment of obscene films; court quoted Rule 1002, and noted that motion pictures are within the ambit of the definition of "photograph" under Rule 1002).

[27] United States v. Rose, 590 F.2d 232, 237 (7th Cir. 1978), *cert. denied*, 442 U.S. 929, 99 S.Ct. 2859, 61 L.Ed. 2d 297 (1979) (where government sought to prove contents of conversation, not contents of tape recording, best evidence rule was inapplicable, citing Treatise). *But cf.*, Daniels v. United States, 393 F.2d 359, 361 (D.C. Cir. 1968) (issue whether police had reasonable cause to arrest defendant because they heard police broadcast describing him in connection with robbery; court stated that although point had not been raised, the government in this kind of case should be required to produce tape or log entry of the broadcast as only the best evidence of the information contained in the broadcast).

Although various foundations must be laid before the exceptions of these Rules may be invoked, each provides for the nonapplication of Rule 1002.

The Advisory Committee's Note to Rule 1002 cites two examples of Acts of Congress which have statutorily created situations in which a copy of a document is to be treated as an original under Rule 1002, *i.e.*, 26 U.S.C. § 7513 allows for the photographic reproduction of tax returns and documents and 44 U.S.C. § 399(a) provides for the photographic copying of documents in the National Archives.[28] These two examples are in no sense the only situations in which Congress has acted in a manner affecting the application of Rule 1002.[29]

Rule 1002 is not superseded by statutes that treat copies as originals. Instead, Rule 1002 merely requires that originals be admitted, including copies statutorily declared to be originals.[30]

[28] *See* Rule 1002, Advisory Committee's Note.

[29] *See* the discussion in 5 WEINSTEIN § 1002[04], at 1002-16 n.1. *See also* 5 LOUISELL & MUELLER, § 571, at 434, n.13.

[30] *See* Rule 1002, Advisory Committee's Note.

Chapter 1003

RULE 1003. ADMISSIBILITY OF DUPLICATES

Rule 1003 reads as follows:

> A duplicate is admissible to the same extent as an original unless (1) a genuine question is raised as to the authenticity of the original or (2) in the circumstances it would be unfair to admit the duplicate in lieu of the original.

§ 1003.1 Duplicates—Admissible as Originals.

The Federal Rules provide both a broad definition of duplicates[1] and a wide authorization for their admission.[2] While, inapplicable with respect to certified copies of public records,[3] Rule 1003 provides that duplicates are generally admissible as originals in all cases except where there is a genuine question of the authenticity of the original or where admission of the duplicate instead of the original would be unfair.[4]

---

[1] See, generally, 1 McCormick §§ 229, 231, 235, 236; 5 Weinstein, ¶¶ 1003[01]-[05]; 5 Louisell & Mueller, §§ 575-77; 4-5 Wigmore, §§ 1177-80, 1190, 1198, 1229, 1232-41, 1249. See also Brown, Authentication and the Contents of Writings, 4 Ariz. St. L.J. 611 (1969); Cleary & Strong, The Best Evidence Rule: An Evaluation in Context, 51 Iowa L. Rev. 825 (1966); Cleary, Evidence—Best Evidence Rule—Admissibility of a Carbon Copy as Primary Evidence, 3 Vill. L. Rev. 217 (1958); Note, Authentication and the Best Evidence Rule Under the Federal Rules of Evidence, 16 Wayne L. Rev. 195 (1969); Comment, The

Best Evidence Rule—A Criticism, 3 Newark L. Rev. 200 (1938).

[2] See Rule 1001(4). See also § 1001.13 of this Treatise.

[3] Rule 1003. See § 1005.1 of this Treatise.

[4] Rule 1003. See also United States v. Tombrello, 666 F.2d 485, 492 (11th Cir. 1982), cert. denied, 458 U.S. 941, 102 S.Ct. 2279, 73 L.Ed. 2d 1291 (1982) (even if exemplified copies of state docket entries were not originals but duplicates, they were admissible because no genuine issue was raised as to authenticity of original, and under circumstances it was unfair to admit them).

The scope and theory of the admissibility of duplicates has been discussed in §§ 1001.13-.16 of this Treatise. As noted, duplicates are generally reliable copies or reproductions of originals produced by methods that tend to ensure accuracy.[5] Duplicates are distinguishable from copies intended by the parties to be originals, *i.e.*, "duplicate originals." As discussed in § 1001.13 of this Treatise, duplicate originals are admissible without regard to the Rule 1003 consideration of authenticity and fairness.[6]

Although Federal law is not completely devoid of authority treating duplicates as admissible in place of originals,[7] Rule 1003 does expand the previously accepted position in some courts that duplicates of originals are only secondary evidence.[8] Rule 1003 provides that a duplicate is admissible without requiring the proponent to make a showing that he cannot produce the original.[9] Instead, the only questions concerning admissibility to be considered by the court pursuant to Rule 1003[10] are (i) whether there is a genuine question of authenticity,[11] and (ii) whether admission of the duplicate in the circumstances would be unfair.[12]

[5] *See* Rule 1003, Advisory Committee's Note; Wharton, *Duplicate Originals and the Best Evidence Rule*, 19 OHIO ST. L.J. 520, 524 (1958). *See, e.g.*, United States v. Barnes, 443 F. Supp. 137, 139 (S.D.N.Y. 1977) (no reason not to admit state court hearing records where no issue had been raised as to their authenticity).

[6] *See* Rule 1003, Advisory Committee's Note; Wharton, *Duplicate Originals and the Best Evidence Rule*, 19 OHIO ST. L.J. 520 (1958).

[7] *See, e.g.*, United States v. Wolf, 455 F.2d 984, 984 (9th Cir. 1972) (alleged refusal to be inducted into armed forces; court summarily dismissed as "nonsense" the defense objection to a "certified copy" of the selective service file, and the claim that the original file should have been offered; court suggested that if defendant had any reason to question the accuracy of the copy, he could have subpoenaed the original); Myrick v. United States, 332 F.2d 279, 282 (5th Cir. 1963), *cert. denied*, 377 U.S. 952, 84 S.Ct. 1630, 12 L.Ed. 2d 497 (alleged fraud; bank photostatic copies of checks properly received); Johns v. United States, 323 F.2d 421, 421-22 (5th Cir. 1963) (rejected defense Best Evidence objection to introduction of rerecording, where counsel conceded openly that the tape was an accurate re-recording of the wire); Sauget v. Johnston, 315 F.2d 816, 817-18 (9th Cir. 1963) (suit for dissolution of joint venture and accounting; court rejected Best Evi-

dence objection to receipt in evidence of a copy of the agreement).

[8] *See, e.g.*, Tampa Shipbuilding & Engineering Co. v. General Construction Co., 43 F.2d 309, 311 (5th Cir. 1930) (criticized receipt of "office copy" in form of carbon duplicate which was not a duplicate original because not so used by the parties; court noted that the original may have been corrected or altered before sending, but found that error was cured by testimony that original order was in fact received).

[9] United States v. Enstam, 622 F.2d 857, 866 (5th Cir. 1980), *cert. denied*, 101 S.Ct. 1351, 67 L.Ed. 2d 336 (1980) (Xerox copy of blank letterhead stationery properly received despite defense objection based in part upon fact that there was no explanation for the disappearance of the original, which had been given to government agents).

[10] *See* § 1008.3 of this Treatise.

[11] *See* § 1003.2 of this Treatise. *See also* United States v. Gipson, 609 F.2d 893, 894-95 (8th Cir. 1979) (alleged theft of barbed wire belonging to government; court rejected defense contention of error in receipt of copies of documents acknowledging receipt by the Government of the barbed wire in question; since defendant raised no objection as to the authenticity of the original, and did not claim any unfairness, receipt of the duplicates was proper under Rule 1003).

[12] *See* § 1003.3 of this Treatise.

Functionally, Rule 1003 provides that duplicates are presumptively the equivalent of originals. Accordingly, the burden is on the opponent of the duplicate to establish conditions requiring the use of the original.

§ 1003.2 Duplicates and Questions of Authenticity.

Duplicates are not admissible as originals where there is a genuine question as to the authenticity of the original. Prevention of fraud is one of the justifications for the best evidence rule,[13] and where there is some question that the original is not authentic, a duplicate may lack its usual degree of reliability. Consequently, admission of the duplicate may be contrary to the resolution of the issue of authenticity. Of course, where the question of the authenticity of the original is so substantial that even the original would be inadmissible, a duplicate would be inadmissible.[14]

At least two types of situations raise questions of authenticity requiring production of the original under Rule 1003. Where there is a question as to whether the original has been altered after the reproduction has been made, whether accidentally, negligently or fraudulently, production of the original should be required.[15] Alternatively, where there is a genuine issue of whether the original is what its proponent claims it to be, a duplicate is inadmissible.[16] A principal reason for inadmissibility of a duplicate in this situation is that it may lack indicia of authenticity which may have derived only from the original, *e.g.*, the watermark of paper used in a letter.[17]

Whether a genuine question of authenticity exists is for the court to decide.[18] Presumably, an unsupported objection by opposing counsel is in-

---

[13] *See* § 1002.2 of this Treatise. *See, generally,* McCormick, § 231; 5 Weinstein, ¶ 1003[01]; 5 Louisell, § 576; 4 Wigmore, §§ 1179, 1180.

[14] 5 Weinstein, ¶ 1003[02] at 1003-9; 5 Louisell & Mueller, § 577, at 451. *See also* Toho Bussan Kaisha, Ltd. v. American President Lines, Ltd., 265 F.2d 418, 420 (2d Cir. 1959) (court feared that photocopies prepared specifically for trial were subject to possibility of fraud). *See e.g.,* Cleary, *Evidence—Best Evidence Rule—Admissibility of a Carbon Copy as Primary Evidence,* 3 Vill. L. Rev. 219 (1958).

[15] 4 Wigmore, § 1190, at 434. *See also* Blade v. Noland, 12 Wend. (N.Y.) 173, 176 (1834) ("no case is to be found, where if a party has deliberately destroyed the higher evidence without explanation, showing affirmatively that the act was done with pure motives, and repelling every suspicion of a fraudulent design, that he had the benefit of it; there is no honest purpose for which a party without any mistake would deliberately destroy the evidence of an existing debt"). *Cf.* People v. Kind, 101 Cal. App. 2d 500, 502, 225 P.2d 950, 952 (1951) (police after re-recording original wire recordings onto tapes erased the originals, held re-recordings not admissible).

[16] *See* United States v. Georgalis, 631 F.2d 1199, 1205 (5th Cir. 1980). *See also* CTS Corp. v. Piher International Corp., 527 F.2d 95, 103-04 (7th Cir. 1975), *cert. denied,* 424 U.S. 978, 96 S.Ct. 1485, 47 L. Ed. 2d 748 (1975) (in bench-tried patent infringement action, trial court excluded evidence of a purchase order in the form of a carbon copy rather than a ribbon copy on basis of plaintiff's Best Evidence objection).

[17] 4 Wigmore, § 1180, at 417.

[18] *See* § 1008.3 of this Treatise.

sufficient to raise a genuine question.[19] Instead, some evidence should be introduced into the record to raise the issue.[20]

§ 1003.3 Duplicates and Questions of Unfairness.

Duplicates are not admissible as originals where admission of the duplicate in lieu of the original would be unfair. The determination of unfairness is for the court.[21]

Although the Rule does not define the concept of unfairness, there are common situations that arise when duplicates of documents should not be admitted into evidence. For example, where a duplicating process fails to reproduce some of the most essential parts of an original, *e.g.*, where reservation clauses are omitted from the photostat of a deed, fairness may require production of the original.[22] Where a rerecording is made highlighting a particular conversation by eliminating background noises, fairness may dictate production of the original.[23] Also, where the duplicate is illegi-

[19] United States v. Georgalis, 631 F.2d 1199, 1199 (5th Cir. 1980) (duplicate may be admitted unless opposing counsel meets the burden of showing that there is a genuine issue as to the authenticity of the unintroduced original).

[20] *Cf.* United States v. Moragan, 555 F.2d 239, 241 (9th Cir. 1977) (the court held duplicate presumptively admissible without evidence in record raising question of authenticity).

[21] *See* § 1008.3 of this Treatise. *See also* United States v. Alexander, 326 F.2d 736, 742 (4th Cir. 1964) (defendant accused of stealing check from mail; court refused to admit thermofax reproduction of check, which because of mechanical error had failed to reproduce the name and address of the payee; the original was not produced nor its absence explained); Hi Hat Elkhorn Coal Co. v. Kelly, 205 F. Supp. 764, 769 (1962) (dispute between Elkhorn, as successor in interest to grantor, and defendants as heirs to grantees, in which Elkhorn claimed that the official record of the deed omitted certain terms found in the actual deed, and

offered a purported office carbon copy as proof; in this bench-tried equity action, court concluded that Elkhorn did not show that the proffer was a copy of the final deed actually conveyed).

[22] *Cf.* Amoco Prod. Co. v. United States, 619 F.2d 1383, 1391 (10th Cir. 1980) (duplicate copy of a deed excluded where reservation clauses omitted).

[23] Fountain v. United States, 384 F.2d 624, 630 (5th Cir. 1967) (court refused to admit re-recording where confused mixture of three or four voices and mechanical interference in the original recording made it impossible to accurately determine whether the rerecording accurately reproduced the conversations transcribed on the original). *See also* United States v. Stephenson, 121 F. Supp. 274, 279 (D.D.C. 1954), *app. dismissed*, 96 App. D.C. 44, 223 F.2d 336 (1955) (court refused to admit transcript of re-recordings which differed with each other and whose accuracy could not be determined due to hearing difficulties with the recording).

ble or unintelligible,[24] the original may justify a court's determination that admission of a duplicate would be unfair.[25]

It should be noted that a situation may arise in which an original has become illegible but the duplicate has not. Rule 1003 fails to be illuminative. Wigmore suggests that in such a case the duplicate can be required.[26] Nevertheless, where the original is illegible and thus effectively destroyed,[27] Rule 1004(1) rejects Wigmore's suggestion and admits any secondary evidence.[28] In such a situation the proponent would likely elect to use the duplicate because of its high probative value, but he is permitted to prove the contents with any available secondary evidence.

[24] *Cf.* Evans v. Holsinger, 242 Iowa 990, 995, 48 N.W.2d 250, 252-53 (1951) (where birth certificate duplicate lacked complete information due to deletion, original required). *See also* Liberty Chair Co. v. Crawford, 193 N.C. 531, 533, 137 S.E. 577, 578 (1927) (court rejected carbon copies of letters because of a lack of proper foundation); Mitchell v. United States, 214 Ga. 473, 475, 105 S.E. 337, 338 (1958) (alleged carbon copy rejected, since no proof of any original and copy contained signature only in type).

[25] *Cf.* Von Bumei v. Whirlpool Corp., 362 F. Supp. 1182, 1187 (N.D. Cal. 1973) (duplicate excluded where discovery orders violated).

[26] 4 WIGMORE, § 1229, at 535.

[27] Falls v. Griffith, Wright 303 (1833).

[28] *See* § 1004.11, *infra.*

Chapter 1004

RULE 1004. ADMISSIBILITY OF OTHER EVIDENCE OF CONTENTS

Rule 1004 reads as follows:

The original is not required, and other evidence of the contents of a writing, recording, or photograph is admissible if—

(1) *Originals lost or destroyed*. All originals are lost or have been destroyed, unless the proponent lost or destroyed them in bad faith; or

(2) *Original not obtainable*. No original can be obtained by any available judicial process or procedure; or

(3) *Original in possession of opponent*. At a time when an original was under the control of the party against whom offered, he was put on notice, by the pleadings or otherwise, that the contents would be a subject of proof at the hearing, and he does not produce the original at the hearing; or

(4) *Collateral matters*. The writing, recording, or photograph is not closely related to a controlling issue.

§ 1004.1　Exceptions to Production of the Original—An Overview.

Rule 1004 lists four general situations in which originals are excused and in which secondary evidence may be used to prove the contents of a writing, recording or photograph.[1] The Rule codifies exceptions traditionally accepted by Federal courts.[2]

If one of the Rule 1004 exceptions applies, a party may prove the contents of a writing, recording or photograph with any secondary evidence.[3] Rule 1004 rejects the concept of degrees of secondary evidence and allows any form of secondary evidence to be used to prove the contents of the original where an exception is satisfied. Accordingly, duplicates need not be produced instead of other secondary evidence where the original is not required.[4]

The broad applicability of Rule 1004 is superseded in certain situations by Rule 1005, and in effect, Rule 1005 does erect a hierarchy of secondary evidence for the proof of contents of public records.[5] Where original public records are unavailable, certified copies are required if available. Rule 1005 also provides for the admission of other secondary evidence where neither

---

[1] *See, generally*, McCORMICK §§ 234-39; 5 WEINSTEIN, ¶¶ 1004(1)[01]-[05], 1004(2)[01], 1004(3)[01], 1004(4)[01]; 5 LOUISELL & MUELLER, §§ 582-87; 4 WIGMORE, §§ 1188, 1189, 1192-1217, 1252-54, 1264-75. *See also* Levin, *Authentication and Contents of Writings*, 10 RUTGERS L. REV. 632 (1956); Note, *Symposium—The Proposed Federal Rules of Evidence: Part II—Authentication and the Best Evidence Rule Under the Federal Rules of Evidence*, 16 WAYNE L. REV. 195 (1969); Note, *Function of Judge and Jury*, 43 HARV. L. REV. 165 (1929); Comment, *Evidence—Degrees of Secondary Evidence—Problems in Application of the So-Called "American Rule"*, 38 MICH. L. REV. 864 (1940); Note, *Evidence—What is Required to Establish a Lost Instrument*, 15 U. DET. L.J. 192 (1952); Note, *Evidence—Documents— "Best Evidence" Rule Applied to Prevent Introduction of a Recording of a Destroyed Recording*, 64 HARV. L. REV. 1369 (1951); Note, *Charred Documents*, 16 Am. Jur., Proof of Facts, 665 (1965).

[2] Renner v. Bank of Columbia, 22 U.S. (9 Wheat.) 257, 260 (1824); McCORMICK, § 237; 4 WIGMORE, §§ 1188, 1189, 1192-98.

[3] United States v. Shoels, 685 F.2d 379, 384 (10th Cir. 1982) (prosecution could introduce photographs of checks taken by FBI when original checks were stolen and no bad faith shown); United States v. Cambindo Valenica, 609 F.2d 603, 633 (2d Cir. 1979), *cert. denied*, 446 U.S. 940, 100 S.Ct. 2163, 64 L.Ed.2d 795 (1980) (citing Treatise); Diplomat Homes, Inc. v. Commercial Standard Insurance Co., 394 F. Supp. 558, 561 (W.D. No. 1975) (citing Rule 1004).

[4] *Cf.* 4 WIGMORE, § 1229, at 535 (allowing secondary evidence on the basis of discretion; noting value of duplicate). *See also* Neville Construction Co. v. Cook Paint and Varnish Co., 671 F.2d 1107, 1110 (8th Cir. 1982) (in breach of warranty action by buyer of insulation for losses suffered as a result of fire, no error in permitting buyer to testify concerning contents of defendant's brochure describing fire retardant characteristics of insulation when fire destroyed brochure; plaintiff did not have to produce similar brochure distributed by defendant since no degrees of secondary evidence are recognized); United States v. Standing Soldier, 538 F.2d 196, 203 (8th Cir. 1976), *cert. denied*, 429 U.S. 1025, 97 S.Ct. 646, 50 L.Ed.2d 627 (1976) (oral testimony of contents of note could be given, since Rule 1004 recognizes no degrees of secondary evidence).

[5] *See* § 1005.4 of this Treatise.

original nor certified copies of public records are available.[6] The Rule 1005 exception provision generally parallels Rule 1004.[7]

Rule 1004 reflects the theory that total exclusion of relevant evidence is less desirable than admission of relevant secondary evidence,[8] and functionally, Rule 1004 requires the party offering the secondary evidence to lay a foundation justifying the nonproduction of the original. Accordingly, the party offering the secondary evidence bears the burden of showing either that the original is unavailable for one of the reasons listed in Rule 1004(1) through (3) or that the original need not be produced because it concerns only a collateral matter. Where the court accepts the adequacy of the foundation, the secondary evidence may be used.[9]

§ 1004.2   Originals Lost or Destroyed—An Overview.

Rule 1004(1) codifies the principle long accepted in the Federal system that where an original is lost or destroyed, secondary evidence of the contents of the original is admissible[10] providing the party offering the secondary evidence has not lost or destroyed the original in bad faith.[11] The Rule, however, allows admission of secondary evidence offered by a party who lost or destroyed the original as long as the action was not taken in bad faith.[12]

Rule 1004(1) reflects the policy of Article X by requiring the best *available* evidence.[13] Because the best evidence, *i.e.* the original, is not being offered, Rule 1004(1) places the burden on the party offering secondary evidence to establish as a foundation that the original has been lost or destroyed.

Although it may be impossible in a particular case to prove directly that all originals have been lost or destroyed, the court may be satisfied by circumstantial evidence that the original has been lost or destroyed.[14] The

---

[6] *See* Rule 1005.

[7] *See* § 1005.4 of this Treatise (noting generally parallel treatment but raising question of dissimilarity where the public record is relevant to a collateral matter only).

[8] *See, generally,* McCormick, § 237.

[9] *See* § 1008.3 of this Treatise (determination of preliminary question of law for court to decide).

[10] *See* Rule 1005, Advisory Committee's Note.

[11] *See* 2 Wigmore, § 291, at 221.

[12] *See* United States v. Balzano, 687 F.2d 6, 7-8 (1st Cir. 1982) (duplicate of tape ad-

missible where tape was knowingly erased by government in order to transfer tape to cassette capable of audio replay; no bad faith and extensive showing of mechanics of original recording); United States v. Conry, 631 F.2d 599, 600 (9th Cir. 1980) (proof of contents of waiver through circumstantial evidence was appropriate).

[13] *See* McCormick, § 237, at 714-15 ("The production of documents rule is principally aimed, not at securing a writing at all hazards and in every instance, but at securing the best *obtainable* evidence of its contents.")

[14] *See* § 1008.3 of this Treatise.

court has substantial discretion in its determination of the adequacy of the foundation establishing the unavailability of the original.[15]

Finally, it should be noted that an original that has been mutilated or has become illegible is treated as one that has been destroyed.[16]

§ 1004.3   Proof of Loss or Destruction.

Courts have traditionally placed the burden for proof of loss or destruction on the party offering secondary evidence.[17] The party offering the secondary evidence has the obligation to lay a foundation satisfactory to the court to show that the original cannot be produced.[18]

Rule 1004(1) does not expressly require that a party offering secondary evidence show that he undertook a reasonable or diligent search where he predicates non-production of the original on loss.[19] Nevertheless, Federal courts have traditionally required such a foundation where loss of the original is offered to justify use of secondary evidence.[20] The traditional requirement of a search will logically have continued applicability because in most situations the only way to prove loss is to show that the original could not be found following a reasonable and diligent search.[21] Of course, in particular circumstances, a showing of a reasonable or diligent search may be inadequate to prove loss or destruction.[22]

[15] Probst v. Trustees of Board of Domestic Missions, 129 U.S. 182, 188, 9 S.Ct. 263, 266, 32 L.Ed. 642, 644 (1889) (conceded that large amount of discretion must be used in trial court to determine whether original was shown to have been lost). *See also* Wright v. Farmers Co-op of Arkansas and Oklahoma, 681 F.2d 549, 553 (8th Cir. 1982); United States v. Covello, 410 F.2d 536, 543 (2d Cir. 1969), *cert. denied*, 396 U.S. 879, 90 S.Ct. 150, 24 L.Ed.2d 136 (1969); United States v. Ross, 321 F.2d 61, 69-70 (2d Cir. 1963), *cert. denied*, 375 U.S. 894, 84 S.Ct. 170, 11 L.Ed.2d 123 (1963); Willhoit v. Commissioner, 308 F.2d 259, 265 (9th Cir. 1962).

[16] 5 WEINSTEIN, ¶ 1004(1)[05], at 1004-22; 5 LOUISELL & MUELLER, § 584, at 487-88. *See also* In re Estate of Marcotte, 170 Kan. 189, 193, 224 P.2d 998, 1001 (1950).

[17] Hacker v. Price, 166 Pa. Super. 404, 407, 71 A.2d 851, 857 (1950). *See also* Woicicky v. Anderson, 95 Conn. 534, 536, 111 A. 986, 988 (1920).

[18] *See* § 1008.3 of this Treatise. Trial courts will require varying degrees of cer-

tainty in establishing the loss or destruction of a document. The proponent, however, will not have to establish the loss or destruction of a document beyond a reasonable doubt. *See* United States v. Sutter, 62 U.S. (21 How.) 170, 175, 16 L.Ed. 119, 123 (1958); Western, Inc. v. United States, 234 F.2d 211, 213 (8th Cir. 1956).

[19] *See* 4 WIGMORE, § 1195 (outlining tests for loss or destruction).

[20] *See, e.g.,* Colvin v. United States, 479 F.2d 998, 1004 (9th Cir. 1973) (wrongful death action brought by surviving spouse; error to permit plaintiff to testify as to decedent's probable income on the basis of daily diary which decedent kept); Nager Electric Co. v. United States, 442 F.2d 936, 951 (Ct. Cl. 1971); Kenner v. Commissioner, 445 F.2d 19, 21-24 (7th Cir. 1971) (tax court sua sponte rejected testimony by physician taxpayer as to amounts he advanced to and obtained by way of reimbursements from a charitable hospital which he operated).

[21] MCCORMICK, § 237, at 715.

[22] *See* DeAddio v. Darling & Co., 112 F. Supp. 166, 167 (N.D. Ohio 1952).

Only where loss can be proven directly, or where the adverse party admits the loss, will the proponent of the secondary evidence be free of the obligation to show that he or she has undertaken a reasonable and diligent search.[23]

§ 1004.4   Bad Faith Loss or Destruction.

Rule 1004(1) does not absolutely bar a proponent from introducing secondary evidence to prove the contents of the original where that party has itself lost or destroyed the original. Rule 1004(1) only prohibits a party from introducing secondary evidence where the party has lost or destroyed the original in bad faith.[24]

Whether bad faith destruction is involved is a question to be decided by the court prior to admission of the secondary evidence.[25] It should be noted that the adequacy of a foundation accounting for nonproduction of an original due to loss or destruction may depend on a party's showing of the absence of bad faith in the loss or destruction of the original.[26]

While Rule 1004(1) does not define "bad faith," it is clear that the term applies to the destruction of an original with the intent of preventing its use as evidence or with the intent of perpetrating a fraud.[27]

§ 1004.5   Unobtainability of an Original.

Rule 1004(2) codifies the traditional federal practice of relieving the proponent from using the original to prove contents where the original is not obtainable by available judicial process.[28] Rule 1004(2) is an acknowledgment that the unobtainability of an original is tantamount to the original's loss or destruction.

Although the Rule does not define the circumstances under which an original is unobtainable, prior case law provides that an original is unavail-

[23] McCormick, § 237, at 715.

[24] See 4 Wigmore, § 1198, at 455; Consolidated Coke Co. v. Commissioner, 25 B.T.A. 345, 357-58 (1932), aff'd, 70 F.2d 446 (3d Cir. 1934) (in Tax Court proceedings, corporate taxpayer offered purported copy of minutes; secondary evidence disregarded since to permit a party to litigation to deliberately destroy evidence and then in his own behalf introduce a copy made by himself and his attorney would subvert the basic principles of the best evidence rule and promote chicanery).

[25] See § 1008.3 of this Treatise.

[26] Estate of Gryder v. Commissioner, 705 F.2d 336, 338; United States v. Shoels, 685 F.2d 379, 384; United States v. Balzano, 687 F.2d 6, 8 (1st Cir. 1982).

[27] McCormick, § 237, at 716.

[28] United States v. Benedict, 647 F.2d 928, 932-33 (9th Cir. 1981), cert. denied, 454 U.S. 1087, 102 S.Ct. 648, 70 L.Ed.2d 624 (1981) (testimony by DEA agents as to business records in Thailand).

able when it is merely shown that the original is outside the court's jurisdiction.[29] Nothing in Rule 1004(2) alters pre-Rule Federal law which admits secondary evidence without any showing of an effort to obtain the original once it has been established that the original is outside the court's jurisdiction.[30] However, Rule 1002(2) requires that the proponent convince the court that no available practicable judicial process or procedure will bring forth the original.

Judge Weinstein suggests, however, that courts should require a party who wishes to obtain a document from a nonparty outside of the court's jurisdiction under Rule 45(e) of the Federal Rules of Civil Procedure, to first attempt to depose the non-party possessing the document. Under Rule 28(a) of the Rules of Civil Procedure, depositions can be taken anywhere in the United States. Additionally, a subpoena duces tecum can then be ordered under Rule 45(d) to require the witness to bring the document to the deposition. If the witness fails to bring the document to the deposition, a sufficient showing has been made under Rule 1004(2). If the witness appears with the document, and will not give up possession of the document, then the party should make a copy and have it admitted in lieu of the original under Rule 1003.[31]

Where, the original at issue is a public record of a foreign jurisdiction, Rule 1004(2) is preempted by Rule 1005 which requires a certified copy to be used where the original cannot be produced.[32]

Unavailability as a basis for justifying use of secondary evidence may arise in a number of diverse situations. Rule 1004(2) is applicable where a third party within the jurisdiction refuses to produce a document.[33] Rule 1004(2) might also be the basis for the admission of secondary evidence of the contents of writings inscribed on objects where the objects cannot be readily produced in court. Accordingly, inscriptions on gravestones could be proven by secondary evidence where the court determines that gravestones are writings.[34] Another basis for nonobtainability of the original is presented where disclosure of the original is prevented by privilege.[35]

---

[29] See, e.g., Hartzell v. United States, 72 F.2d 569, 598 (8th Cir. 1934), cert. denied, 293 U.S. 621, 55 S.Ct. 216, 79 L.Ed. 708 (1934) (since cablegrams were sent from London, England, and the original was out of the jurisdiction of the court, such secondary evidence became admissible).

[30] United States v. Ratliff, 623 F.2d 1293, 1296 (8th Cir. 1980), cert. denied, 449 U.S. 876, 101 S.Ct. 220, 66 L.Ed.2d 98 (1980) (trial court assumed it had no subpoena power over documents in Germany, in absence of demonstration, appellate court did not find court's finding to be clearly erroneous).

[31] 5 WEINSTEIN, ¶ 1004(2)[01], at 1004-24; 5 LOUISELL & MUELLER, § 585, at 498-99.

[32] Rule 1005. See § 1005.4 of this Treatise.

[33] See MCCORMICK, § 238.

[34] See, 4 WIGMORE, § 1214, at 496. See also 1001.4 of this Treatise.

[35] See United States v. Haugen, 58 F.Supp. 436, 438-39 (E.D. Wash. 1944) aff'd, 153 F.2d 850 (9th Cir. 1946) (where original confidential, secondary evidence admitted).

Whether a party has adequately shown that the original is not obtainable is a question for the court.[36] Clearly, the court has considerable discretion in making its determination.[37]

§ 1004.6   Unobtainability and Use of Subpoenas.

Although no showing of an effort to produce the original is required where the original is outside the court's jurisdiction,[38] such an effort must be shown where the original is within the jurisdiction.[39] Essentially, the effort required is that of serving a writ of subpoena duces tecum on the party possessing the original.[40] Civil Rule 45(d)(1) of the Federal Rules of Civil Procedure provides for service of such a writ. Secondary evidence should be admitted where the possessor of the original refuses to obey the subpoena.[41] Of course, failure to obey the subpoena may be deemed contempt of court.[42]

§ 1004.7   Original Possessed by Opponent.

Rule 1004(3) provides that where an adverse party (i) possesses or controls an original, (ii) has received notice that the contents of the original will be an issue at a hearing, and (iii) fails to produce the original, secondary evidence of the original's contents will be admissible if offered by the opponent of the party in possession of the original.[43] Rule 1004(3) codifies the traditional common law rule and effects no change in pre-Rule practice.[44]

It has been suggested that Rule 1004(3) is supported in part by the theory that an original which an adverse party refuses to produce is not more accessible than originals lost, destroyed, or unobtainable.[45] Rule 1004(3) differs from Rule 1004(2), however, in that a party who has provided adequate notice is permitted to offer secondary evidence even though the original could be, but has not been, subpoenaed or otherwise produced in

---

[36] See § 1008.3 of this Treatise.

[37] Id.

[38] See § 1004.1 of this Treatise.

[39] United States v. Taylor, 648 F.2d 565, 570 (9th Cir. 1981), cert. denied, 454 U.S. 866, 102 S.Ct. 329, 70 L.Ed.2d 168 (1981) (trial court did not err in admitting photocopy of crucial letter where government represented that subpoenas requesting the original letter had been served on the parties and the original was not produced, and defendant's counsel failed to object to admission of copy).

[40] Id.

[41] McCORMICK, § 238, at 717.

[42] F.R. Civ. P. 45(f).

[43] See, generally, McCORMICK, § 239; 5 WEINSTEIN, ¶ 1004(3)[01]; 5 LOUISELL & MUELLER, § 586; 4 WIGMORE, § 1199.

[44] See, generally, Hodgson v. Humphries, 454 F.2d 1279, 1282-83 (10th Cir. 1972); Jones v. Atlantic Refining Co., 55 F.Supp. 17, 20-21 (E.D. Pa. 1941).

[45] McCORMICK, § 239, at 718.

discovery.[46] Accordingly, the more impressive justification of Rule 1004(3) is that it is compelled by the nature of the adversary process, *i.e.*, an opponent to the introduction of secondary evidence will not be heard to object where he has possession of the original and has received notice that the contents will be proven at trial.

The question of whether the conditions have been met for admission of secondary evidence is one for the court to decide within a wide range of discretion.[47] The burden for laying the foundation is on the party offering the secondary evidence.[48]

§ 1004.8   Possession or Control.

In its applicability to originals in the possession of the opponent, Rule 1004(3) accepts Wigmore's analysis that an original need not be in the actual personal custody of an adverse party for secondary evidence to be admissible after appropriate notice.[49] Instead, control of the original will suffice.[50]

The burden of proving control of the original by an adverse party is on the party offering the secondary evidence,[51] and the proof must be sufficient to satisfy the trial court.[52]

§ 1004.9   Notice to Opponent.

As a condition precedent to the admission of secondary evidence, Rule 1004(3) requires that the party in possession of the original be given appropriate notice.[53] The notice required, however, need only indicate that proof of the contents of the original will be at issue at the trial or hearing,[54] and Rule 1004(3) does not require notice demanding production of the original.[55] The notice, as McCormick notes, lacks "compulsive force," and it

[46] *See* § 1004.2 of this Treatise.

[47] *See* § 1008.3 of this Treatise.

[48] McCormick, § 239, at 718.

[49] 4 Wigmore, § 1200, at 462.

[50] Transamerica Insurance Co. v. Bloomfield, 401 F.2d 357, 360-61 (6th Cir. 1968) (construction performance bond; trial court did not permit consultant to testify that he had examined the books; court reversed directed verdict which had been entered for defendant since the surety was not required to produce the books of its principles where defendant had testified that his company was a "dummy corporation"; it should be assumed that he was familiar with its books).

[51] 4 Wigmore, § 1201, at 463.

[52] *See* § 1008.3 of this Treatise.

[53] *E.g.*, United States v. Levine, 546 F.2d 658, 668 (5th Cir. 1977), *reh. denied*, 551 F.2d 687 (5th Cir. 1977) (in alleged conspiracy and interstate shipment of obscene films, "release print" of film in question was properly admitted in evidence despite defense Best Evidence objection that "work print" should have been offered).

[54] *See* McCormick, § 239, at 718.

[55] *Id. See also* Comment, *Authentication and the Best Evidence Rule under the Federal Rules of Evidence*, 16 Wayne L. Rev. 195, 230 (1969).

merely provides the party possessing the original with the opportunity to prevent the admission of secondary evidence by production of the original at the trial.[56]

Rule 1004(3) continues the traditional rule which provides that satisfactory notice may be effected through the pleading or through other means.[57] Rule 1004(3) does not require any formal notice. Consequently, where the nature of the action indicates that the adverse party will be charged with possession of a written instrument, formal notice is unnecessary as a condition for the admission of secondary evidence.[58]

Rule 1004(3) does not discard the traditional position that notice must be reasonable. Accordingly, notice usually is not reasonable unless given prior to commencement of trial.[59] Only if it is apparent that the original is present in the courtroom in the personal custody of an adverse party will notice at trial be adequate.[60]

The burden of establishing the adequacy of notice is on the party offering the secondary evidence, and the proof must be sufficient to satisfy the discretion of the court.[61]

§ 1004.10   Failure to Produce the Original.

Simple failure by the adverse party to bring the original to the trial or hearing satisfies the non-production condition of Rule 1004(3). Additionally, the offering by the adverse party of a document denied by the proponent of the secondary evidence to be the original constitutes failure to produce the original.[62]

If an adverse party fails to produce the original when secondary evidence is offered, traditionally that party has been barred from subsequent introduction of the original later in the trial or hearing.[63] Rule 403 provides a similar basis, viz., unfair prejudice, for excluding the original.[64]

§ 1004.11   Secondary Evidence and Collateral Matters.

Rule 1004(4) restates the common law rule that proof of the contents of

---

[56] McCormick, § 239, at 718. See also, TransAmerica Insurance Co. v. Bloomfield, 401 F.2d 357, 357 (6th Cir. 1968).

[57] See, 5 Weinstein, ¶ 1004(3)[01], at 1004-27; McCormick, § 239, at 718; 4 Wigmore, § 1205, at 470.

[58] See United States v. Marcantoni, 590 F.2d 1324, 1329-30 (5th Cir. 1979), cert. denied, 441 U.S. 937, 99 S.Ct. 2063, 60 L.Ed.2d 666 (1979) (court suggested that

defendants were "put on notice" that serial numbers of two $10 bills "would be subject of proof").

[59] 5 Weinstein, ¶ 1004(3)[01], at 1004-27; 4 Wigmore, § 1208, at 480.

[60] Id.

[61] See § 1008.3 of this Treatise.

[62] 4 Wigmore, § 1209, at 483.

[63] Id. at § 1210, at 485.

[64] See § 403.1 et seq. of this Treatise.

writings, recordings, or photographs may be proven by secondary evidence where the contents are not closely related to a controlling issue in the litigation.[65] As Wigmore has noted, when the terms of a document are not the basis of the dispute, considerations of convenience support admission of secondary evidence.[66] The court has discretion in determining whether proof of the contents is collateral to the matter at issue, and it can require production of the original if a genuine question arises as to the original's contents.[67]

§ 1004.12   When Originals are Collateral.

Rule 1004(4) does not provide criteria for determining when the contents of an original are merely collateral to the question at issue. McCormick, however, has suggested that three principal factors should be weighed by the court:

> . . . the centrality of the writing to the principal issues of the litigation; the complexity of the relevant features of the writing; and the existence of genuine dispute as to the contents of the writing.[68]

The respective weight to be accorded these factors is left to the discretion of the court.

Pre-Rule case law provides some indication of standards to be applied in determining when a matter is collateral. For example, one case held that the contents of a patent assignment may be proven by secondary evidence where the issue is the validity of title.[69] Because the patent was issued on the assignment and the title was perfected, the assignment was held to be merely a collateral paper affecting the title.[70]

In the case of *Blachly v. United States*,[71] the court excused the production of the originals of promissory notes which the defendants had acquired from the targets of a fraudulent scheme to sell water softeners. The court held the notes were not introduced to prove their exact terms, but instead were introduced to show the scheme by which the fraud was perpetrated.[72]

---

[65] *See* United States v. Duffy, 454 F.2d 809, 811-12 (5th Cir. 1972); Reistrapper v. United States, 258 F.2d 379, 384 (8th Cir. 1968); Scullin v. Harper, 79 F. 460, 463 (2d Cir. 1897).

[66] 4 Wigmore, § 1253, at 595. *See also* Bouldin v. Massie's Heirs, 20 U.S. 122, 125, 5 L.Ed. 414, 417 (7 Wheat. 1822).

[67] *See* § 1008.3 of this Treatise.

[68] McCormick, § 234, at 710. *See also*, 4 Wigmore, § 1253, at 595.

[69] Bouldin v. Massie's Heirs, 20 U.S. 122, 125, 5 L.Ed. 414, 417 (7 Wheat. 1822).

[70] *Id.*

[71] 380 F.2d 665, 674 (5th Cir. 1967).

[72] *Id.* at 674, n.16.

The Advisory Committee's Note to Rule 1004 provides two additional examples: it is not necessary to produce the original of "a newspaper in an action for the price of publishing [the] defendant's advertisements,"[73] nor is it necessary to produce the original of the "street car transfer of [a] plaintiff claiming status as a passenger."[74]

[73] *See* Rule 1004, Advisory Committee's Note.
[74] *Id.*

Chapter 1005

RULE 1005. PUBLIC RECORDS

SECTION

1005.1   Public records—In general

1005.2   Official records and filed or recorded documents

1005.3   Certification of copies

1005.4   Reasonable diligence and other evidence of contents

Rule 1005 reads as follows:

The contents of an official record, or of a document authorized to be recorded or filed and actually recorded or filed, including data compilations in any form, if otherwise admissible, may be proved by copy, certified as correct in accordance with Rule 902 or testified to be correct by a witness who has compared it with the original. If a copy which complies with the foregoing cannot be obtained by the exercise of reasonable diligence, then other evidence of the contents may be given.

§ 1005.1   Public Records—In General.

Rule 1005 provides that a copy of the public record may be used to prove contents of the original record where the copy is certified as correct in accordance with Rule 902 or authenticated as correct by testimony from a witness who has compared the copy with the original.[1] The Rule also provides that if such a copy cannot be obtained by the exercise of reasonable diligence, "other evidence of the contents may be given."[2]

[1] *See, generally,* McCormick, § 240, 5 Weinstein, ¶¶ 1005[01]-[08]; 5 Louisell & Mueller, §§ 592-93; 4 Wigmore, §§ 1215-18. *See also* Brown, *Authentication and Contents of Writings,* 4 Ariz. St. L.J. 611 (1969); Cleary & Strong, *The Best Evidence Rule: An Evaluation in Context,* 51 Iowa L. Rev. 825 (Summer 1966); Levin, *Authentication and the Content of Writings,* 10 Rutgers L. Rev. 632 (1956); Orfield, *Proof of Official Records in Federal Cases,* 22 Mont. L. Rev. 137 (1961); Tracey, *The In-troduction of Documentary Evidence,* 24 Iowa L. Rev. 436 (1939); Comment, *Authentication and the Best Evidence Rule Under the Federal Rules of Evidence,* Wayne L. Rev. (1969).

[2] United States v. Rodriguez, 524 F.2d 485, 487-88 (5th Cir. 1975), *cert. denied,* 424 U.S. 972, 96 S.Ct. 1474, 47 L.Ed. 2d 741 (Xerox copy of vehicle certificate of title satisfied Rule 1005. *See also* the discussion of Rule 901(b)[03], *supra.*

By establishing a preference for certified copies of official records and filed or recorded documents, Rule 1005 introduces into the Rules the concept of degrees of secondary evidence for public records.[3] Copies of official records that are authenticated by the stipulated requirements are preferred to any other secondary evidence which might be offered to prove the contents of a public record. Accordingly, Rule 1005 preempts Rule 1003's general provision that duplicates are admissible as originals.[4] Additionally, Rule 1005 supersedes Rule 1004 insofar as it allows the use of a copy certified or testified to be correct without any showing that the original is lost, destroyed, unobtainable or pertinent to a collateral matter. It further supersedes Rule 1004 by creating a mandatory preference for the use of certified copies over other types of secondary evidence. Rule 1004 creates no such preference once a prerequisite for dispensing with the original has been shown. Rule 1005 does not, however, supersede or conflict with Rule 1004 or other Rules in Article X when the object of proof is an unfiled original where a copy of the original has been filed or recorded with a public agency.[5] Rule 1005 comes into play only when the contents of the document actually on file are sought to be proved.

The underlying policies of Rule 1005 are convenience and protection of the public. The public would be inconvenienced by the absence of official records from the offices in which they are regularly kept. Additionally, the risk of loss or damage of such records would be present if the originals were required to be offered into evidence.[6] Accordingly, the certification requirement both protects the public and ensures a high degree of reliability of the evidence. Rule 1005 does not require, however, that copies of public records be offered in lieu of originals. Logically, an original is admissible if it is properly authenticated.[7]

---

[3] See 4 WIGMORE, § 1269, at 652.

[4] 5 WEINSTEIN, ¶ 1005[01] at 1005-4; 5 LOUISELL & MUELLER, § 593, at 531. See, e.g., Amoco Production Co. v. United States, 619 F.2d 1383, 1390-91 (10th Cir. 1980) (photocopy of what was purportedly a conformed copy of deed found in case file of the Bureau of Land Management would not necessarily qualify as a "public record" for purposes of authentication or hearsay; court therefore rejected defense contention that the records were authenticated under Federal Rules).

[5] 5 WEINSTEIN, ¶ 1005[01], at 1005-4. The example is given of a deed, the original of which is returned to the owner after a photostat is made for the public record. Under this analysis, "The contents of the origi-nal in the hands of the owner may be proved in any way permitted by Article X." See also, Amoco Production Co. v. United States, 619 F.2d 1383, 1390 (10th Cir. 1980) (original deed is not a public record and Rule 1004 rather than Rule 1005 applies to it).

[6] See, e.g., Seese v. Voltswagenwerk A.G., 648 F.2d 833, 845-46 (3d Cir. 1981), cert. denied, 454 U.S. 867, 102 S.Ct. 330, 70 L.Ed. 2d 168 (1981) (computer printouts of the Fatal Accident Reporting System consisting of statistical information pertaining to fatal accidents maintained by National Highway Traffic and Safety Administration admissible as public records). See also McCORMICK, § 240; 4 WIGMORE, § 1218.

[7] See Rule 901.

§ 1005.2 Official Records and Filed or Recorded Documents.

Rule 1005 applies when the contents of public records or filed or recorded documents are sought to be proven. Public records include "official records" as well as documents "authorized to be recorded or filed and actually recorded or filed."

While not expressly defined, the term "official record" should apply to any document prepared and retained by any agency of government, state or federal, foreign or domestic. Such a broad reading of "official record" is indicated by the policy supporting the Rule discussed in § 1005.3 of this Treatise. Additional guidance as to the scope of the term "official record" is only marginally provided by the Rules of Procedure. Civil Rule 44, which also applies to "official records," and which might provide an indication of the interpretation of that term, has not been treated by the courts as a term of art.[8] In practice, however, the absence of a definition should not be problematic, and the horizon of the term "public record" should be broadly interpreted. The courts have treated the following as public records: court records,[9] weather reports,[10] summaries of foreign census records,[11] selective service records,[12] copies of foreign marriage records,[13] and tax returns.[14]

Rule 1005 also applies to documents "authorized to be filed or recorded and actually filed or recorded," thereby authorizing the proof of the contents of such recorded documents as deeds, leases or mortgages[15] by a copy

[8] *See* 5 WEINSTEIN, ¶ 1005[03] at 1005-7; 5 LOUISELL & MUELLER, § 592, at 524. *See also* Yaich v. United States, 283 F.2d 613, 616-17 (9th Cir. 1960) (interdepartmental memo found to be a "public document"); Cohen v. United States, 258 F. 355, 362 (2d Cir. 1919) (paper kept on file in a designated office which cannot be removed became "official").

[9] United States v. Locke, 425 F.2d 313, 315 (5th Cir. 1970) (jailbreak prosecution; photostatic copy of record of judgment and commitment was properly admitted); Maroon v. Immigration and Naturalization Services, 364 F.2d 982, 984 (8th Cir. 1966) (petition for review of deportation orders; copies of records of indictment, judgment, sentence, and commitment properly admitted).

[10] Celanese Corp. of America v. Vandalia Warehouse Corp., 424 F.2d 1176, 1180 (7th Cir. 1970) (copy of a weather report was not admitted because it lacked the proper certification); H.R. Anderson v. Swift Co., 380 F.2d 988, 990 (6th Cir. 1967) (weather re-

port admitted); Minnehaha County, S.D. v. Kelley, 150 F.2d 356, 361 (8th Cir. 1945) (wrongful death action; summaries of weather records were admitted because the actual records were voluminous and intricate, and were of doubtful intelligibility to the jury without these explanatory summaries).

[11] United States v. Ghaloub, 385 F.2d 567, 571 (2d Cir. 1966) (Syrian census records were official records).

[12] Pardo v. United States, 369 F.2d 922, 925 (5th Cir. 1966) (authenticated by direct testimony of custodian).

[13] United States v. D'Agostino, 338 F.2d 490, 492 (2d Cir. 1964).

[14] United States v. Farris, 517 F.2d 226, 227-28 (7th Cir. 1975), *cert. denied*, 423 U.S. 892, 96 S.Ct. 189, 46 L.Ed 2d 123 (1975) (printouts of computerized tax records).

[15] Amoco Production Co. v. United States, 619 F.2d 1383, 1390 (10th Cir. 1980) (trial court properly applied Rule 1005 in admitting certified copy of recorded deed).

which meets the requisites of the Rule. The Rule pertains to *filed* documents as well as to *recorded* documents.[16] Whether a document is authorized to be filed or recorded will be of little significance if the document is actually filed or recorded because the filing or recording constitutes *prima facie* evidence of authorization.[17] The requirement that documents be authorized for filing or recording encompasses both permissive and mandatory filing or recording.[18]

§ 1005.3　Certification of Copies.

Rule 1005 provides that a copy of a public record may be authenticated by a certification as to its correctness made in compliance with Rule 902 or by testimony that it is correct from a witness who has compared the copy with the original. It should be noted that the required authentication concerns the accuracy of the copy, *i.e.*, the authentication testimony must show that the copy is an accurate reproduction of the original, and the accuracy of the actual contents of the original is not the pertinent issue.[19] Rule 902 provides that certified copies of public records are self-authenticating when the custodian or other person authorized to make a certification respecting a copy of an official report, record or recorded or filed document certifies the copy as correct.[20]

Federal law has long accepted an appropriate witness's testimony as proof of the correctness of a copy of a public record.[21] Nevertheless, the significance of this method of authenticating a copy is diminished by its excessive costs in comparison with the use of a certified copy.[22]

§ 1005.4　Reasonable Diligence and Other Evidence of Contents.

Rule 1005 provides that if, by the exercise of reasonable diligence, a copy that satisfies Rule 1005 cannot be obtained, other evidence of the contents of the public record may be admitted. If a public record is accessible to the public, a copy of that record should ordinarily be obtained by the exercise

---

[16] Cohen v. United States, 258 F. 355, 362 (2d Cir. 1919) (filed document in designated office is official).

[17] 5 Weinstein, ¶ 1005[04], at 1005-11; 5 Louisell & Mueller, § 593, at 533. *See, e.g.*, Amoco Production Co. v. United States, 619 F.2d 1383, 1390 (10th Cir. 1980).

[18] Cohen v. United States, 258 F. 355, 357-62 (2d Cir. 1919).

[19] 5 Weinstein, ¶ 1005[05], at 1005-11; 5 Louisell & Mueller, § 593, at 533.

[20] United States v. Farris, 517 F.2d 226, 227, n.1 (7th Cir. 1975), *cert. denied*, 423 U.S. 892, 96 S.Ct. 189, 46 L.Ed. 2d 123 (1975).

[21] Block v. United States, 7 Ct. Cl. 406, 412 (1871).

[22] 5 Weinstein, ¶ 1005[05], at 1005-11; 5 Louisell & Mueller, § 593, at 532-33.

of reasonable diligence. Nevertheless, failure to obtain a satisfactory copy might occur, for example, in regard to a foreign record where no official publication can be located or where the official transmitting the record fails to do so in a manner that complies with Rule 902. In such a case, if the court finds that the failure has occurred despite the exercise of reasonable diligence, any otherwise admissible secondary evidence may be offered to prove the contents of the document.[23] Secondary evidence might include, for example, an uncertified copy of a document, testimony by someone familiar with the contents of the document, or other documentary evidence, *e.g.*, a written summary of the contents of the official record.

Rule 1005 provides an exception to the requirement of production of a certified or authenticated copy that largely parallels Rule 1004's exception to the requirement of production of the original. In this regard, it might be questioned whether the standards for excusing production of the original set forth in Rule 1004 are incorporated into Rule 1005. The latter, for example, does not explicitly provide for the use of secondary evidence to prove the contents of public records relating to collateral matters as does Rule 1004(4). The possible justification for the differing treatment is the customary ease with which copies of public records can be obtained coupled with the persuasive nature of such records. Of course, it would be appropriate to construe the requirement of reasonable diligence as not requiring great exertion for a collateral matter, and a court would be justified in admitting secondary evidence in such instance.

---

[23] *But see* 4 Wigmore, § 1268, at 649 (stating that a party "must offer a copy, if he has one in his control, in preference to recollection testimony").

Chapter 1006

RULE 1006. SUMMARIES

Rule 1006 reads as follows:

> The contents of voluminous writings, recordings, or photographs which cannot conveniently be examined in court may be presented in the form of a chart, summary, or calculation. The originals, or duplicates, shall be made available for examination or copying, or both, by other parties at [a] reasonable time and place. The court may order that they be produced in court.

§ 1006.1 Summaries, Charts and Calculations—In General.

Rule 1006 codifies the traditional best evidence rule exception,[1] which provides that where writings are voluminous or multifarious, summaries, abstracts or schedules may be admitted in evidence.[2] Just as the best evidence rule has been expanded by the Federal Rules to apply to recordings and photographs,[3] this exception has been extended to apply to voluminous

---

[1] *See, generally,* McCORMICK, § 240, 5 WEINSTEIN, ¶¶ 1006[01]-[09]; 5 LOUISELL & MUELLER, §§ 598-600; 4 WIGMORE, § 1230. *See also* Brown, *Authentication and Contents of Writings,* 4 ARIZ. ST. L.J. 611 (1969); *Symposium on the Proposed Federal Rules of Evidence: Part II,* 16 WAYNE L. REV. 195 (1969); DEWEY, *Best Evidence Rule—Use of Summaries of Voluminous Originals,* 37 MICH. L. REV. 499 (1939); Comment, *Evidence: Best Evidence Rule: Admissibility of Secondary Evidence in Oklahoma,* 20 OKLA. L. REV. 56 (1967).

[2] Burton v. Driggs, 87 U.S. (20 Wall.) 125, 136, 22 L.Ed. 299, 306 (1873) (summary may be used to prove the contents of voluminous books and documents). *See also*

Hodgson v. Humphries, 454 F.2d 1279, 1281 (10th Cir. 1972) (Fair Labor Standards Act; summaries used to speed up trial and avoid unnecessary detailed documentation); Braunstein v. Massachusetts Bank & Trust Co., 443 F.2d 1281, 1284 (1st Cir. 1971) (audit used as summary); Boston Securities, Inc. v. United Bonding Insurance Co., 441 F.2d 1302, 1303 (8th Cir. 1971) (accountant's summary); McGuire v. Davis, 437 F.2d 570, 572 (5th Cir. 1971) (medical expenses); Miami National Bank v. Pennsylvania Insurance Co., 314 F. Supp. 858, 865 (D.C. Fla. 1970) (summaries of bank's records).

[3] *See* Rules 1001(1) and (2).

681

recordings or photographs. Rule 1006 provides that charts or calculations as well as summaries may be used to prove the contents of voluminous documents.

For a summary, calculation or chart to be admissible under Rule 1006, three conditions must be satisfied. First, the writings, recordings or photographs must be voluminous.[4] In keeping with Rule 1008, this is a question to be determined by the court.[5] The requirement that writings, recordings, or photographs be voluminous satisfies the general objective of this Rule, *i.e.*, maximizing the convenience of the presentation of evidence at trial.[6] Additionally, an issue of fairness, undue delay or redundancy under Rule 403 may be involved where the writings, recordings or photographs are not voluminous.[7] Second, a proper foundation must be laid for the introduction of the summary.[8] As a part of this requirement, the originals must be admissible for the summaries, calculations or charts based on those originals to be admissible.[9] Additionally, charts, summaries and calculations may not include information not contained or computed from the originals.[10] Third, the originals or duplicates must be made available to all litigants for examination or copying at a reasonable time and place.[11] This requirement provides all litigants with the opportunity to determine the accuracy, completeness and fairness of the charts, summaries or calculations.

Charts, summaries and calculations may be admissible under other Rules without satisfying the foregoing requirements. For example, where the originals on which a summary, chart or calculation is based are un-

[4] Nichols v. Upjohn Co., 610 F.2d 293, 294 (5th Cir. 1980) (the court admitted a summary of an FDA investigative report of a document of 94,000 pages). *See also* Javelin Investment, S.A. v. Ponce, 645 F.2d 92, 96 (1st Cir. 1981) (reviewing court doubted the need for a summary, since material involved was simple, short, and straight forward, and not the type of voluminous writings which could not conveniently be examined in court).

[5] *See* § 1008.3 of this Treatise.

[6] *See* § 1006.2 of this Treatise.

[7] *See* Rule 403.

[8] Phillips v. United States, 201 F. 259, 269 (8th Cir. 1912) (foundation must be laid before summaries may be introduced).

[9] Ford Motor Co. v. Auto Supply Co., Inc., 661 F.2d 1171, 1175 (8th Cir. 1981) (trademark infringement action; exhibit of summary of figures admissible, since the underlying figures would have been admissible); United States v. Seelig, 622 F.2d 207,

210 (6th Cir. 1980), *cert. denied*, 449 U.S. 869, 101 S.Ct. 206, 66 L.Ed. 2d 89 (1980) (admission of chart purporting to summarize sales activities at other drug stores was reversible error since there was no showing that other stores were the same size, covered same marketing area, charged same prices, etc.; chart therefore irrelevant).

[10] Pritchard v. Liggett & Myers Tobacco Co., 295 F.2d 292, 301 (3d Cir. 1961) (bibliography of original articles was not admissible as summary, since no showing was made that the materials were accurately summarized).

[11] Sylvania Electric Products, Inc. v. Flanagan, 352 F.2d 1005, 1007 (1st Cir. 1965) (admission of summary barred, where there was an inability to satisfactorily explain failure to produce originals); Flame Coal Co. v. United Mine Workers of America, 303 F.2d 39, 45 (6th Cir. 1962) (in absence of showing that missing originals cannot be produced, they must be produced).

available and one of the exceptions of Rule 1004 is satisfied, the summary, chart or calculation may be admissible as secondary evidence.[12] Alternatively, data compilations based on public records may be admissible under Rule 1005.

One apparent difference between Rule 1006 and prior case law is that an expert is no longer required to prepare the chart, summary or calculation.[13] Under Rule 1006, the fact that an expert did or did not prepare the chart, summary or calculation would be a matter affecting the weight of the evidence, not its admissibility. In practice, however, attorneys usually will use experts, such as accountants, when preparing a chart, summary or calculation.

§ 1006.2   Conceptual Basis for Rule 1006.

Unlike the general justification for the best evidence rule,[14] the conceptual basis for Rule 1006 is rooted both in the convenience and the practicability[15] of introducing into evidence the contents of voluminous writings, recordings or photographs. Although courts have been quite willing to admit charts, summaries, or calculations into evidence where such vehicles represent the only practical means of introducing the evidence, Rule 1006 provides that even where introduction of the originals is feasible, summaries may be introduced in any situation where convenience would be served.[16] The only limitation on this doctrine of convenience is imposed by Rule 403's prohibition of undue prejudice, delay and redundancy.[17]

§ 1006.3   Requirement of Availability of Originals or Duplicates.

Rule 1006 requires that either the original or a duplicate be made available to opposing parties for examination or copying at a reasonable time

---

[12] John Irving Shoe Co., Inc. v. Dugan, 93 F.2d 711, 712 (1st Cir. 1937) (secondary evidence of missing records not admissible without proof that they are lost, destroyed, or unavailable); Equitable Life Assur. Soc. of the United States v. Sieg, 53 F.2d 318, 319-20 (6th Cir. 1931) (summary of lost account books admissible as best evidence of their contents). *See also* Burton v. Driggs, 87 U.S. (20 Wall.) 125, 135, 22 L.Ed. 299, 307 (1873) (summary of unavailable bank books acceptable secondary evidence of their contents).

[13] *See* Needham v. White Laboratories, Inc., 639 F.2d 394, 403 (7th Cir. 1981) (but

the chart cannot be used as a foundation to admit articles upon which the chart was based, when the expert has not read all the articles).

[14] *See* § 1002.2 of this Treatise.

[15] 4 Wigmore, § 1230, at 535.

[16] *See* United States v. Denton, 556 F.2d 811, 816 (6th Cir. 1977), *cert. denied*, 434 U.S. 892, 98 S.Ct. 269, 54 L.Ed. 2d 178 (1977) (court approved admission of "composite tape" made from duplicate copies of taped telephone conversations).

[17] *See* Rule 403.

and place. Rule 1006 codifies the modern trend in that it requires only that documents be made available for inspection and copying, and the introduction of summaries is not conditional on the concomitant introduction of the originals or the delivery of the originals to the court for retention.[18] Rule 1006, however, provides for discretionary power in the court to order production of originals or duplicates.

Although Rule 1006 seems to impose an absolute requirement that the charts, summaries and exhibits be made available to all litigants, in light of Rules 102 and 103, it is not illogical to conclude that a party can effectively waive the requirements of Rule 1006 by a failure to object.

The development of liberal discovery and pre-trial conferences provides a framework within which Rule 1006 can effectively operate. Proponents of charts, summaries, and calculations can determine their admissibility by a motion in limine submitted prior to trial. Additionally, Federal Civil Procedure Rule 34 provides for discovery of documents in the possession of a party without court order.[19] Nevertheless, the availability requirement embodied in Rule 1006 is independent of the discovery procedure of Civil Procedure Rule 34.[20]

§ 1006.4   Laying the Proper Foundation.

In order for charts, summaries or calculations to be admitted, either the proponent must lay a proper foundation for their admission or their admissibility must be the subject of stipulation. Federal courts traditionally have required that where charts, summaries or calculations are to be introduced into evidence, the person who prepared the summaries, supervised the originals or controlled the originals, must testify to the foundation.[21]

---

[18] United States v. Clements, 588 F.2d 1030, 1038-39 (5th Cir. 1979), *cert. denied,* 440 U.S. 982, 99 S.Ct. 1792, 60 L.Ed. 2d 243 (1979) (alleged gambling operation; government witness was properly permitted to testify). *Cf.* Solari Furs v. United States, 436 F.2d 683, 685 (8th Cir. 1971) (no error in consideration of summaries of original and genuine business records and papers).

[19] *See* F.R.C.P. 34.

[20] *See* 5 WEINSTEIN, ¶ 1006[04], at 1006-10; 5 LOUISELL & MUELLER, § 600, at 557.

[21] McDaniel v. United States, 343 F.2d 785, 789 (5th Cir. 1965), *cert. denied,* 382 U.S. 826, 86 S.Ct. 59, 15 L.Ed. 2d 71 (1965) (government offered summaries of defendant's records prepared by a Certified Public Accountant, who was a member of SEC and expert; he was allowed to state his conclusions).

The foundation must show that the charts, summaries, or calculations accurately reflect the information included in, or computed from the originals. Accordingly, inadmissible hearsay evidence may not be included in the summary,[22] except in the situation under Rule 703 in which an expert witness is authorized to base his testimony on hearsay evidence.[23]

[22] United States v. Goss, 650 F.2d 1336, 1344 (5th Cir. 1981) (admission of summaries of testimony of out-of-court witness should not have been received over hearsay objection).

[23] *See* Rule 703. *See, generally,* §§ 703.1-.5 of this Treatise.

Chapter 1007

RULE 1007. TESTIMONY OR WRITTEN ADMISSION OF PARTY

SECTION
1007.1   Testimony or written admission of party—An overview
1007.2   Theory of Rule 1007
1007.3   Admissions by party's representatives

Rule 1007 reads as follows:

> Contents of writings, recordings, or photographs may be proved by the testimony or deposition of the party against whom offered or by his written admission, without accounting for the nonproduction of the original.

§ 1007.1   Testimony or Written Admission of Party—An Overview.

Rule 1007 sets forth an exception to the best evidence rule in providing for a method proving contents of a writing, recording or photograph other than through the use of the original.[1] Rule 1007 authorizes proof of contents through the written admission by the party against whom offered or through admissions by such party made in testimony or deposition. Under Rule 1007 there is no necessity of accounting for the nonproduction of the original.

Pre-Rule federal law provided that any oral admission by the party against whom offered, under oath or not, without accounting for nonproduction of the original, as to the contents of a writing or record, may be

---

[1] See, generally, McCORMICK, § 242; 5 WEINSTEIN, ¶¶ 1007[01]-[07]; 5 LOUISELL & MUELLER, §§ 605-606; 4 WIGMORE, § 1255. See also Comment, Symposium on the Proposed Federal Rules of Evidence: Part II, Authentication and the Best Evidence Rule Under the Proposed Rules of Evidence, 16 WAYNE L. REV. 195, 235 (1969); Comment, Evidence—Best Evidence Rule—Admissions of a Party as an Exception, 17 TEX. L. REV. 371 (1939).

used to prove the contents. This rule was established firmly in the leading English case, *Slatterie v. Pooley*,[2] and held that the defendant's out-of-court admission of an existing debt was admissible as original evidence, even though a schedule listing the debt ordinarily would have been the best evidence of the debt. Rule 1007 limits *Slatterie* by requiring the admission of the adverse party to be written or made while under oath in testimony or deposition.[3] Unsworn oral out-of-court admissions occurring outside of hearings or depositions are not admissible to prove the contents of a writing.[4]

Rule 1007 should be interpreted to authorize admissions of the contents of originals made in testimony at grand jury proceedings and at unrelated actions because such admissions being under oath at a formal proceeding satisfy the policies underlying the Rule. Additionally, Civil Procedure Rule 33 provides that answers to interrogatories be made in writing under oath. An admission of the contents of a writing, recording or photograph in response to interrogatories is consequently admissible under Rule 1007 as proof of the contents of a writing.[5]

Civil Procedure Rule 36, which authorizes requests for admissions, may be used by a party to require opposing parties to admit to the authenticity and contents of a writing.[6] The value of this method of proof is diminished by Procedure Rule 36's requirement that a copy of the pertinent document be served on opposing parties with the request, unless it was previously made available.[7] An issue left unresolved by Rule 1007 and Procedure Rule 36 is whether a failure to reply to a Procedure Rule 36 request for admission constitutes an admission satisfying Rule 1007. The policy underlying Rule 1007 would seem to require an actual, express admission rather than one arising by implication.[8]

---

[2] 151 Eng. Rep. 579 (Exch. 1840). *Accord* Metropolitan Life Ins. Co. v. Hogan, 63 F.2d 654, 656 (7th Cir. 1933); City of Cleveland v. Cleveland C.C. & St. L. Ry. 93 F. 113, 124-31 (Cir. Ct. N.D. Ohio 1899). *See also* 4 WIGMORE, § 1256.

[3] *See* Rule 1007, Advisory Committee's Note.

[4] MCCORMICK, § 242.

[5] *See* § 1007.2 of this Treatise. Basically, whenever an admission as to the content of a writing is made under oath and the admission is recorded, there will be little doubt either with respect to the sincerity of the speaker or mistransmission of the evidence.

[6] 5 WEINSTEIN, ¶ 107[05], at 1007-8 to 1007-9; 5 LOUISELL & MUELLER, § 606, at 570-571.

[7] Generally such a copy will be a duplicate, itself admissible in most circumstances (Rule 1003). Of course, inability to obtain the original or copies may trigger the Rule 1004 exceptions. Thus, only convenience is at stake, not the ability to prove the contents.

[8] *See* § 1007.2 of this Treatise. Where reliability and accuracy are essential, admissions by silence are disfavored. Lumpkin v. Meskill, 64 F.R.D. 673, 678-79 (D. Conn. 1974) (without considering question of best evidence, treating failure to admit data on accuracy of statistics in report under Federal Civil Rule 36 as equivalent to admission).

It should be emphasized that contents of the writing, recording or photograph sought to be proven through Rule 1007 need not have been prepared by the party whose admission is offered as a vehicle of proof. Accordingly, this exception to the best evidence rule may be used to prove the contents of, *e.g.*, a writing originally prepared by a person other than the party whose written or testimonial admission is used to prove contents.

Rule 1007 must be read as a limitation on Rule 801(d)(2), and a party's oral, out-of-court admission is generally admissible under Rule 801 unless it concerns the contents of a writing, recording or photograph.[9] In that case, Rule 1007 would exclude the oral admission from evidence.[10] Additionally, the parol evidence rule frequently operates to complement Rule 1007 by limiting oral statements relating to writings.

Finally, it should be noted that Rule 1007 does not operate to preclude the introduction of oral, unsworn admissions by a party as secondary evidence to prove contents where justification for the non-production of the document falls under one of the exceptions contained in Rules 1004, 1005, and 1006.[11]

§ 1007.2   Theory of Rule 1007.

The principle of Rule 1007 has been justified as a rule of convenience generally based on the theory that the admissions of an adverse party are reliable because such admissions are presumptively accurate and reliable.[12] Beyond accuracy, the original common law rule was predicated on the same policy underlying the admission by a party exception to the hearsay rule, *viz.*, estoppel from denial at trial of the truth of admissions made out of court.[13] Not only was the policy of the common law rule identical to the admission exception to the hearsay rule, but the common law rule treated the admission of the contents of a writing as original evidence just like any other admission of a party.[14]

---

[9] *See* § 801.23 of this Treatise.

[10] The best evidence rule is a condition to admissibility independent of and in addition to hearsay considerations.

[11] *See* Rule 1007, Advisory Committee's Note. (The Note refers only to Rule 1004, but clearly other exceptions are equally available.) *Cf.* Prussing v. Jackson, 208 Ill. 85, 88, 69 N.E. 771, 774 (1904) (not followed Maxcy v. Frontier Ford, Inc., 29 Ill. App. 3d 867, 331 N.E. 2d 858) (in defamation suit, error to allow plaintiff to testify that defendant admitted that the printed article, about which plaintiff complained, accurately set out a letter by defendant; it would abrogate the rule that the contents of a written instrument cannot be proved by parol evidence in the absence of proof accounting for and excusing the nonproduction of the writing).

[12] Slatterie v. Pooley, 151 Eng. Rep. 579, 581 (1840) ("what a party himself admits to be true may reasonably be presumed to be so."). *See also* 4 WIGMORE, § 1255, at 599.

[13] *See* § 801.23 *supra*.

[14] *See* Metropolitan Life Ins. Co. v. Hogan, 63 F.2d 654, 656 (7th Cir. 1933) (admissions of defendant insurance company's

While Rule 1007 recognizes the convenience afforded by this exception to the best evidence rule, it places greater emphasis on accuracy and reliability than did the traditional exception by requiring the adverse party's admission to be in writing or in testimony or deposition.[15] The traditional rule admitted evidence twice removed from the writing itself and, consequently, was subject to the dangers both of mistransmission by the witness[16] and of insincerity by the party.[17] A written admission eliminates the possibility of mistransmission, and an admission in testimony or deposition will meet an adequate standard of care on the part of the speaker due to the safeguards and solemnity accompanying the oath and proceedings.

§ 1007.3　Admissions by Party's Representatives.

An issue not expressly resolved in Rule 1007 is whether the Rule applies only to admissions made by the adverse party or whether it also applies to admissions by that party's representative. Under Pre-Rule practice, courts have held corporations and partnerships bound by their representatives.[18]

The best reading of Rule 1007 can be obtained by equating the scope of the admission of a party of Rule 1007 with that of Rule 801(d)(2). Such a reading would authorize the admissibility of admissions even though made by persons other than the adverse party, where such admissions can be attributed to representatives of that party.[19] Additionally, the safeguard of requiring that the admission by a representative of a party be contained in a writing, testimony, or deposition supports a presumption of reliability with respect to representatives to the same extent as to parties.

---

agent admissible to prove contents); York Blouse Corp. v. Kaplowitz Bros., 97 A.2d 465, 467 (D.C. Mun. App. 1957) (testimony of officer of defendant corporation admissible against corporation to prove contents). *See also* 4 Wigmore, § 1255 *et seq.*

[15] McCORMICK, § 242.

[16] Mistransmission could arise due to fraud, faulty memorization or quotation out of context.

[17] *See* 5 WEINSTEIN, ¶ 1007[02], at 1007-5; 5 LOUISELL & MUELLER, § 606, at 569; 4 WIGMORE, § 1255. *See also* Lawless v. Queale, 8 Ir. L. R., 382, 385 (1845) (testimony of witness concerning adverse party's oral, extrajudicial admission of contents held inadmissible because of danger of fraud).

[18] Metropolitan Life Ins. Co. v. Hogan, 63 F.2d 654, 656 (7th Cir. 1933).

[19] *See* § 801.25 of this Treatise.

Chapter 1008

RULE 1008. FUNCTIONS OF COURT AND JURY

Rule 1008 reads as follows:

> When the admissibility of other evidence of contents of writing, recordings, or photographs under these rules depends upon the fulfillment of a condition of fact, the question whether the condition has been fulfilled is ordinarily for the court to determine in accordance with the provisions of Rule 104. However, when an issue is raised (a) whether the asserted writing ever existed, or (b) whether another writing, recording, or photograph produced at the trial is the original, or (c) whether other evidence of contents correctly reflects the contents, the issue is for the trier of fact to determine as in the case of other issues of fact.

§ 1008.1   Functions of the Court and the Jury—In General.

Rule 1008 allocates responsibility for deciding preliminary questions of fact involving the admissibility of evidence other than originals to prove the contents of writings, recordings or photographs. Factual questions otherwise respecting admissibility, which in reality are determinative issues in the case and which generally turn on questions of credibility or the weight to be accorded certain evidence, are allocated to the trier of fact. Other preliminary questions of fact which relate to the admissibility of secondary evidence are within the province of the court.[1] Rule 1008's allocation of

---

[1] *See, generally,* McCORMICK, § 53, at 135-36; 5 WEINSTEIN, ¶¶ 1008[01]-[07]; 5 LOUISELL & MUELLER, §§ 611-13; 4 WIGMORE, § 1192. *See also* Levin, *Authentication and Contents of Writings,* 10 RUTGERS L. REV. 632 (1956); Maguire and Epstein, *Preliminary Questions of Fact in Determining the Admissibility of Evidence,* 40 HARV. L. REV. 392 (1927); Morgan, *The Law of Evidence, 1941-1945,* 59 HARV. L.

determinations as to admissibility is a specialized application of the court's power to determine preliminary matters under Rule 104.[2]

Because the distinction between preliminary factual questions and questions properly left to the jury may not be immediately apparent, Rule 1008 provides that the trier of fact, and not the court, must resolve questions as to (i) whether the original writings asserted to exist ever existed, (ii) which of writings claimed to be an original is such, and (iii) whether the secondary evidence accurately reproduces the contents of the original. The purpose of the allocation is similar to the policy underlying Rule 104(b),[3] *i.e.*, to ensure that issues are not determined prematurely due to the court's negative ruling on the admissibility of secondary evidence as to any one of the three issues enumerated.[4] The court, of course, retains its traditional control over jury determinations of these issues.[5] For example, if the opponent of secondary evidence objects on one of the grounds specified in Rule 1008 but then fails to offer evidence sufficient to support a finding that the challenge is valid, the determination as to the admissibility of secondary evidence remains exclusively within the province of the court. If, on the other hand, an objection is raised and evidence offered as to one of the issues identified in Rule 1008, and a reasonable juror could determine the issue on evidence offered, the court must leave the determination to the jury pursuant to proper instructions.[6] In sum, under Rule 1008 the trial judge is not permitted to make a preliminary determination as to the appropriateness of secondary evidence and exclude the secondary evidence based on a finding which embraces the conclusion that the original never existed, that some other writing, recording or photograph is the original or that the offered secondary evidence is not a faithful reproduction of the original. Such issues may not be taken from the trier of fact.

REV. 481 (1946); Morgan, *Functions of Judge and Jury in Determination of Preliminary Questions of Fact*, 43 HARV. L. REV. 165 (1929); Morgan and Maguire, *Looking Backward and Forward at Evidence*, 50 HARV. L. REV. 909 (1937); Comment, *Authentication and the Best Evidence Rule Under the Federal Rules of Evidence*, 16 WAYNE L. REV. 195 (1969); Comment, *A Critical Appraisal of the Application of the Best Evidence Rule*, 21 RUTGERS L. REV. 526 (1967).

[2] *See* Rule 1008, Advisory Committee's Note. *See also* § 104.3 of this Treatise.

[3] *See* the discussion of Rule 104 in this Treatise at § 104.1.

[4] *See* Rule 1008, Advisory Committee's Note.

[5] *Cf.* Federal Rule 1008, Advisory Committee's Note (stating that decision is not left to the uncontrolled decision of the jury because the jury is subject to traditional controls exercised by the judge). *See, e.g.*, Transamerica Insurance Co. v. Bloomfield, 401 F.2d 357, 360-61 (6th Cir. 1968).

[6] *See* Lewis v. Kepple, 185 F.Supp. 884, 887-88 (W.D. Pa. 1960), *aff'd*, 287 F.2d 409 (3d Cir. 1961). *See also* Nu Car Carriers, Inc. v. Traynor, 125 F.2d 47, 50 (D.C. Cir. 1942) (nonexistence of written release asserted; properly authenticated secondary evidence must therefore be submitted to the jury over the best evidence objection, with the jury deciding the existence issue).

Under the Rule, the court decides all other preliminary questions of admissibility that depend upon the fulfillment of a condition of fact, and the court may exclude secondary evidence on such bases. The primary examples of questions properly determined by the court are the threshold showings required by Rule 1004 as a prerequisite to the admission of secondary evidence to prove the contents of a writing, recording or photograph, *e.g.*, that the original was lost or destroyed or otherwise was not obtainable.[7] Additionally, the court must decide preliminary questions raised by other Rules as to admissibility of secondary evidence, and must decide any question of privilege, for example, that might arise in connection with the offer of secondary evidence.[8]

§ 1008.2   Questions for the Trier of Fact.

Rule 1008 provides that a question as to whether an original ever existed is left to the trier of fact.[9] The issue will usually arise as a question of credibility where witnesses have contradicted one another with respect to the existence of the original.[10] In such instances, the court should admit the secondary evidence and allow the jury to hear the evidence and determine its weight.[11] It should be noted that Rule 1008 comes into play only where a party seeks to prove the *contents* of a writing, recording or photograph by evidence other than the original; the Rule does not apply where the issue is merely whether a writing, recording or photograph exists.[12]

Rule 1008 also accords to the jury the decision as to which of two or more documents is the original.[13] Once a proper showing of authenticity pursuant to Article IX has been made, the competing documents should be admitted.[14] Again, the issue arises under this Rule only where the contents of the original document are at issue.[15]

Finally, Rule 1008 provides that a question as to whether secondary evidence accurately reproduces the original is a question for the trier of

---

[7] *See* Chapter 1004 of this Treatise. *See also* United States v. Gerhart, 538 F.2d 807, 809 (8th Cir. 1976) (photocopy of copy of check properly admitted; government was merely required to demonstrate that the original copy was lost).

[8] Robinson v. United States, 144 F.2d 392, 405 (6th Cir. 1944). *See also* United States v. Collins, 596 F.2d 166, 169 (alleged mail fraud; court rejected defense claim of error in receipt of summary and charts to aid jury's understanding of financial data).

[9] Dunbar v. United States, 156 U.S. 185, 15 S.Ct. 325, 39 L.Ed. 390 (1895); Nu Car

Carriers, Inc. v. Traynor, 125 F.2d 47, 48 (D.C. Cir. 1942).

[10] *E.g.*, Equitable Life Assurance Soc. v. Sieg, 53 F.2d 318, 319 (6th Cir. 1931).

[11] *See* § 104.1-.5 of this Treatise.

[12] *See* § 1002.3 of this Treatise.

[13] 5 WEINSTEIN, § 1008[05], at 1008-20 to 1008-22; 5 LOUISELL & MUELLER, § 613, at 588-89.

[14] 5 WEINSTEIN, § 1008[05], at 1008-20; 5 LOUISELL & MUELLER, § 613, at 588.

[15] *See* Rule 1008, Advisory Committee's Note.

fact.[16] Once the court has determined that nonproduction of the original is justified, the accuracy of the offered secondary evidence is an issue for the trier of fact. Recognizing that this question goes to the weight of the evidence, the Rule does not insist on a particular type of secondary evidence in order to prove the contents of the original. Although Rule 1008 allocates this issue to the trier of fact, the court retains its general power over the determination of factual issues and may, for example, bar the admission of evidence that is prejudicial, confusing or misleading.[17] Additionally, the court has discretion to require the availability or production of originals where the admitted secondary evidence consists of charts, summaries or calculations.[18]

§ 1008.3　Preliminary Decisions for the Court.

Rule 1002 sets forth a general preference for use of the original to prove the contents of a writing, recording or photograph. Use of the original is excused where the proponent shows satisfaction of another Rule or statute which authorizes proof of contents by alternative means. In each case, the admissibility of secondary evidence (i.e., evidence other than the original) depends upon the fulfillment of a preliminary factual condition. Determinations as to whether a party has made the requisite factual showing justifying nonproduction of the original are for the court under Rule 1008.

Rule 1004 specifies four alternative conditions of fact which will satisfy the foundational requirement for use of secondary evidence in order to prove the contents of a writing, recording or photograph. Accordingly, in Rule 1004(1), the preliminary questions for the court concern the adequacy of the foundation for the admission of secondary evidence upon a claim that the original has been lost or destroyed.[19] The court must determine that all originals have suffered either of these fates.[20] The court must also

[16] See Cooper v. Brown, 126 F.2d 874, 877-78 (3d Cir. 1942) (action for accounting of partnership assets; plaintiff claimed that a waiver of interest on a mortgage held by defendant had been executed; testimony of contents should have been excluded, since there had been no showing of personal knowledge; issue of existence and contents were properly kept from the jury).

[17] See Rule 403 and § 403.3 of this Treatise.

[18] See § 1006.3 of this Treatise.

[19] Sylvania Electric Products, Inc. v. Flanagan, 352 F.2d 1005, 1008 (1st Cir. 1965) (contract suit; error to permit plaintiff to testify to content of bills and invoices; burden was on plaintiff to show that he had used all reasonable means to obtain the original).

[20] Willhoit v. Commissioner, 308 F.2d 259, 265 (9th Cir. 1962) (when secondary evidence is offered and the proponent seeks to excuse nonproduction of the original, sufficiency of the preliminary proof of diligence in searching for the original is addressed to the sound discretion of the trial judge); Sellmayer Packaging Co. v. Commissioner, 146 F.2d 707, 710 (4th Cir. 1944) (no error to exclude testimony by taxpayer's accountant as to certain transactions, where tax court ruled that the taxpayer had not borne the burden of showing that the sales slips had ceased to exist).

decide that a diligent search has been made for the original by the proponent where there is no foundational proof as to destruction.[21] Additionally, if a challenge is raised on the issue that the proponent of the secondary evidence actually lost or destroyed the originals in bad faith, the court must determine the validity of the challenge and the concomitant question of admissibility of the secondary evidence. Determination of these preliminary factual questions is within the court's discretion, although, of course, such decisions cannot be arbitrary.[22]

Admission of secondary evidence under Rule 1004(2) requires the court to determine preliminarily whether all originals are beyond the court's jurisdiction and whether any available judicial process or procedure, for example, issuance of a subpoena duces tecum, could produce an original.[23] Again, the determination is within the court's discretion, and where the foundation is inadequate, the court may exclude the secondary evidence.

Under Rule 1004(3), preliminary questions for the court include whether the original is under the control of a party at the time an adverse party seeks to prove its contents, whether adequate notice has been furnished to the adverse party that the contents of the original would be the subject of proof at the hearing, and whether the party in possession of the original has failed to make the original available.[24] In connection with the question of whether the opponent failed to produce an original, the court may have to decide whether the document in question is admissible in view of an opponent's claim that it is protected by constitutional or testimonial privilege.[25] Of course, if the opponent intends to assert a privilege claim, she should nonetheless have the original at the hearing in order for the judge to examine it if necessary, or for use by the proponent if the claim of privilege is rejected.

Rule 1004(4) pertaining to collateral matters raises two preliminary questions for the court: (i) a determination of the controlling issues of a

[21] United States v. Gerhart, 538 F.2d 807, 809 (8th Cir. 1976) (in prosecution for knowingly making a false statement on a loan application, a photocopy of a check was properly admitted against defendant, since government demonstrated that the photocopy was what it purported to be and accurately reflected the contents of the original photocopy).

[22] United States v. Jacobs, 475 F.2d 270, 285 (2d Cir. 1973), cert. denied, 414 U.S. 821, 94 S.Ct. 116, 38 L.Ed. 2d 53 (1974) (alleged dealing in stolen government securities; photocopy of alleged agreement among conspirators was properly received); United States v. Covello, 410 F.2d 536, 543 (2d Cir. 1969), cert. denied 396 U.S. 879, 90 S.Ct. 150, 24 L.Ed. 2d 136 (1969) (alleged interstate gambling and criminal fraud; copies of telephone toll records were properly admitted; diligent search had not uncovered the originals).

[23] Western Inc. v. United States, 234 F.2d 211, 213 (8th Cir. 1956) (bankruptcy proceedings, deposition sufficed to establish that debtor corporation assumed the obligations of a partnership; sufficiency of foundation was laid for admission of secondary evidence).

[24] Transamerica Insurance Company v. Bloomfield, 401 F.2d 357, 360 (6th Cir. 1968); United States v. Pike, 158 F.2d 46, 50-51 (7th Cir. 1946).

[25] See Chapter 501 of this Treatise.

case, and (ii) a determination of whether the contents of the original are closely related to one of those issues.[26] Although the standards for determination of these questions are discretionary with the court, Rule 1004(4) requires a greater connective showing to controlling issues than mere relevancy in order to justify an insistence on use of the original.

In addition to Rule 1004, other Rules involve the court in admissibility determinations regarding proof of contents by means other than the original. For example, in determining the admissibility of duplicates under Rule 1002, it is for the court to decide whether there is a genuine issue as to the authenticity of the original or whether unfairness would result by use of the duplicate in lieu of the original.[27]

Rule 1005 allows proof of contents of official records under certain circumstances, thereby requiring the court to determine whether a copy of a public record is properly certified or adequately authenticated by a witness who has compared the original with the copy.[28] Alternatively, the court must determine whether a copy conforming to those requirements cannot be obtained by the exercise of reasonable diligence prior to admitting other evidence of the contents of public records.[29] Of course, if an issue is raised as to whether an original public record ever existed, the question is ultimately left to the trier of fact.

Rule 1006, allowing use of charts, summaries or calculations to prove contents, raises several preliminary questions for the court: (i) whether the contents of documentary evidence can be conveniently examined in court; (ii) whether the originals or duplicates have been made available to all parties as required by the Rule; and (iii) whether there are special reasons for requiring the actual production of the originals or duplicates in court.[30] In making a determination as to the admissibility of summaries, charts or calculations, the court must necessarily also decide upon the admissibility of the underlying documents.

[26] *See* McCORMICK, § 234, at 709-10.
[27] *See* § 1003.3 of this Treatise.
[28] *See* Chapter 1005 of this Treatise.
[29] *Id.*
[30] United States v. Collins, 596 F.2d 166, 169 (6th Cir. 1979) (alleged mail fraud; court rejected defense claim of error in receipt of summaries and charts to aid jury's understanding of financial data); United States v. Bartone, 400 F.2d 459, 461 (6th Cir. 1968), *cert. denied*, 393 U.S. 1027, 89 S.Ct. 631, 21 L.Ed. 2d 571 (1968) (if summaries are offered, trial judge must carefully examine them in order to determine that everything is supported by proof).

Rule 1007 also involves preliminary questions to be decided by the court. The Rule supersedes Rule 1004 and allows proof of contents by the testimony, deposition, or written admission of the party against whom the evidence is offered, without accounting for nonproduction of the original. The court must consequently decide whether a particular sworn statement is part of the testimony or deposition of a party, or whether a written document is an admission of a party.[31]

[31] *See* Development Corp. of America v. United Bonding Ins. Co., 413 F.2d 823, 825 (5th Cir. 1969), *cert. denied*, 396 U.S. 957, 90 S.Ct. 430, 24 L.Ed. 2d 422 (1969) (performance bond suit; no error in receipt into evidence of photographic copy of bond; defendant admitted the genuineness of the copy of the bond by formal answer to interrogatories).

XI
MISCELLANEOUS RULES

Chapter 1101

RULE 1101. APPLICABILITY OF RULES

Rule 1101 reads as follows:

(a) **Courts and magistrates.** These rules apply to the United States district courts, the District Court of Guam, the District Court of the Virgin Islands, the District Court for the District of the Canal Zone, the United States courts of appeals, the United States Claims Court and to United States magistrates, in the actions, cases, and proceedings and to the extent hereinafter set forth. The terms "judge" and "court" in these rules include United States magistrates.

(b) **Proceedings generally.** These rules apply generally to civil actions and proceedings, including admiralty and maritime cases, to criminal cases and proceedings, to contempt proceedings except those in which the court may act similarly, and to proceedings and cases under title 11, United States Code.

(c) **Rule of privilege.** The rule with respect to privilege applies at all stages of all actions, cases, and proceedings.

(d) **Rules inapplicable.** The rules (other than with respect to privileges) do not apply in the following situations:

(1) *Preliminary questions of fact.* The determination of questions of fact preliminary to admissibility of evidence when the issue is to be determined by the court under rule 104.

(2) *Grand jury.* Proceedings before grand juries.

(3) Miscellaneous proceedings. Proceedings for extradition or rendition; preliminary examinations in criminal cases; sentencing, or granting or revoking probation; issuance of warrants for arrest, criminal summonses, and search warrants; and proceedings with respect to release on bail or otherwise.

(e) Rules applicable in part. In the following proceedings these rules apply to the extent that matters of evidence are not provided for in the statutes which govern procedure therein or in other rules prescribed by the Supreme Court pursuant to statutory authority: the trial of minor and petty offenses by United States magistrates; review of agency actions when the facts are subject to trial de novo under section 706(2)(F) of title 5, United States Code; review of orders of the Secretary of Agriculture under section 2 of the Act entitled "An Act to authorize association of producers of agricultural products" approved February 18, 1922 (7 U.S.C. 292), and under sections 6 and 7(c) of the Perishable Agricultural Commodities Act, 1930 (7 U.S.C. 499f, 499g(c); naturalization and revocation of naturalization under section 310-318 of the Immigration and Nationality Act (8 U.S.C. 1421-1429); prize proceedings in admiralty under sections 7651-7681 of title 10, United States Code; review of orders of the Secretary of the Interior under section 2 of the Act entitled "An Act authorizing associations of producers of aquatic products" approved June 25, 1934 (15 U.S.C. 522); review of orders of petroleum control boards under section 5 of the Act entitled "An Act to regulate interstate and foreign commerce in petroleum and its products by prohibiting the shipment in such commerce of petroleum and its products produced in violation of State Law, and for other purposes," approved February 22, 1935 (15 U.S.C. 715d); actions for fines, penalties, or forfeitures under part V of title IV of the Tariff Act of 1930 (19 U.S.C. 1581-1624), or under the Anti-Smuggling Act (19 U.S.C. 1701-1711); criminal libel for condemnation, exclusion of imports, or other proceedings under the Federal Food, Drug and Cosmetic Act (21 U.S.C. 301-392); disputes between seamen under sections 4079, 4080, and 4081 of the Revised Statutes (22 U.S.C. 256-258); habeas corpus under sections 2241-2254 of title 28, United States Code, motions to vacate, set aside or correct sentence under section 2255 of title 28, United States Code; actions for penalties for refusal to transport destitute seamen under section 4578 of the Revised Statutes (46 U.S.C. 679); actions against the United States under the Act entitled "An Act authorizing suits against the United States in admiralty for damage caused by and salvage service rendered to public vessels belonging to the United States, and for other purposes," approved March 3, 1925 (46 U.S.C. 781-790), as implemented by section 7730 of title 10, United States Code.

§ 1101.1 Rule 1101(a) and Rule 1101(b)—Scope.

Rule 1101(a) initially lists the various courts that are within the Supreme Court's rule-making power and then applies the Federal Rules of Evidence to proceedings within these courts.[1] The Advisory Committee compiled the list of courts contained in Rule 1101(a) from the various enabling acts creating the courts and from Congressional statutes that applied future enacted rules or procedures for specified federal courts.[2] Noticeably, administrative and agency hearings are not subject to the Rules of Evidence under Rule 1101(a).[3]

The Rules of Evidence apply in proceedings before a magistrate or bankruptcy judge,[4] and to judges of the courts listed except in the situations or proceedings identified under Rule 1101(d). Arbitrators are bound by the Rules of Evidence.[5]

Rule 1101(b) contemplates a unitary system of evidence. Thus, the Rule applies to all proceedings, civil and criminal, regardless of whether the issue is tried to the court or to a jury.[6] In certain instances, other Rules draw distinctions between certain types of cases, *i.e.*, civil and criminal cases. For example, under Rule 404 certain applications of character evidence are available only to the criminal accused.[7] Other examples may be found in Rule 104(c) and Rule 608. Where the Rules make a distinction between civil and criminal cases, the difference in treatment is usually supported by long-standing doctrines which seek to foster fundamental protections with a minimal suppression of helpful proof.

---

[1] *See, generally,* 5 Weinstein, ¶¶ 1101[01]-[05]; 5 Louisell & Mueller, §§ 618-23; 1 Wigmore, § 4. *See also,* Albert, *Application of Rules of Evidence to Administrative Proceedings: The Case of the Occupational Safety and Health Review Commission,* 47 Ad. L. Rev. 135 (1975); Friendly, *Some Kind of Hearing,* 123 U. Pa. L. Rev. 1267 (1975); Russell, *Federal Rules of Evidence With Special Emphasis on Bankruptcy Proceedings,* 49 Am. Banker. L.J. 231 (1975); Smith, *Evidence Admissible During the Punishment Stage of a Criminal Trial,* 7 St. Mary's L.J. 38 (1975); Note, *The Constitutionality of Statutes Permitting Increased Sentences for Habitual or Dangerous Criminals,* 89 Harv. L. Rev. 356 (1975).

[2] *See* Rule 1101, Advisory Committee's Note.

[3] Calhoun v. Bailar, 626 F.2d 145, 148-49 (9th Cir. 1980), *cert. denied,* 452 U.S. 906, 101 S.Ct. 3033, 69 L.Ed.2d 407 (1981) (court rejected any per se rule that holds that hearsay can never constitute substantial evidence); E.E.O.C. v. University of Notre Dame du Lac, 551 F.Supp. 737, 740 (N.D. Ind. 1982) (actions to enforce an administrative subpoena are encompassed within the phrase "civil actions and proceedings" making Rule 501 applicable.

[4] Matter of Clifford, 566 F.2d 1023, 1024-25 (5th Cir. 1978) (authentication pursuant to rule 901 in bankruptcy); *In re* Sheehan, 350 F.Supp. 907, 915-16 (W.D. Mo. 1972) (best evidence in bankruptcy proceeding).

[5] *See* Drayer v. Krasner, 572 F.2d 348, 352 (2d Cir. 1978), *cert. denied,* 436 U.S. 948, 98 S.Ct. 2855, 56 L.Ed.2d 791 (1978).

[6] 5 Louisell & Mueller, § 620, at 625.

[7] *See* Rule 404(a). *See also* Michelson v. United States, 335 U.S. 469, 477, 69 S.Ct. 213, 219, 93 L.Ed. 168, 175 (1948).

Whether a specific rule of evidence will apply in a given case cannot be determined solely from the face of Rule 1101. In some instances a court governed by the Federal Rules of Evidence under Rule 1101(a) will be required by other Rules[8] or constitutional principles[9] to apply state evidentiary rules in the determinations of a specific issue arising in a proceeding.

§ 1101.2   Proceedings in Contempt of Court.

Rule 1101(b) excepts from the operation of the Rules contempt proceedings in which the court may act "summarily." The Rules are inapplicable only when the contempt is committed within the view or presence of the court or so near to the court as to disturb its proceedings and impair due respect for its authority.[10] Only in such a contempt situation may a court act summarily. In this sense, the only contempt proceedings exempted from the Rules are those involving charges for "direct" contempt, *i.e.*, obstreperous or disrespectful conduct which occurs in the presence of the court.[11]

In determining what is meant by the limiting phrase, "the presence of the court," it has been held that "the court" consists not simply of the judge, the courtroom, the jury or jury room individually, but of all of these combined. In short, the court is present wherever any one of its constituent parts is engaged in the activity of the judiciary.[12]

To maintain a summary proceeding for contempt, the alleged misbehavior must require immediate punishment or deterrence in order to preserve the court's authority. The contempt must occur in the presence of the judge or before any of its constituent parts, and it must obstruct the administration of justice by impeding or influencing a pending case. In such circumstances, the judge is the "evidence" since she has witnessed the contemptuous conduct. Accordingly, relaxation of the formal Rules of Evidence in summary contempt proceedings is appropriate. In all other contempt proceedings the Rules are fully operative.

§ 1101.3   Privileges.

Federal Rule 1101(c) is direct in its instruction that the law of privileges applies in any proceeding, including, as noted in Rule 1101(c), those pro-

[8] *See* Rules 302, 501, 601, 902(9) and 902.

[9] Erie R.R. Co. v. Tompkins, 304 U.S. 64, 58 S.Ct. 817, 82 L.Ed. 1188 (1938).

[10] *See, generally,* the discussion of Federal Rule of Criminal Procedure 42 in 3 WRIGHT, FEDERAL PRACTICE AND PROCEDURE (CRIMINAL), §§ 701-15 (1969).

[11] *See* 5 LOUISELL & MUELLER, § 620, at 626.

[12] *See* WRIGHT B. MILLER, FEDERAL PRACTICE AND PROCEDURE (CIVIL), § 2960 (1973).

ceedings specifically exempted from the application of the Rules. Thus, a person may assert a privilege at any stage of any proceeding.

The preservation of privileges is, of course, at tension with a system designed to reveal the truth.[13] Nevertheless, time-honored, societal values are fostered by the continuation of privileges. Privileges, however characterized, are not lightly conferred and are not, therefore, expansively construed.

The law of privileges is comprehensively treated in Article V of the Rules of Evidence and in Chapter V of this Treatise.

§ 1101.4   Admissibility Determinations.

Despite the fact that the Rules are, as a whole, designed to elicit the truth by providing an orderly system for the introduction and reception of relevant evidence, their application in some situations would be either overly burdensome or entirely contrary to the nature of the proceeding. Accordingly, Rule 1101(d) excepts certain proceedings from the operation of the Rules where the application of the Rules would be counterproductive or inappropriate.

The first of these exceptions concerns determinations by the court on the admissibility of evidence. Rule 1101(d)(1) excepts such admissibility determinations by reference to Rule 104(a), and Rule 104(a) provides that the court is not bound by the Rules, except with respect to privileges, when ruling on questions of admissibility, qualifications of witnesses or the existence of a privilege. For example, where the admissibility of particular evidence necessarily rests upon the existence of some condition such as the qualification of an expert, responsibility for this threshold determination has traditionally resided with the court. The Rule incorporates this practice.[14] Where the determination is factual, the court may decide the question on the basis of otherwise inadmissible facts.[15]

In addition, the nonprivilege Rules of Evidence do not apply to preliminary hearings in criminal cases where the purpose is to determine whether there exists "probable cause" to hold the accused for further proceedings.[16] The reasoning for this provision is that the nonprivilege Rules of Evidence do not govern grand jury proceedings, and also because it is feared that

---

[13] *See* United States v. Nixon, 418 U.S. 683, 688, 94 S.Ct. 3090, 3095, 41 L.Ed.2d 1039, 1044 (1974). *But see* United States v. Ocanas, 628 F.2d 353, 357, n.1 (5th Cir. 1980), *reh. denied*, 633 F.2d 582 (5th Cir. 1980).

[14] *See* McCORMICK, § 53, at 135.
[15] *Id.*
[16] *See* Federal Rule of Criminal Procedure 5.1(a).

making the rules applicable to preliminary hearings would increase the number of preliminary motions.[17]

The inapplicability of the Rules to admissibility determinations is in part predicated on the principle that any evidence, once admitted, is thereafter subject to attack by the opposing party. Where, for example, expert opinion testimony is admitted over objection, the opposing party retains the right to demonstrate that the expertise of the witness is faulty or that the information used by the expert in arriving at his conclusions is inadequate or inaccurate.

§ 1101.5　　Grand Juries and Miscellaneous Criminal Proceedings.

Except with respect to privileges, Rule 1101(d)(2) specifically exempts proceedings before grand juries from the operation of the Rules. The purpose of the grand jury is to make a preliminary determination of whether there exists reasonable cause to believe that the accused engaged in the conduct complained of, and whether such conduct constitutes a crime under the laws of the United States.[18] These determinations are to be made regardless of the evidence that may eventually be admitted at trial. The duty of the grand jury is to approve or disapprove the government's cause of action in a criminal case, and the issue before the grand jury is whether the government has in its possession certain facts demonstrating the substantive requirements essential to a criminal conviction.[19] Since the determination of ultimate truth of factual allegations is not the province of the grand jury, the system of evidence embodied in the Rules is not essential to the integrity of its proceedings. Accordingly, grand jury proceedings are exempted from the evidentiary dictates of the Rules.[20]

[17] See Notes of the Advisory Committee on the Criminal Rules, 48 F.R.D. 553, 569-73 (1970).

[18] See Kamisar, LaFave, Israel, *Modern Criminal Procedure*, 5th Ed., 1980, at 1025. See also Dong Haw v. Superior Court, 81 Cal. App. 2d 153, 183 P.2d 724 (1947).

[19] Hammond v. Brown, 323 F.Supp. 326, 345-46 (D.C. Cir.), aff'd, 450 F.2d 480 (6th Cir. 1971).

[20] United States v. Calandra, 414 U.S. 338, 346, 94 S.Ct. 613, 619, 38 L.Ed.2d 561, 567 (1974) (while grand jury may consider incompetent evidence, it may not violate a valid privilege, whether established by the constitution, statutes, or the common law); United States v. Costello, 350 U.S. 359, 362, 76 S.Ct. 406, 408, 100 L.Ed. 397,

401-402 (1956) (indictment sufficient even though based entirely on hearsay); United States v. Ocanas, 628 F.2d 353, 357 n.1 (1980), reh. denied, 633 F.2d 582 (5th Cir. 1980) (even if information obtained in violation of appellants' Sixth Amendment right to counsel, that would not be grounds to challenge the indictment). See also United States v. McKenzie, 678 F.2d 629, 631 (5th Cir. 1982), cert. denied, 459 U.S. 1038, 103 S.Ct. 450, 74 L.Ed.2d 604 (1982) (grand juror can visit place mentioned in testimony and discuss findings with fellow jurors); United States v. Mackey, 405 F.Supp. 854 (E.D.N.Y. 1975) (violation of an evidentiary privilege in grand jury proceedings does not justify dismissing indictment).

For much the same reasons, Rule 1101(d)(3) excepts from the Rules certain unique criminal proceedings which need not be attended by the usual evidentiary safeguards. Proceedings in extradition or rendition are essentially administrative in nature.[21] The process involves the surrender of an individual to the jurisdiction where the alleged crime was committed. The proceeding merely seeks to determine the fact of an outstanding warrant and not the facts of the charges levied in the warrant by the petitioning jurisdiction. Consequently, the Rules are inapplicable.[22]

The Rules do not apply to sentencing proceedings. The entire theoretical foundation for sentencing is inconsistent with the system of evidence which seeks to ensure a correct and fair determination of guilt or innocence. Once guilt has been determined, the court is under a duty to pass sentence upon the convicted individual by resorting to information which is essentially irrelevant to the adjudication of his culpability.[23] Accordingly, pre-sentence investigation and reports containing, among other things, information about the accused's past activities are normally prepared with an eye toward placing before the court the life and personality of the accused. Evidence such as hearsay and prior acts are contained in pre-sentence reports. While the Rules might preclude the use of such evidence in determining guilt, the relevant consideration in sentencing is not related to such a determination. Rather, the issue is one of personalized sanctions. Accordingly, evidence concerning prior acts, hearsay evidence, and character evidence are highly probative to the sentencing function.[24] Subjection of this proceeding to the Rules would serve no purpose consistent with prevailing theories of sentencing, and, consequently, sentencing hearings are exempted from the Rules.

The granting of probation is subsumed within the sentencing process discussed above. For the same reasons set forth above, the granting of parole by an executive board is likewise excepted from the Rules of Evidence. As a matter of policy, the prisoner has no legitimate expectation of liberty during the term of his sentence. This policy is extended to apply equally to the continuing incarceration and the conditions imposed upon the parolee

---

[21] See Melia v. United States, 667 F.2d 300, 302 (2d Cir. 1981); Simmons v. Braun, 627 F.2d 635, 636-37 (2d Cir. 1980).

[22] Eain v. Wilkes, 641 F.2d 504, 508-11 (7th Cir. 1981).

[23] Morrissey v. Brewer, 408 U.S. 471, 489, 92 S.Ct. 2593, 2604, 33 L.Ed.2d 484, 499 (1972); United States v. McCallum, 677 F.2d 1024, 1026 (4th Cir. 1982), cert. denied, 459 U.S. 1010, 103 S.Ct. 365, 74 L.Ed.2d 400 (1982).

[24] United States v. Ray, 683 F.2d 1116, 1120-21 (7th Cir. 1982), cert. denied, U.S. 103 S.Ct. 578, 74 L.Ed.2d 938 (1982) (trial court entitled to consider broad range of information, largely unlimited as to kind or source in sentencing); United States v. Torrez-Flores, 624 F.2d 776, 779 (7th Cir. 1980) (only privilege rules apply).

if released.[25] Consequently, parole hearings are not governed by the usual system of proof.

Where either probation or parole is sought to be revoked, however, the government attempts to deprive an individual of a freedom that has once been granted. With respect to parole revocation, significant constitutional guarantees are applicable.[26] The same constitutional protections do not apply with equal force to the revocation of probation proceedings,[27] although Criminal Rule 32.3 does grant the accused the right to counsel prior to the revocation of probation. In regard to both parole and probation revocation, the court is guided by principles of fundamental fairness and not by the formal Rules of Evidence.

The same theories underpinning the exemption from formal Rules of Evidence for grand juries apply with enhanced force to the issuance of criminal summons, arrest warrants and search warrants. Here, the ultimate duty of the court is not to determine the truth of the underlying allegations, but only to determine whether reasonable or probable cause exists to believe that a certain person has committed a crime[28] or that certain contraband is located in a certain place.[29] Accordingly, the evidentiary safeguards contained in the Rules must give way to the overriding consideration of efficient and effective law enforcement.[30] To subject these investigatory proceedings to the formal principles of proof would needlessly impede the paramount process of detection and arrest. If evidence seized pursuant to a defective warrant is tainted, there remains ample time

[25] United States v. Jarrett, 705 F.2d 198, 208 (7th Cir. 1983). *See also* United States v. Francischine, 512 F.2d 827, 830 (5th Cir. 1975), *cert. denied*, 423 U.S. 931, 96 S.Ct. 284, 46 L.Ed.2d 261 (1975) (rules other than with respect to privileges do not apply in proceedings for revoking probation); United States v. Dozier, 543 F.Supp. 880, 891 (M.D. La. 1982) (Rules of Evidence not applicable to probation revocation hearing). *See, e.g.*, United States v. Heyd, 318 F.Supp. 648, 650 (E.D. La. 1970), *aff'd*, 438 F.2d 1027 (5th Cir. 1970), *cert. denied*, 404 U.S. 880, 92 S.Ct. 195, 30 L.Ed.2d 160 (1971) (exclusionary rule does not apply); McArthur v. United States, 434 F.Supp. 163, 167 (S.D. Ind. 1976), *aff'd*, 559 F.2d 1226 (7th Cir. 1977) (rules of evidence do not apply to parole board proceedings).

[26] Morrissey v. Brewer, 408 U.S. 471, 489, 92 S.Ct. 2593, 2604, 33 L.Ed.2d 484, 499 (1972); United States *ex rel.* Vitoratos v. Campbell, 410 F.Supp. 1208, 1211 (D.C. Ohio 1976).

[27] *See* United States v. Francischine, 512 F.2d 827, 828 (5th Cir. 1975); Arciniega v. Freeman, 439 F.2d 776, 778 (9th Cir. 1971), *rev'd on other grounds*, 404 U.S. 4, 92 S.Ct. 22, 30 L.Ed.2d 22 (1971); McArthur v. United States Board of Parole, 434 F.Supp. 163, 167 (S.D. Ind. 1976), *aff'd*, 559 F.2d 1226 (7th Cir. 1977); United States v. Heyd, 318 F.Supp. 648, 651 (E.D. La. 1970), *aff'd*, 438 F.2d 1027 (5th Cir. 1970), *cert. denied*, 404 U.S. 880, 92 S.Ct. 195, 30 L.Ed.2d 160 (1971).

[28] *See* Rule 4(a) and (c) of the Federal Rules of Criminal Procedure. *See also* Eain v. Wilkes, 641 F.2d 504, 507 (7th Cir. 1981), *cert. denied*, 454 U.S. 894, 102 S.Ct. 390, 70 L.Ed.2d 208 (1981) (extradition proceeding).

[29] *See, e.g.*, United States v. Gosser, 339 F.2d 102, 109-10 (6th Cir. 1965).

[30] *See, e.g.*, Coury v. United States, 426 F.2d 1354, 1356 (6th Cir. 1970).

to challenge the admission of such evidence, and it is thought to be more advantageous to society's interests that such errors be raised prior to or during trial than prior to the initial issuance of the arrest or search warrant.

The granting and setting of bail, like sentencing, is a task peculiarly within the province of the court. The overriding policy is that of assuring the accused's appearance at trial.[31] As in sentencing, the facts pertinent to a bail hearing are not probative of the guilt or innocence of the accused. The primary concern is the balancing of the accused's likelihood to appear when properly summoned against the accused's freedom and opportunity to prepare his defense. Given the nature and purpose of the proceeding, in which the court must address the character of the accused and the severity of the charged offense, the Rules of Evidence would do little to aid the court in this highly personalized function. Therefore, bail hearings are excepted from the operation of the Rules.[32]

§ 1101.6   Rule 1101(e)—Scope.

Rule 1101(e) is self-explanatory. It provides that if an Act of Congress, or a rule promulgated by the Supreme Court, governing one of the special types of proceedings listed, specifically deals with evidentiary matters, then the Federal Rules of Evidence apply to the proceeding only to an extent not inconsistent with the statute or rule.[33]

---

[31] *See, generally,* Stack v. Boyle, 342 U.S. 1, 72 S.Ct. 1, 96 L.Ed. 3 (1951).

[32] United States v. Montemayor, 666 F.2d 235, 237-38 (5th Cir. 1982).

[33] *See, generally,* 5 WEINSTEIN, ¶ 1101[03], at 1101-27 n.42; 5 LOUISELL & MUELLER, § 623.

Chapter 1102

RULE 1102. AMENDMENTS

Rule 1102 reads as follows:

Amendments to the Federal Rules of Evidence may be made as provided in section 2076 of title 28 of the United States Code.

Section 2076 of title 28 of the United States Code reads as follows:

The Supreme Court of the United States shall have the power to prescribe amendments to the Federal Rules of Evidence. Such amendments shall not take effect until they have been reported to Congress by the Chief Justice at or after the beginning of a regular session of Congress but not later than the first day of May, and until the expiration of one hundred and eighty days after they have been so reported; but if either House of Congress within that time shall by resolution disapprove any amendment so reported it shall not take effect. The effective date of any amendment so reported may be deferred by either House of Congress to a later date or until approval by Act of Congress. Any rule whether proposed or in force may be amended by Act of Congress. Any provision of law in force at the expiration of such time and in conflict with any such amendment not disapproved shall be of no further force o[r] effect after such amendment has taken effect. Any such amendment creating, abolishing, or modifying a privilege shall have no force or effect unless it shall be approved by Act of Congress.

§ 1102.1   Rule 1102 In General—The Procedure Established in Title 28 U.S.C. § 2076.

Rule 1102 establishes that the procedure by which the Federal Rules of Evidence are to be amended is to be found in 28 U.S.C. § 2076.[1] This section generally provides that the Supreme Court has the power to prescribe amendments to the Federal Rules of Evidence subject to Congressional action.

Under § 2076, a proposed amendment to the Rules of Evidence will be enacted into law 180 days after its submission to the Congress, unless either House of Congress passes a resolution to block the enactment of the amendment. Prior enabling acts contained a shorter period of 90 days within which the Congress could act.[2] Section 2076 further provides that by an act of either House of Congress within the 180 day period, Congress may defer the effective date of a proposed rule for a specified period, or for an indefinite period lasting until the Congress acts on the proposed rule.[3] The section additionally states that the Congress, by a resolution of both Houses, may at any time initiate the amendment of the Rules of Evidence, without a precondition that the Supreme Court first promulgate a rule for the Congress' approval.[4]

Under § 2076, even if the Congress fails to act within the 180 day period, any amendment promulgated by the Supreme Court abolishing or modifying a privilege, will not become effective without Congressional action.[5]

§ 1102.2   Rationale.

Rule 1102 was enacted in a form that refers to a statute for its substantive provision, apparently as an effort to reinforce the Congress' jurisdictional role in the making of Rules of Procedure for the federal court system.[6]

An examination of the report by the House Judiciary Committee provides some insight into the rationale underlying the substance of 28 U.S.C.

[1] *See, generally,* 5 WEINSTEIN, § 1102; 5 LOUISELL & MUELLER, §§ 628-30; *See also,* Degnan, *The Law of Federal Evidence Reform,* 76 HARV. L. REV. 275 (1962); Pound, *Procedure Under Rules of Court in New Jersey,* 66 HARV. L. REV. 28 (1952); WEINSTEIN, *The Uniformity-Conformity Dilemma Facing Draftsmen of Federal Rules of Evidence,* 69 COLUM. L. REV. 353 (1969); WIGMORE, *All Legislative Rules for Judiciary Procedure Are Void Constitutionality,* 23 ILL. L. REV. 276 (1928); Wright, *Proce-*

dural Reform: Its Limitations and Its Future, 1 GA. L. REV. 563 (1967).

[2] House Judiciary Committee Report on 28 U.S.C.S. § 2076.

[3] *See* Rule 28 U.S.C. § 2076.

[4] *Id.*

[5] *Id.*

[6] *See* House Judiciary Committee Report on 28 U.S.C.S. § 2076; Senate Judiciary Committee Report on 28 U.S.C.S. § 2076; 5 LOUISELL & MUELLER, § 628, at 676 n.6.

§ 2076. The House Committee was concerned that the Congress continued to play an appropriate role in the rule-making process.[7] This theme is embodied in the lengthy time period required before a rule automatically becomes law in the absence of congressional action, as well as in the provision recognizing Congress' power to initiate the amendment process.

Another concern of the Judiciary Committee was to disspell any doubt about the legitimacy of the Supreme Court promulgating and amending the Rules of Evidence.[8] Congress did not share the Supreme Court's confidence that prior enabling acts had authorized the Supreme Court to promulgate rules of evidence for the federal courts.[9] The Preamble to Rule 1102 resolves any doubt on this issue.

The Judiciary Committee was also troubled by the prospect that by amending the Federal Rules of Evidence, the Supreme Court would be exercising a legislative power over matters bearing heavily on important social policies. Thus, the last sentence of Rule 1102 is designed to implement a policy that, in areas governing privileges, Congress shall play the key role in formulating changes in the law.[10] The legitimacy of this position is presumably based on an assumption that Congress will make changes in the area of privileges only after a careful examination of the social policies underlying the existence of the privilege.

---

[7] *See* House Report, § 2076.

[8] *Id.*

[9] *See* Rule 1101, Advisory Committee's Note. *See also* 5 LOUISELL & MUELLER, § 628, at 678 n.12; 5 WEINSTEIN, § 1102, at 1102.1.

[10] House Report, § 2076.

Chapter 1103

RULE 1103. TITLE

Rule 1103 reads as follows:

These rules may be known and cited as the Federal Rules of Evidence.

Rule 1103 is self-explanatory. Throughout this Treatise, the author has cited the Federal Rules of Evidence in the form mandated by Rule 1103 or as simply, the Rules of Evidence.

Appendix

ADVISORY COMMITTEE'S NOTES TO THE FEDERAL RULES OF EVIDENCE

ARTICLE I
GENERAL PROVISIONS

Rule 101   Scope

ADVISORY COMMITTEE'S NOTE

Rule 101 specifies in detail the courts, proceedings, questions, and stages of proceedings to which the rules apply in whole or in part.

Rule 102   Purpose and Construction

ADVISORY COMMITTEE'S NOTE

For similar provisions see Rule 2 of the Federal Rules of Criminal Procedure, Rule 1 of the Federal Rules of Civil Procedure, California Evidence Code § 2, and New Jersey Evidence Rule 5. (Neither the Report of the Senate Judiciary Committee, nor the Report of the House/Senate Conferees made comments directed separately toward Rule 102.)

Rule 103   Rulings on Evidence

ADVISORY COMMITTEE'S NOTE

Subdivision (a) states the law as generally accepted today. Rulings on evidence cannot be assigned as error unless (1) a substantial right is affected, and (2) the nature of the error was called to the attention of the judge, so as to alert him to the proper course of action and enable opposing counsel to take proper corrective measures. The objection and the offer of proof are the techniques for accomplishing these objectives. For similar provisions see Uniform Rules 4 and 5; California Evidence Code §§ 353 and 354; Kansas Code of Civil Procedure §§ 60-404 and 60-405. The rule does not purport to change the law with respect to harmless error. See 28 U.S.C. § 2111, F.R. Civ.P. 61, F.R. Crim.P. 52, and decisions construing them. The status of constitutional error as harmless or not is treated in Chapman v. California, 386 U.S. 18, 87 S.Ct. 824, 17 L.Ed.2d 705 (1967), reh. denied id. 937, 87 S.Ct. 1283, 18 L.Ed.2d 241.

Subdivision (b). The first sentence is the third sentence of Rule 43(c) of the Federal Rules of Civil Procedure virtually verbatim. Its purpose is to reproduce for an appellate court, insofar as possible, a true reflection of what occurred in the trial court. The second sentence is in part derived from the final sentence of Rule 43(c). It is designed to resolve doubts as to what testimony the witness would have in fact given, and, in nonjury cases, to provide the appellate court with material for a possible final disposition of the case in the event of reversal of a ruling which excluded evidence. See 5 Morre's Federal Practice, § 43.11 (2d Ed. 1968). Application is made discretionary in view of the practical impossibility of formulating a satisfactory rule in mandatory terms.

Subdivision (c). This subdivision proceeds on the supposition that a ruling which excludes evidence in a jury case is likely to be a pointless procedure if the excluded evidence nevertheless comes to the attention of the jury. Bruton v. United States, 389 U.S. 818, 88 S.Ct. 126, 19 L.Ed.2d 70 (1968). Rule 43(c) of the Federal Rules of Civil Procedure provides: "The Court may require the offer to be made out of the hearing of the jury." In re McConnell, 370 U.S. 230, 82 S.Ct. 1288, 8 L.Ed.2d 434 (1962), left some doubt whether questions on which an offer is based must first be asked in the presence of the jury. The subdivision answers in the negative. The judge can foreclose a particular line of testimony and counsel can protect his record without a series of questions before the jury, designed at best to waste time and at worst "to waft into the jury box" the very matter sought to be excluded.

Subdivision (d). This wording of the plain error principle is from Rule 52(b) of the Federal Rules of Criminal Procedure. While judicial unwillingness to be constricted by mechanical breakdowns of the adversary system has been more pronounced in criminal cases, there is no scarcity of decisions to the same effect in civil cases. In general, see Campbell, Extent to Which Courts of Review Will Consider Questions Not Properly Raised and Presented, 7 Wis. L. Rev. 91, 160 (1932); Vestal, Sua Sponte Consideration in Appellate Review, 27 Fordham L. Rev. 477 (1958-59); 64 Harv. L. Rev. 652 (1951). In the nature of things the application of the plain error will be more likely with respect to the admission of evidence than to exclusion, since failure to comply with normal requirements of offers of proof is likely to produce a record which simply does not disclose the error.

NOTE BY FEDERAL JUDICIAL CENTER

The House bill contains the word "judge." The Senate amendment substitutes the word "court" in order to conform with usage elsewhere in the House bill. The conference adopts the Senate amendment.

Rule 104   Preliminary Questions

ADVISORY COMMITTEE'S NOTE

Subdivision (a). The applicability of a particular rule of evidence often depends upon the existence of a condition. Is the alleged expert a qualified physician? Is a witness whose former testimony is offered unavailable? Was a stranger present during a conversation between attorney and client? In each instance the admissibility of evidence will turn upon the answer to the question of the existence of the condition. Accepted practice, incorporated in the rule, places on the judge the responsibility for these determinations. McCormick § 53; Morgan, Basic Problems of Evidence 45-50 (1962).

To the extent that these inquiries are factual, the judge acts as a trier of fact. Often, however, rulings on evidence call for an evaluation in terms of a legally set standard. Thus when a hearsay statement is offered as a declaration against interest, a decision must be made whether it possesses the required against-interest characteristics. These decisions, too, are made by the judge.

In view of these considerations, this subdivision refers to preliminary requirements generally by the broad term "questions," without attempt at specification.

This subdivision is of general application. It must, however, be read as subject to the special provisions for "conditional relevancy" in subdivision (b) and those for confessions in subdivision (c).

If the question is factual in nature, the judge will of necessity receive evidence pro and con on the issue. The rule provides that the rules of evidence in general do not apply to this process. McCormick § 53, p. 123, n. 8, points out that the authorities are "scattered and inconclusive," and observes:

"Should the exclusionary law of evidence, 'the child of the jury system' in Thayer's phrase, be applied to this hearing before the judge? Sound sense backs the view that it should not, and that the judge should be empowered to hear any relevant evidence, such as affidavits or other reliable hearsay."

This view is reinforced by practical necessity in certain situations. An item, offered and objected to, may itself be considered in ruling on admissibility, though not yet admitted in evidence. Thus the content of an asserted declaration against interest must be considered in ruling whether it is against interest. Again common practice calls for considering the testimony of a witness, particularly a child, in determining competency. Another example is the requirement of Rule 602 dealing with personal knowledge. In the case of hearsay, it is enough, if the declarant "so far as appears [has] had an opportunity to observe the fact declared." McCormick, § 10, p. 19.

If concern is felt over the use of affidavits, by the judge in preliminary hearings on admissibility, attention is directed to the many important judicial determinations made on the basis of affidavits. Rule 47 of the Federal Rules of Criminal Procedure provides:

"An application to the court for an order shall be by motion. . . . It may be supported by affidavit."

The Rules of Civil Procedure are more detailed. Rule 43(c), dealing with motions generally, provides:

"When a motion is based on facts not appearing of record the court may hear the matter on affidavits presented by the respective parties, but the court may direct that the matter be heard wholly or partly on oral testimony or depositions."

Rule 4(g) provides for proof of service by affidavit. Rule 56 provides in detail for the entry of summary judgment based on affidavits. Affidavits may supply the foundation for temporary restraining orders under Rule 65(b).

The study made for the California Law Revision Commission recommended an amendment to Uniform Rule 2 as follows:

"In the determination of the issue aforesaid [preliminary determination], exclusionary rules shall not apply, subject, however, to Rule 45 and any valid claim of privilege." Tentative Recommendation and a Study Relating to the Uniform Rules of Evidence (Article VIII, Hearsay), Cal. Law Revision Comm'n, Rep., Rec. & Studies, 470 (1962). The proposal was not adopted in the California Evidence Code. The Uniform Rules are likewise silent on the subject. However, New Jersey Evidence Rule 8(1), dealing with preliminary inquiry by the judge, provides:

"In his determination the rules of evidence shall not apply except for Rule 4 [exclusion on grounds of confusion, etc.] or a valid claim of privilege."

Subdivision (b). In some situations, the relevancy of an item of evidence, in the large sense, depends upon the existence of a particular preliminary fact. Thus when a spoken statement is relied upon to prove notice to X, it is without probative value unless X heard it. Or if a letter purporting to be from Y is relied upon to establish an admission by him, it has no probative value unless Y wrote or authorized it. Relevance in this sense has been labelled "conditional relevancy." Morgan, Basic Problems of Evidence 45, 46 (1962). Problems arising in connection with it are to be distinguished from problems of logical relevancy, e.g. evidence in a murder case that accused on the day before purchased a weapon of the kind used in the killing, treated in Rule 401.

If preliminary questions of conditional relevancy were determined solely by the judge, as provided in subdivision (a), the functioning of the jury as a trier of fact would be greatly restricted and in some cases virtually destroyed. These are appropriate questions for juries. Accepted treatment, as provided in the rule, is consistent with that given fact questions generally. The judge makes a preliminary determination whether the foundation evidence is sufficient to support a finding of fulfillment of the condition. If so, the item is admitted. If after all the evidence on the issue is in, pro and con, the jury could reasonably conclude that fulfillment of the condition is not established, the issue is for them. If the evidence is not such as to allow a finding, the judge withdraws the matter from their consideration. Morgan, *supra;* California Evidence Code § 403; New Jersey Rule 8(2). See also Uniform Rules 19 and 67.

The order of proof here, as generally, is subject to the control of the judge.

Subdivision (c). Preliminary hearings on the admissibility of confessions must be conducted outside the hearing of the jury. See Jackson v. Denno, 378 U.S. 368, 84 S.Ct. 1774, 12 L.Ed.2d 908 (1964). Otherwise, detailed treatment of when preliminary matters should be heard outside the hearing of the jury is not feasible. The procedure is time consuming. Not infrequently the same evidence which is relevant to the issue of establishment of fulfillment of a condition precedent to admissibility is also relevant to weight or credibility, and time is saved by taking foundation proof in the presence of the jury. Much evidence on preliminary questions, though not relevant to jury issues, may be heard by the jury with no adverse effect. A great deal must be left to the discretion of the judge who will act as the interests of justice require.

NOTE BY FEDERAL JUDICIAL CENTER

The Rule enacted by the Congress is the Rule prescribed by the Supreme Court, amended by substituting "court" in place of "judge," with appropriate pronominal change, and by adding to subdivision (c) the concluding phrase, "or when an accused is a witness, if he so requests."

REPORT OF THE HOUSE COMMITTEE ON THE JUDICIARY

Rule 104(c)

Rule 104(c) as submitted to the Congress provided that hearings on the admissibility of confessions shall be conducted outside the presence of the jury and hearings on all other preliminary matters should be so conducted when the interests of justice require. The Committee amended the Rule to provide that where an accused is a witness as to a preliminary matter, he has the right, upon his request, to be heard outside the jury's presence. Although recognizing that in some cases duplication of evidence would occur and that the procedure could be subject to abuse, the Committee believed that a proper regard for the right of an accused not to testify generally in the case dictates that he be given an option to testify out of the presence of the jury on preliminary matters.

The Committee construes the second sentence of subdivision (c) as applying to civil actions and proceedings as well as to criminal cases, and on this assumption has left the sentence unamended.

ADVISORY COMMITTEE'S NOTE

Subdivision (d). The limitation upon cross-examination is designed to encourage participation by the accused in the determination of preliminary matters. He may testify concerning them without exposing himself to cross-examination generally. The provision is necessary because of the breadth of cross-examination under Rule 611(b).

The rule does not address itself to questions of the subsequent use of testimony given by an accused at a hearing on a preliminary matter. See Walder v. United States, 347 U.S. 62 (1954); Simmons v. United States, 390 U.S. 377 (1968); Harris v. New York, 401 U.S. 222 (1971).

REPORT OF THE SENATE COMMITTEE ON THE JUDICIARY

Rule 104(d). Preliminary Questions: Testimony by accused

Under Rule 104(c) the hearing on a preliminary matter may at times be conducted in front of the jury. Should an accused testify in such a hearing, waiving his privilege against self-incrimination as to the preliminary issue, Rule 104(d) provides that he will not generally be subject to cross-examination as to any other issue. This rule is not, however, intended to immunize the accused from cross-examination where, in testifying about a preliminary issue, he injects other issues into the hearing. If he could not be cross-examined about any issues gratuitously raised by him beyond the scope of the preliminary matters, injustice might result. Accordingly, in order to prevent any such unjust result, the committee intends the rule to be construed to provide that the accused may subject himself to cross-examination as to issues raised by his own testimony upon a preliminary matter before a jury.

ADVISORY COMMITTEE'S NOTE

Subdivision (e). For similar provisions see Uniform Rule 8; California Evidence Code § 406; Kansas Code of Civil Procedure § 60-408; New Jersey Evidence Rule 8(1).

Rule 105   Limited Admissibility

Advisory Committee's Note

A close relationship exists between this rule and Rule 403 which . . . [provides for] exclusion when "probative value is substantially outweighed by the danger of unfair prejudice, confusion of the issues, or misleading the jury." The present rule recognizes the practice of admitting evidence for a limited purpose and instructing the jury accordingly. The availability and effectiveness of this practice must be taken into consideration in reaching a decision whether to exclude for unfair prejudice under Rule 403. In Bruton v. United States, 389 U.S. 818, 88 S.Ct. 126, 19 L.Ed.2d 70 (1968), the Court ruled that a limiting instruction did not effectively protect the accused against the prejudicial effect of admitting in evidence the confession of a codefendant which implicated him. The decision does not, however, bar the use of limited admissibility with an instruction where the risk of prejudice is less serious.

Similar provisions are found in Uniform Rule 6; California Evidence Code § 355; Kansas Code of Civil Procedure § 61-406; New Jersey Evidence Rule 6. The wording of the present rule differs, however, in repelling any implication that limiting or curative instructions are sufficient in all situations.

Report of House Committee on the Judiciary

Rule 106 as submitted by the Supreme Court (now Rule 105 in the bill) dealt with the subject of evidence which is admissible as to one party or for one purpose but is not admissible against another party or for another purpose. The Committee adopted this Rule without change on the understanding that it does not affect the authority of a court to order a severance in a multi-defendant case.

Note by Federal Judicial Center

Because Rule 105 as proposed by the Supreme Court was eliminated by Congress, the number of the Rule was changed from 106, as promulgated by the Supreme Court, to 105. The Rule enacted by the Congress is the Rule prescribed by the Supreme Court as Rule 106, amended by substituting "court" in place of "judge."

Rule 106   Remainder of or Related Writings or Recorded Statements

Advisory Committee's Note

The rule is an expression of the rule of completeness. McCormick § 56. It is manifested as to depositions in Rule 32(a)(1) of the Federal Rules of Civil Procedure, of which the proposed rule is substantially a restatement.

The rule is based on two considerations. The first is the misleading impression created by taking matters out of context. The second is the inadequacy of repair work when delayed to a point later in the trial. See McCormick § 56; California Evidence Code § 356. The rule does not in any way circumscribe the right of the adversary to develop the matter on cross-examination or as part of his own case.

For practical reasons, the rule is limited to writings and recorded statements and does not apply to conversations.

Note by Federal Judicial Center

The Rule enacted by the Congress is the Rule prescribed by the Supreme Court as Rule 107 without change.

ARTICLE II
JUDICIAL NOTICE

Rule 201   Judicial Notice of Adjudicative Facts

ADVISORY COMMITTEE'S NOTE

Subdivision (a). This is the only evidence rule on the subject of judicial notice. It deals only with judicial notice of "adjudicative" facts. No rule deals with judicial notice of "legislative" facts. Judicial notice of matters of foreign law is treated in Rule 44.1 of the Federal Rules of Civil Procedure and Rule 26.1 of the Federal Rules of Criminal Procedure.

The omission of any treatment of legislative facts results from fundamental differences between adjudicative facts and legislative facts. Adjudicative facts are simply the facts of the particular case. Legislative facts, on the other hand, are those which have relevance to legal reasoning and the lawmaking process, whether in the formulation of a legal principle or ruling by a judge or court or in the enactment of a legislative body. The terminology was coined by Professor Kenneth Davis in his article An Approach to Problems of Evidence in the Administrative Process, 55 Harv L Rev 364, 404-407 (1942). The following discussion draws extensively upon his writings. In addition, see the same author's Judicial Notice, 55 Colum L Rev 945 (1955); Administrative Law Treatise, ch. 15 (1958); A System of Judicial Notice Based on Fairness and Convenience, in Perspectives of Law 69 (1964).

The usual method of establishing adjudicative facts is through the introduction of evidence, ordinarily consisting of the testimony of witnesses. If particular facts are outside the area of reasonable controversy, this process is dispensed with as unnecessary. A high degree of indisputability is the essential prerequisite.

Legislative facts are quite different. As Professor Davis says:

"My opinion is that judge-made law would stop growing if judges, in thinking about questions of law and policy, were forbidden to take into account the facts they believe, as distinguished from facts which are 'clearly . . . within the domain of the indisputable.' Facts most needed in thinking about difficult problems of law and policy have a way of being outside the domain of the clearly indisputable." A System of Judicial Notice Based on Fairness and Convenience, supra, at 82.

An illustration is Hawkins v United States, 358 U.S. 74, 79 S.Ct. 136, 3 L.Ed.2d 125 (1958), in which the Court refused to discard the common law rule that one spouse could not testify against the other, saying, "Adverse testimony given in criminal proceedings would, we think, be likely to destroy almost any marriage." This conclusion has a large intermixture of fact, but the factual aspect is scarcely "indisputable." See Hutchins and Slesinger, Some Observations on the Law of Evidence—Family Relations, 13 Minn. L. Rev. 675 (1929). If the destructive effect of the giving of adverse testimony by a spouse is not indisputable, should the Court have refrained from considering it in the absence of supporting evidence?

"If the Model Code or the Uniform Rules had been applicable, the Court would have been barred from thinking about the essential factual ingredient of the problems before it, and such a result would be obviously intolerable. What the law needs at its growing points is more, not less, judicial thinking about the factual ingredients of problems of what the law ought to be, and the needed facts are seldom 'clearly' indisputable." Davis, supra, at 83.

Professor Morgan gave the following description of the methodology of determining domestic law:

"In determining the content or applicability of a rule of domestic law, the judge is unrestricted in his investigation and conclusion. He may reject the propositions of either party or of both parties. He may consult the sources of pertinent data to which they refer, or he may refuse to do so. He may make an independent search for persuasive data or rest content with what he has or what the parties present. . . . [T]he parties do no more than to assist; they control no part of the process." Morgan, Judicial Notice, 57 Harv. L. Rev 269, 270-271 (1944).

This is the view which should govern judicial access to legislative facts. It renders inappropriate any limitation in the form of indisputability, any formal requirements of notice other than those already inherent in affording opportunity to hear and be heard and exchanging briefs, and any requirement of formal findings at any level. It should, however, leave open the possibility of introducing evidence through regular channels in appropriate situations. See Borden's Farm Products Co. v Baldwin, 293 US 194, 55 S.Ct. 187, 79 L.Ed 281 (1934), where the cause was remanded for the taking of evidence as to the economic conditions and trade practices underlying the New York Milk Control Law.

Similar considerations govern the judicial use of non-adjudicative facts in ways other than formulating laws and rules. Thayer described them as a part of the judicial reasoning process.

"In conducting a process of judicial reasoning, as of other reasoning, not a step can be taken without assuming something which has not been proved; and the capacity to do this with competent judgment and efficiency, is imputed to judges and juries as part of their necessary mental outfit." Thayer, Preliminary Treatise on Evidence 279-280 (1898).

As Professor Davis points out, A System of Judicial Notice Based on Fairness and Convenience, in Perspectives of Law 69, 73 (1964), every case involves the use of hundreds or thousands of non-evidence facts. When a witness in an automobile accident case says "car," everyone, judge and jury included, furnishes, from non-evidence sources within himself, the supplementing information that the "car" is an automobile, not a railroad car, that it is self-propelled, probably by an internal combustion engine, that it may be assumed to have four wheels with pneumatic rubber tires, and so on. The judicial process cannot construct every case from scratch, like Descartes creating a world based on the postulate *Cogito, ergo sum*. These items could not possibly be introduced into evidence, and no one suggests that they be. Nor are they appropriate subjects for any formalized treatment of judicial notice of facts. See Levin and Levy, Persuading the Jury with Facts Not in Evidence: The Fiction-Science Spectrum, 105 U.Pa.L.Rev. 139 (1956).

Another aspect of what Thayer had in mind is the use of non-evidence facts to appraise or assess the adjudicative facts of the case. Pairs of cases from two jurisdictions illustrate this use and also the difference between non-evidence facts thus used and adjudicative facts. In People v. Strook, 347 Ill. 460, 179 NE 821 (1932), venue in Cook County had been held not established by testimony that the crime was committed at 7956 South Chicago Avenue, since judicial notice would not be taken that the address was in Chicago. However, the same court subsequently ruled that venue in Cook County was established by testimony that a crime occurred at 8900 South Anthony Avenue, since notice would be taken of the common practice of omitting the name of the city when speaking of local addresses, and the witness was testifying in Chicago. People v. Pride, 16 Ill.2d 82, 156 N.E.2d 551 (1951). And in Hughes v. Vestal, 264 N.C.500, 142 S.E.2d 361 (1965), the Supreme Court of North Carolina disapproved the trial judge's admission in evidence of a state-published table of automobile stopping distances on the basis of judicial notice, though the court itself had referred to the same table in an earlier case in a "rhetorical and illustrative" way in determining that the defendant could not have stopped her car in time to avoid striking a child who suddenly appeared in the highway and that a nonsuit was properly granted. Ennis v. Dupress, 262 N.C.224, 136 S.E.2d 702 (1964). See also Brown v. Hale, 263 NC 176, 139 S.E.2d 210 (1964); Clayton v. Rimmer, 262 N.C. 302, 136 S.E.2d 562 (1964). It is apparent that this use of non-evidence facts in evaluating the adjudicative facts of the case is not an appropriate subject for a formalized judicial notice treatment.

In view of these considerations, the regulation of judicial notice of facts by the present rule extends only to adjudicative facts.

What, then, are "adjudicative" facts? Davis refers to them as those "which relate to the parties," or more fully:

"When a court or an agency finds facts concerning the immediate parties—who did what, where, when, how, and with what motive or intent—the court or agency is performing an adjudicative function, and the facts are conveniently called adjudicative facts. . . .

"Stated in other terms, the adjudicative facts are those to which the law is applied in the process of adjudication. They are the facts that normally go to the jury in a jury case. They relate to the parties, their activities, their properties, their businesses." 2 Administrative Law Treatise 353.

Subdivision (b). With respect to judicial notice of adjudicative facts, the tradition has been one of caution in requiring that the matter be beyond reasonable controversy. This tradition of circumspection appears to be soundly based, and no reason to depart from it is apparent. As Professor Davis says:

"The reason we use trial-type procedure, I think, is that we make the practical judgment, on the basis of experience, that taking evidence, subject to cross-examination and rebuttal, is the best way to resolve controversies involving disputes of adjudicative facts, that is, facts pertaining to the parties. The reason we require a determination on the record is that we think fair procedure in resolving disputes of adjudicative facts calls for giving each party a chance to meet in the appropriate fashion the facts that come to the tribunal's attention, and the appropriate fashion for meeting disputed adjudicative facts includes rebuttal evidence, cross-examination, usually confrontation, and argument (either written or oral or both). The key to a fair trial is opportunity to use the appropriate weapons (rebuttal evidence, cross-examination, and argument) to meet adverse materials that come to the tribunal's attention." A System of Judicial Notice Based on Fairness and Convenience, in Perspectives of Law 69, 93 (1964).

The rule proceeds upon the theory that these considerations call for dispensing with traditional methods of proof only in clear cases. Compare Professor Davis' conclusion that judicial notice should be a matter of convenience, subject to requirements of procedural fairness. Id., 94.

This rule is consistent with Uniform Rule 9(1) and (2) which limit judicial notice of facts to those "so universally known that they cannot reasonably be the subject of dispute," those "so generally known or of such common notoriety within the territorial jurisdiction of the court that they cannot reasonably be the subject of dispute," those "capable of immediate and accurate determination by resort to easily accessible sources of indisputable accuracy." The traditional textbook treatment has included these general categories (matters of common knowledge, facts capable of verification), McCormick §§ 324, 325, and then has passed on into detailed treatment of such specific topics as facts relating to the personnel and records of the court, id. § 327, and other governmental facts, id. § 328. The California draftsmen, with a background of detailed statutory regulation of judicial notice, followed a somewhat similar pattern. California Evidence Code §§ 451, 452. The Uniform Rules, however, were drafted on the theory that these particular matters are included within the general categories and need no specific mention. This approach is followed in the present rule.

The phrase "propositions of generalized knowledge," found in Uniform Rule 9(1) and (2) is not included in the present rule. It was, it is believed, originally included in Model Code Rules 801 and 802 primarily in order to afford some minimum recognition to the right of the judge in his "legislative" capacity (not acting as the trier of fact) to take judical notice of very limited categories of generalized knowledge. The limitations thus imposed have been discarded herein as undesirable, unworkable, and contrary to existing practice. What is left, then, to be considered, is the status of a "proposition of generalized knowledge" as an "adjudicative" fact to be noticed judicially and communicated by the judge to the jury. Thus viewed, it is considered to be lacking practical significance. While judges used judicial notice of "propositions of generalized knowledge" in a variety of situations: determining the validity and meaning of statutes, formulating common law rules, deciding whether evidence should be admitted, assessing the sufficiency and effect of evidence, all are essentially nonadjudicative in nature. When judicial notice is seen as a significant vehicle for progress in the law, these are the areas involved, particularly in developing fields of scientific knowledge. See McCormick 712. It is not believed that judges now instruct juries as to "propositions of generalized knowledge" derived from encyclopedias or other sources, or that they are likely to do so, or, indeed, that it is desirable that they do so. There is a vast difference between ruling on the basis of judicial notice that radar evidence of speed is admissible and explaining to the jury its principles and degree of accuracy, or between using a table of stopping distances of automobiles at various speeds in a judicial evaluation of testimony and telling the jury its precise application in the case. For cases raising doubt as to the propriety of the use of medical texts by lay triers of fact in passing on disability claims in administrative proceedings, see Sayers v. Gardner, 380 F2d 940 (6th Cir. 1967); Ross v. Gardner, 365 F2d 554 (6th Cir. 1966); Sosna v. Celebreeze, 234 F Supp 289 (ED Pa. 1964); Glendenning v. Ribicoff, 213 F Supp 301 (WD Mo. 1962).

Subdivisions (c) and (d). Under subdivision (c) the judge has a discretionary authority to take judicial notice, regardless of whether he is so requested by a party. The taking of judicial notice is mandatory, under subdivision (d), only when a party requests it and the necessary information is supplied. This scheme is believed to reflect existing practice. It is simple and workable. It avoids troublesome distinctions in the many situations in which the process of taking judicial notice is not recognized as such.

Compare Uniform Rule 9 making judicial notice of facts universally known mandatory without request, and making judicial notice of facts generally known in the jurisdiction or capable of determination by resort to accurate sources discretionary in the absence of request but mandatory if request is made and the information furnished. But see Uniform Rule 10(3), which directs the judge to decline to take judicial notice if available information fails to convince him that the matter falls clearly within Uniform Rule 9 or is insufficient to enable him to notice it judicially. Substantially the same approach is found in California Evidence Code §§ 451-453 and in New Jersey Evidence Rule 9. In contrast, the present rule treats alike all adjudicative facts which are subject to judicial notice.

Subdivision (c). Basic considerations of procedural fairness demand an opportunity to be heard on the propriety of taking judicial notice and the tenor of the matter noticed. The rule requires the granting of that opportunity upon request. No formal scheme of giving notice is provided. An adversely affected party may learn in advance that judicial notice is in contemplation, either by virtue of being served with a copy of a request by another party under subdivision (d) that judicial notice be taken, or through an advance indication by the judge. Or he may have no advance notice at all. The likelihood of the latter is enhanced by the frequent failure to recognize judicial notice as such. And in the absence of advance notice, a request made after the fact could not in fairness be considered untimely. See the provision for hearing on timely request in the Administrative Procedure Act, 5 USC § 556(e). See also Revised Model State Administrative Procedure Act (1961), 9C ULA § 10(4) (Supp 1967).

Subdivision (f). In accord with the usual view, judicial notice may be taken at any stage of the proceedings, whether in the trial court or on appeal. Uniform Rule 12; California Evidence Code § 459; Kansas Rules of Evidence § 60-412; New Jersey Evidence Rule 12; McCormick § 330, p. 712.

Subdivision (g). Much of the controversy about judicial notice has centered upon the question whether evidence should be admitted in disproof of facts of which judicial notice is taken.

The writers have been divided. Favoring admissibility are Thayer, Preliminary Treatise on Evidence 308 (1898); 9 Wigmore § 2567; Davis, A System of Judicial Notice Based on Fairness and Convenience, in Perspectives of Law, 69, 76-77 (1964). Opposing admissibility are Keeffe, Landis and Shaad, Sense and Nonsense about Judicial Notice, 2 Stan L Rev 664, 668 (1950); McNaughton, Judicial Notice—Excerpts Relating to the Morgan-Whitmore Controversy, 14 Vand L Rev 779 (1961); Morgan, Judicial Notice, 57 Harv L Rev 269, 279 (1944); McCormick 710-

714. The Model Code and the Uniform Rules are predicated upon indisputability of judicially noticed facts.

The proponents of admitting evidence in disproof have concentrated largely upon legislative facts. Since the present rule deals only with judicial notice of adjudicative facts, arguments directed to legislative facts lose their relevancy.

Within its relatively narrow area of adjudicative facts, the rule contemplates there is to be no evidence before the jury in disproof. The judge instructs the jury to take judicially noticed facts as established. This position is justified by the undesirable effects of the opposite rule in limiting the rebutting party, though not his opponent, to admissible evidence, in defeating the reasons for judicial notice, and in affecting the substantive law to an extent and in ways largely unforeseeable. Ample protection and flexibility are afforded by the broad provision for opportunity to be heard on request, set forth in subdivision (e).

[The following paragraph accompanied only the March, 1969 Draft of Rule 201. See 46 FRD 161, 205 (1969). A different version of this paragraph accompanied the March, 1971 Draft, 51 FRD 315, 335 (1971) and the November, 1972 Draft, 56 FRD 183, 207 (1972). We set forth the 1969 version because the Congress restored essentially the 1969 draft of the provisions to which this paragraph of Notes refers.]

Criminal cases are treated somewhat differently in the rule. While matters falling within the common fund of information supposed to be possessed by jurors need not be proved, *State v Dunn*, 221 Mo 530, 120 SW 1179 (1909), these are not, properly speaking, adjudicative facts but an aspect of legal reasoning. The considerations which underlie the general rule that a verdict cannot be directed against the accused in a criminal case seems to foreclose the judge's directing the jury on the basis of judicial notice to accept as conclusive any adjudicative facts in the case. *State v Main*, 91 RI 338, 180 A2d 814 (1962); *State v Lawrence*, 120 Utah 323, 234 P2d 600 (1951). Cf. *People v Mayes*, 113 Cal 618, 45 P 860 (1896); *Ross v United States*, 374 F2d 97 (8th Cir. 1967). However, this view presents no obstacle to the judge's advising the jury as to a matter judicially noticed, if he instructs them that it need not be taken as conclusive.

REPORT OF THE HOUSE COMMITTEE ON THE JUDICIARY

Rule 201(g) as received from the Supreme Court provided that when judicial notice of a fact is taken, the court shall instruct the jury to accept that fact as established. Being of the view that mandatory instruction to a jury in a criminal case to accept as conclusive any fact judicially noticed is inappropriate because contrary to the spirit of the Sixth Amendment right to a jury trial, the Committee adopted the 1969 Advisory Committee draft of this subsection, allowing a mandatory instruction in civil actions and proceedings and a discretionary instruction in criminal cases.

NOTE BY ADVISORY COMMITTEE ON JUDICIAL NOTICE OF LAW

By rules effective July 1, 1966, the method of invoking the law of a foreign country is covered elsewhere. Rule 44.1 of the Federal Rules of Civil Procedure; Rule 26.1 of the Federal Rules of Criminal Procedure. These two new admirably designed rules are founded upon the assumption that the manner in which law is fed into the judicial process is never a proper concern of the rules of evidence but rather of the rules of procedure. The Advisory Committee on Evidence, believing that this assumption is entirely correct, proposes no evidence rule with respect to judicial notice of law, and suggests that those matters of law which, in addition to foreign-country law, have traditionally been treated as requiring pleading and proof and more recently as the subject of judicial notice be left to the Rules of Civil and Criminal Procedure.

NOTE BY FEDERAL JUDICIAL CENTER

The Rule enacted by the Congress is the rule prescribed by the Supreme Court with the following changes: (1) In subdivisions (c) and (d) the words "judge or" before "court" were deleted. (2) Subdivision (g) as it is shown was substituted in place of, "The judge shall instruct the jury to accept as established any facts judicially noticed." The substituted language is from the 1969 Preliminary Draft, 46 F.R.D. 161, 195.

ARTICLE III
PRESUMPTIONS IN CIVIL ACTIONS AND PROCEEDINGS

Rule 301   Presumptions in General in Civil Actions and Proceedings

ADVISORY COMMITTEE'S NOTE

This rule governs presumptions generally. See Rule 302 for presumptions controlled by state law and Rule 303 for those against an accused in a criminal case.

Presumptions governed by this rule are given the effect of placing upon the opposing party the burden of establishing the nonexistence of the presumed fact, once the party invoking the presumption establishes the basic facts giving rise to it. The same considerations of fairness, policy, and probability which dictate the allocation of the burden of the various elements of a case as between the prima facie case of a plaintiff and affirmative defenses also underlie the creation of presumptions. These considerations are not satisfied by giving a lesser effect to presumptions. Morgan and Maguire, Looking Backward and Forward at Evidence, 50 Harv L Rev 909, 913 (1937); Morgan, Instructing the Jury upon Presumptions and Burden of Proof, 47 Harv L Rev 59, 82 (1933); Cleary, Presuming and Pleading: An Essay on Juristic Immaturity, 12 Stan L Rev 5 (1959).

The so-called "bursting bubble" theory, under which a presumption vanishes upon the introduction of evidence which would support a finding of the nonexistence of the presumed fact, even though not believed, is rejected as according presumptions too "slight and evanescent" an effect. Morgan and Maguire, *supra*, at p. 913.

In the opinion of the Advisory Committee, no constitutional infirmity attends this view of presumptions. In Mobile, J. & K. C. R. Co. v. Turnipseed, 219 US 35, 31 S Ct 136, 55 L Ed 78 (1910), the Court upheld a Mississippi statute which provided that in actions against railroads proof of injury inflicted by the running of trains should be prima facie evidence of negligence by the railroad. The injury in the case had resulted from a derailment. The opinion made the points (1) that the only effect of the statute was to impose on the railroad the duty of producing some evidence to the contrary, (2) that an inference may be supplied by law if there is a rational connection between the fact proved and the fact presumed, as long as the opposite party is not precluded from presenting his evidence to the contrary, and (3) that considerations of public policy arising from the character of the business justified the application in question. Nineteen years later, in Western & Atlantic R. Co. v. Henderson, 279 US 639, 49 S Ct 445, 73 L Ed 884 (1929), the Court overturned a Georgia statute making railroads liable for damages done by trains, unless the railroad made it appear that reasonable care had been used, the presumption being against the railroad. The declaration alleged the death of plaintiff's husband from a grade crossing collision, due to specified acts of negligence by defendant. The jury were instructed that proof of the injury raised a presumption of negligence; the burden shifted to the railroad to prove ordinary care; and unless it did so, they should find for plaintiff. The instruction was held erroneous in an opinion stating (1) that there was no rational connection between the mere fact of collision and negligence on the part of anyone, and (2) that the statute was different from that in *Turnipseed* in imposing a burden upon the railroad. The reader is left in a state of some confusion. Is the difference between a derailment and a grade crossing collision of no significance? Would the *Turnipseed* presumption have been bad if it had imposed a burden of persuasion on defendant, although that would in nowise have impaired its "rational connection"? If *Henderson* forbids imposing a burden of persuasion on defendants, what happens to affirmative defenses?

Two factors serve to explain *Henderson*. The first was that it was common ground that negligence was indispensable to liability. Plaintiff thought so, drafted her complaint accordingly, and relied upon the presumption. But how in logic could the same presumption establish her alternative grounds of negligence that the engineer was so blind he could not see decedent's truck and that he failed to stop after he saw it? Second, take away the basic assumption of no liability without fault, as *Turnipseed* intimated might be done ("considerations of public policy arising out of the character of the business"), and the structure of the decision in *Henderson* fails. No question of logic would have arisen if the statute had simply said: a prima facie case of liability is made by proof of injury by a train; lack of negligence is an affirmative defense, to be pleaded and proved as other affirmative defenses. The problem would be one of economic due process only. While it seems likely that the Supreme Court of 1929 would have voted that due process was denied, that result today would be unlikely. See, for example, the shift in the direction of absolute liability in the consumer cases. Prosser, The Assault upon the Citadel (Strict Liability to the Consumer), 69 Yale LJ 1099 (1960).

Any doubt as to the constitutional permissibility of a presumption imposing a burden of persuasion of the nonexistence of the presumed fact in civil cases is laid at rest by Dick v. New York Life Ins. Co., 359 US 437, 79 S Ct 921, 3 L Ed 2d 935 (1959). The Court unhesitatingly applied the North Dakota rule that the presumption against suicide imposed on defendant the burden of proving that the death of insured, under an accidental death clause, was due to suicide.

"Proof of coverage and of death by gunshot wound shifts the burden to the insurer to establish that the death of the insured was due to his suicide." 359 US at 443, 79 S Ct at 925.

"In a case like this one, North Dakota presumes that death was accidental and places on the insurer the burden of proving that death resulted from suicide." *Id.* at 446, 79 S Ct at 927.

The rational connection requirement survives in criminal cases, Tot v. United States, 319 US 463, 63 S Ct 1241, 87 L Ed 1519 (1943), because the Court has been unwilling to extend into that area the greater-includes-the-lesser theory of Ferry v. Ramsey, 277 US 88, 48 S Ct 443, 72 L Ed 796 (1928). In that case the Court sustained a Kansas statute under which bank directors were personally liable for deposits made with their assent and with knowledge of insolvency, and the fact of insolvency was prima facie evidence of assent and knowledge of insolvency. Mr. Justice Holmes pointed out that the state legislature could have made the directors personally liable to depositors in every case. Since the statute imposed a less stringent liability, "the thing to be considered is the result reached, not the possibly inartificial or clumsy way of reaching it." *Id.* at 94, 48 S Ct at 444. Mr. Justice Sutherland dissented: though the state could have created an absolute liability, it did not purport to do so; a rational connection was necessary, but lacking, between the liability created and the prima facie evidence of it: the result might be different if the basis of the presumption were being open for business.

The Sutherland view has prevailed in criminal cases by virtue of the higher standard of notice there required. The fiction that everyone is presumed to know the law is applied to the substantive law of crimes as an alternative to complete unenforceability. But the need does not extend to criminal evidence and procedure, and the fiction does not encompass them. "Rational connection" is not fictional or artificial, and so it is reasonable to suppose that Gainey should have known that his presence at the site of an illicit still could convict him of being connected with (carrying on) the business, United States v. Gainey, 380 US 68, 85 S Ct 751, 13 L Ed 2d 658 (1965), but not that Romano should have known that his presence at a still could convict him of possessing it, United States v. Romano, 382 US 136, 86 S Ct 279, 15 L Ed 2d 210 (1965).

In his dissent in Gainey, Mr. Justice Black put it more artistically:

"It might be argued, although the Court does not so argue or hold, that Congress if it wished could make presence at a still a crime in itself, and so Congress should be free to create crimes which are called 'possession' and 'carrying on an illegal distillery business' but which are defined in such a way that unexplained presence is sufficient and indisputable evidence in all cases to support conviction for those offenses. See Ferry v Ramsey, 277 US 88, 48 S Ct 443, 72 L Ed 796. Assuming for the sake of argument that Congress could make unexplained presence a criminal act, and ignoring also the refusal of this Court in other cases to uphold a statutory presumption on such a theory, see Heiner v Donnan, 285 US 312, 52 S Ct 358, 76 L Ed 772, there is no indication here that Congress intended to adopt such a misleading method of draftsmanship, nor in my judgment could the statutory provisions if so construed escape condemnation for vagueness, under the principles applied in Lanzetta v New Jersey, 306 US 451, 59 S Ct 618, 83 L Ed 888, and many other cases." 380 US at 84, n 12, 85 S Ct at 766. And the majority opinion in *Romano* agreed with him:

"It may be, of course, that Congress has the power to make presence at an illegal still a punishable crime, but we find no clear indication that it intended to so exercise this power. The crime remains possession, not presence, and with all due deference to the judgment of Congress, the former may not constitutionally be inferred from the latter." 382 US at 144, 86 S Ct at 284.

The rule does not spell out the procedural aspects of its application. Questions as to when the evidence warrants submission of a presumption and what instructions are proper under varying states of fact are believed to present no particular difficulties.

Report of the House Committee on the Judiciary

[The following Report refers to the version of Rule 301 originally passed by the House of Representatives. The enacted version of Rule 301, set forth prior to the Advisory Committee's Note above, differs significantly.]

Rule 301 as submitted by the Supreme Court provided that in all cases a presumption imposes on the party against whom it is directed the burden of proving that the nonexistence of the presumed fact is more probable than its existence. The Committee limited the scope of Rule 301 to "civil actions and proceedings" to effectuate its decision not to deal with the question of presumptions in criminal cases. (See note on Rule 303 in discussion of Rules deleted.) With respect to the weight to be given a presumption in a civil case, the Committee agreed with the judgment implicit in the Court's version that the so-called "bursting bubble" theory of presumptions, whereby a presumption vanishes upon the appearance of any contradicting evidence by the other party, gives to presumptions too slight an effect. On the other hand, the Committee believed that the Rule proposed by the Court, whereby a presumption permanently alters the burden of persuasion, no matter how much contradicting evidence is introduced—a view shared by only a few courts—lends too great a force to presumptions. Accordingly, the Committee amended the Rule to adopt an intermediate position under which a presumption does not vanish upon the introduction of contradicting evidence, and does not change the burden of persuasion; instead it is merely deemed sufficient evidence of the fact presumed, to be considered by the jury or other finder of fact.

REPORT OF THE SENATE COMMITTEE ON THE JUDICIARY

[The following Report refers to the version of Rule 301 which the Congress ultimately enacted.]

This rule governs presumptions in civil cases generally. Rule 302 provides for presumptions in cases controlled by State law.

As submitted by the Supreme Court, presumptions governed by this rule were given the effect of placing upon the opposing party the burden of establishing the nonexistence of the presumed fact, once the party invoking the presumption established the basic facts giving rise to it.

Instead of imposing a burden of persuasion on the party against whom the presumption is directed, the House adopted a provision which shifted the burden of going forward with the evidence. They further provided that "even though met with contradicting evidence, a presumption is sufficient evidence of the fact presumed, to be considered by the trier of fact." The effect of the amendment is that presumptions are to be treated as evidence.

The committee feels the House amendment is ill-advised. As the joint committees (the Standing Committee on Practice and Procedure of the Judicial Conference and the Advisory Committee on the Rules of Evidence) stated: "Presumptions are not evidence, but ways of dealing with evidence." This treatment requires juries to perform the task of considering "as evidence" facts upon which they have no direct evidence and which may confuse them in performance of their duties. California had a rule much like that contained in the House amendment. It was sharply criticized by Justice Traynor in Speck v. Sarcer and was repealed after 93 troublesome years.

Professor McCormick gives a concise and compelling critique of the presumption as evidence rule:

* * * * *

Another solution, formerly more popular than now, is to instruct the jury that the presumption is 'evidence', to be weighed and considered with the testimony in the case. This avoids the danger that the jury may infer that the presumption is conclusive, but it probably means little to the jury, and certainly runs counter to accepted theories of the nature of evidence.

For these reasons the committee has deleted that provision of the House-passed rule that treats presumptions as evidence. The effect of the rule as adopted by the committee is to make clear that while evidence of facts giving rise to a presumption shifts the burden of coming forward with evidence to rebut or meet the presumption, it does not shift the burden of persuasion on the existence of the presumed facts. The burden of persuasion remains on the party to whom it is allocated under the rules governing the allocation in the first instance.

The court may instruct the jury that they may infer the existence of the presumed fact from proof of the basic facts giving rise to the presumption. However, it would be inappropriate under this rule to instruct the jury that the inference they are to draw is conclusive.

Report of the House/Senate Conference Committee

[The "senate amendment" to which the following Report refers, embodies Rule 301 in the form which Congress ultimately enacted.]

The House bill provides that a presumption in civil actions and proceedings shifts to the party against whom it is directed the burden of going forward with evidence to meet or rebut it. Even though evidence contradicting the presumption is offered, a presumption is considered sufficient evidence of the presumed fact to be considered by the jury. The Senate amendment provides that a presumption shifts to the party against whom it is directed the burden of going forward with evidence to meet or rebut the presumption, but it does not shift to that party the burden of persuasion on the existence of the presumed fact.

Under the Senate amendment, a presumption is sufficient to get a party past an adverse party's motion to dismiss made at the end of his case-in-chief. If the adverse party offers no evidence contradicting the presumed fact, the court will instruct the jury that if it finds the basic facts, it may presume the existence of the presumed fact. If the adverse party does offer evidence contradicting the presumed fact, the court cannot instruct the jury that it may *presume* the existence of the presumed fact from proof of the basic facts. The court may, however, instruct the jury that it may infer the existence of the presumed fact from proof of the basic facts.

The Conference adopts the Senate amendment.

Note by Federal Judicial Center

The bill passed by the House substituted a substantially different Rule in place of that prescribed by the Supreme Court. The Senate bill substituted yet a further version, which was accepted by the House, was enacted by the Congress, and is the current Rule.

Rule 302   Applicability of State Law in Civil Actions and Proceedings

Advisory Committee's Note

A series of Supreme Court decisions in diversity cases leaves no doubt of the relevance of Erie Railroad Co. v. Tompkins, 301 US 61, 58 S Ct 817, 82 L Ed 1188 (1938), to questions of burden of proof. These decisions are Cities Service Oil Co. v. Dunlap, 308 US 208, 60 S Ct 201, 84 L Ed 196 (1939), Palmer v. Hoffman, 318

US 109, 63 S Ct 177, 87 L Ed 645 (1943), and Dick v. New York Life Ins. Co., 359 US 437, 79 S Ct 921, 3 L Ed 2d 935 (1959). They involved burden of proof, respectively, as to status as bona fide purchaser, contributory negligence, and non-accidental death (suicide) of an insured. In each instance the state rule was held to be applicable. It does not follow, however, that all presumptions in diversity cases are governed by state law. In each case cited, the burden of proof questioned had to do with a substantive element of the claim or defense. Application of the state law is called for only when the presumption operates upon such an element. Accordingly the rule does not apply state law when the presumption operates upon a lesser aspect of the case, i.e. "tactical" presumptions.

The situations in which the state law is applied have been tagged for convenience in the preceding discussion as "diversity cases." The designation is not a completely accurate one since Erie applies to any claim or issue having its source in state law, regardless of the basis of federal jurisdiction, and does not apply to a federal claim or issue, even though jurisdiction is based on diversity. Vestal, Erie R. R. v. Tompkins: A Projection, 48 Iowa L Rev 248, 257 (1963); Hart and Wechsler, The Federal Courts and the Federal System, 697 (1953); 1A Moore, Federal Practice ¶ 0.305[3] (2d ed., 1965); Wright, Federal Courts, 217-218 (1963). Hence the rule employs, as appropriately descriptive, the phrase "as to which state law supplies the rule of decision." See ALI Study of the Division of Jurisdiction Between State and Federal Courts, § 2344(c), p. 40, PFD No. 1 (1965).

NOTE BY FEDERAL JUDICIAL CENTER

Congress merely added the phrase "and proceedings" after "civil actions." No substantive change was involved. The Rule enacted by the Congress is the Rule prescribed by the Supreme Court, as amended.

ARTICLE IV
RELEVANCY AND ITS LIMITS

Rule 401   Definition of "Relative Evidence"

ADVISORY COMMITTEE'S NOTE

Problems of relevancy call for an answer to the question whether an item of evidence, when tested by the processes of legal reasoning, possesses sufficient probative value to justify receiving it in evidence. Thus, assessment of the probative value of evidence that a person purchased a revolver shortly prior to a fatal shooting with which he is charged is a matter of analysis and reasoning.

The variety of relevancy problems is coextensive with the ingenuity of counsel in using circumstantial evidence as a means of proof. An enormous number of cases fall in no set pattern, and this rule is designed as a guide for handling them. On the other hand, some situations recur with sufficient frequency to create patterns susceptible of treatment by specific rules. Rule 404 and those following it are of that variety; they also serve as illustrations of the application of the present rule as limited by the exclusionary principles of Rule 403.

Passing mention should be made of so-called "conditional" relevancy. Morgan, Basic Problems of Evidence 45-46 (1962). In this situation, probative value depends not only upon satisfying the basic requirement of relevancy as described above but also upon the existence of some matter of fact. For example, if evidence of a spoken statement is relied upon to prove notice, probative value is lacking unless the person sought to be charged heard the statement. The problem is one of fact, and the only rules needed are for the purpose of determining the respective functions of judge and jury. See Rules 101(b) and 901. The discussion which follows in the present note is concerned with relevancy generally, not with any particular problem of conditional relevancy.

Relevancy is not an inherent characteristic of any item of evidence but exists only as a relation between an item of evidence and a matter properly provable in the case. Does the item of evidence tend to prove the matter sought to be proved? Whether the relationship exists depends upon principles evolved by experience or science, applied logically to the situation at hand. James, Relevancy, Probability and the Law, 29 Calif.L.Rev. 689, 696, n. 15 (1911), in Selected Writings on Evidence and Trial 610, 615, n. 15 (Fryer ed. 1957). The rule summarizes this relationship as a "tendency to make the existence" of the fact to be proved "more probable or less probable." Compare Uniform Rule 1(2) which states the crux of relevancy as "a tendency in reason," thus perhaps emphasizing unduly the logical process and ignoring the need to draw upon experience or science to validate the general principle upon which relevancy in a particular situation depends.

The standard of probability under the rule is "more . . . probable than it would be without the evidence." Any more stringent requirement is unworkable and unrealistic. As McCormick § 152, p. 317, says, "A brick is not a wall," or, as Falknor, Extrinsic Policies Affecting Admissibility, 10 Rutgers L. Rev. 574, 576 (1956), quotes Professor McBaine,". . . [I]t is not to be supposed that every witness can make a home run." Dealing with probability in the language of the rule has the added virtue of avoiding confusion between questions of admissibility and questions of the sufficiency of the evidence.

The rule uses the phrase "fact that is of consequence to the determination of the action" to describe the kind of fact to which proof may properly be directed. The language is that of California Evidence Code § 210, it has the advantage of avoiding the loosely used and ambiguous word "material." Tentative Recommendation and a Study Relating to the Uniform Rules of Evidence (Art. I, General Provisions), Cal. Law Revision Comm'n, Rep., Rec. & Studies, 10-11 (1964). The fact to be proved may be ultimate, intermediate, or evidentiary; it matters not, so long as it is of consequence in the determination of the action. Cf. Uniform Rule 1(2) which requires that the evidence relate to a "material" fact.

The fact to which the evidence is directed need not be in dispute. While situations will arise which call for the exclusion of evidence offered to prove a point conceded by the opponent, the ruling should be made on the basis of such considerations as waste of time and undue prejudice (see Rule 403), rather than under any general requirement that evidence is admissible only if directed to matters in dispute. Evidence which is essentially background in nature can scarcely be said to involve disputed matter, yet it is universally offered and admitted as an aid to understanding. Charts, photographs, views of real estate, murder weapons, and many other items of evidence fall in this category. A rule limiting admissibility to evidence directed to a controversial point would invite the exclusion of this helpful evidence, or at least the raising of endless questions over its admission. Cf. California Evidence Code § 210, defining relevant evidence in terms of tendency to prove a disputed fact.

NOTE BY FEDERAL JUDICIAL CENTER

The Rule enacted by the Congress is the Rule prescribed by the Supreme Court without change. Congress made no change in Rule 401; it was not the subject of floor debate. No witnesses at the Hearings before the Special Subcommittee on Criminal Justice of the Committee on the Judiciary expressed any dissatisfaction with the Rule. The Senate Hearings were also free of criticism.

Rule 402   Relevant Evidence Generally Admissible; Irrelevant Evidence Inadmissible

ADVISORY COMMITTEE'S NOTE

The provisions that all relevant evidence is admissible, with certain exceptions, and that evidence which is not relevant is not admissible are "a presupposition involved in the very conception of a rational system of evidence." Thayer, Preliminary Treatise on Evidence 264 (1898). They constitute the foundation upon which the structure of admission and exclusion rests. For similar provisions see California Evidence Code §§ 350, 351. Provisions that all relevant evidence is admissible are found in Uniform Rule 7(f); Kansas Code of Civil Procedure § 60-407(f); and New Jersey Evidence Rule 7(f); but the exclusion of evidence which is not relevant is left to implication.

Not all relevant evidence is admissible. The exclusion of relevant evidence occurs in a variety of situations and may be called for by these rules, by the Rules of Civil and Criminal Procedure, by Bankruptcy Rules, by Act of Congress, or by constitutional considerations.

Succeeding rules in the present article, in response to the demands of particular policies, require the exclusion of evidence despite its relevancy. In addition, Article V recognizes a number of privileges; Article VI imposes limitations upon witnesses and the manner of dealing with them; Article VII specifies requirements with respect to opinions and expert testimony; Article VIII excludes hearsay not falling within an exception; Article IX spells out the handling of authentication and identification; and Article X restricts the manner of proving the contents of writings and recordings.

The Rules of Civil and Criminal Procedure in some instances require the exclusion of relevant evidence. For example, Rules 30(b) and 32(a)(3) of the Rules of Civil Procedure, by imposing requirements of notice and unavailability of the deponent, place limits on the use of relevant depositions. Similarly, Rule 15 of the Rules of Criminal Procedure restricts the use of depositions in criminal cases, even though relevant. And the effective enforcement of the command, originally statutory and now found in Rule 5(a) of the Rules of Criminal Procedure, that an arrested person be taken without unnecessary delay before a commissioner or other similar officer is held to require the exclusion of statements elicited during detention in violation thereof. Mallory v. United States, 354 US 449, 77 S Ct 1356, 1 L Ed 2d 1479 (1957); 18 U.S.C. § 3501(c).

While congressional enactments in the field of evidence have generally tended to expand admissibility beyond the scope of the common law rules, in some particular situations they have restricted the admissibility of relevant evidence. Most of this legislation has consisted of the formulation of a privilege or of a prohibition against disclosure. 8 U.S.C. § 1202(f), records of refusal of visas or permits to enter United States confidential, subject to discretion of Secretary of State to make available to court upon certification of need; 10 U.S.C. § 3693, replacement certificate of honorable discharge from Army not admissible in evidence; 10 U.S.C. § 8693, same as to Air Force; 11 U.S.C. § 25(a) (10), testimony given by bankrupt on his examination not admissible in criminal proceedings against him, except that given in hearing upon objection to discharge; 11 U.S.C. § 205(a), railroad reorganization petition, if dismissed, not admissible in evidence; 11 U.S.C. § 403(a), list of creditors filed with municipal composition plan not an admission; 13 U.S.C. § 9(a), census information confidential, retained copies of reports privileged; 47 U.S.C. § 605, interception and divulgence of wire or radio communications prohibited unless authorized by sender. These statutory provisions would remain undisturbed by the rules.

The rule recognizes but makes no attempt to spell out the constitutional considerations which impose basic limitations upon the admissibility of relevant evidence. Examples are evidence obtained by unlawful search and seizure, Weeks v. United States, 232 US 383, 34 S Ct 341, 58 L Ed 652 (1914); Katz v. United States, 389 US 347, 88 S Ct 507, 19 L Ed 2d 576 (1967); incriminating statement elicited from an accused in violation of right to counsel, Massiah v United States, 377 US 201, 84 S Ct 1199, 12 L Ed 2d 246 (1964).

Rule 402 as submitted to the Congress contained the phrase "or by other rules adopted by the Supreme Court." To accommodate the view that the Congress should not appear to acquiesce in the Court's judgment that it has authority under the existing Rules Enabling Acts to promulgate Rules of Evidence, the Committee amended the above phrase to read "or by other rules prescribed by the Supreme Court pursuant to statutory authority" in this and other Rules where the reference appears.

NOTE BY FEDERAL JUDICIAL CENTER

The Rule enacted by the Congress is the Rule prescribed by the Supreme Court, with the first sentence amended by substituting "prescribed" in place of "adopted," and by adding at the end thereof the phrase "pursuant to statutory authority."

Rule 403   Exclusion of Relevant Evidence on Grounds of Prejudice, Confusion, or Waste of Time

ADVISORY COMMITTEE'S NOTE

The case law recognizes that certain circumstances call for the exclusion of evidence which is of unquestioned relevance. These circumstances entail risks which range all the way from inducing decision on a purely emotional basis, at one extreme, to nothing more harmful than merely wasting time, at the other extreme. Situations in this area call for balancing the probative value of and need for the evidence against the harm likely to result from its admission. Slough, Relevancy Unraveled, 5 Kan.L.Rev. 1, 12-15 (1956); Trautman, Logical or Legal Relevancy—A Conflict in Theory, 5 Van.L.Rev. 385, 392 (1952); McCormick § 152, pp. 319-321. The rules which follow in this Article are concrete applications evolved for particular situations. However, they reflect the policies underlying the present rule, which is designed as a guide for the handling of situations for which no specific rules have been formulated.

Exclusion for risk of unfair prejudice, confusion of issues, misleading the jury, or waste of time, all find ample support in the authorities. "Unfair prejudice" within its context means an undue tendency to suggest decision on an improper basis, commonly, though not necessarily, an emotional one.

The rule does not enumerate surprise as a ground for exclusion, in this respect following Wigmore's view of the common law. 6 Wigmore § 1849. Cf. McCormick § 152, p. 320, n. 29, listing unfair surprise as a ground for exclusion but stating that it is usually "coupled with the danger of prejudice and confusion of issues." While Uniform Rule 45 incorporates surprise as a ground and is followed in Kansas Code of Civil Procedure § 60-445, surprise is not included in California Evidence Code § 352 or New Jersey Rule 4, though both the latter otherwise substantially embody Uniform Rule 45. While it can scarcely be doubted that claims of unfair surprise may still be justified despite procedural requirements of notice and instrumentalities of discovery, the granting of a continuance is a more appropriate remedy than exclusion of the evidence. Tentative Recommendation and a Study Relating to the Uniform Rules of Evidence (Art. VI, Extrinsic Policies Affecting

Admissibility), Cal. Law Revision Comm'n, Rep., Rec. & Studies, 612 (1964). Moreover, the impact of a rule excluding evidence on the ground of surprise would be difficult to estimate.

In reaching a decision whether to exclude on grounds of unfair prejudice, consideration should be given to the probable effectiveness or lack of effectiveness of a limiting instruction. See Rule 106 and Advisory Committee's Note thereunder. The availability of other means of proof may also be an appropriate factor.

NOTE BY FEDERAL JUDICIAL CENTER

The Rule enacted by the Congress is the Rule prescribed by the Supreme Court without change.

Rule 404   Character Evidence not Admissible to Prove Conduct; Exceptions; Other Crimes

ADVISORY COMMITTEE'S NOTE

Subdivision (a) This subdivision deals with the basic question whether character evidence should be admitted. Once the admissibility of character evidence in some form is established under this rule, reference must then be made to Rule 405, which follows, in order to determine the appropriate method of proof. If the character is that of a witness, see Rules 608 and 609 for methods of proof.

Character questions arise in two fundamentally different ways. (1) Character may itself be an element of a crime, claim, or defense. A situation of this kind is commonly referred to as "character in issue." Illustrations are: the chastity of the victim under a statute specifying her chastity as an element of the crime of seduction, or the competency of the driver in an action for negligently entrusting a motor vehicle to an incompetent driver. No problem of the general relevancy of character evidence is involved, and the present rule therefore has no provision on the subject. The only question relates to allowable methods of proof, as to which see Rule 405, immediately following. (2) Character evidence is susceptible of being used for the purpose of suggesting an inference that the person acted on the occasion in question consistently with his character. This use of character is often described as "circumstantial." Illustrations are: evidence of a violent disposition to prove that the person was the aggressor in an affray, or evidence of honesty in disproof of a charge of theft. This circumstantial use of character evidence raises questions of relevancy as well as questions of allowable methods of proof.

In most jurisdictions today, the circumstantial use of character is rejected but with important exceptions: (1) an accused may introduce pertinent evidence of good character (often misleadingly described as "putting his character in issue"), in which event the prosecution may rebut with evidence of bad character; (2) an accused may introduce pertinent evidence of the character of the victim, as in support of a claim of self-defense to a charge of homicide or consent in a case of rape, and the prosecution may introduce similar evidence in rebuttal of the character evidence, or, in a homicide case, to rebut a claim that deceased was the first aggressor, however proved; and (3) the character of a witness may be gone into as bearing on his credibility. McCormick §§ 155-161. This pattern is incorporated in the rule. While its basis lies more in history and experience than in logic an underlying justification can fairly be found in terms of the relative presence and absence of prejudice in the various situations. Falknor, Extrinsic Policies Affecting Admissibility, 10 Rutgers L.Rev. 574, 584 (1956); McCormick § 157. In any event, the criminal rule is so deeply imbedded in our jurisprudence as to assume almost constitutional proportions and to override doubts of the basic relevancy of the evidence.

The limitation to pertinent traits of character, rather than character generally, in paragraphs (1) and (2) is in accordance with the prevailing view. McCormick § 158, p. 334. A similar provision in Rule 608, to which reference is made in paragraph (3), limits character evidence respecting witnesses to the trait of truthfulness or untruthfulness.

The argument is made that circumstantial use of character ought to be allowed in civil cases to the same extent as in criminal cases, i.e. evidence of good (nonprejudicial) character would be admissible in the first instance, subject to rebuttal by evidence of bad character. Falknor, Extrinsic Policies Affecting Admissibility, 10 Rutgers L. Rev. 574, 581-583 (1956); Tentative Recommendation and a Study Relating to the Uniform Rules of Evidence (Art. VI. Extrinsic Policies Affecting Admissibility), Cal. Law Revision Comm'n, Rep., Rec. & Studies, 657-658 (1964). Uniform Rule 47 goes farther, in that it assumes that character evidence in general satisfies the conditions of relevancy, except as provided in Uniform Rule 48. The difficulty with expanding the use of character evidence in civil cases is set forth by the California Law Revision Commission in its ultimate rejection of Uniform Rule 47, id., 615:

"Character evidence is of slight probative value and may be very prejudicial. It tends to distract the trier of fact from the main question of what actually happened on the particular occasion. It subtly permits the trier of fact to reward the good man and to punish the bad man because of their respective characters despite what the evidence in the case shows actually happened."

Much of the force of the position of those favoring greater use of character evidence in civil cases is dissipated by their support of Uniform Rule 48 which excludes the evidence in negligence cases, where it could be expected to achieve its maximum usefulness. Moreover, expanding concepts of "character," which seem of necessity to extend into such areas as psychiatric evaluation and psychological testing, coupled with expanded admissibility, would open up such vistas of mental examinations as caused the Court concern in Schlagenhauf v. Holder, 379 U.S. 104, 85 S.Ct. 234, 13 L.Ed.2d 152 (1964). It is believed that those espousing change have not met the burden of persuasion.

Subdivision (b) deals with a specialized but important application of the general rule excluding circumstantial use of character evidence. Consistently with that rule, evidence of other crimes, wrongs, or acts is not admissible to prove character as a basis for suggesting the inference that conduct on a particular occasion was in conformity with it. However, the evidence may be offered for another purpose, such as proof of motive, opportunity, and so on, which does not fall within the prohibition. In this situation the rule does not require that the evidence be excluded. No mechanical solution is offered. The determination must be made whether the danger of undue prejudice outweighs the probative value of the evidence in view of the availability of other means of proof and other factors appropriate for making decisions of this kind under Rule 403. Slough and Knightly, Other Vices, Other Crimes, 41 Iowa L.Rev. 325 (1956).

REPORT OF THE HOUSE COMMITTEE ON THE JUDICIARY

Rule 404(b)

The second sentence of Rule 404(b) as submitted to the Congress began with the words "This subdivision does not exclude the evidence when offered." The Committee amended this language to read "It may, however, be admissible," the words used in the 1971 Advisory Committee draft, on the ground that this formulation properly placed greater emphasis on admissibility than did the final Court version.

REPORT OF THE SENATE COMMITTEE ON THE JUDICIARY

Rule 404(b). Character Evidence Not Admissible To Prove Conduct: Other crimes, wrongs, or acts

This rule provides that evidence of other crimes, wrongs, or acts is not admissible to prove character but may be admissible for other specified purposes such as proof of motive.

Although your committee sees no necessity in amending the rule itself, it anticipates that the use of the discretionary word "may" with respect to the admissibility of evidence of crimes, wrongs, or acts is not intended to confer any arbitrary discretion on the trial judge. Rather, it is anticipated that with respect to permissible uses for such evidence, the trial judge may exclude it only on the basis of those considerations set forth in Rule 403, i.e. prejudice, confusion or waste of time.

NOTE BY FEDERAL JUDICIAL CENTER

The Rule enacted by the Congress is the Rule prescribed by the Supreme Court, with the second sentence of subdivision (b) amended by substituting "It may, however, be admissible" in place of "This subdivision does not exclude the evidence when offered."

Rule 405   Methods of Proving Character

ADVISORY COMMITTEE'S NOTE

The rule deals only with allowable methods of proving character, not with the admissibility of character evidence, which is covered in Rule 404.

Of the three methods of proving character provided by the rule, evidence of specific instances of conduct is the most convincing. At the same time it possesses the greatest capacity to arouse prejudice, to confuse, to surprise, and to consume time. Consequently the rule confines the use of evidence of this kind to cases in which character is, in the strict sense, in issue and hence deserving of a searching inquiry. When character is used circumstantially and hence occupies a lesser status in the case, proof may be only by reputation and opinion. These latter methods are also available when character is in issue. This treatment is, with respect to specific instances of conduct and reputation, conventional contemporary common law doctrine. McCormick § 153.

In recognizing opinion as a means of proving character, the rule departs from usual contemporary practice in favor of that of an earlier day. See 7 Wigmore § 1986, pointing out that the earlier practice permitted opinion and arguing strongly for evidence based on personal knowledge and belief as contrasted with "the secondhand, irresponsible product of multiplied guesses and gossip which we term 'reputation'." It seems likely that the persistence of reputation evidence is due to its largely being opinion in disguise. Traditionally character has been regarded primarily in moral overtones of good and bad: chaste, peaceable, truthful, honest. Nevertheless, on occasion nonmoral considerations crop up, as in the case of the incompetent driver, and this seems bound to happen increasingly. If character is defined as the kind of person one is, then account must be taken of varying ways of arriving at the estimate. These may range from the opinion of the employer who has found the man honest to the opinion of the psychiatrist based upon examination and testing. No effective dividing line exists between character and mental capacity, and the latter traditionally has been provable by opinion.

According to the great majority of cases, on cross-examination inquiry is allowable as to whether the reputation witness has heard of particular instances of conduct pertinent to the trait in question. Michelson v. United States, 335 U.S. 469, 69 S.Ct. 213, 93 L.Ed. 168 (1948): Annot., 47 A.L.R.2d 1258. The theory is that, since the reputation witness relates what he has heard, the inquiry tends to shed light on the accuracy of his hearing and reporting. Accordingly, the opinion witness would be asked whether he knew, as well as whether he had heard. The fact is, of course, that these distinctions are of slight if any practical significance, and the second sentence of subdivision (a) eliminates them as a factor in formulating questions. This recognition of the propriety of inquiring into specific instances of conduct does not circumscribe inquiry otherwise into the bases of opinion and reputation testimony.

The express allowance of inquiry into specific instances of conduct on cross-examination in subdivision (a) and the express allowance of it as part of a case in chief when character is actually in issue in subdivision (b) contemplate that testimony of specific instances is not generally permissible on the direct examination of an ordinary opinion witness to character. Similarly as to witnesses to the character of witnesses under Rule 608(b). Opinion testimony on direct in these situations ought in general to correspond to reputation testimony as now given, i.e., be confined to the nature and extent of observation and acquaintance upon which the opinion is based. See Rule 701.

NOTE BY FEDERAL JUDICIAL CENTER

The Rule enacted by the Congress is the Rule prescribed by the Supreme Court without change. The bill reported by the House Committee on the Judiciary deleted the provision in subdivision (a) for making proof by testimony in the form of an opinion, but the provision was reinstated on the floor of the House. [120 Cong. Rec. 2370-73 (1974).]

Rule 406   Habit; Routine Practice

ADVISORY COMMITTEE'S NOTE

Subdivision (a). An oft-quoted paragraph, McCormick, § 162, p. 340, describes habit in terms effectively contrasting it with character:

"Character and habit are close akin. Character is a generalized description of one's disposition, or of one's disposition in respect to a general trait, such as honesty, temperance, or peacefulness. 'Habit,' in modern usage, both lay and psychological, is more specific. It describes one's regular response to a repeated specific situation. If we speak of character for care, we think of the person's tendency to act prudently in all the varying situations of life, in business, family life, in handling automobiles and in walking across the street. A habit, on the other hand, is the person's regular practice of meeting a particular kind of situation with a specific type of conduct, such as the habit of going down a particular stairway two stairs at a time, or of giving the hand-signal for a left turn, or of alighting from railway cars while they are moving. The doing of the habitual acts may become semi-automatic."

Equivalent behavior on the part of a group is designated "routine practice of an organization" in the rule.

Agreement is general that habit evidence is highly persuasive as proof of conduct on a particular occasion. Again quoting McCormick § 162, p. 341:

"Character may be thought of as the sum of one's habits though doubtless it is more than this. But unquestionably the uniformity of one's response to habit is far greater than the consistency with which one's conduct conforms to character or disposition. Even though character comes in only exceptionally as evidence of an act, surely any sensible man in investigating whether X did a particular act would be greatly helped in his inquiry by evidence as to whether he was in the habit of doing it."

When disagreement has appeared, its focus has been upon the question what constitutes habit, and the reason for this is readily apparent. The extent to which instances must be multiplied and consistency of behavior maintained in order to rise to the status of habit inevitably gives rise to differences of opinion. Lewan, Rationale of Habit Evidence, 16 Syracuse L. Rev. 39, 49 (1964). While adequacy of sampling and uniformity of response are key factors, precise standards for measuring their sufficiency for evidence purposes cannot be formulated.

The rule is consistent with prevailing views. Much evidence is excluded simply because of failure to achieve the status of habit. Thus, evidence of intemperate "habits" is generally excluded when offered as proof of drunkeness in accident cases, Annot., 46 A.L.R.2d 103, and evidence of other assaults is inadmissible to prove the instant one in a civil assault action, Annot., 66 A.L.R.2d 806. In Levin v. United States, 119 U.S.App.D.C. 156, 338 F.2d 265 (1964), testimony as to the religious "habits" of the accused, offered as tending to prove that he was at home observing the Sabbath rather than out obtaining money through larceny by trick, was held properly excluded:

"It seems apparent to us that an individual's religious practices would not be the type of activities which would lend themselves to the characterization of 'invariable regularity.' [1 Wigmore 520.] Certainly the very volitional basis of the activity raises serious questions as to its invariable nature, and hence its probative value." Id. at 272.

These rulings are not inconsistent with the trend towards admitting evidence of business transactions between one of the parties and a third person as tending to prove that he made the same bargain or proposal in the litigated situation. Slough, Relevancy Unraveled, 6 Kan.L.Rev. 38-41 (1957). Nor are they inconsistent with such cases as Whittemore v. Lockheed Aircraft Corp., 65 Cal.App.2d 737, 151 P.2d 670 (1944), upholding the admission of evidence that plaintiff's intestate had on four other occasions flown planes from defendant's factory for delivery to his employer airline, offered to prove that he was piloting rather than a guest on a plane which crashed and killed all on board while en route for delivery.

A considerable body of authority has required that evidence of the routine practice of an organization be corroborated as a condition precedent to its admission in evidence. Slough, Relevancy Unraveled, 5 Kan.L.Rev 404, 449 (1957). This requirement is specifically rejected by the rule on the ground that it relates to the sufficiency of the evidence rather than admissibility. A similar position is taken in New Jersey Rule 49. The rule also rejects the requirement of the absence of eyewitnesses, sometimes encountered with respect to admitting habit evidence to prove freedom from contributory negligence in wrongful death cases. For comment critical of the requirements see Frank, J., in Cereste v. New York, N. H. & H. R. Co., 231 F.2d 50 (2d Cir. 1956), cert. denied 351 U.S. 951, 76 S.Ct. 848, 100 L.Ed. 1475, 10 Vand.L.Rev. 447 (1957); McCormick § 162, p. 342. The omission of the requirement from the California Evidence Code is said to have effected its elimination. Comment, Cal.Ev.Code § 1105.

Subdivision (b).*Permissible methods of proving habit or routine conduct include opinion and specific instances sufficient in number to warrant a finding that the habit or routine practice in fact existed. Opinion evidence must be "rationally based on the perception of the witness" and helpful, under the provisions of Rule 701. Proof by specific instances may be controlled by the overriding provisions of Rule 403 for exclusion on grounds of prejudice, confusion, misleading the jury, or waste of time. Thus the illustrations following A.L.I. Model Code of Evidence Rule 307 suggests the possibility of admitting testimony by W that on numerous occasions he had been with X when X crossed a railroad track and that on each occasion X had first stopped and looked in both directions, but discretion to exclude offers of 10 witnesses, each testifying to a different occasion.

Similar provisions for proof by opinion or specific instances are found in Uniform Rule 50 and Kansas Code of Civil Procedure § 60-450. New Jersey Rule 50 provides for proof by specific instances but is silent as to opinion. The California Evidence Code is silent as to methods of proving habit, presumably proceeding on the theory that any method is relevant and all relevant evidence is admissible unless otherwise provided. Tentative Recommendation and a Study Relating to the Uniform Rules of Evidence (Art. VI. Extrinsic Policies Affecting Admissibility), Rep., Rec. & Study, Cal. Law Rev. Comm'n, 620 (1964).

* Note that Congress deleted subdivision (b) in enacting Rule 406.

REPORT OF THE HOUSE COMMITTEE ON THE JUDICIARY *PROPOSED RULE*
406(b)

Rule 406 as submitted to Congress contained a subdivision (b) providing that the method of proof of habit or routine practice could be "in the form of an opinion or by specific instances of conduct sufficient in number to warrant a finding that the habit existed or that the practice was routine." The Committee deleted this subdivision believing that the method of proof of habit and routine practice should be left to the courts to deal with on a case-by-case basis. At the same time, the Committee does not intend that its action be construed as sanctioning a general authorization of opinion evidence in this area.

NOTE BY FEDERAL JUDICIAL CENTER

The Rule enacted by the Congress is subdivision (a) of the Rule prescribed by the Supreme Court. Subdivision (b) of the Court's Rule was deleted for reasons stated in the Report of the House Committee on the Judiciary set forth above.

Rule 407   Subsequent Remedial Measures

ADVISORY COMMITTEE'S NOTE

The rule incorporates conventional doctrine which excludes evidence of subsequent remedial measures as proof of an admission of fault. The rule rests on two grounds. (1) The conduct is not in fact an admission, since the conduct is equally consistent with injury by mere accident or through contributory negligence. Or, as Baron Bramwell put it, the rule rejects the notion that "because the world gets wiser as it gets older, therefore it was foolish before." Hart v. Lancashire & Yorkshire Ry. Co., 21 L.T.R. N.S. 261, 263 (1869). Under a liberal theory of relevancy this ground alone would not support exclusion as the inference is still a possible one. (2) The other, and more impressive, ground for exclusion rests on a social policy of encouraging people to take, or at least not discouraging them from taking, steps in furtherance of added safety. The courts have applied this principle to exclude evidence of subsequent repairs, installation of safety devices, changes in company rules, and discharge of employees, and the language of the present rule is broad enough to encompass all of them. See Falknor, Extrinsic Policies Affecting Admissibility, 10 Rutgers L.Rev. 574, 590 (1956).

The second sentence of the rule directs attention to the limitations of the rule. Exclusion is called for only when the evidence of subsequent remedial measures is offered as proof of negligence or culpable conduct. In effect it rejects the suggested inference that fault is admitted. Other purposes are, however, allowable, including ownership or control, existence of duty, and feasibility of precautionary measures, if controverted, and impeachment. 2 Wigmore § 283; Annot., 64 A.L.R.2d 1296. Two recent federal cases are illustrative. Boeing Airplane Co. v. Brown, 291 F.2d 310 (9th Cir. 1961), an action against an airplane manufacturer for using an allegedly defectively designed alternator shaft which caused a plane crash, upheld the admission of evidence of subsequent design modification for the purpose of showing that design changes and safeguards were feasible. And Powers v. J. B. Michael & Co., 329 F.2d 674 (6th Cir. 1964), an action against a road contractor for negligent failure to put out warning signs, sustained the admission of evidence that defendant subsequently put out signs to show that the portion of the road in question was under defendant's control. The requirement that the other purpose be controverted calls for automatic exclusion unless a genuine issue be present and allows the opposing party to lay the groundwork for exclusion by making an admission. Otherwise the factors of undue prejudice, confusion of issues, misleading the jury, and waste of time remain for consideration under Rule 403.

For comparable rules, see Uniform Rule 51; California Evidence Code § 1151; Kansas Code of Civil Procedure § 60-451; New Jersey Evidence Rule 51.

NOTE BY FEDERAL JUDICIAL CENTER

Congress made no change in Rule 407, and it was neither the subject of floor debate, nor the subject of discussion during the course of committee hearings on the Rules in the House of Representatives. Therefore, the Rule enacted by the Congress is the Rule prescribed by the Supreme Court without change.

Rule 408   Compromise and Offers to Compromise

ADVISORY COMMITTEE'S NOTE

As a matter of general agreement, evidence of an offer to compromise a claim is not receivable in evidence as an admission of, as the case may be, the validity or invalidity of the claim. As with evidence of subsequent remedial measures, dealt with in Rule 407, exclusion may be based on two grounds. (1) The evidence is irrelevant, since the offer may be motivated by a desire for peace rather than from any concession of weakness of position. The validity of this position will vary as the amount of the offer varies in relation to the size of the claim and may also be influenced by other circumstances. (2) A more consistently impressive ground is promotion of the public policy favoring the compromise and settlement of disputes. McCormick §§ 76, 251. While the rule is ordinarily phrased in terms of offers of compromise, it is apparent that a similar attitude must be taken with respect to completed compromises when offered against a party thereto. This latter situation will not, of course, ordinarily occur except when a party to the present litigation has compromised with a third person.

The same policy underlies the provision of Rule 68 of the Federal Rules of Civil Procedure that evidence of an unaccepted offer of judgment is not admissible except in a proceeding to determine costs.

The practical value of the common law rule has been greatly diminished by its inapplicability to admissions of fact, even though made in the course of compromise negotiations, unless hypothetical, stated to be "without prejudice," or so connected with the offer as to be inseparable from it. McCormick § 251, pp. 540-541. An inevitable effect is to inhibit freedom of communication with respect to compromise, even among lawyers. Another effect is the generation of controversy over whether a given statement falls within or without the protected area. These considerations account for the expansion of the rule herewith to include evidence of conduct or statements made in compromise negotiations, as well as the offer or completed compromise itself. For similar provisions see California Evidence Code §§ 1152, 1154.

The policy considerations which underlie the rule do not come into play when the effort is to induce a creditor to settle an admittedly due amount for a lessor sum. McCormick § 251, p. 540. Hence the rule requires that the claim be disputed as to either validity or amount.

The final sentence of the rule serves to point out some limitations upon its applicability. Since the rule excludes only when the purpose is proving the validity or invalidity of the claim or its amount, an offer for another purpose is not within the rule. The illustrative situations mentioned in the rule are supported by the authorities. As to proving bias or prejudice of a witness, see Annot., 161 A.L.R. 395, contra, Fenberg v. Rosenthal, 348 Ill.App. 510, 109 N.E.2d 402 (1952), and negativing a contention of lack of due diligence in presenting a claim, 4 Wigmore § 1061. An effort to "buy off" the prosecution or a prosecuting witness in a criminal case is not within the policy of the rule of exclusion. McCormick § 251, p. 542.

For other rules of similar import, see Uniform Rules 52 and 53; California Evidence Code §§ 1152, 1154; Kansas Code of Civil Procedure §§ 60-452, 60-453; New Jersey Evidence Rules 52 and 53.

REPORT OF THE HOUSE COMMITTEE ON THE JUDICIARY

[Note, that the form of the Rule referred to herein was revised by the Senate (see the Senate Committee Report, infra), and the version of the Rule which was enacted is substantially different from the House version herein described.]

Under existing federal law evidence of conduct and statements made in compromise negotiations is admissible in subsequent litigation between the parties. The second sentence of Rule 408 as submitted by the Supreme Court proposed to reverse that doctrine in the interest of further promoting non-judicial settlement of disputes. Some agencies of government expressed the view that the Court formulation was likely to impede rather than assist efforts to achieve settlement of disputes. For one thing, it is not always easy to tell when compromise negotiations begin, and informal dealings end. Also, parties dealing with government agencies would be reluctant to furnish factual information at preliminary meetings; they would wait until "compromise negotiations" began and thus hopefully effect an immunity for themselves with respect to the evidence supplied. In light of these considerations, the Committee recast the Rule so that admissions of liability or opinions given during compromise negotiations continue inadmissible, but evidence of unqualified factual assertions is admissible. The latter aspect of the Rule is drafted, however, so as to preserve other possible objections to the introduction of such evidence. The Committee intends no modification of current law whereby a party may protect himself from future use of his statements by couching them in hypothetical conditional form.

REPORT OF THE SENATE COMMITTEE ON THE JUDICIARY

This rule as reported makes evidence of settlement or attempted settlement of a disputed claim inadmissible when offered as an admission of liability or the amount of liability. The purpose of this rule is to encourage settlements which would be discouraged if such evidence were admissible.

Under present law, in most jurisdictions, statements of fact made during settlement negotiations, however, are excepted from this ban and are admissible. The only escape from admissibility of statements of fact made in a settlement negotiation is if the declarant or his representative expressly states that the statement is hypothetical in nature or i[s] made without prejudice. Rule 408 as submitted by the Court reversed the traditional rule. It would have brought statements of fact within the ban and made them, as well as an offer of settlement, inadmissible.

The House amended the rule and would continue to make evidence of facts disclosed during compromise negotiations admissible. It thus reverted to the traditional rule. The House Committee report states that the Committee intends to preserve current law under which a party may protect himself by couching his statements in hypothetical form.[1] The real impact of this amendment, however, is to deprive the rule of much of its salutary effect. The exception for factual admissions was believed by the Advisory Committee to hamper free communication between parties and thus to constitute an unjustifiable restraint upon efforts to negotiate settlements—the encouragement of which is the purpose of the rule. Further, by protecting hypothetically phrased statements, it constituted a preference for the sophisticated, and a trap for the unwary.

Three States which had adopted rules of evidence patterned after the proposed rules prescribed by the Supreme Court opted for versions of rule 408 identical with the Supreme Court draft with respect to the inadmissibility of conduct or statements made in compromise negotiations.[2]

For these reasons, the committee has deleted the House amendment and restored the Rule to the version submitted by the Supreme Court with one additional amendment. This amendment adds a sentence to insure that evidence, such as documents, is not rendered inadmissible merely because it is presented in the course of compromise negotiations, if the evidence is otherwise discoverable. A party should not be able to immunize from admissibility documents otherwise discoverable merely by offering them in a compromise negotiation.

REPORT OF THE HOUSE/SENATE CONFERENCE COMMITTEE

The House bill provides that evidence of admissions of liability or opinions given during compromise negotiations is not admissible, but that evidence of facts disclosed during compromise negotiations is not inadmissible by virtue of having been first disclosed in the compromise negotiations. The Senate amendment provides that evidence of conduct or statements made in compromise negotiations is not admissible. The Senate amendment also provides that the rule does not require the exclusion of any evidence otherwise discoverable merely because it is presented in the course of compromise negotiations.

The House bill was drafted to meet the objection of executive agencies that under the rule as proposed by the Supreme Court, a party could present a fact during compromise negotiations and thereby prevent an opposing party from offering evidence of that fact at trial even though such evidence was obtained from independent sources. The Senate amendment expressly precludes this result.

The Conference adopts the Senate amendment.

NOTE BY FEDERAL JUDICIAL CENTER

As finally enacted by Congress, Rule 408 is identical to the version promulgated by the Supreme Court with a minor addition (the word "also" in the final sentence between "rule" and "does"), and the insertion of a new third sentence, which

---

1. See Report No. 93-650, dated November 15, 1973.
2. Nev. Rev. Stats., §§ 48, 105; N. Mex. Stats. Anno. (1973 Supp.) § 20-4-408; West's Wis. Stats. Anno. (1973 Supp.) §§ 904.08.

provides: "The rule does not require the exclusion of any evidence otherwise discoverable merely because it is presented in the course of compromise negotiations." Other amendments, proposed by the House bill, were not enacted, for reasons set forth in the Report of the Senate Committee of the Judiciary and in the Report of the House/Senate Conference Committee set forth above.

Rule 409   Payment of Medical and Similar Expenses

ADVISORY COMMITTEE'S NOTE

The considerations underlying this rule parallel those underlying Rules 407 and 408, which deal respectively with subsequent remedial measures and offers of compromise. As stated in Annot., 20 A.L.R.2d 291, 293.

"[G]enerally, evidence of payment of medical, hospital, or similar expenses of an injured party by the opposing party, is not admissible, the reason often given being that such payment or offer is usually made from humane impulses and not from an admission of liability, and that to hold otherwise would tend to discourage assistance to the injured person."

Contrary to Rule 408, dealing with offers of compromise, the present rule does not extend to conduct or statements not a part of the act of furnishing or offering or promising to pay. This difference in treatment arises from fundamental differences in nature. Communication is essential if compromises are to be effected, and consequently broad protection of statements is needed. This is not so in cases of payments or offers or promises to pay medical expenses, where factual statements may be expected to be incidental in nature.

For rules on the same subject, but phrased in terms of "humanitarian motives," see Uniform Rule 52; California Evidence Code § 1152; Kansas Code of Civil Procedure § 60-452; New Jersey Evidence Rule 52.

NOTE BY FEDERAL JUDICIAL CENTER

Congress made no change in Rule 409, and it was neither the subject of floor debate, nor a topic of discussion at the committee hearings; the Rule enacted by Congress is the Rule prescribed by the Supreme Corut without change.

Rule 410   Inadmissibility of Pleas, Plea Discussions, and Related Statements

ADVISORY COMMITTEE'S NOTE

Withdrawn pleas of guilty were held inadmissible in federal prosecutions in Kercheval v. United States, 274 U.S. 220, 47 S.Ct. 582, 71 L.Ed. 1009 (1927). The Court pointed out that to admit the withdrawn plea would effectively set at naught the allowance of withdrawal and place the accused in a dilemma utterly inconsistent with the decision to award him a trial. The New York Court of Appeals, in People v. Spitaleri, 9 N.Y.2d 168, 212 N.Y.S.2d 53, 173 N.E.2d 35 (1961), reexamined and overturned its earlier decisions which had allowed admission. In addition to the reasons set forth in Kercheval, which was quoted at length, the court pointed out that the effect of admitting the plea was to compel defendant to take the stand by way of explanation and to open the way for the prosecution to call the lawyer who had represented him at the time of entering the plea. State court decisions for and against admissibility are collected in Annot., 86 A.L.R.2d 326.

Pleas of *nolo contendere* are recognized by Rule 11 of the Rules of Criminal Procedure, although the law of numerous States is to the contrary. The present rule gives effect to the principal traditional characteristic of the *nolo* plea, i.e. avoiding the admission of guilt which is inherent in pleas of guilty. This position is consistent with the construction of Section 5 of the Clayton Act, 15 U.S.C. § 16(a), recognizing the inconclusive and compromise nature of judgments based on *nolo* pleas. General Electric Co. v. City of San Antonio, 334 F.2d 480 (5th Cir. 1964); Commonwealth Edison Co. v. Allis-Chalmers Mfg. Co., 323 F.2d 412 (7th Cir. 1963), cert. denied 376 U.S. 939, 84 S.Ct. 794, 11 L.Ed.2d 659; Armco Steel Corp. v. North Dakota, 376 F.2d 206 (8th Cir. 1967); City of Burbank v. General Electric Co., 329 F.2d 825 (9th Cir. 1964). See also state court decisions in Annot., 18 A.L.R.2d 1287, 1314.

Exclusion of offers to plead guilty or *nolo* has as its purpose the promotion of disposition of criminal cases by compromise. As pointed out in McCormick § 251, p. 543.

"Effective criminal law administration in many localities would hardly be possible if a large proportion of the charges were not disposed of by such compromises."

See also People v. Hamilton, 60 Cal.2d 105, 32 Cal.Rptr. 4, 383 P.2d 412 (1963), discussing legislation designed to achieve this result. As with compromise offers generally, rule 408, free communication is needed, and security against having an offer of compromise or related statement admitted in evidence effectively encourages it.

Limiting the exclusionary rule to use against the accused is consistent with the purpose of the rule, since the possibility of use for or against other persons will not impair the effectiveness of withdrawing pleas or the freedom of discussion which the rule is designed to foster. See A.B.A. Standards Relating to Pleas of Guilty § 2.2 (1968). See also the narrower provisions of New Jersey Evidence Rule 52(2) and the unlimited exclusion provided in California Evidence Code § 1153.

REPORT OF THE HOUSE COMMITTEE ON THE JUDICIARY

[Note, that the phrase referred to in the following note was enacted with the original version of the Rule, but was deleted from the present version of the Rule, without comment.]

The Committee added the phrase "Except as otherwise provided by Act of Congress" to Rule 410 as submitted by the Court in order to preserve particular congressional policy judgments as to the effect of a plea of guilty or of nolo contendere. See 15 U.S.C. 16(a). The Committee intends that its amendment refers to both present statutes and statutes subsequently enacted.

REPORT OF THE SENATE COMMITTEE ON THE JUDICIARY

[Note, that the present version of Rule 410 differs markedly from the original version, to which the following note refers, and it is clear today that under Rule 410 a plea bargaining statement by the defendant cannot be introduced against him for impeachment purposes if he takes the stand on his own behalf.]

As adopted by the House, rule 410 would make inadmissible pleas of guilty or nolo contendere subsequently withdrawn as well as offers to make such pleas. Such a rule is clearly justified as a means of encouraging pleading. However, the House rule would then go on to render inadmissible for any purpose statements made in connection with these pleas or offers as well.

The committee finds this aspect of the House rule unjustified. Of course, in certain circumstances such statements should be excluded. If, for example, a plea is vitiated because of coercion, statements made in connection with the plea may also have been coerced and should be inadmissible on that basis. In other cases, however, voluntary statements of an accused made in court on the record, in connection with a plea, and determined by a court to be reliable should be admissible even though the plea is subsequently withdrawn. This is particularly true in those cases where, if the House rule were in effect, a defendant would be able to contradict his previous statements and thereby lie with impunity.[3] To prevent such an injustice, the rule has been modified to permit the use of such statements for the limited purposes of impeachment and in subsequent perjury or false statement prosecutions.

REPORT OF THE HOUSE/SENATE CONFERENCE COMMITTEE

[Note, that the version of Rule 410 presently in effect is not the version referred to in the following note.]

The House bill provides that evidence of a guilty or nolo contendere plea, of an offer of either plea, or of statements made in connection with such pleas or offers of such pleas, is inadmissible in any civil or criminal action, case or proceeding against the person making such plea or offer. The Senate amendment makes the rule inapplicable to a voluntary and reliable statement made in court on the record where the statement is offered in a subsequent prosecution of the declarant for perjury or false statement.

The issues raised by Rule 410 are also raised by proposed Rule 11(e)(6) of the Federal Rules of Criminal Procedure presently pending before Congress. This proposed rule, which deals with the admissibility of pleas of guilty or nolo contendere, offers to make such pleas, and statements made in connection with such pleas, was promulgated by the Supreme Court on April 22, 1974, and in the absence of congressional action will become effective on August 1, 1975. The conferees intend to make no change in the presently-existing case law until that date, leaving the courts free to develop rules in this area on a case-by-case basis.

The Conferees further determined that the issues presented by the use of guilty and nolo contendere pleas, offers of such pleas, and statements made in connection with such pleas or offers, can be explored in greater detail during Congressional consideration of Rule 11(c)(6) of the Federal Rules of Criminal Procedure. The Conferees believe, therefore, that it is best to defer its effective date until August 1, 1975. The Conferees intend that Rule 410 would be superseded by any subsequent Federal Rule of Criminal Procedure or Act of Congress with which it is inconsistent, if the Federal Rule of Criminal Procedure or Act of Congress takes effect or becomes law after the date of the enactment of the act establishing the rules of evidence.

---

3. See Harris v. New York, 401 U.S. 222 (1971). [Senate Judiciary Committee's footnote.]

The conference adopts the Senate amendment with an amendment that expresses the above intentions.

Rule 411   Liability Insurance

Advisory Committee's Note

The courts have with substantial unanimity rejected evidence of liability insurance for the purpose of proving fault, and absence of liability insurance as proof of lack of fault. At best the inference of fault from the fact of insurance coverage is a tenuous one, as is its converse. More important, no doubt, has been the feeling that knowledge of the presence or absence of liability insurance would induce juries to decide cases on improper grounds. McCormick § 168; Annot., 4 A.L.R.2d 761. The rule is drafted in broad terms so as to include contributory negligence or other fault of a plaintiff as well as fault of a defendant.

The second sentence points out the limits of the rule, using well established illustrations. *Id.*

For similar rules see Uniform Rule 54; California Evidence Code § 1155; Kansas Code of Civil Procedure § 60-454; New Jersey Evidence Rule 54.

Note by Federal Judicial Center

Congress made no change in Rule 411, and it was neither the subject of floor debate, nor a topic of discussion at the committee hearings. Therefore, the Rule enacted by Congress is the Rule prescribed by the Supreme Court without change.

Rule 412   Rape Cases; Relevance of Victim's Past Behavior

Congressional Action

[Note, that there is no Advisory Committee's Note to this Rule.]

Public Law 95-540, the Privacy Protection for Rape Victims Act of 1978, adds Rule 412 to the Federal Rules of Evidence. Public Law 95-540 was approved by the House of Representatives on October 10, 1978 and by the Senate on October 12, 1978. It was signed by President Carter on October 28, 1978 and accordingly became effective with respect to trials begun after November 28, 1978 since section 3 of Public Law 95-540 provides that:

The amendments made by this Act shall apply to trials which begin more than thirty days after the date of the enactment of this Act.

In case of a retrial begun after this date, the new rule would apply so that evidence admitted at an earlier trial might not be admitted on the retrial. See discussion of "Effective Date" under Rule 1103.

In the House of Representatives, Representatives Holtzman, Mann and Wiggins discussed the bill at length. The following excerpts from their remarks suggests the tenor of the discussion:

Mr. MANN. Mr. Speaker, for many years in this country, evidentiary rules have permitted the introduction of evidence about a rape victim's prior sexual conduct. Defense lawyers were permitted great latitude in bringing out intimate details about a rape victim's life. Such evidence quite often serves no real purpose and only results in embarrassment to the rape victim and unwarranted public intrusion into her private life.

The evidentiary rules that permit such inquiry have in recent years come under question: and the States have taken the lead to change and modernize their evidentiary rules about evidence of a rape victim's prior sexual behavior. The bill before us similarly seeks to modernize the Federal Evidentiary rules.

The present Federal Rules of Evidence reflect the traditional approach. If a defendant in a rape case raises the defense of consent, that defendant may then offer evidence about the victim's prior sexual behavior. Such evidence may be in the form of opinion evidence, evidence of reputation, or evidence of specific instances of behavior. Rule 404(a)(2) of the Federal Rules of Evidence permits the introduction of evidence of a "pertinent character trait." The Advisory Committee note to that rule cites, as an example of what the rule covers, the character of a rape victim when the issue is consent. Rule 405 of the Federal Rules of Evidence permits the use of opinion or reputation evidence or the use of evidence of specific behavior to show a character trait."

Thus, Federal evidentiary rules permit a wide ranging inquiry into the private conduct of a rape victim, even though that conduct may have at best a tenuous connection to the offense for which the defendant is being tried. H.R. 4727 amends the Federal Rules of Evidence to add a new rule, applicable only in criminal cases, to spell out when, and under what conditions, evidence of a rape victim's prior sexual behavior can be admitted. The new rule provides that reputation or opinion evidence about a rape victim's prior sexual behavior is not admissible. The new rule also provides that a court cannot admit evidence of specific instances of a rape victim's prior sexual conduct except in three circumstances.

The first circumstance is where the Constitution requires that the evidence be admitted. This exception is intended to cover those infrequent instances where, because of an unusual chain of circumstances, the general rule of inadmissibility, if followed, would result in denying the defendant a constitutional right.

The second circumstance in which the defendant can offer evidence of specific instances of a rape victim's prior sexual behavior is where the defendant raises the issue of consent and the evidence is of sexual behavior with the defendant. To admit such evidence, however, the court must find that the evidence is relevant and that its probative value outweighs the danger of unfair prejudice.

The third circumstance in which a court can admit evidence of specific instances of a rape victim's prior sexual behavior is where the evidence is of behavior with someone other than the defendant and is offered by the defendant on the issue of whether or not he was the source of semen or injury. Again, such evidence will be admitted only if the court finds that the evidence is relevant and that its probative value outweighs the danger of unfair prejudice.

The new rule further provides that before evidence is admitted under any of these exceptions, there must be an in camera hearing—that is, a proceeding that takes place in the judge's chambers out of the presence of the jury and the general public. At this hearing, the defendant will present the evidence he intends to offer and be able to argue why it should be admitted. The prosecution, of course, will be able to argue against that evidence being admitted.

The purpose of the in camera hearing is twofold. It gives the defendant an opportunity to demonstrate to the court why certain evidence is admissible and ought to be presented to the jury. At the same time, it protects the privacy of the rape victim in those instances when the court finds that evidence is inadmissible. Of course, if the court finds the evidence to be admissible, the evidence will be presented to the jury in open court.

The effect of this legislation, therefore, is to preclude the routine use of evidence of specific instances of a rape victim's prior sexual behavior. Such evidence will be admitted only in clearly and narrowly defined circumstances and only after an in camera hearing. In determining the admissibility of such evidence, the court will consider all of the facts and circumstances surrounding the evidence, such as the amount of time that lapsed between the alleged prior act and the rape charged in the prosecution. The greater the lapse of time, of course, the less likely it is that such evidence will be admitted.

Mr. Speaker, the principal purpose of this legislation is to protect rape victims from the degrading and embarrassing disclosure of intimate details about their private lives. It does so by narrowly circumscribing when such evidence may be admitted. It does not do so, however, by sacrificing any constitutional right possessed by the defendant. The bill before us fairly balances the interests involved—the rape victim's interest in protecting her private life from unwarranted public exposure; the defendant's interest in being able adequately to present a defense by offering relevant and probative evidence; and society's interst in a fair trial, one where unduly prejudicial evidence is not permitted to becloud the issues before the jury.

Mr. WIGGINS. Mr. Speaker, this legislation addresses itself to a subject that is certainly a proper one for our consideration. Many of us have been troubled for years about the indiscriminate and prejudicial use of testimony with respect to a victim's prior sexual behavior in rape and similar cases. This bill deals with that problem. It is not, in my opinion, Mr. Speaker, a perfect bill in the manner in which it deals with the problem, but my objections are not so fundamental as would lead me to oppose the bill.

I think, Mr. Speaker, that it is unwise to adopt a per se rule absolutely excluding evidence of reputation and opinion with respect to the victim— and this bill does that—but it is difficult for me to foresee the specific case in which such evidence might be admissible. The trouble is this, Mr. Speaker: None of us can foresee perfectly all of the various circumstances under which the propriety of evidence might be before the court. If this bill has a defect, in my view it is because it adopts a per se rule with respect to opinion and reputation evidence. Alternatively we might have permitted that evidence to be considered in camera as we do other evidence under the bill.

I should note, however, in fairness, having expressed minor reservations, that the bill before the House at this time does improve significantly upon the bill which was presented to our committee.

I will not detail all of those improvements but simply observe that the bill upon which we shall soon vote is a superior product to that which was initially considered by our subcommittee.

Ms. HOLTZMAN. Too often in this country victims of rape are humiliated and harrassed when they report and prosecute the rape. Bullied and cross-examined about their prior sexual experiences, many find the trial almost as degrading as the rape itself. Since rape trials become inquisitions into the victim's morality, not trials of the defendant's innocence or guilt, it is not surprising that it is the least reported crime. It is estimated that as few as one in ten rapes is ever reported.

Mr. Speaker, over 30 States have taken some action to limit the vulnerability of rape victims to such humiliating cross-examination of their past sexual experiences and intimate personal histories. In federal courts, however, it is permissible still to subject rape victims to brutal cross-examination about their past sexual histories. H.R. 4727 would rectify this problem in Federal Courts and I hope, also serve as a model to suggest to the remaining states that reform of existing rape laws is important to the equity of our criminal justice system.

H.R. 4727 applies only to criminal rape cases in Federal courts. The bill provides that neither the prosecution nor the defense can introduce any reputation or opinion evidence about the victim's past sexual conduct. It does permit, however, the introduction of specific evidence about the victim's past sexual conduct in three very limited circumstances.

First, this evidence can be introduced if it deals with the victim's past sexual relations with the defendant and is relevant to the issue of whether she consented. Second, when the defendant claims he had no relations with the victim, he can use evidence of the victim's past sexual relations with others if the evidence rebuts the victim's claim that the rape caused certain physical consequences, such as semen or injury. Finally, the evidence can be introduced if it is constitutionally required. This last exception, added in subcommittee, will insure that the defendant's constitutional rights are protected.

Before any such evidence can be introduced, however, the court must determine at a hearing in chambers that the evidence falls within one of the exceptions.

Furthermore, unless constitutionally required, the evidence of specific instances of prior sexual conduct cannot be introduced at all if it would be more prejudicial and inflammatory than probative.

Congressional Record, October 10, 1978, H11944-11945

In the Senate, further explanatory remarks were offered by Senators Thurmond, Bayh and Biden.

Mr. THURMOND. . . .

H.R. 4727, as passed by the House, essentially does the following:

First. Prohibits any use of reputation or opinion evidence of the past sexual behavior of the victim in a criminal prosecution for rape or assault with intent to commit rape.

Second. Restricts the use of direct evidence of the past sexual behavior of the victim of rape and assault with intent to commit rape to three situations:

(a) Where the judge finds after a hearing that admission of the evidence is required under the Constitution;

(b) The judge finds after a hearing that the past sexual behavior was with a person other than the accused and is being offered to show that someone other than the accused was the source of semen or injury; and

(c) The judge finds after a hearing that the past sexual behavior was with the accused and is offered by the accused solely on the issue of consent.

Third. Creates notice and hearing procedures on the evidentiary issues delineated by the bill.

. . .

Mr. BAYH. . . .

. . . .Under the provisions of H.R. 4727, a new rule of evidence applicable only in criminal cases would make evidence of prior sexual history inadmissible except under three circumstances.

First, in order to make sure that we are [not] infringing upon a defendant's civil liberties, such evidence may be admissible where it is required under the constitution. Thus exception is intended to cover those instances where, because of an unusual set of circumstances, if the general rule of inadmissiblity were to be followed, it might deprive a defendant of his Constitutional rights.

The second circumstance in which the defendant can offer evidence of a rape victim's prior sexual history is where the defendant raises the issue of consent and the evidence is of sexual behavior with the defendant.

The third circumstance in which a court can admit evidence of prior sexual history is where the evidence may show that sexual relations occurred between the victim and someone other than the defendant.

Evidence which might fall under these exceptions is not automatically admissible however. If the defendant proposed to offer evidence in either category, he must first make a written offer of proof which is submitted to the presiding judge. If the judge then decides after an in camera hearing that such evidence is admissible, he must make a written order specifically identifying the evidence to be admitted and describing exactly the areas of cross-examination to be permitted. This procedure is designed to afford the victim maximum notice of the questioning that may occur.

Mr. BIDEN. . . .

. . .[It] is important that we keep in mind the constitutional rights of the defendant to a fair trial. Therefore this bill has been carefully drafted to keep the reform within constitutional limits.

The bill clearly permits the defendant to offer evidence where it is constitutionally required. Indeed, the bill specifically recognizes two circumstances where the evidence may be admitted. However, the bill also would establish a special in camera procedure whereby the question of admissibility could be litigated without harm to the privacy rights of the victim or the constitutional rights of the defendant.

Congressional Record, October 12, 1978, S18579-S18581.

ARTICLE V
PRIVILEGES

Rule 501   General Rule

[Note, that there is no Advisory Committee's Note to this Rule. The Committee's version of this Rule differed substantially. The Rules enacted by Congress substituted the single Rule 501 in place of the thirteen Rules dealing with privilege prescribed by the Supreme Court as Article V. The reasons given in support of the congressional action are stated in the Report of the House Committee on the Judiciary, the Report of the Senate Committee on the Judiciary, and Report of the House/Senate Conference Committee, set forth below.]

REPORT OF THE HOUSE COMMITTEE ON THE JUDICIARY

Article V as submitted to Congress contained thirteen Rules. Nine of those Rules defined specific non-constitutional privileges which the federal courts must recognize (i.e. required reports, lawyer-client, psychotherapist-patient, husband-wife, communications to clergymen, political vote, trade secrets, secrets of state and other official information, and identity of informer). Another Rule provided that only those privileges set forth in Article V or in some other Act of Congress could be recognized by the federal courts. The three remaining Rules addressed collateral problems as to waiver of privilege by voluntary disclosure, privileged matter disclosed under compulsion or without opportunity to claim privilege, comment upon or inference from a claim of privilege, and jury instruction with regard thereto.

The Committee amended Article V to eliminate all of the Court's specific Rules on privileges. Instead, the Committee, through a single Rule, 501, left the law of privileges in its present state and further provided that privileges shall continue to be developed by the courts of the United States under a uniform standard applicable both in civil and criminal cases. That standard, derived from Rule 26 of the Federal Rules of Criminal Procedure, mandates the application of the principles of the common law as interpreted by the courts of the United States in the light of reason and experience. The words "person, government, State, or political subdivision thereof" were added by the Committee to the lone term "witnesses" used in Rule 26 to make clear that, as under present law, not only witnesses may have privileges. The Committee also included in its amendment a provisio modeled after Rule 302 and similar to language added by the Committee to Rule 601 relating to the competency of witnesses. The proviso is designed to require the application of State privilege law in civil actions and proceedings governed by *Erie R. Co. v. Tompkins*, 304 U.S. 64 (1938), a result in accord with current federal court decisions. See Republic Gear Co. v. Borg-Warner Corp., 381 F2d 551, 555-556 n.2 (2nd Cir. 1967). The Committee deemed the proviso to be necessary in the light of the Advisory Committee's view (see its note to Court Rule 501) that this result is not mandated under *Erie*.

The rationale underlying the proviso is that federal law should not supersede that of the States in substantive areas such as privilege absent a compelling reason.

The Committee believes that in civil cases in the federal courts where an element of a claim or defense is not grounded upon a federal question, there is no federal interest strong enough to justify departure from State policy. In addition, the Committee considered that the Court's proposed Article V would have promoted forum shopping in some civil actions, depending upon differences in the privilege law applied as among the State and federal courts. The Committee's proviso, on the other hand, under which the federal courts are bound to apply the State's privilege law in actions founded upon a State-created right or defense, removes the incentive to "shop."

Report of the Senate Committee on the Judiciary

[The version of Rule 501 recommended in this Report differs in the second sentence from the enacted Rule set forth above.]

Article V as submitted to Congress contained 13 rules. Nine of those rules defined specific nonconstitutional privileges which the Federal courts must recognize (i.e., required reports, lawyer-client, psychotherapist-patient, husband-wife, communications to clergymen, political vote, trade secrets, secrets of state and other official information, and identity of informer.) Many of these rules contained controversial modifications or restrictions upon common law privileges. As noted supra, the House amended article V to eliminate all of the Court's specific rules on privileges. Through a single rule, 501, the House provided that privileges shall be governed by the principles of the common law as interpreted by the courts of the United States in the light of reason and experience (a standard derived from rule 26 of the Federal Rules of Criminal Procedure) except in the case of an element of a civil claim or defense as to which State law supplies the rules of decision, in which event state privilege law was to govern.

The committee agrees with the main thrust of the House amendment: that a federally developed common law based on modern reason and experience shall apply except where the State nature of the issues renders deference to State privilege law the wiser course, as in the usual diversity case. The committee understands that thrust of the House amendment to require that State privilege law be applied in "diversity" cases (actions on questions of State law between citizens of different States arising under 28 U.S.C. § 1332). The language of the House amendment, however, goes beyond this in some respects, and falls short of it in others: State privilege law applies even in nondiversity, Federal question civil cases, where an issue governed by State substantive law is the object of the evidence (such issues do sometimes arise in such cases); and, in all instances where State privilege law is to be applied, e.g., on proof of a State issue in a diversity case, a close reading reveals that State privilege law is not to be applied unless the matter to be proved is an element of that state claim or defense, as distinguished from a step along the way in the proof of it.

The committee is concerned that the language used in the House amendment could be difficult to apply. It provides that "in civil actions . . . with respect to an element of a claim or defense as to which State law supplies the rule of decision," State law on privilege applies. The question of what is an element of a claim or defense is likely to engender considerable litigation. If the matter in question constitutes an element of a claim, State law supplies the privilege rule; whereas if it is a mere item of proof with respect to a claim, then, even though State law might supply the rule of decision, Federal law on the privilege would apply. Further, disputes will arise as to how the rule should be applied in an antitrust action or in a tax case where the Federal statute is silent as to a particular aspect of the substantive law in question, but Federal cases had incorporated State law by reference to State law.[4] Is a claim (or defense) based on such a reference a claim or defense as to which federal or State law supplies the rule of decision?

Another problem not entirely avoidable is the complexity or difficulty the rule introduces into the trial of a Federal case containing a combination of Federal and State claims and defenses, e.g. an action involving Federal antitrust and State unfair competition claims. Two different bodies of privilege law would need to be consulted. It may even develop that the same witness-testimony might be relevant on both counts and privileged as to one but not the other.[5]

The formulation adopted by the House is pregnant with litigious mischief. The committee has, therefore, adopted what we believe will be a clearer and more practical guideline for determining when courts should respect State rules of privilege. Basically, it provides that in criminal and Federal question civil cases, federally evolved rules on privilege should apply since it is Federal policy which is being enforced.[6] Conversely, in diversity cases where the litigation in question turns on a substantive question of State law, and is brought in the Federal courts because the parties reside in different States, the committee believes it is clear that State rules of privilege should apply unless the proof is directed at a claim or defense for which Federal law supplies the rule of decision (a situation which would not commonly arise.)[7] It is intended that the State rules of privilege should apply equally in original diversity actions and diversity actions removed under 28 U.S.C. § 1441(b).

Two other comments on the privilege rule should be made. The committee has received a considerable volume of correspondence from psychiatric organizations and psychiatrists concerning the deletion of rule 504 of the rule submitted by the Supreme Court. It should be clearly understood that, in approving this general rule as to privileges, the action of Congress should not be understood as disapproving any recognition of a psychiatrist-patient, or husband-wife, or any other of the enumerated privileges contained in the Supreme Court rules. Rather, our action should be understood as reflecting the view that the recognition of a privilege

4. For a discussion of reference to State substantive law, see note on Federal Incorporation by Reference of State Law, Hart & Wechster, *The Federal Courts and the Federal System*, pp. 491-94 (2d Ed. 1973).

5. The problems with the House formulation are discussed in Rothstein, "The Propped Amendments to the Federal Rules of Evidence," 62 Georgetown University Law Journal 125 (1973) at notes 25, 26 and 70-74, and accompanying text.

6. It is also intended that the Federal law of privileges should be applied with respect to pendant state law claims when they arise in a Federal question case.

7. While such a situation might require use of two bodies of privilege law, federal and state, in the same case, nevertheless the occasions on which this would be required are considerably reduced as compared with the House version, and confined to situations where the Federal and State interests are such as to justify application of neither privilege law to the case as a whole. If the rule proposed here results in two conflicting bodies of privilege law applying to the same piece of evidence in the same case, it is contemplated that the rule favoring reception of the evidence should be applied. This policy is based on the present rule 43(a) of the Federal Rules of Civil Procedure which provides: In any case, the statute or rule which favors the reception of the evidence governs and the evidence shall be presented according to the most convenient method prescribed in any of the statutes or rules to which reference is herein made.

based on a confidential relationship and other privileges should be determined on a case-by-case basis.

Further, we would understand that the prohibition against spouses testifying against each other is considered a rule of privilege and covered by this rule and not by rule 601 of the competency of witnesses.

Report of House/Senate Conference Committee

Rule 501 deals with the privilege of a witness not to testify. Both the House and Senate bills provide that federal privilege law applies in criminal cases. In civil actions and proceedings, the House bill provides that state privilege law applies "to an element of a claim or defense as to which State law supplies the rule of decision." The Senate bill provides that "in civil actions and proceedings arising under 28 U.S.C. § 1332 or 28 U.S.C. § 1335, or between citizens of different States and removed under 28 U.S.C. § 1441(b) the privilege of a witness, person, government, State or political subdivision thereof is determined in accordance with State law, unless with respect to the particular claim or defense, Federal law supplies the rule of decision."

The wording of the House and Senate bills differs in the treatment of civil actions and proceedings. The rule in the House bill applies to evidence that relates to "an element of a claim or defense." If an item of proof tends to support or defeat a claim or defense, or an element of a claim or defense, and if state privilege law applies to that item of proof.

Under the provision in the House bill, therefore, state privilege law will usually apply in diversity cases. There may be diversity cases, however, where a claim or defense is based upon federal law. In such instances, federal privilege law will apply to evidence relevant to the federal claim or defense. See Sola Electric Co. v. Jefferson Electric Co., 317 U.S. 173 (1942).

In nondiversity jurisdiction civil cases, federal privilege law will generally apply. In those situations where a federal court adopts or incorporates state law to fill interstices or gaps in federal statutory phrases, the court generally will apply federal privilege law. As Justice Jackson has said:

> A federal court sitting in a non-diversity case such as this does not sit as a local tribunal. In some cases it may see fit for special reasons to give the law of a particular state highly persuasive or even controlling effect, but in the last analysis its decision turns upon the law of the United States, not that of any state.

D'Oench, Duhme & Co. v. Federal Deposit Insurance Corp., 315 U.S. 447, 471 (1942) (Jackson, J., concurring). When a federal court chooses to absorb state law, it is applying the state law as a matter of federal common law. Thus, state law does not supply the rule of decision (even though the federal court may apply a rule derived from the decisions), and state privilege law would not apply. See C. A. Wright, *Federal Courts* 251-252 (2d ed. 1970); Holmberg v. Armbrecht, 327 U.S. 392 (1946); DeSylva v. Ballentine, 351 U.S. 570, 581 (1956); 9 Wright & Miller, *Federal Rules and Procedure* § 2408.

In civil actions and proceedings, where the rule of decision as to a claim or defense or as to an element of a claim or defense is supplied by state law, the House provision requires that state privilege law apply.

The Conference adopts the House provision.

ARTICLE VI
WITNESSES

Rule 601   General Rule of Competency

ADVISORY COMMITTEE'S NOTE

[Note, that this Advisory Committee's Note was written before the Congressional changes.]

This general ground-clearing eliminates all grounds of incompetency not specifically recognized in the succeeding rules of this Article. Included among the grounds thus abolished are religious belief, conviction of crime, and connection with the litigation as a party or interested person or spouse of a party or interested person. With the exception of the so-called Dead Man's Acts, American jurisdictions generally have ceased to recognize these grounds.

The Dead Man's Acts are surviving traces of the common law disqualification of parties and interested persons. They exist in variety too great to convey conviction of their wisdom and effectiveness. These rules contain no provision of this kind. * * *

No mental or moral qualifications for testifying as a witness are specified. Standards of mental capacity have proved elusive in actual application. A leading commentator observes that few witnesses are disqualified on that ground. Weihofen, Testimonial Competence and Credibility, 34 Geo.Wash.L.Rev. 53 (1965). Discretion is regularly exercised in favor of allowing the testimony. A witness wholly without capacity is difficult to imagine. The question is one particularly suited to the jury as one of weight and credibility, subject to judicial authority to review the sufficiency of the evidence. 2 Wigmore §§ 501, 509. Standards of moral qualification in practice consist essentially of evaluating a person's truthfulness in terms of his own answers about it. Their principal utility is in affording an opportunity on voir dire examination to impress upon the witness his moral duty. This result may, however, be accomplished more directly, and without haggling in terms of legal standards, by the manner of administering the oath or affirmation under Rule 603.

Admissibility of religious belief as a ground of impeachment is treated in Rule 610. Conviction of crime as a ground of impeachment is the subject of Rule 609. Marital relationship is the basis for privilege under Rule 505. Interest in the outcome of litigation and mental capacity are, of course, highly relevant to credibility and require no special treatment to render them admissible along with other matters bearing upon the perception, memory, and narration of witnesses.

REPORT OF THE HOUSE COMMITTEE ON THE JUDICIARY

Rule 601 as submitted to the Congress provided that "Every person is competent to be a witness except as otherwise provided in these rules." One effect of the Rule as proposed would have been to abolish age, mental capacity, and other grounds recognized in some State jurisdictions as making a person incompetent as a witness. The greatest controversy centered around the Rule's rendering inapplicable in the federal courts the so-called Dead Man's Statutes which exist in some States. Acknowledging that there is substantial disagreement as to the merit of Dead Man's Statutes, the Committee nevertheless believed that where such statutes have been enacted they represent State policy which should not be overturned in the absence of a compelling federal interest. The Committee therefore amended the Rule to make competency in civil actions determinable in accordance with State law with respect to elements of claims or defenses as to which State law supplies the rule of decision. Cf. Courtland v. Walston & Co., Inc., 340 F.Supp. 1076, 1087-1092 (S.D.N.Y.1972).

REPORT OF THE SENATE COMMITTEE ON THE JUDICIARY

The amendment to Rule 601 parallels the treatment accorded Rule 501 discussed immediately above.

REPORT OF THE HOUSE/SENATE CONFERENCE COMMITTEE

Rule 601 deals with competency of witnesses. Both the House and Senate bills provide that federal competency law applies in criminal cases. In civil actions and proceedings, the House bill provides that state competency law applies "to an element of a claim or defense as to which State law supplies the rule of decision." The Senate bill provides that "in civil actions and proceedings arising under 28 U.S.C. § 1332 or 28 U.S.C. § 1335, or between citizens of different States and removed under 28 U.S.C. § 1441(b) the competency of a witness, person, government, State or political subdivision thereof is determined in accordance with State law, unless with respect to the particular claim or defense, Federal law supplies the rule of decision.".

The wording of the House and Senate bills differs in the treatment of civil actions and proceedings. The rule in the House bill applies to evidence that relates to "an element of a claim or defense." If an item of proof tends to support or defeat a claim or defense, or an element of a claim or defense, and if state law supplies the rule of decision for that claim or defense, then state competency law applies to that item of proof.

For reasons similar to those underlying its action on Rule 501, the Conference adopts the House provision.

Rule 602   Lack of Personal Knowledge

ADVISORY COMMITTEE'S NOTE

". . . [T]he rule requiring that a witness who testifies to a fact which can be perceived by the senses must have had an opportunity to observe, and must have actually observed the fact" is a "most pervasive manifestation" of the common law insistence upon "the most reliable sources of information." McCormick § 10, p. 19. These foundation requirements may, of course, be furnished by the testimony of the witness himself; hence personal knowledge is not an absolute but may consist of what the witness thinks he knows from personal perception. 2 Wigmore § 650. It will be observed that the rule is in fact a specialized application of the provisions of Rule 104(b) on conditional relevancy.

This rule does not govern the situation of a witness who testifies to a hearsay statement as such, if he has personal knowledge of the making of the statement.

Rules 801 and 805 would be applicable. This rule would, however, prevent him from testifying to the subject matter of the hearsay statement, as he has no personal knowledge of it.

The reference to Rule 703 is designed to avoid any question of conflict between the present rule and the provisions of that rule allowing an expert to express opinions based on facts of which he does not have personal knowledge.

NOTE BY FEDERAL JUDICIAL CENTER

The Rule enacted by Congress is the Rule prescribed by the Supreme Court without change; the Rule was not the subject of floor debate.

Rule 603　　Oath or Affirmation

ADVISORY COMMITTEE'S NOTE

The rule is designed to afford the flexibility required in dealing with religious adults, atheists, conscientious objectors, mental defectives, and children. Affirmation is simply a solemn undertaking to tell the truth; no special verbal formula is required. As is true generally, affirmation is recognized by federal law. "Oath" includes affirmation, 1 U.S.C. § 1; judges and clerks may administer oaths and affirmations, 28 U.S.C. §§ 459, 953; and affirmations are acceptable in lieu of oaths under Rule 43(d) of the Federal Rules of Civil Procedure. Perjury by a witness is a crime, 18 U.S.C. § 1621.

NOTE BY FEDERAL JUDICIAL CENTER

The Rule enacted by Congress is the Rule prescribed by the Supreme Court without change; the Rule was not the subject of floor debate.

Rule 604　　Interpreters

ADVISORY COMMITTEE'S NOTE

The rule implements Rule 13(f) of the Federal Rules of Civil Procedure and Rule 28(b) of the Federal Rules of Criminal Procedure, both of which contain provisions for the appointment and compensation of interpreters.

NOTE BY FEDERAL JUDICIAL CENTER

The Rule enacted by Congress is the Rule prescribed by the Supreme Court without change; the Rule was not the subject of floor debate.

Rule 605　　Competency of Judge as Witness

ADVISORY COMMITTEE'S NOTE

In view of the mandate of 28 U.S.C. § 455 that a judge disqualify himself in "any case in which he . . . is or has been a material witness," the likelihood that the presiding judge in a federal court might be called to testify in the trial over which he is presiding is slight. Nevertheless the possibility is not totally eliminated.

The solution here presented is a broad rule of incompetency, rather than such alternatives as incompetency only as to material matters, leaving the matter to the discretion of the judge, or recognizing no incompetency. The choice is the result of inability to evolve satisfactory answers to questions which arise when the judge abandons the bench for the witness stand. Who rules on objections? Who compels him to answer? Can he rule impartially on the weight and admissibility of his own testimony? Can he be impeached or cross-examined effectively? Can he, in a jury trial, avoid conferring his seal of approval on one side in the eyes of the jury? Can he, in a bench trial, avoid an involvement destructive of impartiality? The rule of general incompetency has substantial support. See Report of the Special Committee on the Propriety of Judges Appearing as Witnesses, 36 A.B.A.J. 630 (1950); cases collected in Annot. 157 A.L.R. 311; McCormick § 68, p. 147; Uniform Rule 42; California Evidence Code § 703; Kansas Code of Civil Procedure § 60-442; New Jersey Evidence Rule 42. Cf. 6 Wigmore § 1909, which advocates leaving the matter to the discretion of the judge, and statutes to that effect collected in Annot. 157 A.L.R. 311.

The rule provides an "automatic" objection. To require an actual objection would confront the opponent with a choice between not objecting, with the result of allowing the testimony, and objecting, with the probable result of excluding the testimony but at the price of continuing the trial before a judge likely to feel that his integrity had been attacked by the objector.

NOTE BY FEDERAL JUDICIAL CENTER

The Rule enacted by Congress is the Rule prescribed by the Supreme Court without change; the Rule was not the subject of floor debate.

Rule 606   Competency of Juror as Witness

ADVISORY COMMITTEE'S NOTE

Subdivision (a). The considerations which bear upon the permissibility of testimony by a juror in the trial in which he is sitting as juror bear an obvious similarity to those evoked when the judge is called as a witness. See Advisory Committee's Note to Rule 605. The judge is not, however in this instance so involved as to call for departure from usual principles requiring objection to be made; hence the only provision on objection is that opportunity be afforded for its making out of the presence of the jury. Compare Rule 605.

Subdivision (b). Whether testimony, affidavits, or statements of jurors should be received for the purpose of invalidating or supporting a verdict or indictment, and if so, under what circumstances, has given rise to substantial differences of opinion. The familiar rubric that a juror may not impeach his own verdict, dating from Lord Mansfield's time, is a gross oversimplification. The values sought to be promoted by excluding the evidence include freedom of deliberation, stability and finality of verdicts, and protection of jurors against annoyance and embarrassment. McDonald v. Pless, 238 U.S. 264, 35 S.Ct. 785, 59 L.Ed. 1300 (1915). On the other hand, simply putting verdicts beyond effective reach can only promote irregularity and injustice. The rule offers an accommodation between these competing considerations.

The mental operations and emotional reactions of jurors in arriving at a given result would, if allowed as a subject of inquiry, place every verdict at the mercy of jurors and invite tampering and harassment. See Grenz v. Werre, 129 N.W.2d 681 (N.D. 1964). The authorities are in virtually complete accord in excluding the evidence. Fryer, Note on Disqualification of Witnesses, Selected Writings on Evidence and Trial 345, 347 (Fryer ed. 1957); Maguire, Weinstein, et al., Cases on Evidence 887 (5th ed. 1965); 8 Wigmore § 2349 (McNaughton Rev. 1961). As to matters other than mental operations and emotional reactions of jurors, substantial authority refuses to allow a juror to disclose irregularities which occur in the jury room, but allows his testimony as to irregularities occurring outside and allows outsiders to testify as to occurrences both inside and out. 8 Wigmore § 2354 (McNaughton Rev. 1961). However, the door of the jury room is not necessarily a satisfactory dividing point, and the Supreme Court has refused to accept it for every situation. Mattox v. United States, 146 U.S. 140, 13 S.Ct. 50, 36 L.Ed. 917 (1892).

Under the federal decisions the central focus has been upon insulation of the manner in which the jury reached its verdict, and this protection extends to each of the components of deliberation, including arguments, statements, discussions, mental and emotional reactions, votes, and any other feature of the process. Thus testimony or affidavits of jurors have been held incompetent to show a compromise verdict, Hyde v. United States, 225 U.S. 347, 382 (1912); a quotient verdict, McDonald v. Pless, 238 U.S. 264 (1915); speculation as to insurance coverage, Holden v. Porter, 405 F.2d 878 (10th Cir. 1969), Farmers Coop. Elev. Ass'n v. Strand, 382 F.2d 224, 230 (8th Cir. 1967), cert. denied 389 U.S. 1014; misinterpretation of instructions, Farmers Coop. Elev. Ass'n v. Strand, supra; mistake in returning verdict, United States v. Chereton, 309 F.2d 197 (6th Cir. 1962); interpretation of guilty plea by one defendant as implicating others, United States v. Crosby, 294 F.2d 928, 949 (2d Cir. 1961). The policy does not, however, foreclose testimony by jurors as to extraneous prejudicial information or influences injected into or brought to bear upon the deliberative process. Thus a juror is recognized as competent to testify to statements by the bailiff or the introduction of a prejudicial newspaper account into the jury room, Mattox v. United States, 146 U.S. 140 (1892). See also Parker v. Gladden, 385 U.S. 363 (1966).

This rule does not purport to specify the substantive grounds for setting aside verdicts for irregularity; it deals only with the competency of jurors to testify concerning those grounds.

See also Rule 6(e) of the Federal Rules of Criminal Procedure and 18 U.S.C. § 3500, governing the secrecy of grand jury proceedings. The present rule does not relate to secrecy and disclosure but to the competency of certain witnesses and evidence.

REPORT OF THE HOUSE COMMITTEE ON THE JUDICIARY

[Note, that the version of the Rule described in this Report differs substantially from that finally enacted by Congress.]

As proposed by the Court, Rule 606(b) limited testimony by a juror in the course of an inquiry into the validity of a verdict or indictment. He could testify as to the influence of extraneous prejudicial information brought to the jury's attention (e.g. a radio newscast or a newspaper account) or an outside influence which improperly had been brought to bear upon a juror (e.g. a threat to the safety of a member of his family), but he could not testify as to other irregularities which occurred in the jury room. Under this formulation a quotient verdict could not be attacked through the testimony of a juror, nor could a juror testify to the drunken condition of a fellow juror which so disabled him that he could not participate in the jury's deliberations.

The 1969 and 1971 Advisory Committee drafts would have permitted a member of the jury to testify concerning these kinds of irregularities in the jury room. The Advisory Committee note in the 1971 draft stated that "* * * the door of the jury room is not a satisfactory dividing point, and the Supreme Court has refused to accept it." The Advisory Committee further commented that—

> The trend has been to draw the dividing line between testimony as to mental processes, on the one hand, and as to the existence of conditions or occurrences of events calculated improperly to influence the verdict, on the other hand, without regard to whether the happening is within or without the jury room. * * * The jurors are the persons who know what really happened. Allowing them to testify as to matters other than their own reactions involves no particular hazard to the values sought to be protected. The rule is based upon this conclusion. It makes no attempt to specify the substantive grounds for setting aside verdicts for irregularity.

Objective jury misconduct may be testified to in California, Florida, Iowa, Kansas, Nebraska, New Jersey, North Dakota, Ohio, Oregon, Tennessee, Texas, and Washington.

Persuaded that the better practice is that provided for in the earlier drafts, the Committee amended subdivision (b) to read in the text of those drafts.

REPORT OF THE SENATE COMMITTEE ON THE JUDICIARY

As adopted by the House, this rule would permit the impeachment of verdicts by inquiry into, not the mental processes of the jurors, but what happened in terms of conduct in the jury room. This extension of the ability to impeach a verdict is felt to be unwarranted and ill-advised.

The rule passed by the House embodies a suggestion by the Advisory Committee of the Judicial Conference that is considerably broader than the final version adopted by the Supreme Court, which embodied long-accepted Federal law. Although forbidding the impeachment of verdicts by inquiry into the jurors' mental processes, it deletes from the Supreme Court version the proscription against testimony "as to any matter or statement occurring during the course of the jury's deliberations." This deletion would have the effect of opening verdicts up to challenge on the basis of what happened during the jury's internal deliberations, for example, where a juror alleged that the jury refused to follow the trial judge's instructions or that some of the jurors did not take part in deliberations.

Permitting an individual to attack a jury verdict based upon the jury's internal deliberations has long been recognized as unwise by the Supreme Court. In *McDonald v. Pless*, the Court stated:

* * * * *

[L]et it once be established that verdicts solemnly made and publicly returned into court can be attacked and set aside on the testimony of those who took part in their publication and all verdicts could be, and many would be, followed by an inquiry in the hope of discovering something which might invalidate the finding. Jurors would be harassed and beset by the defeated party in an effort to secure from them evidence of facts which might establish misconduct sufficient to set aside a verdict. If evidence thus secured could be thus used, the result would be to make what was intended to be a private deliberation, the constant subject of public investigation—to the destruction of all frankness and freedom of discussion and conference.[8]

* * * * *

As it stands then, the rule would permit the harassment of former jurors by losing parties as well as the possible exploitation of disgruntled or otherwise badly-motivated ex-jurors.

Public policy requires a finality to litigation. And common fairness requires that absolute privacy be preserved for jurors to engage in the full and free debate necessary to the attainment of just verdicts. Jurors will not be able to function effectively if their deliberations are to be scrutinized in post-trial litigation. In the interest of protecting the jury system and the citizens who make it work, Rule 606 should not permit any inquiry into the internal deliberations of the jurors.

REPORT OF THE HOUSE/SENATE CONFERENCE COMMITTEE

Rule 606(b) deals with juror testimony in an inquiry into the validity of a verdict or indictment. The House bill provides that a juror cannot testify about his mental processes or about the effect of anything upon his or another juror's mind as influencing him to assent to or dissent from a verdict or indictment. Thus, the House bill allows a juror to testify about objective matters occurring during the jury's deliberation, such as the misconduct of another juror or the reaching of a quotient verdict. The Senate bill does not permit juror testimony about any matter or statement occurring during the course of the jury's deliberations. The Senate bill does provide, however, that a juror may testify on the question whether extraneous prejudicial information was improperly brought to the jury's attention and on the question whether any outside influence was improperly brought to bear on any juror.

The Conference adopts the Senate amendment. The Conferees believe that jurors should be encouraged to be conscientious in promptly reporting to the court misconduct that occurs during jury deliberations.

NOTE BY FEDERAL JUDICIAL CENTER

The Rule enacted by Congress is the Rule prescribed by the Supreme Court, amended only by the addition of the concluding phrase "for these purposes." The bill originally passed by the House did not contain in the first sentence the prohibition as to matters or statements during the deliberations or the clause beginning "except."

Rule 607   Who May Impeach

ADVISORY COMMITTEE'S NOTE

The traditional rule against impeaching one's own witness is abandoned as based on false premises. A party does not hold out his witnesses as worthy of

8. 238 U.S. 264, at 267 (1944).

belief, since he rarely has a free choice in selecting them. Denial of the right leaves the party at the mercy of the witness and the adversary. If the impeachment is by a prior statement, it is free from hearsay dangers and is excluded from the category of hearsay under Rule 801(d)(1). Ladd, Impeachment of One's Own Witness—New Developments, 4 U.Chi.L.Rev. 69 (1936); McCormick § 38; 3 Wigmore §§ 896-918. The substantial inroads into the old rule made over the years by decisions, rules, and statutes are evidence of doubts as to its basic soundness and workability. Cases are collected in 3 Wigmore § 905. Revised Rule 32(a)(1) of the Federal Rules of Civil Procedure allows any party to impeach a witness by means of his deposition, and Rule 43(b) has allowed the calling and impeachment of an adverse party or person identified with him. Illustrative statutes allowing a party to impeach his own witness under varying circumstances are Ill.Rev.Stats. 1967, c. 110, § 60; Mass.Laws Annot.1959, c. 233 § 23; 20 N.M.Stats.Annot.1953, § 20-2-4; N.Y. CPLR § 4514 (McKinney 1963); 12 Vt.Stats.Annot.1959, §§ 1641a, 1642. Complete judicial rejection of the old rule is found in United States v. Freeman, 302 F.2d 347 (2d Cir.1962). The same result is reached in Uniform Rule 20; California Evidence Code § 785; Kansas Code of Civil Procedure § 60-420. See also New Jersey Evidence Rule 20.

NOTE BY FEDERAL JUDICIAL CENTER

The Rule enacted by Congress is the Rule prescribed by the Supreme Court without change; the Rule was not the subject of floor debate.

Rule 608   Evidence of Character and Conduct of Witness

ADVISORY COMMITTEE'S NOTE

Subdivision (a). In Rule 404(a) the general position is taken that character evidence is not admissible for the purpose of proving that the person acted in conformity therewith, subject, however, to several exceptions, one of which is character evidence of a witness as bearing upon his credibility. The present rule develops that exception.

In accordance with the bulk of judicial authority, the inquiry is strictly limited to character for veracity, rather than allowing evidence as to character generally. The result is to sharpen relevancy, to reduce surprise, waste of time, and confusion, and to make the lot of the witness somewhat less unattractive. McCormick § 44.

The use of opinion and reputation evidence as means of proving the character of witnesses is consistent with Rule 405(a). While the modern practice has purported to exclude opinion, witnesses who testify to reputation seem in fact often to be giving their opinions, disguised somewhat misleadingly as reputation. See McCormick § 44. And even under the modern practice, a common relaxation has allowed inquiry as to whether the witnesses would believe the principal witness under oath. United States v. Walker, 313 F.2d 236 (6th Cir. 1963), and cases cited therein; McCormick § 44, pp. 94-95, n. 3.

Character evidence in support of credibility is admissible under the rule only after the witness' character has first been attacked, as has been the case at common law. Maguire, Weinstein, et al., Cases on Evidence 295 (5th ed. 1965); McCormick § 49, p. 105; 4 Wigmore § 1104. The enormous needless consumption of time which a contrary practice would entail justifies the limitation. Opinion or reputation that the witness is untruthful specifically qualifies as an attack under the rule, and evidence of misconduct, including conviction of crime, and of corruption also fall within this category. Evidence of bias or interest does not. McCormick § 49; 4 Wigmore §§ 1106, 1107. Whether evidence in the form of contradiction is an attack upon the character of the witness must depend upon the circumstances. McCormick § 49. Cf. 4 Wigmore §§ 1108, 1109.

As to the use of specific instances on direct by an opinion witness, see the Advisory Committee's Note to Rule 405, *supra*.

Subdivision (b). In conformity with Rule 405, which forecloses use of evidence of specific incidents as proof in chief of character unless character is an issue in the case, the present rule generally bars evidence of specific instances of conduct of a witness for the purpose of attacking or supporting his credibility. There are, however, two exceptions: (1) specific instances are provable when they have been the subject of criminal conviction, and (2) specific instances may be inquired into on cross-examination of the principal witness or of a witness giving an opinion of his character for truthfulness.

(1) Conviction of crime as a technique of impeachment is treated in detail in Rule 609, and here is merely recognized as an exception to the general rule excluding evidence of specific incidents for impeachment purposes.

(2) Particular instances of conduct, though not the subject of criminal conviction, may be inquired into on cross-examination of the principal witness himself or of a witness who testifies concerning his character for truthfulness. Effective cross-examination demands that some allowance be made for going into matters of this kind, but the possibilities of abuse are substantial. Consequently safeguards are erected in the form of specific requirements that the instances inquired into be probative of truthfulness or its opposite and not remote in time. Also, the overriding protection of Rule 403 requires that probative value not be outweighed by danger of unfair prejudice, confusion of issues, or misleading the jury, and that of Rule 611 bars harassment and undue embarrassment.

The final sentence constitutes a rejection of the doctrine of such cases as People v. Sorge, 301 N.Y. 198, 93 N.E.2d 637 (1950), that any past criminal act relevant to credibility may be inquired into on cross-examination, in apparent disregard of the privilege against self-incrimination. While it is clear that an ordinary witness cannot make a partial disclosure of incriminating matter and then invoke the privilege on cross-examination, no tenable contention can be made that merely by testifying he wiaves his right to foreclose inquiry on cross-examination into criminal activities for the purpose of attacking his credibility. So to hold would reduce the privilege to a nullity. While it is true that an accused, unlike an ordinary witness, has an option whether to testify, if the option can be exercised only at the price of opening up inquiry as to any and all criminal acts committed during his lifetime, the right to testify could scarcely be said to possess much vitality. In Griffin v. California, 380 U.S. 609, 85 S.Ct. 1229, 14 L.Ed.2d 106 (1965), the Court held that allowing comment on the election of an accused not to testify exacted a constitutionally impermissible price, and so here. While no specific provision in terms confers constitutional status on the right of an accused to take the stand in his own defense, the existence of the right is so completely recognized that a denial of it or substantial infringement upon it would surely be of due process dimensions. See Ferguson v. Georgia, 365 U.S. 570, 81 S.Ct. 756, 5 L.Ed.2d 783 (1961); McCormick § 131; 8 Wigmore § 2276 (McNaughton Rev.1961). In any event, wholly aside from constitutional considerations, the provision represents a sound policy.

REPORT OF THE HOUSE COMMITTEE ON THE JUDICIARY

[Note, that the description of Rule 608(a) which follows is one which assumes that "opinion" testimony will be disallowed. As enacted, Rule 608(a) expressly allows opinion testimony.]

Rule 608(a)

Rule 608(a) as submitted by the Court permitted attack to be made upon the character for truthfulness or untruthfulness of a witness either by reputation or opinion testimony. For the same reasons underlying its decision to eliminate the admissibility of opinion testimony in Rule 405(a), the Committee amended Rule 608(a) to delete the reference to opinion testimony.

Rule 608(b)

The second sentence of Rule 608(b) as submitted by the Court permitted specific instances of misconduct of a witness to be inquired into on cross-examination for the purpose of attacking his credibility, if probative of truthfulness or untruthfulness, "and not remote in time." Such cross-examination could be of the witness himself or of another witness who testifies as to "his" character for truthfulness or untruthfulness.

The Committee amended the Rule to emphasize the discretionary power of the Court in permitting such testimony and deleted the reference to remoteness in time as being unnecessary and confusing (remoteness from time of trial or remoteness from the incident involved?). As recast, the Committee amendment also makes clear the antecedent of "his" in the original Court proposal.

NOTE BY FEDERAL JUDICIAL CENTER

The Rule enacted by Congress is the Rule prescribed by the Supreme Court, changed only by amending the second sentence of subdivision (b). The sentence as prescribed by the Court read: "They may, however, if probative of truthfulness or untruthfulness and not remote in time, be inquired into on cross-examination of the witness himself or on cross-examination of a witness who testifies to his character for truthfulness or untruthfulness." The effect of the amendments was to delete the phrase "and not remote in time," to add the phrase "in the discretion of the court," and otherwise only to clarify the meaning of the sentence. The reasons for the amendments are stated in the Report of the House Committee of the Judiciary, set forth above.

Rule 609   Impeachment by Evidence of Conviction of Crime

ADVISORY COMMITTEE'S NOTE

As a means of impeachment, evidence of conviction of crime is significant only because it stands as proof of the commission of the underlying criminal act. There is little dissent from the general proposition that at least some crimes are relevant to credibility but much disagreement among the cases and commentators about which crimes are usable for this purpose. See McCormick § 43: 2 Wright, Federal

Practice and Procedure: Criminal § 416 (1969). The weight of traditional authority has been to allow use of felonies generally, without regard to the nature of the particular offense, and of *crimen falsi* without regard to the grade of the offense. This is the view accepted by Congress in the 1970 amendment of § 14-305 of the District of Columbia Code, P.L. 91-358, 81 Stat. 473. Uniform Rule 21 and Model Code Rule 106 permit only crimes involving "dishonesty or false statement." Others have thought that the trial judge should have discretion to exclude convictions if the probative value of the evidence of the crime is substantially outweighed by the danger of unfair prejudice. Luck v. United States, 121 U.S.App.D.C. 151, 318 F.2d 763 (1965); McGowan, Impeachment of Criminal Defendants by Prior Convictions, 1970 Law & Soc. Order 1. Whatever may be the merits of those views, this rule is drafted to accord with the Congressional policy manifested in the 1970 legislation.

The proposed rule incorporates certain basic safeguards, in terms applicable to all witnesses but of particular significance to an accused who elects to testify. These protections include the imposition of definite time limitations, giving effect to demonstrated rehabilitation, and generally excluding juvenile adjudications.

Subdivision (a). For purposes of impeachment, crimes are divided into two categories by the rule: (1) those of what is generally regarded as felony grade, without particular regard to the nature of the offense, and (2) those involving dishonesty or false statement, without regard to the grade of the offense. Provable convictions are not limited to violations of federal law. By reason of our constitutional structure, the federal catalog of crimes is far from being a complete one, and resort must be had to the laws of the states for the specification of many crimes. For example, simple theft as compared with theft from interstate commerce. Other instances of borrowing are the Assimilative Crimes Act, making the state law of crimes applicable to the special territorial and maritime jurisdiction of the United States, 18 U.S.C. § 13, and the provision of the Judicial Code disqualifying persons as jurors on the grounds of state as well as federal convictions, 28 U.S.C. § 1865. For evaluation of the crime in terms of seriousness, reference is made to the congressional measurement of felony (subject to imprisonment in excess of one year) rather than adopting state definitions which vary considerably. See 28 U.S.C. § 1865, *supra*, disqualifying jurors for conviction in state or federal court of crime punishable by imprisonment for more than year.

Subdivision (b). Few statutes recognize a time limit on impeachment by evidence of conviction. However, practical considerations of fairness and relevancy demand that some boundary be recognized. See Ladd, Credibility Tests—Current Trends, 89 U.Pa.L.Rev. 166, 176-177 (1910). This portion of the rule is derived from the proposal advanced in Recommendation Proposing in Evidence Code, § 788(5), p. 142, Cal.Law Rev.Comm'n (1965), though not adopted. See California Evidence Code § 788.

Subdivision (c). A pardon or its equivalent granted solely for the purpose of restoring civil rights lost by virtue of a conviction has no relevance to an inquiry into character. If, however, the pardon or other proceeding is hinged upon a showing of rehabilitation the situation is otherwise. The result under the rule is to render the conviction inadmissible. The alternative of allowing in evidence both the conviction and the rehabilitation has not been adopted for reasons of policy, economy of time, and difficulties of evaluation.

A similar provision is contained in California Evidence Code § 788. Cf. A.L.I. Model Penal Code, Proposed Official Draft § 306.6(3)(e) (1962), and discussion in A.L.I. Proceedings 310 (1961).

Pardons based on innocence have the effect, of course, of nullifying the conviction *ab initio*.

Subdivision (d). The prevailing view has been that a juvenile adjudication is not usable for impeachment. Thomas v. United States, 74 App.D.C. 167, 121 F.2d 905 (1911); Cotton v. United States, 355 F.2d 480 (10th Cir. 1966). This conclusion was based upon a variety of circumstances. By virtue of its informality, frequently diminished quantum of required proof, and other departures from accepted standards for criminal trials under the theory of *parens patriae*, the juvenile adjudication was considered to lack the precision and general probative value of the criminal conviction. While In re Gault, 387 U.S. 1, 87 S.Ct. 1428, 18 L.Ed.2d 527 (1967), no doubt eliminates these characteristics insofar as objectionable, other obstacles remain. Practical problems of administration are raised by the common provisions in juvenile legislation that records be kept confidential and that they be destroyed after a short time. While *Gault* was skeptical as to the realities of confidentiality of juvenile records, it also saw no constitutional obstacles to improvement. 387 U.S. at 25, 87 S.Ct. 1428. See also Note, Rights and Rehabilitation in the Juvenile Courts, 67 Colum.L.Rev. 281, 289 (1967). In addition, policy considerations much akin to those which dictate exclusion of adult convictions after rehabilitation has been established, strongly suggest a rule of excluding juvenile adjudications. Admittedly, however, the rehabilitative process may in a given case be a demonstrated failure, or the strategic importance of a given witness may be so great as to require the overriding of general policy in the interests of particular justice. See Giles v. Maryland, 386 U.S. 66, 87 S.Ct. 793, 17 L.Ed.2d 737 (1967). Wigmore was outspoken in his condemnation of the disallowance of juvenile adjudications to impeach, especially when the witness is the complainant in a case of molesting a minor. 1 Wigmore § 196; 3 *id*. §§ 924a, 980. The rule recognizes discretion in the judge to effect an accomodation among these various factors by departing from the general principle of exclusion. In deference to the general pattern and policy of juvenile statutes, however, no discretion is accorded when the witness is the accused in a criminal case.

Subdivision (e). The presumption of correctness which ought to attend judicial proceedings supports the position that pendency of an appeal does not preclude use of a conviction for impeachment. United States v. Empire Packing Co., 174 F.2d 16 (7th Cir. 1949), cert. denied 337 U.S. 959, 69 S.Ct. 1534, 93 L.Ed. 1758; Bloch v. United States, 226 F.2d 185 (9th Cir. 1955), cert. denied 350 U.S. 948, 76 S.Ct. 323, 100 L.Ed. 826 and 353 U.S. 959, 77 S.Ct. 868, 1 L.Ed.2d 910; and see Newman v. United States, 331 F.2d 968 (8th Cir. 1964). *Contra*, Campbell v. United States, 85 U.S.App.D.C. 133, 176 F.2d 45 (1949). The pendency of an appeal is, however, a qualifying circumstance properly considerable.

REPORT OF THE HOUSE COMMITTEE ON THE JUDICIARY

[Note, that Rule 609 underwent substantial change in the Senate after this House Report was prepared, particularly with respect to subdivision (a).]

Rule 609(a)

Rule 609(a) as submitted by the Court was modeled after Section 133(a) of Public Law 91-358, 11 D.C. Code 305(b)(1), enacted in 1970. The Rule provided that:

> For the purpose of attacking the credibility of a witness, evidence that he has been convicted of a crime is admissible but only if the crime (1) was punishable by death or imprisonment in excess of one year under the law under which he was convicted or (2) involved dishonesty or false statement regardless of the punishment.

As reported to the Committee by the Subcommittee, Rule 609(a) was amended to read as follows:

> For the purpose of attacking the credibility of a witness, evidence that he has been convicted of a crime is admissible only if the crime (1) was punishable by death or imprisonment in excess of one year, unless the court determines that the danger of unfair prejudice outweighs the probative value of the evidence of the conviction, or (2) involved dishonesty or false statement.

In full committee, the provision was amended to permit attack upon the credibility of a witness by prior conviction only if the prior crime involved dishonesty or false statement. While recognizing that the prevailing doctrine in the federal courts and in most States allows a witness to be impeached by evidence of prior felony convictions without restriction as to type, the Committee was of the view that, because of the danger of unfair prejudice in such practice and the deterrent effect upon an accused who might wish to testify, and even upon a witness who was not the accused, cross-examination by evidence of prior conviction should be limited to those kinds of convictions bearing directly on credibility, *i.e.*, crimes involving dishonesty or false statement.

Rule 609(b)

Rule 609(b) as submitted by the Court was modeled after Section 133(a) of Public Law 91-358, 14 D.C. Code 305(b)(2)(B), enacted in 1970. The Rule provided:

> Evidence of a conviction under this rule is not admissible if a period of more than ten years has elapsed since the date of the release of the witness from confinement imposed for his most recent conviction, or the expiration of the period of his parole, probation, or sentence granted or imposed with respect to his most recent conviction, whichever is the later date.

Under this formulation, a witness' entire past record of criminal convictions could be used for impeachment (provided the conviction met the standard of subdivison (a)), if the witness had been most recently released from confinement, or the period of his parole or probation had expired, within ten years of the conviction.

The Committee amended the Rule to read in the text of the 1971 Advisory Committee version to provide that upon the expiration of ten years from the date of a conviction of a witness, or of his release from confinement for that offense, that conviction may no longer be used for impeachment. The Committee was of the view that after ten years following a person's release from confinement (or from the date of his conviction) the probative value of the conviction with respect to that person's credibility diminished to a point where it should no longer be admissible.

Rule 609(c)

Rule 609(c) as submitted by the Court provided in part that evidence of a witness' prior conviction is not admissible to attack his credibility if the conviction was the subject of a pardon, annulment, or other equivalent procedure, based on a showing of rehabilitation, and the witness has not been convicted of a subsequent crime. The Committee amended the Rule to provide that the "subsequent crime" must have been "punishable by death or imprisonment in excess of one year," on the ground that a subsequent conviction of an offense not a felony is insufficient to rebut the finding that the witness has been rehabilitated. The Committee also intends that the words "based on a finding of the rehabilitation of the person convicted" apply not only to "certificate or rehabilitation, or other equivalent procedure," but also to "pardon" and "annulment."

REPORT OF THE SENATE COMMITTEE ON THE JUDICIARY

[Note, that Rule 609(a) and 609(b) underwent further change in Conference after this Senate Report was prepared.]

Rule 609(a). Impeachment by Evidence of Conviction

As proposed by the Supreme Court, the rule would allow the use of prior convictions to impeach if the crime was a felony or a misdemeanor if the misdemeanor involved dishonesty or false statement. As modified by the House, the rule would admit prior convictions for impeachment purposes only if the offense, whether felony or misdemeanor, involved dishonesty or false statement.

The committee has adopted a modified version of the House-passed rule. In your committee's view, the danger of unfair prejudice is far greater when the accused, as opposed to other witnesses, testifies, because the jury may be prejudiced not merely on the question of credibility but also on the ultimate question of guilt or innocence. Therefore, with respect to defendants, the committee agreed with the House limitation that only offenses involving false statement, or dishonesty may be used. By that phrase, the committee means crimes such as perjury or subornation of perjury, false statement, criminal fraud, embezzlement or false pretense, or any other offense, in the nature of *crimen falsi*, the commission of which involves some element of untruthfulness, deceit or falsification bearing on the accused's propensity to testify truthfully.

With respect to other witnesses, in addition to any prior conviction involving false statement or dishonesty, any other felony may be used to impeach if, and only if, the court finds that the probative value of such evidence outweighs its prejudicial effect against the party offering that witness.

Notwithstanding this provision, proof of any prior offense otherwise admissible under Rule 404 could still be offered for the purposes sanctioned by that rule. Furthermore, the committee intends that notwithstanding this rule, a defendant's misrepresentation regarding the existence or nature of prior convictions may be met by rebuttal evidence, including the record of such prior convictions. Similarly, such records may be offered to rebut representations made by the defendant regarding his attitude toward or willingness to commit a general category of offense, although denials or other representations by the defendant regarding the specific conduct which forms the basis of the charge against him shall not make prior convictions admissible to rebut such statement.

In regard to either type of representation, of course, prior convictions may be offered in rebuttal only if the defendant's statement is made in response to defense counsel's questions or is made gratuitously in the course of cross-examination. Prior convictions may not be offered as rebuttal evidence if the prosecution has sought to circumvent the purpose of this rule by asking questions which elicit such representations from the defendant.

One other clarifying amendment has been added to this subsection, that is, to provide that the admissibility of evidence of a prior conviction is permitted only upon cross-examination of a witness. It is not admissible if a person does not testify. It is to be understood, however, that a court record of a prior conviction is admissible to prove that conviction if the witness has forgotten or denies its existence.

Rule 609(b). Impeachment by Evidence of Conviction of Crime; Time Limit

Although convictions over ten years old generally do not have much probative value, there may be exceptional circumstances under which the conviction substantially bears on the credibility of the witness. Rather than exclude all convictions over 10 years old, the committee adopted an amendment in the form of a final clause to the section granting the court discretion to admit convictions over 10 years old, but only upon a determination by the court that the probative value of the conviction supported by specific facts and circumstances, substantially outweighs its prejudicial effect.

It is intended that convictions over 10 years old will be admitted very rarely and only in exceptional circumstances. The rules provide that the decision be supported by specific facts and circumstances thus requiring the court to make specific findings on the record as to the particular facts and circumstances it has considered in determining that the probative value of the conviction substantially outweighs its prejudicial impact. It is expected that, in fairness, the court will give the party against whom the conviction is introduced a full and adequate opportunity to contest its admission.

REPORT OF THE HOUSE/SENATE CONFERENCE COMMITTEE

Rule 609 defines when a party may use evidence of a prior conviction in order to impeach a witness. The Senate amendments make changes in two subsections of Rule 609.

A. Rule 609(a)—General Rule

The House bill provides that the credibility of a witness can be attacked by proof of prior conviction of a crime only if the crime involves dishonesty or false statement. The Senate amendment provides that a witness' credibility may be attacked if the crime (1) was punishable by death or imprisonment in excess of one year under the law under which he was convicted or (2) involves dishonesty or false statement, regardless of the punishment.

The Conference adopts the Senate amendment with an amendment. The Conference amendment provides that the credibility of a witness, whether a defendant or someone else, may be attacked by proof of a prior conviction but only if the crime: (1) was punishable by death or imprisonment in excess of one year under the law under which he was convicted and the court determines that the probative value of the conviction outweighs its prejudicial effect to the defendant; or (2) involved dishonesty or false statement regardless of the punishment.

By the phrase "dishonesty and false statement" the Conference means crimes such as perjury or subornation of perjury, false statement, criminal fraud, embezzlement, or false pretense, or any other offense in the nature of *crimen falsi*, the commission of which involves some element of deceit, untruthfulness, or falsification bearing on the accused's propensity to testify truthfully.

The admission of prior convictions involving dishonesty and false statement is not within the discretion of the Court. Such convictions are peculiarly probative of credibility and, under this rule, are always to be admitted. Thus, judicial discretion granted with respect to the admissibility of other prior convictions is not applicable to those involving dishonesty or false statement.

With regard to the discretionary standard established by paragraph (1) of Rule 609(a), the Conference determined that the prejudicial effect to be weighed against the probative value of the conviction is specifically the prejudicial effect *to the defendant*. The danger of prejudice to a witness other than the defendant (such as injury to the witness' reputation in his community) was considered and rejected by the Conference as an element to be weighed in determining admissibility. It was the judgment of the Conference that the danger of prejudice to a nondefendant witness is outweighed by the need for the trier of fact to have as much relevant evidence on the issue of credibility as possible. Such evidence should only be excluded where it presents a danger of improperly influencing the outcome of the trial by persuading the trier of fact to convict the defendant on the basis of his prior criminal record.

B. Rule 609(b)—Time Limit

The House bill provides in subsection (b) that evidence of conviction of a crime may not be used for impeachment purposes under subsection (a) if more than ten years have elapsed since the date of the conviction or the date the witness was released from confinement imposed for the conviction, whichever is later. The Senate amendment permits the use of convictions older than ten years, if the court determines, in the interests of justice, that the probative value of the conviction, supported by specific facts and circumstances, substantially outweighs its prejudicial effect.

The Conference adopts the Senate amendment with an amendment requiring notice by a party that he intends to request that the court allow him to use a conviction older than ten years. The Conferees anticipate that a written notice, in order to give the adversary a fair opportunity to contest the use of the evidence, will ordinarily include such information as the date of the conviction, the jurisdiction, and the offense or statute involved. In order to eliminate the possibility that the flexibility of this provision may impair the ability of a party-opponent to prepare for trial, the Conferees intend that the notice provision operate to avoid surprise.

NOTE BY FEDERAL JUDICIAL CENTER

Rule 609 underwent substantial change at the hands of Congress. They are as follows:

Subdivision (a) of the Rule prescribed by the Supreme Court was revised successively in the House, in the Senate, and in the Conference. The nature of the Rule prescribed by the Court, the various amendments, and the reasons therefor are stated in the Report of the House Committee on the Judiciary, the Report of the Senate Committee on the Judiciary, and the Conference Report, set forth above.

Subdivision (b) of the Rule prescribed by the Supreme Court was also revised successively in the House, in the Senate, and in the Conference. The nature of the Rule prescribed by the Court, those amendments and the reasons therefor are likewise stated in the Report of the House Committee on the Judiciary, the Report of the Senate Committee on the Judiciary, and the Conference Report, set forth above.

Subdivision (c) enacted by the Congress is the subdivision prescribed by the Supreme Court, with amendments and reasons therefor stated in the Report of the House Committee on the Judiciary, set forth above.

Subdivision (d) enacted by the Congress is the subdivision prescribed by the Supreme Court, amended in the second sentence by substituting "court" in place of "judge" and by adding the phrase "in a criminal case."

Subdivision (e) enacted by the Congress is the subdivision prescribed by the Supreme Court without change.

Rule 610   Religious Beliefs or Opinions

ADVISORY COMMITTEE'S NOTE

While the rule forecloses inquiry into the religious beliefs or opinions of a witness for the purpose of showing that his character for truthfulness is affected by their nature, an inquiry for the purpose of showing interest or bias because of them is not within the prohibition. Thus disclosure of affiliation with a church which is a party to the litigation would be allowable under the rule. Cf. Tucker v. Reil, 51 Ariz. 357, 77 P.2d 203 (1938). To the same effect, though less specifically worded, is California Evidence Code § 789. See 3 Wigmore § 936.

NOTE BY FEDERAL JUDICIAL CENTER

The Rule enacted by Congress is the Rule prescribed by the Supreme Court without change. Rule 610 is not mentioned in the Report of the Senate Judiciary Committee or the Reports of the House/Senate Conference Committee.

Rule 611   Mode and Order of Interrogation and Presentation

ADVISORY COMMITTEE'S NOTE

Subdivision (a). Spelling out detailed rules to govern the mode and order of interrogating witnesses and presenting evidence is neither desirable nor feasible. The ultimate responsibility for the effective working of the adversary system rests with the judge. The rule sets forth the objectives which he should seek to attain.

Item (1) restates in broad terms the power and obligation of the judge as developed under common law principles. It covers such concerns as whether testimony shall be in the form of a free narrative or responses to specific questions, McCormick § 5, the order of calling witnesses and presenting evidence, 6 Wigmore § 1867, the use of demonstrative evidence, McCormick § 179, and the many other questions arising during the course of a trial which can be solved only by the judge's common sense and fairness in view of the particular circumstances.

Item (2) is addressed to avoidance of needless consumption of time, a matter of daily concern in the disposition of cases. A companion piece is found in the discretion vested in the judge to exclude evidence as a waste of time in Rule 403(b).

Item (3) calls for a judgment under the particular circumstances whether interrogation tactics entail harassment or undue embarrassment. Pertinent circumstances include the importance of the testimony, the nature of the inquiry, its relevance to credibility, waste of time, and confusion. McCormick § 42. In Alford v. United States, 282 U.S. 687, 694, 51 S.Ct. 218, 75 L.Ed. 624 (1931), the Court pointed out that, while the trial judge should protect the witness from questions which "go beyond the bounds of proper cross-examination merely to harass, annoy or humiliate," this protection by no means forecloses efforts to discredit the witness. Reference to the transcript of the prosecutor's cross-examination in Berger v. United States, 295 U.S. 78, 55 S.Ct. 629, 79 L.Ed. 1314 (1935), serves to lay at rest any doubts as to the need for judicial control in this area.

The inquiry into specific instances of conduct of a witness allowed under Rule 608(b) is, of course, subject to this rule.

Subdivision (b). The tradition in the federal courts and in numerous state courts has been to limit the scope of cross-examination to matters testified to on direct, plus matters bearing upon the credibility of the witness. Various reasons have been advanced to justify the rule of limited cross-examination. (1) A party vouches for his own witness but only to the extent of matters elicited on direct. Resurrection Gold Mining Co. v. Fortune Gold Mining Co., 129 F. 668, 675 (8th Cir. 1904), quoted in Maguire, Weinstein, et al., Cases on Evidence 277, n. 38 (5th ed. 1965). But the concept of vouching is discredited, and Rule 607 rejects it. (2) A party cannot ask his own witness leading questions. This is a problem properly solved in terms of what is necessary for a proper development of the testimony rather than by a mechanistic formula similar to the vouching concept. See discussion under subdivision (c). (3) A practice of limited cross-examination promotes orderly presentation of the case. Finch v. Weiner, 109 Conn. 616, 145 A. 31 (1929). While this latter reason has merit, the matter is essentially one of the order of presentation and not one in which involvement at the appellate level is likely to prove fruitful. See, for example, Moyer v. Aetna Life Ins. Co., 126 F.2d 141 (3rd Cir. 1942); Butler v. New York Central R. Co., 253 F.2d 281 (7th Cir. 1958); United States v. Johnson, 285 F.2d 35 (9th Cir. 1960); Union Automobile Indemnity Ass'n v. Capitol Indemnity Ins. Co., 310 F.2d 318 (7th Cir. 1962). In evaluating these considerations, McCormick says:

"The foregoing considerations favoring the wide-open or restrictive rules may well be thought to be fairly evenly balanced. There is another factor, however, which seems to swing the balance overwhelmingly in favor of the wide-open rule. This is the consideration of economy of time and energy. Obviously, the wide-open rule presents little or no opportunity for dispute in its application. The restrictive practice in all its forms, on the other hand, is productive in many court rooms, of continual bickering over the choice of the numerous variations of the 'scope of the direct' criterion, and of their application to particular cross-questions. These controversies are often reventilated on appeal, and reversals for error in their determination are frequent. Observance of these vague and ambiguous restrictions is a matter of constant and hampering concern to the cross-examiner. If these efforts, delays and misprisions were the necessary incidents to the guarding of substantive rights or the fundamentals of fair trial, they might be worth the cost. As the price of the choice of an obviously debatable regulation of the order of evidence, the sacrifice seems misguided. The American Bar Association's Committee for the Improvement of the Law of Evidence for the year 1937-38 said this:

> "The rule limiting cross-examination to the precise subject of the direct examination is probably the most frequent rule (except the Opinion rule) leading in the trial practice today to refined and technical quibbles which obstruct the progress of the trial, confuse the jury, and give rise to appeal on technical grounds only. Some of the instances in which Supreme Courts have ordered new trials for the mere transgression of this rule about the order of evidence have been astounding.
>
> 'We recommend that the rule allowing questions upon any part of the issue known to the witness . . . be adopted. . . .' " McCormick, § 27, p. 51. See also 5 Moore's Federal Practice § 43.10 (2nd ed. 1964).

The provision of the second sentence, that the judge may in the interests of justice limit inquiry into new matters on cross-examination, is designed for those situations in which the result otherwise would be confusion, complication, or protraction of the case, not as a matter of rule but as demonstrable in the actual development of the particular case.

The rule does not purport to determine the extent to which an accused who elects to testify thereby waives his privilege against self-incrimination. The question is a constitutional one, rather than a mere matter of administering the trial. Under Simmons v. United States, 390 U.S. 377, 88 S.Ct. 967, 19 L.Ed.2d 1247 (1968), no general waiver occurs when the accused testifies on such preliminary matters as the validity of a search and seizure or the admissibility of a confession. Rule 104(d), *supra*. When he testifies on the merits, however, can he foreclose inquiry into an aspect or element of the crime by avoiding it on direct? The affirmative answer given in Tucker v. United States, 5 F.2d 818 (8th Cir. 1925), is inconsistent with the description of the waiver as extending to "all other relevant facts" in Johnson v. United States, 318 U.S. 189, 195, 63 S.Ct. 549, 87 L.Ed. 704 (1943). See also Brown v. United States, 356 U.S. 148, 78 S.Ct. 622, 2 L.Ed.2d 589 (1958). The situation of an accused who desires to testify on some but not all counts of a multiple-count indictment is one to be approached, in the first instance at least, as a problem of severance under Rule 14 of the Federal Rules of Criminal Procedure. Cross v. United States, 118 U.S.App.D.C. 324, 335 F.2d 987 (1964). Cf. United States v. Baker, 262 F.Supp. 657, 686 (D.D.C. 1966). In all events, the extent of the waiver of the privilege against self-incrimination ought not to be determined as a by-product of a rule on scope of cross-examination.

Subdivision (c). The rule continues the traditional view that the suggestive powers of the leading question are as a general proposition undesirable. Within this tradition, however, numerous exceptions have achieved recognition: The witness who is hostile, unwilling, or biased; the child witness or the adult with communication problems; the witness whose recollection is exhausted; and undisputed preliminary matters. 3 Wigmore §§ 774-778. An almost total unwillingness to reverse for infractions has been manifested by appellate courts. See cases cited in 3 Wigmore § 770. The matter clearly falls within the area of control by the judge over the mode and order of interrogation and presentation and accordingly is phrased in words of suggestion rather than command.

The rule also conforms to tradition in making the use of leading questions on cross-examination a matter of right. The purpose of the qualification "ordinarily" is to furnish a basis for denying the use of leading questions when the cross-examination is cross-examination in form only and not in fact, as for example the "cross-examination" of a party by his own counsel after being called by the opponent (savoring more of re-direct) or of an insured defendant who proves to be friendly to the plaintiff.

The final sentence deals with categories of witnesses automatically regarded and treated as hostile. Rule 43(b) of the Federal Rules of Civil Procedure has included only "an adverse party or an officer, director, or managing agent of a public or private corporation or of a partnership or association which is an adverse party." This limitation virtually to persons whose statements would stand as admissions is believed to be an unduly narrow concept of those who may safely be regarded as hostile without further demonstration. See, for example, Maryland Casualty Co. v. Kador, 225 F.2d 120 (5th Cir. 1955), and Degelos v. Fidelity and Casualty Co., 313 F.2d 809 (5th Cir. 1963), holding despite the language of Rule 43(b) that an insured fell within it, though not a party in an action under the Louisiana direct action statute. The phrase of the rule, "witness identified with" an adverse party, is designed to enlarge the category of persons thus callable.

REPORT OF THE HOUSE COMMITTEE ON THE JUDICIARY

Rule 611(b)

As submitted by the Court, Rule 611(b) provided:

> A witness may be cross-examined on any matter relevant to any issue in the case, including credibility. In the interests of justice, the judge may limit cross-examination with respect to matters not testified to on direct examination.

The Committee amended this provision to return to the rule which prevails in the federal courts and thirty-nine State jurisdictions. As amended, the Rule is in the text of the 1969 Advisory Committee draft. It limits cross-examination to credibility and to matters testified to on direct examination, unless the judge permits more, in which event the cross-examiner must proceed as if on direct examination. This traditional rule facilitates orderly presentation by each party at trial. Further, in light of existing discovery procedures, there appears to be no need to abandon the traditional rule.

Rule 611(c)

The third sentence of Rule 611(c) as submitted by the Court provided that:

> In civil cases, a party is entitled to call an adverse party or witness identified with him and interrogate by leading questions.

The Committee amended this Rule to permit leading questions to be used with respect to any hostile witness, not only an adverse party or person identified with such adverse party. The Committee also substituted the word "When" for the phrase "In civil cases" to reflect the possibility that in criminal cases a defendant may be entitled to call witnesses identified with the government, in which event the Committee believed the defendant should be permitted to inquire with leading questions.

REPORT OF THE SENATE COMMITTEE ON THE JUDICIARY

Rule 611(b). Mode and Order of Interrogation and Presentation; Scope of Cross-examination

Rule 611(b) as submitted by the Supreme Court permitted a broad scope of cross-examination: "cross-examination on any matter relevant to any issue in the case" unless the judge, in the interests of justice, limited the scope of cross-examination.

The House narrowed the Rule to the more traditional practice of limiting cross-examination to the subject matter of direct examination (and credibility), but with discretion in the judge to permit inquiry into additional matters in situations where that would aid in the development of the evidence or otherwise facilitate the conduct of the trial.

The committee agrees with the House amendment. Although there are good arguments in support of broad cross-examination from prospectives of developing all relevant evidence, we believe the factors of insuring an orderly and predictable development of the evidence weigh in favor of the narrower rule, especially when discretion is given to the trial judge to permit inquiry into additional matters. The committee expressly approves this discretion and believes it will permit sufficient flexibility allowing a broader scope of cross-examination whenever appropriate.

The House amendment providing broader discretionary cross-examination permitted inquiry into additional matters only as if on direct examination. As a general rule, we concur with this limitation, however, we would understand that this limitation would not preclude the utilization of leading questions if the conditions of subsection (c) of this rule were met, bearing in mind the judge's discretion in any case to limit the scope of cross-examination. Further, the committee has received correspondence from Federal judges commenting on the applicability of this rule to section 1407 of title 28. It is the committee's judgment that this rule as reported by the House is flexible enough to provide sufficiently broad cross-examination in appropriate situations in multidistrict litigation.

Rule 611(c). Mode and Order of Interrogation and Presentation; Leading Questions

As submitted by the Supreme Court, the rule provided: "In civil cases, a party is entitled to call an adverse party or witness identified with him and interrogate by leading questions."

The final sentence of subsection (c) was amended by the House for the purpose of clarifying the fact that a "hostile witness"—that is a witness who is hostile in fact—could be subject to interrogation by leading questions. The rule as submitted by the Supreme Court declared certain witnesses hostile as a matter of law and thus subject to interrogation by leading questions without any showing of hostility in fact. These were adverse parties or witnesses identified with adverse parties. However, the wording of the first sentence of subsection (c) while generally prohibiting the use of leading questions on direct examination, also provides "except as may be necessary to develop his testimony." Further, the first paragraph of the Advisory Committee note explaining the subsection makes clear that they intended that leading questions could be asked of a hostile witness or a witness who was unwilling or biased and even though that witness was not associated with an adverse party. Thus, we question whether the House amendment was necessary.

However, concluding that it was not intended to affect the meaning of the first sentence of the subsection and was intended solely to clarify the fact that leading questions are permissible in the interrogation of a witness, who is hostile in fact, the committee accepts that House amendment.

The final sentence of this subsection was also amended by the House to cover criminal as well as civil cases. The committee accepts this amendment, but notes that it may be difficult in criminal cases to determine when a witness is "identified with an adverse party," and thus the rule should be applied with caution.

NOTE BY FEDERAL JUDICIAL CENTER

Subdivision (a) of the Rule enacted by Congress is the subdivision prescribed by the Supreme Court, amended only by substituting "court" in place of "judge."

Subdivision (b) of the Rule enacted by Congress is substantially different from the subdivision prescribed by the Supreme Court. The nature of the changes and the reasons therefor are stated in the Report of the House Committee of the Judiciary, set forth above.

The first two sentences of subdivision (c) of the Rule enacted by Congress are the same as prescribed by the Supreme Court. The third sentence has been amended in the manner and for the reasons stated in the Report of the House Committee of the Judiciary, set forth above.

Rule 612   Writing Used to Refresh Memory

ADVISORY COMMITTEE'S NOTE

The treatment of writings used to refresh recollection while on the stand is in accord with settled doctrine. McCormick § 9, p. 15. The bulk of the case law has, however, denied the existence of any right to access by the opponent when the writing is used prior to taking the stand, though the judge may have discretion in the matter. Goldman v. United States, 316 U.S. 129, 62 S.Ct. 993, 86 L.Ed. 1322 (1942); Needelman v. United States, 261 F.2d 802 (5th Cir. 1958), cert. dismissed 362 U.S. 600, 80 S.Ct. 960, 4 L.Ed.2d 980, rehearing denied 363 U.S. 858, 80 S.Ct. 1606, 4 L.Ed.2d 1739, Annot., 82 A.L.R.2d 473, 562 and 7 A.L.R.3d 181, 247. An increasing group of cases has repudiated the distinction, People v. Scott, 29 Ill.2d 97, 193 N.E.2d 814 (1963); State v. Mucci, 25 N.J. 423, 136 A.2d 761 (1957); State v. Hunt, 25 N.J. 514, 138 A.2d 1 (1958); State v. Deslovers, 40 R.I. 89, 100 A. 64 (1917), and this position is believed to be correct. As Wigmore put it, "the risk of imposition and the need of safeguard is just as great" in both situations. 3 Wigmore § 762, p. 111. To the same effect is McCormick § 9, p. 17.

The purpose of the phrase "for the purpose of testifying" is to safeguard against using the rule as a pretext for wholesale exploration of an opposing party's files and to insure that access is limited only to those writings which may fairly be said in fact to have an impact upon the testimony of the witness.

The purpose of the rule is the same as that of the *Jencks* statute, 18 U.S.C. § 3500; to promote the search of credibility and memory. The same sensitivity to disclosure of government files may be involved; hence the rule is expressly made subject to the statute, subdivision (a) of which provides: "In any criminal prosecution brought by the United States, no statement or report in the possession of the United States which was made by a Government witness or prospective Government witness (other than the defendant) shall be the subject of subpoena, discovery, or inspection until said witness has testified on direct examination in the trial of the case." Items falling within the purview of the statute are producible only as provided by its terms, Palermo v. United States, 360 U.S. 343, 351 (1959), and disclosure under the rule is limited similarly by the statutory conditions. With this limitation in mind, some differences of application may be noted. The *Jencks* statute applies only to statements of witnesses; the rule is not so limited. The statute applies only to criminal cases; the rule applies to all cases. The statute applies only to government witnesses; the rule applies to all witnesses. The statute contains no requirement that the statement be consulted for purposes of refreshment before or while testifying; the rule so requires. Since many writings would qualify under either statute or rule, a substantial overlap exists, but the identity of procedures makes this of no importance.

The consequences of nonproduction by the government in a criminal case are those of the *Jencks* statute, striking the testimony or in exceptional cases a mistrial. 18 U.S.C. § 3500(d). In other cases these alternatives are unduly limited, and such possibilities as contempt, dismissal, finding issues against the offender, and the like are available. See Rule 16(g) of the Federal Rules of Criminal Procedure and Rule 37(b) of the Federal Rules of Civil Procedure for appropriate sanctions.

REPORT OF THE HOUSE COMMITTEE ON THE JUDICIARY

As submitted to Congress, Rule 612 provided that except as set forth in 18 U.S.C. 3500, if a witness uses a writing to refresh his memory for the purpose of testifying, "either before or while testifying," an adverse party is entitled to have the writing produced at the hearing, to inspect it, to cross-examine the witness on it, and to introduce in evidence those portions relating to the witness' testimony. The Committee amended the Rule so as still to require the production of writings used by a witness while testifying, but to render the production of writings used by a witness to refresh his memory before testifying discretionary with the court in the interests of justice, as is the case under existing federal law. See *Goldman v. United States*, 316 U.S. 129 (1942). The Committee considered that permitting an adverse party to require the production of writings used before testifying could result in fishing expeditions among a multitude of papers which a witness may have used in preparing for trial.

The Committee intends that nothing in the Rule be construed as barring the assertion of a privilege with respect to writings used by a witness to refresh his memory.

NOTE BY FEDERAL JUDICIAL CENTER

Rule 612 underwent substantial change at the hands of Congress with respect to the right of the questioner's adversary to inspect and use a writing before he testifies. The Rule was amended by substituting "court" in place of "judge," with appropriate pronominal change, and in the first sentence, by substituting "the writing" in place of "it" before "produced," and by substituting the phrase "(1) while testifying, or (2) before testifying if the Court in its discretion determines it is necessary in the interests of justice" in place of "before or while testifying." The reasons for the latter amendment are stated in the Report of the House Committee of the Judiciary, set forth above.

Rule 613   Prior Statements of Witnesses

ADVISORY COMMITTEE'S NOTE

Subdivision (a). The Queen's Case, 2 Br. & B. 284, 129 Eng.Rep. 976 (1820), laid down the requirement that a cross-examiner, prior to questioning the witness about his own prior statement in writing, must first show it to the witness. Abolished by statute in the country of its origin, the requirement nevertheless gained currency in the United States. The rule abolishes this useless impediment to cross-examination. Ladd, Some Observations on Credibility: Impeachment of Witnesses, 52 Cornell L.Q. 239, 246-247 (1967); McCormick § 28; 4 Wigmore §§ 1259-1260. Both oral and written statements are included.

The provision for disclosure to counsel is designed to protect against unwarranted insinuations that a statement has been made when the fact is to the contrary.

The rule does not defeat the application of Rule 1002 relating to production of the original when the contents of a writing are sought to be proved. Nor does it defeat the application of Rule 26(b)(3) of the Rules of Civil Procedure, as revised, entitling a person on request to a copy of his own statement, though the operation of the latter may be suspended temporarily.

Subdivision (b). The familiar foundation requirement that an impeaching statement first be shown to the witness before it can be proved by extrinsic evidence is preserved but with some modifications. See Ladd, Some Observations on Credibility: Impeachment of Witnesses, 52 Cornell L.Q. 239, 247 (1967). The traditional insistence that the attention of the witness be directed to the statement on cross-examination is relaxed in favor of simply providing the witness an opportunity to explain and the opposite party an opportunity to examine on the statement, with no specification of any particular time or sequence. Under this procedure, several collusive witnesses can be examined before disclosure of a joint prior inconsistent statement. See Comment to California Evidence Code § 770. Also, dangers of oversight are reduced. See McCormick § 37, p. 68.

In order to allow for such eventualities as the witness becoming unavailable by the time the statement is discovered, a measure of discretion is conferred upon the judge. Similar provisions are found in California Evidence Code § 770 and New Jersey Evidence Rule 22(b).

Under principles of *expression unius* the rule does not apply to impeachment by evidence of prior inconsistent conduct. The use of inconsistent statements to impeach a hearsay declaration is treated in Rule 800.

Note by Federal Judicial Center

The Rule enacted by Congress is the Rule prescribed by the Supreme Court, amended only by substituting "nor" in the place of "or" in subdivision (a); Rule 613 was not the subject of floor debate.

Rule 614　　Calling and Interrogation of Witnesses by Court

Advisory Committee's Note

Subdivision (a). While exercised more frequently in criminal than in civil cases, the authority of the judge to call witnesses is well established. McCormick § 8, p. 11; Maguire, Weinstein, et al., Cases on Evidence 303-304 (5th ed. 1965); 9 Wigmore § 2484. One reason for the practice, the old rule against impeaching one's own witness, no longer exists by virtue of Rule 607, *supra*. Other reasons remain, however, to justify the continuation of the practice of calling court's witnesses. The right to cross-examine, with all it implies, is assured. The tendency of juries to associate a witness with the party calling him, regardless of technical aspects of vouching, is avoided. And the judge is not imprisoned within the case as made by the parties.

Subdivision (b). The authority of the judge to question witnesses is also well established. McCormick § 8, pp. 12-13; Maguire, Weinstein, et al., Cases on Evidence 737-739 (5th ed. 1965); 3 Wigmore § 784. The authority is, of course, abused when the judge abandons his proper role and assumes that of advocate, but the manner in which interrogation should be conducted and the proper extent of its exercise are not susceptible of formulation in a rule. The omission in no sense precludes courts of review from continuing to reverse for abuse.

Subdivision (c). The provision relating to objections is designed to relieve counsel of the embarrassment attendant upon objecting to questions by the judge in the presence of the jury, while at the same time assuring that objections are made in apt time to afford the opportunity to take possible corrective measures. Compare the "automatic" objection feature of Rule 605 when the judge is called as a witness.

Note by Federal Judicial Center

The Rule enacted by Congress is the Rule prescribed by the Supreme Court, amended by substituting "court" in place of "judge," with conforming pronominal changes. Rule 614 was not the subject of floor debate.

Rule 615　　Exclusion of Witnesses

Advisory Committee's Note

The efficacy of excluding or sequestering witnesses has long been recognized as a means of discouraging and exposing fabrication, inaccuracy, and collusion. 6 Wigmore §§ 1837-1838. The authority of the judge is admitted, the only question being whether the matter is committed to his discretion or one of right. The rule takes the latter position. No time is specified for making the request.

Several categories of persons are excepted. (1) Exclusion of persons who are parties would raise serious problems of confrontation and due process. Under accepted practice they are not subject to exclusion. 6 Wigmore § 1811. (2) As the equivalent of the right of a natural-person party to be present, a party which is not a natural person is entitled to have a representative present. Most of the cases have involved allowing a police officer who has been in charge of an investigation to remain in court despite the fact that he will be a witness. United States v. Infanzon, 235 F.2d 318 (2d Cir. 1956); Portomene v. United States, 221 F.2d 582 (5th Cir. 1955); Powell v. United States, 208 F.2d 618 (6th Cir. 1953); Jones v. United States, 252 F.Supp. 781 (W.D.Okl.1966). Designation of the representative by the attorney rather than by the client may at first glance appear to be an inversion of the attorney-client relationship, but it may be assumed that the attorney will follow the wishes of the client, and the solution is simple and workable. See California Evidence Code § 777. (3) The category contemplates such persons as an agent who handled the transaction being litigated or an expert needed to advise counsel in the management of the litigation. See 6 Wigmore § 1841, n. 4.

REPORT OF THE SENATE COMMITTEE ON THE JUDICIARY

Many district courts permit government counsel to have an investigative agent at counsel table throughout the trial although the agent is or may be a witness. The practice is permitted as an exception to the rule of exclusion and compares with the situation defense counsel finds himself in—he always has the client with him to consult during the trial. The investigative agent's presence may be extremely important to government counsel, especially when the case is complex or involves some specialized subject matter. The agent, too, having lived with the case for a long time, may be able to assist in meeting trial surprises where the best-prepared counsel would otherwise have difficulty. Yet, it would not seem the Government could often meet the burden under Rule 615 of showing that the agent's presence is essential. Furthermore, it could be dangerous to use the agent as a witness as early in the case as possible, so that he might then help counsel as a nonwitness, since the agent's testimony could be needed in rebuttal. Using another, nonwitness agent from the same investigative agency would not generally meet government counsel's needs.

This problem is solved if it is clear that investigative agents are within the group specified under the second exception made in the rule, for "an officer or employee of a party which is not a natural person designated as its representative by its attorney." It is our understanding that this was the intention of the House committee. It is certainly this committee's construction of the rule.

NOTE BY FEDERAL JUDICIAL CENTER

The Rule enacted by Congress is the Rule prescribed by the Supreme Court, amended only by substituting "court," in place of "judge," with conforming pronominal changes.

ARTICLE VII
OPINIONS AND EXPERT TESTIMONY

Rule 701　Opinion Testimony by Lay Witnesses

ADVISORY COMMITTEE'S NOTE

The rule retains the traditional objective of putting the trier of fact in possession of an accurate reproduction of the event.

Limitation (a) is the familiar requirement of first-hand knowledge or observation.

Limitation (b) is phrased in terms of requiring testimony to be helpful in resolving issues. Witnesses often find difficulty in expressing themselves in language which is not that of an opinion or conclusion. While the courts have made concessions in certain recurring situations, necessity as a standard for permitting opinions and conclusions has proved too elusive and too unadaptable to particular situations for purposes of satisfactory judicial administration. McCormick § 11. Moreover, the practical impossibility of determining by rule what is a "fact," demonstrated by a century of litigation of the question of what is a fact for purposes of pleading under the Field Code, extends into evidence also. 7 Wigmore § 1919. The rule assumes that the natural characteristics of the adversary system will generally lead to an acceptable result, since the detailed account carries more conviction than the broad assertion, and a lawyer can be expected to display his witness to the best advantage. If he fails to do so, cross-examination and argument will point up the weakness. See Ladd, Expert Testimony 5 Vand.L.Rev. 414, 415-417 (1952). If, despite these considerations, attempts are made to introduce meaningless assertions which amount to little more than choosing up sides, exclusion for lack of helpfulness is called for by the rule.

The language of the rule is substantially that of Uniform Rule 56(1). Similar provisions are California Evidence Code § 800; Kansas Code of Civil Procedure § 60-456(a); New Jersey Evidence Rule 56(1).

NOTE BY FEDERAL JUDICIAL CENTER

The Rule enacted by Congress is the Rule prescribed by the Supreme Court without change. Rule 701 was not the subject of floor debate.

Rule 702　Testimony by Experts

ADVISORY COMMITTEE'S NOTE

An intelligent evaluation of facts is often difficult or impossible without the application of some scientific, technical, or other specialized knowledge. The most common source of this knowledge is the expert witness, although there are other techniques for supplying it.

Most of the literature assumes that experts testify only in the form of opinions. The assumption is logically unfounded. The rule accordingly recognizes that an expert on the stand may give a dissertation or exposition of scientific or other principles relevant to the case, leaving the trier of fact to apply them to the facts. Since much of the criticism of expert testimony has centered upon the hypothetical question, it seems wise to recognize that opinions are not indispensable and to encourage the use of expert testimony in nonopinion form when counsel believes the trier can itself draw the requisite inference. The use of opinions is not abolished by the rule, however. It will continue to be permissible for the expert to take the further step of suggesting the inference which should be drawn from applying the specialized knowledge to the facts. See Rules 703 to 705.

Whether the situation is a proper one for the use of expert testimony is to be determined on the basis of assisting the trier. "There is no more certain test for determining when experts may be used than the common sense inquiry whether the untrained layman would be qualified to determine intelligently and to the best possible degree the particular issue without enlightenment from those having a specialized understanding of the subject involved in the dispute." Ladd, Expert Testimony, 5 Vand.L.Rev. 414, 418 (1952). When opinions are excluded, it is because they are unhelpful and therefore superfluous and a waste of time. 7 Wigmore § 1918.

The rule is broadly phrased. The fields of knowledge which may be drawn upon are not limited merely to the "scientific" and "technical" but extend to all "specialized" knowledge. Similarly, the expert is viewed, not in a narrow sense, but as a person qualified by "knowledge, skill, experience, training or education." Thus within the scope of the rule are not only experts in the strictest sense of the word, e.g. physicians, physicists, and architects, but also the large group sometimes called "skilled" witnesses, such as bankers or landowners testifying to land values.

NOTE BY FEDERAL JUDICIAL CENTER

The Rule enacted by Congress is the Rule prescribed by the Supreme Court without change. Rule 702 was not the subject of floor debate.

Rule 703 Bases of Opinion Testimony by Experts

ADVISORY COMMITTEE'S NOTE

Facts or data upon which expert opinions are based may, under the rule, be derived from three possible sources. The first is the firsthand observation of the witness, with opinions based thereon traditionally allowed. A treating physician affords an example. Rheingold, The Basis of Medical Testimony, 15 Vand.L.Rev. 473, 489 (1962). Whether he must first relate his observations is treated in Rule 705. The second source, presentation at the trial, also reflects existing practice. The technique may be the familiar hypothetical question or having the expert attend the trial and hear the testimony establishing the facts. Problems of determining what testimony the expert relied upon, when the latter technique is employed and the testimony is in conflict, may be resolved by resort to Rule 705. The third source contemplated by the rule consists of presentation of data to the expert outside of court and other than by his own perception. In this respect the rule is designed to broaden the basis for expert opinions beyond that current in many jurisdictions and to bring the judicial practice into line with the practice of the experts themselves when not in court. Thus a physician in his own practice bases his diagnosis on information from numerous sources and of considerable variety, including statements by patients and relatives, reports and opinions from nurses, technicians and other doctors, hospital records, and X rays. Most of them are admissible in evidence, but only with the expenditure of substantial time in producing and examining various authenticating witnesses. The physician makes life-and-death decisions in reliance upon them. His validation, expertly performed and subject to cross-examination, ought to suffice for judicial purposes. Rheingold, *supra,* at 531; McCormick § 15. A similar provision is California Evidence Code § 801(b).

The rule also offers a more satisfactory basis for ruling upon the admissibility of public opinion poll evidence. Attention is directed to the validity of the techniques employed rather than to relatively fruitless inquiries whether hearsay is involved. See Judge Feinberg's careful analysis in Zippo Mfg. Co. v. Rogers Imports, Inc., 216 F. Supp. 670 (S.D.N.Y.1963). See also Blum et al., The Art of Opinion Research: A Lawyer's Appraisal of an Emerging Service, 24 U.Chi.L.Rev. 1 (1956); Bonynge, Trademark Surveys and Techniques and Their Use in Litigation, 48 A.B.A.J. 329 (1962); Zeisel, The Uniqueness of Survey Evidence, 45 Cornell L.Q. 322 (1960); Annot., 76 A.L.R.2d 919.

If it be feared that enlargement of permissible data may tend to break down the rules of exclusion unduly, notice should be taken that the rule requires that the facts or data "be of a type reasonably relied upon by experts in the particular field." The language would not warrant admitting in evidence the opinion of an "accidentologist" as to the point of impact in an automobile collision based on statements of bystanders, since this requirement is not satisfied. See Comment, Cal.Law Rev.Comm'n, Recommendation Proposing an Evidence Code 148-150 (1965).

NOTE BY FEDERAL JUDICIAL CENTER

The Rule enacted by Congress is the Rule prescribed by the Supreme Court without change. Rule 703 was not the subject of floor debate.

Rule 704　Opinion on Ultimate Issue

ADVISORY COMMITTEE'S NOTE

The basic approach to opinions, lay and expert, in these rules is to admit them when helpful to the trier of fact. In order to render this approach fully effective and to allay any doubt on the subject, the so-called "ultimate issue" rule is specifically abolished by the instant rule.

The older cases often contained strictures against allowing witnesses to express opinions upon ultimate issues, as a particular aspect of the rule against opinions. The rule was unduly restrictive, difficult of application, and generally served only to deprive the trier of fact of useful information. 7 Wigmore §§ 1920, 1921; McCormick § 12. The basis usually assigned for the rule, to prevent the witness from "usurping the province of the jury," is aptly characterized as "empty rhetoric." 7 Wigmore § 1920, p. 17. Efforts to meet the felt needs of particular situations led to odd verbal circumlocutions which were said not to violate the rule. Thus a witness could express his estimate of the criminal responsibility of an accused in terms of sanity or insanity, but not in terms of ability to tell right from wrong or other more modern standard. And in cases of medical causation, witnesses were sometimes required to couch their opinions in cautious phrases of "might or could," rather than "did," though the result was to deprive many opinions of the positiveness to which they were entitled, accompanied by the hazard of a ruling of insufficiency to support a verdict. In other instances the rule was simply disregarded, and, as concessions to need, opinions were allowed upon such matters as intoxication, speed, handwriting, and value, although more precise coincidence with an ultimate issue would scarcely be possible.

Many modern decisions illustrate the trend to abandon the rule completely. People v. Wilson, 25 Cal.2d 341, 153 P.2d 720 (1944), whether abortion necessary to save life of patient; Clifford-Jacobs Forging Co. v. Industrial Comm., 19 Ill.2d 236, 166 N.E.2d 582 (1960), medical causation; Dowling v. L. H. Shattuck, Inc., 91 N.H. 234, 17 A.2d 529 (1941), proper method of shoring ditch; Schweiger v. Solbeck, 191 Or. 454, 230 P.2d 195 (1951), cause of landslide. In each instance the opinion was allowed.

The abolition of the ultimate issue rule does not lower the bars so as to admit all opinions. Under Rules 701 and 702, opinions must be helpful to the trier of fact, and Rule 403 provides for exclusion of evidence which wastes time. These provisions afford ample assurances against the admission of opinions which would merely tell the jury what result to reach, somewhat in the manner of the oath-helpers of an earlier day. They also stand ready to exclude opinions phrased in terms of inadequately explored legal criteria. Thus the question, "Did T have capacity to make a will?" would be excluded, while the question, "Did T have sufficient mental capacity to know the nature and extent of his property and the natural objects of his bounty and to formulate a rational scheme of distribution?" would be allowed. McCormick § 12.

For similar provisions see Uniform Rule 56(4); California Evidence Code § 805; Kansas Code of Civil Procedure § 60-456(d); New Jersey Evidence Rule 56(3).

NOTE BY FEDERAL JUDICIAL CENTER

The Rule enacted by Congress is the Rule prescribed by the Supreme Court without change. Rule 704 was not the subject of floor debate.

Rule 705 Disclosure of Facts or Data Underlying Expert Opinion

ADVISORY COMMITTEE'S NOTE

The hypothetical question has been the target of a great deal of criticism as encouraging partisan bias, affording an opportunity for summing up in the middle of the case, and as complex and time consuming. Ladd, Expert Testimony, 5 Vand.L.Rev. 414, 426-427 (1952). While the rule allows counsel to make disclosure of the underlying facts or data as a preliminary to the giving of an expert opinion, if he chooses, the instances in which he is required to do so are reduced. This is true whether the expert bases his opinion on data furnished him at secondhand or observed by him at firsthand.

The elimination of the requirement of preliminary disclosure at the trial of underlying facts or data has a long background of support. In 1937 the Commissioners on Uniform State Laws incorporated a provision to this effect in their Model Expert Testimony Act, which furnished the basis for Uniform Rules 57 and 58. Rule 4515, N.Y. CPLR (McKinney 1963), provides:

"Unless the court orders otherwise, questions calling for the opinion of an expert witness need not be hypothetical in form, and the witness may state his opinion and reasons without first specifying the data upon which it is based. Upon cross-examination, he may be required to specify the data. . .."

See also California Evidence Code § 802; Kansas Code of Civil Procedure §§ 60-456, 60-457; New Jersey Evidence Rules 57, 58.

If the objection is made that leaving it to the cross-examiner to bring out the supporting data is essentially unfair, the answer is that he is under no compulsion to bring out any facts or data except those unfavorable to the opinion. The answer assumes that the cross-examiner has the advance knowledge which is essential for effective cross-examination. This advance knowledge has been afforded, though imperfectly, by the traditional foundation requirement. Rule 26(b)(4) of the Rules of Civil Procedure, as revised, provides for substantial discovery in this area, obviating in large measure the obstacles which have been raised in some instances to discovery of findings, underlying data, and even the identity of the experts. Friedenthal, Discovery and Use of an Adverse Party's Expert Information, 14 Stan.L.Rev. 455 (1962).

These safeguards are reinforced by the discretionary power of the judge to require preliminary disclosure in any event.

NOTE BY FEDERAL JUDICIAL CENTER

The Rule enacted by Congress is the Rule prescribed by the Supreme Court, amended only by substituting "court" in place of "judge." Rule 705 was not the subject of floor debate.

Rule 706 Court Appointed Experts

ADVISORY COMMITTEE'S NOTE

The practice of shopping for experts, the venality of some experts, and the reluctance of many reputable experts to involve themselves in litigation, have been matters of deep concern. Though the contention is made that court appointed experts acquire an aura of infallibility to which they are not entitled, Levy, Impartial Medical Testimony—Revisited, 34 Temple L.Q. 416 (1961), the trend is increasingly to provide for their use. While experience indicates that actual appointment is a relatively infrequent occurrence, the assumption may be made that the availability of the procedure in itself decreases the need for resorting to it. The ever-present possibility that the judge *may* appoint an expert in a given case must inevitably exert a sobering effect on the expert witness of a party and upon the person utilizing his services.

The inherent power of a trial judge to appoint an expert of his own choosing is virtually unquestioned. Scott v. Spanjer Bros., Inc., 298 F.2d 928 (2d Cir. 1962); Danville Tobacco Assn. v. Bryant-Buckner Associates, Inc., 333 F.2d 202 (4th Cir. 1964); Sink, The Unused Power of a Federal Judge to Call His Own Expert Witnesses, 29 S.Cal.L.Rev. 195 (1956); 2 Wigmore § 563, 9 *id.* § 2484; Annot., 95 A.L.R.2d 383. Hence the problem becomes largely one of detail.

The New York plan is well known and is described in Report by Special Committee of the Association of the Bar of the City of New York: Impartial Medical Testimony (1956). On recommendation of the Section of Judicial Administration, local adoption of an impartial medical plan was endorsed by the American Bar Association. 82 A.B.A.Rep. 184-185 (1957). Descriptions and analyses of plans in effect in various parts of the country are found in Van Dusen, A United States District Judge's View of the Impartial Medical Expert System, 32 F.R.D. 498 (1963); Wick and Kightlinger, Impartial Medical Testimony Under the Federal Civil Rules: A Tale of Three Doctors, 34 Ins. Counsel J. 115 (1967); and numerous articles collected in Klein, Judicial Administration and the Legal Profession 393 (1963). Statutes and rules include California Evidence Code §§ 730-733; Illinois Supreme Court Rule 215(d), Ill.Rev.Stat.1969, c. 110A, § 215(d); Burns, Indiana Stats.1956, § 9-1702; Wisconsin Stats.Annot.1958, § 957.27.

In the federal practice, a comprehensive scheme for court appointed experts was initiated with the adoption of Rule 28 of the Federal Rules of Criminal Procedure in 1946. The Judicial Conference of the United States in 1953 considered court appointed experts in civil cases, but only with respect to whether they should be compensated from public funds, a proposal which was rejected. Report of the Judicial Conference of the United States 23 (1953). The present rule expands the practice to include civil cases.

Subdivision (a) is based on Rule 28 of the Federal Rules of Criminal Procedure, with a few changes, mainly in the interest of clarity. Language has been added to provide specifically for the appointment either on motion of a party or on the judge's own motion. A provision subjecting the court appointed expert to deposition procedures has been incorporated. The rule has been revised to make definite the right of any party, including the party calling him, to cross-examine.

Subdivision (b) combines the present provision for compensation in criminal cases with what seems to be a fair and feasible handling of civil cases, originally found in the Model Act and carried from there into Uniform Rule 60. See also California Evidence Code §§ 730-731. The special provision for Fifth Amendment compensation cases is designed to guard against reducing constitutionally guaranteed just compensation by requiring the recipient to pay costs. See Rule 71A*(1)* of the Rules of Civil Procedure.

Subdivision (c) seems to be essential if the use of court appointed experts is to be fully effective. Uniform Rule 61 so provides.

Subdivision (d) is in essence the last sentence of Rule 28(a) of the Federal Rules of Criminal Procedure.

NOTE BY FEDERAL JUDICIAL CENTER

The Rule enacted by Congress is the Rule prescribed by the Supreme Court, amended by substituting "court" in place of "judge," with conforming pronominal changes, and, in subdivision (b), by substituting the phrase "and civil actions and proceedings" in place of "and cases" before "involving" in the second sentence. Rule 706 was not the subject of floor debate.

ARTICLE VIII
HEARSAY

Rule 801　Definitions

Advisory Committee's Note to Rule 801(a), (b) and (c)

Subdivision (a). The definition of "statement" assumes importance because the term is used in the definition of hearsay in subdivision (c). The effect of the definition of "statement" is to exclude from the operation of the hearsay rule all evidence of conduct, verbal or nonverbal, not intended as an assertion. The key to the definition is that nothing is an assertion unless intended to be one.

It can scarcely be doubted that an assertion made in words is intended by the declarant to be an assertion. Hence verbal assertions readily fall into the category of "statement." Whether nonverbal conduct should be regarded as a statement for purposes of defining hearsay requires further consideration. Some nonverbal conduct, such as the act of pointing to identify a suspect in a lineup, is clearly the equivalent of words, assertive in nature, and to be regarded as a statement. Other nonverbal conduct, however, may be offered as evidence that the person acted as he did because of his belief in the existence of the condition sought to be proved, from which belief the existence of the condition may be inferred. This sequence is, arguably, in effect an assertion of the existence of the condition and hence properly includable within the hearsay concept. See Morgan, Hearsay Dangers and the Application of the Hearsay Concept, 62 Harv.L.Rev. 177, 214, 217 (1948), and the elaboration in Finman, Implied Assertions as Hearsay: Some Criticisms of the Uniform Rules of Evidence, 14 Stan.L.Rev. 682 (1962). Admittedly evidence of this character is untested with respect to the perception, memory, and narration (or their equivalents) of the actor, but the Advisory Committee is of the view that these dangers are minimal in the absence of an intent to assert and do not justify the loss of the evidence on hearsay grounds. No class of evidence is free of the possibility of fabrication, but the likelihood is less with nonverbal than with assertive verbal conduct. The situations giving rise to the nonverbal conduct are such as virtually to eliminate questions of sincerity. Motivation, the nature of the conduct, and the presence or absence of reliance will bear heavily upon the weight to be given the evidence. Falknor, The "Hear-Say" Rule as a "See-Do" Rule: Evidence of Conduct, 33 Rocky Mt.L.Rev. 133 (1961). Similar considerations govern nonassertive verbal conduct and verbal conduct which is assertive but offered as a basis for inferring something other than the matter asserted, also excluded from the definition of hearsay by the language of subdivision (c).

When evidence of conduct is offered on the theory that it is not a statement, and hence not hearsay, a preliminary determination will be required to determine whether an assertion is intended. The rule is so worded as to place the burden upon the party claiming that the intention existed; ambiguous and doubtful cases will be resolved against him and in favor of admissibility. The determination involves no greater difficulty than many other preliminary questions of fact. Maguire, The Hearsay System: Around and Through the Thicket, 14 Vand.L.Rev. 741, 765-767 (1961).

For similar approaches, see Uniform Rule 62(1); California Evidence Code §§ 225, 1200; Kansas Code of Civil Procedure § 60-459(a); New Jersey Evidence Rule 62(1).

Subdivision (c). The definition follows along familiar lines in including only statements offered to prove the truth of the matter asserted. McCormick § 225; 5 Wigmore § 1361, 6 *id.* § 1766. If the significance of an offered statement lies solely in the fact that it was made, no issue is raised as to the truth of anything asserted, and the statement is not hearsay. Emich Motors Corp. v. General Motors Corp., 181 F.2d 70 (7th Cir. 1950), rev'd on other grounds 340 U.S. 558, 71 S.Ct. 408, 95 L.Ed. 534, letters of complaint from customers offered as a reason for cancellation of dealer's franchise, to rebut contention that franchise was revoked for refusal to finance sales through affiliated finance company. The effect is to exclude from hearsay the entire category of "verbal acts" and "verbal parts of an act," in which the statement itself affects the legal rights of the parties or is a circumstance bearing on conduct affecting their rights.

The definition of hearsay must, of course, be read with reference to the definition of statement set forth in subdivision (a).

Testimony given by a witness in the course of court proceedings is excluded since there is compliance with all the ideal conditions for testifying.

ADVISORY COMMITTEE'S NOTE TO RULE 801 (d)(1)(A)

[Note, that the version of Rule 801 (d)(1)(A) which is discussed below was changed before enactment by the action of Congress. See the Congressional Reports set forth below.]

Subdivision (d). Several types of statements which would otherwise literally fall within the definition are expressly excluded from it:

(1) *Prior statement by witness.* Considerable controversy has attended the question whether a prior out-of-court statement by a person now available for cross-examination concerning it, under oath and in the presence of the trier of fact, should be classed as hearsay. If the witness admits on the stand that he made the statement and that it was true, he adopts the statement and there is no hearsay problem. The hearsay problem arises when the witness on the stand denies having made the statement or admits having made it but denies its truth. The argument in favor of treating these latter statements as hearsay is based upon the ground that the conditions of oath, cross-examination, and demeanor observation did not prevail at the time the statement was made and cannot adequately be supplied by the later examination. The logic of the situation is troublesome. So far as concerns the oath, its mere presence has never been regarded as sufficient to remove a statement from the hearsay category, and it receives much less emphasis than cross-examination as a truth-compelling device. While strong expressions are found to the effect that no conviction can be had or important right taken away on the basis of statements not made under fear of prosecution for perjury, Bridges v. Wixon, 326 U.S. 135, 65 S.Ct. 1443, 89 L.Ed. 2103 (1945), the fact is that, of the many common law exceptions to the hearsay rule, only that for reported testimony has required the statement to have been made under oath. Nor is it satisfactorily explained why cross-examination cannot be conducted subsequently with success. The decisions contending most vigorously for its inadequacy in fact demonstrate quite thorough exploration of the weaknesses and doubts attending

the earlier statement. State v. Saporen, 205 Minn. 358, 285 N.W. 898 (1939); Ruhala v. Roby, 379 Mich. 102, 150 N.W.2d 146 (1967); People v. Johnson, 68 Cal.2d 646, 68 Cal.Rptr. 599, 441 P.2d 111 (1968). In respect to demeanor, as Judge Learned Hand observed in Di Carlo v. United States, 6 F.2d 364 (2d Cir. 1925), when the jury decides that the truth is not what the witness says now, but what he said before, they are still deciding from what they see and hear in court. The bulk of the case law nevertheless has been against allowing prior statements of witnesses to be used generally as substantive evidence. Most of the writers and Uniform Rule 63(1) have taken the opposite position.

The position taken by the Advisory Committee in formulating this part of the rule is founded upon an unwillingness to countenance the general use of prior prepared statements as substantive evidence, but with a recognition that particular circumstances call for a contrary result. The judgment is one more of experience than of logic. The rule requires in each instance, as a general safeguard, that the declarant actually testify as a witness, and it then enumerates three situations in which the statement is excepted from the category of hearsay. Compare Uniform Rule 63(1) which allows any out-of-court statement of a declarant who is present at the trial and available for cross-examination.

(A) Prior inconsistent statements traditionally have been admissible to impeach but not as substantive evidence. Under the rule they are substantive evidence. As has been said by the California Law Revision Commission with respect to a similar provision:

"Section 1235 admits inconsistent statements of witnesses because the dangers against which the hearsay rule is designed to protect are largely nonexistent. The declarant is in court and may be examined and cross-examined in regard to his statements and their subject matter. In many cases, the inconsistent statement is more likely to be true than the testimony of the witness at the trial because it was made nearer in time to the matter to which it relates and is less likely to be influenced by the controversy that gave rise to the litigation. The trier of fact has the declarant before it and can observe his demeanor and the nature of his testimony as he denies or tries to explain away the inconsistency. Hence, it is in as good a position to determine the truth or falsity of the prior statement as it is to determine the truth or falsity of the inconsistent testimony given in court. Moreover, Section 1235 will provide a party with desirable protection against the 'turncoat' witness who changes his story on the stand and deprives the party calling him of evidence essential to his case." Comment, California Evidence Code § 1235. See also McCormick § 39. The Advisory Committee finds these views more convincing than those expressed in People v. Johnson, 68 Cal.2d 646, 68 Cal.Rptr. 599, 441 P.2d 111 (1968). The constitutionality of the Advisory Committee's view was upheld in California v. Green, 399 U.S. 149, 90 S.Ct. 1930, 26 L.Ed.2d 489 (1970). Moreover, the requirement that the statement be inconsistent with the testimony given assures a thorough exploration of both versions while the witness is on the stand and bars any general and indiscriminate use of previously prepared statements.

REPORT OF THE HOUSE COMMITTEE ON THE JUDICIARY

[Note, that the version of Rule 801 (d)(1)(A) which is discussed below was changed before enactment by the action of the Senate and the House/Senate Conference Committee. See the Congressional Report set forth below.]

Present federal law, except in the Second Circuit, permits the use of prior inconsistent statements of a witness for impeachment only. Rule 801(d)(1) as proposed by the Court would have permitted all such statements to be admissible as substantive evidence, an approach followed by a small but growing number of State jurisdictions and recently held constitutional in *California v. Green*, 399 U.S. 149 (1970). Although there was some support expressed for the Court Rule, based largely on the need to counteract the effect of witness intimidation in criminal cases, the Committee decided to adopt a compromise version of the Rule similar to the position of the Second Circuit. The Rule as amended draws a distinction between types of prior inconsistent statements (other than statements of identification of a person made after perceiving him which are currently admissible, see *United States v. Anderson*, 406 F.2d 719, 720 (4th Cir.), cert. denied, 395 U.S. 967 (1969)) and allows only those made while the declarant was subject to cross-examination at a trial or hearing or in a deposition, to be admissible for their truth. Compare *United States v. DeSisto*, 329 F.2d 929 (2nd Cir.), cert. denied, 377 U.S. 979 (1964); *United States v. Cunningham*, 446 F.2d 194 (2nd Cir. 1971) (restricting the admissibility of prior inconsistent statements as substantive evidence to those made under oath in a formal proceeding, but not requiring that there have been an opportunity for cross-examination). The rationale for the Committee's decision is that (1) unlike in most other situations involving unsworn or oral statements, there can be no dispute as to whether the prior statement was made; and (2) the context of a formal proceeding, an oath, and the opportunity for cross-examination provide firm additional assurances of the reliability of the prior statement.

REPORT OF THE SENATE COMMITTEE ON THE JUDICIARY

[Note, that the version of Rule 801 (d)(1)(A) which is discussed below was changed before enactment by the action of the Senate and the House/Senate Conference Committee. See the Conference Report set forth below.]

Rule 801 defines what is and what is not hearsay for the purpose of admitting a prior statement as substantive evidence. A prior statement of a witness at a trial or hearing which is inconsistent with his testimony is, of course, always admissible for the purpose of impeaching the witness' credibility.

As submitted by the Supreme Court, subdivision (d)(1)(A) made admissible as substantive evidence the prior statement of a witness inconsistent with his present testimony.

The House severely limited the admissibility of prior inconsistent statements by adding a requirement that the prior statement must have been subject to cross-examination, thus precluding even the use of grand jury statements. The requirement that the prior statement must have been subject to cross-examination appears unnecessary since this rule comes into play only when the witness testifies in the present trial. At that time, he is on the stand and can explain an earlier position and be cross-examined as to both.

The requirement that the statement be under oath also appears unnecessary. Notwithstanding the absence of an oath contemporaneous with the statement, the witness, when on the stand, qualifying or denying the prior statement, is under oath. In any event, of all the many recognized exceptions to the hearsay rule, only one (former testimony) requires that the out-of-court statement have been made under oath. With respect to the lack of evidence of the demeanor of the witness at the time of the prior statement, it would be difficult to improve upon Judge Learned Hand's observation that when the jury decides that the truth is not what the witness says now but what he said before, they are still deciding from what they see and hear in court.[9]

The rule as submitted by the Court has positive advantages. The prior statement was made nearer in time to the events, when memory was fresher and intervening influences had not been brought into play. A realistic method is provided for dealing with the turncoat witness who changes his story on the stand.[10]

New Jersey, California, and Utah have adopted a rule similar to this one; and Nevada, New Mexico, and Wisconsin have adopted the identical Federal rule.

For all of these reasons, we think the House amendment should be rejected and the rule as submitted by the Supreme Court reinstated.[11]

REPORT OF THE HOUSE/SENATE CONFERENCE COMMITTEE

[Note, that the version of Rule 801 (d)(1)(A) discussed below is the one which Congress enacted.]

The House bill provides that a statement is not hearsay if the declarant testifies and is subject to cross-examination concerning the statement and if the statement is inconsistent with his testimony and was given under oath subject to cross-examination and subject to the penalty of perjury at a trial or hearing or in a deposition. The Senate amendment drops the requirement that the prior statement be given under oath subject to cross-examination and subject to the penalty of perjury at a trial or hearing or in a deposition.

The Conference adopts the Senate amendment with an amendment, so that the rule now requires that the prior inconsistent statement be given under oath subject to the penalty of perjury at a trial, hearing, or other proceeding, or in a deposition. The rule as adopted covers statements before a grand jury. Prior inconsistent statements may, of course, be used for impeaching the credibility of a witness. When the prior inconsistent statement is one made by a defendant in a criminal case, it is covered by Rule 801(d)(2).

9. *Di Carlo v. United States*, 6 F.2d 364 (2d Cir. 1925).
10. *See* Comment, California Evidence Code § 1235; McCormick, Evidence, § 38 (2d ed. 1972).
11. It would appear that some of the opposition to this Rule is based on a concern that a person could be convicted solely upon evidence admissible under this Rule. The Rule, however, is not addressed to the question of the sufficiency of evidence to send a case to the jury, but merely as to its admissibility. Factual circumstances could well arise where, if this were the sole evidence, dismissal would be appropriate.

Advisory Committee's Note to Rule 801 (d)(1)(B)

(B) Prior consistent statements traditionally have been admissible to rebut charges of recent fabrication or improper influence or motive but not as substantive evidence. Under the rule they are substantive evidence. The prior statement is consistent with the testimony given on the stand, and, if the opposite party wishes to open the door for its admission in evidence, no sound reason is apparent why it should not be received generally.

Advisory Committee's Note to Rule 801 (d)(1)(C)

[Note, that originally Congress did not enact the provision discussed below. Several months after enactment of the Rules, however, Congress amended them to add the present Rule 801 (d)(1)(C), which is identical to the provision discussed below.]

(C) The admission of evidence of identification finds substantial support, although it falls beyond a doubt in the category of prior out-of-court statements. Illustrative are People v. Gould, 54 Cal.2d 621, 7 Cal.Rptr. 273, 354 P.2d 865 (1960); Judy v. State, 218 Md. 168, 146 A.2d 29 (1958); State v. Simmons, 63 Wash.2d 17, 385 P.2d 389 (1963); California Evidence Code § 1238; New Jersey Evidence Rule 63(1)(c); N.Y.Code of Criminal Procedure § 393-b. Further cases are found in 4 Wigmore § 1130. The basis is the generally unsatisfactory and inconclusive nature of courtroom identifications as compared with those made at an earlier time under less suggestive conditions. The Supreme Court considered the admissibility of evidence of prior identification in Gilbert v. California, 388 U.S. 263, 87 S.Ct. 1951, 18 L.Ed.2d 1178 (1967). Exclusion of lineup identification was held to be required because the accused did not then have the assistance of counsel. Significantly, the Court carefully refrained from placing its decision on the ground that testimony as to the making of a prior out-of-court identification ("That's the man") violated either the hearsay rule or the right of confrontation because not made under oath, subject to immediate cross-examination, in the presence of the trier. Instead the Court observed:

"There is a split among the States concerning the admissibility of prior extrajudicial identifications, as independent evidence of identity, both by the witness and third parties present at the prior identification. See 71 ALR2d 449. It has been held that the prior identification is hearsay, and, when admitted through the testimony of the identifier, is merely a prior consistent statement. The recent trend, however, is to admit the prior identification under the exception that admits as substantive evidence a prior communication by a witness who is available for cross-examination at the trial. See 5 ALR2d Later Case Service 6.131225-1228 . . . ." 388 U.S. at 272, n. 3, 87 S.Ct. at 1956.

Report of the Senate Committee on the Judiciary

[Note, that this Report refers to the proposed version of Rule 801 (d)(1)(C), which Congress did not enact along with the balance of the Rules. Congress did, however, add the present Rule 801 (d)(1)(C), which is identical to the version originally proposed, at a later date. See the 1975 Reports from the House and Senate Judiciary Committees below.]

As submitted by the Supreme Court and as passed by the House, subdivision (d)(1)(c) of Rule 801 made admissible the prior statement identifying a person made after perceiving him. The committee decided to delete this provision because of the concern that a person could be convicted solely upon evidence admissible under this subdivision.

1974 REPORT OF THE HOUSE/SENATE CONFERENCE COMMITTEE

[Note, that this Report refers to the proposed version of Rule 801 (d)(1)(C), which Congress did not enact along with the balance of the Rules. Congress did, however, add the present Rule 801 (d)(1)(C), which is identical to the version originally proposed, at a later date. See the 1975 Reports from the Senate and House Judiciary Committees below.]

The House bill provides that a statement is not hearsay if the declarant testifies and is subject to cross-examination concerning the statement and the statement is one of identification of a person made after perceiving him. The Senate amendment eliminated this provision.

The Conference adopts the Senate amendment.

1975 REPORT OF THE SENATE COMMITTEE ON THE JUDICIARY

[Note, that this Report refers to the version of Rule 801 (d)(1)(C), which Congress ultimately enacted.]

STATEMENT

The Federal Rules of Evidence, as submitted by the Supreme Court and passed by the House of Representatives, included the following provision in Rule 801(d)(1)(C):

> A statement is not hearsay if * * * the declarant testifies at the trial or hearing and is subject to cross-examination concerning the statement, and the statement is * * * *one of identification of a person made after perceiving him.* [Emphasis supplied.]

A similar provision was contained in the Preliminary Draft of the Proposed Rules (March 1969), the Revised Draft (March 1971), the Judicial Conference Proposed Draft, and the Supreme Court Draft (November 1972).

Senator Philip A. Hart (for himself and Senators Hruska and McClellan) introduced S. 1549 on April 29, 1975, to add a new subparagraph (d)(1) to Rule 801, Definitions, of Article VIII (Hearsay).

The purpose of the provision was to make clear, in line with the recent law in the area, that nonsuggestive lineup, photographic and other identifications are not hearsay and therefore are admissible. In the lineup case of *Gilbert v. California*, 388 U.S. 263, 272 n. 3 (1967), the Supreme Court, noting the split of authority in admitting prior out-of-court identifications, stated, "The recent trend, however, is to admit the prior identification under the exception [to the hearsay rule] that admits as substantive evidence a prior communication by a witness who is available for cross-examination at the trial." And the Federal Courts of Appeals have generally admitted these identifications. See, e.g., *Clemons v. United States*, 408 F. 2d 1230 (D.C. Cir. 1968) *(en banc)*, *cert. denied*, 394 U.S. 964 (1969); *United*

States v. Miller, 381 F.2d 529, 538 (2d Cir. 1967) (Friendly, J.); *Edison v. United States,* 272 F.2d 684, 686 (10th Cir. 1959). See also 4 *Wigmore, Evidence,* Sec. 1130 (Chadbourn rev. 1972) which strongly supports admissibility of prior identifications. Additional authority is collected in Rothstein, *Understanding the New Federal Rules of Evidence,* pp. 385-86, 390, and 669-70 (1975 Supplement).

In the course of processing the Rules of Evidence in the final weeks of the 93d Congress, the provision excluding such statements of identification from the hearsay category was deleted. Although there was no suggestion in the committee report that prior identifications are not probative, concern was there expressed that a conviction could be based upon such unsworn, out-of-court testimony. Upon further reflection, that concern appears misdirected. First, this exception is addressed to the "admissibility" of evidence and not to the "sufficiency" of evidence to prove guilt. Secondly, except for the former testimony exception to the hearsay exclusion, all hearsay exceptions allow into evidence statements which may not have been made under oath. Moreover, under this rule, unlike a significant majority of the hearsay exceptions, the prior identification is admissible only when the person who made it testifies at trial and is subject to cross-examination. This assures that if any discrepancy occurs between the witness' in-court and out-of-court testimony, the opportunity is available to probe, with the witness under oath, the reasons for that discrepancy so that the trier of fact might determine which statement is to be believed.

Upon reflection, then, it appears the rule is desirable. Since these identifications take place reasonably soon after an offense has been committed, the witness' observations are still fresh in his mind. The identification occurs before his recollection has been dimmed by the passage of time. Equally as important, it also takes place before the defendant or some other party has had the opportunity, through bribe or threat, to influence the witness to change his mind.

Both experience and psychological studies suggest that identifications consisting of nonsuggestive lineups, photographic spreads, or similar identifications, made reasonably soon after the offense, are more reliable than in-court identifications. Admitting these prior identifications therefore provides greater fairness to both the prosecution and defense in a criminal trial. See McCormick, Evidence, 602 (2d ed. 1972). Their exclusion would thus be detrimental to the fair administration of justice.

That the trier of fact, whether it be judge or jury, cannot properly perform its function if highly probative and constitutional identification evidence is kept from it has been recognized by the Court of Appeals for the District of Columbia Circuit in an *en banc* decision in *Clemons v. United States,* 408 F.2d at 1243:

> The rationale behind the exclusion of hearsay evidence has little force in the case of witnesses * * * who are available for cross-examination. We also think that juries in criminal cases, before being called upon to decide the awesome question of guilt or innocence, are entitled to know more of the circumstances which culminate in the courtroom identification—an event which, standing alone, often means very little to a conscientious and intelligent juror, who routinely expects the witnesses to identify the defendant in court and who may not attach great weight to such an identification in the absence of corroboration.

For these reasons, evidence of an earlier identification made by a person who is now testifying at the trial should not be treated as inadmissible hearsay.

Again, it should be emphasized that though the rule makes prior identifications admissible, they *still* must meet constitutional muster. In *Gilbert v. California*, 388 U.S. 218 (1967), the Supreme Court held that the Sixth Amendment right to assistance of counsel applied to lineup identifications. Even though the Court held that the right to counsel applied only to post-indictment lineups, *Kirby v. Illinois*, 406 U.S. 682 (1972), other cases make clear that the Due Process Clause is applicable to *all* pretrial lineups and that it forbids a lineup that is unnecessarily suggestive and conducive to mistaken identification. *Stovall v. Denno*, 388 U.S. 293 (1967); *Foster v. California*, 394 U.S. 440 (1969). Having the identifying witness on the stand (which is required by the first clause of Rule 801(d)(1)), coupled with these constitutional safeguards, provide adequate assurances of trustworthiness to warrant the admissibility of such prior identifications.

Finally, the committee notes that several States which have adopted Evidence Codes in the last few years have included a rule which provides for the admissibility of prior identifications. Cal. Evid. Code § 1238 (West 1966); Kan. Civ. Pro. Stat. Ann. § 60-460(a) (Vernon 1964); Nev. Rev. Stat. § 51.035(2)(c) (1973); New Jersey Evidence Rule § 63(1)(c); N.M. Stat. Ann. § 20-4-801(d)(1)(C) (1973); N.Y. Crim. Pro. § 60.25 (McKinney Supp. 1971); Utah Rules of Evidence § 63(1) (1971); Wis. Stat. Ann. § 908.01(1)(a) (Spec. Pamphlet 1974); Proposed Maine Rules of Evidence § 801(d)(1)(C) (Tent. Draft, Dec. 1974).

1975 REPORT OF THE HOUSE COMMITTEE ON THE JUDICIARY

[Note, that this Report refers to the version of Rule 801 (d)(1)(C), which Congress ultimately enacted.]

BACKGROUND

The Federal Rules of Evidence govern proceedings in federal courts and before United States magistrates. Article VIII of those Rules deals with hearsay evidence, and Rule 801 provides general definitions for Article VIII. Subdivision (d)(1) of Rule 801 defines certain statements not to be hearsay and therefore not inadmissible under Rule 802, which makes hearsay statements generally inadmissible.

When the Federal Rules of Evidence bill (H.R. 5463) passed the House on February 6, 1974, by a vote of 377 to 13, it contained the following provision:

> A statement is not hearsay if . . . the defendant testifies at the trial or hearing and is subject to cross-examination concerning the statement, and the statement is . . . (C) *one of identification of a person made after perceiving him*. [Emphasis added.]

The Senate-passed version of H.R. 5463 omitted the italicized language.

The House-Senate Conference Committee on H.R. 5463 met in December 1974 to iron out the differences between the House and Senate versions of the bill. The Senate strenuously insisted upon its version of Rule 801(d)(1); in fact, it was indicated that any compromise that included the House version of the rule would face extended discussion during the Senate debate. In the face of this, the House Conferees agreed to the Senate version of Rule 801(d)(1).

S. 1549, which is cosponsored in the Senate by Senators Philip A. Hart, John L. McClellan and Roman Hruska, seeks to put back into Rule 801(d)(1) the language that was struck at Conference. In other words, the Senate is now acceding to the House version of Rule 801(d)(1).

ANALYSIS OF THE BILL

Rule 801(d)(1)(C), as it is proposed to read, has a precondition to the use of the out-of-court statement of identification. The person who made the statement (the "declarant") must testify at the trial or hearing and must be subject to cross-examination concerning the statement. Even if this precondition is met, the out-of-court statement of identification must still meet constitutional standards. If the precondition is satisfied and the constitutional standards are met, then the out-of-court statement of identification is admissible.

A. *Constitutional Standards*

Out-of-court statements of identification can be made in different contexts. They can be made at a preindictment or a postindictment lineup. They can be made at a one-person showup that takes place shortly after the crime. They can also be made after being shown a series of photographs.

When there is a postindictment lineup, the Constitution requires that the defendant's counsel be present. *United States v. Wade*, 388 U.S. 218 (1967). When there is a preindictment lineup, there is no requirement that defendant's counsel be present. *Kirby v. Illinois*, 406 U.S. 682 (1972). Likewise, when a group of photographs is shown to someone, there is no requirement that the defendant's lawyer be present. *Simmons v. United States*, 390 U.S. 377 (1968).

Out-of-court identification procedures—including lineups, showups and displays of photographs—must meet the due process standard of the Fifth and Fourteenth Amendments to the United States Constitution. *Kirby v. Illinois*, 406 U.S. 682 (1972) (preindictment lineup); *Foster v. California*, 394 U.S. 440 (1969) (preindictment lineup followed by face-to-face showup); *Stovall v. Denno*, 388 U.S. 293 (1967) (one-person showup); *Simmons v. United States*, 390 U.S. 377 (1968) (display of photographs). The due process standard requires looking at the totality of the circumstances to determine whether the identification procedure was "unnecessarily suggestive and conducive to irreparably mistaken identification." *Kirby v. Illinois*, 406 U.S. 682, 691 (1972).

If the identification procedure does not measure up to the Constitutional standard, then the witness' out-of-court statement is not admissible. Furthermore, the witness cannot make an in-court identification unless there is clear and convincing evidence that there is an independent basis for the in-court identification. *United States v. Wade*, 388 U.S. 218 (1967); *Gilbert v. California*, 388 U.S. 263 (1967).

B. *Case Law*

There was a split among the authorities as to whether out-of-court statements of identification are admissible. See Annot., 71 A.L.R.2d 449.

> The recent trend, however, is to admit the prior identification under the exception that admits as substantive evidence a prior communication by a witness who is available for cross-examination at trial.

Gilbert v. California, 388 U.S. 263, 272 n. 3 (1967)

Federal courts admit out-of-court statements of identification. See, e g., *United States v. Miller*, 381 F.2d 529 (2d Cir. 1967) (photographic display); *United States v. Shannon*, 424 F.2d 175 (3d Cir. 1970), cert. denied 400 U.S. 844 (photographic display followed by one-person showup); *Bolling v. United States*, 18 F.2d 863 (4th Cir. 1927) (on-the-scene identification); *United States v. Fabio*, 394 F.2d 132 (4th Cir. 1968) (preindictment lineup); *United States v. Cooper*, 472 F.2d 64 (5th Cir. 1973), cert. denied 111 U.S. 840 (photographic display); *United States v. Lincoln*, 494 F.2d 833 (9th Cir. 1974) (photographic display); *Edison v. United States*, 272 F.2d 684 (10th Cir. 1959) (preindictment lineup); *Clemons v. United States*, 408 F.2d 1230 (D.C. Cir. 1968) (cellblock confrontation).

Thus, Rule 801(d)(1)(C) as proposed in S. 1549 is fully consistent with current Federal case law. Federal case law treats such statements as exceptions to the hearsay rule; Rule 801(d)(1)(C) defines them not to be hearsay. The result is the same in either instance, the statement is admissible if the person who made it testifies and is subject to cross-examination.

C. Rationale

Courtroom identifications can be very suggestive. The defendant is known to be present and generally sits in a certain location. Out-of-court identifications are generally more reliable. They take place relatively soon after the offense, while the incident is still reasonably fresh in the witness' mind. Out-of-court identifications are particularly important in jurisdictions where there may be a long delay between arrest or indictment and trial. As time goes by, a witness' memory will fade and his identification will become less reliable. An early, out-of-court identification provides fairness to defendants by ensuring accuracy of the identification. At the same time, it aids the government by making sure that delays in the criminal justice system do not lead to cases falling through because the witness can no longer recall the identity of the person he saw commit the crime.

The justification for not admitting out-of-court statements of identification was stated in the Senate Report on the Federal Rules of Evidence bill (H.R. 5463) to be a "concern that a person could be convicted solely upon evidence admitted under this [exception]." Senate Report No. 93-1277, at 16. However, Rule 801(d)(1) is not addressed to the issue of the sufficiency of evidence but to the issue of its admissibility. This was pointed out in Senate Report on the Federal Rules of Evidence in reference to subdivision (A) of Rule 801(d)(1).

> It would appear that some of the opposition to this Rule is based on a concern that a person could be convicted solely upon evidence admissible under this Rule. The Rule, however, is not addressed to the question of the sufficiency of evidence to send a case to the jury, but merely to its admissibility.

Senate Report No. 93-1277, at 16 n. 20.

ADVISORY COMMITTEE'S NOTE TO RULE 801 (d)(2)

[Note that this Advisory Committee's Note refers to the version of Rule 801 (d)(2) which Congress did enact, since Congress made no changes.]

(2) Admissions. Admissions by a party-opponent are excluded from the category of hearsay on the theory that their admissibility in evidence is the result of

the adversary system rather than satisfaction of the conditions of the hearsay rule. Strahorn, A Reconsideration of the Hearsay Rule and Admissions, 85 U.Pa.L.Rev. 484, 564 (1937); Morgan, Basic Problems of Evidence 265 (1962); 4 Wigmore § 1048. No guarantee of trustworthiness is required in the case of an admission. The freedom which admissions have enjoyed from technical demands of searching for an assurance of trustworthiness in some against-interest circumstance, and from the restrictive influences of the opinion rule and the rule requiring firsthand knowledge, when taken with the apparently prevalent satisfaction with the results, calls for generous treatment of this avenue to admissibility.

The rule specifies five categories of statements for which the responsibility of a party is considered sufficient to justify reception in evidence against him:

(A) A party's own statement is the classic example of an admission. If he has a representative capacity and the statement is offered against him in that capacity, no inquiry whether he was acting in the representative capacity in making the statement is required; the statement need only be relevant to representative affairs. To the same effect is California Evidence Code § 1220. Compare Uniform Rule 63(7), requiring a statement to be made in a representative capacity to be admissible against a party in a representative capacity.

(B) Under established principles an admission may be made by adopting or acquiescing in the statement of another. While knowledge of contents would ordinarily be essential, this is not inevitably so: "X is a reliable person and knows what he is talking about." See McCormick § 246, p. 527, n. 15. Adoption or acquiescence may be manifested in any appropriate manner. When silence is relied upon, the theory is that the person would, under the circumstances, protest the statement made in his presence, if untrue. The decision in each case calls for an evaluation in terms of probable human behavior. In civil cases, the results have generally been satisfactory. In criminal cases, however, troublesome questions have been raised by decisions holding that failure to deny is an admission: the inference is a fairly weak one, to begin with; silence may be motivated by advice of counsel or realization that "anything you say may be used against you"; unusual opportunity is afforded to manufacture evidence; and encroachment upon the privilege against self-incrimination seems inescapably to be involved. However, recent decisions of the Supreme Court relating to custodial interrogation and the right to counsel appear to resolve these difficulties. Hence the rule contains no special provisions concerning failure to deny in criminal cases.

(C) No authority is required for the general proposition that a statement authorized by a party to be made should have the status of an admission by the party. However, the question arises whether only statements to third persons should be so regarded, to the exclusion of statements by the agent to the principal. The rule is phrased broadly so as to encompass both. While it may be argued that the agent authorized to make statements to his principal does not speak for him, Morgan, Basic Problems of Evidence 273 (1962), communication to an outsider has not generally been thought to be an essential characteristic of an admission. Thus a party's books or records are usable against him, without regard to any intent to disclose to third persons. 5 Wigmore § 1557. See also McCormick § 78, pp. 159-161. In accord is New Jersey Evidence Rule 63(8)(a). Cf. Uniform Rule 63(8)(a) and California Evidence Code § 1222 which limit status as an admission in this regard to statements authorized by the party to be made "for" him, which is perhaps an ambiguous limitation to statements to third persons. Falknor, Vicarious Admissions and the Uniform Rules, 14 Vand.L.Rev. 855, 860-861 (1961).

(D) The tradition has been to test the admissibility of statements by agents, as admissions, by applying the usual test of agency. Was the admission made by the agent acting in the scope of his employment? Since few principals employ agents for the purpose of making damaging statements, the usual result was exclusion of the statement. Dissatisfaction with this loss of valuable and helpful evidence has been increasing. A substantial trend favors admitting statements related to a matter within the scope of the agency or employment. Grayson v. Williams, 256 F.2d 61 (10th Cir. 1958); Koninklijke Luchtvaart Maatschappij N. V. KLM Royal Dutch Airlines v. Tuller, 110 U.S.App.D.C. 282, 292 F.2d 775, 784 (1961); Martin v. Savage Truck Lines, Inc., 121 F.Supp. 417 (D.D.C.1954), and numerous state court decisions collected in 4 Wigmore, 1964 Supp., pp. 66-73, with comments by the editor that the statements should have been excluded as not within scope of agency. For the traditional view see Northern Oil Co. v. Socony Mobil Oil Co., 347 F.2d 81, 85 (2d Cir. 1965) and cases cited therein. Similar provisions are found in Uniform Rule 63(9)(a), Kansas Code of Civil Procedure § 60-460(i)(1), and New Jersey Evidence Rule 63(9)(a).

(E) The limitation upon the admissibility of statements of co-conspirators to those made "during the course and in furtherance of the conspiracy" is in the accepted pattern. While the broadened view of agency taken in item (iv) might suggest wider admissibility of statements of co-conspirators, the agency theory of conspiracy is at best a fiction and ought not to serve as a basis for admissibility beyond that already established. See Levie, Hearsay and Conspiracy, 52 Mich.L. Rev. 1159 (1954); Comment, 25 U.Chi.L.Rev. 530 (1958). The rule is consistent with the position of the Supreme Court in denying admissibility to statements made after the objectives of the conspiracy have either failed or been achieved. Krulewitch v. United States, 336 U.S. 440, 69 S.Ct. 716, 93 L.Ed. 790 (1949); Wong Sun v. United States, 371 U.S. 471, 490, 83 S.Ct. 407, 9 L.Ed.2d 441 (1963). For similarly limited provisions see California Evidence Code § 1223 and New Jersey Rule 63(9)(b). Cf. Uniform Rule 63(9)(b).

REPORT OF THE SENATE COMMITTEE ON THE JUDICIARY

[Note, that this Report refers to the version of Rule 801 (d)(2)(E) which Congress did enact, since Congress made no changes in any part of Rule 801 (d)(2).]

The House approved the long-accepted rule that "a statement by a coconspirator of a party during the course and in furtherance of the conspiracy" is not hearsay as it was submitted by the Supreme Court. While the rule refers to a coconspirator, it is this committee's understanding that the rule is meant to carry forward the universally accepted doctrine that a joint venturer is considered as a coconspirator for the purposes of this rule even though no conspiracy has been charged. United States v. Rinaldi, 393 F.2d 97, 99, cert. denied 393 U.S. 913 (1968); *United States v. Spencer,* 415 F.2d 1301, 1304 (7th Cir. 1969).

Rule 802   Hearsay Rule

Advisory Committee's Note

The provision excepting from the operation of the rule hearsay which is made admissible by other rules adopted by the Supreme Court or by Act of Congress continues the admissibility thereunder of hearsay which would not qualify under these Evidence Rules. The following examples illustrate the working of the exception:

Federal Rules of Civil Procedure

Rule 4(g): proof of service by affidavit.

Rule 32: admissibility of depositions.

Rule 43(e): affidavits when motion based on facts not appearing of record.

Rule 56: affidavits in summary judgment proceedings.

Rule 65(b): showing by affidavit for temporary restraining order.

Federal Rules of Criminal Procedure

Rule 4(a): affidavits to show grounds for issuing warrants.

Rule 12(b)(4): affidavits to determine issues of fact in connection with motions.

Acts of Congress

10 U.S.C. § 7730: affidavits of unavailable witnesses in actions for damages caused by vessel in naval service, or towage or salvage of same, when taking of testimony or bringing of action delayed or stayed on security grounds.

29 U.S.C. § 161(4): affidavit as proof of service in NLRB proceedings.

38 U.S.C. § 5206: affidavit as proof of posting notice of sale of unclaimed property by Veterans Administration.

Note by Federal Judicial Center

The Rule enacted by Congress is the Rule prescribed by the Supreme Court, amended by substituting "prescribed" in place of "adopted" and by inserting the phrase "pursuant to statutory authority."

Rule 803   Hearsay Exceptions; Availability of Declarant Immaterial

Advisory Committee's Rule

The exceptions are phrased in terms of nonapplication of the hearsay rule, rather than in positive terms of admissibility, in order to repel any implication that other possible grounds for exclusion are eliminated from consideration.

The present rule proceeds upon the theory that under appropriate circumstances a hearsay statement may possess circumstantial guarantees of trustworthiness sufficient to justify nonproduction of the declarant in person at the trial even though he may be available. The theory finds vast support in the many exceptions to the hearsay rule developed by the common law in which unavailability of the declarant is not a relevant factor. The present rule is a synthesis of them, with revision where modern developments and conditions are believed to make that course appropriate.

In a hearsay situation, the declarant is, of course, a witness, and neither this rule nor Rule 804 dispenses with the requirement of firsthand knowledge. It may appear from his statement or be inferable from circumstances. See Rule 602.

Exceptions (1) and (2). In considerable measure these two examples overlap, though based on somewhat different theories. The most significant practical difference will lie in the time lapse allowable between event and statement.

The underlying theory of Exception (1) is that substantial contemporaneity of event and statement negative the likelihood of deliberate or conscious misrepresentation. Moreover, if the witness is the declarant, he may be examined on the statement. If the witness is not the declarant, he may be examined as to the circumstances as an aid in evaluating the statement. Morgan, Basic Problems of Evidence 340-341 (1962).

The theory of Exception (2) is simply that circumstances may produce a condition of excitement which temporarily stills the capacity of reflection and produces utterances free of conscious fabrication. 6 Wigmore § 1747, p. 135. Spontaneity is the key factor in each instance, though arrived at by somewhat different routes. Both are needed in order to avoid needless niggling.

While the theory of Exception (2) has been criticized on the ground that excitement impairs accuracy of observation as well as eliminating conscious fabrication, Hutchins and Slesinger, Some Observations on the Law of Evidence: Spontaneous Exclamations, 28 Colum.L.Rev. 432 (1928), it finds support in cases without number. See cases in 6 Wigmore § 1750; Annot. 53 A.L.R.2d 1245 (statements as to cause of or responsibility for motor vehicle accident); Annot., 4 A.L.R.3d 149 (accusatory statements by homicide victims). Since unexciting events are less likely to evoke comment, decisions involving Exception (1) are far less numerouns [sic]. Illustrative are Tampa Elec. Co. v. Getrost, 151 Fla. 558, 10 So.2d 83 (1942); Houston Oxygen Co. v. Davis, 139 Tex. 1, 161 S.W.2d 474 (1942); and cases cited in McCormick § 273, p. 585, n. 4.

With respect to the *time element*, Exception (1) recognizes that in many, if not most, instances precise contemporaneity is not possible, and hence a slight lapse is allowable. Under Exception (2) the standard of measurement is the duration of the state of excitement. "How long can excitement prevail? Obviously there are no pat answers and the character of the transaction or event will largely determine the significance of the time factor." Slough, Spontaneous Statements and State of Mind, 46 Iowa L.Rev. 224, 243 (1961); McCormick § 272, p.580.

Participation by the declarant is not required: a non-participant may be moved to describe what he perceives, and one may be startled by an event in which he is not an actor. Slough, *supra;* McCormick, *supra;* 6 Wigmore § 1755; Annot., 78 A.L.R.2d 300.

Whether *proof of the startling event* may be made by the statement itself is largely an academic question, since in most cases there is present at least circumstantial evidence that something of a startling nature must have occurred. For cases in which the evidence consists of the condition of the declarant (injuries, state of shock), see Insurance Co. v. Mosely, 75 U.S. (8 Wall.) 397, 19 L.Ed. 437

(1869); Wheeler v. United States, 93 U.S.App.D.C. 159, 211 F.2d 19 (1953), cert. denied 347 U.S. 1019, 74 S.Ct. 876, 98 L.Ed. 1140; Wetherbee v. Safety Casualty Co., 219 F.2d 274 (5th Cir. 1955); Lampe v. United States, 97 U.S.App.D.C. 160, 229 F.2d 43 (1956). Nevertheless, on occasion the only evidence may be the content of the statement itself, and rulings that it may be sufficient are described as "increasing," Slough, *supra* at 246, and as the "prevailing practice," McCormick § 272, p. 579. Illustrative are Armour & Co. v. Industrial Commission, 78 Colo. 569, 243 P. 546 (1926); Young v. Stewart, 191 N.C. 297, 131 S.E. 735 (1926). Moreover, under Rule 104(a) the judge is not limited by the hearsay rule in passing upon preliminary questions of fact.

Proof of declarant's perception by his statement presents similar considerations when declarant is identified. People v. Poland, 22 Ill.2d 175, 174 N.E.2d 804 (1961). However, when declarant is an unidentified bystander, the cases indicate hesitancy in upholding the statement alone as sufficient, Garrett v. Howden, 73 N.M. 307, 387 P.2d 874 (1963); Beck v. Dye, 200 Wash. 1, 92 P.2d 1113 (1939), a result which would under appropriate circumstances be consistent with the rule.

Permissible *subject matter* of the statement is limited under Exception (1) to description or explanation of the event or condition, the assumption being that spontaneity, in the absence of a startling event, may extend no farther. In Exception (2), however, the statement need only "relate" to the startling event or condition, thus affording a broader scope of subject matter coverage. 6 Wigmore §§ 1750, 1754. See Sanitary Grocery Co. v. Snead, 67 App.D.C. 129, 90 F.2d 374 (1937), slip-and-fall case sustaining admissibility of clerk's statement, "That has been on the floor for a couple of hours," and Murphy Auto Parts Co., Inc. v. Ball, 101 U.S.App.D.C. 416, 249 F.2d 508 (1957), upholding admission, on issue of driver's agency, of his statement that he had to call on a customer and was in a hurry to get home. Quick, Hearsay, Excitement, Necessity and the Uniform Rules: A Reappraisal of Rule 63(4), 6 Wayne L.Rev. 204, 206-209 (1960).

Similar provisions are found in Uniform Rule 63(4) (a) and (b); California Evidence Code § 1240 (as to Exception (2) only); Kansas Code of Civil Procedure § 60-460(d)(1) and (2); New Jersey Evidence Rule 63(4).

Exception (3) is essentially a specialized application of Exception (1), presented separately to enhance its usefulness and accessibility. See McCormick §§ 265, 268.

The exclusion of "statements of memory or belief to prove the fact remembered or believed" is necessary to avoid the virtual destruction of the hearsay rule which would otherwise result from allowing state of mind, provable by a hearsay statement, to serve as the basis for an inference of the happening of the event which produced the state of mind. Shepard v. United States, 290 U.S. 96, 54 S.Ct. 22, 78 L.Ed. 196 (1933); Maguire, The Hillmon Case—Thirty-three Years After, 38 Harv.L.Rev. 709, 719-731 (1925); Hinton, States of Mind and the Hearsay Rule, 1 U.Chi.L.Rev. 394, 421-423 (1934). The rule of Mutual Life Ins. Co. v. Hillmon, 145 U.S. 285, 12 S.Ct. 909, 36 L.Ed. 706 (1892), allowing evidence of intention as tending to prove the doing of the act intended, is, of course, left undisturbed.

The carving out, from the exclusion mentioned in the preceding paragraph, of declarations relating to the execution, revocation, identification, or terms of declarant's will represents an *ad hoc* judgment which finds ample reinforcement in the decisions, resting on practical grounds of necessity and expediency rather than logic. McCormick § 271, pp. 577-578; Annot., 34 A.L.R.2d 588, 62 A.L.R.2d

855. A similar recognition of the need for and practical value of this kind of evidence is found in California Evidence Code § 1260.

REPORT OF THE HOUSE COMMITTEE ON THE JUDICIARY

Rule 803(3) was approved in the form submitted by the Court to Congress. However, the Committee intends that the Rule be construed to limit the doctrine of *Mutual Life Insurance Co. v. Hillmon*, 145 U.S. 285, 295-300 (1892), so as to render statements of intent by a declarant admissible only to prove his future conduct, not the future conduct of another person.

ADVISORY COMMITTEE'S NOTE TO EXCEPTION (4)

Exception (4). Even those few jurisdictions which have shied away from generally admitting statements of present condition have allowed them if made to a physician for purposes of diagnosis and treatment in view of the patient's strong motivation to be truthful. McCormick § 266, p. 563. The same guarantee of trustworthiness extends to statements of past conditions and medical history, made for purposes of diagnosis or treatment. It also extends to statements as to causation, reasonably pertinent to the same purposes, in accord with the current trend, Shell Oil Co. v. Industrial Commission, 2 Ill.2d 590, 119 N.E.2d 224 (1954); McCormick § 266, p. 564; New Jersey Evidence Rule 63(12)(c). Statements as to fault would not ordinarily qualify under this latter language. Thus a patient's statement that he was struck by an automobile would qualify but not his statement that the car was driven through a red light. Under the exception the statement need not have been made to a physician. Statements to hospital attendants, ambulance drivers, or even members of the family might be included.

Conventional doctrine has excluded from the hearsay exception, as not within its guarantee of truthfulness, statements to a physician consulted only for the purpose of enabling him to testify. While these statements were not admissible as substantive evidence, the expert was allowed to state the basis of his opinion, including statements of this kind. The distinction thus called for was one most unlikely to be made by juries. The rule accordingly rejects the limitation. This position is consistent with the provision of Rule 703 that the facts on which expert testimony is based need not be admissible in evidence if of a kind ordinarily relied upon by experts in the field.

REPORT OF THE HOUSE COMMITTEE ON THE JUDICIARY

After giving particular attention to the question of physical examination made solely to enable a physician to testify, the Committee approved Rule 803(4) as submitted to Congress, with the understanding that it is not intended in any way to adversely affect present privilege rules or those subsequently adopted.

REPORT OF THE SENATE COMMITTEE ON THE JUDICIARY

The House approved this rule as it was submitted by the Supreme Court "with the understanding that it is not intended in any way to adversely affect present privilege rules." We also approve this rule, and we would point out with respect to the question of its relation to privileges, it must be read in conjunction with rule 35 of the Federal Rules of Civil Procedure which provides that whenever the physical or mental condition of a party (plaintiff or defendant) is in controversy, the court may require him to submit to an examination by a physician. It is these examinations which will normally be admitted under this exception.

ADVISORY COMMITTEE'S NOTE TO EXCEPTION (5)

Exception (5). A hearsay exception for recorded recollection is generally recognized and has been described as having "long been favored by the federal and practically all the state courts that have had occasion to decide the question." United States v. Kelly, 349 F.2d 720, 770 (2d Cir. 1965), citing numerous cases and sustaining the exception against a claimed denial of the right of confrontation. Many additional cases are cited in Annot., 82 A.L.R.2d 473, 520. The guarantee of trustworthiness is found in the reliability inherent in a record made while events were still fresh in mind and accurately reflecting them. Owens v. State, 67 Md. 307, 316, 10 A. 210, 212 (1887).

The principal controversy attending the exception has centered, not upon the propriety of the exception itself, but upon the question whether a preliminary requirement of impaired memory on the part of the witness should be imposed. The authorities are divided. If regard be had only to the accuracy of the evidence, admittedly impairment of the memory of the witness adds nothing to it and should not be required. McCormick § 277, p. 593; 3 Wigmore § 738, p. 76; Jordan v. People, 151 Colo. 133, 376 P.2d 699 (1962), cert. denied 373 U.S. 944, 83 S.Ct. 1553, 10 L.Ed.2d 699; Hall v. State, 223 Md. 158, 162 A.2d 751 (1960); State v. Bindhammer, 44 N.J. 372, 209 A.2d 124 (1965). Nevertheless, the absence of the requirement, it is believed, would encourage the use of statements carefully prepared for purposes of litigation under the supervision of attorneys, investigators, or claim adjusters. Hence the example includes a requirement that the witness not have "sufficient recollection to enable him to testify fully and accurately." To the same effect are California Evidence Code § 1237 and New Jersey Rule 63(1)(b), and this has been the position of the federal courts. Vicksburg & Meridian R. R. v. O'Brien, 119 U.S. 99, 7 S.Ct. 118, 30 L.Ed. 299 (1886); Ahern v. Webb, 268 F.2d 45 (10th Cir. 1959); and see N. L. R. B. v. Hudson Pulp and Paper Corp., 273 F.2d 600, 665 (5th Cir. 1960); N. L. R. B. v. Federal Dairy Co., 297 F.2d 487 (1st Cir. 1962). But cf. United States v. Adams, 385 F.2d 548 (2d Cir. 1967).

No attempt is made in the exception to spell out the method of establishing the initial knowledge or the contemporaneity and accuracy of the record, leaving them to be dealt with as the circumstances of the particular case might indicate. Multiple person involvement in the process of observing and recording, as in Rathbun v. Brancatella, 93 N.I.L. 222, 107 A. 279 (1919), is entirely consistent with the exception.

Locating the exception at this place in the scheme of the rules is a matter of choice. There were two other possibilities. The first was to regard the statement as one of the group of prior statements of a testifying witness which are excluded entirely from the category of hearsay by Rule 801(d)(1). That category, however, requires that declarant be "subject to cross-examination," as to which the impaired memory aspect of the exception raises doubts. The other possibility was to include the exception among those covered by Rule 804. Since unavailability is required by that rule and lack of memory is listed as a species of unavailability by the definition of the term in Rule 804(a)(3), that treatment at first impression would seem appropriate. The fact is, however, that the unavailability requirement of the exception is of a limited and peculiar nature. Accordingly, the exception is located at this point rather than in the context of a rule where unavailability is conceived of more broadly.

REPORT OF THE HOUSE COMMITTEE ON THE JUDICIARY

Rule 803(5) as submitted by the Court permitted the reading into evidence of a memorandum or record concerning a matter about which a witness once had knowledge but now has insufficient recollection to enable him to testify accurately and fully, "shown to have been made when the matter was fresh in his memory and to reflect that knowledge correctly." The Committee amended this Rule to add the words "or adopted by the witness" after the phrase "shown to have been made," a treatment consistent with the definition of "statement" in the Jencks Act, 18 U.S.C. 3500. Moreover, it is the Committee's understanding that a memorandum or report, although barred under this Rule, would nonetheless be admissible if it came within another hearsay exception. This last stated principle is deemed applicable to all the hearsay rules.

REPORT OF THE SENATE COMMITTEE ON THE JUDICIARY

Rule 803(5) as submitted by the Court permitted the reading into evidence of a memorandum or record concerning a matter about which a witness once had knowledge but now has insufficient recollection to enable him to testify accurately and fully, "shown to have been made when the matter was fresh in his memory and to reflect that knowledge correctly." The House amended the rule to add the words "or adopted by the witness" after the phrase "shown to have been made," language parallel to the Jencks Act.[12]

The committee accepts the House amendment with the understanding and belief that it was not intended to narrow the scope of applicability of the rule. In fact, we understand it to clarify the rule's applicability to a memorandum adopted by the witness as well as one made by him. While the rule as submitted by the Court was silent on the question of who made the memorandum, we view the House amendment as a helpful clarification; noting, however, that the Advisory Committee's note to this rule suggests that the important thing is the accuracy of the memorandum rather than who made it.

The committee does not view the House amendment as precluding admissibility in situations in which multiple participants were involved.

When the verifying witness has not prepared the report, but merely examined it and found it accurate, he has adopted the report, and it is therefore admissible. The rule should also be interpreted to cover other situations involving multiple participants, e.g., employer dictating to secretary, secretary making memorandum at direction of employer, or information being passed along a chain of persons, as in *Curtis v. Bradley.*[13]

The committee also accepts the understanding of the House that a memorandum or report, although barred under this rule, would nonetheless be admissible if it came within another hearsay exception. We consider this principle to be applicable to all the hearsay rules.

---

12. 18 U.S.C. § 3500.
13. 65 Conn. 99, 31 Atl. 591 (1894). *See also Rathbun v. Brancatella*, 93 N.I.L. 222, 107 Atl. 279 (1919). *See, e.g.*, McCormick on Evidence, § 303 (2d ed. 1972).

Advisory Committee's Note to Exception (6)

Exception (6) represents an area which has received much attention from those seeking to improve the law of evidence. The Commonwealth Fund Act was the result of a study completed in 1927 by a distinguished committee under the chairmanship of Professor Morgan. Morgan et al., The Law of Evidence: Some Proposals for its Reform 63 (1927). With changes too minor to mention, it was adopted by Congress in 1936 as the rule for federal courts. 28 U.S.C. § 1732. A number of states took similar action. The Commissioners on Uniform State Laws in 1936 promulgated the Unform Business Records as Evidence Act, 9A U.L.A. 506, which has acquired a substantial following in the states. Model Code Rule 514 and Uniform Rule 63(13) also deal with the subject. Difference of varying degrees of importance exist among these various treatments.

These reform efforts were largely within the context of business and commercial records, as the kind usually encountered, and concentrated considerable attention upon relaxing the requirement of producing as witnesses, or accounting for the nonproduction of, all participants in the process of gathering, transmitting, and recording information which the common law had evolved as a burdensome and crippling aspect of using records of this type. In their areas of primary emphasis on witnesses to be called and the general admissibility of ordinary business and commercial records, the Commonwealth Fund Act and the Uniform Act appear to have worked well. The exception seeks to preserve their advantages.

On the subject of what witnesses must be called, the Commonwealth Fund Act eliminated the common law requirement of calling or accounting for all participants by failing to mention it. United States v. Mortimer, 118 F.2d 266 (2d Cir. 1941); La Porte v. United States, 300 F.2d 878 (9th Cir. 1962); McCormick § 290, p. 608. Model Code Rule 514 and Uniform Rule 63(13) did likewise. The Uniform Act, however, abolished the common law requirement in express terms, providing that the requisite foundation testimony might be furnished by "the custodian or other qualified witness." Uniform Business Records as Evidence Act, § 2; 9A U.L.A. 506. The exception follows the Uniform Act in this respect.

The element of unusual reliability of business records is said variously to be supplied by systematic checking, by regularity and continuity which produce habits of precision, by actual experience of business in relying upon them, or by a duty to make an accurate record as part of a continuing job or occupation. McCormick §§ 281, 286, 287; Laughlin, Business Entries and the Like, 46 Iowa L.Rev. 276 (1961). The model statutes and rules have sought to capture these factors and to extend their impact by employing the phrase "regular course of business," in conjunction with a definition of "business" far broader than its ordinarily accepted meaning. The result is a tendency unduly to emphasize a requirement of routineness and repetitiveness and an insistence that other types of records be squeezed into the fact patterns which give rise to traditional business records. The rule therefore adopts the phrase "the course of a regularly conducted activity" as capturing the essential basis of the hearsay exception as it has evolved and the essential element which can be abstracted from the various specifications of what is a "business."

Amplification of the kinds of activities producing admissible records has given rise to problems which conventional business records by their nature avoid. They are problems of the source of the recorded information, of entries in opinion form, of motivation, and of involvement as participant in the matters recorded.

Sources of information presented no substantial problem with ordinary business records. All participants, including the observer or participant furnishing the information to be recorded, were acting routinely, under a duty of accuracy, with employer reliance on the result, or in short "in the regular course of business." If, however, the supplier of the information does not act in the regular course, an essential link is broken; the assurance of accuracy does not extend to the information itself, and the fact that it may be recorded with scrupulous accuracy is of no avail. An illustration is the police report incorporating information obtained from a bystander: the officer qualifies as acting in the regular course but the informant does not. The leading case, Johnson v. Lutz, 253 N.Y. 124, 170 N.E. 517 (1930), held that a report thus prepared was inadmissible. Most of the authorities have agreed with the decision. Gencarella v. Fyfe, 171 F.2d 419 (1st Cir. 1948); Gordon v. Robinson, 210 F.2d 192 (3d Cir. 1954); Standard Oil Co. of California v. Moore, 251 F.2d 188, 214 (9th Cir. 1957), cert. denied 356 U.S. 975, 78 S.Ct. 1139, 2 L.Ed.2d 1148; Yates v. Bair Transport, Inc., 249 F.Supp. 681 (S.D.N.Y.1965); Annot., 69 A.L.R.2d 1148. Cf. Hawkins v. Gorea Motor Express, Inc., 360 F.2d 933 (2d Cir. 1966). *Contra*, 5 Wigmore § 1530a, n. 1, pp. 391-392. The point is not dealt with specifically in the Commonwealth Fund Act, the Uniform Act, or Uniform Rule 63(13). However, Model Code Rule 514 contains the requirement "that it was the regular course of that business for one with personal knowledge . . . to make such a memorandum or record or to transmit information thereof to be included in such a memorandum or record . . . ." The rule follows this lead in requiring an informant with knowledge acting in the course of the regularly conducted activity.

Entries in the form of opinions were not encountered in traditional business records in view of the purely factual nature of the items recorded, but they are now commonly encountered with respect to medical diagnoses, prognoses, and test results, as well as occasionally in other areas. The Commonwealth Fund Act provided only for records of an "act, transaction, occurrence, or event," while the Uniform Act, Model Code Rule 514, and Uniform Rule 63(13) merely added the ambiguous term "condition." The limited phrasing of the Commonwealth Fund Act, 28 U.S.C. § 1732, may account for the reluctance of some federal decisions to admit diagnostic entries. New York Life Ins. Co. v. Taylor, 79 U.S.App.D.C. 66, 147 F.2d 297 (1945); Lyles v. United States, 103 U.S.App.D.C. 22, 254 F.2d 725 (1957), cert. denied 356 U.S. 961, 78 S.Ct. 997, 2 L.Ed.2d 1067; England v. United States, 174 F.2d 466 (5th Cir. 1949); Skogen v. Dow Chemical Co., 375 F.2d 692 (8th Cir. 1967). Other federal decisions, however, experienced no difficulty in freely admitting diagnostic entries. Reed v. Order of United Commercial Travelers, 123 F.2d 252 (2d Cir. 1941); Buckminster's Estate v. Commissioner of Internal Revenue, 147 F.2d 331 (2d Cir. 1944); Medina v. Erickson, 226 F.2d 475 (9th Cir. 1955); Thomas v. Hogan, 308 F.2d 355 (4th Cir. 1962); Glawe v. Rulon, 284 F.2d 495 (8th Cir. 1960). In the state courts, the trend favors admissibility. Borucki v. MacKenzie Bros. Co., 125 Conn. 92, 3 A.2d 224 (1938); Allen v. St. Louis Public Service Co., 365 Mo. 677, 285 S.W.2d 663, 55 A.L.R.2d 1022 (1956); People v. Kohlmeyer, 284 N.Y. 366, 31 N.E.2d 490 (1940); Weis v. Weis, 147 OS 416, 72 N.E.2d 245 (1947). In order to make clear its adherence to the latter position, the rule specifically includes both diagnoses and opinions, in addition to acts, events, and conditions, as proper subjects of admissible entries.

Problems of the motivation of the informant have been a source of difficulty and disagreement. In Palmer v. Hoffman, 318 U.S. 109, 63 S.Ct. 477, 87 L.Ed. 645 (1943), exclusion of an accident report made by the since deceased engineer, offered by defendant railroad trustees in a grade crossing collision case, was upheld. The report was not "in the regular course of business," not a record of the systematic conduct of the business as a business, said the Court. The report was prepared for use in litigating, not railroading. While the opinion mentions the motivation of the engineer only obliquely, the emphasis on records of routine operations is significant only by virtue of impact on motivation to be accurate. Absence of routineness raises lack of motivation to be accurate. The opinion of the Court of Appeals had gone beyond mere lack of motive to be accurate: the engineer's statement was "dripping with motivations to misrepresent." Hoffman v. Palmer, 129 F.2d 976, 991 (2d Cir. 1942). The direct introduction of motivation is a disturbing factor, since absence of motive to misrepresent has not traditionally been a requirement of the rule; that records might be self-serving has not been a ground for exclusion. Laughlin, Business Records and the Like, 46 Iowa L.Rev. 276, 285 (1961). As Judge Clark said in his dissent, "I submit that there is hardly a grocer's account book which could not be excluded on that basis." 129 F.2d at 1002. A physician's evaluation report of a personal injury litigant would appear to be in the routine of his business. If the report is offered by the party at whose instance it was made, however, it has been held inadmissible, Yates v. Bair Transport, Inc., 249 F.Supp. 681 (S.D.N.Y.1965), otherwise if offered by the opposite party, Korte v. New York, N. H. & H. R. Co., 191 F.2d 86 (2d Cir. 1951), cert. denied 342 U.S. 868, 72 S.Ct. 108, 96 L.Ed. 652.

The decisions hinge on motivation and which party is entitled to be concerned about it. Professor McCormick believed that the doctor's report or the accident report were sufficiently routine to justify admissibility. McCormick § 287, p. 604. Yet hesitation must be experienced in admitting everything which is observed and recorded in the course of a regularly conducted activity. Efforts to set a limit are illustrated by Hartzog v. United States, 217 F.2d 706 (4th Cir. 1954), error to admit worksheets made by since deceased deputy collector in preparation for the instant income tax evasion prosecution, and United States v. Ware, 247 F.2d 698 (7th Cir. 1957), error to admit narcotics agents' records of purchases. See also Exception (8), *infra* as to the public record aspects of records of this nature. Some decisions have been satisfied as to motivation of an accident report if made pursuant to statutory duty, United States v. New York Foreign Trade Zone Operators, 304 F.2d 792 (2d Cir. 1962); Taylor v. Baltimore & O. R. Co., 344 F.2d 281 (2d Cir. 1965), since the report was oriented in a direction other than the litigation which ensued. Cf. Matthews v. United States, 217 F.2d 409 (5th Cir. 1954). The formulation of specific terms which would assure satisfactory results in all cases is not possible. Consequently the rule proceeds from the base that records made in the course of a regularly conducted activity will be taken as admissible but subject to authority to exclude if "the sources of information or other circumstances indicate lack of trustworthiness."

Occasional decisions have reached for enhanced accuracy by requiring involvement as a participant in matters reported. Clainos v. United States, 82

U.S.App.D.C. 278, 163 F.2d 593 (1947), error to admit police records of convictions; Standard Oil Co. of California v. Moore, 251 F.2d 188 (9th Cir. 1957), cert. denied 356 U.S. 975, 78 S.Ct. 1139, 2 L.Ed.2d 1148, error to admit employees' records of observed business practices of others. The rule includes no requirement of this nature. Wholly acceptable records may involve matters merely observed, e.g. the weather.

The form which the "record" may assume under the rule is described broadly as a "memorandum, report, record, or data compilation, in any form." The expression "data compilation" is used as broadly descriptive of any means of storing information other than the conventional words and figures in written or documentary form. It includes, but is by no means limited to, electronic computer storage. The term is borrowed from revised Rule 34(a) of the Rules of Civil Procedure.

REPORT OF THE HOUSE COMMITTEE ON THE JUDICIARY

Rule 803(6) as submitted by the Court permitted a record made "in the course of a regularly conducted activity" to be admissible in certain circumstances. The Committee believed there were insufficient guarantees of reliability in records made in the course of activities falling outside the scope of "business" activities as that term is broadly defined in 28 U.S.C. 1732. Moreover, the Committee concluded that the additional requirement of Section 1732 that it must have been the regular practice of a business to make the record is a necessary further assurance of its trustworthiness. The Committee accordingly amended the Rule to incorporate these limitations.

REPORT OF THE SENATE COMMITTEE ON THE JUDICIARY

[Note, that the Senate effort to delete references to "business" in the House-passed version of Rule 803 (6), described above, did not survive enactment.]

Rule 803(6) as submitted by the Supreme Court permitted a record made in the course of a regularly conducted activity to be admissible in certain circumstances. This rule constituted a broadening of the traditional business records hearsay exception which has been long advocated by scholars and judges active in the law of evidence.

The House felt there were insufficient guarantees of reliability of records not within a broadly defined business records exception. We disagree. Even under the House definition of "business" including profession, occupation, and "calling of every kind," the records of many regularly conducted activities will, or may be, excluded from evidence. Under the principle of *ejusdem generis*, the intent of "calling of every kind" would seem to be related to work-related endeavors—e.g., butcher, baker, artist, etc.

Thus, it appears that the records of many institutions or groups might not be admissible under the House amendments. For example, schools, and hospitals will not normally be considered businesses within the definition. Yet, these are groups which keep financial and other records on a regular basis in a manner similar to business enterprises. We believe these records are of equivalent trustworthiness and should be admitted into evidence.

Three states, which have recently codified their evidence rules, have adopted the Supreme Court version of Rule 803(6), providing for admission of memoranda of a "regularly conducted activity." None adopted the words "business activity" used in the House amendment.[14]

Therefore, the committee deleted the word "business" as it appears before the word "activity." The last sentence then is unnecessary and was also deleted.

It is the understanding of the committee that the use of the phrase "person with knowledge" is not intended to imply that the party seeking to introduce the memorandum, report, record, or data compilation must be able to produce, or even identify, the specific individual upon whose first-hand knowledge the memorandum, report, record or data compilation was based. A sufficient foundation for the introduction of such evidence will be laid if the party seeking to introduce the evidence is able to show that it was the regular practice of the activity to base such memorandums, reports, records, or data compilations upon a transmission from a person with knowledge, e.g., in the case of the content of a shipment of goods, upon a report from the company's receiving agent or in the case of a computer printout, upon a report from the company's computer programer or one who has knowledge of the particular record system. In short, the scope of the phrase "person with knowledge" is meant to be coterminous with the custodian of the evidence or other qualified witness. The committee believes this represents the desired rule in light of the complex nature of modern business organizations.

REPORT OF THE HOUSE/SENATE CONFERENCE COMMITTEE

The House bill provides in subsection (6) that records of a regularly conducted "business" activity qualify for admission into evidence as an exception to the hearsay rule. "Business" is defined as including "business, profession, occupation and calling of every kind." The Senate amendment drops the requirement that the records be those of a "business" activity and eliminates the definition of "business." The Senate amendment provides that records are admissible if they are records of a regularly conducted "activity."

The Conference adopts the House provision that the records must be those of a regularly conducted "business" activity. The Conferees changed the definition of "business" contained in the House provision in order to make it clear that the records of institutions and associations like schools, churches and hospitals are admissible under this provision. The records of public schools and hospitals are also covered by Rule 803(8), which deals with public records and reports.

ADVISORY COMMITTEE'S NOTE TO EXCEPTION (7)

Exception (7). Failure of a record to mention a matter which would ordinarily be mentioned is satisfactory evidence of its nonexistence. Uniform Rule 63(14), Comment. While probably not hearsay as defined in Rule 801, supra, decisions may be found which class the evidence not only as hearsay but also as not within any exception. In order to set the question at rest in favor of admissibility, it is specifically treated here. McCormick § 289, p. 609; Morgan, Basic Problems of Evidence 314 (1962); 5 Wigmore § 1531; Uniform Rule 63(14); California Evidence Code § 1272; Kansas Code of Civil Procedure § 60-460(n); New Jersey Evidence Rule 63(14).

14. *See* Nev. Rev. Stats. § 15.135; N. Mex. Stats. (1973 Supp.) § 20-4-803 (6); West's Wis. Stats. Anno. (1973 Supp.) w 908.03 (6).

REPORT OF THE HOUSE COMMITTEE ON THE JUDICIARY

Rule 803(7) as submitted by the Court concerned the *absence* of entry in the records of a "regularly conducted activity." The Committee amended this Rule to conform with its action with respect to Rule 803(6).

ADVISORY COMMITTEE'S NOTE TO EXCEPTION (8)

[Note, that Rule 803 (8) was significantly amended on the floor of the House, and that the House-passed amendments were ultimately adopted by Congress in the enacted version of this provision. Those amendments affect clause (b) of Rule 803 (8).]

Exception (8). Public records are a recognized hearsay exception at common law and have been the subject of statutes without number. McCormick § 291. See, for example, 28 U.S.C. § 1733, the relative narrowness of which is illustrated by its nonapplicability to nonfederal public agencies, thus necessitating resort to the less appropriate business record exception to the hearsay rule. Kay v. United States, 255 F.2d 476 (4th Cir. 1958). The rule makes no distinction between federal and nonfederal offices and agencies.

Justification for the exception is the assumption that a public official will perform his duty properly and the unlikelihood that he will remember details independently of the record. Wong Wing Foo v. McGrath, 196 F.2d 120 (9th Cir. 1952), and see Chesapeake & Delaware Canal Co. v. United States, 250 U.S. 123, 39 S.Ct. 407, 63 L.Ed. 889 (1919). As to items (a) and (b), further support is found in the reliability factors underlying records of regularly conducted activities generally. See Exception (6), supra.

(a) Cases illustrating the admissibility of records of the office's or agency's own activities are numerous. Chesapeake & Delaware Canal Co. v. United States, 250 U.S. 123, 39 S.Ct. 407, 63 L.Ed. 889 (1919), Treasury records of miscellaneous receipts and disbursements; Howard v. Perrin, 200 U.S. 71, 26 S.Ct. 195, 50 L.Ed. 374 (1906), General Land Office records; Ballew v. United States, 160 U.S. 187, 16 S.Ct. 263, 40 L.Ed. 388 (1895), Pension Office records.

(b) Cases sustaining admissibility of records of matters observed are also numerous. United States v. Van Hook, 284 F.2d 489 (7th Cir. 1960), remanded for resentencing 365 U.S. 609, 81 S.Ct. 823, 5 L.Ed.2d 821, letter from induction officer to District Attorney, pursuant to army regulations, stating fact and circumstances of refusal to be inducted; T'Kach v. United States, 242 F.2d 937 (5th Cir. 1957), affidavit of White House personnel officer that search of records showed no employment of accused, charged with fraudulently representing himself as an envoy of the President; Minnehaha County v. Kelley, 150 F.2d 356 (8th Cir. 1945); Weather Bureau records of rainfall; United States v. Meyer, 113 F.2d 387 (7th Cir. 1940), cert. denied 311 U.S. 706, 61 S.Ct. 174, 85 L.Ed. 459, map prepared by government engineer from information furnished by men working under his supervision.

(c) The more controversial area of public records is that of the so-called "evaluative" report. The disagreement among the decisions has been due in part, no doubt, to the variety of situations encountered, as well as to differences in principle. Sustaining admissibility are such cases as United States v. Dumas, 149 U.S. 278, 13 S.Ct. 872, 37 L.Ed. 734 (1893), statement of account certified by Postmaster General in action against postmaster; McCarty v. United States, 185 F.2d 520 (5th Cir. 1950), reh. denied 187 F.2d 234, Certificate of Settlement of General Accounting Office showing indebtedness and letter from Army official stating Government had performed, in action on contract to purchase and remove waste food from Army camp; Morgan v. Pittsburgh-Des Moines Steel Co., 183 F.2d 467 (3d Cir. 1950), report of Bureau of Mines as to cause of gas tank explosion; Petition of W___, 164 F.Supp. 659 (E.D.Pa.1958), report by Immigration and Naturalization Service investigator that petitioner was known in community as wife of man to whom she was not married. To the opposite effect and denying admissibility are Franklin v. Skelly Oil Co., 141 F.2d 568 (10th Cir. 1944), State Fire Marshal's report of cause of gas explosion; Lomax Transp. Co. v. United States, 183 F.2d 331 (9th Cir. 1950), Certificate of Settlement from General Accounting Office in action for naval supplies lost in warehouse fire; Yung Jin Teung v. Dulles, 229 F.2d 244 (2d Cir. 1956), "Status Reports" offered to justify delay in processing passport applications. Police reports have generally been excluded except to the extent to which they incorporate firsthand observations of the officer. Annot., 69 A.L.R.2d 1148. Various kinds of evaluative reports are admissible under federal statutes: 7 U.S.C. § 78, findings of Secretary of Agriculture prima facie evidence of true grade of grain; 7 U.S.C. § 210(f), findings of Secretary of Agriculture prima facie evidence in action for damages against stockyard owner; 7 U.S.C. § 292, order by Secretary of Agriculture prima facie evidence in judicial enforcement proceedings against producers association monopoly, 7 U.S.C. § 1622(h), Department of Agriculture inspection certificates of products shipped in interstate commerce prima facie evidence; 8 U.S.C. § 1440(c), separation of alien from military service on conditions other than honorable provable by certificate from department in proceedings to revoke citizenship; 18 U.S.C. § 4245, certificate of Director of Prisons that convicted person has been examined and found probably incompetent at time of trial prima facie evidence in court hearing on competency; 42 U.S.C. § 269(b), bill of health by appropriate official prima facie evidence of vessel's sanitary history and condition and compliance with regulations; 46 U.S.C. § 679, certificate of consul presumptive evidence of refusal of master to transport destitute seamen to United States. While these statutory exceptions to the hearsay rule are left undisturbed, Rule 802, the willingness of Congress to recognize a substantial measure of admissibility for evaluative reports is a helpful guide.

Factors which may be of assistance in passing upon the admissibilty of evaluative reports include: (1) the timeliness of the investigation, McCormick, Can the Courts Make Wider Use of Reports of Official Investigations? 42 Iowa L.Rev. 363 (1957); (2) the special skill or experience of the official, id., (3) whether a hearing was held and the level at which conducted, Franklin v. Skelly Oil Co., 141 F.2d 568 (10th Cir. 1944); (4) possible motivation problems suggested by Palmer v. Hoffman, 318 U.S. 109, 63 S.Ct. 477, 87 L.Ed. 645 (1943). Others no doubt could be added.

The formulation of an approach which would give appropriate weight to all possible factors in every situation is an obvious impossibility. Hence the rule, as in Exception (6), assumes admissibility in the first instance but with ample provision for escape if sufficient negative factors are present. In one respect, however, the rule with respect to evaluative reports under item (c) is very specific: they are admissible only in civil cases and against the government in criminal cases in view of the almost certain collision with confrontation rights which would result from their use against the accused in a criminal case.

REPORT OF THE SENATE COMMITTEE ON THE JUDICIARY

[Note, that the amendment to Rule 803 (8) described below, which was proposed by the Senate Judiciary Committee and which would have added a reference to proposed Rule 804 (b)(5), was ultimately rejected by the Conference Committee, and did not become part of Rule 803 (8) as enacted. The proposed Rule 804 (b)(5) was also rejected by Congress, and is not the Rule 804 (b)(5) which Congress enacted.]

The House approved Rule 803(8), as submitted by the Supreme Court, with one substantive change. It excluded from the hearsay exception reports containing matters observed by police officers and other law enforcement personnel in criminal cases. Ostensibly, the reason for this exclusion is that observations by police officers at the scene of the crime or the apprehension of the defendant are not as reliable as observations by public officials in other cases because of the adversarial nature of the confrontation between the police and the defendant in criminal cases.

The committee accepts the House's decision to exclude such recorded observations where the police officer is available to testify in court about his observation. However, where he is unavailable as unavailability is defined in rule 804 (a)(4) and (a)(5), the report should be admitted as the best available evidence. Accordingly, the committee has amended rule 803(8) to refer to the provision of rule 804(b)(5), which allows the admission of such reports, records or other statements where the police officer or other law enforcement officer is unavailable because of death, then existing physical or mental illness or infirmity, or not being successfully subject to legal process.

The House Judiciary Committee report contained a statement of intent that "the phrase 'factual findings' in subdivision (c) be strictly construed and that evaluations or opinions contained in public reports shall not be admissible under this rule." The committee takes strong exception to this limiting understanding of the application of the rule. We do not think it reflects an understanding of the intended operation of the rule as explained in the Advisory Committee notes to this subsection. The Advisory Committee notes on subsection (c) of this subdivision point out that various kinds of evaluative reports are now admissible under Federal statutes. 7 U.S.C. § 78, findings of Secretary of Agriculture prima facie evidence of true grade of grain; 42 U.S.C. § 269(b), bill of health by appropriate official prima facie evidence of vessel's sanitary history and condition and compliance with regulations. These statutory exceptions to the hearsay rule are preserved. Rule 802. The willingness of Congress to recognize these and other such evaluative reports provides a helpful guide in determining the kind of reports which are intended to be admissible under this rule. We think the restrictive interpretation of the House overlooks the fact that while the Advisory Committee assumes admissibility in the first instance of evaluative reports, they are not admissible if, as the Rule states, "the sources of information or other circumstances indicate lack of trustworthiness."

The Advisory Committee explains the factors to be considered:

* * * * *

Factors which may be assistance in passing upon the admissibility of evaluative reports include: (1) the timeliness of the investigation, McCormick, Can the Courts Make Wider Use of Reports of Official Investigations? 42 Iowa L. Rev. 363 (1957); (2) the special skill or experience of the official, id.; (3) whether a hearing was held and the level at which conducted, Franklin v. Skelly Oil Co., 141 F. 2d 568 (10th Cir. 1944); (4) possible motivation problems suggested by Palmer v. Hoffman, 318 U.S. 109, 63 S. Ct. 477, 87 L. Ed. 645 (1943). Others no doubt could be added.[15]

* * * * *

The committee concludes that the language of the rule together with the explanation provided by the Advisory Committee furnish sufficient guidance on the admissibility of evaluative reports.

Report of the House/Senate Conference Committee

The Senate amendment adds language, not contained in the House bill, that refers to another rule that was added by the Senate in another amendment (Rule 804(b)(5)—Criminal law enforcement records and reports).

In view of its action on Rule 804(b)(5) (Criminal law enforcement records and reports), the Conference does not adopt the Senate amendment and restores the bill to the House version.

Advisory Committee's Note to Exception (9)

Exception (9). Records of vital statistics are commonly the subject of particular statutes making them admissible in evidence, Uniform Vital Statistics Act, 9C U.L.A. 350 (1957). The rule is in principle narrower than Uniform Rule 63(16) which includes reports required of persons performing functions authorized by statute, yet in practical effect the two are substantially the same. Comment Uniform Rule 63(16). The exception as drafted is in the pattern of California Evidence Code § 1281.

Advisory Committee's Note to Exception (10)

Exception (10). The principle of proving nonoccurrence of an event by evidence of the absence of a record which would regularly be made of its occurrence, developed in Exception (7) with respect to regularly conducted activities, is here extended to public records of the kind mentioned in Exceptions (8) and (9). 5 Wigmore § 1633(6), p. 519. Some harmless duplication no doubt exists with Exception (7). For instances of federal statutes recognizing this method of proof, see 8 U.S.C. § 1284(b), proof of absence of alien crewman's name from outgoing manifest prima facie evidence of failure to detain or deport, and 42 U.S.C. § 405(c)(3), (4)(B), (4)(C), absence of HEW record prima facie evidence of no wages or self-employment income.

The rule includes situations in which absence of a record may itself be the ultimate focal point of inquiry, e.g. People v. Love, 310 Ill. 558, 142 N.E. 204 (1923), certificate of Secretary of State admitted to show failure to file documents

---

15.   Advisory Committee's Note to Exception (8).

required by Securities Law, as well as cases where the absence of a record is offered as proof of the nonoccurrence of an event ordinarily recorded.

The refusal of the common law to allow proof by certificate of the lack of a record or entry has no apparent justification, 5 Wigmore § 1678(7), p. 752. The rule takes the opposite position, as do Uniform Rule 63(17); California Evidence Code § 1284; Kansas Code of Civil Procedure § 60-460(c); New Jersey Evidence Rule 63(17). Congress has recognized certification as evidence of the lack of a record. 8 U.S.C. § 1360(d), certificate of Attorney General or other designated officer that no record of Immigration and Naturalization Service of specified nature or entry therein is found, admissible in alien cases.

Advisory Committee's Note to Exception (11)

Exception (11). Records of activities of religious organizations are currently recognized as admissible at least to the extent of the business records exception to the hearsay rule, 5 Wigmore § 1523, p. 371, and Exception (6) would be applicable. However, both the business record doctrine and Exception (6) require that the person furnishing the information be one in the business or activity. The result is such decisions as Daily v. Grand Lodge, 311 Ill. 184, 142 N.E. 478 (1924), holding a church record admissible to prove fact, date, and place of baptism, but not age of child except that he had at least been born at the time. In view of the unlikelihood that false information would be furnished on occasions of this kind, the rule contains no requirement that the informant be in the course of the activity. See California Evidence Code § 1315 and Comment.

Exception (12). The principle of proof by certification is recognized as to public officials in Exceptions (8) and (10), and with respect to authentication in Rule 902. The present exception is a duplication to the extent that it deals with a certificate by a public official, as in the case of a judge who performs a marriage ceremony. The area covered by the rule is, however, substantially larger and extends the certification procedure to clergymen and the like who perform marriages and other ceremonies or administer sacraments. Thus certificates of such matters as baptism or confirmation, as well as marriage, are included. In principle they are as acceptable evidence as certificates of public officers. See 5 Wigmore § 1645, as to marriage certificates. When the person executing the certificate is not a public official, the self-authenticating character of documents purporting to emanate from public officials, see Rule 902, is lacking and proof is required that the person was authorized and did make the certificate. The time element, however, may safely be taken as supplied by the certificate, once authority and authenticity are established, particularly in view of the presumption that a document was executed on the date it bears.

For similar rules, some limited to certificates of marriage, with variations in foundation requirements, see Uniform Rule 63(18); California Evidence Code § 1316; Kansas Code of Civil Procedure § 60-460(p); New Jersey Evidence Rule 63(18).

Exception (13). Records of family history kept in family Bibles have by long tradition been received in evidence. 5 Wigmore §§ 1495, 1496, citing numerous statutes and decisions. See also Regulations, Social Security Administration, 20 C.F.R. § 404.703(c), recognizing family Bible entries as proof of age in the absence of public or church records. Opinions in the area also include inscriptions on tombstones, publicly displayed pedigrees, and engravings on rings. Wigmore, supra. The rule is substantially identical in coverage with California Evidence Code § 1312.

Report of the House Committee on the Judiciary

The Committee approved this Rule in the form submitted by the Court, intending that the phrase "Statements of fact concerning personal or family history" be read to include the specific types of such statements enumerated in Rule 803(11).

Advisory Committee's Note to Exception (14)

Exception (14). The recording of title documents is a purely statutory development. Under any theory of the admissibility of public records, the records would be receivable as evidence of the contents of the recorded document, else the recording process would be reduced to a nullity. When, however, the record is offered for the further purpose of proving execution and delivery, a problem of lack of first-hand knowledge by the recorder, not present as to contents, is presented. This problem is solved, seemingly in all jurisdictions, by qualifying for recording only those documents shown by a specified procedure, either acknowledgement or a form of probate, to have been executed and delivered. 5 Wigmore §§ 1647-1651. Thus what may appear in the rule, at first glance, as endowing the record with an effect independently of local law and inviting difficulties of an Erie nature under Cities Service Oil Co. v. Dunlap, 308 U.S. 208, 60 S.Ct. 201, 84 L.Ed. 196 (1939), is not present, since the local law in fact governs under the example.

Advisory Committee's Note to Exception (15)

Exception (15). Dispositive documents often contain recitals of fact. Thus a deed purporting to have been executed by an attorney in fact may recite the existence of the power of attorney, or a deed may recite that the grantors are all the heirs of the last record owner. Under the rule, these recitals are exempted from the hearsay rule. The circumstances under which dispositive documents are executed and the requirement that the recital be germane to the purpose of the document are believed to be adequate guarantees of trustworthiness, particularly in view of the nonapplicability of the rule if dealings with the property have been inconsistent with the document. The age of the document is of no significance, though in practical application the document will most often be an ancient one. See Uniform Rule 63(29), Comment.

Similar provisions are contained in Uniform Rule 63(29); California Evidence Code § 1330; Kansas Code of Civil Procedure § 60-460(aa); New Jersey Evidence Rule 63(29).

Advisory Committee's Note to Exception (16)

Exception (16). Authenticating a document as ancient, essentially in the pattern of the common law, as provided in Rule 901(b)(8), leaves open as a separate question the admissibility of assertive statements contained therein as against a hearsay objection. 7 Wigmore § 2145a. Wigmore further states that the ancient document technique of authentication is universally conceded to apply to all sorts of documents, including letters, records, contracts, maps, and certificates, in addition to title documents, citing numerous decisions. *Id.* § 2145. Since most of these items are significant evidentially only insofar as they are assertive, their admission in evidence must be as a hearsay exception. But see 5 *id.* § 1573, p. 429, referring to recitals in ancient deeds as a "limited" hearsay exception. The former position is believed to be the correct one in reason and authority. As pointed out in McCormick § 298, danger of mistake is minimized by authentication requirements, and age affords assurance that the writing antedates the present controversy. See Dallas County v. Commercial Union Assurance Co., 286 F.2d 388 (5th Cir. 1961), upholding admissibility of 58-year-old newspaper story. Cf. Morgan, Basic Problems of Evidence 364 (1962), but see *id.* 254.

For a similar provision, but with the added requirement that "the statement has since generally been acted upon as true by persons having an interest in the matter," see California Evidence Code § 1331.

ADVISORY COMMITTEE'S NOTE TO EXCEPTION (17)

Exception (17). Ample authority at common law supported the admission in evidence of items falling in this category. While Wigmore's text is narrowly oriented to lists, etc., prepared for the use of a trade or profession, 6 Wigmore § 1702, authorities are cited which include other kinds of publications, for example, newspaper market reports, telephone directories, and city directories. *Id.* §§ 1702-1706. The basis of trustworthiness is general reliance by the public or by a particular segment of it, and the motivation of the compiler to foster reliance by being accurate.

For similar provisions, see Uniform Rule 63(30); California Evidence Code § 1340; Kansas Code of Civil Procedure § 60-460(bb); New Jersey Evidence Rule 63(30). Uniform Commercial Code § 2-724 provides for admissibility in evidence of "reports in official publications or trade journals or in newspapers or periodicals of general circulation published as the reports of such [established commodity] market."

ADVISORY COMMITTEE'S NOTE TO EXCEPTION (18)

Exception (18). The writers have generally favored the admissibility of learned treatises, McCormick § 296, p. 621; Morgan, Basic Problems of Evidence 366 (1962); 6 Wigmore § 1692, with the support of occasional decisions and rules, City of Dothan v. Hardy, 237 Ala. 603, 188 So. 264 (1939); Lewandowski v. Preferred Risk Mut. Ins. Co., 33 Wis.2d 69, 146 N.W.2d 505 (1966), 66 Mich.L.Rev. 183 (1967); Uniform Rule 63(31); Kansas Code of Civil Procedure § 60-460(cc), but the great weight of authority has been that learned treatises are not admissible as substantive evidence though usable in the cross-examination of experts. The foundation of the minority view is that the hearsay objection must be regarded as unimpressive when directed against treatises since a high standard of accuracy is engendered by various factors: the treatise is written primarily and impartially for professionals, subject to scrutiny and exposure for inaccuracy, with the reputation of the writer at stake. 6 Wigmore § 1692. Sound as this position may be with respect to trustworthiness, there is, nevertheless, an additional difficulty in the likelihood that the treatise will be misunderstood and misapplied without expert assistance and supervision. This difficulty is recognized in the cases demonstrating unwillingness to sustain findings relative to disability on the basis of judicially noticed medical texts. Ross v. Gardner, 365 F.2d 554 (6th Cir. 1966); Sayers v.

Gardner, 380 F.2d 940 (6th Cir. 1967); Colwell v. Gardner, 386 F.2d 56 (6th Cir. 1967); Glendenning v. Ribicoff, 213 F.Supp. 301 (W.D.Mo.1962); Cook v. Celebreeze, 217 F.Supp. 366 (W.D.Mo.1963); Sosna v. Celebreeze, 234 F.Supp 289 (E.D.Pa.1964); and see McDaniel v. Celebrezze, 331 F.2d 426 (4th Cir. 1964). The rule avoids the danger of misunderstanding and misapplication by limiting the use of treatises as substantive evidence to situations in which an expert is on the stand and available to explain and assist in the application of the treatise if desired. The limitation upon receiving the publication itself physically in evidence, contained in the last sentence, is designed to further this policy.

The relevance of the use of treatises on cross-examination is evident. This use of treatises has been the subject of varied views. The most restrictive position is that the witness must have stated expressly on direct his reliance upon the treatise. A slightly more liberal approach still insists upon reliance but allows it to be developed on cross-examination. Further relaxation dispenses with reliance but requires recognition as an authority by the witness, developable on cross-examination. The greatest liberality is found in decisions allowing use of the treatise on cross-examination when its status as an authority is established by any means. Annot., 60 A.L.R.2d 77. The exception is hinged upon this last position, which is that of the Supreme Court, Reilly v. Pinkus, 338 U.S. 269, 70 S.Ct. 110, 94 L.Ed. 63 (1949), and of recent well considered state court decisions, City of St. Petersburg v. Ferguson, 193 So.2d 648 (Fla.App.1967), cert. denied Fla., 201 So.2d 556; Darling v. Charleston Memorial Community Hospital, 33 Ill.2d 326, 211 N.E.2d 253 (1965); Dabroe v. Rhodes Co., 64 Wash.2d 431, 392 P.2d 317 (1964).

In Reilly v. Pinkus, *supra,* the Court pointed out that testing of professional knowledge was incomplete without exploration of the witness' knowledge of and attitude toward established treatises in the field. The process works equally well in reverse and furnishes the basis of the rule.

The rule does not require that the witness rely upon or recognize the treatise as authoritative, thus avoiding the possibility that the expert may at the outset block cross-examination by refusing to concede reliance or authoritativeness. Dabroe v. Rhodes Co., *supra.* Moreover, the rule avoids the unreality of admitting evidence for the purpose of impeachment only, with an instruction to the jury not to consider it otherwise. The parallel to the treatment of prior inconsistent statements will be apparent. See Rules 613(b) and 801(d)(1).

Advisory Committee's Note to Exceptions (19), (20) and (21)

Exceptions (19), (20), and (21). Trustworthiness in reputation evidence is found "when the topic is such that the facts are likely to have been inquired about and that persons having personal knowledge have disclosed facts which have thus been discussed in the community; and thus the community's conclusion, if any has been formed, is likely to be a trustworthy one." 5 Wigmore § 1580, p. 444, and see also § 1583. On this common foundation, reputation as to land boundaries, customs, general history, character, and marriage have come to be regarded as admissible. The breadth of the underlying principle suggests the formulation of an equally broad exception, but tradition has in fact been much narrower and more particularized, and this is the pattern of these exceptions in the rule.

Exception (19) is concerned with matters of personal and family history. Marriage is universally conceded to be a proper subject of proof by evidence of reputation in the community. 5 Wigmore § 1602. As to such items as legitimacy, relationship, adoption, birth, and death, the decisions are divided. *Id.* § 1605. All seem to be susceptible to being the subject of well founded repute. The "world" in which the reputation may exist may be family, associates, or community. This world has proved capable of expanding with changing times from the single uncomplicated neighborhood, in which all activities take place, to the multiple and unrelated worlds of work, religious affiliation, and social activity, in each of which a reputation may be generated. People v. Reeves, 360 Ill. 55, 195 N.E. 443 (1935); State v. Axilrod, 248 Minn. 204, 79 N.W.2d 677 (1956); Mass.Stat. 1947, c. 410, M.G.L.A. c. 233 § 21A; 5 Wigmore § 1616. The family has often served as the point of beginning for allowing community reputation. 5 Wigmore § 1488. For comparable provisions see Uniform Rule 63(26), (27) (c); California Evidence Code §§ 1313, 1314; Kansas Code of Civil Procedure § 60-460(x), (y)(3); New Jersey Evidence Rule 63(26), (27)(c).

The first portion of Exception (20) is based upon the general admissibility of evidence of reputation as to land boundaries and land customs, expanded in this country to include private as well as public boundaries. McCormick § 299, p. 625. The reputation is required to antedate the controversy, though not to be ancient. The second portion is likewise supported by authority, *id.*, and is designed to facilitate proof of events when judicial notice is not available. The historical character of the subject matter dispenses with any need that the reputation antedate the controversy with respect to which it is offered. For similar provisions see Uniform Rule 63(27) (a), (b); California Evidence Code §§ 1320-1322; Kansas Code of Civil Procedure § 60-460(y), (1), (2); New Jersey Evidence Rule 63(27) (a), (b).

Exception (21) recognizes the traditional acceptance of reputation evidence as a means of proving human character. McCormick §§ 44, 158. The exception deals only with the hearsay aspect of this kind of evidence. Limitations upon admissibility based on other grounds will be found in Rules 404, relevancy of character evidence generally, and 608, character of witness. The exception is in effect a reiteration, in the context of hearsay, of Rule 405(a). Similar provisions are contained in Uniform Rule 63(28); California Evidence Code § 1324; Kansas Code of Civil Procedure § 60-460(z); New Jersey Evidence Rule 63(28).

ADVISORY COMMITTEE'S NOTE TO EXCEPTION (22)

Exception (22). When the status of a former judgment is under consideration in subsequent litigation, three possibilities must be noted: (1) the former judgment is conclusive under the doctrine of res judicata, either as a bar or a collateral estoppel; or (2) it is admissible in evidence for what it is worth; or (3) it may be of no effect at all. The first situation does not involve any problem of evidence except in the way that principles of substantive law generally bear upon the relevancy and materiality of evidence. The rule does not deal with the substantive effect of the judgment as a bar or collateral estoppel. When, however, the doctrine of res judicata does not apply to make the judgment either a bar or a collateral estoppel, a choice is presented between the second and third alternatives. The rule adopts the second for judgments of criminal conviction of felony grade. This is the direction of the decisions, Annot., 18 A.L.R.2d 1287, 1299, which manifest an increasing reluctance to reject *in toto* the validity of the law's factfinding processes outside the confines of res judicata and collateral estoppel. While this may leave a jury with the evidence of conviction but without means to evaluate it, as suggested by Judge Hinton, Note 27 Ill.L.Rev. 195 (1932), it seems safe to assume that the jury will give it substantial effect unless defendant offers a satisfactory explanation, a possibility not foreclosed by the provision. But see North River Ins. Co. v. Militello, 104 Colo. 28, 88 P.2d 567 (1939), in which the jury found for plaintiff on a fire policy despite the introduction of his conviction for arson. For supporting federal decisions see Clark, J., in New York & Cuba Mail S. S. Co. v. Continental Cas. Co., 117 F.2d 404, 411 (2d Cir. 1941); Connecticut Fire Ins. Co. v. Farrara, 277 F.2d 388 (8th Cir. 1960).

Practical considerations require exclusion of convictions of minor offenses, not because the administration of justice in its lower echelons must be inferior, but because motivation to defend at this level is often minimal or nonexistent. Cope v. Goble, 39 Cal.App.2d 448, 103 P.2d 598 (1940); Jones v. Talbot, 87 Idaho 498, 394 P.2d 316 (1964); Warren v. Marsh, 215 Minn. 615, 11 N.W.2d 528 (1943); Annot., 18 A.L.R.2d 1287, 1295-1297; 16 Brooklyn L.Rev. 286 (1950); 50 Colum.L.Rev. 529 (1950); 35 Cornell L.Q. 872 (1950). Hence the rule includes only convictions of felony grade, measured by federal standards.

Judgments of conviction based upon pleas of *nolo contendere* are not included. This position is consistent with the treatment of *nolo pleas in Rule 410 and the authorities cited in the Advisory Committee's Note in support thereof.*

While these rules do not in general purport to resolve constitutional issues, they have in general been drafted with a view to avoiding collision with constitutional principles. Consequently the exception does not include evidence of the conviction of a third person, offered against the accused in a criminal prosecution to prove any fact essential to sustain the judgment of conviction. A contrary position would seem clearly to violate the right of confrontation. Kirby v. United States, 174 U.S. 47, 19 S.Ct. 574, 43 L.Ed. 890 (1899), error to convict of possessing stolen postage stamps with the only evidence of theft being the record of conviction of the thieves. The situation is to be distinguished from cases in which conviction of another person is an element of the crime, e.g. 15 U.S.C. § 902(d), interstate shipment of firearms to a known convicted felon, and, as specifically provided, from impeachment.

For comparable provisions see Uniform Rule 63(20); California Evidence Code § 1300; Kansas Code of Civil Procedure § 60-460(r); New Jersey Evidence Rule 63(20).

ADVISORY COMMITTEE'S NOTE TO EXCEPTION (23)

Exception (23). A hearsay exception in this area was originally justified on the ground that verdicts were evidence of reputation. As trial by jury graduated from the category of neighborhood inquests, this theory lost its validity. It was never valid as to chancery decrees. Nevertheless the rule persisted, though the judges and writers shifted ground and began saying that the judgment or decree was as good evidence as reputation. See City of London v. Clerke, Carth. 181, 90 Eng.Rep. 710 (K.B. 1691); Neill v. Duke of Devonshire, 8 App.Cas. 135 (1882). The shift appears to be correct, since the process of inquiry, sifting, and scrutiny which is relied upon to render reputation reliable is present in perhaps greater measure in the process of litigation. While this might suggest a broader area of application, the affinity to reputation is strong, and paragraph (23) goes no further, not even including character.

The leading case in the United States, Patterson v. Gaines, 47 U.S. (6 How.) 550, 599, 12 L.Ed. 553 (1847), follows in the pattern of the English decisions, mentioning as illustrative matters thus provable: manorial rights, public rights of way, immemorial custom, disputed boundary, and pedigree. More recent recognition of the principle is found in Grant Bros. Construction Co. v. United States, 232 U.S. 647, 34 S.Ct. 452, 58 L.Ed. 776 (1914), in action for penalties under Alien Contract Labor Law, decision of board of inquiry of Immigration Service admissible to prove alienage of laborers, as a matter of pedigree; United States v. Mid-Continent Petroleum Corp., 67 F.2d 37 (10th Cir. 1933), records of commission enrolling Indians admissible on pedigree; Jung Yen Loy v. Cahill, 81 F.2d 809 (9th Cir. 1936), board decisions as to citizenship of plaintiff's father admissible in proceeding for declaration of citizenship. *Contra*, In re Estate of Cunha, 49 Haw. 273, 414 P.2d 925 (1966).

ADVISORY COMMITTEE'S NOTE TO EXCEPTION (24)

Exception (24). The preceding 23 exceptions of Rule 803 and the first five exceptions of Rule 804(b), *infra*, are designed to take full advantage of the accumulated wisdom and experience of the past in dealing with hearsay. It would, however, be presumptuous to assume that all possible desirable exceptions to the hearsay rule have been catalogued and to pass the hearsay rule to oncoming generations as a closed system. Exception (24) and its companion provision in Rule 804(b)(6) are accordingly included. They do not contemplate an unfettered exercise of judicial discretion, but they do provide for treating new and presently unanticipated situations which demonstrate a trustworthiness within the spirit of the specifically stated exceptions. Within this framework, room is left for growth and development of the law of evidence in the hearsay area, consistently with the broad purposes expressed in Rule 102. See Dallas County v. Commercial Union Assur. Co., 286 F.2d 388 (5th Cir. 1961).

REPORT OF THE HOUSE COMMITTEE ON THE JUDICIARY

[Note, that the attempt in the House to delete Rule 803(24) below, ultimately failed.]

The proposed Rules of Evidence submitted to Congress contained identical provisions in Rules 803 and 804 (which set forth the various hearsay exceptions), to the effect that the federal courts could admit any hearsay statement not specifically covered by any of the stated exceptions, if the hearsay statement was found to have "comparable circumstantial guarantees of trustworthiness."

The Committee deleted these provisions (proposed Rules 803(24) and 804(b)(6)) as injecting too much uncertainty into the law of evidence and impairing the ability of practitioners to prepare for trial. It was noted that Rule 102 directs the courts to construe the Rules of Evidence so as to promote "growth and development." The Committee believed that if additional hearsay exceptions are to be created, they should be by amendments to the Rules, not on a case-by-case basis.

Report of the Senate Committee on the Judiciary

[Note, that after the Report set forth below was prepared, Rule 803(24) was again amended to add a notice provision.]

The proposed Rules of Evidence submitted to Congress contained identical provisions in rules 803 and 804 (which set forth the various hearsay exceptions), admitting any hearsay statement not specifically covered by any of the stated exceptions, if the hearsay statement was found to have "comparable circumstantial guarantees of trustworthiness." The House deleted these provisions (proposed rules 803(24) and 804(b)(6)) as injecting "too much uncertainty" into the law of evidence and impairing the ability of practitioners to prepare for trial. The House felt that rule 102, which directs the courts to construe the Rules of Evidence so as to promote growth and development, would permit sufficient flexibility to admit hearsay evidence in appropriate cases under various factual situations that might arise.

We disagree with the total rejection of a residual hearsay exception. While we view rule 102 as being intended to provide for a broader construction and interpretation of these rules, we feel that, without a separate residual provision, the specifically enumerated exceptions could become tortured beyond any reasonable circumstances which they were intended to include (even if broadly construed). Moreover, these exceptions, while they reflect the most typical and well recognized exceptions to the hearsay rule, may not encompass every situation in which the reliability and appropriateness of a particular piece of hearsay evidence make clear that it should be heard and considered by the trier of fact.

The committee believes that there are certain exceptional circumstances where evidence which is found by a court to have guarantees of trustworthiness equivalent to or exceeding the guarantees reflected by the presently listed exceptions, and to have a high degree of probativeness and necessity could properly be admissible.

The case of *Dallas County v. Commercial Union Assoc. Co., Ltd.*, 286 F.2d 388 (5th Cir. 1961) illustrates the point. The issue in that case was whether the tower of the county courthouse collapsed because it was struck by lightning (covered by insurance) or because of structural weakness and deterioration of the structure (not covered). Investigation of the structure revealed the presence of charcoal and charred timbers. In order to show that lightning may not have been the cause of the charring, the insurer offered a copy of a local newspaper published over 50 years earlier containing an unsigned article describing a fire in the courthouse while it was under construction. The Court found that the newspaper did not qualify for admission as a business record or an ancient document and did not fit within any other recognized hearsay exception. The court concluded, however, that the article was trustworthy because it was inconceivable that a newspaper reporter in a small town would report a fire in the courthouse if none had occurred. *See also United States v. Barbati*, 284 F. Supp. 409 (E.D.N.Y. 1968).

Because exceptional cases like the *Dallas County* case may arise in the future, the committee has decided to reinstate a residual exception for rules 803 and 804(b).

The committee, however, also agrees with those supporters of the House version who felt that an overly broad residual hearsay exception could emasculate the hearsay rule and the recognized exceptions or vitiate the rationale behind codification of the rules.

Therefore, the committee has adopted a residual exception for rules 803 and 804(b) of much narrower scope and applicability than the Supreme Court version. In order to qualify for admission, a hearsay statement not falling within one of the recognized exceptions would have to satisfy at least four conditions. First, it must have "equivalent circumstantial guarantees of trustworthiness." Second, it must be offered as evidence of a material fact. Third, the court must determine that the statement "is more probative on the point for which it is offered than any other evidence which the proponent can procure through reasonable efforts." This requirement is intended to insure that only statements which have high probative value and necessity may qualify for admission under the residual exceptions. Fourth, the court must determine that "the general purposes of these rules and the interests of justice will best be served by admission of the statement into evidence."

It is intended that the residual hearsay exceptions will be used very rarely, and only in exceptional circumstances. The committee does not intend to establish a broad license for trial judges to admit hearsay statements that do not fall within one of the other exceptions contained in rules 803 and 804(b). The residual exceptions are not meant to authorize major judicial revisions of the hearsay rule, including its present exceptions. Such major revisions are best accomplished by legislative action. It is intended that in any case in which evidence is sought to be admitted under these subsections, the trial judge will exercise no less care, reflection and caution than the courts did under the common law in establishing the now-recognized exceptions to the hearsay rule.

In order to establish a well-defined jurisprudence, the special facts and circumstances which, in the court's judgment, indicates that the statement has a sufficiently high degree of trustworthiness and necessity to justify its admission should be stated on the record. It is expected that the court will give the opposing party a full and adequate opportunity to contest the admission of any statement sought to be introduced under these subsections.

REPORT OF THE HOUSE/SENATE CONFERENCE COMMITTEE

The Senate amendment adds a new subsection, (24), which makes admissible a hearsay statement not specifically covered by any of the previous twenty-three subsections, if the statement has equivalent circumstantial guarantees of trustworthiness and if the court determines that (A) the statement is offered as evidence of a material fact; (B) the statement is more probative on the point for which it is offered than any other evidence the proponent can procure through reasonable efforts; and (C) the general purposes of these rules and the interests of justice will best be served by admission of the statement into evidence.

The House bill eliminated a similar, but broader, provision because of the conviction that such a provision injected too much uncertainty into the law of evidence regarding hearsay and impaired the ability of a litigant to prepare adequately for trial.

The Conference adopts the Senate amendment with an amendment that provides that a party intending to request the court to use a statement under this provision must notify any adverse party of this intention as well as of the particulars of the statement, including the name and address of the declarant. This notice must be given sufficiently in advance of the trial or hearing to provide any adverse party with a fair opportunity to prepare to contest the use of the statement.

Rule 804   Hearsay Exceptions; Declarant Unavailable

ADVISORY COMMITTEE'S NOTE

As to firsthand knowledge on the part of hearsay declarants, see the introductory portion of the Advisory Committee's Note to Rule 803.

Subdivision (a). The definition of unavailability implements the division of hearsay exceptions into two categories by Rules 803 and 804(b).

At common law the unavailability requirement was evolved in connection with particular hearsay exceptions rather than along general lines. For example, see the separate explications of unavailability in relation to former testimony, declarations against interest, and statements of pedigree, separately developed in McCormick §§ 234, 257, and 297. However, no reason is apparent for making distinctions as to what satisfies unavailability for the different exceptions. The treatment in the rule is therefore uniform although differences in the range of process for witnesses between civil and criminal cases will lead to a less exacting requirement under item (5). See Rule 45(e) of the Federal Rules of Civil Procedure and Rule 17(e) of the Federal Rules of Criminal Procedure.

Five instances of unavailability are specified:

(1) Substantial authority supports the position that exercise of a claim of privilege by the declarant satisfies the requirement of unavailability (usually in connection with former testimony). Wyatt v. State, 35 Ala.App. 147, 46 So.2d 837 (1950); State v. Stewart, 85 Kan. 404, 116 P. 489 (1911); Annot., 45 A.L.R.2d 1354; Uniform Rule 62(7)(a); California Evidence Code § 240(a)(1); Kansas Code of Civil Procedure § 60-459(g)(1). A ruling by the judge is required, which clearly implies that an actual claim of privilege must be made.

(2) A witness is rendered unavailable if he simply refuses to testify concerning the subject matter of his statement despite judicial pressures to do so, a position supported by similar considerations of practicality. Johnson v. People, 152 Colo. 586, 384 P.2d 454 (1963); People v. Pickett, 339 Mich. 294, 63 N.W.2d 681, 45 A.L.R.2d 1341 (1954). *Contra,* Pleau v. State, 255 Wis. 362, 38 N.W.2d 496 (1949).

(3) The position that a claimed lack of memory by the witness of the subject matter of his statement constitutes unavailability likewise finds support in the cases, though not without dissent. McCormick § 234, p. 494. If the claim is successful, the practical effect is to put the testimony beyond reach, as in the other instances. In this instance, however, it will be noted that the lack of memory must be established by the testimony of the witness himself, which clearly contemplates his production and subjection to cross-examination.

REPORT OF THE HOUSE COMMITTEE ON THE JUDICIARY

Rule 804(a)(3) was approved in the form submitted by the Court. However, the Committee intends no change in existing federal law under which the court may choose to disbelieve the declarant's testimony as to his lack of memory. See United States v. Insana, 423 F.2d 1165, 1169-1170 (2nd Cir.), cert. denied, 400 U.S. 841 (1970).

Advisory Committee's Note

[Note, that the last sentence in the Note below does not apply to Rule 804 as enacted.]

(4) Death and infirmity find general recognition as grounds. McCormick §§ 234, 257, 297; Uniform Rule 62(7) (c); California Evidence Code § 240(a)(3); Kansas Code of Civil Procedure § 60-459(g)(3); New Jersey Evidence Rule 62(6)(c). See also the provisions on use of depositions in Rule 32(a)(3) of the Federal Rules of Civil Procedure and Rule 15(e) of the Federal Rules of Criminal Procedure.

(5) Absence from the hearing coupled with inability to compel attendance by process or other reasonable means also satisfies the requirement. McCormick § 234; Uniform Rule 62(7)(d) and (e); California Evidence Code § 240(a)(4) and (5); Kansas Code of Civil Procedure § 60-459(g)(4) and (5); New Jersey Rule 62(6) (b) and (d). See the discussion of procuring attendance of witnesses who are nonresidents or in custody in Barber v. Page, 390 U.S. 719, 88 S.Ct. 1318, 20 L.Ed.2d 255 (1968).

If the conditions otherwise constituting unavailability result from the procurement or wrongdoing of the proponent of the statement, the requirement is not satisfied. The rule contains no requirement that an attempt be made to take the deposition of a declarant.

Report of the House Committee on the Judiciary

[Note, that the proposed change discussed in the Committee Report below was in fact adopted, and is in Rule 804(a)(5) as enacted.]

Rule 804(a)(5) as submitted to the Congress provided, as one type of situation in which a declarant would be deemed "unavailable," that he be "absent from the hearing and the proponent of his statement has been unable to procure his attendance by process or other reasonable means." The Committee amended the Rule to insert after the word "attendance" the parenthetical expression "(or, in the case of a hearsay exception under subdivision (b)(2), (3), or (4), his attendance or testimony)." The amendment is designed primarily to require that an attempt be made to depose a witness (as well as to seek his attendance) as a precondition to the witness being deemed unavailable. The Committee, however, recognized the propriety of an exception to this additional requirement when it is the declarant's former testimony that is sought to be admitted under subdivision (b)(1).

Report of the Senate Committee on the Judiciary

[Note, that the position of the Committee set forth below with respect to Rule 804(a)(5) did not prevail. The deposition clause remained in the Rule as enacted.]

Subdivision (a) of rule 804 as submitted by the Supreme Court defined the conditions under which a witness was considered to be unavailable. It was amended in the House.

The purpose of the amendment, according to the report of the House Committee on the Judiciary, is "primarily to require that an attempt be made to depose a witness (as well as to seek his attendance) as a precondition to the witness being unavailable."[15]

15.   H. Rept. 93-650, at p. 15.

Under the House amendment, before a witness is declared unavailable, a party must try to depose a witness (declarant) with respect to dying declarations, declarations against interest, and declarations of pedigree. None of these situations would seem to warrant this needless, impractical and highly restrictive complication. A good case can be made for eliminating the unavailability requirement entirely for declarations against interest cases.[16]

In dying declaration cases, the declarant will usually, though not necessarily, be deceased at the time of trial. Pedigree statements which are admittedly and necessarily based largely on word of mouth are not greatly fortified by a deposition requirement.

Depositions are expensive and time-consuming. In any event, deposition procedures are available to those who wish to resort to them. Moreover, the deposition procedures of the Civil Rules and Criminal Rules are only imperfectly adapted to implementing the amendment. No purpose is served unless the deposition, if taken, may be used in evidence. Under Civil Rule (a)(3) and Criminal Rule 15(e), a deposition, though taken, may not be admissible, and under Criminal Rule 15(a) substantial obstacles exist in the way of even taking a deposition.

For these reasons, the committee deleted the House amendment.

The committee understands that the rule as to unavailability, as explained by the Advisory Committee "contains no requirement that an attempt to be made to take the deposition of a declarent." In reflecting the committee's judgment, the statement is accurate insofar as it goes. Where, however, the proponent of the statement, with knowledge of the existence of the statement, fails to confront the declarant with the statement at the taking of the deposition, then the proponent should not, in fairness, be permitted to treat the declarant as "unavailable" simply because the declarant was not amenable to process compelling his attendance at trial. The committee does not consider it necessary to amend the rule to this effect because such a situation abuses, not conforms to, the rule. Fairness would preclude a person from introducing a hearsay statement on a particular issue if the person taking the deposition was aware of the issue at the time of the deposition but failed to depose the unavailable witness on that issue.

REPORT OF THE HOUSE/SENATE CONFERENCE COMMITTEE

[Note, that the resolution of the controversy recommended below was in fact approved.]

Subsection (a) defines the term "unavailability as a witness." The House bill provides in subsection (a)(5) that the party who desires to use the statement must be unable to procure the declarant's attendance by process or other reasonable means. In the case of dying declarations, statements against interest and statements of personal or family history, the House bill requires that the proponent must also be unable to procure the declarant's testimony (such as by deposition or interrogatories) by process or other reasonable means. The Senate amendment eliminates this latter provision.

The Conference adopts the provision contained in the House bill.

16. Uniform Rule 63 (10); Kan. Stat. Anno. 60-460 (j); 2A N.J. Stats. Anno. 84-63 (10).

ADVISORY COMMITTEE'S NOTE

[Note, that on the "identity of parties" problem discussed in the last two paragraphs of the Committee's note below, Congress differed, and Rule 804(b)(1) was amended accordingly.]

Subdivision (b). Rule 803, *supra,* is based upon the assumption that a hearsay statement falling within one of its exceptions possesses qualities which justify the conclusion that whether the declarant is available or unavailable is not a relevant factor in determining admissibility. The instant rule proceeds upon a different theory: hearsay which admittedly is not equal in quality to testimony of the declarant on the stand may nevertheless be admitted if the declarant is unavailable and if his statement meets a specified standard. The rule expresses preferences: testimony given on the stand in person is preferred over hearsay, and hearsay, if of the specified quality, is preferred over complete loss of the evidence of the declarant. The exceptions evolved at common law with respect to declarations of unavailable declarants furnish the basis for the exceptions enumerated in the proposal. The term "unavailable" is defined in subdivision (a).

Exception (1). Former testimony does not rely upon some set of circumstances to substitute for oath and cross-examination, since both oath and opportunity to cross-examine were present in fact. The only missing one of the ideal conditions for the giving of testimony is the presence of trier and opponent ("demeanor evidence"). This is lacking with all hearsay exceptions. Hence it may be argued that former testimony is the strongest hearsay and should be included under Rule 803, *supra.* However, opportunity to observe demeanor is what in a large measure confers depth and meaning upon oath and cross-examination. Thus in cases under Rule 803 demeanor lacks the significance which it possesses with respect to testimony. In any event, the tradition, founded in experience, uniformly favors production of the witness if he is available. The exception indicates continuation of the policy. This preference for the presence of the witness is apparent also in rules and statutes on the use of depositions, which deal with substantially the same problem.

Under the exception, the testimony may be offered (1) against the party *against* whom it was previously offered or (2) against the party *by* whom it was previously offered. In each instance the question resolves itself into whether fairness allows imposing, upon the party against whom now offered, the handling of the witness on the earlier occasion. (1) If the party against whom now offered is the one against whom the testimony was offered previously, no unfairness is apparent in requiring him to accept his own prior conduct of cross-examination or decision not to cross-examine. Only demeanor has been lost, and that is inherent in the situation. (2) If the party against whom now offered is the one *by* whom the testimony was offered previously, a satisfactory answer becomes somewhat more difficult. One possibility is to proceed somewhat along the line of an adoptive admission, i.e. by offering the testimony proponent in effect adopts it. However, this theory savors of discarded concepts of witnesses' belonging to a party, of litigants' ability to pick and choose witnesses, and of vouching for one's own witnesses. Cf. McCormick § 246, pp. 526-527; 4 Wigmore § 1075. A more direct and acceptable approach is simply to recognize direct and redirect examination of one's own witness as the equivalent of cross-examining an opponent's witness. Falknor, Former Testimony and the Uniform Rules: A Comment, 38 N.Y.U.L.Rev. 651, n. 1 (1963); McCormick § 231, p. 483. See also 5 Wigmore § 1389. Allowable techniques for dealing with hostile, double-crossing, forgetful, and mentally deficient witnesses leave no substance to a claim that one could not adequately develop his own witness at the former hearing. An even less appealing argument is presented when failure to develop fully was the result of a deliberate choice.

The common law did not limit the admissibility of former testimony to that given in an earlier trial of the same case, although it did require identity of issues as a means of insuring that the former handling of the witness was the equivalent of what would now be done if the opportunity were presented. Modern decisions reduce the requirement to "substantial" identity. McCormick § 233. Since identity of issues is significant only in that it bears on motive and interest in developing fully the testimony of the witness, expressing the matter in the latter terms is preferable. *Id.* Testimony given at a preliminary hearing was held in California v. Green, 399 U.S. 149, 90 S.Ct. 1930, 26 L.Ed.2d 489 (1970), to satisfy confrontation requirements in this respect.

As a further assurance of fairness in thrusting upon a party the prior handling of the witness, the common law also insisted upon identity of parties, deviating only to the extent of allowing substitution of successors in a narrowly construed privity. Mutuality as an aspect of identity is now generally discredited, and the requirement of identity of the offering party disappears except as it might affect motive to develop the testimony. Falknor, *supra*, at 652; McCormick § 232, pp. 487-488. The question remains whether strict identity, or privity, should continue as a requirement with respect to the party against whom offered. The rule departs to the extent of allowing substitution of one with the right and opportunity to develop the testimony with similar motive and interest. This position is supported by modern decisions. McCormick § 232, pp. 489-490; 5 Wigmore § 1388.

Provisions of the same tenor will be found in Uniform Rule 63(3)(b); California Evidence Code §§ 1290-1292; Kansas Code of Civil Procedure § 60-460(o)(2); New Jersey Evidence Rule 63(3). Unlike the rule, the latter three provide either that former testimony is not admissible if the right of confrontation is denied or that it is not admissible if the accused was not a party to the prior hearing. The genesis of these limitations is a caveat in Uniform Rule 63(3) Comment that use of former testimony against an accused may violate his right of confrontation. Mattox v. United States, 156 U.S. 237, 15 S.Ct. 337, 39 L.Ed. 409 (1895), held that the right was not violated by the Government's use, on a retrial of the same case, of testimony given at the first trial by two witnesses since deceased. The decision leaves open the questions (1) whether direct and redirect are equivalent to cross-examination for purposes of confrontation, (2) whether testimony given in a different proceeding is acceptable, and (3) whether the accused must himself have been a party to the earlier proceeding or whether a similarly situated person will serve the purpose. Professor Falknor concluded that, if a dying declaration untested by cross-examination is constitutionally admissible, former testimony tested by the cross-examination of one similarly situated does not offend against confrontation. Falknor, *supra*, at 659-660. The constitutional acceptability of dying declarations has often been conceded. Mattox v. United States, 156 U.S. 237, 243, 15 S.Ct. 337,

39 L.Ed. 409 (1895); Kirby v. United States, 174 U.S. 47, 61, 19 S.Ct. 574, 43 L.Ed. 890 (1899); Pointer v. Texas, 380 U.S. 400, 407, 85 S.Ct. 1065, 13 L.Ed.2d 923 (1965).

REPORT OF THE HOUSE COMMITTEE ON THE JUDICIARY

[Note, that the amendment described below was in fact adopted.]

Rule 804(b)(1) as submitted by the Court allowed prior testimony of an unavailable witness to be admissible if the party against whom it is offered or a person "with motive and interest similar" to his had an opportunity to examine the witness. The Committee considered that it is generally unfair to impose upon the party against whom the hearsay evidence is being offered responsibility for the manner in which the witness was previously handled by another party. The sole exception to this, in the Committee's view, is when a party's predecessor in interest in a civil action or proceeding had an opportunity and similar motive to examine the witness. The Committee amended the Rule to reflect these policy determinations.

REPORT OF THE SENATE/COMMITTEE ON THE JUDICIARY

[Note, that the "House Amendment" in which the Senate Committee concurred in the Report below was in fact adopted.]

Former testimony.—Rule 804(b)(1) as submitted by the Court allowed prior testimony of an unavailable witness to be admissible if the party against whom it is offered or a person "with motive and interest similar" to his had an opportunity to examine the witness.

The House amended the rule to apply only to a party's predecessor in interest. Although the committee recognizes considerable merit to the rule submitted by the Supreme Court, a position which has been advocated by many scholars and judges, we have concluded that the difference between the two versions is not great and we accept the House amendment.

ADVISORY COMMITTEE'S NOTE

[Note, that Subdivision (b)(2) as described below would have created an exception for statements of recent perception. This provision was deleted by Congress, and did not become part of Rule 804 as enacted. A qualified version of this exception, available only in civil cases, was approved by the National Conference of Commissioners on Uniform State Laws, and is found in Uniform Rule 804(b)(5). New Mexico, Wisconsin, and Wyoming did adopt an exception for statements of recent perception.]

Exception (2). The rule finds support in several directions. The well known Massachusetts Act of 1898 allows in evidence the declaration of any deceased person made in good faith before the commencement of the action and upon personal knowledge. Mass.G.L., c. 233, § 65. To the same effect is R.I.G.L. § 9-19-11. Under other statutes, a decedent's statement is admissible on behalf of his estate in actions against it, to offset the presumed inequality resulting from allowing a surviving opponent to testify. California Evidence Code § 1261; Conn.G.S., § 52-172; and statutes collected in 5 Wigmore § 1576. See also Va.Code § 8-286, allowing statements made when capable by a party now incapable of testifying.

In 1938 the Committee on Improvements in the Law of Evidence of the American Bar Association recommended adoption of a statute similar to that of Massachusetts but with the concept of unavailability expanded to include, in addition to death, cases of insanity or inability to produce a witness or take his deposition. 63 A.B.A. Reports 570, 584, 600 (1938). The same year saw enactment of the English Evidence Act of 1938, allowing written statements made on personal knowledge, if declarant is deceased or otherwise unavailable or if the court is satisfied that undue delay or expense would otherwise be caused, unless declarant was an interested person in pending or anticipated relevant proceedings. Evidence Act of 1938, 1 & 2 Geo. 6, c. 28; Cross on Evidence 482 (3rd ed. 1967).

Model Code Rule 503(a) provided broadly for admission of any hearsay declaration of an unavailable declarant. No circumstantial guarantees of trustworthiness were required. Debate upon the floor of the American Law Institute did not seriously question the propriety of the rule but centered upon what should constitute unavailability. 18 A.L.I. Proceedings 90-134 (1941).

The Uniform Rules draftsman took a less advanced position, more in the pattern of the Massachusetts statute, and invoked several assurances of accuracy: recency of perception, clarity of recollection, good faith, and antecedence to the commencement of the action. Uniform Rule 63(4)(c).

Opposition developed to the Uniform Rule because of its countenancing of the use of statements carefully prepared under the tutelage of lawyers, claim adjusters, or investigators with a view to pending or prospective litigation. Tentative Recommendation and a Study Relating to the Uniform Rules of Evidence (Art. VIII. Hearsay Evidence), Cal.Law Rev.Comm'n, 318 (1962); Quick, Excitement, Necessity and the Uniform Rules: A Reappraisal of Rule 63(4), 6 Wayne L.Rev. 204, 219-224 (1960). To meet this objection, the rule excludes statements made at the instigation of a person engaged in investigating, litigating, or settling a claim. It also incorporates as safeguards the good faith and clarity of recollection required by the Uniform Rule and the exclusion of a statement by a person interested in the litigation provided by the English act.

With respect to the question whether the introduction of a statement under this exception against the accused in a criminal case would violate his right of confrontation, reference is made to the last paragraph of the Advisory Committee's Note under Exception (1), *supra*.

Report of the House Committee on the Judiciary

[Note, that the position of the Committee described below prevailed. The exception which the Committee deleted never reappeared in Rule 804.]

Rule 804(b)(2), a hearsay exception submitted by the Court, titled "Statement of recent "perception," read[s] as follows:

> A statement, not in response to the instigation of a person engaged in investigating, litigating, or settling a claim, which narrates, describes, or explains an event or condition recently perceived by the declarant, made in good faith, not in contemplation of pending or anticipated litigation in which he was interested, and while his recollection was clear.

The Committee eliminated this Rule as creating a new and unwarranted hearsay exception of great potential breadth. The Committee did not believe that statements of the type referred to bore sufficient guarantees of trustworthiness to justify admissibility.

ADVISORY COMMITTEE'S NOTE

[Note, that the exception for dying declarations, described below as Exception (3), became Exception (2) in Rule 804(b) as enacted. The change in numbering was caused by deletion of the exception for statements of recent perception. The dying declarations exception described below was amended by Congress so as to be available only in civil cases and prosecutions for homicide.]

Exception (3). The exception is the familiar dying declaration of the common law, expanded somewhat beyond its traditionally narrow limits. While the original religious justification for the exception may have lost its conviction for some persons over the years, it can scarcely be doubted that powerful psychological pressures are present. See 5 Wigmore § 1443 and the classic statement of Chief Baron Eyre in Rex v. Woodcock, 1 Leach 500, 502, 168 Eng.Rep. 352, 353 (K.B.1789).

The common law required that the statement be that of the victim, offered in a prosecution for criminal homicide. Thus declarations by victims in prosecutions for other crimes, e.g. a declaration by a rape victim who dies in childbirth, and all declarations in civil cases were outside the scope of the exception. An occasional statute has removed these restrictions, as in Colo.R.S. § 52-1-20, or has expanded the area of offenses to include abortions, 5 Wigmore § 1432, p. 224, n. 4. Kansas by decision extended the exception to civil cases. Thurston v. Fritz, 91 Kan. 468, 138 P. 625 (1914). While the common law exception no doubt originated as a result of the exceptional need for the evidence in homicide cases, the theory of admissibility applies equally in civil cases and in prosecutions for crimes other than homicide. The same considerations suggest abandonment of the limitation to circumstances attending the event in question, yet when the statement deals with matters other than the supposed death, its influence is believed to be sufficiently attenuated to justify the limitation. Unavailability is not limited to death. See subdivision (a) of this rule. Any problem as to declarations phrased in terms of opinion is laid at rest by Rule 701, and continuation of a requirement of first-hand knowledge is assured by Rule 602.

Comparable provisions are found in Uniform Rule 63(5): California Evidence Code § 1242; Kansas Code of Civil Procedure § 60-460(e); New Jersey Evidence Rule 63(5).

REPORT OF THE HOUSE COMMITTEE ON THE JUDICIARY

[Note, that the amendment to the exception for dying declarations described below was to become part of Rule 804(b)(2) as enacted.]

Rule 804(b)(3) as submitted by the Court (now Rule 804(b)(2) in the bill) proposed to expand the traditional scope of the dying declaration exception (i.e. a statement of the victim in a homicide case as to the cause or circumstances of his believed imminent death) to allow such statements in all criminal and civil cases. The Committee did not consider dying declarations as among the most reliable forms of hearsay. Consequently, it amended the provision to limit their admissibility in criminal cases to homicide prosecutions, where exceptional need for the evidence is present. This is existing law. At the same time, the Committee approved the expansion to civil actions and proceedings where the stakes do not involve possible imprisonment, although noting that this could lead to forum shopping in some instances.

ADVISORY COMMITTEE'S NOTE

[Note, that the exception for statements against interest, described below as Exception (4), became Exception (5) in Rule 804(b) as enacted. The change in numbering was caused by the deletion of the exception for statements of recent perception. The against-interest exception was amended by Congress prior to enactment.]

Exception (4). The circumstantial guaranty of reliability for declarations against interest is the assumption that persons do not make statements which are damaging to themselves unless satisfied for good reason that they are true. Hileman v. Northwest Engineering Co., 346 F.2d 668 (6th Cir. 1965). If the statement is that of a party, offered by his opponent, it comes in as an admission, Rule 803(d)(2), and there is no occasion to inquire whether it is against interest, this not being a condition precedent to admissibility of admissions by opponents.

The common law required that the interest declared against be pecuniary or proprietary but within this limitation demonstrated striking ingenuity in discovering an against-interest aspect. Higham v. Ridgway, 10 East 109, 103 Eng.Rep. 717 (K.B.1808); Reg. v. Overseers of Birmingham, 1 B. & S. 763, 121 Eng.Rep. 897 (Q.B.1861); McCormick, § 256, p. 551, nn. 2 and 3.

The exception discards the common law limitation and expands to the full logical limit. One result is to remove doubt as to the admissibility of declarations tending to establish a tort liability against the declarant or to extinguish one which might be asserted by him, in accordance with the trend of the decisions in this country. McCormick § 254, pp. 548-549. Another is to allow statements tending to expose declarant to hatred, ridicule, or disgrace, the motivation here being considered to be as strong as when financial interests are at stake. McCormick § 255, p. 551. And finally, exposure to criminal liability satisfies the against-interest requirement. The refusal of the common law to concede the adequacy of a penal interest was no doubt indefensible in logic, see the dissent of Mr. Justice Holmes in Donnelly v. United States, 228 U.S. 243, 33 S.Ct. 449, 57 L.Ed. 820 (1913), but one senses in the decisions a distrust of evidence of confessions by third persons offered to exculpate the accused arising from suspicions of fabrication either of the fact of the making of the confession or in its contents, enhanced in either instance by the required unavailability of the declarant. Nevertheless, an increasing amount of decisional law recognizes exposure to punishment for crime as a sufficient stake. People v. Spriggs, 60 Cal.2d 868, 36 Cal.Rptr. 841, 389 P.2d 377 (1964); Sutter v. Easterly, 354 Mo. 282, 189 S.W.2d 284 (1945); Band's Refuse Removal, Inc. v. Fairlawn Borough, 62 N.J.Super. 522, 163 A.2d 465 (1960); Newberry v. Commonwealth, 191 Va. 445, 61 S.E.2d 318 (1950); Annot., 162 A.L.R. 446. The requirement of corroboration is included in the rule in order to effect an accommodation between these competing considerations. When the statement is offered by the accused by way of exculpation, the resulting situation is not adapted to control by rulings as to the weight of the evidence, and hence the provision is cast in terms of a requirement preliminary to admissibility. Cf. Rule 406(a). The requirement of corroboration should be construed in such a manner as to effectuate its purpose of circumventing fabrication.

Ordinarily the third-party confession is thought of in terms of exculpating the accused, but this is by no means always or necessarily the case: it may include statements implicating him, and under the general theory of declarations against interest they would be admissible as related statements. Douglas v. Alabama, 380 U.S. 415, 85 S.Ct. 1074, 13 L.Ed.2d 934 (1965), and Bruton v. United States, 389 U.S. 818, 88 S.Ct. 126, 19 L.Ed.2d 70 (1968), both involved confessions by codefendants which implicated the accused. While the confession was not actually offered in evidence in *Douglas*, the procedure followed effectively put it before the jury, which the Court ruled to be error. Whether the confession might have been admissible as a declaration against penal interest was not considered or discussed. *Bruton* assumed the inadmissibility, as against the accused, of the implicating confession of his codefendant, and centered upon the question of the effectiveness of a limiting instruction. These decisions, however, by no means require that all statements implicating another person be excluded from the category of declarations against interest. Whether a statement is in fact against interest must be determined from the circumstances of each case. Thus a statement admitting guilt and implicating another person, made while in custody, may well be motivated by a desire to curry favor with the authorities and hence fail to qualify as against interest. See the dissenting opinion of Mr. Justice White in *Bruton*. On the other hand, the same words spoken under different circumstances, *e.g.*, to an acquaintance, would have no difficulty in qualifying. The rule does not purport to deal with questions of the right of confrontation.

The balancing of self-serving against dissenting aspects of a declaration is discussed in McCormick § 256.

For comparable provisions, see Uniform Rule 63(10); California Evidence Code § 1230; Kansas Code of Civil Procedure § 60-460(j); New Jersey Evidence Rule 63(10).

Report of the House Committee on the Judiciary

[Note, that the exception described below for statements against interest was indeed to be amended, but out of the amendments described in the note below, only the deletion of the reference to "hatred, ridicule, or disgrace" and the change requiring "clearly" corroborative circumstances for third party confessions exculpating the accused were to survive.]

Rule 804(b)(4) as submitted by the Court (now Rule 804(b)(3) in the bill) provided as follows:

> *Statement against interest.*—A statement which was at the time of its making so far contrary to the declarant's pecuniary or proprietary interest or so far tended to subject him to civil or criminal liability or to render invalid a claim by him against another or to make him an object of hatred, ridicule, or disgrace, that a reasonable man in his position would not have made the statement unless he believed it to be true. A statement tending to exculpate the accused is not admissible unless corroborated.

The Committee determined to retain the traditional hearsay exception for statements against pecuniary or proprietary interest. However, it deemed the Court's additional references to statements tending to subject a declarant to civil liability or to render invalid a claim by him against another to be redundant as included within the scope of the reference to statements against pecuniary or proprietary interest. See *Gichner v. Antonio Triano Tile and Marble Co.*, 410 F.2d 238 (D.C. Cir. 1968). Those additional references were accordingly deleted.

The Court's Rule also proposed to expand the hearsay limitation from its present federal limitation to include statements subjecting the declarant to criminal liability and statements tending to make him an object of hatred, ridicule, or disgrace. The Committee eliminated the latter category from the subdivision as lacking sufficient guarantees of reliability. See *United States v. Dovico*, 380 F.2d 325, 327 nn.2,4 (2d Cir.), cert. denied, 389 U.S. 944 (1967). As for statements against penal interest, the Committee shared the view of the Court that some such statements do possess adequate assurances of reliability and should be admissible. It believed, however, as did the Court, that statements of this type tending to exculpate the accused are more suspect and so should have their admissibility conditioned upon some further provision insuring trustworthiness. The proposal in the Court Rule to add a requirement of simple corrob[or]ation was, however, deemed ineffective to accomplish this purpose since the accused's own testimony might suffice while not necessarily increasing the reliability of the hearsay statement. The Committee settled upon the language "unless corroborating circumstances clearly indicate the trustworthiness of the statement" as affording a proper standard and degree of discretion. It was contemplated that the result in such cases as *Donnelly v. United States*, 228 U.S. 243 (1912), where the circumstances plainly indicated reliability, would be changed. The Committee also added to the Rule the final sentence from the 1971 Advisory Committee draft, designed to codify the doctrine of *Bruton v. United States*, 391 U.S. 123 (1968). The Committee does not intend to affect the existing exception to the *Bruton* principle where the codefendant takes the stand and is subject to cross-examination, but believed there was no need to make specific provision for this situation in the Rule, since in that event the declarant would not be "unavailable."

REPORT OF THE SENATE COMMITTEE ON THE JUDICIARY

[Note, that the exception described below for statements against interest was indeed amended by Congress. The Senate view on the reference to "civil liability," described in the third paragraph below, prevailed in the end. So did the Senate view on the sentence which would have put third party confessions implicating the accused beyond reach of the exception.]

The rule defines those statements which are considered to be against interest and thus of sufficient trustworthiness to be admissible even though hearsay. With regard to the type of interest declared against, the version submitted by the Supreme Court included inter alia, statements tending to subject a declarant to civil liability or to invalidate a claim by him against another. The House struck these provisions as redundant. In view of the conflicting case law construing pecuniary or proprietary interests narrowly so as to exclude, e.g., tort cases, this deletion could be misconstrued.

Three States which have recently codified their rules of evidence have followed the Supreme Court's version of this rule, i.e., that a statement is against interest if it tends to subject a declarant to civil liability.[17]

The committee believes that the reference to statements tending to subject a person to civil liability constitutes a desirable clarification of the scope of the rule. Therefore, we have reinstated the Supreme Court language on this matter.

The Court rule also proposed to expand the hearsay limitation from its present federal limitation to include statements subjecting the declarant to statements tending to make him an object of hatred, ridicule, or disgrace. The House eliminated the latter category from the subdivision as lacking sufficient guarantees of reliability. Although there is considerable support for the admissibility of such statements (all three of the State rules referred to supra, would admit such statements), we accept the deletion by the House.

The House amended this exception to add a sentence making inadmissible a statement or confession offered against the accused in a criminal case, made by a codefendant or other person implicating both himself and the accused. The sentence was added to codify the constitutional principle announced in *Bruton v. United States*, 391 U.S. 123 (1968). *Bruton* held that the admission of the extrajudicial hearsay statement of one codefendant inculpating a second codefendant violated the confrontation clause of the Sixth Amendment.

The committee decided to delete this provision because the basic approach of the rules is to avoid codifying, or attempting to codify, constitutional evidentiary principles, such as the fifth amendment's right against self-incrimination and, here, the sixth amendment's right of confrontation. Codification of a constitutional principle is unnecessary and, where the principle is under development, often unwise. Furthermore, the House provision does not appear to recognize the exceptions to the *Bruton* rule, e.g. where the codefendant takes the stand and is subject to cross-examination; where the accused confessed, see *United States v. Mancusi*, 404 F.2d 296 (2d Cir. 1968), cert. denied 397 U.S. 942 (1907); where the accused was placed at the scene of the crime, see *United States v. Zelker*, 452 F.2d 1009 (2d Cir. 1971). For these reasons, the committee decided to delete this provision.

REPORT OF THE HOUSE/SENATE CONFERENCE COMMITTEE

[Note, that the compromise described below with respect to the exception for statements against interest prevailed.]

The Senate amendment to subsection (b)(3) provides that a statement is against interest and not excluded by the hearsay rule when the declarant is unavailable as a witness, if the statement tends to subject a person to civil or criminal liability or renders invalid a claim by him against another. The House bill did not refer specifically to civil liability and to rendering invalid a claim against another. The Senate amendment also deletes from the House bill the provision that subsection (b)(3) does not apply to a statement or confession, made by a codefendant or

---

17. Nev. Rev. Stats. § 51.345; N. Mex. Stats. (1973 Supp.) § 20-4-804(4); West's Wis. Stats. Anno. (1973 Supp.) § 908-045(4).

another, which implicates the accused and the person who made the statement, when that statement or confession is offered against the accused in a criminal case.

The Conference adopts the Senate amendment. The Conferees intend to include within the purview of this rule, statements subjecting a person to civil liability and statements rendering claims invalid. The Conferees agree to delete the provision regarding statements by a codefendant, thereby reflecting the general approach in the Rules of Evidence to avoid attempting to codify constitutional evidentiary principles.

ADVISORY COMMITTEE'S NOTE

[Note, that the exception described below for statements of personal or family history survived in the form discussed here. It is referred to as Exception (5), but because of the deletion of the exception for statements of recent perception, the exception for statements of personal or family history ultimately became Exception (4) to Rule 804(b).]

Exception (5). The general common law requirement that a declaration in this area must have been made *ante litem motam* has been dropped, as bearing more appropriately on weight than admissibility. See 5 Wigmore § 1483. Item (i) specifically disclaims any need of firsthand knowledge respecting declarant's own personal history. In some instances it is self-evident (marriage) and in others impossible and traditionally not required (date of birth). Item (ii) deals with declarations concerning the history of another person. As at common law, declarant is qualified if related by blood or marriage. 5 Wigmore § 1489. In addition, and contrary to the common law, declarant qualifies by virtue of intimate association with the family. *Id.,* § 1487. The requirement sometimes encountered that when the subject of the statement is the relationship between two other persons the declarant must qualify as to both is omitted. Relationship is reciprocal. *Id.,* § 1491.

For comparable provisions, see Uniform Rule 63(23), (24), (25); California Evidence Code §§ 1310, 1311; Kansas Code of Civil Procedure § 60-460(u), (v), (w); New Jersey Evidence Rules 63(23), 63(24), 63(25).

REPORT OF THE HOUSE/SENATE CONFERENCE COMMITTEE

[Note, that the Senate-proposed Rule 804(b)(5) would have created an exception for records and reports by law enforcement personnel. The Senate Committee's view on this exception is stated in its Report on Rule 803(8), which creates an exception for public records. The Conference Committee Report set forth immediately below recommending against adoption of this exception was to prevail, and no such exception is in Rule 804(b).]

Rule 804(b)(5)—Criminal Law Enforcement Records and Reports

The Senate amendment adds a new hearsay exception, not contained in the House bill, which provides that certain law enforcement records are admissible if the officer-declarant is unavailable to testify or be present because of (1) death or physical or mental illness or infirmity or (2) absence from the proceeding and the proponent of the statement has been unable to procure his attendance by process or other reasonable means.

The Conference does not adopt the Senate amendment, preferring instead to leave the bill in the House version, which contained no such provision.

ADVISORY COMMITTEE'S NOTE

[Note, that the catchall exception described below as Exception (6) was renumbered as Exception (5) of Rule 804(b) because of the deletion of the exception for statements of recent perception. The simple provision noted below was amended by Congress.]

REPORT OF THE HOUSE COMMITTEE ON THE JUDICIARY

[The discussion of Rule 804(b)(5) by the Committee is included with its discussion of the identical catchall exception found in Rule 803(24).]

REPORT OF THE SENATE COMMITTEE ON THE JUDICIARY

[The discussion of Rule 804(b)(5) by the committee is included with its discussion of the identical catchall exception found in Rule 803 (24).]

NOTE BY FEDERAL JUDICIAL CENTER

The rule prescribed by the Supreme Court was amended by the Congress in a number of respects as follows:

Subdivision (a). Paragraphs (1) and (2) were amended by substituting "court" in place of "judge," and paragraph (5) was amended by inserting "(or in the case of a hearsay exception under subdivision (b)(2), (3), or (4), his attendance or testimony)."

Subdivision (b). Exception (1) was amended by inserting "the same or" after "course of," and by substituting the phrase "if the party against whom the testimony is now offered, or, in a civil action or proceeding, a predecessor in interest, had an opportunity and similar motive to develop the testimony by direct, cross, or redirect examination" in place of "at the instance of or against a party with an opportunity to develop the testimony by direct, cross, or redirect examination, with motive and interest similar to those of the party against whom now offered."

Exception (2) as prescribed by the Supreme Court, dealing with statements of recent perception, was deleted by the Congress.

. . . Exception (2) as enacted by the Congress is Exception (3) prescribed by the Supreme Court, amended by inserting at the beginning, "In a prosecution for homicide or in a civil action or proceeding."

Exception (3) as enacted by the Congress is Exception (4) prescribed by the Supreme Court, amended in the first sentence by deleting, after "another," the phrase "or to make him an object of hatred, ridicule, or disgrace," and amended in the second sentence by substituting, after "unless," the phrase, "corroborating circumstances clearly indicate the trustworthiness of the statement," in place of "corroborated."

Exception (4) as enacted by the Congress is Exception (5) prescribed by the Supreme Court without change.

Exception (5) as enacted by the Congress is Exception (6) prescribed by the Supreme Court, amended by substituting "equivalent" in place of "comparable" and by adding all after "trustworthiness."

Rule 805   Hearsay Within Hearsay

Advisory Committee's Note

On principle it scarcely seems open to doubt that the hearsay rule should not call for exclusion of a hearsay statement which includes a further hearsay statement when both conform to the requirements of a hearsay exception. Thus a hospital record might contain an entry of the patient's age based on information furnished by his wife. The hospital record would qualify as a regular entry except that the person who furnished the information was not acting in the routine of the business. However, her statement independently qualifies as a statement of pedigree (if she is unavailable) or as a statement made for purposes of diagnosis or treatment, and hence each link in the chain falls under sufficient assurances. Or, further to illustrate, a dying declaration may incorporate a declaration against interest by another declarant. See McCormick § 290, p. 611.

Note by Federal Judicial Center

The Rule enacted by Congress is the Rule prescribed by the Supreme Court without change.

Rule 806   Attacking and Supporting Credibility of Declarant

Advisory Committee's Note

The declarant of a hearsay statement which is admitted in evidence is in effect a witness. His credibility should in fairness be subject to impeachment and support as though he had in fact testified. See Rules 608 and 609. There are, however, some special aspects of the impeaching of a hearsay declarant which require consideration. These special aspects center upon impeachment by inconsistent statement, arise from factual differences which exist between the use of hearsay and an actual witness and also between various kinds of hearsay, and involve the question of applying to declarants the general rule disallowing evidence of an inconsistent statement to impeach a witness unless he is afforded an opportunity to deny or explain. See Rule 613(b).

The principal difference between using hearsay and an actual witness is that the inconsistent statement will in the case of the witness almost inevitably of necessity in the nature of things be a *prior* statement, which it is entirely possible and feasible to call to his attention, while in the case of hearsay the inconsistent statement may well be a *subsequent* one, which practically precludes calling it to the attention of the declarant. The result of insisting upon observation of this impossible requirement in the hearsay situation is to deny the opponent, already barred from cross-examination, any benefit of this important technique of impeachment. The writers favor allowing the subsequent statement. McCormick, § 37, p. 69; 3 Wigmore § 1033. The cases, however, are divided. Cases allowing the impeachment include People v. Collup, 27 Cal.2d 829, 167 P.2d 714 (1946); People v. Rosoto, 58 Cal.2d 304, 23 Cal.Rptr. 779, 373 P.2d 867 (1962); Carver v. United States, 164 U.S. 694, 17 S.Ct. 228, 41 L.Ed. 602 (1897). Contra, Mattox v. United States, 156 U.S. 237, 15 S.Ct. 337, 39 L.Ed. 409 (1895); People v. Hines, 284 N.Y.

93, 29 N.E.2d 483 (1940). The force of *Mattox*, where the hearsay was the former testimony of a deceased witness and the denial of use of a subsequent inconsistent statement was upheld, is much diminished by *Carver*, where the hearsay was a dying declaration and denial of use of a subsequent inconsistent statement resulted in reversal. The difference in the particular brand of hearsay seems unimportant when the inconsistent statement is a *subsequent* one. True, the opponent is not totally deprived of cross-examination when the hearsay is former testimony or a deposition but he is deprived of cross-examining on the statement or along lines suggested by it. Mr. Justice Shiras, with two justices joining him, dissented vigorously in *Mattox*.

When the impeaching statement was made *prior* to the hearsay statement, differences in the kinds of hearsay appear which arguably may justify differences in treatment. If the hearsay consisted of a simple statement by the witness, e.g. a dying declaration or a declaration against interest, the feasibility of affording him an opportunity to deny or explain encounters the same practical impossibility as where the statement is a subsequent one, just discussed, although here the impossibility arises from the total absence of anything resembling a hearing at which the matter could be put to him. The courts by a large majority have ruled in favor of allowing the statement to be used under these circumstances. McCormick § 37, p. 69; 3 Wigmore § 1033. If, however, the hearsay consists of former testimony or a deposition, the possibility of calling the prior statement to the attention of the witness or deponent is not ruled out, since the opportunity to cross-examine was available. It might thus be concluded that with former testimony or depositions the conventional foundation should be insisted upon. Most of the cases involve depositions, and Wigmore describes them as divided. 3 Wigmore § 1031. Deposition procedures at best are cumbersome and expensive, and to require the laying of the foundation may impose an undue burden. Under the federal practice, there is no way of knowing with certainty at the time of taking a deposition whether it is merely for discovery or will ultimately end up in evidence. With respect to both former testimony and depositions the possibility exists that knowledge of the statement might not be acquired until after the time of the cross-examination. Moreover, the expanded admissibility of former testimony and depositions under Rule 804(b)(1) calls for a correspondingly expanded approach to impeachment. The rule dispenses with the requirement in all hearsay situations, which is readily administered and best calculated to lead to fair results.

Notice should be taken that Rule 26(f) of the Federal Rules of Civil Procedure, as originally submitted by the Advisory Committee, ended with the following:

". . . and, without having first called them to the deponent's attention, may show statements contradictory thereto made at any time by the deponent."

This language did not appear in the rule as promulgated in December, 1937. See 4 Moore's Federal Practice ¶¶ 26.01[9], 26.35 (2d ed. 1967). In 1951, Nebraska adopted a provision strongly resembling the one stricken from the federal rule:

"Any party may impeach any adverse deponent by self-contradiction without having laid foundation for such impeachment at the time such deposition was taken." R.S.Neb. § 25-1267.07.

For similar provisions, see Uniform Rule 65; California Evidence Code § 1202; Kansas Code of Civil Procedure § 60-462; New Jersey Evidence Rule 65.

The provision for cross-examination of a declarant upon his hearsay statement is a corollary of general principles of cross-examination. A similar provision is found in California Evidence Code § 1203.

Report of the Senate Committee on the Judiciary

Rule 906 [806], as passed by the House and as proposed by the Supreme Court provides that whenever a hearsay statement is admitted, the credibility of the declarant of the statement may be attacked, and if attacked may be supported, by any evidence which would be admissible for those purposes if the declarant had testified as a witness. Rule 801 defines what is a hearsay statement. While statements by a person authorized by a party-opponent to make a statement concerning the subject, by the party-opponent's agent or by a coconspirator of a party—see rule 801(d)(2)(c), (d) and (e)—are traditionally defined as exceptions to the hearsay rule, rule 801 defines such admission by a party-opponent as statements which are not hearsay. Consequently, rule 806 by referring exclusively to the admission of hearsay statements, does not appear to allow the credibility of the declarant to be attacked when the declarant is a coconspirator, agent or authorized spokesman. The committee is of the view that such statements should open the declarant to attacks on his credibility. Indeed, the reason such statements are excluded from the operation of rule 806 is likely attributable to the drafting technique used to codify the hearsay rule, viz. some statements, instead of being referred to as exceptions to the hearsay rule, are defined as statements which are not hearsay. The phrase "or a statement defined in rule 801(d)(2)(c), (d) and (e)" is added to the rule in order to subject the declarant of such statements, like the declarant of hearsay statements, to attacks on his credibility.[18]

Report of the House/Senate Conference Committee

The Senate amendment permits an attack upon the credibility of the declarant of a statement if the statement is one by a person authorized by a party-opponent to make a statement concerning the subject, only by an agent of a party-opponent, or one by a coconspirator of the party-opponent, as these statements are defined in Rules 801(d)(2)(C), (D) and (E). The House bill has no such provision.

The Conference adopts the Senate amendment. The Senate amendment conforms the rule to present practice.

Note by Federal Judicial Center

The Rule enacted by Congress is the Rule prescribed by the Supreme Court, amended by inserting the phrase "or a statement defined in Rule 801(d)(2), (C), (D) or (E)."

---

18. The Committee considered it unnecessary to include statements contained in Rule 801(d)(2)(A) and (B)—the statement made by the party-opponent himself or the statement of which he has manifested his adoption—because the credibility of the party-opponent is always subject to an attack on his credibility.

ARTICLE IX
AUTHENTICATION AND IDENTIFICATION

Rule 901　　Requirement of Authentication or Identification

Advisory Committee's Note

Subdivision (a). Authentication and identification represent a special aspect of relevancy. Michael and Adler, Real Proof, 5 Vand.L. Rev. 344, 362 (1952); McCormick §§ 179, 185; Morgan, Basic Problems of Evidence 378 (1962). Thus a telephone conversation may be irrelevant because on an unrelated topic or because the speaker is not identified. The latter aspect is the one here involved. Wigmore describes the need for authentication as "an inherent logical necessity." 7 Wigmore § 2129, p. 564.

This requirement of showing authenticity or identity falls in the category of relevancy dependent upon fulfillment of a condition of fact and is governed by the procedure set forth in Rule 104(b).

The common law approach to authentication of documents has been criticized as an "attitude of agnosticism," McCormick, Cases on Evidence 388, n. 4 (3rd ed. 1956), as one which "departs sharply from men's customs in ordinary affairs," and as presenting only a slight obstacle to the introduction of forgeries in comparison to the time and expense devoted to proving genuine writings which correctly show their origin on their face, McCormick § 185, pp. 395, 396. Today, such available procedures as requests to admit and pretrial conference afford the means of eliminating much of the need for authentication or identification. Also, significant inroads upon the traditional insistence on authentication and identification have been made by accepting as at least prima facie genuine items of the kind treated in Rule 902, *infra*. However, the need for suitable methods of proof still remains, since criminal cases pose their own obstacles to the use of preliminary procedures, unforeseen contingencies may arise, and cases of genuine controversy will still occur.

Subdivision (b). The treatment of authentication and identification draws largely upon the experience embodied in the common law and in statutes to furnish illustrative applications of the general principle set forth in subdivision (a). The examples are not intended as an exclusive enumeration of allowable methods but are meant to guide and suggest, leaving room for growth and development in this area of the law.

The examples relate for the most part to documents, with some attention given to voice communications and computer print-outs. As Wigmore noted, no special rules have been developed for authenticating chattels. Wigmore, Code of Evidence § 2086 (3rd ed. 1942).

It should be observed that compliance with requirements of authentication or identification by no means assures admission of an item into evidence, as other bars, hearsay for example, may remain.

Example (1). contemplates a broad spectrum ranging from testimony of a witness who was present at the signing of a document to testimony establishing narcotics as taken from an accused and accounting for custody through the period until trial, including laboratory analysis. See California Evidence Code § 1413, eyewitness to signing.

Example (2). states conventional doctrine as to lay identification of handwriting, which recognizes that a sufficient familiarity with the handwriting of another person may be acquired by seeing him write, by exchanging correspondence, or by other means, to afford a basis for identifying it on subsequent occasions. McCormick § 189. See also California Evidence Code § 1416. Testimony based upon familiarity acquired for purposes of the litigation is reserved to the expert under the example which follows.

Example (3). The history of common law restrictions upon the technique of proving or disproving the genuineness of a disputed specimen of handwriting through comparison with a genuine specimen, by either the testimony of expert witnesses or direct viewing by the triers themselves, is detailed in 7 Wigmore §§ 1991-1994. In breaking away, the English Common Law Procedure Act of 1854, 17 and 18 Vict., c. 125, § 27, cautiously allowed expert or trier to use exemplars "proved to the satisfaction of the judge to be genuine" for purposes of comparison. The language found its way into numerous statutes in this country, e.g., California Evidence Code §§ 1417, 1418. While explainable as a measure of prudence in the process of breaking with precedent in the handwriting situation, the reservation to the judge of the question of the genuineness of exemplars and the imposition of an unusually high standard of persuasion are at variance with the general treatment of relevancy which depends upon fulfillment of a condition of fact. Rule 104(b). No similar attitude is found in other comparison situations, e.g., ballistics comparison by jury, as in Evans v. Commonwealth, 230 Ky. 411, 19 S.W.2d 1091 (1929), or by experts, Annot., 26 A.L.R.2d 892, and no reason appears for its continued existence in handwriting cases. Consequently Example (3) sets no higher standard for handwriting specimens and treats all comparison situations alike, to be governed by Rule 104(b). This approach is consistent with 28 U.S.C. § 1731: "The admitted or proved handwriting of any person shall be admissible, for purposes of comparison, to determine genuineness of other handwriting attributed to such person."

Precedent supports the acceptance of visual comparison as sufficiently satisfying preliminary authentication requirements for admission in evidence. Brandon v. Collins, 267 F.2d 731 (2d Cir. 1959); Wausau Sulphate Fibre Co. v. Commissioner of Internal Revenue, 61 F.2d 879 (7th Cir. 1932); Desimone v. United States, 227 F.2d 864 (9th Cir. 1955).

Example (4). The characteristics of the offered item itself, considered in the light of circumstances, afford authentication techniques in great variety. Thus a document or telephone conversation may be shown to have emanated from a particular person by virtue of its disclosing knowledge of facts known peculiarly to him; Globe Automatic Sprinkler Co. v. Braniff, 89 Okl. 105, 214 P. 127 (1923); California Evidence Code § 1421; similarly, a letter may be authenticated by content and circumstances indicating it was in reply to a duly authenticated one. McCormick § 192; California Evidence Code § 1420. Language patterns may indicate authenticity or its opposite. Magnuson v. State, 187 Wis. 122, 203 N.W. 749 (1925); Arens and Meadow, Psycholinguistics and the Confession Dilemma, 56 Colum.L.Rev. 19 (1956).

Example (5). Since aural voice identification is not a subject of expert testimony, the requisite familiarity may be acquired either before or after the particular speaking which is the subject of the identification, in this respect resembling visual identification of a person rather than identification of handwriting. Cf. Example (2), *supra,* People v. Nichols, 378 Ill. 487, 38 N.E.2d 766 (1942); McGuire v. State, 200 Md. 601, 92 A.2d 582 (1952); State v. McGee, 336 Mo. 1082, 83 S.E.2d 98 (1935).

Example (6). The cases are in agreement that a mere assertion of his identity by a person talking on the telephone is not sufficient evidence of the authenticity of the conversation and that additional evidence of his identity is required. The additional evidence need not fall in any set pattern. Thus the content of his statements or the reply technique, under Example (4), *supra,* or voice identification under Example (5), may furnish the necessary foundation. Outgoing calls made by the witness involve additional factors bearing upon authenticity. The calling of a number assigned by the telephone company reasonably supports the assumption that the listing is correct and that the number is the one reached. If the number is that of a place of business, the mass of authority allows an ensuing conversation if it relates to business reasonably transacted over the telephone, on the theory that the maintenance of the telephone connection is an invitation to do business without further identification. Matton v. Hoover Co., 350 Mo. 506, 166 S.W.2d 557 (1942); City of Pawhuska v. Crutchfield, 147 Okl. 4, 293 P. 1095 (1930); Zurich General Acc. & Liability Ins. Co. v. Baum, 159 Va. 404, 165 S.E. 518 (1932). Otherwise, some additional circumstance of identification of the speaker is required. The authorities divide on the question whether the self-identifying statement of the person answering suffices. Example (6) answers in the affirmative on the assumption that usual conduct respecting telephone calls furnish adequate assurances of regularity, bearing in mind that the entire matter is open to exploration before the trier of fact. In general, see McCormick § 193; 7 Wigmore § 2155; Annot., 71 A.L.R. 5, 105 id. 326.

Example (7). Public records are regularly authenticated by proof of custody, without more. McCormick § 191; 7 Wigmore §§ 2158, 2159. The example extends the principle to include data stored in computers and similar methods, of which increasing use in the public records area may be expected. See California Evidence Code §§ 1532, 1600.

Example (8). The familiar ancient document rule of the common law is extended to include data stored electronically or by other similar means. Since the importance of appearance diminishes in this situation, the importance of custody or place where found increases correspondingly. This expansion is necessary in view of the widespread use of methods of storing data in forms other than conventional written records.

Any time period selected is bound to be arbitrary. The common law period of 30 years is here reduced to 20 years, with some shift of emphasis from the probable unavailability of witnesses to the unlikeliness of a still viable fraud after the lapse of time. The shorter period is specified in the English Evidence Act of 1938, 1 & 2 Geo. 6, c. 28, and in Oregon R.S.1963, § 41.360(34). See also the numerous statutes prescribing periods of less than 30 years in the case of recorded documents. 7 Wigmore § 2143.

The application of Example (8) is not subject to any limitation to title documents or to any requirement that possession, in the case of a title document, has been consistent with the document. See McCormick § 190.

Example (9). is designed for situations in which the accuracy of a result is dependent upon a process or system which produces it. X rays afford a familiar instance. Among more recent developments is the computer, as to which see Transport Indemnity Co. v. Seib, 178 Neb. 253, 132 N.W.2d 871 (1965); States v. Veres, 7 Ariz.App. 117, 436 P.2d 629 (1968); Merrick v. United States Rubber Co., 7 Ariz.App. 433, 440 P.2d 314 (1968); Freed, Computer Print-Outs as Evidence, 16 Am.Jur. Proof of Facts 273; Symposium, Law and Computers in the Mid-Sixties, ALI-ABA (1966); 37 Albany L.Rev 61 (1967). Example (9) does not, of course, foreclose taking judicial notice of the accuracy of the process or system.

Example (10). The example makes clear that methods of authentication provided by Act of Congress and by the Rules of Civil and Criminal Procedure or by Bankruptcy Rules are not intended to be superseded. Illustrative are the provisions for authentication of official records in Civil Procedure Rule 44 and Criminal Procedure Rule 27, for authentication of records of proceedings by court reporters in 28 U.S.C. § 753(b) and Civil Procedure Rule 80(c), and for authentication of depositions in Civil Procedure Rule 30(f).

NOTE BY FEDERAL JUDICIAL CENTER

The Rule enacted by Congress is the Rule prescribed by the Supreme Court, amended in subdivision (b)(10) by substituting "prescribed" in place of "adopted," and by adding "pursuant to statutory authority."

Rule 902 Self Authentication

ADVISORY COMMITTEE'S NOTE

Case law and statutes have, over the years, developed a substantial body of instances in which authenticity is taken as sufficiently established for purposes of admissibility without extrinsic evidence to that effect, sometimes for reasons of policy but perhaps more often because practical considerations reduce the possibility of unauthenticity to a very small dimension. The present rule collects and incorporates these situations, in some instances expanding them to occupy a larger area which their underlying considerations justify. In no instance is the opposite party foreclosed from disputing authenticity.

Paragraph (1). The acceptance of documents bearing a public seal and signature, most often encountered in practice in the form of acknowledgments or certificates authenticating copies of public records, is actually of broad application. Whether theoretically based in whole or in part upon judicial notice, the practical underlying considerations are that forgery is a crime and detection is fairly easy and certain. 7 Wigmore § 2161, p. 638; California Evidence Code § 1452. More than 50 provisions for judicial notice of official seals are contained in the United States Code.

Paragraph (2). While statutes are found which raise a presumption of genuineness of purported official signatures in the absence of an official seal, 7 Wigmore § 2167; California Evidence Code § 1453, the greater ease of effecting a forgery under these circumstances is apparent. Hence this paragraph of the rule calls for authentication by an officer who has a seal. Notarial acts by members of the armed forces and other special situations are covered in paragraph (10).

Paragraph (3). provides a method for extending the presumption of authenticity to foreign official documents by a procedure of certification. It is derived from Rule 44(a)(2) of the Rules of Civil Procedure but is broader in applying to public documents rather than being limited to public records.

Paragraph (4). The common law and innumerable statutes have recognized the procedure of authenticating copies of public records by certificate. The certificate qualifies as a public document, receivable as authentic when in conformity with paragraph (1), (2), or (3). Rule 44(a) of the Rules of Civil Procedure and Rule 27 of the Rules of Criminal Procedure have provided authentication procedures of this nature for both domestic and foreign public records. It will be observed that the certification procedure here provided extends only to public records, reports, and recorded documents, all including data compilations, and does not apply to public documents generally. Hence documents provable when presented in original form under paragraphs (1), (2), or (3) may not be provable by certified copy under paragraph (4).

Paragraph (5). Dispensing with preliminary proof of the genuineness of purportedly official publications, most commonly encountered in connection with statutes, court reports, rules, and regulations, has been greatly enlarged by statutes and decisions. 5 Wigmore § 1684. Paragraph (5), it will be noted, does not confer admissibility upon all official publications; it merely provides a means whereby their authenticity may be taken as established for purposes of admissibility. Rule 44(a) of the Rules of Civil Procedure has been to the same effect.

Paragraph (6). The likelihood of forgery of newspapers or periodicals is slight indeed. Hence no danger is apparent in receiving them. Establishing the authenticity of the publication may, of course, leave still open questions of authority and responsibility for items therein contained. See 7 Wigmore § 2150. Cf. 39 U.S.C. § 4005(b), public advertisement prima facie evidence of agency of person named, in postal fraud order proceeding; Canadian Uniform Evidence Act, Draft of 1936, printed copy of newspaper prima facie evidence that notices or advertisements were authorized.

Paragraph (7). Several factors justify dispensing with preliminary proof of genuineness of commercial and mercantile labels and the like. The risk of forgery is minimal. Trademark infringement involves serious penalties. Great efforts are devoted to inducing the public to buy in reliance on brand names, and substantial protection is given them. Hence the fairness of this treatment finds recognition in the cases. Curtiss Candy Co. v. Johnson, 163 Miss. 426, 141 So. 762 (1932), Baby Ruth candy bar; Doyle v. Continental Baking Co., 262 Mass. 516, 160 N.E. 325 (1928), loaf of bread; Weiner v. Mager & Throne, Inc., 167 Misc. 338, 3 N.Y.S.2d 918 (1938), same. And see W.Va.Code 1966, § 47-3-5, trade-mark on bottle prima facie evidence of ownership. *Contra*, Keegan v. Green Giant Co., 150 Me. 283, 110 A.2d 599 (1954); Murphy v. Campbell Soup Co., 62 F.2d 564 (1st Cir. 1933). Cattle brands have received similar acceptance in the western states. Rev.Code Mont.1947, § 46-606; State v. Wolfley, 75 Kan. 406, 89 P. 1046 (1907); Annot., 11 L.R.A.(N.S.) 87. Inscriptions on trains and vehicles are held to be prima facie evidence of ownership or control. Pittsburgh, Ft. W. & C. Ry. v. Callaghan, 157

Ill. 406, 41 N.E. 909 (1895); 9 Wigmore § 2510a. See also the provision of 19 U.S.C. § 1615(2) that marks, labels, brands, or stamps indicating foreign origin are prima facie evidence of foreign origin of merchandise.

Paragraph (8). In virtually every state, acknowledged title documents are receivable in evidence without further proof. Statutes are collected in 5 Wigmore § 1676. If this authentication suffices for documents of the importance of those affecting titles, logic scarcely permits denying this method when other kinds of documents are involved. Instances of broadly inclusive statutes are California Evidence Code § 1451 and N.Y.CPLR 4538, McKinney's Consol.Laws 1963.

Report of the House Committee on the Judiciary

Rule 902(8) as submitted by the Court referred to certificates of acknowledgment "under the hand and seal of" a notary public or other officer authorized by law to take acknowledgments. The Committee amended the Rule to eliminate the requirement, believed to be inconsistent with the law in some States, that a notary public must affix a seal to a document acknowledged before him. As amended the Rule merely requires that the document be executed in the manner prescribed by State law.

Advisory Committee's Note

Paragraph (9). Issues of the authenticity of commercial paper in federal courts will usually arise in diversity cases, will involve an element of a cause of action or defense, and with respect to presumptions and burden of proof will be controlled by Erie Railroad Co. v. Tompkins, 304 U.S. 64, 58 S.Ct. 817, 82 L.Ed. 1188 (1938). Rule 302, *supra*. There may, however, be questions of authenticity involving lesser segments of a case or the case may be one governed by federal common law. Clearfield Trust Co. v. United States, 318 U.S. 363, 63 S.Ct. 573, 87 L.Ed. 838 (1943). *Cf.* United States v. Yazell, 382 U.S. 341, 86 S.Ct. 500, 15 L.Ed.2d 404 (1966). In these situations, resort to the useful authentication provisions of the Uniform Commercial Code is provided for. While the phrasing is in terms of "general commercial law," in order to avoid the potential complications inherent in borrowing local statutes, today one would have difficulty in determining the general commercial law without referring to the Code. See Williams v. Walker-Thomas Furniture Co., 121 U.S.App.D.C. 315, 350 F.2d 445 (1965). Pertinent Code provisions are sections 1-202, 3-307, and 3-510, dealing with third-party documents, signatures on negotiable instruments, protests, and statements of dishonor.

Report of the House Committee on the Judiciary

The Committee approved Rule 902(9) as submitted by the Court. With respect to the meaning of the phrase "general commercial law," the Committee intends that the Uniform Commercial Code, which has been adopted in virtually every State, will be followed generally, but that federal commercial law will apply where federal commercial paper is involved. See *Clearfield Trust Co. v. United States*, 318 U.S. 363 (1943). Further, in those instances in which the issues are governed by *Erie R. Co. v. Tompkins*, 304 U.S. 64 (1938), State law will apply irrespective of whether it is the Uniform Commercial Code.

ADVISORY COMMITTEE'S NOTE

Paragraph (10). The paragraph continues in effect dispensations with preliminary proof of genuineness provided in various Acts of Congress. See, for example, 10 U.S.C. § 936, signature, without seal, together with title, prima facie evidence of authenticity of acts of certain military personnel who are given notarial powers; 15 U.S.C. § 77f(a), signature on SEC registration presumed genuine; 26 U.S.C. § 6064, signature to tax return prima facie genuine.

NOTE BY FEDERAL JUDICIAL CENTER

The Rule enacted by Congress is the Rule prescribed by the Supreme Court, amended as follows:

Paragraph (4) was amended by substituting "prescribed" in place of "adopted," and by adding "pursuant to statutory authority."

Paragraph (8) was amended by substituting "in the manner provided by law" in place of "under the hand and seal of."

Rule 903   Subscribing Witness' Testimony Unnecessary

ADVISORY COMMITTEE'S NOTE

The common law required that attesting witnesses be produced or accounted for. Today the requirement has generally been abolished except with respect to documents which must be attested to be valid, e.g. wills in some states. McCormick § 188. Uniform Rule 71; California Evidence Code § 1411; Kansas Code of Civil Procedure § 60-468; New Jersey Evidence Rule 71; New York CPLR Rule 4537.

NOTE BY FEDERAL JUDICIAL CENTER

The Rule enacted by Congress is the Rule prescribed by the Supreme Court without change.

ARTICLE X
CONTENTS OF WRITINGS,
RECORDINGS AND PHOTOGRAPHS

Rule 1001   Definitions

ADVISORY COMMITTEE'S NOTE

In an earlier day, when discovery and other related procedures were strictly limited, the misleading named "best evidence rule" afforded substantial guarantees against inaccuracies and fraud by its insistence upon production of original documents. The great enlargement of the scope of discovery and related procedures in recent times has measurably reduced the need for the rule. Nevertheless important areas of usefulness persist: discovery of documents outside the jurisdiction may require substantial outlay of time and money; the unanticipated document may not practically be discoverable; criminal cases have built-in limitations on discovery. Cleary and Strong, The Best Evidence Rule: An Evaluation in Context, 51 Iowa L.Rev. 825 (1966).

Paragraph (1). Traditionally the rule requiring the original centered upon accumulations of data and expressions affecting legal relations set forth in words and figures. This meant that the rule was one essentially related to writings. Present day techniques have expanded methods of storing data, yet the essential form which the information ultimately assumes for usable purposes is words and figures. Hence the considerations underlying the rule dictate its expansion to include computers, photographic systems, and other modern developments.

REPORT OF THE HOUSE COMMITTEE ON THE JUDICIARY

The Committee amended this Rule expressly to include "video tapes" in the definition of "photographs."

ADVISORY COMMITTEE'S NOTE

Paragraph (3). In most instances, what is an original will be self-evident and further refinement will be unnecessary. However, in some instances particularized definition is required. A carbon copy of a contract executed in duplicate becomes an original, as does a sales ticket carbon copy given to a customer. While strictly speaking the original of a photograph might be thought to be only the negative, practicality and common usage require that any print from the negative be regarded as an original. Similarly, practicality and usage confer the status of original upon any computer printout. Transport Indemnity Co. v. Seib, 178 Neb. 253, 132 N.W.2d 871 (1965).

Paragraph (4). The definition describes "copies" produced by methods possessing an accuracy which virtually eliminates the possibility of error. Copies thus produced are given the status of originals in large measure by Rule 1003, *infra*. Copies subsequently produced manually, whether handwritten or typed, are not within the definition. It should be noted that what is an original for some purposes may be a duplicate for others. Thus a bank's microfilm record of checks cleared is the original as a record. However, a print offered as a copy of a check whose contents are in controversy is a duplicate. This result is substantially consistent with 28 U.S.C. § 1732(b). Compare 26 U.S.C. § 7513(c), giving full status as originals to photographic reproductions of tax returns and other documents, made by authority of the Secretary of the Treasury, and 44 U.S.C. § 399(a), giving original status to photographic copies in the National Archives.

Note by Federal Judicial Center

The Rule enacted by Congress is the Rule prescribed by the Supreme Court, amended by inserting "video tapes" in paragraph (2).

Rule 1002　Requirement of Original

Advisory Committee's Note

The rule is the familiar one requiring production of the original of a document to prove its contents, expanded to include writings, recordings, and photographs, as defined in Rule 1001(1) and (2), *supra*.

Application of the rule requires a resolution of the question whether contents are sought to be proved. Thus an event may be proved by nondocumentary evidence, even though a written record of it was made. If, however, the event is sought to be proved by the written record, the rule applies. For example, payment may be proved without producing the written receipt which was given. Earnings may be proved without producing books of account in which they are entered. McCormick § 198; 4 Wigmore § 1245. Nor does the rule apply to testimony that books or records have been examined and found not to contain any reference to a designated matter.

The assumption should not be made that the rule will come into operation on every occasion when use is made of a photograph in evidence. On the contrary, the rule will seldom apply to ordinary photographs. In most instances a party *wishes* to introduce the item and the question raised is the propriety of receiving it in evidence. Cases in which an offer is made of the testimony of a witness as to what he saw in a photograph or motion picture, without producing the same, are most unusual. The usual course is for a witness on the stand to identify the photograph or motion picture as a correct representation of events which he saw or of a scene with which he is familiar. In fact he adopts the picture as his testimony, or, in common parlance, uses the picture to illustrate his testimony. Under these circumstances, no effort is made to prove the contents of the picture, and the rule is inapplicable. Paradis, The Celluloid Witness, 37 U.Colo.L.Rev. 235, 249-251 (1965).

On occasion, however, situations arise in which contents are sought to be proved. Copyright, defamation, and invasion of privacy by photograph or motion picture falls in this category. Similarly as to situations in which the picture is offered as having independent probative value, e.g. automatic photograph of bank robber. See People v. Doggett, 83 Cal.App.2d 405, 188 P.2d 792 (1948), photograph of defendants engaged in indecent act; Mouser and Philbin, Photographic Evidence—Is There a Recognized Basis for Admissibility? 8 Hastings L.J. 310 (1957). The most commonly encountered of this latter group is of course, the X ray, with substantial authority calling for production of the original. Daniels v.

Iowa City, 191 Iowa 811, 183 N.W. 415 (1921); Callamare v. Third Acc. Transit Corp., 273 App.Div. 260, 77 N.Y.S.2d 91 (1948); Patrick & Tilman v. Matkin, 154 Okl. 232, 7 P.2d 414 (1932); Mendoza v. Rivera, 78 P.R.R. 569 (1955).

It should be noted, however, that Rule 703, *supra*, allows an expert to give an opinion based on matters not in evidence, and the present rule must be read as being limited accordingly in its application. Hospital records which may be admitted as business records under Rule 803(6) commonly contain reports interpreting X rays by the staff radiologist, who qualifies as an expert, and these reports need not be excluded from the records by the instant rule.

The reference to Acts of Congress is made in view of such statutory provisions as 26 U.S.C. § 7513, photographic reproductions of tax returns and documents, made by authority of the Secretary of the Treasury, treated as originals, and 44 U.S.C. § 399(a), photographic copies in National Archives treated as originals.

NOTE BY FEDERAL JUDICIAL CENTER

The Rule enacted by Congress is the Rule prescribed by the Supreme Court without change.

Rule 1003 Admissibility of Duplicates

ADVISORY COMMITTEE'S NOTE

When the only concern is with getting the words or other contents before the court with accuracy and precision, then a counterpart serves equally as well as the original, if the counterpart is the product of a method which insures accuracy and genuineness. By definition in Rule 1001(4), *supra*, a "duplicate" possesses this character.

Therefore, if no genuine issue exists as to authenticity and no other reason exists for requiring the original, a duplicate is admissible under the rule. This position finds support in the decisions, Myrick v. United States, 332 F.2d 279 (5th Cir. 1964), no error in admitting photostatic copies of checks instead of original microfilm in absence of suggestion to trial judge that photostats were incorrect; Johns v. United States, 323 F.2d 421 (5th Cir. 1963), not error to admit concededly accurate tape recording made from original wire recording; Sanget v. Johnston, 315 F.2d 816 (9th Cir. 1963), not error to admit copy of agreement when opponent had original and did not on appeal claim any discrepancy. Other reasons for requiring the original may be present when only a part of the original is reproduced and the remainder is needed for cross-examination or may disclose matters qualifying the part offered or otherwise useful to the opposing party. United States v. Alexander, 326 F.2d 736 (4th Cir. 1964). And see Toho Bussan Kaisha, Ltd. v. American President Lines, Ltd., 265 F.2d 418, 76 A.L.R.2d 1344 (2d Cir. 1959).

REPORT OF THE HOUSE COMMITTEE ON THE JUDICIARY

The Committee approved this Rule in the form submitted by the Court, with the expectation that the courts would be liberal in deciding that a "genuine question is raised as to the authenticity of the original."

NOTE BY FEDERAL JUDICIAL CENTER

The Rule enacted by Congress is the Rule prescribed by the Supreme Court without change.

Rule 1004   Admissibility of Other Evidence of Contents

ADVISORY COMMITTEE'S NOTE

Basically the rule requiring the production of the original as proof of contents has developed as a rule of preference: if failure to produce the original is satisfactorily explained, secondary evidence is admissible. The instant rule specifies the circumstances under which production of the original is excused.

The rule recognizes no "degrees" of secondary evidence. While strict logic might call for extending the principle of preference beyond simply preferring the original, the formulation of a hierarchy of preferences and a procedure for making it effective is believed to involve unwarranted complexities. Most, if not all, that would be accomplished by an extended scheme of preferences will, in any event, be achieved through the normal motivation of a party to present the most convincing evidence possible and the arguments and procedures available to his opponent if he does not. Compare McCormick § 207.

Paragraph (1). Loss or destruction of the original, unless due to bad faith of the proponent, is a satisfactory explanation of nonproduction. McCormick § 201.

REPORT OF THE HOUSE COMMITTEE ON THE JUDICIARY

The Committee approved Rule 1004(1) in the form submitted to Congress. However, the Committee intends that loss or destruction of an original by another person at the instigation of the proponent should be considered as tantamount to loss or destruction in bad faith by the proponent himself.

ADVISORY COMMITTEE'S NOTE

Paragraph (2). When the original is in the possession of a third person, inability to procure it from him by resort to process or other judicial procedure is a sufficient explanation of nonproduction. Judicial procedure includes subpoena duces tecum as an incident to the taking of a deposition in another jurisdiction. No further showing is required. See McCormick § 202.

Paragraph (3). A party who has an original in his control has no need for the protection of the rule if put on notice that proof of contents will be made. He can ward off secondary evidence by offering the original. The notice procedure here provided is not to be confused with orders to produce or other discovery procedures, as the purpose of the procedure under this rule is to afford the opposite party an opportunity to produce the original, not to compel him to do so. McCormick § 203.

Paragraph (4). While difficult to define with precision, situations arise in which no good purpose is served by production of the original. Examples are the newspaper in an action for the price of publishing defendant's advertisement, Foster-Holcomb Investment Co. v. Little Rock Publishing Co., 151 Ark. 449, 236 S.W. 597 (1922), and the streetcar transfer of plaintiff claiming status as a passenger, Chicago City Ry. Co. v. Carroll, 206 Ill. 318, 68 N.E. 1087 (1903). Numerous cases are collected in McCormick § 200, p. 412, n. 1.

NOTE BY FEDERAL JUDICIAL CENTER

The Rule enacted by Congress is the Rule prescribed by the Supreme Court without change.

Rule 1005   Public Records

ADVISORY COMMITTEE'S NOTE

Public records call for somewhat different treatment. Removing them from their usual place of keeping would be attended by serious inconvenience to the public and to the custodian. As a consequence judicial decisions and statutes commonly hold that no explanation need be given for failure to produce the original of a public record. McCormick § 204; 4 Wigmore §§ 1215-1228. This blanket dispensation from producing or accounting for the original would open the door to the introduction of every kind of secondary evidence of contents of public records were it not for the preference given certified or compared copies. Recognition of degrees of secondary evidence in this situation is an appropriate *quid pro quo* for not applying the requirement of producing the original.

The provisions of 28 U.S.C. § 1733(b) apply only to departments or agencies of the United States. The rule, however, applies to public records generally and is comparable in scope in this respect to Rule 44(a) of the Rules of Civil Procedure.

NOTE BY FEDERAL JUDICIAL CENTER

The Rule enacted by Congress is the Rule prescribed by the Supreme Court without change.

Rule 1006   Summaries

ADVISORY COMMITTEE'S NOTE

The admission of summaries of voluminous books, records, or documents offers the only practicable means of making their contents available to judge and jury. The rule recognizes this practice, with appropriate safeguards. 4 Wigmore § 1230.

NOTE BY FEDERAL JUDICIAL CENTER

The Rule enacted by Congress is the Rule prescribed by the Supreme Court without change.

Rule 1007   Testimony or Written Admission of Party

ADVISORY COMMITTEE'S NOTE

While the parent case, Slatterie v. Pooley, 6 M. & W. 664, 151 Eng. Rep. 579 (Exch. 1840), allows proof of contents by evidence of an oral admission by the party against whom offered, without accounting for nonproduction of the original, the risk of inaccuracy is substantial and the decision is at odds with the purpose of the rule giving preference to the original. See 4 Wigmore § 1255. The instant rule follows Professor McCormick's suggestion of limiting this use of admissions to those made in the course of giving testimony or in writing. McCormick § 208, p. 424. The limitation, of course, does not call for excluding evidence of an oral admission when nonproduction of the original has been accounted for and secondary evidence generally has become admissible. Rule 1004, *supra*.

A similar provision is contained in New Jersey Evidence Rule 70(1)(h).

NOTE BY FEDERAL JUDICIAL CENTER

The Rule enacted by Congress is the Rule prescribed by the Supreme Court without change.

Rule 1008   Functions of Court and Jury

ADVISORY COMMITTEE'S NOTE

Most preliminary questions of fact in connection with applying the rule preferring the original as evidence of contents are for the judge, under the general principles announced in Rule 1004, *supra*. Thus, the question whether the loss of the originals has been established, or of the fulfillment of other conditions specified in Rule 1004, *supra*, is for the judge. However, questions may arise which go beyond the mere administration of the rule preferring the original and into the merits of the controversy. For example, plaintiff offers secondary evidence of the contents of an alleged contract, after first introducing evidence of loss of the original, and defendant counters with evidence that no such contract was ever executed. If the judge decides that the contract was never executed and excludes the secondary evidence, the case is at an end without ever going to the jury on a central issue. Levin, Authentication and Content of Writings, 10 Rutgers L.Rev. 632, 644 (1956). The latter portion of the instant rule is designed to insure treatment of these situations as raising jury questions. The decision is not one for uncontrolled discretion of the jury but is subject to the control exercised generally by the judge over jury determinations. See Rule 104(b), *supra*.

For similar provisions, see Uniform Rule 70(2); Kansas Code of Civil Procedure § 60-467(b); New Jersey Evidence Rule 70(2), (3).

NOTE BY FEDERAL JUDICIAL CENTER

The Rule enacted by Congress is the Rule prescribed by the Supreme Court, amended by substituting "court" in place of "judge," and by adding at the end of the first sentence the phrase "in accordance with the provisions of Rule 104."

ARTICLE XI
MISCELLANEOUS RULES

Rule 1101   Applicability of Rules

ADVISORY COMMITTEE'S NOTE

Subdivision (a). The various enabling acts contain differences in phraseology in their descriptions of the courts over which the Supreme Court's power to make rules of practice and procedure extends. The act concerning civil actions, as amended in 1966, refers to "the district courts . . . of the United States in civil actions, including admiralty and maritime cases. . . ." 28 U.S.C. § 2072, Pub.L. 89-773, § 1, 80 Stat. 1323. The bankruptcy authorization is for rules of practice and procedure "under the Bankruptcy Act." 28 U.S.C. § 2075, Pub.L. 88-623, § 1, 78 Stat. 1001. The Bankruptcy Act in turn creates bankruptcy courts of "the United States district courts and the district courts of the Territories and possessions to which this title is or may hereafter be applicable." 11 U.S.C. §§ 1(10), 11(a). The provision as to criminal rules up to and including verdicts applies to "criminal cases and proceedings to punish for criminal contempt of court in the United States district courts, in the district courts for the districts of the Canal Zone and Virgin Islands, in the Supreme Court of Puerto Rico, and in proceedings before United States magistrates." 18 U.S.C. § 3771.

These various provisions do not in terms describe the same courts. In congressional usage the phrase "district courts of the United States," without further qualification, traditionally has included the district courts established by Congress in the states under Article III of the Constitution, which are "constitutional" courts, and has not included the territorial courts created under Article IV, Section 3, Clause 2, which are "legislative" courts. Hornbuckle v. Toombs, 85 U.S. 648, 21 L.Ed. 966 (1873). However, any doubt as to the inclusion of the District Court for the District of Columbia in the phrase is laid at rest by the provisions of the Judicial Code constituting the judicial districts, 28 U.S.C. § 81 et seq. creating district courts therein, *id.*, § 132, and specifically providing that the term "district court of the United States" means the courts so constituted. *Id.* § 451. The District of Columbia is included. *Id.* § 88. Moreover, when these provisions were enacted, reference to the District of Columbia was deleted from the original civil rules enabling act. 28 U.S.C. § 2072. Likewise Puerto Rico is made a district, with a district court, and included in the term. *Id.* § 119. The question is simply one of the extent of the authority conferred by Congress. With respect to civil rules it seems clearly to include the district courts in the states, the District Court for the District of Columbia, and the District Court for the District of Puerto Rico.

The bankruptcy coverage is broader. The bankruptcy courts include "the United States district courts," which includes those enumerated above. Bankruptcy courts also include "the district courts of the Territories and possessions to which this title is or may hereafter be applicable." 11 U.S.C. §§ 1(10), 11(a). These courts include the district courts of Guam and the Virgin Islands. 48 U.S.C. §§ 1424(b), 1615. Professor Moore points out that whether the District Court for the District of the Canal Zone is a court of bankruptcy "is not free from doubt in view of the fact that no other statute expressly or inferentially provides for the applicability of the Bankruptcy Act in the Zone." He further observes that while there seems to be little doubt that the Zone is a territory or possession within the meaning of the Bankruptcy Act, 11 U.S.C. § 1(10), it must be noted that the appendix to the Canal Zone Code of 1934 did not list the Act among the laws of the United States applicable to the Zone. 1 Moore's Collier on Bankruptcy ¶ 1.10, pp. 67, 72, n. 25 (14th ed. 1967). The Code of 1962 confers on the district court jurisdiction of:

"(4) actions and proceedings involving laws of the United States applicable to the Canal Zone; and

"(5) other matters and proceedings wherein jurisdiction is conferred by this Code or any other law." Canal Zone Code, 1962, Tit. 3, § 141.

Admiralty jurisdiction is expressly conferred. *Id.* § 142. General powers are conferred on the district court, "if the course of proceeding is not specifically prescribed by this Code, by the statute, or by applicable rule of the Supreme Court of the United States . . ." *Id.* § 279. Neither these provisions nor § 1(10) of the Bankruptcy Act ("district courts of the Territories and possessions to which this title is or may hereafter be applicable") furnishes a satisfactory answer as to the status of the District Court for the District of the Canal Zone as a court of bankruptcy. However, the fact is that this court exercises no bankruptcy jurisdiction in practice.

The criminal rules enabling act specifies United States district courts, district courts for the districts of the Canal Zone and the Virgin Islands, the Supreme Court of the Commonwealth of Puerto Rico, and proceedings before United States commissioners. Aside from the addition of commissioners, now magistrates, this scheme differs from the bankruptcy pattern in that it makes no mention of the District Court of Guam but by specific mention removes the Canal Zone from the doubtful list.

The further difference in including the Supreme Court of the Commonwealth of Puerto Rico seems not to be significant for present purposes, since the Supreme Court of the Commonwealth of Puerto Rico is an appellate court. The Rules of Criminal Procedure have not been made applicable to it, as being unneeded and inappropriate, Rule 54(a) of the Federal Rules of Criminal Procedure, and the same approach is indicated with respect to Rules of Evidence.

If one were to stop at this point and frame a rule governing the applicability of the proposed Rules of Evidence in terms of the authority conferred by the three enabling acts, an irregular pattern would emerge as follows:

Civil actions, including admiralty and maritime cases—district courts in the states, District of Columbia, and Puerto Rico.

Bankruptcy—same as civil actions, plus Guam and Virgin Islands.

Criminal cases—same as civil actions, plus Canal Zone and Virgin Islands (but not Guam).

This irregular pattern need not, however, be accepted. Originally the Advisory Committee on the Rules of Civil Procedure took the position that, although the phrase "district courts of the United States" did not include territorial courts, provisions in the organic laws of Puerto Rico and Hawaii would make the rules applicable to the district courts thereof, though this would not be so as to Alaska, the Virgin Islands, or the Canal Zone, whose organic acts contained no corresponding provisions. At the suggestion of the Court, however, the Advisory Committee struck from its notes a statement to the above effect. 2 Moore's Federal Practice ¶ 1.07 (2nd ed. 1967); 1 Barron and Holtzoff, Federal Practice and Procedure § 121 (Wright ed. 1960). Congress thereafter by various enactments provided that the rules and future amendments thereto should apply to the district courts of Hawaii, 53 Stat. 841 (1939), Puerto Rico, 54 Stat. 22 (1940), Alaska, 63 Stat. 445 (1949), Guam, 64 Stat. 384-390 (1950), and the Virgin Islands, 68 Stat. 497, 507 (1954). The original enabling act for rules of criminal procedure specifically mentioned the district courts of the Canal Zone and the Virgin Islands. The Commonwealth of Puerto Rico was blanketed in by creating its court a "district court of the United States" as previously described. Although Guam is not mentioned in either the enabling act or in the expanded definition of "district court of the United States," the Supreme Court in 1956 amended Rule 54(a) to state that the Rules of Criminal Procedure are applicable in Guam. The Court took this step following the enactment of legislation by Congress in 1950 that rules theretofore or thereafter promulgated by the Court in civil cases, admiralty, criminal cases and bankruptcy should apply to the District Court of Guam, 48 U.S.C. § 1424(b), and two Ninth Circuit decisions upholding the applicability of the Rules of Criminal Procedure to Guam. Pugh v. United States, 212 F.2d 761 (9th Cir. 1954); Hatchett v. Guam, 212 F.2d 767 (9th Cir. 1954); Orfield, The Scope of the Federal Rules of Criminal Procedure, 38 U. of Det.L.J. 173, 187 (1960).

From this history, the reasonable conclusion is that Congressional enactment of a provision that rules and future amendments shall apply in the courts of a territory or possession is the equivalent of mention in an enabling act and that a rule on scope and applicability may properly be drafted accordingly. Therefore the pattern set by Rule 54 of the Federal Rules of Criminal Procedure is here followed.

The substitution of magistrates in lieu of commissioners is made in pursuance of the Federal Magistrates Act, P.L. 90-578, approved October 17, 1968, 82 Stat. 1107.

Subdivision (b). is a combination of the language of the enabling acts, *supra*, with respect to the kinds of proceedings in which the making of rules is authorized. It is subject to the qualifications expressed in the subdivisions which follow.

Subdivision (c). singling out the rules of privilege for special treatment, is made necessary by the limited applicability of the remaining rules.

Subdivision (d). The rule is not intended as an expression as to when due process or other constitutional provisions may require an evidentiary hearing. Paragraph (1) restates, for convenience, the provisions of the second sentence of Rule 104(a), *supra*. See Advisory Committee's Note to that rule.

(2) While some states have statutory requirements that indictments be based on "legal evidence," and there is some case law to the effect that the rules of evidence apply to grand jury proceedings, 1 Wigmore § 4(5), the Supreme Court has not accepted this view. In Costello v. United States, 350 U.S. 359, 76 S.Ct. 406, 100 L.Ed. 397 (1965), the Court refused to allow an indictment to be attacked, for either constitutional or policy reasons, on the ground that only hearsay evidence was presented.

"It would run counter to the whole history of the grand jury institution, in which laymen conduct their inquiries unfettered by technical rules. Neither justice nor the concept of a fair trial requires such a change." *Id.* at 364. The rule as drafted does not deal with the evidence required to support an indictment.

(3) The rule exempts preliminary examinations in criminal cases. Authority as to the applicability of the rules of evidence to preliminary examinations has been meager and conflicting. Goldstein, The State and the Accused: Balance of Advantage in Criminal Procedure, 69 Yale L.J. 1149, 1168, n. 53 (1960); Comment, Preliminary Hearings on Indictable Offenses in Philadelphia, 106 U. of Pa.L.Rev. 589, 592-593 (1958). Hearsay testimony is, however, customarily received in such examinations. Thus in a Dyer Act case, for example, an affidavit may properly be used in a preliminary examination to prove ownership of the stolen vehicle, thus saving the victim of the crime the hardship of having to travel twice to a distant district for the sole purpose of testifying as to ownership. It is believed that the extent of the applicability of the Rules of Evidence to preliminary examinations should be appropriately dealt with by the Federal Rules of Criminal Procedure which regulate those proceedings.

Extradition and rendition proceedings are governed in detail by statute. 18 U.S.C. §§ 3181-3195. They are essentially administrative in character. Traditionally the rules of evidence have not applied. 1 Wigmore § 4(6). Extradition proceedings are accepted from the operation of the Rules of Criminal Procedure. Rule 54(b)(5) of Federal Rules of Criminal Procedure.

The rules of evidence have not been regarded as applicable to sentencing or probation proceedings, where great reliance is placed upon the presentence investigation and report. Rule 32(c) of the Federal Rules of Criminal Procedure requires a presentence investigation and report in every case unless the court otherwise directs. In Williams v. New York, 337 U.S. 241, 69 S.Ct. 1079, 93 L.Ed. 1337 (1949), in which the judge overruled a jury recommendation of life imprisonment and imposed a death sentence, the Court said that due process does not require confrontation or cross-examination in sentencing or passing on probation, and that the judge has broad discretion as to the sources and types of information relied upon. Compare the recommendation that the substance of all derogatory information be disclosed to the defendant, in A.B.A. Project on Minimum Standards for Criminal Justice, Sentencing Alternatives and Procedures § 4.4, Tentative Draft (1967, Sobeloff, Chm.). Williams was adhered to in Specht v. Patterson, 386 U.S. 605, 87 S.Ct. 1209, 18 L.Ed.2d 326 (1967), but not extended to a proceeding under the Colorado Sex Offenders Act, which was said to be a new charge leading in effect to punishment, more like the recidivist statutes where opportunity must be given to be heard on the habitual criminal issue.

Warrants for arrest, criminal summonses, and search warrants are issued upon complaint or affidavit showing probable cause. Rules 4(a) and 41(c) of the Federal Rules of Criminal Procedure. The nature of the proceedings makes application of the formal rules of evidence inappropriate and impracticable.

Criminal contempts are punishable summarily if the judge certifies that he saw or heard the contempt and that it was committed in the presence of the court. Rule 42(a) of the Federal Rules of Criminal Procedure. The circumstances which preclude application of the rules of evidence in this situation are not present, however, in other cases of criminal contempt.

Proceedings with respect to release on bail or otherwise do not call for application of the rules of evidence. The governing statute specifically provides:

"Information stated in, or offered in connection with, any order entered pursuant to this section need not conform to the rules pertaining to the admissibility of evidence in a court of law." 18 U.S.C.A. § 3146(f).

This provision is consistent with the type of inquiry contemplated in A.B.A. Project on Minimum Standards for Criminal Justice, Standards Relating to Pretrial Release, § 4.5(b), (c), p. 16 (1968). The references to the weight of the evidence against the accused, in Rule 46(a) (1), (c) of the Federal Rules of Criminal Procedure and in 18 U.S.C.A. § 3146(b), as a factor to be considered, clearly do not have in view evidence introduced at a hearing under the rules of evidence.

The rule does not exempt habeas corpus proceedings. The Supreme Court held in Walker v. Johnston, 312 U.S. 275, 61 S.Ct. 574, 85 L.Ed. 830 (1941), that the practice of disposing of matters of fact on affidavit, which prevailed in some circuits, did not "satisfy the command of the statute that the judge shall proceed 'to determine the facts of the case, by hearing the testimony and arguments.' " This view accords with the emphasis in Townsend v. Sain, 372 U.S. 293, 83 S.Ct. 745, 9 L.Ed.2d 770 (1963), upon trial-type proceedings, *id.* 311, 83 S.Ct. 745, with demeanor evidence as a significant factor, *id.* 322, 83 S.Ct. 745, in applications by state prisoners aggrieved by unconstitutional detentions. Hence subdivision (e) applies the rules to habeas corpus proceedings to the extent not inconsistent with the statute.

Subdivision (e). In a substantial number of special proceedings, *ad hoc* evaluation has resulted in the promulgation of particularized evidentiary provisions, by Act of Congress or by rule adopted by the Supreme Court. Well adapted to the particular proceedings, though not apt candidates for inclusion in a set of general rules, they are left undisturbed. Otherwise, however, the rules of evidence are applicable to the proceedings enumerated in the subdivision.

REPORT OF THE HOUSE COMMITTEE ON THE JUDICIARY

Subdivision (a) as submitted to the Congress, in stating the courts and judges to which the Rules of Evidence apply, omitted the Court of Claims and commissioners of that Court. At the request of the Court of Claims, the Committee amended the Rule to include the Court and its commissioners within the purview of the Rules.

Subdivision (b) was amended merely to substitute positive law citations for those which were not.

NOTE BY FEDERAL JUDICIAL CENTER

The rule enacted by the Congress is the rule prescribed by the Supreme Court, amended as follows:

Subdivision (a) was amended in the first sentence by inserting "the Court of Claims" and by inserting "actions, cases, and." It was amended in the second sentence by substituting "terms" in place of "word," by inserting the phrase "and 'court'," and by adding "commissioners of the Court of Claims."

Subdivision (b) was amended by substituting "civil actions and proceedings" in place of "civil actions," and by substituting "criminal cases and proceedings" in place of "criminal proceedings."

Subdivision (c) was amended by substituting "rule" in place of "rules" and by changing the verb to the singular.

Subdivision (d) was amended by deleting "those" after "other than" and by substituting "Rule 104" in place of "Rule 104(a)."

Subdivision (e) was amended by substituting "prescribed" in place of "adopted" and by adding "pursuant to statutory authority." The form of the statutory citations was also changed.

Rule 1102   Amendments

REPORT OF THE HOUSE COMMITTEE ON THE JUDICIARY

REPORT ON 28 USCS § 2076

Subsection (a) sets forth the method by which future amendments may be made to the Rules of Evidence. The present Rules Enabling Acts (18 U.S.C. 3771, 3772, 3402; 28 U.S.C. 2072, 2075), which the Supreme Court invoked as the authority pursuant to which it promulgated the Rules of Evidence, provide that the Court may prescribe rules of "practice and procedure" and submit them to Congress. The rules then take effect automatically either at such time as the Court directs, or after ninety days following their submission. An Act of Congress is necessary to prevent any rule so submitted from taking effect.

The Committee believed that many of the Rules of Evidence, particularly in the privilege and hearsay fields, involve substantive policy judgments as to which it is appropriate that the Congress play a greater role than that provided for in the present Enabling Acts. Accordingly, the Committee concluded that it should provide for a new statutory procedure by which amendments to the Rules of Evidence may be made, designed to insure adequate congressional participation in the evidence rule-making process. Section 2(a) as adopted by the Committee adds a new Section 2076, to title 28, United States Code, permitting the Court to prescribe amendments to the Rules of Evidence, which amendments must be reported to the Congress. However, unlike the situation under the present Rules Enabling Acts, either House of Congress may, by resolution, prevent a rule from becoming operative. Moreover, rather than the ninety-day period allowed in the existing Rules Enabling Acts, a one hundred and eighty day period is prescribed for Congressional action.

The committee considered the possibility of requiring Congressional approval of any rule of evidence submitted to it by the Court, and recognized that a similar judgment inhered in Public Law 93-12, pursuant to which the Court's proposed Rules of Evidence were barred from taking effect until approved by Congress. However, the Committee determined that requiring affirmative congressional action was appropriate to this first effort at codifying the Rules of Evidence, but was not needed with respect to subsequent amendments which would likely be of more modest dimension. Indeed, it believed that to require affirmative Congressional action with respect to amendments might well result in some worthwhile amendments not being approved because of other pressing demands on the Congress. The Committee thus concluded that the system of allowing Court-proposed amendments to the Rules of Evidence to take effect automatically unless disapproved by either House strikes a sound balance between the proper role of Congress in the amendatory process and the dictates of convenience and legislative priorities.

Subsection (b) strikes out Section 1732(a) of title 28, United States Code, since its subject matter is covered in Rule 803(6) relating to records of a regularly conducted business activity.

Subsection (c) amends Section 1733 of title 28, United States Code, since that section is largely, if not entirely, encompassed by Rule 803(8) relating to public records and reports. Because of the possibility that Section 1733 may reach some matters not touched by Rule 803(8), subsection (c) does not repeal Section 1733 but merely provides that the Section does not apply to actions, cases, and proceedings to which the Rules of Evidence are applicable.

Report of the Senate Committee on the Judiciary
Report on 28 USCS § 2076

The House, in order to clarify the power of the Supreme Court to issue Rules of Evidence or amendments to them, added a new Section 2076 to title 28, United States Code, specifying the Supreme Court's authority. The present Rules Enabling Acts (18 U.S.C. §§ 3771, 3772, 3402; 28 U.S.C. 2072, 2075), which the Supreme Court invoked as the authority pursuant to which it promulgated the Rules of Evidence, provide that the Court may prescribe rules of "practice and procedure" and submit them to Congress. The rules then take effect automatically either at such time as the Court directs, or after 90 days following their submission. An act of Congress is necessary to prevent any rule so submitted from taking effect.

The House believed that the Rules of Evidence involve policy judgments as to which it is appropriate for the Congress to play a greater role than that provided in the present Enabling Acts. Accordingly, the bill provides for a new statutory procedure by which amendments to the Rules of Evidence may be made, designed to insure adequate congressional participation in the evidence rulemaking process. Section 2(a) adds a new section, 2076, to title 28, United States Code, permitting the Court to prescribe amendments to the Rules of Evidence, which amendments must be reported to the Congress. However, three changes were made with respect to the role of Congress. First, any rule, rather than the entire package of rules may be disapproved. Second, either House of Congress, rather than the both Houses acting together, can prevent a rule from becoming operative. Third, rather than the 90-day period allowed in the existing Rules Enabling Acts, a 180-day period is prescribed for congressional action.

In order to augment the power of Congress to review rules of evidence, the committee made two additional amendments. It decided to extend the review period to 365 days—1 full year—and adopted a provision under which either House of Congress can defer the effective date of a rule to permit further study, either until a later date or until approved by Act of Congress. Thus, either House of Congress can disapprove or defer consideration of any proposed rule or combination of rules. The committee also added one clarifying amendment which provides that either a proposed rule or a rule already in effect may be amended by Act of Congress. While this has been generally understood, the committee feels it should be made clear.

The committee considered the possibility of requiring congressional approval of any rule of evidence submitted to it by the Court. We determined, however, that while requiring affirmative congressional action was appropriate to this first effort at codifying the Rules of Evidence, it was not needed with respect to subsequent amendments which would likely be of more modest dimension. Indeed, the committee believed that to require affirmative congressional action with respect to amendments might well result in some worthwhile amendments not being approved because of other pressing demands on the Congress. The committee thus concluded that the system of allowing Court-proposed amendments to the Rules of Evidence to take effect automatically unless disapproved by either House strikes a sound balance between the proper role of Congress in the amendatory process and the dictates of convenience and legislative priorities.

For the same reasons, the committee has deleted an amendment made on the floor of the House providing that no amendment creating, abolishing or modifying a privilege could take effect until approved by Act of Congress. The basis for the House action was the belief that rules of privilege constitute matters of substance that require affirmative congressional approval. While matters of privilege are, in a sense, substantive, and also involve particularly sensitive issues, the committee does not believe that privileges necessarily require different treatment from other rules, provided there are adequate safeguards so that the Congress retains sufficient review power to review effectively proposed changes in this area, as well as in others. By extending the period of review from 90 to 365 days and by providing that any proposed rule may be disapproved or its effective date deferred by either House of Congress, the committee believes that the Congress does, in fact retain sufficient review power to reflect its views on such matters.

Subsection (b) strikes out section 1732(a) of title 28, United States Code, since its subject matter is covered in rule 803(b) relating to records of a regularly conducted activity.

Subsection (c) amends section 1733 of title 28, United States Code, since that section is largely, if not entirely, encompassed by rule 803(8) relating to public records and reports. Because of the possibility that section 1733 may reach some matters not touched by rule 803(9), subsection (c) does not repeal section 1733 but merely provides that the section does not apply to actions, cases, and proceedings to which the Rules of Evidence are applicable.

REPORT OF THE HOUSE/SENATE CONFERENCE COMMITTEE

REPORT ON 28 USCS § 2076

Section 2 of the bill adds a new section to title 28 of the United States Code that establishes a procedure for amending the rules of evidence in the future. The House bill provides that the Supreme Court may promulgate amendments, and these amendments become effective 180 days after being reported to Congress. However, any amendment that creates, abolishes or modifies a rule of privilege does not become effective until approved by Act of Congress. The Senate amendments changed the length of time that must elapse before an amendment becomes effective to 365 days. The Senate amendments also added language, not contained in the House provision, that (1) either House can defer the effective date of a proposed amendment to a later date or until approved by Act of Congress and (2) an Act of Congress can amend any rule of evidence, whether proposed or in effect. Finally, the Senate amendments struck the provision requiring that amendments creating, abolishing or modifying a privilege be approved by Act of Congress.

The Conference adopts the House provision on the time period (180 days) and the House provision requiring that an amendment creating, abolishing or modifying a rule of privilege cannot become effective until approved by Act of Congress. The Conference adopts the Senate amendment providing that either House can defer the effective date of an amendment to the rules of evidence and that any rule, either proposed or in effect, can be amended by Act of Congress. In making these changes in the enabling Act, Conference recognizes the continuing role of the Supreme Court in promulgating rules of evidence.

NOTE BY FEDERAL JUDICIAL CENTER

The Rule was not included among those prescribed by the Supreme Court. The Rule prescribed by the court as 1102 now appears as 1103.

Rule 1103   Title

NOTE BY FEDERAL JUDICIAL CENTER

The Rule enacted by Congress is the Rule prescribed by the Supreme Court as Rule 1102 without change.

FEDERAL RULES OF EVIDENCE

Effective July 1, 1975

NOTE: These Rules contain amendments that will become effective on October 1, 1987, unless Congress takes other action with respect to them. New matter is underlined and matter to be omitted is lined through.

RULES OF EVIDENCE FOR

UNITED STATES COURTS AND MAGISTRATES

ARTICLE I. GENERAL PROVISIONS

RULE 101. Scope

These rules govern proceedings in the courts of the United States and before United States bankruptcy judges and United States magistrates, to the extent and with the exceptions stated in Rule 1101.

(Amended, eff 10-1-87)

RULE 102. Purpose and Construction

These rules shall be construed to secure fairness in administration, elimination of unjustifiable expense and delay, and promotion of growth and development of the law of evidence to the end that the truth may be ascertained and proceedings justly determined.

RULE 103. Rulings on Evidence

(a) Effect of erroneous ruling. Error may not be predicated upon a ruling which admits or excludes evidence unless a substantial right of the party is affected, and

(1) Objection. In case the ruling is one admitting evidence, a timely objection or motion to strike appears of record, stating the specific ground of objection, if the specific ground was not apparent from the context; or

(2) Offer of proof. In case the ruling is one excluding evidence, the substance of the evidence was made known to the court by offer or was apparent from the context within which questions were asked.

(b) Record of offer and ruling. The court may add any other or further statement which shows the character of the evidence, the form in which it was offered, the objection made, and the ruling thereon. It may direct the making of an offer in question and answer form.

(c) Hearing of jury. In jury cases, proceedings shall be conducted, to the extent practicable, so as to prevent inadmissible evidence from being suggested to the jury by any means, such as making statements or offers of proof or asking questions in the hearing of the jury.

(d) Plain error. Nothing in this rule precludes taking notice of plain errors affecting substantial rights although they were not brought to the attention of the court.

RULE 104. Preliminary Questions

(a) Questions of admissibility generally. Preliminary questions concerning the qualification of a person to be a witness, the existence of a privilege, or the admissibility of evidence shall be determined by the court, subject to the provisions of subdivision (b). In making its determination it is not bound by the rules of evidence except those with respect to privileges.

(b) Relevancy conditioned on fact. When the relevancy of evidence depends upon the fulfillment of a condition of fact, the court shall admit it upon, or subject to, the introduction of evidence sufficient to support a finding of the fulfillment of the condition.

(c) Hearing of jury. Hearings on the admissibility of confessions shall in all cases be conducted out of the hearing of the jury. Hearings on other preliminary matters shall be so conducted when the interests of justice require, or, when an accused is a witness, if he and so requests.

(d) Testimony by accused. The accused does not, by testifying upon a preliminary matter, become subject himself to cross-examination as to other issues in the case.

(e) Weight and credibility. This rule does not limit the right of a party to introduce

875

before the jury evidence relevant to weight or credibility.

(Amended, eff 10-1-87)

RULE 105. Limited Admissibility

When evidence which is admissible as to one party or for one purpose but not admissible as to another party or for another purpose is admitted, the court, upon request, shall restrict the evidence to its proper scope and instruct the jury accordingly.

RULE 106. Remainder of or Related Writings or Recorded Statements

When a writing or recorded statement or part thereof is introduced by a party, an adverse party may require ~~him~~ the introduction at that time of ~~to introduce~~ any other part or any other writing or recorded statement which ought in fairness to be considered contemporaneously with it.

(Amended, eff 10-1-87)

ARTICLE II. JUDICIAL NOTICE

RULE 201. Judicial Notice of Adjudicative Facts

(a) **Scope of rule.** This rule governs only judicial notice of adjudicative facts.

(b) **Kinds of facts.** A judicially noticed fact must be one not subject to reasonable dispute in that it is either (1) generally known within the territorial jurisdiction of the trial court or (2) capable of accurate and ready determination by resort to sources whose accuracy cannot reasonably be questioned.

(c) **When discretionary.** A court may take judicial notice, whether requested or not.

(d) **When mandatory.** A court shall take judicial notice if requested by a party and supplied with the necessary information.

(e) **Opportunity to be heard.** A party is entitled upon timely request to an opportunity to be heard as to the propriety of taking judicial notice and the tenor of the matter noticed. In the absence of prior notification, the request may be made after judicial notice has been taken.

(f) **Time of taking notice.** Judicial notice may be taken at any stage of the proceeding.

(g) **Instructing jury.** In a civil action or proceeding, the court shall instruct the jury to accept as conclusive any fact judicially noticed. In a criminal case, the court shall instruct the jury that it may, but is not required to, accept as conclusive any fact judicially noticed.

ARTICLE III. PRESUMPTIONS IN CIVIL ACTIONS AND PROCEEDINGS

RULE 301. Presumptions in General in Civil Actions and Proceedings

In all civil actions and proceedings not otherwise provided for by Act of Congress or by these rules, a presumption imposes on the party against whom it is directed the burden of going forward with evidence to rebut or meet the presumption, but does not shift to such party the burden of proof in the sense of the risk of nonpersuasion, which re-

mains throughout the trial upon the party on whom it was originally cast.

RULE 302. Applicability of State Law in Civil Actions and Proceedings

In civil actions and proceedings, the effect of a presumption respecting a fact which is an element of a claim or defense as to which State law supplies the rule of decision is determined in accordance with State law.

ARTICLE IV. RELEVANCY AND ITS LIMITS

RULE 401. Definition of "Relevant Evidence"

"Relevant evidence" means evidence having any tendency to make the existence of any fact that is of consequence to the determination of the action more probable or less probable than it would be without the evidence.

RULE 402. Relevant Evidence Generally Admissible; Irrelevant Evidence Inadmissible

All relevant evidence is admissible, except as otherwise provided by the Constitution of the United States, by Act of Congress, by these rules, or by other rules prescribed by the Supreme Court pursuant to statutory authority. Evidence which is not relevant is not admissible.

RULE 403. Exclusion of Relevant Evidence on Grounds of Prejudice, Confusion, or Waste of Time

Although relevant, evidence may be excluded if its probative value is substantially outweighed by the danger of unfair prejudice, confusion of the issues, or misleading the jury, or by considerations of undue delay, waste of time, or needless presentation of cumulative evidence.

RULE 404. Character Evidence Not Admissible To Prove Conduct; Exceptions; Other Crimes

(a) Character evidence generally. Evidence of a person's character or a trait of his character is not admissible for the purpose of proving that he acted action in conformity therewith on a particular occasion, except:

(1) Character of accused. Evidence of a pertinent trait of his character offered by an accused, or by the prosecution to rebut the same;

(2) Character of victim. Evidence of a pertinent trait of character of the victim of the crime offered by an accused, or by the prosecution to rebut the same, or evidence of a character trait of peacefulness of the victim offered by the prosecution in a homicide case to rebut evidence that the victim was the first aggressor;

(3) Character of witness. Evidence of the character of a witness, as provided in rules 607, 608 and 609.

(b) Other crimes, wrongs, or acts. Evidence of other crimes, wrongs, or acts is not admissible to prove the character of a person in order to show that he acted action in conformity therewith. It may, however, be admissible for other purposes, such as proof of motive, opportunity, intent, preparation, plan, knowledge, identity, or absence of mistake or accident.

(Amended, eff 10-1-87)

RULE 405. Methods of Proving Character

(a) Reputation or opinion. In all cases in which evidence of character or a trait of character of a person is admissible, proof may be made by testimony as to reputation or by testimony in the form of an opinion. On cross-examination, inquiry is allowable into relevant specific instances of conduct.

(b) Specific instances of conduct. In cases in which character or a trait of character of a person is an essential element of a charge, claim, or defense, proof may also be made of specific instances of his that person's conduct.

(Amended, eff 10-1-87)

RULE 406. Habit; Routine Practice

Evidence of the habit of a person or of the routine practice of an organization, whether corroborated or not and regardless of the presence of eyewitnesses, is relevant to prove that the conduct of the person or organization on a particular occasion was in conformity with the habit or routine practice.

RULE 407. Subsequent Remedial Measures

When, after an event, measures are taken which, if taken previously, would have made the event less likely to occur, evidence of the subsequent measures is not admissible to prove negligence or culpable conduct in connection with the event. This rule does not require the exclusion of evidence of subsequent measures when offered for another purpose, such as proving ownership, control, or feasibility of precautionary measures, if controverted, or impeachment.

RULE 408. Compromise and Offers to Compromise.

Evidence of (1) furnishing or offering or promising to furnish, or (2) accepting or offering or promising to accept, a valuable consideration in compromising or attempting to compromise a claim which was disputed as to either validity or amount, is not admissible to prove liability for or invalidity of the claim or its amount. Evidence of conduct or statements made in compromise negotiations is likewise not admissible. This rule does not require the exclusion of any evidence otherwise discoverable merely because it is presented in the course of compromise negotiations. This rule also does not require exclusion when the evidence is offered for another purpose, such as proving bias or prejudice of a witness, negativing a contention of undue delay, or proving an effort to obstruct a criminal investigation or prosecution.

RULE 409. Payment of Medical and Similar Expenses

Evidence of furnishing or offering or promising to pay medical, hospital, or similar expenses occasioned by an injury is not admissible to prove liability for the injury.

RULE 410. Inadmissibility of Pleas, Plea Discussions, and Related Statements

Except as otherwise provided in this rule, evidence of the following is not, in any civil or criminal proceeding, admissible against the defendant who made the plea or was a participant in the plea discussions:

(1) a plea of guilty which was later withdrawn;

(2) a plea of nolo contendere;

(3) any statement made in the course of any proceedings under Rule 11 of the Federal Rules of Criminal Procedure or comparable state procedure regarding either of the foregoing pleas; or

(4) any statement made in the course of plea discussions with an attorney for the prosecuting authority which do not result in a plea of guilty or which result in a plea of guilty later withdrawn.

However, such a statement is admissible (i) in any proceeding wherein another statement made in the course of the same plea or plea discussions has been introduced and the statement ought in fairness be considered contemporaneously with it, or (ii) in a criminal proceeding for perjury or false statement if the statement was made by the defendant under oath, on the record and in the presence of counsel.

(Amended 12-12-75; 4-30-79, eff 12-1-80)

RULE 411. Liability Insurance

Evidence that a person was or was not insured against liability is not admissible upon the issue whether he the person acted negligently or otherwise wrongfully. This rule does not require the exclusion of evidence of insurance against liability when offered for another purpose, such as proof of agency, ownership, or control, or bias or prejudice of a witness.

(Amended, eff 10-1-87)

RULE 412. Rape Cases; Relevance of Victim's Past Behavior

(a) Notwithstanding any other provision of law, in a criminal case in which a person is accused of rape or of assault with intent to commit rape, reputation or opinion evidence of the past sexual behavior of an alleged victim of such rape or assault is not admissible.

(b) Notwithstanding any other provision of law, in a criminal case in which a person is accused of rape or of assault with intent to commit rape, evidence of a victim's past sexual behavior other than reputation or opinion evidence is also not admissible, unless such evidence other than reputation or opinion evidence is—

(1) admitted in accordance with subdivisions (c)(1) and (c)(2) and is constitutionally required to be admitted; or

(2) admitted in accordance with subdivision (c) and is evidence of—

(A) past sexual behavior with persons other than accused, offered by the accused upon the issue of whether accused was or was not, with respect to the alleged victim, the source of semen or injury; or

(B) past sexual behavior with the accused and is offered by the accused upon the issue of whether the alleged victim consented to the sexual behavior with respect to which rape or assault is alleged.

(c)(1) If the person accused of committing rape or assault with intent to commit rape intends to offer under subdivision (b) evidence of specific instances of the alleged victim's past sexual behavior, the accused shall make a written motion to offer such evidence not later than fifteen days before the date on which the trial in which such evidence is to be offered is scheduled to begin, except that the court may allow the motion to be made at a later date, including during trial, if the court determines either that the evidence is newly discovered and could not have been obtained earlier through the exercise of due diligence or that the issue to which such evidence relates has newly arisen in the case. Any motion made under this paragraph shall be served on all other parties and on the alleged victim.

(2) The motion described in paragraph (1) shall be accompanied by a written offer of proof. If the court determines that the offer of proof contains evidence described in subdivision (b), the court shall order a hearing in chambers to determine if such evidence is admissible. At such hearing the parties may call witnesses, including the alleged victim, and offer relevant evidence. Notwithstanding subdivision (b) of Rule 104, if the relevancy of the evidence which the accused seeks to offer in the trial depends upon the fulfillment of a condition of fact, the court, at the hearing in chambers or at a subsequent hearing in chambers scheduled for such purpose, shall accept evidence on the issue of whether such condition of fact is fulfilled and shall determine such issue.

(3) If the court determines on the basis of the hearing described in paragraph (2) that the evidence which the accused seeks to offer is relevant and that the probative value of such evidence outweighs the danger of unfair prejudice, such evidence shall be admissible in the trial to the extent an order made by the court specifies evidence which may be offered and areas with respect to which the alleged victim may be examined or cross-examined.

(d) For purposes of this rule, the term "past sexual behavior" means sexual behavior other than the sexual behavior with respect to which rape or assault with intent to commit rape is alleged.

(Added 10-28-78)

ARTICLE V. PRIVILEGES

RULE 501. General Rule

Except as otherwise required by the Constitution of the United States or provided by Act of Congress or in rules prescribed by the Supreme Court pursuant to statutory authority, the privilege of a witness, person, government, State, or political subdivision thereof shall be governed by the principles of the common law as they may be interpreted by the courts of the United States in the light of reason and experience. However, in civil actions and proceedings, with respect to an element of a claim or defense as to which State law supplies the rule of decision, the privilege of a witness, person, government, State, or political subdivision thereof shall be determined in accordance with State law.

ARTICLE VI. WITNESSES

RULE 601. General Rule of Competency

Every person is competent to be a witness except as otherwise provided in these rules. However, in civil actions and proceedings, with respect to an element of a claim or defense as to which State law supplies the rule of decision, the competency of a witness shall be determined in accordance with State law.

RULE 602. Lack of Personal Knowledge

A witness may not testify to a matter unless evidence is introduced sufficient to support a finding that he the witness has personal knowledge of the matter. Evidence to prove personal knowledge may, but need not, consist of the witness' own testimony. of the witness himself. This rule is subject to the provisions of Rule 703, relating to opinion testimony by expert witnesses.

(Amended, eff 10-1-87)

RULE 603. Oath or Affirmation

Before testifying, every witness shall be required to declare that he the witness will testify truthfully, by oath or affirmation administered in a form calculated to awaken his the witness' conscience and impress his the witness' mind with his the duty to do so.

(Amended, eff 10-1-87)

RULE 604. Interpreters

An interpreter is subject to the provisions of these rules relating to qualification as an expert and the administration of an oath or affirmation to that he will make a true translation.

(Amended, eff 10-1-87)

RULE 605. Competency of Judge as Witness

The judge presiding at the trial may not testify in that trial as a witness. No objection need be made in order to preserve the point.

RULE 606. Competency of Juror as Witness

(a) At the trial. A member of the jury may not testify as a witness before that jury in the trial of the case in which he the juror is sitting. as a juror. If he the juror is called so to testify, the opposing party shall be afforded an opportunity to object out of the presence of the jury.

(b) Inquiry into validity of verdict or indictment. Upon an inquiry into the validity of a verdict or indictment, a juror may not testify as to any matter or statement occurring during the course of the jury's deliberations or to the effect of anything upon his that or any other juror's mind or emotions as influencing him the juror to assent to or dissent from the verdict or indictment or concerning his the juror's mental processes in connection therewith, except that a juror may testify on the question whether extraneous prejudicial information was improperly brought to the jury's attention or whether any outside influence was improperly brought to bear upon any juror. Nor may his a juror's affidavit or evidence of any statement by him the juror concerning a matter about which he the juror would be precluded from testifying be received for these purposes.

(Amended, eff 12-12-75; 10-1-87)

RULE 607. Who May Impeach

The credibility of a witness may be attacked by any party, including the party calling ~~him~~ the witness.

(Amended, eff 10-1-87)

RULE 608. Evidence of Character and Conduct of Witness

(a) Opinion and reputation evidence of character. The credibility of a witness may be attacked or supported by evidence in the form of opinion or reputation, but subject to these limitations: (1) the evidence may refer only to character for truthfulness or untruthfulness, and (2) evidence of truthful character is admissible only after the character of the witness for truthfulness has been attacked by opinion or reputation evidence or otherwise.

(b) Specific instances of conduct. Specific instances of the conduct of a witness, for the purpose of attacking or supporting ~~his~~ the witness' credibility, other than conviction of crime as provided in Rule 609, may not be proved by extrinsic evidence. They may, however, in the discretion of the court, if probative of truthfulness or untruthfulness, be inquired into on cross-examination of the witness (1) concerning ~~his~~ the witness' character for truthfulness or untruthfulness, or (2) concerning the character for truthfulness or untruthfulness of another witness as to which character the witness being cross-examined has testified.

The giving of testimony, whether by an accused or by any other witness, does not operate as a waiver of ~~his~~ the accused's or the witness' privilege against self-incrimination when examined with respect to matters which relate only to credibility.

(Amended, eff 10-1-87)

RULE 609. Impeachment by Evidence of Conviction of Crime

(a) General rule. For the purpose of attacking the credibility of a witness, evidence that ~~he~~ the witness has been convicted of a crime shall be admitted if elicited from ~~him~~ the witness or established by public record during cross-examination but only if the crime (1) was punishable by death or imprisonment in excess of one year under the law under which ~~he~~ the witness was convicted, and the court determines that the probative value of admitting this evidence outweighs its prejudicial effect to the defendant, or (2) involved dishonesty or false statement, regardless of the punishment.

(b) Time limit. Evidence of a conviction under this rule is not admissible if a period of more than ten years has elapsed since the date of the conviction or of the release of the witness from the confinement imposed for that conviction, whichever is the later date, unless the court determines, in the interests of justice, that the probative value of the conviction supported by specific facts and circumstances substantially outweighs its prejudicial effect. However, evidence of a conviction more than 10 years old as calculated herein, is not admissible unless the proponent gives to the adverse party sufficient advance written notice of intent to use such evidence to provide the adverse party with a fair opportunity to contest the use of such evidence.

(c) Effect of pardon, annulment, or certificate of rehabilitation. Evidence of a conviction is not admissible under this rule if (1) the conviction has been the subject of a pardon, annulment, certificate of rehabilitation, or other equivalent procedure based on a finding of the rehabilitation of the person convicted, and that person has not been convicted of a subsequent crime which was punishable by death or imprisonment in excess of one year, or (2) the conviction has been the subject of a pardon, annulment, or other equivalent procedure based on a finding of innocence.

(d) Juvenile adjudications. Evidence of juvenile adjudications is generally not admissible under this rule. The court may, however, in a criminal case allow evidence of a juvenile adjudication of a witness other than the accused if conviction of the offense would be admissible to attack the credibility of an adult and the court is satisfied that admission in evidence is necessary for a fair determination of the issue of guilt or innocence.

(e) Pendency of appeal. The pendency of an appeal therefrom does not render evidence of a conviction inadmissible. Evidence of the pendency of an appeal is admissible.

(Amended, eff 10-1-87)

RULE 610. Religious Beliefs or Opinions

Evidence of the beliefs or opinions of a witness on matters of religion is not admissible for the purpose of showing that by reason of their nature ~~his~~ the witness' credibility is impaired or enhanced.

(Amended, eff 10-1-87)

RULE 611. Mode and Order of Interrogation and Presentation

(a) Control by court. The court shall exercise reasonable control over the mode and order of interrogating witnesses and presenting evidence so as to (1) make the interrogation and presentation effective for the ascertainment of the truth, (2) avoid needless consumption of time, and (3) protect witnesses from harassment or undue embarrassment.

(b) Scope of cross-examination. Cross-examination should be limited to the subject matter of the direct examination and matters affecting the credibility of the witness. The court may, in the exercise of discretion, permit inquiry into additional matters as if on direct examination.

(c) Leading questions. Leading questions should not be used on the direct examination of a witness except as may be necessary to develop ~~his~~ the witness' testimony. Ordinarily leading questions should be permitted on cross-examination. When a party calls a hostile witness, an adverse party, or a witness identified with an adverse party, interrogation may be by leading questions.

(Amended, eff 10-1-87)

RULE 612. Writing Used To Refresh Memory

Except as otherwise provided in criminal proceedings by section 3500 of title 18, United States Code, if a witness uses a writing to refresh ~~his~~ memory for the purpose of testifying, either —

(1) while testifying, or

(2) before testifying, if the court in its discretion determines it is necessary in the interests of justice,

an adverse party is entitled to have the writing produced at the hearing, to inspect it, to cross-examine the witness thereon, and to introduce in evidence those portions which relate to the testimony of the witness. If it is claimed that the writing contains matters not related to the subject matter of the testimony the court shall examine the writing in camera, excise any portions not so related, and order delivery of the remainder to the party entitled thereto. Any portion withheld over objections shall be preserved and made available to the appellate court in the event of an appeal. If a writing is not produced or delivered pursuant to order under this rule, the court shall make any order justice requires, except that in criminal cases when the prosecution elects not to comply, the order shall be one striking the testimony or, if the court in its discretion determines that the interests of justice so require, declaring a mistrial.

(Amended, eff 10-1-87)

RULE 613. Prior Statements of Witnesses

(a) Examining witness concerning prior statement. In examining a witness concerning a prior statement made by ~~him~~ the witness, whether written or not, the statement need not be shown nor its contents disclosed to ~~him~~ the witness at that time, but on request the same shall be shown or disclosed to opposing counsel.

(b) Extrinsic evidence of prior inconsistent statement of witness. Extrinsic evidence of a prior inconsistent statement by a witness is not admissible unless the witness is afforded an opportunity to explain or deny the same and the opposite party is afforded an opportunity to interrogate ~~him~~ the witness thereon, or the interests of justice otherwise require. This provision does not apply to admissions of a party-opponent as defined in Rule 801(d)(2).

(Amended, eff 10-1-87)

RULE 614. Calling and Interrogation of Witnesses by Court

(a) Calling by court. The court may, on its own motion or at the suggestion of a party, call witnesses, and all parties are entitled to cross-examine witnesses thus called.

(b) Interrogation by court. The court may interrogate witnesses, whether called by itself or by a party.

(c) Objections. Objections to the calling of witnesses by the court or to interrogation by it may be made at the time or at the next available opportunity when the jury is not present.

RULE 615. Exclusion of Witnesses

At the request of a party the court shall order witnesses excluded so that they cannot hear the testimony of other witnesses, and it may make the order of its own motion. This rule does not authorize exclusion of (1) a party who is a natural person, or (2) an officer or employee of party which is not a natural person designated as its representative by its attorney, or (3) a person whose presence is shown by a party to be essential to the presentation of ~~his~~ the party's cause.

(Amended, eff 10-1-87)

ARTICLE VII. OPINIONS AND EXPERT TESTIMONY

RULE 701. Opinion Testimony by Lay Witnesses

If the witness is not testifying as an expert, ~~his~~ the witness' testimony in the form of opinions or inferences is limited to those opinions or inferences which are (a) rationally based on the perception of the witness and (b) helpful to a clear understanding of ~~his~~ the witness' testimony or the determination of a fact in issue.

(Amended, eff 10-1-87)

RULE 702. Testimony by Experts

If scientific, technical, or other specialized knowledge will assist the trier of fact to understand the evidence or to determine a fact in issue, a witness qualified as an expert by knowledge, skill, experience, training, or education, may testify thereto in the form of an opinion or otherwise.

RULE 703. Bases of Opinion Testimony by Experts

The facts or data in the particular case upon which an expert bases an opinion or inference may be those perceived by or made known to ~~him~~ the expert at or before the hearing. If of a type reasonably relied upon by experts in the particular field in forming opinions or inferences upon the subject, the facts or data need not be admissible in evidence.

(Amended, eff 10-1-87)

RULE 704. Opinion on Ultimate Issue

(a) Except as provided in subdivision (b), testimony in the form of an opinion or inference otherwise admissible is not objectionable because it embraces an ultimate issue to be decided by the trier of fact.

(b) No expert witness testifying with respect to the mental state or condition of a defendant in a criminal case may state an opinion or inference as to whether the defendant did or did not have the mental state or condition constituting an element of the crime charged or of a defense thereto. Such ultimate issues are matters for the trier of fact alone.

(Amended, eff 10-12-84)

RULE 705. Disclosure of Facts or Data Underlying Expert Opinion

The expert may testify in terms of opinion or inference and give his reasons therefore without prior disclosure of the underlying facts or data, unless the court requires otherwise. The expert may in any event be required to disclose the underlying facts or data on cross-examination.

(Amended, eff 10-1-87)

RULE 706. Court Appointed Experts

(a) Appointment. The court may on its own motion or on the motion of any party enter an order to show cause why expert witnesses should not be appointed, and may request the parties to submit nominations. The court may appoint any expert witnesses agreed upon by the parties, and may appoint expert witnesses of its own selection. An expert witness shall not be appointed by the court unless he the witness consents to act. A witness so appointed shall be informed of his the witness' duties by the court in writing, a copy of which shall be filed with the clerk, or at a conference in which the parties shall have opportunity to participate. A witness so appointed shall advise the parties of his the witness' findings, if any; his the witness' deposition may be taken by any party; and he the witness may be called to testify by the court or any party. He The witness shall be subject to cross-examination by each party, including a party calling him as a witness the witness.

(b) Compensation. Expert witnesses so appointed are entitled to reasonable compensation in whatever sum the court may allow. The compensation thus fixed is payable from funds which may be provided by law in criminal cases and civil actions and proceedings involving just compensation under the fifth amendment. In other civil actions and proceedings the compensation shall be paid by the parties in such proportion and at such time as the court directs, and thereafter charged in like manner as other costs.

(c) Disclosure of appointment. In the exercise of its discretion, the court may authorize disclosure to the jury of the fact that the court appointed the expert witness.

(d) Parties' experts of own selection. Nothing in this rule limits the parties in calling expert witnesses of their own selection.

(Amended, eff 10-1-87)

ARTICLE VIII. HEARSAY

RULE 801. Definitions

The following definitions apply under this article:

(a) Statement. A "statement" is (1) an oral or written assertion or (2) nonverbal conduct of a person, if it is intended by him the person as an assertion.

(b) Declarant. A "declarant" is a person who makes a statement.

(c) Hearsay. "Hearsay" is a statement, other than one made by the declarant while testifying at the trial or hearing, offered in evidence to prove the truth of the matter asserted.

(d) Statements which are not hearsay. A statement is not hearsay if—

(1) Prior statement by witness. The declarant testifies at the trial or hearing and is subject to cross-examination concerning the statement, and the statement is (A) inconsistent with his the declarant's testimony, and was given under oath subject to the penalty of perjury at a trial, hearing, or other proceeding, or in a deposition, or (B) consistent with his the declarant's testimony and is offered to rebut an express or implied charge against him the declarant of recent fabrication or improper influence or motive, or (C) one of identification of a person made after perceiving him the person; or

(2) Admission by party-opponent. The statement is offered against a party and is (A) his the party's own statement in either his an individual or a representative capacity or (B) a statement of which he the party has manifested his an adoption

or belief in its truth, or (C) a statement by a person authorized by ~~him~~ the party to make a statement concerning the subject, or (D) a statement by ~~his~~ the party's agent or servant concerning a matter within the scope of ~~his~~ the agency or employment, made during the existence of the relationship, or (E) a statement by a coconspirator of a party during the course and in furtherance of the conspiracy.

(Amended, eff 10-31-75; 10-1-87)

RULE 802. Hearsay Rule

Hearsay is not admissible except as provided by these rules or by other rules prescribed by the Supreme Court pursuant to statutory authority or by Act of Congress.

RULE 803. Hearsay Exceptions; Availability of Declarant Immaterial

The following are not excluded by the hearsay rule, even though the declarant is available as a witness:

(1) Present sense impression. A statement describing or explaining an event or condition made while the declarant was perceiving the event or condition, or immediately thereafter.

(2) Excited utterance. A statement relating to a startling event or condition made while the declarant was under the stress of excitement caused by the event or condition.

(3) Then existing mental, emotional, or physical condition. A statement of the declarant's then existing state of mind, emotion, sensation, or physical condition (such as intent, plan, motive, design, mental feeling, pain, and bodily health), but not including a statement of memory or belief to prove the fact remembered or believed unless it relates to the execution, revocation, identification, or terms of declarant's will.

(4) Statements for purposes of medical diagnosis or treatment. Statements made for purposes of medical diagnosis or treatment and describing medical history, or past or present symptoms, pain, or sensations, or the inception or general character of the cause or external source

thereof insofar as reasonably pertinent to diagnosis or treatment.

(5) Recorded recollection. A memorandum or record concerning a matter about which a witness once had knowledge but now has insufficient recollection to enable ~~him~~ the witness to testify fully and accurately, shown to have been made or adopted by the witness when the matter was fresh in ~~his~~ the witness' memory and to reflect that knowledge correctly. If admitted, the memorandum or record may be read into evidence but may not itself be received as an exhibit unless offered by an adverse party.

(6) Records of regularly conducted activity. A memorandum, report, record, or data compilation, in any form, of acts, events, conditions, opinions, or diagnoses, made at or near the time by, or from information transmitted by, a person with knowledge, if kept in the course of a regularly conducted business activity, and if it was the regular practice of that business activity to make the memorandum, report, record, or data compilation, all as shown by the testimony of the custodian or other qualified witness, unless the source of information or the method or circumstances of preparation indicate lack of trustworthiness. The term "business" as used in this paragraph includes business, institution, association, profession, occupation, and calling of every kind, whether or not conducted for profit.

(7) Absence of entry in records kept in accordance with the provisions of paragraph (6). Evidence that a matter is not included in the memoranda reports, records, or data compilations, in any form, kept in accordance with the provisions of paragraph (6), to prove the nonoccurrence or nonexistence of the matter, if the matter was of a kind of which a memorandum, report, record, or data compilation was regularly made and preserved, unless the sources of information or other circumstances indicate lack of trustworthiness.

(8) Public records and reports. Records, reports, statements, or data compilations, in any form, of public offices or agencies, setting forth (A) the activities of the office or agency, or (B) matters observed pursuant to duty imposed by law as to which matters there was a duty to report, excluding, however, in criminal cases matters observed by police officers and other law enforcement personnel, or (C) in civil actions and proceedings and against the Government in criminal cases, factual findings resulting from an investigation made pursuant to authority granted by law, unless the sources of information or other circumstances indicate lack of trustworthiness.

(9) Records of vital statistics. Records or data compilations, in any form, of births, fetal deaths, deaths, or marriages, if the report thereof was made to a public office pursuant to requirements of law.

(10) Absence of public record or entry. To prove the absence of a record, report, statement, or data compilation, in any form, or the nonoccurrence or nonexistence of a matter of which a record, report, statement, or data compilation, in any form, was regularly made and preserved by a public office or agency, evidence in the form of a certification in accordance with Rule 902, or testimony, that diligent search failed to disclose the record, report, statement, or data compilation, or entry.

(11) Records of religious organizations. Statements of births, marriages, divorces, deaths, legitimacy, ancestry, relationship by blood or marriage, or other similar facts of personal or family history, contained in a regularly kept record of a religious organization.

(12) Marriage, baptismal, and similar certificates. Statements of fact contained in a certificate that the maker performed a marriage or other ceremony or administered a sacrament, made by a clergyman, public official, or other person authorized by the rules or practices of a religious organization or by law to perform the act certified, and purporting to have been issued at the time of the act or within a reasonable time thereafter.

(13) Family records. Statements of fact concerning personal or family history contained in family Bibles, genealogies, charts, engravings on rings, inscriptions on family portraits, engravings on urns, crypts, or tombstones, or the like.

(14) Records of documents affecting an interest in property. The record of a document purporting to establish or affect an interest in property, as proof of the content of the original recorded document and its exceecution and delivery by each person by whom it purports to have been executed, if the record is a record of a public office and an applicable statute authorizes the recording of documents of that kind in that office.

(15) Statements in documents affecting an interest in property. A statement contained in a document purporting to establish or affect an interest in property if the matter stated was relevant to the purpose of the document, unless dealings with the property since the document was made have been inconsistent with the truth of the statement or the purport of the document.

(16) Statements in ancient documents. Statements in a document in existence twenty years or more the authenticity of which is established.

(17) Market reports, commercial publications. Market quotations, tabulations, lists, directories, or other published compilations, generally used and relied upon by the public or by persons in particular occupations.

(18) Learned treatises. To the extent called to the attention of an expert witness upon cross-examination or relied upon by ~~him~~ the expert witness in direct examination, statements contained in published treatises, periodicals, or pamphlets on a subject of history, medicine, or other science or art, established as a reliable authority by the testimony or admission of the witness or by other expert testimony or by judicial notice. If admitted, the statements may be read into evidence but may not be received as exhibits.

(19) Reputation concerning personal or family history. Reputation among members of ~~his~~ a person's family by blood, adoption, or marriage, or among ~~his~~ a person's associates, or in the community, concerning a person's birth, adoption, marriage, divorce, death, legitimacy, relationship by blood, adoption, or marriage, ancestry, or other similar fact of ~~his~~ personal or family history.

(20) Reputation concerning boundaries or general history. Reputation in a community, arising before the controversy, as to boundaries of or customs affecting lands in the community, and reputation as to events of general history important to the community or State or nation in which located.

(21) Reputation as to character. Reputation of a person's character among ~~his~~ associates or in the community.

(22) Judgment of previous conviction. Evidence of a final judgment, entered after a trial or upon a plea of guilty (but not upon a plea of nolo contendere), adjudging a person guilty of a crime punishable by death or imprisonment in excess of one year, to prove any fact essential to sustain the judgment, but not including, when offered by the Government in a criminal prosecution for purposes other than impeachment, judgments against persons other than the accused. The pendency of an appeal may be shown but does not affect admissibility.

(23) Judgment as to personal, family or general history, or boundaries. Judgments as proof of matters of personal, family, or general history, or boundaries, essential to the judgment, if the same would be provable by evidence of reputation.

(24) Other exceptions. A statement not specifically covered by any of the foregoing exceptions but having equivalent circumstantial guarantees of trustworthiness, if the court determines that (A) the statement is offered as evidence of a material fact; (B) the statement is more probative on the point for which it is offered than any other evidence which the proponent can procure through reasonable efforts; and (C) the general purposes of these rules and the interests of justice will best be served by admission of the evidence. However, a statement may not be admitted under this exception unless the proponent of it makes known to the

adverse party sufficiently in advance of the trial or hearing to provide the adverse party with a fair opportunity to prepare to meet it, ~~his~~ the proponent's intention to offer the statement and the particulars of it, including the name and address of the declarant.

(Amended, eff 12-12-75; 10-1-87)

RULE 804. Hearsay Exceptions: Declarant Unavailable

(a) Definition of unavailability. "Unavailability as a witness" includes situations in which the declarant—

(1) is exempted by ruling of the court on the ground of privilege from testifying concerning the subject matter of ~~his~~ the declarant's statement; or

(2) persists in refusing to testify concerning the subject matter of ~~his~~ the declarant's statement despite an order of the court to do so; or

(3) testifies to a lack of memory of the subject matter of ~~his~~ the declarant's statement; or

(4) is unable to be present or to testify at the hearing because of death or then existing physical or mental illness or infirmity; or

(5) is absent from the hearing and the proponent of ~~his~~ a statement has been unable to procure ~~his~~ the declarant's subdivisions (b)(2), (3), or (4), ~~his~~ the declarant's attendance or testimony) by process or other reasonable means.

A declarant is not unavailable as a witness if ~~his~~ exemption, refusal, claim of lack of memory, inability, or absence is due to the procurement or wrongdoing of the proponent of ~~his~~ a statement for the purpose of preventing the witness from attending or testifying.

(b) Hearsay exceptions. The following are not excluded by the hearsay rule if the declarant is unavailable as a witness:

(1) Former testimony. Testimony given as a witness at another hearing of the same or a different proceeding, or in a deposition taken in compliance with law in the course of the same or another proceeding, if the party against whom the testimony is now offered, or, in a civil action or proceeding, a predecessor in interest, had an opportunity and similar motive to develop the testimony by direct, cross, or redirect examination.

(2) Statement under belief of impending death. In a prosecution for homicide or in a civil action or proceeding, a statement made by a declarant while believing that ~~his~~ the declarant's death was imminent, concerning the cause or circumstances of what ~~he~~ the declarant believed to be ~~his~~ impending death.

(3) Statement against interest. A statement which was at the time of its making so far contrary to the declarant's pecuniary or proprietary interest, or so far tended to subject ~~him~~ the declarant to civil or criminal liability, or to render invalid a claim by ~~him~~ the declarant against another, that a reasonable ~~man~~ person in ~~his~~ the declarant's position would not have made the statement unless ~~he be-lieved~~ believing it to be true. A statement tending to expose the declarant to criminal liability and offered to exculpate the accused is not admissible unless corroborating circumstances clearly indicate the trustworthiness of the statement.

(4) Statement of personal or family history. (A) A statement concerning the declarant's own birth, adoption, marriage, divorce, legitimacy, relationship by blood, adoption, or marriage, ancestry, or other similar fact of personal or family history, even though declarant had no means of acquiring personal knowledge of the matter stated; or (B) a statement concerning the foregoing matters, and death also, of another person, if the declarant was related to the other by blood, adoption, or marriage or was so intimately associated with the other's family as to be likely to have accurate information concerning the matter declared.

(5) Other exceptions. A statement not specifically covered by any of the foregoing exceptions but having equivalent circumstantial guarantees of trustworthi-

ness, if the court determines that (A) the statement is offered as evidence of a material fact; (B) the statement is more probative on the point for which it is offered than any other evidence which the proponent can procure through reasonable efforts; and (C) the general purposes of these rules and the interests of justice will best be served by admission of the statement into evidence. However, a statement may not be admitted under this exception unless the proponent of it makes known to the adverse party sufficiently in advance of the trial or hearing to provide the adverse party with a fair opportunity to prepare to meet it, ~~his~~ the proponent's intention to offer the statement and the particulars of it, including the name and address of the declarant.

(Amended, eff 12-12-75; 10-1-87)

RULE 805. Hearsay Within Hearsay

Hearsay included within hearsay is not excluded under the hearsay rule if each part of the combined statements conforms with an exception to the hearsay rule provided in these rules.

RULE 806. Attacking and Supporting Credibility of Declarant

When a hearsay statement, or a statement defined in Rule 801(d)(2),(C),(D), or (E), has been admitted in evidence, the credibility of the declarant may be attacked, and if attacked may be supported, by any evidence which would be admissible for those purposes if declarant had testified as a witness. Evidence of a statement or conduct by the declarant at any time, inconsistent with ~~his~~ the declarant's hearsay statement, is not subject to any requirement that ~~he~~ the declarant may have been afforded an opportunity to deny or explain. If the party against whom a hearsay statement has been admitted calls the declarant as a witness, the party is entitled to examine ~~him~~ the declarant on the statement as if under cross-examination.

(Amended, eff 10-1-87)

ARTICLE IX. AUTHENTICATION AND IDENTIFICATION

RULE 901. Requirement of Authentication or Identification

(a) General provision. The requirement of authentication or identification as a condition precedent to admissibility is satisfied by evidence sufficient to support a finding that the matter in question is what its proponent claims.

(b) Illustrations. By way of illustration only, and not by way of limitation, the following are examples of authentication or identification conforming with the requirements of this rule:

(1) Testimony of witness with knowledge. Testimony that a matter is what it is claimed to be.

(2) Nonexpert opinion on handwriting. Nonexpert opinion as to the genuineness of handwriting, based upon familiarity not acquired for purposes of the litigation.

(3) Comparison by trier or expert witness. Comparison by the trier of fact or by expert witnesses with specimens which have been authenticated.

(4) Distinctive characteristics and the like. Appearance, contents, substance, internal patterns, or other distinctive characteristics, taken in conjunction with circumstances.

(5) Voice identification. Identification of a voice, whether heard firsthand or through mechanical or electronic transmission or recording, by opinion based upon hearing the voice at any time under circumstances connecting it with the alleged speaker.

(6) Telephone conversations. Telephone conversations, by evidence that a call was made to the number assigned at the time by the telephone company to a particular person or business, if (A) in the case of a person, circumstances, including self-identification, show the person answering to be the one called, or (B) in the case of a business, the call was made to a place of business and the conversation related to business reasonably transacted over the telephone.

(7) Public records or reports. Evidence that a writing authorized by law to be recorded or filed and in fact recorded or filed in a public office, or a purported public record, report, statement, or data compilation, in any form, is from the public office where items of this nature are kept.

(8) Ancient documents or data compilation. Evidence that a document or data compilation, in any form, (A) is in such condition as to create no suspicion concerning its authenticity, (B) was in a place where it, if authentic, would likely be, and (C) has been in existence 20 years or more at the time it is offered.

(9) Process or system. Evidence describing a process or system used to produce a result and showing that the process or system produces an accurate result.

(10) Methods provided by statute or rule. Any method of authentication or identification provided by Act of Congress or by other rules prescribed by the Supreme Court pursuant to statutory authority.

RULE 902. Self-authentication

Extrinsic evidence of authenticity as a condition precedent to admissibility is not required with respect to the following:

(1) Domestic public documents under seal. A document bearing a seal purporting to be that of the United States, or of any State, district, Commonwealth, territory, or insular possession thereof, or the Panama Canal Zone, or the Trust Territory of the Pacific Islands, or of a political subdivision, department, officer, or agency thereof, and a signature purporting to be an attestation or execution.

(2) Domestic public documents not under seal. A document purporting to bear the signature in ~~his~~ the official capacity of an officer or employee of any entity included in paragraph (1) hereof, having no seal, if a public officer having a seal and having official duties in the district or political subdivision of the officer or employee certifies under seal that the signer has the official capacity and that the signature is genuine.

(3) Foreign public documents. A document purporting to be executed or attested in ~~his~~ an official capacity by a person authorized by the laws of a foreign country to make the execution or attestation, and accompanied by a final certification as to the genuineness of the signature and official position (A) of the executing or attesting person, or (B) of any foreign official whose certificate of genuineness of signature and official position relates to the execution or attestation or is in a chain of certificates of genuineness of signature and official position relating to the execution or attestation.

(4) Certified copies of public records. A copy of an official record or report or entry therein, or of a document authorized by law to be recorded or filed and actually recorded or filed in a public office, including data compilations in any form, certified as correct by the custodian or other person authorized to make the certification, by certificate complying with paragraph (1), (2), or (3) of this rule or complying with any Act of Congress or rule prescribed by the Supreme Court pursuant to statutory authority.

(5) Official publications. Books, pamphlets, or other publications purporting to be issued by public authority.

(6) Newspapers and periodicals. Printed materials purporting to be newspapers or periodicals.

(7) Trade inscriptions and the like. Inscriptions, signs, tags, or labels purporting to have been affixed in the course of business and indicating ownership, control, or origin.

(8) Acknowledged documents. Documents accompanied by a certificate of acknowledgement executed in the manner provided by law by a notary public or other officer authorized by law to take acknowledgements.

(9) Commercial paper and related documents. Commercial paper, signatures thereon, and documents relating thereto to the extent provided by general commercial law.

(10) Presumptions under Acts of Congress. Any signature, document, or other matter declared by Act of Congress to be presumptively or prima facie genuine or authentic.

(Amended, eff 10-1-87)

RULE 903. Subscribing Witness' Testimony Unnecessary

The testimony of a subscribing witness is not necessary to authenticate a writing unless required by the laws of the jurisdiction whose laws govern the validity of the writing.

ARTICLE X. CONTENTS OF WRITINGS, RECORDINGS, AND PHOTOGRAPHS

RULE 1001. Definitions

For purposes of this article the following definitions are applicable:

(1) Writings and recordings. "Writings" and "recordings" consist of letters, words, or numbers, or their equivalent, set down by handwriting, typewriting, printing, photostating, photographing, magnetic impulse, mechanical or electronic recording, or other form of data compilation.

(2) Photographs. "Photographs" include still photographs, X-ray films, video tapes, and motion pictures.

(3) Original. An "original" of a writing or recording is the writing or recording itself or any counterpart intended to have the same effect by a person executing or issuing it. An "original" of a photograph includes the negative or any print therefrom. If data are stored in a computer or similar device, any printout or other output readable by sight, shown to reflect the data accurately, is an "original."

(4) Duplicate. A "duplicate" is a counterpart produced by the same impression as the original, or from the same matrix, or by means of photography, including enlargements and miniatures, or by mechanical or electronic re-recording, or by chemical reproduction, or by other equivalent techniques which accurately reproduces the original.

RULE 1002. Requirement of Original

To prove the content of a writing, recording, or photograph, the original writing, recording, or photograph is required, except as otherwise provided in these rules or by Act of Congress.

RULE 1003. Admissibility of Duplicates

A duplicate is admissible to the same extent as an original unless (1) a genuine question is raised as to the authenticity of the original or (2) in the circumstances it would be unfair to admit the duplicate in lieu of the original.

RULE 1004. Admissibility of Other Evidence of Contents

The original is not required, and other evidence of the contents of a writing, recording, or photograph is admissible if—

(1) Originals lost or destroyed. All originals are lost or have been destroyed, unless the proponent lost or destroyed them in bad faith; or

(2) Original not obtainable. No original can be obtained by any available judicial process or procedure; or

(3) Original in possession of opponent. At a time when an original was under the control of the party against whom offered, ~~he~~ that party was put on notice, by the pleadings or otherwise, that the contents would be a subject of proof at the hearing, and ~~he~~ that party does not produce the original at the hearing; or

(4) Collateral matters. The writing, recording, or photograph is not closely related to a controlling issue.

(Amended, eff 10-1-87)

RULE 1005. Public Records

The contents of an official record, or of a document authorized to be recorded or filed

and actually recorded or filed, including data compilations in any form, if otherwise admissible, may be proved by copy, certified as correct in accordance with Rule 902 or testified to be correct by a witness who has compared it with the original. If a copy which compiles with the foregoing cannot be obtained by the exercise of reasonable diligence, then other evidence of the contents may be given.

RULE 1006. Summaries

The contents of voluminous writings, recordings, or photographs which cannot conveniently be examined in court may be presented in the form of a chart, summary, or calculation. The originals, or duplicates, shall be made available for examination or copying, or both, by other parties at reasonable time and place. The court may order that they be produced in court.

RULE 1007. Testimony or Written Admission of Party

Contents of writings, recordings, or photographs may be proved by the testimony or deposition of the party against whom offered or by ~~his~~ that party's written admission, without accounting for the nonproduction of the original.

(Amended, eff 10-1-87)

RULE 1008. Functions of Court and Jury

When the admissibility of other evidence of contents of writings, recordings, or photographs under these rules depends upon the fulfillment of a condition of fact, the question whether the condition has been fulfilled is ordinarily for the court to determine in accordance with the provisions of Rule 104. However, when an issue is raised (a) whether the asserted writing ever existed, or (b) whether another writing, recording, or photograph produced at the trial is the original, or (c) whether other evidence of contents correctly reflects the contents, the issue is for the trier of fact to determine as in the case of other issues of fact.

ARTICLE XI. MISCELLANEOUS RULES

RULE 1101. Applicability of Rules

(a) Courts and magistrates. These Rules apply to the United States district courts, the District Court of Guam, the District Court of the Virgin Islands, the District Court for the ~~District of the Canal Zone~~ Northern Mariana Islands, the United States Courts of Appeals, the United States Claims Court, and to United States <u>bankruptcy judges and United States</u> magistrates, in the actions, cases, and proceedings and to the extent hereinafter set forth. The terms "judge" and "court" in these rules include <u>United States bankruptcy judges and</u> United States magistrates.

(b) Proceedings generally. These rules apply generally to civil actions and proceedings, including admiralty and maritime cases, to criminal cases and proceedings, to contempt proceedings except those in which the court may act summarily, and to proceedings and cases under title 11, United States Code.

(c) Rule of privilege. The rule with respect to privileges applies at all stages of all actions, cases, and proceedings.

(d) Rules inapplicable. The rules (other than with respect to privilege) do not apply in the following situations:

(1) Preliminary question of fact. The determination of questions of fact preliminary to admissibility of evidence when the issue is to be determined by the court under Rule 104.

(2) Grand jury. Proceedings before grand juries.

(3) Miscellaneous proceedings. Proceedings for extradition or rendition; preliminary examinations in criminal cases; sentencing, or granting or revoking probation; issuance of warrants for arrest, criminal summonses, and search warrants; and proceedings with respect to release on bail or otherwise.

(e) Rules applicable in part. In the following proceedings these rules apply to the extent that matters of evidence are not provided for in statutes which govern procedure therein or in other rules prescribed by the Supreme Court pursuant to statutory authority: the trial of minor and petty offenses by United States magistrates; review of agency actions when the facts are subject to trial de novo under section 706(2)(F) of title 5, United States Code; review of orders of the Secretary of Agriculture under section 2 of the Act entitled "An Act to authorize association of producers of agricultural products" approved February 18, 1922 (7 U.S.C. 292), and under sections 6 and 7(c) of the Perishable Agricultural Commodities Act, 1930 (7 U.S.C. 499f, 499g(c)); naturalization and revocation of naturalization under sections 310-318 of the Immigration and Nationality Act (8 U.S.C. 1421-1429); prize proceedings in admiralty under sections 7651-7681 of title 10, United States Code; review of orders of the Secretary of the Interior under section 2 of the Act entitled "An Act authorizing associations of producers of aquatic products" approved June 25, 1934 (15 U.S.C. 522); review of orders of petroleum control boards under section 5 of the Act entitled "An Act to regular interstate and foreign commerce in petroleum and its products by prohibiting the shipment in such commerce of petroleum and its products produced in violation of State law, and for other purposes," approved February 22, 1935 (15 U.S.C. 715d); actions for fines, penalties, or forfeitures under part V of title IV of the Tariff Act of 1930 (19 U.S.C. 1581-1624), or under the Anti-Smuggling Act (19 U.S.C. 1701-1711); criminal libel for condemnation, exclusion of imports, or other proceedings under the Federal Food, Drug, and Cosmetic Act (21 U.S.C. 301-392); disputes between seamen under sections 4079, 4080, and 4081 of the Revised Statutes (22 U.S.C. 256-258); habeas corpus under sections 2241-2254 of title 28, United States Code; motions to vacate, set aside or correct sentence under section 2255 of title 28, United States Code; actions for penalties for refusal to transport destitute seamen under section 4578 of the Revised Statutes (46 U.S.C. 679); actions against the United States under the Act entitled "An

Act authorizes suits against the United States in admiralty for damage caused by and salvage service rendered to public vessels belonging to the United States, and for other purposes," approved March 3, 1925 (46 U.S.C. 781-790), as implemented by section 7730 of title 10, United States Code.

(Amended, eff 12-12-75; 11-6-78; 4-2-82; 10-1-87)

RULE 1102. Amendments

Amendments to the Federal Rules of Evidence may be made as provided in section 2076 of title 28 of the United States Code.

RULE 1103. Title.

These rules may be known and cited as the Federal Rules of Evidence.

INDEX

References not otherwise designated are to sections of the Treatise

VITAL STATISTICS
records, *see* HEARSAY EXCEPTIONS

VOICE IDENTIFICATION, 901.23-901.27; EvR 901(b)(5)—*see also* AUTHENTICATION AND IDENTIFICATION

WASTE OF TIME, RELEVANT EVIDENCE EXCLUDED WHEN, 403.5; EvR 403

WILL, ADMISSIBILITY REGARDING MENTAL, PHYSICAL OR EMOTIONAL CONDITION THEN-EXISTING, 803.17; EvR 803(3)

WITNESSES
affirmation, *see* oath or affirmation, this heading
applicability of other rules, 601.4; EvR 601, 602, 605, 606
authentication, *see* AUTHENTICATION AND IDENTIFICATION
character and conduct—
  extrinsic evidence, 608.8; EvR 608(b)
  impeachment—
    knowledge, 608.3; EvR 608(a)(1)
    opinion evidence, 608.2; EvR 405, 608(a)
    reputation evidence, 608.2; EvR 405, 608(a)
    testimony, 608.4; EvR 403, 405, 608(a)(1), 608(b)(2), 611
  in general, 608.1; EvR 404(a), 607-609
  inquiry appropriate, specific instances, 608.9; EvR 608(b)
  opinion evidence, bolstering credibility, 608.5; EvR 608(a)(2), 609
  prior conduct, 608.7; EvR 608(b)
  rehabilitation, 608.6; EvR 608(a)(2)
  reputation, bolstering credibility, 608.5; EvR 608(a)(2), 609
  trial judge, discretion, 608.8; EvR 608(b)
  unrelated inquiry, right to foreclose, 608.10; EvR 608
character, cross-examination, 405.4, 405.5; EvR 105, 403, 405
character evidence, 404.8; EvR 404(a)(3), 607-609
competency, 601.1; EvR 601
court's power to exclude testimony, 601.2; EvR 103(b), 104, 401, 403, 601, 611(a), 614(b)
exclusion of—
  in general, 615.1; EvR 615

WITNESSES—*Continued*
exclusion of—*Concluded*
  person not subject to, 615.2; EvR 615
  separation order, violation of, 615.3; EvR 615
expert testimony—*see* EXPERT TESTIMONY
identification—*see* AUTHENTICATION AND IDENTIFICATION
illustrations—*see* AUTHENTICATION AND IDENTIFICATION
impairment—
  infancy, 601.3; EvR 104(c), 601
  mental, 601.3; EvR 104(c), 601
  physchological, 601.3; EvR 104(c), 601
impeachment—
  annulment, effect of, 609.9; EvR 609(c)
  appeal, pendency of, effect, 609.11; EvR 609(e)
  appropriate convictions, 609.3; EvR 609(a)(1)
  bias, exposure of, 607.4; EvR 607, 613(b)
  capital offenses, 609.2; EvR 609(a)(1)
  character, *see* character and conduct, this heading
  conduct, *see* character and conduct, this heading
  contradiction, 607.5; EvR 403, 607, 613
  conviction, introduction of, 609.7; EvR 609
  conviction of crime, 609.1; EvR 404(b), 609
  convictions without regard to penalty, 609.5; EvR 609(a)(2)
  "conviction", what constitutes, 609.6; EvR 609
  court, power to prohibit impeaching own witness, 607.3; EvR 102, 403, 607, 611, 801
  crimen falsi, offenses in nature of, 609.4; EvR 609(a)(2)
  crimes punishable by imprisonment in excess of one year, 609.2; EvR 609(a)(1)
  impeaching own witness, court's power to prohibit, 607.3; EvR 102, 403, 607, 611, 801
  in general, 607.1; EvR 607-610, 613
  interest, exposure of, 607.4; EvR 607, 613(b)
  juvenile adjudications, 609.10; EvR 609(d)
  mental capacity, defects, 607.6; EvR 403, 602, 607, 608
  operation of EvR 609(a)(2), 609.4
  pardon, effect of, 609.9; EvR 609(c)
  perception, defects, 607.6; EvR 403, 602, 607, 608

WITNESSES—*Continued*

impeachment—*Concluded*

   policy, voucher rule rejected, 607.2; EvR 102, 403, 607, 611, 801(d)(1)(A)

   rehabilitation, certification of, 609.9; EvR 609(c)

   time limit, 609.8; EvR 609(b)

   voucher rule rejected, 607.2; EvR 102, 403, 607, 611, 801(d)(1)(A)

interplay between EvR 601, 104 and 403, 601.2; EvR 104, 403, 601, 611(a), 614(b)

interpreters—

   credibility of, 604.3; EvR 604

   in general, 604.1; EvR 604

   jury, function, 604.3; EvR 604

   trial judge, function, 604.2; EvR 604

interrogation, *see* INTERROGATION OF WITNESSES

judge as witness—

   civil proceedings, 605.2; EvR 605

   competency, 605.1; EvR 605

   criminal proceedings, 605.3; EvR 605

   violation of EvR 605, 605.4

judge's role, 601.5; EvR 601

juror as witness—

   affidavits, 606.5; EvR 602(b), 606

   competency of, 606.1; EvR 605, 606(a)

   extraneous prejudicial information, 606.3; EvR 606(b)

   matters internal to deliberative process, 606.2; EvR 606(b)

   misconduct, procedure in determining, 606.4; EvR 606(b)

   outside influence, 606.3; EvR 606(b)

   statements, 606.5; EvR 602(b), 606

   subsequent proceedings—

      indictment, 606.2; EvR 606(b)

      original verdict, 606.2; EvR 606(b)

   testimony, extent competent, 606.5; EvR 602(b), 606

oath or affirmation, 603.1; EvR 603

   operation of, 603.2; EvR 603

   testimony, absence of, 603.3; EvR 603

WITNESSES—*Concluded*

personal knowledge—

   competency versus weight, 602.3; EvR 602

   foundation as to, 602.2; EvR 104, 602

   general requirements, 602.1; EvR 602

   other rules, 602.4; EvR 602, 701, 703

prior statement of—

   admissions, party-opponent, 613.8; EvR 613, 801(d)(2)

   collateral matter doctrine, 613.5; EvR 613

   denial, necessity of, 613.6; EvR 613

   explanation requirement, discretion to dispense with, 613.4; EvR 613(b)

   extrinsic evidence, 613.3; EvR 613(b)

   inconsistent, 613.3; EvR 613(b)

   inconsistency, degree required for impeachment, 613.7; EvR 613

   in general, 613.1; EvR 613

   interrogation, 613.2; EvR 613(a)

   party-opponent, admissions, 613.8; EvR 613, 801(d)(2)

religious beliefs or opinions—

   credibility affected, 610.1; EvR 610

      admissible evidence, 610.2; EvR 610

state law, application of, 601.6; EvR 601

subscribing, testimony unnecessary to authenticate writing, when, 903.1 et seq; EvR 903

testimony, court's power to exclude, 601.2; EvR 103(b), 104, 401, 403, 601, 611(a), 614(b)

WRITINGS—*see* RECORDS, WRITINGS AND PHOTOGRAPHS

WRITINGS—*see* RECORDS, WRITINGS AND PHOTOGRAPHS

X-RAY FILM, PROOF OF CONTENTS, 1001.8; EvR 1001(2)